Random House Webster's
Pocket
Spanish
Dictionary

Third Edition

Spanish • English
English • Spanish
español • inglés
inglés • español

Edited by
Donald F. Solá
CORNELL UNIVERSITY

Revised by
David L. Gold
Doctor in Romance Philology
UNIVERSITY OF BARCELONA

RANDOM HOUSE
NEW YORK

Random House Webster's
Pocket Spanish Dictionary, Third Edition

Copyright © 2000, 1995 by Random House, Inc.

Library of Congress Cataloging-in-Publication Number: 99-66702

Visit the Random House Reference Web site:
www.randomwords.com

Typeset by Random House Reference and Seaside Press

Typeset and printed in the United States of America

Third Edition
0 9 8 7 6 5
November 2001
ISBN: 0-375-70566-X

New York   Toronto   London   Sydney   Auckland

Pronunciation Key for Spanish

IPA Symbols	Key Words	Approximate Equivalents
a	alba, banco, cera	father, depart
e	esto, del, parte, mesa	bet; like rain when **e** ends syllable and is not followed by **r**, **rr**, or **t**
i	ir, fino, adiós, muy	like beet, but shorter
o	oler, flor, grano	like vote, but shorter
u	un, luna, cuento, vergüenza, guarda	fool, group
b	bajo, ambiguo, vaca	by, abet
β	hablar, escribir, lavar	like vehicle, but with lips almost touching
d	dar, desde, andamio, dueña	deal, adept
ð	pedir, edredón, verdad	that, gather
f	fecha, afectar, golf	fan, after
g	gato, grave, gusto, largo, guerra	garden, ugly
h	gemelo, giro, junta, bajo	horse
k	cacao, claro, cura, cuenta, que, quinto	kind, actor
l	lado, lente, habla, papel	lot, altar
ʎ	(in Spain) llama, calle, olla	like million, but with tongue behind teeth
m	mal, amor	more, commit

IPA Symbols	Key Words	Approximate Equivalents
n	nada, nuevo, mano, bien	not, enter
ɲ	ñapa, año	canyon, companion
ŋ	angosto, aunque	ring, anchor
p	peso, guapo	pill, applaud
r	real, faro, deber	like rice, but with single flap of tongue on roof of mouth
rr	perro, sierra	like rice, but with trill, or vibration of tongue, against upper teeth
s	sala, espejo, mas; (in Latin America) cena, hacer, vez	say, clasp
θ	(in Spain) cena, hacer, cierto, cine, zarzuela, lazo, vez	thin, myth
t	tocar, estado, cenit	table, attract
y	ya, ayer; (in Latin America) llama, calle	you, voyage
tʃ	chica, mucho	chill, batch

Diphthongs

ai	baile, hay	high, rye
au	audacia, laudable	out, round
ei	veinte, seis, rey	ray
ie	miel, tambien	fiesta
oi	estoico, hoy	coin, loyal
ua	cuanto	quantity
ue	buena, suerte	sway, quaint

Spanish Stress

In a number of words, spoken stress is marked by an accent (´): *nación, país, médico, día.*

Words which are not so marked are, generally speaking, stressed on the next-to-the-last syllable if they end in a vowel, *n*, or *s*; and on the last syllable if they end in a consonant other than *n* or *s*.

Note: An accent is placed over some words to distinguish them from others having the same spelling and pronunciation but differing in meaning.

Spanish Alphabetization

In Spanish, *ch* and *ll* are no longer considered to be separate letters of the alphabet. They are now alphabetized as they would be in English. However, words with *ñ* are alphabetized after *n*.

Guía de Pronunciación del inglés

Símbolos del AFI	Ejemplos
/æ/	*ingl.* hat; como la **a** de *esp.* paro, pero más cerrada
/ei/	*ingl.* stay; *esp.* reina
/ɛə/ [followed by /r/]	*ingl.* hair; *esp.* ver
/ɑ/	*ingl.* father; similar a las **a**s de *esp.* casa, pero más larga
/ɛ/	*ingl.* bet; *esp.* entre
/i/	*ingl.* bee; como la **i** de *esp.* vida, pero más larga
/ɪə/ [followed by /r/]	*ingl.* hear; como la **i** de *esp.* venir, pero menos cerrada
/ɪ/	*ingl.* sit; como la **i** de *esp.* Chile, pero menos cerrada
/ai/	*ingl.* try; *esp.* hay
/ɒ/	*ingl.* hot; *esp.* poner
/ou/	*ingl.* boat; similar a la **o** de *esp.* saco, pero más cerrada
/ɔ/	*ingl.* saw; similar a la **o** de *esp.* corte, pero más cerrada
/ɔi/	*ingl.* toy; *esp.* hoy
/ʊ/	*ingl.* book; como la **u** de *esp.* insulto, pero menos cerrada
/u/	*ingl.* too; como la **u** de *esp.* luna, pero más larga
/au/	*ingl.* cow; *esp.* pausa
/ʌ/	*ingl.* up; entre la **o** de *esp.* borde y la **a** de *esp.* barro
/ɜ/ [followed by /r/]	*ingl.* burn; *fr.* fleur
/ə/	*ingl.* alone; *fr.* demain
/ᵊ/	*ingl.* fire (fiᵊr); *fr.* bastille
/b/	*ingl.* boy; como la **b** de *esp.* boca, pero más aspirada
/tʃ/	*ingl.* child; *esp.* mucho
/d/	*ingl.* dad; *esp.* dar
/f/	*ingl.* for; *esp.* fecha
/g/	*ingl.* give; *esp.* gato

Símbolos del AFI	**Ejemplos**
/h/	*ingl.* **h**appy; como la **j** de *esp.* **j**abón, pero más aspirada y menos aspera
/dʒ/	*ingl.* **j**ust; *it.* **g**iorno
/k/	*ingl.* **k**ick; similar a la **k** de *esp.* **k**ilogramo, pero más aspirada
/l/	*ingl.* **l**ove; *esp.* **l**ibro
/m/	*ingl.* **m**other; *esp.* li**m**bo
/n/	*ingl.* **n**ow; *esp.* **n**oche
/ŋ/	*ingl.* si**ng**; *esp.* bla**n**co
/p/	*ingl.* **p**ot; como las **ps** de *esp.* **p**a**p**a, pero más aspirada
/r/	*ingl.* **r**ead; como la **r** de *esp.* pa**r**a, pero con la lengua elevada hacia el paladar, sin tocarlo
/s/	*ingl.* **s**ee; *esp.* ha**s**ta
/ʃ/	*ingl.* **sh**op; *fr.* **ch**ercher
/t/	*ingl.* **t**en; similar a la **t** de *esp.* **t**omar, pero más aspirada
/θ/	*ingl.* **th**ing; *esp.* (en España) **c**erdo, **z**apato
/ð/	*ingl.* fa**th**er; *esp.* co**d**o
/v/	*ingl.* **v**ictory; como la **b** de *esp.* ha**b**a, pero es labiodental en vez de bilabial
/w/	*ingl.* **w**itch; como la **u** de *esp.* p**u**esto, pero con labios más cerrados
/y/	*ingl.* **y**es; *esp.* **y**acer
/z/	*ingl.* **z**ipper; *fr.* **z**éro
/ʒ/	*ingl.* plea**s**ure; *fr.* **j**eune

Las consonantes /l̩/, /m̩/, y /n̩/ son similar a las **l**, **m**, y **n** del español, pero alargada y resonante.

English Abbreviations/
Abreviaturas inglesas

a.	adjective	*Govt.*	government
abbr.	abbreviation	*Gram.*	grammar
adv.	adverb	*interj.*	interjection
Aero.	aeronautics	*interrog.*	interrogative
Agr.	agriculture	*Leg.*	legal
Anat.	anatomy	*m.*	masculine
art.	article	*Mech.*	mechanics
Auto.	automotive	*Mex.*	Mexico
Biol.	biology	*Mil.*	military
Bot.	botany	*Mus.*	music
Carib.	Caribbean	*n.*	noun
Chem.	chemistry	*Naut.*	nautical
Colloq.	colloquial	*Phot.*	photography
Com.	commerce	*pl.*	plural
conj.	conjunction	*Pol.*	politics
dem.	demonstrative	*prep.*	preposition
Econ.	economics	*pron.*	pronoun
Elec.	electrical	*Punct.*	punctuation
esp.	especially	*rel.*	relative
f.	feminine	*Relig.*	religion
Fig.	figurative	*S.A.*	Spanish America
Fin.	finance	*Theat.*	theater
Geog.	geography	*v.*	verb

Note: If a main entry term is repeated in a boldface subentry in exactly the same form, it is abbreviated. Example: **comedor** *n.m.* dining room. **coche c.,** dining car.

A

a /a/ *prep.* to; at.

abacería /aβaθe'ria; aβase'ria/ *n. f.* grocery store.

abacero /aβa'θero; aβa'sero/ *n. m.* grocer.

ábaco /'aβako/ *n. m.* abacus.

abad /a'βað/ *n. m.* abbot.

abadía /aβa'ðia/ *n. f.* abbey.

abajar /aβa'har/ *v.* lower; go down.

abajo /a'βaho/ *adv.* down; downstairs.

abandonar /aβando'nar/ *v.* abandon.

abandono /aβan'dono/ *n. m.* abandonment.

abanico /aβa'niko/ *n. m.* fan. —**abanicar,** *v.*

abaratar /aβara'tar/ *v.* cheapen.

abarcar /aβar'kar/ *v.* comprise; clasp.

abastecer /aβaste'θer; aβaste'ser/ *v.* supply, provide.

abatido /aβa'tiðo/ *a.* dejected, despondent.

abatir /aβa'tir/ *v.* knock down; dismantle; depress, dishearten.

abdicación /aβðika'θion; aβðika'sion/ *n. f.* abdication.

abdicar /aβði'kar/ *v.* abdicate.

abdomen /aβ'ðomen/ *n. m.* abdomen.

abdominal /aβðomi'nal/ *a.* **1.** abdominal. —*n.* **2.** *m.* sit-up.

abecé /aβe'θe; aβe'se/ *n. m.* ABCs, rudiments.

abecedario /aβeθe'ðario; aβese'ðario/ *n. m.* alphabet; reading book.

abeja /a'βeha/ *n. f.* bee.

abejarrón /aβeha'rron/ *n. m.* bumblebee.

aberración /aβerra'θion; aβerra'sion/ *n. f.* aberration.

abertura /aβer'tura/ *n. f.* opening, aperture, slit.

abeto /a'βeto/ *n. m.* fir.

abierto /a'βierto/ *a.* open; overt.

abismal /aβis'mal/ *a.* abysmal.

abismo /a'βismo/ *n. m.* abyss, chasm.

ablandar /aβlan'dar/ *v.* soften.

abnegación /aβnega'θion; aβnega'sion/ *n. f.* abnegation.

abochornar /aβot∫or'nar/ *v.* overheat; embarrass.

abogado /aβo'gaðo/ **-da** *n.* lawyer, attorney.

abolengo /aβo'lengo/ *n. m.* ancestry.

abolición /aβoli'θion; aβoli'sion/ *n. f.* abolition.

abolladura /aβoʎa'ðura; aβoya'ðura/ *n. f.* dent. —**abollar,** *v.*

abominable /aβomi'naβle/ *a.* abominable.

abominar /aβomi'nar/ *v.* abhor.

abonado /aβo'naðo/ **-da** *n. m.* & *f.* subscriber.

abonar /aβo'nar/ *v.* pay; fertilize.

abonarse /aβo'narse/ *v.* subscribe.

abono /a'βono/ *n. m.* fertilizer; subscription; season ticket.

aborigen /aβo'rihen/ *a.* & *n.* aboriginal.

aborrecer /aβorre'θer; aβorre'ser/ *v.* hate, loathe, abhor.

abortar /aβor'tar/ *v.* abort, miscarry.

aborto /a'βorto/ *n. m.* abortion.

abovedar /aβoβe'ðar/ *v.* vault.

abrasar /aβra'sar/ *v.* burn.

abrazar /aβra'θar; aβra'sar/ *v.* embrace; clasp.

abrazo /a'βraθo; a'βraso/ *n. m.* embrace.

abrelatas /aβre'latas/ *n. m.* can opener.

abreviar /aβre'βiar/ *v.* abbreviate, abridge, shorten.

abreviatura /aβreβia'tura/ *n. f.* abbreviation.

abrigar /aβri'gar/ *v.* harbor, shelter.

abrigarse /aβri'garse/ *v.* bundle up.

abrigo /a'βrigo/ *n. m.* overcoat; shelter; (*pl.*) wraps.

abril /a'βril/ *n. m.* April.

abrir /a'βrir/ *v.* open; *Med.* lance.

abrochar /aβro't∫ar/ *v.* clasp.

abrogación /aβroga'θion; aβroga'sion/ *n. f.* abrogation, repeal.

abrogar /aβro'gar/ *v.* abrogate.

abrojo /a'βroho/ *n. m.* thorn.

abrumar /aβru'mar/ *v.* overwhelm, crush, swamp.

absceso /aβ'sθeso; aβ'sseso/ *n. m.* abscess.

absolución /aβsolu'θion; aβsolu'sion/ *n. f.* absolution; acquittal.

absoluto /aβso'luto/ a. absolute; downright.

absolver /aβsol'βer/ v. absolve, pardon.

absorbente /aβsor'βente/ a. absorbent.

absorber /aβsor'βer/ v. absorb.

absorción /aβsor'θion; aβsor'sion/ n. f. absorption.

abstemio /aβs'temio/ a. abstemious.

abstenerse /aβste'nerse/ v. abstain; refrain.

abstinencia /aβsti'nenθia; aβsti'nensia/ n. f. abstinence.

abstracción /aβstrak'θion; aβstrak'sion/ n. f. abstraction.

abstracto /aβ'strakto/ a. abstract.

abstraer /aβstra'er/ v. abstract.

absurdo /aβ'surðo/ a. **1.** absurd. —n. **2.** m. absurdity.

abuchear /aβutʃe'ar/ v. boo.

abuela /a'βuela/ n. f. grandmother.

abuelo /a'βuelo/ n. m. grandfather; (pl.) grandparents.

abultado /aβul'taðo/ a. bulky.

abultamiento /aβulta'miento/ n. m. bulge. —**abultar,** v.

abundancia /aβun'danθia; aβun'dansia/ n. f. abundance, plenty.

abundante /aβun'dante/ a. abundant, plentiful.

abundar /aβun'dar/ v. abound.

aburrido /aβu'rriðo/ a. boring, tedious.

aburrimiento /aβurri'miento/ n. m. boredom.

aburrir /aβu'rrir/ v. bore.

abusar /aβu'sar/ v. abuse, misuse.

abusivo /aβu'siβo/ a. abusive.

abuso /a'βuso/ n. m. abuse.

abyecto /aβ'yekto/ a. abject, low.

a.C., abbr. (antes de Cristo) BC.

acá /a'ka/ adv. here.

acabar /aka'βar/ v. finish. **a. de...,** to have just....

acacia /a'kaθia; a'kasia/ n. f. acacia.

academia /aka'ðemia/ n. f. academy.

académico /aka'ðemiko/ a. academic.

acaecer /akae'θer; akae'ser/ v. happen.

acanalar /akana'lar/ v. groove.

acaparar /akapa'rar/ v. hoard; monopolize.

acariciar /akari'θiar; akari'siar/ v. caress, stroke.

acarrear /akarre'ar/ v. cart, transport; occasion, entail.

acaso /a'kaso/ n. m. chance. **por si a,** just in case.

acceder /akθe'ðer; akse'ðer/ v. accede.

accesible /akθe'siβle; akse'siβle/ a. accessible.

acceso /ak'θeso; ak'seso/ n. m. access, approach.

accesorio /akθe'sorio; akse'sorio/ a. accessory.

accidentado /akθiðen'taðo; aksiðen'taðo/ a. hilly.

accidental /akθiðen'tal; aksiðen'tal/ a. accidental.

accidente /akθi'ðente; aksi'ðente/ n. m. accident, wreck.

acción /ak'θion; ak'sion/ n. f. action, act; Com. share of stock.

accionista /akθio'nista; aksio'nista/ n. m. & f. shareholder.

acechar /aθe'tʃar; ase'tʃar/ v. ambush, spy on.

acedia /a'θeðia; a'seðia/ n. f. heartburn.

aceite /a'θeite; a'seite/ n. m. oil.

aceite de hígado de bacalao /a'θeite de i'gaðo de baka'lao; a'seite/ cod-liver oil.

aceitoso /aθei'toso; asei'toso/ a. oily.

aceituna /aθei'tuna; asei'tuna/ n. f. olive.

aceleración /aθelera'θion; aselera'sion/ n. f. acceleration.

acelerar /aθele'rar; asele'rar/ v. accelerate, speed up.

acento /a'θento; a'sento/ n. m. accent.

acentuar /aθen'tuar; asen'tuar/ v. accent, accentuate, stress.

acepillar /aθepi'ʎar; asepi'yar/ v. brush; plane (wood).

aceptable /aθep'taβle; asep'taβle/ a. acceptable.

aceptación /aθepta'θion; asepta'sion/ n. f. acceptance.

aceptar /aθep'tar; asep'tar/ v. accept.

acequia /a'θekia; a'sekia/ n. f. ditch.

acera /a'θera; a'sera/ n. f. sidewalk.

acerca de /a'θerka de; a'serka de/ prep. about, concerning.

acercar /aθer'kar; aser'kar/ v. bring near.

acercarse /aθer'karse; aser'karse/ *v.* approach, come near, go near.

acero /a'θero; a'sero/ *n. m.* steel.

acero inoxidable /a'θero inoksi-'ðaβle; a'sero inoksi'ðaβle/ stainless steel.

acertar /aθer'tar; aser'tar/ *v.* guess right. **a. en,** hit (a mark).

acertijo /aθer'tiho; aser'tiho/ *n. m.* puzzle, riddle.

achicar /atʃi'kar/ *v.* diminish; dwarf; humble.

acidez /aθi'ðeθ; asi'ðes/ *n. f.* acidity.

ácido /'aθiðo; 'asiðo/ *a.* sour. —*n.* **2.** *m.* acid.

aclamación /aklama'θion; aklama'sion/ *n. f.* acclamation.

aclamar /akla'mar/ *v.* acclaim.

aclarar /akla'rar/ *v.* brighten; clarify, clear up.

acoger /ako'her/ *v.* welcome, receive.

acogida /ako'hiða/ *n. f.* welcome, reception.

acometer /akome'ter/ *v.* attack.

acomodador /akomoða'ðor/ *n. m.* usher.

acomodar /akomo'ðar/ *v.* accommodate, fix up.

acompañamiento /akompaɲa'miento/ *n. m.* accompaniment; following.

acompañar /akompa'ɲar/ *v.* accompany.

acondicionar /akondiθio'nar; akondisio'nar/ *v.* condition.

aconsejable /akonse'haβle/ *a.* advisable.

aconsejar /akonse'har/ *v.* advise.

acontecer /akonte'θer; akonte'ser/ *v.* happen.

acontecimiento /akonteθi'miento; akontesi'miento/ *n. m.* event, happening.

acorazado /akora'θaðo; akora'saðo/ *n.* **1.** *m.* battleship. —*a.* **2.** armor-plated, ironclad.

acordarse /akor'ðarse/ *v.* remember, recollect.

acordeón /akorðe'on/ *n. m.* accordion.

acordonar /akorðo'nar/ *v.* cordon off.

acortar /akor'tar/ *v.* shorten.

acosar /ako'sar/ *v.* beset, harry.

acostar /akos'tar/ *v.* lay down; put to bed.

acostarse /akos'tarse/ *v.* lie down; go to bed.

acostumbrado /akostum'braðo/ *a.* accustomed; customary.

acostumbrar /akostum'brar/ *v.* accustom.

acrecentar /akreθen'tar; akresen'tar/ *v.* increase.

acreditar /akreði'tar/ *v.* accredit.

acreedor /akree'ðor/ **-ra** *n.* creditor.

acróbata /a'kroβata/ *n. m. & f.* acrobat.

acrobático /akro'βatiko/ *a.* acrobatic.

actitud /akti'tuð/ *n. f.* attitude.

actividad /aktiβi'ðað/ *n. f.* activity.

activista /akti'βista/ *a. & n.* activist.

activo /ak'tiβo/ *a.* active.

acto /'akto/ *n. m.* act.

actor /ak'tor/ *n. m.* actor.

actriz /ak'triθ; ak'tris/ *n. f.* actress.

actual /ak'tual/ *a.* present; present day.

actualidades /aktuali'ðaðes/ *n. f.pl.* current events.

actualmente /aktual'mente/ *adv.* at present; nowadays.

actuar /ak'tuar/ *v.* act.

acuarela /akua'rela/ *n. f.* watercolor.

acuario /a'kuario/ *n. m.* aquarium.

acuático /a'kuatiko/ *a.* aquatic.

acuchillar /akutʃi'ʎar; akutʃi'yar/ *v.* slash, knife.

acudir /aku'ðir/ *v.* rally; hasten; be present.

acuerdo /a'kuerðo/ *n. m.* accord, agreement; settlement. **de a.,** in agreement, agreed.

acumulación /akumula'θion; akumula'sion/ *n. f.* accumulation.

acumular /akumu'lar/ *v.* accumulate.

acuñar /aku'ɲar/ *v.* coin, mint.

acupuntura /akupun'tura/ *n. f.* acupuncture.

acusación /akusa'θion; akusa'sion/ *n. f.* accusation, charge.

acusado /aku'saðo/ **-da** *a. & n.* accused; defendant.

acusador /akusa'ðor/ **-ra** *n.* accuser.

acusar /aku'sar/ *v.* accuse; acknowledge.

acústica /a'kustika/ *n. f.* acoustics.

adaptación /aðapta'θion/ aðap-ta'sion/ n. f. adaptation.

adaptador /aðapta'ðor/ n. m. adapter.

adaptar /aðap'tar/ v. adapt.

adecuado /aðe'kuaðo/ a. adequate.

adelantado /aðelan'taðo/ a. advanced; fast (clock).

adelantamiento /aðelanta-'miento/ n. m. advancement, promotion.

adelantar /aðelan'tar/ v. advance.

adelante /aðe'lante/ adv. ahead, forward, onward, on.

adelanto /aðe'lanto/ n. m. advancement, progress, improvement.

adelgazar /aðelga'θar; aðelga'sar/ v. make thin.

ademán /aðe'man/ n. m. attitude; gesture.

además /aðe'mas/ adv. in addition, besides, also.

adentro /a'ðentro/ adv. in, inside.

adepto /a'ðepto/ a. adept.

aderezar /aðere'θar; aðere'sar/ v. prepare; trim.

adherirse /aðe'rirse/ v. adhere, stick.

adhesivo /aðe'siβo/ a. adhesive.

adicción /aðik'θion; aðik'sion/ n. f. adiction.

adición /aði'θion; aði'sion/ n. f. addition.

adicional /aðiθio'nal; aðisio'nal/ a. additional, extra.

adicto /a'ðikto/ **-ta** a. & n. addicted; addict.

adinerado /aðine'raðo/ **-a** a. wealthy.

adiós /aðios/ n. m. & interj. goodbye, farewell.

adivinar /aðiβi'nar/ v. guess.

adjetivo /aðhe'tiβo/ n. m. adjective.

adjunto /að'hunto/ a. enclosed.

administración /aðministra'θion; aðministra'sion/ n. f. administration.

administrador /aðministra'ðor/ **-ra** n. administrator.

administrar /aðminis'trar/ v. administer; manage.

administrativo /aðministra'tiβo/ a. administrative.

admirable /aðmi'raβle/ a. admirable.

admiración. /aðmira'θion; að-

mira'sion/ n. f. admiration; wonder.

admirar /aðmi'rar/ v. admire.

admisión /aðmi'sion/ n. f. admission.

admitir /aðmi'tir/ v. admit, acknowledge.

ADN, abbr. (**ácido deoxirribonucleico**) DNA (deoxyribonucleic acid).

adobar /aðo'βar/ v. marinate.

adolescencia /aðoles'θenθia; aðoles'sensia/ n. f. adolescence, youth.

adolescente /aðoles'θente; aðoles'sente/ a. & n. adolescent.

adónde /a'ðonde/ adv. where.

adondequiera /a,ðonde'kiera/ conj. wherever.

adopción /aðop'θion; aðop'sion/ n. f. adoption.

adoptar /aðop'tar/ v. adopt.

adoración /aðora'θion; aðora'sion/ n. f. worship, love, adoration. **—adorar,** v.

adormecer /aðorme'θer; aðorme'ser/ v. drowse.

adornar /aðor'nar/ v. adorn; decorate.

adorno /a'ðorno/ n. m. adornment, trimming.

adquirir /aðki'rir/ v. acquire, obtain.

adquisición /aðkisi'θion; aðkisi'sion/ n. f. acquisition, attainment.

aduana /a'ðuana/ n. f. custom house, customs.

adujada /aðu'haða/ n. f. Naut. coil of rope.

adulación /aðula'θion; aðula'sion/ n. f. flattery.

adular /aðu'lar/ v. flatter.

adulterar /aðulte'rar/ v. adulterate.

adulterio /aðul'terio/ n. m. adultery.

adulto /a'ðulto/ **-ta** a. & n. adult.

adusto /a'ðusto/ a. gloomy; austere.

adverbio /að'βerβio/ n. m. adverb.

adversario /aðβer'sario/ n. m. adversary.

adversidad /aðβersi'ðað/ n. f. adversity.

adverso /að'βerso/ a. adverse.

advertencia /aðβer'tenθia; aðβer'tensia/ n. f. warning.

advertir /aðβer'tir/ v. warn; notice.

adyacente /aðya'θente; aðya'sente/ a. adjacent.

aéreo /a'ereo/ a. aerial; air.

aerodeslizador /aeroðesliða'ðor; aeroðeslisa'ðor/ n. m. hovercraft.

aeromoza /aero'moθa; aero'mosa/ n. f. stewardess, flight attendant.

aeroplano /aero'plano/ n. m. light plane.

aeropuerto /aero'puerto/ n. m. airport.

aerosol /aero'sol/ n. m. aerosol, spray.

afable /a'faβle/ a. affable, pleasant.

afanarse /afa'narse/ v. toil.

afear /afe'ar/ v. deface, mar, deform.

afectación /afekta'θion; afekta'sion/ n. f. affectation.

afectar /afek'tar/ v. affect.

afecto /a'fekto/ n. m. affection, attachment.

afeitada /afei'taða/ n. f. shave. —**afeitarse**, v.

afeminado /afemi'naðo/ a. effeminate.

afición /afi'θion; afi'sion/ n. f. fondness, liking; hobby.

aficionado /afiθio'naðo; afisio'naðo/ a. fond.

aficionado -da /afiθio'naðo; afisio'naðo/ n. fan, devotee; amateur.

aficionarse a /afiθio'narse a; afisio'narse a/ v. become fond of.

afilado /afi'laðo/ a. sharp.

afilar /afi'lar/ v. sharpen.

afiliación /afilia'θion; afilia'sion/ n. f. affiliation.

afiliado -da /afi'liaðo/ -da n. affiliate. —**afiliar**, v.

afinar /afi'nar/ v. polish; tune up.

afinidad /afini'ðað/ n. f. relationship, affinity.

afirmación /afirma'θion; afirma'sion/ n. f. affirmation, statement.

afirmar /afir'mar/ v. affirm, assert.

afirmativa /afirma'tiβa/ n. f. affirmative. —**afirmativo**, a.

aflicción /aflik'θion; aflik'sion/ n. f. affliction; sorrow, grief.

afligido /afli'hiðo/ a. sorrowful, grieved.

afligir /afli'hir/ v. grieve, distress.

aflojar /aflo'har/ v. loosen.

afluencia /a'fluenθia; a'fluensia/ n. f. influx.

afortunado /afortu'naðo/ a. fortunate, successful, lucky.

afrenta /a'frenta/ n. f. insult, outrage, affront. —**afrentar**, v.

afrentoso /afren'toso/ a. shameful.

africano /afri'kano/ -na a. & n. African.

afuera /a'fuera/ adv. out, outside.

afueras /a'fueras/ n. f.pl. suburbs.

agacharse /aga't∫arse/ v. squat, crouch; cower.

agarrar /aga'rrar/ v. seize, grasp, clutch.

agarro /a'garro/ n. m. clutch, grasp.

agencia /a'henθia; a'hensia/ n. f. agency.

agencia de colocaciones /a'henθia de koloka'θiones; a'hensia de koloka'siones/ employment agency.

agencia de viajes /a'henθia de 'biahes; a'hensia de 'biahes/ travel agency.

agente /a'hente/ n. m. & f. agent, representative.

agente de aduana /a'hente de a'ðuana/ mf. customs officer.

agente inmobiliario /a'hente imoβi'liario/ -ria n. real-estate agent.

ágil /'ahil/ a. agile, spry.

agitación /ahita'θion; ahita'sion/ mf. agitation, ferment.

agitado /ahi'taðo/ a. agitated; excited.

agitador /ahita'ðor/ n. m. agitator.

agitar /ahi'tar/ v. shake, agitate, excite.

agobiar /ago'βiar/ v. oppress, burden.

agosto /a'gosto/ n. m. August.

agotamiento /a,gota'miento/ n. m. exhaustion.

agotar /ago'tar/ v. exhaust, use up, sap.

agradable /agra'ðaβle/ a. agreeable, pleasant.

agradar /agra'ðar/ v. please.

agradecer /agraðe'θer; agraðe'ser/ v. thank; appreciate, be grateful for.

agradecido /agraðe'θiðo; agraðe'siðo/ a. grateful, thankful.

agradecimiento /agraðeθi'miento; agraðesi'miento/ n. m. gratitude, thanks.

agravar /agra'βar/ v. aggravate, make worse.

agravio /a'graβio/ n. m. wrong. **—agraviar,** v.

agregado /agre'gaðo/ a. & n. aggregate; Pol. attaché.

agregar /agre'gar/ v. add; gather.

agresión /agre'sion/ n. f. aggression; Leg. battery.

agresivo /agre'siβo/ a. aggressive.

agresor /agre'sor/ -ra n. aggressor.

agrícola /a'grikola/ a. agricultural.

agricultor /agrikul'tor/ n. m. farmer.

agricultura /agrikul'tura/ n. f. agriculture, farming.

agrio /'agrio/ a. sour.

agrupar /agru'par/ v. group.

agua /'agua/ n. f. water. **—aguar,** v.

aguacate /agua'kate/ n. m. avocado, alligator pear.

aguafuerte /,agua'fuerte/ n. f. etching.

agua mineral /'agua mine'ral/ mineral water.

aguantar /aguan'tar/ v. endure, stand, put up with.

aguardar /aguar'ðar/ v. await; expect.

aguardiente /aguar'ðiente/ n. m. brandy.

aguas abajo /'aguas a'βaho/ adv. downriver, downstream.

aguas arriba /'aguas a'rriβa/ adv. upriver, upstream.

agudo /a'guðo/ a. sharp, keen, shrill, acute.

agüero /a'guero/ n. m. omen.

águila /'agila/ n. f. eagle.

aguja /a'guha/ n. f. needle.

agujero /agu'hero/ n. m. hole.

aguzar /agu'θar; agu'sar/ v. sharpen.

ahí /a'i/ adv. there.

ahogar /ao'gar/ v. drown; choke; suffocate.

ahondar /aon'dar/ v. deepen.

ahora /a'ora/ adv. now.

ahorcar /aor'kar/ v. hang (execute).

ahorrar /ao'rrar/ v. save, save up; spare.

ahorros /a'orros/ n. m.pl. savings.

ahumar /au'mar/ v. smoke.

airado /ai'raðo/ a. angry, indignant.

aire /'aire/ n. m. air. **—airear,** v.

aire acondicionado /'aire akondi-θio'naðo; 'aire akondisio'naðo/ air conditioning.

aislamiento /aisla'miento/ n. m. isolation.

aislar /ais'lar/ v. isolate.

ajedrez /ahe'ðreθ; ahe'ðres/ n. m. chess.

ajeno /a'heno/ a. alien; someone else's.

ajetreo /ahe'treo/ n. m. hustle and bustle.

ají /a'hi/ n. m. chili.

ajo /'aho/ n. m. garlic.

ajustado /ahus'taðo/ a. adjusted; trim; exact.

ajustar /ahus'tar/ v. adjust.

ajuste /a'huste/ n. m. adjustment, settlement.

al /al/ contr. of **a + el.**

ala /'ala/ n. f. wing; brim (of hat).

alabanza /ala'βanθa; ala'βansa/ n. f. praise. **—alabar,** v.

alabear /alaβe'ar/ v. warp.

ala delta /'ala 'delta/ hang glider.

alambique /alam'bike/ n. m. still.

alambre /a'lambre/ n. m. wire. **a. de púas,** barbed wire.

alarde /a'larðe/ n. m. boasting, ostentation.

alargar /alar'gar/ v. lengthen; stretch out.

alarma /a'larma/ n. f. alarm. **—alarmar,** v.

alba /'alβa/ n. f. daybreak, dawn.

albanega /alβa'nega/ n. f. hair net.

albañil /alβa'ɲil/ n. m. bricklayer; mason.

albaricoque /alβari'koke/ n. m. apricot.

alberca /al'βerka/ n. f. swimming pool.

albergue /al'βerge/ n. m. shelter. **—albergar,** v.

alborotar /alβoro'tar/ v. disturb, make noise, brawl, riot.

alboroto /alβo'roto/ n. m. brawl, disturbance, din, tumult.

álbum /'alβum/ n. m. album.

álbum de recortes /'alβum de rre'kortes/ scrapbook.

alcachofa /alka'tʃofa/ n. f. artichoke.

alcalde /al'kalde/ n. m. mayor.

alcance /al'kanθe; al'kanse/ n. m. reach; range, scope.

alcanfor /alkan'for/ n. m. camphor.

alcanzar /alkan'θar; alkan'sar/ v. reach, overtake, catch.

alojarse

alcayata /alka'yata/ *n. f.* spike.
alce /'alθe; 'alse/ *n. m.* elk.
alcoba /al'koβa/ *n. f.* bedroom; alcove.
alcoba de huéspedes /al'koβa de 'uespeðes/ guest room.
alcoba de respeto /al'koβa de rres'peto/ guest room.
alcohol /al'kool/ *n. m.* alcohol.
alcohólico /alko'oliko/ **-ca** *a. & n.* alcoholic.
aldaba /al'daβa/ *n. f.* latch.
aldea /al'dea/ *n. f.* village.
alegación /alega'θion; alega'sion/ *n. f.* allegation.
alegar /ale'gar/ *v.* allege.
alegrar /ale'grar/ *v.* make happy, brighten.
alegrarse /ale'grarse/ *v.* be glad.
alegre /a'legre/ *a.* glad, cheerful, merry.
alegría /ale'gria/ *n. f.* gaiety, cheer.
alejarse /ale'harse/ *v.* move away, off.
alemán /ale'man/ **-ana** *a. & n.* German.
Alemania /ale'mania/ *n. f.* Germany.
alentar /alen'tar/ *v.* cheer up, encourage.
alergia /aler'hia/ *n. f.* allergy.
alerta /a'lerta/ *adv.* on the alert.
aleve /a'leβe/ **alevoso** *a.* treacherous.
alfabeto /alfa'βeto/ *n. m.* alphabet.
alfalfa /al'falfa/ *n. f.* alfalfa.
alfarería /alfare'ria/ *n. f.* pottery.
alférez /al'fereθ; al'feres/ *n. m.* (naval) ensign.
alfil /al'fil/ *n. m.* (chess) bishop.
alfiler /alfi'ler/ *n. m.* pin.
alfombra /al'fombra/ *n. f.* carpet, rug.
alforja /al'forha/ *n. f.* knapsack; saddlebag.
alga /'alga/ *n. f.* seaweed.
alga marina /'alga ma'rina/ seaweed.
algarabía /algara'βia/ *n. f.* jargon; din.
álgebra /'alheβra/ *n. f.* algebra.
algo /'algo/ *pron. & adv.* something, somewhat; anything.
algodón /algo'ðon/ *n. m.* cotton.
algodón hidrófilo /algo'ðon i'ðrofilo/ absorbent cotton.
alguien /'algien/ *pron.* somebody, someone; anybody, anyone.

algún /al'gun/ **-no -na** *a. & pron.* some; any.
alhaja /al'aha/ *n. f.* jewel.
aliado /a'liaðo/ **-da** *a. & n.* allied; ally. **—aliar,** *v.*
alianza /a'lianθa; a'liansa/ *n. f.* alliance.
alicates /ali'kates/ *n. m.pl.* pliers.
aliento /a'liento/ *n. m.* breath.
dar a., encourage.
aligerar /alihe'rar/ *v.* lighten.
alimentar /alimen'tar/ *v.* feed, nourish.
alimento /ali'mento/ *n. m.* nourishment, food.
alinear /aline'ar/ *v.* line up; *Pol.* align.
aliñar /ali'ɲar/ *v.* dress (a salad).
aliño /a'liɲo/ *n. m.* salad dressing.
alisar /ali'sar/ *v.* smooth.
alistamiento /alista'miento/ *n. m.* enlistment.
alistar /alis'tar/ *v.* make ready, prime.
alistarse /alis'tarse/ *v.* get ready; *Mil.* enlist.
aliviar /ali'βiar/ *v.* alleviate, relieve, ease.
alivio /a'liβio/ *n. m.* relief.
allá /a'ʎa; a'ya/ *adv.* there. **más a.,** beyond, farther on.
allanar /aʎa'nar; aya'nar/ *v.* flatten, smooth, plane.
allí /a'ʎi; a'yi/ *adv.* there. **por a.,** that way.
alma /'alma/ *n. f.* soul.
almacén /alma'θen; alma'sen/ *n. m.* department store; storehouse, warehouse.
almacenaje /almaθe'nahe; almase'nahe/ *n. m.* storage.
almacenar /almaθe'nar; almase'nar/ *v.* store.
almanaque /alma'nake/ *n. m.* almanac.
almeja /al'meha/ *n. f.* clam.
almendra /al'mendra/ *n. f.* almond.
almíbar /al'miβar/ *n. m.* syrup.
almidón /almi'ðon/ *n. m.* starch. **—almidonar,** *v.*
almirante /almi'rante/ *n. m.* admiral.
almohada /almo'aða/ *n. f.* pillow.
almuerzo /al'muerθo; al'muerso/ *n. m.* lunch. **—almorzar,** *v.*
alojamiento /aloha'miento/ *n. m.* lodging, accommodations.
alojar /alo'har/ *v.* lodge, house.
alojarse /alo'harse/ *v.* stay, room.

alquiler /alki'ler/ n. m. rent.
—**alquilar,** v.

alrededor /alreðe'ðor/ adv.
around.

alrededores /alreðe'ðores/
m.pl. environs.

altanero /alta'nero/ a. haughty.

altar /al'tar/ n. m. altar.

altavoz /ˌalta'βoθ; ˌalta'βos/ n. m.
loudspeaker.

alteración /altera'θion; altera-
'sion/ n. f. alteration.

alterar /alte'rar/ v. alter.

alternativa /alterna'tiβa/ n. f. alternative. —**alternativo,** a.

alterno /al'terno/ a. alternate.
—**alternar,** v.

alteza /al'teθa; al'tesa/ n. f. high-
ness.

altivo /al'tiβo/ a. proud, haughty,
lofty.

alto /'alto/ a. **1.** high, tall; loud.
—n. **2.** m. height, story (house).

altura /al'tura/ n. f. height, altitude.

alud /a'luð/ n. m. avalanche.

aludir /alu'ðir/ v. allude.

alumbrado /alum'braðo/ n. m.
lighting.

alumbrar /alum'brar/ v. light.

aluminio /alu'minio/ n. m. aluminum.

alumno /a'lumno/ **-na** n. student,
pupil.

alusión /alu'sion/ n. f. allusion.

alza /'alθa; 'alsa/ n. f. rise; boost.

alzar /al'θar; al'sar/ v. raise, lift.

ama /'ama/ n. f. housewife, mistress (of house). **a. de llaves,**
housekeeper.

amable /a'maβle/ a. kind; pleasant, sweet.

amalgamar /amalga'mar/ v. amalgamate.

amamantar /amaman'tar/ v.
suckle, nurse.

amanecer /amane'θer; amane'ser/
n. **1.** m. dawn, daybreak. —v. **2.**
dawn; awaken.

amante /a'mante/ n. m. & f.
lover.

amapola /ama'pola/ n. f. poppy.

amar /a'mar/ v. love.

amargo /a'margo/ a. bitter.

amargón /amar'gon/ n. m. dandelion.

amargura /amar'gura/ n. f. bitterness.

amarillo /ama'riʎo; ama'riyo/ a.
yellow.

amarradero /amarra'ðero/ n. m.
mooring.

amarrar /ama'rrar/ v. hitch, moor,
tie up.

amartillar /amarti'ʎar; amarti'yar/
v. hammer; cock (a gun).

amasar /ama'sar/ v. knead, mold.

ámbar /'ambar/ n. m. amber.

ambarino /amba'rino/ a. amber.

ambición /ambi'θion; ambi'sion/
n. f. ambition.

ambicionar /ambiθio'nar; ambi-
sio'nar/ v. aspire to.

ambicioso /ambi'θioso; ambi-
'sioso/ a. ambitious.

ambientalista /ambienta'lista/ n.
m. & f. environmentalist.

ambiente /am'biente/ n. m. environment, atmosphere.

ambigüedad /ambigue'ðað/ n. f.
ambiguity.

ambiguo /am'biguo/ a. ambiguous.

ambos /'ambos/ a. & pron. both.

ambulancia /ambu'lanθia;
ambu'lansia/ n. f. ambulance.

amenaza /ame'naθa; ame'nasa/
n. f. threat, menace.

amenazar /amena'θar; amena'sar/
v. threaten, menace.

ameno /a'meno/ a. pleasant.

americana /ameri'kana/ n. f. suit
coat.

americano /ameri'kano/ **-na** a. &
n. American.

ametralladora /ametraʎa'ðora;
ametraya'ðora/ n. f. machine
gun.

amigable /ami'gaβle/ a. amicable,
friendly.

amígdala /a'migðala/ n. f. tonsil.

amigo /a'migo/ **-ga** n. friend.

aminorar /amino'rar/ v. lessen, reduce.

amistad /amis'tað/ n. f. friendship.

amistoso /amis'toso/ a. friendly.

amniocéntesis /amnioθen'tesis/
amniosen'tesis/ n. m. amniocentesis.

amo /'amo/ n. m. master.

amonestaciones /amonesta-
'θiones; amonesta'siones/ n. f.pl.
banns.

amonestar /amones'tar/ v. admonish.

amoníaco /amo'niako/ n. m. ammonia.

amontonar /amonto'nar/ v.
amass, pile up.

anteojos

amor /a'mor/ n. m. love. **a. propio,** self-esteem.

amorío /amo'rio/ n. m. romance, love affair.

amoroso /amo'roso/ a. amorous, loving.

amortecer /amorte'θer; amorte-'ser/ v. deaden.

amparar /ampa'rar/ v. aid, befriend; protect, shield.

amparo /am'paro/ n. m. protection.

ampliar /amp'liar/ v. enlarge; elaborate.

amplificar /amplifi'kar/ v. amplify.

amplio /'amplio/ a. ample, roomy.

ampolla /am'poʎa; am'poya/ n. f. bubble; bulb; blister.

amputar /ampu'tar/ v. amputate.

amueblar /amue'βlar/ v. furnish.

analfabeto /analfa'βeto/ **-ta** a. & n. illiterate.

analgésico /anal'hesiko/ n. m. pain killer.

análisis /a'nalisis/ n. m. analysis.

analizar /anali'θar; anali'sar/ v. analyze.

analogía /analo'hia/ n. f. analogy.

análogo /a'nalogo/ a. similar, analogous.

anarquía /anar'kia/ n. f. anarchy.

anatomía /anato'mia/ n. f. anatomy.

ancho /'antʃo/ a. wide, broad.

anchoa /an'tʃoa/ n. f. anchovy.

anchura /an'tʃura/ n. f. width, breadth.

anciano /an'θiano; an'siano/ **-na** a. & n. old, aged (person).

ancla /'ankla/ n. f. anchor. **—anclar,** v.

anclaje /an'klahe/ n. m. anchorage.

andamio /an'damio/ n. m. scaffold.

andar /an'dar/ v. walk; move, go.

andén /an'den/ n. m. (railroad) platform.

andrajoso /andra'hoso/ a. ragged, uneven.

anécdota /a'nekðota/ n. f. anecdote.

anegar /ane'gar/ v. flood, drown.

anestesia /anes'tesia/ n. f. anesthetic.

anexar /anek'sar/ v. annex.

anexión /anek'sion/ n. f. annexation.

anfitrión /anfitri'on/ **-na** n. host.

ángel /'anhel/ n. m. angel.

angosto /aŋ'gosto/ a. narrow.

anguila /aŋ'gila/ n. f. eel.

angular /aŋgu'lar/ a. angular.

ángulo /'aŋgulo/ n. m. angle.

angustia /aŋ'gustia/ n. f. anguish, agony.

angustiar /aŋgus'tiar/ v. distress.

anhelar /ane'lar/ v. long for.

anidar /ani'ðar/ v. nest, nestle.

anillo /a'niʎo; a'niyo/ n. m. ring; circle.

animación /anima'θion; anima-'sion/ n. f. animation; bustle.

animado /ani'maðo/ a. animated, lively; animate.

animal /ani'mal/ a. & n. animal.

ánimo /'animo/ n. m. state of mind, spirits; courage.

aniquilar /aniki'lar/ v. annihilate, destroy.

aniversario /aniβer'sario/ n. m. anniversary.

anoche /a'notʃe/ adv. last night.

anochecer /anotʃe'θer; anotʃe'ser/ n. **1.** twilight, nightfall. —v. **2.** get dark.

anónimo /a'nonimo/ a. anonymous.

anorexia /ano'reksia/ n. f. anorexia.

anormal /anor'mal/ a. abnormal.

anotación /anota'θion; anota'sion/ n. f. annotation.

anotar /ano'tar/ v. annotate.

ansia /'ansia/ **ansiedad** n. f. anxiety.

ansioso /an'sioso/ a. anxious.

antagonismo /antago'nismo/ n. m. antagonism.

antagonista /antago'nista/ n. m. & f. antagonist, opponent.

anteayer /antea'yer/ adv. day before yesterday.

antebrazo /ante'βraθo; ante-'βraso/ n. m. forearm.

antecedente /anteθe'ðente; antese'ðente/ a. & m. antecedent.

anteceder /anteθe'ðer; antese'ðer/ v. precede.

antecesor /anteθe'sor; antese'sor/ n. m. ancestor.

antemano /ante'mano/ de a., in advance.

antena /an'tena/ n. f. antenna.

antena parabólica /an'tena para'βolika/ satellite dish.

anteojos /ante'ohos/ n. m.pl. eyeglasses.

antepasado /antepa'saðo/ n. m. ancestor.

antepenúltimo /antepe'nultimo/ a. antepenultimate.

anterior /ante'rior/ a. previous, former.

antes /'antes/ adv. before; formerly.

antibala /anti'bala/ a. bulletproof.

anticipación /antiθipa'θion; antisipa'sion/ n. f. anticipation.

anticipar /antiθi'par; antisi'par/ v. anticipate; advance.

anticonceptivo /antikonθep'tiβo; antikonsep'tiβo/ a. & n. contraceptive.

anticongelante /antikonge'lante/ n. m. antifreeze.

anticuado /anti'kuaðo/ a. antiquated, obsolete.

antídoto /an'tiðoto/ n. m. antidote.

antigüedad /antigue'ðað/ n. f. antiquity; antique.

antiguo /an'tiguo/ a. former; old; antique.

antihistamínico /antiista'miniko/ n. m. antihistamine.

antílope /an'tilope/ n. m. antelope.

antinuclear /antinukle'ar/ a. antinuclear.

antipatía /antipa'tia/ n. f. antipathy.

antipático /anti'patiko/ a. disagreeable, nasty.

antiséptico /anti'septiko/ a. & m. antiseptic.

antojarse /anto'harse/ v. **se me antoja...** etc., I desire..., take a fancy to..., etc.

antojo /an'toho/ n. m. whim, fancy.

antorcha /an'tortʃa/ n. f. torch.

antracita /antra'θita; antra'sita/ n. f. anthracite.

anual /a'nual/ a. annual, yearly.

anudar /anu'ðar/ v. knot; tie.

anular /anu'lar/ v. annul, void.

anunciar /anun'θiar; anun'siar/ v. announce; proclaim; advertise.

anuncio /a'nunθio; a'nunsio/ n. m. announcement; advertisement.

añadir /aɲa'ðir/ v. add.

añil /a'ɲil/ n. m. bluing; indigo.

año /'aɲo/ n. m. year.

apacible /apa'θiβle; apa'siβle/ a. peaceful, peaceable.

apaciguamiento /a,paθigua'miento; a,pasigua'miento/ n. m. appeasement.

apaciguar /apaθi'guar; apasi'guar/ v. appease; placate.

apagado /apa'gaðo/ a. dull.

apagar /apa'gar/ v. extinguish, quench, put out.

apagón /apa'gn/ n. m. blackout.

aparador /apara'ðor/ n. m. buffet, cupboard.

aparato /apa'rato/ n. m. apparatus; machine; appliance, set.

aparcamiento /aparka'miento/ n. m. parking lot; parking space.

aparecer /apare'θer; apare'ser/ v. appear, show up.

aparejo /apa'reho/ n. m. rig.
—**aparejar**, v.

aparentar /aparen'tar/ v. pretend; profess.

aparente /apa'rente/ a. apparent.

apariencia /apa'rienθia; apa'riensia/ **aparición** n. f. appearance.

apartado /apar'taðo/ a. **1.** aloof; separate. —n. **2.** m. post-office box.

apartamento /aparta'mento/ n. m. apartment. **a. en propiedad,** condominium.

apartar /apar'tar/ v. separate; remove.

aparte /a'parte/ adv. apart; aside.

apartheid /apar'teið/ n. m. apartheid.

apasionado /apasio'naðo/ a. passionate.

apatía /apa'tia/ n. f. apathy.

apearse /ape'arse/ v. get off, alight.

apedrear /apeðre'ar/ v. stone.

apelación /apela'θion; apela'sion/ n. f. appeal. —**apelar**, v.

apellido /ape'ʎiðo; ape'yiðo/ n. m. family name.

apellido materno /ape'ʎiðo ma'terno; ape'yiðo ma'terno/ mother's family name.

apellido paterno /ape'ʎiðo pa'terno; ape'yiðo pa'terno/ father's family name.

apenas /a'penas/ adv. scarcely, hardly.

apéndice /a'pendiθe; a'pendise/ n. m. appendix.

apercibir /aperθi'βir; apersi'βir/ v. prepare, warn.

aperitivo /aperi'tiβo/ n. m. appetizer.

aperos /a'peros/ n. m.pl. implements.

apestar /apes'tar/ v. infect; stink.

apetecer /apete'θer/ apete'ser/ v. desire, have appetite for.

apetito /ape'tito/ n. m. appetite.

ápice /'apiθe/ 'apise/ n. m. apex.

apilar /api'lar/ v. stack.

apio /'apio/ n. m. celery.

aplacar /apla'kar/ v. appease; placate.

aplastar /aplas'tar/ v. crush, flatten.

aplaudir /aplau'ðir/ v. applaud, cheer.

aplauso /a'plauso/ n. m. applause.

aplazar /apla'θar/ apla'sar/ v. postpone, put off.

aplicable /apli'kaβle/ a. applicable.

aplicado /apli'kaðo/ a. industrious, diligent.

aplicar /apli'kar/ v. apply.

aplomo /a'plomo/ n. m. aplomb, poise.

apoderado /apoðe'raðo/ **-da** n. attorney.

apoderarse de /apoðe'rarse de/ v. get hold of, seize.

apodo /a'poðo/ n. m. nickname. —**apodar,** v.

apologético /apolo'hetiko/ a. apologetic.

apoplejía /apople'hia/ n. f. apoplexy.

aposento /apo'sento/ n. m. room, flat.

apostar /apos'tar/ v. bet, wager.

apóstol /a'postol/ n. m. apostle.

apoyar /apo'yar/ v. support; prop; lean.

apoyo /a'poyo/ n. m. support; prop; aid; approval.

apreciable /apre'θiaβle/ apre'siaβle/ a. appreciable.

apreciar /apre'θiar/ apre'siar/ v. appreciate, prize.

aprecio /a'preθio/ a'presio/ n. m. appreciation, regard.

apremio /a'premio/ n. m. pressure, compulsion.

aprender /apren'der/ v. learn.

aprendiz /apren'diθ/ apren'dis/ n. m. apprentice.

aprendizaje /aprendi'θahe/ aprendi'sahe/ n. m. apprenticeship.

aprensión /apren'sion/ n. f. apprehension.

aprensivo /apren'siβo/ a. apprehensive.

apresurado /apresu'raðo/ a. hasty, fast.

apresurar /apresu'rar/ v. hurry, speed up.

apretado /apre'taðo/ a. tight.

apretar /apre'tar/ v. squeeze, press; tighten.

apretón /apre'ton/ n. m. squeeze.

aprieto /a'prieto/ n. m. plight, predicament.

aprobación /aproβa'θion/ aproβa'sion/ n. f. approbation, approval.

aprobar /apro'βar/ v. approve.

apropiación /apropia'θion/ apropia'sion/ n. f. appropriation.

apropiado /apro'piaðo/ a. appropriate. —**apropiar,** v.

aprovechar /aproβe'tʃar/ v. profit by.

aprovecharse /aproβe'tʃarse/ v. take advantage.

aproximado /aproksi'maðo/ a. approximate.

aproximarse a /aproksi'marse a/ v. approach.

aptitud /apti'tuð/ n. f. aptitude.

apto /'apto/ a. apt.

apuesta /a'puesta/ n. f. bet, wager, stake.

apuntar /apun'tar/ v. point, aim; prompt; write down.

apunte /a'punte/ n. m. annotation, note; promptings, cue.

apuñalar /apuɲa'lar/ v. stab.

apurar /apu'rar/ v. hurry; worry.

apuro /a'puro/ n. m. predicament, scrape, trouble.

aquel /a'kel/ **aquella** dem. a. that.

aquél /a'kel/ **aquélla** dem. pron. that (one); the former.

aquello /a'keʎo/ a'keyo/ dem. pron. that.

aquí /a'ki/ adv. here. **por a.,** this way.

aquietar /akie'tar/ v. allay; lull; pacify.

ara /'ara/ n. f. altar.

árabe /'araβe/ a. & n. Arab, Arabic.

arado /a'raðo/ n. m. plow. —**arar,** v.

arándano /a'randano/ n. m. cranberry.

araña /a'raɲa/ n. f. spider. **a. de luces,** chandelier.

arbitración /arβitra'θion/ arβitra'sion/ n. f. arbitration.

arbitrador /arβitraˈðor/ **-ra** n. arbitrator.

arbitraje /arβiˈtrahe/ n. m. arbitration.

arbitrar /arβiˈtrar/ v. arbitrate.

arbitrario /arβiˈtrario/ a. arbitrary.

árbitro /ˈarβitro/ n. m. arbiter, umpire, referee.

árbol /ˈarβol/ n. m. tree; mast.

árbol genealógico /ˈarβol heneaˈlohiko/ family tree.

arbusto /arˈβusto/ n. m. bush, shrub.

arca /ˈarka/ n. f. chest; ark.

arcada /arˈkaða/ n. f. arcade.

arcaico /arˈkaiko/ a. archaic.

arce /ˈarθe; ˈarse/ n. m. maple.

archipiélago /artʃiˈpielago/ n. m. archipelago.

archivador /artʃiβaˈðor/ n. m. file cabinet.

archivo /arˈtʃiβo/ n. m. archive; file. **—archivar,** v.

arcilla /arˈθiʎa; arˈsiya/ n. f. clay.

arco /ˈarko/ n. m. arc; arch; (archer's) bow. **a. iris,** rainbow.

arder /arˈðer/ v. burn.

ardid /arˈðið/ n. m. stratagem, cunning.

ardiente /arˈðiente/ a. ardent, burning, fiery.

ardilla /arˈðiʎa; arˈðiya/ n. f. squirrel.

ardor /arˈðor/ n. m. ardor, fervor.

ardor de estómago /arˈðor de esˈtomago/ heartburn.

arduo /ˈarðuo/ a. arduous.

área /ˈarea/ n. f. area.

arena /aˈrena/ n. f. sand; arena.

arenoso /areˈnoso/ a. sandy.

arenque /aˈrenke/ n. m. herring.

arete /aˈrete/ n. earring.

argentino /arhenˈtino/ **-na** a. & n. Argentine.

argüir /arˈguir/ v. dispute, argue.

árido /ˈariðo/ a. arid.

aristocracia /aristoˈkraθia; aristoˈkrasia/ n. f. aristocracy.

aristócrata /arisˈtokrata/ n. f. aristocrat.

aristocrático /aristoˈkratiko/ a. aristocratic.

aritmética /aritˈmetika/ n. f. arithmetic.

arma /ˈarma/ n. f. weapon, arm.

armadura /armaˈðura/ n. f. armor; reinforcement; framework.

armamento /armaˈmento/ n. m. armament.

armar /arˈmar/ v. arm.

armario /arˈmario/ n. m. cabinet, bureau, wardrobe.

armazón /armaˈθon; armaˈson/ n. m. framework, frame.

armería /armeˈria/ n. f. armory.

armisticio /armisˈtiθio; armisˈtisio/ n. m. armistice.

armonía /armoˈnia/ n. f. harmony.

armonioso /armoˈnioso/ a. harmonious.

armonizar /armoniˈθar; armoniˈsar/ v. harmonize.

arnés /arˈnes/ n. m. harness.

aroma /aˈroma/ n. f. aroma, fragrance.

aromático /aroˈmatiko/ a. aromatic.

arpa /ˈarpa/ n. f. harp.

arquear /arkeˈar/ v. arch.

arquitecto /arkiˈtekto/ n. m. architect.

arquitectura /arkitekˈtura/ n. f. architecture.

arquitectural /arkitektuˈral/ a. architectural.

arrabal /arraˈβal/ n. m. suburb.

arraigar /arraiˈgar/ v. take root, settle.

arrancar /arranˈkar/ v. pull out, tear out; start up.

arranque /aˈrranke/ n. m. dash, sudden start; fit of anger.

arrastrar /arrasˈtrar/ v. drag.

arrebatar /arreβaˈtar/ v. snatch, grab.

arrebato /arreˈβato/ n. m. sudden attack, fit of anger.

arrecife /arreˈθife; arreˈsife/ n. m. reef.

arreglar /arreˈglar/ v. arrange; repair, fix; adjust, settle.

arreglárselas /arreˈglarselas/ v. manage, shift for oneself.

arreglo /aˈrreglo/ n. m. arrangement, settlement.

arremangarse /arremanˈgarse/ v. roll up one's sleeves; roll up one's pants.

arremeter /arremeˈter/ v. attack.

arrendar /arrenˈdar/ v. rent.

arrepentimiento /arrepentiˈmiento/ n. m. repentance.

arrepentirse /arrepenˈtirse/ v. repent.

arrestar /arresˈtar/ v. arrest.

arriba /aˈrriβa/ adv. up; upstairs.

arriendo /aˈrriendo/ n. m. lease.

arriero /aˈrriero/ n. m. muleteer.

arriesgar /arriesˈgar/ v. risk.

arrimarse /arriˈmarse/ v. lean.

arrodillarse /arroði'ʎarse; arroði-'yarse/ v. kneel.

arrogancia /arro'ganθia; arro-'gansia/ n. f. arrogance.

arrogante /arro'gante/ a. arrogant.

arrojar /arro'har/ v. throw, hurl; shed.

arrollar /arro'ʎar; arro'yar/ v. roll, coil.

arroyo /a'rroyo/ n. m. brook; gully; gutter.

arroz /a'rroθ; a'rros/ n. m. rice.

arruga /a'rruga/ n. f. ridge; wrinkle.

arrugar /arru'gar/ v. wrinkle, crumple.

arruinar /arrui'nar/ v. ruin, destroy, wreck.

arsenal /arse'nal/ n. m. arsenal; armory.

arsénico /ar'seniko/ n. m. arsenic.

arte /'arte/ n. m. (f. in pl.) art, craft; wiliness.

arteria /ar'teria/ n. f. artery.

artesa /ar'tesa/ n. f. trough.

artesano /arte'sano/ **-na** n. artisan, craftsman.

ártico /'artiko/ a. arctic.

articulación /artikula'θion; artikula'sion/ n. f. articulation; joint.

articular /artiku'lar/ v. articulate.

artículo /ar'tikulo/ n. m. article.

artífice /ar'tifiθe; ar'tifise/ n. m. & f. artisan.

artificial /artifi'θial; artifi'sial/ a. artificial.

artificio /artifi'θio; artifi'sio/ n. m. artifice, device.

artificioso /artifi'θioso; artifi-'sioso/ a. affected.

artillería /artiʎe'ria; artiye'ria/ n. f. artillery.

artista /ar'tista/ n. m. & f. artist.

artístico /ar'tistiko/ a. artistic.

artritis /ar'tritis/ n. f. arthritis.

arzobispo /arθo'βispo; arso'βispo/ n. m. archbishop.

as /as/ n. m. ace.

asado /a'saðo/ a. & n. roast.

asaltador /asalta'ðor/ **-ra** n. assailant.

asaltante /asal'tante/ n. m. & f. mugger.

asaltar /asal'tar/ v. assail, attack.

asalto /a'salto/ n. m. assault. **—asaltar,** v.

asamblea /asam'βlea/ n. f. assembly.

asar /a'sar/ v. roast; broil, cook (meat).

asaz /a'saθ; a'sas/ adv. enough; quite.

ascender /asθen'der; assen'der/ v. ascend, go up; amount.

ascenso /as'θenso; as'senso/ n. m. ascent.

ascensor /asθen'sor; assen'sor/ n. m. elevator.

ascensorista /asθenso'rista; assenso'rista/ n. m. & f. (elevator) operator.

asco /'asko/ n. m. nausea; disgusting thing. **qué a.,** how disgusting!

aseado /ase'aðo/ a. tidy. **—asear,** v.

asediar /ase'ðiar/ v. besiege.

asedio /ase'ðio/ n. m. siege.

asegurar /asegu'rar/ v. assure; secure.

asegurarse /asegu'rarse/ v. make sure.

asemejarse a /aseme'harse a/ v. resemble.

asentar /asen'tar/ v. settle; seat.

asentimiento /asenti'miento/ n. m. assent. **—asentir,** v.

aseo /a'seo/ n. m. neatness, tidiness.

aseos /a'seos/ n. m.pl. restroom.

asequible /ase'kiβle/ a. attainable; affordable.

aserción /aser'θion; aser'sion/ n. f. assertion.

aserrar /ase'rrar/ v. saw.

asesinar /asesi'nar/ v. assassinate; murder, slay.

asesinato /asesi'nato/ n. m. assassination; murder.

asesino /ase'sino/ **-na** n. murderer, assassin.

aseveración /aseβera'θion; aseβera'sion/ n. f. assertion.

aseverar /aseβe'rar/ v. assert.

asfalto /as'falto/ n. m. asphalt.

así /a'si/ adv. so, thus, this way, that way. **a. como,** as well as. **a. que,** as soon as.

asiático /a'siatiko/ **-ca** a. & n. Asiatic.

asiduo /a'siðuo/ a. assiduous.

asiento /a'siento/ n. m. seat; chair; site.

asiento delantero /a'siento de-lan'tero/ front seat.

asiento trasero /a'siento tra'sero/ back seat.

asignar /asiɡ'nar/ v. assign; allot.

asilo /a'silo/ n. m. asylum, sanctuary.

asimilar /asimi'lar/ v. assimilate.

asir /a'sir/ v. grasp.

asistencia /asis'tenθia; asistensia/ n. f. attendance, presence.

asistir /asis'tir/ v. be present, attend.

asno /'asno/ n. m. donkey.

asociación /asoθia'θion; asosia-'sion/ n. f. association.

asociado /aso'θiaðo; aso'siaðo/ n. m. associate, partner.

asociar /aso'θiar; aso'siar/ v. associate.

asolar /aso'lar/ v. desolate; burn, parch.

asoleado /asole'aðo/ a. sunny.

asomar /aso'mar/ v. appear, loom up, show up.

asombrar /asom'βrar/ v. astonish, amaze.

asombro /a'sombro/ n. m. amazement, astonishment.

aspa /'aspa/ n. f. reel. —**aspar**, v.

aspecto /as'pekto/ n. m. aspect.

aspereza /aspe'reθa; aspe'resa/ n. f. harshness.

áspero /'aspero/ a. rough, harsh.

aspiración /aspira'θion; aspira-'sion/ n. f. aspiration.

aspirador /aspira'ðor/ n. m. vacuum cleaner.

aspirar /aspi'rar/ v. aspire.

aspirina /aspi'rina/ n. f. aspirin.

asqueroso /aske'roso/ a. dirty, nasty, filthy.

asta /'asta/ n. f. shaft.

asterisco /aste'risko/ n. m. asterisk.

astilla /as'tiʎa; as'tiya/ n. f. splinter, chip. —**astillar**, v.

astillero /asti'ʎero; asti'yero/ n. m. dry dock.

astro /'astro/ n. m. star.

astronauta /astro'nauta/ n. m. & f. astronaut.

astronave /astro'naβe/ n. f. spaceship.

astronomía /astrono'mia/ n. f. astronomy.

astucia /as'tuθia; as'tusia/ n. f. cunning.

astuto /as'tuto/ a. astute, sly, shrewd.

asumir /asu'mir/ v. assume.

asunto /a'sunto/ n. m. matter, affair, business; subject.

asustar /asus'tar/ v. frighten, scare, startle.

atacar /ata'kar/ v. attack, charge.

atajo /a'taho/ n. m. shortcut.

ataque /a'take/ n. m. attack, charge; spell, stroke.

ataque cardíaco /a'take kar'ðiako/ heart attack.

atar /a'tar/ v. tie, bind, fasten.

atareado /atare'aðo/ a. busy.

atascar /atas'kar/ v. stall, stop, obstruct.

atasco /a'tasko/ n. m. traffic jam.

ataúd /ata'uð/ n. m. casket, coffin.

atavío /ata'βio/ n. m. dress; gear, equipment.

atemorizar /atemori'θar; atemori'sar/ v. frighten.

atención /aten'θion; aten'sion/ n. f. attention.

atender /aten'der/ v. heed; attend to, wait on.

atenerse a /ate'nerse a/ v. count on, depend on.

atentado /aten'taðo/ n. m. crime, offense.

atento /a'tento/ a. attentive, courteous.

ateo /a'teo/ n. m. atheist.

aterrizaje /aterri'θahe; aterri'sahe/ n. m. landing (of aircraft).

aterrizaje forzoso /aterri'θahe for'θoso; aterri'sahe for'soso/ emergency landing, forced landing.

aterrizar /aterri'θar; aterri'sar/ v. land.

atesorar /ateso'rar/ v. hoard.

atestar /ates'tar/ v. witness.

atestiguar /atesti'guar/ v. attest, testify.

atinar /ati'nar/ v. hit upon.

atisbar /atis'βar/ v. scrutinize, pry.

Atlántico /at'lantiko/ n. m. Atlantic.

atlántico a. Atlantic.

atlas /'atlas/ n. m. atlas.

atleta /at'leta/ n. m. & f. athlete.

atlético /at'letiko/ a. athletic.

atletismo /atle'tismo/ n. m. athletics.

atmósfera /at'mosfera/ n. f. atmosphere.

atmosférico /atmos'feriko/ a. atmospheric.

atolladero /atoʎa'ðero; atoya'ðero/ n. m. dead end, impasse.

atómico /a'tomiko/ a. atomic.

átomo /'atomo/ n. m. atom.

atormentar /atormen'tar/ v. torment, plague.

atornillar /atorni'ʎar; atorni'yar/ v. screw.

atracción /atrak'θion; atrak'sion/ n. f. attraction.

atractivo /atrak'tiβo/ a. **1.** attractive. —n. **2.** m. attraction.

atraer /atra'er/ v. attract; lure.

atrapar /atra'par/ v. trap, catch.

atrás /a'tras/ adv. back; behind.

atrasado /atra'saðo/ a. belated; backward; slow (clock).

atrasar /atra'sar/ v. delay, retard; be slow.

atraso /a'traso/ n. m. delay; backwardness; (pl.) arrears.

atravesar /atraβe'sar/ v. cross.

atreverse /atre'βerse/ v. dare.

atrevido /atre'βiðo/ a. daring, bold.

atrevimiento /atreβi'miento/ n. m. boldness.

atribuir /atri'βuir/ v. attribute, ascribe.

atributo /atri'βuto/ n. m. attribute.

atrincherar /atrintʃe'rar/ v. entrench.

atrocidad /atroθi'ðað; atrosi'ðað/ n. f. atrocity, outrage.

atronar /atro'nar/ v. deafen.

atropellar /atrope'ʎar; atrope'yar/ v. trample; fell.

atroz /a'troθ; a'tros/ a. atrocious.

atún /a'tun/ n. m. tuna.

aturdir /atur'ðir/ v. daze, stun, bewilder.

audacia /au'ðaθia; au'ðasia/ n. f. audacity.

audaz /au'ðaθ; au'ðas/ a. audacious, bold.

audible /au'ðiβle/ a. audible.

audífono /au'ðifono/ n. m. hearing aid.

audiovisual /auðioβi'sual/ a. audiovisual.

auditorio /auði'torio/ n. m. audience.

aula /'aula/ n. f. classroom, hall.

aullar /au'ʎar; au'yar/ v. howl, bay.

aullido /au'ʎiðo; au'yiðo/ n. m. howl.

aumentar /aumen'tar/ v. augment; increase, swell.

aun /a'un/ **aún** adv. still; even. **a. cuando,** even though, even if.

aunque /'aunke/ conj. although, though.

áureo /'aureo/ a. golden.

aureola /aure'ola/ n. f. halo.

auriculares /auriku'lares/ n. m.pl. headphones.

aurora /au'rora/ n. f. dawn.

ausencia /au'senθia; au'sensia/ n. f. absence.

ausentarse /ausen'tarse/ v. stay away.

ausente /au'sente/ a. absent.

auspicio /aus'piθio; aus'pisio/ n. m. auspice.

austeridad /austeri'ðað/ n. f. austerity.

austero /aus'tero/ a. austere.

austríaco /aus'triako/ **-ca** a. & n. Austrian.

auténtico /au'tentiko/ a. authentic.

auto /'auto/ **automóvil** n. m. auto, automobile.

autobús /auto'βus/ n. m. bus.

autocine /auto'θine; auto'sine/ **autocinema** n. m. drive-in (movie theater).

automático /auto'matiko/ a. automatic.

autonomía /autono'mia/ n. f. autonomy.

autopista /auto'pista/ n. f. expressway.

autor /au'tor/ n. m. author.

autoridad /autori'ðað/ n. f. authority.

autoritario /autori'tario/ a. authoritarian; authoritative.

autorizar /autori'θar; autori'sar/ v. authorize.

autostop /auto'stop/ n. m. hitchhiking. **hacer a.,** to hitchhike.

auxiliar /auksi'liar/ a. **1.** auxiliary. —v. **2.** assist, aid.

auxilio /auk'silio/ n. m. aid, assistance.

avaluar /aβa'luar/ v. evaluate, appraise.

avance /a'βaŋθe; a'βanse/ n. m. advance. —**avanzar,** v.

avaricia /aβa'riθia; aβa'risia/ n. f. avarice.

avariento /aβa'riento/ a. miserly, greedy.

avaro /a'βaro/ **-ra** a. & m. miser; miserly.

ave /'aβe/ n. f. bird.

avellana /aβe'ʎana; aβe'yana/ n. f. hazelnut.

Ave María /aβema'ria/ *n. m.* Hail Mary.

avena /a'βena/ *n. f.* oat.

avenida /aβe'niða/ *n. f.* avenue; flood.

avenirse /aβe'nirse/ *v.* compromise; agree.

aventajar /aβenta'har/ *v.* surpass, get ahead of.

aventar /aβen'tar/ *v.* fan; scatter.

aventura /aβen'tura/ *n. f.* adventure.

aventurar /aβentu'rar/ *v.* venture, risk, gamble.

aventurero /aβentu'rero/ **-ra** *a.* & *n.* adventurous; adventurer.

avergonzado /aβergon'θaðo; aβergon'saðo/ *a.* ashamed, abashed.

avergonzar /aβergon'θar; aβergon'sar/ *v.* shame, abash.

avería /aβe'ria/ *n. f.* damage.
—**averiar,** *v.*

averiguar /aβeri'guar/ *v.* ascertain, find out.

aversión /aβer'sion/ *n. f.* aversion.

avestruz /aβes'truθ; aβes'trus/ *n. m.* ostrich.

aviación /aβia'θion; aβia'sion/ *n. f.* aviation.

aviador /aβia'ðor/ **-ra** *n.* aviator.

ávido /a'βiðo/ *a.* avid; eager.

avión /a'βion/ *n. m.* airplane.

avisar /aβi'sar/ *v.* notify, let know; warn, advise.

aviso /a'βiso/ *n. m.* notice, announcement; advertisement; warning.

avispa /a'βispa/ *n. f.* wasp.

avivar /aβi'βar/ *v.* enliven, revive.

axila /ak'sila/ *n. f.* armpit.

aya /'aya/ *n. f.* governess.

ayatolá /aya'tola/ *n. m.* ayatollah.

ayer /a'yer/ *adv.* yesterday.

ayuda /a'yuða/ *n. f.* help, aid.
—**ayudar,** *v.*

ayudante /ayu'ðante/ *a.* assistant, helper; adjutant.

ayuno /a'yuno/ *n. m.* fast.
—**ayunar,** *v.*

ayuntamiento /ayunta'miento/ *n. m.* city hall.

azada /a'θaða; a'saða/ *n. f.,* **azadón,** *m.* hoe.

azafata /aθa'fata; asa'fata/ *n. f.* stewardess, flight attendant.

azar /a'θar; a'sar/ *n. m.* hazard, chance. **al a.,** at random.

azotar /aθo'tar; aso'tar/ *v.* whip, flog; belabor.

azote /a'θote; a'sote/ *n. m.* scourge, lash.

azúcar /a'θukar; a'sukar/ *n. m.* sugar.

azucarero /aθuka'rero; asuka'rero/ *n. m.* sugar bowl.

azúcar moreno /a'θukar mo'reno; a'sukar mo'reno/ brown sugar.

azul /a'θul; a'sul/ *a.* blue.

azulado /aθu'laðo; asu'laðo/ *a.* blue, bluish.

azulejo /aθu'leho; asu'leho/ *n. m.* tile; bluebird.

azul marino /a'θul ma'rino; a'sul ma'rino/ navy blue.

B

baba /'baβa/ *n. f.* drivel.
—**babear,** *v.*

babador /baβa'ðor, ba'βero/ *n. m.* bib.

babucha /ba'βutʃa/ *n. f.* slipper.

bacalao /baka'lao/ *n. m.* codfish.

bachiller /batʃi'yer; batʃi'yer/ **-ra** *n.* bachelor (degree).

bacía /ba'θia; ba'sia/ *n. f.* washbasin.

bacterias /bak'terias/ *n. f.pl.* bacteria.

bacteriología /bakteriolo'hia/ *n. f.* bacteriology.

bahía /ba'ia/ *n. f.* bay.

bailador /baila'ðor/ **-ra** *n.* dancer.

bailar /bai'lar/ *v.* dance.

bailarín /baila'rin/ **-ina** *n.* dancer.

baile /'baile/ *n. m.* dance.

baja /'baha/ *n. f.* fall (in price); *Mil.* casualty.

bajar /ba'har/ *v.* lower; descend.

bajeza /ba'heθa; ba'hesa/ *n. f.* baseness.

bajo /'baho/ *prep.* **1.** under, below. —*a.* **2.** low; short; base.

bala /'bala/ *n. f.* bullet; ball; bale.

balada /ba'laða/ *n. f.* ballad.

balancear /balanθe'ar; balanse'ar/ *v.* balance; roll, swing, sway.

balanza /ba'lanθa; ba'lansa/ *n. f.* balance; scales.

balbuceo /balβu'θeo; balβu'seo/ *n. m.* stammer; babble.
—**balbucear,** *v.*

Balcanes /bal'kanes/ *n. m.pl.* Balkans.

balcón /bal'kon/ *n. m.* balcony.

balde /'balde/ *n. m.* bucket, pail. **de b.**, gratis. **en b.**, in vain.

balística /ba'listika/ *n. f.* ballistics.

ballena /ba'ʎena; ba'yena/ *n. f.* whale.

balneario /balne'ario/ *n. m.* bathing resort; spa.

balompié /balom'pie/ *n. m.* football.

balón /ba'lon/ *n. m.* football; *Auto.* balloon tire.

baloncesto /balon'θesto; balon-'sesto/ *n. m.* basketball.

balota /ba'lota/ *n. f.* ballot, vote. **—balotar,** *v.*

balsa /'balsa/ *n. f.* raft.

bálsamo /'balsamo/ *n. m.* balm.

baluarte /ba'luarte/ *n. m.* bulwark.

bambolearse /bambole'arse/ *v.* sway.

bambú /bam'βu/ *n.* bamboo.

banal /ba'nal/ *a.* banal, trite.

banana /ba'nana/ *n. f.* banana.

banano /ba'nano/ *n. m.* banana tree.

bancarrota /banka'rrota/ *n. f.* bankruptcy.

banco /'banko/ *n. m.* bank; bench; school of fish.

banco cooperativo /'banko koopera'tiβo/ credit union.

banda /'banda/ *n. f.* band.

bandada /ban'daða/ *n. f.* covey, flock.

banda sonora /'banda so'nora/ *n. f.* soundtrack.

bandeja /ban'deha/ *n. f.* tray.

bandera /ban'dera/ *n. f.* flag; banner; ensign.

bandido /ban'diðo/ **-da** *n.* bandit.

bando /'bando/ *n. m.* faction.

bandolero /bando'lero/ **-ra** *n.* bandit, robber.

banquero /ban'kero/ **-ra** *n.* banker.

banqueta /ban'keta/ *n. f.* stool; (Mex.) sidewalk.

banquete /ban'kete/ *n. m.* feast, banquet.

banquillo /ban'kiʎo; ban'kiyo/ *n. m.* stool.

bañar /ba'ɲar/ *v.* bathe.

bañera /ba'ɲera/ *n. f.* bathtub.

baño /'baɲo/ *n. m.* bath; bathroom.

bar /bar/ *n. m.* bar, pub.

baraja /ba'raha/ *n. f.* pack of cards; game of cards.

baranda /ba'randa/ *n. f.* railing, banister.

barato /ba'rato/ *a.* cheap.

barba /'barβa/ *n. f.* beard; chin.

barbacoa /barβa'koa/ *n. f.* barbecue; stretcher.

barbaridad /barβari'ðað/ *n. f.* barbarity; *Colloq.* excess (in anything).

bárbaro /'barβaro/ *a.* barbarous; crude.

barbería /barβe'ria/ *n. f.* barbershop.

barbero /bar'βero/ *n. m.* barber.

barca /'barka/ *n. f.* (small) boat.

barcaza /bar'kaθa; bar'kasa/ *n. f.* barge.

barco /'barko/ *n. m.* ship, boat.

barniz /bar'niθ; bar'nis/ *n. m.* varnish. **—barnizar,** *v.*

barómetro /ba'rometro/ *n. m.* barometer.

barón /ba'ron/ *n. m.* baron.

barquilla /bar'kiʎa; bar'kiya/ *n. f. Naut.* log.

barra /'barra/ *n. f.* bar.

barraca /ba'rraka/ *n. f.* hut, shed.

barrear /barre'ar/ *v.* bar, barricade.

barreno /ba'rreno/ *n. m.* blast, blasting. **—barrenar,** *v.*

barrer /ba'rrer/ *v.* sweep.

barrera /ba'rrera/ *n. f.* barrier.

barricada /barri'kaða/ *n. f.* barricade.

barriga /ba'rriga/ *n. f.* belly.

barril /ba'rril/ *n. m.* barrel; cask.

barrio /'barrio/ *n. m.* district, ward, quarter.

barro /'barro/ *n. m.* clay, mud.

base /'base/ *n. f.* base; basis.

base de datos /'base de 'datos/ database.

bastante /bas'tante/ *a.* **1.** enough, plenty of. *—adv.* **2.** enough; rather, quite.

bastar /bas'tar/ *v.* suffice, be enough.

bastardo /bas'tarðo/ **-a** *a. & n.* bastard.

bastear /baste'ar/ *v.* baste.

bastidor /basti'ðor/ *n. m.* wing (in theater).

bastón /bas'ton/ *n. m.* (walking) cane.

bastos /'bastos/ *n. m.pl.* clubs (cards).

basura /ba'sura/ *n. f.* refuse, dirt; garbage; junk.

basurero /basu'rero/ **-ra** *n.* scavenger.

batalla /ba'taʎa; ba'taya/ *n. f.* battle. —**batallar,** *v.*

batallón /bata'ʎon; bata'yon/ *n. m.* battalion.

batata /ba'tata/ *n. f.* sweet potato.

bate /'bate/ *n. m.* bat. —**batear,** *v.*

batería /bate'ria/ *n. f.* battery.

batido /ba'tiðo/ *n. m.* (cooking) batter; milkshake.

batidora /bati'ðora/ *n. f.* mixer (for food).

batir /ba'tir/ *v.* beat; demolish; conquer.

baúl /ba'ul/ *n. m.* trunk.

bautismo /bau'tismo/ *n. m.* baptism.

bautista /bau'tista/ *n. m. & f.* Baptist.

bautizar /bauti'θar; bauti'sar/ *v.* christen, baptize.

bautizo /bau'tiθo; bau'tiso/ *n. m.* baptism.

baya /'baia/ *n. f.* berry.

bayoneta /bayo'neta/ *n. f.* bayonet.

beato /be'ato/ *a.* blessed.

bebé /be'βe/ *n. m.* baby.

beber /be'βer/ *v.* drink.

bebible /be'βiβle/ *a.* drinkable.

bebida /be'βiða/ *n. f.* drink, beverage.

beca /'beka/ *n. f.* grant, scholarship.

becado /be'kaðo/ **-da** *n.* scholar.

becerro /be'θerro; be'serro/ *n. m.* calf; calfskin.

beldad /bel'dað/ *n. f.* beauty.

belga /'belga/ *a. & n.* Belgian.

Bélgica /'belxika/ *n. f.* Belgium.

belicoso /beli'koso/ *a.* warlike.

beligerante /belixe'rante/ *a. & n.* belligerent.

bellaco /be'ʎako; be'yako/ *a.* **1.** sly, roguish. —*n.* **2.** rogue.

bellas artes /'beʎas 'artes; 'beyas 'artes/ *n. f.pl.* fine arts.

belleza /be'ʎeθa; be'yesa/ *n. f.* beauty.

bello /'beʎo; 'beyo/ *a.* beautiful.

bellota /be'ʎota; be'yota/ *n. f.* acorn.

bendecir /bende'θir; bende'sir/ *v.* bless.

bendición /bendi'θion; bendi'sion/ *n. f.* blessing, benediction.

bendito /ben'dito/ *a.* blessed.

beneficio /bene'fiθio; bene'fisio/ *n. m.* benefit. —**beneficiar,** *v.*

beneficioso /benefi'θioso; benefi'sioso/ *a.* beneficial.

benevolencia /beneβo'lenθia; beneβo'lensia/ *n. f.* benevolence.

benévolo /be'neβolo/ *a.* benevolent.

benigno /be'nigno/ *a.* benign.

beodo /be'oðo/ **-da** *a. & n.* drunk.

berenjena /beren'hena/ *n. f.* eggplant.

beso /'beso/ *n. m.* kiss. —**besar,** *v.*

bestia /'bestia/ *n. f.* beast, brute.

betabel /beta'βel/ *n. m.* beet.

Biblia /'biβlia/ *n. f.* Bible.

bíblico /'biβliko/ *a.* Biblical.

biblioteca /biβlio'teka/ *n. f.* library.

bicarbonato /bikarβo'nato/ *n. m.* bicarbonate.

bicicleta /biθi'kleta; bisi'kleta/ *n. f.* bicycle.

bien /bien/ *adv.* **1.** well. —*n.* **2.** good; (*pl.*) possessions.

bienes inmuebles /'bienes i'mueβles/ *n. m.pl.* real estate.

bienestar /bienes'tar/ *n. m.* well-being, welfare.

bienhechor /biene'tʃor/ **-ra** *n.* benefactor.

bienvenida /biembe'niða/ *n. f.* welcome.

bienvenido /biembe'niðo/ *a.* welcome.

biftec /bif'tek/ *n. m.* steak.

bifurcación /bifurka'θion; bifurka'sion/ *n. f.* fork. —**bifurcar,** *v.*

bigamia /bi'gamia/ *n. f.* bigamy.

bígamo /'bigamo/ **-a** *n.* bigamist.

bigotes /bi'gotes/ *n. m.pl.* mustache.

bikini /bi'kini/ *n. m.* bikini.

bilingüe /bi'lingue/ *a.* bilingual.

bilingüismo /bilin'guismo/ *n. m.* bilingualism.

bilis /'bilis/ *n. f.* bile.

billar /bi'ʎar; bi'yar/ *n. m.* billiards.

billete /bi'ʎete; bi'yete/ *n. m.* ticket; bank note, bill.

billete de banco /bi'ʎete de 'banko; bi'yete de 'banko/ bank note.

billón /bi'ʎon; bi'yon/ n. m. billion.

bingo /'biŋgo/ n. m. bingo.

biodegradable /bioðegra'ðaβle/ a. biodegradable.

biografía /biogra'fia/ n. f. biography.

biología /biolo'hia/ n. f. biology.

biombo /'biombo/ n. m. folding screen.

bisabuela /bisa'βuela/ n. f. great-grandmother.

bisabuelo /bisa'βuelo/ n. m. great-grandfather.

bisel /bi'sel/ n. m. bevel. —**biselar,** v.

bisonte /bi'sonte/ n. m. bison.

bisté /bis'te/ **bistec** n. m. steak.

bisutería /bisute'ria/ n. f. costume jewelry.

bizarro /bi'θarro; bi'sarro/ a. brave; generous; smart.

bizco /'biθko; 'bisko/ **-ca** n. **1.** cross-eyed person. —a. **2.** cross-eyed, squinting.

bizcocho /biθ'kotʃo; bis'kotʃo/ n. m. biscuit, cake.

blanco /'blanko/ a. **1.** white; blank. —n. **2.** m. white; target.

blandir /blan'dir/ v. brandish, flourish.

blando /'blando/ a. soft.

blanquear /blanke'ar/ v. whiten; bleach.

blasfemar /blasfe'mar/ v. blaspheme, curse.

blasfemia /blas'femia/ n. f. blasphemy.

blindado /blin'daðo/ a. armored.

blindaje /blin'dahe/ n. m. armor. —**blindar,** v.

bloque /'bloke/ n. m. block. —**bloquear,** v.

bloqueo /blo'keo/ n. m. blockade. —**bloquear,** v.

blusa /'blusa/ n. f. blouse.

bobada /bo'βaða/ n. f. stupid, silly thing.

bobo /'boβo/ **-ba** a. & n. fool; foolish.

boca /'boka/ n. f. mouth.

bocado /bo'kaðo/ n. m. bit; bite, mouthful.

bocanada /boka'naða/ n. f. puff (of smoke); mouthful (of liquor).

bocazas /bo'kaθas/ n. m. & f. Colloq. bigmouth.

bochorno /bo'tʃorno/ n. m. sultry weather; embarrassment.

bocina /bo'θina; bo'sina/ n. f. horn.

boda /'boða/ n. f. wedding.

bodega /bo'ðega/ n. f. wine cellar; Naut. hold; (Carib.) grocery store.

bofetada /bofe'taða/ n. f. **bofetón,** n. m. slap.

boga /'boga/ n. f. vogue; fad.

bogar /bo'gar/ v. row (a boat).

bohemio /bo'emio/ **-a** a. & n. Bohemian.

boicoteo /boiko'teo/ n. m. boycott. —**boicotear,** v.

boina /'boina/ n. f. beret.

bola /'bola/ n. f. ball.

bola de nieve /'bola de 'nieβe/ snowball.

bolas de billar /'bolas de bi'ʎar; 'bolas de bi'yar/ billiard balls.

bolera /bo'lera/ n. f. bowling alley.

boletín /bole'tin/ n. m. bulletin.

boletín informativo /bole'tin informa'tiβo/ news bulletin.

boleto /bo'leto/ n. m. ticket. **b. de embarque,** boarding pass.

boliche /bo'litʃe/ n. m. bowling alley.

bolígrafo /bo'ligrafo/ n. m. ballpoint pen.

boliviano /boli'βiano/ **-a** a. & n. Bolivian.

bollo /'boʎo; 'boyo/ n. m. bun, loaf.

bolos /'bolos/ n. m.pl. bowling.

bolsa /'bolsa/ n. f. purse; stock exchange.

bolsa de agua caliente /'bolsa de 'agua ka'liente/ hot-water bottle.

bolsillo /bol'siʎo; bol'siyo/ n. m. pocket.

bomba /'bomba/ n. f. pump; bomb; gas station.

bombardear /bombarðe'ar/ v. bomb; bombard, shell.

bombear /bombe'ar/ v. pump.

bombero /bom'βero/ n. m. fireman.

bombilla /bom'βiʎa; bom'βiya/ n. f. (light) bulb.

bonanza /bo'nanθa; bo'nansa/ n. f. prosperity; fair weather.

bondad /bon'dað/ n. f. kindness; goodness.

bondadoso /bonda'ðoso/ a. kind, kindly.

bongó /boŋ'go/ n. m. bongo drum.

bonito /bo'nito/ a. pretty.

bono /'bono/ n. m. bonus; Fin. bond.

boqueada /boke'aða/ n. f. gasp; gape. —**boquear**, v.

boquilla /bo'kiʎa; bo'kiya/ n. f. cigarette holder.

bordado /bor'ðaðo/ n. m., **bordadura**, f. embroidery.

bordar /bor'ðar/ v. embroider.

borde /'borðe/ n. m. border, rim, edge, brink, ledge.

borde de la carretera /'borðe de la karre'tera/ roadside.

borla /'borla/ n. f. tassel.

borracho /bo'rratʃo/ -a a. & n. drunk.

borrachón /borra'tʃon/ -na n. drunkard.

borrador /borra'ðor/ n. m. eraser.

borradura /borra'ðura/ n. f. erasure.

borrar /bo'rrar/ v. erase, rub out.

borrasca /bo'rraska/ n. f. squall, storm.

borrico /bo'rriko/ n. m. donkey.

bosque /'boske/ n. m. forest, wood.

bosquejo /bos'keho/ n. m. sketch, draft. —**bosquejar**, v.

bostezo /bos'teθo; bos'teso/ n. m. yawn. —**bostezar**, v.

bota /'bota/ n. f. boot.

botalón /bota'lon/ n. m. Naut. boom.

botánica /bo'tanika/ n. f. botany.

botar /bo'tar/ v. throw out, throw away.

bote /'bote/ n. m. boat; can, box.

bote salvavidas /'bote salβa-'βiðas/ lifeboat.

botica /bo'tika/ n. f. pharmacy, drugstore.

boticario /boti'kario/ n. m. pharmacist, druggist.

botín /bo'tin/ n. m. booty, plunder, spoils.

botiquín /boti'kin/ n. m. medicine chest.

boto /'boto/ a. dull, stupid.

botón /bo'ton/ n. m. button.

botones /bo'tones/ n. m. bellboy (in a hotel).

bóveda /'boβeða/ n. f. vault.

boxeador /boksea'ðor/ n. m. boxer.

boxeo /bok'seo/ n. m. boxing. —**boxear**, v.

boya /'boya/ n. f. buoy.

boyante /bo'yante/ a. buoyant.

bozal /bo'θal; bo'sal/ n. m. muzzle.

bragas /'bragas/ n. f.pl. panties.

bramido /bra'miðo/ n. m. roar, bellow. —**bramar**, v.

brasa /'brasa/ n. f. embers, grill. —**brasear**, v.

brasileño /brasi'leɲo/ -ña a. & n. Brazilian.

bravata /bra'βata/ n. f. bravado.

bravear /braβe'ar/ v. bully.

braza /'braθa; 'brasa/ n. f. fathom.

brazada /bra'θaða; bra'saða/ n. f. (swimming) stroke.

brazalete /braθa'lete; brasa'lete/ n. m. bracelet.

brazo /'braθo; 'braso/ n. m. arm.

brea /'brea/ n. f. tar, pitch.

brecha /'bretʃa/ n. f. gap, breach.

brécol /'brekol/ n. m. broccoli.

bregar /bre'gar/ v. scramble.

breña /'breɲa/ n. f. rough country with brambly shrubs.

Bretaña /bre'taɲa/ n. f. Britain.

breve /'breβe/ a. brief, short. **en b.**, shortly, soon.

brevedad /breβe'ðað/ n. f. brevity.

bribón /bri'βon/ -na n. rogue, rascal.

brida /'briða/ n. f. bridle.

brigada /bri'gaða/ n. f. brigade.

brillante /bri'ʎante; bri'yante/ a. **1.** brilliant, shiny. —n. **2.** m. diamond.

brillo /'briʎo; 'briyo/ n. m. shine, glitter. —**brillar**, v.

brinco /'brinko/ n. m. jump; bounce, skip. —**brincar**, v.

brindis /'brindis/ n. m. toast. —**brindar**, v.

brío /'brio/ n. m. vigor.

brioso /'brioso/ a. vigorous, spirited.

brisa /'brisa/ n. f. breeze.

brisa marina /'brisa ma'rina/ sea breeze.

británico /bri'taniko/ a. British.

brocado /bro'kaðo/ -da a. & n. brocade.

brocha /'brotʃa/ n. f. brush.

broche /'brotʃe/ n. m. brooch, clasp, pin.

broma /'broma/ n. f. joke. —**bromear**, v.

bronca /'bronka/ n. f. Colloq. quarrel, row, fight.

bronce /'bronθe; 'bronse/ n. m. bronze; brass.

bronceador /bronθea'ðor; bronsea'ðor/ n. m. suntan lotion, suntan oil.

bronquitis /bron'kitis/ n. f. bronchitis.

brotar /bro'tar/ v. gush; sprout; bud.

brote /'brote/ n. m. bud, shoot.

bruja /'bruha/ n. f. witch.

brújula /'bruhula/ n. f. compass.

bruma /'bruma/ n. f. mist.

brumoso /bru'moso/ a. misty.

brusco /'brusko/ a. brusque; abrupt, curt.

brutal /bru'tal/ a. savage, brutal.

brutalidad /brutali'ðað/ n. f. brutality.

bruto /'bruto/ **-ta** a. **1.** brutish; ignorant. —n. **2.** blockhead.

bucear /buθe'ar/ buse'ar/ v. dive.

bueno /'bueno/ a. good, fair; well (in health).

buey /buei/ n. m. ox, steer.

búfalo /'bufalo/ n. m. buffalo.

bufanda /bu'fanda/ n. f. scarf.

bufón /bu'fon/ **-ona** a. & n. fool, buffoon, clown.

búho /'buo/ n. m. owl.

buhonero /buo'nero/ n. m. peddler, vendor.

bujía /bu'hia/ n. f. spark plug.

bulevar /bule'βar/ n. m. boulevard.

bulimia /bu'limia/ n. f. bulimia.

bullicio /bu'ʎiθio/ bu'yisio/ n. m. bustle, noise.

bullicioso /buʎi'θioso/ buyi'sioso/ a. boisterous, noisy.

bulto /'bulto/ n. m. bundle; lump.

buñuelo /bu'ɲuelo/ n. m. bun.

buque /'buke/ n. m. ship.

buque de guerra /'buke de 'gerra/ warship.

buque de pasajeros /'buke de pasa'heros/ passenger ship.

burdo /'burðo/ a. coarse.

burgués /bur'ges/ **-esa** a. & n. bourgeois.

burla /'burla/ n. f. mockery; fun.

burlador /burla'ðor/ **-ra** n. trickster, jokester.

burlar /bur'lar/ v. mock, deride.

burlarse de /bur'larse de/ v. scoff at; make fun of.

burro /'burro/ n. m. donkey.

busca /'buska/ n. f. search, pursuit, quest.

buscar /bus'kar/ v. seek, look for; look up.

busto /'busto/ n. m. bust.

butaca /bu'taka/ n. f. armchair; *Theat.* orchestra seat.

buzo /'buθo/ 'buso/ n. m. diver.

buzón /bu'θon/ bu'son/ n. m. mailbox.

C

cabal /ka'βal/ a. exact; thorough.

cabalgar /kaβal'gar/ v. ride horseback.

caballeresco /kaβaʎe'resko/ kaβaye'resko/ a. gentlemanly, chivalrous.

caballería /kaβaʎe'ria/ kaβaye'ria/ n. f. cavalry; chivalry.

caballeriza /kaβaʎe'riθa/ kaβaye'risa/ n. f. stable.

caballero /kaβa'ʎero/ kaβa'yero/ n. m. gentleman; knight.

caballete /kaβa'ʎete/ kaβa'yete/ n. m. sawhorse; easel; ridge (of roof).

caballo /ka'βaʎo/ ka'βayo/ n. m. horse.

cabaña /ka'βaɲa/ n. f. cabin; booth.

cabaré /kaβa're/ n. m. nightclub.

cabaretero /kaβare'tero/ **-a** n. m. & f. nightclub owner.

cabecear /kaβeθe'ar/ kaβese'ar/ v. pitch (as a ship).

cabecera /kaβe'θera/ kaβe'sera/ f. head (of bed, table).

cabello /ka'βeʎo/ ka'βeyo/ n. m. hair.

caber /ka'βer/ v. fit into, be contained in. **no cabe duda,** there is no doubt.

cabeza /ka'βeθa/ ka'βesa/ n. f. head; warhead.

cabildo /ka'βildo/ n. m. city hall.

cabildo abierto /ka'βildo a'βierto/ town meeting.

cabizbajo /kaβiβ'βaho/ kaβis-'βaho/ a. downcast.

cablegrama /kaβle'grama/ n. m. cablegram.

cabo /'kaβo/ n. m. end; *Geog.* cape; *Mil.* corporal. **llevar a c.,** carry out, accomplish.

cabra /'kaβra/ n. f. goat.

cacahuete /kaka'uete/ n. m. peanut.

cacao /ka'kao/ n. m. cocoa; chocolate.

cacerola /kaθe'rola; kase'rola/ n. f. pan, casserole.

cachondeo /katʃon'deo/ n. m. fun, hilarity.

cachondo /ka'tʃondo/ a. funny; *Colloq.* horny.

cachorro /ka'tʃorro/ n. m. cub; puppy.

cada /'kaða/ a. each, every.

cadáver /ka'ðaβer/ n. m. corpse.

cadena /ka'ðena/ n. f. chain.

cadera /ka'ðera/ n. f. hip.

cadete /ka'ðete/ n. m. cadet.

caer /ka'er/ v. fall.

café /ka'fe/ n. m. coffee; café.

café exprés /ka'fe eks'pres/ espresso.

café soluble /ka'fe so'luβle/ instant coffee.

cafetal /kafe'tal/ n. m. coffee plantation.

cafetera /kafe'tera/ n. f. coffee pot.

caída /ka'iða/ n. f. fall, drop; collapse.

caimán /kai'man/ n. m. alligator.

caja /'kaha/ n. f. box, case; checkout counter.

caja de ahorros /'kaha de a'orros/ savings bank.

caja de cerillos /'kaha de θe'riλos; 'kaha de se'riλos/ matchbox.

caja de fósforos /'kaha de 'fosforos/ matchbox.

caja torácica /'kaha to'raθika; 'kaha to'rasika/ rib cage.

cajero /ka'hero/ **-ra** n. cashier.

cajón /ka'hon/ n. m. drawer.

cal /kal/ n. f. lime.

calabaza /kala'βaθa; kala'βasa/ n. f. calabash, pumpkin.

calabozo /kala'βoθo; kala'βoso/ n. m. jail, cell.

calambre /ka'lambre/ n. m. cramp.

calamidad /kalami'ðað/ n. f. calamity, disaster.

calcetín /kalθe'tin; kalse'tin/ n. m. sock.

calcio /'kalθio; 'kalsio/ n. m. calcium.

calcular /kalku'lar/ v. calculate, figure.

cálculo /'kalkulo/ n. m. calculation, estimate.

caldera /kal'dera/ n. f. kettle, caldron; boiler.

caldo /'kaldo/ n. m. broth.

calefacción /kalefak'θion; kalefak'sion/ n. f. heat, heating.

calendario /kalen'dario/ n. m. calendar.

calentar /kalen'tar/ v. heat, warm.

calidad /kali'ðað/ n. f. quality, grade.

caliente /ka'liente/ a. hot, warm.

calificar /kalifi'kar/ v. qualify.

callado /ka'ʎaðo; ka'yaðo/ a. silent, quiet.

callarse /ka'ʎarse; ka'yarse/ v. quiet down; keep still; stop talking.

calle /'kaʎe; 'kaye/ n. f. street.

callejón /kaʎe'hon; kaye'hon/ n. m. alley.

calle sin salida /'kaʎe sin sa'liða; 'kaye sin sa'liða/ dead end.

callo /'kaʎo; 'kayo/ n. m. callus, corn.

calma /'kalma/ n. f. calm, quiet.

calmado /kal'maðo/ a. calm.

calmante /kal'mante/ a. soothing, calming.

calmar /kal'mar/ v. calm, quiet, lull, soothe.

calor /ka'lor/ n. heat, warmth. **tener c.,** to be hot, warm; feel hot, warm. **hacer c.,** to be hot, warm (weather).

calorífero /kalo'rifero/ a. **1.** heat-producing. —n. **2.** m. radiator.

calumnia /ka'lumnia/ n. f. slander. —**calumniar,** v.

caluroso /kalu'roso/ a. warm, hot.

calvario /kal'βario/ n. m. Calvary.

calvo /'kalβo/ a. bald.

calzado /kal'θaðo; kal'saðo/ n. m. footwear.

calzar /kal'θar; kal'sar/ v. wear (as shoes).

calzoncillos /kalθon'θiʎos; kalson'siyos/ n. m.pl. shorts.

calzones /kal'θones; kal'sones/ n. m.pl. trousers.

cama /'kama/ n. f. bed.

cámara /'kamara/ n. f. chamber; camera.

camarada /kama'raða/ n. m. & f. comrade.

camarera /kama'rera/ n. f. chambermaid; waitress.

camarero /kama'rero/ n. m. steward; waiter.

camarón /kama'ron/ n. m. shrimp.

camarote /kama'rote/ n. m. stateroom, berth.

cambiar /kam'βiar/ v. exchange, change, trade; cash.

cambio /kam'bio/ n. m. change, exchange. **en c.,** on the other hand.

cambista /kam'βista/ n. m. & f. money changer; banker, broker.

cambur /kam'βur/ n. m. banana.

camello /ka'meʎo; ka'meyo/ n. m. camel.

camilla /ka'miʎa; ka'miya/ n. f. stretcher.

caminar /kami'nar/ v. walk.

caminata /kami'nata/ n. f. tramp, hike.

camino /ka'mino/ n. m. road; way.

camión /ka'mion/ n. m. truck.

camisa /ka'misa/ n. f. shirt.

camisería /kamise'ria/ n. f. haberdashery.

camiseta /kami'seta/ n. f. undershirt; T-shirt.

campamento /kampa'mento/ n. m. camp.

campana /kam'pana/ n. f. bell.

campanario /kampa'nario/ n. m. bell tower, steeple.

campaneo /kampa'neo/ n. m. chime.

campaña /kam'paɲa/ n. f. campaign.

campeón /kampe'on/ -na n. champion.

campeonato /kampeo'nato/ n. m. championship.

campesino /kampe'sino/ -na n. peasant.

campestre /kam'pestre/ a. country, rural.

campo /'kampo/ n. m. field; (the) country.

campo de concentración /'kampo de konθen'traθion; 'kampo de konsentra'sion/ concentration camp.

campo de golf /'kampo de 'golf/ golf course.

Canadá /kana'ða/ n. m. Canada.

canadiense /kana'ðiense/ a. & n. Canadian.

canal /ka'nal/ n. m. canal; channel.

Canal de la Mancha /ka'nal de la 'mantʃa/ n. m. English Channel.

canalla /ka'naʎa; ka'naya/ n. f. rabble.

canario /ka'nario/ n. m. canary.

canasta /ka'nasta/ n. f. basket.

cáncer /'kanθer; 'kanser/ n. m. cancer.

cancha de tenis /'kantʃa de 'tenis/ n. f. tennis court.

canciller /kanθi'ʎer; kansi'yer/ n. m. chancellor.

canción /kan'θion; kan'sion/ n. f. song.

candado /kan'daðo/ n. m. padlock.

candela /kan'dela/ n. f. fire; light; candle.

candelero /kande'lero/ n. m. candlestick.

candidato /kandi'ðato/ -ta n. candidate; applicant.

candidatura /kandiða'tura/ n. f. candidacy.

canela /ka'nela/ n. f. cinnamon.

cangrejo /kaŋ'greho/ n. m. crab.

caníbal /ka'niβal/ n. m. cannibal.

caniche /ka'nitʃe/ n. m. poodle.

canje /'kanhe/ n. m. exchange, trade. —**canjear,** v.

cano /'kano/ a. gray.

canoa /ka'noa/ n. f. canoe.

cansado /kan'saðo/ a. tired, weary.

cansancio /kan'sanθio; kan'sansio/ n. m. fatigue.

cansar /kan'sar/ v. tire, fatigue, wear out.

cantante /kan'tante/ n. m. & f. singer.

cantar /kan'tar/ n. **1.** m. song. —v. **2.** sing.

cántaro /'kantaro/ n. m. pitcher.

cantera /kan'tera/ n. f. (stone) quarry.

cantidad /kanti'ðað/ n. f. quantity, amount.

cantina /kan'tina/ n. f. bar, tavern; restaurant.

canto /'kanto/ n. m. chant, song, singing; edge.

caña /'kaɲa/ n. f. cane, reed; sugar cane; small glass of beer.

cañón /ka'ɲon/ n. m. canyon; cannon; gun barrel.

caoba /ka'oβa/ n. f. mahogany.

caos /'kaos/ n. m. chaos.

caótico /ka'otiko/ a. chaotic.

capa /'kapa/ n. f. cape, cloak; coat (of paint).

capacidad /kapaθi'ðað; kapasi'ðað/ n. f. capacity; capability.

capacitar /kapaθi'tar; kapasi'tar/ v. enable.

capataz /kapa'taθ; kapa'tas/ n. m. foreman.

capaz /ka'paθ; ka'pas/ *a.* capable, able.

capellán /kape'ʎan; kape'yan/ *n. m.* chaplain.

caperuza /kape'ruθa; kape'rusa/ *n. f.* hood.

capilla /ka'piʎa; ka'piya/ *n. f.* chapel.

capital /kapi'tal/ *n.* **1.** *m.* capital. **2.** *f.* capital (city).

capitalista /kapita'lista/ *a. & n.* capitalist.

capitán /kapi'tan/ *n. m.* captain.

capitular /kapitu'lar/ *v.* yield.

capítulo /ka'pitulo/ *n. m.* chapter.

capota /ka'pota/ *n. f.* hood.

capricho /ka'pritʃo/ *n. m.* caprice; fancy, whim.

caprichoso /kapri'tʃoso/ *a.* capricious.

cápsula /'kapsula/ *n. f.* capsule.

capturar /kaptu'rar/ *v.* capture.

capucha /ka'putʃa/ *n. f.* hood.

capullo /ka'puʎo; ka'puyo/ *n. m.* cocoon.

cara /'kara/ *n. f.* face.

caracol /kara'kol/ *n. m.* snail.

carácter /ka'rakter/ *n. m.* character.

característica /karakte'ristika/ *n. f.* characteristic.

característico /karakte'ristiko/ *a.* characteristic.

caramba /ka'ramba/ mild exclamation.

caramelo /kara'melo/ *n. m.* caramel; candy.

carátula /ka'ratula/ *n. f.* dial.

caravana /kara'βana/ *n. f.* caravan.

carbón /kar'βon/ *n. m.* carbon; coal.

carbonizar /karβoni'θar; karβoni'sar/ *v.* char.

carburador /karβura'ðor/ *n. m.* carburetor.

carcajada /karka'haða/ *n. f.* burst of laughter.

cárcel /'karθel; 'karsel/ *n. f.* prison, jail.

carcelero /karθe'lero; karse'lero/ *n. m.* jailer.

carcinogénico /karθino'heniko; karsino'heniko/ *a.* carcinogenic.

cardenal /karðe'nal/ *n. m.* cardinal.

cardiólogo /kar'ðiologo/ *-a* *m & f* cardiologist.

carecer /kare'θer; kare'ser/ *v.* lack.

carestía /kares'tia/ *n. f.* scarcity; famine.

carga /'karga/ *n. f.* cargo; load, burden; freight.

cargar /kar'gar/ *v.* carry; load; charge.

cargo /'kargo/ *n. m.* load; charge, office.

caricatura /karika'tura/ *n. f.* caricature; cartoon.

caricaturista /karikatu'rista/ *n. m. & f.* caricaturist; cartoonist.

caricia /ka'riθia; ka'risia/ *n. f.* caress.

caridad /kari'ðað/ *n. f.* charity.

cariño /ka'riɲo/ *n. m.* affection, fondness.

cariñoso /kari'ɲoso/ *a.* affectionate, fond.

carisma /ka'risma/ *n. m.* charisma.

caritativo /karita'tiβo/ *a.* charitable.

carmesí /karme'si/ *a. & m.* crimson.

carnaval /karna'βal/ *n. m.* carnival.

carne /'karne/ *n. f.* meat, flesh; pulp.

carne acecinada /'karne aθe-θi'naða; 'karne asesi'naða/ *n. f.* corned beef.

carnero /kar'nero/ *n. m.* ram; mutton.

carnicería /karniθe'ria; karnise'ria/ *n. f.* meat market; massacre.

carnicero /karni'θero; karni'sero/ **-ra** *n.* butcher.

carnívoro /kar'niβoro/ *a.* carnivorous.

caro /'karo/ *a.* dear, costly, expensive.

carpa /'karpa/ *n. f.* tent.

carpeta /kar'peta/ *n. f.* folder; briefcase.

carpintero /karpin'tero/ *n. m.* carpenter.

carrera /ka'rrera/ *n. f.* race; career.

carrera de caballos /ka'rrera de ka'βaʎos; ka'rrera de ka'βayos/ horse race.

carreta /ka'rreta/ *n. f.* wagon, cart.

carrete /ka'rrete/ *n. m.* reel, spool.

carretera /karre'tera/ *n. f.* road, highway.

carril /ka'rril/ *n. m.* rail.

carrillo /ka'rriʎo; ka'rriyo/ *n. m.* cart (for baggage or shopping).

carro /'karro/ *n. m.* car, automobile; cart.

carroza /ka'rroθa; ka'rrosa/ *n. f.* chariot.

carruaje /ka'rruahe/ *n. m.* carriage.

carta /'karta/ *n. f.* letter; (*pl.*) cards.

cartel /kar'tel/ *n. m.* placard, poster; cartel.

cartelera /karte'lera/ *n. f.* billboard.

cartera /kar'tera/ *n. f.* pocketbook, handbag, wallet; portfolio.

cartero /kar'tero/ **(-ra)** *n. m.* mail carrier.

cartón /kar'ton/ *n. m.* cardboard.

cartón piedra /kar'ton 'pieðra/ *n. m.* papier-mâché.

cartucho /kar'tutʃo/ *n. m.* cartridge; cassette.

casa /'kasa/ *n. f.* house, dwelling; home.

casaca /ka'saka/ *n. f.* dress coat.

casa de pisos /'kasa de 'pisos/ apartment house.

casado /ka'saðo/ *a.* married.

casamiento /kasa'miento/ *n. m.* marriage.

casar /ka'sar/ *v.* marry, marry off.

casarse /ka'sarse/ *v.* get married. **c. con**, marry.

cascabel /kaska'βel/ *n. m.* jingle bell.

cascada /kas'kaða/ *n. f.* waterfall, cascade.

cascajo /kas'kaho/ *n. m.* gravel.

cascanueces /kaska'nueθes; kaska'nueses/ *n. m.* nutcracker.

cascar /kas'kar/ *v.* crack, break, burst.

cáscara /kaskara/ *n. f.* shell, rind, husk.

casco /'kasko/ *n. m.* helmet; hull.

casera /ka'sera/ *n. f.* landlady; housekeeper.

caserío /kase'rio/ *n. m.* settlement.

casero /ka'sero/ *a.* **1.** homemade. —*n.* **2.** *m.* landlord, superintendent.

caseta /ka'seta/ *n. f.* cottage, hut.

casi /'kasi/ *adv.* almost, nearly.

casilla /ka'siʎa; ka'siya/ *n. f.* booth; ticket office; pigeonhole.

casimir /kasi'mir/ *n. m.* cashmere.

casino /ka'sino/ *n. m.* club; clubhouse.

caso /'kaso/ *n. m.* case. **hacer c. a**, pay attention to.

casorio /ka'sorio/ *n. m.* informal wedding.

caspa /kaspa/ *n. f.* dandruff.

casta /'kasta/ *n. f.* caste.

castaña /kas'tana/ *n. f.* chestnut.

castaño /kas'tano/ *a.* **1.** brown. —*n.* **2.** *m.* chestnut tree.

castañuela /kasta'ɲuela/ *n. f.* castanet.

castellano /kaste'ʎano; kaste'yano/ **-na** *a.* & *n.* Castilian.

castidad /kasti'ðað/ *n. f.* chastity.

castigar /kasti'gar/ *v.* punish, castigate.

castigo /kas'tigo/ *n. m.* punishment.

castillo /kas'tiʎo; kas'tiyo/ *n. m.* castle.

castizo /kas'tiθo; kas'tiso/ *a.* pure, genuine; noble.

casto /'kasto/ *a.* chaste.

castor /kas'tor/ *n. m.* beaver.

casual /ka'sual/ *adj.* accidental, coincidental.

casualidad /kasuali'ðað/ *n. f.* coincidence. **por c.**, by chance.

casuca /ka'suka/ *n. f.* hut, shanty, hovel.

cataclismo /kata'klismo/ *n. m.* cataclysm.

catacumba /kata'kumba/ *n. f.* catacomb.

catadura /kata'ðura/ *n. f.* act of tasting; appearance.

catalán /kata'lan/ **-na** *a.* & *n.* Catalonian.

catálogo /ka'talogo/ *n. m.* catalogue. —**catalogar,** *v.*

cataputta /kata'putta/ *n. f.* catapult.

catar /ka'tar/ *v.* taste; examine, try; bear in mind.

catarata /kata'rata/ *n. f.* cataract, waterfall.

catarro /ka'tarro/ *n. m.* head cold, catarrh.

catástrofe /ka'tastrofe/ *n. f.* catastrophe.

catecismo /kate'θismo; kate'sismo/ *n. m.* catechism.

cátedra /kate'ðra/ *n. f.* professorship.

catedral /kate'ðral/ *n. f.* cathedral.

catedrático /kate'ðratiko/ **-ca** *n.* professor.

categoría /katego'ria/ *n. f.* category.

categórico /kate'goriko/ a. categorical.

catequismo /kate'kismo/ n. m. catechism.

catequizar /kateki'θar; kateki'sar/ v. catechize.

cátodo /'katoðo/ n. m. cathode.

catolicismo /katoli'θismo; katoli'sismo/ n. m. Catholicism.

católico /ka'toliko/ **-ca** a. & n. Catholic.

catorce /ka'torθe; ka'torse/ a. & pron. fourteen.

catre /'katre/ n. m. cot.

cauce /'kauθe; 'kause/ n. m. riverbed; ditch.

cauchal /kau'tʃal/ n. m. rubber plantation.

caucho /'kautʃo/ n. m. rubber.

caución /kau'θion; kau'sion/ n. f. precaution; security, guarantee.

caudal /kau'ðal/ n. m. means, fortune; (pl.) holdings.

caudaloso /kauða'loso/ a. prosperous, rich.

caudillaje /kauði'ʎahe; kauði'yahe/ n. m. leadership; tyranny.

caudillo /kau'ðiʎo; kau'ðiyo/ n. m. leader, chief.

causa /'kausa/ n. f. cause.
—**causar**, v.

cautela /kau'tela/ n. f. caution.

cauteloso /kaute'loso/ a. cautious.

cautivar /kauti'βar/ v. captivate.

cautiverio /kauti'βerio/ n. m. captivity.

cautividad /kautiβi'ðað/ n. f. captivity.

cautivo /kau'tiβo/ **-va** a. & n. captive.

cauto /'kauto/ a. cautious.

cavar /ka'βar/ v. dig.

caverna /ka'βerna/ n. f. cavern, cave.

cavernoso /kaβer'noso/ a. cavernous.

cavidad /kaβi'ðað/ n. f. cavity, hollow.

cavilar /kaβi'lar/ v. criticize, cavil.

cayado /ka'yaðo/ n. m. shepherd's staff.

cayo /'kayo/ n. m. small rocky islet, key.

caza /'kaθa; 'kasa/ n. f. hunting, pursuit, game.

cazador /kaθa'ðor; kasa'ðor/ n. m. hunter.

cazar /ka'θar; ka'sar/ v. hunt.

cazatorpedero /kaθatorpe'ðero;

kasatorpe'ðero/ n. m. torpedo-boat, destroyer.

cazo /'kaθo; 'kaso/ n. m. ladle, dipper; pot.

cazuela /ka'θuela; ka'suela/ n. f. crock.

cebada /θe'βaða; se'βaða/ n. f. barley.

cebiche /θe'bitʃe/ n. m. dish of marinated raw fish.

cebo /'θeβo; 'seβo/ n. m. bait.
—**cebar**, v.

cebolla /θe'βoʎa; se'βoya/ n. f. onion.

cebolleta /θeβo'ʎeta; seβo'yeta/ n. f. spring onion.

ceceo /θe'θeo; se'seo/ n. m. lisp.
—**cecear**, v.

cecina /θe'θina; se'sina/ n. f. dried beef.

cedazo /θe'ðaθo; se'ðaso/ n. m. sieve, sifter.

ceder /θe'ðer; se'ðer/ v. cede; transfer; yield.

cedro /'θeðro; 'seðro/ n. m. cedar.

cédula /'θeðula; 'seðula/ n. f. decree. **c. personal,** identification card.

céfiro /'θefiro; 'sefiro/ n. m. zephyr.

cegar /θe'gar; se'gar/ v. blind.

ceguedad /θege'ðað, θe'gera; sege'ðað, se'gera/ **ceguera** n. f. blindness.

ceja /'θeha; 'seha/ n. f. eyebrow.

cejar /θe'har; se'har/ v. go backwards; yield, retreat.

celada /θe'laða; se'laða/ n. f. trap; ambush.

celaje /θe'lahe; se'lahe/ n. m. appearance of the sky.

celar /θe'lar; se'lar/ v. watch carefully, guard.

celda /'θelda; 'selda/ n. f. cell.

celebración /θeleβra'θion; seleβra'sion/ n. f. celebration.

celebrante /θele'βrante; sele'βrante/ n. m. officiating priest.

celebrar /θele'βrar; sele'βrar/ v. celebrate, observe.

célebre /'θeleβre; 'seleβre/ a. celebrated, noted, famous.

celebridad /θeleβri'ðað; seleβri'ðað/ n. f. fame; celebrity; pageant.

celeridad /θeleri'ðað; seleri'ðað/ n. f. speed, rapidity.

celeste /θe'leste; se'leste/ a. celestial.

celestial /θeles'tial; seles'tial/ a. heavenly.

celibato /θeli'βato; seli'βato/ n. m. celibacy.

célibe /'θeliβe; 'seliβe/ a. **1.** unmarried. —n. **2.** m. & f. unmarried person.

celista /θe'lista; se'lista/ n. m. & f. cellist.

cellisca /θe'ʎiska; se'yiska/ n. f. sleet. —**cellisquear,** v.

celo /'θelo; 'selo/ n. m. zeal; (pl.) jealousy.

celofán /θelo'fan; selo'fan/ n. m. cellophane.

celosía /θelo'sia; selo'sia/ n. f. Venetian blind.

celoso /θe'loso; se'loso/ a. jealous; zealous.

céltico /'θeltiko; 'seltiko/ a. Celtic.

célula /'θelula; 'selula/ n. f. Biol. cell.

celuloide /θelu'loiðe; selu'loiðe/ n. m. celluloid.

cementar /θemen'tar; semen'tar/ v. cement.

cementerio /θemen'terio; semen'terio/ n. m. cemetery.

cemento /θe'mento; se'mento/ n. m. cement.

cena /'θena; 'sena/ n. f. supper.

cenagal /θena'gal; sena'gal/ n. m. swamp, marsh.

cenagoso /θena'goso; sena'goso/ a. swampy, marshy, muddy.

cenar /θe'nar; se'nar/ v. dine, sup.

cencerro /θen'θerro; sen'serro/ n. m. cowbell.

cendal /θen'dal; sen'dal/ n. m. thin, light cloth; gauze.

cenicero /θeni'θero; seni'sero/ n. m. ashtray.

ceniciento /θeni'θiento; seni'siento/ a. ashen.

cenit /'θenit; 'senit/ n. m. zenith.

ceniza /θe'niθa; se'nisa/ n. f. ash, ashes.

censo /'θenso; 'senso/ n. m. census.

censor /θen'sor; sen'sor/ n. m. censor.

censura /θen'sura; sen'sura/ n. f. reproof, censure; censorship.

censurable /θensu'raβle; sensu'raβle/ a. objectionable.

censurar /θensu'rar; sensu'rar/ v. censure, criticize.

centavo /θen'taβo; sen'taβo/ n. m. cent.

centella /θen'teʎa; sen'teya/ n. f. thunderbolt, lightning.

centellear /θente'ʎe'ar; sente'ye'ar/ v. twinkle, sparkle.

centelleo /θente'ʎeo; sente'yeo/ n. m. sparkle.

centenar /θente'nar; sente'nar/ n. (a) hundred.

centenario /θente'nario; sente-'nario/ n. m. centennial, centenary.

centeno /θen'teno; sen'teno/ n. m. rye.

centigrado /θen'tigraðo; sen'tigraðo/ a. centigrade.

centímetro /θen'ti'metro; senti'metro/ n. m. centimeter.

céntimo /'θentimo; 'sentimo/ n. m. cent.

centinela /θenti'nela; senti'nela/ n. m. sentry, guard.

central /θen'tral; sen'tral/ a. central.

centralita /θentra'lita; sentra'lita/ n. f. switchboard.

centralizar /θentrali'θar; sentrali'sar/ v. centralize.

centrar /θen'trar; sen'trar/ v. center.

céntrico /'θentriko; 'sentriko/ a. central.

centro /'θentro; 'sentro/ n. m. center.

centroamericano /θentro-ameri'kano; sentroameri'kano/ **-na** a. & n. Central American.

centro de mesa /'θentro de 'mesa; 'sentro de 'mesa/ centerpiece.

ceñidor /θeɲi'ðor; seɲi'ðor/ n. m. belt, sash; girdle.

ceñir /θe'ɲir; se'ɲir/ v. gird.

ceño /'θeɲo; 'seɲo/ n. m. frown.

ceñudo /θe'ɲuðo; se'ɲuðo/ a. frowning, grim.

cepa /'θepa; 'sepa/ n. f. stump.

cepillo /θe'piʎo; se'piyo/ n. m. brush; plane. —**cepillar,** v.

cera /'θera; 'sera/ n. f. wax.

cerámica /θe'ramika; se'ramika/ n. f. ceramics.

cerámico /θe'ramiko; se'ramiko/ a. ceramic.

cerca /'θerka; 'serka/ adv. **1.** near. —n. **2.** f. fence, hedge.

cercado /θer'kaðo; ser'kaðo/ n. m. enclosure; garden.

cercamiento /θerka'miento; serka'miento/ n. m. enclosure.

cercanía /θerka'nia; serka'nia/ n. f. proximity.

cercano /θer'kano; ser'kano/ a. near, nearby.

cercar /θer'kar; ser'kar/ v. surround.

cercenar /θerθe'nar; serse'nar/ v. clip; lessen, reduce.

cerciorar /θerθio'rar; sersio'rar/ v. make sure; affirm.

cerco /'θerko; 'serko/ n. m. hoop; siege.

cerda /'θerða; 'serða/ n. f. bristle.

cerdo /'θerðo; 'serðo/ **-da** n. hog.

cerdoso /θer'ðoso; ser'ðoso/ a. bristly.

cereal /θere'al; sere'al/ a. & m. cereal.

cerebro /θe'reβro; se'reβro/ n. m. brain.

ceremonia /θere'monia; sere-'monia/ n. f. ceremony.

ceremonial /θeremo'nial; seremo'nial/ a. & m. ceremonial, ritual.

ceremonioso /θeremo'nioso; seremo'nioso/ a. ceremonious.

cereza /θe'reθa; se'resa/ n. f. cherry.

cerilla /θe'riʎa; se'riya/ n. f., **cerillo,** m. match.

cerner /θer'ner; ser'ner/ v. sift.

cero /'θero; 'sero/ n. m. zero.

cerrado /θe'rraðo; se'rraðo/ a. closed; cloudy; obscure; taciturn.

cerradura /θerra'ðura; serra'ðura/ n. f. lock.

cerrajero /θerra'hero; serra'hero/ n. m. locksmith.

cerrar /θe'rrar; se'rrar/ v. close, shut.

cerro /'θerro; 'serro/ n. m. hill.

cerrojo /θe'rroho; se'rroho/ n. m. latch, bolt.

certamen /θer'tamen; ser'tamen/ n. m. contest; competition.

certero /θer'tero; ser'tero/ a. accurate, exact; certain, sure.

certeza /θer'teθa; ser'tesa/ n. f. certainty.

certidumbre /θerti'ðumbre; serti'ðumbre/ n. f. certainty.

certificado /θertifi'kaðo; sertifi'kaðo/ n. m. certificate.

certificado de compra /θertifi'kaðo de 'kompra; sertifi'kaðo de 'kompra/ proof of purchase.

certificar /θertifi'kar; sertifi'kar/ v. certify; register (a letter).

cerúleo /θe'ruleo; se'ruleo/ a. cerulean, sky-blue.

cervecería /θerβeθe'ria; serβese'ria/ n. f. brewery; beer saloon.

cervecero /θerβe'θero; serβe'sero/ n. m. brewer.

cerveza /θer'βeθa; ser'βesa/ n. f. beer.

cesante /θe'sante; se'sante/ a. unemployed.

cesar /θe'sar; se'sar/ v. cease.

césped /'θespeð; 'sespeð/ n. m. sod, lawn.

cesta /'θesta; 'sesta/ n. f., **cesto,** m. basket.

cetrino /θe'trino; se'trino/ a. yellow, lemon-colored.

cetro /'θetro; 'setro/ n. m. scepter.

chabacano /tʃaβa'kano/ a. vulgar.

chacal /tʃa'kal/ n. m. jackal.

chacó /'tʃako/ n. m. shako.

chacona /tʃa'kona/ n. f. chaconne.

chacota /tʃa'kota/ n. f. fun, mirth.

chacotear /tʃakote'ar/ v. joke.

chacra /'tʃakra/ n. f. small farm.

chafallar /tʃafa'ʎar; tʃafa'yar/ v. mend badly.

chagra /'tʃagra/ n. m. rustic; rural person.

chal /tʃal/ n. m. shawl.

chalán /tʃa'lan/ n. m. horse trader.

chaleco /tʃa'leko/ n. m. vest.

chaleco salvavidas /tʃa'leko salβa'βiðas/ life jacket.

chalet /tʃa'le; tʃa'let/ n. m. chalet.

challí /tʃa'ʎi; tʃa'yi/ n. m. challis.

chamada /tʃa'maða/ n. f. brushwood.

chamarillero /tʃamari'ʎero; tʃamari'yero/ n. m. gambler.

chamarra /tʃa'marra/ n. f. coarse linen jacket.

chambelán /tʃambe'lan/ n. m. chamberlain.

champaña /tʃam'paɲa/ n. m. champagne.

champú /tʃam'pu/ n. m. shampoo.

chamuscar /tʃamus'kar/ v. scorch.

chancaco /tʃan'kako/ a. brown.

chance /'tʃanθe/ n. m. & f. opportunity, break.

chancear /tʃanθe'ar; tʃanse'ar/ v. jest, joke.

canciller /tʃanθiˈʎer; tʃansiˈyer/ *n. m.* chancellor.

cancillería /tʃanθiʎeˈria; tʃansiye'ria/ *n. f.* chancery.

chancla /'tʃankla/ *n. f.* old shoe.

chancleta /tʃanˈkleta/ *n. f.* slipper.

chanclos /'tʃanklos/ *n. m.pl.* galoshes.

chancro /'tʃankro/ *n. m.* chancre.

changador /tʃanɡaˈðor/ *n. m.* porter; handyman.

chantaje /tʃanˈtahe/ *n. m.* blackmail.

chantajista /tʃantaˈhista/ *n. m. & f.* blackmailer.

chantejear /tʃantehe'ar/ *v.* blackmail.

chanto /'tʃanto/ *n. m.* flagstone.

chantre /'tʃantre/ *n. m.* precentor.

chanza /'tʃanθa; tʃansa/ *n. f.* joke, jest. **—chancear,** *v.*

chanzoneta /tʃanθoˈneta; tʃanso'neta/ *n. f.* chansonette.

chapa /'tʃapa/ *n. f.* (metal) sheet, plate; lock.

chapado en oro /tʃaˈpaðo en 'oro/ *a.* gold-plated.

chapado en plata /tʃaˈpaðo en 'plata/ *a.* silver-plated.

chaparrada /tʃapaˈrraða/ *n. f.* downpour.

chaparral /tʃapaˈrral/ *n. m.* chaparral.

chaparreras /tʃapaˈrreras/ *n. f.pl.* chaps.

chaparrón /tʃapaˈrron/ *n. m.* downpour.

chapear /tʃapeˈar/ *v.* veneer.

chapeo /tʃaˈpeo/ *n. m.* hat.

chapero /tʃaˈpero/ *n. m. Colloq.* male homosexual prostitute.

chapitel /tʃapiˈtel/ *n. m.* spire, steeple; (architecture) capital.

chapodar /tʃapoˈðar/ *v.* lop.

chapón /tʃaˈpon/ *n. m.* inkblot.

chapotear /tʃapoteˈar/ *v.* paddle or splash in the water.

chapoteo /tʃapoˈteo/ *n. m.* splash.

chapucear /tʃapuθeˈar; tʃapuse'ar/ *v.* fumble, bungle.

chapucero /tʃapuˈθero; tʃapu'sero/ *a.* sloppy, bungling.

chapurrear /tʃapurreˈar/ *v.* speak (a language) brokenly.

chapuz /tʃaˈpuθ; tʃa'pus/ *n. m.* dive; ducking.

chapuzar /tʃapuˈθar; tʃapu'sar/ *v.* dive; duck.

chaqueta /tʃaˈketa/ *n. f.* jacket, coat.

chaqueta deportiva /tʃaˈketa deporˈtiβa/ *sport* jacket.

charada /tʃaˈraða/ *n. f.* charade.

charamusca /tʃaraˈmuska/ *n. f.* twisted candy stick.

charanga /tʃaˈraŋɡa/ *n. f.* military band.

charanguero /tʃaraŋˈɡuero/ *n. m.* peddler.

charca /'tʃarka/ *n. f.* pool, pond.

charco /'tʃarko/ *n. m.* pool, puddle.

charla /'tʃarla/ *n. f.* chat; chatter, prattle. **—charlar,** *v.*

charladuría /tʃarlaðuˈria/ *n. f.* chatter.

charlatán /tʃarlaˈtan/ **-ana** *n.* charlatan.

charlatanismo /tʃarlataˈnismo/ *n. m.* charlatanism.

charol /tʃaˈrol/ *n. m.* varnish.

charolar /tʃaroˈlar/ *v.* varnish; polish.

charquear /tʃarkeˈar/ *v.* jerk (beef).

charquí /tʃarˈki/ *n. m.* jerked beef.

charrán /tʃaˈrran/ *a.* roguish.

chascarillo /tʃaskaˈriʎo; tʃaska'riyo/ *n.* risqué story.

chasco /'tʃasko/ *n. m.* disappointment, blow; practical joke.

chasis /'tʃasis/ *n. m.* chassis.

chasquear /tʃaskeˈar/ *v.* fool, trick; disappoint; crack (a whip).

chasquido /tʃasˈkiðo/ *n. m.* crack (sound).

chata /'tʃata/ *n. f.* bedpan.

chatear /tʃateˈar/ *v.* chat (on the Internet).

chato /'tʃato/ *a.* flat-nosed, pug-nosed.

chauvinismo /tʃauβiˈnismo/ *n. m.* chauvinism.

chauvinista /tʃauβiˈnista/ *n. & a.* chauvinist.

chelín /tʃeˈlin/ *n. m.* shilling.

cheque /'tʃeke/ *n. m.* (bank) check.

chica /'tʃika/ *n. f.* girl.

chicana /tʃiˈkana/ *n. f.* chicanery.

chicha /'tʃitʃa/ *n. f.* an alcoholic drink.

chícharo /'tʃitʃaro/ *n. f.* pea.

chicharra /tʃiˈtʃarra/ *n. f.* cicada; talkative person.

chicharrón /tʃitʃaˈrron/ *n. m.* crisp fried scrap of meat.

chichear /tʃitʃe'ar/ v. hiss in disapproval.

chichón /tʃi'tʃon/ n. m. bump, bruise, lump.

chicle /'tʃikle/ n. m. chewing gum.

chico /'tʃiko/ a. **1.** little. —n. **2.** m. boy.

chicote /tʃi'kote/ n. m. cigar; cigar butt.

chicotear /tʃikote'ar/ v. whip, flog.

chifladura /tʃifla'ðura/ n. f. mania; whim; jest.

chiflar /tʃi'flar/ v. whistle; become insane.

chiflido /tʃi'fliðo/ n. m. shrill whistle.

chile /'tʃile/ n. m. chili.

chileno /tʃi'leno/ **-na** a. & n. Chilean.

chillido /tʃi'ʎiðo; tʃi'yiðo/ n. m. shriek, scream, screech. **—chillar,** v.

chillón /tʃi'ʎon; tʃi'yon/ a. shrill.

chimenea /tʃime'nea/ n. f. chimney, smokestack; fireplace.

china /'tʃina/ n. f. pebble; maid; Chinese woman.

chinarro /tʃi'narro/ n. m. large pebble, stone.

chinche /'tʃintʃe/ n. f. bedbug; thumbtack.

chincheta /tʃin'tʃeta/ n. f. thumbtack.

chinchilla /tʃin'tʃiʎa; tʃin'tʃiya/ n. f. chinchilla.

chinchorro /tʃin'tʃorro/ n. m. fishing net.

chinela /tʃi'nela/ n. f. slipper.

chinero /tʃi'nero/ n. m. china closet.

chino /'tʃino/ **-na** a. & n. Chinese.

chipirón /tʃipi'ron/ n. m. baby squid.

chiquero /tʃi'kero/ n. m. pen for pigs, goats, etc.

chiquito /tʃi'kito/ **-ta** a. **1.** small, tiny. —n. **2.** m. & f. small child.

chiribitil /tʃiriβi'til/ n. m. small room, den.

chirimía /tʃiri'mia/ n. f. flageolet.

chiripa /tʃi'ripa/ n. f. stroke of good luck.

chirla /'tʃirla/ n. f. mussel.

chirle /'tʃirle/ a. insipid.

chirona /tʃi'rona/ n. f. prison, jail.

chirrido /tʃi'rriðo/ n. m. squeak, chirp. **—chirriar,** v.

chis /tʃis/ interj. hush!

chisgarabís /tʃisgara'βis/ n. meddler; unimportant person.

chisguete /tʃis'gete/ n. m. squirt, splash.

chisme /'tʃisme/ n. m. gossip. **—chismear,** v.

chismero /tʃis'mero/ **-ra** n. gossiper.

chismoso /tʃis'moso/ adj. gossiping.

chispa /'tʃispa/ n. f. spark.

chispeante /tʃispe'ante/ a. sparkling.

chispear /tʃispe'ar/ v. sparkle.

chisporrotear /tʃisporrote'ar/ v. emit sparks.

chistar /tʃis'tar/ v. speak.

chiste /'tʃiste/ n. m. joke, gag; witty saying.

chistera /tʃis'tera/ n. f. fish basket; top hat.

chistoso /tʃis'toso/ a. funny, comic, amusing.

chito /'tʃito/ interj. hush!

chiva /'tʃiβa/ n. f. female goat.

chivato /tʃi'βato/ n. m. kid, young goat.

chivo /'tʃiβo/ n. m. male goat.

chocante /tʃo'kante/ a. striking; shocking; unpleasant.

chocar /tʃo'kar/ v. collide, clash, crash; shock.

chocarrear /tʃokarre'ar/ v. joke, jest.

chochear /tʃotʃe'ar/ v. be in one's dotage.

chochera /tʃo'tʃera/ n. f. dotage, senility.

choclo /'tʃoklo/ n. m. clog; overshoe; ear of corn.

chocolate /tʃoko'late/ n. m. chocolate.

chocolate con leche /tʃoko'late kon 'letʃe/ milk chocolate.

chocolatería /tʃokolate'ria/ n. f. chocolate shop.

chofer /'tʃofer/ **chófer** n. m. chauffeur, driver.

chofeta /tʃo'feta/ n. f. chafing dish.

cholo /'tʃolo/ n. m. half-breed.

chopo /'tʃopo/ n. m. black poplar.

choque /'tʃoke/ n. m. collision, clash, crash; shock.

chorizo /tʃo'riθo; tʃo'riso/ n. m. sausage.

chorrear /tʃorre'ar/ v. spout; drip.

chorro /'tʃorro/ n. m. spout; spurt, jet. **llover a chorros,** to pour (rain).

choto /'tʃoto/ n. m. calf, kid.

choza /'tʃoθa; 'tʃosa/ n. f. hut, cabin.

chozno /'tʃoθno; 'tʃosno/ **-na** n. great-great-great-grandchild.

chubasco /tʃu'βasko/ n. m. shower, squall.

chubascoso /tʃuβas'koso/ a. squally.

chuchería /tʃutʃe'ria/ n. f. trinket, knickknack.

chucho /'tʃutʃo/ n. m. Colloq. mutt.

chulería /tʃule'ria/ n. f. pleasant manner.

chuleta /tʃu'leta/ n. f. chop, cutlet.

chulo /'tʃulo/ n. m. rascal, rogue; joker.

chupa /'tʃupa/ n. f. jacket.

chupada /tʃu'paða/ n. f. suck, sip.

chupado /tʃu'paðo/ a. very thin.

chupaflor /tʃupa'flor/ n. m. hummingbird.

chupar /tʃu'par/ v. suck.

churrasco /tʃu'rrasko/ n. m. roasted meat.

churros /'tʃuros/ n. m.pl. long, slender fritters.

chuscada /tʃus'kaða/ n. f. joke, jest.

chusco /'tʃusko/ a. funny, humorous.

chusma /'tʃusma/ n. f. mob, rabble.

chuzo /'tʃuθo; 'tʃuso/ n. m. pike.

CI, abbr. (coeficiente intelectual) IQ (intelligence quotient).

ciberespacio /θiβeres'paθio/ n. m. cyberspace.

cibernauta /θiβer'nauta/ n. m. & f. cybernaut.

cicatero /θika'tero; sika'tero/ a. stingy.

cicatriz /θika'triθ; sika'tris/ n. f. scar.

cicatrizar /θikatri'θar; sikatri'sar/ v. heal.

ciclamato /θi'klamato; si'klamato/ n. m. cyclamate.

ciclista /θi'klista; si'klista/ m & f cyclist.

ciclo /'θiklo; 'siklo/ n. m. cycle.

ciclón /θi'klon; si'klon/ n. m. cyclone.

ciego /'θiego; 'siego/ **-ga** a. **1.** blind. —n. **2.** blind person.

cielo /'θielo; 'sielo/ n. m. heaven; sky, heavens; ceiling.

ciempiés /θiem'pies; siem'pies/ n. m. centipede.

cien /θien; sien/ **ciento** a. & pron. hundred. **por c.,** per cent.

ciénaga /'θienaga; 'sienaga/ n. f. swamp, marsh.

ciencia /'θienθia; 'siensia/ n. f. science.

cieno /'θieno; 'sieno/ n. m. mud.

científico /θien'tifiko; sien'tifiko/ **-ca** a. **1.** scientific. —n. **2.** scientist.

cierre /'θierre; 'sierre/ n. m. fastener, snap, clasp.

cierto /'θierto; 'sierto/ a. certain, sure, true.

ciervo /'θierβo; 'sierβo/ n. m. deer.

cierzo /'θierθo; 'sierso/ n. m. northerly wind.

cifra /'θifra; 'sifra/ n. f. cipher, number. —**cifrar,** v.

cigarra /θi'garra; si'garra/ n. f. locust.

cigarrera /θiga'rrera; siga'rrera/ **cigarrillera** f. cigarette case.

cigarrillo /θiga'rriʎo; siga'rriyo/ n. m. cigarette.

cigarro /θi'garro; si'garro/ n. m. cigar; cigarette.

cigüeña /θi'gueɲa; si'gueɲa/ n. f. stork.

cilíndrico /θi'lindriko; si'lindriko/ a. cylindrical.

cilindro /θi'lindro; si'lindro/ n. m. cylinder.

cima /'θima; 'sima/ n. f. summit, peak.

cimarrón /θima'rron; sima'rron/ a. **1.** wild, untamed. —n. **2.** m. runaway slave.

címbalo /'θimbalo; 'simbalo/ n. m. cymbal.

cimbrar /θim'βrar, θimbre'ar; sim'βrar, simbre'ar/ v. shake, brandish.

cimientos /θi'mientos; si'mientos/ n. m.pl. foundation.

cinc /θink; sink/ n. m. zinc.

cincel /θin'θel; sin'sel/ n. m. chisel. —**cincelar,** v.

cincha /'θintʃa; 'sintʃa/ n. f. (harness) cinch. —**cinchar,** v.

cinco /'θinko; 'sinko/ a. & pron. five.

cincuenta /θin'kuenta; sin'kuenta/ a. & pron. fifty.

cine /'θine; 'sine/ n. m. movies; movie theater.

cíngulo /'θiŋgulo; 'siŋgulo/ n. m. cingulum.

cínico /'θiniko; 'siniko/ **-ca** a. & n. cynical; cynic.

cinismo /θi'nismo; si'nismo/ n. m. cynicism.

cinta /'θinta; 'sinta/ n. f. ribbon, tape; (movie) film.

cintilar /θinti'lar; sinti'lar/ v. glitter, sparkle.

cinto /'θinto; 'sinto/ n. m. belt; girdle.

cintura /θin'tura; sin'tura/ n. f. waist.

cinturón /θintu'ron; sintu'ron/ n. m. belt.

cinturón de seguridad /θintu'ron de seguri'ðað; sintu'ron de seguri'ðað/ safety belt.

ciprés /θi'pres; si'pres/ n. m. cypress.

circo /'θirko; 'sirko/ n. m. circus.

circuito /θir'kuito; sir'kuito/ n. m. circuit.

circulación /θirkula'θion; sirkula-'sion/ n. f. circulation.

circular /θirku'lar; sirku'lar/ a. & m. **1.** circular. —v. **2.** circulate.

círculo /'θirkulo; 'sirkulo/ n. m. circle, club.

circundante /θirkun'dante; sirkun'dante/ a. surrounding.

circundar /θirkun'dar; sirkun'dar/ v. encircle, surround.

circunferencia /θirkunfe'renθia; sirkunfe'rensia/ n. f. circumference.

circunlocución /θirkunloku'θion; sirkunloku'sion/ n. f. circumlocution.

circunscribir /θirkunskri'βir; sirkunskri'βir/ v. circumscribe.

circunspección /θirkunspek'θion; sirkunspek'sion/ n. decorum, propriety.

circunspecto /θirkuns'pekto; sirkuns'pekto/ a. circumspect.

circunstancia /θirkuns'tanθia; sirkuns'tansia/ n. f. circumstance.

circunstante /θirkuns'tante; sirkuns'tante/ n. m. bystander.

circunvecino /θirkumbe'θino; sirkumbe'sino/ a. neighboring, adjacent.

cirio /'θirio; 'sirio/ n. m. candle.

cirrosis /θi'rrosis; si'rrosis/ n. f. cirrhosis.

ciruela /θi'ruela; si'ruela/ n. f. plum; prune.

cirugía /θiru'hia; siru'hia/ n. f. surgery.

cirujano /θiru'hano; siru'hano/ n. m. surgeon.

cisne /'θisne; 'sisne/ n. m. swan.

cisterna /θis'terna; sis'terna/ n. f. cistern.

cita /'θita; 'sita/ n. f. citation; appointment, date.

citación /θita'θion; sita'sion/ n. f. citation; (legal) summons.

citar /θi'tar; si'tar/ v. cite, quote; summon; make an appointment with.

cítrico /'θitriko; 'sitriko/ a. citric.

ciudad /θiu'ðað; siu'ðað/ n. f. city.

ciudadanía /θiuðaða'nia; siuðaða'nia/ n. f. citizenship.

ciudadano /θiuða'ðano; siu-ða'ðano/ **-na** n. citizen.

ciudadela /θiuða'ðela; siuða'ðela/ n. f. fortress, citadel.

cívico /'θiβiko; 'siβiko/ a. civic.

civil /θi'βil; si'βil/ a. & n. civil; civilian.

civilidad /θiβili'ðað; siβili'ðað/ n. f. politeness, civility.

civilización /θiβiliθa'θion; siβilisa'sion/ n. f. civilization.

civilizador /θiβiliθa'ðor; siβilisa-'ðor/ a. civilizing.

civilizar /θiβili'θar; siβili'sar/ v. civilize.

cizallas /θi'θaʎas; si'sayas/ n. f.pl. shears. —**cizallar**, v.

cizaña /θi'θaɲa; si'saɲa/ n. f. weed; vice.

clamar /kla'mar/ v. clamor.

clamor /kla'mor/ n. m. clamor.

clamoreo /klamo'reo/ n. m. persistent clamor.

clamoroso /klamo'roso/ a. clamorous.

clandestino /klandes'tino/ a. secret, clandestine.

clara /'klara/ n. f. white (of egg).

claraboya /klara'βoya/ n. m. skylight; bull's-eye.

clara de huevo /'klara de 'ueβo/ egg white.

clarear /klare'ar/ v. clarify; become light, dawn.

clarete /kla'rete/ n. m. claret.

claridad /klari'ðað/ n. f. clarity.

clarificar /klarifi'kar/ v. clarify.

clarín /kla'rin/ n. m. bugle, trumpet.

clarinete /klari'nete/ n. m. clarinet.

clarividencia /klariβi'ðenθia; klariβi'ðensia/ *n. f.* clairvoyance.

clarividente /klariβi'ðente/ *a.* clairvoyant.

claro /'klaro/ *a.* clear; bright; light (in color); of course.

clase /'klase/ *n. f.* class; classroom; kind, sort.

clase nocturna /'klase nok'turna/ evening class.

clásico /'klasiko/ *a.* classic, classical.

clasificar /klasifi'kar/ *v.* classify, rank.

claustro /'klaustro/ *n. m.* cloister.

claustrofobia /klaustro'foβia/ *n. f.* claustrophobia.

cláusula /'klausula/ *n. f.* clause.

clausura /klau'sura/ *n. f.* cloister; inner sanctum; closing.

clavado /kla'βaðo/ *a.* **1.** nailed. —*n.* **2.** *m.* & *f.* dive.

clavar /kla'βar/ *v.* nail, peg, pin.

clave /'klaβe/ *n. f.* code; *Mus.* key.

clavel /kla'βel/ *n. m.* carnation.

clavetear /klaβete'ar/ *v.* nail.

clavícula /kla'βikula/ *n. f.* collarbone.

clavija /kla'βiha/ *n. f.* pin, peg.

clavo /'klaβo/ *n. m.* nail, spike; clove.

clemencia /kle'menθia; kle'mensia/ *n. f.* clemency.

clemente /kle'mente/ *a.* merciful.

clementina /klemen'tina/ *n. f.* tangerine.

clerecía /klere'θia; klere'sia/ *n. f.* clergy.

clerical /kleri'kal/ *a.* clerical.

clérigo /'klerigo/ *n. m.* clergyman.

clero /'klero/ *n. m.* clergy.

cliente /'kliente/ *n. m.* & *f.* customer, client.

clientela /klien'tela/ *n. f.* clientele, practice.

clima /'klima/ *n. m.* climate.

clímax /'klimaks/ *n. m.* climax.

clínca de reposo /'klinka de rre'poso/ convalescent home.

clínica /'klinika/ *n. f.* clinic.

clínico /'kliniko/ *a.* clinical.

clíper /'kliper/ *n. m.* clipper ship.

cloaca /klo'aka/ *n. f.* sewer.

cloquear /kloke'ar/ *v.* cluck, cackle.

cloqueo /klo'keo/ *n. m.* cluck.

cloro /'kloro/ *n. m.* chlorine.

club /kluβ/ *n. m.* club, association.

club juvenil /kluβ huβe'nil/ youth club.

clueca /'klueka/ *n. f.* brooding hen.

coacción /koak'θion; koak'sion/ *n.* compulsion.

coagular /koagu'lar/ *v.* coagulate, clot.

coágulo /ko'agulo/ *n. m.* clot.

coalición /koali'θion; koali'sion/ *n. f.* coalition.

coartada /koar'taða/ *n. f.* alibi.

coartar /koar'tar/ *v.* limit.

cobarde /ko'βarðe/ *n.* & *a.* cowardly; coward.

cobardía /koβar'ðia/ *n. f.* cowardice.

cobayo /ko'βayo/ *n. m.* guinea pig.

cobertizo /koβer'tiθo; koβer'tiso/ *n. m.* shed.

cobertor /koβer'tor/ *n. m.*, **cobija**, *f.* blanket.

cobertura /koβer'tura/ *n. f.* cover, wrapping.

cobijar /koβi'har/ *v.* cover; protect.

cobrador /koβra'ðor/ *n. m.* collector.

cobranza /ko'βranθa; ko'βransa/ *n. f.* collection or recovery of money.

cobrar /ko'βrar/ *v.* collect; charge; cash.

cobre /'koβre/ *n. m.* copper.

cobrizo /ko'βriθo; ko'βriso/ *a.* coppery.

cobro /'koβro/ *n. m.* collection or recovery of money.

coca /'koka/ *n. f.* coca leaves.

cocaína /koka'ina/ *n. f.* cocaine.

cocal /ko'kal/ *n. m.* coconut plantation.

cocear /koθe'ar; kose'ar/ *v.* kick; resist.

cocer /ko'θer; ko'ser/ *v.* cook, boil, bake.

coche /'kotʃe/ *n. m.* coach; car; automobile.

cochecito de niño /kotʃe'θito de 'niɲo; kotʃe'sito de 'niɲo/ baby carriage.

coche de choque /'kotʃe de 'tʃoke/ dodgem.

cochera /ko'tʃera/ *n. f.* garage.

cochero /ko'tʃero/ *n. m.* coachman; cab driver.

cochinada /kotʃi'naða/ *n. f.* filth; herd of swine.

cochino /ko'tʃino/ n. m. pig, swine.

cocido /ko'θiðo; ko'siðo/ n. m. stew.

cociente /ko'θiente; ko'siente/ n. m. quotient.

cocimiento /koθi'miento; kosi'miento/ n. m. cooking.

cocina /ko'θina; ko'sina/ n. f. kitchen.

cocinar /koθi'nar; kosi'nar/ v. cook.

cocinero /koθi'nero; kosi'nero/ -ra n. cook.

coco /'koko/ n. m. coconut; coconut tree.

cocodrilo /koko'ðrilo/ n. m. crocodile.

cóctel /kok'tel/ n. m. cocktail.

codazo /ko'ðaθo; ko'ðaso/ n. m. nudge with the elbow.

codicia /ko'ðiθia; ko'ðisia/ n. f. avarice, greed; lust.

codiciar /koðiθi'ar; koðisi'ar/ v. covet.

codicioso /koðiθi'oso; koðisi'oso/ a. covetous; greedy.

código /'koðigo/ n. m. (law) code.

codo /'koðo/ n. m. elbow.

codorniz /koðor'niθ; koðor'nis/ n. f. quail.

coeficiente /koefi'θiente; koefi'siente/ n. m. quotient.

coeficiente intelectual /koefi'θiente intelek'tual; koefi'siente intelek'tual/ intelligence quotient.

coetáneo /koe'taneo/ a. contemporary.

coexistir /koeksis'tir/ v. coexist.

cofrade /ko'fraðe/ n. m. fellow member of a club, etc.

cofre /'kofre/ n. m. coffer; chest; trunk.

coger /ko'her/ v. catch; pick; take.

cogote /ko'gote/ n. m. nape.

cohecho /ko'etʃo/ n. m. bribe. —**cohechar,** v.

coheredero /koere'ðero/ -ra n. coheir.

coherente /koe'rente/ a. coherent.

cohesión /koe'sion/ n. f. cohesion.

cohete /ko'ete/ n. m. firecracker; rocket.

cohibición /koiβi'θion; koiβi'sion/ n. f. restraint; repression.

cohibir /koi'βir/ v. restrain; repress.

coincidencia /koinθi'ðenθia; koinsi'ðensia/ n. f. coincidence.

coincidir /koinθi'ðir; koinsi'ðir/ v. coincide.

cojear /kohe'ar/ v. limp.

cojera /ko'hera/ n. f. limp.

cojín /ko'hin/ n. m. cushion.

cojinete /kohi'nete/ n. m. small cushion, pad.

cojo /'koho/ -a a. **1.** lame. —n. **2.** lame person.

col /kol/ n. f. cabbage.

cola /'kola/ n. f. tail; glue; line, queue.

colaboración /kolaβora'θion; kolaβora'sion/ n. f. collaboration.

colaborar /kolaβo'rar/ v. collaborate.

cola de caballo /'kola de ka'βaλo; 'kola de ka'βayo/ ponytail.

coladera /kola'ðera/ n. f. strainer.

colador /kola'ðor/ n. m. colander, strainer.

colapso /ko'lapso/ n. m. collapse, prostration.

colar /ko'lar/ v. strain; drain.

colateral /kolate'ral/ a. collateral.

colcha /'koltʃa/ n. f. bedspread, quilt.

colchón /kol'tʃon/ n. m. mattress.

colear /kole'ar/ v. wag the tail.

colección /kolek'θion; kolek'sion/ n. f. collection, set.

coleccionar /kolekθio'nar; koleksio'nar/ v. collect.

colecta /ko'lekta/ n. f. collection; collect (a prayer).

colectivo /kolek'tiβo/ a. collective.

colector /kolek'tor/ n. m. collector.

colega /ko'lega/ n. & f. colleague.

colegial /kole'hial/ n. m. college student.

colegiatura /kolehia'tura/ n. f. scholarship; tuition.

colegio /ko'lehio/ n. m. (private) school, college.

colegir /kole'hir/ v. infer, deduce.

cólera /'kolera/ n. **1.** f. rage, wrath. **2.** m. cholera.

colérico /ko'leriko/ adj. angry, irritated.

colesterol /koleste'rol/ n. m. cholesterol.

coleta /ko'leta/ n. f. pigtail; postscript.

coleto /ko'leto/ n. m. leather jacket.

colgado /kol'gaðo/ **-da** *n.* **1.** crazy person.—*a.* **2.** hanging, pending.

colgador /kolga'ðor/ *n. m.* rack, hanger.

colgaduras /kolga'ðuras/ *n. f.pl.* drapery.

colgante /kol'gante/ *a.* hanging.

colgar /kol'gar/ *v.* hang up, suspend.

colibrí /koli'βri/ *n. f.* hummingbird.

coliflor /koli'flor/ *n. f.* cauliflower.

coligarse /koli'garse/ *v.* band together, unite.

colilla /ko'liʎa; ko'liya/ *n. f.* butt of a cigar or cigarette.

colina /ko'lina/ *n. f.* hill, hillock.

colinabo /koli'naβo/ *n. m.* turnip.

colindante /kolin'dante/ *a.* neighboring, adjacent.

colindar /kolin'dar/ *v.* neighbor, abut.

coliseo /koli'seo/ *n. m.* theater; coliseum.

colisión /koli'sion/ *n. f.* collision; clash.

collado /ko'ʎaðo; ko'yaðo/ *n. m.* hillock.

collar /ko'ʎar; ko'yar/ *n. m.* necklace; collar.

colmar /kol'mar/ *v.* heap up, fill liberally.

colmena /kol'mena/ *n. f.* hive.

colmillo /kol'miʎo; kol'miyo/ *n. m.* eyetooth; tusk; fang.

colmo /'kolmo/ *n. m.* height, peak, extreme.

colocación /koloka'θion; koloka-'sion/ *n. f.* place, position; employment, job; arrangement.

colocar /kolo'kar/ *v.* place, locate, put, set.

colombiano /kolom'biano/ **-na** *a.* & *n.* Colombian.

colon /'kolon/ *n. m.* colon (of intestines).

colonia /ko'lonia/ *n. f.* colony; eau de Cologne.

Colonia *n. f.* Cologne.

colonial /kolo'nial/ *a.* colonial.

colonización /koloniθa'θion; kolonisa'sion/ *n. f.* colonization.

colonizador /koloniθa'ðor; kolonisa'ðor/ **-ra** *n.* colonizer.

colonizar /koloni'θar; koloni'sar/ *v.* colonize.

colono /ko'lono/ *n. m.* colonist; tenant farmer.

coloquio /ko'lokio/ *n. m.* conversation, talk.

color /ko'lor/ *n. m.* color.
—**colorar,** *v.*

coloración /kolora'θion; kolora-'sion/ *n. f.* coloring.

colorado /kolo'raðo/ *a.* red, ruddy.

colorar /kolo'rar/ *v.* color, paint; dye.

colorete /kolo'rete/ *n. m.* rouge.

colorformo /kolor'formo/ *n. m.* chloroform.

colorido /kolo'riðo/ *n. m.* color, coloring.—**colorir,** *v.*

colosal /kolo'sal/ *a.* colossal.

columbrar /kolum'brar/ *v.* discern.

columna /ko'lumna/ *n. f.* column, pillar, shaft.

columpiar /kolum'piar/ *v.* swing.

columpio /ko'lumpio/ *n. m.* swing.

coma /'koma/ *n. f.* coma; comma.

comadre /ko'maðre/ *n. f.* midwife; gossip; close friend.

comadreja /koma'ðreha/ *n. f.* weasel.

comadrona /koma'ðrona/ *n. f.* midwife.

comandancia /koman'danθia; koman'dansia/ *n. f.* command; command post.

comandante /koman'dante/ *n. m.* commandant; commander; major.

comandar /koman'dar/ *v.* command.

comandita /koman'dita/ *n. f.* silent partnership.

comanditario /komandi'tario/ **-ra** *n.* silent partner.

comando /ko'mando/ *n. m.* command.

comarca /ko'marka/ *n. f.* region; border, boundary.

comba /'komba/ *n. f.* bulge.

combar /kom'bar/ *v.* bend; bulge.

combate /kom'bate/ *n. m.* combat.—**combatir,** *v.*

combatiente /komba'tiente/ *a.* & *m.* combatant.

combinación /kombina'θion; kombina'sion/ *n. f.* combination; slip (garment).

combinar /kombi'nar/ *v.* combine.

combustible /kombus'tiβle/ *a.* **1.** combustible.—*n.* **2.** *m.* fuel.

combustión /kombus'tion/ *n. f.* combustion.

comedero /kome'ðero/ *n. m.* trough.

comedia /ko'meðia/ n. f. comedy; play.

comediante /kome'ðiante/ n. m. actor; comedian.

comedido /kome'ðiðo/ a. polite, courteous; obliging.

comedirse /kome'ðirse/ v. to be polite or obliging.

comedor /kome'ðor/ n. m. dining room. **coche c.,** dining car.

comendador /komenda'ðor/ n. m. commander.

comensal /komen'sal/ n. m. table companion.

comentador /komenta'ðor/ -ra n. commentator.

comentario /komen'tario/ n. m. commentary.

comento /ko'mento/ n. m. comment. —**comentar,** v.

comenzar /komen'θar; komen'sar/ v. begin, start, commence.

comer /ko'mer/ v. eat, dine.

comercial /komer'θial; komer'sial/ a. commercial.

comercializar /komerθiali'θar; komersiali'sar/ v. market.

comerciante /komer'θiante; komer'siante/ -ta n. merchant, trader, businessperson.

comerciar /komer'θiar; komer'siar/ v. trade, deal, do business.

comercio /ko'merθio; ko'mersio/ n. m. commerce, trade, business; store.

comestible /komes'tiβle/ a. **1.** edible. —n. **2.** m. (pl.) groceries, provisions.

cometa /ko'meta/ n. **1.** m. comet. **2.** f. kite.

cometer /kome'ter/ v. commit.

cometido /kome'tiðo/ n. m. commission; duty; task.

comezón /kome'θon; kome'son/ n. f. itch.

comicios /ko'miθios; ko'misios/ n. m.pl. primary elections.

cómico /'komiko/ -ca a. & n. comic, comical; comedian.

comida /ko'miða/ n. f. food; dinner; meal.

comidilla /komi'ðiʎa; komi'ðiya/ n. f. light meal; gossip.

comienzo /ko'mienθo; ko'mienso/ n. m. beginning.

comilitona /komili'tona/ n. f. spread, feast.

comillas /ko'miʎas; ko'miyas/ n. f.pl. quotation marks.

comilón /komi'lon/ -na n. glutton; heavy eater.

comisario /komi'sario/ n. m. commissary.

comisión /komi'sion/ n. f. commission. —**comisionar,** v.

comisionado /komisio'naðo/ -da n. agent, commissioner.

comisionar /komisio'nar/ v. commission.

comiso /ko'miso/ n. m. (law) confiscation of illegal goods.

comistrajo /komis'traho/ n. m. mess, hodgepodge.

comité /komi'te/ n. m. committee.

comitiva /komi'tiβa/ n. f. retinue.

como /'komo/ conj. & adv. like, as.

cómo adv. how.

cómoda /'komoða/ n. f. bureau, chest (of drawers).

cómodamente /komoða'mente/ adv. conveniently.

comodidad /komoði'ðað/ n. f. convenience, comfort; commodity.

comodín /komo'ðin/ n. m. joker (playing card).

cómodo /'komoðo/ a. comfortable; convenient.

comodoro /komo'ðoro/ n. m. commodore.

compacto /kom'pakto/ a. compact.

compadecer /kompaðe'θer; kompaðe'ser/ v. be sorry for, pity.

compadraje /kompa'ðrahe/ n. m. clique.

compadre /kom'paðre/ n. m. close friend.

compaginar /kompahi'nar/ v. put in order; arrange.

compañerismo /kompaɲe'rismo/ n. m. companionship.

compañero /kompa'ɲero/ -ra n. companion, partner.

compañía /kompa'ɲia/ n. f. company.

comparable /kompa'raβle/ a. comparable.

comparación /kompara'θion; kompara'sion/ n. f. comparison.

comparar /kompa'rar/ v. compare.

comparativamente /komparatiβa'mente/ adv. comparatively.

comparativo /kompara'tiβo/ a. comparative.

comparecer /kompare'θer; kompare'ser/ v. appear.

comparendo /kompa'rendo/ n. m. summons.

comparsa /kom'parsa/ n. f. carnival masquerade; retinue.

compartimiento /komparti'miento/ n. m. compartment.

compartir /kompar'tir/ v. share.

compás /kom'pas/ n. m. compass; beat, rhythm.

compasar /kompa'sar/ v. measure exactly.

compasión /kompa'sion/ n. f. compassion.

compasivo /kompa'siβo/ a. compassionate.

compatibilidad /kompatiβili'ðað/ n. f. compatibility.

compatible /kompa'tiβle/ a. compatible.

compatriota /kompa'triota/ n. m. & f. compatriot.

compeler /kompe'ler/ v. compel.

compendiar /kompen'diar/ v. summarize; abridge.

compendiariamente /kompendiaria'mente/ adv. briefly.

compendio /kom'pendio/ n. m. summary; abridgment.

compendiosamente /kompendiosa'mente/ adv. briefly.

compensación /kompensa'θion; kompensa'sion/ n. f. compensation.

compensar /kompen'sar/ v. compensate.

competencia /kompe'tenθia; kompe'tensia/ n. f. competence; competition.

competente /kompe'tente/ a. competent.

competentemente /kompetente'mente/ adv. competently.

competición /kompeti'θion; kompeti'sion/ n. f. competition.

competidor /kompeti'ðor/ **-ra** a. & n. competitive; competitor.

competir /kompe'tir/ v. compete.

compilación /kompila'θion; kompila'sion/ n. f. compilation.

compilar /kompi'lar/ v. compile.

compinche /kom'pintʃe/ n. m. pal.

complacencia /kompla'θenθia; kompla'sensia/ n. f. complacency.

complacer /kompla'θer; kompla'ser/ v. please, oblige, humor.

complaciente /kompla'θiente; kompla'siente/ a. pleasing, obliging.

complejidad /komplehi'ðað/ n. f. complexity.

complejo /kom'pleho/ **-ja** a. & n. complex.

complemento /komple'mento/ n. m. complement; *Gram.* object.

completamente /kompleta'mente/ adv. completely.

completamiento /kompleta'miento/ n. m. completion, finish.

completar /komple'tar/ v. complete.

completo /kom'pleto/ a. complete, full, perfect.

complexión /komplek'sion/ n. f. nature, temperament.

complicación /komplika'θion; komplika'sion/ n. f. complication.

complicado /kompli'kaðo/ a. complicated.

complicar /kompli'kar/ v. complicate.

cómplice /'kompliθe; 'komplise/ n. m. & f. accomplice, accessory.

complicidad /kompliθi'ðað; komplisi'ðað/ n. f. complicity.

complot /kom'plot/ n. m. conspiracy.

componedor /kompone'ðor/ **-ra** n. typesetter.

componenda /kompo'nenda/ n. f. compromise; settlement.

componente /kompo'nente/ a. & n. m. component.

componer /kompo'ner/ v. compose; fix, repair.

componible /kompo'niβle/ a. reparable.

comportable /kompor'taβle/ a. endurable.

comportamiento /komporta'miento/ n. m. behavior.

comportarse /kompor'tarse/ v. behave.

comporte /kom'porte/ n. m. behavior.

composición /komposi'θion; komposi'sion/ n. f. composition.

compositivo /komposi'tiβo/ a. synthetic; composite.

compositor /komposi'tor/ **-ra** n. composer.

compost /kom'post/ n. m. compost.

compostura /kompos'tura/ n. f. composure; repair; neatness.

compota /kom'pota/ n. f. (fruit) sauce.

compra /'kompra/ n. f. purchase.
ir de compras, to go shopping.

comprador /kompra'ðor/ **-ra** n.
buyer, purchaser.

comprar /kom'prar/ v. buy, purchase.

comprender /kompren'der/ v.
comprehend, understand; include,
comprise.

comprensibilidad /komprensiβili'ðað/ n. f. comprehensibility.

comprensible /kompren'siβle/ a.
understandable.

comprensión /kompren'sion/ n. f.
comprehension, understanding.

comprensivo /kompren'siβo/ a.
m. comprehensive.

compresa /kom'presa/ n. f. medical compress.

compresión /kompre'sion/ n. f.
compression.

comprimir /kompri'mir/ v. compress; restrain, control.

comprobación /komproβa'θion;
komproβa'sion/ n. f. proof.

comprobante /kompro'βante/ a.
1. proving. —n. **2.** m. proof.

comprobar /kompro'βar/ v. prove;
verify, check.

comprometer /komprome'ter/ v.
compromise.

comprometerse /komprome-
'terse/ v. become engaged.

compromiso /kompro'miso/ n. m.
compromise; engagement.

compuerta /kom'puerta/ n. f.
floodgate.

compuesto /kom'puesto/ n. m.
composition; compound.

compulsión /kompul'sion/ n. f.
compulsion.

compulsivo /kompul'siβo/ a. compulsive.

compunción /kompun'θion; kompun'sion/ n. f. compunction.

compungirse /kompuŋ'girse/ v.
regret, feel remorse.

computación /komputa'θion;
komputa'sion/ n. f. computation.

computador /komputa'ðor/ n. m.
computer.

computadora de sobremesa
/komputa'ðora de soβre'mesa/ n.
f. desktop computer.

computadora doméstica /komputa'ðora do'mestika/ n. f. home
computer.

computar /kompu'tar/ v. compute.

cómputo /'komputo/ n. m. computation.

comulgar /komul'gar/ v. take
communion.

comulgatorio /komulga'torio/
m. communion altar.

común /ko'mun/ a. common,
usual.

comunal /komu'nal/ a. communal.

comunero /komu'nero/ n. m.
commoner.

comunicable /komuni'kaβle/ a.
communicable.

comunicación /komunika'θion;
komunika'sion/ n. f. communication.

comunicante /komuni'kante/ n.
m. & f. communicant.

comunicar /komuni'kar/ v. communicate; convey.

comunicativo /komunika'tiβo/ a.
communicative.

comunidad /komuni'ðað/ n. f.
community.

comunión /komu'nion/ n. f. communion.

comunismo /komu'nismo/ n. m.
communism.

comunista /komu'nista/ a. & n.
communistic; communist.

comúnmente /komu'mente/ adv.
commonly; usually; often.

con /kon/ prep. with.

concavidad /konkaβi'ðað/ n. f.
concavity.

cóncavo /'konkaβo/ a. **1.** concave.
—n. **2.** m. concavity.

concebible /konθe'βiβle; konse-
'βiβle/ a. conceivable.

concebir /konθe'βir; konse'βir/ v.
conceive.

conceder /konθe'ðer; konse'ðer/
v. concede.

concejal /konθe'hal; konse'hal/ n.
m. councilman.

concejo /kon'θeho; kon'seho/ n.
m. city council.

concento /kon'θento; kon'sento/
n. m. harmony (of singing
voices).

concentración /konθentra'θion;
konsentra'sion/ n. f. concentration.

concentrar /konθen'trar; konsen'trar/ v. concentrate.

concepción /konθep'θion; konsep'sion/ n. f. conception.

conceptible /konθep'tiβle; konsep'tiβle/ a. conceivable.

concepto /kon'θepto; kon'septo/
n. m. concept; opinion.

concerniente /konθer'niente; konser'niente/ *a.* concerning.

concernir /konθer'nir; konser'nir/ *v.* concern.

concertar /konθer'tar; konser'tar/ *v.* arrange.

concertina /konθer'tina; konser'tina/ *n. f.* concertina.

concesión /konθe'sion; konse'sion/ *n. f.* concession.

concha /'kontʃa; *n. f.* S.A. shell.

conciencia /konθien'θia; kon'siensia/ *n. f.* conscience; consciousness; conscientiousness.

concienzudo /konθien'θuðo; konsien'suðo/ *a.* conscientious.

concierto /kon'θierto; kon'sierto/ *n. m.* concert.

conciliación /konθilia'θion; konsilia'sion/ *n. f.* conciliation.

conciliador /konθilia'ðor; konsilia'ðor/ **-ra** *a.* conciliatory.

conciliar /konθi'liar; konsi'liar/ *v.* conciliate.

concilio /kon'θilio; kon'silio/ *n. m.* council.

concisión /konθi'sion; konsi'sion/ *n. f.* conciseness.

conciso /kon'θiso; kon'siso/ *a.* concise.

concitar /konθi'tar; konsi'tar/ *v.* instigate, stir up.

conciudadano /konθiuða'ðano; konsiuða'ðano/ **-na** *n.* fellow citizen.

concluir /kon'kluir/ *v.* conclude.

conclusión /konklu'sion/ *n. f.* conclusion.

conclusivo /konklu'siβo/ *a.* conclusive.

concluso /kon'kluso/ *a.* concluded; closed.

concluyentemente /konkluyente'mente/ *adv.* conclusively.

concomitante /konkomi'tante/ *a.* concomitant, attendant.

concordador /konkorða'ðor/ **-ra** *n.* moderator; conciliator.

concordancia /konkor'ðanθia; konkor'ðansia/ *n. f.* agreement, concord.

concordar /konkor'ðar/ *v.* agree; put or be in accord.

concordia /kon'korðia/ *n. f.* concord, agreement.

concretamente /konkreta'mente/ *adv.* concretely.

concretar /konkre'tar/ *v.* summarize; make concrete.

concretarse /konkre'tarse/ *v.* limit oneself to.

concreto /kon'kreto/ *a. & m.* concrete.

concubina /konku'βina/ *n. f.* concubine, mistress.

concupiscente /konkupis'θente; konkupis'sente/ *a.* lustful.

concurrencia /konku'rrenθia; konku'rrensia/ *n. f.* assembly; attendance; competition.

concurrente /konku'rrente/ *a.* concurrent.

concurrido /konku'rriðo/ *a.* heavily attended or patronized.

concurrir /konku'rrir/ *v.* concur; attend.

concurso /kon'kurso/ *n. m.* contest, competition; meeting.

conde /'konde/ *n. m.* (title) count.

condecente /konde'θente; konde'sente/ *a.* appropriate, proper.

condecoración /kondekora'θion; kondekora'sion/ *n. f.* decoration; medal; badge.

condecorar /kondeko'rar/ *v.* decorate with a medal.

condena /kon'dena/ *n. f.* prison sentence.

condenación /kondena'θion; kondena'sion/ *n. f.* condemnation.

condenar /konde'nar/ *v.* condemn; damn; sentence.

condensación /kondensa'θion; kondensa'sion/ *n. f.* condensation.

condensar /konden'sar/ *v.* condense.

condesa /kon'desa/ *n. f.* countess.

condescendencia /kondesθen'denθia; kondessen'densia/ *n. f.* condescension.

condescender /kondesθen'der; kondessen'der/ *v.* condescend, deign.

condescendiente /kondesθen'diente; kondessen'diente/ *a.* condescending.

condición /kondi'θion; kondi'sion/ *n. f.* condition.

condicional /kondiθio'nal; kondi'sio'nal/ *a.* conditional.

condicionalmente /kondiθional'mente; kondisional'mente/ *adv.* conditionally.

condimentar /kondimen'tar/ *v.* season, flavor.

condimento /kondi'mento/ *n. m.* condiment, seasoning, dressing.

condiscípulo /kondis'θipulo; kondis'sipulo/ **-la** n. schoolmate.

condolencia /kondo'lenθia; kondo'lensia/ n. f. condolence, sympathy.

condolerse de /kondo'lerse de/ v. sympathize with.

condominio /kondo'minio/ n. m. condominium.

condómino /kon'domino/ n. m. co-owner.

condonar /kondo'nar/ v. condone.

cóndor /'kondor/ n. m. condor (bird).

conducción /konduk'θion; konduk'sion/ n. f. conveyance.

conducente /kondu'θente; kondu'sente/ a. conducive.

conducir /kondu'θir; kondu'sir/ v. conduct, escort, lead; drive.

conducta /kon'dukta/ n. f. conduct, behavior.

conducto /kon'dukto/ n. m. pipe, conduit; sewer.

conductor /konduk'tor/ **-ra** n. driver; conductor.

conectar /konek'tar/ v. connect.

conejera /kone'hera/ n. f. rabbit warren; place of ill repute.

conejillo de Indias /kone'hiʎo de 'indias; kone'hiyo de 'indias/ guinea pig.

conejo /ko'neho/ **-ja** n. rabbit.

conexión /konek'sion/ n. f. connection; coupling.

conexivo /konek'siβo/ a. connective.

conexo /ko'nekso/ a. connected, united.

confalón /konfa'lon/ n. m. ensign, standard.

confección /konfek'θion; konfek'sion/ n. f. workmanship; ready-made article; concoction.

confeccionar /konfekθio'nar; konfeksio'nar/ v. concoct.

confederación /konfeðera'θion; konfeðera'sion/ n. f. confederation.

confederado /konfeðe'raðo/ **-da** a. & n. confederate.

confederar /konfeðe'rar/ v. confederate, unite, ally.

conferencia /konfe'renθia; konfe'rensia/ n. f. lecture; conference. **c. interurbana**, long-distance call.

conferenciante /konferen'θiante; konferen'siante/ n. m. & f. lecturer, speaker.

conferenciar /konferen'θiar; konferen'siar/ v. confer.

conferencista /konferen'θista; konferen'sista/ n. m. & f. lecturer, speaker.

conferir /konfe'rir/ v. confer.

confesar /konfe'sar/ v. confess.

confesión /konfe'sion/ n. f. confession.

confesionario /konfesio'nario/ n. m. confessional.

confesor /konfe'sor/ **-ra** n. confessor.

confeti /kon'feti/ n. m.pl. confetti.

confiable /kon'fiaβle/ a. dependable.

confiado /kon'fiado/ a. confident; trusting.

confianza /kon'fianθa; kon'fiansa/ n. f. confidence, trust, faith.

confiar /kon'fiar/ v. entrust; trust, rely.

confidencia /konfi'ðenθia; konfi'ðensia/ n. f. confidence, secret.

confidencial /konfiðen'θial; konfiðen'sial/ a. confidential.

confidente /konfi'ðente/ n. m. & f. confidant.

confidentemente /konfiðente'mente/ adv. confidently.

confín /kon'fin/ n. m. confine.

confinamiento /konfina'miento/ n. m. confinement.

confinar /konfi'nar/ v. confine, imprison; border on.

confirmación /konfirma'θion; konfirma'sion/ n. f. confirmation.

confirmar /konfir'mar/ v. confirm.

confiscación /konfiska'θion; konfiska'sion/ n. f. confiscation.

confiscar /konfis'kar/ v. confiscate.

confitar /konfi'tar/ v. sweeten; make into candy or jam.

confite /kon'fite/ n. m. candy.

confitería /konfite'ria/ n. f. confectionery; candy store.

confitura /konfi'tura/ n. f. confection.

conflagración /konflagra'θion; konflagra'sion/ n. f. conflagration.

conflicto /kon'flikto/ n. m. conflict.

confluencia /kon'fluenθia; kon'fluensia/ n. f. confluence, junction.

confluir /kon'fluir/ v. flow into each other.

conformación /konforma'θion;

konforma'sion/ n. f. conformation.

conformar /konfor'mar/ v. conform.

conforme /kon'forme/ a. 1. acceptable, right, as agreed; in accordance, in agreement. —conj. 2. according, as.

conformidad /konformi'ðað/ n. f. conformity; agreement.

conformismo /konfor'mismo/ n. m. conformism.

conformista /konfor'mista/ n. m. & f. conformist.

confortar /konfor'tar/ v. comfort.

confraternidad /konfraterni'ðað/ n. f. brotherhood, fraternity.

confricar /konfri'kar/ v. rub vigorously.

confrontación /konfronta'θion; konfronta'sion/ n. f. confrontation.

confrontar /konfron'tar/ v. confront.

confucianismo /konfuθia'nismo; konfusia'nismo/ n. m. Confucianism.

confundir /konfun'dir/ v. confuse; puzzle, mix up.

confusamente /konfusa'mente/ adv. confusedly.

confusión /konfu'sion/ n. f. confusion, mix-up; clutter.

confuso /kon'fuso/ a. confused; confusing.

confutación /konfuta'θion; konfuta'sion/ n. f. disproof.

confutar /konfu'tar/ v. refute, disprove.

congelable /konge'laβle/ a. congealable.

congelación /konhela'θion; konhela'sion/ n. f. congealment; deep freeze.

congelado /konge'laðo/ a. frozen, congealed.

congelar /konhe'lar/ v. congeal, freeze.

congenial /konge'nial/ a. congenial; analogous.

congeniar /konhe'niar/ v. be congenial.

congestión /konhes'tion/ n. f. congestion.

conglomeración /konglomera-'θion; konglomera'sion/ n. f. conglomeration.

congoja /kon'goha/ n. f. grief, anguish.

congraciamiento /kongraθia-

'miento; kongrasia'miento/ n. m. flattery; ingratiation.

congraciar /kongra'θiar; kongra-'siar/ v. flatter; ingratiate oneself.

congratulación /kongratula'θion; kongratula'sion/ n. f. congratulation.

congratular /kongratu'lar/ v. congratulate.

congregación /kongrega'θion; kongrega'sion/ n. f. congregation.

congregar /kongre'gar/ v. congregate.

congresista /kongre'sista/ n. m. & f. congressional representative.

congreso /kon'greso/ n. m. congress; conference.

conjetura /konhe'tura/ n. f. conjecture. —conjeturar, v.

conjetural /konhetu'ral/ a. conjectural.

conjugación /konhuga'θion; konhuga'sion/ n. f. conjugation.

conjugar /konhu'gar/ v. conjugate.

conjunción /konhun'θion; konhun'sion/ n. f. union; conjunction.

conjuntamente /konhunta'mente/ adv. together, jointly.

conjunto /kon'hunto/ a. 1. joint, unified. —n. 2. m. whole.

conjuración /konhura'θion; konhura'sion/ n. f. conspiracy, plot.

conjurado /konhu'raðo/ -da n. conspirator, plotter.

conjurar /konhu'rar/ v. conjure.

conjuro /kon'huro/ n. m. exorcism; spell; plea.

conllevador /konʎeβa'ðor; konyeβa'ðor/ n. m. helper, aide.

conmemoración /komemora'θion; komemora'sion/ n. f. commemoration; remembrance.

conmemorar /komemo'rar/ v. commemorate.

conmemorativo /komemora'tiβo/ a. commemorative, memorial.

conmensal /komen'sal/ n. m. messmate.

conmigo /ko'migo/ adv. with me.

conmilitón /komili'ton/ n. m. fellow soldier.

conminación /komina'θion; komina'sion/ n. f. threat, warning.

conminar /komi'nar/ v. threaten.

conminatorio /komina'torio/ a. threatening, warning.

conmiseración /komiseraˈθion; komiseraˈsion/ n. f. sympathy.

conmoción /komoˈθion; komoˈsion/ n. f. commotion, stir.

conmovedor /komoβeˈðor/ a. moving, touching.

conmover /komoˈβer/ v. move, affect, touch.

conmutación /komutaˈθion; komutaˈsion/ n. f. commutation.

conmutador /komutaˈðor/ n. m. electric switch.

conmutar /komuˈtar/ v. exchange.

connatural /konnatuˈral/ a. innate, inherent.

connotación /konnotaˈθion; konnotaˈsion/ n. f. connotation.

connotar /konnoˈtar/ v. connote.

connubial /konnuˈβial/ a. connubial.

connubio /koˈnnuβio/ n. m. matrimony.

cono /ˈkono/ n. m. cone.

conocedor /konoθeˈðor; konoseˈðor/ -ra n. expert, connoisseur.

conocer /konoˈθer; konoˈser/ v. know, be acquainted with; meet, make the acquaintance of.

conocible /konoˈθiβle; konoˈsiβle/ a. knowable.

conocido /konoˈθiðo; konoˈsiðo/ -da a. 1. familiar, well-known. —n. 2. acquaintance, person known.

conocimiento /konoθiˈmiento; konosiˈmiento/ n. m. knowledge, acquaintance; consciousness.

conque /ˈkonke/ conj. so then; and so.

conquista /konˈkista/ n. f. conquest.

conquistador /konkistaˈðor/ -ra n. conqueror.

conquistar /konkisˈtar/ v. conquer.

consabido /konsaˈβiðo/ a. aforesaid.

consagración /konsagraˈθion; konsagraˈsion/ n. f. consecration.

consagrado /konsaˈgraðo/ a. consecrated.

consagrar /konsaˈgrar/ v. consecrate, dedicate, devote.

consanguinidad /konsaŋguiniˈðað/ n. f. consanguinity.

consciente /konsˈθiente; konsˈsiente/ a. conscious, aware.

conscientemente /konsθiente-ˈmente; konssienteˈmente/ adv. consciously.

conscripción /konskripˈθion; konskripˈsion/ n. f. conscription for military service.

consecución /konsekuˈθion; konsekuˈsion/ n. f. attainment.

consecuencia /konseˈkuenθia; konseˈkuensia/ n. f. consequence.

consecuente /konseˈkuente/ a. consequent; consistent.

consecuentemente /konsekuenteˈmente/ adv. consequently.

consecutivamente /konsekutiβaˈmente/ adv. consecutively.

consecutivo /konsekuˈtiβo/ a. consecutive.

conseguir /konseˈgir/ v. obtain, get, secure; succeed in, manage to.

conseja /konˈseha/ n. f. fable.

consejero /konseˈhero/ -ra n. adviser, counselor.

consejo /konˈseho/ n. m. council; counsel; (piece of) advice. **c. de redacción**, editorial board.

consenso /konˈsenso/ n. m. consensus.

consentido /konsenˈtiðo/ a. spoiled, bratty.

consentimiento /konsentiˈmiento/ n. m. consent.

consentir /konsenˈtir/ v. allow, permit.

conserje /konˈserhe/ n. m. superintendent, keeper.

conserva /konˈserβa/ n. f. conserve, preserve.

conservación /konserβaˈθion; konserβaˈsion/ n. f. conservation.

conservador /konserβaˈðor/ -ra a. & n. conservative.

conservar /konserˈβar/ v. conserve.

conservativo /konserβaˈtiβo/ a. conservative, preservative.

conservatorio /konserβaˈtorio/ n. m. conservatory.

considerable /konsiðeˈraβle/ a. considerable, substantial.

considerablemente /konsiðeraβleˈmente/ adv. considerably.

consideración /konsiðeraˈθion; konsiðeraˈsion/ n. f. consideration.

consideradamente /konsiðeraðaˈmente/ adv. considerably.

considerado /konsiðeˈraðo/ a. considerate; considered.

considerando /konsiðe'rando/ *conj.* whereas.

considerar /konsiðe'rar/ *v.* consider.

consigna /kon'signa/ *n. f.* watchword.

consignación /konsigna'θion; konsigna'sion/ *n. f.* consignment.

consignar /konsig'nar/ *v.* consign.

consignatorio /konsigna'torio/ **-ria** *n.* consignee; trustee.

consigo /kon'sigo/ *adv.* with herself, with himself, with oneself, with themselves, with yourself, with yourselves.

consiguiente /konsi'giente/ *a.* **1.** consequent. —*n.* **2.** *m.* consequence.

consiguientemente /konsigiente'mente/ *adv.* consequently.

consistencia /konsis'tenθia; konsis'tensia/ *n. f.* consistency.

consistente /konsis'tente/ *a.* consistent.

consistir /konsis'tir/ *v.* consist.

consistorio /konsis'torio/ *n. m.* consistory.

consocio /kon'soθio; kon'sosio/ *m.* associate; partner; comrade.

consola /kon'sola/ *n. f.* console.

consolación /konsola'θion; konsola'sion/ *n. f.* consolation.

consolar /konso'lar/ *v.* console.

consolativo /konsola'tiβo/ *a.* consolatory.

consolidación /konsoliða'θion; konsoliða'sion/ *n.* consolidation.

consolidado /konsoli'ðaðo/ *a.* consolidated.

consolidar /konsoli'ðar/ *v.* consolidate.

consonancia /konso'nanθianb; konso'nansia/ *n. f.* agreement, accord, harmony.

consonante /konso'nante/ *a. & f.* consonant.

consonar /konso'nar/ *v.* rhyme.

consorte /kon'sorte/ *n. m. & f.* consort, mate.

conspicuo /kons'pikuo/ *a.* conspicuous.

conspiración /konspira'θion; konspira'sion/ *n. f.* conspiracy, plot.

conspirador /konspira'ðor/ **-ra** *n.* conspirator.

conspirar /konspi'rar/ *v.* conspire, plot.

constancia /kons'tanθia; kons'tansia/ *n. f.* perseverance; record.

constante /kons'tante/ *a.* constant.

constantemente /konstante'mente/ *adv.* constantly.

constar /kons'tar/ *v.* consist; be clear, be on record.

constelación /konstela'θion; konstela'sion/ *n. f.* constellation.

consternación /konsterna'θion; konsterna'sion/ *n. f.* consternation.

consternar /konster'nar/ *v.* dismay.

constipación /konstipa'θion; konstipa'sion/ *n. f.* head cold.

constipado /konsti'paðo/ *a.* **1.** having a head cold. —*n.* **2.** *m.* head cold.

constitución /konstitu'θion; konstitu'sion/ *n. f.* constitution.

constitucional /konstituθio'nal; konstitusio'nal/ *a.* constitutional.

constitucionalidad /konstituθionali'ðað; konstitusionali'ðað/ *n. f.* constitutionality.

constituir /konsti'tuir/ *v.* constitute.

constitutivo /konstitu'tiβo/ *n. m.* constituent.

constituyente /konstitu'yente, konstitu'tiβo/ *a.* constituent.

constreñidamente /konstreɲiða'mente/ *adv.* compulsively; with constraint.

constreñimiento /konstreɲi'miento/ *n. m.* compulsion; constraint.

constreñir /konstre'ɲir/ *v.* constrain.

constricción /konstrik'θion; konstrik'sion/ *n. f.* constriction.

construcción /konstruk'θion; konstruk'sion/ *n. f.* construction.

constructivo /konstruk'tiβo/ *a.* constructive.

constructor /konstruk'tor/ **-ra** *n.* builder.

construir /kons'truir/ *v.* construct, build.

consuelo /kon'suelo/ *n. m.* consolation.

cónsul /'konsul/ *n. m.* consul.

consulado /konsu'laðo/ *n. m.* consulate.

consular /konsu'lar/ *a.* consular.

consulta /kon'sulta/ *n. f.* consultation.

consultación /konsulta'θion; konsulta'sion/ *n. f.* consultation.

consultante /konsul'tante/ *n. m. & f.* consultant.

consultar /konsul'tar/ *v.* consult.

consultivo /konsul'tiβo/ *a.* consultative.

consultor /konsul'tor/ **-ra** *n.* adviser.

consumación /konsuma'θion; konsuma'sion/ *n. f.* consummation; end.

consumado /konsu'maðo/ *a.* consummate, downright.

consumar /konsu'mar/ *v.* consummate.

consumidor /konsumi'ðor/ **-ra** *n.* consumer.

consumir /konsu'mir/ *v.* consume.

consumo /kon'sumo/ *n. m.* consumption.

consunción /konsun'θion; konsun'sion/ *n. m.* consumption, tuberculosis.

contabilidad /kontaβili'ðað/ *n. f.* accounting, bookkeeping.

contabilista /kontaβi'lista; **contable** *n. m. & f.* accountant.

contacto /kon'takto/ *n. m.* contact.

contado /kon'taðo/ *n. m.* **al c.,** (for) cash.

contador /konta'ðor/ **-ra** *n.* accountant, bookkeeper; meter.

contagiar /konta'hiar/ *v.* infect.

contagio /kon'tahio/ *n. m.* contagion.

contagioso /konta'hioso/ *a.* contagious.

contaminación /kontamina'θion; kontamina'sion/ *n. f.* contamination, pollution. **c. del aire, c. atmosférica,** air pollution.

contaminar /kontami'nar/ *v.* contaminate, pollute.

contar /kon'tar/ *v.* count; relate, recount, tell. **c. con,** count on.

contemperar /kontempe'rar/ *v.* moderate.

contemplación /kontempla'θion; kontempla'sion/ *n. f.* contemplation.

contemplador /kontempla'ðor/ **-ra** *n.* thinker.

contemplar /kontem'plar/ *v.* contemplate.

contemplativamente /kontemplatiβa'mente/ *adv.* thoughtfully.

contemplativo /kontempla'tiβo/ *a.* contemplative.

contemporáneo /kontempo'raneo/ **-nea** *a. & n.* contemporary.

contención /konten'θion; konten'sion/ *n. f.* contention.

contencioso /konten'θioso; konten'sioso/ *a.* quarrelsome; argumentative.

contender /konten'der/ *v.* cope, contend; conflict.

contendiente /konten'diente/ *n. m. & f.* contender.

contenedor /kontene'ðor/ *n. m.* container.

contener /konte'ner/ *v.* contain; curb, control.

contenido /konte'niðo/ *n. m.* contents.

contenta /kon'tenta/ *n. f.* endorsement.

contentamiento /kontenta'miento/ *n. m.* contentment.

contentar /konten'tar/ *v.* content, satisfy.

contentible /konten'tiβle/ *a.* contemptible.

contento /kon'tento/ *a.* **1.** contented, happy. —*n.* **2.** *m.* contentment, satisfaction, pleasure.

contérmino /kon'termino/ *a.* adjacent, abutting.

contestable /kontes'taβle/ *a.* disputable.

contestación /kontesta'θion; kontesta'sion/ *n. f.* answer. —**contestar,** *v.*

contestador automático /kontesta'ðor auto'matiko/ *n. m.* answering machine.

contextura /konteks'tura/ *n. f.* texture.

contienda /kon'tienda/ *n. f.* combat; match; strife.

contigo /kon'tigo/ *adv.* with you.

contiguamente /kontigua'mente/ *adv.* contiguously.

contiguo /kon'tiguo/ *a.* adjoining, next.

continencia /konti'nenθia; konti'nensia/ *n. f.* continence, moderation.

continental /konti'nental/ *a.* continental.

continente /konti'nente/ *n. m.* continent; mainland.

continentemente /kontinente'mente/ *adv.* in moderation.

contingencia /kontin'henθia; kontin'hensia/ *n. f.* contingency.

contingente /kontin'hente/ *a.* contingent; incidental.

continuación /kontinua'θion; kontinua'sion/ *n. f.* continuation. **a c.,** thereupon, hereupon.

continuamente /kontinua'mente/ *adv.* continuously.

continuar /konti'nuar/ *v.* continue, keep on.

continuidad /kontinui'ðað/ *n. f.* continuity.

continuo /kon'tinuo/ *a.* continual; continuous.

contorcerse /kontor'θerse; kontor'serse/ *v.* writhe, twist.

contorción /kontor'θion; kontor'sion/ *n. f.* contortion.

contorno /kon'torno/ *n. m.* contour; profile, outline; neighborhood.

contra /'kontra/ *prep.* against.

contraalmirante /kontraalmi-'rante/ *n. m.* rear admiral.

contraataque /kontraa'take/ *n. m.* counterattack.

contrabajo /kontra'βaho/ *n. m.* double bass.

contrabalancear /kontraβalanθe'ar; kontraβalanse'ar/ *v.* counterbalance.

contrabandear /kontraβande'ar/ *v.* smuggle.

contrabandista /kontraβan'dista/ *n. m. & f.* smuggler.

contrabando /kontra'βando/ *n. m.* contraband, smuggling.

contracción /kontrak'θion; kontrak'sion/ *n. f.* contraction.

contracepción /kontraθep'θion; kontrasep'sion/ *n. f.* contraception, birth control.

contractual /kontrak'tual/ *a.* contractual.

contradecir /kontraðe'θir; kontraðe'sir/ *v.* contradict.

contradicción /kontraðik'θion; kontraðik'sion/ *n. f.* contradiction.

contradictorio /kontraðik'torio/ *adj.* contradictory.

contraer /kontra'er/ *v.* contract; shrink.

contrahacedor /kontraaθe'ðor; kontraase'ðor/ **-ra** *n.* imitator.

contrahacer /kontraa'θer; kontraa'ser/ *v.* forge.

contralor /kontra'lor/ *n. m.* comptroller.

contramandar /kontraman'dar/ *v.* countermand.

contraorden /kontra'orðen/ *n. f.* countermand.

contraparte /kontra'parte/ *n. f.* counterpart.

contrapesar /kontrape'sar/ *v.* counterbalance; offset.

contrapeso /kontra'peso/ *n. m.* counterweight.

contraproducente /kontraproðu'θente; kontraproðu'sente/ *a.* counterproductive.

contrapunto /kontra'punto/ *n. m.* counterpoint.

contrariamente /kontraria'mente/ *adv.* contrarily.

contrariar /kontra'riar/ *v.* contradict; vex; antagonize; counteract.

contrariedad /kontrarie'ðað/ *n. f.* contrariness; opposition; contradiction; disappointment; trouble.

contrario /kon'trario/ *a. & m.* contrary, opposite.

contrarrestar /kontrarres'tar/ *v.* resist; counteract.

contrasol /kontra'sol/ *n. m.* sunshade.

contraste /kon'traste/ *n. m.* contrast. —**contrastar,** *v.*

contratar /kontra'tar/ *v.* engage, contract.

contratiempo /kontra'tiempo/ *n. m.* accident; misfortune.

contratista /kontra'tista/ *n. m. & f.* contractor.

contrato /kon'trato/ *n. m.* contract.

contribución /kontriβu'θion; kontriβu'sion/ *n. f.* contribution; tax.

contribuir /kontri'βuir/ *v.* contribute.

contribuyente /kontriβu'yente/ *n. m. & f.* contributor; taxpayer.

contrición /kontri'θion; kontri'sion/ *n. f.* contrition.

contristar /kontris'tar/ *v.* afflict.

contrito /kon'trito/ *a.* contrite, remorseful.

control /kon'trol/ *n. m.* control. —**controlar,** *v.*

controlador aéreo /kontrola'ðor a'ereo/ *n. m.* air traffic controller.

controversia /kontro'βersia/ *n. f.* controversy.

controversista /kontroβer'sista/ *n. m. & f.* controversialist.

controvertir /kontroβer'tir/ *v.* dispute.

contumacia /kontu'maθia; kontu'masia/ *n. f.* stubbornness.

contumaz /kontu'maθ; kontu'mas/ *adj.* stubborn.

contumelia /kontu'melia/ n. f. contumely; abuse.

conturbar /kontur'βar/ v. trouble, disturb.

contusión /kontu'sion/ n. f. contusion; bruise.

convalecencia /kombale'θenθia; kombale'sensia/ n. f. convalescence.

convalecer /kombale'θer; kombale'ser/ v. convalesce.

convaleciente /kombale'θiente; kombale'siente/ a. convalescent.

convecino /kombe'θino; kombe'sino/ —n. **2.** near, close. neighbor.

convencedor /kombenθe'ðor; kombense'ðor/ adj. convincing.

convencer /komben'θer; komben'ser/ v. convince.

convencimiento /kombenθi-'miento; kombensi'miento/ n. m. conviction, firm belief.

convención /komben'θion; komben'sion/ n. f. convention.

convencional /kombenθio'nal; kombensio'nal/ a. conventional.

conveniencia /kombe'nienθia; kombe'niensia/ n. f. suitability; advantage, interest.

conveniente /kombe'niente/ a. suitable; advantageous, opportune.

convenio /kom'benio/ n. m. pact, treaty; agreement.

convenir /kombe'nir/ v. assent, agree, concur; be suitable, fitting, convenient.

convento /kom'bento/ n. m. convent.

convergencia /komber'henθia; komber'hensia/ n. f. convergence.

convergir /komber'hir/ v. converge.

conversación /kombersa'θion; kombersa'sion/ n. f. conversation.

conversar /komber'sar/ v. converse.

conversión /komber'sion/ n. f. conversion.

convertible /komber'tiβle/ a. convertible.

convertir /komber'tir/ v. convert.

convexidad /kombeksi'ðað/ n. f. convexity.

convexo /kom'bekso/ a. convex.

convicción /kombik'θion; kombik'sion/ n. f. conviction.

convicto /kom'bikto/ a. found guilty.

convidado /kombi'ðaðo/ **-da** n. guest.

convidar /kombi'ðar/ v. invite.

convincente /kombin'θente; kombin'sente/ a. convincing.

convite /kom'bite/ n. m. invitation, treat.

convocación /komboka'θion; komboka'sion/ n. f. convocation.

convocar /kombo'kar/ v. convoke, assemble.

convoy /kom'boi/ n. m. convoy, escort.

convoyar /kombo'yar/ v. convey; escort.

convulsión /kombul'sion/ n. f. convulsion.

convulsivo /kombul'siβo/ a. convulsive.

conyugal /konyu'gal/ a. conjugal.

cónyuge /'konyuhe/ n. m. & f. spouse, mate.

coñac /ko'nak/ n. m. cognac, brandy.

cooperación /koopera'θion; koopera'sion/ n. f. cooperation.

cooperador /koopera'ðor/ a. cooperative.

cooperar /koope'rar/ v. cooperate.

cooperativa /koopera'tiβa/ n. f. (food, etc.) cooperative, co-op.

cooperativo /koopera'tiβo/ a. cooperative.

coordinación /koorðina'θion; koorðina'sion/ n. f. coordination.

coordinar /koorði'nar/ v. coordinate.

copa /'kopa/ n. f. goblet.

copartícipe /kopar'tiθipe; kopar'tisipe/ m & f. partner.

copete /ko'pete/ n. m. tuft; toupee.

copia /'kopia/ n. f. copy. —**copiar,** v.

copiadora /kopia'ðora/ n. f. copier.

copioso /ko'pioso/ a. copious.

copista /ko'pista/ n. m. & f. copyist.

copla /'kopla/ n. f. popular song.

coplero /kop'lero/ n. m. poetaster.

cópula /'kopula/ n. f. connection.

coqueta /ko'keta/ n. f. flirt. —**coquetear,** v.

coraje /ko'rahe/ n. m. courage, bravery; anger.

coral /ko'ral/ a. **1.** choral. —n. **2.** m. coral.

coralino /kora'lino/ a. coral.

Corán /ko'ran/ n. m. Koran.

corazón /kora'θon; kora'son/ n. m. heart.

corazonada /koraθo'naða; koraso'naða/ n. f. foreboding.

corbata /kor'βata/ n. f. necktie.

corbeta /kor'βeta/ n. f. corvette.

corcho /'kortʃo/ n. m. cork.

corcova /kor'koβa/ n. f. hump, hunchback.

corcovado /korko'βaðo/ **-da** a. & n. hunchback.

cordaje /kor'ðahe/ n. m. rigging.

cordel /kor'ðel/ n. m. string, cord.

cordero /kor'ðero/ n. m. lamb.

cordial /kor'ðial/ a. cordial; hearty.

cordialidad /korðiali'ðað/ n. f. cordiality.

cordillera /korði'ʎera; korði'yera/ n. f. mountain range.

cordón /kor'ðon/ n. m. cord; (shoe) lace.

cordura /kor'ðura/ n. f. sanity.

Corea /ko'rea/ n. f. Korea.

coreano /kore'ano/ **-a** a. & n. Korean.

coreografía /koreogra'fia/ n. f. choreography.

corista /ko'rista/ n. f. chorus girl.

corneja /kor'neha/ n. f. crow.

córneo /'korneo/ a. horny.

corneta /kor'neta/ n. f. bugle, horn, cornet.

corniforme /korni'forme/ a. horn-shaped.

cornisa /kor'nisa/ n. f. cornice.

cornucopia /kornu'kopia/ n. f. cornucopia.

coro /'koro/ n. m. chorus; choir.

corola /ko'rola/ n. f. corolla.

corolario /koro'lario/ n. m. corollary.

corona /ko'rona/ n. f. crown; halo; wreath.

coronación /korona'θion; korona'sion/ n. f. coronation.

coronamiento /korona'miento/ n. m. completion of a task.

coronar /koro'nar/ v. crown.

coronel /koro'nel/ n. m. colonel.

coronilla /koro'niʎa; koro'niya/ n. f. crown, top of the head.

corporación /korpora'θion; korpora'sion/ n. f. corporation.

corporal /korpo'ral/ adj. corporeal, bodily.

corpóreo /kor'poreo/ a. corporeal.

corpulencia /korpu'lenθia; korpu'lensia/ n. f. corpulence.

corpulento /korpu'lento/ a. corpulent, stout.

corpuscular /korpusku'lar/ a. corpuscular.

corpúsculo /kor'puskulo/ n. m. corpuscle.

corral /ko'rral/ n. m. corral, pen, yard.

correa /ko'rrea/ n. f. belt, strap.

correa transportadora /korrea transporta'ðora/ conveyor belt.

corrección /korrek'θion; korrek'sion/ n. f. correction.

correcto /ko'rrekto/ a. correct, proper, right.

corrector /korrek'tor/ **-ra** n. corrector, proofreader.

corredera /korre'ðera/ n. f. race course.

corredizo /korre'ðiθo; korre'ðiso/ a. easily untied.

corredor /korre'ðor/ n. m. corridor; runner.

corregible /korre'hiβle/ a. corrigible.

corregidor /korrehi'ðor/ n. m. corrector; magistrate, mayor.

corregir /korre'hir/ v. correct.

correlación /korrela'θion; korrela'sion/ n. f. correlation.

correlacionar /korrelaθio'nar; korrelasio'nar/ v. correlate.

correlativo /korrela'tiβo/ a. correlative.

correo /ko'rreo/ n. m. mail.

correoso /korre'oso/ a. leathery.

correr /ko'rrer/ v. run.

correría /korre'ria/ n. f. raid; escapade.

correspondencia /korrespon'denθia; korrespon'densia/ n. f. correspondence.

corresponder /korrespon'der/ v. correspond.

correspondiente /korrespon'diente/ a. & m. corresponding; correspondent.

corresponsal /korrespon'sal/ n. m. correspondent.

corretaje /korre'tahe/ n. m. brokerage.

correvedile /korreβe'ðile/ n. m. tale bearer; gossip.

corrida /ko'rriða/ n. f. race. **c. (de toros),** bullfight.

corrido /ko'rriðo/ a. abashed; expert.

corriente /ko'rriente/ a. **1.** current, standard. —n. **2.** f. current, stream. **3.** m. **al c.,** informed, up to date. **contra la c.,** against the current; upriver, upstream.

corroboración /korroβora'θion; korroβora'sion/ n. f. corroboration.

corroborar /korroβo'rar/ v. corroborate.

corroer /korro'er/ v. corrode.

corromper /korrom'per/ v. corrupt.

corrompido /korrom'piðo/ a. corrupt.

corrupción /korrup'θion; korrup'sion/ n. f. corruption.

corruptela /korrup'tela/ n. f. corruption; vice.

corruptibilidad /korruptiβili'ðað/ n. f. corruptibility.

corruptor /korrup'tor/ **-ra** n. corrupter.

corsario /kor'sario/ n. m. corsair.

corsé /kor'se/ n. m. corset.

corso /'korso/ n. m. piracy.

cortacésped /korta'θespeð; korta'sespeð/ n. m. lawnmower.

cortadillo /korta'ðiλo; korta'ðiyo/ n. m. small glass.

cortado /kor'taðo/ a. cut.

cortadura /korta'ðura/ n. f. cut.

cortante /kor'tante/ a. cutting, sharp, keen.

cortapisa /korta'pisa/ n. f. obstacle.

cortaplumas /korta'plumas/ n. m. penknife.

cortar /kor'tar/ v. cut, cut off, cut out.

corte /'korte/ n. f. court, m. cut.

cortedad /korte'ðað/ n. f. smallness; shyness.

cortejar /korte'har/ v. pay court to, woo.

cortejo /kor'teho/ n. m. court; courtship; sweetheart.

cortés /kor'tes/ a. civil, courteous, polite.

cortesana /korte'sana/ n. f. courtesan.

cortesano. 1. /korte'sano/ a. **1.** courtly, courteous. —n **2.** m. courtier.

cortesía /korte'sia/ n. f. courtesy.

corteza /kor'teθa; kor'tesa/ n. f. bark; rind; crust.

cortijo /kor'tiho/ n. m. farmhouse.

cortina /kor'tina/ n. f. curtain.

corto /'korto/ a. short.

corva /'korβa/ n. f. back of the knee.

cosa /'kosa/ n. f. thing. **c. de,** a matter of, roughly.

cosecha /ko'setʃa/ n. f. crop, harvest. —**cosechar,** v.

coser /ko'ser/ v. sew, stitch.

cosmético /kos'metiko/ a. & m. cosmetic.

cósmico /'kosmiko/ a. cosmic.

cosmonauta /kosmo'nauta/ n. m. & f. cosmonaut.

cosmopolita /kosmopo'lita/ a. & n. cosmopolitan.

cosmos /'kosmos/ n. m. cosmos.

coso /'koso/ n. m. arena for bull fights.

cosquilla /kos'kiλa; kos'kiya/ n. f. tickle. —**cosquillar,** v.

cosquilloso /koski'λoso; koski'yoso/ a ticklish.

costa /'kosta/ n. f. coast; cost, expense.

costado /kos'taðo/ n. m. side.

costal /kos'tal/ n. m. sack, bag.

costanero /kosta'nero/ a. coastal.

costar /kos'tar/ v. cost.

costarricense /kostarri'θense; kostarri'sense/ a. & n. Costa Rican.

coste /'koste/ n. m. cost, price.

costear /koste'ar/ v. defray, sponsor; sail along the coast of.

costilla /kos'tiλa; kos'tiya/ n. f. rib; chop.

costo /'kosto/ n. m. cost, price.

costoso /kos'toso/ a. costly.

costra /'kostra/ n. f. crust.

costumbre /kos'tumbre/ n. f. custom, practice, habit.

costura /kos'tura/ n. f. sewing; seam.

costurera /kostu'rera/ n. f. seamstress, dressmaker.

costurero /kostu'rero/ n. m. sewing basket.

cota de malla /'kota de 'maλa; 'kota de 'maya/ coat of mail.

cotejar /kote'har/ v. compare.

cotidiano /koti'ðiano/ a. daily; everyday.

cotillón /koti'λon; koti'yon/ n. m. cotillion.

cotización /kotiθa'θion; kotisa'sion/ n. f. quotation.

cotizar /koti'θar; koti'sar/ v. quote (a price).

coto /'koto/ n. m. enclosure; boundary.

cotón /ko'ton/ n. m. printed cotton cloth.

cotufa /ko'tufa/ n. f. Jerusalem artichoke.

coturno /ko'turno/ n. m. buskin.

covacha /ko'βatʃa/ n. f. small cave.

coxal /kok'sal/ a. of the hip.

coy /koi/ n. hammock.

coyote /ko'yote/ n. m. coyote.

coyuntura /koyun'tura/ n. f. joint; juncture.

coz /koθ/ n. m. kick.

crac /krak/ n. m. failure.

cráneo /'kraneo/ n. m. skull.

craniano /kra'niano/ a. cranial.

crapuloso /krapu'loso/ a. drunken.

crasiento /kra'siento/ a. greasy, oily.

craso /'kraso/ a. fat; gross.

cráter /'krater/ n. m. crater.

craza /'kraθa/ /'krasa/ n. f. crucible.

creación /krea'θion/ krea'sion/ n. f. creation.

creador /krea'ðor/ **-ra** n. & a. creative; creator.

crear /krea'r/ v. create.

creativo /krea'tiβo/ a. creative.

crébol /'kreβol/ n. m. holly tree.

crecer /kre'θer/ kre'ser/ v. grow, grow up; increase.

creces /'kreθes/ 'kreses/ n. f.pl. increase, addition.

crecidamente /kreθiða'mente/ kresiða'mente/ adv. abundantly.

crecido /kre'θiðo/ kre'siðo/ a. increased, enlarged; swollen.

creciente /kre'θiente/ kre'siente/ a. **1.** growing. —n. **2.** m. crescent.

crecimiento /kreθi'miento/ kresi'miento/ n. m. growth.

credenciales /kreðen'θiales/ kreðen'siales/ f.pl. credentials.

credibilidad /kreðiβili'ðað/ n. f. credibility.

crédito /'kreðito/ n. m. credit.

credo /'kreðo/ n. m. creed, belief.

crédulamente /kreðula'mente/ adv. credulously, gullibly.

credulidad /kreðuli'ðað/ n. f. credulity.

crédulo /'kreðulo/ a. credulous.

creedero /kree'ðero/ a. credible.

creedor /kree'ðor/ a. credulous, believing.

creencia /kre'enθia/ kre'ensia/ n. f. belief.

creer /kre'er/ v. believe; think.

creíble /kre'iβle/ a. credible, believable.

crema /'krema/ n. f. cream.

cremación /krema'θion/ krema'sion/ n. f. cremation.

crema dentífrica /'krema den'tifrika/ toothpaste.

cremallera /krema'ʎera/ krema'yera/ n. f. zipper.

crémor tártaro /'kremor 'tartaro/ n. m. cream of tartar.

cremoso /kre'moso/ a. creamy.

creosota /kreo'sota/ n. f. creosote.

crepitar /krepi'tar/ v. crackle.

crepuscular /krepusku'lar/ a. of or like the dawn or dusk; crepuscular.

crepúsculo /kre'puskulo/ n. m. dusk, twilight.

crescendo /kres'θendo/ kres'sendo/ n. m. crescendo.

crespo /'krespo/ a. curly.

crespón /kres'pon/ n. m. crepe.

cresta /'kresta/ n. f. crest; heraldic crest.

crestado /kres'taðo/ a. crested.

creta /'kreta/ n. f. chalk.

cretáceo /kre'taθeo/ kre'taseo/ a. chalky.

cretinismo /kreti'nismo/ n. m. cretinism.

cretino /kre'tino/ **-na** n. & a. cretin.

cretona /kre'tona/ n. f. cretonne.

creyente /kre'yente/ a. **1.** believing. —n. **2.** believer.

creyón /kre'yon/ n. m. crayon.

cría /'kria/ n. f. (stock) breeding; young (of an animal), litter.

criada /'kriaða/ n. f. maid.

criadero /kria'ðero/ n. m. Agr. nursery.

criado /kria'ðo/ **-da** n. servant.

criador /kria'ðor/ a. fruitful, prolific.

crianza /kri'anθa/ kri'ansa/ n. f. breeding; upbringing.

criar /kri'ar/ v. raise, rear; breed.

criatura /kria'tura/ n. f. creature; infant.

criba /'kriβa/ n. f. sieve.

cribado /kri'βaðo/ a. sifted.

cribar /kri'βar/ v. sift.

crimen /'krimen/ n. m. crime.

criminal /krimi'nal/ a. & n. criminal.

criminalidad /kriminali'ðað/ n. f. criminality.

criminalmente /kriminal'mente/ adv. criminally.

criminología /kriminolo'hia/ n. f. criminology.

criminoso /krimi'noso/ a. criminal.

crines /'krines/ n. f.pl. mane of a horse.

crinolina /krino'lina/ n. f. crinoline.

criocirugía /krioθiru'hia; kriosiru-'hia/ n. f. cryosurgery.

criollo /kri'oʎo; 'krioyo/ **-lla** a. & n. native; Creole.

cripta /'kripta/ n. f. crypt.

criptografía /kriptogra'fia/ n. f. cryptography.

crisantemo /krisan'temo/ n. m. chrysanthemum.

crisis /'krisis/ n. f. crisis.

crisis nerviosa /krisis ner'βiosa/ nervous breakdown.

crisma /'krisma/ n. m. chrism.

crisol /kri'sol/ n. m. crucible.

crispamiento /krispa'miento/ n. m. twitch, contraction.

crispar /kris'par/ v. contract (the muscles); twitch.

cristal /kris'tal/ n. m. glass; crystal; lens.

cristalería /kristale'ria/ n. f. glassware.

cristalino /krista'lino/ a. crystalline.

cristalización /kristaliθa'θion; kristalisa'sion/ n. f. crystallization.

cristalizar /kristali'θar; kristali'sar/ v. crystallize.

cristianar /kristia'nar/ v. baptize.

cristiandad /kristian'dað/ n. f. Christendom.

cristianismo /kristia'nismo/ n. m. Christianity.

cristiano /kris'tiano/ **-na** a. & n. Christian.

Cristo /'kristo/ n. m. Christ.

criterio /kri'terio/ n. m. criterion; judgment.

crítica /'kritika/ n. f. criticism; critique.

criticable /kriti'kaβle/ a. blameworthy.

criticador /kritika'ðor/ a. critical.

criticar /kriti'kar/ v. criticize.

crítico /'kritiko/ **-ca** a. & n. critical; critic.

croar /kro'ar/ v. croak.

crocante /kro'kante/ n. m. almond brittle.

crocitar /kroθi'tar; krosi'tar/ v. crow.

cromático /kro'matiko/ a. chromatic.

cromo /'kromo/ n. m. chromium.

cromosoma /kromo'soma/ n. m. chromosome.

cromotipia /kromo'tipia/ n. f. color printing.

crónica /'kronika/ n. f. chronicle.

crónico /'kroniko/ a. chronic.

cronicón /kroni'kon/ n. m. concise chronicle.

cronista /kro'nista/ n. m. & f. chronicler.

cronología /kronolo'hia/ n. f. chronology.

cronológicamente /kronolo-hika'mente/ adv. chronologically.

cronológico /krono'lohiko/ a. chronologic.

cronometrar /kronome'trar/ v. time.

cronómetro /kro'nometro/ n. m. stopwatch; chronometer.

croqueta /kro'keta/ n. f. croquette.

croquis /'krokis/ n. m. sketch; rough outline.

crótalo /'krotalo/ n. m. rattlesnake; castanet.

cruce /'kruθe; 'kruse/ n. m. crossing, crossroads, junction.

crucero /kru'θero; kru'sero/ n. m. cruiser.

crucífero /kru'θifero; kru'sifero/ a. cross-shaped.

crucificado /kruθifi'kaðo; krusi-fi'kaðo/ a. crucified.

crucificar /kruθifi'kar; krusifi'kar/ v. crucify.

crucifijo /kruθi'fiho; krusi'fiho/ n. m. crucifix.

crucifixión /kruθifik'sion; krusi-fik'sion/ n. f. crucifixion.

crucigrama /kruθi'grama; krusi-'grama/ n. m. crossword puzzle.

crudamente /kruða'mente/ adv. crudely.

crudeza /kru'ðeθa; kru'ðesa/ n. f. crudeness.

crudo /'kruðo/ a. crude, raw.

cruel /kruel/ a. cruel.

crueldad /kruel'dað/ n. f. cruelty.

cruelmente /kruel'mente/ adv. cruelly.

cruentamente /kruenta'mente/ adv. bloodily.

cruento /'kruento/ a. bloody.

crujía /kru'hia/ n. f. corridor.

crujido /kru'hiðo/ n. m. creak.

crujir /kru'hir/ v. crackle; creak; rustle.

cruórico /'kruoriko/ a. bloody.

crup /krup/ *n. m.* croup.

crupié /kru'pie/ *n. m. & f.* croupier.

crustáceo /krus'taθeo; krus'taseo/ *n. & a.* crustacean.

cruz /kruθ; krus/ *n. f.* cross.

cruzada /kru'θaða; kru'saða/ *n. f.* crusade.

cruzado /kru'θaðo; kru'saðo/ **-da** *n.* crusader.

cruzamiento /kruθa'miento; krusa'miento/ *n. m.* crossing.

cruzar /kru'θar; kru'sar/ *v.* cross.

cruzarse con /kru'θarse kon; kru'sarse kon/ *v.* to (meet and) pass.

cuaderno /kua'ðerno/ *n. m.* notebook.

cuadra /'kuaðra/ *n. f.* block; (hospital) ward.

cuadradamente /kuaðraða'mente/ *adv.* exactly, precisely; completely, in full.

cuadradillo /kuaðra'ðiλo; kuaðra'ðiyo/ *n. m.* lump of sugar.

cuadrado /kua'ðraðo/ **-da** *& a.* square.

cuadrafónico /kuaðra'foniko/ *a.* quadraphonic.

Cuadragésima /kuaðra'hesima/ *n. f.* Lent.

cuadragesimal /kuaðrahesi'mal/ *a.* Lenten.

cuadrángulo /kua'ðrangulo/ *n. m.* quadrangle.

cuadrante /kua'ðrante/ *n. m.* quadrant; dial.

cuadrar /kua'ðrar/ *v.* square; suit.

cuadricular /kuaðriku'lar/ *a.* in squares.

cuadrilátero /kuaðri'latero/ *a.* quadrilateral.

cuadrilla /kua'ðriλa; kua'ðriya/ *n. f.* band, troop, gang.

cuadro /'kuaðro/ *n. m.* picture; painting; frame. **a cuadros,** checked, plaid.

cuadro de servicio /'kuaðro de ser'βiθio; 'kuaðro de ser'βisio/ timetable.

cuadrupedal /kuaðrupe'ðal/ *a.* quadruped.

cuádruplo /'kuaðruplo/ *a.* fourfold.

cuajada /kua'haða/ *n. f.* curd.

cuajamiento /kuaha'miento/ *n. m.* coagulation.

cuajar /kua'har/ *v.* coagulate; overdecorate.

cuajo /'kuaho/ *n. m.* rennet; coagulation.

cual /kual/ *rel. pron.* which.

cuál /kual/ *a. & pron.* what, which.

cualidad /kuali'ðað/ *n. f.* quality.

cualitativo /kualita'tiβo/ *a.* qualitative.

cualquiera /kual'kiera/ *a. & pron.* whatever, any; anyone.

cuando /'kuando/ *conj.* when.

cuando *adv.* when. **de cuando en cuando,** from time to time.

cuantía /kuan'tia/ *n. f.* quantity; amount.

cuantiar /kuan'tiar/ *v.* estimate.

cuantiosamente /kuantiosa'mente/ *adv.* abundantly.

cuantioso /kuan'tioso/ *a.* abundant.

cuantitativo /kuantita'tiβo/ *a.* quantitative.

cuanto /'kuanto/ *a., adv. & pron.* as much as, as many as; all that which. **en c.,** as soon as. **en c a,** as for. **c. antes,** as soon as possible. **c. más... tanto más,** the more... the more. **unos cuantos,** a few.

cuánto *a & adv.* how much, how many.

cuaquerismo /kuake'rismo/ *n. m.* Quakerism.

cuáquero /'kuakero/ **-ra** *n. & a.* Quaker.

cuarenta /kua'renta/ *a. & pron.* forty.

cuarentena /kuaren'tena/ *n. f.* quarantine.

cuaresma /kua'resma/ *n. f.* Lent.

cuaresmal /kuares'mal/ *a.* Lenten.

cuarta /'kuarta/ *n. f.* quarter; quadrant; quart.

cuartear /kuarte'ar/ *v.* divide into quarters.

cuartel /kuar'tel/ *n. m.* Mil. quarters; barracks; *Naut.* hatch. **c. general,** headquarters. **sin c.,** giving no quarter.

cuartelada /kuarte'laða/ *n. f.* military uprising.

cuarterón /kuarte'ron/ *n. & a.* quadroon.

cuarteto /kuar'teto/ *n. m.* quartet.

cuartillo /kuar'tiλo; kuar'tiyo/ *n. m.* pint.

cuarto /'kuarto/ *a.* **1.** fourth. —*n.* **2.** *m.* quarter; room.

cuarto de baño /'kuarto de 'baɲo/ bathroom.

cuarto de dormir /'kuarto de dor'mir/ bedroom.

cuarto para invitados /'kuarto para imbi'taðos/ guest room.

cuarzo /ku'barθo; 'kuarso/ n. m. quartz.

cuasi /'kuasi/ adv. almost, nearly.

cuate /'kuate/ a. & n. twin.

cuatrero /kua'trero/ n. m. cattle rustler.

cuatrillón /kuatri'ʎon; kuatri'yon/ n. m. quadrillion.

cuatro /'kuatro/ a. & pron. four.

cuatrocientos /kuatro'θientos; kuatro'sientos/ a. & pron. four hundred.

cuba /'kuβa/ n. f. cask, tub, vat.

cubano /ku'βano/ **-na** a. & n. Cuban.

cubero /ku'βero/ n. m. cooper.

cubeta /ku'βeta/ n. f. small barrel, keg.

cúbico /'kuβiko/ a. cubic.

cubículo /ku'βikulo/ n. m. cubicle.

cubierta /ku'βierta/ n. f. cover; envelope; wrapping; tread (of a tire); deck.

cubiertamente /kuβierta'mente/ adv. secretly, stealthily.

cubierto /ku'βierto/ n. m. place (at table).

cubil /ku'βil/ n. m. lair.

cubismo /ku'βismo/ n. m. cubism.

cubito de hielo /ku'βito de 'ielo/ n. m. ice cube.

cubo /'kuβo/ n. m. cube; bucket.

cubo de la basura /'kuβo de la ba'sura/ trash can.

cubrecama /kuβre'kama/ n. f. bedspread.

cubrir /ku'βrir/ v. cover.

cubrirse /ku'βrirse/ v. put on one's hat.

cucaracha /kuka'ratʃa/ n. f. cockroach.

cuchara /ku'tʃara/ n. f. spoon, tablespoon.

cucharada /kutʃa'raða/ n. f. spoonful.

cucharita /kutʃa'rita/ **cucharilla** n. f. teaspoon.

cucharón /kutʃa'ron/ n. m. dipper, ladle.

cuchicheo /kutʃi'tʃeo/ n. m. whisper. —**cuchichear,** v.

cuchilla /ku'tʃiʎa/ n. f. cleaver.

cuchillada /kutʃi'ʎaða; kutʃi'yaða/ n. f. slash.

cuchillería /kutʃiʎe'ria; kutʃiye-'ria/ n. f. cutlery.

cuchillo /ku'tʃiʎo; ku'tʃiyo/ n. m. knife.

cucho /'kutʃo/ n. m. fertilizer.

cuchufleta /kutʃu'fleta/ n. f. jest.

cuclillo /ku'kliθo; ku'kliyo/ n. m. cuckoo.

cuco /'kuko/ a. sly.

cuculla /ku'kuʎa; ku'kuya/ n. f. hood, cowl.

cuelga /'kuelga/ n. f. cluster, bunch.

cuelgacapas /kuelga'kapas/ n. m. coat rack.

cuello /'kueʎo; 'kueyo/ n. m. neck; collar.

cuenca /'kuenka/ n. f. socket; (river) basin; wooden bowl.

cuenco /'kuenko/ n. m. earthen bowl.

cuenta /'kuenta/ n. f. account; bill. **darse c.,** to realize. **tener en c.,** to keep in mind.

cuenta bancaria /'kuenta ban-'karia/ bank account.

cuenta de ahorros /'kuenta de a'orros/ savings account.

cuentagotas /kuenta'gotas/ n. m. dropper (for medicine).

cuentista /kuen'tista/ n. m. & f. storyteller; informer.

cuento /'kuento/ n. m. story, tale.

cuerda /'kuerða/ n. f. cord; chord; rope; string; spring (of clock). **dar c. a,** to wind (clock).

cuerdamente /kuerða'mente/ adv. sanely; prudently.

cuerdo /'kuerðo/ a. sane; prudent.

cuerno /'kuerno/ n. m. horn.

cuero /'kuero/ n. m. leather; hide.

cuerpo /'kuerpo/ n. m. body; corps.

cuervo /'kuerβo/ n. m. crow, raven.

cuesco /'kuesko/ n. m. pit, stone (of fruit).

cuesta /'kuesta/ n. f. hill, slope. **llevar a cuestas,** to carry on one's back.

cuestación /kuesta'θion; kuesta-'sion/ n. f. solicitation for charity.

cuestión /kues'tion/ n. f. question; affair; argument.

cuestionable /kuestio'naβle/ a. questionable.

cuestionar /kuestio'nar/ v. question; discuss; argue.

cuestionario /kuestio'nario/ n. m. questionnaire.

cuete /'kuete/ n. m. firecracker.

cueva /'kueβa/ n. f. cave; cellar.

cuguar /ku'ɣuar/ n. m. cougar.

cugujada /kuɣu'haða/ n. f. lark.

cuidado /kui'ðaðo/ n. m. care, caution, worry. **tener c.**, to be careful.

cuidadosamente /kuiðaðosa'mente/ adv. carefully.

cuidadoso /kuiða'ðoso/ a. careful, painstaking.

cuidante /kui'ðante/ n. caretaker, custodian.

cuidar /kui'ðar/ v. take care of.

cuita /'kuita/ n. f. trouble, care; grief.

cuitado /kui'taðo/ a. unfortunate; shy, timid.

cuitamiento /kuita'miento/ n. m. timidity.

culata /ku'lata/ n. f. haunch, buttock; butt of a gun.

culatada /kula'taða/ n. f. recoil.

culatazo /kula'taθo; kula'taso/ n. m. blow with the butt of a gun; recoil.

culebra /ku'leβra/ n. f. snake.

culero /ku'lero/ a. lazy, indolent.

culinario /kuli'nario/ a. culinary.

culminación /kulmina'θion; kulmina'sion/ n. f. culmination.

culminar /kulmi'nar/ v. culminate.

culpa /'kulpa/ n. f. fault, guilt, blame. **tener la c.**, to be at fault. **echar la culpa a**, to blame.

culpabilidad /kulpaβili'ðað/ n. f. guilt, fault, blame.

culpable /kul'paβle/ a. at fault, guilty, to blame, culpable.

culpar /kul'par/ v. blame, accuse.

cultamente /kulta'mente/ adv. politely, elegantly.

cultivable /kulti'βaβle/ a. arable.

cultivación /kultiβa'θion; kultiβa'sion/ n. f. cultivation.

cultivador /kultiβa'ðor/ **-ra** n. cultivator.

cultivar /kulti'βar/ v. cultivate.

cultivo /kul'tiβo/ n. m. cultivation; (growing) crop.

culto /'kulto/ a. **1.** cultured, cultivated. —n. **2.** m. cult; worship.

cultura /kul'tura/ n. f. culture; refinement.

cultural /kultu'ral/ a. cultural.

culturar /kultu'rar/ v. cultivate.

culturismo /kultu'rismo/ n. m. body building.

culturista /kultu'rista/ n. m. & f. body builder.

cumbre /'kumbre/ n. m. summit, peak.

cumpleaños /kumple'aɲos/ n. m.pl. birthday.

cumplidamente /kumpliða'mente/ adv. courteously, correctly.

cumplido /kum'pliðo/ a. polite, polished.

cumplimentar /kumplimen'tar/ v. compliment.

cumplimiento /kumpli'miento/ n. m. fulfillment; compliment.

cumplir /kum'plir/ v. comply; carry out, fulfill; reach (years of age).

cumulativo /kumula'tiβo/ a. cumulative.

cúmulo /'kumulo/ n. m. heap, pile.

cuna /'kuna/ n. f. cradle.

cundir /kun'dir/ v. spread; expand; propagate.

cuneiforme /kunei'forme/ a. cuneiform, wedge-shaped.

cuneo /'ku'neo/ n. m. rocking.

cuña /'kuɲa/ n. f. wedge.

cuñada /ku'ɲaða/ n. f. sister-in-law.

cuñado /ku'ɲaðo/ n. m. brother-in-law.

cuñete /ku'ɲete/ n. m. keg.

cuota /'kuota/ n. f. quota; dues.

cuotidiano /kuoti'ðiano/ a. daily.

cupé /ku'pe/ n. m. coupé.

Cupido /ku'piðo/ n. m. Cupid.

cupo /'kupo/ n. m. share; assigned quota.

cupón /ku'pon/ n. m. coupon.

cúpula /'kupula/ n. f. dome.

cura /'kura/ n. m. priest; f. treatment, (medical) care. **c. de urgencia**, first aid.

curable /ku'raβle/ a. curable.

curación /kura'θion; kura'sion/ n. f. healing; cure; (surgical) dressing.

curado /ku'raðo/ a. cured, healed.

curador /kura'ðor/ **-ra** n. healer.

curandero /kuran'dero/ **-ra** n. healer, medicine man.

curar /ku'rar/ v. cure, heal, treat.

curativo /kura'tiβo/ a. curative, healing.

curia /'kuria/ n. f. ecclesiastical court.

curiosear /kuriose'ar/ v. snoop, pry, meddle.

curiosidad /kuriosi'ðað/ n. f. curiosity.

curioso /ku'rioso/ a. curious.

curro /'kurro/ a. showy, loud, flashy.

cursante /kur'sante/ n. student.

cursar /kur'sar/ v. frequent; attend.

cursi /'kursi/ a. vulgar, shoddy, in bad taste.

curso /'kurso/ n. m. course.

curso por correspondencia /'kurso por korrespon'denθia; 'kurso por korrespon'densia/ n. m. correspondence course.

cursor /kur'sor/ n. m. cursor.

curtidor /kurti'ðor/ n. m. tanner.

curtir /kur'tir/ v. tan.

curva /'kurβa/ n. f. curve; bend.

curvatura /kurβa'tura, kurβi'ðað/ n. f. curvature.

cúspide /'kuspiðe/ n. f. top, peak.

custodia /kus'toðia/ n. f. custody.

custodiar /kusto'ðiar/ v. guard, watch.

custodio /kus'toðio/ n. m. custodian.

cutáneo /ku'taneo/ a. cutaneous.

cutícula /ku'tikula/ n. f. cuticle.

cutis /'kutis/ n. m. or f. skin, complexion.

cutre /'kutre/ a. shoddy.

cuyo /'kuyo/ a. whose.

D

dable /'daβle/ a. possible.

dactilógrafo /dakti'lografo/ **-fa** n. typist.

dádiva /'daðiβa/ n. f. gift.

dadivosamente /daðiβosa'mente/ adv. generously.

dadivoso /daði'βoso/ a. generous, bountiful.

dado /'daðo/ n. m. die.

dador /da'ðor/ **-ra** n. giver.

dados /'daðos/ n. m.pl. dice.

daga /'daga/ n. f. dagger.

dalia /'dalia/ n. f. dahlia.

dallador /daʎa'ðor; daya'ðor/ n. m. lawn mower.

dallar /da'ʎar; da'yar/ v. mow.

daltonismo /dalto'nismo/ n. m. color blindness.

dama /'dama/ n. f. lady.

damasco /da'masko/ n. m. apricot; damask.

damisela /dami'sela/ n. f. young lady, girl.

danés /da'nes/ **-esa** & n. Danish, Dane.

danza /'danθa; 'dansa/ n. f. (the) dance. —**danzar,** v.

danzante /dan'θante; dan'sante/ **-ta** n. dancer.

dañable /da'ɲaβle/ a. condemnable.

dañar /da'ɲar/ v. hurt, harm; damage.

dañino /da'ɲino/ a. harmful.

daño /'daɲo/ n. m. damage; harm.

dañoso /da'ɲoso/ a. harmful.

dar /dar/ v. give; strike (clock). **d. a,** face, open on. **d. con,** find, locate. **¡Dalo por hecho!** Consider it done!

dardo /'darðo/ n. m. dart.

dársena /'darsena/ n. f. dock.

datar /'datar/ v. date.

dátil /'datil/ n. m. date (fruit).

dativo /da'tiβo/ n. m. & a. dative.

datos /'datos/ n. m.pl. data.

de /de/ prep. of; from; than.

debajo /de'βaho/ adv. underneath. **d. de,** under.

debate /de'βate/ n. m. debate.

debatir /deβa'tir/ v. debate, argue.

debe /'deβe/ n. m. debit.

debelación /deβela'θion; deβela'sion/ n. f. conquest.

debelar /deβe'lar/ v. conquer.

deber /de'βer/ v. **1.** owe; must; be to, be supposed to. —**2.** m. obligation.

deberes /de'βeres/ n. m.pl. homework.

debido /de'βiðo/ a. due.

débil /'deβil/ a. weak, faint.

debilidad /deβili'ðað/ n. f. weakness.

debilitación /deβilita'θion; deβilitasion/ n. f. weakness.

debilitar /deβili'tar/ v. weaken.

débito /'deβito/ n. m. debit.

debutar /deβu'tar/ v. make a debut.

década /'dekaða/ n. f. decade.

decadencia /deka'ðenθia; deka'ðensia/ n. f. decadence, decline, decay.

decadente /deka'ðente/ a. decadent, declining, decaying.

decaer /deka'er/ v. decay, decline.

decalitro /deka'litro/ n. m. decaliter.

decálogo /de'kalogo/ n. m. m. decalogue.

decámetro /de'kametro/ n. m. decameter.

decano /de'kano/ n. m. dean.

decantado /dekan'taðo/ a. much discussed; overexalted.

decapitación /dekapita'θion; dekapitasion/ n. f. beheading.

decapitar /dekapi'tar/ v. behead.

decencia /de'θenθia; de'sensia/ n. f. decency.

decenio /de'θenio; de'senio/ n. m. decade.

decente /de'θente; de'sente/ a. decent.

decentemente /deθente'mente; desente'mente/ adv. decently.

decepción /deθep'θion; desep'sion/ n. f. disappointment, letdown; delusion.

decepcionar /deθepθio'nar; desepsio'nar/ v. disappoint, disillusion.

dechado /de'tʃaðo/ n. m. model; sample; pattern; example.

decibelio /deθi'βelio; desi'βelio/ n. m. decibel.

decididamente /deθiðiða'mente; desiðiða'mente/ adv. decidedly.

decidir /deθi'ðir; desi'ðir/ v. decide.

decigramo /deθi'gramo; desi'gramo/ n. m. decigram.

decilitro /deθi'litro; desi'litro/ n. m. deciliter.

décima /'deθima; 'desima/ n. f. ten-line stanza.

decimal /deθi'mal; desi'mal/ a. decimal.

décimo /'deθimo; 'desimo/ a. tenth.

decir /de'θir; de'sir/ v. tell, say. **es d.,** that is (to say).

decisión /deθi'sion; desi'sion/ n. f. decision.

decisivamente /deθisiβa'mente; desisiβa'mente/ adv. decisively.

decisivo /deθi'siβo; desi'siβo/ a. decisive.

declamación /deklama'θion; deklama'sion/ n. f. declamation, speech.

declamar /dekla'mar/ v. declaim.

declaración /deklara'θion; deklara'sion/ n. f. declaration; statement; plea.

declaración de la renta /dekla'raθion de la 'rrenta; dekla'rasion de la 'rrenta/ tax return.

declarar /dekla'rar/ v. declare, state.

declarativo /deklara'tiβo, deklara'torio/ a. declarative.

declinación /deklina'θion; deklina'sion/ n. f. descent; decay; decline; declension.

declinar /dekli'nar/ v. decline.

declive /de'kliβe,/ n. m. declivity, slope.

decocción /dekok'θion; dekok'sion/ n. f. decoction.

decomiso /deko'miso/ n. m. seizure, confiscation.

decoración /dekora'θion; dekora'sion/ n. f. decoration, trimming.

decorado /deko'raðo/ n. m. Theat. scenery, set.

decorar /deko'rar/ v. decorate, trim.

decorativo /dekora'tiβo/ a. decorative, ornamental.

decoro /de'koro/ n. m. decorum; decency.

decoroso /deko'roso/ a. decorous.

decrecer /dekre'θer; dekre'ser/ v. decrease.

decrépito /de'krepito/ a. decrepit.

decreto /de'kreto/ n. m. decree. —**decretar,** v.

dedal /de'ðal/ n. m. thimble.

dédalo /'deðalo/ n. m. labyrinth.

dedicación /deðika'θion; deðika'sion/ n. f. dedication.

dedicar /deði'kar/ v. devote; dedicate.

dedicatoria /deðika'toria/ n. f. dedication, inscription.

dedo /'deðo/ n. m. finger, toe.

dedo anular /'deðo anu'lar/ ring finger.

dedo corazón /'deðo kora'θon; 'deðo kora'son/ middle finger.

dedo índice /'deðo 'indiθe; 'deðo 'indise/ index finger.

dedo meñique /'deðo me'nike/ little finger, pinky.

dedo pulgar /'deðo pul'gar/ thumb.

deducción /deðuk'θion; deðuk'sion/ n. f. deduction.

deducir /deðu'θir; deðu'sir/ v. deduce; subtract.

defectivo /defek'tiβo/ a. defective.

defecto /de'fekto/ n. m. defect, flaw.

defectuoso /defek'tuoso/ a. defective, faulty.

defender /defen'der/ v. defend.

defensa /de'fensa,/ n. f. defense.

defensivo /defen'siβo/ a. defensive.

defensor /defen'sor/ **-ra** n. defender.

deferencia /defe'renθia; deferen'sia/ n. f. deference.

deferir /defe'rir/ v. defer.

deficiente /defi'θiente; defi'siente/ a. deficient.

déficit /'defiθit; 'defisit/ n. m. deficit.

definición /defini'θion; defini'sion/ n. f. definition.

definido /defi'niðo/ a. definite.

definir /defi'nir/ v. define; establish.

definitivamente /definitiβa'mente/ adv. definitely.

definitivo /defini'tiβo/ a. definitive.

deformación /deforma'θion; deforma'sion/ n. f. deformation.

deformar /defor'mar/ v. deform.

deforme /de'forme/ a. deformed; ugly.

deformidad /deformi'ðað/ n. f. deformity.

defraudar /defrau'ðar/ v. defraud.

defunción /defun'θion; defun'sion/ n. f. death.

degeneración /dehenera'θion; dehenera'sion/ n. f. degeneration.

degenerado /dehene'raðo/ a. degenerate. —**degenerar,** v.

deglutir /deglu'tir/ v. swallow.

degollar /dego'ʎar; dego'yar/ v. behead.

degradación /degraða'θion; degraða'sion/ n. f. degradation.

degradar /degra'ðar/ v. degrade, debase.

deidad /dei'ðað/ n. f. deity.

deificación /deifika'θion; deifika'sion/ n. f. deification.

deificar /deifi'kar/ v. deify.

deífico /de'ifiko/ a. divine, deific.

deísmo /de'ismo/ n. m. deism.

dejadez /deha'ðeθ; deha'ðes/ n. f. neglect, untidiness; laziness.

dejado /de'haðo/ a. untidy; lazy.

dejar /de'har/ v. let, allow; leave. **d. de,** stop, leave off. **no d. de,** not fail to.

dejo /'deho/ n. m. abandonment; negligence; aftertaste; accent.

del /del/ contr. of de + el.

delantal /delan'tal/ n. m. apron; pinafore. **delantal de niña,** pinafore.

delante /de'lante/ adv. ahead, forward; in front.

delantero /delan'tero/ a. forward, front, first.

delator /dela'tor/ n. m. informer; accuser.

delegación /delega'θion; delega'sion/ n. f. delegation.

delegado /dele'gaðo/ **-da** n. delegate. —**delegar,** v.

deleite /de'leite/ n. m. delight. —**deleitar,** v.

deleitoso /delei'toso/ a. delightful.

deletrear /deletre'ar/ v. spell; decipher.

delfín /del'fin/ n. m. dolphin; dauphin.

delgadez /delga'ðeθ; delgaðes/ n. f. thinness, slenderness.

delgado /del'gaðo/ a. thin, slender, slim, slight.

deliberación /deliβera'θion; deliβera'sion/ n. f. deliberation.

deliberadamente /deliβeraða'mente/ adv. deliberately.

deliberar /deliβe'rar/ v. deliberate.

deliberativo /deliβera'tiβo/ a. deliberative.

delicadamente /delikaða'mente/ adv. delicately.

delicadeza /delika'ðeθa; delika'ðesa/ n. f. delicacy.

delicado /deli'kaðo/ a. delicate, dainty.

delicia /de'liθia; deli'sia/ n. f. delight; deliciousness.

delicioso /deli'θioso; deli'sioso/ a. delicious.

delincuencia /delin'kuenθia; delin'kuensia/ n. f. delinquency.

delincuencia de menores /delin'kuenθia de me'nores; delin'kuensia de me'nores/ **delincuencia juvenil** juvenile delinquency.

delincuente /delin'kuente/ n. & a. delinquent; culprit, offender.

delineación /delinea'θion; delinea'sion/ n. f. delineation, sketch.

delinear /deline'ar/ v. delineate, sketch.

delirante /deli'rante/ a. delirious.

delirar /deli'rar/ v. rave, be delirious.

delirio /de'lirio/ n. m. delirium; rapture, bliss.

delito /de'lito/ n. m. crime, offense.

delta /'delta/ *n. m.* delta (of river); hang glider.

demacrado /dema'kraðo/ *a.* emaciated.

demagogia /dema'gohia/ *n. f.* demagogy.

demagogo /dema'gogo/ *n. m.* demagogue.

demanda /de'manda/ *n. f.* demand, claim.

demandador /demanda'ðor/ **-ra** *n.* plaintiff.

demandar /deman'dar/ *v.* sue; demand.

demarcación /demarka'θion; demarka'sion/ *n. f.* demarcation.

demarcar /demar'kar/ *v.* demarcate, limit.

demás /de'mas/ *a. & n.* other; (the) rest (of). **por d.,** too much.

demasía /dema'sia/ *n. f.* excess; audacity; iniquity.

demasiado /dema'siaðo/ *a. & adv.* too; too much; too many.

demencia /de'menθia; de'mensia/ *n. f.* dementia; insanity.

demente /de'mente/ *a.* demented.

democracia /demo'kraθia; demo-'krasia/ *n. f.* democracy.

demócrata /de'mokrata/ *n. m. & f.* democrat.

democrático /demo'kratiko/ *a.* democratic.

demoler /demo'ler/ *v.* demolish, tear down.

demolición /demoli'θion; demoli-'sion/ *n. f.* demolition.

demonio /de'monio/ *n. m.* demon, devil.

demontre /de'montre/ *n. m.* devil.

demora /de'mora/ *n. f.* delay, **—demorar,** *v.*

demostración /demostra'θion; demostra'sion/ *n. f.* demonstration.

demostrador /demostra'ðor/ **-ra** *n.* demonstrator.

demostrar /demos'trar/ *v.* demonstrate, show.

demostrativo /demostra'tiβo/ *a.* demonstrative.

demudar /demu'ðar/ *v.* change; disguise, conceal.

denegación /denega'θion; denega'sion/ *n. f.* denial; refusal.

denegar /dene'gar/ *v.* deny; refuse.

dengue /'dengue/ *n. m.* prudishness; dengue.

denigración /denigra'θion; deni-gra'sion/ *n. f.* defamation, disgrace.

denigrar /deni'grar/ *v.* defame, disgrace.

denodado /deno'ðaðo/ *a.* brave, dauntless.

denominación /denomina'θion; denomina'sion/ *n. f.* denomination.

denominar /denomi'nar/ *v.* name, call.

denotación /denota'θion; denota-'sion/ *n. f.* denotation.

denotar /deno'tar/ *v.* denote, betoken, express.

densidad /densi'ðað/ *n. f.* density.

denso /'denso/ *a.* dense.

dentado /den'taðo/ *a.* toothed; serrated; cogged.

dentadura /denta'ðura/ *n. f.* set of teeth.

dentadura postiza /denta'ðura pos'tiθa; denta'ðura pos'tisa/ false teeth, dentures.

dental /den'tal/ *a.* dental.

dentífrico /den'tifriko/ *n. m.* dentifrice, toothpaste.

dentista /den'tista/ *n. m. & f.* dentist.

dentistería /dentiste'ria/ *n. f.* dentistry.

dentro /'dentro/ *adv.* within, inside. **d. de poco,** in a short while.

dentudo /den'tuðo/ *a.* toothy (person).

denuedo /de'nueðo/ *n. m.* bravery, courage.

denuesto /de'nuesto/ *n. m.* insult, offense.

denuncia /de'nunθia; de'nunsia/ *n. f.* denunciation; declaration; complaint.

denunciación /denunθia'θion; denunsia'sion/ *n. f.* denunciation.

denunciar /denun'θiar; denun'siar/ *v.* denounce.

deparar /depa'rar/ *v.* offer; grant.

departamento /departa'mento/ *n. m.* department, section.

departir /depar'tir/ *v.* talk, chat.

dependencia /depen'denθia; depen'densia/ *n. f.* dependence; branch office.

depender /depen'der/ *v.* depend.

dependiente /depen'diente/ *a. & m.* dependent; clerk.

depilar /depi'lar/ *v.* depilate, pluck.

depilatorio /depila'torio/ *a. & n.* depilatory.

depistar *v.* mislead, put off the track.

deplorable /deplo'raβle/ *a.* deplorable, wretched.

deplorablemente /deploraβle-'mente/ *adv.* deplorably.

deplorar /deplo'rar/ *v.* deplore.

deponer /depo'ner/ *v.* depose.

deportación /deporta'θion; deporta'sion/ *n. f.* deportation; exile.

deportar /depor'tar/ *v.* deport.

deporte /de'porte/ *n. m.* sport. —**deportivo,** *a.*

deposición /deposi'θion; deposi'sion/ *n. f.* assertion, deposition; removal; movement.

depositante /deposi'tante/ *n. m. & f.* depositor.

depósito /de'posito/ *n. m.* deposit. —**depositar,** *v.*

depravado /depra'βaðo/ *a.* depraved, wicked.

depravar /depra'βar/ *v.* deprave, corrupt, pervert.

depreciación /depreθia'θion; depresia'sion/ *n. f.* depreciation.

depreciar /depre'θiar; depre'siar/ *v.* depreciate.

depredación /depreða'θion; predra'sion/ *n. f.* depredation.

depredar /depre'ðar/ *v.* pillage, depredate.

depresión /depre'sion/ *n. f.* depression.

depresivo /depre'siβo/ *a.* depressive.

deprimir /depri'mir/ *v.* depress.

depurar /depu'rar/ *v.* purify.

derecha /de'retʃa/ *n. f.* right (hand, side).

derechera /dere'tʃera/ *n. f.* shortcut.

derecho /de'retʃo/ *a.* **1.** right; straight. —*n.* **2.** right; (the) law. **derechos,** *Com.* duty.

derechos civiles /de'retʃos θi'βiles; de'retʃos si'βiles/ *n. m.pl.* civil rights.

derechos de aduana /de'retʃos de a'ðuana/ *n. m.pl.* customs duty.

derechura /dere'tʃura/ *n. f.* straightness.

derelicto /dere'likto/ *a.* abandoned, derelict.

deriva /de'riβa/ *n. f. Naut.* drift.

derivación /deriβa'θion; deriβa-'sion/ *n. f.* derivation.

derivar /deri'βar/ *v.* derive.

dermatólogo /derma'tologo/ **-a** *n.* dermatologist, skin doctor.

derogar /dero'gar/ *v.* derogate; repeal, abrogate.

derramamiento /derrama'miento; *n. m.* overflow.

derramar /derra'mar/ *v.* spill, pour, scatter.

derrame /de'rrame/ *n. m.* overflow; discharge.

derretir /derre'tir/ *v.* melt, dissolve.

derribar /derri'βar/ *v.* demolish, knock down; bowl over, floor, fell.

derrocamiento /derroka'miento; *n. m.* overthrow.

derrocar /derro'kar/ *v.* overthrow; oust; demolish.

derrochar /derro'tʃar/ *v.* waste.

derroche /de'rrotʃe/ *n. m.* waste.

derrota /de'rrota/ *n. f.* rout, defeat. —**derrotar,** *v.*

derrotismo /derro'tismo/ *n. m.* defeatism.

derrumbamiento /derrumba-'miento/ **derrumbe** *m.* collapse; landslide.

derrumbarse /derrum'βarse/ *v.* collapse, tumble.

derviche /der'βitʃe/ *n. m.* dervish.

desabotonar /desaβoto'nar/ *v.* unbutton.

desabrido /desa'βriðo/ *a.* insipid, tasteless.

desabrigar /desaβri'gar/ *v.* uncover.

desabrochar /desaβro'tʃar/ *v.* unbutton, unclasp.

desacato /desa'kato/ *n. m.* disrespect, lack of respect.

desacierto /desa'θierto; desa-'sierto/ *n. m.* error.

desacobardar /desakoβar'ðar/ *v.* remove fear; embolden.

desacomodadamente /desako-moðaða'mente/ *adv.* inconveniently.

desacomodado /desakomo'ðaðo/ *a.* unemployed.

desacomodar /desakomo'ðar/ *v.* molest; inconvenience; dismiss.

desacomodo /desako'moðo/ *n. m.* loss of employment.

desaconsejar /desakonse'har/ v. dissuade (someone); advise against (something).

desacordadamente /desakorða-ða'mente/ adv. unadvisedly.

desacordar /desakor'ðar/ v. differ, disagree; be forgetful.

desacorde /desa'korðe/ a. discordant.

desacostumbradamente /de-sakostumbraða'mente/ adv. unusually.

desacostumbrado /desakostum-'braðo/ a. unusual, unaccustomed.

desacostumbrar /desakostum-'brar/ v. give up a habit or custom.

desacreditar /desakreði'tar/ v. discredit.

desacuerdo /desa'kuerðo/ n. m. disagreement.

desadeudar /desaðeu'ðar/ v. pay one's debts.

desadormecer /desaðorme'θer; desaðorme'ser/ v. waken, rouse.

desadornar /desaðor'nar/ v. divest of ornament.

desadvertidamente /desaðβer-tiða'mente/ adv. inadvertently.

desadvertido /desaðβer'tiðo/ a. imprudent.

desadvertimiento /desaðβerti-'miento/ n. m. imprudence, rashness.

desadvertir /desaðβer'tir/ v. act imprudently.

desafección /desafek'θion; de-safek'sion/ n. f. disaffection.

desafecto /desa'fekto/ a. disaffected.

desafiar /desa'fiar/ v. defy; challenge.

desafinar /desafi'nar/ v. be out of tune.

desafío /desa'fio/ n. m. defiance; challenge.

desaforar /desafo'rar/ v. infringe one's rights; be outrageous.

desafortunado /desafortu'naðo/ a. unfortunate.

desafuero /desa'fuero/ n. m. violation of the law; outrage.

desagraciado /desagra'θiaðo; de-sagra'siaðo/ a. graceless.

desagradable /desagra'ðaβle/ a. disagreeable, unpleasant.

desagradablemente /desagra-ðaβle'mente/ adv. disagreeably.

desagradecido /desagraðe'θiðo; desagraðe'siðo/ a. ungrateful.

desagradecimiento /desagraðe-θi'miento; desagraðesimiento/ n. m. ingratitude.

desagrado /desa'graðo/ n. m. displeasure.

desagraviar /desagra'βiar/ v. make amends.

desagregar /desagre'gar/ v. separate, disintegrate.

desagriar /desa'griar/ v. mollify, appease.

desaguadero /desagua'ðero/ n. m. drain, outlet; cesspool; sink.

desaguador /desagua'ðor/ n. m. water pipe.

desaguar /desa'guar/ v. drain.

desaguisado /desagi'saðo/ n. m. offense; injury.

desahogadamente /desaogaða-'mente/ adv. impudently; brazenly.

desahogado /desao'gaðo/ a. impudent, brazen; cheeky.

desahogar /desao'gar/ v. relieve.

desahogo /desa'ogo/ n. m. relief; nerve, cheek.

desahuciar /desau'θiar; desau'siar/ v. give up hope for; despair of.

desairado /desai'raðo/ a. graceless.

desaire /des'aire/ n. m. slight; scorn. —**desairar**, v.

desajustar /desahus'tar/ v. mismatch, misfit; make unfit.

desalar /desa'lar/ v. hurry, hasten.

desalentar /desalen'tar/ v. make out of breath; discourage.

desaliento /desa'liento/ n. m. discouragement.

desaliñar /desali'ɲar/ v. disarrange; make untidy.

desaliño /desa'liɲo/ n. m. slovenliness, untidiness.

desalivar /desali'βar/ v. remove saliva from.

desalmadamente /desalmaða-'mente/ adv. mercilessly.

desalmado /desal'maðo/ a. merciless.

desalojamiento /desaloha'miento/ n. m. displacement; dislodging.

desalojar /desalo'har/ v. dislodge.

desalquilado /desalki'laðo/ a. vacant, unrented.

desamar /desa'mar/ v. cease loving.

desamasado /desama'saðo/ a. dissolved, disunited, undone.

desamistarse /desamis'tarse/ v. quarrel, disagree.

desamor /desa'mor/ n. m. disaffection, dislike; hatred.

desamorado /desamo'raðo/ a. cruel; harsh; rude.

desamparador /desampara'ðor/ n. m. deserter.

desamparar /desampa'rar/ v. desert, abandon.

desamparo /desam'paro/ n. m. desertion, abandonment.

desamueblado /desamue'βlaðo/ a. unfurnished.

desamueblar /desamue'βlar/ v. remove furniture from.

desandrajado /desandra'haðo/ a. shabby, ragged.

desanimadamente /desanimaða'mente/ adv. in a discouraged manner; spiritlessly.

desanimar /desani'mar/ v. dishearten, discourage.

desánimo /des'animo/ n. m. discouragement.

desanudar /desanu'ðar/ v. untie; loosen; disentangle.

desapacible /desapa'θiβle; desapa'siβle/ a. rough, harsh; unpleasant.

desaparecer /desapare'θer; desapare'ser/ v. disappear.

desaparición /desapari'θion; desapari'sion/ n. f. disappearance.

desapasionadamente /desapasionaða'mente/ adv. dispassionately.

desapasionado /desapasio'naðo/ a. dispassionate.

desapego /desa'pego/ n. m. impartiality.

desapercibido /desaperθi'βiðo; desapersi'βiðo/ a. unnoticed; unprepared.

desapiadado /desapia'ðaðo/ a. merciless, cruel.

desaplicación /desaplika'θion; desaplika'sion/ n. f. indolence, laziness; negligence.

desaplicado /desapli'kaðo/ a. indolent, lazy; negligent.

desaposesionar /desaposesio'nar/ v. dispossess.

desapreciar /desapre'θiar; desapre'siar/ v. depreciate.

desapretador /desapreta'ðor/ n. m. screwdriver.

desapretar /desapre'tar/ v. loosen; relieve, ease.

desaprisionar /desaprisio'nar/ v. set free, release.

desaprobación /desaproβa'θion; desaproβa'sion/ n. f. disapproval.

desaprobar /desapro'βar/ v. disapprove.

desaprovechado /desaproβe-'tʃaðo/ a. useless, profitless; backward.

desaprovechar /desaproβe'tʃar/ v. waste; be backward.

desarbolar /desarβo'lar/ v. unmast.

desarmado /desar'maðo/ a. disarmed, defenseless.

desarmar /desar'mar/ v. disarm.

desarme /de'sarme/ n. m. disarmament.

desarraigado /desarrai'gaðo/ a. rootless.

desarraigar /desarrai'gar/ v. uproot; eradicate; expel.

desarreglar /desarre'glar/ v. disarrange, mess up.

desarrollar /desarro'ʎar; desarro-'yar/ v. develop.

desarrollo /desa'rroʎo; des-'arroyo/ n. m. development.

desarropar /desarro'par/ v. undress; uncover.

desarrugar /desarru'gar/ v. remove wrinkles from.

desaseado /desase'aðo/ a. dirty; disorderly.

desasear /desase'ar/ v. make dirty or disorderly.

desaseo /desa'seo/ n. m. dirtiness; disorder.

desasir /desa'sir/ v. loosen; disengage.

desasociable /desaso'θiaβle; desaso'siaβle/ a. unsociable.

desasosegar /desasose'gar/ v. disturb.

desasosiego /desaso'siego/ n. m. uneasiness.

desastrado /desas'traðo/ a. ragged, wretched.

desastre /de'sastre/ n. m. disaster.

desastroso /desas'troso/ a. disastrous.

desatar /desa'tar/ v. untie, undo.

desatención /desaten'θion; desaten'sion/ n. f. inattention; disrespect; rudeness.

desatender /desaten'der/ v. ignore; disregard.

desatentado /desaten'taðo/ a. inconsiderate; imprudent.

desatinado /desati'naðo/ a. foolish; insane, wild.

desatino /desa'tino/ n. m. blunder. **—desatinar,** v.

desatornillar /desatorni'ʎar; desatorni'yar/ v. unscrew.

desavenencia /desaβe'nenθia; desaβe'nensia/ n. f. disagreement, discord.

desaventajado /desaβenta'haðo/ a. disadvantageous.

desayuno /desa'yuno/ n. m. breakfast. **—desayunar,** v.

desazón /desa'θon; desa'son/ n. f. insipidity; uneasiness.

desazonado /desaθo'naðo; desaso'naðo/ a. insipid; uneasy.

desbandada /desβan'daða/ n. f. disbanding.

desbandarse /desβan'darse/ v. disband.

desbarajuste /desβara'huste/ n. m. disorder, confusion.

desbaratar /desβara'tar/ v. destroy.

desbastar /desβas'tar/ v. plane, smoothen.

desbocado /desβo'kaðo/ a. foulspoken, indecent.

desbocarse /desβo'karse/ v. use obscene language.

desbordamiento /desβorða'miento/ n. m. overflow; flood.

desbordar /desβor'ðar/ v. overflow.

desbrozar /desβro'θar; desβro'sar/ v. clear away rubbish.

descabal /deska'βal/ a. incomplete.

descabalar /deskaβa'lar/ v. render incomplete; impair.

descabellado /deskaβe'ʎaðo; deskaβe'yaðo/ a. absurd, preposterous.

descabezar /deskaβe'θar; deskaβe'sar/ v. behead.

descaecimiento /deskaeθi'miento; deskaesi'miento/ n. m. weakness; dejection.

descafeinado /deskafei'naðo/ a. decaffeinated.

descalabrar /deskala'βrar/ v. injure, wound (esp. the head).

descalabro /deska'laβro/ n. m. accident, misfortune.

descalzarse /deskal'θarse; deskal'sarse/ v. take off one's shoes.

descalzo /des'kalθo; des'kalso/ a. shoeless; barefoot.

descaminado /deskami'naðo/ a. wrong, misguided.

descaminar /deskami'nar/ v. mislead; lead into error.

descamisado /deskami'saðo/ a. shirtless; shabby.

descansillo /deskan'siʎo; deskan'siyo/ n. m. landing (of stairs).

descanso /des'kanso/ n. m. rest. **—descansar,** v.

descarado /deska'raðo/ a. saucy, fresh.

descarga /des'karga/ n. f. discharge.

descargar /deskar'gar/ v. discharge, unload, dump.

descargo /des'kargo/ n. m. unloading; acquittal.

descarnar /deskar'nar/ v. skin.

descaro /des'karo/ n. m. gall, effrontery.

descarriar /deska'rriar/ v. lead or go astray.

descarrilamiento /deskarrila'miento/ n. m. derailment.

descarrilar /deskarri'lar/ v. derail.

descartar /deskar'tar/ v. discard.

descascarar /deskaska'rar/ v. peel; boast, brag.

descendencia /desθen'denθia; dessen'densia/ n. f. descent, origin; progeny.

descender /desθen'der; dessen'der/ v. descend.

descendiente /desθen'diente; dessen'diente/ n. m. & f. descendant.

descendimiento /desθendi'miento; dessendi'miento/ n. m. descent.

descenso /des'θenso; des'senso/ n. m. descent.

descentralización /desθentraliθa'θion; dessentralisa'sion/ n. f. decentralization.

descifrar /desθi'frar; dessi'frar/ v. decipher, puzzle out.

descoco /des'koko/ n. m. boldness, brazenness.

descolgar /deskol'gar/ v. take down.

descollar /desko'ʎar; desko'yar/ v. stand out; excel.

descolorar /deskolo'rar/ v. discolor.

descolorido /deskolo'riðo/ a. pale, faded.

descomedido /deskome'ðiðo/ a. disproportionate; rude.

descomedirse /deskome'ðirse/ v. be rude.

descomponer /deskompo'ner/ v. decompose; break down, get out of order.

descomposición /deskomposi'θion; deskomposi'sion/ n. f. discomposure; disorder, confusion.

descompuesto /deskom'puesto/ a. impudent, rude.

descomulgar /deskomul'gar/ v. excommunicate.

descomunal /deskomu'nal/ a. extraordinary, huge.

desconcertar /deskonθer'tar; deskonser'tar/ v. disconcert, baffle.

desconcierto /deskon'θierto; deskon'sierto/ n. m. confusion, disarray.

desconectar /deskonek'tar/ v. disconnect.

desconfiado /deskon'fiaðo/ a. distrustful.

desconfianza /deskon'fianθa; deskon'fiansa/ n. f. distrust.

desconfiar /deskon'fiar/ v. distrust, mistrust; suspect.

descongelar /deskoŋge'lar/ v. defrost.

descongestionante /deskoŋgestio'nante/ n. decongestant.

desconocer /deskono'θer; deskono'ser/ v. ignore, fail to recognize.

desconocido /deskono'θiðo; deskonos'iðo/ **-da** n. stranger.

desconocimiento /deskonoθi-'miento; deskonosi'miento/ n. m. ingratitude; ignorance.

desconsejado /deskonse'haðo/ a. imprudent, ill advised, rash.

desconsolado /deskonso'laðo/ a. disconsolate, wretched.

desconsuelo /deskon'suelo/ n. m. grief.

descontar /deskon'tar/ v. discount, subtract.

descontentar /deskonten'tar/ v. dissatisfy.

descontento /deskon'tento/ a. discontent.

descontinuar /deskonti'nuar/ v. discontinue.

desconvenir /deskombe'nir/ v. disagree.

descorazonar /deskoraθo'nar; deskoraso'nar/ v. dishearten.

descorchar /deskor'tʃar/ v. uncork.

descortés /deskor'tes/ a. discourteous, impolite, rude.

descortesía /deskorte'sia/ n. f. discourtesy, rudeness.

descortezar /deskorte'θar; deskorte'sar/ v. peel.

descoyuntar /deskoyun'tar/ v. dislocate.

descrédito /des'kreðito/ n. m. discredit.

describir /deskri'βir/ v. describe.

descripción /deskrip'θion; deskrip'sion/ n. f. description.

descriptivo /deskrip'tiβo/ a. descriptive.

descuartizar /deskuarti'θar; deskuarti'sar/ v. dismember, disjoint.

descubridor /deskuβri'ðor/ **-ra** n. discoverer.

descubrimiento /deskuβri'miento/ n. m. discovery.

descubrir /desku'βrir/ v. discover; uncover; disclose.

descubrirse /desku'βrirse/ v. take off one's hat.

descuento /des'kuento/ n. m. discount.

descuidado /deskui'ðaðo/ a. reckless, careless; slack.

descuido /des'kuiðo/ n. m. neglect. **—descuidar,** v.

desde /'desðe/ prep. since; from. **d. luego,** of course.

desdén /des'ðen/ n. m. disdain. **—desdeñar,** v.

desdeñoso /desðe'ɲoso/ a. contemptuous, disdainful, scornful.

desdicha /des'ðitʃa/ n. f. misfortune.

deseable /dese'aβle/ a. desirable.

desear /dese'ar/ v. desire, wish.

desecar /dese'kar/ v. dry, desiccate.

desechable /dese'tʃaβle/ a. disposable.

desechar /dese'tʃar/ v. scrap, reject.

desecho /de'setʃo/ n. m. remainder, residue; (pl.) waste.

desembalar /desemba'lar/ v. unpack.

desembarazado /desembara-'θaðo; desembara'saðo/ a. free; unrestrained.

desembarazar /desembara'θar; desembara'sar/ v. free; extricate; unburden.

desembarcar /desembar'kar/ v. disembark, go ashore.

desembocar /desembo'kar/ v. flow into.

desembolsar /desembol'sar/ v. disburse; expend.

desembolso /desem'bolso/ n. m. disbursement.

desemejante /deseme'hante/ a. unlike, dissimilar.

desempacar /desempa'kar/ v. unpack.

desempeñar /desempe'ɲar/ v. carry out; redeem.

desempeño /desem'peɲo/ n. m. fulfillment.

desencajar /desenka'har/ v. disjoint; disturb.

desencantar /desenkan'tar/ v. disillusion.

desencanto /desen'kanto/ n. m. disillusion.

desencarcelar /desenkarθe'lar; desenkarse'lar/ v. set free; release.

desenchufar /desentʃu'far/ v. unplug.

desenfadado /desenfa'ðaðo/ a. free; unembarrassed; spacious.

desenfado /desen'faðo/ n. m. freedom; ease; calmness.

desenfocado /desenfo'kaðo/ a. out of focus.

desengaño /deseŋ'gaɲo/ m. disillusion. —**desengañar** v.

desenlace /desen'laθe; desen'lase/ n. m. outcome, conclusion.

desenredar /desenre'ðar/ v. disentangle.

desensartar /desensar'tar/ v. unthread (pearls).

desentenderse /desenten'derse/ v. overlook; avoid noticing.

desenterrar /desente'rrar/ v. disinter, exhume.

desenvainar /desembai'nar/ v. unsheath.

desenvoltura /desembol'tura/ n. f. confidence; impudence; boldness.

desenvolver /desembol'βer/ v. evolve, unfold.

deseo /de'seo/ n. m. wish, desire, urge.

deseoso /dese'oso/ a. desirous.

deserción /deser'θion; deser'sion/ n. f. desertion.

desertar /deser'tar/ v. desert.

desertor /deser'tor/ **-ra** n. deserter.

desesperación /desespera'θion; desespera'sion/ n. f. despair, desperation.

desesperado /desespe'raðo/ a. desperate; hopeless.

desesperar /desespe'rar/ v. despair.

desfachatez /desfatʃa'teθ; desfatʃa'tes/ n. f. cheek (gall).

desfalcar /desfal'kar/ v. embezzle.

desfase horario /des'fase o'rario/ n. m. jet lag.

desfavorable /desfaβo'raβle/ a. unfavorable.

desfigurar /desfigu'rar/ v. disfigure, mar.

desfiladero /desfila'ðero/ n. m. defile.

desfile /des'file/ n. m. parade. —**desfilar**, v.

desfile de modas /des'file de 'moðas/ fashion show.

desgaire /des'gaire/ n. m. slovenliness.

desgana /des'gana/ n. f. lack of appetite; unwillingness; repugnance.

desgarrar /desga'rrar/ v. tear, lacerate.

desgastar /desgas'tar/ v. wear away; waste; erode.

desgaste /des'gaste/ n. m. wear; erosion.

desgracia /des'graθia; des'grasia/ n. f. misfortune.

desgraciado /desgra'θiaðo; desgra'siaðo/ a. unfortunate.

desgranar /desgra'nar/ v. shell.

desgreñar /desgre'ɲar/ v. dishevel.

deshacer /desa'θer; desa'ser/ v. undo, take apart, destroy.

deshacerse de /desa'θerse de; desa'serse de/ v. get rid of, dispose of.

deshecho /des'etʃo/ a. undone; wasted.

deshelar /dese'lar/ v. thaw; melt.

desheredamiento /desereða'miento/ n. m. disinheriting.

desheredar /desere'ðar/ v. disinherit.

deshielo /des'ielo/ n. m. thaw, melting.

deshinchar /desin'tʃar/ v. reduce a swelling.

deshojarse /deso'harse/ v. shed (leaves).

deshonestidad /desonesti'ðað/ n. f. dishonesty.

deshonesto /deso'nesto/ a. dishonest.

deshonra /de'sonra/ n. f. dishonor.

deshonrar /deson'rar/ v. disgrace; dishonor.

deshonroso /deson'roso/ a. dishonorable.

desierto /de'sierto/ n. m. desert, wilderness.

designar /desig'nar/ v. appoint, name.

designio /de'signio/ n. m. purpose, intent.

desigual /desi'gual/ a. uneven, unequal.

desigualdad /desigual'dað/ n. f. inequality.

desilusión /desilu'sion/ n. f. disappointment.

desinfección /desinfek'θion; desinfek'sion/ n. f. disinfection.

desinfectar /desinfek'tar/ v. disinfect.

desintegrar /desinte'grar/ v. disintegrate, zap.

desinterés /desinte'res/ n. m. indifference.

desinteresado /desintere'saðo/ a. disinterested, unselfish.

desistir /desis'tir/ v. desist, stop.

desleal /desle'al/ a. disloyal.

deslealtad /desleal'tað/ n. f. disloyalty.

desleír /desle'ir/ v. dilute, dissolve.

desligar /desli'gar/ v. untie, loosen; free, release.

deslindar /deslin'dar/ v. make the boundaries of.

deslinde /des'linde/ n. m. demarcation.

desliz /des'liθ; des'lis/ n. m. slip; false step; weakness.

deslizarse /desli'θarse; desli'sarse/ v. slide; slip; glide; coast.

deslumbramiento /deslumbra'miento/ n. m. dazzling glare; confusion.

deslumbrar /deslumb'rar/ v. dazzle; glare.

deslustre /des'lustre/ n. m. tarnish. —**deslustrar**, v.

desmán /des'man/ n. m. mishap; misbehavior; excess.

desmantelar /desmante'lar/ v. dismantle.

desmañado /desma'ɲaðo/ a. awkward, clumsy.

desmaquillarse /desmaki'ʎarse; desmaki'yarse/ v. remove one's makeup.

desmayar /desma'yar/ v. depress, dishearten.

desmayo /des'mayo/ n. m. faint. —**desmayarse**, v.

desmejorar /desmeho'rar/ v. make worse; decline.

desmembrar /desmem'brar/ v. dismember.

desmemoria /desme'moria/ n. f. forgetfulness.

desmemoriado /desmemo'riaðo/ a. forgetful.

desmentir /desmen'tir/ v. contradict, disprove.

desmenuzable /desmenu'θaβle; desmenu'saβle/ a. crisp, crumbly.

desmenuzar /desmenu'θar; desmenu'sar/ v. crumble, break into bits.

desmesurado /desmesu'raðo/ a. excessive.

desmobilizar /desmoβili'θar; desmoβili'sar/ v. demobilize.

desmonetización /desmonetiθa'θion; desmonetisa'sion/ n. f. demonetization.

desmonetizar /desmoneti'θar; desmoneti'sar/ v. demonetize.

desmontado /desmon'taðo/ a. dismounted.

desmontar /desmon'tar/ v. dismantle.

desmontarse /desmon'tarse/ v. dismount.

desmoralización /desmoraliθa'θion; desmoralisa'sion/ n. f. demoralization.

desmoralizar /desmorali'θar; desmorali'sar/ v. demoralize.

desmoronar /desmoro'nar/ v. crumble, decay.

desmovilizar /desmoβili'θar; desmoβili'sar/ v. demobilize.

desnatar /desna'tar/ v. skim.

desnaturalización /desnaturaliθa'θion; desnaturalisa'sion/ n. f. denaturalization.

desnaturalizar /desnaturali'θar; desnaturali'sar/ v. denaturalize.

desnegamiento /desnega'miento/ n. m. denial, contradiction.

desnervar /desner'βar/ v. enervate.

desnivel /desni'βel/ n. m. unevenness or difference in elevation.

desnudamente /desnuða'mente/ *adv.* nakedly.

desnudar /desnu'ðar/ *v.* undress.

desnudez /desnu'ðeθ; desnu'ðes/ *n. f.* bareness, nudity.

desnudo /des'nuðo/ *a.* bare, naked.

desnutrición /desnutri'θion; desnutri'sion/ *n. f.* malnutrition.

desobedecer /desoβeðe'θer; desoβeðe'ser/ *v.* disobey.

desobediencia /desoβeðien'θia; desoβeðien'sia/ *n. f.* disobedience.

desobediente /desoβe'ðiente/ *a.* disobedient.

desobedientemente /desoβeðiente'mente/ *adv.* disobediently.

desobligar /desoβli'gar/ *v.* release from obligation; offend.

desocupado /desoku'paðo/ *a.* idle, not busy; vacant.

desocupar /desoku'par/ *v.* vacate.

desolación /desola'θion; desola-'sion/ *n. f.* desolation; ruin.

desolado /deso'laðo/ *a.* desolate. —**desolar,** *v.*

desollar /deso'ʎar; deso'yar/ *v.* skin.

desorden /de'sorðen/ *n. m.* disorder.

desordenar /desorðe'nar/ *v.* disarrange.

desorganización /desorganiθa-'θion; desorganisa'sion/ *n. f.* disorganization.

desorganizar /desorgani'θar; desorgani'sar/ *v.* disorganize.

despabilado /despaβi'laðo/ *a.* vigilant, watchful; lively.

despachar /despa'tʃar/ *v.* dispatch, ship, send.

despacho /des'patʃo/ *n. m.* shipment; dispatch, promptness; office.

despacio /des'paθio; des'pasio/ *adv.* slowly.

desparpajo /despar'paho/ *n. m.* glibness; fluency of speech.

desparramar /desparra'mar/ *v.* scatter.

despavorido /despaβo'riðo/ *a.* terrified.

despecho /des'petʃo/ *n. m.* spite.

despedazar /despeða'θar; despeða'sar/ *v.* tear up.

despedida /despe'ðiða/ *n. f.* farewell; leave-taking; discharge.

despedir /despe'ðir/ *v.* dismiss, discharge; see off.

despedirse de /despe'ðirse de/ *v.* say good-bye to, take leave of.

despegar /despe'gar/ *v.* unglue; separate; *Aero.* take off.

despego /des'pego/ *n. m.* indifference; disinterest.

despejar /despe'har/ *v.* clear, clear up.

despejo /des'peho/ *n. m.* sprightliness; clarity; without obstruction.

despensa /des'pensa/ *n. f.* pantry.

despensero /despen'sero/ *n. m.* butler.

despeñar /despe'ɲar/ *v.* throw down.

desperdicio /desper'ðiθio; desper'ðisio/ *n. m.* waste. —**desperdiciar,** *v.*

despertador /desperta'ðor/ *n. m.* alarm clock.

despertar /desper'tar/ *v.* wake, wake up.

despesar /despe'sar/ *n. m.* dislike.

despicar /despi'kar/ *v.* satisfy.

despidida /despi'ðiða/ *n. f.* gutter.

despierto /des'pierto/ *a.* awake; alert, wide-awake.

despilfarrado /despilfa'rraðo/ *a.* wasteful, extravagant.

despilfarrar /despilfa'rrar/ *v.* waste, squander.

despilfarro /despil'farro/ *n. m.* waste, extravagance.

despique /des'pike/ *n. m.* revenge.

despistar /despis'tar/ *v.* mislead, put off the track.

desplazamiento /desplaθa-'miento; desplasa'miento/ *n. m.* displacement.

desplegar /desple'gar/ *v.* display; unfold.

desplome /des'plome/ *n. m.* collapse. —**desplomarse,** *v.*

desplumar /desplu'mar/ *v.* defeather, pluck.

despoblar /despo'βlar/ *v.* depopulate.

despojar /despo'har/ *v.* strip; despoil, plunder.

despojo /des'poho/ *n. m.* plunder, spoils; (*pl.*) remains, debris.

desposado /despo'saðo/ *a.* newly married.

desposar /despo'sar/ *v.* marry.

desposeer /despose'er/ *v.* dispossess.

déspota /'despota/ *n. m. & f.* despot.

despótico /des'potiko/ a. despotic.

despotismo /despo'tismo/ n. m. despotism, tyranny.

despreciable /despre'θiaβle; despre'siaβle/ a. contemptible.

despreciar /despre'θiar; despre'siar/ v. spurn, despise, scorn.

desprecio /des'preθio; des'presio/ n. m. scorn, contempt.

desprender /despren'der/ v. detach, unfasten.

desprenderse /despren'derse/ v. loosen, come apart. **d. de**, get rid of; part with.

desprendido /despren'diðo/ a. disinterested.

despreocupado /despreoku'paðo/ a. unconcerned; unprejudiced.

desprevenido /despreβe'niðo/ a. unprepared, unready.

desproporción /despropor'θion; despropor'sion/ n. f. disproportion.

despropósito /despro'posito/ n. m. nonsense.

desprovisto /despro'βisto/ a. devoid.

después /des'pues/ adv. afterwards, later; then; next. **d. de, d. que**, after.

despuntar /despun'tar/ v. blunt; remove the point of.

desquiciar /deski'θiar; deski'siar/ v. unhinge; disturb, unsettle.

desquitar /deski'tar/ v. get revenge, retaliate.

desquite /des'kite/ n. m. revenge, retaliation.

desrazonable /desraβo'naβle; desraso'naβle/ a. unreasonable.

destacamento /destaka'mento/ n. m. Mil. detachment.

destacarse /desta'karse/ v. stand out, be prominent.

destajero /desta'hero/ **-a** n. **destajista**, m. & f. pieceworker.

destapar /desta'par/ v. uncover.

destello /des'teλo; deste'yo/ n. m. sparkle, gleam.

destemplar /destem'plar/ v. Mus. untune; disturb, upset.

desteñir /deste'nir/ v. fade, discolor.

desterrado /deste'rraðo/ **-da** n. exile.

desterrar /deste'rrar/ v. banish, exile.

destetar /deste'tar/ v. wean.

destierro /des'tierro/ n. m. banishment, exile.

destilación /destila'θion; destila-'sion/ n. f. distillation.

destilar /desti'lar/ v. distill.

destilería /destile'ria/ n. f. distillery.

destilería de petróleo /destile'ria de pe'troleo/ oil refinery.

destinación /destina'θion; destina'sion/ n. f. destination.

destinar /desti'nar/ v. destine, intend.

destinatario /destina'tario/ **-ria** n. addressee (mail); payee (money).

destino /des'tino/ n. m. destiny, fate; destination.

destitución /destitu'θion; destitu'sion/ n. f. dismissal; abandonment.

destituido /desti'tuiðo/ a. destitute.

destorcer /destor'θer; destor'ser/ v. undo, straighten out.

destornillado /destorni'λaðo; destorni'yaðo/ a. reckless, careless.

destornillador /destorni'λaðor; destorni'yaðor/ n. m. screwdriver.

destraillar /destrai'λar; destrai'yar/ v. unleash; set loose.

destral /des'tral/ n. m. hatchet.

destreza /des'treθa; des'tresa/ n. f. cleverness; dexterity, skill.

destripar /destri'par/ v. eviscerate, disembowel.

destrísimo /des'trisimo/ a. extremely dexterous.

destronamiento /destrona-'miento/ n. m. dethronement.

destronar /destro'nar/ v. dethrone.

destrozador /destroθa'ðor; destrosa'ðor/ n. m. destroyer, wrecker.

destrozar /destro'θar; destro'sar/ v. destroy, wreck.

destrozo /des'troθo; des'troso/ n. m. destruction, ruin.

destrucción /destruk'θion; destruk'sion/ n. f. destruction.

destructibilidad /destruktiβili-'ðað/ n. f. destructibility.

destructible /destruk'tiβle/ a. destructible.

destructivamente /destruktiβa-'mente/ adv. destructively.

destructivo /destruk'tiβo/ a. destructive.

destruir /destruir/ v. destroy; wipe out.

desuello /desue'ʎo; desue'yo/ n. m. impudence.

desunión /desu'nion/ n. f. disunion; discord; separation.

desunir /desu'nir/ v. disconnect, sever.

desusadamente /desusaða'mente/ adv. unusually.

desusado /desu'saðo/ a. archaic; obsolete.

desuso /de'suso/ n. m. disuse.

desvalido /desβa'liðo/ a. helpless; destitute.

desvalijador /desβaliha'ðor/ n. m. highwayman.

desván /des'βan/ n. m. attic.

desvanecerse /desβane'θerse; desβane'serse/ v. vanish; faint.

desvariado /desβa'riaðo/ a. delirious; disorderly.

desvarío /desβa'rio/ n. m. raving. —**desvariar,** v.

desvedado /desβe'ðaðo/ a. free; unrestrained.

desveladamente /desβelaða-'mente/ adv. watchfully, alertly.

desvelado /desβe'laðo/ a. watchful; alert.

desvelar /desβe'lar/ v. be watchful; keep awake.

desvelo /des'βelo/ n. m. vigilance; uneasiness; insomnia.

desventaja /desβen'taha/ n. f. disadvantage.

desventar /desβen'tar/ v. let air out of.

desventura /desβen'tura/ n. f. misfortune.

desventurado /desβentu'raðo/ a. unhappy; unlucky.

desvergonzado /desβergon'θaðo; desβergonsaðo/ a. shameless, brazen.

desvergüenza /desβer'guenθa; desβer'guensa/ n. f. shamelessness.

desvestir /desβes'tir/ v. undress.

desviación /desβia'θion; desβia-'sion/ n. f. deviation.

desviado /des'βiaðo/ a. deviant; remote.

desviar /des'βiar/ v. divert; deviate, detour.

desvío /des'βio/ n. m. detour; side track; indifference.

desvirtuar /desβir'tuar/ v. decrease the value of.

deszumar /desθu'mar; dessu'mar/ v. remove the juice from.

detalle /de'taʎe; de'taye/ n. m. detail. —**detallar,** v.

detective /detek'tiβe/ n. m. & f. detective.

detención /deten'θion; deten'sion/ n. f. detention, arrest.

detenedor /detene'ðor/ -ra n. stopper; catch.

detener /dete'ner/ v. detain, stop; arrest.

detenidamente /detenida'mente/ adv. carefully, slowly.

detenido /dete'niðo/ adv. stingy; thorough.

detergente /deter'hente/ a. detergent.

deterioración /deteriora'θion; deteriora'sion/ n. f. deterioration.

deteriorar /deterio'rar/ v. deteriorate.

determinable /determi'naβle/ a. determinable.

determinación /determina'θion; determina'sion/ n. f. determination.

determinar /determi'nar/ v. determine, settle, decide.

determinismo /determi'nismo/ n. m. determinism.

determinista /determi'nista/ n. & a. determinist.

detestable /detes'taβle/ a. detestable, hateful.

detestablemente /detestaβle-'mente/ adv. detestably, hatefully, abhorrently.

detestación /detesta'θion; detesta'sion/ n. f. detestation, hatefulness.

detestar /detes'tar/ v. detest.

detonación /detona'θion; detona'sion/ n. f. detonation.

detonar /deto'nar/ v. detonate, explode.

detracción /detrak'θion; detrak-'sion/ n. f. detraction, defamation.

detractar /detrak'tar/ v. detract, defame, vilify.

detraer /detra'er/ v. detract.

detrás /de'tras/ adv. behind; in back.

detrimento /detri'mento/ n. m. detriment, damage.

deuda /'deuða/ n. f. debt.

deudo /'deuðo/ -da n. relative, kin.

deudor /deu'ðor/ -ra n. debtor.

Deuteronomio /deutero'nomio/ n. m. Deuteronomy.

devalar /deβa'lar/ v. drift off course.

devanar /deβa'nar/ v. to wind, as on a spool.

devanear /deβane'ar/ v. talk deliriously, rave.

devaneo /deβa'neo/ n. m. frivolity; idle pursuit; delirium.

devastación /deβasta'θion; deβasta'sion/ n. f. devastation, ruin, havoc.

devastador /deβasta'ðor/ a. devastating.

devastar /deβas'tar/ v. devastate.

devenir /deβe'nir/ v. happen, occur; become.

devoción /deβo'θion; deβo'sion/ n. f. devotion.

devocionario /deβoθio'nario; deβosio'nario/ n. m. prayer book.

devocionero /deβoθio'nero; deβosio'nero/ a. devotional.

devolver /deβol'βer/ v. return, give back.

devorar /deβo'rar/ v. devour.

devotamente /deβota'mente/ adv. devotedly, devoutly, piously.

devoto /de'βoto/ a. devoted.

deyección /deiek'θion; deiek'sion/ n. f. depression, dejection.

día /dia/ n. m. day. **buenos días,** good morning.

diabetes /dia'βetes/ n. f. diabetes.

diabético /dia'βetiko/ a. diabetic.

diablear /diaβle'ar/ v. play pranks.

diablo /'diaβlo/ n. m. devil.

diablura /dia'βlura/ n. f. mischief.

diabólicamente /diaβolika'mente/ adv. diabolically.

diabólico /dia'βoliko/ a. diabolic, devilish.

diaconato /diako'nato/ n. m. deaconship.

diaconía /diako'nia/ n. f. deaconry.

diácono /'diakono/ n. m. deacon.

diacrítico /dia'kritiko/ a. diacritic.

diadema /dia'ðema/ n. f. diadem; crown.

diáfano /'diafano/ a. transparent.

diafragma /dia'fragma/ n. m. diaphragm.

diagnosticar /diagnosti'kar/ v. diagnose.

diagonal /diago'nal/ n. f. diagonal.

diagonalmente /diagonal'mente/ adv. diagonally.

diagrama /dia'grama/ n. m. diagram.

dialectal /dialek'tal/ a. dialectal.

dialéctico /dia'lektiko/ a. dialectic.

dialecto /dia'lekto/ n. m. dialect.

diálogo /'dialogo/ n. m. dialogue.

diamante /dia'mante/ n. m. diamond.

diamantista /diaman'tista/ n. m. & f. diamond cutter; jeweler.

diametral /diame'tral/ a. diametric.

diametralmente /diametral'mente/ adv. diametrically.

diámetro /'diametro/ n. m. diameter.

diana /'diana/ n. f. reveille; dartboard.

diapasón /diapa'son/ n. m. standard pitch; tuning fork.

diaplejía /diaple'hia/ n. f. paralysis.

diariamente /diaria'mente/ adv. daily.

diario /'diario/ a. & m. daily; daily paper; diary; journal.

diarrea /dia'rrea/ n. f. diarrhea.

diatriba /dia'triβa/ n. f. diatribe, harangue.

dibujo /di'βuho/ n. m. drawing, sketch. —**dibujar,** v.

dicción /dik'θion; dik'sion/ n. f. diction.

diccionario /dikθio'nario; diksio'nario/ n. m. dictionary.

diccionarista /dikθiona'rista; diksiona'rista/ n. m. & f. lexicographer.

dicha /'ditʃa/ n. f. happiness.

dicho /'ditʃo/ n. m. saying.

dichoso /di'tʃoso/ a. happy; fortunate.

diciembre /di'θiembre; di'siembre/ n. m. December.

dicotomía /dikoto'mia/ n. f. dichotomy.

dictado /dik'taðo/ n. m. dictation.

dictador /dikta'ðor/ -ra n. dictator.

dictadura /dikta'ðura/ n. f. dictatorship.

dictamen /dik'tamen/ n. m. dictate.

dictar /dik'tar/ v. dictate; direct.

dictatorial /diktato'rial/ **dictatorio** a. dictatorial.

didáctico /di'ðaktiko/ a. didactic.

diecinueve /dieθi'nueβe; diesi-'nueβe/ *a.* & *pron.* nineteen.

dieciocho /die'θiotʃo; die'siotʃo/ *a.* & *pron.* eighteen.

dieciseis /dieθi'seis; diesi'seis/ *a.* & *pron.* sixteen.

diecisiete /dieθi'siete; diesi'siete/ *a.* & *pron.* seventeen.

diente /'diente/ *n. m.* tooth.

diestramente /diestra'mente/ *adv.* skillfully, ably; ingeniously.

diestro /'diestro/ *a.* dexterous, skillful; clever.

dieta /'dieta/ *n. f.* diet; allowance.

dietética /die'tetika/ *n. f.* dietetics.

dietético /die'tetiko/ *a.* **1.** dietetic; dietary. —*n.* **2. -ca,** dietician.

diez /dieθ; dies/ *a.* & *pron.* ten.

diezmal /dieθ'mal; dies'mal/ *a.* decimal.

diezmar /dieθ'mar; dies'mar/ *v.* decimate.

difamación /difama'θion; difama'sion/ *n. f.* defamation, smear.

difamar /difa'mar/ *v.* defame, smear, libel.

difamatorio /difama'torio/ *a.* defamatory.

diferencia /dife'renθia; dife'rensia/ *n. f.* difference.

diferencial /diferen'θial; diferen-'sial/ *a.* & *f.* differential.

diferenciar /diferen'θiar; diferen-'siar/ *v.* differentiate, distinguish.

diferente /dife'rente/ *a.* different.

diferentemente /diferente'mente/ *adv.* differently.

diferir /dife'rir/ *v.* differ; defer, put off.

difícil /di'fiθil; di'fisil/ *a.* difficult, hard.

difícilmente /difiθil'mente; difisil'mente/ *adv.* with difficulty or hardship.

dificultad /difikul'tað/ *n. f.* difficulty.

dificultar /difikul'tar/ *v.* make difficult.

dificultoso /difikul'toso/ *a.* difficult, hard.

difidencia /difi'ðenθia; difi'ðensia/ *n. f.* diffidence.

difidente /difi'ðente/ *a.* diffident.

difteria /dif'teria/ *n. f.* diphtheria.

difundir /difun'dir/ *v.* diffuse, spread.

difunto /di'funto/ *a.* **1.** deceased, dead, late. —*n.* **2. -ta,** deceased person.

difusamente /difusa'mente/ *adv.* diffusely.

difusión /difu'sion/ *n. f.* diffusion, spread.

digerible /dihe'riβle/ *a.* digestible.

digerir /dihe'rir/ *v.* digest.

digestible /dihes'tiβle/ *a.* digestible.

digestión /dihes'tion/ *n. f.* digestion.

digestivo /dihes'tiβo/ *a.* digestive.

digesto /di'hesto/ *n. m.* digest or code of laws.

digitado /dihi'taðo/ *a.* digitate.

digital /dihi'tal/ *a.* **1.** digital. —*n.* **2.** *f.* foxglove, digitalis.

dignación /digna'θion; digna'sion/ *f.* condescension; deigning.

dignamente /digna'mente/ *adv.* with dignity.

dignarse /dig'narse/ *v.* condescend, deign.

dignatario /digna'tario/ **-ra** *n.* dignitary.

dignidad /digni'ðað/ *n. f.* dignity.

dignificar /dignifi'kar/ *v.* dignify.

digno /'digno/ *a.* worthy; dignified.

digresión /digre'sion/ *n. f.* digression.

digresivo /digre'siβo/ *a.* digressive.

dij, dije /dih; 'dihe/ *n. m.* trinket, piece of jewelry.

dilación /dila'θion; dila'sion/ *n. f.* delay.

dilapidación /dilapiða'θion; dilapi-'ðasion/ *n. f.* dilapidation.

dilapidado /dilapi'ðaðo/ *a.* dilapidated.

dilatación /dilata'θion; dilata'sion/ *n. f.* dilatation, enlargement.

dilatar /dila'tar/ *v.* dilate; delay; expand.

dilatoria /dila'toria/ *n. f.* delay.

dilatorio /dila'torio/ *a.* dilatory.

dilecto /di'lekto/ *a.* loved.

dilema /di'lema/ *n. m.* dilemma.

diligencia /dili'henθia; dili'hensia/ *n. f.* diligence, industriousness.

diligente /dili'hente/ *a.* diligent, industrious.

diligentemente /dilihente'mente/ *adv.* diligently.

dilogía /dilo'hia/ *n. f.* ambiguous meaning.

dilución /dilu'θion; dilu'sion/ *n. f.* dilution.

diluir /dilu'ir/ *v.* dilute.

diluvial /dilu'βial/ *a.* diluvial.

diluvio /di'luβio/ n. m. flood, deluge.

dimensión /dimen'sion/ n. f. dimension; measurement.

diminución /diminu'θion; diminu'sion/ n. f. diminution.

diminuto /dimi'nuto/ a. diminutive, little.

dimisión /dimi'sion/ n. f. resignation.

dimitir /dimi'tir/ v. resign.

Dinamarca /dina'marka/ n. f. Denmark.

dinamarqués /dinamar'kes/ **-esa** a. & n. Danish, Dane.

dinámico /di'namiko/ a. dynamic.

dinamita /dina'mita/ n. f. dynamite.

dinamitero /dinami'tero/ **-ra** n. dynamiter.

dinamo /'dinamo/ n. m. dynamo.

dinasta /di'nasta/ n. m. dynast, king, monarch.

dinastía /dinas'tia/ n. f. dynasty.

dinástico /di'nastiko/ a. dynastic.

dinero /di'nero/ n. m. money, currency.

dinosauro /dino'sauro/ n. m. dinosaur.

diócesis /'dioθesis; 'diosesis/ n. f. diocese.

Dios /dios/ n. m. God.

dios **-sa** n. god, goddess.

diploma /di'ploma/ n. m. diploma.

diplomacia /diplo'maθia; diplo'masia/ n. f. diplomacy.

diplomado /diplo'maðo/ **-da** n. graduate.

diplomarse /diplo'marse/ v. graduate (from a school).

diplomática /diplo'matika/ n. f. diplomacy.

diplomático /diplo'matiko/ **-ca** a. & n. diplomat; diplomatic.

dipsomanía /dipsoma'nia/ n. f. dipsomania.

diptongo /dip'toŋgo/ n. m. diphthong.

diputación /diputa'θion; diputa'sion/ n. f. deputation, delegation.

diputado /dipu'taðo/ **-da** n. deputy; delegate.

diputar /dipu'tar/ v. depute, delegate; empower.

dique /'dike/ n. m. dike; dam.

dirección /direk'θion; direk'sion/ n. f. direction; address; guidance; Com. management.

directamente /direkta'mente/ adv. directly.

directo /di'rekto/ a. direct.

director /direk'tor/ **-ra** n. director; manager.

directorio /direk'torio/ n. m. directory.

dirigente /diri'hente/ a. directing, controlling, managing.

dirigible /diri'hiβle/ n. m. dirigible.

dirigir /diri'hir/ v. direct; lead; manage.

dirigirse a /diri'hirse a/ v. address; approach, turn to; head for.

dirruir /di'rruir/ v. destroy, devastate.

disanto /di'santo/ n. m. holy day.

discantar /diskan'tar/ v. sing (esp. in counterpoint); discuss.

disceptación /disθepta'θion; dissepta'sion/ n. f. argument, quarrel.

disceptar /disθep'tar; dissep'tar/ v. argue, quarrel.

discernimiento /disθerni'miento; disserni'miento/ n. m. discernment.

discernir /disθer'nir; disser'nir/ v. discern.

disciplina /disθi'plina; dissi'plina/ n. f. discipline.

disciplinable /disθipli'naβle; dissipli'naβle/ a. disciplinable.

disciplinar /disθipli'nar; dissipli'nar/ v. discipline, train, teach.

discípulo /dis'θipulo; dis'sipulo/ **-la** n. disciple, follower; pupil.

disco /'disko/ n. m. disk; (phonograph) record.

disco compacto /'disko kom'pakto/ compact disk.

disco duro /'disko 'duro/ hard disk.

disco flexible /'disko flek'siβle/ floppy disk.

discontinuación /diskontinua-'θion; diskontinua'sion/ n. f. discontinuation.

discontinuar /diskonti'nuar/ v. discontinue, break off, cease.

discordancia /diskor'ðanθia; diskor'ðansia/ n. f. discordance.

discordar /diskor'ðar/ v. disagree, conflict.

discordia /dis'korðia/ n. f. discord.

discoteca /disko'teka/ n. f. disco, discotheque.

discreción /diskre'θion; diskre-'sion/ *n. f.* discretion.

discrecional /diskreθio'nal; diskre-sio'nal/ *a.* optional.

discrecionalmente /diskreθional-'mente; diskresional'mente/ *adv.* optionally.

discrepancia /diskre'panθia; dis-kre'pansia/ *n. f.* discrepancy.

discretamente /diskreta'mente/ *adv.* discreetly.

discreto /dis'kreto/ *a.* discreet.

discrimen /dis'krimen/ *n. m.* risk, hazard.

discriminación /diskrimina'θion; diskrimina'sion/ *n. f.* discrimina-tion.

discriminar /diskrimi'nar/ *v.* dis-criminate.

disculpa /dis'kulpa/ *n. f.* excuse; apology.

disculpar /diskul'par/ *v.* excuse; exonerate.

disculparse /diskul'parse/ *v.* apol-ogize.

discurrir /disku'rrir/ *v.* roam; flow; think; plan.

discursante /diskur'sante/ *n.* lec-turer, speaker.

discursivo /diskur'siβo/ *a.* discur-sive.

discurso /dis'kurso/ *n. m.* speech, talk.

discusión /disku'sion/ *n. f.* discus-sion.

discutible /disku'tiβle/ *a.* debata-ble.

discutir /disku'tir/ *v.* discuss; de-bate; contest.

disecación /diseka'θion; diseka-'sion/ *n. f.* dissection.

disecar /dise'kar/ *v.* dissect.

disección /disek'θion; disek'sion/ *n. f.* dissection.

diseminación /disemina'θion; dis-emina'sion/ *n. f.* dissemination.

diseminar /disemi'nar/ *v.* dissemi-nate, spread.

disensión /disen'sion/ *n. f.* dissen-sion.

disenso /di'senso/ *n. m.* dissent.

disentería /disente'ria/ *n. f.* dys-entery.

disentir /disen'tir/ *v.* disagree, dis-sent.

diseñador /diseɲa'ðor/ **-ra** *n.* de-signer.

diseño /di'seɲo/ *n. m.* design. —**diseñar**, *v.*

disertación /diserta'θion; diserta-'sion/ *n. f.* dissertation.

disertar /diser'tar/ *v.* dissertate.

disforme /dis'forme/ *a.* deformed, monstrous, ugly.

disformidad /disformi'ðað/ *n. f.* deformity.

disfraz /dis'fraθ; dis'fras/ *n. m.* disguise. —**disfrazar**, *v.*

disfrutar /disfru'tar/ *v.* enjoy.

disfrute /dis'frute/ *n. m.* enjoy-ment.

disgustar /disgus'tar/ *v.* displease; disappoint.

disgusto /dis'gusto/ *n. m.* dis-pleasure; disappointment.

disidencia /disi'ðenθia; disi-'ðensia/ *n. f.* dissidence.

disidente /disi'ðente/ *a.* & *n.* dis-sident.

disímil /di'simil/ *a.* unlike.

disimilitud /disimili'tuð/ *n. f.* dis-similarity.

disimulación /disimula'θion; disi-mula'sion/ *n. f.* dissimulation.

disimulado /disimu'laðo/ *a.* dis-sembling, feigning; sly.

disimular /disimu'lar/ *v.* hide; dis-semble.

disimulo /di'simulo/ *n. m.* pre-tense.

disipación /disipa'θion; disi-pa'sion/ *n. f.* dissipation.

disipado /disi'paðo/ *a.* dissipated; wasted; scattered.

disipar /disi'par/ *v.* waste; scatter.

dislexia /dis'leksia/ *n. f.* dyslexia.

disléxico /dis'leksiko/ *a.* dyslexic.

dislocación /disloka'θion; dislo-ka'sion/ *n. f.* dislocation.

dislocar /dislo'kar/ *v.* dislocate; displace.

disminuir /dismi'nuir/ *v.* diminish, lessen, reduce.

disociación /disoθia'θion; disosia-'sion/ *n. f.* dissociation.

disociar /diso'θiar; diso'siar/ *v.* dissociate.

disolubilidad /disoluβili'ðað/ *n. f.* dissolubility.

disoluble /diso'luβle/ *a.* dissolu-ble.

disolución /disolu'θion; disolu-'sion/ *n. f.* dissolution.

disolutamente /disoluta'mente/ *adv.* dissolutely.

disoluto /diso'luto/ *a.* dissolute.

disolver /disol'βer/ *v.* dissolve.

disonancia /diso'nanθia; diso-'nansia/ *n. f.* dissonance; discord.

disonante

disonante /diso'nante/ *a.* disonant; discordant.

disonar /diso'nar/ *v.* be discordant; clash in sound.

dísono /di'sono/ *a.* dissonant.

dispar /dis'par/ *a.* unlike.

disparadamente /disparaða'mente/ *adv.* hastily, hurriedly.

disparar /dispa'rar/ *v.* shoot, fire (a weapon).

disparatado /dispara'taðo/ *a.* nonsensical.

disparatar /dispara'tar/ *v.* talk nonsense.

disparate /dispa'rate/ *n. m.* nonsense, tall tale.

disparejo /dispa'reho/ *a.* uneven, unequal.

disparidad /dispari'ðað/ *n. f.* disparity.

disparo /dis'paro/ *n. m.* shot.

dispendio /dis'pendio/ *n. m.* extravagance.

dispendioso /dispen'dioso/ *a.* expensive; extravagant.

dispensa /dis'pensa/ **dispensación** *n. f.* dispensation.

dispensable /dispen'saβle/ *a.* dispensable; excusable.

dispensar /dispen'sar/ *v.* dispense, excuse; grant.

dispensario /dispen'sario/ *n. m.* dispensary.

dispepsia /dis'pepsia/ *n. f.* dyspepsia.

dispéptico /dis'peptiko/ *a.* dyspeptic.

dispersar /disper'sar/ *v.* scatter; dispel; disband.

dispersión /disper'sion/ *n. f.* dispersion, dispersal.

disperso /dis'perso/ *a.* dispersed.

displicente /displi'θente; displi'sente/ *a.* unpleasant.

disponer /dispo'ner/ *v.* dispose. **d. de,** have at one's disposal.

disponible /dispo'niβle/ *a.* available.

disposición /disposi'θion; disposi'sion/ *n. f.* disposition; disposal.

dispuesto /dis'puesto/ *a.* disposed, inclined; attractive.

disputa /dis'puta/ *n. f.* dispute, argument.

disputable /dispu'taβle/ *a.* disputable.

disputador /disputa'ðor/ **-ra** *n.* disputant.

disputar /dispu'tar/ *v.* argue; dispute.

disquete /dis'kete/ *n. m.* diskette.

disquetera /diske'tera/ *n. f.* disk drive.

disquisición /diskisi'θion; diskisi'sion/ *n. f.* disquisition.

distancia /dis'tanθia; dis'tansia/ *n. f.* distance.

distante /dis'tante/ *a.* distant.

distantemente /distante'mente/ *adv.* distantly.

distar /dis'tar/ *v.* be distant, be far.

distender /disten'der/ *v.* distend, swell, enlarge.

distensión /disten'sion/ *n. f.* distension, swelling.

dístico /'distiko/ *n. m.* couplet.

distinción /distin'θion; distin'sion/ *n. f.* distinction, difference.

distingo /dis'tiŋgo/ *n. m.* restriction.

distinguible /distiŋ'guiβle/ *a.* distinguishable.

distinguido /distiŋ'guiðo/ *a.* distinguished, prominent.

distinguir /distiŋ'guir/ *v.* distinguish; make out, spot.

distintamente /distinta'mente/ *adv.* distinctly, clearly; differently.

distintivo /distin'tiβo/ *a.* distinctive.

distintivo del país /distin'tiβo del pa'is/ country code.

distinto /dis'tinto/ *a.* distinct; different.

distracción /distrak'θion; distrak'sion/ *n. f.* distraction, pastime; absent-mindedness.

distraer /distra'er/ *v.* distract.

distraídamente /distraiða'mente/ *adv.* absent-mindedly, distractedly.

distraído /distra'iðo/ *a.* absent-minded; distracted.

distribución /distriβu'θion; distriβu'sion/ *n. f.* distribution.

distribuidor /distriβui'ðor/ **-ra** *n.* distributor.

distribuir /distri'βuir/ *v.* distribute.

distributivo /distriβu'tiβo/ *a.* distributive.

distributor /distriβu'tor/ *n. m.* distributor.

distrito /dis'trito/ *n. m.* district.

disturbar /distur'βar/ *v.* disturb, trouble.

disturbio /dis'turβio/ *n. m.* disturbance, outbreak; turmoil.

disuadir /disua'ðir/ *v.* dissuade.

disuasión /disua'sion/ n. f. dissuasion; deterrence.

disuasivo /disua'siβo/ a. dissuasive.

disyunción /disyun'θion; disyun-'sion/ n. f. disjunction.

ditirambo /diti'rambo/ n. m. dithyramb.

diurno /di'urno/ a. diurnal.

diva /'diβa/ n. f. diva, prima donna.

divagación /diβaga'θion; diβaga-'sion/ n. f. digression.

divagar /diβa'gar/ v. digress, ramble.

diván /di'βan/ n. m. couch.

divergencia /diβer'henθia; diβer-'hensia/ n. f. divergence.

divergente /diβer'hente/ a. divergent, differing.

divergir /diβer'hir/ v. diverge.

diversamente /diβersa'mente/ adv. diversely.

diversidad /diβersi'ðað/ n. f. diversity.

diversificar /diβersifi'kar/ v. diversify, vary.

diversión /diβer'sion/ n. f. diversion, pastime.

diverso /di'βerso/ a. diverse, different; (pl.) various, several.

divertido /diβer'tiðo/ a. humorous, amusing.

divertimiento /diβerti'miento/ n. m. diversion; amusement.

divertir /diβer'tir/ v. entertain, amuse.

divertirse /diβer'tirse/ v. enjoy oneself, have a good time.

dividendo /diβi'ðendo/ n. m. dividend.

divididero /diβiði'ðero/ a. to be divided.

dividido /diβi'ðiðo/ a. divided.

dividir /diβi'ðir/ v. divide; separate.

divieso /di'βieso/ n. m. Med. boil.

divinamente /diβina'mente/ adv. divinely.

divinidad /diβini'ðað/ n. f. divinity.

divinizar /diβini'θar; diβini'sar/ v. deify.

divino /di'βino/ a. divine; heavenly.

divisa /di'βisa/ n. f. badge, emblem.

divisar /diβi'sar/ v. sight, make out.

divisibilidad /diβisiβili'ðað/ n. f. divisibility.

divisible /diβi'siβle/ a. divisible.

división /diβi'sion/ n. f. division.

divisivo /diβi'siβo/ a. divisive.

divo /'diβo/ n. m. movie star.

divorcio /di'βorθio; di'βorsio/ n. m. divorce. —**divorciar**, v.

divulgable /diβul'gaβle/ a. divulgable.

divulgación /diβulga'θion; diβulga'sion/ n. f. divulgation.

divulgar /diβul'gar/ v. divulge, reveal.

dobladamente /doβlaða'mente/ adv. doubly.

dobladillo /doβla'ðiλo; doβla-'ðiyo/ n. m. hem of a skirt or dress.

dobladura /doβla'ðura/ n. f. fold; bend.

doblar /do'βlar/ v. fold; bend.

doble /'doβle/ a. double.

doblegable /doβle'gaβle/ a. flexible, foldable.

doblegar /doβle'gar/ v. fold, bend; yield.

doblez /do'βleθ; doβles/ n. m. fold; duplicity.

doblón /do'βlon/ n. m. doubloon.

doce /'doθe; 'dose/ a. & pron. twelve.

docena /do'θena; do'sena/ n. f. dozen.

docente /do'θente; do'sente/ a. educational.

dócil /'doθil; dosil/ a. docile.

docilidad /doθili'ðað; dosili'ðað/ n. f. docility, tractableness.

dócilmente /doθil'mente; dosil-'mente/ adv. docilely, meekly.

doctamente /dokta'mente/ adv. learnedly, profoundly.

docto /'dokto/ a. learned, expert.

doctor /dok'tor/ **-ra** n. doctor.

doctorado /dokto'raðo/ n. m. doctorate.

doctoral /dokto'ral/ a. doctoral.

doctrina /dok'trina/ n. f. doctrine.

doctrinador /doktrina'ðor/ **-ra** n. teacher.

doctrinal /doktri'nal/ n. m. doctrinal.

doctrinar /doktri'nar/ v. teach.

documentación /dokumenta'θion; dokumenta'sion/ n. f. documentation.

documental /dokumen'tal/ a. documentary.

documento /doku'mento/ n. m. document.

dogal /do'gal/ n. m. noose.

dogma /'dogma/ n. m. dogma.

dogmáticamente /dog'matika-'mente/ adv. dogmatically.

dogmático /dog'matiko/ n. m. dogmatic.

dogmatismo /dogma'tismo/ n. m. dogmatism.

dogmatista /dogma'tista/ n. m. & f. dogmatist.

dogo /'dogo/ n. m. bulldog.

dolar /'dolar/ v. cut, chop, hew.

dólar n. m. dollar.

dolencia /do'lenθia; do'lensia/ n. f. pain; disease.

doler /do'ler/ v. ache, hurt, be sore.

doliente /do'liente/ a. ill; aching.

dolor /do'lor/ n. m. pain; grief, sorrow, woe.

dolor de cabeza /do'lor de ka-'βeθa; do'lor de ka'βesa/ headache.

dolor de espalda /do'lor de es-'palda/ backache.

dolor de estómago /do'lor de es-'tomago/ stomachache.

dolorido /dolo'riðo/ a. painful, sorrowful.

dolorosamente /dolorosa'mente/ adv. painfully, sorrowfully.

doloroso /dolo'roso/ a. painful, sorrowful.

dolosamente /dolosa'mente/ adv. deceitfully.

doloso /do'loso/ a. deceitful.

domable /do'maβle/ a. that can be tamed or managed.

domar /do'mar/ v. tame; subdue.

dombo /'dombo/ n. m. dome.

domesticable /domesti'kaβle/ a. that can be domesticated.

domesticación /domestika'θion; domestika'sion/ n. f. domestication.

domésticamente /domestika-'mente/ adv. domestically.

domesticar /domesti'kar/ v. tame, domesticate.

domesticidad /domestiθi'ðað; domestisi'ðað/ n. f. domesticity.

doméstico /do'mestiko/ a. domestic.

domicilio /domi'θilio; domi'silio/ n. m. dwelling, home, residence, domicile.

dominación /domina'θion; domina'sion/ n. f. domination.

dominador /domina'ðor/ a. dominating.

dominante /domi'nante/ a. dominant.

dominar /domi'nar/ v. rule, dominate; master.

dómine /'domine/ n. m. teacher.

domingo /do'mingo/ n. m. Sunday.

dominio /do'minio/ n. m. domain; rule; power.

dominó /domi'no/ n. m. domino.

domo /'domo/ n. m. dome.

Don /don/ title used before a man's first name.

don n. m. gift.

donación /dona'θion; dona'sion/ n. f. donation.

donador /dona'ðor/ -ra n. giver, donor.

donaire /do'naire/ n. m. grace.

donairosamente /donairosa-'mente/ adv. gracefully.

donairoso /donai'roso/ a. graceful.

donante /do'nante/ n. giver, donor.

donar /do'nar/ v. donate.

donativo /dona'tiβo/ n. m. donation, contribution; gift.

doncella /don'θeʎa; don'seya/ n. f. lass; maid.

donde /'donde/ **dónde** conj. & adv. where.

dondequiera /donde'kiera/ adv. wherever, anywhere.

donosamente /donosa'mente/ adv. gracefully; wittily.

donoso /do'noso/ a. graceful; witty.

donosura /dono'sura/ n. f. gracefulness; wittiness.

Doña /'doɲa/ title used before a lady's first name.

dopar /do'par/ v. drug, dope.

dorado /do'raðo/ a. gilded.

dorador /dora'ðor/ -ra n. gilder.

dorar /do'rar/ v. gild.

dórico /'doriko/ a. Doric.

dormidero /dormi'ðero/ a. sleep-inducing; soporific.

dormido /dor'miðo/ a. asleep.

dormir /dor'mir/ v. sleep.

dormirse /dor'mirse/ v. fall asleep, go to sleep.

dormitar /dormi'tar/ v. doze.

dormitorio /dormi'torio/ n. m. dormitory; bedroom.

dorsal /dor'sal/ a. dorsal.

dorso /'dorso/ n. m. spine.

dos /dos/ *a. & pron.* two. **los d.,** both.

dosañal /dosa'ɲal/ *a.* biennial.

doscientos /dos'θientos; dos-'sientos/ *a. & pron.* two hundred.

dosel /do'sel/ *n. m.* canopy; platform, dais.

dosificación /dosifika'θion; dosifika'sion/ *n. f.* dosage.

dosis /'dosis/ *n. f.* dose.

dotación /dota'θion; dota'sion/ *n. f.* endowment; *Naut.* crew.

dotador /dota'ðor/ **-ra** *n.* donor.

dotar /do'tar/ *v.* endow; give a dowry to.

dote /'dote/ *n. f.* dowry; (*pl.*) talents.

dragaminas /draga'minas/ *n. m.* mine sweeper.

dragar /dra'gar/ *v.* dredge; sweep.

dragón /dra'gon/ *n. m.* dragon; dragoon.

dragonear /dragone'ar/ *v.* pretend to be.

drama /'drama/ *n. m.* drama; play.

dramática /dra'matika/ *n. f.* drama, dramatic art.

dramáticamente /dramatika'mente/ *adv.* dramatically.

dramático /dra'matiko/ *a.* dramatic.

dramatizar /dramati'θar; dramati'sar/ *v.* dramatize.

dramaturgo /drama'turgo/ **-ga** *n.* playwright, dramatist.

drástico /'drastiko/ *a.* drastic.

drenaje /dre'nahe/ *n. m.* drainage.

dríada /'driaða/ *n. f.* dryad.

dril /dril/ *n. m.* denim.

driza /'driθa; 'drisa/ *n. f.* halyard.

droga /'droga/ *n. f.* drug.

drogadicto /droga'ðikto/ **-ta** *n.* drug addict.

droguería /droge'ria/ *n. f.* drugstore.

droguero /dro'gero/ *n. m.* druggist.

dromedario /drome'ðario/ *n. m.* dromedary.

druida /'druiða/ *n. m. & f.* Druid.

dualidad /duali'ðað/ *n. f.* duality.

dubitable /duβi'taβle/ *a.* doubtful.

dubitación /duβita'θion; duβita'sion/ *n. f.* doubt.

ducado /du'kaðo/ *n. m.* duchy.

ducal /du'kal/ *a.* ducal.

ducha /'dutʃa/ *n. f.* shower (bath).

ducharse /du'tʃarse/ *v.* take a shower.

dúctil /'duktil/ *a.* ductile.

ductilidad /duktili'ðað/ *n. f.* ductility.

duda /'duða/ *n. f.* doubt.

dudable /du'ðaβle/ *a.* doubtful.

dudar /du'ðar/ *v.* doubt; hesitate; question.

dudosamente /duðosa'mente/ *adv.* doubtfully.

dudoso /du'ðoso/ *a.* dubious; doubtful.

duela /'duela/ *n. f.* stave.

duelista /due'lista/ *n. m. & f.* duelist.

duelo /'duelo/ *n. m.* duel; grief; mourning.

duende /'duende/ *n. m.* elf, hobgoblin.

dueño /'dueɲo/ **-ña** *n.* owner; landlord -lady; master, mistress.

dulce /'dulθe; dulse/ *a.* **1.** sweet. **agua d.,** fresh water. —*n.* **2.** *m.* piece of candy; (*pl.*) candy.

dulcedumbre /dulθe'ðumbre; dulse'ðumbre/ *n. f.* sweetness.

dulcemente /dulθe'mente; dulse'mente/ *adv.* sweetly.

dulcería /dulθe'ria; dulse'ria/ *n. f.* confectionery; candy shop.

dulcificar /dulθifi'kar; dulsifi'kar/ *v.* sweeten.

dulzura /dul'θura; dul'sura/ *n. f.* sweetness; mildness.

duna /'duna/ *n. f.* dune.

dúo /'duo/ *n. m.* duo, duet.

duodenal /duoðe'nal/ *a.* duodenal.

duplicación /duplika'θion; duplika'sion/ *n. f.* duplication; doubling.

duplicadamente /duplikaða'mente/ *adv.* doubly.

duplicado /dupli'kaðo/ *a. & m.* duplicate.

duplicar /dupli'kar/ *v.* double, duplicate, repeat.

duplicidad /dupliθi'ðað; duplisi'ðað/ *n. f.* duplicity.

duplo /'duplo/ *a.* double.

duque /'duke/ *n. m.* duke.

duquesa /du'kesa/ *n. f.* duchess.

durabilidad /duraβili'ðað/ *n. f.* durability.

durable /du'raβle/ *a.* durable.

duración /dura'θion; dura'sion/ *n. f.* duration.

duradero /dura'ðero/ *a.* lasting, durable.

durante /du'rante/ *adv.*
harshly, roughly.

durante /du'rante/ *prep.* during.

durar /du'rar/ *v.* last.

durazno /du'raɵno; du'rasno/ *n.
m.* peach; peach tree.

dureza /du'reɵa; du'resa/ *n. f.*
hardness.

durmiente /dur'miente/ *a.* sleeping.

duro /'duro/ *a.* hard; stiff; stern;
stale.

dux /duks/ *n. m.* doge.

E

e /e/ *conj.* and.

ebanista /eβa'nista/ *n. m. & f.*
cabinetmaker.

ebanizar /eβani'ɵar; eβani'sar/ *v.*
give an ebony finish to.

ébano /'eβano/ *n. m.* ebony.

ebonita /eβo'nita/ *n. f.* ebonite.

ebrio /'eβrio/ *a.* drunken, inebri-
ated.

ebullición /eβuʎi'ɵion; eβuyi'sion/
n. f. boiling.

echada /e'tʃaða/ *n. f.* throw.

echadillo /etʃa'ðiʎo; etʃa'ðiyo/ *n.
m.* foundling; orphan.

echar /e'tʃar/ *v.* throw, toss; pour.
e. a, start to. **e. a perder,** spoil,
ruin. **e. de menos,** miss.

echarse /e'tʃarse/ *v.* lie down.

eclecticismo /eklekti'ɵismo;
eklekti'sismo/ *n. m.* eclecticism.

ecléctico /e'klektiko/ *a. &.*
eclectic.

eclesiástico /ekle'siastiko/ *a. & m.*
ecclesiastic.

eclipse /e'klipse/ *n. m.* eclipse.
—**eclipsar,** *v.*

écloga /'ekloga/ *n. f.* eclogue.

eco /'eko/ *n. m.* echo.

ecología /ekolo'hia/ *n. f.* ecology.

ecológico /eko'lohiko/ *n. f.*
ecological.

ecologista /ekolo'hista/ *n. m. & f.*
ecologist.

economía /ekono'mia/ *n. f.* economy; thrift; economics. **e. política,** political economy.

económicamente /ekonomika-
'mente/ *adv.* economically.

económico /eko'nomiko/ *a.* economic; economical, thrifty; inexpensive.

economista /ekono'mista/ *n. m.
& f.* economist.

economizar /ekonomi'ɵar; eko-
nomi'sar/ *v.* save, economize.

ecuación /ekua'ɵion; ekua'sion/ *n.
f.* equation.

ecuador /ekua'ðor/ *n. m.* equator.

ecuanimidad /ekuanimi'ðað/ *n. f.*
equanimity.

ecuatorial /ekuato'rial/ *a.* equatorial.

ecuatoriano /ekuato'riano/ **-na** *a.
& n.* Ecuadorian.

ecuestre /e'kuestre/ *a.* equestrian.

ecuménico /eku'meniko/ *a.* ecumenical.

edad /e'ðað/ *n. f.* age.

edecán /eðe'kan/ *n. m.* aide-de-
camp.

Edén /e'ðen/ *n. m.* Eden.

edición /eði'ɵion; eði'sion/ *n. f.*
edition; issue.

edicto /e'ðikto/ *n. m.* edict, decree.

edificación /eðifika'ɵion; eðifika-
'sion/ *n. f.* construction; edifica-
tion.

edificador /eðifika'ðor/ *n.* constructor; builder.

edificar /eðifi'kar/ *v.* build.

edificio /eði'fiɵio; eði'fisio/ *n. m.*
edifice, building.

editar /eði'tar/ *v.* publish, issue;
edit.

editor /eði'tor/ *n. m.* publisher;
editor.

editorial /eðito'rial/ *n. m.* editorial; publishing house.

edredón /eðre'ðon/ *n. m.* quilt.

educación /eðuka'ɵion; eðu-
ka'sion/ *n. f.* upbringing, breeding; education.

educado /eðu'kaðo/ *a.* well-mannered; educated.

educador /eðuka'ðor/ **-ra** *n.* educator.

educar /eðu'kar/ *v.* educate; bring
up; train.

educativo /eðuka'tiβo/ *a.* educational.

educción /eðuk'ɵion; eðuk'sion/ *n.
f.* deduction.

educir /eðu'ɵir; eðu'sir/ *v.* educe.

efectivamente /efektiβa'mente/
adv. actually, really.

efectivo /efek'tiβo/ *a.* effective;
actual, real. **en e.,** *Com.* in cash.

efecto /e'fekto/ *n. m.* effect.

efecto invernáculo /e'fekto imber'nakulo/ greenhouse effect.

efectuar /efek'tuar/ v. effect; cash.

eferente /efe'rente/ a. efferent.

efervescencia /eferβes'θenθia; eferβes'sensia/ n. f. effervescence; zeal.

eficacia /efi'kaθia; efi'kasia/ n. f. efficacy.

eficaz /efi'kaθ; efi'kas/ a. efficient, effective.

eficazmente /efikaθ'mente; efikas'mente/ adv. efficaciously.

eficiencia /efi'θienθia; efi'siensia/ n. f. efficiency.

eficiente /efi'θiente; efi'siente/ a. efficient.

efigie /e'fihie/ n. f. effigy.

efímera /efi'mera/ n. f. mayfly.

efímero /e'fimero/ a. ephemeral, passing.

efluvio /e'fluβio/ n. m. effluvium.

efundir /efun'dir/ v. effuse; pour out.

efusión /efu'sion/ n. f. effusion.

egipcio /e'hipθio; e'hipsio/ **-cia** a. & n. Egyptian.

Egipto /e'hipto/ n. m. Egypt.

egoísmo /ego'ismo/ n. m. egoism, egotism, selfishness.

egoísta /ego'ista/ a. & n. selfish, egoistic; egoist.

egotismo /ego'tismo/ n. m. egotism.

egotista /ego'tista/ n. m. & f. egotist.

egreso /e'greso/ n. m. expense, outlay.

eje /'ehe/ n. m. axis; axle.

ejecución /eheku'θion; eheku'sion/ n. f. execution; performance; enforcement.

ejecutar /eheku'tar/ v. execute; enforce; carry out.

ejecutivo /eheku'tiβo/ **-va** a. & n. executive.

ejecutor /eheku'tor/ **-ra** n. executor.

ejemplar /ehem'plar/ a. **1.** exemplary. —n. **2.** copy.

ejemplificación /ehemplifika'θion; ehemplifika'sion/ n. f. exemplification.

ejemplificar /ehemplifi'kar/ v. illustrate.

ejemplo /e'hemplo/ n. m. example.

ejercer /eher'θer; eher'ser/ v. exert; practice.

ejercicio /eher'θiθio; eher'sisio/ n. m. exercise, drill.

ejercitación /eherθita'θion; ehersita'sion/ n. f. exercise, training, drill.

ejercitar /eherθi'tar; ehersi'tar/ v. exercise, train, drill.

ejército /e'herθito; e'hersito/ n. m. army.

ejotes /e'hotes/ n. m.pl. string beans.

el /el/ art. & pron. the; the one.

él pron. he, him; it.

elaboración /elaβora'θion; elaβora'sion/ n. f. elaboration; working up.

elaborado /elaβo'raðo/ a. elaborate.

elaborador /elaβora'ðor/ n. m. manufacturer, maker.

elaborar /elaβo'rar/ v. elaborate; manufacture; brew.

elación /ela'θion; ela'sion/ n. f. elation; magnanimity; turgid style.

elasticidad /elastiθi'ðað; elastisi'ðað/ n. f. elasticity.

elástico /e'lastiko/ n. m. elastic.

elección /elek'θion; elek'sion/ n. f. election; option, choice.

electivo /elek'tiβo/ a. elective.

electo /e'lekto/ a. elected, chosen, appointed.

electorado /elekto'raðo/ n. m. electorate.

electoral /elekto'ral/ a. electoral.

electricidad /elektriθi'ðað; elektrisi'ðað/ n. f. electricity.

electricista /elektri'θista; elektri'sista/ n. m. & f. electrician.

eléctrico /e'lektriko/ a. electric.

electrización /elektriθa'θion; elektrisa'sion/ n. f. electrification.

electrocardiograma /e,lektrokarðio'grama/ n. m. electrocardiogram.

electrocución /elektroku'θion; elektroku'sion/ n. f. electrocution.

electrocutar /elektroku'tar/ v. electrocute.

electrodo /elek'troðo/ n. m. electrode.

electrodoméstico /e,lektroðoi'umestiko/ n. m. electrical appliance, home appliance.

electroimán /elektroi'man/ n. m. electromagnet.

electrólisis /elek'trolisis/ n. f. electrolysis.

electrólito /elek'trolito/ n. m. electrolyte.

electrón /elek'tron/ n. m. electron.

electrónico /elek'troniko/ a. electronic.

elefante /ele'fante/ n. m. elephant.

elegancia /ele'ganθia; ele'gansia/ n. f. elegance.

elegante /ele'gante/ a. elegant, smart, stylish, fine.

elegantemente /elegante'mente/ adv. elegantly.

elegía /ele'hia/ n. f. elegy.

elegibilidad /elehiβili'ðað/ n. f. eligibility.

elegible /ele'hiβle/ a. eligible.

elegir /ele'hir/ v. select, choose; elect.

elemental /elemen'tal/ a. elementary.

elementalmente /elemental-'mente/ adv. elementally; fundamentally.

elemento /ele'mento/ n. m. element.

elepé /ele'pe/ n. m. long-playing (record), LP.

elevación /eleβa'θion; eleβa'sion/ n. f. elevation; height.

elevador /eleβa'ðor/ n. m. elevator.

elevamiento /eleβa'miento/ n. m. elevation.

elevar /ele'βar/ v. elevate; erect, raise.

elidir /eli'ðir/ v. elide.

eliminación /elimina'θion; elimina'sion/ n. f. elimination.

eliminar /elimi'nar/ v. eliminate.

elipse /e'lipse/ n. f. ellipse.

elipsis /e'lipsis/ n. f. ellipsis.

elíptico /e'liptiko/ a. elliptic.

ella /'eʎa; 'eya/ pron. she, her; it.

ello /'eʎo; 'eyo/ pron. it.

ellos /'eʎos; 'eyos/ -as pron. pl. they, them.

elocuencia /elo'kuenθia; elo'kuensia/ n. f. eloquence.

elocuente /elo'kuente/ a. eloquent.

elocuentemente /elokuente-'mente/ adv. eloquently.

elogio /e'lohio/ n. m. praise, compliment. —**elogiar**, v.

elucidación /eluθiða'θion; elusiða-'sion/ n. f. elucidation.

elucidar /eluθi'ðar; elusi'ðar/ v. elucidate.

eludir /elu'ðir/ v. elude.

emanar /ema'nar/ v. emanate, stem.

emancipación /emanθipa'θion; emansipa'sion/ n. f. emancipation; freeing.

emancipador /emanθipa'ðor; emansipa'ðor/ -ra n. emancipator.

emancipar /emanθi'par; emansi'par/ v. emancipate; free.

embajada /emba'haða/ n. f. embassy; legation; Colloq. errand.

embajador /embaha'ðor/ -ra n. ambassador.

embalar /emba'lar/ v. pack, bale.

embaldosado /embaldo'saðo/ n. m. tile floor.

embalsamador /embalsama'ðor/ n. m. embalmer.

embalsamar /embalsa'mar/ v. embalm.

embarazada /embara'θaða; embara'saða/ a. pregnant.

embarazadamente /embaraθaða-'mente; embarasaða'mente/ adv. embarrassedly.

embarazar /embara'θar; embara'sar/ v. make pregnant; embarrass.

embarazo /emba'raθo; emba'raso/ n. m. embarrassment; pregnancy.

embarbascado /embarβas'kaðo/ a. difficult; complicated.

embarcación /embarka'θion; embarka'sion/ n. f. boat, ship; embarkation.

embarcadero /embarka'ðero/ n. m. wharf, pier, dock.

embarcador /embarka'ðor/ n. m. shipper, loader, stevedore.

embarcar /embar'kar/ v. embark, board ship.

embarcarse /embar'karse/ v. embark; sail.

embargador /embarga'ðor/ n. m. one who impedes; one who orders an embargo.

embargante /embar'gante/ a. impeding, hindering.

embargar /embar'gar/ v. impede, restrain; Leg. seize, embargo.

embargo /em'bargo/ n. m. seizure, embargo. **sin e.**, however, nevertheless.

embarnizar /embarni'θar; embarni'sar/ v. varnish.

embarque /em'barke/ n. m. shipment.

embarrador /embarra'ðor/ -ra n. plasterer.

embarrancar /embarran'kar/ v.

get stuck in mud; *Naut.* run aground.

embarrar /emba'rrar/ *v.* plaster; besmear with mud.

embasamiento /embasa'miento/ *n. m.* foundation of a building.

embastecer /embaste'θer; embaste'ser/ *v.* get fat.

embaucador /embauka'ðor/ **-ra** *n.* impostor.

embaucar /embau'kar/ *v.* deceive, trick, hoax.

embaular /embau'lar/ *v.* pack in a trunk.

embausamiento /embausa'miento/ *n. m.* amazement.

embebecer /embeβe'θer; embeβe'ser/ *v.* amaze, astonish; entertain.

embeber /embe'βer/ *v.* absorb; incorporate; saturate.

embelecador /embeleka'ðor/ **-ra** *n.* impostor.

embeleco /embe'leko/ *n. m.* fraud, perpetration.

embeleñar /embele'ɲar/ *v.* fascinate, charm.

embelesamiento /embelesa'miento/ *n. m.* rapture.

embelesar /embele'sar/ *v.* fascinate, charm.

embeleso /embe'leso/ *n. m.* rapture, bliss.

embellecer /embeʎe'θer; embeye'ser/ *v.* beautify, embellish.

embestida /embes'tiða/ *n. f.* violent assault; attack.

emblandecer /emblande'θer; emblande'ser/ *v.* soften; moisten; move to pity.

emblema /em'blema/ *n. m.* emblem.

emblemático /emble'matiko/ *a.* emblematic.

embocadura /emboka'ðura/ *n. f.* narrow entrance; mouth of a river.

embocar /embo'kar/ *v.* eat hastily; gorge.

embolia /em'bolia/ *n. f.* embolism.

émbolo /'embolo/ *n. m.* piston.

embolsar /embol'sar/ *v.* pocket.

embonar /embo'nar/ *v.* improve, fix, repair.

emborrachador /emborratʃa'ðor/ *a.* intoxicating.

emborrachar /emborra'tʃar/ *v.* get drunk.

emboscada /embos'kaða/ *n. f.* ambush.

emboscar /embos'kar/ *v.* put or lie in ambush.

embotado /embo'taðo/ *a.* blunt, dull (edged). —**embotar**, *v.*

embotadura /embota'ðura/ *n. f.* bluntness; dullness.

embotellamiento /emboteʎa'miento; emboteya'miento/ *n. m.* bottling (liquids); traffic jam.

embotellar /embote'ʎar; embote'yar/ *v.* put in bottles.

embozado /embo'θaðo; embo'saðo/ *v.* muzzled; muffled.

embozar /embo'θar; embo'sar/ *v.* muzzle; muffle.

embozo /em'boθo; em'boso/ *n. m.* muffler.

embrague /em'brage/ *n. m. Auto.* clutch.

embravecer /embraβe'θer; embraβe'ser/ *v.* be or make angry.

embriagado /embria'gaðo/ *a.* drunken, intoxicated.

embriagar /embria'gar/ *v.* intoxicate.

embriaguez /embria'geθ; embria'ges/ *n. f.* drunkenness.

embrión /em'brion/ *n. m.* embryo.

embrionario /embrio'nario/ *a.* embryonic.

embrochado /embro'tʃaðo/ *a.* embroidered.

embrollo /em'broʎo; em'broyo/ *n. m.* muddle. —**embrollar**, *v.*

embromar /embro'mar/ *v.* tease; joke.

embuchado /embu'tʃaðo/ *n. m.* pork sausage.

embudo /em'buðo/ *n. m.* funnel.

embuste /em'buste/ *n. m.* lie, fib.

embustear /embuste'ar/ *v.* lie, fib.

embustero /embus'tero/ **-ra** *n.* liar.

embutir /embu'tir/ *v.* stuff, cram.

emergencia /emer'henθia; emer'hensia/ *n. f.* emergency.

emérito /e'merito/ *a.* emeritus.

emético /e'metiko/ *n. m. & a.* emetic.

emigración /emigra'θion; emigra'sion/ *n. f.* emigration.

emigrante /emi'grante/ *a. & n.* emigrant.

emigrar /emi'grar/ *v.* emigrate.

eminencia /emi'nenθia; emi'nensia/ *n. f.* eminence, height.

eminente /emi'nente/ a. eminent.

emisario /emi'sario/ **-ria** n. emissary, spy; outlet.

emisión /emi'sion/ n. f. issue; emission.

emisor /emi'sor/ n. m. radio transmitter.

emitir /emi'tir/ v. emit.

emoción /emo'θion/ emo'sion/ n. f. feeling, emotion, thrill.

emocional /emo'θional/ emo'sional/ a. emotional.

emocionante /emoθio'nante/ emosio'nante/ a. exciting.

emocionar /emoθio'nar/ emosio'nar/ v. touch, move, excite.

emolumento /emolu'mento/ n. m. emolument; perquisite.

empacar /empa'kar/ v. pack.

empacho /em'patʃo/ n. m. shyness, timidity; embarrassment.

empadronamiento /empaðrona'miento/ n. m. census; list of taxpayers.

empalizada /empali'θaða/ empali'saða/ n. f. palisade, stockade.

empanada /empa'nada/ n. f. meat pie.

empañar /empa'ɲar/ v. blur; soil, sully.

empapar /empa'par/ v. soak.

empapelado /empape'laðo/ n. m. wallpaper.

empapelar /empape'lar/ v. wallpaper.

empaque /em'pake/ n. m. packing; appearance, mien.

empaquetar /empake'tar/ v. pack, package.

emparedado /empare'ðaðo/ n. m. sandwich.

emparejarse /empare'harse/ v. match, pair off; level, even off.

emparentado /emparen'taðo/ a. related by marriage.

emparrado /empa'rraðo/ n. m. arbor.

empastadura /empasta'ðura/ n. f. (dental) filling.

empastar /empas'tar/ v. fill (a tooth); paste.

empate /em'pate/ n. m. tie, draw. —**empatarse**, v.

empecer /empe'θer/ empe'ser/ v. hurt, harm, injure; prevent.

empedernir /empeðer'nir/ v. harden.

empeine /em'peine/ n. m. groin; instep; hoof.

empellar /empe'ʎar/ empe'yar/ v. shove, jostle.

empellón /empe'ʎon/ empe'yon/ n. m. hard push, shove.

empeñar /empe'ɲar/ v. pledge; pawn.

empeñarse en /empe'ɲarse en/ v. persist in, be bent on.

empeño /em'peɲo/ n. m. persistence; pledge; pawning.

empeoramiento /empeora'miento/ n. m. deterioration.

empeorar /empeo'rar/ v. get worse.

emperador /empera'ðor/ n. m. emperor.

emperatriz /empera'triθ/ empera'tris/ n. f. empress.

empernar /emper'nar/ v. bolt.

empero /em'pero/ conj. however; but.

emperramiento /emperra'miento/ n. m. stubbornness.

empezar /empe'θar/ empe'sar/ v. begin, start.

empinado /empi'naðo/ a. steep.

empinar /empi'nar/ v. raise; exalt.

empíreo /em'pireo/ a. celestial, heavenly; divine.

empíricamente /empirika'mente/ adv. empirically.

empírico /em'piriko/ a. empirical.

empirismo /empi'rismo/ n. m. empiricism.

emplastarse /emplas'tarse/ v. get smeared.

emplasto /em'plasto/ n. m. salve.

emplazamiento /emplaθa'miento/ emplasa'miento/ n. m. court summons.

emplazar /empla'θar/ empla'sar/ v. summon to court.

empleado /emple'aðo/ **-da** n. employee.

emplear /em'plear/ v. employ; use.

empleo /em'pleo/ n. m. employment, job; use.

empobrecer /empoβre'θer/ empoβre'ser/ v. impoverish.

empobrecimiento /empoβreθi'miento/ empoβresi'miento/ n. m. impoverishment.

empollador /empoʎa'ðor/ empoya'ðor/ n. m. incubator.

empollar /empo'ʎar/ empo'yar/ v. hatch.

empolvado /empol'βaðo/ a. dusty.

empolvar /empol'βar/ v. powder.

emporcar /empor'kar/ v. soil, make dirty.

emporio /em'porio/ n. m. emporium.

emprendedor /emprende'ðor/ a. enterprising.

emprender /empren'der/ v. undertake.

empreñar /empre'ɲar/ v. make pregnant; beget.

empresa /em'presa/ n. f. enterprise, undertaking; company.

empresario /empre'sario/ **-ria** n. businessperson; impresario.

empréstito /em'prestito/ n. m. loan.

empujón /empu'hon/ n. m. push, shove. **—empujar,** v.

empuñar /empu'ɲar/ v. grasp, seize; wield.

emulación /emula'θion; emula-'sion/ n. f. emulation; envy; rivalry.

emulador /emula'ðor/ n. m. emulator; rival.

émulo /'emulo/ a. rival.
—emular, v.

emulsión /emul'sion/ n. f. emulsion.

emulsionar /emulsio'nar/ v. emulsify.

en /en/ prep. in, on, at.

enaguas /e'naguas/ n. f.pl. petticoat; skirt.

enajenable /enahe'naβle/ a. alienable.

enajenación /enahena'θion; enahena'sion/ n. f. alienation; derangement, insanity.

enajenar /enahe'nar/ v. alienate.

enamoradamente /enamoraða-'mente/ adv. lovingly.

enamorado /enamo'raðo/ a. in love.

enamorador /enamora'ðor/ n. m. wooer; suitor; lover.

enamorarse /enamo'rarse/ v. fall in love.

enano /e'nano/ **-na** n. midget; dwarf.

enardecer /enarðe'θer; enarðe'ser/ v. inflame.

enastado /enas'taðo/ a. horned.

encabestrar /enkaβe'strar/ v. halter.

encabezado /enkaβe'θaðo; enka-βe'saðo/ n. m. headline.

encabezamiento /enkaβeθa-'miento; enkaβesa'miento/ n. m. title; census; tax roll.

encabezar /enkaβe'θar; enkaβe-'sar/ v. head.

encachar /enka'tʃar/ v. hide.

encadenamiento /enkaðena-'miento/ n. m. connection, linkage.

encadenar /enkaðe'nar/ v. chain; link, connect.

encajar /enka'har/ v. fit in, insert.

encaje /en'kahe/ n. m. lace.

encalar /enka'lar/ v. whitewash.

encallarse /enka'ʎarse; enka'yarse/ v. be stranded.

encallecido /enkaʎe'θiðo; en-kaye'siðo/ a. hardened; calloused.

encalvecer /enkalβe'θer; enkalβe-'ser/ v. lose one's hair.

encaminar /enkami'nar/ v. guide; direct; be on the way to.

encandilar /enkandi'lar/ v. dazzle; daze.

encantación /enkanta'θion; enkanta'sion/ n. f. incantation.

encantado /enkan'taðo/ a. charmed, fascinated, enchanted.

encantador /enkanta'ðor/ a. charming, delightful.

encante /en'kante/ n. m. public auction.

encanto /en'kanto/ n. m. charm, delight. **—encantar,** v.

encapillado /enkapi'ʎaðo; enkapi-'yaðo/ n. m. clothes one is wearing.

encapotar /enkapo'tar/ v. cover, cloak; muffle.

encaprichamiento /enkapritʃa-'miento/ n. m. infatuation.

encararse /enkara'marse/ v. perch; climb.

encararse con /enka'rarse kon/ v. face.

encarcelación /enkarθela'θion; enkarsela'sion/ n. f. imprisonment.

encarcelar /enkarθe'lar; enkarse-'lar/ v. jail, imprison.

encarecer /enkare'θer; enkare'ser/ v. recommend; extol.

encarecidamente /enkareθi-ða'mente; enkaresiða'mente/ adv. extremely; ardently.

encargado /enkar'gaðo/ **-da** n. agent; attorney; representative.

encargar /enkar'gar/ v. entrust; order.

encargarse /enkar'garse/ v. take charge, be in charge.

encargo /en'kargo/ n. m. errand; assignment; Com. order.

encarnación /enkarna'θion; en-karna'sion/ n. f. incarnation.

encarnado /enkar'naðo/ a. red.

encarnar /enkar'nar/ v. embody.

encarnecer /enkarne'θer; enkarne-'ser/ v. grow fat or heavy.

encarnizado /enkarni'θaðo; en-karni'saðo/ a. bloody, fierce.

encarrilar /enkarri'lar/ v. set right; put on the track.

encartar /enkar'tar/ v. ban, outlaw; summon.

encastar /enkas'tar/ v. improve by crossbreeding.

encastillar /enkasti'ʎar; enkasti-'yar/ v. be obstinate or unyielding.

encatarrado /enkata'rraðo/ a. suffering from a cold.

encausar /enkau'sar/ v. prosecute; take legal action against.

encauzar /enkau'θar; enkau'sar/ v. channel; direct.

encefalitis /enθefa'litis; ensefa-'litis/ n. f. encephalitis.

encelamiento /enθela'miento; ense-la'miento/ n. m. envy, jealousy.

encelar /enθe'lar; ense'lar/ v. make jealous.

encenagar /enθena'gar; ensena-'gar/ v. wallow in mud.

encendedor /enθende'ðor; en-sende'ðor/ n. m. lighter.

encender /enθen'der; ensen'der/ v. light; set fire to, kindle; turn on.

encendido /enθen'diðo; ensen-'diðo/ n. m. ignition.

encerado /enθe'raðo; ense'raðo/ n. m. oilcloth; tarpaulin.

encerar /enθe'rar; ense'rar/ v. wax.

encerrar /enθe'rrar; ense'rrar/ v. enclose; confine, shut in.

enchapado /entʃa'paðo/ n. m. veneer.

enchufe /en'tʃufe/ n. m. Elec. plug, socket.

encia /en'θia; en'sia/ n. f. gum.

encíclico /en'θikliko; en'sikliko/ a. **1.** encyclic. —n. **2.** f. encyclical.

enciclopedia /enθiklo'peðia; en-siklo'peðia/ n. f. encyclopedia.

enciclopédico /enθiklo'peðiko; en-siklo'peðiko/ a. encyclopedic.

encierro /en'θierro; en'sierro/ n. m. confinement, prison.

encima /en'θima; en'sima/ adv. on top. **e. de,** on. **por e. de,** above.

encina /en'θina; en'sina/ n. f. oak.

encinta /en'θinta; en'sinta/ a. pregnant.

enclavar /enkla'βar/ v. nail.

enclenque /en'klenke/ a. frail, weak, sickly.

encogerse /enko'herse/ v. shrink. **e. de hombros,** shrug the shoulders.

encogido /enko'hiðo/ a. shy, bashful, timid.

encojar /enko'har/ v. make or become lame; cripple.

encolar /enko'lar/ v. glue, paste, stick.

encolerizar /enkoleri'θar; enkole-ri'sar/ v. make or become angry.

encomendar /enkomen'dar/ v. commend; recommend.

encomiar /enko'miar/ v. praise, laud, extol.

encomienda /enko'mienda/ n. f. commission, charge; (postal) package.

encomio /en'komio/ n. m. encomium, eulogy.

enconar /enko'nar/ v. irritate, annoy, anger.

encono /en'kono/ n. m. rancor, resentment.

enconoso /enko'noso/ a. rancorous, resentful.

encontrado /enkon'traðo/ a. opposite.

encontrar /enkon'trar/ v. find; meet.

encorajar /enkora'har/ v. encourage; incite.

encornar /enkor'nar/ v. gore.

encorralar /enkorra'lar/ v. corral.

encorvadura /enkorβa'ðura/ n. f. bend, curvature.

encorvar /enkor'βar/ v. arch, bend.

encorvarse /enkor'βarse/ v. stoop.

encrucijada /enkruθi'haða; enkru-si'haða/ n. f. crossroads.

encuadrar /enkuað'rar/ v. frame.

encubierta /enku'βierta/ a. **1.** secret, fraudulent. —n. **2.** f. fraud.

encubrir /enku'βrir/ v. hide, conceal.

encuentro /en'kuentro/ n. m. encounter; match, bout.

encurtido /enkur'tiðo/ n. m. pickle.

endeble /en'deβle/ a. rail, weak, sickly.

enderezar /endere'θar/ v. endere-'sar/ v. straighten; redress.

endeudarse /endeu'ðarse/ v. get into debt.

endiablado /endia'βlaðo/ a. devilish.

endibia /en'diβia/ n. f. endive.

endiosar /endio'sar/ v. deify.

endorso /en'dorso/ **endoso** n. m. endorsement.

endosador /endosa'ðor/ **-ra** n. endorser.

endosar /endo'sar/ v. endorse.

endosatario /endosa'tario/ **-ria** n. endorsee.

endulzar /endul'θar; endul'sar/ v. sweeten; soothe.

endurar /endu'rar/ v. harden.

endurecer /endure'θer; endure'ser/ v. harden.

enemigo /ene'miɣo/ **-ga** n. foe, enemy.

enemistad /enemis'tað/ n. f. enmity.

éneo /'eneo/ a. brass.

energía /ener'hia/ n. f. energy.

energía nuclear /ener'hia nukle-'ar/ atomic energy, nuclear energy.

energía vital /ener'hia bi'tal/ élan vital, vitality.

enérgicamente /e'nerhikamente/ adv. energetically.

enérgico /e'nerhiko/ a. forceful; energetic.

enero /e'nero/ n. m. January.

enervación /enerβa'θion; enerβa-'sion/ n. f. enervation.

enfadado /enfa'ðaðo/ a. angry.

enfadar /enfa'ðar/ v. anger, vex.

enfado /en'faðo/ n. m. anger, vexation.

énfasis /'enfasis/ n. m. or f. emphasis, stress.

enfáticamente /en'fatikamente/ adv. emphatically.

enfático /en'fatiko/ a. emphatic.

enfermar /enfer'mar/ v. make ill; fall ill.

enfermedad /enferme'ðað/ n. f. illness, sickness, disease.

enfermera /enfer'mera/ n. f. nurse.

enfermería /enferme'ria/ n. f. sanatorium.

enfermo /en'fermo/ **-ma** a. & n. ill, sick; sickly; patient.

enfilar /enfi'lar/ v. line up; put in a row.

enflaquecer /enflake'θer; enflake-'ser/ v. make thin; grow thin.

enfoque /en'foke/ n. m. focus. —**enfocar,** v.

enfrascamiento /enfraska'miento/ n. m. entanglement.

enfrascar /enfras'kar/ v. bottle; entangle oneself.

enfrenar /enfre'nar/ v. bridle; curb; restrain.

enfrentamiento /enfrenta'miento/ n. m. clash, confrontation.

enfrente /en'frente/ adv. across, opposite; in front.

enfriadera /enfria'ðera/ n. f. icebox; cooler.

enfriar /enf'riar/ v. chill, cool.

enfurecer /enfure'θer; enfure'ser/ v. infuriate, enrage.

engalanar /engala'nar/ v. adorn, trim.

enganchar /engan't∫ar/ v. hook, hitch, attach.

engañar /enga'ɲar/ v. deceive, cheat.

engaño /en'gaɲo/ n. m. deceit; delusion.

engañoso /enga'ɲoso/ a. deceitful.

engarce /en'garθe; engarse/ n. m. connection, link.

engastar /engas'tar/ v. to put (gems) in a setting.

engaste /en'gaste/ n. m. setting.

engatusar /engatu'sar/ v. deceive, trick.

engendrar /enhen'drar/ v. engender, beget, produce.

engendro /en'hendro/ n. m. fetus, embryo.

englobar /englo'βar/ v. include.

engolfar /engol'far/ v. be deeply absorbed.

engolosinar /engolosi'nar/ v. allure, charm, entice.

engomar /engo'mar/ v. gum.

engordador /engor'ðaðor/ a. fattening.

engordar /engor'ðar/ v. fatten; grow fat.

engranaje /engra'nahe/ n. m. Mech. gear.

engranar /engra'nar/ v. gear; mesh together.

engrandecer /engrande'θer; engrande'ser/ v. increase, enlarge; exalt; exaggerate.

engrasación /engrasa'θion; engrasa'sion/ n. f. lubrication.

engrasar /engra'sar/ v. grease, lubricate.

engreído /engre'iðo/ a. conceited.

engreimiento /eŋgreiˈmiento/ n. m. conceit.

engullidor /eŋguʎiˈðor/; enguyiˈðor/ -ra n. devourer.

engullir /eŋguˈʎir/; enguˈyir/ v. devour.

enhebrar /eneˈβrar/ v. thread.

enhestadura /enestaˈðura/ n. f. raising.

enhestar /enesˈtar/ v. raise, erect, set up.

enhiesto /enˈiesto/ a. erect, upright.

enhorabuena /enoraˈβuena/ n. f. congratulations.

enigma /eˈnigma/ n. m. enigma, puzzle.

enigmáticamente /enigmatikaˈmente/ adv. enigmatically.

enigmático /enigˈmatiko/ a. enigmatic.

enjabonar /enhaβoˈnar/ v. soap, lather.

enjalbegar /enhalβeˈgar/ v. whitewash.

enjambradera /enhambraˈðera/ n. f. queen bee.

enjambre /enˈhambre/ n. m. swarm. —**enjambrar,** v.

enjaular /enhauˈlar/ v. cage, coop up.

enjebe /enˈheβe/ n. m. lye.

enjuagar /enhuaˈgar/ v. rinse.

enjuague bucal /enˈhuage buˈkal/ n. m. mouthwash.

enjugar /enhuˈgar/ v. wipe, dry off.

enjutez /enhuˈteθ; enhuˈtes/ n. f. dryness.

enjuto /enˈhuto/ a. dried; lean, thin.

enlace /enˈlaθe; enˈlase/ n. m. attachment; involvement; connection.

enladrillador /enlaðriʎaˈðor; enlaðriyaˈðor/ -ra n. bricklayer.

enlardar /enlarˈðar/ v. baste.

enlatado /enlaˈtaðo/ -da a. canned (food).

enlatar /enlaˈtar/ v. can (food).

enlazar /enlaˈθar; enlaˈsar/ v. lace; join, connect; wed.

enlodar /enloˈðar/ v. cover with mud.

enloquecer /enlokeˈθer; enlokeˈser/ v. go insane; drive crazy.

enloquecimiento /enlokeθiˈmiento; enlokesiˈmiento/ n. m. insanity.

enlustrecer /enlustreˈθer; enlustreˈser/ v. polish, brighten.

enmarañar /emaraˈɲar/ v. entangle.

enmendación /enmendaˈθion; enmendaˈsion/ n. f. emendation.

enmendador /enmendaˈðor/ -ra n. emender, reviser.

enmendar /enmenˈdar/ v. amend, correct.

enmienda /enˈmienda/ n. f. amendment; correction.

enmohecer /enmoeˈθer; enmoeˈser/ v. rust; mold.

enmohecido /enmoeˈθiðo; enmoeˈsiðo/ a. rusty; moldy.

enmudecer /enmuðeˈθer; enmuðeˈser/ v. silence; become silent.

ennegrecer /ennegreˈθer; ennegreˈser/ v. blacken.

ennoblecer /ennoβleˈθer; ennoβleˈser/ v. ennoble.

enodio /eˈnoðio/ n. m. young deer.

enojado /enoˈhaðo/ a. angry, cross.

enojarse /enoˈharse/ v. get angry.

enojo /eˈnoho/ n. m. anger. —**enojar,** v.

enojosamente /enohosaˈmente/ adv. angrily.

enorme /eˈnorme/ a. enormous, huge.

enormemente /enormeˈmente/ adv. enormously; hugely.

enormidad /enormiˈðað/ n. f. enormity; hugeness.

enraizar /enraiˈθar; enraiˈsar/ v. take root, sprout.

enramada /enraˈmaða/ n. f. bower.

enredadera /enreðaˈðera/ n. f. climbing plant.

enredado /enreˈðaðo/ a. entangled, snarled.

enredar /enreˈðar/ v. entangle, snarl; mess up.

enredo /enˈreðo/ n. m. tangle, entanglement.

enriquecer /enrikeˈθer; enrikeˈser/ v. enrich.

enrojecerse /enroheˈθerse; enroheˈserse/ v. color; blush.

enrollar /enroˈʎar; enroˈyar/ v. wind, coil, roll up.

enromar /enroˈmar/ v. make dull, blunt.

enronquecimiento /enronkeθiˈmiento; enronkesiˈmiento/ n. m. hoarseness.

enroscar /enros'kar/ v. twist, curl, wind.

ensacar /ensa'kar/ v. put in a bag.

ensalada /ensa'laða/ n. f. salad.

ensaladera /ensala'ðera/ n. f. salad bowl.

ensalmo /en'salmo/ n. m. charm, enchantment.

ensalzamiento /ensalθa'miento; ensalsa'miento/ n. m. praise.

ensalzar /ensal'θar; ensal'sar/ v. praise, laud, extol.

ensamblar /ensam'blar/ v. join; unite; connect.

ensanchamiento /ensantʃa'miento/ n. m. widening, expansion, extension.

ensanchar /ensan'tʃar/ v. widen, expand, extend.

ensangrentado /ensaŋgren'taðo/ a. bloody; bloodshot.

ensañar /ensa'ɲar/ v. enrage, infuriate; rage.

ensayar /ensa'yar/ v. try out; rehearse.

ensayista /ensa'yista/ n. m. & f. essayist.

ensayo /ensa'yo/ n. m. attempt; trial; rehearsal.

ensenada /ense'naða/ n. f. cove.

enseña /en'seɲa/ n. f. ensign, standard.

enseñador /enseɲa'ðor/ **-ra** n. teacher.

enseñanza /ense'ɲanθa; enseɲan-sa/ n. f. education; teaching.

enseñar /ense'ɲar/ v. teach, train; show.

enseres /en'seres/ n. m.pl. household goods.

ensilaje /ensi'lahe/ n. m. ensilage.

ensillar /ensi'ʎar; ensi'yar/ v. saddle.

ensordecedor /ensorðeθe'ðor; ensorðese'ðor/ a. deafening.

ensordecer /ensorðe'θer; ensorðe'ser/ v. deafen.

ensordecimiento /ensorðeθi'miento; ensorðesi'miento/ n. m. deafness.

ensuciar /ensu'θiar; ensu'siar/ v. dirty, muddy, soil.

ensueño /en'sueɲo/ n. m. illusion, dream.

entablar /enta'βlar/ v. board up; initiate, begin.

entallador /entaʎa'ðor; enta-ya'ðor/ n. m. sculptor, carver.

entapizar /entapi'θar; entapi'sar/ v. upholster.

ente /'ente/ n. m. being.

entenada /ente'naða/ n. f. stepdaughter.

entenado /ente'naðo/ n. m. stepson.

entender /enten'der/ v. understand.

entendimiento /entendi'miento/ n. m. understanding.

entenebrecer /enteneβre'θer; enteneβre'ser/ v. darken.

enterado /ente'raðo/ a. aware, informed.

enteramente /entera'mente/ adv. entirely, completely.

enterar /ente'rar/ v. inform.

enterarse /ente'rarse/ v. find out.

entereza /ente'reθa; ente'resa/ f. entirety; integrity; firmness.

entero /en'tero/ a. entire, whole, total.

enterramiento /enterra'miento/ n. m. burial, interment.

enterrar /ente'rrar/ v. bury.

entestado /entes'taðo/ a. stubborn, willful.

entibiar /enti'βiar/ v. to cool; moderate.

entidad /enti'ðað/ n. f. entity.

entierro /en'tierro/ n. m. interment, burial.

entonación /entona'θion; entona-'sion/ n. f. intonation.

entonamiento /entona'miento/ n. m. intonation.

entonar /ento'nar/ v. chant; harmonize.

entonces /en'tonθes; entonses/ adv. then.

entono /en'tono/ n. m. intonation; arrogance; affectation.

entortadura /entorta'ðura/ n. f. crookedness.

entortar /entor'tar/ v. make crooked; bend.

entrada /en'traða/ n. f. entrance; admission, admittance.

entrambos /en'trambos/ a. & pron. both.

entrante /en'trante/ a. coming, next.

entrañable /entra'ɲaβle/ a. affectionate.

entrañas /en'traɲas/ n. f.pl. entrails, bowels; womb.

entrar /en'trar/ v. enter, go in, come in.

entre /'entre/ prep. among; between.

entreabierto /entrea'βierto/ a. ajar, half-open.

entreabrir /entrea'βrir/ v. set ajar.

entreacto /entre'akto/ n. m. intermission.

entrecejo /entre'θeho; entre'seho/ n. m. frown; space between the eyebrows.

entrecuesto /entre'kuesto/ n. m. spine, backbone.

entredicho /entre'ðitʃo/ n. m. prohibition.

entrega /en'trega/ n. f. delivery.

entregar /entre'gar/ v. deliver, hand; hand over.

entrelazar /entrela'θar; entrela-'sar/ v. intertwine, entwine.

entremedias /entre'meðias/ adv. meanwhile; halfway.

entremés /entre'mes/ n. m. side dish.

entremeterse /entreme'terse/ v. meddle, intrude.

entremetido /entreme'tiðo/ -da n. meddler.

entrenador /entrena'ðor/ -ra n. coach. —**entrenar,** v.

entrenarse /entre'narse/ v. train.

entrepalado /entrepa'laðo/ a. variegated; spotted.

entrerenglonar /entrereŋlo'nar/ v. interline.

entresacar /entresa'kar/ v. select, choose; sift.

entresuelo /entre'suelo/ n. m. mezzanine.

entretanto /entre'tanto/ adv. meanwhile.

entretenedor /entretene'ðor/ -ra n. entertainer.

entretener /entrete'ner/ v. entertain, amuse; delay.

entretenimiento /entreteni-'miento/ n. m. entertainment, amusement.

entrevista /entre'βista/ n. f. interview. —**entrevistar,** v.

entrevistador /entreβista'ðor/ -ra n. interviewer.

entristecedor /entristeθe'ðor; entristese'ðor/ a. sad.

entristecer /entriste'θer; entriste-'ser/ v. sadden.

entronar /entro'nar/ v. enthrone.

entroncar /entroŋ'kar/ v. be related or connected.

entronización /entroniθa'θion; entronisa'sion/ n. f. enthronement.

entronque /entroŋ'ke/ n. m. relationship; connection.

entumecer /entume'θer; entume-'ser/ v. become or be numb; swell.

entusiasmado /entusias'maðo/ a. enthusiastic.

entusiasmo /entu'siasmo/ n. m. enthusiasm.

entusiasta /entu'siasta/ n. m. & f. enthusiast.

entusiástico /entu'siastiko/ a. enthusiastic.

enumeración /enumera'θion; enumera'sion/ n. f. enumeration.

enumerar /enume'rar/ v. enumerate.

enunciación /enunθia'θion; enunsia'sion/ n. f. enunciation; statement.

enunciar /enun'θiar; enun'siar/ v. enunciate.

envainar /embai'nar/ v. sheathe.

envalentonar /embalento'nar/ v. encourage, embolden.

envanecimiento /embaneθi-miento; embanesi'miento/ n. m. conceit, vanity.

envasar /emba'sar/ v. put in a container; bottle.

envase /em'base/ n. m. container.

envejecer /embehe'θer; embehe-'ser/ v. age, grow old.

envejecimiento /embeheθi-'miento; embehesi'miento/ n. m. oldness, aging.

envenenar /embene'nar/ v. poison.

envés /em'bes/ n. m. wrong side; back.

envestir /embes'tir/ v. put in office; invest.

enviada /em'biaða/ n. f. shipment.

enviado /em'biaðo/ -da n. envoy.

enviar /em'biar/ v. send; ship.

envidia /em'biðia/ n. f. envy. —**envidiar,** v.

envidiable /embi'ðiaβle/ a. enviable.

envidioso /embi'ðioso/ a. envious.

envilecer /embile'θer; embile'ser/ v. vilify, debase; disgrace.

envío /em'bio/ n. m. shipment.

envión /em'bion/ n. m. shove.

envoltura /embol'tura/ n. f. wrapping.

envolver /embol'βer/ v. wrap, wrap up.

enyesar /enye'sar/ v. plaster.

enyugar /enyu'gar/ v. yoke.

eperlano /eper'lano/ *n. m.* smelt (fish).

épica /'epika/ *n. f.* epic.

épico /'epiko/ *a.* epic.

epicureísmo /epikure'ismo/ *n. m.* epicureanism.

epicúreo /epi'kureo/ *n.* & *a.* epicurean.

epidemia /epi'ðemia/ *n. f.* epidemic.

epidémico /epi'ðemiko/ *a.* epidemic.

epidermis /epi'ðermis/ *n. f.* epidermis.

epigrama /epi'grama/ *n. m.* epigram.

epigramático /epigra'matiko/ **-ca** *a.* epigrammatic.

epilepsia /epi'lepsia/ *n. f.* epilepsy.

epiléptico /epi'leptiko/ **-ca** *n.* & *a.* epileptic.

epílogo /e'pilogo/ *n. m.* epilogue.

episcopado /episko'paðo/ *n. m.* bishopric; episcopate.

episcopal /episko'pal/ *a.* episcopal.

episódico /epi'soðiko/ *a.* episodic.

episodio /epi'soðio/ *n. m.* episode.

epístola /e'pistola/ *n. f.* epistle, letter.

epitafio /epi'tafio/ *n. m.* epitaph.

epitomadamente /epitomaða-'mente/ *adv.* concisely.

epitomar /epito'mar/ *v.* epitomize, summarize.

época /'epoka/ *n. f.* epoch, age.

epopeya /epo'peya/ *n. f.* epic.

epsomita /epso'mita/ *n. f.* Epsom salts.

equidad /eki'ðað/ *n. f.* equity.

equilibrado /ekili'βraðo/ *a.* stable.

equilibrio /eki'liβrio/ *n. m.* equilibrium, balance.

equinoccio /eki'nokθio; ekinoksio/ *n. m.* equinox.

equipaje /eki'pahe/ *n. m.* luggage, baggage. **e. de mano,** luggage.

equipar /eki'par/ *v.* equip.

equiparar /ekipa'rar/ *v.* compare.

equipo /e'kipo/ *n. m.* equipment; team.

equitación /ekita'θion; ekita'sion/ *f.* horsemanship; horseback riding, riding.

equitativo /ekita'tiβo/ *a.* fair, equitable.

equivalencia /ekiβa'lenθia; ekiβa'lensia/ *n. f.* equivalence.

equivalente /ekiβa'lente/ *a.* equivalent.

equivaler /ekiβa'ler/ *v.* equal, be equivalent.

equivocación /ekiβoka'θion; ekiβoka'sion/ *n. f.* mistake.

equivocado /ekiβo'kaðo/ *a.* wrong, mistaken.

equivocarse /ekiβo'karse/ *v.* make a mistake, be wrong.

equívoco /e'kiβoko/ *a.* equivocal, ambiguous.

era /'era/ *n. f.* era, age.

erario /e'rario/ *n. m.* exchequer.

erección /erek'θion; erek'sion/ *n. f.* erection; elevation.

eremita /ere'mita/ *n. m.* hermit.

erguir /er'gir/ *v.* erect; straighten up.

erigir /eri'hir/ *v.* erect, build.

erisipela /erisi'pela/ *n. f.* erysipelas.

erizado /eri'θaðo; eri'saðo/ *a.* bristly.

erizarse /eri'θarse; eri'sarse/ *v.* bristle.

erizo /e'riθo; e'riso/ *n. m.* hedgehog; sea urchin.

ermita /er'mita/ *n. f.* hermitage.

ermitaño /ermi'taɲo/ *n. m.* hermit.

erogación /eroga'θion; eroga'sion/ *n. f.* expenditure. **—erogar,** *v.*

erosión /ero'sion/ *n. f.* erosion.

erótico /e'rotiko/ *a.* erotic.

erradicación /erraðika'θion; erra-ðika'sion/ *n. f.* eradication.

erradicar /erraði'kar/ *v.* eradicate.

errado /e'rraðo/ *a.* mistaken, erroneous.

errante /e'rrante/ *a.* wandering, roving.

errar /e'rrar/ *v.* be mistaken.

errata /e'rrata/ *n. f.* erratum.

errático /e'rratiko/ *a.* erratic.

erróneamente /erronea'mente/ *adv.* erroneously.

erróneo /e'rroneo/ *a.* erroneous.

error /e'rror/ *n. m.* error, mistake.

eructo /e'rukto/ *n. m.* belch.
—eructar, *v.*

erudición /eruði'θion; eruði'sion/ *n. f.* scholarship, learning.

eruditamente /eruðita'mente/ *adv.* learnedly.

erudito /eru'ðito/ **-ta** *n.* **1.** scholar. **—a. 2.** scholarly.

erupción /erup'θion; erup'sion/ *n. f.* eruption; rash.

eruptivo /erup'tiβo/ *a.* eruptive.

esbozo /es'βoθo; es'βoso/ n. m. outline, sketch. **—esbozar,** v.

escabechar /eskaβe't∫ar/ v. pickle; preserve.

escabeche /eska'βet∫e/ n. m. brine.

escabel /eska'βel/ n. m. small stool or bench.

escabroso /eska'βroso/ a. rough, irregular; craggy; rude.

escabullirse /eskaβu'λirse; eskaβu'yirse/ v. steal away, sneak away.

escala /es'kala/ n. f. scale; ladder. **hacer e.,** to make a stop.

escalada /eska'laða/ n. f. escalation.

escalador /eskala'ðor/ **-ra** n. climber.

escalar /eska'lar/ v. climb; scale.

escaldar /eskal'dar/ v. scald.

escalera /eska'lera/ n. f. stairs, staircase; ladder.

escalfado /eskal'faðo/ a. poached.

escalofriado /eskalo'friaðo/ a. chilled.

escalofrío /eskalo'frio/ n. m. chill.

escalón /eska'lon/ n. m. step.

escalonar /eskalo'nar/ v. space out, stagger.

escaloña /eska'loɲa/ n. f. scallion.

escalpar /eskal'par/ v. scalp.

escalpelo /eskal'pelo/ n. m. scalpel.

escama /es'kama/ n. f. (fish) scale. **—escamar,** v.

escamondar /eskamon'dar/ v. trim, cut; prune.

escampada /eskam'paða/ n. f. break in the rain, clear spell.

escandalizar /eskandali'θar; eskandali'sar/ v. shock, scandalize.

escandalizativo /eskandaliθa'tiβo; eskandalisa'tiβo/ a. scandalous.

escándalo /es'kandalo/ n. m. scandal.

escandaloso /eskanda'loso/ a. scandalous; disgraceful.

escandinavo /eskandi'naβo/ **-va** n. & a. Scandinavian.

escandir /eskan'dir/ v. scan.

escanear /eskane'ar/ v. scan (on a computer).

escáner /es'kaner/ n. m. scanner (of a computer).

escanilla /eska'niλa; eska'niya/ n. f. cradle.

escañuelo /eska'ɲuelo/ n. m. small footstool.

escapada /eska'paða/ n. f. escapade.

escapar /eska'par/ v. escape.

escaparate /eskapa'rate/ n. m. shop window, store window.

escape /es'kape/ n. m. escape; Auto. exhaust.

escápula /es'kapula/ n. f. scapula.

escarabajo /eskara'βaho/ n. m. black beetle; scarab.

escaramucear /eskaramuθe'ar; eskaramuse'ar/ v. skirmish; dispute.

escarbadientes /eskarβa'ðientes/ n. m. toothpick.

escarbar /eskar'βar/ v. scratch; poke.

escarcha /es'kart∫a/ n. f. frost.

escardar /eskar'ðar/ v. weed.

escarlata /eskar'lata/ n. f. scarlet.

escarlatina /eskarla'tina/ n. f. scarlet fever.

escarmentar /eskarmen'tar/ v. correct severely.

escarnecedor /eskarneθe'ðor; eskarnese'ðor/ **-ra** n. scoffer; mocker.

escarnecer /eskarne'θer; eskarne'ser/ v. mock, make fun of.

escarola /eska'rola/ n. f. endive.

escarpa /es'karpa/ n. m. escarpment.

escarpado /eskar'paðo/ a. **1.** steep. **—2.** m. bluff.

escasamente /eskasa'mente/ adv. scarcely; sparingly; barely.

escasear /eskase'ar/ v. be scarce.

escasez /eska'seθ; eska'ses/ n. f. shortage, scarcity.

escaso /es'kaso/ a. scant; scarce.

escatimar /eskati'mar/ v. be stingy; skimp; save.

escatimoso /eskati'moso/ a. malicious; sly, cunning.

escena /es'θena; es'sena/ n. f. scene; stage.

escenario /esθe'nario; esse'nario/ n. m. stage (of theater); scenario.

escénico /es'θeniko; es'seniko/ a. scenic.

escépticamente /esθeptika'mente; esseptika'mente/ adv. skeptically.

escepticismo /esθepti'θismo; essepti'sismo/ n. m. skepticism.

escéptico /es'θeptiko; es'septiko/ **-ca** a. & n. skeptic; skeptical.

esclarecer /esklare'θer; esklare'ser/ v. clear up.

esclavitud /esklaβi'tuð/ n. f. slavery; bondage.

esclavizar /esklaβi'θar; esklaβi-'sar/ v. enslave.

esclavo /es'klaβo/ **-va** n. slave.

escoba /es'koβa/ n. f. broom.

escocés /esko'θes; esko'ses/ **-esa** a. & n. Scotch, Scottish; Scot.

Escocia /es'koθia; es'kosia/ n. f. Scotland.

escofinar /eskofi'nar/ v. rasp.

escoger /esko'her/ v. choose, select.

escogido /esko'hiðo/ a. chosen, selected.

escogimiento /eskohi'miento/ n. m. choice.

escolar /esko'lar/ a. **1.** scholastic, (of) school. —n. **2.** m.& f. student.

escolasticismo /eskolasti'θismo; eskolasti'sismo/ n. m. scholasticism.

escollo /es'koʎo; es'koyo/ n. m. reef.

escolta /es'kolta/ n. f. escort. —**escoltar,** v.

escombro /es'kombro/ n. m. mackerel.

escombros /es'kombros/ n. m. pl. debris, rubbish.

esconce /es'konθe; es'konse/ n. m. corner.

escondedero /eskonde'ðero/ n. m. hiding place.

esconder /eskon'der/ v. hide, conceal.

escondidamente /eskondiða-'mente/ adv. secretly.

escondimiento /eskondi'miento/ n. m. concealment.

escondrijo /eskon'driho/ n. m. hiding place.

escopeta /esko'peta/ n. f. shotgun.

escopetazo /eskope'taθo; eskope-'taso/ n. m. gunshot.

escoplo /es'koplo/ n. m. chisel.

escorbuto /eskor'βuto/ n. m. scurvy.

escorpena /eskor'pena/ n. f. grouper.

escorpión /eskor'pion/ n. m. scorpion.

escorzón /eskor'θon; eskor'son/ n. m. toad.

escotado /esko'taðo/ a. low-cut, with a low neckline.

escote /es'kote/ n. m. low neckline.

escribiente /eskri'βiente/ n. m. & f. clerk.

escribir /eskri'βir/ v. write.

escritor /eskri'tor/ **-ra** n. writer, author.

escritorio /eskri'torio/ n. m. desk.

escritura /eskri'tura/ n. f. writing, handwriting.

escrófula /es'krofula/ n. f. scrofula.

escroto /es'kroto/ n. m. scrotum.

escrúpulo /es'krupulo/ n. m. scruple.

escrupuloso /eskrupu'loso/ a. scrupulous.

escrutinio /eskru'tinio/ n. m. scrutiny; examination.

escuadra /es'kuaðra/ n. f. squad; fleet.

escuadrón /eskuað'ron/ n. m. squadron.

escualidez /eskuali'ðeθ; eskuali-'ðes/ n. f. squalor; poverty; emaciation.

escuálido /es'kualiðo/ a. squalid.

escualo /es'kualo/ n. m. shark.

escuchar /esku'tʃar/ v. listen; listen to.

escudero /esku'ðero/ n. m. squire.

escudo /es'kuðo/ n. m. shield; protection; coin of certain countries.

escuela /es'kuela/ n. f. school.

escuela nocturna /es'kuela nok-'turna/ night school.

escuela por correspondencia /es'kuela por korrespon'denθia; es'kuela por korrespon'densia/ correspondence school.

escuerzo /es'kuerθo; es'kuerso/ n. m. toad.

esculpir /eskul'pir/ v. carve, sculpture.

escultor /eskul'tor/ **-ra** n. sculptor.

escultura /eskul'tura/ n. f. sculpture.

escupidera /eskupi'ðera/ n. f. cuspidor.

escupir /esku'pir/ v. spit.

escurridero /eskurri'ðero/ n. m. drain board.

escurridor /eskurri'ðor/ n. m. colander, strainer.

escurrir /esku'rrir/ v. drain off; wring out.

escurrirse /esku'rrirse/ v. slip; sneak away.

ese /'ese/ **esa** dem. a. that.

ése, ésa dem. pron. that (one).

esencia /e'senθia; e'sensia/ n. f. essence; perfume.

esencial /esen'θial; esen'sial/ a. essential.

esencialmente /esenθial'mente; esensial'mente/ adv. essentially.

esfera /es'fera/ n. f. sphere.

esfinge /es'finxe/ n. f. sphinx.

esforzar /esfor'θar; esfor'sar/ v. strengthen.

esforzarse /esfor'θarse; esfor'sarse/ v. strive, exert oneself.

esfuerzo /es'fuerθo; es'fuerso/ n. m. effort, attempt; vigor.

esgrima /es'grima/ n. f. fencing.

esguince /es'ginθe; es'ginse/ n. m. sprain.

eslabón /esla'βon/ n. m. link (of a chain).

eslabonar /eslaβo'nar/ v. link, join, connect.

eslavo /es'laβo/ -va a. & n. Slavic; Slav.

esmalte /es'malte/ n. m. enamel, polish. —esmaltar, v.

esmerado /esme'raðo/ a. careful, thorough.

esmeralda /esme'ralda/ n. f. emerald.

esmerarse /esme'rarse/ v. take pains, do one's best.

esmeril /esme'ril/ n. m. emery.

eso /'eso/ dem. pron. that.

esófago /e'sofago/ n. m. esophagus.

esotérico /eso'teriko/ a. esoteric.

espacial /espa'θial; espa'sial/ a. spatial.

espacio /es'paθio; es'pasio/ n. m. space. —espaciar, v.

espaciosidad /espaθiosi'ðað; espasiosi'ðað/ n. f. spaciousness.

espacioso /espa'θioso; espa'sioso/ a. spacious.

espada /es'paða/ n. f. sword; spade (in cards).

espadarte /espa'ðarte/ n. m. swordfish.

espaguetis /espa'getis/ n. m.pl. spaghetti.

espalda /es'palda/ n. f. back.

espaldera /espal'dera/ n. f. espalier.

espantar /espan'tar/ v. frighten, scare; scare away.

espanto /es'panto/ n. m. fright.

espantoso /espan'toso/ a. frightening, frightful.

España /es'paɲa/ n. f. Spain.

español /espa'ɲol/ -ola a. & n. Spanish; Spaniard.

esparcir /espar'θir; espar'sir/ v. scatter, disperse.

espárrago /es'parrago/ n. m. asparagus.

espartano /espar'tano/ -na n. & a. Spartan.

espasmo /es'pasmo/ n. m. spasm.

espasmódico /espas'moðiko/ a. spasmodic.

espata /es'pata/ n. f. spathe.

espato /es'pato/ n. m. spar (mineral).

espátula /es'patula/ n. f. spatula.

especia /es'peθia; es'pesia/ n. f. spice. —especiar, v.

especial /espe'θial; espe'sial/ a. special, especial.

especialidad /espeθiali'ðað; espesiali'ðað/ n. f. specialty.

especialista /espeθia'lista; espesia'lista/ n. m. & f. specialist.

especialización /espeθialiθa'θion; espesialisa'sion/ n. f. specialization.

especialmente /espeθial'mente; espesial'mente/ adv. especially.

especie /es'peθie; es'pesie/ n. f. species; sort.

especiería /espeθie'ria; espesie'ria/ n. f. grocery store; spice store.

especiero /espe'θiero; espe'siero/ -ra n. spice dealer; spice box.

especificar /espeθifi'kar; espesifi'kar/ v. specify.

específico /espe'θifiko; espe'sifiko/ a. specific.

espécimen /es'peθimen; es'pesimen/ n. m. specimen.

especioso /espe'θioso; espe'sioso/ a. neat; polished; specious.

espectacular /espektaku'lar/ a. spectacular.

espectáculo /espek'takulo/ n. m. spectacle, show.

espectador /espekta'ðor/ -ra n. spectator.

espectro /es'pektro/ n. m. specter, ghost.

especulación /espekula'θion; espekula'sion/ n. f. speculation.

especulador /espekula'ðor/ -ra n. speculator.

especular /espeku'lar/ v. speculate.

especulativo /espekula'tiβo/ a. speculative.

espejo /es'peho/ n. m. mirror.

espelunca /espe'lunka/ n. f. dark cave, cavern.

espera /es'pera/ n. f. wait.

esperanza /espe'ranθa; espe'ransa/ n. f. hope, expectation.

esperar /espe'rar/ v. hope; expect; wait, wait for, watch for.

espesar /espe'sar/ v. thicken.

espeso /es'peso/ a. thick, dense, bushy.

espesor /espe'sor/ n. m. thickness, density.

espía /es'pia/ n. m. & f. spy. —**espiar,** v.

espigón /espi'gon/ n. m. bee sting.

espina /es'pina/ n. f. thorn.

espinaca /espi'naka/ n. f. spinach.

espina dorsal /es'pina dor'sal/ spine.

espinal /espi'nal/ a. spinal.

espinazo /espi'naθo; espi'naso/ n. m. backbone.

espineta /espi'neta/ n. f. spinet.

espino /es'pino/ n. m. briar.

espinoso /espi'noso/ a. spiny, thorny.

espión /es'pion/ n. m. spy.

espionaje /espio'nahe/ n. m. espionage.

espiral /espi'ral/ a. & m. spiral.

espirar /espi'rar/ v. expire; breathe, exhale.

espíritu /es'piritu/ n. m. spirit.

espiritual /espiri'tual/ a. spiritual.

espiritualidad /espirituali'ðað/ n. f. spirituality.

espiritualmente /espiritual-'mente/ adv. spiritually.

espita /es'pita/ n. f. faucet, spigot.

espléndido /es'plendiðo/ a. splendid.

esplendor /esplen'dor/ n. m. splendor.

espolear /espole'ar/ v. incite, spur on.

espoleta /espo'leta/ n. f. wishbone.

esponja /es'ponha/ n. f. sponge.

esponjoso /espon'hoso/ a. spongy.

esponsales /espon'sales/ n. m.pl. engagement, betrothal.

esponsalicio /esponsa'liθio; esponsa'lisio/ a. nuptial.

espontáneamente /espontanea-'mente/ adv. spontaneously.

espontaneidad /espontanei'ðað/ n. f. spontaneity.

espontáneo /espon'taneo/ a. spontaneous.

espora /es'pora/ n. f. spore.

esporádico /espo'raðiko/ a. sporadic.

esposa /es'posa/ n. f. wife.

esposar /espo'sar/ v. shackle; handcuff.

esposo /es'poso/ n. m. husband.

espuela /es'puela/ n. f. spur. —**espolear,** v.

espuma /es'puma/ n. f. foam. —**espumar,** v.

espumadera /espuma'ðera/ n. f. whisk; skimmer.

espumajear /espumahe'ar/ v. foam at the mouth.

espumajo /espu'maho/ n. m. foam.

espumar /espu'mar/ v. foam, froth; skim.

espumoso /espu'moso/ a. foamy; sparkling (wine).

espurio /es'purio/ a. spurious.

esputar /espu'tar/ v. spit, expectorate.

esputo /es'puto/ n. m. spit, saliva.

esquela /es'kela/ n. f. note.

esqueleto /eske'leto/ n. m. skeleton.

esquema /es'kema/ n. m. scheme; diagram.

esquero /es'kero/ n. m. leather sack, leather pouch.

esquiar /es'kiar/ v. ski.

esquiciar /eski'θiar; eski'siar/ v. outline, sketch.

esquicio /es'kiθio; es'kisio/ n. m. rough sketch, rough outline.

esquife /es'kife/ n. m. skiff.

esquilar /eski'lar/ v. fleece, shear.

esquilmo /es'kilmo/ n. m. harvest.

esquimal /eski'mal/ n. & a. Eskimo.

esquina /es'kina/ n. f. corner.

esquivar /eski'βar/ v. evade, shun.

estabilidad /estaβili'ðað/ n. f. stability.

estable /es'taβle/ a. stable.

establecedor /estaβleθe'ðor; estaβlese'ðor/ n. m. founder, originator.

establecer /estaβle'θer; estaβle-'ser/ v. establish, set up.

establecimiento /estaβleθi-'miento; estaβlesi'miento/ n. m. establishment.

establero /esta'βˈlero/ n. m. groom.

establo /es'taβlo/ n. m. stable.

estaca /es'taka/ n. f. stake.

estación /esta'θion; esta'sion/ n. f. station; season.

estacionamiento /estaθiona-'miento; estasiona'miento/ n. m. parking; parking lot; parking space.

estacionar /estaθio'nar; estasio-'nar/ v. station; park (a vehicle).

estacionario /estaθio'nario; esta-sio'nario/ a. stationary.

estación de servicio /esta'θion de ser'βiθio; esta'sion de ser'βisio/ service station.

estación de trabajo /esta'θion de tra'βaho; esta'sion de tra'βaho/ work station.

estadista /esta'δista/ n. m. & f. statesman.

estadística /esta'δistika/ n. f. statistics.

estadístico /esta'δistiko/ a. statistical.

estado /es'taδo/ n. m. state; condition; status.

Estados Unidos /es'taδos u'niδos/ n. m.pl. United States.

estafa /es'tafa/ n. f. swindle, fake. —**estafar,** v.

estafeta /esta'feta/ n. f. post office.

estagnación /estagna'θion; estagna'sion/ n. f. stagnation.

estallar /esta'ʎar; esta'yar/ v. explode; burst; break out.

estallido /esta'ʎiδo; esta'yiδo/ n. m. crash; crack; explosion.

estampa /es'tampa/ n. f. stamp. —**estampar,** v.

estampado /estam'paδo/ n. m. printed cotton cloth.

estampida /estam'piδa/ n. f. stampede.

estampilla /estam'piʎa; estam-'piya/ n. f. (postage) stamp.

estancado /estan'kaδo/ a. stagnant.

estancar /estan'kar/ v. stanch, stop, check.

estancia /es'tanθia; es'tansia/ n. f. stay; (S.A.) small farm.

estanciero /estan'θiero; estan-'siero/ -ra n. small farmer.

estandarte /estan'darte/ n. m. banner.

estanque /es'tanke/ n. m. pool; pond.

estante /es'tante/ n. m. shelf.

estaño /es'taɲo/ n. m. tin. —**estañar,** v.

estar /es'tar/ v. be; stand; look.

estática /es'tatika/ n. f. static.

estático /es'tatiko/ a. static.

estatua /es'tatua/ n. f. statue.

estatura /esta'tura/ n. f. stature.

estatuto /esta'tuto/ n. m. statute, law.

este /'este/ n. m. east.

este, esta dem. a. this.

éste, ésta dem. pron. this (one); the latter.

estelar /este'lar/ a. stellar.

estenografía /estenogra'fia/ n. f. stenography.

estenógrafo /este'nografo/ **-fa** n. stenographer.

estera /es'tera/ n. f. mat, matting.

estereofónico /estereo'foniko/ a. stereophonic.

estéril /es'teril/ a. barren; sterile.

esterilidad /esterili'δaδ/ n. f. sterility, fruitlessness.

esterilizar /esterili'θar; esterili'sar/ v. sterilize.

esternón /ester'non/ n. m. breastbone.

estética /es'tetika/ n. f. esthetics.

estético /es'tetiko/ a. esthetic.

estetoscopio /estetos'kopio/ n. m. stethoscope.

estibador /estiβa'δor/ n. m. stevedore.

estiércol /es'tierkol/ n. m. dung, manure.

estigma /es'tigma/ n. m. stigma; disgrace.

estilarse /esti'larse/ v. be in fashion, be in vogue.

estilo /es'tilo/ n. m. style; sort.

estilográfica /estilo'grafika/ n. f. (fountain) pen.

estima /es'tima/ n. f. esteem.

estimable /esti'maβle/ a. estimable, worthy.

estimación /estima'θion; estima'sion/ n. f. estimation.

estimar /esti'mar/ v. esteem; value; estimate; gauge.

estimular /estimu'lar/ v. stimulate.

estímulo /es'timulo/ n. m. stimulus.

estío /es'tio/ n. m. summer.

estipulación /estipula'θion; estipula'sion/ n. f. stipulation.

estipular /estipu'lar/ v. stipulate.

estirar /esti'rar/ v. stretch.

estirpe /es'tirpe/ n. m. stock, lineage.

esto /'esto/ dem. pron. this.

estocada /esto'kaða/ n. f. stab, thrust.

estofado /esto'faðo/ n. m. stew. —**estofar,** v.

estoicismo /estoi'θismo; estoi-'sismo/ n. m. stoicism.

estoico /es'toiko/ n. & a. stoic.

estómago /es'tomaɣo/ n. m. stomach.

estorbar /estor'βar/ v. bother, hinder, interfere with.

estorbo /es'torβo/ n. m. hindrance.

estornudo /estor'nuðo/ n. m. sneeze. —**estornudar,** v.

estrabismo /estra'βismo/ n. m. strabismus.

estrago /es'traɣo/ n. m. devastation, havoc.

estrangulación /estraŋgula'θion; estraŋgula'sion/ n. f. strangulation.

estrangular /estraŋgu'lar/ v. strangle.

estraperlista /estraper'lista/ n. m. & f. black marketeer.

estraperlo /estra'perlo/ n. m. black market.

estratagema /estrata'hema/ n. f. stratagem.

estrategia /estra'tehia/ n. f. strategy.

estratégico /estra'tehiko/ a. strategic.

estrato /es'trato/ n. m. stratum.

estrechar /estre'tʃar/ v. tighten; narrow.

estrechez /estre'tʃeθ; estre'tʃes/ n. f. narrowness; tightness.

estrecho /es'tretʃo/ a. **1.** narrow, tight. —n. **2.** m. strait.

estregar /estre'ɣar/ v. scour, scrub.

estrella /es'treʎa; es'treya/ n. f. star.

estrellamar /estreʎa'mar; estreya'mar/ n. f. starfish.

estrellar /estre'ʎar; estre'yar/ v. shatter, smash.

estremecimiento /estremeθi-'miento; estremesi'miento/ n. m. shudder. —**estremecerse,** v.

estrenar /estre'nar/ v. wear for the first time; open (a play).

estreno /es'treno/ n. m. debut, first performance.

estrenuo /es'trenuo/ a. strenuous.

estreñido /estre'ɲiðo/ **-da** a. constipated.

estreñimiento /estreɲi'miento/ n. m. constipation.

estreñir /estre'ɲir/ v. constipate.

estrépito /es'trepito/ n. m. din.

estreptococo /estrepto'koko/ n. m. streptococcus.

estría /es'tria/ n. f. groove.

estribillo /estri'βiʎo; estri'βiyo/ n. m. refrain.

estribo /es'triβo/ n. m. stirrup.

estribor /estri'βor/ n. m. starboard.

estrictamente /estrikta'mente/ adv. strictly.

estrictez /estrik'teθ; estrik'tes/ n. f. strictness.

estricto /es'trikto/ a. strict.

estrofa /es'trofa/ n. f. stanza.

estropajo /estro'paho/ n. m. mop.

estropear /estrope'ar/ v. cripple, damage, spoil.

estructura /estruk'tura/ n. f. structure.

estructural /estruktu'ral/ a. structural.

estruendo /es'truendo/ n. m. din, clatter.

estuario /es'tuario/ n. m. estuary.

estuco /es'tuko/ n. m. stucco.

estudiante /estu'ðiante/ **-ta** n. student.

estudiar /estu'ðiar/ v. study.

estudio /es'tuðio/ n. m. study; studio.

estudioso /estu'ðioso/ a. studious.

estufa /es'tufa/ n. f. stove.

estufa de aire /es'tufa de 'aire/ fan heater.

estulto /es'tulto/ a. foolish.

estupendo /estu'pendo/ a. wonderful, grand, fine.

estupidez /estupi'ðeθ; estupi'ðes/ n. f. stupidity.

estúpido /es'tupiðo/ a. stupid.

estupor /estu'por/ n. m. stupor.

estuque /es'tuke/ n. m. stucco.

esturión /estu'rion/ n. m. sturgeon.

etapa /e'tapa/ n. f. stage.

éter /'eter/ n. m. ether.

etéreo /e'tereo/ a. ethereal.

eternal /eter'nal/ a. eternal.

eternidad /eterni'ðað/ n. f. eternity.

eterno /e'terno/ a. eternal.

ética /'etika/ n. f. ethics.

ético /'etiko/ a. ethical.

etimología /etimolo'hia/ *n. f.* etymology.

etiqueta /eti'keta/ *n. f.* etiquette; tag, label.

étnico /'etniko/ *a.* ethnic.

etrusco /e'trusko/ **-ca** *n. & a.* Etruscan.

eucaristía /eukaris'tia/ *n. f.* Eucharist.

eufemismo /eufe'mismo/ *n. m.* euphemism.

eufonía /eufo'nia/ *n. f.* euphony.

Europa /eu'ropa/ *n. f.* Europe.

europeo /euro'peo/ **-pea** *a. & n.* European.

eutanasia /euta'nasia/ *n. f.* euthanasia.

evacuación /eβakua'θion; eβakua-'sion/ *n. f.* evacuation.

evacuar /eβa'kuar/ *v.* evacuate.

evadir /eβa'ðir/ *v.* evade.

evangélico /eβan'heliko/ *a.* evangelical.

evangelio /eβan'helio/ *n. m.* gospel.

evangelista /eβanhe'lista/ *n. m.* evangelist.

evaporación /eβapora'θion; eβapora'sion/ *n. f.* evaporation.

evaporarse /eβapo'rarse/ *v.* evaporate.

evasión /eβa'sion, eβa'siβa/ *n. f.* evasion.

evasivamente /eβasiβa'mente/ *adv.* evasively.

evasivo /eβa'siβo/ *a.* evasive.

evento /e'βento/ *n. m.* event, occurrence.

eventual /eβen'tual/ *a.* eventual.

eventualidad /eβentuali'ðað/ *n. f.* eventuality.

evicción /eβik'θion; eβik'sion/ *n. f.* eviction.

evidencia /eβi'ðenθia; eβiðensia/ *n. f.* evidence.

evidenciar /eβiðen'θiar; eβiðen'siar/ *v.* prove, show.

evidente /eβi'ðente/ *a.* evident.

evitación /eβita'θion; eβita'sion/ *n. f.* avoidance.

evitar /eβi'tar/ *v.* avoid, shun.

evocación /eβoka'θion; eβoka'sion/ *n. f.* evocation.

evocar /eβo'kar/ *v.* evoke.

evolución /eβolu'θion; eβolu'sion/ *n. f.* evolution.

exacerbar /eksaθer'βar; eksaser-'βar/ *v.* irritate deeply; exacerbate.

exactamente /eksakta'mente/ *adv.* exactly.

exactitud /eksakti'tuð/ *n. f.* precision, accuracy.

exacto /ek'sakto/ *a.* exact, accurate.

exageración /eksahera'θion; eksahera'sion/ *n. f.* exaggeration.

exagerar /eksahe'rar/ *v.* exaggerate.

exaltación /eksalta'θion; eksalta-'sion/ *n. f.* exaltation.

exaltamiento /eksalta'miento/ *n. m.* exaltation.

exaltar /eksal'tar/ *v.* exalt.

examen /ek'samen/ *n. m.* test, examination.

examen de ingreso /ek'samen de iŋ'greso/ entrance examination.

examinar /eksami'nar/ *v.* test, examine.

exánime /eksa'nime/ *a.* spiritless, weak.

exasperación /eksaspera'θion; eksaspera'sion/ *n. f.* exasperation.

exasperar /eksaspe'rar/ *v.* exasperate.

excavación /ekskaβa'θion; ekskaβa'sion/ *n. f.* excavation.

excavar /ekska'βar/ *v.* excavate.

exceder /eksθe'ðer; eksse'ðer/ *v.* exceed, surpass; outrun.

excelencia /eksθe'lenθia; eksse-'lensia/ *n. f.* excellence.

excelente /eksθe'lente; eksse-'lente/ *a.* excellent.

excéntrico /eks'θentriko; eks-'sentriko/ *a.* eccentric.

excepción /eksθep'θion; ekssep-'sion/ *n. f.* exception.

excepcional /eksθepθio'nal; ekssepsio'nal/ *a.* exceptional.

excepto /eks'θepto; eks'septo/ *prep.* except, except for.

exceptuar /eksθep'tuar; ekssep'tuar/ *v.* except.

excesivamente /eksθesiβa'mente; ekssesiβa'mente/ *adv.* excessively.

excesivo /eksθe'siβo; eksse'siβo/ *a.* excessive.

exceso /eks'θeso; eks'seso/ *n. m.* excess.

excitabilidad /eksθitaβili'ðað; ekssitaβili'ðað/ *n. f.* excitability.

excitación /eksθita'θion; ekssita'sion/ *n. f.* excitement.

excitar /eksθi'tar; ekssi'tar/ *v.* excite.

exclamación /eksklama'θion; eksklama'sion/ n. f. exclamation.

exclamar /ekskla'mar/ v. exclaim.

excluir /eksk'luir/ v. exclude, bar, shut out.

exclusión /eksklu'sion/ n. f. exclusion.

exclusivamente /eksklusiβa-'mente/ adv. exclusively.

exclusivo /eksklu'siβo/ a. exclusive.

excomulgar /ekskomul'gar/ v. excommunicate.

excomunión /ekskomu'nion/ n. f. excommunication.

excreción /ekskre'θion; ekskre-'sion/ n. f. excretion.

excremento /ekskre'mento/ n. m. excrement.

excretar /ekskre'tar/ v. excrete.

exculpar /ekskul'par/ v. exonerate.

excursión /ekskur'sion/ n. f. excursion.

excursionista /ekskursio'nista/ n. m. & f. excursionist; tourist.

excusa /eks'kusa/ n. f. excuse.
—**excusar,** v.

excusado /eksku'saðo/ n. m. toilet.

excusarse /eksku'sarse/ v. apologize.

exención /eksen'θion; eksen'sion/ n. f. exemption.

exento /ek'sento/ a. exempt.
—**exentar,** v.

exhalación /eksala'θion; eksala-'sion/ n. f. exhalation.

exhalar /eksa'lar/ v. exhale, breathe out.

exhausto /ek'sausto/ a. exhausted.

exhibición /eksiβi'θion; eksiβi-'sion/ n. f. exhibit, exhibition.

exhibir /eksi'βir/ v. exhibit, display.

exhortación /eksorta'θion; eksorta'sion/ n. f. exhortation.

exhortar /eksor'tar/ v. exhort, admonish.

exhumación /eksuma'θion; eksuma'sion/ n. f. exhumation.

exhumar /eksu'mar/ v. exhume.

exigencia /eksi'henθia; eksi'hensia/ n. f. requirement, demand.

exigente /eksi'hente/ a. exacting, demanding.

exigir /eksi'hir/ v. require, exact, demand.

eximir /eksi'mir/ v. exempt.

existencia /eksis'tenθia; eksis-'tensia/ n. f. existence; Econ. supply.

existente /eksis'tente/ a. existent.

existir /eksis'tir/ v. exist.

éxito /'eksito/ n. m. success.

éxodo /'eksoðo/ n. m. exodus.

exoneración /eksonera'θion; eksonera'sion/ n. f. exoneration.

exonerar /eksone'rar/ v. exonerate, acquit.

exorar /ekso'rar/ v. beg, implore.

exorbitancia /eksorβi'tanθia; eksorβi'tansia/ n. f. exorbitance.

exorbitante /eksorβi'tante/ a. exorbitant.

exorcismo /eksor'θismo; eksor-'sismo/ n. m. exorcism.

exornar /eksor'nar/ v. adorn, decorate.

exótico /ek'sotiko/ a. exotic.

expansibilidad /ekspansiβili'ðað/ n. f. expansibility.

expansión /ekspan'sion/ n. f. expansion.

expansivo /ekspan'siβo/ a. expansive; effusive.

expatriación /ekspatria'θion; ekspatria'sion/ n. f. expatriation.

expatriar /ekspatri'ar/ v. expatriate.

expectación /ekspekta'θion; ekspekta'sion/ n. f. expectation.

expectorar /ekspekto'rar/ v. expectorate.

expedición /ekspeði'θion; ekspeði'sion/ n. f. expedition.

expediente /ekspe'ðiente/ n. m. expedient; means.

expedir /ekspe'ðir/ v. send off, ship; expedite.

expeditivo /ekspeði'tiβo/ a. speedy, prompt.

expedito /ekspe'ðito/ a. speedy, prompt.

expeler /ekspe'ler/ v. expel, eject.

expendedor /ekspende'ðor/ -ra n. dealer.

expender /ekspen'der/ v. expend.

expensas /ek'spensas/ n. f.pl. expenses, costs.

experiencia /ekspe'rienθia; ekspe'riensia/ n. f. experience.

experimentado /eksperimen'taðo/ a. experienced.

experimental /eksperimen'tal/ a. experimental.

experimentar /eksperimen'tar/ v. experience.

experimento /eksperi'mento/ *n. m.* experiment.

expertamente /eksperta'mente/ *adv.* expertly.

experto /ek'sperto/ **-ta** *a. & n.* expert.

expiación /ekspia'θion; ekspia'sion/ *n. f.* atonement.

expiar /eks'piar/ *v.* atone for.

expiración /ekspira'θion; ekspira'sion/ *n. f.* expiration.

expirar /ekspi'rar/ *v.* expire.

explanación /eksplana'θion; eksplana'sion/ *n. f.* explanation.

explanar /ekspla'nar/ *v.* make level.

expletivo /eksple'tiβo/ *n. & a.* expletive.

explicable /ekspli'kaβle/ *a.* explicable.

explicación /eksplika'θion; eksplika'sion/ *n. f.* explanation.

explicar /ekspli'kar/ *v.* explain.

explicativo /eksplika'tiβo/ *a.* explanatory.

explícitamente /ekspliθita'mente; eksplisita'mente/ *adv.* explicitly.

explícito /eks'pliθito; eks'plisito/ *adj.* explicit.

exploración /eksplora'θion; eksplorasion/ *n. f.* exploration.

explorador /eksplora'ðor/ **-ra** *n.* explorer; scout.

explorar /eksplo'rar/ *v.* explore; scout.

exploratorio /eksplora'torio/ *a.* exploratory.

explosión /eksplo'sion/ *n. f.* explosion; outburst.

explosivo /eksplo'siβo/ *a. & m.* explosive.

explotación /eksplota'θion; eksplota'sion/ *n. f.* exploitation.

explotar /eksplo'tar/ *v.* exploit.

exponer /ekspo'ner/ *v.* expose; set forth.

exportación /eksporta'θion; eksporta'sion/ *n. f.* exportation; export.

exportador /eksporta'ðor/ **-ra** *n.* exporter.

exportar /ekspor'tar/ *v.* export.

exposición /eksposi'θion; eksposi'sion/ *n. f.* exhibit; exposition; exposure.

expósito /eks'posito/ **-ta** *n.* foundling; orphan.

expresado /ekspre'saðo/ *a.* aforesaid.

expresamente /ekspresa'mente/ *adv.* clearly, explicitly.

expresar /ekspre'sar/ *v.* express.

expresión /ekspre'sion/ *n. f.* expression.

expresivo /ekspre'siβo/ *a.* expressive; affectionate.

expreso /eks'preso/ *a. & m.* express.

exprimidera de naranjas /eksprimi'ðera de na'ranhas/ *n. f.* orange squeezer.

exprimir /ekspri'mir/ *v.* squeeze.

expropiación /ekspropia'θion; ekspropia'sion/ *n. f.* expropriation.

expropiar /ekspro'piar/ *v.* expropriate.

expulsar /ekspul'sar/ *v.* expel, eject; evict.

expulsión /ekspul'sion/ *n. f.* expulsion.

expurgación /ekspurga'θion; ekspurga'sion/ *n. f.* expurgation.

expurgar /ekspur'gar/ *v.* expurgate.

exquisitamente /ekskisita'mente/ *adv.* exquisitely.

exquisito /eks'kisito/ *a.* exquisite.

éxtasis /'ekstasis/ *n. m.* ecstasy.

extemporáneo /ekstempo'raneo/ *a.* extemporaneous, impromptu.

extender /eksten'der/ *v.* extend; spread; widen; stretch.

extensamente /ekstensa'mente/ *adv.* extensively.

extensión /eksten'sion/ *n. f.* tension, spread, expanse.

extenso /eks'tenso/ *a.* extensive, widespread.

extenuación /ekstenua'θion; ekstenua'sion/ *n. f.* weakening; emaciation.

extenuar /ekste'nuar/ *v.* extenuate.

exterior /ekste'rior/ *a. & m.* exterior; foreign.

exterminar /ekstermi'nar/ *v.* terminate.

exterminio /ekster'minio/ *n. m.* extermination, ruin.

extinción /ekstin'θion; ekstin'sion/ *n. f.* extinction.

extinguir /ekstiŋ'guir/ *v.* extinguish.

extinto /eks'tinto/ *a.* extinct.

extintor /ekstin'tor/ *n. m.* fire extinguisher.

extirpar /ekstir'par/ *v.* eradicate.

extorsión /ekstor'sion/ n. f. extortion.

extra /'ekstra/ n. extra.

extracción /ekstrak'θion; ekstrak'sion/ n. f. extraction.

extractar /ekstrak'tar/ v. summarize.

extracto /eks'trakto/ n. m. extract; summary.

extradición /ekstraði'θion; ekstraði'sion/ n. f. extradition.

extraer /ekstra'er/ v. extract.

extranjero /ekstran'hero/ -ra a. **1.** foreign. —n. **2.** foreigner; stranger.

extrañar /ekstra'nar/ v. surprise; miss.

extraño /eks'trano/ a. strange, queer.

extraordinariamente /,ekstraorðinaria'mente/ adv. extraordinarily.

extraordinario /ekstraorði'nario/ a. extraordinary.

extravagancia /ekstraβa'ganθia; ekstraβa'gansia/ n. f. extravagance.

extravagante /ekstraβa'gante/ a. extravagant.

extraviado /ekstra'βiaðo/ a. lost, misplaced.

extraviarse /ekstra'βiarse/ v. stray, get lost.

extravío /ekstra'βio/ n. m. misplacement; aberration, deviation.

extremadamente /ekstremaða'mente/ adv. extremely.

extremado /ekstre'maðo/ a. extreme.

extremaunción /ekstremaun'θion; ekstremaun'sion/ n. f. extreme unction.

extremidad /ekstremi'ðað/ n. f. extremity.

extremista /ekstre'mista/ n. & a. extremist.

extremo /eks'tremo/ a. & m. extreme, end.

extrínseco /ekstrin'seko/ a. extrinsic.

exuberancia /eksuβe'ranθia; eksuβeransia/ n. f. exuberance.

exuberante /eksuβe'rante/ a. exuberant.

exudación /eksuða'θion; eksuða'sion/ n. f. exudation.

exudar /eksu'ðar/ v. exude, ooze.

exultación /eksulta'θion; eksulta'sion/ n. f. exultation.

eyaculación /eyakula'θion; eyakula'sion/ n. f. ejaculation.

eyacular /eyaku'lar/ v. ejaculate.

eyección /eyek'θion; eyek'sion/ n. f. ejection.

eyectar /eyek'tar/ v. eject.

F

fábrica /'faβrika/ n. f. factory.

fabricación /faβrika'θion; faβrika'sion/ n. f. manufacture, manufacturing.

fabricante /faβri'kante/ n. m. & f. manufacturer, maker.

fabricar /faβri'kar/ v. manufacture, make.

fabril /fa'βril/ a. manufacturing, industrial.

fábula /'faβula/ n. f. fable, myth.

fabuloso /faβu'loso/ a. fabulous.

facción /fak'θion; fak'sion/ n. f. faction, party; (pl.) features.

faccioso /fak'θioso; fak'sioso/ a. factious.

fachada /fa't∫aða/ n. f. façade, front.

fácil /'faθil; 'fasil/ a. easy.

facilidad /faθili'ðað; fasili'ðað/ n. f. facility, ease.

facilitar /faθili'tar; fasili'tar/ v. facilitate, make easy.

fácilmente /,faθil'mente; ,fasil'mente/ adv. easily.

facsímile /fak'simile/ n. m. facsimile.

factible /fak'tiβle/ a. feasible.

factor /fak'tor/ n. m. factor.

factótum /fak'totum/ n. m. factotum; jack of all trades.

factura /fak'tura/ n. f. invoice, bill.

facturar /faktu'rar/ v. bill; check (baggage).

facultad /fakulta'ð/ n. f. faculty; ability.

facultativo /fakulta'tiβo/ a. optional.

faena /fa'ena/ n. f. task; work.

faisán /fai'san/ n. m. pheasant.

faja /'faha/ n. f. band; sash; zone.

falacia /fa'laθia; fa'lasia/ n. f. fallacy; deceitfulness.

falda /'falda/ n. f. skirt; lap.

falibilidad /faliβili'ðað/ *n. f.* fallibility.

falla /'faʎa; faya/ /'faʎa; 'faya/ *n. f.* failure; fault.

fallar /fa'ʎar; fa'yar/ *v.* fail.

fallecer /faʎe'θer; faye'ser/ *v.* pass away, die.

fallo /'faʎo; 'fayo/ *n. m.* verdict; shortcoming.

falsear /false'ar/ *v.* falsify, counterfeit; forge.

falsedad /false'ðað/ *n. f.* falsehood; lie; falseness.

falsificación /falsifika'θion; falsifika'sion/ *n. f.* falsification; forgery.

falsificar /falsifi'kar/ *v.* falsify, counterfeit, forge.

falso /'falso/ *a.* false; wrong.

falta /'falta/ *n. f.* error, mistake; fault; lack. **hacer f.**, to be lacking, to be necessary. **sin f.**, without fail.

faltar /fal'tar/ *v.* be lacking, be missing; be absent.

faltriquera /faltri'kera/ *n. f.* pocket.

fama /'fama/ *n. f.* fame; reputation; glory.

familia /fa'milia/ *n. f.* family; household.

familiar /fami'liar/ *a.* familiar; domestic; (of) family.

familiaridad /familiari'ðað/ *n. f.* familiarity, intimacy.

familiarizar /familiari'θar; familiari'sar/ *v.* familiarize, acquaint.

famoso /fa'moso/ *a.* famous.

fanal /fa'nal/ *n. m.* lighthouse; lantern, lamp.

fanático /fa'natiko/ **-ca** *& n.* fanatic.

fanatismo /fana'tismo/ *n. m.* fanaticism.

fanfarria /fan'farria/ *n. f.* bluster. **—fanfarrear**, *v.*

fango /'faŋgo/ *n. m.* mud.

fantasía /fanta'sia/ *n. f.* fantasy; fancy, whim.

fantasma /fan'tasma/ *n. m.* phantom; ghost.

fantástico /fan'tastiko/ *a.* fantastic.

faquín /fa'kin/ *n. m.* porter.

faquir /fa'kir/ *n. m.* fakir.

farallón /fara'ʎon; fara'yon/ *n. m.* cliff.

Faraón /fara'on/ *n. m.* Pharaoh.

fardel /far'ðel/ *n. m.* bag; package.

fardo /far'ðo/ /'farðo/ *n. m.* bundle.

farináceo /fari'naθeo; fari'naseo/ *a.* farinaceous.

faringe /fa'rinhe/ *n. f.* pharynx.

fariseo /fari'seo/ *n. m.* pharisee, hypocrite.

farmacéutico /farma'θeutiko; farma'seutiko/ **-ca 1.** pharmaceutical. **—2.** pharmacist.

farmacia /far'maθia; far'masia/ *n. f.* pharmacy.

faro /'faro/ *n. m.* beacon; lighthouse; headlight.

farol /fa'rol/ *n. m.* lantern; (street) light, street lamp.

farra /'farra/ *n. f.* spree.

fárrago /'farrago/ *n. m.* medley; hodgepodge.

farsa /'farsa/ *n. f.* farce.

fascinación /fasθina'θion; fassina'sion/ *n. f.* fascination.

fascinar /fasθi'nar; fassi'nar/ *v.* fascinate, bewitch.

fase /'fase/ *n. f.* phase.

fastidiar /fasti'ðiar/ *v.* disgust; irk, annoy.

fastidio /fasti'ðio/ *n. m.* disgust; annoyance.

fastidioso /fasti'ðioso/ *a.* annoying; tedious.

fasto /'fasto/ *a.* happy, fortunate.

fatal /fa'tal/ *a.* fatal.

fatalidad /fatali'ðað/ *n. f.* fate; calamity, bad luck.

fatalismo /fata'lismo/ *n. m.* fatalism.

fatalista /fata'lista/ *n. & a.* fatalist.

fatiga /fa'tiga/ *n. f.* fatigue. **—fatigar**, *v.*

fauna /'fauna/ *n. f.* fauna.

fauno /'fauno/ *n. m.* faun.

favor /fa'βor/ *n. m.* favor; behalf. **por f.**, please. **¡Favor!** Puh-lease!

favorable /faβo'raβle/ *a.* favorable.

favorablemente /faβoraβle'mente/ *adv.* favorably.

favorecer /faβore'θer; faβore'ser/ *v.* favor; flatter.

favoritismo /faβori'tismo/ *n. m.* favoritism.

favorito /faβo'rito/ **-ta** *& n.* favorite.

fax /faks/ *n. f.* fax.

faz /faθ; fas/ *n. f.* face.

fe /fe/ *n. f.* faith.

fealdad /feal'dað/ n. f. ugliness, homeliness.

febrero /fe'βrero/ n. m. February.

febril /fe'βril/ a. feverish.

fecha /'fetʃa/ n. f. date. **—fechar,** v.

fecha de caducidad /'fetʃa de kaðuθi'ðað; 'fetʃa de kaðusi'ðað/ expiration date.

fécula /'fekula/ n. f. starch.

fecundar /fekun'dar/ v. fertilize.

fecundidad /fekundi'ðað/ n. f. fecundity, fertility.

fecundo /fe'kundo/ a. fecund, fertile.

federación /feðera'θion; feðera-'sion/ n. f. federation.

federal /feðe'ral/ a. federal.

felicidad /feliθi'ðað; felisi'ðað/ n. f. happiness; bliss.

felicitación /feliθita'θion; felisita-'sion/ n. f. congratulation.

felicitar /feliθi'tar; felisi'tar/ v. congratulate.

feligrés /feli'gres/ **-esa** n. parishioner.

feliz /fe'liθ; fe'lis/ a. happy; fortunate.

felón /fe'lon/ n. m. felon.

felonía /felo'nia/ n. f. felony.

felpa /'felpa/ n. f. plush.

felpudo /fel'puðo/ n. m. doormat.

femenino /feme'nino/ a. feminine.

feminismo /femi'nismo/ n. m. feminism.

feminista /femi'nista/ n. m. & f. feminist.

fenecer /fene'θer; fene'ser/ v. conclude; die.

fénix /'feniks/ n. m. phoenix; model.

fenomenal /fenome'nal/ a. phenomenal.

fenómeno /fe'nomeno/ n. m. phenomenon.

feo /'feo/ a. ugly, homely.

feracidad /feraθi'ðað; ferasi'ðað/ n. f. feracity, fertility.

feraz /fe'raθ; fe'ras/ a. fertile, fruitful; copious.

feria /'feria/ n. f. fair; market.

feriado /fe'riaðo/ a. **día f.,** holiday.

fermentación /fermenta'θion; fermenta'sion/ n. f. fermentation.

fermento /fer'mento/ n. m. ferment. **—fermentar,** v.

ferocidad /feroθi'ðað; ferosi'ðað/ n. f. ferocity, fierceness.

feroz /fe'roθ; fe'ros/ a. ferocious, fierce.

férreo /'ferreo/ a. of iron.

ferrería /ferre'ria/ n. f. ironworks.

ferretería /ferrete'ria/ n. f. hardware; hardware store.

ferrocarril /ferroka'rril/ n. m. railroad.

fértil /'fertil/ a. fertile.

fertilidad /fertili'ðað/ n. f. fertility.

fertilizar /fertili'θar; fertili'sar/ v. fertilize.

férvido /'ferβiðo/ a. fervid, ardent.

ferviente /fer'βiente/ a. fervent.

fervor /fer'βor/ n. m. fervor, zeal.

fervoroso /ferβo'roso/ a. zealous, eager.

festejar /feste'har/ v. entertain, fete.

festejo /feste'ho/ n. m. feast.

festín /fes'tin/ n. m. feast.

festividad /festiβi'ðað/ n. f. festivity.

festivo /fes'tiβo/ a. festive.

fétido /'fetiðo/ adj. fetid.

feudal /feu'ðal/ a. feudal.

feudo /'feuðo/ n. m. fief; manor.

fiado /'fiaðo, al/ adj. on trust, on credit.

fiambrera /fiam'brera/ n. f. lunch box.

fianza /'fianθa; 'fiansa/ n. f. bail.

fiar /fi'ar/ v. trust, sell on credit; give credit.

fiarse de /'fiarse de/ v. trust (in), rely on.

fiasco /'fiasko/ n. m. fiasco.

fibra /'fiβra/ n. f. fiber; vigor.

fibroso /fi'βroso/ a. fibrous.

ficción /fik'θion; fik'sion/ n. f. fiction.

ficha /'fitʃa/ n. f. slip, index card; chip.

fichero /fi'tʃero/ n. m. computer file, filing cabinet, card catalog.

ficticio /fik'tiθio; fik'tisio/ a. fictitious.

fidedigno /fiðe'ðigno/ a. trustworthy.

fideicomisario /fiðeikomi'sario/ **-ria** n. trustee.

fideicomiso /fiðeiko'miso/ n. m. trust.

fidelidad /fiðeli'ðað/ n. f. fidelity.

fideo /fi'ðeo/ n. m. noodle.

fiebre /'fieβre/ n. f. fever.

fiebre del heno /'fieβre del 'eno/ hayfever.

fiel /fiel/ a. faithful.

fieltro /'fieltro/ *n. m.* felt.

fiera /'fiera/ *n. f.* wild animal.

fiereza /fie'reθa; fie'resa/ *n. f.* fierceness, wildness.

fiero /'fiero/ *a.* fierce; wild.

fiesta /'fiesta/ *n. f.* festival, feast; party.

figura /fi'gura/ *n. f.* figure. —**figurar,** *v.*

figurarse /figu'rarse/ *v.* imagine.

figurón /figu'ron/ *n. m.* dummy.

fijar /fi'har/ *v.* fix; set, establish, post.

fijarse en /fi'harse en/ *v.* notice.

fijeza /fi'heθa; fi'hesa/ *n. f.* firmness.

fijo /'fiho/ *a.* fixed, stationary, permanent, set.

fila /'fila/ *n. f.* row, rank, file, line.

filantropía /filantro'pia/ *n. f.* philanthropy.

filatelia /fila'telia/ *n. f.* philately, stamp collecting.

filete /fi'lete/ *n. m.* fillet; steak.

film /film/ *n. m.* film. —**filmar,** *v.*

filo /'filo/ *n. m.* (cutting) edge.

filón /fi'lon/ *n. m.* vein (of ore).

filosofía /filoso'fia/ *n. f.* philosophy.

filosófico /filo'sofiko/ *a.* philosophical.

filósofo /fi'losofo/ **-fa** *n.* philosopher.

filtro /'filtro/ *n. m.* filter. —**filtrar,** *v.*

fin /fin/ *n. m.* end, purpose, goal. **a f. de que,** in order that. **en f.,** in short. **por f.,** finally, at last.

final /fi'nal/ *a.* **1.** final. —*n.* **2.** end.

finalidad /finali'ðað/ *n. f.* finality.

finalmente /final'mente/ *adv.* at last.

financiero /finan'θiero; finan-'siero/ **-ra** *a.* **1.** financial. —*n.* **2.** financier.

finca /'finka/ *n. f.* real estate; estate; farm.

finés /fi'nes/ **-esa** *a. & n.* Finnish; Finn.

fineza /fi'neθa; fi'nesa/ *n. f.* courtesy, politeness; fineness.

fingimiento /finhi'miento/ *n. m.* pretense.

fingir /fin'hir/ *v.* feign, pretend.

fino /'fino/ *a.* fine; polite, courteous.

firma /'firma/ *n. f.* signature; *Com.* firm.

firmamento /firma'mento/ *n. m.* firmament, heavens.

firmar /fir'mar/ *v.* sign.

firme /'firme/ *a.* firm, fast, steady, sound.

firmemente /firme'mente/ *adv.* firmly.

firmeza /fir'meθa; fir'mesa/ *n. f.* firmness.

fisco /'fisko/ *n. m.* exchequer, treasury.

física /'fisika/ *n. f.* physics.

físico /'fisiko/ **-ca** *a. & n.* physical; physicist.

fisiología /fisiolo'hia/ *n. f.* physiology.

fláccido /'flakθiðo; 'flaksiðo/ *a.* flaccid, soft.

flaco /'flako/ *a.* thin, gaunt.

flagelación /flahela'θion; flahela'sion/ *n. f.* flagellation.

flagelar /flahe'lar/ *v.* flagellate, whip.

flagrancia /fla'granθia; fla'gransia/ *n. f.* flagrancy.

flagrante /fla'grante/ *a.* flagrant.

flama /'flama/ *n. f.* flame; ardor, zeal.

flamante /fla'mante/ *a.* flaming.

flamenco /fla'menko/ *n. m.* flamingo.

flan /flan/ *n. m.* custard.

flanco /'flanko/ *n. m.* side; *Mil.* flank.

flanquear /flanke'ar/ *v.* flank.

flaqueza /fla'keθa; fla'kesa/ *n. f.* thinness; weakness.

flauta /'flauta/ *n. f.* flute.

flautín /flau'tin/ *n. m.* piccolo.

flautista /flau'tista/ *n. m. & f.* flutist, piper.

flecha /'fletʃa/ *n. f.* arrow.

flechazo /fle'tʃaθo; fle'tʃaso/ *n. m.* love at first sight.

flechero /fle'tʃero/ **-ra** *n.* archer.

fleco /'fleko/ *n. m.* fringe; flounce.

flema /'flema/ *n. f.* phlegm.

flemático /fle'matiko/ *a.* phlegmatic.

flequillo /fle'kiʎo; fle'kiyo/ *n. m.* fringe; bangs (of hair).

flete /'flete/ *n. m.* freight. —**fletar,** *v.*

flexibilidad /fleksiβili'ðað/ *n. f.* flexibility.

flexible /fle'ksiβle/ *a.* flexible, pliable.

flirtear /flirte'ar/ *v.* flirt.

flojo /'floho/ a. limp; loose, flabby, slack.

flor /flor/ n. f. flower; compliment.

flora /'flora/ n. f. flora.

floral /flo'ral/ a. floral.

florecer /flore'θer; flore'ser/ v. flower, bloom; flourish.

floreo /flo'reo/ n. m. flourish.

florero /flo'rero/ n. m. flower pot; vase.

floresta /flo'resta/ n. f. forest.

florido /flo'riðo/ a. flowery; flowering.

florista /flo'rista/ n. m. & f. florist.

flota /'flota/ n. f. fleet.

flotante /flo'tante/ a. floating.

flotar /flo'tar/ v. float.

flotilla /flo'tiʎa; flo'tiya/ n. f. flotilla, fleet.

fluctuación /fluktua'θion; fluktua'sion/ n. f. fluctuation.

fluctuar /fluktu'ar/ v. fluctuate.

fluente /'fluente/ a. fluent; flowing.

fluidez /flui'ðeθ; flui'ðes/ n. f. fluency.

flúido /'fluiðo/ a. & m. fluid, liquid.

fluir /flu'ir/ v. flow.

flujo /'fluho/ n. m. flow, flux.

fluor /fluor/ n. m. fluorine.

fluorescencia /fluores'θenθia; fluores'sensia/ n. f. fluorescence.

fluorescente /fluores'θente; fluores'sente/ a. fluorescent.

fobia /'foβia/ n. f. phobia.

foca /'foka/ n. f. seal.

foco /'foko/ n. m. focus, center; floodlight.

fogata /fo'gata/ n. f. bonfire.

fogón /fo'gon/ n. m. hearth, fireplace.

fogosidad /fogosi'ðað/ n. f. vehemence, ardor.

fogoso /fo'goso/ a. vehement, ardent.

folclore /fol'klore/ n. m. folklore.

follaje /fo'ʎahe; fo'yahe/ n. m. foliage.

folleto /fo'ʎeto; fo'yeto/ n. m. pamphlet, booklet.

follón /fo'ʎon; fo'yon/ n. m. mess, chaos.

fomentar /fomen'tar/ v. develop, promote, further, foster.

fomento /fo'mento/ n. m. fomentation.

fonda /'fonda/ n. f. eating house, inn.

fondo /'fondo/ n. m. bottom; back (part); background; (pl.) funds; finances. **a f.,** thoroughly.

fonética /fo'netika/ n. f. phonetics.

fonético /fo'netiko/ a. phonetic.

fonógrafo /fo'nografo/ n. m. phonograph.

fontanero /fonta'nero/ **-era** n. plumber.

forastero /foras'tero/ **-ra** a. **1.** foreign, exotic. —n. **2.** stranger.

forjar /for'har/ v. forge.

forma /'forma/ n. f. form, shape. —**formar,** v.

formación /forma'θion; forma'sion/ n. f. formation.

formal /for'mal/ a. formal.

formaldehido /formalde'iðo/ n. m. formaldehyde.

formalidad /formali'ðað/ n. f. formality.

formalizar /formali'θar; formali'sar/ v. finalize; formulate.

formidable /formi'ðaβle/ a. formidable.

formidablemente /formiðaβle-'mente/ adv. formidably.

formón /for'mon/ n. m. chisel.

fórmula /'formula/ n. f. formula.

formular /formu'lar/ v. formulate, draw up.

formulario /formu'lario/ n. m. form.

foro /'foro/ n. m. forum.

forrado /fo'rraðo/ a. stuffed; Colloq. filthy rich.

forraje /fo'rrahe/ n. m. forage, fodder.

forrar /fo'rrar/ v. line.

forro /'forro/ n. m. lining; condom.

fortalecer /fortale'θer; fortale'ser/ v. fortify.

fortaleza /forta'leθa; forta'lesa/ n. f. fort, fortress; fortitude.

fortificación /fortifika'θion; fortifika'sion/ n. f. fortification.

fortitud /forti'tuð/ n. f. fortitude.

fortuitamente /fortuita'mente/ adv. fortuitously.

fortuito /for'tuito/ a. fortuitous.

fortuna /for'tuna/ n. f. fortune; luck.

forúnculo /fo'runkulo/ n. m. boil.

forzar /for'θar; for'sar/ v. force, compel, coerce.

forzosamente /forθosa'mente/

forsosa'mente/ adv. compulsorily; forcibly.

forzoso /for'θoso; for'soso/ a. compulsory; necessary. **paro f.,** unemployment.

forzudo /for'θuðo; for'suðo/ a. powerful, vigorous.

fosa /'fosa/ n. f. grave; pit.

fósforo /'fosforo/ n. m. match; phosphorus.

fósil /'fosil/ n. m. fossil.

foso /'foso/ n. m. ditch, trench; moat.

fotocopia /foto'kopia/ n. f. photocopy.

fotocopiadora /fotokopia'ðora/ n. f. photocopier.

fotografía /fotogra'fia/ n. f. photograph; photography.
—**fotografiar,** v.

frac /frak/ n. m. dress coat.

fracasar /fraka'sar/ v. fail.

fracaso /fra'kaso/ n. m. failure.

fracción /frak'θion; frak'sion/ n. f. fraction.

fractura /frak'tura/ n. f. fracture, break.

fragancia /fra'ganθia; fra'gansia/ n. f. fragrance; perfume; aroma.

fragante /fra'gante/ a. fragrant.

frágil /'frahil/ a. fragile, breakable.

fragilidad /frahili'ðað/ n. f. fragility.

fragmentario /fragmen'tario/ a. fragmentary.

fragmento /frag'mento/ n. m. fragment, bit.

fragor /fra'gor/ n. m. noise, clamor.

fragoso /fra'goso/ a. noisy.

fragua /'fragua/ n. f. forge.
—**fraguar,** v.

fraile /'fraile/ n. m. monk.

frambuesa /fram'buesa/ n. f. raspberry.

francamente /franka'mente/ adv. frankly, candidly.

francés /fran'θes; fran'ses/ **-esa** a. & n. French; Frenchman, Frenchwoman.

Francia /'franθia; 'fransia/ n. f. France.

franco /'franko/ a. frank.

franela /fra'nela/ n. f. flannel.

frangible /fraŋ'giβle/ a. breakable.

franqueo /fran'keo/ n. m. postage.

franqueza /fran'keθa; fran'kesa/ n. f. frankness.

franquicia /fran'kiθia; fran'kisia/ n. f. franchise.

frasco /'frasko/ n. m. flask, bottle.

frase /'frase/ n. f. phrase; sentence.

fraseología /fraseolo'hia/ n. f. phraseology; style.

fraternal /frater'nal/ a. fraternal, brotherly.

fraternidad /fraterni'ðað/ n. f. fraternity, brotherhood.

fraude /'fraude/ n. m. fraud.

fraudulento /frauðu'lento/ a. fraudulent.

frazada /fra'θaða; fra'saða/ n. f. blanket.

frecuencia /fre'kuenθia; fre'kuensia/ n. f. frequency.

frecuente /fre'kuente/ a. frequent.

frecuentemente /frekuente'mente/ adv. frequently, often.

fregadero /frega'ðero/ n. m. sink.

fregadura /frega'ðura/ n. f. scouring, scrubbing.

fregar /fre'gar/ v. scour, scrub, mop.

fregona /fre'gona/ n. f. mop.

freír /fre'ir/ v. fry.

fréjol /'frehol/ n. m. kidney bean.

frenazo /fre'naθo; fre'naso/ n. m. sudden braking, slamming on the brakes.

frenesí /frene'si/ n. m. frenzy.

frenéticamente /fre'netikamente/ adv. frantically.

frenético /fre'netiko/ a. frantic, frenzied.

freno /'freno/ n. m. brake.
—**frenar,** v.

freno de auxilio /'freno de auk-'silio/ emergency brake.

freno de mano /'freno de 'mano/ hand brake.

frente /'frente/ 1. n. f. forehead. **2.** m. front. **en f., al f.,** opposite, across. **f. a,** in front of.

fresa /'fresa/ n. f. strawberry.

fresca /'freska/ n. f. fresh, cool air.

fresco /'fresko/ a. fresh; cool; crisp.

frescura /fres'kura/ n. f. coolness, freshness.

fresno /'fresno/ n. m. ash tree.

fresquería /freske'ria/ n. f. soda fountain.

friabilidad /friaβili'ðað/ n. f. brittleness.

friable /'friaβle/ a. brittle.

frialdad /frial'dað/ n. f. coldness.

fríamente /fria'mente/ adv. coldly; coolly.

frícandó /frikando/ n. m. fricandeau.

fricar /fri'kar/ v. rub together.

fricción /frik'θion; frik'sion/ n. f. friction.

friccionar /frikθio'nar; friksio'nar/ v. rub.

friega /'friega/ n. f. friction; massage.

frigidez /frihi'ðeθ; frihi'ðes/ n. f. frigidity.

frígido /'frihiðo/ a. frigid.

frijol /fri'hol/ n. m. bean.

frío /'frio/ a. & n. cold. **tener f.,** to be cold, feel cold. **hacer f.,** to be cold (weather).

friolento /frio'lento/ a. chilly; sensitive to cold.

friolera /frio'lera/ n. f. trifle, trinket.

friso /'friso/ n. m. frieze.

fritillas /fri'tiʎas; fri'tiyas/ n. f.pl. fritters.

frito /'frito/ a. fried.

fritura /fri'tura/ n. f. fritter.

frívolamente /friβola'mente/ adv. frivolously.

frivolidad /friβoli'ðað/ n. f. frivolity.

frívolo /'friβolo/ a. frivolous.

frondoso /fron'doso/ a. leafy.

frontera /fron'tera/ n. f. frontier; border.

frotar /fro'tar/ v. rub.

fructífero /fruk'tifero/ a. fruitful.

fructificar /fruktifi'kar/ v. bear fruit.

fructuosamente /fruktuosa-'mente/ adv. fruitfully.

fructuoso /fruk'tuoso/ a. fruitful.

frugal /fru'gal/ a. frugal; thrifty.

frugalidad /frugali'ðað/ n. f. frugality; thrift.

frugalmente /frugal'mente/ adv. frugally, thriftily.

fruncir /frun'θir; frun'sir/ v. gather, contract. **f. el entrecejo,** frown.

fruslería /frusle'ria/ n. f. trinket.

frustrar /frus'trar/ v. frustrate, thwart.

fruta /'fruta/ n. f. fruit.

frutería /frute'ria/ n. f. fruit store.

fruto /'fruto/ n. m. fruit; product; profit.

fucsia /'fuksia/ n. f. fuchsia.

fuego /'fuego/ n. m. fire.

fuelle /'fueʎe; 'fueye/ n. m. bellows.

fuente /'fuente/ n. f. fountain; source; platter.

fuera /'fuera/ adv. without, outside.

fuero /'fuero/ n. m. statute.

fuerte /'fuerte/ a. **1.** strong; loud. —n. **2.** m. fort.

fuertemente /fuerte'mente/ adv. strongly; loudly.

fuerza /'fuerθa; 'fuersa/ n. f. force, strength.

fuga /'fuga/ n. f. flight, escape.

fugarse /fu'garse/ v. flee, escape.

fugaz /fu'gaθ; fu'gas/ a. fugitive, passing.

fugitivo /fuhi'tiβo/ **-va** a. & n. fugitive.

fulano /fu'lano/ **-na** n. Mr., Mrs. so-and-so.

fulcro /fulkro/ n. m. fulcrum.

fulgor /ful'gor/ n. m. gleam, glow. **—fulgurar,** v.

fulminante /fulmi'nante/ a. explosive.

fumador /fuma'ðor/ **-ra** n. smoker.

fumar /fu'mar/ v. smoke.

fumigación /fumiga'θion; fumiga'sion/ n. f. fumigation.

fumigador /fumiga'ðor/ **-ra** n. fumigator.

fumigar /fumi'gar/ v. fumigate.

fumoso /fu'moso/ a. smoky.

función /fun'θion; fun'sion/ n. f. function; performance, show.

funcionar /funθio'nar; funsio'nar/ v. function; work, run.

funcionario /funθio'nario; funsio'nario/ **-ria** n. official, functionary.

funda /'funda/ n. f. case, sheath, slipcover.

fundación /funda'θion; funda'sion/ n. f. foundation.

fundador /funda'ðor/ **-ra** n. founder.

fundamental /funda'mental/ a. fundamental, basic.

fundamentalmente /fundamental'mente/ adv. fundamentally.

fundamento /funda'mento/ n. m. base, basis, foundation.

fundar /fun'dar/ v. found, establish.

fundición /fundi'θion; fundi'sion/ *n. f.* foundry; melting; meltdown.

fundir /fun'dir/ *v.* fuse; smelt.

fúnebre /'funeβre/ *a.* dismal.

funeral /fune'ral/ *n. m.* funeral.

funeraria /fune'raria/ *n. f.* funeral home, funeral parlor.

funestamente /funesta'mente/ *adv.* sadly.

fungo /'fungo/ *n. m.* fungus.

furente /fu'rente/ *a.* furious, enraged.

furgoneta /furgo'neta/ *n. f.* van.

furia /'furia/ *n. f.* fury.

furiosamente /furiosa'mente/ *adv.* furiously.

furioso /fu'rioso/ *a.* furious.

furor /fu'ror/ *n. m.* furor; fury.

furtivamente /furtiβa'mente/ *adv.* furtively.

furtivo /fur'tiβo/ *a.* furtive, sly.

furúnculo /fu'runkulo/ *n. m.* boil.

fusibilidad /fusiβili'ðað/ *n. f.* fusibility.

fusible /fu'siβle/ *n. m.* fuse.

fusil /fu'sil/ *n. m.* rifle, gun.

fusilar /fusi'lar/ *v.* shoot, execute.

fusión /fu'sion/ *n. f.* fusion; merger.

fusionar /fusio'nar/ *v.* unite, fuse, merge.

fútbol /'futβol/ *n. m.* football, soccer.

fútil /'futil/ *a.* trivial.

futilidad /futili'ðað/ *n. f.* triviality.

futuro /fu'turo/ *a. & m.* future.

futurología /futurolo'hia/ *n. f.* futurology.

G

gabán /ga'βan/ *n. m.* overcoat.

gabardina /gaβar'ðina/ *n. f.* raincoat.

gabinete /gaβi'nete/ *n. m.* closet; cabinet; study.

gacela /ga'θela; ga'sela/ *n. f.* gazelle.

gaceta /ga'θeta; ga'seta/ *n. f.* gazette, newspaper.

gacetilla /gaθe'tiʎa; gase'tiya/ *n. f.* personal news section of a newspaper.

gaélico /ga'eliko/ *a.* Gaelic.

gafas /'gafas/ *n. f.pl.* eyeglasses.

gaguear /gage'ar/ *v.* stutter, stammer.

gaita /'gaita/ *n. f.* bagpipes.

gaje /'gahe/ *n. m.* salary; fee.

gala /'gala/ *n. f.* gala, ceremony; (*pl.*) regalia. **tener a g.,** be proud of.

galán /ga'lan/ *n. m.* gallant.

galano /ga'lano/ *a.* stylishly dressed; elegant.

galante /ga'lante/ *a.* gallant.

galantería /galante'ria/ *n. f.* gallantry, compliment.

galápago /ga'lapago/ *n. m.* freshwater turtle.

galardón /galar'ðon/ *n. m.* prize; reward.

gáleo /'galeo/ *n. m.* swordfish.

galera /ga'lera/ *n. f.* wagon; shed; galley.

galería /gale'ria/ *n. f.* gallery, *Theat.* balcony.

galés /'gales/ **-esa** *a. & n.* Welsh; Welshman, Welshwoman.

galgo /'galgo/ *n. m.* greyhound.

galillo /ga'liʎo; ga'liyo/ *n. m.* uvula.

galimatías /galima'tias/ *n. m.* gibberish.

gallardete /gaʎar'ðete; gayar-'ðete/ *n. m.* pennant.

galleta /ga'ʎeta; ga'yeta/ *n. f.* cracker.

gallina /ga'ʎina; ga'yina/ *n. f.* hen.

gallinero /gaʎi'nero; gayi'nero/ *n. m.* chicken coop.

gallo /'gaʎo; ga'yo/ *n. m.* rooster.

galocha /ga'lotʃa/ *n. f.* galosh.

galón /ga'lon/ *n. m.* gallon; *Mil.* stripe.

galope /ga'lope/ *n. m.* gallop. **—galopar,** *v.*

galopín /galo'pin/ *n. m.* ragamuffin, urchin (child).

gamba /'gamba/ *n. f.* prawn.

gamberro /gam'βerro/ **-ra** *n.* hooligan.

gambito /gam'βito/ *n. m.* gambit.

gamuza /ga'muθa; ga'musa/ *n. f.* chamois.

gana /'gana/ *n. f.* desire, wish, mind (to). **de buena g.,** willingly. **tener ganas de,** to feel like.

ganado /ga'naðo/ *n. m.* cattle.

ganador /gana'ðor/ **-ra** *n.* winner.

ganancia /ga'nanθia; ga'nansia/ *n. f.* gain, profit; (*pl.*) earnings.

ganapán /gana'pan/ n. m. drudge.

ganar /ga'nar/ v. earn; win; beat.

ganchillo /gan'tʃiʎo; gan'tʃiyo/ n. m. crochet work.

gancho /'gantʃo/ n. m. hook, hanger, clip, hairpin.

gandul /gan'dul/ -la n. idler, tramp, hobo.

ganga /'ganga/ n. f. bargain.

gangrena /gaŋ'grena/ n. f. gangrene.

gansarón /gansa'ron/ n. m. gosling.

ganso /'ganso/ n. m. goose.

garabato /gara'βato/ n. m. hook; scrawl, scribble.

garaje /ga'rahe/ n. m. garage.

garantía /garan'tia/ n. f. guarantee; collateral, security.

garantizar /garanti'θar; garanti'sar/ v. guarantee, secure, pledge.

garbanzo /gar'βanθo; gar'βanso/ n. m. chickpea.

garbo /'garβo/ n. m. grace.

garboso /gar'βoso/ a. graceful, sprightly.

gardenia /gar'ðenia/ n. f. gardenia.

garfa /'garfa/ n. f. claw, talon.

garganta /gar'ganta/ n. f. throat.

gárgara /'gargara/ n. f. gargle. —**gargarizar,** v.

garita /ga'rita/ n. f. sentry box.

garito /ga'rito/ n. m. gambling house.

garlopa /gar'lopa/ n. f. carpenter's plane.

garra /'garra/ n. f. claw.

garrafa /ga'rrafa/ n. f. decanter, carafe.

garrideza /garri'ðeθa; garri'ðesa/ n. f. elegance, handsomeness.

garrido /ga'rriðo/ a. elegant, handsome.

garrote /ga'rrote/ n. m. club, cudgel.

garrotillo /garro'tiʎo; garro'tiyo/ n. m. croup.

garrudo /ga'rruðo/ a. powerful, brawny.

garza /'garθa; 'garsa/ n. f. heron.

gas /gas/ n. m. gas.

gasa /'gasa/ n. f. gauze.

gaseosa /gase'osa/ n. f. carbonated water.

gaseoso /gase'oso/ a. gaseous.

gasolina /gaso'lina/ n. f. gasoline.

gasolinera /gasoli'nera/ n. f. gas station.

gastar /gas'tar/ v. spend; use up, wear out; waste.

gastritis /gas'tritis/ n. f. gastritis.

gastrómano /gas'tromano/ n. m. glutton.

gastrónomo /gas'tronomo/ -ma n. gourmet, epicure, gastronome.

gatear /gate'ar/ v. creep.

gatillo /ga'tiʎo; ga'tiyo/ n. m. trigger.

gato /'gato/ -ta n. cat.

gaucho /'gautʃo/ n. m. Argentine cowboy.

gaveta /ga'βeta/ n. f. drawer.

gavilla /ga'βiʎa; ga'βiya/ n. f. sheaf.

gaviota /ga'βiota/ n. f. seagull.

gayo /'gayo/ a. merry, gay.

gayola /ga'yola/ n. f. cage; Colloq. prison.

gazapera /gaθa'pera; gasa'pera/ n. f. rabbit warren.

gazapo /ga'θapo; ga'sapo/ n. m. rabbit.

gazmoñada /gaθmo'ɲaða; gasmo-'ɲaða/ n. f. prudishness.

gazmoño /gaθ'moɲo; gas'moɲo/ n. m. prude.

gaznate /gaθ'nate; gas'nate/ n. m. windpipe.

gazpacho /gaθ'patʃo; gas'patʃo/ n. m. cold tomato soup; gazpacho.

gelatina /hela'tina/ n. f. gelatine.

gemelo /he'melo/ -la n. twin.

gemelos /he'melos/ n. m.pl. cuff links; opera glasses; **-as,** twins.

gemido /he'miðo/ n. m. moan, groan, wail. —**gemir,** v.

genciana /hen'θiana; hen'siana/ n. f. gentian.

genealogía /henealo'hia/ n. f. genealogy, pedigree.

generación /henera'θion; henera-'sion/ n. f. generation.

generador /henera'ðor/ n. m. generator.

general /hene'ral/ a. & n. general.

generalidad /henerali'ðað/ n. f. generality.

generalización /heneraliθa'θion; heneralisa'sion/ n. f. generalization.

generalizar /henerali'θar; henerali'sar/ v. generalize.

generalmente /heneral'mente/ adv. generally.

género /'henero/ n. **1.** m. gender; kind. **2.** (pl.) goods, material.

generosidad /henerosi'ðað/ n. f. generosity.

generoso /hene'roso/ a. generous.

génesis /'henesis/ n. m. genesis.

genético /he'netiko/ a. genetic.

genial /he'nial/ a. genial; brilliant.

genio /'henio/ n. m. genius; temper; disposition.

genitivo /heni'tiβo/ n. m. genitive.

genocidio /heno'θiðio; heno'siðio/ n. m. genocide.

gente /'hente/ n. f. people, folk.

gentil /hen'til/ a. gracious; graceful.

gentileza /henti'leθa; henti'lesa/ n. f. grace, graciousness.

gentío /hen'tio/ n. m. mob, crowd.

genuino /he'nuino/ a. genuine.

geografía /heogra'fia/ n. f. geography.

geográfico /heo'grafiko/ a. geographical.

geométrico /heo'metriko/ a. geometric.

geranio /he'ranio/ n. m. geranium.

gerencia /he'renθia; he'rensia/ n. f. management.

gerente /he'rente/ n. m. & f. manager, director.

germen /'hermen/ n. m. germ.

germinar /hermi'nar/ v. germinate.

gerundio /he'rundio/ n. m. gerund.

gesticulación /hestikula'θion; hestikula'sion/ n. f. gesticulation.

gesticular /hestiku'lar/ v. gesticulate, gesture.

gestión /hes'tion/ n. f. conduct; effort; action.

gesto /'hesto/ n. m. gesture, facial expression.

gigante /hi'gante/ a. & n. gigantic, giant.

gigantesco /higan'tesko/ a. gigantic, huge.

gilipollas /gili'poʎas; gili'poyas/ n. m. & f. Colloq. fool, idiot.

gimnasio /him'nasio/ n. m. gymnasium.

gimnástica /him'nastika/ n. f. gymnastics.

gimotear /himote'ar/ v. whine.

ginebra /hi'neβra/ n. f. gin.

ginecólogo /hine'kologo/ **-ga** n. gynecologist.

gira /'hira/ n. f. tour, trip.

girado /hi'raðo/ **-da** n. Com. drawee.

girador /hira'ðor/ **-ra** n. Com. drawer.

girar /hi'rar/ v. revolve, turn, spin, whirl.

giratorio /hira'torio/ a. rotary, revolving.

giro /'hiro/ n. m. whirl, turn, spin; Com. draft. **g. postal**, money order.

gitano /hi'tano/ **-na** a. & n. Gypsy.

glacial /gla'θial; gla'sial/ a. glacial, icy.

glaciar /gla'θiar; gla'siar/ n. m. glacier.

gladiador /glaðia'ðor/ n. m. gladiator.

glándula /'glandula/ n. f. gland.

glándula endocrina /'glandula endo'krina/ endocrine gland.

glándula pituitaria /'glandula pitui'taria/ pituitary gland.

glándula prostática /'glandula pros'tatika/ prostate gland.

glasé /gla'se/ n. m. glacé.

glicerina /gliθe'rina; glise'rina/ n. f. glycerine.

globo /'gloβo/ n. m. globe; balloon.

gloria /'gloria/ n. f. glory.

glorieta /glo'rieta/ n. f. bower.

glorificación /glorifika'θion; glorifika'sion/ n. f. glorification.

glorificar /glorifi'kar/ v. glorify.

glorioso /glo'rioso/ a. glorious.

glosa /'glosa/ n. f. gloss. —*glosar*, v.

glosario /glo'sario/ n. m. glossary.

glotón /glo'ton/ **-ona** a. & n. gluttonous; glutton.

glucosa /glu'kosa/ n. f. glucose.

gluten /'gluten/ n. m. gluten; glue.

gobernación /goβerna'θion; goβerna'sion/ n. f. government.

gobernador /goβerna'ðor/ **-ra** n. governor.

gobernalle /goβer'naʎe; goβer'naye/ n. m. rudder, tiller, helm.

gobernante /goβer'nante/ n. m. & f. ruler.

gobernar /goβer'nar/ v. govern.

gobierno /go'βierno/ n. m. government.

goce /'goθe; 'gose/ n. m. enjoyment.

gola /'gola/ n. f. throat.

golf /golf/ n. m. golf.

golfista /gol'fista/ n. m. & f. golfer.

golfo /'golfo/ n. m. gulf.

gollete /go'ʎete; go'yete/ n. m. upper portion of one's throat.

golondrina /golon'drina/ n. f. swallow.

golosina /golo'sina/ n. f. delicacy.

goloso /go'loso/ a. sweet-toothed.

golpe /'golpe/ n. m. blow, stroke. **de g.,** suddenly.

golpear /golpe'ar/ v. strike, beat, pound.

goma /'goma/ n. f. rubber; gum; glue; eraser.

góndola /'ɡondola/ n. f. gondola.

gordo /'ɡorðo/ a. fat.

gordura /ɡor'ðura/ n. f. fatness.

gorila /ɡo'rila/ n. m. gorilla.

gorja /'ɡorha/ n. f. gorge.

gorjeo /ɡor'heo/ n. m. warble, chirp. **—gorjear,** v.

gorrión /ɡo'rrion/ n. m. sparrow.

gorro /'ɡorro/ n. m. cap.

gota /'ɡota/ n. f. drop (of liquid).

gotear /ɡote'ar/ v. drip, leak.

goteo /ɡo'teo/ n. m. leak.

gotera /ɡo'tera/ n. f. leak; gutter.

gótico /'ɡotiko/ a. Gothic.

gozar /ɡo'θar; ɡo'sar/ v. enjoy.

gozne /'ɡoθne; 'ɡosne/ n. m. hinge.

gozo /'ɡoθo; 'ɡoso/ n. m. enjoyment, delight, joy.

gozoso /ɡo'θoso; ɡo'soso/ a. joyful, joyous.

grabado /ɡra'βaðo/ n. **1.** engraving, cut, print. —a. **2.** recorded.

grabador /ɡraβa'ðor/ n. m. engraver.

grabadora /ɡraβa'ðora/ n. f. tape recorder.

grabar /ɡra'βar/ v. engrave; record.

gracia /'ɡraθia; 'ɡrasia/ n. f. grace; wit, charm. **hacer g.,** to amuse, strike as funny. **tener g.,** to be funny, to be witty.

gracias /'ɡraθias; 'ɡrasias/ n. f.pl. thanks, thank you.

gracioso /ɡra'θioso; ɡra'sioso/ a. witty, funny.

grada /'ɡraða/ n. f. step.

gradación /ɡraða'θion; ɡraða'sion/ n. f. gradation.

grado /'ɡraðo/ n. m. grade; rank; degree.

graduado /ɡra'ðuaðo/ **-da** n. graduate.

gradual /ɡra'ðual/ a. gradual.

graduar /ɡra'ðuar/ v. grade; graduate.

gráfico /'ɡrafiko/ a. graphic, vivid.

grafito /ɡra'fito/ n. m. graphite.

grajo /'ɡraho/ n. m. jackdaw.

gramática /ɡra'matika/ n. f. grammar.

gramo /'ɡramo/ n. m. gram.

gran /ɡran/ **grande** a. big, large; great.

granada /ɡra'naða/ n. f. grenade; pomegranate.

granar /ɡra'nar/ v. seed.

grandes almacenes /'ɡrandes alma'θenes; 'ɡrandes alma'senes/ n. m.pl. department store.

grandeza /ɡran'deθa; ɡran'desa/ n. f. greatness.

grandiosidad /ɡrandiosi'ðað/ n. f. grandeur.

grandioso /ɡran'dioso/ a. grand, magnificent.

grandor /ɡran'dor/ n. m. size.

granero /ɡra'nero/ n. m. barn; granary.

granito /ɡra'nito/ n. m. granite.

granizada /ɡrani'θaða; ɡrani'saða/ n. f. hailstorm.

granizo /ɡra'niθo; ɡra'niso/ n. m. hail. **—granizar,** v.

granja /'ɡranha/ n. f. grange; farm; farmhouse.

granjear /ɡranhe'ar/ v. earn, gain; get.

granjero /ɡran'hero/ **-era** n. farmer.

grano /'ɡrano/ n. m. grain; kernel.

granuja /ɡra'nuha/ n. m. waif, urchin.

grapa /'ɡrapa/ n. f. clamp, clip.

grapadora /ɡrapa'ðora/ n. f. stapler.

grasa /'ɡrasa/ n. f. grease, fat.

grasiento /ɡra'siento/ a. greasy.

gratificación /ɡratifika'θion; ɡratifika'sion/ n. f. gratification; reward; tip.

gratificar /ɡratifi'kar/ v. gratify; reward; tip.

gratis /'ɡratis/ adv. gratis, free.

gratitud /ɡrati'tuð/ n. f. gratitude.

grato /'ɡrato/ a. grateful; pleasant.

gratuito /ɡra'tuito/ a. gratuitous; free.

gravamen /ɡra'βamen/ n. m. tax; burden; obligation.

grave /'graβe/ a. grave, serious, severe.

gravedad /graβe'ðað/ n. f. gravity, seriousness.

gravitación /graβita'θion; graβita'sion/ n. f. gravitation.

gravitar /graβi'tar/ v. gravitate.

gravoso /gra'βoso/ a. burdensome.

graznido /graθ'niðo; gras'niðo/ n. m. croak. **—graznar,** v.

Grecia /'greθia; 'gresia/ n. f. Greece.

greco /'greko/ **-ca** a. & n. Greek.

greda /'greða/ n. f. clay.

gresca /'greska/ n. f. revelry; quarrel.

griego /'griego/ **-ga** a. & n. Greek.

grieta /'grieta/ n. f. opening; crevice, crack.

grifo /'grifo/ n. m. faucet.

grillo /'griʎo; 'griyo/ n. m. cricket.

grima /'grima/ n. f. fright.

gringo /'gringo/ **-ga** n. foreigner (usually North American).

gripa /'gripa/ **gripe** /'gripe/ n. f. grippe.

gris /gris/ a. gray.

grito /'grito/ n. m. shout, scream, cry. **—gritar,** v.

grosella /gro'seʎa; gro'seya/ n. f. currant.

grosería /grose'ria/ n. f. grossness; coarseness.

grosero /gro'sero/ a. coarse, vulgar, discourteous.

grotesco /gro'tesko/ a. grotesque.

grúa /'grua/ n. f. crane; tow truck.

gruesa /'gruesa/ n. f. gross.

grueso /'grueso/ a. **1.** bulky; stout; coarse, thick. **—n. 2.** m. bulk.

grulla /'gruʎa; 'gruya/ n. f. crane.

gruñido /gru'ɲiðo/ n. m. growl, snarl, mutter. **—gruñir,** v.

grupo /'grupo/ n. m. group, party.

gruta /'gruta/ n. f. cavern.

guacamol /guaka'mol/ **guacamole** n. m. avocado sauce; guacamole.

guadaña /gua'ðaɲa/ n. f. scythe. **—guadañar,** v.

guagua /'guagua/ n. f. (S.A.) baby; (Carib.) bus.

gualdo /'gualdo/ n. m. yellow, golden.

guano /'guano/ n. m. guano (fertilizer).

guante /'guante/ n. m. glove.

guantera /guan'tera/ n. f. glove compartment.

guapo /'guapo/ a. handsome.

guarda /'guarða/ n. m. or f. guard.

guardabarros /guarða'βarros/ n. m. fender.

guardacostas /guarða'kostas/ n. m. revenue ship.

guardaespaldas /guarðaes'paldas/ n. m. & f. bodyguard.

guardameta /guarða'meta/ n. m. & f. goalkeeper.

guardar /guar'ðar/ v. keep, store, put away; guard.

guardarropa /guarða'rropa/ n. f. coat room.

guardarse de /guar'ðarse de/ v. beware of, avoid.

guardia /'guarðia/ n. **1.** f. guard; watch. **—n. 2.** m. policeman.

guardián /guar'ðian/ **-na** n. guardian, keeper, watchman.

guardilla /guar'ðiʎa; guar'ðiya/ n. f. attic.

guarida /gua'riða/ n. f. den.

guarismo /gua'rismo/ n. m. number, figure.

guarnecer /guarne'θer; guarne'ser/ v. adorn.

guarnición /guarni'θion; guarni'sion/ n. f. garrison; trimming.

guasa /'guasa/ n. f. joke, jest.

guayaba /gua'yaβa/ n. f. guava.

gubernativo /guβerna'tiβo/ a. governmental.

guerra /'gerra/ n. f. war.

guerrero /ge'rrero/ **-ra** n. warrior.

guía /'gia/ n. **1.** m. & f. guide. **2.** f. guidebook, directory.

guiar /giar/ v. guide; steer, drive.

guija /'giha/ n. f. pebble.

guillotina /giʎo'tina; giyo'tina/ n. f. guillotine.

guindar /gin'dar/ v. hang.

guinga /'ginga/ n. f. gingham.

guiñada /gi'ɲaða/ n. f., **guiño,** m. wink. **—guiñar,** v.

guión /gi'on/ n. m. dash, hyphen; script.

guirnalda /gir'nalda/ n. f. garland, wreath.

guisa /'gisa/ n. f. guise, manner.

guisado /gi'saðo/ n. m. stew.

guisante /gi'sante/ n. m. pea.

guisar /gi'sar/ v. cook.

guiso /'giso/ n. m. stew.

guita /'gita/ n. f. twine.

guitarra /gi'tarra/ n. f. guitar.

guitarrista /gita'rrista/ n. m. & f. guitarist.

gula /'gula/ n. f. gluttony.

gurú /gu'ru/ n. m. guru.

gusano /gu'sano/ n. m. worm, caterpillar.

gustar /gus'tar/ v. please; taste.

gustillo /gus'tiʎo; gus'tiyo/ n. m. aftertaste, slight pleasure.

gusto /'gusto/ n. m. pleasure; taste; liking.

gustoso /gus'toso/ a. pleasant; tasteful.

gutural /gutu'ral/ a. guttural.

H

haba /'aβa/ n. f. bean.

habanera /aβa'nera/ n. f. Cuban dance melody.

haber /a'βer/ v. have. **h. de,** be to, be supposed to.

haberes /a'βeres/ n. m.pl. property; worldly goods.

habichuela /aβi't'ʃuela/ n. f. bean.

hábil /'aβil/ a. skillful; capable; clever.

habilidad /aβili'ðað/ n. f. ability; skill; talent.

habilidoso /aβili'ðoso/ a. able, skillful, talented.

habilitado /aβili'taðo/ **-da** n. paymaster.

habilitar /aβili'tar/ v. qualify; supply, equip.

hábilmente /'aβilmente/ adv. ably.

habitación /aβita'θion; aβita'sion/ n. f. dwelling; room. **h. individual,** single room.

habitante /aβi'tante/ n. m. & f. inhabitant.

habitar /aβi'tar/ v. inhabit; dwell.

hábito /'aβito/ n. m. habit; custom.

habitual /aβi'tual/ a. habitual.

habituar /aβi'tuar/ v. accustom, habituate.

habla /'aβla/ n. f. speech.

hablador /aβla'ðor/ a. talkative.

hablar /a'βlar/ v. talk, speak.

haca /'aka/ n. f. pony.

hacedor /aθe'ðor; ase'ðor/ n. m. maker.

hacendado /aθen'daðo; asen'daðo/ **-da** n. hacienda owner; farmer.

hacendoso /aθen'doso; asen'doso/ a. industrious.

hacer /a'θer; a'ser/ v. do; make. **hace dos años,** etc., two years ago, etc.

hacerse /a'θerse; a'serse/ v. become, get to be.

hacha /'atʃa/ n. f. ax, hatchet.

hacia /'aθia; 'asia/ prep. toward.

hacienda /a'θienda; a'sienda/ n. f. property; estate; ranch; farm; Govt. treasury.

hada /'aða/ n. f. fairy.

hado /'aðo/ n. m. fate.

halagar /ala'gar/ v. flatter.

halar /a'lar/ v. haul, pull.

halcón /al'kon/ n. m. hawk, falcon.

haleche /a'letʃe/ n. m. anchovy.

hallado /a'ʎaðo; a'yaðo/ a. found. **bien h.,** welcome. **mal h.,** uneasy.

hallar /a'ʎar; a'yar/ v. find, locate.

hallarse /a'ʎarse; a'yarse/ v. be located; happen to be.

hallazgo /a'ʎaθgo; a'yasgo/ n. m. find, thing found.

hamaca /a'maka/ n. f. hammock.

hambre /'ambre/ n. f. hunger. **tener h., estar con h.,** to be hungry.

hambrear /ambre'ar/ v. hunger; starve.

hambriento /am'briento/ a. starving, hungry.

hamburguesa /ambur'gesa/ n. f. beefburger, hamburger.

haragán /ara'gan/ **-na** n. idler, lazy person.

haraganear /aragane'ar/ v. loiter.

harapo /a'rapo/ n. m. rag, tatter.

haraposo /ara'poso/ a. ragged, shabby.

harén /a'ren/ n. m. harem.

harina /a'rina/ n. f. flour, meal.

harnero /ar'nero/ n. m. sieve.

hartar /ar'tar/ v. satiate.

harto /'arto/ a. stuffed; fed up.

hartura /ar'tura/ n. f. superabundance, glut.

hasta /'asta/ prep. **1.** until, till; as far as, up to. **h. luego,** good-bye, so long. —adv. **2.** even.

hastío /as'tio/ n. m. distaste, loathing.

hato /'ato/ n. m. herd.

hay /ai/ v. there is, there are. **h. que,** it is necessary to. **no h. de**

qué, you're welcome, don't mention it.

haya /'aya/ n. f. beech tree.

haz /aθ/ as; n. f. bundle, sheaf; face.

hazaña /a'θaɲa; a'saɲa/ n. f. deed; exploit, feat.

hebdomadario /eβðoma'ðario/ a. weekly.

hebilla /e'βiʎa; e'βiya/ n. f. buckle.

hebra /'eβra/ n. f. thread, string.

hebreo /e'βreo/ **-rea** a. & n. Hebrew.

hechicero /etʃi'θero; etʃi'sero/ **-ra** n. wizard, witch.

hechizar /etʃi'θar; etʃi'sar/ v. bewitch.

hechizo /e'tʃiθo; e'tʃiso/ n. m. spell.

hecho /'etʃo/ n. m. fact; act; deed.

hechura /e'tʃura/ n. f. workmanship, make.

hediondez /eðion'deθ; eðion'des/ n. f. stench.

hégira /'ehira/ n. f. hegira.

helada /e'laða/ n. f. frost.

heladería /elaðe'ria/ n. f. ice-cream parlor.

helado /e'laðo/ n. m. ice cream.

helar /e'lar/ v. freeze.

helecho /e'letʃo/ n. m. fern.

hélice /'eliθe; 'elise/ n. f. propeller; helix.

helicóptero /eli'koptero/ n. m. helicopter.

helio /'elio/ n. m. helium.

hembra /'embra/ n. f. female.

hemisferio /emis'ferio/ n. m. hemisphere.

hemoglobina /emoglo'βina/ n. f. hemoglobin.

hemorragia /emo'rrahia/ n. f. hemorrhage.

hemorragia nasal /emo'rrahia na'sal/ nosebleed.

henchir /en'tʃir/ v. stuff.

hendedura /ende'ðura/ n. f. crevice, crack.

hendido /en'diðo/ a. cloven, cleft (lip).

heno /'eno/ n. m. hay.

hepática /e'patika/ n. f. liverwort.

hepatitis /epa'titis/ n. f. hepatitis.

heraldo /e'raldo/ n. m. herald.

herbáceo /er'βaθeo; er'βaseo/ a. herbaceous.

herbívoro /er'βiβoro/ a. herbivorous.

heredar /ere'ðar/ v. inherit.

heredero /ere'ðero/ **-ra** n. heir; successor.

hereditario /ereði'tario/ a. hereditary.

hereje /e'rehe/ n. m. & f. heretic.

herejía /ere'hia/ n. f. heresy.

herencia /e'renθia; e'rensia/ n. f. inheritance; heritage.

herético /e'retiko/ a. heretical.

herida /e'riða/ n. f. wound, injury.

herir /e'rir/ v. wound, injure.

hermafrodita /ermafro'ðita/ a. & n. hermaphrodite.

hermana /er'mana/ n. f. sister.

hermano /er'mano/ n. m. brother.

hermético /er'metiko/ a. airtight.

hermoso /er'moso/ a. beautiful, handsome.

hermosura /ermo'sura/ n. f. beauty.

hernia /'ernia/ n. f. hernia, rupture.

héroe /'eroe/ n. m. hero.

heroico /e'roiko/ a. heroic.

heroína /ero'ina/ n. f. heroine.

heroísmo /ero'ismo/ n. m. heroism.

herradura /erra'ðura/ n. f. horseshoe.

herramienta /erra'mienta/ n. f. tool; implement.

herrería /erre'ria/ n. f. blacksmith's shop.

herrero /e'rrero/ n. m. blacksmith.

herrumbre /e'rrumbre/ n. f. rust.

hertzio /'ertθio; 'ertsio/ n. m. hertz.

hervir /er'βir/ v. boil.

hesitación /esita'θion; esita'sion/ n. f. hesitation.

heterogéneo /etero'heneo/ a. heterogeneous.

heterosexual /eterosek'sual/ a. heterosexual.

hexagonal /eksago'nal/ a. hexagonal.

hexágono /e'ksagono/ n. m. hexagon.

hez /eθ; es/ n. f. dregs, sediment.

híbrido /'iβriðo/ **-da** n. & a. hybrid.

hidalgo /i'ðalgo/ **-ga** & n. noble.

hidalguía /iðal'gia/ n. f. nobility; generosity.

hidráulico /i'ðrauliko/ a. hydraulic.

hidroavión /iðroa'βion/ *n. m.* seaplane, hydroplane.

hidrofobia /iðro'foβia/ *n. f.* rabies.

hidrógeno /i'ðroheno/ *n. m.* hydrogen.

hidropesía /iðrope'sia/ *n. f.* dropsy.

hiedra /'ieðra/ *n. f.* ivy.

hiel /iel/ *n. f.* gall.

hielo /'ielo/ *n. m.* ice.

hiena /'iena/ *n. f.* hyena.

hierba /'ierβa/ *n. f.* grass; herb; marijuana.

hierbabuena /ierβa'βuena/ *n. f.* mint.

hierro /'ierro/ *n. m.* iron.

hígado /'iɣaðo/ *n. m.* liver.

higiene /i'hiene/ *n. f.* hygiene.

higiénico /i'hieniko/ *a.* sanitary, hygienic.

higo /'iɣo/ *n. m.* fig.

higuera /i'ɣera/ *n. f.* fig tree.

hija /'iha/ *n. f.* daughter.

hija adoptiva /'iha aðop'tiβa/ adopted daughter.

hijastro /i'hastro/ **-tra** *n.* stepchild.

hijo /'iho/ *n. m.* son.

hijo adoptivo /'iho aðop'tiβo/ *n. m.* adopted child, adopted son.

hila /'ila/ *n. f.* line.

hilandero /ilan'dero/ **-ra** *n.* spinner.

hilar /i'lar/ *v.* spin.

hilera /i'lera/ *n. f.* row, line, tier.

hilo /'ilo/ *n. m.* thread; string; wire; linen.

himno /'imno/ *n. m.* hymn.

hincar /in'kar/ *v.* drive, thrust; sink into.

hincarse /in'karse/ *v.* kneel.

hinchar /in'tʃar/ *v.* swell.

hindú /in'du/ *n.* & *a.* Hindu.

hinojo /i'noho/ *n. m.* knee.

hiperenlace /iperen'laθe, iperen-'lase/ *n. m.* hyperlink.

hipermercado /ipermer'kaðo/ *n. m.* hypermarket.

hipertexto /iper'teksto/ *n. m.* hypertext.

hipnótico /ip'notiko/ *a.* hypnotic.

hipnotismo /ipno'tismo/ *n. m.* hypnotism.

hipnotista /ipno'tista/ *n. m.* & *f.* hypnotist.

hipnotizar /ipnoti'θar/ ipnoti'sar/ *v.* hypnotize.

hipo /'ipo/ *n. m.* hiccough.

hipocresía /ipokre'sia/ *n. f.* hypocrisy.

hipócrita /i'pokrita/ *a.* & *n.* hypocritical; hypocrite.

hipódromo /i'poðromo/ *n. m.* race track.

hipoteca /ipo'teka/ *n. f.* mortgage. **—hipotecar,** *v.*

hipótesis /i'potesis/ *n. f.* hypothesis.

hirsuto /ir'suto/ *a.* hairy, hirsute.

hispano /is'pano/ *a.* Hispanic, Spanish American.

Hispanoamérica /ispanoa'merika/ *f.* Spanish America.

hispanoamericano /ispanoameri-'kano/ **-na** *a.* & *n.* Spanish American.

histerectomía /isterekto'mia/ *n. f.* hysterectomy.

histeria /is'teria/ *n. f.* hysteria.

histérico /is'teriko/ *a.* hysterical.

historia /is'toria/ *n. f.* history; story.

historiador /istoria'ðor/ **-ra** *n.* historian.

histórico /is'toriko/ *a.* historic, historical.

histrión /is'trion/ *n. m.* actor.

hocico /o'θiko; o'siko/ *n. m.* snout, muzzle.

hogar /o'ɣar/ *n. m.* hearth; home.

hoguera /o'ɣera/ *n. f.* bonfire, blaze.

hoja /'oha/ *n. f.* leaf; sheet (of paper); pane; blade.

hoja de cálculo /'oha de 'kalkulo/ spreadsheet.

hoja de inscripción /'oha de ins-krip'θion; 'oha de inskrip'sion/ entry blank.

hoja de pedidos /'oha de pe-'ðiðos/ order blank.

hoja informativa /'oha informa-'tiβa/ newsletter.

hojalata /oha'lata/ *n. f.* tin.

hojalatero /ohala'tero/ **-ra** *n.* tinsmith.

hojear /ohe'ar/ *v.* scan, skim through.

hola /'ola/ *interj.* hello.

Holanda /o'landa/ *n. f.* Holland, Netherlands.

holandés /olan'des/ **-esa** *a.* & *n.* Dutch; Hollander.

holganza /ol'ɡanθa; ol'ɡansa/ *n. f.* leisure; diversion.

holgazán /olɡa'θan; olɡa'san/ **-ana** *a.* **1.** idle, lazy. **—** *n.* **2.** *m.* idler, loiterer, tramp.

holgazanear /olɡaθane'ar; olɡasane'ar/ v. idle, loiter.

hollín /o'ʎin; o'yin/ n. m. soot.

holografía /oloɡra'fia/ n. f. holography.

holograma /olo'ɡrama/ n. m. hologram.

hombre /'ombre/ n. m. man.

hombría /om'βria/ n. f. manliness.

hombro /'ombro/ n. m. shoulder.

hombruno /om'bruno/ a. mannish, masculine (woman).

homenaje /ome'nahe/ n. m. homage.

homeópata /ome'opata/ n. m. homeopath.

homicidio /omi'θiðio; omi'siðio/ n. m. homicide.

homilía /omi'lia/ n. f. homily.

homosexual /omose'ksual/ a. homosexual, gay.

honda /'onda/ n. f. sling.

hondo /'ondo/ a. deep.

hondonada /ondo'naða/ n. f. ravine.

hondura /on'dura/ n. f. depth.

honestidad /onesti'ðað/ n. f. modesty, unpretentiousness.

honesto /o'nesto/ a. honest; pure; just.

hongo /'onɡo/ n. m. fungus; mushroom.

honor /o'nor/ n. m. honor.

honorable /ono'raβle/ a. honorable.

honorario /ono'rario/ a. **1.** honorary. —n. **2.** m. honorarium, fee.

honorífico /ono'rifiko/ a. honorary.

honra /'onra/ n. f. honor.
—**honrar,** v.

honradez /onra'ðeθ; onra'ðes/ n. f. honesty.

honrado /on'raðo/ a. honest, honorable.

hora /'ora/ n. f. hour; time (of day).

horadar /ora'ðar/ v. perforate.

hora punta /'ora 'punta/ rush hour.

horario /o'rario/ n. m. timetable, schedule.

horca /'orka/ n. f. gallows; pitchfork.

horda /'orða/ n. f. horde.

horizontal /oriθon'tal; orison'tal/ a. horizontal.

horizonte /ori'θonte; ori'sonte/ n. m. horizon.

hormiga /or'miɡa/ n. f. ant.

hormiguear /ormiɡe'ar/ v. itch.

hormiguero /ormi'ɡero/ n. m. ant hill.

hornero /or'nero/ -ra n. baker.

hornillo /or'niʎo; or'niyo/ n. m. stove.

horno /'orno/ n. m. oven; kiln.

horóscopo /o'roskopo/ n. m. horoscope.

horrendo /o'rrendo/ a. dreadful, horrendous.

horrible /o'rriβle/ a. horrible, hideous, awful.

hórrido /'orriðo/ a. horrid.

horror /o'rror/ n. m. horror.

horrorizar /orrori'θar; orrori'sar/ v. horrify.

horroroso /orro'roso/ a. horrible, frightful.

hortelano /orte'lano/ n. m. horticulturist.

hospedaje /ospe'ðahe/ n. m. lodging.

hospedar /ospe'ðar/ v. give or take lodgings.

hospital /ospi'tal/ n. m. hospital.

hospitalario /ospita'lario/ a. hospitable.

hospitalidad /ospitali'ðað/ n. f. hospitality.

hospitalmente /ospital'mente/ adv. hospitably.

hostia /'ostia/ n. f. host; Colloq. hit, blow.

hostil /os'til/ a. hostile.

hostilidad /ostili'ðað/ n. f. hostility.

hotel /o'tel/ n. m. hotel.

hoy /oi/ adv. today. **h. día, h. en día,** nowadays.

hoya /'oya/ n. f. dale, valley.

hoyo /'oyo/ n. m. pit, hole.

hoyuelo /o'yuelo/ n. m. dimple.

hoz /oθ; os/ n. f. sickle.

hucha /'utʃa/ n. f. chest, money box; savings.

hueco /'ueko/ a. **1.** hollow, empty. —n. **2.** m. hole, hollow.

huelga /'uelɡa/ n. f. strike.

huelguista /uel'hista/ n. m. & f. striker.

huella /'ueʎa; 'ueya/ n. f. track, trace; footprint.

huérfano /'uerfano/ **-na** a. & n. orphan.

huero /'uero/ a. empty.

huerta /'uerta/ n. f. (vegetable) garden.

huerto /'uerto/ n. m. orchard.

hueso /'ueso/ n. m. bone; fruit pit.

huésped /'uespeð/ n. m. & f. guest.

huesudo /ue'suðo/ a. bony.

huevo /'ueβo/ n. m. egg.

huída /'uiða/ n. f. flight, escape.

huir /uir/ v. flee.

hule /'ule/ n. m. oilcloth.

humanidad /umani'ðað/ n. f. humanity, mankind; humaneness.

humanista /uma'nista/ n. m. & f. humanist.

humanitario /umani'tario/ a. humane.

humano /u'mano/ a. human; humane.

humareda /uma'reða/ n. f. dense cloud of smoke.

humear /ume'ar/ v. emit smoke or steam.

humedad /ume'ðað/ n. f. humidity, moisture, dampness.

humedecer /umeðe'θer/ umeðe-'ser/ v. moisten, dampen.

húmedo /'umeðo/ a. humid, moist, damp.

humildad /umil'dað/ n. f. humility, meekness.

humilde /u'milde/ a. humble, meek.

humillación /umiʎa'θion/ umiya-'sion/ n. f. humiliation.

humillar /umi'ʎar/ umi'yar/ v. humiliate.

humo /'umo/ n. m. smoke; (pl.) airs, affectation.

humor /u'mor/ n. m. humor, mood.

humorista /umo'rista/ n. m. & f. humorist.

hundimiento /undi'miento/ n. m. collapse.

hundir /un'dir/ v. sink; collapse.

húngaro /'ungaro/ -ra a. & n. Hungarian.

Hungría /uŋ'gria/ n. f. Hungary.

huracán /ura'kan/ n. m. hurricane.

huraño /u'rano/ a. shy, bashful.

hurgar /ur'gar/ v. stir.

hurón /u'ron/ n. m. ferret.

hurtadillas /urta'ðiʎas/ urta'ðiyas/ n. f.pl. **a h.,** on the sly.

hurtador /urta'ðor/ -ra n. thief.

hurtar /ur'tar/ v. steal, rob of; hide.

hurtarse /ur'tarse/ v. hide; withdraw.

husmear /usme'ar/ v. scent, smell.

huso /'uso/ n. m. spindle; bobbin.

huso horario /'uso o'rario/ time zone.

I

ibérico /i'βeriko/ a. Iberian.

iberoamericano /iβeroameri'kano/ **-na** a. & n. Latin American.

ida /'iða/ n. f. departure; trip out. **i. y vuelta,** round trip.

idea /i'ðea/ n. f. idea.

ideal /i'ðeal/ a. & m. ideal.

idealismo /iðea'lismo/ n. m. idealism.

idealista /iðea'lista/ n. m. & f. idealist.

idear /iðe'ar/ v. plan, conceive.

idéntico /i'ðentiko/ a. identical.

identidad /iðenti'ðað/ n. f. identity; identification.

identificar /iðentifi'kar/ v. identify.

idilio /i'ðilio/ n. m. idyll.

idioma /i'ðioma/ n. m. language.

idiota /i'ðiota/ a. & n. idiotic; idiot.

idiotismo /iðio'tismo/ n. m. idiocy.

idolatrar /iðola'trar/ v. idolize, adore.

ídolo /'iðolo/ n. m. idol.

idóneo /i'ðoneo/ a. suitable, fit, apt.

iglesia /i'glesia/ n. f. church.

ignición /igni'θion/ igni'sion/ n. f. ignition.

ignominia /igno'minia/ n. f. ignominy, shame.

ignominioso /ignomi'nioso/ a. ignominious, shameful.

ignorancia /igno'ranθia/ igno-'ransia/ n. f. ignorance.

ignorante /igno'rante/ a. ignorant.

ignorar /igno'rar/ v. be ignorant of, not know.

ignoto /ig'noto/ a. unknown.

igual /i'gual/ a. equal; the same; (pl.) alike. **m.** equal.

igualar /igua'lar/ v. equal; equalize; match.

igualdad /igual'dað/ n. f. equality; sameness.

ijada /i'haða/ n. f. flank (of an animal).

ilegal /ile'gal/ a. illegal.

ilegítimo /ile'hitimo/ a. illegitimate.

ileso /i'leso/ a. unharmed.

ilícito /i'liθito; i'lisito/ a. illicit, unlawful.

iluminación /ilumina'θion; ilumina'sion/ n. f. illumination.

iluminar /ilumi'nar/ v. illuminate.

ilusión /ilu'sion/ n. f. illusion.

ilusión de óptica /ilu'sion de 'optika/ optical illusion.

ilusorio /ilu'sorio/ a. illusive.

ilustración /ilustra'θion; ilustra-'sion/ n. f. illustration; learning.

ilustrador /ilustra'ðor/ **-ra** n. illustrator.

ilustrar /ilus'trar/ v. illustrate.

ilustre /i'lustre/ a. illustrious, honorable, distinguished.

imagen /i'mahen/ n. f. image.

imaginación /imahina'θion; imahina'sion/ n. f. imagination.

imaginar /imahi'nar/ v. imagine.

imaginario /imahi'nario/ a. imaginary.

imaginativo /imahina'tiβo/ a. imaginative.

imán /i'man/ n. m. magnet; imam.

imbécil /im'beθil; im'besil/ a. & n. imbecile; stupid, foolish; fool.

imbuir /im'buir/ v. imbue, instil.

imitación /imita'θion; imita'sion/ n. f. imitation.

imitador /imita'ðor/ **-ra** n. imitator.

imitar /imi'tar/ v. imitate.

impaciencia /impa'θienθia; impa-'siensia/ n. f. impatience.

impaciente /impa'θiente; impa-'siente/ a. impatient.

impar /im'par/ a. unequal, uneven, odd.

imparcial /impar'θial; impar'sial/ a. impartial.

impasible /impa'siβle/ a. impassive, unmoved.

impávido /im'paβiðo/ adj. fearless, intrepid.

impedimento /impeði'mento/ n. m. impediment, obstacle.

impedir /impe'ðir/ v. impede, hinder, stop, obstruct.

impeler /impe'ler/ v. impel; incite.

impensado /impen'saðo/ a. unexpected.

imperar /impe'rar/ v. reign; prevail.

imperativo /impera'tiβo/ a. imperative.

imperceptible /imperθep'tiβle; impersep'tiβle/ a. imperceptible.

imperdible /imper'ðiβle/ n. m. safety pin.

imperecedero /impere'θeðero; imperese'ðero/ a. imperishable.

imperfecto /imper'fekto/ a. imperfect, faulty.

imperial /impe'rial/ a. imperial.

imperialismo /imperia'lismo/ n. m. imperialism.

impericia /impe'riθia; impe'risia/ n. f. inexperience.

imperio /im'perio/ n. m. empire.

imperioso /impe'rioso/ a. imperious, domineering.

impermeable /imperme'aβle/ a. waterproof. n. raincoat.

impersonal /imperso'nal/ a. impersonal.

impertinencia /impertinen'θia; impertinen'sia/ n. f. impertinence.

ímpetu /'impetu/ n. m. impulse; impetus.

impetuoso /impe'tuoso/ a. impetuous.

impiedad /impie'ðað/ n. f. impiety.

impío /im'pio/ a. impious.

implacable /impla'kaβle/ a. implacable, unrelenting.

implicar /impli'kar/ v. implicate, involve.

implorar /implo'rar/ v. implore.

imponente /impo'nente/ a. impressive.

imponer /impo'ner/ v. impose.

impopular /impopu'lar/ a. unpopular.

importación /importa'θion; importa'sion/ n. f. importation, importing.

importador /importa'ðor/ **-ra** n. importer.

importancia /impor'tanθia; impor'tansia/ n. f. importance.

importante /impor'tante/ a. important.

importar /impor'tar/ v. be important, matter; import.

importe /im'porte/ n. m. value; amount.

importunar /importu'nar/ v. beg, importune.

imposibilidad /imposiβili'ðað/ n. f. impossibility.

imposibilitado /imposiβili'taðo/ a. helpless.

imposible /impo'siβle/ a. impossible.

inicuo /ini'kuo/ *a.* wicked.

iniquidad /iniki'ðað/ *n. f.* iniquity; sin.

injuria /in'huria/ *n. f.* insult.
—**injuriar,** *v.*

injusticia /inhus'tiθia; inhus'tisia/ *n. f.* injustice.

injusto /in'husto/ *a.* unjust, unfair.

inmaculado /imaku'laðo/ *a.* immaculate; pure.

inmediato /ime'ðiato/ *a.* immediate.

inmensidad /imensi'ðað/ *n. f.* immensity.

inmenso /i'menso/ *a.* immense.

inmersión /imer'sion/ *n. f.* immersion.

inmigración /imigra'θion; imigra'sion/ *n. f.* immigration.

inmigrante /imi'grante/ *a. & n.* immigrant.

inmigrar /imi'grar/ *v.* immigrate.

inminente /imi'nente/ *a.* imminent.

inmoderado /imoðe'raðo/ *a.* immoderate.

inmodesto /imo'ðesto/ *a.* immodest.

inmoral /imo'ral/ *a.* immoral.

inmoralidad /imorali'ðað/ *n. f.* immorality.

inmortal /imor'tal/ *a.* immortal.

inmortalidad /imortali'ðað/ *n. f.* immortality.

inmóvil /i'moβil/ *a.* immobile, motionless.

inmundicia /imun'diθia; imun'disia/ *n. f.* dirt, filth.

inmune /i'mune/ *a.* immune; exempt.

inmunidad /imuni'ðað/ *n. f.* immunity.

innato /in'nato/ *a.* innate, inborn.

innecesario /inneθe'sario; innese'sario/ *a.* unnecessary, needless.

innegable /inne'gaβle/ *a.* undeniable.

innoble /in'noβle/ *a.* ignoble.

innocuo /inno'kuo/ *a.* innocuous.

innovación /innoβa'θion; innoβa'sion/ *n. f.* innovation.

innumerable /innume'raβle/ *a.* innumerable, countless.

inocencia /ino'θenθia; ino'sensia/ *n. f.* innocence.

inocentada /inoθen'taða; inosen'taða/ *n. f.* practical joke.

inocente /ino'θente; ino'sente/ *a.* innocent.

inocular /inoku'lar/ *v.* inoculate.

inodoro /ino'ðoro/ *n. m.* toilet.

inofensivo /inofen'siβo/ *a.* inoffensive, harmless.

inolvidable /inolβi'ðaβle/ *a.* unforgettable.

inoportuno /inopor'tuno/ *a.* inopportune.

inoxidable /inoksi'ðaβle/ *a.* stainless.

inquietante /inkie'tante/ *a.* disturbing, worrisome, worrying, upsetting.

inquietar /inkie'tar/ *v.* disturb, worry, trouble.

inquieto /in'kieto/ *a.* anxious, uneasy, worried; restless.

inquietud /inkie'tuð/ *n. f.* concern, anxiety, worry; restlessness.

inquilino /inki'lino/ **-na** *n.* occupant, tenant.

inquirir /inki'rir/ *v.* inquire into, investigate.

inquisición /inkisi'θion; inkisi'sion/ *n. f.* inquisition, investigation.

insaciable /insa'θiaβle; insa'siaβle/ *a.* insatiable.

insalubre /insa'luβre/ *a.* unhealthy.

insano /in'sano/ *a.* insane.

inscribir /inskri'βir/ *v.* inscribe; record.

inscribirse /inskri'βirse/ *v.* register, enroll.

inscripción /inskrip'θion; inskrip'sion/ *n. f.* inscription; registration.

insecticida /insekti'θiða; insekti'siða/ *n. m.* insecticide.

insecto /in'sekto/ *n. m.* insect.

inseguro /inse'guro/ *a.* unsure, uncertain; insecure, unsafe.

insensato /insen'sato/ *a.* stupid, senseless.

insensible /insen'siβle/ *a.* unfeeling, heartless.

inseparable /insepa'raβle/ *a.* inseparable.

inserción /inser'θion; inser'sion/ *n. f.* insertion.

insertar /inser'tar/ *v.* insert.

inservible /inser'βiβle/ *a.* useless.

insidioso /insi'ðioso/ *a.* insidious, crafty.

insigne /in'signe/ *a.* famous, noted.

insignia /in'signia/ *n. f.* insignia, badge.

insignificante /insignifi'kante/ *a.* insignificant, negligible.

insincero /insin'θero; insin'sero/ *a.* insincere.

insinuación /insinua'θion; insinua'sion/ *n. f.* insinuation; hint.

insinuar /insi'nuar/ *v.* insinuate, suggest, hint.

insipidez /insipi'ðeθ; insipi'ðes/ *n. f.* insipidity.

insípido /in'sipiðo/ *a.* insipid.

insistencia /insis'tenθia; insis'tensia/ *n. f.* insistence.

insistente /insis'tente/ *a.* insistent.

insistir /insis'tir/ *v.* insist.

insolación /insola'θion; insola'sion/ *n. f.* sunstroke.

insolencia /inso'lenθia; inso'lensia/ *n. f.* insolence.

insolente /inso'lente/ *a.* insolent.

insólito /in'solito/ *a.* unusual.

insolvente /insol'βente/ *a.* insolvent.

insomnio /in'somnio/ *n. m.* insomnia.

insonorizado /insonori'θaðo; insonori'saðo/ *a.* soundproof.

insonorizar /insonori'θar; insonori'sar/ *v.* soundproof.

insoportable /insopor'taβle/ *a.* unbearable.

inspección /inspek'θion; inspek'sion/ *n. f.* inspection.

inspeccionar /inspekθio'nar; inspeksio'nar/ *v.* inspect, examine.

inspector /inspek'tor/ **-ra** *n.* inspector.

inspiración /inspira'θion; inspira'sion/ *n. f.* inspiration.

inspirar /inspi'rar/ *v.* inspire.

instalación /instala'θion; instala'sion/ *n. f.* installation, fixture.

instalar /insta'lar/ *v.* install, set up.

instantánea /instan'tanea/ *n. f.* snapshot.

instantáneo /instan'taneo/ *a.* instantaneous.

instante /ins'tante/ *a. & m.* instant. **al i.,** at once.

instar /ins'tar/ *v.* coax, urge.

instigar /insti'gar/ *v.* instigate, urge.

instintivo /instin'tiβo/ *a.* instinctive.

instinto /ins'tinto/ *n. m.* instinct. **por i.,** by instinct, instinctively.

institución /institu'θion; institu'sion/ *n. f.* institution.

instituto /insti'tuto/ *n. m.* institute. **—instituir,** *v.*

institutriz /institu'triθ; institu'tris/ *n. f.* governess.

instrucción /instruk'θion; instruk'sion/ *n. f.* instruction; education.

instructivo /instruk'tiβo/ *a.* instructive.

instructor /instruk'tor/ **-ra** *n.* instructor.

instruir /ins'truir/ *v.* instruct, teach.

instrumento /instru'mento/ *n. m.* instrument.

insuficiente /insufi'θiente; insufi'siente/ *a.* insufficient.

insufrible /insu'friβle/ *a.* intolerable.

insular /insu'lar/ *a.* island, insular.

insulto /in'sulto/ *n. m.* insult. **—insultar,** *v.*

insuperable /insupe'raβle/ *a.* insuperable.

insurgente /insur'hente/ *n. & a.* insurgent, rebel.

insurrección /insurrek'θion; insurrek'sion/ *n. f.* insurrection, revolt.

insurrecto /insu'rrekto/ **-ta** *a. & n.* insurgent.

intacto /in'takto/ *a.* intact.

integral /inte'gral/ *a.* integral.

integridad /integri'ðað/ *n. f.* integrity; entirety.

íntegro /'integro/ *a.* entire; upright.

intelecto /inte'lekto/ *n. m.* intellect.

intelectual /intelek'tual/ *a. & n.* intellectual.

inteligencia /inteli'henθia; inteli'hensia/ *n. f.* intelligence.

inteligente /inteli'hente/ *a.* intelligent.

inteligible /inteli'hiβle/ *a.* intelligible.

intemperie /intem'perie/ *n. f.* bad weather.

intención /inten'θion; inten'sion/ *n. f.* intention.

intendente /inten'dente/ *n. m.* manager.

intensidad /intensi'ðað/ *n. f.* intensity.

intensificar /intensifi'kar/ *v.* intensify.

intensivo /inten'siβo/ *a.* intensive.

intenso /in'tenso/ *a.* intense.

intentar /inten'tar/ *v.* attempt, try.

intento /in'tento/ *n. m.* intent; attempt.

intercambiable /interkam'biaβle/ *a.* interchangeable.

intercambiar /interkam'βiar/ *v.* exchange, interchange.

interceptar /interθep'tar; intersep'tar/ *v.* intercept.

intercesión /interθe'sion; interse-'sion/ *n. f.* intercession.

interés /inte'res/ *n. m.* interest; concern; appeal.

interesante /intere'sante/ *a.* interesting.

interesar /intere'sar/ *v.* interest, appeal to.

interfaz /inter'faθ; inter'fas/ *n. f.* interface.

interferencia /interfe'renθia; interfe'rensia/ *n. f.* interference.

interino /inte'rino/ *a.* temporary.

interior /inte'rior/ *a.* **1.** interior, inner. —*n.* **2.** *m.* interior.

interjección /interhek'θion; interhek'sion/ *n. f.* interjection.

intermedio /inter'meðio/ *a.* **1.** intermediate. —*n.* **2.** *m.* intermediary; intermission.

interminable /intermi'naβle/ *a.* interminable, endless.

intermisión /intermi'sion/ *n. f.* intermission.

intermitente /intermi'tente/ *a.* intermittent.

internacional /internaθio'nal; internasio'nal/ *a.* international.

internarse en /inter'narse en/ *v.* enter into, go into.

Internet, el /inter'net/ *n. m.* the Internet.

interno /in'terno/ *a.* internal.

interpelar /interpe'lar/ *v.* ask questions; implore.

interponer /interpo'ner/ *v.* interpose.

interpretación /interpreta'θion; interpreta'sion/ *n. f.* interpretation.

interpretar /interpre'tar/ *v.* interpret; construe.

intérprete /in'terprete/ *n. m. & f.* interpreter; performer.

interrogación /interroga'θion; interroga'sion/ *n. f.* interrogation.

interrogar /interro'gar/ *v.* question, interrogate.

interrogativo /interroga'tiβo/ *a.* interrogative.

interrumpir /interrum'pir/ *v.* interrupt.

interrupción /interrup'θion; interrup'sion/ *n. f.* interruption.

intersección /intersek'θion; intersek'sion/ *n. f.* intersection.

intervalo /inter'βalo/ *n. m.* interval.

intervención /interβen'θion; interβen'sion/ *n. f.* intervention.

intervenir /interβe'nir/ *v.* intervene, interfere.

intestino /intes'tino/ *n. m.* intestine.

intimación /intima'θion; intima-'sion/ *n. f.* intimation, hint.

intimar /inti'mar/ *v.* suggest, hint.

intimidad /intimi'ðað/ *n. f.* intimacy.

intimidar /intimi'ðar/ *v.* intimidate.

íntimo /'intimo/ **-ma** *a. & n.* intimate.

intolerable /intole'raβle/ *a.* intolerable.

intolerancia /intole'ranθia; intole-'ransia/ *n. f.* intolerance, bigotry.

intolerante /intole'rante/ *a.* intolerant.

intoxicación alimenticia /intoksika'θion alimen'tiθia; intoksika'sion alimen'tisia/ *n. f.* food poisoning.

intranquilo /intran'kilo/ *a.* uneasy.

intravenoso /intraβe'noso/ *a.* intravenous.

intrepidez /intrepi'ðeθ; intrepi'ðes/ *n. f.* daring.

intrépido /in'trepiðo/ *a.* intrepid.

intriga /in'triga/ *n. f.* intrigue, plot, scheme. —**intrigar,** *v.*

intrincado /intrin'kaðo/ *a.* intricate, involved; impenetrable.

introducción /introðuk'θion; introðuk'sion/ *n. f.* introduction.

introducir /introðu'θir; introðu'sir/ *v.* introduce.

intruso /in'truso/ **-sa** *n.* intruder.

intuición /intui'θion; intui'sion/ *n. f.* intuition.

inundación /inunda'θion; inunda'sion/ *n. f.* flood. —**inundar,** *v.*

inútil /i'nutil/ *a.* useless.

invadir /imba'ðir/ *v.* invade.

inválido /im'baliðo/ **-da** *a. & n.* invalid.

invariable /imba'riaβle/ *a.* constant.

invasión /imba'sion/ *n. f.* invasion.

invasor /imba'sor/ **-ra** *n.* invader.

invencible /imben'θiβle; imben-'siβle/ *a.* invincible.

invención /imben'θion; imben-'sion/ *n. f.* invention.

inventar /imben'tar/ *v.* invent; devise.

inventario /imben'tario/ *n. m.* inventory.

inventivo /imben'tiβo/ *a.* inventive.

invento /im'bento/ *n. m.* invention.

inventor /imben'tor/ **-ra** *n.* inventor.

invernáculo /imber'nakulo/ *n. m.* greenhouse.

invernal /imber'nal/ *a.* wintry.

inverosímil /imbero'simil/ *a.* improbable, unlikely.

inversión /imber'sion; imber'sion/ *n. f.* inversion. *Com.* investment.

inverso /im'berso/ *a.* inverse, reverse.

inversor /imber'sor/ **-ra** *n.* investor.

invertir /imber'tir/ *v.* invert; reverse; *Com.* invest.

investigación /imbestiga'θion; imbestiga'sion/ *n. f.* investigation.

investigador /imbestiga'ðor/ **-ra** *n.* investigator; researcher.

investigar /imbesti'gar/ *v.* investigate.

invierno /im'bierno/ *n. m.* winter.

invisible /imbi'siβle/ *a.* invisible.

invitación /imbita'θion; imbita-'sion/ *n. f.* invitation.

invitar /imbi'tar/ *v.* invite.

invocar /imbo'kar/ *v.* invoke.

involuntario /imbolun'tario/ *a.* involuntary.

inyección /inyek'θion; inyek'sion/ *n. f.* injection.

inyectar /inyek'tar/ *v.* inject.

ir /ir/ *v.* go. **irse,** go away, leave.

ira /'ira/ *n. f.* anger, ire.

iracundo /ira'kundo/ *a.* wrathful, irate.

iris /'iris/ *n. m.* iris. **arco i.,** rainbow.

Irlanda /ir'landa/ *n. f.* Ireland.

irlandés /irlan'des/ **-esa** *a. & n.* Irish; Irishman, Irishwoman.

ironía /iro'nia/ *n. f.* irony.

irónico /i'roniko/ *a.* ironical.

irracional /irraθio'nal; irrasio'nal/ *a.* irrational; insane.

irradiación /irraðia'θion; irraðia-'sion/ *n. f.* irradiation.

irradiar /irra'ðiar/ *v.* radiate.

irrazonable /irraθo'naβle; irraso-'naβle/ *a.* unreasonable.

irregular /irregu'lar/ *a.* irregular.

irreligioso /irreli'hioso/ *a.* irreligious.

irremediable /irreme'ðiaβle/ *a.* remediable, hopeless.

irresistible /irresis'tiβle/ *a.* irresistible.

irresoluto /irreso'luto/ *a.* irresolute, wavering.

irrespetuoso /irrespe'tuoso/ *a.* disrespectful.

irreverencia /irreβe'renθia; irreβe'rensia/ *n. f.* irreverence.

irreverente /irreβe'rente/ *adj.* irreverent.

irrigación /irriga'θion; irriga'sion/ *n. f.* irrigation.

irrigar /irri'gar/ *v.* irrigate.

irritación /irrita'θion; irrita'sion/ *n. f.* irritation.

irritar /irri'tar/ *v.* irritate.

irrupción /irrup'θion; irrup'sion/ *n. f.* raid, attack.

isla /'isla/ *n. f.* island.

isleño /is'leɲo/ **-ña** *n.* islander.

israelita /israe'lita/ *a. & n.* Israelite.

Italia /i'talia/ *n. f.* Italy.

italiano /ita'liano/ **-na** *a. & n.* Italian.

itinerario /itine'rario/ *n. m.* itinerary; timetable.

IVA, *abbrev.* (**impuesto sobre el valor añadido**) VAT (value-added tax).

izar /i'θar; i'sar/ *v.* hoist.

izquierda /iθ'kierða; is'kierða/ *n. f.* left (hand, side).

izquierdista /iθkier'ðista; iskier'ðista/ *n. & a.* leftist.

izquierdo /iθ'kierðo; is'kierðo/ *a.* left.

J

jabalí /haβa'li/ *n. m.* wild boar.
jabón /ha'βon/ *n. m.* soap. **j. en polvo,** soap powder.
jabonar /haβo'nar/ *v.* soap.
jaca /'haka/ *n. f.* nag.
jacinto /ha'θinto; ha'sinto/ *n. m.* hyacinth.
jactancia /hak'tanθia; hak'tansia/ *n. f.* boast. **—jactarse,** *v.*
jactancioso /haktan'θioso; haktan'sioso/ *a.* boastful.
jadear /haðe'ar/ *v.* pant, puff.
jaez /ha'eθ; ha'es/ *n. m.* harness; kind.
jalar /ha'lar/ *v.* haul, pull.
jalea /ha'lea/ *n. f.* jelly.
jaleo /ha'leo/ *n. m.* row, uproar; hassle.
jamás /ha'mas/ *adv.* never, ever.
jamón /ha'mon/ *n. m.* ham.
Japón /ha'pon/ *n. m.* Japan.
japonés /hapo'nes/ **-esa** *a. & n.* Japanese.
jaqueca /ha'keka/ *n. f.* headache.
jarabe /ha'raβe/ *n. m.* syrup.
jaranear /harane'ar/ *v.* jest; carouse.
jardín /har'ðin/ *n. m.* garden.
jardín de infancia /har'ðin de in'fanθia; har'ðin de in'fansia/ nursery school.
jardinero /harði'nero/ **-ra** *n.* gardener.
jarra /'harra/ *n. f.* jar; pitcher.
jarro /'harro/ *n. m.* jug, pitcher.
jaspe /'haspe/ *n. m.* jasper.
jaula /'haula/ *n. f.* cage; coop.
jauría /hau'ria/ *n. f.* pack of hounds.
jazmín /haθ'min; has'min/ *n. m.* jasmine.
jefatura /hefa'tura/ *n. f.* headquarters.
jefe /'hefe/ **-fa** *n.* chief, boss.
jefe de comedor /'hefe de kome'ðor/ headwaiter.
jefe de sala /'hefe de 'sala/ maître d'.
jefe de taller /'hefe de ta'ʎer; 'hefe de taʎer/ foreman.
Jehová /heo'βa/ *n. m.* Jehovah.
jengibre /hen'hiβre/ *n. m.* ginger.
jerez /he'reθ; he'res/ *n. m.* sherry.
jerga /'herga/ *n. f.* slang.
jergón /her'gon/ *n. m.* straw mattress.

jerigonza /heri'gonθa; heri'gonsa/ *n. f.* jargon.
jeringa /he'ringa/ *n. f.* syringe.
jeringar /herin'gar/ *v.* inject; annoy.
jeroglífico /hero'glifiko/ *n. m.* hieroglyph.
jersey /her'sei/ *n. m.* pullover; **j. de cuello alto,** turtleneck sweater.
Jerusalén /herusa'len/ *n. m.* Jerusalem.
jesuita /he'suita/ *n. m.* Jesuit.
Jesús /he'sus/ *n. m.* Jesus.
jeta /'heta/ *n. f.* snout.
jícara /'hikara/ *n. f.* cup.
jinete /hi'nete/ *n. m.* horseman.
jingoísmo /higgo'ismo/ *n. m.* jingoism.
jingoísta /higgo'ista/ *n. & a.* jingoist.
jira /'hira/ *n. f.* picnic; outing.
jirafa /hi'rafa/ *n. f.* giraffe.
jiu-jitsu /hiu'hitsu/ *n. m.* jujitsu.
jocundo /ho'kundo/ *a.* jovial.
jornada /hor'naða/ *n. f.* journey; day's work.
jornal /hor'nal/ *n. m.* day's wage.
jornalero /horna'lero/ *n. m.* day laborer, workman.
joroba /ho'roβa/ *n. f.* hump.
jorobado /horo'βaðo/ *a.* humpbacked.
joven /'hoβen/ *a.* **1.** young. **2.** *m. & f.* young person.
jovial /ho'βial/ *a.* jovial, jolly.
jovialidad /hoβiali'ðað/ *n. f.* joviality.
joya /'hoia/ *n. f.* jewel, gem.
joyas de fantasía /'hoias de fanta'sia/ *n. f.pl.* costume jewelry.
joyelero /hoie'lero/ *n. m.* jewel box.
joyería /hoie'ria/ *n. f.* jewelry; jewelry store.
joyero /ho'iero/ *n. m.* jeweler; jewel case.
juanete /hua'nete/ *n. m.* bunion.
jubilación /huβila'θion; huβila'sion/ *n. f.* retirement; pension.
jubilar /huβi'lar/ *v.* retire, pension.
jubileo /huβi'leo/ *n. m.* jubilee, public festivity.
júbilo /'huβilo/ *n. m.* glee, rejoicing.
jubiloso /huβi'loso/ *a.* joyful, gay.
judaico /hu'ðaiko/ *a.* Jewish.

judaísmo /huða'ismo/ *n. m.* Judaism.

judía /hu'ðia/ *n. f.* bean, string bean.

judicial /huði'θial; huði'sial/ *a.* judicial.

judío /hu'ðio/ **-día** *a. & n.* Jewish; Jew.

juego /'huego/ *n. m.* game; play; gambling; set. **j. de damas,** checkers. **j. limpio,** fair play. **Juegos Olímpicos** /huegos o'limpikos/ *n. m.pl.* Olympic Games.

juerga /'huerga/ *n. f.* spree.

jueves /'hueβes/ *n. m.* Thursday.

juez /hueθ; hues/ *n. m.* judge.

jugador /huga'ðor/ **-ra** *n.* player.

jugar /hu'gar/ *v.* play; gamble.

juglar /hug'lar/ *n. m.* minstrel.

jugo /'hugo/ *n. m.* juice. **j. de naranja,** orange juice.

jugoso /hu'goso/ *a.* juicy.

juguete /hu'gete/ *n. m.* toy, plaything.

juguetear /hugete'ar/ *v.* trifle.

juguetón /huge'ton/ *a.* playful.

juicio /'huiθio; 'huisio/ *n. m.* sense, wisdom, judgment; sanity; trial.

juicioso /hui'θioso; hui'sioso/ *a.* wise, judicious.

julio /'hulio/ *n. m.* July.

jumento /hu'mento/ *n. m.* donkey.

junco /'hunko/ *n. m.* reed, rush.

jungla /'huŋgla/ *n. f.* jungle.

junio /'hunio/ *n. m.* June.

junípero /hu'nipero/ *n. m.* juniper.

junquillo /hun'kiʎo; hun'kiyo/ *n. m.* jonquil.

junta /'hunta/ *n. f.* board, council; joint, coupling.

juntamente /hunta'mente/ *adv.* jointly.

juntar /hun'tar/ *v.* join; connect; assemble.

junto /'hunto/ *a.* together. **j. a,** next to.

juntura /hun'tura/ *n. f.* joint, juncture.

jurado /hu'raðo/ *n. m.* jury.

juramento /hura'mento/ *n. m.* oath.

jurar /hu'rar/ *v.* swear.

jurisconsulto /huriskon'sulto/ *n. m.* jurist.

jurisdicción /hurisðik'θion; hurisðik'sion/ *n. f.* jurisdiction; territory.

jurisprudencia /hurispru'ðenθia; hurispru'ðensia/ *n. f.* jurisprudence.

justa /'husta/ *n. f.* joust. **—justar,** *v.*

justicia /hus'tiθia; hus'tisia/ *n. f.* justice, equity.

justiciero /husti'θiero; husti'siero/ *a.* just.

justificación /hustifika'θion; hustifika'sion/ *n. f.* justification.

justificadamente /hustifika-ða'mente/ *adv.* justifiably.

justificar /hustifi'kar/ *v.* justify, warrant.

justo /'husto/ *a.* right; exact; just; righteous.

juvenil /huβe'nil/ *a.* youthful.

juventud /huβen'tuð/ *n. f.* youth.

juzgado /huθ'gaðo; hus'gaðo/ *n. m.* court.

juzgar /huθ'gar; hus'gar/ *v.* judge, estimate.

K L

káiser /'kaiser/ *n. m.* kaiser.

karate /ka'rate/ *n. m.* karate.

kepis /'kepis/ *n. m.* military cap.

kerosena /kero'sena/ *n. f.* kerosene.

kilo /'kilo/ **kilogramo** *n. m.* kilogram.

kilohercio /kilo'erθio; kilo'ersio/ *n. m.* kilohertz.

kilolitro /kilo'litro/ *n. m.* kiloliter.

kilometraje /kilome'trahe/ *n. m.* mileage.

kilómetro /ki'lometro/ *n. m.* kilometer.

kiosco /'kiosko/ *n. m.* newsstand; pavilion.

la /la/ *art. & pron.* **1.** the; the one. **—pron. 2.** her, it, you; (*pl.*) them, you.

laberinto /laβe'rinto/ *n. m.* labyrinth, maze.

labia /'laβia/ *n. f.* eloquence, fluency.

labio /'laβio/ *n. m.* lip.

labor /la'βor/ *n. f.* labor, work.

laborar /laβo'rar/ *v.* work; till.

laboratorio /laβora'torio/ *n. m.* laboratory.

laborioso /laβo'rioso/ a. industrious.

labrador /laβra'ðor/ n. m. farmer.

labranza /la'βranθa; la'βransa/ n. f. farming; farmland.

labrar /la'βrar/ v. work, till.

labriego /la'βriego/ **-ga** n. peasant.

laca /'laka/ n. f. shellac.

lacio /'laθio; 'lasio/ a. withered; limp; straight.

lactar /lak'tar/ v. nurse, suckle.

lácteo /'lakteo/ a. milky.

ladear /laðe'ar/ v. tilt, tip; sway.

ladera /la'ðera/ n. f. slope.

ladino /la'ðino/ a. cunning, crafty.

lado /'laðo/ n. m. side. **al l. de,** beside. **de l.,** sideways.

ladra /'laðra/ n. f. barking.
—**ladrar,** v.

ladrillo /la'ðriʎo; la'ðriyo/ n. m. brick.

ladrón /la'ðron/ **-ona** n. thief, robber.

lagarto /la'garto/ n. m. lizard; (Mex.) alligator.

lago /'lago/ n. m. lake.

lágrima /'lagrima/ n. f. tear.

lagrimear /lagrime'ar/ v. weep, cry.

laguna /la'guna/ n. f. lagoon; gap.

laico /'laiko/ a. lay.

laja /'laha/ n. f. stone slab.

lamentable /lamen'taβle/ a. lamentable.

lamentación /lamenta'θion; lamenta'sion/ n. f. lamentation.

lamentar /lamen'tar/ v. lament; wail; regret, be sorry.

lamento /la'mento/ n. m. lament, wail.

lamer /la'mer/ v. lick; lap.

lámina /'lamina/ n. f. print, illustration.

lámpara /'lampara/ n. f. lamp.

lampiño /lam'piɲo/ a. beardless.

lana /'lana/ n. f. wool.

lanar /la'nar/ a. woolen.

lance /'lanθe; 'lanse/ n. m. throw; episode; quarrel.

lancha /'lantʃa/ n. f. launch; small boat.

lanchón /lan'tʃon/ n. m. barge.

langosta /laŋ'gosta/ n. f. lobster; locust.

langostino /laŋgos'tino/ n. m. king prawn.

languidecer /laŋgiðe'θer; laŋgiðe'ser/ v. languish, pine.

languidez /laŋgi'ðeθ; laŋgi'ðes/ n. f. languidness.

lánguido /'laŋgiðo/ a. languid.

lanza /'lanθa; 'lansa/ n. f. lance, spear.

lanzada /lan'θaða; lan'saða/ n. f. thrust, throw.

lanzar /lan'θar; lan'sar/ v. throw, hurl; launch.

lañar /la'ɲar/ v. cramp; clamp.

lapicero /lapi'θero; lapi'sero/ n. m. mechanical pencil.

lápida /'lapiða/ n. f. stone; tombstone.

lápiz /'lapiθ; 'lapis/ n. m. pencil.

lápiz de ojos /'lapiθ de 'ohos; 'lapis de 'ohos/ n. m. eyeliner.

lapso /'lapso/ n. m. lapse.

lardo /'larðo/ n. m. lard.

largar /lar'gar/ v. loosen; free.

largo /'largo/ a. **1.** long. **a lo l. de,** along. —n. **2.** length.

largometraje /largome'trahe/ n. m. feature film.

largor /lar'gor/ n. m. length.

largueza /lar'geθa; lar'gesa/ n. f. generosity; length.

largura /lar'gura/ n. f. length.

laringe /la'rinhe/ n. f. larynx.

larva /'larβa/ n. f. larva.

lascivia /las'θiβia; las'siβia/ n. f. lasciviousness.

lascivo /las'θiβo; las'siβo/ a. lascivious.

láser /'laser/ n. m. laser.

laso /'laso/ a. weary.

lástima /'lastima/ n. f. pity. **ser l.,** to be a pity, to be too bad.

lastimar /lasti'mar/ v. hurt, injure.

lastimoso /lasti'moso/ a. pitiful.

lastre /'lastre/ n. m. ballast.
—**lastrar,** v.

lata /'lata/ n. f. tin can; tin (plate); *Colloq.* annoyance, bore.

latente /la'tente/ a. latent.

lateral /late'ral/ a. lateral, side.

latigazo /lati'gaθo; lati'gaso/ n. m. lash, whipping.

látigo /'latigo/ n. m. whip.

latín /la'tin/ n. m. Latin (language).

latino /la'tino/ a. Latin.

latir /la'tir/ v. beat, pulsate.

latitud /lati'tuð/ n. f. latitude.

latón /la'ton/ n. m. brass.

laúd /la'uð/ n. m. lute.

laudable /lau'ðaβle/ a. laudable.

láudano /'lauðano/ n. m. laudanum.

laurel /lau'rel/ *n. m.* laurel.

lava /'laβa/ *n. f.* lava.

lavabo /la'βaβo/ *lavamanos* *n. m.* washroom, lavatory.

lavadora /laβa'ðora/ *n. f.* washing machine.

lavandera /laβan'dera/ *n. f.* washerwoman, laundress.

lavandería /laβande'ria/ *n. f.* laundry; laundromat.

lavaplatos /laβa'platos/ *n.* **1.** *m.* dishwasher (machine). —*n.* **2.** *m. & f.* dishwasher (person).

lavar /la'βar/ *v.* wash.

lavatorio /laβa'torio/ *n. m.* lavatory.

laya /'laia/ *n. f.* spade. —**layar,** *v.*

lazar /la'θar; la'sar/ *v.* lasso.

lazareto /laθa'reto; lasa'reto/ *n. m.* isolation hospital; quarantine station.

lazo /'laθo; 'laso/ *n. m.* tie, knot; bow; loop.

le /le/ *pron.* him, her, you; (*pl.*) them, you.

leal /le'al/ *a.* loyal.

lealtad /leal'tað/ *n. f.* loyalty, allegiance.

lebrel /le'βrel/ *n. m.* greyhound.

lección /lek'θion; lek'sion/ *n. f.* lesson.

leche /'letʃe/ *n. f.* milk.

lechería /letʃe'ria/ *n. f.* dairy.

lechero /le'tʃero/ *n. m.* milkman.

lecho /'letʃo/ *n. m.* bed; couch.

lechón /le'tʃon/ *n. m.* pig.

lechoso /le'tʃoso/ *a.* milky.

lechuga /le'tʃuɣa/ *n. f.* lettuce.

lechuza /le'tʃuθa; le'tʃusa/ *n. f.* owl.

lecito /le'θito; le'sito/ *n. m.* yolk.

lector /lek'tor/ **-ra** *n.* reader.

lectura /lek'tura/ *n. f.* reading.

leer /le'er/ *v.* read.

legación /leɣa'θion; leɣa'sion/ *n. f.* legation.

legado /le'ɣaðo/ *n. m.* bequest.

legal /le'ɣal/ *a.* legal, lawful.

legalizar /leɣali'θar; leɣali'sar/ *v.* legalize.

legar /le'ɣar/ *v.* bequeath, leave, will.

legible /le'hiβle/ *a.* legible.

legión /le'hion/ *n. f.* legion.

legislación /lehisla'θion; lehisla-'sion/ *n. f.* legislation.

legislador /lehisla'ðor/ **-ra** *n.* legislator.

legislar /lehis'lar/ *v.* legislate.

legislativo /lehisla'tiβo/ *a.* legislative.

legislatura /lehisla'tura/ *n. f.* legislature.

legítimo /le'hitimo/ *a.* legitimate.

lego /'leɣo/ *n. m.* layman.

legua /'leɣua/ *n. f.* league (measure).

legumbre /le'ɣumbre/ *n. f.* vegetable.

lejano /le'hano/ *a.* distant, far-off.

lejía /le'hia/ *n. f.* lye.

lejos /'lehos/ *adv.* far. **a lo l.,** in the distance.

lelo /'lelo/ *a.* stupid, foolish.

lema /'lema/ *n. m.* theme; slogan.

lengua /'leŋgua/ *n. f.* tongue; language.

lenguado /leŋ'guaðo/ *n. m.* sole, flounder.

lenguaje /leŋ'guahe/ *n. m.* speech; language.

lenguaraz /leŋgua'raθ; leŋgua'ras/ *a.* talkative.

lente /'lente/ *n.* **1.** *m. or f.* lens. **2.** *m.pl.* eyeglasses.

lenteja /len'teha/ *n. f.* lentil.

lentilla /len'tiʎa; len'tiya/ *n. f.* contact lens.

lentitud /lenti'tuð/ *n. f.* slowness.

lento /'lento/ *a.* slow.

leña /'leɲa/ *n. f.* wood, firewood.

león /le'on/ *n. m.* lion.

leopardo /leo'parðo/ *n. m.* leopard.

lerdo /'lerðo/ *a.* dull-witted.

lesbiana /les'βiana/ *n. f.* lesbian.

lesión /le'sion/ *n. f.* wound; damage.

letanía /leta'nia/ *n. f.* litany.

letárgico /le'tarhiko/ *a.* lethargic.

letargo /le'targo/ *n. m.* lethargy.

letra /'letra/ *n. f.* letter (of alphabet); print; words (of a song).

letrado /le'traðo/ *a.* **1.** learned. —*n.* **2.** *m.* lawyer.

letrero /le'trero/ *n. m.* sign, poster.

leva /'leβa/ *n. f. Mil.* draft.

levadura /leβa'ðura/ *n. f.* yeast, leavening, baking powder.

levantador /leβanta'ðor/ *n. m.* lifter; rebel, mutineer.

levantar /leβan'tar/ *v.* raise, lift.

levantarse /leβan'tarse/ *v.* rise, get up; stand up.

levar /le'βar/ *v.* weigh (anchor).

leve /'leβe/ *a.* slight, light.

levita /le'βita/ *n. f.* frock coat.

léxico /'leksiko/ n. m. lexicon, dictionary.

ley /lei/ n. f. law, statute.

leyenda /le'ienda/ n. f. legend.

lezna /'leθna; 'lesna/ n. f. awl.

libación /liβa'θion; liβa'sion/ n. f. libation.

libelo /li'βelo/ n. m. libel.

libélula /li'βelula/ n. f. dragonfly.

liberación /liβera'θion; liβera'sion/ n. f. liberation, release.

liberal /liβe'ral/ a. liberal.

libertad /liβer'tað/ n. f. liberty, freedom.

libertador /liβerta'ðor/ **-ra** n. liberator.

libertar /liβer'tar/ v. free, liberate.

libertinaje /liβerti'nahe/ n. m. licentiousness.

libertino /liβer'tino/ **-na** n. libertine.

libídine /li'βiðine/ n. f. licentiousness; lust.

libidinoso /liβiði'noso/ a. libidinous; lustful.

libra /'liβra/ n. f. pound.

libranza /li'βranθa; li'βransa/ n. f. draft, bill of exchange.

librar /li'βrar/ v. free, rid.

libre /'liβre/ a. free, unoccupied.

librería /liβre'ria/ n. f. bookstore.

librero /li'βrero/ **-ra** n. bookseller.

libreta /li'βreta/ n. f. notebook; booklet.

libreto /li'βreto/ n. m. libretto.

libro /'liβro/ n. m. book.

libro de texto /'liβro de 'teksto/ textbook.

licencia /li'θenθia; li'sensia/ n. f. permission, license, leave; furlough. **l. de armas,** gun permit.

licenciado /liθen'θiaðo; lisen'siaðo/ **-da** n. graduate.

licencioso /liθen'θioso; lisen'sioso/ a. licentious.

lícito /'liθito; 'lisito/ a. lawful.

licor /li'kor/ n. m. liquor.

licuadora /likua'ðora/ n. f. blender (for food).

lid /lid/ n. f. fight. —**lidiar,** v.

líder /'liðer/ n. m. leader.

liebre /'lieβre/ n. f. hare.

lienzo /'lienθo; 'lienso/ n. m. linen.

liga /'liga/ n. f. league, confederacy; garter.

ligadura /liga'ðura/ n. f. ligature.

ligar /li'gar/ v. tie, bind, join.

ligero /li'hero/ a. light; fast, nimble.

ligustro /li'gustro/ n. m. privet.

lija /'liha/ n. f. sandpaper.

lijar /li'har/ v. sandpaper.

lima /'lima/ n. f. file; lime.

limbo /'limbo/ n. m. limbo.

limitación /limita'θion; limita'sion/ n. f. limitation.

límite /'limite/ n. m. limit. —**limitar,** v.

limo /'limo/ n. m. slime.

limón /li'mon/ n. m. lemon.

limonada /limo'naða/ n. f. lemonade.

limonero /limo'nero/ n. m. lemon tree.

limosna /li'mosna/ n. f. alms.

limosnero /limos'nero/ **-ra** n. beggar.

limpiabotas /limpia'βotas/ n. m. bootblack.

limpiadientes /limpia'ðientes/ n. m. toothpick.

limpiar /lim'piar/ v. clean, wash, wipe.

límpido /'limpiðo/ a. limpid, clear.

limpieza /lim'pieθa; lim'piesa/ n. f. cleanliness.

limpio /'limpio/ a. m. clean.

limusina /limu'sina/ n. f. limousine.

linaje /li'nahe/ n. m. lineage, ancestry.

linaza /li'naθa; li'nasa/ n. f. linseed.

lince /'linθe; 'linse/ a. sharp-sighted, observing.

linchamiento /lintʃa'miento/ n. m. lynching.

linchar /lin'tʃar/ v. lynch.

lindar /lin'dar/ v. border, bound.

linde /'linde/ n. f. boundary; landmark.

lindero /lin'dero/ n. m. boundary.

lindo /'lindo/ a. pretty, lovely, nice.

línea /'linea/ n. f. line.

línea de puntos /'linea de 'puntos/ dotted line.

lineal /line'al/ a. lineal.

linfa /'linfa/ n. f. lymph.

lingüista /liŋ'guista/ n. m. & f. linguist.

lingüístico /liŋ'guistiko/ a. linguistic.

linimento /lini'mento/ n. m. liniment.

lino /'lino/ n. m. linen; flax.

linóleo /li'noleo/ n. m. linoleum.

linterna /lin'terna/ n. f. lantern; flashlight.

lío

128

lío /'lio/ *n. m.* pack, bundle; mess, scrape; hassle.

liquidación /likiða'θion; likiða-'sion/ *n. f.* liquidation.

liquidar /liki'ðar/ *v.* liquidate; settle up.

líquido /'likiðo/ *a. & m.* liquid.

lira /'lira/ *n. f.* lyre.

lírico /'liriko/ *a.* lyric.

lirio /'lirio/ *n. m.* lily.

lirismo /li'rismo/ *n. m.* lyricism.

lis /lis/ *n. f.* lily.

lisiar /li'siar/ *v.* cripple, lame.

liso /'liso/ *a.* smooth, even.

lisonja /li'sonha/ *n. f.* flattery.

lisonjear /lisonhe'ar/ *v.* flatter.

lisonjero /lison'hero/ **-ra** *a.* flatterer.

lista /'lista/ *n. f.* list; stripe; menu.

lista negra /'lista 'negra/ blacklist.

listar /lis'tar/ *v.* list; put on a list.

listo /'listo/ *a.* ready; smart, clever.

listón /lis'ton/ *n. m.* ribbon.

litera /li'tera/ *n. f.* litter, bunk, berth.

literal /lite'ral/ *a.* literal.

literario /lite'rario/ *a.* literary.

literato /lite'rato/ *n. m.* literary person, writer.

literatura /litera'tura/ *n. f.* literature.

litigación /litiga'θion; litiga'sion/ *n. f.* litigation.

litigio /li'tihio/ *n. m.* litigation; lawsuit.

litoral /lito'ral/ *n. m.* coast.

litro /'litro/ *n. m.* liter.

liturgia /li'turhia/ *n. f.* liturgy.

liviano /li'βiano/ *a.* light (in weight).

lívido /'liβiðo/ *a.* livid.

llaga /'ʎaga/ *n. f.* sore.

llama /'ʎama/ *n. f.* flame; llama.

llamada /ʎa'maða/ *n. f.* call; knock. —**llamar**, *v.*

llamarse /ʎa'marse/ *v.* be called, be named. **se llama...** etc., his name is... etc.

llamativo /ʎama'tiβo/ *a.* gaudy, showy.

llamear /ʎame'ar/ *v.* blaze.

llaneza /ʎa'neθa/ *n. f.* simplicity.

llano /'ʎano/ *a.* **1.** flat, level; plain. —*n.* **2.** *m.* plain.

llanta /'ʎanta/ *n. f.* tire.

llanto /'ʎanto; 'yanto/ *n. m.* crying, weeping.

llanura /ʎa'nura; ya'nura/ *n. f.* prairie, plain.

llave /'ʎaβe; 'yaβe/ *n. f.* key; wrench; faucet; *Elec.* switch. **ll. inglesa,** monkey wrench.

llegada /ʎe'gaða; ye'gaða/ *n. f.* arrival.

llegar /ʎe'gar; ye'gar/ *v.* arrive; reach. **ll. a ser,** become, come to be.

llenar /ʎe'nar; ye'nar/ *v.* fill.

lleno /'ʎeno; 'yeno/ *a.* full.

llenura /ʎe'nura; ye'nura/ *n. f.* abundance.

llevadero /ʎeβa'ðero; yeβa'ðero/ *a.* tolerable.

llevar /ʎe'βar; ye'βar/ *v.* take, carry, bear; wear (clothes). **ll. a cabo,** carry out.

llevarse /ʎe'βarse; ye'βarse/ *v.* take away, run away with. **ll. bien,** get along well.

llorar /ʎo'rar; yo'rar/ *v.* cry, weep.

lloroso /ʎo'roso; yo'roso/ *a.* sorrowful, tearful.

llover /ʎo'βer; yo'βer/ *v.* rain.

llovido /ʎo'βiðo; yo'βiðo/ *n. m.* stowaway.

llovizna /ʎo'βiθna; yo'βisna/ *n. f.* drizzle, sprinkle. —**lloviznar,** *v.*

lluvia /'ʎuβia; 'yuβia/ *n. f.* rain.

lluvia ácida /'ʎuβia 'aθiða; 'yuβia 'asiða/ acid rain.

lluvioso /ʎu'βioso; yu'βioso/ *a.* rainy.

lo /lo/ *pron.* him, it, you; (*pl.*) them, you.

loar /lo'ar/ *v.* praise, laud.

lobina /lo'βina/ *n. f.* striped bass.

lobo /'loβo/ *n. m.* wolf.

lóbrego /'loβrego/ *a.* murky; dismal.

local /lo'kal/ *a.* **1.** local. —*n.* **2.** *m.* site.

localidad /lokali'ðað/ *n. f.* locality, location; seat (in theater).

localizar /lokali'θar; lokali'sar/ *v.* localize.

loción /lo'θion; lo'sion/ *n. f.* lotion.

loco /'loko/ **-ca** *a.* **1.** crazy, insane, mad. —*n.* **2.** lunatic.

locomotora /lokomo'tora/ *n. f.* locomotive.

locuaz /lo'kuaθ; lo'kuas/ *a.* loquacious.

locución /loku'θion; loku'sion/ *n. f.* locution, expression.

locura /lo'kura/ n. f. folly; madness, insanity.

lodo /'lodo/ n. m. mud.

lodoso /lo'ðoso/ a. muddy.

lógica /'lohika/ n. f. logic.

lógico /'lohiko/ a. logical.

lograr /lo'grar/ v. achieve; succeed in.

logro /'logro/ n. m. accomplishment.

lombriz /lom'βriθ; lom'βris/ n. f. earthworm.

lomo /'lomo/ n. m. loin; back (of an animal).

lona /'lona/ n. f. canvas, tarpaulin.

longevidad /lonheβi'ðað/ n. f. longevity.

longitud /lonhi'tuð/ n. f. longitude; length.

lonja /'lonha/ n. f. shop; market.

lontananza /lonta'nanθa; lonta'nansa/ n. f. distance.

loro /'loro/ n. m. parrot.

losa /'losa/ n. f. slab.

lote /'lote/ n. m. lot, share.

lotería /lote'ria/ n. f. lottery.

loza /'loθa; 'losa/ n. f. china, crockery.

lozanía /loθa'nia; losa'nia/ n. f. freshness, vigor.

lozano /lo'θano; lo'sano/ a. fresh, spirited.

lubricación /luβrika'θion; luβrika'sion/ n. f. lubrication.

lubricar /luβri'kar/ v. lubricate.

lucero /lu'θero; lu'sero/ n. m. (bright) star.

lucha /'lutʃa/ n. f. fight, struggle; wrestling. —**luchar**, v.

luchador /lutʃa'ðor/ -ra n. fighter, wrestler.

lúcido /lu'θiðo; lu'siðo/ a. lucid, clear.

luciente /lu'θiente; lu'siente/ a. shining, bright.

luciérnaga /lu'θiernaga; lu'siernaga/ n. f. firefly.

lucimiento /luθi'miento; lusi'miento/ n. m. success; splendor.

lucir /lu'θir; lu'sir/ v. shine, sparkle; show off.

lucrativo /lukra'tiβo/ a. lucrative, profitable.

luego /'luego/ adv. right away; afterwards, next. **l. que,** as soon as. **desde l.,** of course. **hasta l.,** good-bye, so long.

lugar /lu'gar/ n. m. place, spot; space, room.

lúgubre /'luguβre/ a. gloomy; dismal.

lujo /'luho/ n. m. luxury. **de l.,** deluxe.

lujoso /lu'hoso/ a. luxurious.

lumbre /'lumbre/ n. f. fire; light.

luminoso /lumi'noso/ a. luminous.

luna /'luna/ n. f. moon.

lunar /lu'nar/ n. m. beauty mark, mole; polka dot.

lunático /lu'natiko/ -ca a. & n. lunatic.

lunes /'lunes/ n. m. Monday.

luneta /lu'neta/ n. f. Theat. orchestra seat.

lupa /'lupa/ n. f. magnifying glass.

lustre /'lustre/ n. m. polish, shine. —**lustrar**, v.

lustroso /lus'troso/ a. shiny.

luto /'luto/ n. m. mourning.

luz /luθ; lus/ n. f. light. **dar a l.,** give birth to.

M

maca /'maka/ n. f. blemish, flaw.

macaco /ma'kako/ a. ugly, horrid.

macareno /maka'reno/ a. boasting.

macarrones /maka'rrones/ n. m.pl. macaroni.

macear /maθe'ar; mase'ar/ v. molest, push around.

macedonia de frutas /maθe'ðonia de 'frutas; mase'ðonia de 'frutas/ n. f. fruit salad.

maceta /ma'θeta; ma'seta/ n. f. vase; mallet.

machacar /matʃa'kar/ v. pound; crush.

machina /ma'tʃina/ n. f. derrick.

machista /ma'tʃista/ a. macho.

macho /'matʃo/ n. m. male.

machucho /ma'tʃutʃo/ a. mature, wise.

macizo /ma'θiθo; ma'siso/ a. **1.** solid. —n. **2. m.** bulk; flower bed.

macular /maku'lar/ v. stain.

madera /ma'ðera/ n. f. lumber; wood.

madero /ma'ðero/ n. m. beam, timber.

madrastra /ma'ðrastra/ n. f. stepmother.

madre /'maðre/ n. f. mother. **m. política**, mother-in-law.

madreperla /maðre'perla/ n. f. mother-of-pearl.

madriguera /maðri'gera/ n. f. burrow; lair, den.

madrina /ma'ðrina/ n. f. godmother.

madroncillo /maðron'θiλo; maðron'siyo/ n. m. strawberry.

madrugada /maðru'gaða/ n. f. daybreak.

madrugar /maðru'gar/ v. get up early.

madurar /maðu'rar/ v. ripen.

madurez /maðu'reθ; maðu'res/ f. maturity.

maduro /ma'ðuro/ a. ripe; mature.

maestría /maes'tria/ n. f. mastery; master's degree.

maestro /ma'estro/ n. m. master; teacher.

mafia /'mafia/ n. f. mafia.

maganto /ma'ganto/ a. lethargic, dull.

magia /'mahia/ n. f. magic.

mágico /'mahiko/ a. & m. magic; magician.

magistrado /mahis'traðo/ n. m. magistrate.

magnánimo /mag'nanimo/ a. magnanimous.

magnético /mag'netiko/ a. magnetic.

magnetismo /magne'tismo/ n. m. magnetism.

magnetófono /magne'tofono/ n. m. tape recorder.

magnificar /magnifi'kar/ v. magnify.

magnificencia /magnifi'θenθia; magnifi'sensia/ n. f. magnificence.

magnífico /mag'nifiko/ a. magnificent.

magnitud /magni'tuð/ n. f. magnitude.

magno /'magno/ a. great, grand.

magnolia /mag'nolia/ n. f. magnolia.

mago /'mago/ n. m. magician; wizard.

magosto /ma'gosto/ n. m. chestnut roast; picnic fire for roasting chestnuts.

magro /'magro/ a. meager; thin.

magullar /magu'λar; magu'yar/ v. bruise.

mahometano /maome'tano/ n. & a. Mohammedan.

mahometismo /maome'tismo/ n. m. Mohammedanism.

maíz /ma'iθ; ma'is/ n. m. corn.

majadero /maha'ðero/ -ra a. & n. foolish; fool.

majar /ma'har/ v. mash.

majestad /mahes'tað/ n. f. majesty.

majestuoso /mahes'tuoso/ a. majestic.

mal /mal/ adv. **1.** badly; wrong. —n. **2.** m. evil, ill; illness.

mala /'mala/ n. f. mail.

malacate /mala'kate/ n. m. hoist.

malandanza /malan'danθa; malan'dansa/ n. f. misfortune.

malaventura /malaβen'tura/ n. f. misfortune.

malcomido /malko'miðo/ a. underfed; malnourished.

malcontento /malkon'tento/ a. disssatisfied.

maldad /mal'dað/ n. f. badness; wickedness.

maldecir /malde'θir; malde'sir/ v. curse, damn.

maldición /maldi'θion; maldi'sion/ n. f. curse.

maldito /mal'dito/ a. accursed, damned.

malecón /male'kon/ n. m. embankment.

maledicencia /maleði'θenθia; maleði'sensia/ n. f. slander.

maleficio /male'fiθio; male'fisio/ n. m. spell, charm.

malestar /males'tar/ n. m. indisposition.

maleta /ma'leta/ n. f. suitcase, valise.

malévolo /ma'leβolo/ a. malevolent.

maleza /ma'leθa; ma'lesa/ n. f. weeds; underbrush.

malgastar /malgas'tar/ v. squander.

malhechor /male'tʃor/ -ra n. malefactor, evildoer.

malhumorado /malumo'raðo/ a. morose, ill-humored.

malicia /ma'liθia; ma'lisia/ n. f. malice.

maliciar /mali'θiar; mali'siar/ v. suspect.

malicioso /mali'θioso; mali'sioso/ a. malicious.

maligno /ma'ligno/ a. malignant, evil.

malla /'maʎa; 'maya/ n. f. mesh, net.

mallas /'maʎas; 'mayas/ n. f.pl. leotard.

mallete /ma'ʎete; ma'yete/ n. m. mallet.

malo /'malo/ a. bad; evil, wicked; naughty; ill.

malograr /malo'grar/ v. miss, lose.

malparto /mal'parto/ n. m. abortion, miscarriage.

malquerencia /malke'renθia; malke'rensia/ n. f. hatred.

malquerer /malke'rer/ v. dislike; bear ill will.

malsano /mal'sano/ a. unhealthy; unwholesome.

malsín /mal'sin/ n. m. malicious gossip.

malta /'malta/ n. f. malt.

maltratar /maltra'tar/ v. mistreat.

malvado /mal'baðo/ **-da** a. **1.** wicked. —n. **2.** villain.

malversar /malβer'sar/ v. embezzle.

malvís /mal'βis/ n. m. redwing.

mamá /ma'ma/ n. f. mama, mother.

mamar /ma'mar/ v. suckle; suck.

mamífero /ma'mifero/ n. m. mammal.

mampara /mam'para/ n. f. screen.

mampostería /mamposte'ria/ n. f. masonry.

mamut /ma'mut/ n. m. mammoth.

manada /ma'naða/ n. f. flock, herd, drove.

manantial /manan'tial/ n. m. spring (of water).

manar /ma'nar/ v. gush, flow out.

mancebo /man'θeβo; man'seβo/ n. m. young man.

mancha /'mantʃa/ n. f. stain, smear, blemish, spot. —**manchar**, v.

mancilla /man'θiʎa; man'siya/ n. f. stain; blemish.

manco /'manko/ a. armless; one-armed.

mandadero /manda'ðero/ n. m. messenger.

mandado /man'daðo/ n. m. order, command.

mandamiento /manda'miento/ n. m. commandment; command.

mandar /man'dar/ v. send; order, command.

mandatario /manda'tario/ n. m. attorney; representative.

mandato /man'dato/ n. m. mandate, command.

mandíbula /man'diβula/ n. f. jaw; jawbone.

mando /'mando/ n. m. command, order; leadership.

mando a distancia /'mando a dis'tanθia; 'mando a dis'tansia/ remote control.

mandón /man'don/ a. domineering.

mandril /man'dril/ n. m. baboon.

manejar /mane'har/ v. handle, manage; drive (a car).

manejo /ma'neho/ n. m. management; horsemanship.

manera /ma'nera/ n. f. way, manner, means. **de m. que,** so, as a result.

manga /'maŋga/ n. f. sleeve.

mangana /maŋ'gana/ n. f. lariat, lasso.

manganeso /maŋga'neso/ n. m. manganese.

mango /'maŋgo/ n. m. handle; mango (fruit).

mangosta /maŋ'gosta/ n. f. mongoose.

manguera /maŋ'guera/ n. f. hose.

manguito /maŋ'guito/ n. m. muff.

maní /ma'ni/ n. m. peanut.

manía /ma'nia/ n. f. mania, madness; hobby.

maníaco /ma'niako/ **-ca, maniático -ca** a. & n. maniac.

manicomio /mani'komio/ n. m. insane asylum.

manicura /mani'kura/ n. f. manicure.

manifactura /manifak'tura/ n. f. manufacture.

manifestación /manifesta'θion; manifesta'sion/ n. f. manifestation.

manifestar /manifes'tar/ v. manifest, show.

manifiesto /mani'fiesto/ a. & m. manifest.

manija /ma'niha/ n. f. handle; crank.

maniobra /ma'nioβra/ n. f. maneuver. —**maniobrar**, v.

manipulación /manipula'θion; manipula'sion/ n. f. manipulation.

manipular /manipu'lar/ v. manipulate.

maniquí /mani'ki/ n. m. mannequin.

manivela /mani'βela/ n. f. Mech. crank.

manjar /man'har/ n. m. food, dish.

manlieve /man'lieβe/ n. m. swindle.

mano /'mano/ n. f. hand.

manojo /ma'noho/ n. m. handful; bunch.

manómetro /ma'nometro/ n. m. gauge.

manopla /ma'nopla/ n. f. gauntlet.

manosear /manose'ar/ v. handle, feel, touch.

manotada /mano'taða/ n. f. slap, smack. —**manotear**, v.

mansedumbre /manse'ðumbre/ n. f. meekness, tameness.

mansión /man'sion/ n. f. mansion; abode.

manso /'manso/ a. tame, gentle.

manta /'manta/ n. f. blanket.

manteca /man'teka/ n. f. fat, lard; butter.

mantecado /mante'kaðo/ n. m. ice cream.

mantecoso /mante'koso/ a. buttery.

mantel /man'tel/ n. m. tablecloth.

mantener /mante'ner/ v. maintain, keep; sustain; support.

mantenimiento /manteni'miento/ n. m. maintenance.

mantequera /mante'kera/ n. f. butter dish; churn.

mantequilla /mante'kiʎa/ mante'kiʎa/ n. f. butter.

mantilla /man'tiʎa/ n. f. mantilla; baby clothes.

mantillo /man'tiʎo/ n. m. humus; manure.

manto /'manto/ n. m. mantle, cloak.

manual /ma'nual/ a. & m. manual.

manubrio /ma'nuβrio/ n. m. handle; crank.

manufacturar /manufaktu'rar/ v. manufacture; make.

manuscrito /manus'krito/ n. m. manuscript.

manzana /man'θana/ man'sana/ n. f. apple; block (of street).

manzanilla /manθa'niʎa/ mansa'niʎa/ n. f. dry sherry.

manzano /man'θano/ man'sano/ n. m. apple tree.

maña /'maɲa/ n. f. skill; cunning; trick.

mañana /ma'ɲana/ adv. **1.** tomorrow. —n. **2.** f. morning.

mañanear /maɲane'ar/ v. rise early in the morning.

mañero /ma'ɲero/ a. clever; skillful; lazy.

mapa /'mapa/ n. m. map, chart.

mapache /ma'patʃe/ n. m. raccoon.

mapurito /mapu'rito/ n. m. skunk.

máquina /'makina/ n. f. machine. **m. de coser,** sewing machine. **m. de lavar,** washing machine.

maquinación /makina'θion/ makina'sion/ n. f. machination; plot.

maquinador /makina'ðor/ **-ra** n. plotter, schemer.

maquinal /maki'nal/ a. mechanical.

maquinar /maki'nar/ v. scheme, plot.

maquinaria /maki'naria/ n. f. machinery.

maquinista /maki'nista/ n. machinist; engineer.

mar /mar/ n. m. or f. sea.

marabú /mara'βu/ n. m. marabou.

maraña /ma'raɲa/ n. f. tangle; maze; snarl; plot.

maravilla /mara'βiʎa/ mara'βiya/ n. f. marvel, wonder. —**maravillarse,** v.

maravilloso /maraβi'ʎoso/ maraβi'yoso/ a. marvelous, wonderful.

marbete /mar'βete/ n. m. tag, label; check.

marca /'marka/ n. f. mark, sign; brand, make.

marcador /marka'ðor/ n. m. highlighter.

marcapáginas /marka'pahinas/ n. m. bookmark.

marcar /mar'kar/ v. mark; observe, note.

marcha /'martʃa/ n. f. march; progress. —**marchar,** v.

marchante /mar'tʃante/ n. m. merchant; customer.

marcharse /mar'tʃarse/ v. go away, depart.

marchitable /martʃi'taβle/ a. perishable.

marchitar /martʃi'tar/ v. fade, wilt, wither.

marchito /mar'tʃito/ a. faded, withered.

marcial /mar'θial/ mar'sial/ a. martial.

marco /'marko/ n. m. frame.

marea /ma'rea/ n. f. tide.

mareado /mare'aðo/ a. seasick.

marearse /mareˈarse/ v. get dizzy; be seasick.
mareo /maˈreo/ n. m. dizziness; seasickness.
marfil /marˈfil/ n. m. ivory.
margarita /margaˈrita/ n. f. pearl; daisy.
margen /ˈmarhen/ n. m. or f. margin, edge, rim.
marido /maˈriðo/ n. m. husband.
marijuana /mariˈhuana/ n. f. marijuana.
marimacha /mariˈmatʃa/ n. f. lesbian.
marimacho /mariˈmatʃo/ n. m. mannish woman.
marimba /maˈrimba/ n. f. marimba.
marina /maˈrina/ n. f. navy; seascape.
marinero /mariˈnero/ n. m. sailor, seaman.
marino /maˈrino/ a. & m. marine, (of) sea; mariner, seaman.
marión /maˈrion/ n. m. sturgeon.
mariposa /mariˈposa/ n. f. butterfly.
mariquita /mariˈkita/ n. f. ladybird.
mariscal /marisˈkal/ n. m. marshal.
marisco /maˈrisko/ n. m. shellfish; mollusk.
marital /mariˈtal/ a. marital.
marítimo /maˈritimo/ a. maritime.
marmita /marˈmita/ n. f. pot, kettle.
mármol /ˈmarmol/ n. m. marble.
marmóreo /marˈmoreo/ a. marble.
maroma /maˈroma/ n. f. rope.
marqués /marˈkes/ n. m. marquis.
marquesa /marˈkesa/ n. f. marquise.
Marruecos /maˈrruekos/ n. m. Morocco.
Marte /ˈmarte/ n. m. Mars.
martes /ˈmartes/ n. m. Tuesday.
martillo /marˈtiʎo/ mar'tiyo/ n. m. hammer. **—martillar,** v.
mártir /ˈmartir/ n. m. & f. martyr.
martirio /marˈtirio/ n. m. martyrdom.
martirizar /martiriˈθar; martiriˈsar/ v. martyrize.
marzo /ˈmarθo; ˈmarso/ n. m. March.
mas /mas/ conj. but.
más a. & adv. more, most; plus. **no m.,** only; no more.

masa /ˈmasa/ n. f. mass; dough.
masaje /maˈsahe/ n. m. massage.
mascar /masˈkar/ v. chew.
máscara /ˈmaskara/ n. f. mask.
mascarada /maskaˈraða/ n. f. masquerade.
mascota /masˈkota/ n. f. mascot; good-luck charm.
masculino /maskuˈlino/ a. masculine.
mascullar /maskuˈʎar; maskuˈyar/ v. mumble.
masón /maˈson/ n. m. Freemason.
masticar /mastiˈkar/ v. chew.
mástil /masˈtil/ n. m. mast; post.
mastín /masˈtin/ n. m. mastiff.
mastín danés /masˈtin daˈnes/ Great Dane.
mastuerzo /masˈtuerθo; masˈtuerso/ n. m. fool, ninny.
mata /ˈmata/ n. f. plant; bush.
matadero /mataˈðero/ n. m. slaughterhouse.
matador /mataˈðor/ -ra n. matador.
matafuego /mataˈfuego/ n. m. fire extinguisher.
matanza /maˈtanθa; maˈtansa/ n. f. killing, bloodshed, slaughter.
matar /maˈtar/ v. kill, slay; slaughter.
matasanos /mataˈsanos/ n. m. quack.
mate /ˈmate/ n. m. checkmate; Paraguayan tea.
matemáticas /mateˈmatikas/ n. f.pl. mathematics.
matemático /mateˈmatiko/ a. mathematical.
materia /maˈteria/ n. f. material; subject (matter).
material /mateˈrial/ a. & m. material.
materialismo /materiaˈlismo/ n. m. materialism.
materializar /materialiˈθar; materialiˈsar/ v. materialize.
maternal /materˈnal/ **materno** a. maternal.
maternidad /materniˈðað/ n. f. maternity; maternity hospital.
matiné /matiˈne/ n. f. matinee.
matiz /maˈtiθ; maˈtis/ n. m. hue, shade.
matizar /matiˈθar; matiˈsar/ v. blend; tint.
matón /maˈton/ n. m. bully.
matorral /matoˈrral/ n. m. thicket.
matoso /maˈtoso/ a. weedy.

matraca /ma'traka/ n. f. rattle.
—**matraquear,** v.

matrícula /ma'trikula/ n. f. registration; tuition.

matricularse /matriku'larse/ v. enroll, register.

matrimonio /matri'monjo/ n. m. matrimony, marriage; married couple.

matriz /ma'triθ/ n. f. womb; *Mech.* die, mold.

matrona /ma'trona/ n. f. matron.

maullar /mau'ʎar/ mau'jar/ v. mew.

máxima /'maksima/ n. f. maxim.

máxime /'maksime/ a. principally.

máximo /'maksimo/ a. & m. maximum.

maya /'maya/ n. f. daisy.

mayo /'mayo/ n. m. May.

mayonesa /mayo'nesa/ n. f. mayonnaise.

mayor /ma'yor/ a. larger, largest; greater, greatest; elder, eldest; senior. **m. de edad,** major, of age. **al por m.,** at wholesale. m. major.

mayoral /mayo'ral/ n. m. head shepherd; boss; foreman.

mayordomo /mayor'ðomo/ n. m. manager; butler, steward.

mayoría /mayo'ria/ n. f. majority, bulk.

mayorista /mayo'rista/ n. m. & f. wholesaler.

mayúscula /ma'yuskula/ n. f. capital letter, upper-case letter.

mazmorra /maθ'morra; mas-'morra/ n. f. dungeon.

mazorca /ma'θorka; ma'sorka/ n. f. ear of corn.

me /me/ pron. me; myself.

mecánico /me'kaniko/ -ca a. & n. mechanical; mechanic.

mecanismo /meka'nismo/ n. m. mechanism.

mecanizar /mekani'θar; mekani-'sar/ v. mechanize.

mecanografía /mekanogra'fia/ n. f. typewriting.

mecanógrafo /meka'nografo/ -fa n. typist.

mecedor /meθe'ðor; mese'ðor/ n. m. swing.

mecedora /meθe'ðora; mese'ðora/ n. f. rocking chair.

mecer /me'θer; me'ser/ v. rock; swing, sway.

mecha /'metʃa/ n. f. wick; fuse.

mechón /me'tʃon/ n. m. lock (of hair).

medalla /me'ðaʎa; me'ðaja/ n. f. medal.

médano /'meðano/ n. m. sand dune.

media /'meðia/ n. f. stocking.

mediación /meðia'θion; meðia-'sion/ n. f. mediation.

mediador /meðia'ðor/ **-ra** n. mediator.

mediados /me'ðiaðos/ n. m.pl. **a m. de,** about the middle of (a period of time).

medianero /meðia'nero/ n. m. mediator.

medianía /meðia'nia/ n. f. mediocrity.

mediano /me'ðiano/ a. medium; moderate; mediocre.

medianoche /meðia'notʃe/ n. f. midnight.

mediante /me'ðiante/ prep. by means of.

mediar /me'ðiar/ v. mediate.

medicamento /meðika'mento/ n. m. medicine, drug.

medicastro /meði'kastro/ n. m. quack.

medicina /meði'θina; meði'sina/ n. f. medicine.

medicinar /meðiθi'nar; meðisi'nar/ v. treat (as a doctor).

médico /'meðiko/ a. **1.** medical. —n. **2.** m. & f. doctor, physician.

medida /me'ðiða/ n. f. measure, step.

medidor /meði'ðor/ n. m. meter.

medieval /meðie'βal/ a. medieval.

medio /'meðio/ a. **1.** half; mid, middle of. —n. **2.** m. middle; means.

mediocre /me'ðiokre/ a. mediocre.

mediocridad /meðiokri'ðað/ n. f. mediocrity.

mediodía /meðio'ðia/ n. m. midday, noon.

medir /me'ðir/ v. measure, gauge.

meditación /meðita'θion; meðita'sion/ n. f. meditation.

meditar /meði'tar/ v. meditate.

mediterráneo /meðite'rraneo/ a. Mediterranean.

medrar /me'ðrar/ v. thrive; grow.

medroso /me'ðroso/ a. fearful, cowardly.

megáfono /me'gafono/ n. m. megaphone.

megahercio /mega'erθio; mega-'ersio/ n. f. megahertz.

mejicano /mehi'kano/ **-na** a. & n. Mexican.

mejilla /me'hiʎa; me'hiya/ n. f. cheek.

mejillón /mehi'ʎon; mehi'yon/ n. m. mussel.

mejor /me'hor/ a. & adv. better; best. **a lo m.**, perhaps.

mejora /me'hora/ n. f., **mejora-miento**, m. improvement.

mejorar /meho'rar/ v. improve, better.

mejoría /meho'ria/ n. f. improvement; superiority.

melancolía /melanko'lia/ n. f. melancholy.

melancólico /melan'koliko/ a. melancholy.

melaza /me'laθa; me'lasa/ n. f. molasses.

melena /me'lena/ n. f. mane; long or loose hair.

melenudo /mele'nuðo/ **-da** a. long-haired.

melindroso /melin'droso/ a. fussy.

mella /'meʎa; 'meya/ n. f. notch; dent. —**mellar,** v.

mellizo /me'ʎiθo; me'yiso/ **-za** n. & a. twin.

melocotón /meloko'ton/ n. m. peach.

melodía /melo'ðia/ n. f. melody.

melodioso /melo'ðioso/ a. melodious.

melón /me'lon/ n. m. melon.

meloso /me'loso/ a. like honey.

membrana /mem'brana/ n. f. membrane.

membrete /mem'brete/ n. m. memorandum; letterhead.

membrillo /mem'briʎo; mem-'briyo/ n. m. quince.

membrudo /mem'bruðo/ a. strong, muscular.

memorable /memo'raβle/ a. memorable.

memorándum /memo'randum/ n. m. memorandum; notebook.

memoria /me'moria/ n. f. memory; memoir; memorandum.

mención /men'θion; men'sion/ n. f. mention. —**mencionar,** v.

mendigar /mendi'gar/ v. beg (for alms).

mendigo /men'digo/ **-a** n. beggar.

mendrugo /men'drugo/ n. m. (hard) crust, chunk.

menear /mene'ar/ v. shake, wag; stir.

menester /menes'ter/ n. m. need, want; duty, task. **ser m.**, to be necessary.

menesteroso /meneste'roso/ a. needy.

mengua /'meŋgua/ n. f. decrease; lack; poverty.

menguar /meŋ'guar/ v. abate, decrease.

meningitis /meniŋ'gitis/ n. f. meningitis.

menopausia /meno'pausia/ n. f. menopause.

menor /me'nor/ a. smaller, smallest; lesser, least; younger, youngest, junior. **m. de edad,** minor, under age. **al por m.,** at retail.

menos /'menos/ a. & adv. less, least; minus. **a m. que,** unless. **echar de m.,** to miss.

menospreciar /menospre'θiar; menospre'siar/ v. cheapen; despise; slight.

mensaje /men'sahe/ n. m. message.

mensajero /mensa'hero/ **-ra** n. messenger.

menstruar /menstru'ar/ v. menstruate.

mensual /men'sual/ a. monthly.

mensualidad /mensuali'ðað/ n. f. monthly income or allowance; monthly payment.

menta /'menta/ n. f. mint, peppermint.

mentado /men'taðo/ a. famous.

mental /men'tal/ a. mental.

mentalidad /mentali'ðað/ n. f. mentality.

menta romana /'menta rro'mana/ spearmint.

mente /'mente/ n. f. mind.

mentecato /mente'kato/ a. foolish, stupid.

mentir /men'tir/ v. lie, tell a lie.

mentira /men'tira/ n. f. lie, falsehood. **parece m.,** it seems impossible.

mentiroso /menti'roso/ a. lying, untruthful.

mentol /'mentol/ n. m. menthol.

menú /me'nu/ n. m. menu.

menudeo /menu'ðeo/ n. m. retail.

menudo /me'nuðo/ a. small, minute. **a m.,** often.

meñique /me'ɲike/ a. tiny.

meple /'meple/ n. m. maple.

merca /'merka/ n. f. purchase.

mercader /merka'ðer/ *n. m.* merchant.

mercaderías /merkaðe'rias/ *n. f.pl.* merchandise, commodities.

mercado /mer'kaðo/ *n. m.* market.

Mercado Común /mer'kaðo ko'mun/ Common Market.

mercado negro /mer'kaðo 'negro/ black market.

mercancía /merkan'θia; merkan'sia/ *n. f.* merchandise; (*pl.*) wares.

mercante /mer'kante/ *a.* merchant.

mercantil /merkan'til/ *a.* mercantile.

merced /mer'θeð; mer'seð/ *n. f.* mercy, grace.

mercenario /merθe'nario; merse'nario/ **-ria** *a. & n.* mercenary.

mercurio /mer'kurio/ *n. m.* mercury.

merecedor /mereθe'ðor; merese'ðor/ *a.* worthy.

merecer /mere'θer; mere'ser/ *v.* merit, deserve.

merecimiento /mereθi'miento; meresi'miento/ *n. m.* merit.

merendar /meren'dar/ *v.* eat lunch; snack.

merendero /meren'dero/ *n. m.* lunchroom.

meridional /meriðio'nal/ *a.* southern.

merienda /me'rienda/ *n. f.* midday meal, lunch; afternoon snack.

mérito /'merito/ *n. m.* merit, worth.

meritorio /meri'torio/ *a.* meritorious.

merla /'merla/ *n. f.* blackbird.

merluza /mer'luθa; mer'lusa/ *n. f.* haddock.

mermelada /merme'laða/ *n. f.* marmalade.

mero /'mero/ *a.* mere.

merodeador /meroðea'ðor/ **-ra** *n.* prowler.

mes /'mes/ *n. m.* month.

mesa /'mesa/ *n. f.* table.

meseta /me'seta/ *n. f.* plateau.

mesón /me'son/ *n. m.* inn.

mesonero /meso'nero/ **-ra** *n.* innkeeper.

mestizo /mes'tiθo; mes'tiso/ **-za** *a. & n.* half-caste.

meta /'meta/ *n. f.* goal, objective.

metabolismo /metaβo'lismo/ *n. m.* metabolism.

metafísica /meta'fisika/ *n. f.* metaphysics.

metáfora /me'tafora/ *n. f.* metaphor.

metal /me'tal/ *n. m.* metal.

metálico /me'taliko/ *a.* metallic.

metalurgia /metalur'hia/ *n. f.* metallurgy.

meteoro /mete'oro/ *n. m.* meteor.

meteorología /meteorolo'hia/ *n. f.* meteorology.

meter /me'ter/ *v.* put (in).

meterse /me'terse/ *v.* interfere, meddle; go into.

metódico /me'toðiko/ *a.* methodic.

método /'metoðo/ *n. m.* method, approach.

metralla /me'traʎa; me'traya/ *n. f.* shrapnel.

métrico /'metriko/ *a.* metric.

metro /'metro/ *n. m.* meter (measure); subway.

metrópoli /me'tropoli/ *n. f.* metropolis.

mexicano /meksi'kano/ **-na** *a. & n.* Mexican.

mezcla /'meθkla; 'meskla/ *n. f.* mixture; blend.

mezclar /meθ'klar; mes'klar/ *v.* mix; blend.

mezcolanza /meθko'lanθa; mesko'lansa/ *n. f.* mixture; hodgepodge.

mezquino /meθ'kino; mes'kino/ *a.* stingy; petty.

mezquita /meθ'kita; mes'kita/ *n. f.* mosque.

mi /'mi/ *a.* my.

mí /'mi/ *pron. me;* myself.

microbio /mi'kroβio/ *n. m.* microbe, germ.

microbús /mikro'βus/ *n. m.* minibus.

microchip /mikro't'ʃip/ *n. m.* microchip.

microficha /mikro'fitʃa/ *n. f.* microfiche.

micrófono /mi'krofono/ *n. m.* microphone.

microforma /mikro'forma/ *n. f.* microform.

microscópico /mikros'kopiko/ *a.* microscopic.

microscopio /mikros'kopio/ *n. m.* microscope.

microtaxi /mikro'taksi/ *n. m.* minicab.

miedo /'mieðo/ *n. m.* fear. **tener m.,** fear, be afraid.

miedoso /mie'ðoso/ *a.* fearful.

miel /miel/ *n. f.* honey.

miembro /mi'embro/ *n. m. & f.* member; limb.

mientras /mientras/ *conj.* while. **m. tanto,** meanwhile. **m. más... más,** the more... the more.

miércoles /mi'erkoles/ *n. m.* Wednesday.

miércoles de ceniza /mi'erkoles de 'θe'nisa; 'mierkoles de se'nisa/ Ash Wednesday.

miga /'miga/ **migaja** /mi'gaxa/ *n. f.* scrap; crumb.

migración /migra'θion; migra'sion/ *n. f.* migration.

migratorio /migra'torio/ *a.* migratory.

mil /mil/ *a. & pron.* thousand.

milagro /mi'lagro/ *n. m.* miracle.

milagroso /mila'groso/ *a.* miraculous.

milicia /mi'liθia; mi'lisia/ *n. f.* militia.

militante /mili'tante/ *a.* militant.

militar /mili'tar/ *a.* **1.** military. —*n.* **2.** *m.* military man.

militarismo /milita'rismo/ *n. m.* militarism.

milla /'miʎa; 'miya/ *n. f.* mile.

millar /mi'ʎar; mi'yar/ *n. m.* (a) thousand.

millón /mi'ʎon; mi'yon/ *n. m.* million.

millonario /miʎo'nario; miyo'nario/ **-ria** *n.* millionaire.

mimar /mi'mar/ *v.* pamper, spoil (a child).

mimbre /'mimbre/ *n. m.* willow; wicker.

mímico /'mimiko/ *a.* mimic.

mimo /'mimo/ *n. m.* mime, mimic.

mina /'mina/ *n. f.* mine. —**minar,** *v.*

mineral /mine'ral/ *a. & m.* mineral.

minero /mi'nero/ **-ra** *n.* miner.

miniatura /minia'tura/ *n. f.* miniature.

miniaturizar /miniaturi'θar; miniaturi'sar/ *v.* miniaturize.

mínimo /'minimo/ *a. & m.* minimum.

ministerio /minis'terio/ *n. m.* ministry; cabinet.

ministro /mi'nistro/ **-a** *n. Govt.* minister, secretary.

minoría /mino'ria/ *n. f.* minority.

minoridad /minori'ðað/ *n. f.* minority (of age).

minucioso /minu'θioso; minu'sioso/ *a.* minute; thorough.

minué /mi'nue/ *n. m.* minuet.

minúscula /mi'nuskula/ *n. f.* lower-case letter, small letter.

minuta /mi'nuta/ *n. f.* draft.

mío /'mio/ *a.* mine.

miopía /mio'pia/ *n. f.* myopia.

mira /'mira/ *n. f.* gunsight.

mirada /mi'raða/ *n. f.* look; gaze, glance.

miramiento /mira'miento/ *n. m.* consideration; respect.

mirar /mi'rar/ *v.* look, look at; watch. **m. a,** face.

miríada /mi'riaða/ *n. f.* myriad.

mirlo /'mirlo/ *n. m.* blackbird.

mirón /mi'ron/ **-ona** *n.* bystander, observer.

mirra /'mirra/ *n. f.* myrrh.

mirto /'mirto/ *n. m.* myrtle.

misa /'misa/ *n. f.* mass, church service.

misceláneo /misθe'laneo; misse-'laneo/ *a.* miscellaneous.

miserable /mise'raβle/ *a.* miserable, wretched.

miseria /mi'seria/ *n. f.* misery.

misericordia /miseri'korðia/ *n. f.* mercy.

misericordioso /miserikor'ðioso/ *a.* merciful.

misión /mi'sion/ *n. f.* assignment; mission.

misionario /misio'nario/ **-ria, misionero -ra** *n.* missionary.

mismo /'mismo/ *a. & pron.* **1.** same; -self, -selves. —*adv.* **2.** right, exactly.

misterio /mis'terio/ *n. m.* mystery.

misterioso /miste'rioso/ *a.* mysterious, weird.

místico /'mistiko/ **-ca** *a. & n.* mystical, mystic.

mitad /mi'tað/ *n. f.* half.

mítico /'mitiko/ *a.* mythical.

mitigar /miti'gar/ *v.* mitigate.

mitin /'mitin/ *n. m.* meeting; rally.

mito /'mito/ *n. m.* myth.

mitón /mi'ton/ *n. m.* mitten.

mitra /'mitra/ *n. f.* miter (bishop's).

mixto /'miksto/ *a.* mixed.

mixtura /miks'tura/ *n. f.* mixture.

mobiliario /moβi'liario/ *n. m.* household goods.

mocasín /moka'sin/ *n. m.* moccasin.

mocedad /moθe'ðað; mose'ðað/ n. f. youthfulness.

mochila /mo'tʃila/ n. f. knapsack, backpack.

mocho /'motʃo/ a. cropped, trimmed, shorn.

moción /mo'θion; mo'sion/ n. f. motion.

mocoso /mo'koso/ a. & -sa n. brat.

moda /'moða/ n. f. mode, fashion, style.

modales /mo'ðales/ n. m.pl. manners.

modelo /mo'ðelo/ n. m. model, pattern.

módem /'moðem/ n. m. modem.

moderación /moðera'θion; moðerasion/ n. f. moderation.

moderado /moðe'raðo/ a. moderate. **—moderar,** v.

modernizar /moðerni'θar; moðerni'sar/ v. modernize.

moderno /mo'ðerno/ a. modern.

modestia /mo'ðestia/ n. f. modesty.

modesto /mo'ðesto/ a. modest.

módico /'moðiko/ a. reasonable, moderate.

modificación /moðifika'θion; moðifika'sion/ n. f. modification.

modificar /moðifi'kar/ v. modify.

modismo /mo'ðismo/ n. m. Gram. idiom.

modista /mo'ðista/ n. f. dressmaker; milliner.

modo /'moðo/ n. m. way, means.

modular /moðu'lar/ v. modulate.

mofarse /mo'farse/ v. scoff, sneer.

mofletudo /mofle'tuðo/ a. fat-cheeked.

mohín /mo'in/ n. m. grimace.

moho /'moo/ n. m. mold, mildew.

mohoso /mo'oso/ a. moldy.

mojar /mo'har/ v. wet.

mojón /mo'hon/ n. m. landmark; heap.

molde /'molde/ n. m. mold, form.

molécula /mo'lekula/ n. f. molecule.

moler /mo'ler/ v. grind, mill.

molestar /moles'tar/ v. molest, bother, disturb, annoy, trouble.

molestia /mo'lestia/ n. f. bother, annoyance, trouble; hassle.

molesto /mo'lesto/ a. bothersome; annoyed; uncomfortable.

molicie /mo'liθie; mo'lisie/ n. f. softness.

molinero /moli'nero/ n. m. miller.

molino /mo'lino/ n. m. mill. **m. de viento,** windmill.

mollera /mo'ʎera; mo'yera/ n. f. top of the head.

molusco /mo'lusko/ n. m. mollusk.

momentáneo /momen'taneo/ a. momentary.

momento /mo'mento/ n. m. moment.

mona /'mona/ n. f. female monkey.

monarca /mo'narka/ n. m. & f. monarch.

monarquía /monar'kia/ n. f. monarchy.

monarquista /monar'kista/ n. & a. monarchist.

monasterio /mona'sterio/ n. m. monastery.

mondadientes /monda'ðientes/ n. m. toothpick.

moneda /mo'neða/ n. f. coin; money.

monetario /mone'tario/ a. monetary.

monición /moni'θion; moni'sion/ n. m. warning.

monigote /moni'gote/ n. m. puppet.

monja /'monha/ n. f. nun.

monje /'monhe/ n. m. monk. *Colloq.* cute. **—***n.* **2.** *m.* & *f.* monkey.

monólogo /mo'nologo/ n. m. monologue.

monopatín /monopa'tin/ n. m. skateboard.

monopolio /mono'polio/ n. m. monopoly.

monopolizar /monopoli'θar; monopoli'sar/ v. monopolize.

monosílabo /mono'silaβo/ n. m. monosyllable.

monotonía /monoto'nia/ n. f. monotony.

monótono /mo'notono/ a. monotonous, dreary.

monstruo /'monstruo/ n. m. monster.

monstruosidad /monstruosi'ðað/ n. f. monstrosity.

monstruoso /mons'truoso/ a. monstrous.

monta /'monta/ n. f. amount; price.

montaña /mon'taɲa/ n. f. mountain.

montañoso /monta'ɲoso/ a. mountainous.

montar /mon'tar/ *v.* mount, climb; amount; *Mech.* assemble. **m. a caballo,** ride horseback.

montaraz /monta'raθ; monta'ras/ *a.* wild, barbaric.

monte /'monte/ *n. m.* mountain; forest.

montón /mon'ton/ *n. m.* heap, pile.

montuoso /mon'tuoso/ *a.* mountainous.

montura /mon'tura/ *n. f.* mount; saddle.

monumental /monumen'tal/ *a.* monumental.

monumento /monu'mento/ *n. m.* monument.

mora /'mora/ *n. f.* blackberry.

morada /mo'raða/ *n. f.* residence, dwelling.

morado /mo'raðo/ *a.* purple.

moral /mo'ral/ *a.* 1. moral. —*n.* 2. *f.* morale.

moraleja /mora'leha/ *n. f.* moral.

moralidad /morali'ðað/ *n. f.* morality, morals.

moralista /mora'lista/ *n. m. & f.* moralist.

morar /mo'rar/ *v.* dwell, live, reside.

mórbido /'morβiðo/ *a.* morbid.

mordaz /mor'ðaθ; mor'ðas/ *a.* caustic; sarcastic.

mordedura /morðe'ðura/ *n. f.* bite.

morder /mor'ðer/ *v.* bite.

moreno /mo'reno/ **-na** *a. & n.* brown; dark-skinned; dark-haired, brunette.

morfina /mor'fina/ *n. f.* morphine.

moribundo /mori'βundo/ *a.* dying.

morir /mo'rir/ *v.* die.

morisco /mo'risko/ **-ca, moro -ra** *a. & n.* Moorish; Moor.

morriña /mo'rriɲa/ *n. f.* sadness.

morro /'morro/ *n. m.* bluff; snout.

mortaja /mor'taha/ *n. f.* shroud.

mortal /mor'tal/ *a. & n.* mortal.

mortalidad /mortali'ðað/ *n. f.* mortality.

mortero /mor'tero/ *n. m.* mortar.

mortífero /mor'tifero/ *a.* fatal, deadly.

mortificar /mortifi'kar/ *v.* mortify.

mortuorio /mor'tuorio/ *a.* funereal.

mosaico /mo'saiko/ *a. & m.* mosaic.

mosca /'moska/ *n. f.* fly.

mosquito /mos'kito/ *n. m.* mosquito.

mostacho /mos'tatʃo/ *n. m.* mustache.

mostaza /mos'taθa; mos'tasa/ *n. f.* mustard.

mostrador /mostra'ðor/ *n. m.* counter; showcase.

mostrar /mos'trar/ *v.* show, display.

mote /'mote/ *n. m.* nickname; alias.

motel /mo'tel/ *n. m.* motel.

motín /mo'tin/ *n. m.* mutiny; riot.

motivo /mo'tiβo/ *n. m.* motive, reason.

motocicleta /motoθi'kleta; motosi'kleta/ *n. f.* motorcycle.

motociclista /motoθi'klista; motosi'klista/ *n. m. & f.* motorcyclist.

motor /mo'tor/ *n. m.* motor.

motorista /moto'rista/ *n. m. & f.* motorist.

movedizo /moβe'ðiθo; moβe'ðiso/ *a.* movable; shaky.

mover /mo'βer/ *v.* move; stir.

movible /mo'βiβle/ *a.* movable.

móvil /'moβil/ *a.* mobile.

movilización /moβiliθa'θion; moβilisa'sion/ *n. f.* mobilization.

movilizar /moβili'θar; moβili'sar/ *v.* mobilize.

movimiento /moβi'miento/ *n. m.* movement, motion.

mozo /'moθo; 'moso/ *n. m.* boy; servant, waiter, porter.

muaré /mua're/ *n. m.* moiré.

muchacha /mu'tʃatʃa/ *n. f.* girl, youngster; maid (servant).

muchachez /mutʃa'tʃeθ; mutʃa'tʃes/ *n. f.* boyhood, girlhood.

muchacho /mu'tʃatʃo/ *n. m.* boy; youngster.

muchedumbre /mutʃe'ðumbre/ *n. f.* crowd, mob.

mucho /'mutʃo/ *a.* 1. much, many. —*adv.* 2. much.

mucoso /mu'koso/ *a.* mucous.

muda /'muða/ *n. f.* change.

mudanza /mu'ðanθa; mu'ðansa/ *n. f.* change; change of residence.

mudar /mu'ðar/ *v.* change, shift.

mudarse /mu'ðarse/ *v.* change residence, move.

mudo /'muðo/ **-da** *a. & n.* mute.

mueble /'mueβle/ *n. m.* piece of furniture; (*pl.*) furniture.

mueca /'mueka/ *n. f.* grimace.

muela /'muela/ *n. f.* (back) tooth.

muelle /'mueʎe; 'mueye/ n. m. pier, wharf; Mech. spring.
muerte /'muerte/ n. f. death.
muerto /'muerto/ -ta a. 1. dead. —n. 2. dead person.
muesca /'mueska/ n. f. notch; groove.
muestra /'muestra/ n. f. sample, specimen; sign.
mugido /mu'hiðo/ n. m. lowing; mooing.
mugir /mu'hir/ v. low, moo.
mugre /'mugre/ n. f. filth, dirt.
mugriento /mu'griento/ a. dirty.
mujer /mu'her/ f. woman; wife. **m. de la limpieza**, cleaning lady, charwoman.
mujeril /muhe'ril/ a. womanly, feminine.
mula /'mula/ n. f. mule.
mulato /mu'lato/ -ta a. & n. mulatto.
muleta /mu'leta/ n. f. crutch; prop.
mulo /'mulo/ -la n. mule.
multa /'multa/ n. f. fine, penalty.
multicolor /multiko'lor/ a. many-colored.
multinacional /multinaθio'nal; multinasio'nal/ a. multinational.
múltiple /'multiple/ a. multiple.
multiplicación /multiplika'θion; multiplika'sion/ n. f. multiplication.
multiplicar /multipli'kar/ v. multiply.
multiplicidad /multipliθi'ðað; multiplisi'ðað/ n. f. multiplicity.
multitud /multi'tuð/ n. f. multitude, crowd.
mundanal /munda'nal/ a. worldly.
mundano /mun'dano/ a. worldly, mundane.
mundial /mun'dial/ a. worldwide; (of the) world.
mundo /'mundo/ n. m. world.

munición /muni'θion; muni'sion/ n. f. ammunition.
municipal /muniθi'pal; munisi'pal/ a. municipal.
municipio /muni'θipio; muni'sipio/ n. m. city hall.
muñeca /mu'ɲeka/ n. f. doll; wrist.
muñeco /mu'ɲeko/ n. m. doll; puppet.
mural /mu'ral/ a. & m. mural.
muralla /mu'raʎa; mu'raya/ n. f. wall.
murciélago /mur'θielago; mur'sielago/ n. m. bat.
murga /'murga/ n. f. musical band.
murmullo /mur'muʎo; mur'muyo/ n. m. murmur; rustle.
murmurar /murmu'rar/ v. murmur; rustle; grumble.
musa /'musa/ n. f. muse.
muscular /musku'lar/ a. muscular.
músculo /'muskulo/ n. m. muscle.
muselina /muse'lina/ n. f. muslin.
museo /mu'seo/ n. m. museum.
música /'musika/ n. f. music.
musical /musi'kal/ a. musical.
músico /'musiko/ -ca a. & n. musical; musician.
muslo /'muslo/ n. m. thigh.
mustio /'mustio/ a. sad.
musulmano /musul'mano/ -na a. & n. Muslim.
muta /'muta/ n. f. pack of hounds.
mutabilidad /mutaβili'ðað/ n. f. mutability.
mutación /muta'θion; muta'sion/ n. f. mutation.
mutilación /mutila'θion; mutila-'sion/ n. f. mutilation.
mutilar /muti'lar/ v. mutilate; mangle.
mutuo /'mutuo/ a. mutual.
muy /'mui/ adv. very.

N Ñ

nabo /'naβo/ n. m. turnip.
nácar /'nakar/ n. m. mother-of-pearl.
nacarado /naka'raðo, na'kareo/ a. pearly.
nacer /na'θer; na'ser/ v. be born.
naciente /na'θiente; na'siente/ a. rising; nascent.
nacimiento /naθi'miento; nasi-'miento/ n. m. birth.

nación /na'θion; na'sion/ n. f. nation.
nacional /naθio'nal; nasio'nal/ a. national.
nacionalidad /naθionali'ðað; nasionali'ðað/ n. f. nationality.
nacionalismo /naθiona'lismo; nasiona'lismo/ n. m. nationalism.
nacionalista /naθiona'lista; nasiona'lista/ n. & a. nationalist.

nacionalización /naθionaliθa'θion; nasionalisa'sion/ n. f. nationalization.

nacionalizar /naθionali'θar; nasionali'sar/ v. nationalize.

Naciones Unidas /na'θiones u'niðas; na'siones u'niðas/ n. f.pl. United Nations.

nada /'naða/ pron. **1.** nothing; anything. **de n.,** you're welcome. —adv. **2.** at all.

nadador /naða'ðor; -ra n. swimmer.

nadar /na'ðar/ v. swim.

nadie /'naðie/ pron. no one, nobody; anyone, anybody.

nafta /'nafta/ n. f. naphtha.

naipe /'naipe/ n. m. (playing) card.

naranja /na'ranha/ n. f. orange.

naranjada /naran'haða/ n. f. orangeade.

naranjo /na'ranho/ n. m. orange tree.

narciso /nar'θiso; nar'siso/ n. m. daffodil; narcissus.

narcótico /nar'kotiko/ a. & m. narcotic.

nardo /'nardo/ n. m. spikenard.

nariz /na'riθ; na'ris/ n. f. nose; (pl.) nostrils.

narración /narra'θion; narra'sion/ n. f. account.

narrador /narra'ðor; -ra n. narrator.

narrar /na'rrar/ v. narrate.

narrativa /narra'tiβa/ n. f. narrative.

nata /'nata/ n. f. cream.

nata batida /'nata ba'tiða/ whipped cream.

natación /nata'θion; nata'sion/ n. f. swimming.

natal /na'tal/ a. native; natal.

natalicio /nata'liθio; nata'lisio/ n. m. birthday.

natalidad /natali'ðað/ n. f. birth rate.

natillas /na'tiλas; na'tiyas/ n. f.pl. custard.

nativo /na'tiβo/ a. native; innate.

natural /natu'ral/ a. **1.** natural. —n. **2.** m. & f. native. **3.** m. nature, disposition.

naturaleza /natura'leθa; natura'lesa/ n. f. nature.

naturalidad /naturali'ðað/ n. f. naturalness; nationality.

naturalista /natura'lista/ n. a. & n. naturalistic; naturalist.

naturalización /naturaliθa'θion; naturalisa'sion/ n. f. naturalization.

naturalizar /naturali'θar; naturali'sar/ v. naturalize.

naufragar /naufra'gar/ v. be shipwrecked; fail.

naufragio /nau'frahio/ n. m. shipwreck; disaster.

náufrago /'naufrago/ -ga a. & n. shipwrecked (person).

nausea /'nausea/ n. f. nausea.

nausear /nause'ar/ v. feel nauseous.

náutico /'nautiko/ a. nautical.

navaja /na'βaha/ n. f. razor; pen knife.

naval /na'βal/ a. naval.

navasca /na'βaska/ n. f. blizzard, snowstorm.

nave /'naβe/ n. f. ship.

nave espacial /'naβe espa'θial; 'naβe es'pasial/ spaceship.

navegable /naβe'gaβle/ a. navigable.

navegación /naβega'θion; naβega'sion/ n. f. navigation.

navegador /naβega'ðor/ -ra n. navigator.

navegante /naβe'gante/ n. m. & f. navigator.

navegar /naβe'gar/ v. sail; navigate.

Navidad /naβi'ðað/ n. f. Christmas.

navío /na'βio/ n. m. ship.

neblina /ne'βlina/ n. f. mist, fog.

nebuloso /neβu'loso/ a. misty; nebulous.

necedad /neθe'ðað; nese'ðað/ n. f. stupidity; nonsense.

necesario /neθe'sario; nese'sario/ a. necessary.

necesidad /neθesi'ðað; nesesi'ðað/ n. f. necessity, need, want.

necesitado /neθesi'taðo; nesesi'taðo/ a. needy; poor.

necesitar /neθesi'tar; nesesi'tar/ v. need.

necio /'neθio; 'nesio/ -cia a. **1.** stupid, silly. —n **2.** fool.

néctar /'nektar/ n. m. nectar.

nectarina /nekta'rina/ n. f. nectarine.

nefando /ne'fando/ a. nefarious.

nefasto /ne'fasto/ a. unlucky, ill-fated.

negable /ne'gaβle/ a. deniable.

negación /nega'θion; nega'sion/ n. f. denial, negation.

negar /ne'gar/ v. deny.

negarse /ne'garse/ v. refuse, decline.

negativa /nega'tiβa/ n. f. negative, refusal.

negativamente /negatiβa'mente/ adv. negatively.

negativo /nega'tiβo/ a. negative.

negligencia /negli'henθia; negli'hensia/ n. f. negligence, neglect.

negligente /negli'hente/ a. negligent.

negociación /negoθia'θion; negosia'sion/ n. f. negotiation, deal.

negociador /negoθia'ðor; negosia'ðor/ -ra n. negotiator.

negociante /nego'θiante; nego'siante/ -ta n. businessperson.

negociar /nego'θiar; nego'siar/ v. negotiate, trade.

negocio /ne'goθio; ne'gosio/ n. m. trade; business.

negro /'negro/ -gra a. 1. black. —n. 2. m. Black.

nene /'nene/ -na n. baby.

neo /'neo/ **neón** /ne'on/ n. m. neon.

nervio /'nerβio/ n. m. nerve.

nerviosamente /nerβiosa'mente/ adv. nervously.

nervioso /ner'βioso/ a. nervous.

nesciencia /nesθien'θia; nessien'sia/ n. f. ignorance.

nesciente /nes'θiente; nes'siente/ a. ignorant.

neto /'neto/ a. net.

neumático /neu'matiko/ a. 1. pneumatic. —n. 2. m. (pneumatic) tire.

neumático de recambio /neu'matiko de rre'kambio/ spare tire.

neumonía /neumo'nia/ n. f. pneumonia.

neurótico /neu'rotiko/ a. neurotic.

neutral /neu'tral/ a. neutral.

neutralidad /neutrali'ðað/ n. f. neutrality.

neutro /'neutro/ a. neuter; neutral.

neutrón /neu'tron/ n. m. neutron.

nevada /ne'βaða/ n. f. snowfall.

nevado /ne'βaðo/ a. snow-white; snow-capped.

nevar /ne'βar/ v. snow.

nevera /ne'βera/ n. f. icebox.

nevoso /ne'βoso/ a. snowy.

ni /ni/ conj. 1. nor. **ni... ni**, neither... nor. —adv. 2. not even.

nicho /'nitʃo/ n. m. recess; niche.

nido /'niðo/ n. m. nest.

niebla /'nieβla/ n. f. fog; mist.

nieto /'nieto/ -ta n. grandchild.

nieve /'nieβe/ n. f. snow.

nilón /ni'lon/ n. m. nylon.

nimio /'nimio/ adj. stingy.

ninfa /'ninfa/ n. f. nymph.

ningún /nin'gun/ **-no -na** a. & pron. no, none, neither (one); any, either (one).

niñera /ni'ɲera/ n. f. nursemaid, nanny.

niñez /ni'ɲeθ; ni'ɲes/ n. f. childhood.

niño /'niɲo/ **-ña 1.** a. **1.** young; childish; childlike. —n. **2.** child.

níquel /'nikel/ n. m. nickel.

niquelado /nike'laðo/ a. nickel-plated.

nítido /'nitiðo/ a. neat, clean, bright.

nitrato /ni'trato/ n. m. nitrate.

nitro /'nitro/ n. m. niter.

nitrógeno /ni'troheno/ n. m. nitrogen.

nivel /ni'βel/ n. m. level; grade. —**nivelar,** v.

no /no/ adv. **1.** not. **no más,** only. —interj. **2.** no.

noble /'noβle/ a. & m. noble; nobleman.

nobleza /no'βleθa; no'βlesa/ n. f. nobility; nobleness.

noche /'notʃe/ n. f. night; evening.

Nochebuena /notʃe'βuena/ n. f. Christmas Eve.

noción /no'θion; no'sion/ n. f. notion, idea.

nocivo /no'θiβo; no'siβo/ a. harmful.

noctiluca /nokti'luka/ n. f. glowworm.

nocturno /nok'turno/ a. nocturnal.

nodriza /no'ðriθa; no'ðrisa/ n. f. wet nurse.

no fumador /no fuma'ðor/ -ra n. m. & f. nonsmoker.

nogal /no'gal/ n. m. walnut.

nombradía /nom'braðia/ n. f. fame.

nombramiento /nombra'miento/ n. m. appointment, nomination.

nombrar /nom'βrar/ v. name, appoint, nominate; mention.

nombre /'nombre/ n. m. name; noun.

nombre y apellidos /'nombre i ape'ʎiðos; 'nombre i ape'yiðos/ (person's) full name.

nómina /'nomina/ n. f. list; pay-roll.

nominación /nomina'θion; nomina'sion/ n. f. nomination.

nominal /nomi'nal/ a. nominal.

nominar /nomi'nar/ v. nominate.

non /non/ a. uneven, odd.

nonada /no'naða/ n. f. trifle.

nordeste /nor'ðeste/ n. m. north-east.

nórdico /'norðiko/ a. Nordic; northerly.

norma /'norma/ n. f. norm, standard.

normal /nor'mal/ a. normal, standard.

normalidad /normali'ðað/ n. f. normality.

normalizar /normali'θar; normali-'sar/ v. normalize; standardize.

noroeste /noro'este/ n. m. north-west.

norte /'norte/ n. m. north.

norteamericano /norteameri-'kano/ -na a. & n. North American.

Noruega /no'ruega/ n. f. Norway.

noruego /no'ruego/ -ga a. & n. Norwegian.

nos /nos/ pron. us; ourselves.

nosotros /no'sotros; no'sotras/ -as pron. we, us; ourselves.

nostalgia /nos'talhia/ n. f. nostalgia, homesickness.

nostálgico /nos'talhiko/ a. nostalgic.

nota /'nota/ n. f. note; grade, mark.

notable /no'taβle/ a. notable, remarkable.

notación /nota'θion; nota'sion/ n. f. notation; note.

notar /no'tar/ v. note, notice.

notario /no'tario/ -ria n. notary.

noticia /no'tiθia; no'tisia/ n. f. notice; piece of news; (pl.) news.

noticia de última hora /no'tiθia de 'ultima 'ora; no'tisia de 'ultima 'ora/ news flash.

notificación /notifika'θion; notifika'sion/ n. f. notification.

notificación de reclutamiento /notifika'θion de rrekluta'miento; notifika'sion de rrekluta'miento/ draft notice.

notificar /notifi'kar/ v. notify.

notorio /no'torio/ a. well-known.

novato /no'βato/ -ta n. novice.

novecientos /noβe'θientos; noβe-'sientos/ a. & pron. nine hundred.

novedad /noβe'ðað/ n. f. novelty; piece of news.

novel /no'βel/ a. new; inexperienced.

novela /no'βela/ n. f. novel.

novelista /noβe'lista/ n. m. & f. novelist.

novena /no'βena/ n. f. novena.

noveno /no'βeno/ a. ninth.

noventa /no'βenta/ a. & pron. ninety.

novia /'noβia/ n. f. bride; sweetheart; fiancée.

noviazgo /no'βiaθgo; no'βiasgo/ n. m. engagement.

novicio /no'βiθio; no'βisio/ -cia n. novice, beginner.

noviembre /no'βiembre/ n. m. November.

novilla /no'βiʎa; no'βiya/ n. f. heifer.

novio /'noβio/ n. m. bridegroom; sweetheart; fiancé.

nube /'nuβe/ n. f. cloud.

núbil /'nuβil/ a. marriageable.

nublado /nu'βlaðo/ a. cloudy.

nuclear /nukle'ar/ a. nuclear.

núcleo /'nukleo/ n. m. nucleus.

nudo /'nuðo/ n. m. knot.

nuera /'nuera/ n. f. daughter-in-law.

nuestro /'nuestro/ a. our, ours.

nueva /'nueβa/ n. f. news.

nueve /'nueβe/ a. & pron. nine.

nuevo /'nueβo/ a. new. **de n.,** again, anew.

nuez /nueθ; nues/ n. f. nut; walnut.

nulidad /nuli'ðað/ n. f. nonentity; nullity.

nulo /'nulo/ a. null, void.

numeración /numera'θion; numera'sion/ n. f. numeration.

numerar /nume'rar/ v. number.

numérico /nu'meriko/ a. numerical.

número /'numero/ n. m. number; size (of shoe, etc.). **n. impar,** odd number. **n. par,** even number.

numeroso /nume'roso/ a. numerous.

numismática /numis'matika/ n. f. numismatics.

nunca /'nunka/ adv. never; ever.

nupcial /nup'θial; nup'sial/ a. nuptial.

nupcias /'nupθias; 'nupsias/ n. f.pl. nuptials, wedding.

nutrición /nutri'θion; nutri'sion/ n. f. nutrition.

nutrimento /nutri'mento/ n. m. nourishment.

nutrir /nu'trir/ v. nourish.

nutritivo /nutri'tiβo/ a. nutritious.

nylon /'nilon/ n. m. nylon.

ñame /'ɲame/ n. m. yam.

ñapa /'ɲapa/ n. f. something extra.

ñoñería /ɲoɲe'ria/ n. f. dotage.

ñoño /'ɲoɲo/ a. feeble-minded, senile.

O

o /o/ conj. or. **o... o**, either... or.

oasis /o'asis/ n. m. oasis.

obedecer /oβeðe'θer; oβeðe'ser/ v. obey, mind.

obediencia /oβe'ðienθia; oβe'ðiensia/ n. f. obedience.

obediente /oβe'ðiente/ a. obedient.

obelisco /oβe'lisko/ n. m. obelisk.

obertura /oβer'tura/ n. f. overture.

obeso /o'βeso/ a. obese.

obispo /o'βispo/ n. m. bishop.

obituario /oβi'tuario/ n. m. obituary.

objeción /oβhe'θion; oβhe'sion/ n. f. objection.

objetivo /oβhe'tiβo/ a. & m. objective.

objeto /oβ'heto/ n. m. object. —**objetar**, v.

objetor de conciencia /oβhe'tor de kon'θienθia; oβhe'tor de kon'siensia/ n. m. conscientious objector.

oblicuo /o'βlikuo/ a. oblique.

obligación /oβliga'θion; oβliga'sion/ n. f. obligation, duty.

obligar /oβli'gar/ v. oblige, require, compel; obligate.

obligatorio /oβliga'torio/ a. obligatory, compulsory.

oblongo /o'βlongo/ a. oblong.

oboe /o'βoe/ n. m. oboe.

obra /'oβra/ n. f. work. —**obrar**, v.

obrero /o'βrero/ -ra n. worker, laborer.

obscenidad /oβsθeni'ðað; oβsseni'ðað/ n. f. obscenity.

obsceno /oβs'θeno; oβs'seno/ a. obscene.

obscurecer /oβskure'θer; oβskure'ɪ'aprim;ser/ v. obscure; darken.

obscuridad /oβskuri'ðað/ n. f. obscurity; darkness.

obscuro /oβs'kuro/ a. obscure; dark.

obsequiar /oβse'kiar/ v. court; make presents to, fete.

obsequio /oβ'sekio/ n. m. obsequiousness; gift; attention.

observación /oβserβa'θion; oβserβa'sion/ n. f. observation.

observador /oβserβa'ðor/ -ra n. observer.

observancia /oβser'βanθia; oβser'βansia/ n. f. observance.

observar /oβser'βar/ v. observe, watch.

observatorio /oβserβa'torio/ n. m. observatory.

obsesión /oβse'sion/ n. f. obsession.

obstáculo /oβs'takulo/ n. m. obstacle.

obstante /oβs'tante/ adv. **no o.**, however, yet, nevertheless.

obstar /oβs'tar/ v. hinder, obstruct.

obstetricia /oβste'triθia; oβste'trisia/ n. f. obstetrics.

obstinación /oβstina'θion; oβstina'sion/ n. f. obstinacy.

obstinado /oβsti'naðo/ a. obstinate, stubborn.

obstinarse /oβsti'narse/ v. persist, insist.

obstrucción /oβstruk'θion; oβstruk'sion/ n. f. obstruction.

obstruir /oβs'truir/ v. obstruct, clog, block.

obtener /oβte'ner/ v. obtain, get, secure.

obtuso /oβ'tuso/ a. obtuse.

obvio /'oββio/ a. obvious.

ocasión /oka'sion/ n. f. occasion; opportunity, chance. **de o.**, secondhand.

ocasional /okasio'nal/ a. occasional.

ocasionalmente /okasional'mente/ adv. occasionally.

ocasionar /okasio'nar/ v. cause, occasion.

occidental /okθiðen'tal; oksiðen'tal/ a. western.

occidente /okθi'ðente; oksi'ðente/ n. m. west.

océano /o'θeano; o'seano/ n. m. ocean.

Océano Atlántico /o'θeano a'tlantiko; o'seano a'tlantiko/ Atlantic Ocean.

Océano Pacífico /o'θeano pa'θifiko; o'seano pa'sifiko/ Pacific Ocean.

ocelote /oθe'lote; ose'lote/ *n. m.* ocelot.

ochenta /o'tʃenta/ *a. & pron.* eighty.

ocho /'otʃo/ *a. & pron.* eight.

ochocientos /otʃo'θientos; otʃo'sientos/ *a. & pron.* eight hundred.

ocio /'oθio; 'osio/ *n. m.* idleness, leisure.

ociosidad /oθiosi'ðað; osiosi'ðað/ *n. f.* idleness, laziness.

ocioso /o'θioso; o'sioso/ *a.* idle, lazy.

ocre /'okre/ *n. m.* ochre.

octagonal /okta'gonal/ *a.* octagonal.

octava /ok'taβa/ *n. f.* octave.

octavo /ok'taβo/ *a.* eighth.

octubre /ok'tuβre/ *n. m.* October.

oculista /oku'lista/ *n. m. & f.* oculist.

ocultación /okulta'θion; okulta-'sion/ *n. f.* concealment.

ocultar /okul'tar/ *v.* hide, conceal.

oculto /o'kulto/ *a.* hidden.

ocupación /okupa'θion; okupa-'sion/ *n. f.* occupation.

ocupado /oku'paðo/ *a.* occupied; busy.

ocupante /oku'pante/ *n. m. & f.* occupant.

ocupar /oku'par/ *v.* occupy.

ocuparse de /oku'parse de/ *v.* take care of, take charge of.

ocurrencia /oku'rrenθia; oku'rren-sia/ *n. f.* occurrence.

ocurrente /oku'rrente/ *a.* witty.

ocurrir /oku'rrir/ *v.* occur, happen.

oda /'oða/ *n. f.* ode.

odio /'oðio/ *n. m.* hate. —**odiar,** *v.*

odiosidad /oðiosi'ðað/ *n. f.* odiousness; hatred.

odioso /o'ðioso/ *a.* obnoxious, odious.

odisea /oði'sea/ *n. f.* odyssey.

OEA, *abbr.* (Organización de los Estados Americanos). OAS (**Organization of American States**).

oeste /o'este/ *n. m.* west.

ofender /ofen'der/ *v.* offend, wrong.

ofenderse /ofen'derse/ *v.* be offended, take offense.

ofensa /o'fensa/ *n. f.* offense.

ofensiva /ofen'siβa/ *n. f.* offensive.

ofensivo /ofen'siβo/ *a.* offensive.

ofensor /ofen'sor/ -**ra** *a.* offender.

oferta /o'ferta/ *n. f.* offer, proposal.

ofertorio /ofer'torio/ *n. m.* offertory.

oficial /ofi'θial; ofi'sial/ *a. & m.* official; officer.

oficialmente /ofiθial'mente; ofisial'mente/ *adv.* officially.

oficiar /ofi'θiar; ofi'siar/ *v.* officiate.

oficina /ofi'θina; ofi'sina/ *n. f.* office.

oficio /o'fiθio; o'fisio/ *n. m.* office; trade; church service.

oficioso /ofi'θioso; ofi'sioso/ *a.* officious.

ofrecer /ofre'θer; ofre'ser/ *v.* offer.

ofrecimiento /ofreθi'miento; ofresi'miento/ *n. m.* offer, offering. **o. de presentación,** introductory offer.

ofrenda /o'frenda/ *n. f.* offering.

oftalmía /oftal'mia/ *n. f.* ophthalmia.

ofuscamiento /ofuska'miento/ *n. m.* obfuscation; bewilderment.

ofuscar /ofus'kar/ *v.* obfuscate; bewilder.

ogro /'ogro/ *n. m.* ogre.

oído /o'iðo/ *n. m.* ear; hearing.

oír /o'ir/ *v.* hear; listen.

ojal /o'hal/ *n. m.* buttonhole.

ojalá /oha'la/ *interj.* expressing wish or hope. **o. que...** would that.

ojeada /ohe'aða/ *n. f.* glance; peep; look.

ojear /ohe'ar/ *v.* eye, look at, glance at, stare at.

ojeriza /ohe'riθa; ohe'risa/ *n. f.* spite; grudge.

ojiva /o'hiβa/ *n. f.* pointed arch, ogive.

ojo /'oho/ *n. m.* eye. **¡Ojo!** Look out!

ola /'ola/ *n. f.* wave.

olaje /o'lahe/ *n. m.* surge of waves.

oleada /ole'aða/ *n. f.* swell.

óleo /'oleo/ *n. m.* oil; holy oil; extreme unction.

oleoducto /oleo'ðukto/ *n. m.* pipeline.

oleomargarina /oleomarga'rina/ n. f. oleomargarine.

oleoso /ole'oso/ a. oily.

oler /o'ler/ v. smell.

olfatear /olfate'ar/ v. smell.

olfato /ol'fato/ n. m. scent, smell.

oliva /o'liβa/ n. f. olive.

olivar /oli'βar/ n. m. olive grove.

olivo /o'liβo/ n. m. olive tree.

olla /'oλa; 'oya/ n. f. pot, kettle. **o. podrida**, stew.

olmo /'olmo/ n. m. elm.

olor /o'lor/ n. m. odor, smell, scent.

oloroso /olo'roso/ a. fragrant, scented.

olvidadizo /olβiδa'δiθo; olβiδa-'δiso/ a. forgetful.

olvidar /olβi'δar/ v. forget.

olvido /ol'βiδo/ n. m. omission; forgetfulness.

ombligo /om'βligo/ n. m. navel.

ominar /omi'nar/ v. foretell.

ominoso /omi'noso/ a. ominous.

omisión /omi'sion/ n. f. omission.

omitir /omi'tir/ v. omit, leave out.

ómnibus /'omniβus/ n. m. bus.

omnipotencia /omnipo'tenθia; omnipo'tensia/ n. f. omnipotence.

omnipotente /omnipo'tente/ a. almighty.

omnipresencia /omnipre'senθia; omnipre'sensia/ n. f. omnipresence.

omnisciencia /omnis'θienθia; omnis'siensia/ n. f. omniscience.

omnívoro /om'niβoro/ a. omnivorous.

omóplato /omo'plato/ n. m. shoulder blade.

once /'onθe; 'onse/ a. & pron. eleven.

onda /'onda/ n. f. wave, ripple.

ondear /onde'ar/ v. ripple.

ondulación /ondula'θion; ondula-'sion/ n. f. wave, undulation.

ondular /ondu'lar/ v. undulate, ripple.

onza /'onθa; 'onsa/ n. f. ounce.

opaco /o'pako/ a. opaque.

ópalo /'opalo/ n. m. opal.

opción /op'θion; op'sion/ n. f. option.

ópera /'opera/ n. f. opera.

operación /opera'θion; opera'sion/ n. f. operation.

operar /ope'rar/ v. operate; operate on.

operario /ope'rario/ **-ria** n. operator; (skilled) worker.

operarse /ope'rarse/ v. have an operation.

operativo /opera'tiβo/ a. operative.

opereta /ope'reta/ n. f. operetta.

opiato /o'piato/ n. m. opiate.

opinar /opi'nar/ v. opine.

opinión /opi'nion/ n. f. opinion, view.

opio /'opio/ n. m. opium.

oponer /opo'ner/ v. oppose.

Oporto /o'porto/ n. m. port (wine).

oportunidad /oportuni'δaδ/ n. f. opportunity.

oportunismo /oportu'nismo/ n. m. opportunism.

oportunista /oportu'nista/ n. & a. opportunist.

oportuno /opor'tuno/ a. opportune, expedient.

oposición /oposi'θion; oposi'sion/ n. f. opposition.

opresión /opre'sion/ n. f. oppression.

opresivo /opre'siβo/ a. oppressive.

oprimir /opri'mir/ v. oppress.

oprobio /o'proβio/ n. m. infamy.

optar /op'tar/ v. select, choose.

óptica /'optika/ n. f. optics.

óptico /'optiko/ a. optic.

optimismo /opti'mismo/ n. m. optimism.

optimista /opti'mista/ a. & n. optimistic; optimist.

óptimo /'optimo/ a. best.

opuesto /o'puesto/ a. opposite; opposed.

opugnar /opug'nar/ v. attack.

opulencia /opu'lenθia; opu'lensia/ n. f. opulence, wealth.

opulento /opu'lento/ a. opulent, wealthy.

oración /ora'θion; ora'sion/ n. f. sentence; prayer; oration.

oráculo /o'rakulo/ n. m. oracle.

orador /ora'δor/ **-ra** n. orator, speaker.

oral /o'ral/ a. oral.

orangután /orangu'tan/ n. m. orangutan.

orar /o'rar/ v. pray.

oratoria /ora'toria/ n. f. oratory.

oratorio /ora'torio/ a. oratorical.

orbe /'orβe/ n. m. orb; globe.

órbita /'orβita/ n. f. orbit.

orden /'orδen/ n. m. order.

ordenador /orδena'δor/ n. m. computer; regulator.

ordenador de sobremesa /orðena'ðor de soβre'mesa/ desktop computer.

ordenador doméstico /ordena-'ðor do'mestiko/ home computer.

ordenanza /orðe'nanθa; orðe-'nansa/ n. f. ordinance.

ordenar /orðe'nar/ v. order; put in order; ordain.

ordeñar /orðe'ɲar/ v. milk.

ordinal /orði'nal/ a. & m. ordinal.

ordinario /orði'nario/ a. ordinary; common, usual.

oreja /o'reha/ n. f. ear.

orejera /ore'hera/ n. f. earmuff.

orfanato /orfa'nato/ n. m. orphanage.

organdí /organ'di/ n. m. organdy.

orgánico /or'ganiko/ a. organic.

organigrama /organi'grama/ n. m. flow chart.

organismo /orga'nismo/ n. m. organism.

organista /orga'nista/ n. m. & f. organist.

organización /organiθa'θion; organisa'sion/ n. f. organization.

organizar /organi'θar; organi'sar/ v. organize.

órgano /'organo/ n. m. organ.

orgía /or'hia/ n. f. orgy, revel.

orgullo /or'guʎo; or'guyo/ n. m. pride.

orgulloso /orgu'ʎoso; orgu'yoso/ a. proud.

orientación /orienta'θion; orienta'sion/ n. f. orientation.

oriental /orien'tal/ a. Oriental; eastern.

orientar /orien'tar/ v. orient.

oriente /o'riente/ n. m. orient, east.

orificación /orifika'θion; orifika'sion/ n. f. gold filling (for tooth).

origen /o'rihen/ n. m. origin; parentage, descent.

original /orihi'nal/ a. original.

originalidad /orihinali'ðað/ n. f. originality.

originalmente /orihinal'mente/ adv. originally.

originar /orihi'nar/ v. originate.

orilla /o'riʎa; o'riya/ n. f. shore; bank; edge.

orín /o'rin/ n. m. rust.

orina /o'rina/ n. f. urine.

orinar /ori'nar/ v. urinate.

orines /o'rines/ n. m.pl. urine.

oriol /o'riol/ n. m. oriole.

orla /'orla/ n. f. border; edging.

ornado /or'naðo/ a. ornate.

ornamentación /ornamenta'θion; ornamenta'sion/ n. f. ornamentation.

ornamento /orna'mento/ n. m. ornament. **—ornamentar,** v.

ornar /or'nar/ v. ornament, adorn.

oro /'oro/ n. m. gold.

oropel /oro'pel/ n. m. tinsel.

orquesta /or'kesta/ n. f. orchestra.

ortiga /or'tiga/ n. f. nettle.

ortodoxo /orto'ðokso/ a. orthodox.

ortografía /ortogra'fia/ n. f. orthography, spelling.

ortóptero /or'toptero/ a. orthopterous.

oruga /o'ruga/ n. f. caterpillar.

orzuelo /or'θuelo; or'suelo/ n. m. sty.

os /os/ pron. you (pl.); yourselves.

osadía /osa'ðia/ n. f. daring.

osar /o'sar/ v. dare.

oscilación /osθila'θion; ossila'sion/ n. f. oscillation.

oscilar /osθi'lar; ossi'lar/ v. oscillate, rock.

ósculo /'oskulo/ n. m. kiss.

oscurecer /oskure'θer; oskure'ser/ v. obscure. **oscuridad,** n. obscurity; darkness. **oscuro,** adj. obscure; dark.

oso /'oso/ osa n. f. bear.

oso de felpa /'oso de 'felpa/ teddy bear.

ostentación /ostenta'θion; ostenta'sion/ n. f. ostentation, showiness.

ostentar /osten'tar/ v. show off.

ostentoso /osten'toso/ a. ostentatious, flashy.

ostra /'ostra/ n. f. oyster.

ostracismo /ostra'θismo; ostra-'sismo/ n. m. ostracism.

otalgia /o'talhia/ n. f. earache.

otero /o'tero/ n. m. hill, knoll.

otoño /o'toɲo/ n. m. autumn, fall.

otorgar /otor'gar/ v. grant, award.

otro /'otro/ a. & pron. other, another. **o. vez,** again. **el uno al o.,** one another, each other.

ovación /oβa'θion; oβa'sion/ n. f. ovation.

oval /o'βal/ **ovalado** a. oval.

óvalo /'oβalo/ n. m. oval.

ovario /o'βario/ n. m. ovary.

oveja /o'βeha/ n. f. sheep.

ovejero /oβe'hero/ n. m. sheep dog.

ovillo /o'βiʎo; o'βiyo/ n. m. ball of yarn.

OVNI /'oβni/ abbr. (objeto volador no identificado) UFO (unidentified flying object).

oxidación /oksiða'θion; oksiða-'sion/ n. f. oxidation.

oxidar /oksi'ðar/ v. oxidize; rust.

óxido /'oksiðo/ n. m. oxide.

oxígeno /ok'siheno/ n. m. oxygen.

oyente /o'iente/ n. m. & f. hearer; (pl.) audience.

ozono /o'θono; o'sono/ n. m. ozone.

P

pabellón /paβe'ʎon; paβe'yon/ n. m. pavilion. **p. de deportes,** sports center.

pabilo /pa'βilo/ n. m. wick.

paciencia /pa'θienθia; pa'siensia/ n. f. patience.

paciente /pa'θiente; pa'siente/ a. & n. patient.

pacificar /paθifi'kar; pasifi'kar/ v. pacify.

pacífico /pa'θifiko; pa'sifiko/ a. pacific.

pacifismo /paθi'fismo; pasi'fismo/ n. m. pacifism.

pacifista /paθi'fista; pasi'fista/ n. & a. pacifist.

pacto /'pakto/ n. m. pact, treaty.

padecer /paðe'θer; paðe'ser/ v. suffer. **p. del corazón,** have heart trouble.

padrastro /pa'ðrastro/ n. m. stepfather.

padre /'paðre/ n. m. father; priest; (pl.) parents.

padrenuestro /paðre'nuestro/ n. m. paternoster, Lord's Prayer.

padrino /pa'ðrino/ n. m. godfather; sponsor.

paella /pa'eʎa; pa'eya/ n. f. dish of rice with meat or chicken.

paga /'paɣa/ n. f. pay, wages. **p. extra,** bonus.

pagadero /paɣa'ðero/ a. payable.

pagador /paɣa'ðor/ -ra n. payer.

paganismo /paɣa'nismo/ n. m. paganism.

pagano /pa'ɣano/ -na a. & n. heathen, pagan.

pagar /pa'ɣar/ v. pay, pay for. **p. en metálico,** pay cash.

página /'pahina/ n. f. page.

pago /'paɣo/ n. m. pay, payment.

país /pa'is/ n. m. country, nation.

paisaje /pai'sahe/ n. m. landscape, scenery, countryside.

paisano /pai'sano/ -na n. countryman; compatriot; civilian.

paja /'paha/ n. f. straw.

pajar /pa'har/ n. m. barn.

pajarita /paha'rita/ n. f. bow tie.

pájaro /'paharo/ n. m. bird.

paje /pahe/ n. m. page (person).

pala /'pala/ n. f. shovel, spade.

palabra /pa'laβra/ n. f. word.

palabrero /pala'βrero/ a. talkative; wordy.

palabrista /pala'βrista/ n. m. & f. talkative person.

palacio /pa'laθio; pa'lasio/ n. m. palace.

paladar /pala'ðar/ n. m. palate.

paladear /palaðe'ar/ v. taste; relish.

palanca /pa'lanka/ n. f. lever. **p. de cambio,** gearshift.

palangana /palaŋ'gana/ n. f. washbasin.

palco /'palko/ n. m. theater box.

palenque /pa'lenke/ n. m. palisade.

paleta /pa'leta/ n. f. mat, pallet.

paletilla /pale'tiʎa; pale'tiya/ n. f. shoulder blade.

palidecer /paliðe'θer; paliðe'ser/ v. turn pale.

palidez /pali'ðeθ; pali'ðes/ n. f. paleness.

pálido /'paliðo/ a. pale.

paliza /pa'liθa; pa'lisa/ n. f. beating.

palizada /pali'θaða; pali'saða/ n. m. palisade.

palma /'palma/ **palmera** n. f. palm (tree).

palmada /pal'maða/ n. f. slap, clap.

palmear /palme'ar/ v. applaud.

palo /'palo/ n. m. pole, stick; suit (in cards); Naut. mast.

paloma /pa'loma/ n. f. dove, pigeon.

palpar /pal'par/ v. touch, feel.

palpitación /palpita'θion; palpita-'sion/ n. f. palpitation.

palpitar /palpi'tar/ v. palpitate.

paludismo /palu'ðismo/ n. m. malaria.

pampa /'pampa/ n. f. (S.A.) prairie, plain.

pan /pan/ n. m. bread; loaf. **p. de centeno,** rye bread.

pana /'pana/ n. f. corduroy.

panacea /pana'θea; pana'sea/ n. f. panacea.

panadería /panaðe'ria/ n. f. bakery.

panadero /pana'ðero/ **-ra** n. baker.

panameño /pana'meɲo/ **-ña** a. & n. Panamanian, of Panama.

panamericano /panameri'kano/ a. Pan-American.

páncreas /'pankreas/ n. m. pancreas.

pandeo /pan'deo/ n. m. bulge.

pandilla /pan'diʎa; pan'diya/ n. f. band, gang.

panecillo /pane'θiʎo; pane'siyo/ n. m. roll, muffin.

panegírico /pane'hiriko/ n. m. panegyric.

pánico /'paniko/ n. m. panic.

panocha /pa'notʃa/ n. f. ear of corn.

panorama /pano'rama/ n. m. panorama.

panorámico /pano'ramiko/ a. panoramic.

pantalla /pan'taʎa; pan'taya/ n. f. (movie) screen; lamp shade.

pantalones /panta'lones/ n. m.pl. trousers, pants.

pántano /'pantano/ n. m. bog, marsh, swamp.

pantanoso /panta'noso/ a. swampy, marshy.

pantera /pan'tera/ n. f. panther.

pantomima /panto'mima/ n. f. pantomime.

pantorrilla /panto'rriʎa; panto-'rriya/ n. f. calf (of body).

panza /'panθa; 'pansa/ n. f. belly, paunch.

pañal /pa'ɲal/ n. m. diaper.

paño /'paɲo/ n. m. piece of cloth.

pañuelo /pa'ɲuelo/ n. m. handkerchief.

Papa /'papa/ n. m. Pope.

papa n. f. potato.

papá n. m. papa, father.

papagayo /papa'gaio/ n. m. parrot.

papal /pa'pal/ a. papal.

Papá Noel /pa'pa no'el/ n. m. Santa Claus.

papel /pa'pel/ n. m. paper; role, part.

papel crespón /pa'pel kres'pon/ crepe paper.

papel de aluminio /pa'pel de alu'minio/ aluminum foil.

papel de escribir /pa'pel de es-kri'βir/ writing paper.

papel de estaño /pa'pel de es'taɲo/ tin foil.

papel de lija /pa'pel de 'liha/ sandpaper.

papelera /pape'lera/ n. f. file cabinet; wastepaper basket.

papelería /papele'ria/ n. f. stationery store.

papel moneda /pa'pel mo'neða/ paper money.

paperas /pa'peras/ n. f.pl. mumps.

paquete /pa'kete/ n. m. package.

par /par/ a. **1.** even, equal. —n. **2.** m. pair; equal, peer. **abierto de p. en p.,** wide open.

para /'para/ prep. for; in order to. **p. que,** in order that. **estar p.,** to be about to.

parabién /para'βien/ n. m. congratulation.

parabrisa /para'βrisa/ n. f. windshield.

paracaídas /paraka'iðas/ n. m. parachute.

parachoques /para'tʃokes/ n. m. Auto. bumper.

parada /pa'raða/ n. f. stop, halt; stopover; parade.

paradero /para'ðero/ n. m. whereabouts; stopping place.

paradigma /para'ðigma/ n. m. paradigm.

paradoja /para'ðoha/ n. f. paradox.

parafina /para'fina/ n. f. paraffin.

parafrasear /parafrase'ar/ v. paraphrase.

paraguas /pa'raguas/ n. m. umbrella.

paraguayano /paragua'yano/ **-na** n. & a. Paraguayan.

paraíso /para'iso/ n. m. paradise.

paralelo /para'lelo/ a. & m. parallel.

parálisis /pa'ralisis/ n. f. paralysis.

paralizar /parali'θar; parali'sar/ v. paralyze.

paramédico /para'meðiko/ n. m. paramedic.

parámetro /pa'rametro/ n. m. parameter.

parapeto /para'peto/ n. m. parapet.

parar /pa'rar/ v. stop, stem, ward off; stay.

pararse /pa'rarse/ v. stop; stand up.

parasítico /para'sitiko/ a. parasitic.

parásito /pa'rasito/ n. m. parasite.

parcela /par'θela; par'sela/ n. f. plot of ground.

parcial /par'θial; par'sial/ a. partial.

parcialidad /parθiali'ðað; parsiali'ðað/ n. f. partiality; bias.

parcialmente /parθial'mente; parsial'mente/ adv. partially.

pardo /'parðo/ a. brown.

parear /pare'ar/ v. pair; match; mate.

parecer /pare'θer; pare'ser/ v. **1.** m. opinion. —v. **2.** seem, appear, look.

parecerse /pare'θerse; pare'serse/ v. look alike. **p. a,** look like.

parecido /pare'θiðo; pare'siðo/ a. similar.

pared /pa'reð/ n. f. wall.

pareja /pa'reha/ n. f. pair, couple; (dancing) partner.

parentela /paren'tela/ n. f. kinfolk.

parentesco /paren'tesko/ n. m. parentage, lineage; kin.

paréntesis /pa'rentesis/ n. m. parenthesis.

paria /'paria/ n. m. outcast, pariah.

participante /pariθi'pante; parisi'pante/ n. & f. participant.

paridad /pari'ðað/ n. f. parity.

pariente /pa'riente/ n. m. & f. relative.

parir /pa'rir/ v. give birth.

parisiense /pari'siense/ n. & a. Parisian.

parlamentario /parlamen'tario/ a. parliamentary.

parlamento /parla'mento/ n. m. parliament.

paro /'paro/ n. m. stoppage; strike. **p. forzoso,** unemployment.

parodia /pa'roðia/ n. f. parody.

parodista /paro'ðista/ n. m. & f. parodist.

paroxismo /parok'sismo/ n. m. paroxysm.

párpado /'parpaðo/ n. m. eyelid.

parque /'parke/ n. m. park.

parquímetro /par'kimetro/ n. m. parking meter.

parra /'parra/ n. f. grapevine.

párrafo /'parrafo/ n. m. paragraph.

parranda /pa'rranda/ n. f. spree.

parrandear /parrande'ar/ v. carouse.

parrilla /pa'rriʎa; pa'rriya/ n. f. grill; grillroom.

párroco /'parroko/ n. m. parish priest.

parroquia /pa'rrokia/ n. f. parish.

parroquial /parro'kial/ a. parochial.

parsimonia /parsi'monia/ n. f. economy, thrift.

parsimonioso /parsimo'nioso/ a. economical, thrifty.

parte /'parte/ n. f. part. **de p. de,** on behalf of. **alguna p.,** somewhere. **por otra p.,** on the other hand. **dar p. a,** to notify.

partera /par'tera/ n. f. midwife.

partición /parti'θion; parti'sion/ n. f. distribution.

participación /partiθipa'θion; partisipa'sion/ n. f. participation.

participar /partiθi'par; partisi'par/ v. participate; announce.

participio /parti'θipio; parti'sipio/ n. m. participle.

partícula /par'tikula/ n. f. particle.

particular /partiku'lar/ a. **1.** particular; private. —n. **2.** m. particular; detail; individual.

particularmente /partikular'mente/ adv. particularly.

partida /par'tiða/ n. f. departure; Mil. party; (sport) game.

partida de defunción /par'tiða de defun'θion; par'tiða de defun'sion/ death certificate.

partida de matrimonio /par'tiða de matri'monio/ marriage certificate.

partida de nacimiento /par'tiða de naθi'miento; par'tiða de nasi'miento/ birth certificate.

partidario /parti'ðario/ -ria n. partisan.

partido /par'tiðo/ n. m. side, party, faction; game, match.

partir /par'tir/ v. leave, depart; part, cleave, split.

parto /'parto/ n. m. delivery, childbirth.

pasa /'pasa/ n. f. raisin.

pasado /pa'saðo/ *a.* **1.** past; last. —*n.* **2.** *m.* past.

pasaje /pa'sahe/ *n. m.* passage, fare.

pasajero /pasa'hero/ **-ra** *a.* **1.** passing, transient. —*n.* **2.** passenger.

pasamano /pasa'mano/ *n. m.* banister.

pasaporte /pasa'porte/ *n. m.* passport.

pasar /pa'sar/ *v.* pass; happen; spend (time). **p. por alto,** overlook. **p. lista,** call the roll. **p. sin,** do without.

pasatiempo /pasa'tiempo/ *n. m.* pastime; hobby.

pascua /'paskua/ *n. f.* religious holiday; (*pl.*) Christmas (season). **P. Florida,** Easter.

pase de modelos /'pase de mo'ðelos/ *n. m.* fashion show.

paseo /pa'seo/ *n. m.* walk, stroll; drive. —**pasear,** *v.*

pasillo /pa'siʎo; pa'siyo/ *n. m.* aisle; hallway.

pasión /pa'sion/ *n. f.* passion.

pasivo /pa'siβo/ *a.* passive.

pasmar /pas'mar/ *v.* astonish, astound, stun.

pasmo /'pasmo/ *n. m.* spasm; wonder.

paso /'paso/ *a.* **1.** dried (fruit). —*n.* **2.** *m.* pace, step; (mountain) pass.

paso cebra /'paso 'θeβra; 'paso 'seβra/ crosswalk.

paso de ganso /'paso de 'ganso/ goose step.

paso de peatones /'paso de pea'tones/ pedestrian crossing.

pasta /'pasta/ *n. f.* paste; batter; plastic.

pasta dentífrica /'pasta den'tifrika/ toothpaste.

pastar /pas'tar/ *v.* graze.

pastel /pas'tel/ *n. m.* pastry; pie.

pastelería /pastele'ria/ *n. f.* pastry; pastry shop.

pasteurización /pasteuriθa'θion; pasteurisa'sion/ *n. f.* pasteurization.

pasteurizar /pasteuri'θar; pasteuri'sar/ *v.* pasteurize.

pastilla /pas'tiʎa; pas'tiya/ *n. f.* tablet, lozenge, coughdrop.

pasto /'pasto/ *n. m.* pasture; grass.

pastor /pas'tor/ *n. m.* pastor; shepherd.

pastorear /pastore'ar/ *v.* pasture, tend (a flock).

pastrón /pas'tron/ *n. m.* pastrami.

pastura /pas'tura/ *n. f.* pasture.

pata /'pata/ *n. f.* foot (of animal).

patada /pa'taða/ *n. f.* kick.

patán /pa'tan/ *n. m.* boor.

patanada /pata'naða/ *n. f.* rudeness.

patata /pa'tata/ *n. f.* potato. **p. asada,** baked potato.

patear /pate'ar/ *v.* stamp, tramp, kick.

patente /pa'tente/ *a. & m.* patent. —**patentar,** *v.*

paternal /pater'nal/ **paterno** *a.* paternal.

paternidad /paterni'ðað/ *n. f.* paternity, fatherhood.

patético /pa'tetiko/ *a.* pathetic.

patíbulo /pa'tiβulo/ *n. m.* scaffold; gallows.

patín /pa'tin/ *n. m.* skate. —**patinar,** *v.*

patín de ruedas /pa'tin de 'rrueðas/ roller skate.

patio /'patio/ *n. m.* yard, court, patio.

pato /'pato/ *n. m.* duck.

patria /'patria/ *n. f.* native land.

patriarca /pa'triarka/ *n. m. & f.* patriarch.

patrimonio /patri'monio/ *n. m.* inheritance.

patriota /pa'triota/ *n. m. & f.* patriot.

patriótico /pa'triotiko/ *a.* patriotic.

patriotismo /patrio'tismo/ *n. m.* patriotism.

patrocinar /patroθi'nar; patrosi'nar/ *v.* patronize, sponsor.

patrón /pa'tron/ **-ona** *n.* patron; boss; (dress) pattern.

patrulla /pa'truʎa; pa'truya/ *n. f.* patrol. —**patrullar,** *v.*

paulatino /paula'tino/ *a.* gradual.

pausa /'pausa/ *n. f.* pause. —**pausar,** *v.*

pausa para el café /'pausa 'para el ka'fe/ coffee break.

pauta /'pauta/ *n. f.* guideline.

pavesa /pa'βesa/ *n. f.* spark, cinder.

pavimentar /paβimen'tar/ *v.* pave.

pavimento /paβi'mento/ *n. m.* pavement.

pavo /'paβo/ *n. m.* turkey. **p. real,** peacock.

pavor /pa'βor/ n. m. terror.

payaso /pa'iaso/ **-sa** n. clown.

paz /paθ/ pas/ n. f. peace.

peatón /pea'ton/ **-na** n. pedestrian.

peca /'peka/ n. f. freckle.

pecado /pe'kaðo/ n. m. sin. —**pecar,** v.

pecador /peka'ðor/ **-ra** a. & n. sinful; sinner.

pecera /pe'θera/ n. f. aquarium, fishbowl.

pechera /pe'tʃera/ n. f. shirt front.

pecho /'petʃo/ n. m. chest; breast; bosom.

pechuga /pe'tʃuga/ n. f. breast (of fowl).

pecoso /pe'koso/ a. freckled, freckly.

peculiar /peku'liar/ a. peculiar.

peculiaridad /pekuliari'ðað/ n. f. peculiarity.

pedagogía /peðago'hia/ n. f. pedagogy.

pedagogo /peða'gogo/ **-ga** n. pedagogue, teacher.

pedal /pe'ðal/ n. m. pedal.

pedantesco /peðan'tesko/ a. pedantic.

pedazo /pe'ðaθo/ n. m. piece.

pedernal /peðer'nal/ n. m. flint.

pedestal /peðes'tal/ n. m. pedestal.

pediatra /pe'ðiatra/ n. m. & f. pediatrician.

pediatría /peðia'tria/ n. f. pediatrics.

pedicuro /peði'kuro/ n. m. chiropodist.

pedir /pe'ðir/ v. ask, ask for, request; apply for; order.

pedo /'peðo/ n. m. fart; intoxication.

pedregoso /peðre'goso/ a. rocky.

pegajoso /pega'hoso/ a. sticky.

pegamento /pega'mento/ n. m. glue.

pegar /pe'gar/ v. beat, strike; adhere, fasten, stick.

peinado /pei'naðo/ n. m. coiffure, hairdo.

peine /'peine/ n. m. comb. —**peinar,** v.

peineta /pei'neta/ n. f. (ornamental) comb.

pelagra /pe'lagra/ n. f. pellagra.

pelar /pe'lar/ v. skin, pare, peel.

pelea /pe'lea/ n. f. fight, row. —**pelearse,** v.

pelícano /pe'likano/ n. m. pelican.

película /pe'likula/ n. f. movie, motion picture, film. **p. de terror** horror film.

peligrar /peli'grar/ v. be in danger.

peligro /pe'ligro/ n. m. peril, danger.

peligroso /peli'groso/ a. perilous, dangerous.

pelirrojo /peli'rroho/ **-ja** a. & n. redhead.

pellejo /pe'ʎeho/ n. m. skin; peel (of fruit).

pellizco /pe'ʎiθko/ n. m. pinch. —**pellizcar,** v.

pelo /'pelo/ n. m. hair.

pelota /pe'lota/ n. f. ball.

peltre /'peltre/ n. m. pewter.

peluca /pe'luka/ n. f. wig.

peludo /pe'luðo/ a. hairy.

peluquería /peluke'ria/ n. f. hairdresser's shop, beauty parlor.

peluquero /pelu'kero/ **-ra** n. hairdresser.

pena /'pena/ n. f. pain, grief, trouble, woe; penalty. **valer la p.,** to be worthwhile.

penacho /pe'natʃo/ n. m. plume.

penalidad /penali'ðað/ n. f. trouble; penalty.

pender /pen'der/ v. hang, dangle; be pending.

pendiente /pen'diente/ a. **1.** hanging; pending. —n. **2.** m. incline, slope; earring; pendant.

pendón /pen'don/ n. m. pennant, flag.

penetración /penetra'θion/ penetra'sion/ n. f. penetration.

penetrar /pene'trar/ v. penetrate, pierce.

penicilina /peniθi'lina/ penisi'lina/ n. f. penicillin.

península /pe'ninsula/ n. f. peninsula.

penitencia /peni'tenθia/ peni'tensia/ n. f. penitence, penance.

penitenciaría /penitenθia'ria/ penitensia'ria/ n. f. penitentiary.

penoso /pe'noso/ a. painful, troublesome, grievous, distressing.

pensador /pensa'ðor/ **-ra** n. thinker.

pensamiento /pensa'miento/ n. m. thought.

pensar /pen'sar/ v. think; intend, plan.

pensativo /pensa'tiβo/ a. pensive, thoughtful.

pensión /pen'sion/ n. f. pension; boardinghouse.

pensionista /pensio'nista/ n. m. & f. boarder.

pentagonal /pentago'nal/ a. pentagonal.

penúltimo /pe'nultimo/ a. next-to-the-last, last but one, penultimate.

penuria /pe'nuria/ n. f. penury, poverty.

peña /'peɲa/ n. f. rock.

peñascoso /peɲas'koso/ a. rocky.

peñón /pe'ɲon/ n. m. rock, crag. **Peñón de Gibraltar** /pe'ɲon de hiβral'tar/ Rock of Gibraltar.

peón /pe'on/ n. m. unskilled laborer; infantryman.

peonada /peo'naða/ n. f. group of laborers.

peonía /peo'nia/ n. f. peony.

peor /pe'or/ a. worse, worst.

pepino /pe'pino/ n. m. cucumber.

pepita /pe'pita/ n. f. seed (in fruit).

pequeñez /peke'ɲeθ; peke'ɲes/ n. f. smallness; trifle.

pequeño /pe'keɲo/ **-ña** a. **1.** small, little, short, slight. —n. **2.** child.

pera /'pera/ n. f. pear.

peral /pe'ral/ n. m. pear tree.

perca /'perka/ n. f. perch (fish).

percal /per'kal/ n. m. calico, percale.

percance /per'kanθe; per'kanse/ n. m. mishap, snag, hitch.

percepción /perθep'θion; persep'sion/ n. f. perception.

perceptivo /perθep'tiβo; persep'tiβo/ a. perceptive.

percha /'pertʃa/ n. f. perch; clothes hanger, rack.

percibir /perθi'βir; persi'βir/ v. perceive, sense; collect.

perder /per'ðer/ v. lose; miss; waste. **echar a p.,** spoil. **p. el conocimiento,** lose consciousness.

perdición /perði'θion; perði'sion/ n. f. perdition, downfall.

pérdida /'perðiða/ n. f. loss.

perdiz /per'ðiθ; per'ðis/ n. f. partridge.

perdón /per'ðon/ n. m. pardon, forgiveness.

perdonar /perðo'nar/ v. forgive, pardon; spare.

perdurable /perðu'raβle/ a. enduring, everlasting.

perdurar /perðu'rar/ v. endure, last.

perecedero /pereθe'ðero; perese'ðero/ a. perishable.

perecer /pere'θer; pere'ser/ v. perish.

peregrinación /peregrina'θion; peregrina'sion/ n. f. peregrination; pilgrimage.

peregrino /pere'grino/ **-na** n. pilgrim.

perejil /pere'hil/ n. m. parsley.

perenne /pe'renne/ a. perennial.

pereza /pe'reθa; pe'resa/ n. f. laziness.

perezoso /pere'θoso; pere'soso/ a. lazy, sluggish.

perfección /perfek'θion; perfek'sion/ n. f. perfection.

perfeccionar /perfekθio'nar; perfeksio'nar/ v. perfect.

perfeccionista /perfekθio'nista; perfeksio'nista/ a. & n. perfectionist.

perfectamente /perfekta'mente/ adv. perfectly.

perfecto /per'fekto/ a. perfect.

perfidia /per'fiðia/ n. f. falseness, perfidy.

pérfido /'perfiðo/ a. perfidious.

perfil /per'fil/ n. m. profile.

perforación /perfora'θion; perfora'sion/ n. f. perforation.

perforar /perfo'rar/ v. pierce, perforate.

perfume /per'fume/ n. m. perfume, scent. —**perfumar,** v.

pergamino /perga'mino/ n. m. parchment.

pericia /pe'riθia/ n. f. skill, expertness.

perico /pe'riko/ n. m. parakeet.

perímetro /pe'rimetro/ n. m. perimeter.

periódico /pe'rioðiko/ a. **1.** periodic. —n. **2.** m. newspaper.

periodista /perio'ðista/ n. m. & f. journalist.

período /pe'rioðo/ n. m. period.

periscopio /peris'kopio/ n. m. periscope.

perito /pe'rito/ **-ta** a. & n. experienced; expert, connoisseur.

perjudicar /perhuði'kar/ v. damage, hurt; impair.

perjudicial /perhuði'θial; perhuði'sial/ a. harmful, injurious.

perjuicio /per'huiθio; per'huisio/ *n. m.* injury, damage.

perjurar /perhu'rar/ *v.* commit perjury.

perjurio /per'hurio/ *n. m.* perjury.

perla /'perla/ *n. f.* pearl.

permanecer /permane'θer; permane'ser/ *v.* remain, stay.

permanencia /perma'nenθia; perma'nensia/ *n. f.* permanence; stay.

permanente /perma'nente/ *a.* permanent.

permiso /per'miso/ *n. m.* permission; permit; furlough.

permitir /permi'tir/ *v.* permit, enable, let, allow.

permuta /per'muta/ *n. f.* exchange, barter.

pernicioso /perni'θioso; perni'sioso/ *a.* pernicious.

perno /'perno/ *n. m.* bolt.

pero /'pero/ *conj.* but.

peróxido /pe'roksiðo/ *n. m.* peroxide.

perpendicular /perpendiku'lar/ *n. m. & a.* perpendicular.

perpetración /perpetra'θion; perpetra'sion/ *n. f.* perpetration.

perpetrar /perpe'trar/ *v.* perpetrate.

perpetuar /perpe'tuar/ *v.* perpetuate.

perpetuidad /perpetui'ðað/ *n. f.* perpetuity.

perpetuo /per'petuo/ *a.* perpetual.

perplejo /per'pleho/ *a.* perplexed, puzzled.

perrito caliente /pe'rrito ka'liente/ *n. m.* hot dog.

perro /'perro/ **-rra** *n.* dog.

persecución /perseku'θion; perseku'sion/ *n. f.* persecution.

perseguir /perse'gir/ *v.* pursue, persecute.

perseverancia /perseβe'ranθia; perseβe'ransia/ *n. f.* perseverance.

perseverar /perseβe'rar/ *v.* persevere.

persiana /per'siana/ *n. f.* shutter, Venetian blind.

persistente /persis'tente/ *a.* persistent.

persistir /persis'tir/ *v.* persist.

persona /per'sona/ *n. f.* person.

personaje /perso'nahe/ *n. m.* personage; *Theat.* character.

personal /perso'nal/ *a.* **1.** personal. —*n.* **2.** *m.* personnel, staff.

personalidad /personali'ðað/ *n. f.* personality.

personalmente /personal'mente/ *adv.* personally.

perspectiva /perspek'tiβa/ *n. f.* perspective; prospect.

perspicaz /perspi'kaθ; perspi'kas/ *a.* perspicacious, acute.

persuadir /persua'ðir/ *v.* persuade.

persuasión /persua'sion/ *n. f.* persuasion.

persuasivo /persua'siβo/ *a.* persuasive.

pertenecer /pertene'θer; pertene'ser/ *v.* pertain; belong.

pertinencia /perti'nenθia; perti'nensia/ *n. f.* pertinence.

pertinente /perti'nente/ *a.* pertinent; relevant.

perturbar /pertur'βar/ *v.* perturb, disturb.

peruano /pe'ruano/ **-na** *a. & n.* Peruvian.

perversidad /perβersi'ðað/ *n. f.* perversity.

perverso /per'βerso/ *a.* perverse.

pesadez /pesa'ðeθ; pesa'ðes/ *n. f.* dullness.

pesadilla /pesa'ðiʎa; pesa'ðiya/ *n. f.* nightmare.

pesado /pe'saðo/ *a.* heavy; dull, dreary, boring.

pésame /'pesame/ *n. m.* condolence.

pesar /pe'sar/ *n. m.* sorrow; regret. **a p. de**, in spite of. *v.* weigh.

pesca /'peska/ *n. f.* fishing; catch (of fish).

pescadería /peskaðe'ria/ *n. f.* fish store.

pescado /pes'kaðo/ *n. m.* fish. —**pescar**, *v.*

pescador /peska'ðor/ *n. m.* fisherman.

pesebre /pe'seβre/ *n. m.* stall, manger; crib.

peseta /pe'seta/ *n. f.* peseta (monetary unit).

pesimismo /pesi'mismo/ *n. m.* pessimism.

pesimista /pesi'mista/ *a. & n.* pessimistic; pessimist.

pésimo /'pesimo/ *a.* awful, terrible, very bad.

peso /'peso/ *n. m.* weight; load; peso (monetary unit).

pesquera /pes'kera/ *n. f.* fishery.

pesquisa /pes'kisa/ n. f. investigation.

pestaña /pes'taɲa/ n. f. eyelash.

pestañeo /pesta'ɲeo/ n. m. wink, blink. —**pestañear,** v.

peste /'peste/ n. f. plague.

pesticida /pesti'θiða; pesti'siða/ n. m. pesticide.

pestilencia /pesti'lenθia; pesti'lensia/ n. f. pestilence.

pétalo /'petalo/ n. m. petal.

petardo /pe'tarðo/ n. m. firecracker.

petición /peti'θion; peti'sion/ n. f. petition.

petirrojo /peti'rroho/ n. m. robin.

petrel /pe'trel/ n. m. petrel.

pétreo /'petreo/ a. rocky.

petrificar /petrifi'kar/ v. petrify.

petróleo /pe'troleo/ n. m. petroleum.

petrolero /petro'lero/ n. m. oil tanker.

petunia /pe'tunia/ n. f. petunia.

pez /peθ; pes/ n. **1.** m. fish (in the water). —n. **2.** f. pitch, tar.

pezuña /pe'θuɲa; pe'suɲa/ n. f. hoof.

piadoso /pia'ðoso/ a. pious; merciful.

pianista /pia'nista/ n. m. & f. pianist.

piano /'piano/ n. m. piano.

picadero /pika'ðero/ n. m. riding school.

picadura /pika'ðura/ n. f. sting, bite, prick.

picamaderos /pikama'ðeros/ n. m. woodpecker.

picante /pi'kante/ a. hot, spicy.

picaporte /pika'porte/ n. m. latch.

picar /pi'kar/ v. sting, bite, prick; itch; chop up, grind up.

pícaro /'pikaro/ **-ra** a. **1.** knavish, mischievous. —n. **2.** rogue, rascal.

picarse /pi'karse/ v. be offended, piqued.

picazón /pika'θon; pika'son/ n. f. itch.

picea /'piθea; 'pisea/ n. f. spruce.

pichón /pi'tʃon/ n. m. pigeon, squab.

pico /'piko/ n. m. beak; pick; beak; spout; small amount.

picotazo /piko'taðo; piko'taso/ n. m. peck. —**picotear,** v.

pictórico /pik'toriko/ a. pictorial.

pie /pie/ n. m. foot. **al p. de la letra,** literally; thoroughly.

piedad /pie'ðað/ n. f. piety; pity; mercy.

piedra /'pieðra/ n. f. stone.

piel /piel/ n. f. skin, hide; fur.

pienso /'pienso/ n. m. fodder.

pierna /'pierna/ n. f. leg.

pieza /'pieθa; 'piesa/ n. f. piece; room; Theat. play.

pijama /pi'hama/ n. m. or m.pl. pajamas.

pila /'pila/ n. f. pile, stack; battery; sink.

pilar /pi'lar/ n. m. pillar, column.

píldora /'pildora/ n. f. pill.

pillo /'piʎo; 'piʝo/ **-a** n. thief; rascal.

piloto /pi'loto/ n. m. & f. pilot.

pimentón /pimen'ton/ n. m. paprika.

pimienta /pi'mienta/ n. f. pepper (spice).

pimiento /pi'miento/ n. m. pepper (vegetable).

pináculo /pi'nakulo/ n. m. pinnacle.

pincel /pin'θel; pin'sel/ n. m. (artist's) brush.

pinchadiscos /pintʃa'ðiskos/ m. & f. disk jockey.

pinchazo /pin'tʃaθo; pin'tʃaso/ n. m. puncture; prick. —**pinchar,** v.

pingajo /piŋ'gaho/ n. m. rag, tatter.

pino /'pino/ n. m. pine.

pinta /'pinta/ n. f. pint.

pintar /pin'tar/ v. paint; portray, depict.

pintor /pin'tor/ **-ra** n. painter.

pintoresco /pinto'resko/ a. picturesque.

pintura /pin'tura/ n. f. paint; painting.

pinzas /'pinθas; 'pinsas/ n. f.pl. pincers, tweezers; claws.

piña /'piɲa/ n. f. pineapple.

pío /'pio/ a. pious; merciful.

piojo /'pioho/ n. m. louse.

pionero /pio'nero/ **-ra** n. pioneer.

pipa /'pipa/ n. f. tobacco pipe.

pique /'pike/ n. m. resentment, pique. **echar a p.,** sink (ship).

pira /'pira/ n. f. pyre.

piragua /pi'ragua/ n. f. canoe.

piragüismo /pira'guismo/ n. m. canoeing.

piragüista /pira'guista/ n. m. canoeist.

pirámide /pi'ramiðe/ n. f. pyramid.

pirata /pi'rata/ n. m. & f. pirate.
p. de aviones, hijacker.
pisada /pi'saða/ n. f. tread, step.
—**pisar,** v.
pisapapeles /pisapa'peles/ n. m.
paperweight.
piscina /pis'θina; pis'sina/ n. f.
fishpond; swimming pool.
piso /'piso/ n. m. floor.
pista /'pista/ n. f. trace, clue,
track; racetrack.
pista de tenis /'pista de 'tenis/
tennis court.
pistola /pis'tola/ n. f. pistol.
pistón /pis'ton/ n. m. piston.
pitillo /pi'tiλo; pi'tiyo/ n. m. cigarette.
pito /'pito/ n. m. whistle. —**pitar,**
v.
pizarra /pi'θarra; pi'sarra/ n. f.
slate; blackboard.
pizca /'piθka; 'piska/ n. f. bit,
speck; pinch.
pizza /'piθθa; 'pissa/ n. f. pizza.
placentero /plaθen'tero; plasen-
'tero/ a. pleasant.
placer /pla'θer; pla'ser/ n. **1.** m.
pleasure. —v. **2.** please.
plácido /'plaθiðo; 'plasiðo/ a.
placid.
plaga /'plaga/ n. f. plague,
scourge.
plagio /'plahio/ n. m. plagiarism;
(S.A.) kidnapping.
plan /plan/ n. m. plan. —**planear,**
v.
plancha /'plantʃa/ n. f. plate;
slab, flatiron.
planchar /plan'tʃar/ v. iron, press.
planeta /pla'neta/ n. m. planet.
planificación /planifika'θion;
planifika'sion/ n. f. planning.
planificar /planifi'kar/ v. plan.
plano /'plano/ a. **1.** level, flat.
—n. **2.** m. plan; plane.
planta /'planta/ n. f. plant; sole
(of foot).
planta baja /'planta 'baha/ n. f.
ground floor.
plantación /planta'θion; planta-
'sion/ n. f. plantation.
plantar /plan'tar/ v. plant.
plantear /plante'ar/ v. pose, present.
plantel /plan'tel/ n. m. educational institution; Agr. nursery.
plasma /'plasma/ n. m. plasma.
plástico /'plastiko/ a. & m. plastic.

plata /'plata/ n. f. silver; Colloq.
money.
plataforma /plata'forma/ n. f.
platform.
plátano /'platano/ n. m. plantain;
banana.
platel /pla'tel/ n. m. platter.
plática /'platika/ n. f. chat, talk.
—**platicar,** v.
platillo /pla'tiλo; pla'tiyo/ n. m.
saucer.
platillo volante /pla'tiλo bo'lante;
pla'tiyo bo'lante/ flying saucer.
plato /'plato/ n. m. plate, dish.
playa /'plaia/ n. f. beach, shore.
plaza /'plaθa; 'plasa/ n. f. square.
p. de toros, bullring.
plazo /'plaθo; 'plaso/ n. m. term,
deadline; installment.
plebe /'pleβe/ n. f. common people; masses.
plebiscito /pleβis'θito; pleβis'sito/
n. m. plebiscite.
plegable /ple'gaβle/ a. foldable,
folding.
plegadura /plega'ðura/ n. f. fold,
pleat. —**plegar,** v.
pleito /'pleito/ n. m. lawsuit; dispute.
plenitud /pleni'tuð/ n. f. fullness;
abundance.
pleno /'pleno/ a. full. **en pleno...**
in the middle of...
pliego /'pliego/ n. m. sheet of paper.
pliegue /'pliege/ n. m. fold, pleat,
crease.
plomería /plome'ria/ n. f. plumb-
ing.
plomero /plo'mero/ n. m.
plumber.
plomizo /plo'miθo; plo'miso/ a.
leaden.
plomo /'plomo/ n. m. lead; fuse.
pluma /'pluma/ n. f. feather;
(writing) pen.
pluma estilográfica /'pluma es-
tiglo'grafika/ fountain pen.
plumafuente /pluma'fuente/ n. f.
fountain pen.
plumaje /plu'mahe/ n. m. plumage.
plumero /plu'mero/ n. m. feather
duster; plume.
plumoso /plu'moso/ a. feathery.
plural /plu'ral/ a. & m. plural.
pluriempleo /pluriem'pleo/ n. m.
moonlighting.
PNB, abbr. (producto nacional

bruto), GNP (gross national product).

población /poβla'θion; poβla'sion/ n. f. population; town.

poblador /poβla'ðor; -ra/ n. settler.

poblar /po'βlar/ v. populate; settle.

pobre /'poβre/ a. & n. poor; poor person.

pobreza /po'βreθa; po'βresa/ n. f. poverty, need.

pocilga /po'θilga; po'silga/ n. f. pigpen.

poción /po'θion; po'sion/ n. f. drink; potion.

poco /'poko/ a. & adv. **1.** little, not much, (pl.) few. **por p., ** almost, nearly. —n. **2.** un **p.** **(de),** a little, a bit (of).

poder /po'ðer/ n. **1.** power. —v. **2.** be able to, can; be possible, may, might. **no p. menos de,** not be able to help.

poder adquisitivo /po'ðer aðkisi'tiβo/ purchasing power.

poderío /poðe'rio/ n. m. power, might.

poderoso /poðe'roso/ a. powerful, mighty, potent.

podrido /po'ðriðo/ a. rotten.

poema /po'ema/ n. m. poem.

poesía /poe'sia/ n. f. poetry; poem.

poeta /po'eta/ n. m. & f. poet.

poético /po'etiko/ a. poetic.

polaco /po'lako/ **-ca** a. & n. Polish; Pole.

polar /po'lar/ a. polar.

polaridad /polari'ðað/ n. f. polarity.

polea /po'lea/ n. f. pulley.

polen /'polen/ n. m. pollen.

policía /poli'θia; poli'sia/ n. **1.** f. police. —n. **2.** m. policeman.

polideportivo /poliðepor'tiβo/ n. m. sports center.

poliéster /poli'ester/ n. m. polyester.

poligamia /poli'gamia/ n. f. polygamy.

polígloto /poli'gloto/ **-ta** n. polyglot.

polígono industrial /po'ligono industrial/ n. m. industrial park.

polilla /po'liʎa; po'liya/ n. f. moth.

política /po'litika/ n. f. politics; policy.

político /po'litiko/ **-ca** a. & n. political; politician.

póliza /'poliθa; 'polisa/ n. f. (insurance) policy; permit, ticket.

polizonte /poli'θonte; poli'sonte/ n. m. policeman.

pollada /po'ʎaða; po'yaða/ n. f. brood.

pollería /poʎe'ria; poye'ria/ n. f. poultry shop.

pollino /po'ʎino; po'yino/ n. m. donkey.

pollo /'poʎo; 'poyo/ n. m. chicken.

polo /'polo/ n. m. pole; polo; popsicle.

polonés /polo'nes/ a. Polish.

Polonia /po'lonia/ n. f. Poland.

polvera /pol'βera/ n. f. powder box; powder puff.

polvo /'polβo/ n. m. powder; dust.

pólvora /'polβora/ n. f. gunpowder.

pompa /'pompa/ n. f. pomp.

pomposo /pom'poso/ a. pompous.

pómulo /'pomulo/ n. m. cheekbone.

ponche /'pontʃe/ n. m. punch (beverage).

ponchera /pon'tʃera/ n. f. punch bowl.

ponderar /ponde'rar/ v. ponder.

ponderoso /ponde'roso/ a. ponderous.

poner /po'ner/ v. put, set, lay, place.

ponerse /po'nerse/ v. put on; become, get; set (sun). **p. a,** start to.

poniente /po'niente/ n. m. west.

pontífice /pon'tifiθe; pon'tifise/ n. m. pontiff.

popa /'popa/ n. f. stern.

popular /popu'lar/ a. popular.

popularidad /populari'ðað/ n. f. popularity.

populazo /popu'laθo; popu'laso/ n. m. populace; masses.

por /por/ prep. by, through, because of; via; for. **p. qué,** why?

porcelana /porθe'lana; porse'lana/ n. f. porcelain, chinaware.

porcentaje /porθen'tahe; porsen'tahe/ n. m. percentage.

porche /'portʃe/ n. m. porch; portico.

porción /por'θion; por'sion/ n. f. portion, lot.

porfiar /por'fiar/ v. persist; argue.

pormenor /porme'nor/ n. m. detail.

pornografía /pornogra'fia/ n. f. pornography.

poro /'poro/ n. m. pore.

poroso /po'roso/ a. porous.

porque /'porke/ conj. because.

porqué n. m. reason, motive.

porra /'porra/ n. f. stick, club.

porrazo /po'rraθo; po'rraso/ n. m. blow.

porro /'porro/ n. m. Colloq. joint (marijuana).

portaaviones /portaa'βiones/ n. m. aircraft carrier.

portador /porta'ðor/ **-ra** n. bearer.

portal /por'tal/ n. m. portal.

portar /por'tar/ v. carry.

portarse /por'tarse/ v. behave, act.

portátil /por'tatil/ a. portable.

portavoz /porta'βoθ; porta'βos/ n. **1.** m. megaphone. **2.** m. & f. spokesperson.

porte /'porte/ n. m. bearing; behavior; postage.

portero /por'tero/ n. m. porter; janitor.

pórtico /'portiko/ n. m. porch.

portorriqueño /portorri'keɲo/ **-ña** n. & a. Puerto Rican.

portugués /portu'ges/ **-esa** a. & n. Portuguese.

posada /po'saða/ n. f. lodge, inn.

posar /po'sar/ v. pose.

posdata /pos'ðata/ n. f. postscript.

poseer /pose'er/ v. possess, own.

posesión /pose'sion/ n. f. possession.

posibilidad /posiβili'ðað/ n. f. possibility.

posible /po'siβle/ a. possible.

posiblemente /posiβle'mente/ adv. possibly.

posición /posi'θion; posi'sion/ n. f. position, stand.

positivo /posi'tiβo/ a. positive.

posponer /pospo'ner/ v. postpone.

postal /pos'tal/ a. postal; postcard.

poste /'poste/ n. m. post, pillar.

posteridad /posteri'ðað/ n. f. posterity.

posterior /poste'rior/ a. posterior, rear.

postizo /pos'tiθo; pos'tiso/ a. false, artificial.

postrado /pos'traðo/ a. prostrate. **—postrar**, v.

postre /'postre/ n. m. dessert.

póstumo /'postumo/ a. posthumous.

postura /pos'tura/ n. f. posture, pose; bet.

potable /po'taβle/ a. drinkable.

potaje /po'tahe/ n. m. porridge; pot stew.

potasa /po'tasa/ n. f. potash.

potasio /po'tasio/ n. m. potassium.

pote /'pote/ n. m. pot, jar.

potencia /po'tenθia; po'tensia/ n. f. potency, power.

potencial /poten'θial; poten'sial/ a. & m. potential.

potentado /poten'taðo/ n. m. potentate.

potente /po'tente/ a. potent, powerful.

potestad /potes'tað/ n. f. power.

potro /'potro/ n. m. colt.

pozo /'poθo; 'poso/ n. m. well.

práctica /'praktika/ n. f. practice. **—practicar**, v.

práctico /'praktiko/ a. practical.

pradera /pra'ðera/ n. f. prairie, meadow.

prado /'praðo/ n. m. meadow; lawn.

pragmatismo /pragma'tismo/ n. m. pragmatism.

preámbulo /pre'ambulo/ n. m. preamble.

precario /pre'kario/ a. precarious.

precaución /prekau'θion; prekau'sion/ n. f. precaution.

precaverse /preka'βerse/ v. beware.

precavido /preka'βiðo/ a. cautious, guarded, wary.

precedencia /preθe'ðenθia; prese'ðensia/ n. f. precedence, priority.

precedente /preθe'ðente; prese'ðente/ a. & m. preceding; precedent.

preceder /preθe'ðer; prese'ðer/ v. precede.

precepto /pre'θepto; pre'septo/ n. m. precept.

preciar /pre'θiar; pre'siar/ v. value, prize.

preciarse de /pre'θiarse de; pre'siarse de/ v. take pride in.

precio /'preθio; 'presio/ n. m. price. **p. del billete de avión** air fare. **p. del cubierto** cover charge.

precioso /pre'θioso; pre'sioso/ *a.* precious; beautiful, gorgeous.

precipicio /preθi'piθio; presi'pisio/ *n. m.* precipice, cliff.

precipitación /preθipita'θion; presipita'sion/ *n. f.* precipitation.

precipitar /preθipi'tar; presipi'tar/ *v.* precipitate, rush; throw headlong.

precipitoso /preθipi'toso; presipi'toso/ *a.* precipitous; rash.

precisar /preθi'sar; presi'sar/ *v.* fix, specify; be necessary.

precisión /preθi'sion; presi'sion/ *n. f.* precision; necessity.

preciso /pre'θiso; pre'siso/ *a.* precise; necessary.

precocidad /prekoθi'ðað; prekosi'ðað/ *n. f.* precocity.

precocinado /prekoθi'naðo; prekosi'naðo/ *a.* precooked, ready-cooked.

precoz /pre'koθ; pre'kos/ *a.* precocious.

precursor /prekur'sor/ **-ra** *a.* **1.** preceding. —*n.* **2.** precursor, forerunner.

predecesor /preðeθe'sor; preðese'sor/ **-ra** *a. & n.* predecessor.

predecir /preðe'θir; preðe'sir/ *v.* predict, foretell.

predicación /preðika'θion; preðika'sion/ *n. f.* sermon.

predicador /preðika'ðor/ **-ra** *n.* preacher.

predicar /preði'kar/ *v.* preach.

predicción /preðik'θion; preðik'sion/ *n. f.* prediction.

predilecto /preði'lekto/ *a.* favorite, preferred.

predisponer /preðispo'ner/ *v.* predispose.

predisposición /preðisposi'θion; preðisposi'sion/ *n. f.* predisposition; bias.

predominante /preðomi'nante/ *a.* prevailing, prevalent, predominant.

predominar /preðomi'nar/ *v.* prevail, predominate.

predominio /preðo'minio/ *n. m.* predominance, sway.

prefacio /pre'faθio; pre'fasio/ *n. m.* preface.

preferencia /prefe'renθia; prefe'rensia/ *n. f.* preference.

preferentemente /preferente'mente/ *adv.* preferably.

preferible /prefe'riβle/ *a.* preferable.

preferir /prefe'rir/ *v.* prefer.

prefijo /pre'fiho/ *n. m.* prefix; area code, dialing code. —**prefijar**, *v.*

pregón /pre'gon/ *n. m.* proclamation; street cry.

pregonar /prego'nar/ *v.* proclaim; cry out.

pregunta /pre'gunta/ *n. f.* question, inquiry. **hacer una p.,** to ask a question.

preguntar /pregun'tar/ *v.* ask, inquire.

preguntarse /pregun'tarse/ *v.* wonder.

prehistórico /preis'toriko/ *a.* prehistoric.

prejuicio /pre'huiθio; pre'huisio/ *n. m.* prejudice.

prelacía /prela'θia; prela'sia/ *n. f.* prelacy.

preliminar /prelimi'nar/ *a. & m.* preliminary.

preludio /pre'luðio/ *n. m.* prelude.

prematuro /prema'turo/ *a.* premature.

premeditación /premeðita'θion; premeðita'sion/ *n. f.* premeditation.

premeditar /premeði'tar/ *v.* premeditate.

premiar /pre'miar/ *v.* reward; award a prize to.

premio /'premio/ *n. m.* prize; award; reward. **p. de consuelo,** consolation prize.

premisa /pre'misa/ *n. f.* premise.

premura /pre'mura/ *n. f.* pressure; urgency.

prenda /'prenda/ *n. f.* jewel; (personal) quality. **p. de vestir,** garment.

prender /pren'der/ *v.* seize, arrest, catch; pin, clip. **p. fuego a,** set fire to.

prensa /'prensa/ *n. f.* printing press; (the) press.

prensar /pren'sar/ *v.* press, compress.

preñado /pre'ɲaðo/ *a.* pregnant.

preocupación /preokupa'θion; preokupa'sion/ *n. f.* worry, preoccupation.

preocupar /preoku'par/ *v.* worry, preoccupy.

preparación /prepara'θion; para'sion/ *n. f.* preparation.

preparar /prepa'rar/ v. prepare.

preparativo /prepara'tiβo/ n. m. preparation.

preparatorio /prepara'torio/ n. m. preparatory.

preponderante /preponde'rante/ a. preponderant.

preposición /preposi'θion; preposi'sion/ n. f. preposition.

prerrogativa /prerroga'tiβa/ n. f. prerogative, privilege.

presa /'presa/ n. f. capture; (water) dam.

presagiar /presa'hiar/ v. presage, forebode.

presbiteriano /presβite'riano/ -na n. & a. Presbyterian.

presbítero /pres'βitero/ n. m. priest.

prescindir de /presθin'dir de; pressin'dir de/ v. dispense with; omit.

prescribir /preskri'βir/ v. prescribe.

prescripción /preskrip'θion; preskrip'sion/ n. f. prescription.

presencia /pre'senθia; pre'sensia/ n. f. presence.

presenciar /presen'θiar; presen'siar/ v. witness, be present at.

presentable /presen'taβle/ a. presentable.

presentación /presenta'θion; presenta'sion/ n. f. presentation; introduction.

presentar /presen'tar/ v. present; introduce.

presente /pre'sente/ a. & m. present.

presentimiento /presenti'miento/ n. m. premonition.

preservación /preserβa'θion; preserβa'sion/ n. f. preservation.

preservar /preser'βar/ v. preserve, keep.

preservativo /preserβa'tiβo/ a. & m. preservative; condom.

presidencia /presi'δenθia; presi'δensia/ n. f. presidency.

presidencial /presiδen'θial; presiδen'sial/ a. presidential.

presidente /presi'δente/ -ta n. president.

presidiario /presi'δiario/ -ria n. m. & f. prisoner.

presidio /pre'siδio/ n. m. prison; garrison.

presidir /presi'δir/ v. preside.

presión /pre'sion/ n. f. pressure.

presión arterial /pre'sion arte-'rial/ blood pressure.

preso /'preso/ -sa n. prisoner.

presta /'presta/ n. f. mint (plant).

prestador /presta'δor/ -ra n. lender.

prestamista /presta'mista/ n. m. & f. money lender.

préstamo /'prestamo/ n. m. loan.

prestar /pres'tar/ v. lend.

presteza /pres'teθa; pres'tesa/ n. f. haste, promptness.

prestidigitación /prestiδihita-'θion; prestiδihita'sion/ n. f. sleight of hand.

prestigio /pres'tihio/ n. m. prestige.

presto /'presto/ a. **1.** quick, prompt; ready. —adv. **2.** quickly; at once.

presumido /presu'miδo/ a. conceited, presumptuous.

presumir /presu'mir/ v. presume; boast; claim; be conceited.

presunción /presun'θion; presun-'sion/ n. f. presumption; conceit.

presunto /pre'sunto/ a. presumed; prospective.

presuntuoso /presun'tuoso/ a. presumptuous.

presupuesto /presu'puesto/ n. m. premise; budget.

pretender /preten'der/ v. pretend; intend; aspire.

pretendiente /preten'diente/ n. m. suitor; pretender (to throne).

pretensión /preten'sion/ n. f. pretension; claim.

pretérito /pre'terito/ a. & m. preterit, past tense.

pretexto /pre'teksto/ n. m. pretext.

prevalecer /preβale'θer; preβale-'ser/ v. prevail.

prevención /preβen'θion; preβen-'sion/ n. f. prevention.

prevenir /preβe'nir/ v. prevent; forewarn; prearrange.

preventivo /preβen'tiβo/ a. preventive.

prever /pre'βer/ v. foresee.

previamente /preβia'mente/ adv. previously.

previo /'preβio/ a. previous.

previsible /preβi'siβle/ a. predictable.

previsión /preβi'sion/ n. f. foresight. **p. social**, social security.

prieto /'prieto/ a. blackish, very dark.

primacía /prima'θia; prima'sia/ *n. f.* primacy.

primario /pri'mario/ *a.* primary.

primavera /prima'βera/ *n. f.* spring (season).

primero /pri'mero/ *a. & adv.* first.

primitivo /primi'tiβo/ *a.* primitive.

primo /'primo/ **-ma** *n.* cousin.

primor /pri'mor/ *n. m.* beauty; excellence; lovely thing.

primoroso /primo'roso/ *a.* exquisite, elegant; graceful.

princesa /prin'θesa; prin'sesa/ *f.* princess.

principal /prinθi'pal; prinsi'pal/ *a.* **1.** principal, main. —*n.* **2.** *m.* chief, head, principal.

principalmente /prinθipal'mente; prinsipal'mente/ *adv.* principally.

príncipe /'prinθipe; 'prinsipe/ *n. m.* prince.

Príncipe Azul /'prinθipe a'θul; 'prinsipe a'sul/ Prince Charming.

principiar /prinθi'piar; prinsi'piar/ *v.* begin, initiate.

principio /prin'θipio; prin'sipio/ *n. m.* beginning, start; principle.

pringado /prin'gaðo/ *n. m.* low-life, loser.

prioridad /priori'ðað/ *n. f.* priority.

prisa /'prisa/ *n. f.* hurry, haste. **darse p.,** hurry, hasten. **tener p.,** be in a hurry.

prisión /pri'sion/ *n. f.* prison; imprisonment.

prisionero /prisio'nero/ **-ra** *n.* captive, prisoner.

prisma /'prisma/ *n. m.* prism.

prismático /pris'matiko/ *a.* prismatic.

privación /priβa'θion; priβa'sion/ *n. f.* privation, want.

privado /pri'βaðo/ *a.* private, secret; deprived.

privar /pri'βar/ *v.* deprive.

privilegio /priβi'lehio/ *n. m.* privilege.

pro /pro/ *n. m. or f.* benefit, advantage. **en p. de,** in behalf of. **en p. y en contra,** pro and con.

proa /'proa/ *n. f.* prow, bow.

probabilidad /proβaβili'ðað/ *n. f.* probability.

probable /pro'βaβle/ *a.* probable, likely.

probablemente /proβaβle'mente/ *adv.* probably.

probador /proβa'ðor/ *n. m.* fitting room.

probar /pro'βar/ *v.* try, sample; taste; test; prove.

probarse /pro'βarse/ *v.* try on.

probidad /proβi'ðað/ *n. f.* honesty, integrity.

problema /pro'βlema/ *n. m.* problem.

probo /'proβo/ *a.* honest.

procaz /pro'kaθ; pro'kas/ *a.* impudent, saucy.

proceder /proθe'ðer; prose'ðer/ *v.* proceed.

procedimiento /proθeði'miento; proseði'miento/ *n. m.* procedure.

procesar /proθe'sar; prose'sar/ *v.* prosecute; sue; process.

procesión /proθe'sion; prose'sion/ *n. f.* procession.

proceso /pro'θeso; pro'seso/ *n. m.* process; (court) trial.

proclama /pro'klama/ **proclamación** *n. f.* proclamation.

proclamar /prokla'mar/ *v.* proclaim.

procreación /prokrea'θion; prokrea'sion/ *n. f.* procreation.

procrear /prokre'ar/ *v.* procreate.

procurar /proku'rar/ *v.* try; see to it; get; procure.

prodigalidad /proðigali'ðað/ *n. f.* prodigality.

prodigar /proði'gar/ *v.* lavish; squander, waste.

prodigio /pro'ðihio/ *n. m.* prodigy.

pródigo /'proðigo/ *a.* prodigal; profuse; lavish.

producción /proðuk'θion; proðuk'sion/ *n. f.* production.

producir /proðu'θir; proðu'sir/ *v.* produce.

productivo /proðuk'tiβo/ *a.* productive.

producto /pro'ðukto/ *n. m.* product.

producto nacional bruto /pro'ðukto naθio'nal 'bruto; pro'ðukto nasio'nal 'bruto/ gross national product.

proeza /pro'eθa; pro'esa/ *n. f.* prowess.

profanación /profana'θion; profana'sion/ *n. f.* profanation.

profanar /profa'nar/ *v.* defile, desecrate.

profanidad /profani'ðað/ *n. f.* profanity.

profano /pro'fano/ *a.* profane.

profecía /profe'θia; profe'sia/ *n. f.* prophecy.

proferir /profe'rir/ v. utter, express.

profesar /profe'sar/ v. profess.

profesión /profe'sion/ n. f. profession.

profesional /profesio'nal/ a. professional.

profesor /profe'sor/ **-ra** n. professor, teacher.

profeta /pro'feta/ n. m. prophet.

profético /pro'fetiko/ a. prophetic.

profetizar /profeti'θar; profeti'sar/ v. prophesy.

proficiente /profi'θiente; profi'siente/ a. proficient.

profundamente /profunda'mente/ adv. profoundly, deeply.

profundidad /profundi'ðað/ n. f. profundity, depth.

profundizar /profundi'θar; profundi'sar/ v. deepen.

profundo /pro'fundo/ a. profound, deep.

profuso /pro'fuso/ a. profuse.

progenie /pro'henie/ n. f. progeny, offspring.

programa /pro'grama/ n. m. program; schedule.

programador /programa'ðor/ **-ra** n. (computer) programmer.

progresar /progre'sar/ v. progress, advance.

progresión /progre'sion/ n. f. progression.

progresista /progre'sista/ **progresivo** a. progressive.

progreso /pro'greso/ n. m. progress.

prohibición /proiβi'θion; proiβi'sion/ n. f. prohibition.

prohibir /proi'βir/ v. prohibit, forbid.

prohibitivo /proiβi'tiβo, proiβi'torio/ a. prohibitive.

prole /'prole/ n. f. progeny.

proletariado /proleta'riaðo/ n. m. proletariat.

proliferación /prolifera'θion; prolifera'sion/ n. f. proliferation.

prolijo /pro'liho/ a. prolix, tedious; long-winded.

prólogo /'prologo/ n. m. prologue; preface.

prolongar /proloŋ'gar/ v. prolong.

promedio /pro'meðio/ n. m. average.

promesa /pro'mesa/ n. f. promise.

prometer /prome'ter/ v. promise.

prometido /prome'tiðo/ a. promised; engaged (to marry).

prominencia /promi'nenθia; promi'nensia/ n. f. prominence.

promiscuamente /promiskua'mente/ adv. promiscuously.

promiscuo /pro'miskuo/ a. promiscuous.

promisorio /promi'sorio/ a. promissory.

promoción /promo'θion; promo'sion/ n. f. promotion.

promocionar /promoθio'nar; promosio'nar/ v. advertise, promote.

promover /promo'βer/ v. promote, further.

promulgación /promulga'θion; promulga'sion/ n. f. promulgation.

promulgar /promul'gar/ v. promulgate.

pronombre /pro'nombre/ n. m. pronoun.

pronosticación /pronostika'θion; pronostika'sion/ n. f. prediction, forecast.

pronosticar /pronosti'kar/ v. predict, forecast.

pronóstico /pro'nostiko/ n. m. prediction.

prontamente /pronta'mente/ adv. promptly.

prontitud /pronti'tuð/ n. f. promptness.

pronto /'pronto/ a. **1.** prompt; ready. —adv. **2.** soon; quickly. **de p.,** abruptly.

pronunciación /pronunθia'θion; pronunsia'sion/ n. f. pronunciation.

pronunciar /pronun'θiar; pronun'siar/ v. pronounce.

propagación /propaga'θion; propaga'sion/ n. f. propagation.

propaganda /propa'ganda/ n. f. propaganda.

propagandista /propagan'dista/ n. m. & f. propagandist.

propagar /propa'gar/ v. propagate.

propicio /pro'piθio; pro'pisio/ a. propitious, auspicious, favorable.

propiedad /propie'ðað/ n. f. property.

propietario /propie'tario/ **-ria** n. proprietor; owner; landlord, landlady.

propina /pro'pina/ n. f. gratuity, tip.

propio /'propio/ a. proper, suitable; typical; (one's) own; -self.

proponer /propo'ner/ v. propose.

proporción /propor'θion; propor'sion/ n. f. proportion.

proporcionado /proporθio'naðo; proporsio'naðo/ a. proportionate.

proporcionar /proporθio'nar; proporsio'nar/ v. provide with, supply, afford.

proposición /proposi'θion; proposi'sion/ n. f. proposition, offer; proposal.

propósito /pro'posito/ n. m. purpose; plan; **a p.,** by the way, apropos; on purpose.

propuesta /pro'puesta/ n. f. proposal, motion.

prorrata /pro'rrata/ n. f. quota.

prórroga /'prorroga/ n. f. renewal, extension.

prorrogar /prorro'gar/ v. renew, extend.

prosa /'prosa/ n. f. prose.

prosaico /pro'saiko/ a. prosaic.

proscribir /proskri'βir/ v. prohibit, proscribe, ban.

prosecución /proseku'θion; proseku'sion/ n. f. prosecution.

proseguir /prose'gir/ v. pursue, proceed, go on.

prosélito /pro'selito/ **-ta** n. proselyte.

prospecto /pros'pekto/ n. m. prospectus.

prosperar /prospe'rar/ v. prosper, thrive, flourish.

prosperidad /prosperi'ðað/ n. f. prosperity.

próspero /'prospero/ a. prosperous, successful.

prosternado /proster'naðo/ a. prostrate.

prostitución /prostitu'θion; prostitu'sion/ n. f. prostitution.

prostituir /prosti'tuir/ v. prostitute; debase.

prostituta /prosti'tuta/ n. f. prostitute.

protagonista /protago'nista/ n. m. & f. protagonist, hero, heroine.

protección /protek'θion; protek'sion/ n. f. protection.

protector /protek'tor/ **-ra** a. & n. protective; protector.

proteger /prote'her/ v. protect, safeguard. **p. contra escritura,** write-protect (diskette).

protegido /prote'hiðo/ **-da** n. **1.**

protégé. —a. 2. protected. **p. contra escritura,** write-protected.

proteína /prote'ina/ n. f. protein.

protesta /pro'testa/ n. f. protest. **—protestar,** v.

protestante /protes'tante/ a. & n. Protestant.

protocolo /proto'kolo/ n. m. protocol.

protuberancia /protuβe'ranθia; protuβe'ransia/ n. f. protuberance, lump.

protuberante /protuβe'rante/ a. bulging.

provecho /pro'βetʃo/ n. m. profit, gain, benefit. **¡Buen provecho!** May you enjoy your meal!

provechoso /proβe'tʃoso/ a. beneficial, advantageous, profitable.

proveer /proβe'er/ v. provide, furnish.

provenir de /proβe'nir de/ v. originate in, be due to, come from.

proverbial /proβer'βial/ a. proverbial.

proverbio /pro'βerβio/ n. m. proverb.

providencia /proβi'ðenθia; proβi'ðensia/ n. f. providence.

providente /proβi'ðente/ a. provident.

provincia /pro'βinθia; pro'βinsia/ n. f. province.

provincial /proβin'θial; proβin'sial/ a. provincial.

provinciano /proβin'θiano; proβin'siano/ **-na** a. & n. provincial.

provisión /proβi'sion/ n. f. provision, supply, stock.

provisional /proβisio'nal/ a. provisional.

provocación /proβoka'θion; proβoka'sion/ n. f. provocation.

provocador /proβoka'ðor/ **-ra** n. provoker.

provocar /proβo'kar/ v. provoke, excite.

provocativo /proβoka'tiβo/ a. provocative.

proximidad /proksimi'ðað/ n. f. proximity, vicinity.

próximo /'proksimo/ a. next; near.

proyección /proiek'θion; proiek'sion/ n. f. projection.

proyectar /proiek'tar/ v. plan, project.

proyectil /proyek'til/ n. m. projectile, missile, shell.

proyecto /pro'iekto/ *n. m.* plan, project, scheme.

proyector /proiek'tor/ *n. m.* projector.

prudencia /pru'ðenθia/ *n. f.* prudence.

prudente /pru'ðente/ *a.* prudent.

prueba /'prueβa/ *n. f.* proof; trial; test.

psicoanálisis /psikoa'nalisis/ *n. m.* psychoanalysis.

psicoanalista /psikoana'lista/ *n. m. & f.* psychoanalyst.

psicodélico /psiko'ðeliko/ *a.* psychedelic.

psicología /psikolo'hia/ *n. f.* psychology.

psicológico /psiko'lohiko/ *a.* psychological.

psicólogo /psi'kologo/ **-ga** *n.* psychologist.

psiquiatra /psi'kiatra/ *n. m. & f.* psychiatrist.

psiquiatría /psikia'tria/ *n. f.* psychiatry.

publicación /puβlika'θion/ *n. f.* publication.

publicar /puβli'kar/ *v.* publish.

publicidad /puβliði'ðað/ *n. f.* publicity.

publicista /puβli'θista/ *n. m. & f.* publicity agent.

público /'puβliko/ *a. & m.* public.

puchero /pu'tʃero/ *n. m.* pot.

pudiente /pu'ðiente/ *a.* powerful; wealthy.

pudin /pu'ðin/ *n. m.* pudding.

pudor /pu'ðor/ *n. m.* modesty.

pudoroso /puðo'roso/ *a.* modest.

pudrirse /pu'ðrirse/ *v.* rot.

pueblo /'pueβlo/ *n. m.* town, village; (the) people.

puente /'puente/ *n. m.* bridge.

puente para peatones /'puente para pea'tones/ *n. m.* footbridge.

puerco /'puerko/ **-ca** *n.* pig.

puericultura /puerikul'tura/ *n. f.* pediatrics.

pueril /pue'ril/ *a.* childish.

puerilidad /puerili'ðað/ *n. f.* puerility.

puerta /'puerta/ *n. f.* door; gate.

puerta giratoria /'puerta hira'toria/ revolving door.

puerta principal /'puerta prinθi'pal/ 'puerta prinsi'pal/ front door.

puerto /'puerto/ *n. m.* port, harbor.

puertorriqueño /puertorri'keɲo/ **-ña** *a. & n.* Puerto Rican.

pues /pues/ *adv.* **1.** well... —*conj.* **2.** as, since, for.

puesto /'puesto/ *n. m.* appointment, post, job; place; stand. **p. que,** since.

pugilato /puhi'lato/ *n. m.* boxing.

pugna /'pugna/ *n. f.* conflict.

pugnacidad /pugnaθi'ðað/ pugnasi'ðað/ *n. f.* pugnacity.

pugnar /pug'nar/ *v.* fight; oppose.

pulcritud /pulkri'tuð/ *n. f.* neatness; exquisitness.

pulga /'pulga/ *n. f.* flea.

pulgada /pul'gaða/ *n. f.* inch.

pulgar /pul'gar/ *n. m.* thumb.

pulir /pu'lir/ *v.* polish; beautify.

pulmón /pul'mon/ *n. m.* lung.

pulmonía /pulmo'nia/ *n. f.* pneumonia.

pulpa /'pulpa/ *n. f.* pulp.

púlpito /'pulpito/ *n. m.* pulpit.

pulque /'pulke/ *n. m.* pulque (fermented maguey juice).

pulsación /pulsa'θion/ pulsa'sion/ *n. f.* pulsation, beat.

pulsar /pul'sar/ *v.* pulsate, beat.

pulsera /pul'sera/ *n. f.* wristband; bracelet.

pulso /'pulso/ *n. m.* pulse.

pulverizar /pulβeri'θar/ pulβeri'sar/ *v.* pulverize.

puma /'puma/ *n. m.* puma.

pundonor /pundo'nor/ *n. m.* point of honor.

punta /'punta/ *n. f.* point, tip, end.

puntada /pun'taða/ *n. f.* stitch.

puntapié /punta'pie/ *n. m.* kick.

puntería /punte'ria/ *n. f.* (marksman's) aim.

puntiagudo /puntia'guðo/ *a.* sharp-pointed.

puntillas /pun'tiʎas/ pun'tiyas/ *n. f.pl.* **de p., en p.,** on tiptoe.

punto /'punto/ *n. m.* point; period; dot, dote. **dos puntos,** *Punct.* colon. **a p. de,** about to. **al p.,** instantly.

punto de admiración /'punto de aðmira'θion/ 'punto de aðmira'sion/ exclamation mark.

punto de congelación /'punto de koŋgela'θion/ 'punto de koŋgela'sion/ freezing point.

punto de ebullición /'punto de eβuʎi'θion/ 'punto de eβuyi'sion/ boiling point.

punto de vista /'punto de 'bista/ point of view, viewpoint.

puntuación /puntua'θion; puntua-'sion/ n. f. punctuation.

puntual /pun'tual/ a. punctual, prompt.

puntuar /pun'tuar/ v. punctuate.

puñada /pu'naða/ n. f. punch.

puñado /pu'naðo/ n. m. handful.

puñal /pu'nal/ n. m. dagger.

puñalada /puna'laða/ n. f. stab.

puñetazo /pune'taθo; pune'taso/ n. m. punch, fist blow.

puño /'puno/ n. m. fist; cuff; handle.

pupila /pu'pila/ n. f. pupil (of eye).

pupitre /pu'pitre/ n. m. writing desk, school desk.

pureza /pu'reθa; pu'resa/ n. f. purity; chastity.

purgante /pur'gante/ n. m. laxative.

purgar /pur'gar/ v. purge, cleanse.

purgatorio /purga'torio/ n. m. purgatory.

puridad /puri'ðað/ n. f. secrecy.

purificación /purifika'θion; puri-fika'sion/ n. f. purification.

purificar /purifi'kar/ v. purify.

purismo /pu'rismo/ n. m. purism.

purista /pu'rista/ n. m. & f. purist.

puritanismo /purita'nismo/ n. m. puritanism.

puro /'puro/ a. **1.** pure. —n. **2.** m. cigar.

púrpura /'purpura/ n. f. purple.

purpúreo /pur'pureo/ a. purple.

purulencia /puru'lenθia; puru-'lensia/ n. f. purulence.

purulento /puru'lento/ a. purulent.

pus /pus/ n. m. pus.

pusilánime /pusi'lanime/ a. pusillanimous.

puta /'puta/ -**to** n. prostitute.

putrefacción /putrefak'θion; putrefak'sion/ n. f. putrefaction, rot.

putrefacto /putre'fakto/ a. putrid, rotten.

pútrido /'putriðo/ a. putrid.

puya /'puya/ n. f. goad.

Q R

que /ke/ rel. pron. **1.** who, whom; that, which. —conj. **2.** than.

qué /ke/ a. & pron. what. **por q., para q.,** why? adv. how.

quebrada /ke'βraða/ n. f. ravine, gully, gulch; stream.

quebradizo /keβra'ðiθo; keβra-'ðiso/ a. fragile, brittle.

quebraley /keβra'lei/ n. m. & f. lawbreaker, outlaw.

quebrar /ke'βrar/ v. break.

queda /'keða/ n. f. curfew.

quedar /ke'ðar/ v. remain, be located; be left. **q. bien a,** be becoming to.

quedarse /ke'ðarse/ v. stay, remain. **q. con,** keep, hold on to; remain with.

quedo /'keðo/ a. quiet; gentle.

quehacer /kea'θer; kea'ser/ n. m. task; chore.

queja /'keha/ n. f. complaint.

quejarse /ke'harse/ v. complain, grumble.

quejido /ke'hiðo/ n. m. moan.

quejoso /ke'hoso/ a. complaining.

quema /'kema/ n. f. burning.

quemadura /kema'ðura/ n. f. burn.

quemar /ke'mar/ v. burn.

querella /ke'reʎa; ke'reya/ n. f. quarrel; complaint.

querencia /ke'renθia; ke'rensia/ n. f. affection, liking.

querer /ke'rer/ v. want, wish; will; love (a person). **q. decir,** mean. **sin q.,** without meaning to; unwillingly.

querido /ke'riðo/ a. dear, loved, beloved.

quesería /kese'ria/ n. f. dairy.

queso /'keso/ n. m. cheese.

queso crema /'keso 'krema/ cream cheese.

quetzal /ket'θal; ket'sal/ n. m. quetzal.

quiche /'kitʃe/ n. f. quiche.

quiebra /'kieβra/ n. f. break, fracture; damage; bankruptcy.

quien /kien/ rel. pron. who, whom.

quién interrog. pron. who, whom.

quienquiera /kien'kiera/ pron. whoever, whomever.

quietamente /kieta'mente/ adv. quietly.

quieto /'kieto/ a. quiet, still.

quietud /kie'tuð/ n. f. quiet, quietude.

quijada /ki'haða/ n. f. jaw.

quijotesco /kiho'tesko/ a. quixotic.

quilate /ki'late/ n. m. carat.

quilla /'kiʎa/ n. f. keel.

quimera /ki'mera/ n. f. chimera; vision; quarrel.

química /'kimika/ n. f. chemistry.

químico /'kimiko/ **-ca** a. & n. chemical; chemist.

quimoterapia /kimote'rapia/ n. f. chemotherapy.

quincalla /kin'kaʎa; kin'kaya/ n. f. (computer) hardware.

quincallería /kinkaʎe'ria; kinkaye-'ria/ n. f. hardware store.

quince /'kinθe; 'kinse/ a. & pron. fifteen.

quinientos /ki'nientos/ a. & pron. five hundred.

quinina /ki'nina/ n. f. quinine.

quintana /kin'tana/ n. f. country home.

quinto /'kinto/ a. fifth.

quirúrgico /ki'rurhiko/ a. surgical.

quiste /'kiste/ n. m. cyst.

quitamanchas /kita'mantʃas/ n. m. stain remover.

quitanieves /kita'nieβes/ n. m. snowplow.

quitar /ki'tar/ v. take away, remove.

quitarse /ki'tarse/ v. take off; get rid of.

quitasol /kita'sol/ n. m. parasol, umbrella.

quitasueño /kita'sueɲo/ n. m. Colloq. nightmare; worry.

quizá /ki'θa; ki'sa/ **quizás** adv. perhaps, maybe.

quórum /'korum/ n. m. quorum.

rábano /'rraβano/ n. m. radish.

rabí /rra'βi/ **rabino** n. m. rabbi.

rabia /'rraβia/ n. f. rage; grudge; rabies.

rabiar /rra'βiar/ v. rage, be furious.

rabieta /rra'βieta/ n. f. tantrum.

rabioso /rra'βioso/ a. furious; rabid.

rabo /'rraβo/ n. m. tail.

racha /'rratʃa/ n. f. streak.

racimo /rra'θimo; rra'simo/ n. m. bunch, cluster.

ración /rra'θion; rra'sion/ n. f. ration. —**racionar,** v.

racionabilidad /rraθionaβili'ðað; rrasionaβili'ðað/ n. f. rationality.

racional /rraθio'nal; rrasio'nal/ a. rational.

racionalismo /rraθiona'lismo; rrasiona'lismo/ n. m. rationalism.

racionalmente /rraθional'mente; rrasional'mente/ adv. rationally.

radar /rra'ðar/ n. m. radar.

radiación /rraðia'θion; rraðia'sion/ n. f. radiation.

radiador /rraðia'ðor/ n. m. radiator.

radiante /rra'ðiante/ a. radiant.

radical /rraði'kal/ a. & n. radical.

radicalismo /rraðika'lismo/ n. m. radicalism.

radicoso /rraði'koso/ a. radical.

radio /'rraðio/ n. m. or f. radio.

radioactividad /rraðioaktiβi'ðað/ n. f. radioactivity.

radioactivo /rraðioak'tiβo/ a. radioactive.

radiocasete /rraðioka'sete/ n. m. radio cassette.

radiodifundir /rraðioðifun'dir/ v. broadcast.

radiodifusión /rraðioðifu'sion/ n. f. (radio) broadcasting.

radiografía /rraðiogra'fia/ n. f. X-ray.

radiografiar /rraðiogra'fiar/ v. X-ray.

ráfaga /'rrafaga/ n. f. gust (of wind).

raíz /rra'iθ; rra'is/ n. f. root.

raja /'rraha/ n. f. rip; split, crack. —**rajar,** v.

ralea /rra'lea/ n. f. stock, breed.

ralo /'rralo/ a. thin, scattered.

rama /'rrama/ n. f. branch, bough.

ramillete /rrami'ʎete; rrami'yete/ n. m. bouquet.

ramo /'rramo/ n. m. branch, bough; bouquet.

ramonear /rramone'ar/ v. browse.

rampa /'rrampa/ n. f. ramp.

rana /'rrana/ n. f. frog.

ranchero /rran'tʃero/ **-ra** n. small farmer.

rancho /'rrantʃo/ n. m. ranch.

rancidez /rranθi'ðeθ; rransi'ðes/ n. f. rancidity.

rancio /'rranθio; 'rransio/ a. rancid, rank, stale, sour.

rango /'rrango/ n. m. rank.

ranúnculo /rra'nunkulo/ n. m. ranunculus; buttercup.

ranura /rra'nura/ n. f. slot.

ranura de expansión /rra'nura de ekspan'sion/ expansion slot.

rapacidad /rrapaθi'ðað; rrapasi-'ðað/ n. f. rapacity.

rapaz /rra'paθ; rra'pas/ a. **1.** rapacious. —n. **2.** young boy.

rapé /'rrape/ n. m. snuff.

rápidamente /rrapiða'mente/ adv. rapidly.

rapidez /rrapi'ðeθ; rrapi'ðes/ n. f. rapidity, speed.

rápido /'rrapiðo/ a. **1.** rapid, fast, speedy. —n. **2.** express (train).

rapiña /rra'piɲa/ n. f. robbery, plundering.

rapsodia /rrap'soðia/ n. f. rhapsody.

rapto /'rrapto/ n. m. kidnapping.

raquero /rra'kero/ **-ra** n. beachcomber.

raqueta /rra'keta/ n. f. (tennis) racket.

rareza /rra'reθa; rra'resa/ n. f. rarity; freak.

raridad /rrari'ðað/ n. f. rarity.

raro /'rraro/ a. rare, strange, unusual, odd, queer.

rasar /rra'sar/ v. skim.

rascacielos /rraska'θielos; rraska'sielos/ n. m. skyscraper.

rascar /rras'kar/ v. scrape; scratch.

rasgadura /rrasga'ðura/ n. f. tear, rip. —**rasgar,** v.

rasgo /'rrasgo/ n. m. trait.

rasgón /rras'gon/ n. m. tear.

rasguño /rras'guɲo/ n. m. scratch. —**rasguñar,** v.

raso /'rraso/ a. **1.** plain. **soldado r.,** Mil. private. —n. **2.** satin.

raspar /rras'par/ v. scrape; erase.

rastra /'rrastra/ n. f. trail, track. —**rastrear,** v.

rastrillar /rrastri'ʎar; rrastri'yar/ v. rake.

rastro /'rrastro/ n. m. track, trail, trace; rake; flea market.

rata /'rrata/ n. f. rat.

ratificación /rratifika'θion; rratifika'sion/ n. f. ratification.

ratificar /rratifi'kar/ v. ratify.

rato /'rrato/ n. m. while, spell, short time.

ratón /rra'ton/ n. m. mouse.

ratonera /rrato'nera/ n. f. mousetrap.

raya /'rraya/ n. f. dash, line, streak, stripe.

rayar /rra'yar/ v. rule, stripe; scratch; cross out.

rayo /'rrayo/ n. m. lightning bolt; ray; flash.

rayón /rra'yon/ n. m. rayon.

raza /'rraθa; 'rrasa/ n. f. race; breed, stock.

razón /rra'θon; rra'son/ n. f. reason; ratio. **a r. de,** at the rate of. **tener r.,** to be right.

razonable /rraθo'naβle; rraso'naβle/ a. reasonable, sensible.

razonamiento /rraθona'miento; rrasona'miento/ n. m. argument.

razonar /rraθo'nar; rraso'nar/ v. reason.

reacción /rreak'θion; rreak'sion/ n. f. reaction.

reaccionar /rreakθio'nar; rreaksio'nar/ v. react.

reaccionario /rreakθio'nario; rreaksio'nario/ **-ria** a. & n. reactionary.

reacondicionar /rreakondiθio'nar; rreakondisio'nar/ v. recondition.

reactivo /rreak'tiβo/ a. & m. reactive; Chem. reagent.

reactor /rreak'tor/ n. m. reactor.

real /rre'al/ a. royal, regal; real, actual.

realdad /rreal'dað/ n. f. royal authority.

realeza /rrea'leθa; rrea'lesa/ n. f. royalty.

realidad /rreali'ðað/ n. f. reality.

realidad virtual /rreali'ðað βir'tual/ virtual reality.

realista /rrea'lista/ a. & n. realistic; realist.

realización /rrealiθa'θion; rrealisa'sion/ n. f. achievement, accomplishment.

realizar /rreali'θar; rreali'sar/ v. accomplish; fulfill; effect; Com. realize.

realmente /rreal'mente/ adv. in reality, really.

realzar /rreal'θar; rreal'sar/ v. enhance.

reata /rre'ata/ n. f. rope; lasso, lariat.

rebaja /rre'βaha/ n. f. reduction.

rebajar /rreβa'har/ v. cheapen; reduce (in price); lower.

rebanada /rreβa'naða/ n. f. slice. —**rebanar,** v.

rebaño /rre'βaɲo/ n. m. flock, herd.

rebato /rre'βato/ n. m. alarm; sudden attack.

rebelarse /rreβe'larse/ v. rebel, revolt.

rebelde /rre'βelde/ a. & n. rebellious; rebel.

rebelión /rreβe'lion/ n. f. rebellion, revolt.

reborde /rre'βorðe/ n. m. border.

rebotar /rreβo'tar/ v. rebound.

rebozo /rre'βoθo; rre'βoso/ n. m. shawl.

rebuscar /rreβus'kar/ v. search thoroughly.

rebuznar /rreβuθ'nar; rreβus'nar/ v. bray.

recado /rre'kaðo/ n. m. message; errand.

recaída /rreka'iða/ n. f. relapse. **—recaer,** v.

recalcar /rrekal'kar/ v. stress, emphasize.

recalentar /rrekalen'tar/ v. reheat.

recámara /rre'kamara/ n. f. (Mex.) bedroom.

recapitulación /rrekapitula'θion; rrekapitula'sion/ n. f. recapitulation.

recapitular /rrekapitu'lar/ v. recapitulate.

recatado /rreka'taðo/ n. m. coy; prudent.

recaudador /rrekauða'ðor/ **-ra** n. tax collector.

recelar /rreθe'lar; rrese'lar/ v. fear, distrust.

receloso /rreθe'loso; rrese'loso/ a. distrustful.

recepción /rreθep'θion; rresep-'sion/ n. f. reception.

recepcionista /rreθepθio'nista; rresepsio'nista/ n. m. & f. desk clerk.

receptáculo /rreθep'takulo; rresep'takulo/ n. m. receptacle.

receptividad /rreθeptiβi'ðað; rreseptiβi'ðað/ n. f. receptivity.

receptivo /rreθep'tiβo; rresep-'tiβo/ a. receptive.

receptor /rreθep'tor; rresep'tor/ n. m. receiver.

receta /rre'θeta; rre'seta/ n. f. recipe; prescription.

recetar /rreθe'tar; rrese'tar/ v. prescribe.

rechazar /rretʃa'θar; rretʃa'sar/ v. reject, spurn, discard.

rechinar /rretʃi'nar/ v. chatter.

recibimiento /rreθiβi'miento; rresiβi'miento/ n. m. reception; welcome; anteroom.

recibir /rreθi'βir; rresi'βir/ v. receive.

recibo /rre'θiβo; rre'siβo/ n. m. receipt.

reciclaje /rreθi'klahe; resi'klahe/ n. m. recycling.

reciclar /rreθi'klar; rresi'klar/ v. recycle.

recidiva /rreθi'ðiβa; rresi'ðiβa/ n. f. relapse.

recién /rre'θien; rre'sien/ adv. recently, newly, just.

reciente /rre'θiente; rre'siente/ a. recent.

recinto /rre'θinto; rre'sinto/ n. m. enclosure.

recipiente /rreθi'piente; rresi-'piente/ n. m. recipient.

reciprocación /rreθiproka'θion; rresiproka'sion/ n. f. reciprocation.

recíprocamente /rreθiproka-'mente; rresiproka'mente/ adv. reciprocally.

reciprocar /rreθipro'kar; rresipro-'kar/ v. reciprocate.

reciprocidad /rreθiproθi'ðað; rresiprosi'ðað/ n. f. reciprocity.

recitación /rreθita'θion; rresita-'sion/ n. f. recitation.

recitar /rreθi'tar; rresi'tar/ v. recite.

reclamación /rreklama'θion; rreklama'sion/ n. f. claim; complaint.

reclamar /rrekla'mar/ v. claim; complain.

reclamo /rre'klamo/ n. m. claim; advertisement, advertising; decoy.

reclinar /rrekli'nar/ v. recline, repose, lean.

recluta /rre'kluta/ n. m. & f. recruit.

reclutar /rreklu'tar/ v. recruit, draft.

recobrar /rreko'βrar/ v. recover, salvage, regain.

recobro /rre'koβro/ n. m. recovery.

recoger /rreko'her/ v. gather; collect; pick up. **r. el conocimiento,** regain consciousness.

recogerse /rreko'herse/ v. retire (for night).

recolectar /rrekolek'tar/ v. gather, assemble; harvest.

recomendación /rrekomenda-'θion; rrekomenda'sion/ n. f. recommendation; commendation.

recomendar /rrekomen'dar/ v. recommend; commend.

recompensa /rrekom'pensa/ n. f. recompense; compensation.

recompensar /rrekompen'sar/ v. reward; compensate.

reconciliación /rrekonθilia'θion; rrekonsilia'sion/ n. f. reconciliation.

reconciliar /rrekonθi'liar; rrekon-si'liar/ *v.* reconcile.

reconocer /rrekono'θer; rrekono-'ser/ *v.* recognize; acknowledge; inspect, examine; *Mil.* reconnoiter.

reconocimiento /rrekonoθi'miento; rrekonosi'miento/ *n. m.* recognition; appreciation, gratitude.

reconstituir /rrekonsti'tuir/ *v.* reconstitute.

reconstruir /rrekons'truir/ *v.* reconstruct, rebuild.

record /'rrekorð/ *n. m.* (sports) record.

recordar /rrekor'ðar/ *v.* recall, recollect; remind.

recorrer /rreko'rrer/ *v.* go over; read over; cover (distance).

recorte /rre'korte/ *n. m.* clipping, cutting.

recostarse /rrekos'tarse/ *v.* recline, lean back, rest.

recreación /rrekrea'θion; rrekrea-'sion/ *n. f.* recreation.

recreo /rre'kreo/ *n. m.* recreation.

recriminación /rrekrimina'θion; rrekrimina'sion/ *n. f.* recrimination.

rectangular /rrektaŋgu'lar/ *a.* rectangular.

rectángulo /rrek'taŋgulo/ *n. m.* rectangle.

rectificación /rrektifika'θion; rrektifika'sion/ *n. f.* rectification.

rectificar /rrektifi'kar/ *v.* rectify.

recto /'rrekto/ *a.* straight; just, fair. **ángulo r.,** right angle.

recuento /rre'kuento/ *n. m.* recount.

recuerdo /rre'kuerðo/ *n. m.* memory; souvenir; remembrance; (*pl.*) regards.

reculada /rreku'laða/ *n. f.* recoil. —**recular,** *v.*

recuperación /rrekupera'θion; rrekupera'sion/ *n. f.* recuperation.

recuperar /rrekupe'rar/ *v.* recuperate.

recurrir /rreku'rrir/ *v.* revert; resort, have recourse.

recurso /rre'kurso/ *n. m.* resource; recourse.

red /rreð/ *n. f.* net; trap. **r. local** local area network.

redacción /rreðak'θion; rreðak-'sion/ *n. f.* (editorial) staff; composition (of written material).

redactar /rreðak'tar/ *v.* draft, draw up; edit.

redactor /rreðak'tor/ **-ra** *n.* editor.

redada /rre'ðaða/ *n. f.* netful, catch, haul.

redargución /rreðarguˈθion; rreðargu'sion/ *n. f.* retort. —**redargüir,** *v.*

redención /rreðen'θion; rreðen-'sion/ *n. f.* redemption, salvation.

redentor /rreðen'tor/ *n. m.* redeemer.

redimir /rreði'mir/ *v.* redeem.

redoblante /rreðo'βlante/ *n. m.* snare drum; snare dummer.

redonda /rre'ðonda/ *n. f.* neighborhood, vicinity.

redondo /rre'ðondo/ *a.* round, circular.

reducción /rreðuk'θion; rreðuk-'sion/ *n. f.* reduction.

reducir /rreðu'θir; rreðu'sir/ *v.* reduce.

reembolso /rreem'βolso/ *n. m.* refund. —**reembolsar,** *v.*

reemplazar /rreempla'θar; rreempla'sar/ *v.* replace, supersede.

reencarnación /rreenkarna'θion; rreenkarna'sion/ *n. f.* reincarnation.

reexaminar /rreeksami'nar/ *v.* reexamine.

reexpedir /rreekspe'ðir/ *v.* forward (mail).

referencia /rrefe'renθia; rrefe-'rensia/ *n. f.* reference.

referéndum /rrefe'rendum/ *n. m.* referendum.

referir /rrefe'rir/ *v.* relate, report on.

referirse /rrefe'rirse/ *v.* refer.

refinamiento /rrefina'miento/ *n. m.* refinement.

refinar /rrefi'nar/ *v.* refine.

refinería /rrefine'ria/ *n. f.* refinery.

reflejar /rrefle'har/ *v.* reflect; think, ponder.

reflejo /rre'fleho/ *n. m.* reflection; glare.

reflexión /rreflek'sion/ *n. f.* reflection, thought.

reflexionar /rrefleksio'nar/ *v.* reflect, think.

reflujo /rre'fluho/ *n. m.* ebb; ebb tide.

reforma /rre'forma/ *n. f.* reform. —**reformar,** *v.*

reformación /rreforma'θion; rreforma'sion/ *n. f.* reformation.

reformador /rreforma'ðor/ **-ra** *n.* reformer.

reforma tributaria /rre'forma triβu'taria/ tax reform.

reforzar /rrefor'θar; refor'sar/ v. reinforce, strengthen; encourage.

refractario /rrefrak'tario/ a. refractory.

refrán /rre'fran/ n. m. proverb, saying.

refrenar /rrefre'nar/ v. curb, rein; restrain.

refrescar /rrefres'kar/ v. refresh, freshen, cool.

refresco /rre'fresko/ n. m. refreshment; cold drink.

refrigeración /rrefrihera'θion; rre-frihera'sion/ n. f. refrigeration.

refrigerador /rrefrihera'ðor/ n. m. refrigerator.

refrigerar /rrefrihe'rar/ v. refrigerate.

refuerzo /rre'fuerθo; rre'fuerso/ n. m. reinforcement.

refugiado /refu'hiaðo/ -da refugee.

refugiarse /refu'hiarse/ v. take refuge.

refugio /rre'fuhio/ n. m. refuge, asylum, shelter.

refulgencia /rreful'henθia; rre-ful'hensia/ n. f. refulgence.

refulgente /rreful'hente/ a. refulgent.

refulgir /rreful'hir/ v. shine.

refunfuñar /rrefunfu'nar/ v. mutter, grumble, growl.

refutación /rrefuta'θion; rrefuta-'sion/ n. f. refutation; rebuttal.

refutar /rrefu'tar/ v. refute.

regadera /rrega'ðera/ n. f. watering can.

regadizo /rrega'ðiθo; rrega'ðiso/ a. irrigable.

regadura /rrega'ðura/ n. f. irrigation.

regalar /rrega'lar/ v. give (a gift), give away.

regaliz /rrega'liθ; rrega'lis/ n. m. licorice.

regalo /rre'galo/ n. m. gift, present, **con r.,** in luxury.

regañar /rrega'nar/ v. reprove; scold.

regaño /rre'gano/ n. m. reprimand; scolding.

regar /rre'gar/ v. water, irrigate.

regatear /rregate'ar/ v. haggle.

regateo /rrega'teo/ n. m. bargaining, haggling.

regazo /rre'gaθo; rre'gaso/ n. m. lap.

regencia /rre'henθia; rre'hensia/ n. f. regency.

regeneración /rrehenera'θion; rre-henera'sion/ n. f. regeneration.

regenerar /rrehene'rar/ v. regenerate.

regente /rre'hente/ **-ta** a. & n. regent.

régimen /'rrehimen/ n. m. regime; diet.

regimentar /rrehimen'tar/ v. regiment.

regimiento /rrehi'miento/ n. m. regiment.

región /rre'hion/ n. f. region.

regional /rrehio'nal/ a. regional, sectional.

regir /rre'hir/ v. rule; be in effect.

registrar /rrehis'trar/ v. register; record; search.

registro /rre'histro/ n. m. register; record; search.

regla /'rregla/ n. f. rule, regulation. **en r.,** in order.

reglamento /rregla'mento/ n. m. code of regulations.

regocijarse /rrego'θiharse; rrego-si'harse/ v. rejoice, exult.

regocijo /rrego'θiho; rrego'siho/ n. f. rejoicing; merriment, joy.

regordete /rregor'ðete/ a. chubby, plump.

regresar /rregre'sar/ v. go back, return.

regresión /rregre'sion/ n. f. regression.

regresivo /rregre'siβo/ a. regressive.

regreso /rre'greso/ n. m. return.

regulación /rregula'θion; rregula-'sion/ n. f. regulation.

regular /rregu'lar/ a. **1.** regular; fair, middling. —v. **2.** regulate.

regularidad /rregulari'ðað/ n. f. regularity.

regularmente /rregular'mente/ adv. regularly.

rehabilitación /rreaβilita'θion; rreaβilita'sion/ n. f. rehabilitation.

rehabilitar /rreaβili'tar/ v. rehabilitate.

rehén /rre'en/ n. m. hostage.

rehogar /rreo'gar/ v. brown.

rehusar /rreu'sar/ v. refuse; decline.

reina /'rreina/ n. f. queen.

reinado /rrei'naðo/ n. m. reign. —**reinar,** v.

reino /'rreino/ n. m. kingdom; realm; reign.

reír /rre'ir/ v. laugh.

reiteración /rreitera'θion; rreitera'sion/ n. f. reiteration.

reiterar /rreite'rar/ v. reiterate.

reja /'rreha/ n. f. grating, grillwork.

relación /rrela'θion; rrela'sion/ n. f. relation; account, report.

relacionar /rrelaθio'nar; rrelasio'nar/ v. relate, connect.

relajamiento /rrelaha'miento/ n. m. laxity, laxness.

relajar /rrela'har/ v. relax, slacken.

relámpago /rre'lampago/ n. m. lightning; flash (of lightning).

relatador /rrelata'ðor/ -ra n. teller.

relatar /rrela'tar/ v. relate, recount.

relativamente /rrelatiβa'mente/ adv. relatively.

relatividad /rrelatiβi'ðað/ n. f. relativity.

relativo /rrela'tiβo/ a. relative.

relato /rre'lato/ n. m. account, story.

relegación /rrelega'θion; rrelega'sion/ n. f. relegation.

relegar /rrele'gar/ v. relegate.

relevar /rrele'βar/ v. relieve.

relicario /rreli'kario/ n. m. reliquary; locket.

relieve /rre'lieβe/ n. m. (sculpture) relief.

religión /rreli'hion/ n. f. religion.

religiosidad /rrelihiosi'ðað/ n. f. religiosity.

religioso /rreli'hioso/ **-sa** a. **1.** religious. —n. **2.** m. member of a religious order.

reliquia /rre'likia/ n. f. relic.

rellenar /rreʎe'nar/ v. refill; fill up, stuff.

relleno /rre'ʎeno; rre'yeno/ n. m. filling; stuffing.

reloj /rre'loh/ n. m. clock; watch.

reloj de pulsera /rre'loh de pul'sera/ wrist watch.

relojería /rreloxe'ria/ n. f. watchmaker's shop.

relojero /rrelo'hero/ -ra n. watchmaker.

relucir /rrelu'θir; rrelu'sir/ v. glow, shine; excel.

relumbrar /rrelum'βrar/ v. glitter, sparkle.

remache /rre'matʃe/ n. m. rivet. **—remachar,** v.

remar /rre'mar/ v. row (a boat).

rematado /rrema'taðo/ a. finished; sold.

remate /rre'mate/ n. m. end, finish; auction. **de r.,** utterly.

remedador /rremeða'ðor/ -ra n. imitator.

remedar /rreme'ðar/ v. imitate.

remedio /rre'meðio/ n. m. remedy. **—remediar,** v.

remendar /rremen'dar/ v. mend, patch.

remesa /rre'mesa/ n. f. shipment; remittance.

remiendo /rre'miendo/ n. m. patch.

remilgado /rremil'gaðo/ a. prudish; affected.

reminiscencia /rreminis'θenθia; rreminis'sensia/ n. f. reminiscence.

remitir /rremi'tir/ v. remit.

remo /'rremo/ n. m. oar.

remolacha /rremo'latʃa/ n. f. beet.

remolcador /rremolka'ðor/ n. m. tug (boat); tow truck.

remolino /rremo'lino/ n. m. whirl; whirlpool; whirlwind.

remolque /rre'molke/ n. m. tow. **—remolcar,** v.

remontar /rremon'tar/ v. ascend, go up.

remontarse /rremon'tarse/ v. get excited; soar. **r. a,** date from; go back to (in time).

remordimiento /rremorði'miento/ n. m. remorse.

remotamente /rremota'mente/ adv. remotely.

remoto /rre'moto/ a. remote.

remover /rremo'βer/ v. remove; stir; shake; loosen.

rempujar /rrempu'har/ v. jostle.

remuneración /rremunera'θion; rremunera'sion/ n. f. remuneration.

remunerar /rremune'rar/ v. remunerate.

renacido /rrena'θiðo; rrena'siðo/ a. reborn, born-again.

renacimiento /rrenaθi'miento; rrenasi'miento/ n. m. rebirth; renaissance.

rencor /rren'kor/ n. m. rancor, bitterness, animosity; grudge.

rencoroso /rrenko'roso/ a. rancorous, bitter.

rendición /rrendi'θion; rrendi'sion/ n. f. surrender.

rendido /rren'diðo/ *a.* weary, worn out.

rendir /rren'dir/ *v.* yield; surrender, give up; win over.

renegado /rrene'gaðo/ **-da** *n.* renegade.

renglón /rren'glon/ *n. m.* line; Com. item.

reno /'rreno/ *n. m.* reindeer.

renombre /rre'nombre/ *n. m.* renowned.

renovación /rrenoβa'θion; rrenoβa'sion/ *f.* renovation, renewal.

renovar /rreno'βar/ *v.* renew; renovate.

renta /'rrenta/ *n. f.* income; rent.

rentar /rren'tar/ *v.* yield; rent.

renuencia /rrenu'enθia; rre'nuensia/ *n. f.* reluctance.

renuente /rre'nuente/ *a.* reluctant.

renuncia /rre'nunθia; rre'nunsia/ *n. f.* resignation; renunciation.

renunciar /rrenun'θiar; rrenun'siar/ *v.* resign; renounce, give up.

reñir /rre'ɲir/ *v.* scold, berate; quarrel, wrangle.

reo /'rreo/ *a. & n.* criminal; convict.

reorganizar /rreorgani'θar; rreorgani'sar/ *v.* reorganize.

reparación /rrepara'θion; rrepara'sion/ *n. f.* reparation, atonement; repair.

reparar /rrepa'rar/ *v.* repair; mend; stop, stay over. **r. en,** notice; consider.

reparo /rre'paro/ *n. m.* repair; remark; difficulty; objection.

repartición /rreparti'θion; rreparti'sion/ *n. f.*, **repartimiento, reparto,** *m.* division, distribution.

repartir /rrepar'tir/ *v.* divide, apportion, distribute; Theat. cast.

repaso /rre'paso/ *n. m.* review. —**repasar,** *v.*

repatriación /rrepatria'θion; rrepatria'sion/ *n. f.* repatriation.

repatriar /rrepa'triar/ *v.* repatriate.

repeler /rrepe'ler/ *v.* repel.

repente /rre'pente/ *n. m.* **de r.,** suddenly; unexpectedly.

repentinamente /rrepentina'mente/ *adv.* suddenly.

repentino /rrepen'tino/ *a.* sudden.

repercusión /rreperku'sion/ *n. f.* repercussion.

repertorio /rreper'torio/ *n. m.* repertoire.

repetición /rrepeti'θion; rrepeti'sion/ *n. f.* repetition; action replay.

repetidamente /rrepetiða'mente/ *adv.* repeatedly.

repetir /rrepe'tir/ *v.* repeat.

repisa /rre'pisa/ *n. f.* shelf.

réplica /'rreplika/ *n. f.* reply; objection; replica.

replicar /rrepli'kar/ *v.* reply; answer back.

repollo /rre'poʎo; rre'poyo/ *n. m.* cabbage.

reponer /rrepo'ner/ *v.* replace; repair.

reponerse /rrepo'nerse/ *v.* recover, get well.

reporte /rre'porte/ *n. m.* report; news.

repórter /rre'porter/ **reportero -ra** *n.* reporter.

reposado /rrepo'saðo/ *a.* tranquil, peaceful, quiet.

reposo /rre'poso/ *n. m.* repose, rest. —**reposar,** *v.*

reposte /rre'poste/ *n. f.* pantry.

represalia /rrepre'salia/ *n. f.* reprisal.

representación /rrepresenta'θion; rrepresenta'sion/ *n. f.* representation; Theat. performance.

representante /rrepresen'tante/ *n. m. & f.* representative, agent.

representar /rrepresen'tar/ *v.* represent; depict; Theat. perform.

representativo /rrepresenta'tiβo/ *a.* representative.

represión /rrepre'sion/ *n. f.* repression.

represivo /rrepre'siβo/ *a.* repressive.

reprimenda /rrepri'menda/ *n. f.* reprimand.

reprimir /rrepri'mir/ *v.* repress, quell.

reproche /rre'protʃe/ *n. m.* reproach. —**reprochar,** *v.*

reproducción /rreproðuk'θion; rreproðuk'sion/ *n. f.* reproduction.

reproducir /rreproðu'θir; rreproðu'sir/ *v.* reproduce.

reptil /rrep'til/ *n. m.* reptile.

república /rre'puβlika/ *n. f.* republic.

republicano /rrepuβli'kano/ **-na** *a. & n.* republican.

repudiación /rrepuðia'θion; rrepuðia'sion/ *n. f.* repudiation.

repudiar /rrepu'ðiar/ v. repudiate; disown.

repuesto /rre'puesto/ n. m. spare part. **de r.**, spare.

repugnancia /rrepug'nanθia; rrepug'nansia/ n. f. repugnance.

repugnante /rrepug'nante/ a. disgusting, repugnant, repulsive, revolting.

repugnar /rrepug'nar/ v. disgust.

repulsa /rre'pulsa/ n. f. refusal; repulse.

repulsivo /rrepul'siβo/ a. repulsive.

reputación /rreputa'θion; rreputa'sion/ n. f. reputation.

reputar /rrepu'tar/ v. repute; appreciate.

requerir /rreke'rir/ v. require.

requesón /rreke'son/ n. m. cottage cheese.

requisición /rrekisi'θion; rrekisi'sion/ n. f. requisition.

requisito /rreki'sito/ n. m. requisite, requirement.

res /rres/ n. f. head of cattle.

resaca /rre'saka/ n. f. hangover.

resbalar /rresβa'lar/ v. slide; slip.

resbaloso /rresβa'loso/ a. slippery.

rescate /rres'kate/ n. m. rescue; ransom. —**rescatar**, v.

rescindir /rresθin'dir; rressin'dir/ v. rescind.

resentimiento /rresenti'miento/ n. m. resentment.

resentirse /rresen'tirse/ v. resent. —**reservar**, v.

reserva /rre'serβa/ n. f. reserve. —**reservar**, v.

reservación /rreserβa'θion; rreserβa'sion/ n. f. reservation.

resfriado /rres'friaðo/ n. m. Med. cold.

resfriarse /rres'friarse/ v. catch cold.

resguardar /rresguar'ðar/ v. guard, protect.

residencia /rresi'ðenθia; rresi'ðensia/ n. f. residence; seat, headquarters.

residente /rresi'ðente/ a. & n. resident.

residir /rresi'ðir/ v. reside.

residuo /rre'siðuo/ n. m. remainder.

resignación /rresigna'θion; rresigna'sion/ n. f. resignation.

resignar /rresig'nar/ v. resign.

resina /rre'sina/ n. f. resin; rosin.

resistencia /rresis'tenθia; rresis'tensia/ n. f. resistance.

resistir /rresis'tir/ v. resist; endure.

resolución /rresolu'θion; rresolu'sion/ n. f. resolution.

resolutivamente /rresolutiβa'mente/ adv. resolutely.

resolver /rresol'βer/ v. resolve; solve.

resonante /rreso'nante/ a. resonant.

resonar /rreso'nar/ v. resound.

resorte /rre'sorte/ n. m. Mech. spring.

respaldar /rrespal'dar/ v. endorse; back.

respaldo /rres'paldo/ n. m. back (of a seat).

respectivo /rrespek'tiβo/ a. respective.

respecto /rres'pekto/ n. m. relation, proportion; **r. a**, concerning, regarding.

respetabilidad /rrespetaβili'ðað/ n. f. respectability.

respetable /rrespe'taβle/ a. respectable.

respeto /rres'peto/ n. m. respect. —**respetar**, v.

respetuosamente /rrespetuosa'mente/ adv. respectfully.

respetuoso /rrespe'tuoso/ a. respectful.

respiración /rrespira'θion; rrespira'sion/ n. f. respiration, breath.

respirar /rrespi'rar/ v. breathe.

resplandeciente /rresplande'θiente; rresplande'siente/ a. resplendent.

resplandor /rresplan'dor/ n. m. brightness, glitter.

responder /rrespon'der/ v. respond, answer.

responsabilidad /rresponsaβili'ðað/ n. f. responsibility.

responsable /rrespon'saβle/ a. responsible.

respuesta /rres'puesta/ n. f. answer, response, reply.

resquicio /rres'kiθio; rres'kisio/ n. m. crack, slit.

resta /'rresta/ n. f. subtraction; remainder.

restablecer /rrestaβle'θer; rrestaβle'ser/ v. restore; reestablish.

restablecerse /rrestaβle'θerse; rrestaβle'serse/ v. recover, get well.

restar /rres'tar/ v. remain; subtract.

restauración /rrestaura'θion; rrestaura'sion/ n. f. restoration.

restaurante /rrestau'rante/ n. m. restaurant.

restaurar /rrestau'rar/ v. restore.

restitución /rrestitu'θion; rrestitu'sion/ n. f. restitution.

restituir /rresti'tuir/ v. restore, give back.

resto /'rresto/ n. m. remainder, rest; (pl.) remains.

restorán /rresto'ran/ n. m. restaurant.

restregar /rrestre'gar/ v. rub hard; scrub.

restricción /rrestrik'θion; rrestrik'sion/ n. f. restriction.

restrictivo /rrestrik'tiβo/ a. restrictive.

restringir /rrestriŋ'gir/ v. restrict, curtail.

resucitar /rresuθi'tar; rresusi'tar/ v. revive, resuscitate.

resuelto /rre'suelto/ a. resolute.

resultado /rresul'taðo/ n. m. result.

resultar /rresul'tar/ v. result; turn out; ensue.

resumen /rre'sumen/ n. m. résumé, summary, **en r.,** in brief.

resumir /rresu'mir/ v. sum up.

resurgir /rresur'hir/ v. resurge, reappear.

resurrección /rresurrek'θion; rresurrek'sion/ n. f. resurrection.

retaguardia /rreta'guarðia/ n. f. rear guard.

retal /rre'tal/ n. m. remnant.

retardar /rretar'ðar/ v. retard, slow.

retardo /rre'tarðo/ n. m. delay.

retención /rreten'θion; rreten'sion/ n. f. retention.

retener /rrete'ner/ v. retain, keep; withhold.

reticencia /rretiθen'θia; rretisen'sia/ n. f. reticence.

reticente /rreti'θente; rreti'sente/ a. reticent.

retirada /rreti'raða/ n. f. retreat, retirement.

retirar /rreti'rar/ v. retire, retreat, withdraw.

retiro /rre'tiro/ n. m. retirement.

retorcer /rretor'θer; rretor'ser/ v. wring.

retórica /rre'torika/ n. f. rhetoric.

retórico /rre'toriko/ a. rhetorical.

retorno /rre'torno/ n. m. return.

retozo /rre'toθo; rre'toso/ n. m. frolic, romp. **—retozar,** v.

retozón /rreto'θon; rreto'son/ a. frisky.

retracción /rretrak'θion; rretrak'sion/ n. f. retraction.

retractar /rretrak'tar/ v. retract.

retrasar /rretra'sar/ v. delay, set back.

retrasarse /rretra'sarse/ v. be slow.

retraso /rre'traso/ n. m. delay, lag, slowness.

retratar /rretra'tar/ v. portray; photograph.

retrato /rre'trato/ n. m. portrait; picture, photograph.

retreta /rre'treta/ n. f. Mil. retreat.

retrete /rre'trete/ n. m. toilet.

retribución /rretriβu'θion; rretriβu'sion/ n. f. retribution.

retroactivo /rretroak'tiβo/ a. retroactive.

retroalimentación /rretroalimenta'θion; rretroalimenta'sion/ n. f. feedback.

retroceder /rretroθe'ðer; rretrose'ðer/ v. recede, go back, draw back, back up

retumbar /rretum'βar/ v. resound, rumble.

reumático /rreu'matiko/ a. rheumatic.

reumatismo /rreuma'tismo/ n. m. rheumatism.

reunión /rreu'nion/ n. f. gathering, meeting, party; reunion.

reunir /rreu'nir/ v. gather, collect, bring together.

reunirse /rreu'nirse/ v. meet, assemble, get together.

reutilizar /rreutili'zar/ v. reuse.

revelación /rreβela'θion; rreβela'sion/ n. f. revelation.

revelar /rreβe'lar/ v. reveal; betray; Phot. develop.

reventa /rre'βenta/ n. f. resale.

reventar /rreβen'tar/ v. burst; split apart.

reventón /rreβen'ton/ n. m. blowout (of tire).

reverencia /rreβeren'θia; rreβeren'sia/ n. f. reverence.

reverendo /rreβe'rendo/ a. reverend.

reverente /rreβe'rente/ a. reverent.

revertir /rreβer'tir/ v. revert.

revés /rre'βes/ *n. m.* reverse; back, wrong side. **al r.,** just the opposite; inside out.

revisar /rreβi'sar/ *v.* revise; review.

revisión /rreβi'sion/ *n. f.* revision.

revista /rre'βista/ *n. f.* magazine, periodical; review.

revivir /rreβi'βir/ *v.* revive.

revocación /rreβoka'θion/ rreβoka'sion/ *n. f.* revocation.

revocar /rreβo'kar/ *v.* revoke, reverse.

revolotear /rreβolote'ar/ *v.* hover.

revolución /rreβolu'θion/ rreβolu'sion/ *n. f.* revolution.

revolucionario /rreβoluθio'nario/ rreβolusio'nario/ **-ria** *a. & n.* revolutionary.

revolver /rreβol'βer/ *v.* revolve, stir, agitate.

revólver *n. m.* revolver, pistol.

revuelta /rre'βuelta/ *n. f.* revolt; turn.

rey /rrei/ *n. m.* king.

reyerta /rre'yerta/ *n. f.* quarrel, wrangle.

rezar /rre'θar/ rre'sar/ *v.* pray.

rezongar /rreθoŋ'gar/ reson'gar/ *v.* grumble; mutter.

ría /'rria/ *n. f.* estuary.

riachuelo /rria't∫uelo/ *n. m.* creek.

riba /'rriβa/ *n. f.* embankment.

rico /'rriko/ *a.* rich, wealthy; delicious.

ridículamente /rri'ðikulamente/ *adv.* ridiculously.

ridiculizar /rriðikuli'θar/ rriðikuli'sar/ *v.* ridicule.

ridículo /rri'ðikulo/ *a. & m.* ridiculous; ridicule.

riego /'rriego/ *n. m.* irrigation.

rienda /'rrienda/ *n. f.* rein.

riesgo /'rriesgo/ *n. m.* risk, gamble.

rifa /'rrifa/ *n. f.* raffle; lottery; scuffle.

rifle /'rrifle/ *n. m.* rifle.

rigidamente /rrihiðamente/ *adv.* rigidly.

rigidez /rrihi'ðeθ/ rrihi'ðes/ *n. f.* rigidity.

rígido /'rrihiðo/ *a.* rigid, stiff.

rigor /rri'gor/ *n. m.* rigor.

riguroso /rrigu'roso/ *a.* rigorous, strict.

rima /'rrima/ *n. f.* rhyme. **—rimar,** *v.*

rimel /rri'mel/ *n. f.* mascara.

rincón /rrin'kon/ *n. m.* corner, nook.

rinoceronte /rrinoθe'ronte/ rrino-se'ronte/ *n. m.* rhinoceros.

riña /'rriɲa/ *n. f.* quarrel, feud.

riñón /rri'ɲon/ *n. m.* kidney.

río /'rrio/ *n. m.* river. **r. abajo** downstream, downriver. **r. arriba,** upstream, upriver.

ripio /'rripio/ *n. m.* debris.

riqueza /rri'keθa/ rri'kesa/ *n. f.* wealth.

risa /'rrisa/ *n. f.* laugh; laughter.

risco /'rrisko/ *n. m.* cliff.

risibilidad /rrisiβili'ðað/ *n. f.* risibility.

risotada /rriso'taða/ *n. f.* peal of laughter.

risueño /rri'sueɲo/ *a.* cheerful, smiling.

rítmico /'rritmiko/ *a.* rhythmical.

ritmo /'rritmo/ *n. m.* rhythm.

rito /'rrito/ *n. m.* rite.

ritual /rri'tual/ *a. & m.* ritual.

rivalidad /rriβali'ðað/ *n. f.* rivalry.

rivera /rri'βera/ *n. f.* brook.

rizado /rri'θaðo/ rri'saðo/ *a.* curly.

rizo /'rriθo/ 'rriso/ *n. m.* curl. **—rizar,** *v.*

robar /rro'βar/ *v.* rob, steal.

roble /'rroβle/ *n. m.* oak.

roblón /rro'βlon/ *n. m.* rivet. **—roblar,** *v.*

robo /'rroβo/ *n. m.* robbery, theft.

robustamente /rroβusta'mente/ *adv.* robustly.

robusto /rro'βusto/ *a.* robust.

roca /'rroka/ *n. f.* rock; cliff.

rociada /rro'θiaða/ rro'siaða/ *n. f.* spray, sprinkle. **—rociar,** *v.*

rocío /rro'θio/ 'rrosio/ *n. m.* dew.

rocoso /rro'koso/ *a.* rocky.

rodar /rro'ðar/ *v.* roll; roam.

rodear /rroðe'ar/ *v.* surround, encircle.

rodeo /rro'ðeo/ *n. m.* turn, winding; roundup.

rodilla /rro'ðiʎa/ rro'ðiya/ *n. f.* knee.

rodillo /rro'ðiʎo/ rro'ðiyo/ *n. m.* roller.

rodio /'rroðio/ *n. m.* rhodium.

rododendro /rroðo'ðendro/ *n. m.* rhododendron.

roedor /rroe'ðor/ *n. m.* rodent.

roer /rro'er/ *v.* gnaw.

rogación /rroga'θion/ rroga'sion/ *n. f.* request, entreaty.

rogar /rro'gar/ *v.* beg, plead with, supplicate.

rojizo /rro'hiθo; rro'hiso/ a. reddish.

rojo /'rroho/ a. red.

rollizo /rro'ʎiθo; rro'yiso/ a. chubby.

rollo /'rroʎo; 'rroyo/ n. m. roll; coil.

romadizo /rroma'ðiθo; roma-'ðiso/ n. m. head cold.

romance /rro'manθe; rro'manse/ n. m. romance; ballad.

románico /rro'maniko/ a. Romance.

romano /rro'mano/ -na a. & n. Roman.

romántico /rro'mantiko/ a. romantic.

romería /rrome'ria/ n. f. pilgrimage; picnic.

romero /rro'mero/ -ra n. pilgrim.

rompecabezas /rrompeka'βeθas; rrompeka'βesas/ n. m. puzzle (pastime).

romper /rrom'per/ v. break, smash, shatter; sever; tear.

rompible /rrom'piβle/ a. breakable.

ron /rron/ n. m. rum.

roncar /rron'kar/ v. snore.

ronco /'rronko/ a. hoarse.

ronda /'rronda/ n. f. round.

rondar /rron'dar/ v. prowl.

ronquido /rron'kiðo/ n. m. snore.

ronronear /rronrone'ar/ v. purr.

ronzal /rron'θal; rron'sal/ n. m. halter.

roña /'rroɲa/ n. f. scab; filth.

ropa /'rropa/ n. f. clothes, clothing. **r. blanca,** linen. **r. interior,** underwear.

ropa de marca /'rropa de 'marka/ designer clothing.

ropero /rro'pero/ n. m. closet.

rosa /'rrosa/ n. f. rose. **r. náutica,** compass.

rosado /rro'saðo/ a. pink, rosy.

rosal /rro'sal/ n. m. rose bush.

rosario /rro'sario/ n. m. rosary.

rosbif /rros'βif/ n. m. roast beef.

rosca /'rroska/ n. f. thread (of screw).

róseo /'rroseo/ a. rosy.

rostro /'rrostro/ n. m. face, countenance.

rota /'rrota/ n. f. defeat; Naut. course.

rotación /rrota'θion; rrota'sion/ n. f. rotation.

rotatorio /rrota'torio/ a. rotary.

rótula /'rrotula/ n. f. kneecap.

rotulador /rrotula'ðor/ n. m. felt-tipped pen.

rótulo /'rrotulo/ n. m. label. —**rotular,** v.

rotundo /rro'tundo/ a. round; sonorous.

rotura /rro'tura/ n. f. break, fracture, rupture.

rozar /rro'θar; rro'sar/ v. rub against, chafe; graze.

rubí /rru'βi/ n. m. ruby.

rubio /'rruβio/ -bia a. & n. blond.

rubor /rru'βor/ n. m. blush; bashfulness.

rúbrica /'rruβrika/ n. f. caption; scroll.

rucho /'rrutʃo/ n. m. donkey.

rudeza /rru'ðeθa; rru'ðesa/ n. f. rudeness; roughness.

rudimentario /rruðimen'tario/ a. rudimentary.

rudimento /rruði'mento/ n. m. rudiment.

rudo /'rruðo/ a. rude, rough.

rueda /'rrueða/ n. f. wheel.

rueda de feria /'rrueða de 'feria/ Ferris wheel.

ruego /'rruego/ n. m. plea; entreaty.

rufián /rru'fian/ n. m. ruffian.

rufo /'rrufo/ a. sandy haired.

rugir /rru'hir/ v. bellow, roar.

rugoso /rru'goso/ a. wrinkled.

ruibarbo /rrui'βarβo/ n. m. rhubarb.

ruido /'rruiðo/ n. m. noise.

ruidoso /rrui'ðoso/ a. noisy.

ruina /'rruina/ n. f. ruin, wreck.

ruinar /rrui'nar/ v. ruin, destroy.

ruinoso /rrui'noso/ a. ruinous.

ruiseñor /rruise'ɲor/ n. m. nightingale.

ruleta /rru'leta/ n. f. roulette.

rumba /'rrumba/ n. f. rumba (dance or music).

rumbo /'rrumbo/ n. m. course, direction.

rumor /rru'mor/ n. m. rumor; murmur.

runrún /rrun'run/ n. m. rumor.

ruptura /rrup'tura/ n. f. rupture, break.

rural /rru'ral/ a. rural.

Rusia /'rrusia/ n. f. Russia.

ruso /'rruso/ -sa a. & n. Russian.

rústico /'rrustiko/ -ca a. & n. rustic. **en rústica,** paperback f.

ruta /'rruta/ n. f. route.

rutina /rru'tina/ n. f. routine.

rutinario /rruti'nario/ a. routine.

S

sábado /'saβaðo/ *n. m.* Saturday.

sábalo /'saβalo/ *n. m.* shad.

sábana /'saβana/ *n. f.* sheet.

sabañon /saβa'ɲon/ *n. m.* chilblain.

saber /sa'βer/ *n.* **1.** knowledge. —*v.* **2.** know; learn, find out; know how to; taste. **a s.**, namely, to wit.

sabiduría /saβiðu'ria/ *n. f.* wisdom; learning.

sabio /'saβio/ *-a* **1.** wise; scholarly. —*n.* **2.** sage; scholar.

sable /'saβle/ *n. m.* saber.

sabor /sa'βor/ *n. m.* flavor, taste, savor.

saborear /saβore'ar/ *v.* savor, relish.

sabotaje /saβo'tahe/ *n. m.* sabotage.

sabroso /sa'βroso/ *a.* savory, tasty.

sabueso /sa'βueso/ *n. m.* hound.

sacacorchos /saka'kortʃos/ *n. m.* corkscrew.

sacapuntas /saka'puntas/ *n. f.* pencil sharpener.

sacar /sa'kar/ *v.* draw out; take out; take.

sacerdocio /saθer'ðoθio; saser'ðosio/ *n. m.* priesthood.

sacerdote /saθer'ðote; saser'ðote/ *n. m.* priest.

saciar /sa'θiar; sa'siar/ *v.* satiate.

saco /'sako/ *n. m.* sack, bag, pouch; suit coat, jacket.

sacramento /sakra'mento/ *n. m.* sacrament.

sacrificio /sakri'fiθio; sakri'fisio/ *n. m.* sacrifice. —**sacrificar,** *v.*

sacrilegio /sakri'lehio/ *n. m.* sacrilege.

sacristán /sakris'tan/ *n. m.* sexton.

sacro /'sakro/ *a.* sacred, holy.

sacrosanto /sakro'santo/ *a.* sacrosanct.

sacudir /saku'ðir/ *v.* shake, jerk, jolt.

sádico /'saðiko/ *a.* sadistic.

sadismo /sa'ðismo/ *n. m.* sadism.

sagacidad /sagaθi'ðað; sagasi'ðað/ *n. f.* sagacity.

sagaz /sa'gaθ; sa'gas/ *a.* sagacious, sage.

sagrado /sa'graðo/ *a.* sacred, holy.

sal /sal/ *n. f.* salt; *Colloq.* wit.

sala /'sala/ *n. f.* room; living room, parlor; hall, auditorium.

salado /sa'laðo/ *a.* salted, salty; *Colloq.* witty.

salar /sa'lar/ *v.* salt; steep in brine.

salario /sa'lario/ *n. m.* salary, wages.

salchicha /sal'tʃitʃa/ *n. f.* sausage.

sal de la Higuera /sal de la i'gera/ Epsom salts.

saldo /'saldo/ *n. m.* remainder, balance; (bargain) sale.

saldo acreedor /'saldo akree'ðor/ credit balance.

saldo deudor /'saldo deu'ðor/ debit balance.

salero /sa'lero/ *n. m.* salt shaker.

salida /sa'liða/ *n. f.* exit, outlet; departure.

salida de urgencia /sa'liða de ur'henθia; sa'liða de ur'hensia/ emergency exit, fire exit.

salir /sa'lir/ *v.* go out, come out; set out, leave, start; turn out, result.

salirse de /sa'lirse de/ *v.* get out of. **s. con la suya,** have one's own way.

salitre /sa'litre/ *n. m.* saltpeter.

saliva /sa'liβa/ *n. f.* saliva.

salmo /'salmo/ *n. m.* psalm.

salmón /sal'mon/ *n. m.* salmon.

salmonete /salmo'nete/ *n. m.* red mullet.

salmuera /sal'muera/ *n. f.* pickle; brine.

salobre /sa'loβre/ *a.* salty.

salón /sa'lon/ *n. m.* parlor, living room; hall. **s. de baile,** dance hall. **s. de belleza** beauty parlor.

salpicar /salpi'kar/ *v.* spatter, splash.

salpullido /salpu'ʎiðo; salpu'yiðo/ *n. m.* rash.

salsa /'salsa/ *n. f.* sauce; gravy.

saltamontes /salta'montes/ *n. m.* grasshopper.

salteador /saltea'ðor/ *n. m.* highwayman.

saltear /salte'ar/ *v.* hold up, rob; sauté.

salto /'salto/ *n. m.* jump, leap, spring. —**saltar,** *v.*

saltón /sal'ton/ *n. m.* grasshopper.

salubre /sa'luβre/ a. salubrious, healthful.

salubridad /saluβri'ðað/ n. f. health.

salud /sa'luð/ n. f. health.

saludable /salu'ðaβle/ a. healthful, wholesome.

saludar /salu'ðar/ v. greet; salute.

saludo /sa'luðo/ n. m. greeting; salutation; salute.

salutación /saluta'θion; saluta-'sion/ n. f. salutation.

salva /'salβa/ n. f. salvo.

salvación /salβa'θion; salβa'sion/ n. f. salvation; deliverance.

salvador /salβa'ðor/ -ra n. savior; rescuer.

salvaguardia /salβa'guarðia/ n. m. safeguard.

salvaje /sal'βahe/ a. & n. savage, wild (person).

salvamento /salβa'mento/ n. m. salvation; rescue.

salvar /sal'βar/ v. save; salvage; rescue; jump over.

salvavidas /salβa'βiðas/ n. m. life preserver.

salvia /'salβia/ n. f. sage (plant).

salvo /'salβo/ a. 1. safe. —prep. 2. except, save (for). **s. que**, unless.

San /san/ title. Saint.

sanar /sa'nar/ v. heal, cure.

sanatorio /sana'torio/ n. m. sanatorium.

sanción /san'θion; san'sion/ n. f. sanction. —**sancionar**, v.

sancochar /sanko'tʃar/ v. parboil.

sandalia /san'dalia/ n. f. sandal.

sandez /san'deθ; san'des/ n. f. stupidity.

sandía /san'dia/ n. f. watermelon.

saneamiento /sanea'miento/ n. m. sanitation.

sangrar /saŋ'grar/ v. bleed.

sangre /'saŋgre/ n. f. blood.

sangriento /saŋ'griento/ a. bloody.

sanguinario /saŋgi'nario/ a. bloodthirsty.

sanidad /sani'ðað/ n. f. health.

sanitario /sani'tario/ a. sanitary.

sano /'sano/ a. healthy, sound, sane; healthful, wholesome.

santidad /santi'ðað/ n. f. sanctity, holiness.

santificar /santifi'kar/ v. sanctify.

santo /'santo/ -ta a. 1. holy, saintly. —n. 2. m. saint.

Santo -ta title. Saint.

santuario /san'tuario/ n. m. sanctuary, shrine.

saña /'saɲa/ n. f. rage, anger.

sapiente /sa'piente/ a. wise.

sapo /'sapo/ n. m. toad.

saquear /sake'ar/ v. sack; ransack; plunder.

sarampión /saram'pion/ n. m. measles.

sarape /sa'rape/ n. m. (Mex.) woven blanket; shawl.

sarcasmo /sar'kasmo/ n. m. sarcasm.

sarcástico /sar'kastiko/ a. sarcastic.

sardina /sar'ðina/ n. f. sardine.

sargento /sar'hento/ n. m. sergeant.

sarna /'sarna/ n. f. itch.

sartén /sar'ten/ n. f. frying pan.

sastre /'sastre/ n. m. tailor.

satánico /sa'taniko/ a. satanic.

satélite /sa'telite/ n. m. satellite.

sátira /'satira/ n. f. satire.

satírico /sa'tiriko/ a. & m. satirical; satirist.

satirizar /satiri'θar; satiri'sar/ v. satirize.

satiro /'satiro/ n. m. satyr.

satisfacción /satisfak'θion; satisfak'sion/ n. f. satisfaction.

satisfacer /satisfa'θer; satisfa'ser/ v. satisfy.

satisfactorio /satisfak'torio/ a. satisfactory.

saturación /satura'θion; satura-'sion/ n. f. saturation.

saturar /satu'rar/ v. saturate.

sauce /'sauθe; 'sause/ n. m. willow.

sauna /'sauna/ n. f. sauna.

savia /'saβia/ n. f. sap.

saxofón /sakso'fon/ **saxófono** /sa'ksofono/ n. m. saxophone.

saya /'saya/ n. f. skirt.

sazón /sa'θon; sa'son/ n. f. season; seasoning. **a la s.**, at that time.

sazonar /saθo'nar; saso'nar/ v. flavor, season.

se /se/ pron. -self, -selves.

seca /'seka/ n. f. drought.

secador /seka'ðor/ **secador de pelo** n. m. hair dryer.

secante /se'kante/ a. **papel s.**, blotting paper.

secar /se'kar/ v. dry.

sección /sek'θion; sek'sion/ n. f. section.

seco /'seko/ a. dry; curt.

secreción /sekre'θion; sekre'sion/ *n. f.* secretion.

secretar /sekre'tar/ *v.* secrete.

secretaría /sekreta'ria/ *n. f.* secretary's office; secretariat.

secretario /sekre'tario/ **-ra** *n.* secretary.

secreto /se'kreto/ *a. & m.* secret.

secta /'sekta/ *n. f.* denomination; sect.

secuela /se'kuela/ *n. f.* result; sequel.

secuestrar /sekues'trar/ *v.* abduct, kidnap; hijack.

secuestro /se'kuestro/ *n. m.* abduction, kidnapping.

secular /seku'lar/ *a.* secular.

secundario /sekun'dario/ *a.* secondary.

sed /seð/ *n. f.* thirst. **tener s., estar con s.,** to be thirsty.

seda /'seða/ *n. f.* silk.

sedar /se'ðar/ *v.* quiet, allay.

sedativo /seða'tiβo/ *a. & m.* sedative.

sede /'seðe/ *n. f.* seat, headquarters.

sedentario /seðen'tario/ *a.* sedentary.

sedición /seði'θion; seði'sion/ *n. f.* sedition.

sedicioso /seði'θioso; seði'sioso/ *a.* seditious.

sediento /se'ðiento/ *a.* thirsty.

sedimento /seði'mento/ *n. m.* sediment.

sedoso /se'ðoso/ *a.* silky.

seducir /seðu'θir; seðu'sir/ *v.* seduce.

seductivo /seðuk'tiβo/ *a.* seductive, alluring.

segar /se'gar/ *v.* reap, harvest; mow.

seglar /se'glar/ *n. m. & f.* layman; laywoman.

segmento /seg'mento/ *n. m.* segment.

segregar /segre'gar/ *v.* segregate.

seguida /se'giða/ *n. f.* succession. **en s.,** right away, at once.

seguido /se'giðo/ *a.* consecutive.

seguir /se'gir/ *v.* follow; continue, keep on, go on.

según /se'gun/ *prep.* **1.** according to. —*conj.* **2.** as.

segundo /se'gundo/ *a. & m.* second. —**segundar,** *v.*

seguridad /seguri'ðað/ *n. f.* safety, security; assurance.

seguro /se'guro/ *a.* **1.** safe, secure; sure, certain. —*n.* **2.** *m.* insurance.

seis /seis/ *a. & pron.* six.

seiscientos /seis'θientos; seis'sientos/ *a. & pron.* six hundred.

selección /selek'θion; selek'sion/ *n. f.* selection, choice.

seleccionar /selekθio'nar; seleksio'nar/ *v.* select, choose.

selecto /se'lekto/ *a.* select, choice, elite.

sello /'seʎo; 'seyo/ *n. m.* seal; stamp. —**sellar,** *v.*

selva /'selβa/ *n. f.* forest; jungle.

selvoso /sel'βoso/ *a.* sylvan.

semáforo /se'maforo/ *n. m.* semaphore; traffic light.

semana /se'mana/ *n. f.* week.

semana inglesa /se'mana iŋ'glesa/ five-day work week.

semanal /sema'nal/ *a.* weekly.

semana laboral /se'mana laβo'ral/ work week.

semántica /se'mantika/ *n. f.* semantics.

semblante /sem'βlante/ *n. m.* look, expression.

sembrado /sem'βraðo/ *n. m.* sown field.

sembrar /sem'βrar/ *v.* sow, seed.

semejante /seme'hante/ *a.* **1.** like, similar; such (a). —*n.* **2.** *m.* fellow man.

semejanza /seme'hanθa; seme'hansa/ *n. f.* similarity, likeness.

semejar /seme'har/ *v.* resemble.

semilla /se'miʎa; se'miya/ *n. f.* seed.

seminario /semi'nario/ *n. m.* seminary.

sémola /'semola/ *n. f.* semolina.

senado /se'naðo/ *n. m.* senate.

senador /sena'ðor/ **-ra** *n.* senator.

sencillez /senθi'ʎeθ; sensi'yes/ *n. f.* simplicity; naturalness.

sencillo /sen'θiʎo; sen'siyo/ *a.* simple, natural; single.

senda /'senda/ *n. f.* **sendero,** *m.* path, footpath.

senectud /senek'tuð/ *n. f.* old age.

senil /se'nil/ *a.* senile.

seno /'seno/ *n. m.* breast, bosom.

sensación /sensa'θion; sensa'sion/ *n. f.* sensation.

sensacional /sensaθio'nal; sensasio'nal/ *a.* sensational.

sensato /sen'sato/ *a.* sensible, wise.

sensibilidad /sensiβili'ðað/ n. f. sensibility; sensitiveness.

sensible /sen'siβle/ a. sensitive; emotional.

sensitivo /sensi'tiβo/ a. sensitive.

sensual /sen'sual/ a. sensual.

sensualidad /sensuali'ðað/ n. f. sensuality.

sentar /sen'tar/ v. seat. **s. bien,** fit well, be becoming.

sentarse /sen'tarse/ v. sit, sit down.

sentencia /sen'tenθia; sen'tensia/ n. f. (court) sentence.

sentidamente /sentiða'mente/ adv. feelingly.

sentido /sen'tiðo/ n. m. meaning, sense; consciousness.

sentido común /sen'tiðo ko'mun/ common sense.

sentimental /sentimen'tal/ a. sentimental.

sentimiento /senti'miento/ n. m. sentiment, feeling.

sentir /sen'tir/ v. feel, sense; hear; regret, be sorry.

seña /'seɲa/ n. f. sign, indication; (pl.) address.

señal /se'ɲal/ n. f. sign, signal; mark.

señalar /seɲa'lar/ v. designate, point out; mark.

señal de marcar /se'ɲal de mar'kar/ dial tone.

señor /se'ɲor/ n. m. gentleman; lord; (title) Mr., Sir.

señora /se'ɲora/ n. f. lady; wife; (title) Mrs., Madam.

señora de la limpieza /se'ɲora de la lim'pieθa; se'ɲora de la lim'piesa/ cleaning woman.

señorita /seɲo'rita/ n. f. young lady; (title) Miss.

sépalo /'sepalo/ n. m. sepal.

separación /separa'θion; separa'sion/ n. f. separation, parting.

separadamente /separaða'mente/ adv. separately.

separado /sepa'raðo/ a. separate; separated. **—separar,** v.

septentrional /septentrio'nal/ a. northern.

septiembre /sep'tiembre/ n. m. September.

séptimo /'septimo/ a. seventh.

sepulcro /se'pulkro/ n. m. sepulcher.

sepultar /sepul'tar/ v. bury, entomb.

sepultura /sepul'tura/ n. f. grave.

sequedad /seke'ðað/ n. f. dryness.

sequía /se'kia/ n. f. drought.

ser /ser/ v. be.

serenata /sere'nata/ n. f. serenade.

serenidad /sereni'ðað/ n. f. serenity.

sereno /se'reno/ a. **1.** serene, calm. **—n. 2.** m. dew; watchman.

ser humano /ser u'mano/ n. human being.

serie /'serie/ n. f. series, sequence.

seriedad /serie'ðað/ n. f. seriousness.

serio /'serio/ a. serious. **en s.,** seriously.

sermón /ser'mon/ n. m. sermon.

seroso /se'roso/ a. watery.

serpiente /ser'piente/ n. f. serpent, snake.

serpiente de cascabel /ser'piente de kaska'βel/ rattlesnake.

serrano /se'rrano/ a. **-na** n. mountaineer.

serrar /se'rrar/ v. saw.

serrín /se'rrin/ n. m. sawdust.

servicial /serβi'θial; serβi'sial/ a. helpful, of service.

servicio /ser'βiθio; ser'βisio/ n. m. service; toilet.

servidor /serβi'ðor/ **-ra** n. servant.

servidumbre /serβi'ðumbre/ n. f. bondage; staff of servants.

servil /ser'βil/ a. servile, menial.

servilleta /serβi'ʎeta; serβi'yeta/ n. f. napkin.

servir /ser'βir/ v. serve. **s. para,** be good for.

servirse /ser'βirse/ v. help oneself.

sesenta /se'senta/ a. & pron. sixty.

sesgo /'sesgo/ n. m. slant. **—sesgar,** v.

sesión /se'sion/ n. f. session; sitting.

seso /'seso/ n. m. brain.

seta /'seta/ n. f. mushroom.

setecientos /sete'θientos; sete'sientos/ a. & pron. seven hundred.

setenta /se'tenta/ a. & pron. seventy.

seto /'seto/ n. m. hedge.

severamente /seβera'mente/ adv. severely.

severidad /seβeri'ðað/ n. f. severity.

severo /se'βero/ a. severe, strict, stern.

sexismo /sek'sismo/ n. m. sexism.

sexista /sek'sista/ a. & n. sexist.

sexo /'sekso/ n. m. sex.

sexto /'seksto/ a. sixth.

sexual /sek'sual/ a. sexual.

si /si/ conj. if; whether.

sí pron. **1.** -self, -selves. —interj. **2.** yes.

sico-. See psicoanálisis, psicología, etc.

sicómoro /siko'moro/ n. m. sycamore.

SIDA /'siða/ n. m. AIDS.

sidra /'siðra/ n. f. cider.

siempre /'siempre/ adv. always. **para s.,** forever. **s. que,** whenever; provided that.

sierra /'sierra/ n. f. saw; mountain range.

siervo /'sierβo/ **-va** n. slave; serf.

siesta /'siesta/ n. f. (afternoon) nap.

siete /'siete/ a. & pron. seven.

sifón /si'fon/ n. m. siphon; siphon bottle.

siglo /'siglo/ n. m. century.

signatura /signa'tura/ n. f. Mus. signature.

significación /signifika'θion; signifika'sion/ n. f. significance.

significado /signifi'kaðo/ n. m. meaning.

significante /signifi'kante/ a. significant.

significar /signifi'kar/ v. signify, mean.

significativo /signifika'tiβo/ a. significant.

signo /'signo/ n. m. sign, symbol; mark.

siguiente /si'giente/ a. following, next.

silaba /'silaβa/ n. f. syllable.

silbar /sil'βar/ v. whistle; hiss, boo.

silbato /sil'βato/ **silbido** n. m. whistle.

silencio /si'lenθio; si'lensio/ n. m. silence, stillness.

silenciosamente /silenθiosa'mente; silensiosa'mente/ a. silently.

silencioso /silen'θioso; silen'sioso/ a. silent, still.

silicato /sili'kato/ n. m. silicate.

silicio /si'liθio; si'lisio/ n. m. silicon.

silla /'siʎa; 'siya/ n. f. chair; saddle.

sillón /si'ʎon; si'yon/ n. m. armchair.

silueta /si'lueta/ n. f. silhouette.

silvestre /sil'βestre/ a. wild, uncultivated. **fauna s.,** wildlife.

sima /'sima/ n. f. chasm; cavern.

simbólico /sim'boliko/ a. symbolic.

símbolo /'simbolo/ n. m. symbol.

simetría /sime'tria/ n. f. symmetry.

simétrico /si'metriko/ a. symmetrical.

simil /'simil/ similar a. similar, alike.

similitud /simili'tuð/ n. f. similarity.

simpatía /simpa'tia/ n. f. congeniality; friendly feeling.

simpático /sim'patiko/ a. likeable, nice, congenial.

simple /'simple/ a. simple.

simpleza /sim'pleθa; sim'plesa/ n. f. silliness; trifle.

simplicidad /simpliθi'ðað; simplisi'ðað/ n. f. simplicity.

simplificación /simplifika'θion; simplifika'sion/ n. f. simplification.

simplificar /simplifi'kar/ v. simplify.

simular /simu'lar/ v. simulate.

simultáneo /simul'taneo/ a. simultaneous.

sin /sin/ prep. without. **s. sentido,** meaningless.

sinagoga /sina'goga/ n. f. synagogue.

sinceridad /sinθeri'ðað; sinseri'ðað/ n. f. sincerity.

sincero /sin'θero; sin'sero/ a. sincere.

sincronizar /sinkroni'θar; sinkroni'sar/ v. synchronize.

sindicato /sindi'kato/ n. m. syndicate; labor union.

síndrome /'sindrome/ n. m. syndrome.

sinfonía /sinfo'nia/ n. f. symphony.

sinfónico /sin'foniko/ a. symphonic.

singular /siŋgu'lar/ a. & a. singular.

siniestro /si'niestro/ a. sinister, ominous.

sino /'sino/ conj. but.

sinónimo /si'nonimo/ *n. m.* synonym.

sinrazón /sinra'θon; sinra'son/ *n. f.* wrong, injustice.

sinsabor /sinsa'βor/ *n. m.* displeasure, distaste; trouble.

sintaxis /sin'taksis/ *n. f.* syntax.

sintesis /'sintesis/ *n. f.* synthesis.

sintético /sin'tetiko/ *a.* synthetic.

síntoma /'sintoma/ *n. m.* symptom.

siquiera /si'kiera/ *adv.* **ni s.,** not even.

sirena /si'rena/ *n. f.* siren.

sirviente /sir'βiente/ **-ta** *n.* servant.

sistema /sis'tema/ *n. m.* system.

sistemático /siste'matiko/ *a.* systematic.

sistematizar /sistemati'θar; sistemati'sar/ *v.* systematize.

sitiar /si'tiar/ *v.* besiege.

sitio /'sitio/ *n. m.* site, location, place, spot.

situación /situa'θion; situa'sion/ *n. f.* situation; location.

situar /si'tuar/ *v.* situate; locate.

smoking /'smoking/ *n. m.* tuxedo, dinner jacket.

so /so/ *prep.* under.

soba /'soβa/ *n. f.* massage. **—sobar,** *v.*

sobaco /so'βako/ *n. m.* armpit.

sobaquero /soβa'kero/ *n. f.* armhole.

soberano /soβe'rano/ **-na** *a. & n.* sovereign.

soberbia /so'βerβia/ *n. f.* arrogance.

soberbio /so'βerβio/ *a.* superb; arrogant.

soborno /so'βorno/ *n. m.* bribe. **—sobornar,** *v.*

sobra /'soβra/ *n. f.* excess, surplus. **de sobra,** to spare.

sobrado /so'βrado/ *n. m.* attic.

sobrante /so'βrante/ *a. & m.* surplus.

sobras /'soβras/ *n. f.pl.* leftovers.

sobre /'soβre/ *prep.* **1.** about; above, over. **—n. 2.** envelope.

sobrecama /soβre'kama/ *n. f.* bedspread.

sobrecargo /soβre'kargo/ *n. m.* supercargo.

sobredicho /soβre'ðitʃo/ *a.* aforesaid.

sobredosis /soβre'ðosis/ *n. f.* overdose.

sobrehumano /soβreu'mano/ *a.* superhuman.

sobrenatural /soβrenatu'ral/ *a.* supernatural, weird.

sobrepasar /soβrepa'sar/ *v.* surpass.

sobresalir /soβresa'lir/ *v.* excel.

sobretodo /soβre'toðo/ *n. m.* overcoat.

sobrevivir /soβreβi'βir/ *v.* survive, outlive.

sobriedad /soβrie'ðað/ *n. f.* sobriety; moderation.

sobrina /so'βrina/ *n. f.* niece.

sobrino /so'βrino/ *n. m.* nephew.

sobrio /'soβrio/ *a.* sober, temperate.

socarrén /soka'rren/ *n. m.* eaves.

sociable /so'θiaβle; so'siaβle/ *a.* sociable.

social /so'θial; so'sial/ *a.* social.

socialismo /soθia'lismo; sosia-'lismo/ *n. m.* socialism.

socialista /soθia'lista; sosia'lista/ *a. & n.* socialist.

sociedad /soθie'ðað; sosie'ðað/ *n. f.* society; association.

sociedad de consumo /soθie'ðað de kon'sumo; sosie'ðað de kon'sumo/ consumer society.

socio /'soθio; 'sosio/ **-cia** *n.* associate, partner; member.

sociología /soθiolo'hia; sosiolo-'hia/ *n. f.* sociology.

sociológico /soθio'lohiko; sosio-'lohiko/ *a.* sociological.

sociólogo /so'θiologo; so'siologo/ **-ga** *n.* sociologist.

socorrista /soko'rrista/ *n. m. & f.* lifeguard.

socorro /so'korro/ *n. m.* help, aid. **—socorrer,** *v.*

soda /'soða/ *n. f.* soda.

sodio /'soðio/ *n. m.* sodium.

soez /so'eθ; so'es/ *a.* vulgar.

sofá /so'fa/ *n. m.* sofa, couch.

sofisma /so'fisma/ *n. m.* sophism.

sofista /so'fista/ *n. m. & f.* sophist.

sofocación /sofoka'θion; sofoka-'sion/ *n. f.* suffocation.

sofocar /sofo'kar/ *v.* smother, suffocate, stifle, choke.

sofrito /so'frito/ *n. m.* sauce of sautéed tomatoes, peppers, onions, and garlic.

software /'sofwer/ *n. m.* software.

soga /'soga/ *n. f.* rope.

soja /'soha/ *n. f.* soya.

sol /sol/ *n. m.* sun.

solada /so'laða/ *n. f.* dregs.

solanera /sola'nera/ *n. f.* sunburn.

solapa /so'lapa/ *n. f.* lapel.

solar /so'lar/ *a.* **1.** solar. —*n.* **2.** *m.* building lot.

solaz /so'laθ/ *n. m.* solace, comfort. —**solazar,** *v.*

soldado /sol'daðo/ *n. m.* soldier.

soldar /sol'dar/ *v.* solder, weld.

soledad /sole'ðað/ *n. f.* solitude, privacy.

solemne /so'lemne/ *a.* solemn.

solemnemente /solemne'mente/ *adv.* solemnly.

solemnidad /solemni'ðað/ *n. f.* solemnity.

soler /so'ler/ *v.* be in the habit of.

solicitador /soliθita'ðor; solisita-'ðor/ **-ra** *n.* applicant, petitioner.

solicitar /soliθi'tar; solisi'tar/ *v.* solicit; apply for.

solícito /so'liθito; so'lisito/ *a.* solicitous.

solicitud /soliθi'tuð; solisi'tuð/ *n. f.* solicitude; application.

sólidamente /soliða'mente/ *adv.* solidly.

solidaridad /soliðari'ðað/ *n. f.* solidarity.

solidez /soli'ðeθ; soli'ðes/ *n. f.* solidity.

solidificar /soliðifi'kar/ *v.* solidify.

sólido /'soliðo/ *a. & m.* solid.

soliloquio /soli'lokio/ *n. m.* soliloquy.

solitario /soli'tario/ *a.* solitary, lone.

sollozo /so'ʎoθo; so'yoso/ *n. m.* sob. —**sollozar,** *v.*

solo /'solo/ *a.* **1.** only; single; alone; lonely. **a solas,** alone. —*n.* **2.** *m. Mus.* solo.

sólo /'solo/ *adv.* only, just.

solomillo /solo'miʎo; solo'miyo/ *n. m.* sirloin.

soltar /sol'tar/ *v.* release; loosen.

soltero /sol'tero/ **-ra** *a. & n.* single, unmarried (person).

soltura /sol'tura/ *n. f.* poise, ease, facility.

solubilidad /soluβili'ðað/ *n. f.* solubility.

solución /solu'θion; solu'sion/ *n. f.* solution.

solucionar /soluθio'nar; solusio-'nar/ *v.* solve, settle.

solvente /sol'βente/ *a.* solvent.

sombra /'sombra/ *n. f.* shade; shadow. —**sombrear,** *v.*

sombra de ojos /'sombra de 'ohos/ eye shadow.

sombrerera /sombre'rera/ *n. f.* hatbox.

sombrero /som'βrero/ *n. m.* hat.

sombrilla /som'βriʎa; som'βriya/ *n. f.* parasol.

sombrío /som'βrio/ *a.* somber, bleak, gloomy.

sombroso /som'βroso/ *a.* very shady.

someter /some'ter/ *v.* subject; submit.

somnífero /som'nifero/ *n. m.* sleeping pill.

somnolencia /somno'lenθia; somno'lensia/ *n. f.* drowsiness.

son /son/ *n. m.* sound. —**sonar,** *v.*

sonata /so'nata/ *n. f.* sonata.

sondar /son'dar/ *v.* sound, fathom.

sonido /so'niðo/ *n. m.* sound.

sonoridad /sonori'ðað/ *n. f.* sonority.

sonoro /so'noro/ *a.* sonorous.

sonrisa /son'risa/ *n. f.* smile. —**sonreír,** *v.*

sonrojo /son'roho/ *n. m.* flush, blush. —**sonrojarse,** *v.*

soñador /soɲa'ðor/ **-ra** *a. & n.* dreamy; dreamer.

soñar /so'ɲar/ *v.* dream.

soñoliento /soɲo'liento/ *a.* sleepy.

sopa /'sopa/ *n. f.* soup.

soplar /so'plar/ *v.* blow.

soplete /so'plete/ *n. m.* blowtorch.

soplo /'soplo/ *n. m.* breath; puff, gust.

soportar /sopor'tar/ *v.* abide, bear, stand.

soprano /so'prano/ *n. m. & f.* soprano.

sorbete /sor'βete/ *n. m.* sherbet.

sorbo /'sorβo/ *n. m.* sip. —**sorber,** *v.*

sordera /sor'ðera/ *n. f.* deafness.

sórdidamente /sorðiða'mente/ *adv.* sordidly.

sordidez /sorði'ðeθ; sorði'ðes/ *n. f.* sordidness.

sórdido /'sorðiðo/ *a.* sordid.

sordo /'sorðo/ *a.* deaf; muffled, dull.

sordomudo /sorðo'muðo/ **-da** *a. & n.* deaf-mute.

sorpresa /sor'presa/ *n. f.* surprise. —**sorprender,** *v.*

sorteo /sor'teo/ n. m. drawing lots; raffle.

sortija /sor'tiha/ n. f. ring.

sosa /'sosa/ n. f. Chem. soda.

soso /'soso/ a. dull, insipid, tasteless.

sospecha /sos'petʃa/ n. f. suspicion.

sospechar /sospe'tʃar/ v. suspect.

sospechoso /sospe'tʃoso/ a. suspicious.

sostén /sos'ten/ n. m. bra, brassiere; support.

sostener /soste'ner/ v. hold, support; maintain.

sostenimiento /sosteni'miento/ n. m. sustenance.

sota /'sota/ n. f. jack (in cards).

sótano /'sotano/ n. m. basement, cellar.

soto /'soto/ n. m. grove.

soviet /so'βiet/ n. m. soviet.

soya /'soya/ n. f. soybean.

su /su/ a. his, her, its, their, your.

suave /'suaβe/ a. smooth; gentle, soft, mild.

suavidad /suaβi'ðað/ n. f. smoothness; gentleness, softness, mildness.

suavizar /suaβi'θar; suaβi'sar/ v. soften.

subalterno /suβal'terno/ **-na** a. & n. subordinate.

subasta /su'βasta/ n. f. auction.

subcampeón /suβkampe'on/ **-na** n. runner-up.

subconsciencia /suβkons'θienθia; suβkons'siensia/ n. f. subconscious.

súbdito /'suβðito/ **-ta** n. m. subject.

subestimar /suβesti'mar/ v. underestimate.

subida /su'βiða/ n. f. ascent, rise.

subilla /su'βiʎa; su'βiya/ n. f. awl.

subir /su'βir/ v. rise, climb, ascend, mount. **s. a,** amount to.

súbito /'suβito/ a. sudden.

subjetivo /suβhe'tiβo/ a. subjective.

subjuntivo /suβhun'tiβo/ a. & m. subjunctive.

sublimación /suβlima'θion; suβlima'sion/ n. f. sublimation.

sublimar /suβli'mar/ v. elevate; sublimate.

sublime /su'βlime/ a. sublime.

submarinismo /suβmari'nismo/ n. m. scuba diving.

submarino /suβma'rino/ a. & m. submarine.

subordinación /suβorðina'θion; suβorðina'sion/ n. f. subordination.

subordinado /suβorði'naðo/ **-da** a. & n. subordinate.
—**subordinar,** v.

subrayar /suβra'yar/ v. underline; sign one's name.

subscribirse /suβskri'βirse/ v. subscribe; sign one's name.

subscripción /suβskrip'θion; suβskrip'sion/ n. f. subscription.

subsecuente /suβse'kuente/ a. subsequent.

subsidiario /suβsi'ðiario/ a. subsidiary.

subsiguiente /suβsi'giente/ a. subsequent.

substancia /suβs'tanθia; suβs'tansia/ n. f. substance.

substancial /suβs'tanθial; suβs'tansial/ a. substantial.

substantivo /suβstan'tiβo/ n. m. substantive, noun.

substitución /suβstitu'θion; suβstitu'sion/ n. f. substitution.

substituir /suβsti'tuir/ v. replace; substitute.

substitutivo /suβstitu'tiβo/ a. substitute.

substituto /suβsti'tuto/ **-ta** n. substitute.

substraer /suβstra'er/ v. subtract.

subsuelo /suβ'suelo/ n. m. subsoil.

subterfugio /suβter'fuhio/ n. m. subterfuge.

subterráneo /suβter'rraneo/ a. **1.** subterranean, underground. —m. **2.** m. place underground; subway.

subtítulo /suβ'titulo/ n. m. subtitle.

suburbio /su'βurβio/ n. m. suburb.

subvención /suββen'θion; suββen'sion/ n. f. subsidy, grant.

subversión /suββer'sion/ n. f. subversion.

subversivo /suββer'siβo/ a. subversive.

subvertir /suββer'tir/ v. subvert.

subyugación /suβyuga'θion; suβyuga'sion/ n. f. subjugation.

subyugar /suβyu'gar/ v. subjugate, quell.

succión /suk'θion; suk'sion/ n. f. suction.

suceder /suθe'ðer; suse'ðer/ v. happen, occur, befall. **s. a,** succeed, follow.

sucesión /suθe'sion; suse'sion/ *n. f.* succession.

sucesivo /suθe'siβo; suse'siβo/ *a.* successive. **en lo s.,** in the future.

suceso /su'θeso; su'seso/ *n. m.* event.

sucesor /suθe'sor; suse'sor/ **-ra** *n.* successor.

suciedad /suθie'ðað; susie'ðað/ *n. f.* filth, dirt.

sucio /su'θio; 'susio/ *a.* filthy, dirty.

suculento /suku'lento/ *a.* succulent.

sucumbir /sukum'βir/ *v.* succumb.

sud /suð/ *n. m.* south.

sudadera /suða'ðera/ *n. f.* sweatshirt.

Sudáfrica /su'ðafrika/ *n. f.* South Africa.

sudafricano /suðafri'kano/ **-na** *a.* & *n.* South African.

sudamericano /suðameri'kano/ **-na** *a.* & *n.* South American.

sudar /su'ðar/ *v.* perspire, sweat.

sudeste /su'ðeste/ *n. m.* southeast.

sudoeste /suðo'este/ *n. m.* southwest.

sudor /su'ðor/ *n. m.* perspiration, sweat.

Suecia /su'eθia; su'esia/ *n. f.* Sweden.

sueco /su'eko/ **-ca** *a.* & *n.* Swedish; Swede.

suegra /su'egra/ *n. f.* mother-in-law.

suegro /su'egro/ *n. m.* father-in-law.

suela /'suela/ *n. f.* sole.

sueldo /'sueldo/ *n. m.* salary, wages.

suelo /'suelo/ *n. m.* soil; floor; ground.

suelto /'suelto/ *a.* **1.** loose; free; odd, separate. —*n.* **2.** loose change.

sueño /su'eɲo/ *n. m.* sleep; sleepiness; dream. **tener s.,** to be sleepy.

suero /su'ero/ *n. m.* serum.

suerte /su'erte/ *n. f.* luck; chance; lot.

suéter /su'eter/ *n. m.* sweater.

suficiente /sufi'θiente; sufi'siente/ *a.* sufficient.

sufragio /su'frahio/ *n. m.* suffrage.

sufrimiento /sufri'miento/ *n. m.* suffering, agony.

sufrir /su'frir/ *v.* suffer; undergo; endure.

sugerencia /suhe'renθia; suhe'rensia/ *n. f.* suggestion.

sugerir /suhe'rir/ *v.* suggest.

sugestión /suhes'tion/ *n. f.* suggestion.

sugestionar /suhestio'nar/ *v.* influence; hypnotize.

suicida /sui'θiða; sui'siða/ *n. m.* & *f.* suicide (person).

suicidarse /suiθi'ðarse; suisi'ðarse/ *v.* commit suicide.

suicidio /sui'θiðio; sui'siðio/ *n. m.* (act of) suicide.

Suiza /'suiθa; 'suisa/ *n. f.* Switzerland.

suizo /'suiθo; 'suiso/ **-za** *a.* & *n.* Swiss.

sujeción /suhe'θion; suhe'sion/ *n. f.* subjection.

sujetador /suheta'ðor/ *n. m.* bra, brassiere.

sujetapapeles /su'hetapa'peles/ *n. m.* paper clip.

sujetar /suhe'tar/ *v.* hold, fasten, clip.

sujeto /su'heto/ *a.* **1.** subject, liable. —*n.* **2.** *Gram.* subject.

sulfato /sul'fato/ *n. m.* sulfate.

sulfuro /sul'furo/ *n. m.* sulfide.

sultán /sul'tan/ *n. m.* sultan.

suma /'suma/ *n. f.* sum, amount. **en s.,** in short. **s. global,** lump sum.

sumar /su'mar/ *v.* add up.

sumaria /su'maria/ *n. f.* indictment.

sumario /su'mario/ *a.* & *m.* summary.

sumergir /sumer'hir/ *v.* submerge.

sumersión /sumer'sion/ *n. f.* submersion.

sumisión /sumi'sion/ *n. f.* submission.

sumiso /su'miso/ *a.* submissive.

sumo /'sumo/ *a.* great, high, utmost.

suntuoso /sun'tuoso/ *a.* sumptuous.

superar /supe'rar/ *v.* overcome, surpass.

superficial /superfi'θial; superfi'sial/ *a.* superficial, shallow.

superficie /super'fiθie; super'fisie/ *n. f.* surface.

superfluo /su'perfluo/ *a.* superfluous.

superhombre /super'ombre/ *n. m.* superman.

superintendente /superinten-'dente/ n. m. & f. superintendent.

superior /supe'rior/ a. **1.** superior; upper, higher. —**2.** m. superior.

superioridad /superiori'ðað/ n. f. superiority.

superlativo /superla'tiβo/ n. m. & a. superlative.

superstición /supersti'θion; supersti'sion/ n. f. superstition.

supersticioso /supersti'θioso; supersti'sioso/ a. superstitious.

supervisar /superβi'sar/ v. supervise.

supervivencia /superβi'βenθia; superβi'βensia/ n. f. survival.

suplantar /suplan'tar/ v. supplant.

suplementario /suplemen'tario/ a. supplementary.

suplemento /suple'mento/ n. m. supplement. —**suplementar,** v.

suplente /su'plente/ a. & n. substitute.

súplica /'suplika/ n. f. request, entreaty, plea.

suplicación /suplika'θion; suplika-'sion/ n. f. supplication; request, entreaty.

suplicar /supli'kar/ v. request, entreat; implore.

suplicio /su'pliθio; su'plisio/ n. m. torture, ordeal.

suplir /su'plir/ v. supply.

suponer /supo'ner/ v. suppose, pressume, assume.

suposición /suposi'θion; suposi-'sion/ n. f. supposition, assumption.

supositorio /suposi'torio/ n. m. suppository.

supremacía /suprema'θia; suprema'sia/ n. f. supremacy.

supremo /su'premo/ a. supreme.

supresión /supre'sion/ n. f. suppression.

suprimir /supri'mir/ v. suppress; abolish.

supuesto /su'puesto/ a. supposed. **por s.,** of course.

sur /sur/ n. m. south.

surco /'surko/ n. m. furrow. —**surcar,** v.

surgir /sur'hir/ v. arise; appear suddenly.

surtido /sur'tiðo/ n. m. assortment; supply, stock.

surtir /sur'tir/ v. furnish, supply.

susceptibilidad /susθeptiβili'ðað; susseptiβili'ðað/ n. f. susceptibility.

susceptible /susθep'tiβle; sussep-'tiβle/ a. susceptible.

suscitar /susθi'tar; sussi'tar/ v. stir up.

suscri- = subscri-

suspender /suspen'der/ v. withhold; suspend; fail (in a course).

suspensión /suspen'sion/ n. f. suspension.

suspenso /sus'penso/ n. m. failing grade. **en s.,** in suspense.

suspicacia /suspi'kaθia; suspi-'kasia/ n. f. suspicion, distrust.

suspicaz /suspi'kaθ; suspi'kas/ a. suspicious.

suspicazmente /suspika'θmente; suspikas'mente/ adv. suspiciously.

suspiro /sus'piro/ n. m. sigh. —**suspirar,** v.

sustan- = substan-

sustentar /susten'tar/ v. sustain, support.

sustento /sus'tento/ n. m. sustenance, support, living.

susti- = substi-

susto /'susto/ n. m. fright, scare.

sustraer /sustra'er/ = substraer.

susurro /su'surro/ n. m. rustle; whisper. —**susurrar,** v.

sutil /'sutil/ a. subtle.

sutileza /suti'leθa, sutili'ðað/ **sutilesa, sutili'ðað/ sutilidad** n. f. subtlety.

sutura /su'tura/ n. f. suture.

suyo /'suyo/ a. his, hers, theirs, yours.

T

tabaco /ta'βako/ *n. m.* tobacco.

tábano /'taβano/ *n. m.* horsefly.

tabaquería /taβake'ria/ *n. f.* tobacco shop.

taberna /ta'βerna/ *n. f.* tavern, bar.

tabernáculo /taβer'nakulo/ *n. m.* tabernacle.

tabique /ta'βike/ *n. m.* dividing wall, partition.

tabla /'taβla/ *n. f.* board, plank; table, list. **t. de planchar**, ironing board.

tablado /ta'βlaðo/ *n. m.* stage, platform.

tablero /ta'βlero/ *n. m.* panel.

tableta /ta'βleta/ *n. f.* tablet.

tablilla /ta'βliʎa; ta'βliya/ *n. f.* bulletin board.

tabú /ta'βu/ *n. m.* taboo.

tabular /taβu'lar/ *a.* tabular.

tacaño /ta'kaɲo/ *a.* stingy.

tacha /'tatʃa/ *n. f.* fault, defect.

tachar /ta'tʃar/ *v.* find fault with; cross out.

tachuela /ta'tʃuela/ *n. f.* tack.

tácitamente /taθita'mente; 'tasi-tamente/ *adv.* tacitly.

tácito /'taθito; 'tasito/ *a.* tacit.

taciturno /taθi'turno; tasi'turno/ *a.* taciturn.

taco /'tako/ *n. m.* heel (of shoe); billiard cue.

tacón /ta'kon/ *n. m.* heel (of shoe).

táctico /'taktiko/ *a.* tactical.

tacto /'takto/ *n. m.* (sense of) touch; tact.

tafetán /tafe'tan/ *n. m.* taffeta.

taimado /tai'maðo/ *a.* sly.

tajada /ta'haða/ *n. f.* cut, slice. —**tajar**, *v.*

tajea /ta'hea/ *n. f.* channel.

tal /tal/ *a.* such. **con t. que—**, provided that. **t. vez**, perhaps.

taladrar /tala'ðrar/ *v.* drill.

taladro /ta'laðro/ *n. m. Mech.* drill.

talante /ta'lante/ *n. m.* humor, disposition.

talco /'talko/ *n. m.* talc.

talega /ta'lega/ *n. f.* bag, sack.

talento /ta'lento/ *n. m.* talent.

talla /'taʎa; 'taya/ *n. f.* engraving; stature; size (of suit).

tallador /taʎa'ðor; taya'ðor/ -ra *n.* engraver; dealer (at cards).

talle /'taʎe; 'taye/ *n. m.* figure; waist; fit.

taller /ta'ʎer; ta'yer/ *n. m.* workshop, factory.

tallo /'taʎo; 'tayo/ *n. m.* stem, stalk.

talón /ta'lon/ *n. m.* heel (of foot); (baggage) check, stub.

tamal /ta'mal/ *n. m.* tamale.

tamaño /ta'maɲo/ *n. m.* size.

tambalear /tambale'ar/ *v.* stagger, totter.

también /tam'bien/ *adv.* also, too.

tambor /tam'bor/ *n. m.* drum.

tamiz /ta'miθ; ta'mis/ *n. m.* sieve, sifter.

tampoco /tam'poko/ *adv.* neither, either.

tan /tan/ *adv.* so.

tanda /'tanda/ *n. f.* turn, relay.

tándem /'tandem/ *n. m.* tandem; pair.

tangencia /taŋ'genθia; taŋ'gensia/ *n. f.* tangency.

tangible /taŋ'giβle/ *a.* tangible.

tango /'taŋgo/ *n. m.* tango (dance or music).

tanque /'taŋke/ *n. m.* tank.

tanteo /tan'teo/ *n. m.* estimate. —**tantear**, *v.*

tanto /'tanto/ *a. & pron.* **1.** so much, so many; as much as, many. **entre t., mientras t.**, meanwhile. **por lo t.**, therefore. **un t.**, somewhat, a bit. —*n.* **2.** point (in games) **3.** (*pl.*) score. **estar al t.**, to be up to date.

tañer /ta'ɲer/ *v.* play (an instrument); ring (bells).

tapa /'tapa/ *n. f.* cap, cover; snack served in a bar. —**tapar**, *v.*

tapadero /tapa'ðero/ *n. m.* stopper, lid.

tápara /'tapara/ *n. f.* caper.

tapete /ta'pete/ *n. m.* small rug, mat, cover.

tapia /'tapia/ *n. f.* wall.

tapicería /tapiθe'ria; tapise'ria/ *n. f.* tapestry.

tapioca /ta'pioka/ *n. f.* tapioca.

tapiz /ta'piθ; ta'pis/ *n. m.* tapestry; carpet.

tapizado (de pared) /tapi'θaðo de pa'reð; tapi'saðo de pa'reð/ *n. m.* (wall) covering.

tapón /ta'pon/ *n. m.* plug; cork.

taquigrafía /takigra'fia/ n. f. shorthand.

taquilla /ta'kiʎa; ta'kiya/ n. f. ticket office; box office; ticket window.

tara /'tara/ n. f. hang-up.

tarántula /ta'rantula/ n. f. tarantula.

tararear /tarare'ar/ v. hum.

tardanza /tar'ðanθa; tar'ðansa/ n. f. delay; lateness.

tardar /tar'ðar/ v. delay; be late; take (of time). **a más t.,** at the latest.

tarde /'tarðe/ adv. **1.** late. —n. **2.** f. afternoon.

tardío /tar'ðio/ a. late, belated.

tarea /ta'rea/ n. f. task, assignment.

tarifa /ta'rifa/ n. f. rate; tariff; price list.

tarjeta /tar'heta/ n. f. card.

tarjeta bancaria /tar'heta ban'karia/ bank card.

tarjeta de crédito /tar'heta de 'kreðito/ credit card.

tarjeta de embarque /tar'heta de em'βarke/ boarding pass.

tarta /'tarta/ n. f. tart.

tartamudear /tartamuðe'ar/ v. stammer, falter.

tasa /'tasa/ n. f. rate.

tasación /tasa'θion; tasa'sion/ n. f. valuation.

tasar /ta'sar/ v. assess, appraise.

tasca /'taska/ n. f. bar, pub.

tasugo /ta'sugo/ n. m. badger.

tatuar /tatu'ar/ v. tattoo.

tautología /tautolo'hia/ n. f. tautology.

taxi /'taksi/ **taxímetro** /tak'simetro/ n. m. taxi.

taxista /tak'sista/ n. m. & f. taxi driver.

taxonomía /taksono'mia/ n. f. taxonomy.

taza /'taθa; 'tasa/ n. f. cup.

te /te/ pron. you; yourself.

té n. m. tea.

team /tim/ n. m. team.

teatrico /te'atriko/ a. theatrical.

teatro /te'atro/ n. m. theater.

tebeo /te'βeo/ n. m. comic book.

techo /'tetʃo/ n. m. roof. —**techar,** v.

tecla /'tekla/ n. f. key (of a piano, etc.).

teclado /te'klaðo/ n. m. keyboard.

teclado numérico /te'klaðo nu'meriko/ numeric keypad.

técnica /'teknika/ n. f. technique.

técnicamente /'teknikamente/ adv. technically.

técnico /'tekniko/ a. **1.** technical. —m. **2.** repairman, technician.

tecnología /teknolo'hia/ n. f. technology.

tedio /'teðio/ n. m. tedium, boredom.

tedioso /te'ðioso/ a. tedious.

teísmo /te'ismo/ n. m. theism.

teja /'teha/ n. f. tile.

tejado /te'haðo/ n. m. roof.

tejano /te'hano/ **-na** a. & n. Texan.

tejanos /te'hanos/ n. m.pl. jeans.

tejer /te'her/ v. weave; knit.

tejido /te'hiðo/ n. m. fabric; weaving.

tejón /te'hon/ n. m. badger.

tela /'tela/ n. f. cloth, fabric, web. **t. metálica,** screen; screening. **t. vaquera,** denim.

telar /te'lar/ n. m. loom.

telaraña /tela'raɲa/ n. f. cobweb, spiderweb.

telefonista /telefo'nista/ n. m. & f. (telephone) operator.

teléfono /te'lefono/ n. m. telephone. —**telefonear,** v.

teléfono gratuito /te'lefono gra'tuito/ toll-free number.

teléfono público /te'lefono 'puβliko/ pay phone, public telephone.

teléfono rojo /te'lefono 'rroho/ hotline.

telégrafo /te'legrafo/ n. m. telegraph. —**telegrafiar,** v.

telegrama /tele'grama/ n. m. telegram.

telescopio /teles'kopio/ n. m. telescope.

televisión /teleβi'sion/ n. f. television.

telón /te'lon/ n. m. *Theat.* curtain.

telurio /te'lurio/ n. m. tellurium.

tema /'tema/ n. m. theme, subject.

temblar /tem'blar/ v. tremble, quake; shake, shiver.

temblor /tem'blor/ n. m. tremor; shiver.

temer /te'mer/ v. fear, be afraid of, dread.

temerario /teme'rario/ a. rash.

temeridad /temeri'ðað/ n. f. temerity.

temerosamente /temerosa'mente/ adv. timorously.

temeroso /teme'roso/ a. fearful.

temor /te'mor/ n. m. fear.

témpano /'tempano/ n. m. kettledrum; iceberg.

temperamento /tempera'mento/ n. m. temperament.

temperancia /tempe'ranθia; tempe'ransia/ n. f. temperance.

temperatura /tempera'tura/ n. f. temperature.

tempestad /tempes'tað/ n. f. tempest, storm.

tempestuoso /tempes'tuoso/ a. tempestuous, stormy.

templado /tem'plaðo/ a. temperate, mild, moderate.

templanza /tem'planθa; tem'plansa/ n. f. temperance; mildness.

templar /tem'plar/ v. temper; tune (an instrument).

templo /'templo/ n. m. temple.

temporada /tempo'raða/ n. f. season, time, spell.

temporal /tempo'ral/ **temporáneo** a. temporary.

temprano /tem'prano/ a. & adv. early.

tenacidad /tenaθi'ðað; tenasi'ðað/ n. f. tenacity.

tenaz /te'naθ; te'nas/ a. tenacious, stubborn.

tenazmente /tenaθ'mente; tenas'mente/ adv. tenaciously.

tendencia /ten'denθia; tendensia/ n. f. tendency, trend.

tender /ten'der/ v. stretch, stretch out.

tendero /ten'dero/ **-ra** n. shopkeeper, storekeeper.

tendón /ten'don/ n. m. tendon, sinew.

tenebrosidad /teneβrosi'ðað/ n. f. gloom.

tenebroso /tene'βroso/ a. dark, gloomy.

tenedor /tene'ðor/ n. **1.** m. & f. keeper; holder. **2.** m. fork.

tener /te'ner/ v. have; own; hold. **t. que,** have to, must.

teniente /te'niente/ n. m. lieutenant.

tenis /'tenis/ n. m. tennis; (pl.) sneakers.

tenor /te'nor/ n. m. tenor.

tensión /ten'sion/ n. f. tension, stress, strain.

tenso /'tenso/ a. tense.

tentación /tenta'θion; tenta'sion/ n. f. temptation.

tentáculo /ten'takulo/ n. m. tentacle.

tentador /tenta'ðor/ a. alluring, tempting.

tentar /ten'tar/ v. tempt, lure; grope, probe.

tentativa /tenta'tiβa/ n. f. attempt.

tentativo /tenta'tiβo/ a. tentative.

teñir /te'ɲir/ v. tint, dye.

teología /teolo'hia/ n. f. theology.

teológico /teo'lohiko/ a. theological.

teoría /teo'ria/ n. f. theory.

teórico /te'oriko/ a. theoretical.

terapéutico /tera'peutiko/ a. therapeutic.

tercero /ter'θero; ter'sero/ a. third.

tercio /'terθio; 'tersio/ n. m. third.

terciopelo /terθio'pelo; tersio'pelo/ n. m. velvet.

terco /'terko/ a. obstinate, stubborn.

termal /ter'mal/ a. thermal.

terminación /termina'θion; termina'sion/ n. f. termination; completion.

terminal aérea /termi'nal 'airea/ n. f. air terminal.

terminar /termi'nar/ v. terminate, finish.

término /'termino/ n. m. term; end.

terminología /terminolo'hia/ n. f. terminology.

termómetro /ter'mometro/ n. m. thermometer.

termos /'termos/ n. m. thermos.

termostato /ter'mostato/ n. m. thermostat.

ternero /ter'nero/ **-ra** n. calf.

ternura /ter'nura/ n. f. tenderness.

terquedad /terke'ðað/ n. f. stubbornness.

terraza /te'rraθa; te'rrasa/ n. f. terrace.

terremoto /terre'moto/ n. m. earthquake.

terreno /te'rreno/ a. **1.** earthly, terrestrial. —n. **2.** m. ground, terrain; lot, plot.

terrible /te'rriβle/ a. terrible, awful.

terrífico /te'rrifiko/ a. terrifying.

territorio /terri'torio/ n. m. territory.

terrón /te'rron/ n. m. clod, lump; mound.

terror 190

terror /te'rror/ n. m. terror.

terso /'terso/ a. smooth, glossy; terse.

tertulia /ter'tulia/ n. f. social gathering, party.

tesis /'tesis/ n. f. thesis.

tesorería /tesore'ria/ n. f. treasury.

tesorero /teso'rero/ **-ra** n. treasurer.

tesoro /te'soro/ n. m. treasure.

testamento /testa'mento/ n. m. will, testament.

testarudo /testa'ruðo/ a. stubborn.

testificar /testifi'kar/ v. testify.

testigo /tes'tigo/ n. m. & f. witness.

testimonial /testimo'nial/ a. testimonial.

testimonio /testi'monio/ n. m. testimony.

teta /'teta/ n. f. teat.

tetera /te'tera/ n. f. teapot.

tétrico /'tetriko/ a. sad; gloomy.

texto /'teksto/ n. m. text.

textura /teks'tura/ n. f. texture.

tez /teθ; tes/ n. f. complexion.

ti /ti/ pron. you; yourself.

tía /'tia/ n. f. aunt.

tibio /'tiβio/ a. lukewarm.

tiburón /tiβu'ron/ n. m. shark.

tiemblo /'tiemblo/ n. m. aspen.

tiempo /'tiempo/ n. m. time; weather; Gram. tense.

tienda /'tienda/ n. f. shop, store; tent.

tientas /'tientas/ n. f.pl. **andar a t.,** to grope (in the dark).

tierno /'tierno/ a. tender.

tierra /'tierra/ n. f. land; ground; earth, dirt, soil.

tieso /'tieso/ a. taut, stiff, hard, strong.

tiesto /'tiesto/ n. m. flower pot.

tiesura /tie'sura/ n. f. stiffness; harshness.

tifo /'tifo/ n. m. typhus.

tifoideo /tifoi'ðeo/ n. m. typhoid fever.

tigre /'tigre/ n. m. tiger.

tijeras /ti'heras/ n. f.pl. scissors.

tila /'tila/ n. f. linden.

timbre /'timbre/ n. m. seal, stamp; tone; (electric) bell.

tímidamente /'timiðamente/ adv. timidly.

timidez /timi'deθ; timi'ðes/ n. f. timidity.

tímido /'timiðo/ a. timid, shy.

timón /ti'mon/ n. m. rudder, helm.

tímpano /'timpano/ n. m. kettledrum; eardrum.

tina /'tina/ n. f. tub, vat.

tinaja /ti'naha/ n. f. jar.

tinta /'tinta/ n. f. ink.

tinte /'tinte/ n. m. tint, shade.

tintero /tin'tero/ n. m. inkwell.

tinto /'tinto/ a. wine-colored; red (of wine).

tintorería /tintore'ria/ n. f. dry cleaning shop.

tintorero /tinto'rero/ **-ra** n. dyer; dry cleaner.

tintura /tin'tura/ n. f. tincture; dye.

tiñoso /ti'ɲoso/ a. scabby; stingy.

tío /'tio/ n. m. uncle.

tiovivo /tio'βiβo/ n. m. merry-go-round.

típico /'tipiko/ a. typical.

tipo /'tipo/ n. m. type, sort; (interest) rate; Colloq. guy, fellow.

tipo de cambio /'tipo de 'kambio/ exchange rate.

tipo de interés /'tipo de inte'res/ interest rate.

tira /'tira/ n. f. strip.

tirabuzón /tiraβu'θon; tiraβu'son/ n. m. corkscrew.

tirada /ti'raða/ n. f. edition.

tirado /ti'raðo/ **-da** a. dirt-cheap.

tiranía /tira'nia/ n. f. tyranny.

tiránico /ti'raniko/ a. m. tyrannical.

tirano /ti'rano/ **-na** n. tyrant.

tirante /ti'rante/ a. **1.** tight, taut; tense. —n. **2.** m.pl. suspenders.

tirar /ti'rar/ v. throw; draw; pull; fire (a weapon).

tiritar /tiri'tar/ v. shiver.

tiro /'tiro/ n. m. throw; shot.

tirón /ti'ron/ n. m. pull. **de un t.,** at a stretch, all in one stroke.

tísico /'tisiko/ n. & a. consumptive.

tisis /'tisis/ n. f. consumption, tuberculosis.

titanio /ti'tanio/ n. m. titanium.

títere /'titere/ n. m. puppet.

titilación /titila'θion; titila'sion/ n. f. twinkle.

titubear /tituβe'ar/ v. stagger; totter; waver.

titulado /titu'laðo/ a. entitled; socalled.

titular /titu'lar/ a. **1.** titular. —v. **2.** entitle.

título /'titulo/ n. m. title, headline.

tiza /'tiθa; 'tisa/ n. f. chalk.

tosco

tiznar /tiθ'nar; tis'nar/ v. smudge; stain.

toalla /to'aʎa; to'aya/ n. f. towel. **t. sanitaria,** sanitary napkin.

toalleta /toa'ʎeta; toa'yeta/ n. f. small towel.

tobillo /to'βiʎo; to'βiyo/ n. m. ankle.

tobogán /toβo'gan/ n. m. toboggan.

tocadiscos /toka'ðiskos/ n. m. record player.

tocadiscos compacto /toka'ðiskos kom'pakto/ **tocadiscos digital** CD player.

tocado /to'kaðo/ n. m. hairdo.

tocador /toka'ðor/ n. m. boudoir; dressing table.

tocante /to'kante/ a. touching. **t. a,** concerning, relative to.

tocar /to'kar/ v. touch; play (an instrument). **t. a uno,** be one's turn; be up to one.

tocayo /to'kayo/ **-ya** n. namesake.

tocino /to'θino/ n. m. bacon.

tocólogo /to'kologo/ **-ga** n. obstetrician.

todavía /toða'βia/ adv. yet, still.

todo /'toðo/ a. **1.** all, whole. **todos los,** every. —pron. **2.** all, everything. **con t.,** still, however. **del t.,** wholly; at all.

todopoderoso /toðopoðe'roso/ a. almighty.

toldo /'toldo/ n. m. awning.

tolerancia /tole'ranθia; tole'ransia/ n. f. tolerance.

tolerante /tole'rante/ a. tolerant.

tolerar /tole'rar/ v. tolerate.

toma /'toma/ n. f. taking, capture, seizure.

tomaína /to'maina/ n. f. ptomaine.

tomar /to'mar/ v. take; drink. **t. el sol,** sunbathe.

tomate /to'mate/ n. m. tomato.

tomillo /to'miʎo; to'miyo/ n. m. thyme.

tomo /'tomo/ n. m. volume.

tonada /to'naða/ n. f. tune.

tonel /to'nel/ n. m. barrel, cask.

tonelada /tone'laða/ n. f. ton.

tonelaje /tone'lahe/ n. m. tonnage.

tónico /'toniko/ a. & m. tonic.

tono /'tono/ n. m. tone, pitch, shade. **darse t.,** to put on airs.

tonsila /ton'sila/ n. f. tonsil.

tonsilitis /tonsi'litis/ n. f. tonsilitis.

tontería /tonte'ria/ n. f. nonsense, foolishness.

tontifútbol /tonti'futβol/ n. m. excessively defensive strategy (in soccer).

tonto /'tonto/ **-ta** a. & n. foolish, silly; fool.

topacio /to'paθio; to'pasio/ n. m. topaz.

topar /to'par/ v. run into. **t. con,** come upon.

tópico /'topiko/ a. **1.** topical. —n. **2.** n. cliché.

topo /'topo/ n. m. mole (animal).

toque /'toke/ n. m. touch.

tórax /'toraks/ n. m. thorax.

torbellino /torβe'ʎino; torβe'yino/ n. m. whirlwind.

torcer /tor'θer; tor'ser/ v. twist; wind; distort.

toreador /torea'ðor/ **-a** n. toreador.

torero /to'rero/ **-ra** n. bullfighter.

torio /'torio/ n. m. thorium.

tormenta /tor'menta/ n. f. storm.

tormento /tor'mento/ n. m. torment.

tornado /tor'naðo/ n. m. tornado.

tornar /tor'nar/ v. return; turn.

tornarse en /tor'narse en/ v. turn into, become.

torneo /tor'neo/ n. m. tournament.

tornillo /tor'niʎo; tor'niyo/ n. m. screw.

toro /'toro/ n. m. bull.

toronja /to'ronha/ n. f. grapefruit.

torpe /'torpe/ a. awkward, clumsy; sluggish.

torpedero /torpe'ðero/ n. m. torpedo boat.

torpedo /tor'peðo/ n. m. torpedo.

torre /'torre/ n. f. tower.

torre de mando /'torre de 'mando/ control tower.

torrente /to'rrente/ n. m. torrent.

tórrido /'torriðo/ a. torrid.

torta /'torta/ n. f. cake; loaf.

tortilla /tor'tiʎa; tor'tiya/ n. f. omelet; (Mex.) tortilla, pancake.

tórtola /'tortola/ n. f. dove.

tortuga /tor'tuga/ n. f. turtle.

tortuoso /tor'tuoso/ a. tortuous.

tortura /tor'tura/ n. f. torture. —**torturar,** v.

tos /tos/ n. m. cough. —**toser,** v.

tosco /'tosko/ a. coarse, rough, uncouth.

tosquedad /toske'ðaθ/ n. f. coarseness, roughness.

tostador /tosta'ðor/ n. m. toaster.

tostar /tos'tar/ v. toast; tan.

total /to'tal/ a. & n. m. total.

totalidad /totali'ðaθ/ n. f. totality, entirety, whole.

totalitario /totali'tario/ a. totalitarian.

totalmente /total'mente/ adv. totally; entirely.

tótem /'totem/ n. m. totem.

tóxico /'toksiko/ a. toxic.

toxicómano /toksi'komano/ **-na** n. m. & f. drug addict.

trabajador /traβaxa'ðor/ **-ra** a. **1.** hardworking. —n. **2.** worker.

trabajo /tra'βaxo/ n. m. work; labor. —**trabajar**, v.

trabar /tra'βar/ v. fasten, shackle; grasp; strike up.

tracción /trak'θion/ trak'sion/ n. f. traction.

tracto /'trakto/ n. m. tract.

tractor /trak'tor/ n. m. tractor.

tradición /traði'θion/ traði'sion/ n. f. tradition.

tradicional /traðiθio'nal/ traðisio'nal/ a. traditional.

traducción /traðuk'θion/ traðuk'sion/ n. f. translation.

traducir /traðu'θir/ traðu'sir/ v. translate.

traductor /traðuk'tor/ **-ra** n. translator.

traer /tra'er/ v. bring; carry; wear.

tráfico /'trafiko/ n. m. traffic. —**traficar**, v.

tragaperras /traga'perras/ n. f. slot machine, one-armed bandit.

tragar /tra'gar/ v. swallow.

tragedia /tra'heðia/ n. f. tragedy.

trágicamente /'traxikamente/ adv. tragically.

trágico /'traxiko/ **-ca** a. **1.** tragic. —n. **2.** tragedian.

trago /'trago/ n. m. swallow; drink.

traición /trai'θion/ trai'sion/ n. f. treason, betrayal.

traicionar /traiθio'nar/ traisio'nar/ v. betray.

traidor /trai'ðor/ **-ra** a. & n. traitorous; traitor.

traje /'trahe/ n. m. suit; dress; garb, apparel.

traje de baño /'trahe ðe 'baɲo/ bathing suit.

trama /'trama/ n. f. plot (of a story).

tramador /trama'ðor/ **-ra** n. weaver; plotter.

tramar /tra'mar/ v. weave; plot, scheme.

trámite /'tramite/ n. m. (business) deal, transaction.

tramo /'tramo/ n. m. span, stretch, section.

trampa /'trampa/ n. f. trap, snare.

trampista /tram'pista/ n. m. & f. cheater; swindler.

trance /'tranθe/ 'transe/ n. m. critical moment or stage. **a todo t.,** at any cost.

tranco /'tranko/ n. m. stride.

tranquilidad /trankili'ðaθ/ n. f. tranquility, calm, quiet.

tranquilizante /trankili'θante/ trankili'sante/ n. m. tranquilizer.

tranquilizar /trankili'θar/ trankili'sar/ v. quiet, calm down.

tranquilo /tran'kilo/ a. tranquil, calm.

transacción /transak'θion/ transak'sion/ n. f. transaction.

transbordador /transβorða'ðor/ n. m. ferry.

transbordador espacial /transβorða'ðor espa'θial/ transβorða'ðor espa'sial/ space shuttle.

transcribir /transkri'βir/ v. transcribe.

transcripción /transkrip'θion/ transkrip'sion/ n. f. transcription.

transcurrir /transku'rrir/ v. elapse.

transeúnte /tran'seunte/ a. & n. transient; passerby.

transexual /transek'sual/ a. transsexual.

transferencia /transfe'renθia/ transfe'rensia/ n. f. transference.

transferir /transfe'rir/ v. transfer.

transformación /transforma'θion/ transforma'sion/ n. f. transformation.

transformar /transfor'mar/ v. transform.

transfusión /transfu'sion/ n. f. transfusion.

transgresión /transgre'sion/ n. f. transgression.

transgresor /transgre'sor/ **-ra** n. transgressor.

transición /transi'θion/ transi'sion/ n. f. transition.

transigir /transi'hir/ v. compromise, settle; agree.

transistor /transis'tor/ n. m. transistor.

transitivo /transi'tiβo/ *a.* transitive.

tránsito /'transito/ *n. m.* transit, passage.

transitorio /transi'torio/ *a.* transitory.

transmisión /transmi'sion/ *n. f.* transmission; broadcast.

transmisora /transmi'sora/ *n. f.* broadcasting station.

transmitir /transmi'tir/ *v.* transmit; broadcast.

transparencia /transpa'renθia/ transpa'rensia/ *n. f.* transparency.

transparente /transpa'rente/ *a.* **1.** transparent. —*n.* **2.** *m.* (window) shade.

transportación /transporta'θion/ transporta'sion/ *n. f.* transportation.

transportar /transpor'tar/ *v.* transport, convey.

transporte /trans'porte/ *n. m.* transportation; transport.

tranvía /tram'bia/ *n. m.* streetcar, trolley.

trapacero /trapa'θero/ trapa'sero/ -ra *n.* cheat; swindler.

trapo /'trapo/ *n. m.* rag.

tráquea /'trakea/ *n. f.* trachea.

tras /tras/ *prep.* after; behind.

trasegar /trase'gar/ *v.* upset, overturn.

trasero /tra'sero/ *a.* rear, back.

traslado /tras'laðo/ *n. m.* transfer. —**trasladar,** *v.*

traslapo /tras'lapo/ *n. m.* overlap. —**traslapar,** *v.*

trasnochar /trasno'tʃar/ *v.* stay up all night.

traspalar /traspa'lar/ *v.* shovel.

traspasar /traspa'sar/ *v.* go beyond; cross; violate; pierce.

trasquilar /traski'lar/ *v.* shear; clip.

trastornar /trastor'nar/ *v.* overturn, overthrow, upset.

trastorno /tras'torno/ *m.* overthrow; upheaval.

trastorno mental /tras'torno men'tal/ mental disorder.

trasvasar /trasβa'sar/ *v.* download; download.

tratado /tra'taðo/ *n. m.* treaty; treatise.

tratamiento /trata'miento/ *n. m.* treatment.

tratar /tra'tar/ *v.* treat, handle. **t. de,** deal with; try to; call (a name).

tratarse de /tra'tarse de/ *v.* be a question of.

trato /'trato/ *n. m.* treatment; manners; *Com.* deal.

través /tra'βes/ *adv.* **a t. de,** through, across. **de t.,** sideways.

travesía /traβe'sia/ *n. f.* crossing; voyage.

travesti /tra'βesti/ *m.* transvestite.

travestido /traβes'tiðo/ *a.* disguised.

travesura /traβe'sura/ *n. f.* prank; mischief.

travieso /tra'βieso/ *a.* naughty, mischievous.

trayectoria /trayek'toria/ *n. f.* trajectory.

trazar /tra'θar/ tra'sar/ *v.* plan, devise; trace; draw.

trazo /'traθo/ 'traso/ *n. m.* plan, outline; line, stroke.

trébol /'treβol/ *n. m.* clover.

trece /'treθe/ 'trese/ *a. & pron.* thirteen.

trecho /'tretʃo/ *n. m.* space, distance, stretch.

tregua /'tregua/ *n. f.* truce; respite, lull.

treinta /'treinta/ *a. & pron.* thirty.

tremendo /tre'mendo/ *a.* tremendous.

tremer /tre'mer/ *v.* tremble.

tren /tren/ *n. m.* train.

trenza /'trenθa/ 'trensa/ *n. f.* braid. —**trenzar,** *v.*

trepar /tre'par/ *v.* climb, mount.

trepidación /trepiða'θion/ trepiða'sion/ *n. f.* trepidation.

tres /tres/ *a. & pron.* three.

trescientos /tres'θientos/ tres'sientos/ *a. & pron.* three hundred.

triángulo /tri'angulo/ *n. m.* triangle.

triar /triar/ *v.* sort, separate.

tribu /'triβu/ *n. f.* tribe.

tribulación /triβula'θion/ triβula'sion/ *n. f.* tribulation.

tribuna /tri'βuna/ *n. f.* rostrum, stand; (*pl.*) grandstand.

tribunal /triβu'nal/ *n. m.* court, tribunal.

tributario /triβu'tario/ *a. & m.* tributary.

tributo /tri'βuto/ *n. m.* tribute.

triciclo /tri'θiklo/ tri'siklo/ *n. m.* tricycle.

trigo /'trigo/ *n. m.* wheat.

trigonometría /trigonome'tria/ *n. f.* trigonometry.

trigueño /tri'geɲo/ *a.* swarthy, dark.

trilogía /trilo'hia/ *n. f.* trilogy.

trimestral /trimes'tral/ *a.* quarterly.

trinchar /trin'tʃar/ *v.* carve (meat).

trinchera /trin'tʃera/ *n. f.* trench, ditch.

trineo /tri'neo/ *n. m.* sled; sleigh.

trinidad /trini'ðað/ *n. f.* trinity.

tripa /'tripa/ *n. f.* tripe, entrails.

triple /'triple/ *a.* triple. —**triplicar**, *v.*

trípode /'tripoðe/ *n. m.* tripod.

tripulación /tripula'θion; tripula-'sion/ *n. f.* crew.

tripulante /tripu'lante/ *m & f.* crew member.

tripular /tripu'lar/ *v.* man.

triste /'triste/ *a.* sad, sorrowful; dreary.

tristemente /triste'mente/ *adv.* sadly.

tristeza /tris'teθa; tris'tesa/ *n. f.* sadness; gloom.

triunfal /triun'fal/ *a.* triumphal.

triunfante /triun'fante/ *a.* triumphant.

triunfo /'triunfo/ *n. m.* triumph; trump. —**triunfar**, *v.*

trivial /tri'βial/ *a.* trivial, commonplace.

trivialidad /triβiali'ðað/ *n. f.* triviality.

trocar /tro'kar/ *v.* exchange, switch; barter.

trofeo /tro'feo/ *n. m.* trophy.

trombón /trom'bon/ *n. m.* trombone.

trompa /'trompa/ **trompeta** *n. f.* trumpet, horn.

tronada /tro'naða/ *n. f.* thunderstorm.

tronar /tro'nar/ *v.* thunder.

tronco /'tronko/ *n. m.* trunk, stump.

trono /'trono/ *n. m.* throne.

tropa /'tropa/ *n. f.* troop.

tropel /tro'pel/ *n. m.* crowd, throng.

tropezar /trope'θar; trope'sar/ *v.* trip, stumble. **t. con**, come upon, run into.

trópico /'tropiko/ *a.* & *m.* tropical; tropics.

tropiezo /tro'pieθo; tro'pieso/ *n. m.* stumble; obstacle; slip, error.

trote /'trote/ *n. m.* trot. —**trotar**, *v.*

trovador /troβa'ðor/ *n. m.* troubadour.

trozo /'troθo; 'troso/ *n. m.* piece, portion, fragment; selection, passage.

trucha /'trutʃa/ *n. f.* trout.

trueco /'trueko/ **trueque** *n. m.* exchange, barter.

trueno /'trueno/ *n. m.* thunder.

trufa /'trufa/ *n. f.* truffle.

tu /tu/ *a.* your.

tú *pron.* you.

tuberculosis /tuβerku'losis/ *n. f.* tuberculosis.

tubo /'tuβo/ *n. m.* tube, pipe.

tubo de ensayo /'tuβo de en'sayo/ test tube.

tubo de escape /'tuβo de es'kape/ exhaust pipe.

tuerca /'tuerka/ *n. f. Mech.* nut.

tulipán /tuli'pan/ *n. m.* tulip.

tumba /'tumba/ *n. f.* tomb, grave.

tumbar /tum'bar/ *v.* knock down.

tumbarse /tum'βarse/ *v.* lie down.

tumbo /'tumbo/ *n. m.* tumble; somersault.

tumbona /tum'βona/ *n. f.* deck chair.

tumor /tu'mor/ *n. m.* tumor; growth.

tumulto /tu'multo/ *n. m.* tumult, commotion.

tumultuoso /tumul'tuoso/ *a.* tumultuous, boisterous.

tunante /tu'nante/ *n. m.* rogue.

tunda /'tunda/ *n. f.* spanking; whipping.

túnel /'tunel/ *n. m.* tunnel.

túnel de Canal de la Mancha /'tunel de ka'nal de la 'mantʃa/ Channel Tunnel, Chunnel.

tungsteno /tuŋgs'teno/ *n. m.* tungsten.

túnica /'tunika/ *n. f.* tunic, robe.

tupir /tu'pir/ *v.* pack tight, stuff; stop up.

turbación /turβa'θion; turβa'sion/ *n. f.* confusion, turmoil.

turbamulta /turβa'multa/ *n. f.* mob, disorderly crowd.

turbar /tur'βar/ *v.* disturb, upset; embarrass.

turbina /tur'βina/ *n. f.* turbine.

turbio /'turβio/ *a.* turbid; muddy.

turco /'turko/ **-ca** *a.* & *n.* Turkish; Turk.

turismo /tu'rismo/ *n. m.* touring, (foreign) travel, tourism.

turista /tu'rista/ *n. m. & f.* tourist.
turno /'turno/ *n. m.* turn; (work) shift.
turquesa /tur'kesa/ *n. f.* turquoise.
Turquía /tur'kia/ *n. f.* Turkey.
turrón /tu'rron/ *n. m.* nougat.
tusa /'tusa/ *n. f.* corncob; corn.

tutear /tute'ar/ *v.* address as **tú**, etc.
tutela /tu'tela/ *n. f.* guardianship; aegis.
tutor /tu'tor/ **-ra** *n.* tutor; guardian.
tuyo /'tuyo/ *a.* your, yours.

U V Y Z

u /u/ *conj.* or.
ubre /'uβre/ *n. f.* udder.
Ucrania /u'krania/ *n. f.* Ukraine.
ucranio /u'kranio/ **-ia** *a. & n.* Ukrainian.
ufano /u'fano/ *a.* proud, haughty.
úlcera /'ulθera/ *n. f.* ulcer.
ulterior /ulte'rior/ *a.* ulterior.
último /'ultimo/ *a.* last, final; ultimate; latest. **por ú.,** finally. **ú. minuto,** last minute, eleventh hour.
ultraje /ul'trahe/ *n. m.* outrage. —**ultrajar,** *v.*
ultrasónico /ultra'soniko/ *a.* ultrasonic.
umbral /um'bral/ *n. m.* threshold.
umbroso /um'broso/ *a.* shady.
un /un/ **una** *art. & a.* a, an; one; (*pl.*) some.
unánime /u'nanime/ *a.* unanimous.
unanimidad /unanimi'ðað/ *n. f.* unanimity.
unción /un'θion/ *n. f.* unction.
ungüento /uŋ'guento/ *n. m.* ointment, salve.
único /'uniko/ *a.* only, sole; unique.
unicornio /uni'kornio/ *n. m.* unicorn.
unidad /uni'ðað/ *n. f.* unit; unity.
unidad de cuidados intensivos /uni'ðað de kui'ðaðos inten'siβos/ **unidad de vigilancia intensiva** intensive-care unit.
unidad de disco /uni'ðað de 'disko/ disk drive.
unificar /unifi'kar/ *v.* unify.
uniforme /uni'forme/ *a. & m.* uniform.
uniformidad /uniformi'ðað/ *n. f.* uniformity.
unión /u'nion/ *n. f.* union; joining.
unir /u'nir/ *v.* unite, join.
universal /uniβer'sal/ *a.* universal.
universalidad /uniβersali'ðað/ *n. f.* universality.

universidad /uniβersi'ðað/ *n. f.* university; college.
universo /uni'βerso/ *n. m.* universe.
uno /'uno/ **una** *pron.* one; (*pl.*) some.
untar /un'tar/ *v.* spread; grease; anoint.
uña /'uɲa/ *n. f.* fingernail.
urbanidad /urβani'ðað/ *n. f.* urbanity; good breeding.
urbanismo /urβa'nismo/ *n. m.* city planning.
urbano /ur'βano/ *a.* urban; urbane; well-bred.
urbe /'urβe/ *n. f.* large city.
urgencia /ur'henθia/ *n. f.* urgency.
urgente /ur'hente/ *a.* urgent, pressing. **entrega u.,** special delivery.
urgir /ur'hir/ *v.* be urgent.
urna /'urna/ *n. f.* urn; ballot box; (*pl.*) polls.
urraca /u'rraka/ *n. f.* magpie.
usanza /u'sanθa/ usansa/ *n. f.* usage, custom.
usar /u'sar/ *v.* use; wear.
uso /'uso/ *n. m.* use; usage; wear.
usted /us'teð/ *pron.* you.
usual /u'sual/ *a.* usual.
usualmente /usual'mente/ *adv.* usually.
usura /u'sura/ *n. f.* usury.
usurero /usu'rero/ **-ra** *n.* usurer.
usurpación /usurpa'θion/ *n. f.* usurpation.
usurpar /usur'par/ *v.* usurp.
utensilio /uten'silio/ *n. m.* utensil.
útero /'utero/ *n. m.* uterus.
útil /'util/ *a.* useful, handy.
utilidad /utili'ðað/ *n. f.* usefulness.
utilizar /utili'θar/ utili'sar/ *v.* use, utilize.
útilmente /util'mente/ *adv.* usefully.
utópico /u'topiko/ *a.* utopian.
uva /'uβa/ *n. f.* grape.
vaca /'baka/ *n. f.* cow; beef.
vacaciones /baka'θiones/ baka-

'siones/ n. f.pl. vacation, holidays.

vacancia /ba'kanθia; ba'kansia/ n. f. vacancy.

vacante /ba'kante/ a. **1.** vacant. —n. **2.** f. vacancy.

vaciar /ba'θiar; ba'siar/ v. empty; pour out.

vacilación /baθila'θion; basila'sion/ n. f. vacillation.

vacilante /baθi'lante; basi'lante/ a. vacillating.

vacilar /baθi'lar; basi'lar/ v. falter, hesitate; waver; stagger.

vacío /ba'θio; ba'sio/ a. **1.** empty. —n. **2.** m. void, empty space.

vacuna /ba'kuna/ n. f. vaccine.

vacunación /bakuna'θion; bakuna'sion/ n. f. vaccination.

vacunar /baku'nar/ v. vaccinate.

vacuo /ba'kuo/ a. **1.** empty, vacant. —n. **2.** m. vacuum.

vadear /baðe'ar/ v. ford.

vado /ba'ðo/ n. m. ford.

vagabundo /baga'βundo/ **-da** a. & n. vagabond.

vagar /ba'gar/ v. wander; loiter.

vago /ba'go/ **-ga** a. **1.** vague, hazy; wandering, vagrant. —n. **2.** vagrant, tramp.

vagón /ba'gon/ n. m. railroad car.

vahído /ba'iðo/ n. m. dizziness.

vaina /'baina/ n. f. sheath; pod.

vainilla /bai'niʎa; bai'niya/ n. f. vanilla.

vaivén /bai'βen/ n. m. vibration, sway.

vajilla /ba'hiʎa; ba'hiya/ n. f. (dinner) dishes.

valentía /balen'tia/ n. f. valor, courage.

valer /ba'ler/ v. **1.** worth. —v. **2.** be worth.

valerse de /ba'lerse de/ v. make use of, avail oneself of.

valía /ba'lia/ n. f. value.

validez /bali'ðeθ; bali'ðes/ n. f. validity.

válido /ba'liðo/ a. valid.

valiente /ba'liente/ a. valiant.

valija /ba'liha/ n. f. valise.

valioso /ba'lioso/ a. valuable.

valla /'baʎa; 'baya/ n. f. fence, barrier.

valle /'baʎe; 'baye/ n. m. valley.

valor /ba'lor/ n. m. value, worth; bravery, valor; (pl., Com.) securities.

valoración /balora'θion; balora'sion/ n. f. appraisal.

valorar /balo'rar/ v. value, appraise.

vals /bals/ n. m. waltz.

valsar /bal'sar/ v. waltz.

valuación /balua'θion; balua'sion/ n. f. valuation.

valuar /balu'ar/ v. value; rate.

válvula /'balβula/ n. f. valve.

válvula de seguridad /'balβula de seguri'ðað/ safety valve.

vandalismo /banda'lismo/ n. m. vandalism.

vándalo /'bandalo/ **-la** n. vandal.

vanidad /bani'ðað/ n. f. vanity.

vanidoso /bani'ðoso/ a. vain, conceited.

vano /'bano/ a. vain; inane.

vapor /ba'por/ n. m. vapor; steam; steamer, steamship.

vaquero /ba'kero/ **-ra** n. cowboy.

vara /'bara/ n. f. wand, stick, switch.

varadero /bara'ðero/ n. m. shipyard.

varar /ba'rar/ v. launch; be stranded; run aground.

variable /ba'riaβle/ a. variable.

variación /baria'θion; baria'sion/ n. f. variation.

variar /ba'riar/ v. vary.

varicela /bari'θela; bari'sela/ n. f. chicken pox.

variedad /barie'ðað/ n. f. variety.

varios /'barios/ a. & pron. pl. various; several.

variz /ba'riθ; ba'ris/ n. f. varicose vein.

varón /ba'ron/ n. m. man; male.

varonil /baro'nil/ a. manly, virile.

vasallo /ba'saʎo; ba'sayo/ n. m. vassal.

vasectomía /basekto'mia/ n. f. vasectomy.

vasija /ba'siha/ n. f. bowl, container (for liquids).

vaso /'baso/ n. m. water glass; vase. **v. de papel,** paper cup.

vástago /'bastago/ n. m. bud, shoot; twig; offspring.

vasto /'basto/ a. vast.

vecindad /beθin'dað; besin'dað/ n. f. vecindario, n. m. neighborhood, vicinity.

vecino /be'θino; be'sino/ **-na** a. & n. neighboring; neighbor.

vedar /be'ðar/ v. forbid; impede.

vega /'bega/ n. f. meadow.

vegetación /beheta'θion; beheta'sion/ n. f. vegetation.

vegetal /behe'tal/ n. m. vegetable.

vehemente /bee'mente/ *a.* vehement.

vehículo /be'ikulo/ *n. m.* vehicle; conveyance.

veinte /'beinte/ *a. & pron.* twenty.

vejez /be'heθ; be'hes/ *n. f.* old age.

vejiga /be'higa/ *n. f.* bladder.

vela /'bela/ *n. f.* vigil, watch; candle; sail.

velar /be'lar/ *v.* stay up, sit up; watch over.

vellón /be'ʎon; be'yon/ *n. m.* fleece.

velloso /be'ʎoso; be'yoso/ *a.* hairy; fuzzy.

velludo /be'ʎuðo; be'yuðo/ *a.* downy.

velo /'belo/ *n. m.* veil.

velocidad /beloθi'ðað; belosi'ðað/ *n. f.* velocity, speed; rate. **v. máxima,** speed limit.

velomotor /belomo'tor/ *n. m.* motorbike, moped.

veloz /be'loθ; be'los/ *a.* speedy, fast, swift.

vena /'bena/ *n. f.* vein.

venado /be'naðo/ *n. m.* deer.

vencedor /benθe'ðor; bense'ðor/ **-ra** *n.* victor.

vencer /ben'θer; ben'ser/ *v.* defeat, overcome, conquer; *Com.* become due, expire.

vencimiento /benθi'miento; bensi'miento/ *n. m.* defeat; expiration.

venda /'benda/ *n. f.* **vendaje,** *m.* bandage. —**vendar,** *v.*

vendedor /bende'ðor/ **-ra** *n.* seller, trader; sales clerk.

vender /ben'der/ *v.* sell.

vendimia /ben'dimia/ *n. f.* vintage; grape harvest.

Venecia /be'neθia; be'nesia/ *n. f.* Venice.

veneciano /bene'θiano; bene'siano/ **-na** *a. & n.* Venetian.

veneno /be'neno/ *n. m.* poison.

venenoso /bene'noso/ *a.* poisonous.

veneración /benera'θion; benera'sion/ *n. f.* veneration.

venerar /bene'rar/ *v.* venerate, revere.

venero /be'nero/ *n. m.* spring; origin.

véneto /'beneto/ *a.* Venetian.

venezolano /beneθo'lano; beneso'lano/ **-na** *a. & n.* Venezuelan.

vengador /benga'ðor/ **-ra** *n.* avenger.

venganza /beŋ'ganθa; beŋ'gansa/ *n. f.* vengeance, revenge.

vengar /beŋ'gar/ *v.* avenge.

venida /be'niða/ *n. f.* arrival, advent, coming.

venidero /beni'ðero/ *a.* future; coming.

venir /be'nir/ *v.* come.

venta /'benta/ *n. f.* sale; sales.

ventaja /ben'taha/ *n. f.* advantage; profit.

ventajoso /benta'hoso/ *a.* advantageous; profitable.

ventana /ben'tana/ *n. f.* window.

ventero /ben'tero/ **-ra** *n.* innkeeper.

ventilación /bentila'θion; bentila'sion/ *n. f.* ventilation.

ventilador /bentila'ðor/ *n. m.* ventilator, fan.

ventilar /benti'lar/ *v.* ventilate, air.

ventisquero /bentis'kero/ *n. m.* snowdrift; glacier.

ventoso /ben'toso/ *a.* windy.

ventura /ben'tura/ *n. f.* venture; happiness; luck.

ver /ber/ *v.* see. **tener que v. con,** have to do with.

vera /'bera/ *n. f.* edge.

veracidad /beraθi'ðað; berasi'ðað/ *n. f.* truthfulness, veracity.

verano /be'rano/ *n. m.* summer. —**veranear,** *v.*

veras /'beras/ *n. f.pl.* **de v.,** really, truly.

veraz /be'raθ; be'ras/ *a.* truthful.

verbigracia /berβi'graθia; berβi'grasia/ *adv.* for example.

verbo /'berβo/ *n. m.* verb.

verboso /ber'βoso/ *a.* verbose.

verdad /ber'ðað/ *n. f.* truth. **ser v.,** to be true.

verdadero /berða'ðero/ *a.* true, real.

verde /'berðe/ *a.* green; risqué; off-color.

verdor /ber'ðor/ *n. m.* greenness; verdure.

verdugo /ber'ðugo/ *n. m.* hangman.

verdura /ber'ðura/ *n. f.* verdure, vegetation; (*pl.*) vegetables.

vereda /be'reða/ *n. f.* path.

veredicto /bere'ðikto/ *n. m.* verdict.

vergonzoso /bergon'θoso; bergon'soso/ *a.* shameful, embarrassing; shy, bashful.

vergüenza /ber'güenθa; ber-

'guensa /n. f. shame; disgrace; embarrassment.

verificar /beri'kar/ v. verify, check.

verja /'berha/ n. f. grating, railing.

verosímil /bero'simil/ a. likely, plausible.

verraco /be'rrako/ n. m. boar.

verruga /be'rruga/ n. f. wart.

versátil /ber'satil/ a. versatile.

verse /'berse/ v. look, appear.

versión /ber'sion/ n. f. version.

verso /'berso/ n. m. verse, stanza; line (of poetry).

verter /ber'ter/ v. pour, spill; shed; empty.

vertical /berti'kal/ a. vertical.

vertiente /ber'tiente/ n. f. slope; watershed.

vertiginoso /bertihi'noso/ a. dizzy.

vértigo /'bertigo/ n. m. vertigo, dizziness.

vestíbulo /bes'tiβulo/ n. m. vestibule, lobby.

vestido /bes'tiðo/ n. m. dress; clothing.

vestigio /bes'tihio/ n. m. vestige, trace.

vestir /bes'tir/ v. dress, clothe.

veterano /bete'rano/ **-na** a. & n. veteran.

veterinario /beteri'nario/ **-ria** a. **1.** veterinary. —n. **2.** veterinarian.

veto /'beto/ n. m. veto.

vetusto /be'tusto/ a. ancient, very old.

vez /beθ/ n. f. time; turn. **tal v.,** perhaps. **a la v.,** at the same time. **en v. de,** instead of. **una v.,** once. **otra v.,** again.

vía /'bia/ n. f. track; route, way.

viaducto /bia'ðukto/ n. m. viaduct.

viajante /bia'hante/ a. & n. traveling; traveler.

viajar /bia'har/ v. travel; journey; tour.

viaje /'biahe/ n. m. trip, journey, voyage; (pl.) travels.

viaje de estudios /'biahe de es'tuðios/ field trip.

viajero /bia'hero/ **-ra** n. traveler; passenger.

viaje todo incluido /'biahe 'toðo in'kluiðo/ package tour.

viandas /'biandas/ n. f.pl. victuals, food.

víbora /'biβora/ n. f. viper.

vibración /biβra'θion; biβra'sion/ n. f. vibration.

vibrar /bi'βrar/ v. vibrate.

vicepresidente /biθepresi'ðente; bisepresi'ðente/ n. m. vice president.

vicio /'biθio; 'bisio/ n. m. vice.

vicioso /bi'θioso; bi'sioso/ a. vicious; licentious.

víctima /'biktima/ n. f. victim.

victoria /bik'toria/ n. f. victory.

victorioso /bikto'rioso/ a. victorious.

vid /bið/ n. f. grapevine.

vida /'biða/ n. f. life; living.

vídeo /bi'ðeo/ n. m. videotape.

videocámara /biðeo'kamara/ n. f. video camera.

videodisco /biðeo'ðisko/ n. m. videodisc.

videojuego /biðeo'huego/ n. m. video game.

vidrio /'biðrio/ n. m. glass.

viejo /'bieho/ **-ja** a. & n. old; old person.

viento /'biento/ n. m. wind. **hacer v.,** to be windy.

vientre /'bientre/ n. m. belly.

viernes /'biernes/ n. m. Friday.

viga /'biga/ n. f. beam, rafter.

vigente /bi'hente/ a. in effect (prices, etc.).

vigilante /bihi'lante/ a. & m. vigilant, watchful; watchman.

vigilante nocturno /bihi'lante nok'turno/ night watchman.

vigilar /bihi'lar/ v. guard, watch over.

vigilia /bi'hilia/ n. f. vigil, watchfulness; Relig. fast.

vigor /bi'gor/ n. m. vigor. **en v.,** in effect, in force.

vil /bil/ a. vile, low, contemptible.

vileza /bi'leθa; bi'lesa/ n. f. baseness; vileness.

villa /'biʎa; 'biya/ n. f. town; country house.

villancico /biʎan'θiko; biyan'siko/ n. m. Christmas carol.

villanía /biʎa'nia; biya'nia/ n. f. villainy.

villano /bi'ʎano; bi'yano/ n. m. boor.

vinagre /bi'nagre/ n. m. vinegar.

vinagrera /bina'grera/ n. f. cruet.

vínculo /'binkulo/ n. m. link. **—vincular,** v.

vindicar /bindi'kar/ v. vindicate.

vino /'bino/ n. m. wine.

viña /'biɲa/ n. f. vineyard.

violación /biola'θion; biola'sion/ n. f. violation; rape.

violador /biola'ðor/ **-ra** n. m. & f. rapist.

violar /bio'lar/ v. violate; rape.

violencia /bio'lenθia; bio'lensia/ n. f. violence.

violento /bio'lento/ a. violent; impulsive.

violeta /bio'leta/ n. f. violet.

violín /bio'lin/ n. m. violin.

violón /bio'lon/ n. m. bass viol.

virar /bi'rar/ v. veer, change course.

virgen /bir'hen/ n. f. virgin.

viril /bi'ril/ a. virile, manly.

virilidad /birili'ðað/ n. f. virility, manhood.

virtual /bir'tual/ a. virtual.

virtud /bir'tuð/ n. f. virtue; efficacy, power.

virtuoso /bir'tuoso/ a. virtuous.

viruela /bi'ruela/ n. f. smallpox.

viruelas locas /bi'ruelas 'lokas/ n. f.pl. chicken pox.

virus /'birus/ n. m. virus.

visa /'bisa/ n. f. visa.

visaje /bi'sahe/ n. m. grimace.

visera /bi'sera/ n. f. visor.

visible /bi'siβle/ a. visible.

visión /bi'sion/ n. f. vision.

visionario /bisio'nario/ **-ria** a. & n. visionary.

visita /bi'sita/ n. f. visit; m. & f. visitor, caller. **v. con guía, v. explicada, v. programada,** guided tour.

visitación /bisita'θion; bisita'sion/ n. f. visitation.

visitante /bisi'tante/ a. & n. visiting; visitor.

visitar /bisi'tar/ v. visit; inspect, examine.

vislumbrar /bislum'βrar/ v. glimpse.

vislumbre /bis'lumbre/ n. f. glimpse.

viso /'biso/ n. m. looks; outlook.

víspera /'bispera/ n. f. eve, day before.

vista /'bista/ n. f. view; scene; sight.

vista de pájaro /'bista de 'paharo/ bird's-eye view.

vistazo /bis'taθo; bis'taso/ n. m. glance, glimpse.

vistoso /bis'toso/ a. beautiful; showy.

visual /bi'sual/ a. visual.

vital /bi'tal/ a. vital.

vitalidad /bitali'ðað/ n. f. vitality.

vitamina /bita'mina/ n. f. vitamin.

vitando /bi'tando/ a. hateful.

vituperar /bitupe'rar/ v. vituperate; revile.

viuda /'biuða/ n. f. widow.

viudo /'biuðo/ n. m. widower.

vivaz /bi'βaθ; bi'βas/ a. vivacious, buoyant; clever.

víveres /'biβeres/ n. m.pl. provisions.

viveza /bi'βeθa; bi'βesa/ n. f. animation, liveliness.

vívido /bi'βiðo/ a. vivid, bright.

vivienda /bi'βienda/ n. f. (living) quarters, dwelling.

vivificar /biβifi'kar/ v. vivify, enliven.

vivir /bi'βir/ v. live.

vivo /'biβo/ a. live, alive, living; vivid; animated, brisk.

vocablo /bo'kaβlo/ n. m. word.

vocabulario /bokaβu'lario/ n. m. vocabulary.

vocación /boka'θion; boka'sion/ n. f. vocation, calling.

vocal /bo'kal/ a. **1.** vocal. —n. **2.** f. vowel.

vocear /boθe'ar; bose'ar/ v. vociferate.

vodca /'boðka/ n. m. vodka.

vodevil /boðe'βil/ n. m. vaudeville.

volante /bo'lante/ a. **1.** flying. —n. **2.** m. memorandum; (steering) wheel.

volar /bo'lar/ v. fly; explode.

volcán /bol'kan/ n. m. volcano.

volcar /bol'kar/ v. upset, capsize.

voltaje /bol'tahe/ n. m. voltage.

voltear /bolte'ar/ v. turn, whirl; overturn.

voltio /'boltio/ n. m. volt.

volumen /bo'lumen/ n. m. volume.

voluminoso /bolumi'noso/ a. voluminous.

voluntad /bolun'tað/ n. f. will. **buena v.** goodwill.

voluntario /bolun'tario/ **-ria** a. & n. voluntary; volunteer.

voluntarioso /bolunta'rioso/ a. willful.

volver /bol'βer/ v. turn; return, go back, come back. **v. a hacer** (etc.), do (etc.) again.

volverse /bol'βerse/ v. turn around; turn, become.

vómito /'bomito/ n. m. vomit. —**vomitar,** v.

voracidad /boraθi'ðað; borasi'ðað/ *n. f.* voracity; greed.

voraz /bo'raθ; bo'ras/ *a.* greedy, ravenous.

vórtice /'bortiθe; 'bortise/ *n. m.* whirlpool.

vosotros /bo'sotros, bo'sotras/ **-as** *pron.pl.* you; yourselves.

votación /bota'θion; bota'sion/ *n. f.* voting; vote.

voto /'boto/ *n. m.* vote; vow. **—votar,** *v.*

voz /boθ; bos/ *n. f.* voice; word. **a voces,** by shouting. **en v. alta,** aloud.

vuelco /'buelko/ *n. m.* upset.

vuelo /'buelo/ *n. m.* flight. **v. libre,** hang gliding.

vuelo chárter /'buelo 'tʃarter/ charter flight.

vuelo regular /'buelo regu'lar/ scheduled flight.

vuelta /'buelta/ *n. f.* turn, bend; return. **a la v. de,** around. **dar una v.,** to take a walk.

vuestro /'buestro/ *a.* your, yours.

vulgar /bul'gar/ *a.* vulgar, common.

vulgaridad /bulgari'ðað/ *n. f.* vulgarity.

vulgo /'bulgo/ *n. m.* (the) masses, (the) common people.

vulnerable /bulne'raβle/ *a.* vulnerable.

y /i/ *conj.* and.

ya /ya/ *adv.* already; now; at once. **y. no,** no longer, any more. **y. que,** since.

yacer /ya'θer; ya'ser/ *v.* lie.

yacimiento /yaθi'miento; yasi'miento/ *n. m.* deposit.

yanqui /'yanki/ *a. & n.* North American.

yate /'yate/ *n. m.* yacht.

yegua /'yegua/ *n. f.* mare.

yelmo /'yelmo/ *n. m.* helmet.

yema /'yema/ *n. f.* yolk (of an egg).

yerba /'yerβa/ *n. f.* grass; herb.

yerno /'yerno/ *n. m.* son-in-law.

yerro /'yerro/ *n. m.* error, mistake.

yeso /'yeso/ *n. m.* plaster.

yídish /'yiðis/ *n. m.* Yiddish.

yo /yo/ *pron.* I.

yodo /'yodo/ *n. m.* iodine.

yoduro /jo'ðuro/ *n. m.* iodide.

yonqui /'yonki/ *n. & f. Colloq.* drug addict, junkie.

yugo /'yugo/ *n. m.* yoke.

yunque /'yunke/ *n. m.* anvil.

yunta /'yunta/ *n. f.* team (of animals).

zafarse /θa'farse; sa'farse/ *v.* run away, escape. **z. de,** get rid of.

zafio /'θafio; 'safio/ *a.* coarse, uncivil.

zafiro /θa'firo; sa'firo/ *n. m.* sapphire.

zaguán /θa'guan; sa'guan/ *n. m.* vestibule, hall.

zalamero /θala'mero; sala'mero/ **-ra** *n.* flatterer; wheedler.

zambullir /θambu'ʎir; sambu'yir/ *v.* plunge, dive.

zampar /θam'par; sam'par/ *v. Colloq.* gobble down, wolf down.

zanahoria /θana'oria; sana'oria/ *n. f.* carrot.

zanja /'θanha; 'sanha/ *n. f.* ditch, trench.

zapatería /θapate'ria; sapate'ria/ *n. f.* shoe store; shoemaker's shop.

zapatero /θapa'tero; sapa'tero/ *n. m.* shoemaker.

zapato /θa'pato; sa'pato/ *n. m.* shoe.

zar /θar; sar/ *n. m.* czar.

zaraza /θa'raθa; sa'rasa/ *n. f.* calico; chintz.

zarza /'θarθa; 'sarsa/ *n. f.* bramble.

zarzuela /θar'θuela; sar'suela/ *n. f.* musical comedy.

zodíaco /θo'ðiako; so'ðiako/ *n. m.* zodiac.

zona /'θona; 'sona/ *n. f.* zone.

zoología /θoolo'hia; soolo'hia/ *n. f.* zoology.

zoológico /θoo'lohiko; soo'lohiko/ *a.* zoological.

zorro /'θorro; 'sorro/ **-rra** *n.* fox.

zozobra /θo'θoβra; so'soβra/ *n. f.* worry, anxiety; capsizing.

zozobrar /θoθo'βrar; soso'βrar/ *v.* capsize; worry.

zumba /'θumba; 'sumba/ *n. f.* spanking.

zumbido /θum'βiðo; sum'βiðo/ *n. m.* buzz, hum. **—zumbar,** *v.*

zumo /'θumo; 'sumo/ *n. m.* juice. **z. de naranja,** orange juice.

zurcir /θur'θir; sur'sir/ *v.* darn, mend.

zurdo /'θurðo; 'surðo/ *a.* left-handed.

zurrar /θu'rrar; su'rrar/ *v.* flog, drub.

n. **1.** desen-
... mo *m.* —*v.* **2.** aban-
, desamparar.

abandoned /ə'bændənd/ *a.* abandonado.
abandonment /ə'bændənmənt/ *n.*
abandono, desamparo *m.*
abase /ə'beis/ *v.* degradar, humillar.
abasement /ə'beismənt/ *n.* degradación, humillación *f.*
abash /ə'bæʃ/ *v.* avergonzar.
abate /ə'beit/ *v.* menguar, mode-
rarse.
abatement /ə'beitmənt/ *n.* disminución *f.*
abbess /'æbis/ *n.* abadesa *f.*
abbey /'æbi/ *n.* abadía *f.*
abbot /'æbət/ *n.* abad *m.*
abbreviate /ə'brivi,eit/ *v.* abreviar.
abbreviation /ə,brivi'eiʃən/ *n.*
abreviatura *f.*
abdicate /'æbdi,keit/ *v.* abdicar.
abdication /,æbdi'keiʃən/ *n.* abdicación *f.*
abdomen /'æbdəmən/ *n.* abdomen *m.*
abdominal /æb'dɒmənl/ *a.* abdominal.
abduct /æb'dʌkt/ *v.* secuestrar.
abduction /æb'dʌkʃən/ *n.* secues-
tración *f.*
abductor /æb'dʌktər/ *n.* secuestrador -ra.
aberrant /ə'berənt, 'æbər-/ *a.*
aberrante.
aberration /,æbə'reiʃən/ *n.* aberración *f.*
abet /ə'bet/ *v.* apoyar, favorecer.
abetment /ə'betmənt/ *n.* apoyo
m.
abettor /ə'betər/ *n.* cómplice *m.*
& *f.*
abeyance /ə'beiəns/ *n.* suspensión
f.
abhor /æb'hɔr/ *v.* abominar,
odiar.
abhorrence /æb'hɔrəns/ *n.* detestación *f.*; aborrecimiento *m.*
abhorrent /æb'hɔrənt/ *a.* detestable, aborrecible.
abide /ə'baid/ *v.* soportar. **to a.
by,** cumplir con.

abiding /ə'baidiŋ/ *a.* perdurable.
ability /ə'biliti/ *n.* habilidad *f.*
abject /'æbdʒekt/ *a.* abyecto;
desanimado.
abjuration /,æbdʒə'reiʃən/ *n.* renuncia *f.*
abjure /æb'dʒʊr/ *v.* renunciar.
ablative /'æblətiv/ *a.* & *n. Gram.*
ablativo *m.*
ablaze /ə'bleiz/ *a.* en llamas.
able /'eibəl/ *a.* capaz; competente.
to be a., poder.
able-bodied /'eibəl 'bɒdid/ *a.* robusto.
ablution /ə'bluʃən/ *n.* ablución *f.*
ably /'eibli/ *adv.* hábilmente.
abnegate /'æbni,geit/ *v.* repudiar;
negar.
abnegation /,æbni'geiʃən/ *n.* abnegación; repudiación *f.*
abnormal /æb'nɔrməl/ *a.* anormal.
abnormality /,æbnɔr'mæliti/ *n.*
anormalidad, deformidad *f.*
abnormally /æb'nɔrməli/ *adv.*
anormalmente.
aboard /ə'bɔrd/ *adv.* a bordo.
abode /ə'boud/ *n.* residencia *f.*
abolish /ə'bɒliʃ/ *v.* suprimir.
abolishment /ə'bɒliʃmənt/ *n.*
abolición *f.*
abolition /,æbə'liʃən/ *n.* abolición
f.
abominable /ə'bɒmənəbəl/ *a.*
abominable.
abominate /ə'bɒmə,neit/ *v.*
abominar, detestar.
abomination /ə,bɒmə'neiʃən/ *n.*
abominación *f.*
aboriginal /,æbə'ridʒənl/ *a.* & *n.*
aborigen *f.*
abortion /ə'bɔrʃən/ *n.* aborto *m.*
abortive /ə'bɔrtiv/ *a.* abortivo.
abound /ə'baund/ *v.* abundar.
about /ə'baut/ *adv.* **1.** como.
about to, para; a punto de.
—*prep.* **2.** de, sobre, acerca de.
about-face /ə'baut,feis, ə'baut-
'feis/ *n. Mil.* media vuelta.
above /ə'bʌv/ *adv.* **1.** arriba.
—*prep.* **2.** sobre; por encima de.
aboveboard /ə'bʌv,bɔrd/ *a.* &
adv. sincero, franco.
abrasion /ə'breiʒən/ *n.* raspadura
f.; *Med.* abrasión *f.*
abrasive /ə'breisiv/ *a.* raspante.
n. abrasivo *f.*
abreast /ə'brest/ *adv.* de frente.

abridge /ə'brɪdʒ/ v. abreviar.

abridgment /ə'brɪdʒmənt/ n. abreviación f.; compendio m.

abroad /ə'brɔd/ adv. en el extranjero, al extranjero.

abrogate /'æbrə,geɪt/ v. abrogar, revocar.

abrogation /,æbrə'geɪʃən/ n. abrogación, revocación f.

abrupt /ə'brʌpt/ a. repentino; brusco.

abruptly /ə'brʌptli/ adv. bruscamente, precipitadamente.

abruptness /ə'brʌptnɪs/ n. precipitación; brusquedad f.

abscess /'æbsɛs/ n. absceso m.

abscond /æb'skɒnd/ v. fugarse.

absence /'æbsəns/ n. ausencia, falta f.

absent /'æbsənt/ a. ausente.

absentee /,æbsən'ti/ a. & n. ausente m. & f.

absent-minded /'æbsənt 'maɪndɪd/ a. distraído.

absinthe /'æbsɪnθ/ n. absenta f.

absolute /'æbsə,lut/ a. absoluto.

absolutely /,æbsə'lutli/ adv. absolutamente.

absoluteness /,æbsə'lutnɪs/ n. absolutismo m.

absolution /,æbsə'luʃən/ n. absolución f.

absolutism /'æbsəlu,tɪzəm/ n. absolutismo, despotismo m.

absolve /æb'zɒlv/ v. absolver.

absorb /æb'sɔrb/ v. absorber; preocupar.

absorbed /æb'sɔrbd/ a. absorbido; absorto.

absorbent /æb'sɔrbənt/ a. absorbente.

absorbent cotton algodón hidrófilo m.

absorbing /æb'sɔrbɪŋ/ a. interesante.

absorption /æb'sɔrpʃən/ n. absorción; preocupación f.

abstain /æb'steɪn/ v. abstenerse.

abstemious /æb'stimiəs/ a. abstemio, sobrio.

abstinence /'æbstənəns/ n. abstinencia f.

abstract /a, v æb'strækt, 'æbstrækt; n 'æbstrækt/ a. **1.** abstracto. —n. **2.** resumen m. —v. **3.** abstraer.

abstracted /æb'stræktɪd/ a. distraído.

abstraction /æb'strækʃən/ n. abstracción f.

abstruse /æb'strus/ a.

absurd /æb'sɜrd/ a. absurdo, ridículo.

absurdity /æb'sɜrdɪti/ n. absurdo m.

absurdly /æb'sɜrdli/ adv. absurdamente.

abundance /ə'bʌndəns/ n. abundancia f.

abundant /ə'bʌndənt/ a. abundante.

abundantly /ə'bʌndəntli/ adv. abundantemente.

abuse /n ə'byus; v ə'byuz/ n. **1.** abuso m. —v. **2.** abusar de; maltratar.

abusive /ə'byusɪv/ a. abusivo.

abusively /ə'byusɪvli/ adv. abusivamente, ofensivamente.

abutment /ə'bʌtmənt/ n. (building) estribo, contrafuerte m.

abut (on) /ə'bʌt/ v. terminar (en); lindar (con).

abyss /ə'bɪs/ n. abismo m.

Abyssinian /,æbə'sɪniən/ a. & n. abisinio -nia.

acacia /ə'keɪʃə/ n. acacia f.

academic /,ækə'dɛmɪk/ a. académico.

academy /ə'kædəmi/ n. academia f.

acanthus /ə'kænθəs/ n. Bot. acanto m.

accede /æk'sid/ v. acceder; consentir.

accelerate /æk'sɛlə,reɪt/ v. acelerar.

acceleration /æk,sɛlə'reɪʃən/ n. aceleración f.

accelerator /æk'sɛlə,reɪtər/ n. Auto. acelerador m.

accent /'æksɛnt/ n. **1.** acento m. —v. **2.** acentuar.

accentuate /æk'sɛntʃu,eɪt/ v. acentuar.

accept /æk'sɛpt/ v. aceptar.

acceptability /æk,sɛptə'bɪlɪti/ n. aceptabilidad f.

acceptable /æk'sɛptəbəl/ a. aceptable.

acceptably /æk'sɛptəbli/ adv. aceptablemente.

acceptance /æk'sɛptəns/ n. aceptación f.

access /'æksɛs/ n. acceso m., entrada f.

accessible /æk'sɛsəbəl/ a. accesible.

accessory /æk'sɛsəri/ a. **1.** accesorio. —n. **2.** cómplice m. & f.

accident /'æksɪdənt/ n. accidente m. **by a.,** por casualidad.

accidental /,æksɪ'dentḷ/ a. accidental.

accidentally /,æksɪ'dentḷi/ adv. accidentalmente, casualmente.

acclaim /ə'kleim/ v. aclamar.

acclamation /,æklə'meiʃən/ n. aclamación f.

acclimate /'æklə,meit/ v. aclimatar.

acclivity /ə'klɪvɪti/ n. subida f.

accolade /'ækə,leid/ n. acolada f.

accommodate /ə'kɒmə,deit/ v. acomodar.

accommodating /ə'kɒmə,deitɪŋ/ a. bondadoso, complaciente.

accommodation /ə,kɒmə'deiʃən/ n. servicio m.; (pl.) alojamiento m.

accompaniment /ə'kʌmpənimənt/ n. acompañamiento m.

accompanist /ə'kʌmpənɪst/ n. acompañante m. & f.

accompany /ə'kʌmpəni/ v. acompañar.

accomplice /ə'kɒmplɪs/ n. cómplice m. & f.

accomplish /ə'kɒmplɪʃ/ v. llevar a cabo; realizar.

accomplished /ə'kɒmplɪʃt/ a. acabado, cumplido; culto.

accomplishment /ə'kɒmplɪʃmənt/ n. realización f.; logro m.

accord /ə'kɔrd/ n. 1. acuerdo m. —v. 2. otorgar.

accordance /ə'kɔrdns/ n.: **in a. with,** de acuerdo con.

accordingly /ə'kɔrdɪŋli/ adv. en conformidad.

according to /ə'kɔrdɪŋ/ prep. según.

accordion /ə'kɔrdiən/ n. acordeón m.

accost /ə'kɔst/ v. dirigirse a.

account /ə'kaunt/ n. 1. relato m.; Com. cuenta f. **on a. of,** a causa de. **on no a.,** de ninguna manera. —v. 2. **a. for,** explicar.

accountable /ə'kauntəbəl/ a. responsable.

accountant /ə'kauntṇt/ n. contador -ra.

accounting /ə'kauntɪŋ/ n. contabilidad f.

accouter /ə'kutər/ v. equipar, ataviar.

accouterments /ə'kutərmənts/ n. equipo, atavío m.

accredit /ə'kredɪt/ v. acreditar.

accretion /ə'kriʃən/ n. aumento m.

accrual /ə'kruəl/ n. aumento, incremento m.

accrue /ə'kru/ v. provenir; acumularse.

accumulate /ə'kyumyə,leit/ v. acumular.

accumulation /ə,kyumyə'leiʃən/ n. acumulación f.

accumulative /ə'kyumyə,leitɪv/ a. acumulativo.

accumulator /ə'kyumyə,leitər/ n. acumulador m.

accuracy /'ækyərəsi/ n. exactitud, precisión f.

accurate /'ækyərɪt/ a. exacto.

accursed /ə'kɜrsɪd, ə'kɜrst/ a. maldito.

accusation /,ækyu'zeiʃən/ n. acusación f., cargo m.

accusative /ə'kyuzətɪv/ a. & n. acusativo m.

accuse /ə'kyuz/ v. acusar.

accused /ə'kyuzd/ a. & n. acusado -da, procesado -da.

accuser /ə'kyuzər/ n. acusador -ra.

accustom /ə'kʌstəm/ v. acostumbrar.

accustomed /ə'kʌstəmd/ a. acostumbrado.

ace /eis/ n. 1. sobresaliente. —n. 2. as m.

acerbity /ə'sɜrbɪti/ n. acerbidad, amargura f.

acetate /'æsɪ,teit/ n. Chem. acetato m.

acetic /ə'sitɪk/ a. acético.

acetylene /ə'setḷ,in/ a. 1. acetilénico. —n. 2. Chem. acetileno m.

ache /eik/ n. 1. dolor m. —v. 2. doler.

achieve /ə'tʃiv/ v. lograr, llevar a cabo.

achievement /ə'tʃivmənt/ n. realización f.; hecho notable m.

acid /'æsɪd/ a. & n. ácido m.

acidify /ə'sɪdə,fai/ v. acidificar.

acidity /ə'sɪdɪti/ n. acidez f.

acidosis /,æsɪ'dousɪs/ n. Med. acidismo m.

acid rain lluvia ácida f.

acid test prueba decisiva.

acidulous /ə'sɪdʒələs/ a. agrio, acídulo.

acknowledge /æk'nɒlɪdʒ/ v. admitir; (receipt) acusar.

acme /'ækmi/ n. apogeo, colmo m.

acne /'ækni/ n. Med. acné m. & f.

acolyte /'ækə,laɪt/ n. acólito m.

acorn /'eɪkɔrn/ n. bellota f.

acoustics /ə'kustɪks/ n. acústica f.

acquaint /ə'kweɪnt/ v. familiarizar. **to be acquainted with,** conocer.

acquaintance /ə'kweɪntns/ n. conocimiento m.; (person known) conocido -da. **to make the a. of,** conocer.

acquiesce /,ækwi'es/ v. consentir.

acquiescence /,ækwi'esəns/ n. consentimiento m.

acquire /ə'kwaɪr/ v. adquirir.

acquirement /ə'kwaɪrmənt/ n. adquisición f.; (pl.) conocimientos m.pl.

acquisition /,ækwə'zɪʃən/ n. adquisición f.

acquisitive /ə'kwɪzɪtɪv/ a. adquisitivo.

acquit /ə'kwɪt/ v. exonerar, absolver.

acquittal /ə'kwɪtl/ n. absolución f.

acre /'eɪkər/ n. acre m.

acreage /'eɪkərɪdʒ/ número de acres.

acrid /'ækrɪd/ a. acre, punzante.

acrimonious /,ækrə'mouniəs/ a. acrimonioso, mordaz.

acrimony /'ækrə,mouni/ n. acrimonia, aspereza f.

acrobat /'ækrə,bæt/ n. acróbata m. & f.

acrobatic /,ækrə'bætɪk/ a. acrobático.

across /ə'krɔs/ adv. **1.** a través, al otro lado. —prep. **2.** al otro lado de, a través de.

acrostic /ə'krɔstɪk/ n. acróstico m.

act /ækt/ n. **1.** acción f.; acto m. —v. **2.** actuar, portarse. **act as,** hacer de. **act on,** decidir sobre.

acting /'æktɪŋ/ a. **1.** interino. —n. **2.** acción f.; Theat. representación f.

actinism /'æktə,nɪzəm/ n. actinismo m.

actinium /æk'tɪniəm/ n. Chem. actinio m.

action /'ækʃən/ n. acción f. **take a.,** tomar medidas.

action replay /'ri,pleɪ/ repetición f.

activate /'æktə,veɪt/ v. activar.

activation /,æktə'veɪʃən/ n. activación f.

activator /'æktə,veɪtər/ n. Chem. activador m.

active /'æktɪv/ a. activo.

activity /æk'tɪvɪti/ n. actividad f.

actor /'æktər/ n. actor m.

actress /'æktrɪs/ n. actriz f.

actual /'æktʃuəl/ a. real, efectivo.

actuality /,æktʃu'ælɪti/ n. realidad, actualidad f.

actually /'æktʃuəli/ adv. en realidad.

actuary /'æktʃu,eri/ n. actuario m.

actuate /'æktʃu,eit/ v. impulsar, mover.

acumen /ə'kyumən/ n. cacumen m., perspicacia f.

acupuncture /'ækyu,pʌŋktʃər/ n. acupuntura f.

acute /ə'kyut/ a. agudo; perspicaz.

acutely /ə'kyutli/ adv. agudamente.

acuteness /ə'kyutnɪs/ n. agudeza f.

adage /'ædɪdʒ/ n. refrán, proverbio m.

adamant /'ædəmənt/ a. firme.

Adam's apple /'ædəmz/ nuez de la garganta.

adapt /ə'dæpt/ v. adaptar.

adaptability /ə,dæptə'bɪlɪti/ n. adaptabilidad f.

adaptable /ə'dæptəbəl/ a. adaptable.

adaptation /,ædəp'teɪʃən/ n. adaptación f.

adapter /ə'dæptər/ n. Elec. adaptador m.; Mech. ajustador m.

adaptive /ə'dæptɪv/ a. adaptable, acomodable.

add /æd/ v. agregar, añadir. **a. up,** sumar.

adder /'ædər/ n. víbora; serpiente f.

addict /'ædɪkt/ n. adicto -ta; (fan) aficionado -da.

addition /ə'dɪʃən/ n. adición f. **in a. to,** además de.

additional /ə'dɪʃənl/ a. adicional.

addle /'ædl/ v. confundir.

address /n ə'dres, 'ædres; v ə'dres/ n. **1.** dirección f.; señas f.pl.; (speech) discurso m. —v. **2.** dirigirse a.

addressee /,ædre'si/ n. destinatario -ia.

adduce /ə'dus/ v. aducir.

adenoid /'ædn,ɔɪd/ a. adenoidea.

adept /ə'dept/ a. adepto.

adeptly /ə'dɛptli/ adv. diestramente.

adeptness /ə'dɛptnɪs/ n. destreza f.

adequacy /'ædɪkwəsi/ n. suficiencia f.

adequate /'ædɪkwɪt/ a. adecuado.

adequately /'ædɪkwɪtli/ adv. adecuadamente.

adhere /æd'hɪər/ v. adherirse, pegarse.

adherence /æd'hɪərəns/ n. adhesión f.; apego m.

adherent /æd'hɪərənt/ n. adherente m., partidario -ria.

adhesion /æd'hiʒən/ n. adhesión f.

adhesive /æd'hisɪv/ a. adhesivo. **a. tape,** esparadrapo m.

adhesiveness /æd'hisɪvnɪs/ n. adhesividad f.

adieu /ə'du/ interj. **1.** adiós. —n. **2.** despedida f.

adjacent /ə'dʒeisənt/ a. adyacente.

adjective /'ædʒɪktɪv/ n. adjetivo m.

adjoin /ə'dʒɔɪn/ v. lindar (con).

adjoining /ə'dʒɔɪnɪŋ/ a. contiguo.

adjourn /ə'dʒɜrn/ v. suspender, levantar.

adjournment /ə'dʒɜrnmənt/ n. suspensión f.; Leg. espera f.

adjunct /'ædʒʌŋkt/ n. adjunto m.; Gram. atributo m.

adjust /ə'dʒʌst/ v. ajustar, acomodar; arreglar.

adjuster /ə'dʒʌstər/ n. ajustador -ra.

adjustment /ə'dʒʌstmənt/ n. ajuste; arreglo m.

adjutant /'ædʒətənt/ n. Mil. ayudante m.

administer /æd'mɪnəstər/ v. administrar.

administration /æd,mɪnə'streiʃən/ n. administración f.; gobierno m.

administrative /æd'mɪnə,streitɪv/ a. administrativo.

administrator /æd'mɪnə,streitər/ n. administrador -ra.

admirable /ə'dmərəbəl/ a. admirable.

admirably /'ædmərəbli/ adv. admirablemente.

admiral /'ædmərəl/ n. almirante m.

admiralty /'ædmərəlti/ n. Ministerio de Marina.

admiration /,ædmə'reiʃən/ n. admiración f.

admire /æd'maiər/ v. admirar.

admirer /æd'maiərər/ n. admirador -ra; enamorado -da.

admiringly /æd'maiərɪŋli/ adv. admirativamente.

admissible /æd'mɪsəbəl/ a. admisible, aceptable.

admission /æd'mɪʃən/ n. admisión; entrada f.

admit /æd'mɪt/ v. admitir.

admittance /æd'mɪtns/ n. entrada f.

admittedly /æd'mɪtɪdli/ adv. reconocidamente.

admixture /æd'mɪkstʃər/ n. mezcla f.

admonish /æd'mɒnɪʃ/ v. amonestar.

admonition /,ædmə'nɪʃən/ n. admonición f.

adolescence /,ædl'ɛsəns/ n. adolescencia f.

adolescent /,ædl'ɛsənt/ n. & a. adolescente.

adopt /ə'dɒpt/ v. adoptar.

adopted child /ə'dɒptɪd/ hija adoptiva f., hijo adoptivo m.

adoption /ə'dɒpʃən/ n. adopción f.

adorable /ə'dɔrəbəl/ a. adorable.

adoration /,ædə'reiʃən/ n. adoración f.

adore /ə'dɔr/ v. adorar.

adorn /ə'dɔrn/ v. adornar.

adornment /ə'dɔrnmənt/ n. adorno m.

adrenalin /ə'drɛnlɪn/ n. adrenalina f.

adrift /ə'drɪft/ adv. a la ventura.

adroit /ə'drɔɪt/ a. diestro.

adulate /'ædʒə,leit/ v. adular.

adulation /,ædʒə'leiʃən/ n. adulación f.

adult /ə'dʌlt/ a. & n. adulto -a.

adulterant /ə'dʌltərənt/ a. & n. adulterante m.

adulterate /ə'dʌltə,reit/ v. adulterar.

adulterer /ə'dʌltərər/ n. adúltero -ra.

adulteress /ə'dʌltərɪs/ n. adúltera f.

adultery /ə'dʌltəri/ n. adulterio m.

advance /æd'væns/ n. **1.** avance; adelanto m. **in a.,** de antemano, antes. —v. **2.** avanzar, adelantar.

advanced /æd'vænst/ a. avanzado, adelantado.

advancement /æd'vænsmənt/ n. adelantamiento m.; promoción f.

advantage /æd'væntɪdʒ/ n. ventaja f. **take a. of**, aprovecharse de.

advantageous /,ædvən'teidʒəs/ a. provechoso, ventajoso.

advantageously /,ædvən'teidʒəsli/ adv. ventajosamente.

advent /'ædvɛnt/ n. venida, llegada f.

adventitious /,ædvən'tɪʃəs/ a. adventicio, espontáneo.

adventure /æd'vɛntʃər/ n. aventura f.

adventurer /æd'vɛntʃərər/ n. aventurero -ra.

adventurous /æd'vɛntʃərəs/ a. aventurero, intrépido.

adventurously /æd'vɛntʃərəsli/ adv. arriesgadamente.

adverb /'ædvɜrb/ n. adverbio m.

adverbial /æd'vɜrbiəl/ a. adverbial.

adversary /'ædvər,sɛri/ n. adversario -a.

adverse /æd'vɜrs/ a. adverso.

adversely /æd'vɜrsli/ adv. adversamente.

adversity /æd'vɜrsiti/ n. adversidad f.

advert /æd'vɜrt/ v. hacer referencia a.

advertise /'ædvər,taiz/ v. avisar, anunciar; (promote) promocionar.

advertisement /,ædvər'taizmənt, æd'vɜrtismənt/ n. aviso, anuncio m.

advertiser /'ædvər,taizər/ n. anunciante m. & f., avisador -ra.

advertising /'ædvər,taiziŋ/ n. publicidad f.

advice /æd'vais/ n. consejos m.pl.

advisability /æd,vaizə'bɪliti/ n. prudencia, propiedad f.

advisable /æd'vaizəbəl/ a. aconsejable, prudente.

advisably /æd'vaizəbli/ adv. prudentemente.

advise /æd'vaiz/ v. aconsejar. **a. against**, desaconsejar.

advisedly /æd'vaizidli/ adv. avisadamente, prudentemente.

advisement /æd'vaizmənt/ n. consideración f.; **take under a.**, someter a estudio.

adviser /æd'vaizər/ n. consejero -ra.

advocacy /'ædvəkəsi/ n. abogacía; defensa f.

advocate /n 'ædvəkɪt; v -,keit/ n. **1.** abogado -da. —v. **2.** apoyar.

aegis /'idʒɪs/ n. amparo m.

aerate /'ɛəreit/ v. airear, ventilar.

aeration /,ɛə'reiʃən/ n. aeración, ventilación f.

aerial /'ɛəriəl/ a. aéreo.

aerie /'ɛəri/ n. nido de águila.

aeronautics /,ɛərə'nɔtiks/ n. aeronáutica f.

aerosol bomb /'ɛərə,sɔl/ bomba insecticida.

afar /ə'fɑr/ adv. lejos. **from a.**, de lejos, desde lejos.

affability /,æfə'bɪliti/ n. afabilidad, amabilidad f.

affable /'æfəbəl/ a. afable.

affably /'æfəbli/ adv. afablemente.

affair /ə'fɛər/ n. asunto m. **love a.**, aventura amorosa.

affect /ə'fɛkt/ v. afectar; (emotionally) conmover.

affectation /,æfɛk'teiʃən/ n. afectación f.

affected /ə'fɛktɪd/ a. artificioso.

affecting /ə'fɛktiŋ/ a. conmovedor.

affection /ə'fɛkʃən/ n. cariño m.

affectionate /ə'fɛkʃənit/ a. afectuoso, cariñoso.

affectionately /ə'fɛkʃənitli/ adv. afectuosamente, con cariño.

affiance /ə'faiəns/ v. dar palabra de casamiento; **become affianced**, comprometerse.

affidavit /,æfi'deivit/ n. Leg. declaración, deposición f.

affiliate /n ə'fɪli,it; v ə'fɪli,eit/ n. **1.** afiliado -da. —v. **2.** afiliar.

affiliation /ə,fɪli'eiʃən/ n. afiliación f.

affinity /ə'fɪniti/ n. afinidad f.

affirm /ə'fɜrm/ v. afirmar.

affirmation /,æfər'meiʃən/ n. afirmación, aserción f.

affirmative /ə'fɜrmətiv/ n. **1.** afirmativa f. —a. **2.** afirmativo.

affirmatively /ə'fɜrmətivli/ adv. afirmativamente, aseveradamente.

affix /n 'æfiks; v ə'fiks/ n. **1.** Gram. afijo m. —v. **2.** fijar, pegar, poner.

afflict /ə'flɪkt/ v. afligir.

affliction /ə'flɪkʃən/ n. aflicción f.; mal m.

affluence /'æfluəns/ n. abundancia, opulencia f.

affluent /'æfluənt/ a. opulento, afluente.

afford /ə'fɔrd/ v. proporcionar. **be able to a.,** tener con que comprar.

affordable /ə'fɔrdəbəl/ a. asequible.

affront /ə'frʌnt/ n. 1. afrenta f. —v. 2. afrentar, insultar.

afield /ə'fild/ adv. lejos de casa; lejos del camino; lejos del asunto.

afire /ə'faiᵊr/ adv. ardiendo.

afloat /ə'flout/ adv. Naut. a flote.

aforementioned /ə'fɔr,mɛnʃənd/ a. dicho, susodicho.

afraid /ə'freid/ a. **to be a.,** tener miedo, temer.

African /'æfrikən/ n. & a. africano -na.

aft /æft/ adv. Naut. a popa, en popa.

after /'æftər/ prep. 1. después de. —conj. 2. después que.

aftermath /'æftər,mæθ/ n. resultados m.pl., consecuencias f.pl.

afternoon /,æftər'nun/ n. tarde f. **good a.,** buenas tardes.

aftertaste /'æftər,teist/ n. gustillo m.

afterthought /'æftər,θɔt/ n. idea tardía.

afterward(s) /'æftərwərd/ adv. después.

again /ə'gɛn/ adv. otra vez, de nuevo. **to do a.,** volver a hacer.

against /ə'gɛnst/ prep. contra; en contra de.

agape /ə'geip/ adv. con la boca abierta.

agate /'ægit/ n. ágata f.

age /eidʒ/ n. 1. edad f. **of a.,** mayor de edad. **old a.,** vejez f. —v. 2. envejecer.

aged /eidʒd/ a. viejo, anciano, añejo.

ageism /'eidʒizəm/ n. discriminación contra las personas de edad.

ageless /'eidʒlis/ a. sempiterno.

agency /'eidʒənsi/ n. agencia f.

agenda /ə'dʒɛndə/ n. agenda f., orden m.

agent /'eidʒənt/ n. agente; representante m. & f.

agglutinate /ə'glutn,eit/ v. aglutinar.

agglutination /ə,glutn'eiʃən/ n. aglutinación f.

aggrandize /ə'grændaiz/ v. agrandar; elevar.

aggrandizement /ə'grændizmənt/ n. engrandecimiento m.

aggravate /'ægrə,veit/ v. agravar; irritar.

aggravation /,ægrə'veiʃən/ n. agravamiento; empeoramiento m.

aggregate /'ægrigit, -,geit/ a. & n. agregado m.

aggregation /,ægri'geiʃən/ n. agregación f.

aggression /ə'grɛʃən/ n. agresión f.

aggressive /ə'grɛsiv/ a. agresivo.

aggressively /ə'grɛsivli/ adv. agresivamente.

aggressiveness /ə'grɛsivnis/ n. agresividad f.

aggressor /ə'grɛsər/ n. agresor -ra.

aghast /ə'gæst/ a. horrorizado.

agile /'ædʒəl/ a. ágil.

agility /ə'dʒɪlɪti/ n. agilidad, ligereza, prontitud f.

agitate /'ædʒɪ,teit/ v. agitar.

agitation /,ædʒɪ'teiʃən/ n. agitación f.

agitator /'ædʒɪ,teitər/ n. agitador -ra.

agnostic /æg'nɒstik/ a. & n. agnóstico -ca.

ago /ə'gou/ adv. hace. **two days a.,** hace dos días.

agonized /'ægə,naizd/ a. angustioso.

agony /'ægəni/ n. sufrimiento m.; angustia f.

agrarian /ə'grɛəriən/ a. agrario.

agree /ə'gri/ v. estar de acuerdo; convenir. **a. with one,** sentar bien.

agreeable /ə'griəbəl/ a. agradable.

agreeably /ə'griəbli/ adv. agradablemente.

agreement /ə'grimənt/ n. acuerdo m.

agriculture /'ægri,kʌltʃər/ n. agricultura f.

ahead /ə'hɛd/ adv. adelante.

aid /eid/ n. 1. ayuda f. —v. 2. ayudar.

aide /eid/ n. ayudante -ta.

AIDS /eidz/ n. SIDA m.

ailing /'eiliŋ/ adj. enfermo.

ailment /'eilmənt/ n. enfermedad f.

aim /eim/ n. 1. puntería f.; (purpose) propósito m. —v. 2. apuntar.

aimless /'eimlis/ a. sin objeto.

air /ɛɑr/ n. **1.** aire m. **by a.** por avión. —v. **2.** ventilar, airear.

airbag /'ɛɑr,bæg/ n. (in automobiles) saco de aire m.

air-conditioned /ɛɑr kən,dɪʃənd/ a. con aire acondicionado.

air-conditioning /ɛɑr kən,dɪʃənɪŋ/ acondicionamiento del aire.

aircraft /'ɛɑr,kræft/ n. avión m.

aircraft carrier portaaviones m.

airfare /'ɛɑr,fɛɑr/ n. precio del billete de avión m.

airing /'ɛɑrɪŋ/ n. ventilación f.

airline /'ɛɑr,laɪn/ n. línea aérea f.

airliner /'ɛɑr,laɪnər/ n. avión de pasajeros.

airmail /'ɛɑr,meɪl/ n. correo aéreo.

airplane /'ɛɑr,pleɪn/ n. avión, aeroplano m.

air pollution contaminación atmosférica, contaminación del aire.

airport /'ɛɑr,pɔrt/ n. aeropuerto m.

air pressure presión atmosférica.

air raid ataque aéreo.

airsick /'ɛɑr,sɪk/ a. mareado.

air terminal terminal aérea f.

airtight /'ɛɑr,taɪt/ a. hermético.

air traffic controller controlador aéreo m.

aisle /aɪl/ n. pasillo m.

ajar /ə'dʒɑr/ a. entreabierto.

akin /ə'kɪn/ a. emparentado, semejante.

alacrity /ə'lækrɪti/ n. alacridad, presteza f.

alarm /ə'lɑrm/ n. **1.** alarma f. —v. **2.** alarmar.

alarmist /ə'lɑrmɪst/ n. alarmista m. & f.

albino /æl'baɪnou/ n. albino -na.

album /'ælbəm/ n. álbum m.

alcohol /'ælkə,hɔl/ n. alcohol m.

alcoholic /,ælkə'hɔlɪk/ a. alcohólico.

alcove /'ælkouv/ n. alcoba f.

ale /eɪl/ n. cerveza inglesa.

alert /ə'lɜrt/ n. **1.** alarma f. **on the a.,** alerta, sobre aviso. —a. **2.** listo, vivo. —v. **3.** poner sobre aviso.

alfalfa /æl'fælfə/ n. alfalfa f.

algebra /'ældʒəbrə/ n. álgebra f.

alias /'eɪliəs/ n. alias m.

alibi /'ælə,baɪ/ n. excusa f.; Leg. coartada f.

alien /'eɪliən/ a. **1.** ajeno, extranjero. —n. **2.** extranjero -ra.

alienate /'eɪliə,neɪt/ v. enajenar.

alight /ə'laɪt/ v. bajar, apearse.

align /ə'laɪn/ v. alinear.

alike /ə'laɪk/ a. **1.** semejante, igual. —adv. **2.** del mismo modo, igualmente.

alimentary canal /,ælə'mɛntəri/ n. tubo digestivo m.

alive /ə'laɪv/ a. vivo; animado.

alkali /'ælkə,laɪ/ n. Chem. álcali, cali m.

alkaline /'ælkə,laɪn/ a. alcalino.

all /ɔl/ a. & pron. todo. **not at a.,** de ninguna manera, nada.

allay /ə'leɪ/ v. aquietar.

allegation /,ælɪ'geɪʃən/ n. alegación f.

allege /ə'lɛdʒ/ v. alegar; pretender.

allegiance /ə'lidʒəns/ n. lealtad f.; (to country) homenaje m.

allegory /'ælə,gɔri/ n. alegoría f.

allergy /'ælərdʒi/ n. alergia f.

alleviate /ə'livi,eɪt/ v. aliviar.

alley /'æli/ n. callejón m. **bowling a.,** bolera f., boliche m.

alliance /ə'laɪəns/ n. alianza f.

allied /'ælaɪd/ a. aliado.

alligator /'ælɪ,geɪtər/ n. caimán m.; (Mex.) lagarto m. **a. pear,** aguacate m.

allocate /'ælə,keɪt/ v. colocar, asignar.

allot /ə'lɒt/ v. asignar.

allotment /ə'lɒtmənt/ n. lote, porción f.

allow /ə'laʊ/ v. permitir, dejar.

allowance /ə'laʊəns/ n. abono m.; dieta f. **make a. for,** tener en cuenta.

alloy /'æblɔɪ/ n. mezcla f.; (metal) aleación f.

all right está bien.

allude /ə'lud/ v. aludir.

allure /ə'lʊr/ n. **1.** atracción f. —v. **2.** atraer, tentar.

alluring /ə'lʊrɪŋ/ a. tentador, seductivo.

allusion /ə'luʒən/ n. alusión f.

ally /n. 'æla, v ə'laɪ/ n. **1.** aliado -da. —v. **2.** aliar.

almanac /'ɔlmə,næk/ n. almanaque m.

almighty /ɔl'maɪti/ a. todopoderoso.

almond /'ɑmənd/ n. almendra f.

almost /'ɔlmoust/ adv. casi.

alms /ɑmz/ n. limosna f.

aloft /ə'lɔft/ adv. arriba, en alto.

alone /ə'loun/ adv. solo, a solas. **to leave a.,** dejar en paz.

along /ə'lɔŋ/ *prep.* por; a lo largo de. **a. with,** junto con.

alongside /ə'lɔŋ'said/ *adv.* **1.** al lado. —*prep.* **2.** junto a.

aloof /ə'luf/ *a.* apartado.

aloud /ə'laud/ *adv.* en voz alta.

alpaca /æl'pækə/ *n.* alpaca *f.*

alphabet /'ælfə,bɛt/ *n.* alfabeto *m.*

alphabetical /,ælfə'bɛtɪkəl/ *a.* alfabético.

alphabetize /'ælfəbɪ,taiz/ *v.* alfabetizar.

already /ɔl'rɛdi/ *adv.* ya.

also /'ɔlsou/ *adv.* también.

altar /'ɔltər/ *n.* altar *m.*

alter /'ɔltər/ *v.* alterar.

alteration /,ɔltə'reiʃən/ *n.* alteración *f.*

alternate /*a, n* 'ɔltərnɪt; *v* -,neit/ *a.* **1.** alterno. —*n.* **2.** substituto -ta. —*v.* **3.** alternar.

alternative /ɔl'tɜrnətɪv/ *a.* **1.** alternativo. —*n.* **2.** alternativa *f.*

although /ɔl'ðou/ *conj.* aunque.

altitude /'æltɪ,tud/ *n.* altura *f.*

alto /'æltou/ *n.* altar *m.*

altogether /,ɔltə'gɛðər/ *adv.* en junto; enteramente.

altruism /'æltru,ɪzəm/ *n.* altruismo *m.*

alum /'æləm/ *n.* alumbre *m.*

aluminum /ə'lumənəm/ *n.* aluminio *m.*

aluminum foil papel de aluminio *m.*

always /'ɔlweiz/ *adv.* siempre.

amalgam /ə'mælgəm/ *n.* amalgama *f.*

amalgamate /ə'mælgə,meit/ *v.* amalgamar.

amass /ə'mæs/ *v.* amontonar.

amateur /'æmə,tʃur/ *n.* aficionado -da.

amaze /ə'meiz/ *v.* asombrar; sorprender.

amazement /ə'meizmənt/ *n.* asombro *m.*

amazing /ə'meiziŋ/ *a.* asombroso, pasmoso.

ambassador /æm'bæsədər/ *n.* embajador -ra.

amber /'æmbər/ *a.* **1.** ambarino. —*n.* **2.** ámbar *m.*

ambidextrous /,æmbɪ'dɛkstrəs/ *a.* ambidextro.

ambiguity /,æmbɪ'gyuiti/ *n.* ambigüedad *f.*

ambiguous /æm'bɪgyuəs/ *a.* ambiguo.

ambition /æm'bɪʃən/ *n.* ambición *f.*

ambitious /æm'bɪʃəs/ *a.* ambicioso.

ambulance /'æmbyələns/ *n.* ambulancia *f.*

ambush /'æmbuʃ/ *n.* **1.** emboscada *f.* —*v.* **2.** acechar.

ameliorate /ə'milyə,reit/ *v.* mejorar.

amenable /ə'minəbəl/ *a.* tratable, dócil.

amend /ə'mɛnd/ *v.* enmendar.

amendment /ə'mɛndmənt/ *n.* enmienda *f.*

amenity /ə'mɛniti/ *n.* amenidad *f.*

American /ə'mɛrikən/ *a. & n.* americano -na, norteamericano -na.

amethyst /'æməθɪst/ *n.* amatista *f.*

amiable /'eimiəbəl/ *a.* amable.

amicable /'æmikəbəl/ *a.* amigable.

amid /ə'mɪd/ *prep.* entre, en medio de.

amidships /ə'mɪd,ʃɪps/ *adv. Naut.* en medio del navío.

amiss /ə'mɪs/ *adv.* mal. **to take a.,** llevar a mal.

amity /'æmiti/ *n.* amistad, armonía *f.*

ammonia /ə'mounyə/ *n.* amoníaco *m.*

ammunition /,æmyə'nɪʃən/ *n.* municiones *f.pl.*

amnesia /æm'niʒə/ *n.* amnesia *f.*

amnesty /'æmnəsti/ *n.* amnistía *f.*, indulto *m.*

amniocentesis /,æmniousɛn'tisis/ *n.* amniocéntesis *f.*

amoeba /ə'mibə/ *n.* amiba *f.*

among /ə'mʌŋ/ *prep.* entre.

amoral /ei'mɔrəl/ *a.* amoral.

amorous /'æmərəs/ *a.* amoroso.

amorphous /ə'mɔrfəs/ *a.* amorfo.

amortize /'æmər,taiz/ *v. Com.* amortizar.

amount /ə'maunt/ *n.* **1.** cantidad, suma *f.* —*v.* **2. a. to,** subir a.

ampere /'æmpiər/ *n. Elec.* amperio *m.*

amphibian /æm'fɪbiən/ *a. & n.* anfibio *m.*

amphitheater /'æmfə,θiətər/ *n.* anfiteatro, circo *m.*

ample /'æmpəl/ *a.* amplio; suficiente.

amplify /'æmplə,fai/ *v.* amplificar.

amputate /'æmpyu,teit/ *v.* amputar.

amuse /ə'myuz/ v. entretener, divertir.

amusement /ə'myuzmənt/ n. diversión f.

an /ən, when stressed an/ art. un, una.

anachronism /ə'nækrə,nɪzəm/ n. anacronismo m.

analogous /ə'næləgəs/ a. análogo, parecido.

analogy /ə'nælədʒi/ n. analogía f.

analysis /ə'næləsɪs/ n. análisis m.

analyst /'ænlɪst/ n. analista m. & f.

analytic /,ænl'ɪtɪk/ a. analítico.

analyze /'ænl,aɪz/ v. analizar.

anarchy /'ænərki/ n. anarquía f.

anatomy /ə'nætəmi/ n. anatomía f.

ancestor /'ænsestər/ n. antepasado m.

ancestral /æn'sestrəl/ a. de los antepasados, hereditario.

ancestry /'ænsestri/ n. linaje, abolengo m.

anchor /'æŋkər/ n. **1.** ancla f. **weigh a.,** levar el ancla. —v. **2.** anclar.

anchorage /'æŋkərɪdʒ/ n. Naut. ancladero, anclaje m.

anchovy /'æntʃouvi/ n. anchoa f.

ancient /'einʃənt/ a. & n. antiguo -ua.

and /ænd, ənd/ conj. y, (before i-, hi-) e.

anecdote /'ænɪk,dout/ n. anécdota f.

anemia /ə'nimiə/ n. Med. anemia f.

anesthetic /,ænəs'θetɪk/ n. anestesia f.

anew /ə'nu/ adv. de nuevo.

angel /'eindʒəl/ n. ángel m.

anger /'æŋgər/ n. **1.** ira f., enojo m. —v. **2.** enfadar, enojar.

angle /'æŋgəl/ n. ángulo m.

angry /'æŋgri/ a. enojado, enfadado.

anguish /'æŋgwɪʃ/ n. angustia f.

angular /'æŋgyələr/ a. angular.

aniline /'ænlɪn/ n. Chem. anilina f.

animal /'ænəməl/ a. & n. animal m.

animate /v 'ænə,meit; a -mɪt/ v. **1.** animar. —a. **2.** animado.

animated /'ænə,meitɪd/ a. vivo, animado.

animation /,ænə'meiʃən/ n. animación, viveza f.

animosity /,ænə'mɒsɪti/ n. rencor m.

anise /'ænɪs/ n. anís m.

ankle /'æŋkəl/ n. tobillo m.

annals /'ænlz/ n.pl. anales m.pl.

annex /n 'æneks; v ə'neks, 'æneks/ n. **1.** anexo m., adición f. —v. **2.** anexar.

annexation /,ænɪk'seiʃən/ n. anexión, adición f.

annihilate /ə'naɪə,leit/ v. aniquilar, destruir.

anniversary /,ænə'vɜrsəri/ n. aniversario m.

annotate /'ænə,teit/ v. anotar.

annotation /,ænə'teiʃən/ n. anotación f., apunte m.

announce /ə'nauns/ v. anunciar.

announcement /ə'naunsmənt/ n. anuncio, aviso m.

announcer /ə'naunsər/ n. anunciador -ra; (radio) locutor -ra.

annoy /ə'nɔi/ v. molestar.

annoyance /ə'nɔiəns/ n. molestia, incomodidad f.

annual /'ænyuəl/ a. anual.

annuity /ə'nuiti/ n. anualidad, pensión f.

annul /ə'nʌl/ v. anular, invalidar.

anode /'ænoud/ n. Elec. ánodo m.

anoint /ə'nɔint/ v. untar; Relig. ungir.

anomalous /ə'nɒmələs/ a. anómalo, irregular.

anonymous /ə'nɒnəməs/ a. anónimo.

anorexia /,ænə'rɛksiə/ n. anorexia f.

another /ə'nʌðər/ a. & pron. otro.

answer /'ænsər, 'ɑn-/ n. **1.** contestación, respuesta f. —v. **2.** contestar, responder. **a. for,** ser responsable de.

answerable /'ænsərəbəl/ a. discutible, refutable.

answering machine /'ænsərɪŋ/ contestador automático m.

ant /ænt/ n. hormiga f.

antacid /ænt'æsɪd/ a. & n. antiácido m.

antagonism /æn'tægə,nɪzəm/ n. antagonismo m.

antagonist /æn'tægənɪst/ n. antagonista m. & f.

antagonistic /æn,tægə'nɪstɪk/ a. antagónico, hostil.

antagonize /æn'tægə,naiz/ v. contrariar.

antarctic /ænt'ɑrktɪk/ a. & n. antártico m.

antecedent /ˌæntə'sidnt/ a. & n. antecedente m.

antedate /'ænti,deit/ v. antedatar.

antelope /'æntl,oup/ n. antílope m., gacela f.

antenna /æn'tɛnə/ n. antena f.

antepenultimate /ˌæntipi'nʌltəmit/ a. antepenúltimo.

anterior /æn'tiəriər/ a. anterior.

anteroom /'ænti,rum/ n. antecámara f.

anthem /'ænθəm/ n. himno m.; (religious) antífona f.

anthology /æn'θɒlədʒi/ n. antología f.

anthracite /'ænθrə,sait/ n. antracita f.

anthrax /'ænθræks/ n. Med. ántrax m.

anthropology /ˌænθrə'pɒlədʒi/ n. antropología f.

antiaircraft /ˌænti'ɛər,kræft, ˌæntai-/ a. antiaéreo.

antibody /'ænti,bɒdi/ n. anticuerpo m.

anticipate /æn'tɪsə,peit/ v. esperar, anticipar.

anticipation /æn,tɪsə'peiʃən/ n. anticipación f.

anticlerical /ˌænti'klɛrikəl, ˌæntai-/ a. anticlerical.

anticlimax /ˌænti'klaimæks, ˌæntai-/ n. anticlímax m.

antidote /'ænti,dout/ n. antídoto m.

antifreeze /'ænti,friz/ n. anticongelante m.

antihistamine /ˌænti'histə,min, -,min, ˌæntai-/ n. antihistamínico m.

antimony /'æntə,mouni/ n. antimonio m.

antinuclear /ˌænti'nukliər, æntai-/ a. antinuclear.

antipathy /æn'tɪpəθi/ n. antipatía f.

antiquated /'ænti,kweitid/ a. anticuado.

antique /æn'tik/ a. **1.** antiguo. —n. **2.** antigüedad f.

antiquity /æn'tikwiti/ n. antigüedad f.

antiseptic /ˌænti'sɛptik/ a. & n. antiséptico m.

antisocial /ˌænti'souʃəl, ˌæntai-/ a. antisocial.

antitoxin /ˌænti'tɒksin/ n. Med. antitoxina f.

antler /'æntlər/ n. asta f.

anvil /'ænvil/ n. yunque m.

anxiety /æŋ'zaiiti/ n. ansia, ansiedad f.

anxious /'æŋkʃəs, 'æŋʃəs/ a. inquieto, ansioso.

any /'ɛni/ a. alguno; (at all) cualquiera; (after not) ninguno.

anybody /'ɛni,bɒdi/ pron. alguien; (at all) cualquiera; (after not) nadie.

anyhow /'ɛni,hau/ adv. de todos modos; en todo caso.

anyone /'ɛni,wʌn/ pron. = anybody.

anything /'ɛni,θiŋ/ pron. algo; (at all) cualquier cosa; (after not) nada.

anyway /'ɛni,wei/ adv. = anyhow.

anywhere /'ɛni,wɛər/ adv. en alguna parte; (at all) dondequiera; (after not) en ninguna parte.

apart /ə'pɑrt/ adv. aparte. **to take a.,** deshacer.

apartheid /ə'pɑrtheit, -hait/ n. apartheid m.

apartment /ə'pɑrtmənt/ n. apartamento, piso m.

apartment house casa de pisos f.

apathetic /ˌæpə'θɛtik/ a. apático.

apathy /'æpəθi/ n. apatía f.

ape /eip/ n. **1.** mono -na. —v. **2.** imitar.

aperture /'æpərtʃər/ n. abertura f.

apex /'eipɛks/ n. ápice m.

aphorism /'æfə,rizəm/ n. aforismo m.

apiary /'eipi,ɛri/ n. colmenario, abejar m.

apiece /ə'pis/ adv. por persona; cada uno.

apologetic /ə,pɒlə'dʒɛtik/ a. apologético.

apologist /ə'pɒlədʒist/ n. apologista m. & f.

apologize /ə'pɒlə,dʒaiz/ v. excusarse, disculparse.

apology /ə'pɒlədʒi/ n. excusa; apología f.

apoplectic /ˌæpə'plɛktik/ a. apopléctico.

apoplexy /'æpə,plɛksi/ n. apoplejía f.

apostate /ə'pɒsteit/ n. apóstata m. & f.

apostle /ə'pɒsəl/ n. apóstol m.

apostolic /ˌæpə'stɒlik/ a. apostólico.

appall /ə'pɔl/ v. horrorizar; consternar.

apparatus /ˌæpəˈrætəs/ n. aparato m.

apparel /əˈpærəl/ n. ropa f.

apparent /əˈpærənt/ a. aparente; claro.

apparition /ˌæpəˈrɪʃən/ n. aparición f.; fantasma m.

appeal /əˈpil/ n. **1.** súplica f.; interés m.; Leg. apelación f. —v. **2.** apelar, suplicar; interesar.

appear /əˈpɪər/ v. aparecer, asomar; (seem) parecer; Leg. comparecer.

appearance /əˈpɪrəns/ n. apariencia f., aspecto m.; aparición f.

appease /əˈpiz/ v. aplacar, apaciguar.

appeasement /əˈpizmənt/ n. apaciguamiento m.

appeaser /əˈpizər/ n. apaciguador -ra, pacificador -ra.

appellant /əˈpɛlənt/ n. apelante, demandante m. & f.

appellate /əˈpɛlɪt/ a. Leg. de apelación.

appendage /əˈpɛndɪdʒ/ n. añadidura f.

appendectomy /ˌæpənˈdɛktəmi/ n. apendectomía f.

appendicitis /ə,pɛndəˈsaitɪs/ n. apendicitis f.

appendix /əˈpɛndɪks/ n. apéndice m.

appetite /ˈæpɪ,tait/ n. apetito m.

appetizer /ˈæpɪ,taizər/ n. aperitivo m.

appetizing /ˈæpɪ,taiziŋ/ a. apetitoso.

applaud /əˈplɔd/ v. aplaudir.

applause /əˈplɔz/ n. aplauso m.

apple /ˈæpəl/ n. manzana f. **a. tree,** manzano m.

applesauce /ˈæpəl,sɔs/ n. compota de manzana.

appliance /əˈplaiəns/ n. aparato m.

applicable /ˈæplɪkəbəl/ a. aplicable.

applicant /ˈæplɪkənt/ n. suplicante m. & f.; candidato -ta.

application /ˌæplɪˈkeiʃən/ n. solicitud f., (computer) programa m.

applied /əˈplaid/ a. aplicado. **a. for,** pedido.

appliqué /ˌæplɪˈkei/ n. (sewing) aplicación f.

apply /əˈplai/ v. aplicar. **a. for,** solicitar, pedir.

appoint /əˈpɔint/ v. nombrar.

appointment /əˈpɔintmənt/ n. nombramiento m.; puesto m.

apportion /əˈpɔrʃən/ v. repartir.

apposition /ˌæpəˈzɪʃən/ n. Gram. aposición f.

appraisal /əˈpreizəl/ n. valoración f.

appraise /əˈpreiz/ v. evaluar; tasar; estimar.

appreciable /əˈpriʃiəbəl/ a. apreciable; notable.

appreciate /əˈpriʃi,eit/ v. apreciar, estimar.

appreciation /ə,priʃiˈeiʃən/ n. aprecio; reconocimiento m.

apprehend /ˌæprɪˈhɛnd/ v. prender, capturar.

apprehension /ˌæprɪˈhɛnʃən/ n. aprensión f.; detención f.

apprehensive /ˌæprɪˈhɛnsɪv/ a. aprensivo.

apprentice /əˈprɛntɪs/ n. aprendiz -iza.

apprenticeship /əˈprɛntɪs,ʃɪp/ n. aprendizaje m.

apprise /əˈpraiz/ v. informar.

approach /əˈproutʃ/ n. **1.** acceso; método m. —v. **2.** acercarse.

approachable /əˈproutʃəbəl/ a. accesible.

approbation /ˌæprəˈbeiʃən/ n. aprobación f.

appropriate /a əˈprouprit; v -,eit/ a. **1.** apropiado. —v. **2.** apropiar.

appropriation /ə,proupriˈeiʃən/ n. apropiación f.

approval /əˈpruvəl/ n. aprobación f.

approve /əˈpruv/ v. aprobar.

approximate /a əˈprɒksəmit; v -,meit/ a. **1.** aproximado. —v. **2.** aproximar.

approximately /əˈprɒksəmitli/ adv. aproximadamente.

approximation /ə,prɒksəˈmeiʃən/ n. aproximación f.

appurtenance /əˈpɜrtənəns/ n. dependencia f.

apricot /ˈæpri,kɒt/ n. albaricoque, damasco m.

April /ˈeiprəl/ n. abril m.

apron /ˈeiprən/ n. delantal m.

apropos /ˌæprəˈpou/ adv. a propósito.

apt /æpt/ a. apto; capaz.

aptitude /ˈæptɪ,tud/ n. aptitud; facilidad f.

aquarium /əˈkwɛəriəm/ n. acuario m., pecera f.

aquatic /əˈkwætɪk/ a. acuático.

aqueduct /'ækwɪ,dʌkt/ n. acueducto m.

aqueous /'ækwɪəs/ a. ácueo, acuoso, aguoso.

aquiline /'ækwə,laɪn/ a. aquilino, aguileño.

Arab /'ærəb/ a. & n. árabe m. & f.

arable /'ærəbəl/ a. cultivable.

arbitrary /'ɑrbɪ,treri/ a. arbitrario.

arbitrate /'ɑrbɪ,treɪt/ v. arbitrar.

arbitration /,ɑrbɪ'treɪʃən/ n. arbitraje m., arbitración f.

arbitrator /'ɑrbɪ,treɪtər/ n. arbitrador -ra.

arbor /'ɑrbər/ n. emparrado m.

arboreal /ɑr'bɔriəl/ a. arbóreo.

arc /ɑrk/ n. arco m.

arch /ɑrtʃ/ n. **1.** arco m. —v. **2.** arquear, encorvar.

archaeology /,ɑrki'ɒlədʒi/ n. arqueología f.

archaic /ɑr'keɪɪk/ a. arcaico.

archbishop /'ɑrtʃ'bɪʃəp/ n. arzobispo m.

archdiocese /,ɑrtʃ'daɪə,sis, -sɪs-/ n. archidiócesis f.

archduke /'ɑrtʃ'duk/ n. archiduque m.

archer /'ɑrtʃər/ n. arquero m.

archery /'ɑrtʃəri/ n. ballestería f.

archipelago /,ɑrkə'pelə,gou/ n. archipiélago m.

architect /'ɑrkɪ,tekt/ n. arquitecto -ta.

architectural /,ɑrkɪ'tektʃərəl/ a. arquitectural.

architecture /'ɑrkɪ,tektʃər/ n. arquitectura f.

archive /'ɑrkaɪv/ n. archivo m.

archway /'ɑrtʃ,weɪ/ n. arcada f.

arctic /'ɑrktɪk, 'ɑrtɪk/ a. ártico.

ardent /'ɑrdnt/ a. ardiente.

ardor /'ɑrdər/ n. ardor m., pasión f.

arduous /'ɑrdʒuəs/ a. arduo, difícil.

area /'ɛəriə/ n. área; extensión f.

area code prefijo m.

arena /ə'rinə/ n. arena f.

Argentine /'ɑrdʒəntin, -,taɪn/ a. & n. argentino -na.

argue /'ɑrgyu/ v. disputar; sostener.

argument /'ɑrgyəmənt/ n. disputa f.; razonamiento m.

argumentative /,ɑrgyə'mentətɪv/ a. argumentoso.

aria /'ɑriə/ n. aria f.

arid /'ærɪd/ a. árido, seco.

arise /ə'raɪz/ v. surgir; alzarse.

aristocracy /,ærə'stɒkrəsi/ n. aristocracia f.

aristocrat /ə'rɪstə,kræt/ n. aristócrata m.

aristocratic /ə,rɪstə'krætɪk/ a. aristocrático.

arithmetic /ə'rɪθmətɪk/ n. aritmética f.

ark /ɑrk/ n. arca f.

arm /ɑrm/ n. **1.** brazo m.; (weapon) arma f. —v. **2.** armar.

armament /'ɑrməmənt/ n. armamento m.

armchair /'ɑrm,tʃɛər/ n. sillón m., butaca f.

armed forces /ɑrmd 'fɔrsɪz/ fuerzas militares.

armful /'ɑrm,fʊl/ n. brazada f.

armhole /'ɑrm,houl/ n. (sew.) sobaquera f.

armistice /'ɑrməstɪs/ n. armisticio m.

armor /'ɑrmər/ n. armadura f., blindaje m.

armored /'ɑrmərd/ a. blindado.

armory /'ɑrməri/ n. armería f., arsenal m.

armpit /'ɑrm,pɪt/ n. axila f., sobaco m.

army /'ɑrmi/ n. ejército m.

arnica /'ɑrnɪkə/ n. árnica f.

aroma /ə'roumə/ n. fragancia f.

aromatic /,ærə'mætɪk/ a. aromático.

around /ə'raund/ prep. alrededor de, a la vuelta de; cerca de. **a. here,** por aquí.

arouse /ə'rauz/ v. despertar; excitar.

arraign /ə'reɪn/ v. Leg. procesar criminalmente.

arrange /ə'reɪndʒ/ v. arreglar; concertar; Mus. adaptar.

arrangement /ə'reɪndʒmənt/ n. arreglo; orden m.

array /ə'reɪ/ n. **1.** orden; adorno m. —v. **2.** adornar.

arrears /ə'rɪərz/ n. atrasos m.pl.

arrest /ə'rɛst/ n. **1.** detención f. —v. **2.** detener, arrestar.

arrival /ə'raɪvəl/ n. llegada f.

arrive /ə'raɪv/ v. llegar.

arrogance /'ærəgəns/ n. arrogancia f.

arrogant /'ærəgənt/ a. arrogante.

arrogate /'ærə,geɪt/ v. arrogarse, usurpar.

arrow /'ærou/ n. flecha f.

arrowhead /'ærou,hed/ n. punta de flecha f.

arsenal /'arsənl/ n. arsenal m.

arsenic /'arsənɪk/ n. arsénico m.

arson /'arsən/ n. incendio premeditado.

art /art/ arte m. (f. in pl.); (skill) maña f.

arterial /ar'tɪəriəl/ a. arterial.

arteriosclerosis /ar,tɪəriouskləʻrousɪs/ n. arteriosclerosis f.

artery /'artəri/ n. arteria f.

artesian well /ar'tiʒən/ pozo artesiano.

artful /'artfəl/ a. astuto.

arthritis /ar'θraitɪs/ n. artritis f.

artichoke /'artɪ,tʃouk/ n. alcachofa f.

article /'artɪkəl/ n. artículo m.

articulate /ar'tɪkyə,leit/ v. articular.

articulation /ar,tɪkyə'leiʃən/ n. articulación f.

artifice /'artəfɪs/ n. artificio m.

artificial /,artə'fɪʃəl/ a. artificial.

artificially /,artə'fɪʃəli/ adv. artificialmente.

artillery /ar'tɪləri/ n. artillería f.

artisan /'artəzən/ n. artesano -na.

artist /'artɪst/ n. artista m. & f.

artistic /ar'tɪstɪk/ a. artístico.

artistry /'artɪstri/ n. arte m. & f.

artless /'artlɪs/ a. natural, cándido.

as /æz/ adv. & conj. como; **as... as** tan... como.

asbestos /æs'bɛstəs/ n. asbesto m.

ascend /ə'sɛnd/ v. ascender.

ascendancy /ə'sɛndənsi/ n. ascendiente m.

ascendant /ə'sɛndənt/ a. ascendente.

ascent /ə'sɛnt/ n. subida f., ascenso m.

ascertain /,æsər'tein/ v. averiguar.

ascetic /ə'sɛtɪk/ a. **1.** ascético. —n. **2.** asceta m. & f.

ascribe /ə'skraib/ v. atribuir.

ash /æʃ/ n. ceniza f.

ashamed /ə'ʃeimd/ a. avergonzado.

ashen /'æʃən/ a. pálido.

ashore /ə'ʃɔr/ adv. a tierra. **go a.** desembarcar.

ashtray /'æʃ,trei/ n. cenicero m.

Ash Wednesday miércoles de ceniza m.

Asiatic /,eiʒi'ætɪk/ a. & n. asiático -ca.

aside /ə'said/ adv. al lado. **a. from.** aparte de.

ask /æsk/ v. preguntar; invitar; (request) pedir. **a. for,** pedir. **a. a question,** hacer una pregunta.

askance /ə'skæns/ adv. de soslayo; con recelo.

asleep /ə'slip/ a. dormido. **to fall a.,** dormirse.

asparagus /ə'spærəgəs/ n. espárrago m.

aspect /'æspɛkt/ n. aspecto m., apariencia f.

asperity /ə'spɛrɪti/ n. aspereza f.

aspersion /ə'spərʒən/ n. calumnia f.

asphalt /'æsfɔlt/ n. asfalto m.

asphyxia /æs'fɪksiə/ n. asfixia f.

asphyxiate /æs'fɪksi,eit/ v. asfixiar, sofocar.

aspirant /'æspərənt/ a. & n. aspirante m. & f.

aspirate /'æspə,reit/ v. aspirar.

aspiration /,æspə'reiʃən/ n. aspiración f.

aspirator /'æspə,reitər/ n. aspirador m.

aspire /ə'spaiər/ v. aspirar. **a. to,** ambicionar.

aspirin /'æspərɪn/ n. aspirina f.

ass /æs/ n. asno, burro m.

assail /ə'seil/ v. asaltar, acometer.

assailant /ə'seilənt/ n. asaltador -ra.

assassin /ə'sæsɪn/ n. asesino -na.

assassinate /ə'sæsə,neit/ v. asesinar.

assassination /ə,sæsə'neiʃən/ n. asesinato m.

assault /ə'sɔlt/ n. **1.** asalto m. —v. **2.** asaltar, atacar.

assay /'æsei/ v. examinar; ensayar.

assemblage /ə'sɛmblɪdʒ/ n. asamblea f.

assemble /ə'sɛmbəl/ v. juntar, convocar; (mechanism) montar.

assembly /ə'sɛmbli/ n. asamblea, concurrencia f.

assent /ə'sɛnt/ n. **1.** asentimiento m. —v. **2.** asentir, convenir.

assert /ə'sɜrt/ v. afirmar, aseverar. **a. oneself,** hacerse sentir.

assertion /ə'sɜrʃən/ n. aserción, aseveración f.

assertive /ə'sɜrtɪv/ a. asertivo.

assess /ə'sɛs/ v. tasar, evaluar.

assessor /ə'sɛsər/ n. asesor -ra.

asset /'æsɛt/ n. ventaja f. **assets,** Com. capital m.

asseverate /ə'sɛvə,reit/ v. aseverar, afirmar.

asseveration /əˌsɛvəˈreɪʃən/ n. as-everacinewlin f.

assiduous /əˈsɪdʒuəs/ a. asiduo.

assiduously /əˈsɪdʒuəsli/ adv. asi-duamente.

assign /əˈsaɪn/ v. asignar; destinar.

assignable /əˈsaɪnəbəl/ a. asigna-ble, transferible.

assignation /ˌæsɪɡˈneɪʃən/ n. asignación f.

assignment /əˈsaɪnmənt/ n. mi-sión; tarea f.

assimilate /əˈsɪməˌleɪt/ v. asimilar.

assimilation /əˌsɪməˈleɪʃən/ n. asimilación f.

assimilative /əˈsɪməlɑtɪv/ a. asi-milativo.

assist /əˈsɪst/ v. ayudar, auxiliar.

assistance /əˈsɪstəns/ n. ayuda f., auxilio m.

assistant /əˈsɪstənt/ n. ayudante -ta, asistente -ta.

associate /əˈsoʊsiɪt/ v -siˌeɪt/ n. **1.** socio -cia. —v. **2.** asociar.

association /əˌsoʊsiˈeɪʃən/ n. aso-ciación; sociedad f.

assonance /ˈæsənəns/ n. asonan-cia f.

assort /əˈsɔrt/ v. surtir con varie-dad.

assorted /əˈsɔrtɪd/ a. variado, sur-tido.

assortment /əˈsɔrtmənt/ n. sur-tido m.

assuage /əˈsweɪdʒ/ v. mitigar, ali-viar.

assume /əˈsum/ v. suponer; asu-mir.

assuming /əˈsumɪŋ/ a. presun-tuoso. **a. that,** dado que.

assumption /əˈsʌmpʃən/ n. supo-sición; Relig. asunción f.

assurance /əˈʃʊrəns/ n. seguridad; confianza f.; garantía f.

assure /əˈʃʊr/ v. asegurar; dar confianza.

assured /əˈʃʊrd/ a. **1.** seguro. —a. & n. **2.** Com. asegurado -da.

assuredly /əˈʃʊrɪdli/ adv. cierta-mente.

aster /ˈæstər/ n. aster f.

asterisk /ˈæstərɪsk/ n. asterisco m.

astern /əˈstɜrn/ adv. Naut. a popa.

asteroid /ˈæstəˌrɔɪd/ n. asteroide m.

asthma /ˈæzmə/ n. Med. asma f.

astigmatism /əˈstɪɡməˌtɪzəm/ n. astigmatismo m.

astir /əˈstɜr/ adv. en movimiento.

astonish /əˈstɒnɪʃ/ v. asombrar, pasmar.

astonishment /əˈstɒnɪʃmənt/ n. asombro m., sorpresa f.

astound /əˈstaʊnd/ v. pasmar, sorprender.

astral /ˈæstrəl/ a. astral, estelar.

astray /əˈstreɪ/ a. desviado.

astride /əˈstraɪd/ adv. a horcaja-das.

astringent /əˈstrɪndʒənt/ a. & n. astringente m.

astrology /əˈstrɒlədʒi/ n. as-trología f.

astronaut /ˈæstrəˌnɔt/ n. as-tronauta m. & f.

astronomy /əˈstrɒnəmi/ n. astro-nomía f.

astute /əˈstut/ a. astuto; agudo.

asunder /əˈsʌndər/ adv. en dos.

asylum /əˈsaɪləm/ n. asilo, refugio m.

asymmetry /eɪˈsɪmɪtri/ n. asi-metría f.

at /æt/ prep. a, en; cerca de.

ataxia /əˈtæksiə/ n. Med. ataxia f.

atheist /ˈeɪθiɪst/ n. ateo -tea.

athlete /ˈæθlit/ n. atleta m. & f.

athletic /æθˈlɛtɪk/ a. atlético.

athletics /æθˈlɛtɪks/ n. atletismo m., deportes m.pl.

athwart /əˈθwɔrt/ prep. a través de.

Atlantic /ætˈlæntɪk/ a. **1.** atlán-tico. —n. **2.** Atlántico m.

Atlantic Ocean Océano Atlántico m.

atlas /ˈætləs/ n. atlas m.

atmosphere /ˈætməsˌfɪər/ n. at-mósfera f.; Fig. ambiente m.

atmospheric /ˌætməsˈfɛrɪk/ a. at-mosférico.

atoll /ˈætɔl/ n. atolón m.

atom /ˈætəm/ n. átomo m.

atomic /əˈtɒmɪk/ a. atómico.

atomic bomb bomba atómica f.

atomic energy energía atómica, energía nuclear f.

atomic theory teoría atómica f.

atomic weight peso atómico m.

atonal /eɪˈtoʊnəl/ a. Mus. atonal.

atone /əˈtoʊn/ v. expiar, compen-sar.

atonement /əˈtoʊnmənt/ n. expia-ción; reparación f.

atrocious /əˈtroʊʃəs/ a. atroz.

atrocity /əˈtrɒsɪti/ n. atrocidad f.

atrophy /ˈætrəfi/ n. **1.** Med. atro-fia f. —v. **2.** atrofiar.

atropine /ˈætrəˌpin, -pɪn/ n. atropina f.

attach /əˈtætʃ/ v. juntar; prender; (hook) enganchar; Fig. atribuir.

attaché /ˌætæˈʃeɪ/ n. agregado -da.

attachment /əˈtætʃmənt/ n. enlace m.; accesorio m.; (emotional) afecto, cariño m.

attack /əˈtæk/ n. **1.** ataque m. —v. **2.** atacar.

attacker /əˈtækər/ n. asaltador -ra.

attain /əˈteɪn/ v. lograr, alcanzar.

attainable /əˈteɪnəbəl/ a. accesible, realizable.

attainment /əˈteɪnmənt/ n. logro; (pl.) dotes f.pl.

attempt /əˈtɛmpt/ n. **1.** ensayo; esfuerzo m.; tentativa f. —v. **2.** ensayar, intentar.

attend /əˈtɛnd/ v. atender; (a meeting) asistir a.

attendance /əˈtɛndəns/ n. asistencia; presencia f.

attendant /əˈtɛndənt/ a. **1.** concomitante. —n. **2.** servidor -ra.

attention /əˈtɛnʃən/ n. atención f.; obsequio m. **to pay a. to,** hacer caso a.

attentive /əˈtɛntɪv/ a. atento.

attentively /əˈtɛntɪvli/ adv. atentamente.

attenuate /əˈtɛnyuˌeɪt/ v. atenuar, adelgazar.

attest /əˈtɛst/ v. confirmar, atestiguar.

attic /ˈætɪk/ n. desván m., guardilla f.

attire /əˈtaɪ˞/ n. **1.** traje m. —v. **2.** vestir.

attitude /ˈætɪˌtud/ n. actitud f., ademán m.

attorney /əˈtɜrni/ n. abogado -da, apoderado -da.

attract /əˈtrækt/ v. atraer. **a. attention,** llamar la atención.

attraction /əˈtrækʃən/ n. atracción f., atractivo m.

attractive /əˈtræktɪv/ a. atractivo; simpático.

attributable /əˈtrɪbyʊtəbəl/ a. atribuible, imputable.

attribute /n ˈætrəˌbyut; v əˈtrɪbyʊt/ n. **1.** atributo m. —v. **2.** atribuir.

attrition /əˈtrɪʃən/ n. roce, desgaste m.; atrición f.

attune /əˈtun/ v. armonizar.

auction /ˈɔkʃən/ n. subasta f., S.A. venduta f.

auctioneer /ˌɔkʃəˈnɪr/ n. subastador -ra, S.A. martillero -ra.

audacious /ɔˈdeɪʃəs/ a. audaz.

audacity /ɔˈdæsɪti/ n. audacia f.

audible /ˈɔdəbəl/ a. audible.

audience /ˈɔdiəns/ n. auditorio, público m.; entrevista f.

audiovisual /ˌɔdiouˈvɪʒuəl/ a. audiovisual.

audit /ˈɔdɪt/ n. **1.** revisión de cuentas f. —v. **2.** revisar cuentas.

audition /ɔˈdɪʃən/ n. audición f.

auditor /ˈɔdɪtər/ n. interventor -ora, revisor -ora.

auditorium /ˌɔdɪˈtɔriəm/ n. sala f.; teatro m.

auditory /ˈɔdɪˌtɔri/ a. & n. auditorio m.

augment /ɔgˈmɛnt/ v. aumentar.

augur /ˈɔgər/ v. augurar, pronosticar.

August /ˈɔgəst/ n. agosto m.

aunt /ænt, ɑnt/ n. tía f.

auspice /ˈɔspɪs/ n. auspicio m.

auspicious /ɔˈspɪʃəs/ a. favorable; propicio.

austere /ɔˈstɪər/ a. austero.

austerity /ɔˈstɛrɪti/ n. austeridad, severidad f.

Austrian /ˈɔstriən/ a. & n. austríaco -ca.

authentic /ɔˈθɛntɪk/ a. auténtico.

authenticate /ɔˈθɛntɪˌkeɪt/ v. autenticar.

authenticity /ˌɔθɛnˈtɪsɪti/ n. autenticidad f.

author /ˈɔθər/ n. autor -ra, escritor -ra.

authoritarian /əˌθɔrɪˈtɛəriən/ a. & n. autoritario -ria.

authoritative /əˈθɔrɪˌteɪtɪv/ a. autoritativo; autorizado.

authoritatively /əˈθɔrɪˌteɪtɪvli/ adv. autoritativamente.

authority /əˈθɔrɪti/ n. autoridad f.

authorization /ˌɔθərəˈzeɪʃən/ n. autorización f.

authorize /ˈɔθəˌraɪz/ v. autorizar.

auto /ˈɔtou/ n. auto, automóvil m.

autobiography /ˌɔtəbaɪˈɒgrəfi/ n. autobiografía f.

autocracy /ɔˈtɒkrəsi/ n. autocracia f.

autocrat /ˈɔtəˌkræt/ n. autócrata m. & f.

autograph /ˈɔtəˌgræf/ n. autógrafo m.

automatic /ˌɔtəˈmætɪk/ a. automático.

automatically /,ɔtə'mætɪkəli/ adv. automáticamente.

automobile /,ɔtəmə'bil/ n. automóvil, coche m.

automotive /,ɔtə'moutɪv/ a. automotriz.

autonomy /ɔ'tɒnəmi/ n. autonomía f.

autopsy /'ɔtɒpsi/ n. autopsia f.

autumn /'ɔtəm/ n. otoño m.

auxiliary /ɔg'zɪlyəri/ a. auxiliar.

avail /ə'veil/ v. **1.** of no a., en vano. —v. **2. a. oneself of,** aprovecharse.

available /ə'veiləbəl/ a. disponible.

avalanche /'ævə,læntʃ/ n. alud m.

avarice /'ævərɪs/ n. avaricia, codicia f.

avariciously /,ævə'rɪʃəsli/ adv. avaramente.

avenge /ə'vendʒ/ v. vengar.

avenger /ə'vendʒər/ n. vengador -ra.

avenue /'ævə,nu/ n. avenida f.

average /'ævərɪdʒ/ a. **1.** medio; común. —n. **2.** promedio, término medio m. —v. **3.** calcular el promedio.

averse /ə'vɜrs/ a. **to be a. to,** tener antipatía a, opuesto a.

aversion /ə'vɜrʒən/ n. aversión f.

avert /ə'vɜrt/ v. desviar; impedir.

aviary /'eivi,eri/ n. pajarera, avería f.

aviation /,eivi'eiʃən/ n. aviación f.

aviator /'eivi,eitər/ n. aviador -ra.

aviatrix /,eivi'eitrɪks/ n. aviatriz f.

avid /'ævɪd/ a. ávido.

avocado /,ævə'kɑdou, ,ɑvə-/ n. aguacate m.

avocation /,ævə'keiʃən/ n. pasatiempo f.

avoid /ə'vɔid/ v. evitar.

avoidable /ə'vɔidəbəl/ a. evitable.

avoidance /ə'vɔidns/ n. evitación f.; Leg. anulación f.

avow /ə'vau/ v. declarar; admitir.

avowal /ə'vauəl/ n. admisión f.

avowed /ə'vaud/ a. reconocido; admitido.

avowedly /ə'vauidli/ adv. reconocidamente; confesadamente.

await /ə'weit/ v. esperar, aguardar.

awake /ə'weik/ a. despierto.

awaken /ə'weikən/ v. despertar.

award /ə'wɔrd/ n. **1.** premio m. —v. **2.** otorgar.

aware /ə'wɛər/ a. enterado, consciente.

awash /ə'wɒʃ/ a. & adv. Naut. a flor de agua.

away /ə'wei/ adv. (see under verb: **go away, put away, take away,** etc.)

awe /ɔ/ n. pavor m.

awesome /'ɔsəm/ a. pavoroso; aterrador.

awful /'ɔfəl/ a. horrible, terrible, muy malo, pésimo.

awhile /ə'wail/ adv. por un rato.

awkward /'ɔkwərd/ a. torpe, desmañado; Fig. delicado, embarazoso.

awning /'ɔnɪŋ/ n. toldo m.

awry /ə'rai/ a. oblicuo, torcido.

ax /æks/ n. hacha f.

axiom /'æksiəm/ n. axioma m.

axis /'æksɪs/ n. eje m.

axle /'æksəl/ n. eje m.

ayatollah /,ayə'toulə/ n. ayatolá f.

azure /'æʒər/ a. azul.

B

babble /'bæbəl/ n. **1.** balbuceo, murmullo m. —v. **2.** balbucear.

babbler /'bæblər/ n. hablador -ra, charlador -ra.

baboon /bæ'bun/ n. mandril m.

baby /'beibi/ n. nene, bebé m.

baby carriage cochecito de niño m.

babyish /'beibiʃ/ a. infantil.

baby squid /skwɪd/ chipirón m.

bachelor /'bætʃələr/ n. soltero m.

bacillus /bə'sɪləs/ n. bacilo, microbio m.

back /bæk/ adv. **1.** atrás. **to be**

b., estar de vuelta. **b. of,** detrás de. —n. **2.** espalda f.; (of animal) lomo m.

backache /bæk,eik/ n. dolor de espalda m.

backbone /bæk,boun/ n. espinazo m.; Fig. firmeza f.

backer /'bækər/ n. sostenedor -ra.

background /bæk,graund/ n. fondo m. antecedentes m.pl.

backing /'bækɪŋ/ n. apoyo m., garantía f.

backlash /'bæk,læʃ/ n. repercusión negativa.

backlog /'bæk,lɒg/ n. atrasos m.pl.

backpack /'bæk,pæk/ n. mochila f.

back seat asiento trasero m.

backstage /'bæk'steidʒ/ n. entre bastidores m.

backup /'bæk,ʌp/ n. copia de seguridad f.

backward /'bækwərd/ a. 1. atrasado. —adv. 2. hacia atrás.

backwardness /'bækwərdnɪs/ n. atraso m.

backwater /'bæk,wɒtər/ n. parte de río estancada f.

backwoods /'bæk'wʊdz/ n. región del monte apartada f.

bacon /'beikən/ n. tocino m.

bacteria /bæk'tɪəriə/ n. bacterias f.pl.

bacteriologist /bæk,tɪəri'ɒlədʒɪst/ n. bacteriólogo -a.

bacteriology /bæk,tɪəri'ɒlədʒi/ n. bacteriología f.

bad /bæd/ a. malo.

badge /bædʒ/ n. insignia, divisa f.

badger /'bædʒər/ n. 1. tejón m. —v. 2. atormentar.

badly /'bædli/ adv. mal.

badness /'bædnɪs/ n. maldad f.

bad-tempered /'bæd'tempərd/ a. de mal humor.

baffle /'bæfəl/ v. desconcertar.

bafflement /'bæfəlmənt/ n. contrariedad; confusión f.

bag /bæg/ n. 1. saco m.; bolsa f. —v. 2. ensacar, cazar.

baggage /'bægɪdʒ/ n. equipaje m. **b. check,** talón m.

baggage cart (airport) carrillo para llevar equipaje.

baggy /'bægi/ a. abotagado; bolsudo; hinchado.

bagpipe /'bæg,paip/ n. gaita f.

bail /beil/ n. 1. fianza f. —v. 2. desaguar.

bailiff /'beilɪf/ n. alguacil m.

bait /beit/ n. 1. cebo m. —v. 2. cebar.

bake /beik/ v. cocer en horno.

baked potato /beikt/ patata asada f.

baker /'beikər/ n. panadero -ra, hornero -ra.

bakery /'beikəri, 'beikri/ n. panadería f.

baking /'beikɪŋ/ n. hornada f. **b. powder,** levadura f.

balance /'bæləns/ n. balanza f.; equilibrio m.; Com. saldo m.

balcony /'bælkəni/ n. balcón m.; Theat. galería f.

bald /bɔld/ a. calvo.

baldness /'bɔldnɪs/ n. calvicie f.

bale /beil/ n. 1. bala f. —v. 2. embalar.

balk /bɔk/ v. frustrar; rebelarse.

Balkans /'bɔlkənz/ n.pl. Balcanes m.pl.

balky /'bɔki/ a. rebelón.

ball /bɔl/ n. bola, pelota f.; (dance) baile m.

ballad /'bæləd/ n. romance, m.; balada f.

ballast /'bæləst/ n. 1. lastre m. —v. 2. lastrar.

ball bearing cojinete de bolas m.

ballerina /,bælə'rinə/ n. bailarina f.

ballet /bæ'lei/ n. danza f.; ballet m.

ballistics /bə'lɪstɪks/ n. balística f.

balloon /bə'lun/ n. globo m. **b. tire,** neumático de balón m.

ballot /'bælət/ n. 1. balota f., voto m. —v. 2. balotar, votar.

ballpoint pen /'bɔl,pɔint/ bolígrafo m.

ballroom /'bɔl,rum/ n. salón de baile m.

balm /bɑm/ n. bálsamo; ungüento m.

balmy /'bɑmi/ a. fragante; reparador; calmante.

balsa /'bɔlsə/ n. balsa f.

balsam /'bɔlsəm/ n. bálsamo m.

balustrade /'bælə,streid/ n. barandilla f.

bamboo /bæm'bu/ n. bambú m.; caña f.

ban /bæn/ n. 1. prohibición f. —v. 2. prohibir; proscribir.

banal /bə'næl/ a. trivial; vulgar.

banana /bə'nænə/ n. banana f., cambur m. **b. tree,** banano, plátano m.

band /bænd/ n. 1. banda f.; (of men) banda, cuadrilla, partida f. —v. 2. asociarse.

bandage /'bændɪdʒ/ n. 1. vendaje m. —v. 2. vendar.

bandanna /bæn'dænə/ n. pañuelo (grande) m.; banda f.

bandbox /'bænd,bɒks/ n. caja de cartón.

bandit /'bændɪt/ n. bandido -da.

bandmaster /'bænd,mæstər/ n. director de una banda musical m.

bandstand /'bænd,stænd/ n. kiosco de música.

bang /bæŋ/ *interj.* **1.** ¡pum! —*n.* **2.** ruido de un golpe. —*v.* **3.** golpear ruidosamente.

banish /'bænɪʃ/ *v.* desterrar.

banishment /'bænɪʃmənt/ *n.* destierro *m.*

banister /'bænəstər/ *n.* pasamanos *m.pl.*

bank /bæŋk/ *n.* **1.** banco *m.*; (of a river) margen *f.* —*v.* **2.** depositar.

bank account cuenta bancaria *f.*

bankbook /'bæŋk,bʊk/ *n.* libreta de depósitos *f.*

bank card tarjeta bancaria *f.*

banker /'bæŋkər/ *n.* banquero -ra.

banking /'bæŋkɪŋ/ *n.* banca *f.*

bank note billete de banco *m.*

bankrupt /'bæŋkrʌpt/ *a.* insolvente.

bankruptcy /'bæŋkrʌptsi/ *n.* bancarrota *f.*

banner /'bænər/ *n.* bandera *f.*; estandarte *m.*

banquet /'bæŋkwɪt/ *n.* banquete *m.*

banter /'bæntər/ *n.* **1.** choteo *m.*; zumba; burla *f.* —*v.* **2.** chotear; zumbar; burlarse.

baptism /'bæptɪzəm/ *n.* bautismo, bautizo *m.*

baptismal /bæp'tɪzməl/ *a.* bautismal.

Baptist /'bæptɪst/ *n.* bautista *m. & f.*

baptize /bæp'taiz, 'bæptaiz/ *v.* bautizar.

bar /bɑr/ *n.* **1.** barra *f.*; obstáculo *m.*; (tavern) taberna *f.*, bar *m.* —*v.* **2.** barrear; prohibir, excluir.

barbarian /bɑr'bɛəriən/ *a.* bárbaro. *n.* bárbaro -ra.

barbarism /barbə,rɪzəm/ *n.* barbarismo *m.*, barbaridad *f.*

barbarous /'barbərəs/ *a.* bárbaro, cruel.

barbecue /'barbɪ,kyu/ *n.* animal asado entero; (Mex.) barbacoa *f.*

barber /'barbər/ *n.* barbero *m.* **b. shop,** barbería *f.*

barbiturate /bar'bɪtʃərɪt/ *n.* barbitúrico *m.*

bar code código de barras *m.*

bare /bɛər/ *a.* **1.** desnudo; descubierto. —*v.* **2.** desnudar; descubrir.

bareback /'bɛər,bæk/ *adv.* sin silla.

barefoot(ed) /'bɛər,fʊtɪd/ *a.* descalzo.

barely /'bɛərli/ *adv.* escasamente, apenas.

bareness /'bɛərnɪs/ *n.* desnudez *f.*; pobreza *f.*

bargain /'bargən/ *n.* **1.** ganga *f.*, compra ventajosa *f.*; contrato *m.* —*v.* **2.** regatear; negociar.

barge /bardʒ/ *n.* lanchón *m.*, barcaza *f.*

baritone /'bærɪ,toun/ *n.* barítono *m.*

barium /'bɛəriəm/ *n.* bario *m.*

bark /bark/ *n.* **1.** corteza *f.*; (of dog) ladrido *m.* —*v.* **2.** ladrar.

barley /'barli/ *n.* cebada *f.*

barn /barn/ *n.* granero *m.*

barnacle /'barnəkəl/ *n.* lapa *f.*

barnyard /'barn,yard/ *n.* corral *m.*

barometer /bə'romɪtər/ *n.* barómetro *m.*

barometric /,bærə'mɛtrɪk/ *a.* barométrico.

baron /'bærən/ *n.* barón *m.*

baroness /'bærənɪs/ *n.* baronesa *f.*

baronial /bə'rouniəl/ *a.* baronial.

baroque /bə'rouk/ *a.* barroco.

barracks /'bærəks/ *n.* cuartel *m.*

barrage /bə'rɑʒ/ *n.* cortina de fuego *f.*

barred /bard/ *a.* excluído; prohibido.

barrel /'bærəl/ *n.* barril *m.*; (of gun) cañón *m.*

barren /'bærən/ *a.* estéril.

barrenness /'bærən,nɪs/ *n.* esterilidad *f.*

barricade /'bærɪ,keid/ *n.* barricada, barrera *f.*

barrier /'bæriər/ *n.* barrera *f.*; obstáculo *m.*

barroom /'bar,rum, -,rʊm/ *n.* cantina *f.*

bartender /'bar,tɛndər/ *n.* tabernero; cantinero *m.*

barter /'bartər/ *n.* **1.** cambio, trueque *m.* —*v.* **2.** cambiar, trocar.

base /beis/ *a.* **1.** bajo, vil. —*n.* **2.** base *f.* —*v.* **3.** basar.

baseball /'beis,bɔl/ *n.* béisbol *m.*

baseboard /'beis,bɔrd/ *n.* tabla de resguardo.

basement /'beismənt/ *n.* sótano *m.*

baseness /'beisnɪs/ *n.* bajeza, vileza *f.*

bashful /'bæʃfəl/ *a.* vergonzoso, tímido.

bashfully /'bæʃfəli/ *adv.* tímidamente; vergonzosamente.

bashfulness /'bæʃfəlnis/ n. vergüenza; timidez f.

basic /'beisik/ a. fundamental, básico.

basin /'beisən/ n. bacía f.; (of river) cuenca f.

basis /'beisis/ n. base f.

bask /bæsk/ v. tomar el sol.

basket /'bæskit/ n. cesta, canasta f.

bass /bæs; beis/ n. (fish) lobina f.; Mus. bajo profundo m. **b. viol.** violín m.

bassinet /,bæsə'nɛt/ n. bacinete m.

bassoon /bæ'sun/ n. bajón m.

bastard /'bæstərd/ a. & n. bastardo -da; hijo -a natural.

baste /beist/ v. (sew) bastear; (cooking) pringar.

bat /bæt/ n. **1.** (animal) murciélago m.; (baseball) bate m. —v. **2.** batear.

batch /bætʃ/ n. cantidad de cosas.

bath /bæθ/ n. baño m.

bathe /beið/ v. bañar, bañarse.

bather /'beiðər/ n. bañista m. & f.

bathing resort /'beiðiŋ/ balneario m.

bathing suit /'beiðiŋ/ traje de baño.

bathrobe /'bæθ,roub/ n. bata de baño f.

bathroom /'bæθ,rum, -,rʊm/ n. cuarto de baño.

bathtub /'bæθ,tʌb/ n. bañera f.

baton /bə'tɒn/ n. bastón m.; Mus. batuta f.

battalion /bə'tælyən/ n. batallón m.

batter /'bætər/ n. **1.** (cooking) batido m.; (baseball) voleador m. —v. **2.** batir; derribar.

battery /'bætəri/ n. batería; Elec. pila f.

batting /'bætiŋ/ n. agramaje, moldeaje m.

battle /'bætl/ n. **1.** batalla f.; combate m. —v. **2.** batallar.

battlefield /'bætl,fild/ n. campo de batalla.

battleship /'bætl,ʃip/ n. acorazado m.

bauxite /'bɒksait, 'bouzait/ n. bauxita f.

bawl /bɒl/ v. gritar; vocear.

bay /bei/ n. bahía f. v. aullar.

bayonet /'beiənɛt/ n. bayoneta f.

bazaar /bə'zɑr/ n. bazar m., feria f.

BC abbr. (**before Christ**) a.C. (antes de Cristo).

be /bi/ v. ser; estar. (See hacer; hay; tener in Sp.-Eng. section).

beach /bitʃ/ n. playa f.

beachcomber /'bitʃ,koumər/ n. raquero -ra m. & f.

beacon /'bikən/ n. faro m.

bead /bid/ n. cuenta f.; pl. Relig. rosario m.

beading /'bidiŋ/ n. abalorio m.

beady /'bidi/ a. globuloso; burbujoso.

beak /bik/ n. pico m.

beaker /'bikər/ n. vaso con pico m.

beam /bim/ n. viga f.; (of wood) madero m.; (of light) rayo m.

beaming /'bimiŋ/ a. radiante.

bean /bin/ n. haba, habichuela f., frijol m.

bear /bɛər/ n. **1.** oso -sa. —v. **2.** llevar; (endure) aguantar.

bearable /'bɛərəbəl/ a. sufrible; soportable.

beard /biərd/ n. barba f.

bearded /'biərdid/ a. barbado; barbudo.

beardless /'biərdlis/ a. lampiño; imberbe.

bearer /'bɛərər/ n. portador -ra.

bearing /'bɛəriŋ/ n. porte, aguante m.

bearskin /'bɛər,skin/ n. piel de oso f.

beast /bist/ n. bestia f.; bruto -ta.

beat /bit/ v. golpear; batir; pulsar; (in games) ganar, vencer.

beaten /'bitn/ a. vencido; batido.

beatify /bi'ætə,fai/ v. beatificar.

beating /'bitiŋ/ n. paliza f.

beau /bou/ n. novio m.

beautiful /'byutəfəl/ a. hermoso, bello.

beautifully /'byutəfəli/ adv. bellamente.

beautify /'byutə,fai/ v. embellecer.

beauty /'byuti/ n. hermosura, belleza f. **b. parlor,** salón de belleza.

beaver /'bivər/ n. castor m.

becalm /bi'kɑm/ v. calmar; sosegar; encalmarse.

because /bi'kɒz/ conj. porque. **b. of,** a causa de.

beckon /'bɛkən/ v. hacer señas.

become /bi'kʌm/ v. hacerse; ponerse.

becoming /bi'kʌmiŋ/ a. propio,

correcto; **be b.,** quedar bien, sentar bien.

bed /bed/ n. cama f.; lecho m.; (of river) cauce m.

bedbug /ˈbedˌbʌg/ n. chinche m.

bedclothes /ˈbedˌklouz, -ˌklouðz/ n. ropa de cama f.

bedding /ˈbedɪŋ/ n. colchones m.pl.

bedfellow /ˈbedˌfelou/ n. compañero -ra de cama.

bedizen /bɪˈdaizən, -ˈdɪzən/ v. adornar; aderezar.

bedridden /ˈbedˌrɪdn/ a. postrado (en cama).

bedrock /ˈbedˌrɒk/ n. (mining) lecho de roca m.; Fig. fundamento m.

bedroom /ˈbedˌrum/ n. alcoba f.; (Mex.) recámara f.

bedside /ˈbedˌsaid/ n. al lado de una cama f.

bedspread /ˈbedˌspred/ n. cubrecama, sobrecama f.

bedstead /ˈbedˌsted/ n. armadura de cama f.

bedtime /ˈbedˌtaim/ n. hora de acostarse.

bee /bi/ n. abeja f.

beef /bif/ n. carne de vaca.

beefburger /ˈbifˌbɜrgər/ n. hamburguesa f.

beefsteak /ˈbifˌsteik/ n. bistec, bisté m.

beehive /ˈbiˌhaiv/ n. colmena f.

beer /bɪər/ n. cerveza f.

beeswax /ˈbizˌwæks/ n. cera de abejas.

beet /bit/ n. remolacha f.; (Mex.) betabel m.

beetle /ˈbitl/ n. escarabajo m.

befall /bɪˈfɔl/ v. suceder, sobrevenir.

befitting /bɪˈfɪtɪŋ/ a. conveniente; propio; digno.

before /bɪˈfɔr/ adv. antes. prep. antes de; (in front of) delante de. conj. antes que.

beforehand /bɪˈfɔrˌhænd/ adv. de antemano.

befriend /bɪˈfrend/ v. amparar.

befuddle /bɪˈfʌdl/ v. confundir; aturdir.

beg /beg/ v. rogar, suplicar; (for alms) mendigar.

beget /bɪˈget/ v. engendrar; producir.

beggar /ˈbegər/ n. mendigo -ga; S.A. limosnero -ra.

beggarly /ˈbegərli/ a. pobre, miserable.

begin /bɪˈgɪn/ v. empezar, comenzar, principiar.

beginner /bɪˈgɪnər/ n. principiante -ta.

beginning /bɪˈgɪnɪŋ/ n. principio, comienzo m.

begrudge /bɪˈgrʌdʒ/ v. envidiar.

behalf /bɪˈhæf/ n.: **in, on b. of,** a favor de, en pro de.

behave /bɪˈheiv/ v. portarse, comportarse.

behavior /bɪˈheivyər/ n. conducta f.; comportamiento m.

behead /bɪˈhed/ v. decapitar.

behind /bɪˈhaind/ adv. atrás, detrás. prep. detrás de.

behold /bɪˈhould/ v. contemplar.

beige /beiʒ/ a. beige.

being /ˈbiɪŋ/ n. existencia f.; (person) ser m.

bejewel /bɪˈdʒuəl/ v. adornar con joyas.

belated /bɪˈleitɪd/ a. atrasado, tardío.

belch /beltʃ/ n. **1.** eructo m. —v. **2.** vomitar; eructar.

belfry /ˈbelfri/ n. campanario m.

Belgian /ˈbeldʒən/ a. & n. belga m. & f.

Belgium /ˈbeldʒəm/ n. Bélgica f.

belie /bɪˈlai/ v. desmentir.

belief /bɪˈlif/ n. creencia f.; parecer m.

believable /bɪˈlivəbəl/ a. creíble.

believe /bɪˈliv/ v. creer.

believer /bɪˈlivər/ n. creyente m. & f.

belittle /bɪˈlɪtl/ v. dar poca importancia f.

bell /bel/ n. campana f.; (of house) campanilla f.; (electric) timbre m.

bellboy /ˈbelˌbɔi/ n. mozo, botones m.

bellicose /ˈbelɪˌkous/ a. guerrero.

belligerence /bəˈlɪdʒərəns/ n. beligerancia f.

belligerent /bəˈlɪdʒərənt/ a. & n. beligerante m.

belligerently /bəˈlɪdʒərəntli/ adv. belicosamente.

bellow /ˈbelou/ v. bramar, rugir.

bellows /ˈbelouz/ n. fuelle m.

belly /ˈbeli/ n. vientre m.; panza, barriga f.

belong /bɪˈlɔŋ/ v. pertenecer.

belongings /bɪˈlɔŋɪŋz/ n. propiedad f.

beloved /bɪˈlʌvɪd/ a. querido, amado.

below /bɪˈlou/ adv. **1.** debajo, abajo. —prep. **2.** debajo de.

belt /belt/ n. cinturón m.

bench /bentʃ/ n. banco m.

bend /bend/ n. vuelta; curva f. v. encorvar, doblar.

beneath /bɪˈniθ/ adv. **1.** debajo, abajo. —prep. **2.** debajo de.

benediction /ˌbenɪˈdɪkʃən/ n. bendición f.

benefactor /ˈbenəˌfæktər/ n. bienhechor -ra.

benefactress /ˈbenəˌfæktrɪs/ n. bienhechora f.

beneficial /ˌbenəˈfɪʃəl/ a. provechoso, beneficioso.

beneficiary /ˌbenəˈfɪʃiˌeri/ n. beneficiario -ria, beneficiado -da.

benefit /ˈbenəfɪt/ n. **1.** provecho, beneficio m. —v. **2.** beneficiar.

benevolence /bəˈnevələns/ n. benevolencia f.

benevolent /bəˈnevələnt/ a. benévolo.

benevolently /bəˈnevələntli/ adv. benignamente.

benign /bɪˈnain/; bɪˈnignənt/ a. benigno.

benignity /bɪˈnignɪti/ n. benignidad; bondad f.

bent /bent/ a. **1.** encorvado. **b. on,** resuelto a. —n. **2.** inclinación f.

benzene /ˈbenzin/, benˈzin/ n. benceno m.

bequeath /bɪˈkwið/ v. legar.

bequest /bɪˈkwest/ n. legado m.

berate /bɪˈreit/ v. reñir, regañar.

bereave /bɪˈriv/ v. despojar; desolar.

bereavement /bɪˈrivmənt/ n. privación f.; despojo m.; (mourning) luto m.

berry /ˈberi/ n. baya f.

berth /bɜrθ/ n. camarote m.; Naut. litera f.; (for vessel) amarradero m.

beseech /bɪˈsitʃ/ v. suplicar; implorar.

beseechingly /bɪˈsitʃiŋli/ adv. suplicantemente.

beset /bɪˈset/ v. acosar; rodear.

beside /bɪˈsaid/ prep. al lado de.

besides /bɪˈsaidz/ adv. además, por otra parte.

besiege /bɪˈsidʒ/ v. sitiar; asediar.

besieged /bɪˈsidʒd/ a. sitiado.

besieger /bɪˈsidʒər/ n. sitiador -ra.

besmirch /bɪˈsmɜrtʃ/ v. manchar; deshonrar.

best /best/ a. & adv. mejor. **at b.,** a lo más.

bestial /ˈbestʃəl/ a. bestial; brutal.

bestir /bɪˈstɜr/ v. incitar; intrigar.

best man n. padrino de boda.

bestow /bɪˈstou/ v. conferir.

bestowal /bɪˈstouəl/ n. dádiva; presentación f.

bet /bet/ n. **1.** apuesta f. —v. **2.** apostar.

betoken /bɪˈtoukən/ v. presagiar, anunciar.

betray /bɪˈtrei/ v. traicionar; revelar.

betrayal /bɪˈtreiəl/ n. traición f.

betroth /bɪˈtrouð/ v. contraer esponsales; prometerse.

betrothal /bɪˈtrouðəl/ n. esponsales m.pl.

better /ˈbetər/ a. & adv. **1.** mejor. —v. **2.** mejorar.

between /bɪˈtwin/ prep. entre, en medio de.

bevel /ˈbevəl/ n. **1.** cartabón m. —v. **2.** cortar al sesgo.

beverage /ˈbevərɪdʒ/ n. bebida f.; (cold) refresco m.

bewail /bɪˈweil/ v. llorar; lamentar.

beware /bɪˈwɛər/ v. guardarse; precaverse.

bewilder /bɪˈwɪldər/ v. aturdir.

bewildered /bɪˈwɪldərd/ a. descarriado.

bewildering /bɪˈwɪldərɪŋ/ a. aturdente.

bewilderment /bɪˈwɪldərmənt/ n. aturdimiento m.; perplejidad f.

bewitch /bɪˈwɪtʃ/ v. hechizar; embrujar.

beyond /bɪˈɒnd/ prep. más allá de.

biannual /baiˈænyuəl/ a. semianual; semestral.

bias /ˈbaiəs/ n. **1.** parcialidad f.; prejuicio m. **on the b.,** al sesgo. —v. **2.** predisponer, influir.

bib /bɪb/ n. babador m.

Bible /ˈbaibəl/ n. Biblia f.

Biblical /ˈbɪblɪkəl/ a. bíblico.

bibliography /ˌbɪbliˈɒɡrəfi/ n. bibliografía f.

bicarbonate /baiˈkɑrbənɪt/ n. bicarbonato m.

bicentennial /ˌbaisenˈteniəl/ a. & n. bicentenario f.

biceps /ˈbaiseps/ n. bíceps m.

bicker /ˈbɪkər/ v. altercar.

bicycle /'baisikəl/ n. bicicleta f.

bicyclist /'baisiklist/ n. biciclista m. & f.

bid /bid/ n. **1.** proposición, oferta f. —v. **2.** mandar; ofrecer.

bidder /'bidər/ n. postor -ra.

bide /baid/ v. aguardar; esperar.

bier /biər/ n. ataúd m.

bifocal /bai'foukəl/ a. bifocal.

big /big/ a. grande.

bigamist /'bigəmist/ n. bígamo -ma.

bigamy /'bigəmi/ n. bigamia f.

bigot /'bigət/ n. persona intolerante.

bigotry /'bigətri/ n. intolerancia f.

bikini /bi'kini/ n. bikini n.

bilateral /bai'lætərəl/ a. bilateral.

bile /bail/ n. bilis f.

bilingual /bai'liŋgwəl/ a. bilingüe.

bilingualism /bai'liŋgwə,lizəm/ n. bilingüismo m.

bilious /'bilyəs/ a. bilioso.

bill /bil/ n. **1.** cuenta, factura f.; (money) billete m.; (of bird) pico m. —v. **2.** facturar.

billboard /'bil,bɔrd/ n. cartelera f.

billet /'bilit/ n. **1.** billete m.; Mil. boleta f. —v. **2.** aposentar.

billfold /'bil,fould/ n. cartera f.

billiard balls /'bilyərd bɔlz/ bolas de billar.

billiards /'bilyərdz/ n. billar m.

billion /'bilyən/ n. billón m.

bill of health n. certificado de sanidad.

bill of lading /'leidiŋ/ n. conocimiento de embarque.

bill of sale n. escritura de venta.

billow /'bilou/ n. ola; oleada f.

bimetallic /,baimə'tælik/ a. bimetálico.

bimonthly /bai'mʌnθli/ a. & adv. bimestral.

bin /bin/ n. hucha f.; depósito m.

bind /baind/ v. atar; obligar; (book) encuadernar.

bindery /'baindəri/ n. taller de encuadernación f.

binding /'baindiŋ/ n. encuadernación f.

bingo /'biŋgou/ n. bingo m.

binocular /bə'nɒkyələr/ a. binocular. n.pl. gemelos m.pl.

biochemistry /,baiou'kemɒstri/ n. bioquímica f.

biodegradable /,baioudi'greidəbəl/ a. biodegradable.

biofeedback /,baiou'fid,bæk/ n. biofeedback.

biographer /bai'ɒgrəfər/ n. biógrafo -fa.

biographical /,baiə'græfikəl/ a. biográfico.

biography /,baiə'lɒdʒikəl/ n. biografía f.

biological /,baiə'lɒdʒikəl/ a. biológico.

biologically /,baiə'lɒdʒikəli/ adv. biológicamente.

biology /bai'ɒlədʒi/ n. biología f.

bipartisan /bai'pɑrtəzən/ a. bipartito.

biped /'baiped/ n. bípedo m.

bird /bɜrd/ n. pájaro m.; ave f.

birdie /'bɜrdi/ n. (golf) una bajo par m.

bird of prey n. ave de rapiña f.

bird's-eye view /'bɜrdz,ai/ n. vista de pájaro f.

birth /bɜrθ/ n. nacimiento m. **give b. to,** dar a luz.

birth certificate partida de nacimiento f.

birth control n. contracepción f.

birthday /'bɜrθ,dei/ n. cumpleaños m.

birthmark /'bɜrθ,mɑrk/ n. marca de nacimiento f.

birthplace /'bɜrθ,pleis/ n. natalicio m.

birth rate n. natalidad f.

birthright /'bɜrθ,rait/ n. primogenitura f.

biscuit /'biskit/ n. bizcocho m.

bisect /bai'sɛkt/ v. bisecar.

bishop /'biʃəp/ n. obispo m.; (chess) alfil m.

bishopric /'biʃəprik/ n. obispado m.

bismuth /'bizməθ/ n. bismuto m.

bison /'baisən/ n. bisonte m.

bit /bit/ n. pedacito m.; Mech. taladro m.; (for horse) bocado m.; (computer) bit m.

bitch /bitʃ/ n. perra f.

bite /bait/ v. **1.** bocado m.; picada f. —v. **2.** morder; picar.

biting /'baitiŋ/ a. penetrante; mordaz.

bitter /'bitər/ a. amargo.

bitterly /'bitərli/ adv. amargamente; agriamente.

bitterness /'bitərnis/ n. amargura f.; rencor m.

bivouac /'bivu,æk/ n. **1.** vivaque m. —v. **2.** vivaquear.

biweekly /bai'wikli/ a. quincenal.

black /blæk/ a. negro.

Black /blæk/ n. (person) negro -gra; persona de color.

blackberry /'blæk,beri/ n. mora f.

blackbird /'blæk,bərd/ n. mirlo m.

blackboard /'blæk,bord/ n. pizarra f.

blacken /'blækən/ v. ennegrecer.

black eye /n. ojo amoratado.

blackguard /'blægərd/ n. tunante; pillo m.

blacklist /'blæk,lıst/ n. lista negra f.

blackmail /'blæk,meil/ n. **1.** chantaje m. —v. **2.** amenazar con chantaje, chantajear.

black market mercado negro, estraperlo m.

black marketeer /,mɑrkɪ'tir/ estraperlista mf.

blackout /'blæk,aut/ n. oscurecimiento, apagamiento m.

blacksmith /'blæk,smɪθ/ n. herrero -ra.

bladder /'blædər/ n. vejiga f.

blade /bleid/ n. (sword) hoja f.; (oar) pala f.; (grass) brizna f.

blame /bleim/ v. culpar, echar la culpa a.

blameless /'bleimlɪs/ a. inculpable.

blanch /blæntʃ/ v. blanquear; escaldar.

bland /blænd/ a. blando.

blank /blæŋk/ a. & n. en blanco.

blanket /'blæŋkɪt/ n. manta f.; cobertor m.

blare /bleər/ n. sonido de trompeta. v. sonar como trompeta.

blaspheme /blæs'fim/ v. blasfemar.

blasphemer /blæs'fimər/ n. blasfemo -ma, blasfemador -ra.

blasphemous /'blæsfəməs/ a. blasfemo, impío.

blasphemy /'blæsfəmi/ n. blasfemia f.

blast /blæst/ n. **1.** barreno m.; (wind) ráfaga f. —v. **2.** barrenar.

blatant /'bleitnt/ a. bramante; descarado.

blaze /bleiz/ n. **1.** llama, hoguera f. —v. **2.** encenderse en llama.

blazing /'bleizıŋ/ a. flameante.

bleach /blitʃ/ n. **1.** lejía, blanqueador. —v. **2.** blanquear.

bleachers /'blitʃərz/ n. asientos al aire libre.

bleak /blik/ a. frío y sombrío.

bleakness /'bliknıs/ n. desolación f.

bleed /blid/ v. sangrar.

blemish /'blemɪʃ/ n. **1.** mancha f.; lunar m. —v. **2.** manchar.

blend /blend/ n. **1.** mezcla f. —v. **2.** mezclar, combinar.

blended /'blendɪd/ a. mezclado.

blender /'blendər/ n. (for food) licuadora f.

bless /bles/ v. bendecir.

blessed /'blesid/ a. bendito.

blessing /'blesıŋ/ a. bendición f.

blight /blait/ n. **1.** plaga f.; tizón m. —v. **2.** atizonar.

blind /blaind/ a. ciego.

blindfold /'blaind,fould/ v. vendar los ojos.

blinding /'blaindıŋ/ a. deslumbrante; ofuscante.

blindly /'blaindli/ adv. ciegamente.

blindness /'blaindnıs/ n. ceguedad, ceguera f.

blink /blıŋk/ n. **1.** guiñada f. —v. **2.** guiñar.

bliss /blıs/ n. felicidad f.

blissful /'blısfəl/ a. dichoso; bienaventurado.

blissfully /'blısfəli/ adv. felizmente.

blister /'blıstər/ n. ampolla f.

blithe /blaið/ a. alegre; jovial; gozoso.

blizzard /'blızərd/ n. nevasca f.

bloat /blout/ v. hinchar.

bloc /blɒk/ n. grupo (político); bloc.

block /blɒk/ n. **1.** bloque m.; (street) manzana, cuadra f. —v. **2.** bloquear.

blockade /blɒ'keid/ n. **1.** bloqueo m. —v. **2.** bloquear.

blond /blɒnd/ a. & n. rubio -ia.

blood /blʌd/ n. sangre f.; parentesco, linaje m.

bloodhound /'blʌd,haund/ n. sabueso m.

bloodless /'blʌdlıs/ a. exangüe; desangrado.

blood poisoning /'pɔizənıŋ/ envenenamiento de sangre.

blood pressure presión arterial.

bloodshed /'blʌd,ʃed/ n. matanza f.

bloodthirsty /'blʌd,θərsti/ a. cruel, sanguinario.

bloody /'blʌdi/ a. ensangrentado, sangriento.

bloom /blum/ n. **1.** flor f. —v. **2.** florecer.

blooming /'blumıŋ/ a. lozano; fresco; floreciente.

blossom /'blɒsəm/ n. **1.** flor f.
—v. **2.** florecer.

blot /blɒt/ n. **1.** mancha f. —v. **2.**
manchar.

blotch /blɒtʃ/ n. **1.** mancha,
roncha f. —v. **2.** manchar.

blotter /'blɒtər/ n. papel secante.

blouse /blaus/ n. blusa f.

blow /blou/ n. **1.** golpe m.; Fig.
chasco m. —v. **2.** soplar.

blowout /'blou,aut/ n. reventón
de neumático m.

blubber /'blʌbər/ n. grasa de ballena.

bludgeon /'blʌdʒən/ n. porra f. v.
apalear.

blue /blu/ a. azul; triste, melancólico.

bluebird /'blu,bərd/ n. azulejo m.

blue jeans jeans; vaqueros m.pl.

blueprint /'blu,prɪnt/ n. heliografía f.

bluff /blʌf/ n. risco m. v. alardear; baladronar.

bluing /bluɪŋ/ n. añil m.

blunder /'blʌndər/ n. **1.** desatino
m. —v. **2.** desatinar.

blunderer /'blʌndərər/ n. desatinado -da.

blunt /blʌnt/ a. embotado; descortés. v. embotar.

bluntly /'blʌntli/ a. bruscamente.

bluntness /'blʌntnɪs/ n. grosería
f.; brusquedad.

blur /blər/ n. **1.** trazo confuso.
—v. **2.** hacer indistinto.

blush /blʌʃ/ n. **1.** rubor, sonrojo
m. —v. **2.** sonrojarse.

bluster /'blʌstər/ n. **1.** fanfarria f.
—v. **2.** fanfarrear.

boar /bɔr/ n. verraco m. **wild b.,**
jabalí.

board /bɔrd/ n. **1.** tabla f; Govt.
consejo m.; junta f. **b. and room,**
cuarto y comida, casa y comida.
—v. **2.** (ship) abordar.

boarder /'bɔrdər/ n. pensionista
m. & f.

boardinghouse /'bɔrdɪŋ/ n. pensión f., casa de huéspedes.

boarding pass /'bɔrdɪŋ/ boleto de
embarque m., tarjeta de embarque f.

boast /boust/ n. **1.** jactancia f.
—v. **2.** jactarse.

boaster /'boustər/ n. fanfarrón
-na.

boastful /'boustfəl/ a. jactancioso.

boastfulness /'boustfəlnɪs/ n. jactancia f.

boat /bout/ n. barco, buque, bote
m.

boathouse /'bout,haus/ n. casilla
de botes f.

boatswain /'bousən/ n. contramaestre m.

bob /bɒb/ v. menear.

bobbin /'bɒbɪn/ n. bobina f.

bobby pin /'bɒbi/ n. gancho m.,
horquilla f.

bodice /'bɒdɪs/ n. corpiño m.

bodily /'bɒdli/ a. corporal.

body /'bɒdi/ n. cuerpo m.

body builder culturista mf.

body building culturismo m.

bodyguard /'bɒdi,gard/ n. guardaespaldas.

bog /bɒg/ n. pantano m.

bogey /'bougi/ n. (golf) uno sobre
par m.

Bohemian /bou'himiən/ a. & n.
bohemio -mia.

boil /bɔil/ n. **1.** hervor m.; Med.
divieso m. —v. **2.** hervir.

boiler /'bɔilər/ n. marmita f; caldera
f.

boiling point /'bɔilɪŋ/ punto de
ebullición f.

boisterous /'bɔistərəs/ a. tumultuoso.

boisterously /'bɔistərəsli/ adv. tumultuosamente.

bold /bould/ a. atrevido, audaz.

boldface /'bould,feis/ n. (type)
letra negra.

boldly /'bouldli/ adv. audazmente;
descaradamente.

boldness /'bouldnɪs/ n. atrevimiento m.; osadía f.

Bolivian /bou'livian/ a. & n. boliviano -na.

bologna /bə'louni/ n. salchicha f.,
mortadela.

bolster /'boulstər/ n. **1.** travesero,
cojín m. —v. **2.** apoyar, sostener.

bolt /boult/ n. perno m.; (of door)
cerrojo m.; (lightning) rayo m. v.
acerrojar.

bomb /bɒm/ n. **1.** bomba f. —v.
2. bombardear.

bombard /bɒm'bard/ v. bombardear.

bombardier /,bɒmbar'dɪər/ n.
bombardero -ra.

bombardment /bɒm'bardmənt/ n.
bombardeo m.

bomber /'bɒmər/ n. avión de
bombardeo.

bombproof /'bɒm,pruf/ a. a
prueba de granadas.

bombshell /'bɒm‚ʃɛl/ n. bomba f.

bonbon /'bɒn‚bɒn/ n. dulce, bombón m.

bond /bɒnd/ n. lazo m.; *Com.* bono m.

bondage /'bɒndɪdʒ/ n. esclavitud, servidumbre f.

bonded /'bɒndɪd/ a. garantizado.

bone /boun/ n. hueso m.

boneless /'bounlɪs/ a. sin huesos.

bonfire /'bɒn‚faɪʳr/ n. hoguera, fogata f.

bonnet /'bɒnɪt/ n. gorra f.

bonus /'bounəs/ n. sobrepaga f.

bony /'bouni/ a. huesudo.

boo /bu/ v. abuchear.

book /bʊk/ n. libro m.

bookbinder /'bʊk‚baɪndər/ n. encuadernador -ora.

bookcase /'bʊk‚keɪs/ n. armario para libros.

bookkeeper /'bʊk‚kipər/ n. tenedor -ra de libros.

bookkeeping /'bʊk‚kipɪŋ/ n. contabilidad f.

booklet /'bʊklɪt/ n. folleto m., libreta f.

bookmark /'bʊk‚mɑrk/ n. marcapáginas m.

bookseller /'bʊk‚sɛlər/ n. librero -ra.

bookstore /'bʊk‚stɔr/ n. librería f.

boom /bum/ n. *Naut.* botalón m.; prosperidad repentina.

boon /bun/ n. dádiva f.

boor /bʊr/ n. patán, rústico m.

boorish /'bʊrɪʃ/ a. villano.

boost /bust/ n. **1.** alza; ayuda f. —v. **2.** levantar, alzar; fomentar.

booster /'bustər/ n. fomentador m.

boot /but/ n. bota f.

bootblack /'but‚blæk/ n. limpiabotas m.

booth /buθ/ n. cabaña; casilla f.

booty /'buti/ n. botín m.

border /'bɔrdər/ n. **1.** borde m.; frontera f. —v. **2. b. on,** lindar con.

borderline /'bɔrdər‚laɪn/ a. marginal. n. margen m.

bore /bɔr/ n. lata f.; persona pesada. v. aburrir, fastidiar; *Mech.* taladrar.

boredom /'bɔrdəm/ n. aburrimiento m.

boric acid /'bɔrɪk/ n. ácido bórico m.

boring /'bɔrɪŋ/ a. aburrido, pesado.

born /bɔrn/ a. nacido. **be born,** nacer.

born-again /'bɔrn ə'gɛn/ a. renacido.

borrow /'bɒrou/ v. pedir prestado.

bosom /'bʊzəm/ v. seno, pecho m.

boss /bɒs/ n. jefe, patrón m.

botany /'bɒtn̩i/ n. botánica f.

both /bouθ/ pron. & a. ambos, los dos.

bother /'bɒðər/ n. molestia f. v. molestar, incomodar.

bothersome /'bɒðərsəm/ a. molesto.

bottle /'bɒtl/ n. **1.** botella f. —v. **2.** embotellar.

bottling /'bɒtlɪŋ/ n. embotellamiento m.

bottom /'bɒtəm/ n. fondo m.

boudoir /'budwɑr/ n. tocador m.

bough /bau/ n. rama f.

boulder /'bouldər/ n. canto rodado.

boulevard /'bulə‚vɑrd/ n. bulevar m.

bounce /bauns/ n. **1.** brinco m. —v. **2.** brincar; hacer saltar.

bound /baund/ n. **1.** salto m. —v. **2.** saltar.

boundary /'baundəri/ n. límite, lindero m.

bouquet /bou'keɪ, bu-/ n. ramillete de flores.

bourgeois /bʊr'ʒwɑ/ a. & n. burgués -esa.

bout /baut/ n. encuentro; combate m.

bow /n bau, bou; v bau/ n. **1.** saludo m.; (of ship) proa f.; (archery) arco m.; (ribbon) lazo m. —v. **2.** saludar, inclinar.

bowels /'bauəlz/ n. intestinos m.pl.; entrañas f.pl.

bowl /boul/ n. **1.** vasija f.; platón m. —v. **2.** jugar a los bolos. **b. over,** derribar.

bowlegged /'bou‚lɛgɪd/ a. perniabierto.

bowling /'boulɪŋ/ n. bolos m.pl.

bow tie /bou/ pajarita f.

box /bɒks/ n. **1.** caja f.; *Theat.* palco m. —v. **2.** (sports) boxear.

boxcar /'bɒks‚kɑr/ n. vagón m.

boxer /'bɒksər/ n. boxeador -ra, pugilista m.

boxing /'bɒksɪŋ/ n. boxeo m.

box office n. taquilla f.

boy /bɔɪ/ n. muchacho, chico, niño m.

boycott /ˈbɔɪkɒt/ n. **1.** boicoteo m. —v. **2.** boicotear.

boyhood /ˈbɔɪhʊd/ n. muchachez f.

boyish /ˈbɔɪʃ/ a. pueril.

boyishly /ˈbɔɪʃli/ adv. puerilmente.

bra /brɑ/ n. sujetador, sostén m.

brace /breɪs/ n. **1.** grapón m.; pl. tirantes m.pl. —v. **2.** reforzar.

bracelet /ˈbreɪslɪt/ n. brazalete m., pulsera f.

bracket /ˈbrækɪt/ n. ménsula f.

brag /bræg/ v. jactarse.

braggart /ˈbrægərt/ a. **1.** jactancioso. —n. **2.** jaque m.

braid /breɪd/ n. **1.** trenza f. —v. **2.** trenzar.

brain /breɪn/ n. cerebro, seso m.

brainy /ˈbreɪni/ a. sesudo, inteligente.

brake /breɪk/ n. **1.** freno m. —v. **2.** frenar.

bran /bræn/ n. salvado m.

branch /bræntʃ, brɑntʃ/ n. ramo m.; (of tree) rama f.

brand /brænd/ n. marca f.

brandish /ˈbrændɪʃ/ v. blandir.

brand-new /ˈbrænˈnu/ a. enteramente nuevo.

brandy /ˈbrændi/ n. aguardiente, coñac m.

brash /bræʃ/ a. impetuoso.

brass /bræs/ n. bronce, latón m.

brassiere /brəˈzɪər/ n. corpiño, sujetador, sostén m.

brat /bræt/ n. mocoso m.

bravado /brəˈvɑdoʊ/ n. bravata f.

brave /breɪv/ a. valiente.

bravery /ˈbreɪvəri/ n. valor m.

brawl /brɔl/ n. alboroto m. v. alborotar.

brawn /brɔn/ n. músculo m.

bray /breɪ/ v. rebuznar.

brazen /ˈbreɪzən/ a. desvergonzado.

Brazil /brəˈzɪl/ n. Brasil m.

Brazilian /brəˈzɪlyən/ a. & n. brasileño -ña.

breach /britʃ/ n. rotura; infracción f.

breach of contract incumplimiento de contrato m.

bread /brɛd/ n. pan m.

breadth /brɛdθ/ n. anchura f.

break /breɪk/ n. **1.** rotura; pausa f. —v. **2.** quebrar, romper.

breakable /ˈbreɪkəbəl/ a. rompible, frágil.

breakage /ˈbreɪkɪdʒ/ n. rotura f., destrozo m.

breakfast /ˈbrɛkfəst/ n. **1.** desayuno, almuerzo m. —v. **2.** desayunar, almorzar.

breakneck /ˈbreɪkˌnɛk/ a. rápido, precipitado, atropellado.

breast /brɛst/ n. (of human) pecho, seno m.; (of fowl) pechuga f.

breastbone /ˈbrɛstˌboʊn/ n. esternón m.

breath /brɛθ/ n. aliento; soplo m.

breathe /brið/ v. respirar.

breathless /ˈbrɛθlɪs/ a. desalentado.

breathlessly /ˈbrɛθlɪsli/ adv. jadeantemente, intensamente.

bred /brɛd/ a. criado; educado.

breeches /ˈbrɪtʃɪz/ n.pl. calzones; pantalones, m.pl.

breed /brid/ n. **1.** raza f. —v. **2.** engendrar; criar.

breeder /ˈbridər/ n. criador -ra.

breeding /ˈbridɪŋ/ n. cría f.

breeze /briz/ n. brisa f.

breezy /ˈbrizi/ a.: **it is b.**, hace brisa.

brevity /ˈbrɛvɪti/ n. brevedad f.

brew /bru/ v. fraguar; elaborar.

brewer /ˈbruər/ n. cervecero -ra.

brewery /ˈbruəri/ n. cervecería f.

bribe /braɪb/ n. **1.** soborno, cohecho m. —v. **2.** sobornar, cohechar.

briber /ˈbraɪbər/ n. sobornador -ra.

bribery /ˈbraɪbəri/ n. soborno, cohecho m.

brick /brɪk/ n. ladrillo m.

bricklayer /ˈbrɪkˌleɪər/ n. albañil m.

bridal /ˈbraɪdl/ a. nupcial.

bride /braɪd/ n. novia f.

bridegroom /ˈbraɪdˌgrum/ n. novio m.

bridesmaid /ˈbraɪdzˌmeɪd/ n. madrina de boda.

bridge /brɪdʒ/ n. puente m.

bridged /brɪdʒd/ a. conectado.

bridgehead /ˈbrɪdʒˌhɛd/ n. Mil. cabeza de puente.

bridle /ˈbraɪdl/ n. brida f.

brief /brif/ a. breve.

briefcase /ˈbrifˌkeɪs/ n. maletín m.

briefly /ˈbrifli/ adv. brevemente.

briefness /ˈbrifnɪs/ n. brevedad f.

brier /ˈbraɪər/ n. zarza f.

brig /brɪg/ n. bergantín m.

brigade /brɪˈgeɪd/ n. brigada f.

bright /brait/ *a.* claro, brillante.

brighten /'braitn/ *v.* abrillantar; alegrar.

brightness /'braitnis/ *n.* resplandor *m.*

brilliance /'brilyəns/ *n.* brillantez *f.*

brilliant /'brilyənt/ *a.* brillante.

brim /brim/ *n.* borde *m.*; (of hat) ala *f.*

brine /brain/ *n.* escabeche, *m.* salmuera *f.*

bring /briŋ/ *v.* traer. **b. about,** efectuar, llevar a cabo.

brink /briŋk/ *n.* borde *m.*

briny /'braini/ *a.* salado.

brisk /brisk/ *a.* vivo; enérgico.

briskly /'briskli/ *adv.* vivamente.

briskness /'brisknis/ *n.* viveza *f.*

bristle /'brisəl/ *n.* cerda *f.*

bristly /'brisli/ *a.* hirsuto.

Britain /'britn/ *n.* **Great B.,** Gran Bretaña *f.*

British /'britiʃ/ *a.* británico.

British Empire imperio británico *m.*

British Isles /ailz/ islas británicas *f.*

Briton /'britn/ *n.* inglés *m.*

brittle /'britl/ *a.* quebradizo, frágil.

broad /brɔd/ *a.* ancho.

broadcast /'brɔd,kæst/ *n.* **1.** radiodifusión *f.* —*v.* **2.** radiodifundir.

broadcaster /'brɔd,kæstər/ *n.* locutor -ra.

broadcloth /'brɔd,klɔθ/ *n.* paño fino.

broaden /'brɔdn/ *v.* ensanchar.

broadly /'brɔdli/ *adv.* ampliamente.

broadminded /'brɔd'maindid/ *a.* tolerante, liberal.

brocade /brou'keid/ *n.* brocado *m.*

brocaded /brou'keidid/ *a.* espolinado.

broccoli /'brɒkəli/ *n.* brécol *m.*

broil /brɔil/ *v.* asar.

broiler /'brɔilər/ *n.* parrilla *f.*

broken /'broukən/ *a.* roto, quebrado.

broken-hearted /'broukən'hɑrtid/ *a.* angustiado.

broker /'broukər/ *n.* corredor -ra, bolsista *m. & f.*

brokerage /'broukəridʒ/ *n.* corretaje *m.*

bronchial /'brɒŋkiəl/ *a.* bronquial.

bronchitis /brɒŋ'kaitis/ *n.* bronquitis *f.*

bronze /brɒnz/ *n.* bronce *m.*

brooch /broutʃ/ *n.* broche *m.*

brood /brud/ *n.* **1.** cría, progenie *f.* —*v.* **2.** empollar; cobijar.

brook /bruk/ *n.* arroyo *m.*, quebrada *f.*

broom /brum/ *n.* escoba *f.*

broomstick /'brum,stik/ *n.* palo de escoba.

broth /brɔθ/ *n.* caldo *m.*

brothel /'brɒθəl/ *n.* burdel *m.*

brother /'brʌðər/ *n.* hermano *m.*

brotherhood /'brʌðər,hʊd/ *n.* fraternidad *f.*

brother-in-law /'brʌðər in ,lɔ/ *n.* cuñado *m.*

brotherly /'brʌðərli/ *a.* fraternal.

brow /brau/ *n.* ceja; frente *f.*

brown /braun/ *a.* pardo, moreno; marrón. *v.* rehogar.

brown sugar azúcar moreno *m.*

browse /brauz/ *v.* curiosear; ramonear.

browser /'brauzər/ *n.* (Internet) nagegador *m.*, visualizador *m.*, visor *m.*

bruise /bruz/ *n.* **1.** contusión *f.* —*v.* **2.** magullar.

brunette /bru'net/ *a. & n.* moreno -na, trigueño -ña.

brush /brʌʃ/ *n.* **1.** cepillo *m.*; brocha *f.* —*v.* **2.** cepillar.

brushwood /'brʌʃ,wʊd/ *n.* matorral *m.*

brusque /brʌsk/ *a.* brusco.

brusquely /'brʌskli/ *adv.* bruscamente.

brutal /'brutl/ *a.* brutal.

brutality /bru'tæliti/ *n.* brutalidad *f.*

brutalize /'brutl,aiz/ *v.* embrutecer.

brute /brut/ *n.* bruto -ta, bestia *f.*

bubble /'bʌbəl/ *n.* ampolla *f.*

bucket /'bʌkit/ *n.* cubo *m.*

buckle /'bʌkəl/ *n.* hebilla *f.*

buckram /'bʌkrəm/ *n.* bucarán *m.*

bucksaw /'bʌk'sɔ/ *n.* sierra de bastidor.

buckshot /'bʌk,ʃɒt/ *n.* posta *f.*

buckwheat /'bʌk,wit/ *n.* trigo sarraceno.

bud /bʌd/ *n.* **1.** brote *m.* —*v.* **2.** brotar.

budding /'bʌdiŋ/ *a.* en capullo.

budge /bʌdʒ/ *v.* moverse.

budget /'bʌdʒit/ *n.* presupuesto *m.*

buffalo /'bʌfə,lou/ n. búfalo m.

buffer /'bʌfər/ n. parachoques m.

buffet /bə'feɪ/ n. bufet m.; (furniture) aparador m.

buffoon /bə'fun/ n. bufón m.

bug /bʌg/ n. insecto m.; (computer) error m.

bugle /'byugəl/ n. clarín m.; corneta f.

build /bɪld/ v. construir.

builder /'bɪldər/ n. constructor -ra.

building /'bɪldɪŋ/ n. edificio m.

bulb /bʌlb/ n. bulbo m.; (of lamp) bombilla, ampolla f.

bulge /bʌldʒ/ n. abultamiento m. v. abultar.

bulging /'bʌldʒɪŋ/ a. protuberante.

bulimia /bu'limiə/ n. bulimia f.

bulk /bʌlk/ n. masa f.; grueso m.; mayoría f.

bulkhead /'bʌlk,hɛd/ n. frontón m.

bulky /'bʌlki/ a. grueso, abultado.

bull /bʊl/ n. toro m.

bulldog /'bʊl,dɔg/ n. perro de presa.

bullet /'bʊlɪt/ n. bala f.

bulletin /'bʊlɪtɪn/ n. boletín m.

bulletproof /'bʊlɪt,pruf/ a. a prueba de bala.

bullfight /'bʊl,faɪt/ n. corrida de toros.

bullfighter /'bʊl,faɪtər/ n. torero -ra.

bullfinch /'bʊl,fɪntʃ/ n. pinzón real m.

bully /'bʊli/ n. **1.** rufián m. —v. **2.** bravear.

bulwark /'bʊlwərk/ n. baluarte m.

bum /bʌm/ n. holgazán m.

bump /bʌmp/ n. **1.** golpe, choque m. —v. **2. b. into,** chocar contra.

bumper /'bʌmpər/ n. parachoques m.

bun /bʌn/ n. bollo m.

bunch /bʌntʃ/ n. racimo; montón m.

bundle /'bʌndl/ n. **1.** bulto m. —v. **2. b. up,** abrigar.

bungalow /'bʌŋgə,lou/ n. casa de un solo piso.

bungle /'bʌŋgəl/ v. estropear.

bunion /'bʌnyən/ n. juanete m.

bunk /bʌŋk/ n. litera f.

bunny /'bʌni/ n. conejito -ta.

bunting /'bʌntɪŋ/ n. lanilla; banderas f.

buoy /'buɪ/ n. boya f.

buoyant /'bɔɪənt/ a. boyante; vivaz.

burden /'bɔrdn/ n. **1.** carga f. —v. **2.** cargar.

burdensome /'bɔrdnsəm/ a. gravoso.

bureau /'byʊrou/ n. (furniture) cómoda f.; departamento m.

burglar /'bɔrglər/ n. ladrón -ona.

burglarize /'bɔrglə,raɪz/ v. robar.

burglary /'bɔrgləri/ n. robo m.

burial /'bɛriəl/ n. entierro m.

burlap /'bɔrlæp/ n. arpillera f.

burly /'bɔrli/ a. corpulento.

burn /bɔrn/ v. quemar; arder.

burner /'bɔrnər/ n. mechero m.

burning /'bɔrnɪŋ/ a. ardiente.

burnish /'bɔrnɪʃ/ v. pulir; acicalar.

burrow /'bɔrou/ v. minar; horadar.

burst /bɔrst/ v. reventar.

bury /'bɛri/ v. enterrar.

bus /bʌs/ n. autobús m.

bush /bʊʃ/ n. arbusto m.

bushy /'bʊʃi/ a. matoso; peludo.

business /'bɪznɪs/ n. negocios m.pl.; comercio m.

businesslike /'bɪznɪs,laɪk/ a. directo, práctico.

businessman /'bɪznɪs,mæn/ n. hombre de negocios, comerciante m.

businesswoman /'bɪznɪs,wʊmən/ n. mujer de negocios.

bust /bʌst/ n. busto; pecho m.

bustle /'bʌsəl/ n. bullicio m.; animación f.

busy /'bɪzi/ a. ocupado, atareado.

busybody /'bɪzi,bɒdi/ n. entremetido m.

but /bʌt/ conj. pero; sino.

butcher /'bʊtʃər/ n. carnicero -ra.

butchery /'bʊtʃəri/ n. carnicería; matanza f.

butler /'bʌtlər/ n. mayordomo m.

butt /bʌt/ n. punta f.; cabo extremo m.

butter /'bʌtər/ n. manteca, mantequilla f.

buttercup /'bʌtər,kʌp/ n. ranúnculo m.

butterfat /'bʌtər,fæt/ n. mantequilla f.

butterfly /'bʌtər,flaɪ/ n. mariposa f.

buttermilk /'bʌtər,mɪlk/ n. suero (de leche) m.

button /'bʌtn/ n. botón m.

buttonhole /'bʌtn,houl/ n. ojal m.

buttress /'bʌtrɪs/ n. sostén; refuerzo m.

buxom /'bʌksəm/ a. regordete.

buy /bai/ v. comprar.

buyer /'baiər/ n. comprador -ra.

buzz /bʌz/ n. **1.** zumbido m. **2.** zumbar.

buzzard /'bʌzərd/ n. gallinazo m.

buzzer /'bʌzər/ n. zumbador m.; timbre m.

buzz saw n. sierra circular f.

by /bai/ prep. por; (near) cerca de, al lado de; (time) para.

by-and-by /,baiən'bai/ adv. pronto; luego.

bygone /'bai,gɔn/ a. pasado.

bylaw /'bai,lɔ/ n. estatuto, reglamento m.

bypass /'bai,pæs/ n. desvío m.

byproduct /'bai,prɑdʌkt/ n. subproducto m.

bystander /'bai,stændər/ n. espectador -ra; mirón -na.

byte /bait/ n. en teoría de la información: ocho bits, byte m.

byway /'bai,wei/ n. camino desviado m.

C

cab /kæb/ n. taxi, coche de alquiler m.

cabaret /,kæbə'rei/ n. cabaret m.

cabbage /'kæbidʒ/ n. repollo m.

cabin /'kæbin/ n. cabaña f.

cabinet /'kæbənit/ n. gabinete; ministerio m.

cabinetmaker /'kæbənit,meikər/ n. ebanista m.

cable /'keibəl/ n. cable m.

cablegram /'keibəl,græm/ n. cablegrama m.

cache /kæʃ/ n. escondite m.

cackle /'kækəl/ n. charla f.; cacareo m. v. cacarear.

cacophony /kə'kɒfəni/ n. cacofonía f.

cactus /'kæktəs/ n. cacto m.

cad /kæd/ n. persona vil.

cadaver /kə'dævər/ n. cadáver m.

cadaverous /kə'dævərəs/ a. cadavérico.

caddie /'kædi/ n. (golf) ayudante m. & f.

cadence /'keidns/ n. cadencia f.

cadet /kə'dɛt/ n. cadete m.

cadmium /'kædmiəm/ n. cadmio m.

cadre /'kædri, 'kɑdrei/ n. núcleo; Mil. cuadro m.

café /kæ'fei/ n. café m., cantina f.

cafeteria /,kæfɪ'tɪəriə/ n. cafetería f.

caffeine /'kæ'fin/ n. cafeína f.

cage /keidʒ/ n. jaula f. v. enjaular.

caged /keidʒd/ a. enjaulado.

caisson /'keisɒn, -sən/ n. arcón m.; Mil. furgón m.

cajole /kə'dʒoul/ v. lisonjear; adular.

cake /keik/ n. torta f.; bizcocho m.

calamitous /kə'læmitəs/ a. calamitoso.

calamity /kə'læmiti/ n. calamidad f.

calcify /'kælsə,fai/ v. calcificar.

calcium /'kælsiəm/ n. calcio m.

calculable /'kælkyələbəl/ a. calculable.

calculate /'kælkyə,leit/ v. calcular.

calculating /'kælkyə,leitiŋ/ a. interesado.

calculation /,kælkyə'leifən/ n. calculación f.; cálculo m.

calculus /'kælkyələs/ n. cálculo m.

caldron /'kɔldrən/ n. caldera f.

calendar /'kæləndər/ n. calendario m.

calf /kæf/ n. ternero m. (animal); pantorrilla f. (of the body).

calfskin /'kæf,skin/ n. piel de becerro.

caliber /'kælibər/ n. calibre m.

calico /'kæli,kou/ n. calicó m.

caliper /'kælipər/ n. calibrador m.

calisthenics /,kæləs'θɛniks/ n. calistenia, gimnasia f.

calk /kɔk/ v. calafatear; rellenar.

calker /'kɔkər/ n. calafate -ta.

call /kɔl/ n. **1.** llamada f. —v. **2.** llamar.

calligraphy /kə'lɪgrəfi/ n. caligrafía f.

calling /'kɔliŋ/ n. vocación f.

calling card n. tarjeta (de visita) f.

callously /'kæləsli/ adv. insensiblemente.

callow /'kælou/ a. sin experiencia.

callus /'kæləs/ n. callo m.

calm /kɑm/ a. **1.** tranquilo, calmado. —n. **2.** calma f. —v. **3.** calmar.

calmly /'kɑmli/ adv. serenamente.

calmness /'kɑmnis/ n. calma f.

caloric /kəˈlɔrɪk/ *a.* calórico.

calorie /ˈkælərɪ/ *n.* caloría *f.*

calorimeter /ˌkæləˈrɪmɪtər/ *n.* calorímetro *m.*

calumniate /kəˈlʌmniˌeɪt/ *v.* calumniar.

calumny /ˈkæləmni/ *n.* calumnia *f.*

Calvary /ˈkælvəri/ *n.* Calvario *m.*

calve /kæv/ *v.* parir (la vaca).

calyx /ˈkeɪlɪks/ *n.* cáliz *m.*

camaraderie /ˌkɑməˈrɑdəri/ *n.* compañerismo *m.,* compadrería *f.*

cambric /ˈkeɪmbrɪk/ *n.* batista *f.*

camcorder /ˈkæmˌkɔrdər/ *n.* videocámara *f.*

camel /ˈkæməl/ *n.* camello -lla.

camellia /kəˈmilyə/ *n.* camelia *f.*

camel's hair /ˈkæməlz/ pelo de camello.

cameo /ˈkæmiˌoʊ/ *n.* camafeo *m.*

camera /ˈkæmərə/ *n.* cámara *f.*

camouflage /ˈkæməˌflɑʒ/ *n.* camuflaje *m.*

camouflaging /ˈkæməˌflɑʒɪŋ/ *n.* simulacro, disfraz *m.*

camp /kæmp/ *n.* **1.** campamento *m.* —*v.* **2.** acampar.

campaign /kæmˈpeɪn/ *n.* campaña *f.*

camper /ˈkæmpər/ *n.* acampado *m.*

campfire /ˈkæmpˌfaɪr/ *n.* fogata de campamento.

camphor /ˈkæmfər/ *n.* alcanfor *m.*

camphor ball bola de alcanfor.

campus /ˈkæmpəs/ *n.* campo de colegio (o universidad), campus *m.*

can /kæn/ *v.* (be able) poder.

can /kæn/ *n.* **1.** lata *f.* —*v.* **2.** conservar en latas, enlatar.

Canada /ˈkænədə/ *n.* Canadá *m.*

Canadian /kəˈneɪdiən/ *a. & n.* canadiense.

canal /kəˈnæl/ *n.* canal *m.*

canalize /ˈkænlˌaɪz/ *v.* canalizar.

canard /kəˈnɑrd/ *n.* embuste *m.*

canary /kəˈnɛəri/ *n.* canario -ria.

cancel /ˈkænsəl/ *v.* cancelar.

cancellation /ˌkænsəˈleɪʃən/ *n.* cancelación *f.*

cancer /ˈkænsər/ *n.* cáncer *m.*

candelabrum /ˌkændlˈɑbrəm/ *n.* candelabro *m.*

candid /ˈkændɪd/ *a.* cándido, sincero.

candidacy /ˈkændɪdəsi/ *n.* candidatura *f.*

candidate /ˈkændɪˌdeɪt/ *n.* candidato -ta.

candidly /ˈkændɪdli/ *adv.* cándidamente.

candidness /ˈkændɪdnɪs/ *n.* candidez; sinceridad *f.*

candied /ˈkændid/ *a.* garapiñado.

candle /ˈkændl/ *n.* vela *f.*

candlestick /ˈkændlˌstɪk/ *n.* candelero *m.*

candor /ˈkændər/ *n.* candor *m.*; sinceridad *f.*

candy /ˈkændi/ *n.* dulces *m.pl.*

cane /keɪn/ *n.* caña *f.*; (for walking) bastón *m.*

canine /ˈkeɪnaɪn/ *a.* canino.

canister /ˈkænəstər/ *n.* frasco *m.*; lata *f.*

canker /ˈkæŋkər/ *n.* llaga; úlcera *f.*

cankerworm /ˈkæŋkərˌwɜrm/ *n.* oruga *f.*

canned /kænd/ *a.* envasado, enlatado.

canner /ˈkænər/ *n.* envasador *m.*

cannery /ˈkænəri/ *n.* fábrica de conservas alimenticias *f.*

cannibal /ˈkænəbəl/ *n.* caníbal *m. & f.*

cannon /ˈkænən/ *n.* cañón *m.*

cannonade /ˌkænəˈneɪd/ *n.* cañoneo *m.*

cannoneer /ˌkænəˈnɪər/ *n.* cañonero -ra.

canny /ˈkæni/ *a.* sagaz; prudente.

canoe /kəˈnu/ *n.* canoa, piragua *f.*

canoeing /kəˈnuɪŋ/ *n.* piragüismo *m.*

canoeist /kəˈnuɪst/ *n.* piragüista *m. & f.*

canon /ˈkænən/ *n.* canon *m.*; *Relig.* canónigo *m.*

canonical /kəˈnɒnɪkəl/ *a.* canónico.

canonize /ˈkænəˌnaɪz/ *v.* canonizar.

can opener /ˈoʊpənər/ abrelatas *m.*

canopy /ˈkænəpi/ *n.* dosel *m.*

cant /kænt/ *n.* hipocresía *f.*

cantaloupe /ˈkæntlˌoʊp/ *n.* melón *m.*

canteen /kænˈtin/ *n.* cantina *f.*

canter /ˈkæntər/ *n.* **1.** medio galope *m.* —*v.* **2.** galopar.

cantonment /kænˈtɒnmənt/ *n. Mil.* acuartelamiento *m.*

canvas /ˈkænvəs/ *n.* lona *f.*

canyon /ˈkænyən/ *n.* cañón, desfiladero *m.*

cap /kæp/ *n.* **1.** tapa *f.*; (headwear) gorro *m.* —*v.* **2.** tapar.

capability /ˌkeipə'biliti/ n. capacidad f.

capable /'keipəbəl/ a. capaz.

capably /'keipəbli/ adv. hábilmente.

capacious /kə'peiʃəs/ a. espacioso.

capacity /kə'pæsiti/ n. capacidad f.

cape /keip/ n. capa f., Geog. cabo m.

caper /'keipər/ n. zapateta f.; Bot. alcaparra f.

capillary /'kæpəˌleri/ a. capilar.

capital /'kæpitl/ n. capital m.; Govt. capital f.

capitalism /'kæpitlˌizəm/ n. capitalismo m.

capitalist /'kæpitlist/ n. capitalista m. & f.

capitalistic /ˌkæpitl'istik/ a. capitalista.

capitalization /ˌkæpitlə'zeiʃən/ n. capitalización f.

capitalize /'kæpitlˌaiz/ v. capitalizar.

capital letter n. mayúscula f.

capitulate /kə'pitʃəˌleit/ v. capitular.

capon /'keipɒn/ n. capón m.

caprice /kə'pris/ n. capricho m.

capricious /kə'priʃəs/ a. caprichoso.

capriciously /kə'priʃəsli/ adv. caprichosamente.

capriciousness /kə'priʃəsnis/ n. capricho m.

capsize /'kæpsaiz/ v. zozobrar, volcar.

capsule /'kæpsəl/ n. cápsula f.

captain /'kæptən/ n. capitán -tana.

caption /'kæpʃən/ n. título m.; (motion pictures) subtítulo m.

captious /'kæpʃəs/ a. capcioso.

captivate /'kæptəˌveit/ v. cautivar.

captivating /'kæptəˌveitiŋ/ a. encantador.

captive /'kæptiv/ n. cautivo -va, prisionero -ra.

captivity /kæp'tiviti/ n. cautividad f.

captor /'kæptər/ n. apresador -ra.

capture /'kæptʃər/ n. **1.** captura f. —v. **2.** capturar.

car /kar/ n. coche, carro m.; (of train) vagón, coche m. **baggage c.**, vagón de equipajes. **parlor c.**, coche salón.

carafe /kə'ræf/ n. garrafa f.

caramel /'kærəməl/ n. caramelo m.

carat /'kærət/ n. quilate m.

caravan /'kærəˌvæn/ n. caravana f.

caraway /'kærəˌwei/ n. alcaravea f.

carbide /'karbaid/ n. carburo m.

carbine /'karbin/ n. carabina f.

carbohydrate /ˌkarbou'haidreit/ n. hidrato de carbono.

carbon /'karbən/ n. carbón m.

carbon dioxide /dai'ɒksaid/ anhídrido carbónico.

carbon monoxide /mɒn'ɒksaid/ monóxido de carbono.

carbon paper papel carbón m.

carbuncle /'karbʌŋkəl/ n. carbúnculo m.

carburetor /'karbəˌreitər/ n. carburador m.

carcinogenic /ˌkarsənə'dʒenik/ a. carcinogénico.

card /kard/ n. tarjeta f. **playing c.**, naipe m.

cardboard /'kardˌbɔrd/ n. cartón m.

cardiac /'kardiˌæk/ a. cardíaco.

cardigan /'kardigən/ n. chaqueta de punto.

cardinal /'kardnḷ/ a. **1.** cardinal. —n. **2.** cardenal m.

cardiologist /ˌkardi'ɒlədʒist/ n. cardiólogo, -ga m. & f.

care /kɛər/ n. **1.** cuidado. —v. **2.** **c. for,** cuidar.

careen /kə'rin/ v. carenar; echarse de costado.

career /kə'riər/ n. carrera f.

carefree /'kɛərˌfri/ a. descuidado.

careful /'kɛərfəl/ a. cuidadoso. **be. c.,** tener cuidado.

carefully /'kɛərfəli/ adv. cuidadosamente.

carefulness /'kɛərfəlnis/ n. esmero; cuidado m.; cautela f.

careless /'kɛərlis/ a. descuidado.

carelessly /'kɛərlisli/ adv. descuidadamente; negligentemente.

carelessness /'kɛərlisnis/ n. descuido m.

caress /kə'rɛs/ n. **1.** caricia f. —v. **2.** acariciar.

caretaker /'kɛərˌteikər/ n. guardián -ana.

cargo /'kargou/ n. carga f.

caricature /'kærikətʃər/ n. caricatura f.

caricaturist /'kærıkə,tʃʊrıst/ n. caricaturista m. & f.

caries /'kɛərIz/ n. caries f.

carjacking /'kɑr,dʒækɪŋ/ n. robo de coche m.

carload /'kɑr,loud/ a. furgonada, vagonada.

carnal /'kɑrnḷ/ a. carnal.

carnation /kɑr'neıʃən/ n. clavel m.

carnival /'kɑrnəvəl/ n. carnaval m.

carnivorous /kɑr'nıvərəs/ a. carnívoro.

carol /'kærəl/ n. villancico m.

carouse /kə'rauz/ v. parrandear.

carpenter /'kɑrpəntər/ n. carpintero -ra.

carpet /'kɑrpıt/ n. alfombra f.

carpeting /'kɑrpıtıŋ/ n. alfombrado m.

car pool /'kɑr,pul/ uso habitual, por varias personas, de un automóvil perteneciente a una de ellas.

carriage /'kærıdʒ/ n. carruaje; (bearing) porte m.

carrier /'kærıər/ n. portador -ra.

carrier pigeon paloma mensajera.

carrot /'kærət/ n. zanahoria f.

carrousel /,kærə'sɛl/ n. volantín, carrusel m.

carry /'kæri/ v. llevar, cargar. **c. out**, cumplir, llevar a cabo.

cart /kɑrt/ n. carreta f.

cartage /'kɑrtıdʒ/ n. acarreo, carretaje m.

cartel /kɑr'tɛl/ n. cartel m.

cartilage /'kɑrtḷıdʒ/ n. cartílago m.

carton /'kɑrtṇ/ n. caja de cartón.

cartoon /kɑr'tun/ n. caricatura f.

cartoonist /kɑr'tunıst/ n. caricaturista m. & f.

cartridge /'kɑrtrıdʒ/ n. cartucho m.

carve /kɑrv/ v. esculpir; (meat) trinchar.

carver /'kɑrvər/ n. tallador -ra; grabador -ra.

carving /'kɑrvıŋ/ n. entalladura f.; arte de trinchar. **c. knife**, cuchillo de trinchar.

cascade /kæs'keıd/ n. cascada f.

case /keıs/ n. caso m.; (box) caja f. **in any c.**, sea como sea.

cash /kæʃ/ n. **1.** dinero contante. —v. **2.** efectuar, cambiar.

cashier /kæ'ʃıər/ n. cajero -ra.

cashmere /'kæʒmıər/ n. casimir m.

casino /kə'sinou/ n. casino m.

cask /kæsk/ n. barril m.

casket /'kæskıt/ n. ataúd m.

casserole /'kæsə,roul/ n. cacerola f.

cassette /kə'sɛt/ n. cassette m., cartucho m.

cast /kæst/ n. **1.** Theat. reparto de papeles. —v. **2.** echar; Theat. repartir.

castanet /,kæstə'nɛt/ n. castañuela f.

castaway /'kæstə,weı/ n. náufrago -ga.

caste /kæst/ n. casta f.

caster /'kæstər/ n. tirador m.

castigate /'kæstı,geıt/ v. castigar.

Castilian /kæ'stıljən/ n. castellano.

cast iron n. hierro colado m.

castle /'kæsəl/ n. castillo m.

castoff /'kæst,ɔf/ a. descartado.

casual /'kæʒuəl/ a. casual.

casually /'kæʒuəli/ adv. casualmente.

casualness /'kæʒuəlnıs/ n. casualidad f.

casualty /'kæʒuəlti/ n. víctima f.; Mil. baja f.

cat /kæt/ n. gato -ta.

cataclysm /'kætə,klızəm/ n. cataclismo m.

catacomb /'kætə,koum/ n. catacumba f.

catalogue /'kætḷ,ɔg/ n. catálogo m.

catapult /'kætə,pʌlt/ n. catapulta f.

cataract /'kætə,rækt/ n. catarata f.

catarrh /kə'tɑr/ n. catarro m.

catastrophe /kə'tæstrəfi/ n. catástrofe f.

catch /kætʃ/ v. alcanzar, atrapar, coger.

catchy /'kætʃi/ a. contagioso.

catechism /'kætı,kızəm/ n. catequismo m.

catechize /'kætı,kaız/ v. catequizar.

categorical /,kætı'gɔrıkəl/ a. categórico.

category /'kætı,gɔri/ n. categoría f.

cater /'keıtər/ v. abastecer; proveer. **c. to**, complacer.

caterpillar /'kætə,pılər/ n. gusano m.

catgut /'kæt,gʌt/ n. cuerda (de tripa).

catharsis /kə'θɑrsɪs/ n. catarsis, purga f.

cathartic /kə'θɑrtɪk/ a. **1.** catártico; purgante. —n. **2.** purgante m.

cathedral /kə'θidrəl/ n. catedral f.

cathode /'kæθoud/ n. cátodo m.

Catholic /'kæθəlɪk/ a. católico & n. católico -ca.

Catholicism /kə'θɒlə,sɪzəm/ n. catolicismo m.

catnap /'kæt,næp/ n. siesta corta.

catsup /'kætsəp, 'kɛtʃəp/ n. salsa de tomate.

cattle /'kætl/ n. ganado m.

cattleman /'kætlmən, -,mæn/ n. ganadero m.

cauliflower /'kɔlə,flauər/ n. coliflor m.

causation /kɔ'zeɪʃən/ n. causalidad f.

cause /kɔz/ n. causa f.

causeway /'kɔz,weɪ/ n. calzada elevada f.; terraplén m.

caustic /'kɔstɪk/ a. cáustico.

cauterize /'kɔtə,raɪz/ v. cauterizar.

cautery /'kɔtəri/ n. cauterio f.

caution /'kɔʃən/ n. cautela f.

cautious /'kɔʃəs/ a. cauteloso.

cavalcade /,kævəl'keɪd/ n. cabalgata f.

cavalier /,kævə'lɪər/ n. caballero m.

cavalry /'kævəlri/ n. caballería f.

cave /keɪv/ **cavern** n. caverna, gruta f.

cave-in /keɪv ,ɪn/ n. hundimiento m.

caviar /'kævi,ɑr/ n. caviar m.

cavity /'kævɪti/ n. hueco m.

cayman /'keɪmən/ n. caimán m.

CD player tocadiscos compacto, tocadiscos digital m.

cease /sis/ v. cesar.

ceaseless /'sislɪs/ a. incesante.

cedar /'sidər/ n. cedro m.

cede /sid/ v. ceder.

ceiling /'silɪŋ/ n. techo; cielo m.

celebrant /'sɛləbrənt/ n. celebrante -ta.

celebrate /'sɛlə,breɪt/ v. celebrar.

celebration /,sɛlə'breɪʃən/ n. celebración f.

celebrity /sə'lɛbrɪti/ n. celebridad f.

celerity /sə'lɛrɪti/ n. celeridad; prontitud f.

celery /'sɛləri/ n. apio m.

celestial /sə'lɛstʃəl/ a. celeste.

celibacy /'sɛləbəsi/ n. celibato -ta.

celibate /'sɛləbɪt/ a. célibe m. & f.

cell /sɛl/ n. celda f.; Biol. célula f.

cellar /'sɛlər/ n. sótano m.

cellist /'tʃɛlɪst/ a. celista m. & f.

cello /'tʃɛlou/ n. violonchelo m.

cellophane /'sɛlə,feɪn/ n. celofán m.

cellular /'sɛlyələr/ a. celular.

cellular phone /foun/ teléfono móvil m.

celluloid /'sɛlyə,lɔɪd/ n. celuloide m.

cellulose /'sɛlyə,lous/ a. **1.** celuloso. —n. **2.** celulosa f.

Celtic /'kɛltɪk, 'sɛl-/ a. céltico.

cement /sɪ'mɛnt/ n. cemento m.

cemetery /'sɛmɪ,tɛri/ n. cementerio m.; campo santo m.

censor /'sɛnsər/ n. censor -ra.

censorious /sɛn'sɔriəs/ a. severo; crítico.

censorship /'sɛnsər,ʃɪp/ n. censura f.

censure /'sɛnʃər/ n. **1.** censura f. —v. **2.** censurar.

census /'sɛnsəs/ n. censo m.

cent /sɛnt/ n. centavo, céntimo m.

centenary /sɛn'tɛnəri/ a. & n. centenario m.

centennial /sɛn'tɛniəl/ a. & n. centenario m.

center /'sɛntər/ n. centro m.

centerfold /'sɛntər,fould/ n. página central desplegable en una revista.

centerpiece /'sɛntər,pis/ n. centro de mesa.

centigrade /'sɛnti,greɪd/ a. centígrado.

centigrade thermometer termómetro centígrado.

central /'sɛntrəl/ a. central.

Central American a. & n. centroamericano -na.

centralize /'sɛntrə,laɪz/ v. centralizar.

century /'sɛntʃəri/ n. siglo m.

century plant maguey m.

ceramic /sə'ræmɪk/ a. cerámico.

ceramics /sə'ræmɪks/ n. cerámica f.

cereal /'sɪəriəl/ n. cereal m.

cerebral /sə'ribrəl/ a. cerebral.

ceremonial /,sɛrə'mouniəl/ a. ceremonial.

ceremonious /,sɛrə'mouniəs/ a. ceremonioso.

ceremony /'sɛrəˌmouni/ n. ceremonia f.

certain /'sɜrtn/ a. cierto, seguro.

certainly /'sɜrtnli/ adv. sin duda, seguramente.

certainty /'sɜrtnti/ n. certeza f.

certificate /sər'tɪfɪkɪt/ n. certificado m.

certification /ˌsɜrtəfɪ'keɪʃən, sərˌtɪfə-/ n. certificación f.

certified /'sɜrtəˌfaɪd/ a. certificado.

certify /'sɜrtəˌfaɪ/ v. certificar.

certitude /'sɜrtɪˌtyud/ n. certeza f.

cessation /sɛ'seɪʃən/ n. cesación, descontinuación f.

cession /'sɛʃən/ n. cesión f.

chafe /tʃeɪf/ v. irritar.

chafing dish /'tʃeɪfɪŋ/ n. escalfador m.

chagrin /ʃə'grɪn/ n. disgusto m.

chain /tʃeɪn/ n. **1.** cadena f. —v. **2.** encadenar.

chair /tʃɛər/ n. silla f.

chairman /'tʃɛərmən/ n. presidente -ta.

chairperson /'tʃɛərˌpɜrsən/ n. presidente -ta; persona que preside.

chalk /tʃɔk/ n. tiza f.

challenge /'tʃælɪndʒ/ n. **1.** desafío m. —v. **2.** desafiar.

challenger /'tʃælɪndʒər/ n. desafiador -ra.

chamber /'tʃeɪmbər/ n. cámara f.

chamberlain /'tʃeɪmbərlɪn/ n. camarero m.

chambermaid /'tʃeɪmbərˌmeɪd/ n. camarera f.

chameleon /kə'miliən/ n. camaleón m.

chamois /'ʃæmi/ n. gamuza f.

champagne /ʃæm'peɪn/ n. champán m., champaña f.

champion /'tʃæmpiən/ n. **1.** campeón -ona f. —v. **2.** defender.

championship /'tʃæmpiənˌʃɪp/ n. campeonato m.

chance /tʃæns/ n. oportunidad, ocasión f. **by c.,** por casualidad, por acaso. **take a c.,** aventurarse.

chancel /'tʃænsəl/ n. antealtar m.

chancellery /'tʃænsələri/ n. cancillería f.

chancellor /'tʃænsələr/ n. canciller m.

chandelier /ˌʃændl'ɪər/ n. araña de luces.

change /tʃeɪndʒ/ n. **1.** cambio; (from a bill) moneda f. —v. **2.** cambiar.

changeability /ˌtʃeɪndʒə'bɪliti/ n. mutabilidad f.

changeable /'tʃeɪndʒəbəl/ a. variable, inconstante.

changer /'tʃeɪndʒər/ n. cambiador m.

channel /'tʃænl/ n. **1.** canal m. —v. **2.** encauzar.

Channel Tunnel túnel del Canal de la Mancha m.

chant /tʃænt/ n. **1.** canto llano m. —v. **2.** cantar.

chaos /'keɪɒs/ n. caos m.

chaotic /keɪ'ɒtɪk/ a. caótico.

chap /tʃæp/ n. **1.** Colloq. tipo m. —v. **2.** rajar.

chapel /'tʃæpəl/ n. capilla f.

chaperon /'ʃæpəˌroʊn/ n. acompañante -ta de señorita.

chaplain /'tʃæplɪn/ n. capellán m.

chapter /'tʃæptər/ n. capítulo m.

char /tʃɑr/ v. carbonizar.

character /'kærɪktər/ n. carácter m.

characteristic /ˌkærɪktə'rɪstɪk/ a. **1.** característico. —n. **2.** característica f.

characterization /ˌkærɪktərə-'zeɪʃən/ n. caracterización f.

characterize /'kærɪktəˌraɪz/ v. caracterizar.

charcoal /'tʃɑrˌkoʊl/ n. carbón leña.

charge /tʃɑrdʒ/ n. **1.** acusación f.; ataque m. —v. **2.** cargar; acusar; atacar.

chariot /'tʃæriət/ n. carroza f.

charisma /kə'rɪzmə/ n. carisma m.

charitable /'tʃærɪtəbəl/ a. caritativo.

charitableness /'tʃærɪtəbəlnɪs/ n. caridad f.

charitably /'tʃærɪtəbli/ adv. caritativamente.

charity /'tʃærɪti/ n. caridad f.; (alms) limosna f.

charlatan /'ʃɑrlətn/ n. charlatán -na.

charlatanism /'ʃɑrlətnˌɪzəm/ n. charlatanería f.

charm /tʃɑrm/ n. **1.** encanto m.; (witchcraft) hechizo m. —v. **2.** encantar; hechizar.

charming /'tʃɑrmɪŋ/ a. encantador.

charred /tʃɑrd/ a. carbonizado.

chart /tʃɑrt/ n. tabla, esquema f.

charter /'tʃɑrtər/ n. **1.** carta f. —v. **2.** alquilar.

charter flight vuelo chárter m.

charwoman /'tʃɑr,wʊmən/ n. mujer de la limpieza f.

chase /tʃeis/ n. **1.** caza f. —v. **2.** cazar; perseguir.

chaser /'tʃeisər/ n. perseguidor -ra.

chasm /'kæzəm/ n. abismo m.

chassis /'tʃæsi/ n. chasis m.

chaste /tʃeist/ a. casto.

chasten /'tʃeisən/ v. corregir, castigar.

chastise /tʃæs'taiz/ v. castigar.

chastisement /tʃæs'taizmənt/ n. castigo m.

chastity /'tʃæstɪti/ n. castidad, pureza f.

chat /tʃæt/ n. **1.** plática, charla f. —v. **2.** platicar, charlar.

chateau /ʃæ'tou/ n. castillo m.

chattels /'tʃætəlz/ n.pl. bienes m.

chatter /'tʃætər/ v. **1.** cotorrear; (teeth) rechinar. —n. **2.** cotorreo m.

chatterbox /'tʃæt,ər bɒks/ n. charlador -ra.

chauffeur /'ʃoufər/ n. chofer m.

cheap /tʃip/ a. barato.

cheapen /'tʃipən/ v. rebajar, menospreciar.

cheaply /'tʃipli/ adv. barato.

cheapness /'tʃipnɪs/ n. baratura f.

cheat /tʃit/ v. engañar.

cheater /'tʃitər/ n. engañador -ra.

check /tʃɛk/ n. **1.** verificación f.; (bank) cheque m.; (restaurant) cuenta f.; (chess) jaque m. —v. **2.** verificar.

checkers /'tʃɛkərz/ n. juego de damas.

checkmate /'tʃɛk,meit/ v. dar mate.

checkout counter /'tʃɛk,aut/ caja f.

cheek /tʃik/ n. mejilla f. (of face), desfachatez f. (gall).

cheekbone /'tʃik,boun/ n. pómulo m.

cheeky /'tʃiki/ a. fresco, descarado, chulo.

cheer /tʃir/ n. **1.** alegría f.; aplauso m. —v. **2.** alegrar; aplaudir.

cheerful /'tʃirfəl/ a. alegre.

cheerfully /'tʃirfəli/ adv. alegremente.

cheerfulness /'tʃirfəlnɪs/ n. alegría f.

cheerless /'tʃirlɪs/ a. triste.

cheery /'tʃiri/ a. alegre.

cheese /tʃiz/ n. queso m. **cottage c.,** requesón m.

chef /ʃɛf/ n. cocinero en jefe.

chemical /'kɛmɪkəl/ a. **1.** químico. —n. **2.** reactivo m.

chemically /'kɛmɪkli/ adv. químicamente.

chemist /'kɛmɪst/ n. químico -ca.

chemistry /'kɛməstri/ n. química f.

chemotherapy /,kimou'θɛrəpi/ n. quimioterapia f.

chenille /ʃə'nil/ n. felpilla f.

cherish /'tʃɛrɪʃ/ v. apreciar.

cherry /'tʃɛri/ n. cereza f.

cherub /'tʃɛrəb/ n. querubín m.

chess /tʃɛs/ n. ajedrez m.

chest /tʃɛst/ n. arca f.; (physiology) pecho m.

chestnut /'tʃɛs,nʌt/ n. castaña f.

chevron /'ʃɛvrən/ n. sardineta f.

chew /tʃu/ v. mascar, masticar.

chewer /'tʃuər/ n. mascador -ra.

chic /ʃik/ a. elegante, paquete.

chicanery /ʃɪ'keinəri/ n. trampería f.

chick /tʃik/ n. pollito -ta.

chicken /'tʃikən/ n. pollo m., gallina f.

chicken-hearted /'tʃikən 'hɑrtɪd/ a. cobarde.

chicken pox /pɒks/ viruelas locas, varicela f.

chicle /'tʃikəl/ n. chicle m.

chicory /'tʃikəri/ n. achicoria f.

chide /tʃaid/ v. regañar, reprender.

chief /tʃif/ a. **1.** principal. —n. **2.** jefe -fa.

chiefly /'tʃifli/ adv. principalmente, mayormente.

chieftain /'tʃiftən/ n. caudillo m.; (Indian c.) cacique m.

chiffon /ʃɪ'fɒn/ n. chifón m., gasa f.

chilblain /'tʃɪlblein/ n. sabañón m.

child /tʃaild/ n. niño -ña; hijo -ja.

childbirth /'tʃaild,bərθ/ n. parto m.

childhood /'tʃaildhʊd/ n. niñez f.

childish /'tʃaildɪʃ/ a. pueril.

childishness /'tʃaildɪʃnɪs/ n. puerilidad f.

childless /'tʃaildlɪs/ a. sin hijos.

childlike /'tʃaild,laik/ a. infantil.

Chilean /'tʃɪliən/ a. & n. chileno -na.

chili /'tʃɪli/ n. chile, ají m.

chill /tʃɪl/ n. **1.** frío; escalofrío m. —v. **2.** enfriar.

chilliness /'tʃɪlinɪs/ n. frialdad f.

chilly /'tʃɪli/ a. frío; friolento.

chimes /tʃaimz/ n. juego de campanas.

chimney /'tʃɪmni/ n. chimenea f.

chimpanzee /,tʃɪmpæn'zi, tʃɪm-'pænzi/ n. chimpancé m.

chin /tʃɪn/ n. barba f.

china /'tʃainə/ n. loza f.

chinchilla /tʃɪn'tʃɪlə/ n. chinchilla f.

Chinese /tʃai'niz/ a. & n. chino -na.

chink /tʃɪŋk/ n. grieta f.

chintz /tʃɪnts/ n. zaraza f.

chip /tʃɪp/ n. **1.** astilla f. —v. **2.** astillar.

chiropodist /kɪ'rɒpədɪst/ n. pedicuro -ra.

chiropractor /'kairə,præktər/ n. quiropráctico -ca.

chirp /tʃɜrp/ n. chirrido m. —v. **2.** chirriar, piar.

chisel /'tʃɪzəl/ n. **1.** cincel m. —v. **2.** cincelar, talar.

chivalrous /'ʃɪvəlrəs/ a. caballeroso.

chivalry /'ʃɪvəlri/ n. caballería f.

chive /tʃaiv/ n. cebollino m.

chloride /'klɔraid/ n. cloruro m.

chlorine /'klɔrin/ n. cloro m.

chloroform /'klɔrə,fɔrm/ n. cloroformo m.

chlorophyll /'klɔrəfɪl/ n. clorofila f.

chock-full /'tʃɒk'fʊl/ a. repleto, colmado.

chocolate /'tʃɔkəlɪt/ n. chocolate m.

choice /tʃɔis/ a. **1.** selecto, escogido. —n. **2.** selección f.; escogimiento m.

choir /kwaiɚr/ n. coro m.

choke /tʃouk/ v. sofocar, ahogar.

cholera /'kɒlərə/ n. cólera f.

choleric /'kɒlərɪk/ a. colérico, irascible.

cholesterol /kə'lɛstə,roul/ n. colesterol m.

choose /tʃuz/ v. elegir, escoger.

chop /tʃɒp/ n. **1.** chuleta, costilla f. —v. **2.** tajar; cortar.

chopper /'tʃɒpər/ n. tajador -ra.

choppy /'tʃɒpi/ a. agitado.

choral /'kɔrəl/ a. coral.

chord /kɔrd/ n. cuerda f.; acorde m.

chore /tʃɔr/ n. tarea f., quehacer m.

choreography /,kɔri'ogrəfi, ,kour-/ n. coreografía f.

chorister /'kɔrəstər/ n. corista m.

chorus /'kɔrəs/ n. coro m.

christen /'krɪsən/ v. bautizar.

Christendom /'krɪsəndəm/ n. cristiandad f.

Christian /'krɪsʃən/ a. & n. cristiano -na.

Christianity /,krɪsʃi'ænɪti/ n. cristianismo m.

Christmas /'krɪsməs/ n. Navidad, Pascua f. **Merry C.,** felices Pascuas. **C. Eve,** Nochebuena f.

chromatic /krou'mætɪk/ a. cromático.

chromium /'kroumiəm/ n. cromo m.

chromosome /'kroumə,soum/ n. cromosoma m.

chronic /'krɒnɪk/ a. crónico.

chronicle /'krɒnɪkəl/ n. crónica f.

chronological /,krɒnl'ɒdʒɪkəl/ a. cronológico.

chronology /krə'nɒlədʒi/ n. cronología f.

chrysalis /'krɪsəlɪs/ n. crisálida f.

chrysanthemum /krɪ'sænθəməm/ n. crisantemo m.

chubby /'tʃʌbi/ a. regordete, rollizo.

chuck /tʃʌk/ v. (cluck) cloquear; (throw) echar, tirar.

chuckle /'tʃʌkəl/ v. reír entre dientes.

chum /tʃʌm/ n. amigo -ga; compinche m.

chummy /'tʃʌmi/ a. íntimo.

chunk /tʃʌŋk/ n. trozo m.

chunky /'tʃʌŋki/ a. fornido, trabado.

Chunnel /'tʃʌnl/ n. túnel del Canal de la Mancha m.

church /tʃɜrtʃ/ n. iglesia f.

churchman /'tʃɜrtʃmən/ n. eclesiástico m.

churchyard /'tʃɜrtʃ,yard/ n. cementerio m.

churn /tʃɜrn/ n. **1.** mantequera f. —v. **2.** agitar, revolver.

chute /ʃut/ n. conducto; canal m.

cicada /sɪ'keidə/ n. cigarra, chicharra f.

cider /'saidər/ n. sidra f.

cigar /sɪ'gar/ n. cigarro, puro m.

cigarette /,sɪgə'rɛt/ n. cigarrillo, cigarro, pitillo m. **c. case,** cigarrillera f. **c. lighter,** encendedor m.

cinchona /sɪŋ'kounə/ n. cinchona f.

cinder /'sɪndər/ n. ceniza f.

cinema /'sɪnəmə/ n. cine m.

cinnamon /'sɪnəmən/ n. canela f.

cipher /'saifər/ n. cifra f.

circle /'sərkəl/ n. círculo m.

circuit /'sərkɪt/ n. circuito m.

circuitous /sər'kyuɪtəs/ a. tortuoso.

circuitously /sər'kyuɪtəsli/ adv. tortuosamente.

circular /'sərkyələr/ a. circular, redondo.

circularize /'sərkyələ,raiz/ v. hacer circular.

circulate /'sərkyə,leit/ v. circular.

circulation /,sərkyə'leiʃən/ n. circulación f.

circulator /'sərkyə,leitər/ n. diseminador -ra.

circulatory /'sərkyələ,tori/ a. circulatorio.

circumcise /'sərkəm,saiz/ v. circuncidar.

circumcision /,sərkəm'sɪʒən/ n. circuncisión f.

circumference /sər'kʌmfərəns/ n. circunferencia f.

circumlocution /,sərkəmlou'kyuʃən/ n. circunlocución f.

circumscribe /'sərkəm,skraib/ v. circunscribir; limitar.

circumspect /'sərkəm,spekt/ a. discreto.

circumstance /'sərkəm,stæns/ n. circunstancia f.

circumstantial /,sərkəm'stænʃəl/ a. circunstancial, indirecto.

circumstantially /,sərkəm'stænʃəli/ adv. minuciosamente.

circumvent /,sərkəm'vent/ v. evadir, evitar.

circumvention /,sərkəm'venʃən/ n. trampa f.

circus /'sərkəs/ n. circo m.

cirrhosis /sɪ'rousɪs/ n. cirrosis f.

cistern /'sɪstərn/ n. cisterna f.

citadel /'sɪtədl/ n. ciudadela f.

citation /sai'teiʃən/ n. citación f.

cite /sait/ v. citar.

citizen /'sɪtəzən/ n. ciudadano -na.

citizenship /'sɪtəzən,ʃɪp/ n. ciudadanía f.

citric /'sɪtrɪk/ a. cítrico.

city /'sɪti/ n. ciudad f.

city hall ayuntamiento, municipio m.

city planning urbanismo m.

civic /'sɪvɪk/ a. cívico.

civics /'sɪvɪks/ n. ciencia del gobierno civil.

civil /'sɪvəl/ a. civil; cortés.

civilian /sɪ'vɪlyən/ a. & n. civil m. & f.

civility /sɪ'vɪlɪti/ n. cortesía f.

civilization /,sɪvələ'zeiʃən/ n. civilización f.

civilize /'sɪvə,laiz/ v. civilizar.

civil rights /raits/ derechos civiles m. pl.

civil service n. servicio civil oficial m.

civil war n. guerra civil f.

clabber /'klæbər/ n. **1.** cuajo m. —v. **2.** cuajarse.

clad /klæd/ a. vestido.

claim /kleim/ n. **1.** demanda; pretensión f. —v. **2.** demandar, reclamar.

claimant /'kleimənt/ n. reclamante -ta.

clairvoyance /klɛr'vɔiəns/ n. clarividencia f.

clairvoyant /klɛr'vɔiənt/ a. clarividente.

clam /klæm/ n. almeja f.

clamber /'klæmbər/ v. trepar.

clamor /'klæmər/ n. **1.** clamor f. —v. **2.** clamar.

clamorous /'klæmərəs/ a. clamoroso.

clamp /klæmp/ n. **1.** prensa de sujeción f. —v. **2.** asegurar, sujetar.

clan /klæn/ n. tribu f., clan m.

clandestine /klæn'destɪn/ a. clandestino.

clandestinely /klæn'destɪnli/ adv. clandestinamente.

clangor /'klæŋər, 'klæŋgər/ n. estruendo m., estrépito m.

clannish /'klænɪʃ/ a. unido; exclusivista.

clap /klæp/ v. aplaudir.

clapboard /'klæbərd, 'klæp,bɔrd/ n. chilla f.

claque /klæk/ n. claque f.

claret /'klærɪt/ n. clarete m.

clarification /,klærəfə'keiʃən/ n. clarificación f.

clarify /'klærə,fai/ v. clarificar.

clarinet /,klærə'net/ n. clarinete m.

clarinetist /,klærə'netɪst/ n. clarinetista m. & f.

clarity /'klærɪti/ n. claridad f.

clash /klæʃ/ n. **1.** choque m., enfrentamiento m. —v. **2.** chocar.

clasp /klæsp/ n. **1.** broche m. —v. **2.** abrochar.

class /klæs/ n. clase f.

classic, /'klæsɪk/ **classical** a. clásico.

classicism /'klæsə,sɪzəm/ n. clasicismo m.

classifiable /'klæsə,faiəbəl/ a. clasificable, calificable.

classification /,klæsəfɪ'keiʃən/ n. clasificación f.

classify /'klæsə,fai/ v. clasificar.

classmate /'klæs,meit/ n. compañero -ra de clase.

classroom /'klæs,rum, -,rʊm/ n. sala de clase.

clatter /'klætər/ n. **1.** alboroto m. —v. **2.** alborotar.

clause /klɔz/ n. cláusula f.

claustrophobia /,klɔstrə'foubiə/ n. claustrofobia f.

claw /klɔ/ n. garra f.

clay /klei/ n. arcilla f.; barro m.

clean /klin/ a. **1.** limpio. —v. **2.** limpiar.

cleaner /'klinər/ n. limpiador -ra.

cleaning lady, cleaning woman /'klinɪŋ/ señora de la limpieza, mujer de la limpieza.

cleanliness /'klɛnlinɪs/ n. limpieza f.

cleanse /klɛnz/ v. limpiar, purificar.

cleanser /'klɛnzər/ n. limpiador m., purificador m.

clear /klɪər/ a. claro.

clearance /'klɪərəns/ n. espacio libre. **c. sale,** venta de liquidación f.

clearing /'klɪərɪŋ/ n. despejo m.; desmonte m.

clearly /'klɪərli/ adv. claramente, evidentemente.

clearness /'klɪərnɪs/ n. claridad f.

cleavage /'klividʒ/ n. resquebradura f.

cleaver /'klivər/ n. partidor m.; hacha f.

clef /klɛf/ n. clave, llave f.

clemency /'klɛmənsi/ n. clemencia f.

clench /klɛntʃ/ v. agarrar.

clergy /'klɜrdʒi/ n. clero m.

clergyman /'klɜrdʒimən/ n. clérigo m.

clerical /'klɛrɪkəl/ a. clerical. **c. work,** trabajo de oficina.

clericalism /'klɛrɪkə,lɪzəm/ n. clericalismo m.

clerk /klɜrk/ n. dependiente, escribiente m.

clerkship /'klɜrkʃɪp/ n. escribanía f., secretaría f.

clever /'klɛvər/ a. diestro, hábil.

cleverly /'klɛvərli/ adv. diestramente, hábilmente.

cleverness /'klɛvərnɪs/ n. destreza f.

cliché /kli'ʃei/ n. tópico m.

client /'klaiənt/ n. cliente -ta.

clientele /,klaiən'tɛl/ n. clientela f.

cliff /klɪf/ n. precipicio, risco m.

climate /'klaimɪt/ n. clima m.

climatic /klai'mætɪk/ a. climático.

climax /'klaimæks/ n. colmo m., culminación f.

climb /klaim/ v. escalar; subir.

climber /'klaimər/ n. trepador -ra, escalador -ra f.; Bot. enredadera f.

climbing plant /'klaimɪŋ/ enredadera f.

clinch /klɪntʃ/ v. afirmar.

cling /klɪŋ/ v. pegarse.

clinic /'klɪnɪk/ n. clínica f.

clinical /'klɪnɪkəl/ a. clínico.

clinically /'klɪnɪkəli/ adv. clínicamente.

clip /klɪp/ n. **1.** grapa f. **paper c.,** gancho m. —v. **2.** prender; (shear) trasquilar.

clipper /'klɪpər/ n. recortador m.; Aero. clíper m.

clipping /'klɪpɪŋ/ n. recorte m.

clique /klik/ n. camarilla f., compadraje m.

cloak /klouk/ n. capa f., manto m.

clock /klɒk/ n. reloj m. **alarm c.,** despertador m.

clod /klɒd/ n. terrón m.; césped m.

clog /klɒg/ v. obstruir.

cloister /'klɔistər/ n. claustro m.

clone /kloun/ n. clon m. & f. v. clonar.

close /a, adv. klous; v klouz/ a. **1.** cercano. —adv. **2.** cerca. **c. to,** cerca de. —v. **3.** cerrar; tapar.

closely /'klousli/ adv. (near) de cerca; (tight) estrechamente; (care) cuidadosamente.

closeness /'klousnɪs/ n. contigüidad f., apretamiento m.; (airless) falta de ventilación f.

closet /'klɒzɪt/ n. gabinete m. **clothes c.,** ropero m.

clot /klɒt/ n. **1.** coágulo f. —v. **2.** coagularse.

cloth /klɔθ/ n. paño m.; tela f.

clothe /kloud/ v. vestir.

clothes /klouz/ n. ropa f.

clothing /'klouðɪŋ/ n. vestidos m., ropa f.

cloud /klaud/ n. nube f.

cloudburst /'klaud,bərst/ n. chaparrón m.

cloudiness /'klaudɪnɪs/ n. nebulosidad f.; obscuridad f.

cloudless /'klaudlɪs/ a. despejado, sin nubes.

cloudy /'klaudi/ a. nublado.

clove /klouv/ n. clavo m.

clover /'klouvər/ n. trébol m.

clown /klaun/ n. bufón -na, payaso -sa.

clownish /'klaunɪʃ/ a. grosero; bufonesco.

cloy /klɔi/ v. saciar, empalagar.

club /klʌb/ n. **1.** porra f.; (social) círculo, club m.; (cards) basto m. —v. **2.** golpear con una porra.

clubfoot /'klʌb,fut/ n. pateta m., pie zambo m.

clue /klu/ n. seña, pista f.

clump /klʌmp/ n. grupo m., masa f.

clumsiness /'klʌmzinɪs/ n. tosquedad f.; desmaña f.

clumsy /'klʌmzi/ a. torpe, desmañado.

cluster /'klʌstər/ n. **1.** grupo m.; (fruit) racimo m. —v. **2.** agrupar.

clutch /klʌtʃ/ n. **1.** Auto. embrague m. —v. **2.** agarrar.

clutter /'klʌtər/ n. **1.** confusión f. —v. **2.** poner en desorden.

coach /koutʃ/ n. **1.** coche, vagón m.; coche ordinario; (sports) entrenador m. —v. **2.** entrenar.

coachman /'koutʃmən/ n. cochero -ra.

coagulate /kou'ægyə,leit/ v. coagular.

coagulation /kou,ægyə'leiʃən/ n. coagulación f.

coal /koul/ n. carbón m.

coalesce /,kouə'les/ v. unirse, soldarse.

coalition /,kouə'lɪʃən/ n. coalición f.

coal oil n. petróleo m.

coal tar n. alquitrán m.

coarse /kɔrs/ a. grosero, burdo; (material) tosco, grueso.

coarsen /'kɔrsən/ v. vulgarizar.

coarseness /'kɔrsnɪs/ n. grosería; tosquedad f.

coast /koust/ n. **1.** costa f., litoral m. —v. **2.** deslizarse.

coastal /'koustl̩/ a. costanero.

coast guard guardacostas m. & f.

coat /kout/ n. **1.** saco m., chaqueta f.; (paint) capa f. —v. **2.** cubrir.

coat of arms /ɑrmz/ n. escudo m.

coax /kouks/ v. instar.

cobalt /'koubɔlt/ n. cobalto m.

cobbler /'kɒblər/ n. zapatero -ra.

cobblestone /'kɒbəl,stoun/ n. guijarro m.

cobra /'koubrə/ n. cobra f.

cobweb /'kɒb,wɛb/ n. telaraña f.

cocaine /kou'kein/ n. cocaína f.

cock /kɒk/ n. (rooster) gallo m.; (water, etc.) llave f.; (gun) martillo m.

cockfight /'kɒk,fait/ n. riña de gallos f.

cockpit /'kɒk,pit/ n. gallera f.; reñidero de gallos m.; Aero. cabina f.

cockroach /'kɒk,routʃ/ n. cucaracha f.

cocktail /'kɒk,teil/ n. cóctel m.

cocky /'kɒki/ a. confiado, atrevido.

cocoa /'koukou/ n. cacao m.

coconut /'koukə,nʌt/ n. coco m.

cocoon /kə'kun/ n. capullo m.

cod /kɒd/ n. bacalao m.

code /koud/ n. código m.; clave f.

codeine /'koudin/ n. codeína f.

codfish /'kɒd,fiʃ/ n. bacalao m.

codify /'kɒdə,fai/ v. compilar.

cod-liver oil /'kɒd 'livər/ aceite de hígado de bacalao m.

coeducation /,kouɛdʒu'keiʃən/ n. coeducación f.

coequal /kou'ikwəl/ a. mutuamente igual.

coerce /kou'ərs/ v. forzar.

coercion /kou'ərʃən/ n. coerción f.

coercive /kou'ərsiv/ a. coercitivo.

coexist /,kouɪg'zɪst/ v. coexistir.

coffee /'kɔfi/ n. café m. **c. plantation**, cafetal m. **c. shop**, café m.

coffee break pausa para el café f.

coffer /'kɔfər/ n. cofre m.

coffin /'kɔfin/ n. ataúd m.

cog /kɒg/ n. diente de rueda m.

cogent /'koudʒənt/ a. convincente.

cogitate /'kɒdʒɪ,teit/ v. pensar, reflexionar.

cognizance /'kɒgnəzəns/ n. conocimiento m., comprensión f.

cognizant /'kɒgnəzənt/ a. conocedor, informado.

cogwheel /'kɒg,wil/ n. rueda dentada f.

cohere /kou'hɪər/ v. pegarse.

coherent /kou'hɪərənt/ a. coherente.

cohesion /kou'hiʒən/ n. cohesión f.

cohesive /kou'hisɪv/ a. cohesivo.

cohort /'kouhɔrt/ n. cohorte f.

coiffure /kwɑ'fyur/ n. peinado, tocado m.

coil /kɔil/ n. **1.** rollo m.; Naut. adujada f. —v. **2.** enrollar.

coin /kɔin/ n. moneda f.

coinage /'kɔinɪdʒ/ n. sistema monetario m.

coincide /,kouɪn'said/ v. coincidir.

coincidence /kou'ɪnsɪdəns/ n. coincidencia; casualidad f.

coincident /kou'ɪnsɪdənt/ a. coincidente.

coincidental /kou,ɪnsɪ'dɛntḷ/ a. coincidental.

coincidentally /kou,ɪnsɪ'dɛntḷi/ adv. coincidentalmente, al mismo tiempo.

colander /'kɒləndər/ n. colador m.

cold /kould/ a. & n. frío -a; Med. resfriado m. **to be c.,** tener frío; (weather) hacer frío.

coldly /'kouldli/ adv. fríamente.

coldness /'kouldnɪs/ n. frialdad f.

collaborate /kə'læbə,reit/ v. colaborar.

collaboration /kə,læbə'reiʃən/ n. colaboración f.

collaborator /kə'læbə,reitər/ n. colaborador -ra.

collapse /kə'læps/ n. **1.** desplome m.; Med. colapso m. —v. **2.** desplomarse.

collar /'kɒlər/ n. cuello m.

collarbone /'kɒlər,boun/ n. clavícula f.

collate /kou'leit/ v. comparar.

collateral /kə'lætərəl/ a. **1.** colateral. —n. **2.** garantía f.

collation /kou'leiʃən/ n. comparación f.; (food) colación f., merienda f.

colleague /'kɒlig/ n. colega m. & f.

collect /kə'lɛkt/ v. cobrar; recoger; coleccionar.

collection /kə'lɛkʃən/ n. colección f.

collective /kə'lɛktɪv/ a. colectivo.

collectively /kə'lɛktɪvli/ adv. colectivamente, en masa.

collector /kə'lɛktər/ n. colector -ra; coleccionista m. & f.

college /'kɒlɪdʒ/ n. colegio m.; universidad f.

collegiate /kə'lidʒɪt/ n. colegiado m.

collide /kə'laid/ v. chocar.

collision /kə'lɪʒən/ n. choque m.

colloquial /kə'loukwiəl/ a. familiar.

colloquially /kə'loukwiəli/ adv. familiarmente.

colloquy /'kɒləkwi/ n. conversación f., coloquio m.

collusion /kə'luʒən/ n. colusión f., connivencia f.

Cologne /kə'loun/ n. Colonia f.

Colombian /kə'lʌmbiən/ a. & n. colombiano -na.

colon /'koulən/ n. colon m.; Punct. dos puntos.

colonel /'kɜrnḷ/ n. coronel m.

colonial /kə'lounɪəl/ a. colonial.

colonist /'kɒlənɪst/ n. colono -na.

colonization /,kɒlənə'zeiʃən/ n. colonización f.

colonize /'kɒlə,naiz/ v. colonizar.

colony /'kɒləni/ n. colonia f.

color /'kʌlər/ n. **1.** color; colorido m. —v. **2.** colorar; colorir.

coloration /,kʌlə'reiʃən/ n. colorido m.

colored /'kʌlərd/ a. de color.

colorful /'kʌlərfəl/ a. vívido.

colorless /'kʌlərlɪs/ a. descolorido, sin color.

colossal /kə'lɒsəl/ a. colosal.

colt /koult/ n. potro m.

column /'kɒləm/ n. columna f.

coma /'koumə/ n. coma m.

comb /koum/ n. **1.** peine m. —v. **2.** peinar.

combat /n 'kɒmbæt; v kəm'bæt/ n. **1.** combate m. —v. **2.** combatir.

combatant /kəm'bætṇt/ n. combatiente -ta.

combative /kəm'bætɪv/ a. combativo.

combination /,kɒmbə'neiʃən/ n. combinación f.

combine /kəm'bain/ v. combinar.

combustible /kəm'bʌstəbəl/ a. & n. combustible m.

combustion /kəm'bʌstʃən/ n. combustión f.

come /kʌm/ v. venir. **c. back,** volver. **c. in,** entrar. **c. out,** salir. **c. up,** subir. **c. upon,** encontrarse con.

comedian /kə'midiən/ n. cómico -ca.

comedienne /kə,midi'ɛn/ n. cómica f., actriz f.

comedy /'kɒmɪdi/ n. comedia f.

comet /'kɒmɪt/ n. cometa m.

comfort /'kʌmfərt/ n. **1.** confort m.; solaz m. —v. **2.** confortar; solazar.

comfortable /'kʌmftəbəl/ a. cómodo.

comfortably /'kʌmftəbli/ adv. cómodamente.

comforter /'kʌmfərtər/ n. colcha f.

comfortingly /'kʌmfərtɪŋli/ adv. confortantemente.

comfortless /'kʌmfərtlɪs/ a. sin consuelo; sin comodidades.

comic /'kɒmɪk/ **comical** a. cómico.

comic book n. tebeo m.

coming /'kʌmɪŋ/ n. **1.** venida f., llegada f. —a. **2.** próximo, que viene, entrante.

comma /'kɒmə/ n. coma f.

command /kə'mænd/ n. **1.** mando m. —v. **2.** mandar.

commandeer /,kɒmən'dɪər/ v. reclutir forzosamente, expropiar.

commander /kə'mændər/ n. comandante -ta.

commander in chief n. generalísimo, jefe supremo.

commandment /kə'mændmənt/ n. mandato; mandamiento m.

commemorate /kə'mɛmə,reit/ v. conmemorar.

commemoration /kə,mɛmə'reiʃən/ n. conmemoración f.

commemorative /kə'mɛmə,reitɪv/ a. conmemorativo.

commence /kə'mɛns/ v. comenzar, principiar.

commencement /kə'mɛnsmənt/ n. comienzo m.; graduación f.

commend /kə'mɛnd/ v. encomendar; elogiar.

commendable /kə'mɛndəbəl/ a. recomendable.

commendably /kə'mɛndəbli/ adv. loablemente.

commendation /,kɒmən'deiʃən/ n. recomendación f.; elogio m.

commensurate /kə'mɛnsərɪt/ a. proporcionado.

comment /'kɒmɛnt/ n. **1.** comentario m. —v. **2.** comentar.

commentary /'kɒmən,tɛri/ n. comentario m.

commentator /'kɒmən,teitər/ n. comentador -ra.

commerce /'kɒmərs/ n. comercio m.

commercial /kə'mɜrʃəl/ a. comercial.

commercialism /kə'mɜrʃə,lɪzəm/ n. comercialismo m.

commercialize /kə'mɜrʃə,laiz/ v. mercantilizar, explotar.

commercially /kə'mɜrʃəli/ a. & adv. comercialmente.

commiserate /kə'mɪzə,reit/ v. compadecerse.

commissary /'kɒmə,sɛri/ n. comisario m.

commission /kə'mɪʃən/ n. **1.** comisión f. —v. **2.** comisionar.

commissioner /kə'mɪʃənər/ n. comisario -ria.

commit /kə'mɪt/ v. cometer.

commitment /kə'mɪtmənt/ n. compromiso m.

committee /kə'mɪti/ n. comité m.

commodious /kə'moudiəs/ a. cómodo.

commodity /kə'mɒdɪti/ n. mercadería f.

common /'kɒmən/ a. común; ordinario.

commonly /'kɒmənli/ adv. comúnmente, vulgarmente.

Common Market Mercado Común m.

commonplace /'kɒmən,pleis/ a. trivial, banal.

common sense sentido común m.

commonwealth /'kɒmən,wɛlθ/ n. estado m.; nación f.

commotion /kə'mouʃən/ n. tumulto m.

communal /kə'myunl/ a. comunal, público.

commune /'kɒmyun/ n. **1.** distrito municipal m.; comuna f. —v. **2.** conversar.

communicable /kə'myunɪkəbəl/ a. comunicable; Med. transmisible.

communicate /kə'myunɪ,keit/ v. comunicar.

communication /kə,myunɪ'keiʃən/ n. comunicación f.

communicative /kə'myunɪ,keitɪv/ a. comunicativo.

communion /kə'myunyən/ n. comunión f. **take c.,** comulgar.

communiqué /kə,myunɪ'kei/ n. comunicación f.

communism /'kɒmyə,nɪzəm/ n. comunismo m.

communist /'kɒmyənɪst/ n. comunista m. & f.

communistic /ˌkɒmjəˈnɪstɪk/ a. comunístico.

community /kəˈmyuniti/ n. comunidad f.

commutation /ˌkɒmyəˈteɪʃən/ n. conmutación f.

commuter /kəˈmyutər/ n. empleado que viaja diariamente desde su domicilio hasta la ciudad donde trabaja.

compact /a 'kɒmpækt; n 'kɒmpækt/ a. **1.** compacto. —n. **2.** pacto m.; (lady's) polvera f.

compact disk disco compacto m.

companion /kəmˈpænyən/ n. compañero -ra.

companionable /kəmˈpænyənəbəl/ a. sociable.

companionship /kəmˈpænyənˌʃɪp/ n. compañerismo m.

company /ˈkʌmpəni/ n. compañía f.

comparable /ˈkɒmpərəbəl/ a. comparable.

comparative /kəmˈpærətɪv/ a. comparativo.

comparatively /kəmˈpærətɪvli/ a. relativamente.

compare /kəmˈpeər/ v. comparar.

comparison /kəmˈpærəsən/ n. comparación f.

compartment /kəmˈpɑrtmənt/ n. compartimiento m.

compass /ˈkʌmpəs/ n. compás m.; Naut. brújula f.

compassion /kəmˈpæʃən/ n. compasión f.

compassionate /kəmˈpæʃənɪt/ a. compasivo.

compassionately /kəmˈpæʃənɪtli/ adv. compasivamente.

compatible /kəmˈpætəbəl/ a. compatible.

compatriot /kəmˈpeɪtriət/ n. compatriota m. & f.

compel /kəmˈpel/ v. obligar.

compensate /ˈkɒmpənˌseɪt/ v. compensar.

compensation /ˌkɒmpənˈseɪʃən/ n. compensación f.

compensatory /kəmˈpensəˌtɔri/ a. compensatorio.

compete /kəmˈpit/ v. competir.

competence /ˈkɒmpɪtəns/ n. competencia f.

competent /ˈkɒmpɪtənt/ a. competente, capaz.

competently /ˈkɒmpɪtəntli/ adv. competentemente.

competition /ˌkɒmpɪˈtɪʃən/ n. concurrencia f.; concurso m.

competitive /kəmˈpetɪtɪv/ a. competidor.

competitor /kəmˈpetɪtər/ n. competidor -ra.

compile /kəmˈpail/ v. compilar.

complacency /kəmˈpleɪsənsi/ n. complacencia f.

complacent /kəmˈpleɪsənt/ a. complaciente.

complacently /kəmˈpleɪsəntli/ adv. complacientemente.

complain /kəmˈplein/ v. quejarse.

complaint /kəmˈpleint/ n. queja f.

complement /ˈkɒmpləmənt/ n. complemento m.

complete /kəmˈplit/ a. **1.** completo —v. **2.** completar.

completely /kəmˈplitli/ adv. completamente, enteramente.

completeness /kəmˈplitnɪs/ n. integridad f.

completion /kəmˈpliʃən/ n. terminación f.

complex /kəmˈpleks/ a. complejo.

complexion /kəmˈplekʃən/ n. tez f.

complexity /kəmˈpleksɪti/ n. complejidad f.

compliance /kəmˈplaiəns/ n. consentimiento m. **in c. with,** de acuerdo con.

compliant /kəmˈplaiənt/ a. dócil; complaciente.

complicate /ˈkɒmplɪˌkeit/ v. complicar.

complicated /ˈkɒmplɪˌkeitɪd/ a. complicado.

complication /ˌkɒmplɪˈkeiʃən/ n. complicación f.

complicity /kəmˈplɪsɪti/ n. complicidad f.

compliment /n 'kɒmpləmənt; v -ˌment/ n. **1.** elogio m. Fig. —v. **2.** felicitar; echar flores.

complimentary /ˌkɒmpləˈmentəri/ a. galante, obsequioso, regaloso.

comply /kəmˈplai/ v. cumplir.

component /kəmˈpounənt/ a. & n. componente m.

comport /kəmˈpɔrt/ v. portarse.

compose /kəmˈpouz/ v. componer.

composed /kəmˈpouzd/ a. tranquilo; (made up) compuesto.

composer /kəmˈpouzər/ n. compositor -ra.

composite /kəmˈpɒzɪt/ a. compuesto.

composition /ˌkɒmpəˈzɪʃən/ n. composición f.

composure /kəmˈpouʒər/ n. serenidad f.; calma f.

compote /ˈkɒmpout/ n. compota f.

compound /ˈkɒmpaund/ a. & n. compuesto m.

comprehend /ˌkɒmprɪˈhɛnd/ v. comprender.

comprehensible /ˌkɒmprɪˈhɛnsəbəl/ a. comprensible.

comprehension /ˌkɒmprɪˈhɛnʃən/ n. comprensión f.

comprehensive /ˌkɒmprɪˈhɛnsɪv/ a. comprensivo.

compress /n ˈkɒmprɛs; v kəmˈprɛs/ n. 1. cabezal m. —v. 2. comprimir.

compressed /kəmˈprɛst/ a. comprimido.

compression /kəmˈprɛʃən/ n. compresión f.

compressor /kəmˈprɛsər/ n. compresor m.

comprise /kəmˈpraɪz/ v. comprender; abarcar.

compromise /ˈkɒmprəˌmaɪz/ n. 1. compromiso m. —v. 2. comprometer.

compromiser /ˈkɒmprəˌmaɪzər/ n. compromisario m.

compulsion /kəmˈpʌlʃən/ n. compulsión f.

compulsive /kəmˈpʌlsɪv/ a. compulsivo.

compulsory /kəmˈpʌlsəri/ a. obligatorio.

compunction /kəmˈpʌŋkʃən/ n. compunción f.; escrúpulo m.

computation /ˌkɒmpyuˈteɪʃən/ n. computación f.

compute /kəmˈpyut/ v. computar, calcular.

computer /kəmˈpyutər/ n. computadora f., ordenador m.

computerize /kəmˈpyutəˌraɪz/ v. procesar en computadora, computerizar.

computer programmer /ˈprougræmər/ programador -ra de ordenadores.

computer science informática f.

comrade /ˈkɒmræd/ n. camarada m. & f.; compañero -ra.

comradeship /ˈkɒmrædˌʃɪp/ n. camaradería f.

concave /kɒnˈkeɪv/ a. cóncavo.

conceal /kənˈsil/ v. ocultar, esconder.

concealment /kənˈsilmənt/ n. ocultación f.

concede /kənˈsid/ v. conceder.

conceit /kənˈsit/ n. amor propio; engreimiento m.

conceited /kənˈsitɪd/ a. engreído.

conceivable /kənˈsivəbəl/ a. concebible.

conceive /kənˈsiv/ v. concebir.

concentrate /ˈkɒnsənˌtreɪt/ v. concentrar.

concentration /ˌkɒnsənˈtreɪʃən/ n. concentración f.

concentration camp campo de concentración m.

concept /ˈkɒnsɛpt/ n. concepto m.

conception /kənˈsɛpʃən/ n. concepción f.; concepto m.

concern /kənˈsɜrn/ n. 1. interés m.; inquietud f.; Com. negocio m. —v. 2. concernir.

concerning /kənˈsɜrnɪŋ/ prep. respecto a.

concert /ˈkɒnsərt/ n. concierto m.

concerted /kənˈsɜrtɪd/ a. convenido.

concession /kənˈsɛʃən/ n. concesión f.

conciliate /kənˈsɪliˌeɪt/ v. conciliar.

conciliation /kənˌsɪliˈeɪʃən/ n. conciliación f.

conciliator /kənˈsɪliˌeɪtər/ n. conciliador -ra.

conciliatory /kənˈsɪliəˌtɔri/ a. conciliatorio.

concise /kənˈsaɪs/ a. conciso.

concisely /kənˈsaɪsli/ adv. concisamente.

conciseness /kənˈsaɪsnɪs/ n. concisión f.

conclave /ˈkɒnkleɪv/ n. conclave m.

conclude /kənˈklud/ v. concluir.

conclusion /kənˈkluʒən/ n. conclusión f.

conclusive /kənˈklusɪv/ a. conclusivo, decisivo.

conclusively /kənˈklusɪvli/ adv. concluyentemente.

concoct /kɒnˈkɒkt/ v. confeccionar.

concomitant /kɒnˈkɒmɪtənt/ n. & a. concomitante m.

concord /ˈkɒnkɔrd/ n. concordia f.

concordat /kɒnˈkɔrdæt/ n. concordato m.

concourse /ˈkɒnkɔrs/ n. concurso m.; confluencia f.

concrete /ˈkɒnkrit/ a. concreto.

concretely /kɒnˈkritli/ *adv.* concretamente.

concubine /ˈkɒŋkyəˌbain/ *n.* concubina, amiga *f.*

concur /kənˈkər/ *v.* concurrir.

concurrence /kənˈkərəns/ *n.* concurrencia *f.*; casualidad *f.*

concurrent /kənˈkərənt/ *a.* concurrente.

concussion /kənˈkʌʃən/ *n.* concusión *f.*; (c. of the brain) conmoción cerebral *f.*

condemn /kənˈdɛm/ *v.* condenar.

condemnable /kənˈdɛmnəbəl/ *a.* culpable, condenable.

condemnation /ˌkɒndɛmˈneiʃən/ *n.* condenación *f.*

condensation /ˌkɒndɛnˈseiʃən/ *n.* condensación *f.*

condense /kənˈdɛns/ *v.* condensar.

condenser /kənˈdɛnsər/ *n.* condensador *m.*

condescend /ˌkɒndəˈsɛnd/ *v.* condescender.

condescension /ˌkɒndəˈsɛnʃən/ *n.* condescendencia *f.*

condiment /ˈkɒndəmənt/ *n.* condimento *m.*

condition /kənˈdiʃən/ *n.* **1.** condición *f.*; estado *m.* —*v.* **2.** acondicionar.

conditional /kənˈdiʃənl/ *a.* condicional.

conditionally /kənˈdiʃənli/ *adv.* condicionalmente.

condole /kənˈdoul/ *v.* condolerse.

condolence /kənˈdouləns/ *n.* pésame *m.*

condom /ˈkɒndəm/ *n.* forro, preservativo *m.*

condominium /ˌkɒndəˈminiəm/ *n.* condominio *m.*

condone /kənˈdoun/ *v.* condonar.

conducive /kənˈdusiv, -ˈdyu-/ *a.* conducente.

conduct /n ˈkɒndʌkt; v kənˈdʌkt/ *n.* **1.** conducta *f.* —*v.* **2.** conducir.

conductivity /ˌkɒndʌkˈtiviti/ *n.* conductividad *f.*

conductor /kənˈdʌktər/ *n.* conductor *m.*

conduit /ˈkɒnduit/ *n.* caño *m.*, canal *f.*; conducto *m.*

cone /koun/ *n.* cono *m.* **ice-cream c.**, barquillo de helado.

confection /kənˈfɛkʃən/ *n.* confitura *f.*

confectioner /kənˈfɛkʃənər/ *n.* confitero -ra.

confectionery /kənˈfɛkʃəˌnɛri/ *n.* dulcería *f.*

confederacy /kənˈfɛdərəsi/ *n.* federación *f.*

confederate /kənˈfɛdərit/ *a.* & *n.* confederado *m.*

confederation /kənˌfɛdəˈreiʃən/ *n.* confederación *f.*

confer /kənˈfər/ *v.* conferenciar; conferir.

conference /ˈkɒnfərəns/ *n.* conferencia *f.*; congreso *m.*

confess /kənˈfɛs/ *v.* confesar.

confession /kənˈfɛʃən/ *n.* confesión *f.*

confessional /kənˈfɛʃənl/ *n.* confesionario *m.* —*a.* **2.** confesional.

confessor /kənˈfɛsər/ *n.* confesor *m.*

confetti /kənˈfɛti/ *n.* confetti *m.*

confidant /ˈkɒnfiˌdænt/ **confidante** /n. confidente *m.* & *f.*

confide /kənˈfaid/ *v.* confiar.

confidence /ˈkɒnfidəns/ *n.* confianza *f.*

confident /ˈkɒnfidənt/ *a.* confiado; cierto.

confidential /ˌkɒnfiˈdɛnʃəl/ *a.* confidencial.

confidentially /ˌkɒnfiˈdɛnʃəli/ *adv.* confidencialmente, en secreto.

confidently /ˈkɒnfidəntli/ *adv.* confiadamente.

confine /kənˈfain/ *n.* **1.** confín *m.* —*v.* **2.** confinar; encerrar.

confirm /kənˈfərm/ *v.* confirmar.

confirmation /ˌkɒnfərˈmeiʃən/ *n.* confirmación *f.*

confiscate /ˈkɒnfəˌskeit/ *v.* confiscar.

confiscation /ˌkɒnfəˈskeiʃən/ *n.* confiscación *f.*

conflagration /ˌkɒnfləˈgreiʃən/ *n.* incendio *m.*

conflict /n ˈkɒnflikt; v kənˈflikt/ *n.* **1.** conflicto *m.* —*v.* **2.** oponerse; estar en conflicto.

conform /kənˈfɔrm/ *v.* conformar.

conformation /ˌkɒnfɔrˈmeiʃən/ *n.* conformación *f.*

conformer /kənˈfɔrmər/ *n.* conformista *m.* & *f.*

conformist /kənˈfɔrmist/ *n.* conformista *m.* & *f.*

conformity /kənˈfɔrmiti/ *n.* conformidad *f.*

confound /kɒnˈfaund/ *v.* confundir.

confront /kən'frʌnt/ v. confrontar.

confrontation /ˌkɒnfrən'teiʃən/ n. enfrentamiento m.

confuse /kən'fyuz/ v. confundir.

confusion /kən'fyuʒən/ n. confusión f.

congeal /kən'dʒil/ v. congelar, helar.

congealment /kən'dʒilmənt/ n. congelación f.

congenial /kən'dʒinyəl/ a. congenial.

congenital /kən'dʒenɪtl/ a. congénito.

congenitally /kən'dʒenɪtli/ adv. congenitalmente.

congestion /kən'dʒestʃən/ n. congestión f.

conglomerate /v kən'glomə,reit; a, n kən'glomərɪt/ v. **1.** conglomerar. —a. & n. **2.** conglomerado.

conglomeration /kən,glomə'reiʃən/ n. conglomeración f.

congratulate /kən'grætʃə,leit/ v. felicitar.

congratulation /kən,grætʃə'leiʃən/ n. felicitación f.

congratulatory /kən'grætʃələ,tɔri/ a. congratulatorio.

congregate /'koŋgrɪ,geit/ v. congregar.

congregation /,koŋgrɪ'geiʃən/ n. congregación f.

congress /'koŋgrɪs/ n. congreso m.

conic /'konɪk/ n. **1.** cónica f. —a. **2.** cónico.

conjecture /kən'dʒektʃər/ n. **1.** conjetura f. —v. **2.** conjeturar.

conjugal /'kondʒəgəl/ a. conyugal, matrimonial.

conjugate /'kondʒə,geit/ v. conjugar.

conjugation /,kondʒə'geiʃən/ n. conjugación f.

conjunction /kən'dʒʌŋkʃən/ n. conjunción f.

conjunctive /kən'dʒʌŋktɪv/ n. **1.** Gram. conjunción f. —a. **2.** conjuntivo.

conjunctivitis /kən,dʒʌŋktə'vaitɪs/ n. conjuntivitis f.

conjure /'kondʒər/ v. conjurar.

connect /kə'nekt/ v. juntar; relacionar.

connection /kə'nekʃən/ n. conexión f.

connivance /kə'naivəns/ n. consentimiento m.

connive /kə'naiv/ v. disimular.

connoisseur /ˌkonə'sɜr/ n. perito -ta.

connotation /ˌkonə'teiʃən/ n. connotación f.

connote /kə'nout/ v. connotar.

connubial /kə'nubiəl/ a. conyugal.

conquer /'koŋkər/ v. conquistar.

conquerable /'koŋkərəbəl/ a. conquistable, vencible.

conqueror /'koŋkərər/ n. conquistador -ra.

conquest /'konkwest/ n. conquista f.

conscience /'konʃəns/ n. conciencia f.

conscientious /ˌkonʃi'enʃəs/ a. concienzudo.

conscientiously /ˌkonʃi'enʃəsli/ adv. escrupulosamente.

conscientious objector /ɒb'dʒektər/ objetor de conciencia.

conscious /'konʃəs/ a. consciente.

consciously /'konʃəsli/ adv. con conocimiento.

consciousness /'konʃəsnɪs/ n. conciencia f.

conscript /n 'konskrɪpt; v kən'skrɪpt/ n. **1.** conscripto m., recluta m. —v. **2.** reclutar, alistar.

conscription /kən'skrɪpʃən/ n. conscripción f., alistamiento m.

consecrate /ˌkonsɪ,kreit/ v. consagrar.

consecration /,konsɪ'kreiʃən/ n. consagración f.

consecutive /kən'sekyətɪv/ a. consecutivo, seguido.

consecutively /kən'sekyətɪvli/ adv. consecutivamente, de seguida.

consensus /kən'sensəs/ n. consenso m., acuerdo general m.

consent /kən'sent/ n. **1.** consentimiento m. —v. **2.** consentir.

consequence /'konsɪ,kwens/ n. consecuencia f.

consequent /'konsɪ,kwent/ a. consiguiente.

consequential /,konsɪ'kwenʃəl/ a. importante.

consequently /'konsɪ,kwentli/ adv. por lo tanto, por consiguiente.

conservation /,konsər'veiʃən/ n. conservación f.

conservatism /kən'sɜrvə,tizəm/ n. conservatismo m.

conservative /kən'sɜrvətɪv/ a. conservador, conservativo.

conservatory /kən'sərvə,tori/ n.
(plants) invernáculo m.; (school)
conservatorio m.

conserve /kən'sərv/ v. conservar.

consider /kən'sidər/ v. considerar.
C. it done! ¡Dalo por hecho!

considerable /kən'sidərəbəl/ a.
considerable.

considerably /kən'sidərəbli/ adv.
considerablemente.

considerate /kən'sidərit/ a. considerado.

considerately /kən'sidəritli/ adv.
consideradamente.

consideration /kən,sidə'reiʃən/ n.
consideración f.

considering /kən'sidəriŋ/ prep.
visto que, en vista de.

consign /kən'sain/ v. consignar.

consignment /kən'sainmənt/ n.
consignación f., envío m.

consist /kən'sist/ v. consistir.

consistency /kən'sistənsi/ n. consistencia f.

consistent /kən'sistənt/ a. consistente.

consolation /,kɒnsə'leiʃən/ n.
consolación f.

consolation prize premio de consuelo m.

console /kən'soul/ v. consolar.

consolidate /kən'sɒli,deit/ v. consolidar.

consommé /,kɒnsə'mei/ n. caldo
m.

consonant /'kɒnsənənt/ n. consonante f.

consort /n 'kɒnsɔrt, v kən'sɔrt/ n.
1. cónyuge m. & f.; socio. —v. **2.**
asociarse.

conspicuous /kən'spikyuəs/ a.
conspicuo.

conspicuously /kən'spikyuəsli/
adv. visiblemente, llamativa-
mente.

conspicuousness /kən'spik-
yuəsnis/ n. visibilidad f.; evidencia f.; fama f.

conspiracy /kən'spirəsi/ n. conspiración f.; complot m.

conspirator /kən'spirətər/ n.
conspirador -ra.

conspire /kən'spaiər/ v. conspirar.

conspirer /kən'spaiərər/ n. conspi-
rante m. & f.

constancy /'kɒnstənsi/ n. constancia f., lealtad f.

constant /'kɒnstənt/ a. constante.

constantly /'kɒnstəntli/ adv. constantemente, de continuo.

constellation /,kɒnstə'leiʃən/ n.
constelación f.

consternation /,kɒnstər'neiʃən/ n.
consternación f.

constipate /'kɒnstə,peit/ v. estreñir.

constipated /'kɒnstə,peitid/ a. estreñido, m.

constipation /,kɒnstə'peiʃən/ n.
estreñimiento, m.

constituency /kən'stitʃuənsi/ n.
distrito electoral m.

constituent /kən'stitʃuənt/ a. **1.**
constituyente. —n. **2.** elector m.

constitute /'kɒnsti,tut/ v. constituir.

constitution /,kɒnsti'tuʃən/ n.
constitución f.

constitutional /,kɒnsti'tuʃənl/ a.
constitucional.

constrain /kən'strein/ v. constreñir.

constraint /kən'streint/ n. constreñimiento m., compulsión f.

constrict /kən'strikt/ v. apretar,
estrechar.

construct /kən'strʌkt/ v. construir.

construction /kən'strʌkʃən/ n.
construcción f.

constructive /kən'strʌktiv/ a.
constructivo.

constructively /kən'strʌktivli/
adv. constructivamente; por deducción.

constructor /kən'strʌktər/ n.
constructor m.

construe /kən'stru/ v. interpretar.

consul /'kɒnsəl/ n. cónsul m.

consular /'kɒnsələr/ a. consular.

consulate /'kɒnsəlit/ n. consulado
m.

consult /kən'sʌlt/ v. consultar.

consultant /kən'sʌltənt/ n. consultor -ora.

consultation /,kɒnsəl'teiʃən/ n.
consulta f.

consume /kən'sum/ v. consumir.

consumer /kən'sumər/ n. consumidor -ra.

consumer society sociedad de
consumo f.

consummation /,kɒnsə'meiʃən/ n.
consumación f.

consumption /kən'sʌmpʃən/ n.
consumo m.; Med. tisis.

consumptive /kən'sʌmptiv/ n. **1.**
tísico m. —a. **2.** consuntivo.

contact /'kɒntækt/ n. **1.** contacto

m. —*v.* **2.** ponerse en contacto con.

contact lens lentilla *f.*

contagion /kən'teidʒən/ *n.* contagio *m.*

contagious /kən'teidʒəs/ *a.* contagioso.

contain /kən'tein/ *v.* contener.

container /kən'teinər/ *n.* envase *m.*

contaminate /kən'tæmə,neit/ *v.* contaminar.

contemplate /'kɒntəm,pleit/ *v.* contemplar.

contemplation /,kɒntəm'pleiʃən/ *n.* contemplación *f.*

contemplative /kən'templətiv/ *a.* contemplativo.

contemporary /kən'tempə,reri/ *n.* & *a.* contemporáneo -nea.

contempt /kən'tempt/ *n.* desprecio *m.*

contemptible /kən'temptəbəl/ *a.* vil, despreciable.

contemptuous /kən'temptʃuəs/ *a.* desdeñoso.

contemptuously /kən'temptʃuəsli/ *adv.* desdeñosamente.

contend /kən'tend/ *v.* contender; competir.

contender /kən'tendər/ *n.* competidor -ra.

content /*a, v* kən'tent; *n* 'kɒntent/ *a.* **1.** contento. —*n.* **2.** contenido *m.* —*v.* **3.** contentar.

contented /kən'tentid/ *a.* contento.

contention /kən'tenʃən/ *n.* contención *f.*

contentment /kən'tentmənt/ *n.* contentamiento *m.*

contest /*n* 'kɒntest; *v* kən'test/ *n.* **1.** concurso *m.* —*v.* **2.** disputar.

contestable /kən'testəbəl/ *a.* contestable.

context /'kɒntekst/ *n.* contexto *m.*

contiguous /kən'tigyuəs/ *a.* contiguo.

continence /'kɒntn̩əns/ *n.* continencia *f.*, castidad *f.*

continent /'kɒntn̩ənt/ *n.* continente *m.*

continental /,kɒntn̩'entl/ *a.* continental.

contingency /kən'tindʒənsi/ *n.* eventualidad *f.*, casualidad *f.*

contingent /kən'tindʒənt/ *a.* contingente.

continual /kən'tinyuəl/ *a.* continuo.

continuation /kən,tinyu'eiʃən/ *n.* continuación *f.*

continue /kən'tinyu/ *v.* continuar.

continuity /,kɒntn̩'uiti/ *n.* continuidad *f.*

continuous /kən'tinyuəs/ *a.* continuo.

continuously /kən'tinyuəsli/ *adv.* continuamente.

contour /'kɒntur/ *n.* contorno *m.*

contraband /'kɒntrə,bænd/ *n.* contrabando *m.*

contraception /,kɒntrə'sepʃən/ *n.* contracepción *f.*

contraceptive /,kɒntrə'septiv/ *a.* & *n.* anticeptivo *m.*

contract /*n* 'kɒntrækt; *v* kən'trækt/ *n.* **1.** contrato *m.* —*v.* **2.** contraer.

contraction /kən'trækʃən/ *n.* contracción *f.*

contractor /'kɒntræktər/ *n.* contratista *m.* & *f.*

contradict /,kɒntrə'dikt/ *v.* contradecir.

contradiction /,kɒntrə'dikʃən/ *n.* contradicción *f.*

contradictory /,kɒntrə'diktəri/ *a.* contradictorio.

contralto /kən'træltou/ *n.* contralto *m.*

contrary /'kɒntreri/ *a.* & *n.* contrario -ria.

contrast /*n* 'kɒntræst; *v* kən'træst/ *n.* **1.** contraste *m.* —*v.* **2.** contrastar.

contribute /kən'tribyut/ *v.* contribuir.

contribution /,kɒntrə'byuʃən/ *n.* contribución *f.*

contributor /kən'tribyətər/ *n.* contribuidor -ra.

contributory /kən'tribyə,tori/ *a.* contribuyente.

contrite /kən'trait/ *a.* contrito.

contrition /kən'triʃən/ *n.* contrición *f.*

contrivance /kən'traivəns/ *n.* aparato *m.*; estratagema *f.*

contrive /kən'traiv/ *v.* inventar, tramar; darse maña.

control /kən'troul/ *n.* **1.** control *m.* —*v.* **2.** controlar.

controllable /kən'trouləbəl/ *a.* controlable, dominable.

controller /kən'troulər/ *n.* interventor -ra; contralor -ra.

control tower torre de mando *f.*

controversial /ˌkɒntrəˈvərʃəl/ a. contencioso.

controversy /ˈkɒntrəˌvərsi/ n. controversia f.

contusion /kənˈtuʒən/ n. contusión f.

convalesce /ˌkɒnvəˈlɛs/ v. convalecer.

convalescence /ˌkɒnvəˈlɛsəns/ n. convalecencia f.

convalescent /ˌkɒnvəˈlɛsənt/ n. convaleciente m. & f.

convalescent home clínica de reposo f.

convene /kənˈvin/ v. juntarse; convocar.

convenience /kənˈvinyəns/ n. comodidad f.

convenient /kənˈvinyənt/ a. cómodo; oportuno.

conveniently /kənˈvinyəntli/ adv. cómodamente.

convent /ˈkɒnvɛnt/ n. convento m.

convention /kənˈvɛnʃən/ n. convención f.

conventional /kənˈvɛnʃənl/ a. convencional.

conventionally /kənˈvɛnʃənli/ adv. convencionalmente.

converge /kənˈvərdʒ/ v. convergir.

convergence /kənˈvərdʒəns/ n. convergencia f.

convergent /kənˈvərdʒənt/ a. convergente.

conversant /kənˈvərsənt/ a. versado; entendido (de).

conversation /ˌkɒnvərˈseiʃən/ n. conversación, plática f.

conversational /ˌkɒnvərˈseiʃənl/ a. de conversación.

conversationalist /ˌkɒnvərˈseiʃənlɪst/ n. conversador -ra.

converse /kənˈvərs/ v. conversar.

conversely /kənˈvərsli/ adv. a la inversa.

convert /n ˈkɒnvərt; v kənˈvərt/ n. **1.** convertido da. —v. **2.** convertir.

converter /kənˈvərtər/ n. convertidor m.

convertible /kənˈvərtəbəl/ a. convertible.

convex /kɒnˈvɛks/ a. convexo.

convey /kənˈvei/ v. transportar; comunicar.

conveyance /kənˈveiəns/ n. transporte; vehículo m.

conveyor /kənˈveiər/ n. conductor m.; Mech. transportador m.

conveyor belt correa transportadora f.

convict /n ˈkɒnvɪkt; v kənˈvɪkt/ n. **1.** reo m. —v. **2.** declarar culpable.

conviction /kənˈvɪkʃən/ n. convicción f.

convince /kənˈvɪns/ v. convencer.

convincing /kənˈvɪnsɪŋ/ a. convincente.

convivial /kənˈvɪviəl/ a. convival.

convocation /ˌkɒnvəˈkeiʃən/ n. convocación; asamblea f.

convoke /kənˈvouk/ v. convocar, citar.

convoy /ˈkɒnvɔi/ n. convoy m.; escolta f.

convulse /kənˈvʌls/ v. convulsionar; agitar violentamente.

convulsion /kənˈvʌlʃən/ n. convulsión f.

convulsive /kənˈvʌlsɪv/ a. convulsivo.

cook /kuk/ n. **1.** cocinero -ra. —v. **2.** cocinar, cocer.

cookbook /ˈkuk.buk/ n. libro de cocina m.

cookie /ˈkuki/ n. galleta dulce f.

cool /kul/ a. **1.** fresco. —v. **2.** refrescar.

cooler /ˈkulər/ n. enfriadera f.

coolness /ˈkulnɪs/ n. frescura f.

coop /kup/ n. **1.** jaula f. **chicken c.,** gallinero m. —v. **2.** enjaular.

cooperate /kouˈɒpəˌreit/ v. cooperar.

cooperation /kouˌɒpəˈreiʃən/ n. cooperación f.

cooperative /kouˈɒpərətɪv/ a. cooperativo.

cooperatively /kouˈɒpərətɪvli/ adv. cooperativamente.

coordinate /kouˈɔrdnˌeit/ v. coordinar.

coordination /kouˌɔrdnˈeiʃən/ n. coordinación f.

coordinator /kouˈɔrdnˌeitər/ n. coordinador -ra.

cope /koup/ v. contender. **c. with,** superar, hacer frente a.

copier /ˈkɒpiər/ n. copiadora f.

copious /ˈkoupiəs/ a. copioso, abundante.

copiously /ˈkoupiəsli/ adv. copiosamente.

copiousness /ˈkoupiəsnɪs/ n. abundancia f.

copper /ˈkɒpər/ n. cobre m.

copy /'kɒpi/ *n.* **1.** copia *f.*; ejemplar *m.* —*v.* **2.** copiar.

copyist /'kɒpiɪst/ *n.* copista *m. & f.*

copyright /'kɒpi,rait/ *n.* derechos de propiedad literaria *m.pl.*

coquetry /'koukɪtri/ *n.* coquetería *f.*

coquette /kou'kɛt/ *n.* coqueta *f.*

coral /'kɒrəl/ *n.* coral *m.*

cord /kɒrd/ *n.* cuerda *f.*

cordial /'kɒrdʒəl/ *a.* cordial.

cordiality /kɒr'dʒæliti/ *n.* cordialidad *f.*

cordially /'kɒrdʒəli/ *adv.* cordialmente.

cordon off /'kɒrdn 'ɔf/ acordonar.

cordovan /'kɒrdəvən/ *n.* cordobán *m.*

corduroy /'kɒrdə,rɔi/ *n.* pana *f.*

core /kɒr/ *n.* corazón *m.*; centro *m.*

cork /kɒrk/ *n.* corcho *m.*

corkscrew /'kɔrk,skru/ *n.* tirabuzón *m.*

corn /kɒrn/ *n.* maíz *m.*

cornea /'kɒrniə/ *n.* córnea *f.*

corned beef /'kɒrnd/ carne acecinada *f.*

corner /'kɒrnər/ *n.* rincón *m.*; (of street) esquina *f.*

cornet /kɒr'nɛt/ *n.* corneta *f.*

cornetist /kɒr'nɛtɪst/ *n.* cornetín *m.*

cornice /'kɒrnɪs/ *n.* cornisa *f.*

cornstarch /'kɒrn,stɑrtʃ/ *n.* maicena *f.*

corollary /'kɒrə,lɛri/ *n.* corolario *m.*

coronary /'kɒrə,nɛri/ *a.* coronario.

coronation /,kɒrə'neiʃən/ *n.* coronación *f.*

corporal /'kɒrpərəl/ *a.* **1.** corpóreo. —*n.* **2.** cabo *m.*

corporate /'kɒrpərɪt/ *a.* corporativo.

corporation /,kɒrpə'reiʃən/ *n.* corporación *f.*

corps /kɒr/ *n.* cuerpo *m.*

corpse /kɒrps/ *n.* cadáver *m.*

corpulent /'kɒrpyələnt/ *a.* corpulento.

corpuscle /'kɒrpəsəl/ *n.* corpúsculo *m.*

corral /kə'ræl/ *n.* **1.** corral *m.* —*v.* **2.** acorralar.

correct /kə'rɛkt/ *a.* **1.** correcto. —*v.* **2.** corregir.

correction /kə'rɛkʃən/ *n.* corrección; enmienda *f.*

corrective /kə'rɛktɪv/ *n. & a.* correctivo.

correctly /kə'rɛktli/ *adv.* correctamente.

correctness /kə'rɛktnɪs/ *n.* exactitud *f.*

correlate /'kɒrə,leit/ *v.* correlacionar.

correlation /,kɒrə'leiʃən/ *n.* correlación *f.*

correspond /,kɒrə'spɒnd/ *v.* corresponder.

correspondence /,kɒrə'spɒndəns/ *n.* correspondencia *f.*

correspondence course curso por correspondencia *m.*

correspondence school escuela por correspondencia *f.*

correspondent /,kɒrə'spɒndənt/ *a. & n.* correspondiente *m. & f.*

corresponding /,kɒrə'spɒndɪŋ/ *a.* correspondiente.

corridor /'kɒridər/ *n.* corredor, pasillo *m.*

corroborate /kə'rɒbə,reit/ *v.* corroborar.

corroboration /kə,rɒbə'reiʃən/ *n.* corroboración *f.*

corroborative /kə'rɒbə,reitɪv/ *a.* corroborativo.

corrode /kə'roud/ *v.* corroer.

corrosion /kə'rouʒən/ *n.* corrosión *f.*

corrugate /'kɒrə,geit/ *v.* arrugar; ondular.

corrupt /kə'rʌpt/ *a.* **1.** corrompido. —*v.* **2.** corromper.

corruptible /kə'rʌptəbəl/ *a.* corruptible.

corruption /kə'rʌpʃən/ *n.* corrupción *f.*

corruptive /kə'rʌptɪv/ *a.* corruptivo.

corset /'kɒrsɪt/ *n.* corsé *m.*, (girdle) faja *f.*

cortege /kɒr'tɛʒ/ *n.* comitiva *f.*, séquito *m.*

corvette /kɒr'vɛt/ *n.* corbeta *f.*

cosmetic /kɒz'mɛtɪk/ *a. & n.* cosmético *m.*

cosmic /'kɒzmɪk/ *a.* cósmico.

cosmonaut /'kɒzmə,nɔt/ *n.* cosmonauta *m. & f.*

cosmopolitan /,kɒzmə'pɒlitn/ *a. & n.* cosmopolita *m. & f.*

cosmos /'kɒzməs/ *n.* cosmos *m.*

cost /kɒst/ *n.* **1.** coste *m.*; costa *f.* —*v.* **2.** costar.

Costa Rican /'kɒstə'rikən/ *a. & n.* costarricense *m. & f.*

costly /'kɔstli/ *a.* costoso, caro.

costume /ˈkɒstum/ n. traje; disfraz m.

costume jewelry bisutería f., joyas de fantasía f.pl.

cot /kɒt/ n. catre m.

coterie /ˈkoʊtəri/ n. camarilla f.

cotillion /kəˈtɪlyən/ n. cotillón m.

cottage /ˈkɒtɪdʒ/ n. casita f.

cottage cheese requesón m.

cotton /ˈkɒtn/ n. algodón m.

cottonseed /ˈkɒtnˌsid/ n. semilla del algodón f.

couch /kaʊtʃ/ n. sofá m.

cougar /ˈkuɡər/ n. puma m.

cough /kɔf/ n. 1. tos f. —v. 2. toser.

council /ˈkaʊnsəl/ n. consejo, concilio m.

counsel /ˈkaʊnsəl/ n. 1. consejo; (law) abogado -da. —v. 2. aconsejar. **to keep one's c.,** no decir nada.

counselor /ˈkaʊnsələr/ n. consejero -ra; (law) abogado -da.

count /kaʊnt/ n. 1. cuenta f.; (title) conde m. —v. 2. contar.

countenance /ˈkaʊntənəns/ n. 1. aspecto m.; cara f. —v. 2. aprobar.

counter /ˈkaʊntər/ adv. 1. **c. to,** contra, en contra de. —n. 2. mostrador m.

counteract /ˌkaʊntərˈækt/ v. contrarrestar.

counteraction /ˌkaʊntərˈækʃən/ n. neutralización f.

counterbalance /ˈkaʊntərˌbæləns/ n. 1. contrapeso m. —v. 2. contrapesar.

counterfeit /ˈkaʊntərˌfɪt/ a. 1. falsificado. —v. 2. falsear.

countermand /ˌkaʊntərˈmænd/ v. contramandar.

counteroffensive /ˌkaʊntərəˈfɛnsɪv/ n. contraofensiva f.

counterpart /ˈkaʊntərˌpɑrt/ n. contraparte f.

counterproductive /ˌkaʊntərprəˈdʌktɪv/ a. contraproducente.

countess /ˈkaʊntɪs/ n. condesa f.

countless /ˈkaʊntlɪs/ a. innumerable.

country /ˈkʌntri/ n. campo m.; Pol. país m.; (homeland) patria f.

country code distintivo del país m.

countryman /ˈkʌntrimən/ n. paisano m. **fellow c.,** compatriota m.

countryside /ˈkʌntriˌsaɪd/ n. campo, paisaje m.

county /ˈkaʊnti/ n. condado m.

coupé /kup/ n. cupé m.

couple /ˈkʌpəl/ n. 1. par m. —v. 2. unir.

coupon /ˈkupɒn/ n. cupón, talón m.

courage /ˈkɜrɪdʒ/ n. valor m.

courageous /kəˈreɪdʒəs/ a. valiente.

course /kɔrs/ n. curso m. **of c.,** por supuesto, desde luego.

court /kɔrt/ n. 1. corte f.; cortejo m.; (of law) tribunal m. —v. 2. cortejar.

courteous /ˈkɜrtiəs/ a. cortés.

courtesy /ˈkɜrtəsi/ n. cortesía f.

courthouse /ˈkɔrtˌhaʊs/ n. palacio de justicia m., tribunal m.

courtier /ˈkɔrtiər/ n. cortesano m.

courtly /ˈkɔrtli/ a. cortés, galante.

courtroom /ˈkɔrtˌrum, -ˌrʊm/ n. sala de justicia f.

courtship /ˈkɔrtʃɪp/ n. cortejo m.

courtyard /ˈkɔrtˌyɑrd/ n. patio m.

cousin /ˈkʌzən/ n. primo -ma.

covenant /ˈkʌvənənt/ n. contrato, convenio m.

cover /ˈkʌvər/ n. 1. cubierta, tapa f. —v. 2. cubrir, tapar.

cover charge precio del cubierto m.

covet /ˈkʌvɪt/ v. ambicionar, suspirar por.

covetous /ˈkʌvɪtəs/ a. codicioso, avaro.

cow /kaʊ/ n. vaca f.

coward /ˈkaʊərd/ n. cobarde m. & f.

cowardice /ˈkaʊərdɪs/ n. cobardía f.

cowardly /ˈkaʊərdli/ a. cobarde.

cowboy /ˈkaʊˌbɔɪ/ n. vaquero, gaucho m.

cower /ˈkaʊər/ v. agacharse (de miedo).

cowhide /ˈkaʊˌhaɪd/ n. cuero m.

coy /kɔɪ/ a. recatado, modesto.

coyote /kaɪˈoʊti/ n. coyote m.

cozy /ˈkoʊzi/ a. cómodo y agradable.

crab /kræb/ n. cangrejo m.

crab apple n. manzana silvestre f.

crack /kræk/ n. 1. hendedura f.; (noise) crujido m. —v. 2. hender; crujir.

cracker /ˈkrækər/ n. galleta f.

cradle /ˈkreɪdl/ n. cuna f.

craft /kræft/ n. arte m.

craftsman /ˈkræftsmən/ n. artesano -na.

craftsmanship /ˈkræftsmənˌʃip/ n. artesanía f.

crafty /ˈkræfti/ a. ladino.

crag /kræg/ n. despeñadero m.; peña f.

cram /kræm/ v. rellenar, hartar.

cramp /kræmp/ n. calambre m.

cranberry /ˈkrænˌberi/ n. arándano m.

crane /krein/ n. (bird) grulla f.; Mech. grúa f.

cranium /ˈkreiniəm/ n. cráneo m.

crank /kræŋk/ n. Mech. manivela f.

cranky /ˈkræŋki/ a. chiflado, caprichoso.

crash /kræʃ/ n. **1.** choque; estallido m. —v. **2.** estallar.

crate /kreit/ n. canasto m.

crater /ˈkreitər/ n. cráter m.

crave /kreiv/ v. desear; anhelar.

craven /ˈkreivən/ a. cobarde.

craving /ˈkreiviŋ/ n. sed m., anhelo m.

crawl /krɔl/ v. andar a gatas, arrastrarse.

crayon /ˈkreiən/ n. creyón; lápiz m.

crazy /ˈkreizi/ a. loco.

creak /krik/ v. crujir.

creaky /ˈkriki/ a. crujiente.

cream /krim/ n. crema f.

cream cheese queso crema m.

creamery /ˈkriməri/ n. lechería f.

creamy /ˈkrimi/ a. cremoso.

crease /kris/ n. **1.** pliegue m. —v. **2.** plegar.

create /kriˈeit/ v. crear.

creation /kriˈeiʃən/ n. creación f.

creative /kriˈeitiv/ a. creativo, creador.

creator /kriˈeitər/ n. creador -ra.

creature /ˈkritʃər/ n. criatura f.

credence /ˈkridns/ n. creencia f.

credentials /krɪˈdɛnʃəlz/ n. credenciales f.pl.

credibility /ˌkrɛdəˈbɪlɪti/ n. credibilidad f.

credible /ˈkrɛdəbəl/ a. creíble.

credit /ˈkrɛdɪt/ n. **1.** crédito m. **on c.,** al fiado. —v. **2.** Com. abonar.

creditable /ˈkrɛdɪtəbəl/ a. fidedigno.

credit balance saldo acreedor m.

credit card n. tarjeta de crédito f.

creditor /ˈkrɛdɪtər/ n. acreedor -ra.

credit union banco cooperativo m.

credo /ˈkridou/ n. credo m.

credulity /krəˈdulɪti/ n. credulidad f.

credulous /ˈkrɛdʒələs/ a. crédulo.

creed /krid/ n. credo m.

creek /krik/ n. riachuelo m.

creep /krip/ v. gatear.

cremate /ˈkrimeit/ v. incinerar.

crematory /ˈkriməˌtɔri/ n. crematorio m.

creosote /ˈkriəˌsout/ n. creosota f.

crepe /kreip/ n. crespón f.

crepe paper papel crespón m.

crescent /ˈkrɛsnt/ a. & n. creciente f.

crest /krɛst/ n. cresta; cima f.; (heraldry) timbre m.

cretonne /ˈkrɪtɒn/ n. cretona f.

crevice /ˈkrɛvɪs/ n. grieta f.

crew /kru/ n. tripulación f.

crew member tripulante m. & f.

crib /krɪb/ n. pesebre m.; cuna f.

cricket /ˈkrɪkɪt/ n. grillo m.

crime /kraim/ n. crimen m.

criminal /ˈkrɪmənl/ a. & n. criminal m. & f.

criminologist /ˌkrɪməˈnɒlədʒɪst/ n. criminólogo -ga, criminalista m. & f.

criminology /ˌkrɪməˈnɒlədʒi/ n. criminología f.

crimson /ˈkrɪmzən, -sən/ a. & n. carmesí m.

cringe /krɪndʒ/ v. encogerse, temblar.

cripple /ˈkrɪpəl/ n. **1.** lisiado -da. —v. **2.** estropear, lisiar.

crisis /ˈkraisɪs/ n. crisis f.

crisp /krɪsp/ a. crespo, fresco.

crispness /ˈkrɪspnɪs/ n. encrespadura f.

crisscross /ˈkrɪsˌkrɔs/ a. entrelazado f.

criterion /kraiˈtɪəriən/ n. criterio m.

critic /ˈkrɪtɪk/ n. crítico -ca.

critical /ˈkrɪtɪkəl/ a. crítico.

criticism /ˈkrɪtəˌsɪzəm/ n. crítica; censura f.

criticize /ˈkrɪtəˌsaiz/ v. criticar; censurar.

critique /krɪˈtik/ n. crítica f.

croak /krouk/ n. **1.** graznido m. —v. **2.** graznar.

crochet /krouˈʃei/ n. **1.** crochet m. —v. **2.** hacer crochet.

crochet work ganchillo m.

crock /krɒk/ n. cazuela f.; olla de barro.

crockery /ˈkrɒkəri/ n. loza f.

crocodile /'krɒkə,dail/ n. cocodrilo m.

crony /'krouni/ n. compinche m.

crooked /'krʊkɪd/ a. encorvado; deshonesto.

croon /krun/ v. canturrear.

crop /krɒp/ n. cosecha f.

croquet /krou'kei/ n. juego de croquet m.

croquette /krou'kɛt/ n. croqueta f.

cross /krɔs/ a. **1.** enojado, mal humorado. —n. **2.** cruz f. —v. **3.** cruzar, atravesar.

crossbreed /'krɔs,brid/ n. **1.** mestizo m. —a. **2.** cruzar (animales o plantas).

cross-examine /'krɔs ɪg,zæmɪn/ v. interrogar.

cross-eyed /'krɔs ,aid/ a. bizco.

cross-fertilization /'krɔs ,fɜrtlə-'zeiʃən/ n. alogamia f.

crossing /'krɔsɪŋ/ n. cruce m.

crossroads /'krɔs,roudz/ n. cruce m.

cross section corte transversal m.

crosswalk /'krɔs,wɔk/ n. paso cebra m.

crossword puzzle /'krɔs ,wɜrd/ crucigrama m.

crotch /krɒtʃ/ n. bifurcación f.; Anat. bragadura f.

crouch /krautʃ/ v. agacharse.

croup /krup/ n. Med. crup m.

croupier /'krupiər/ n. crupié m. & f.

crow /krou/ n. cuervo m.

crowd /kraud/ n. **1.** muchedumbre f.; tropel m. —v. **2.** apretar.

crowded /'kraudɪd/ a. lleno de gente.

crown /kraun/ n. **1.** corona f. —v. **2.** coronar.

crown prince príncipe heredero m.

crucial /'kruʃəl/ a. crucial.

crucible /'krusəbəl/ n. crisol m.

crucifix /'krusəfiks/ n. crucifijo m.

crucifixion /,krusə'fikʃən/ n. crucifixión f.

crucify /'krusə,fai/ v. crucificar.

crude /krud/ a. crudo; (oil) bruto.

crudeness /'krudnɪs/ a. crudeza f.

cruel /'kruəl/ a. cruel.

cruelty /'kruəlti/ n. crueldad f.

cruet /'kruɪt/ n. vinagrera f.

cruise /kruz/ v. **1.** viaje por mar. —v. **2.** navegar.

cruiser /'kruzər/ n. crucero m.

crumb /krʌm/ n. miga; migaja f.

crumble /'krʌmbəl/ v. desmigajar; desmoronar.

crumple /'krʌmpəl/ v. arrugar; encogerse.

crusade /kru'seid/ n. cruzada f.

crusader /kru'seidər/ n. cruzado m.

crush /krʌʃ/ v. aplastar.

crust /krʌst/ n. costra; corteza f.

crustacean /krʌ'steiʃən/ n. crustáceo m.

crutch /krʌtʃ/ n. muleta f.

cry /krai/ n. **1.** grito m. —v. **2.** gritar; (weep) llorar.

cryosurgery /,kraiou'sɜrdʒəri/ n. criocirugía f.

crypt /krɪpt/ n. gruta f., cripta f.

cryptic /'krɪptɪk/ a. secreto.

cryptography /krɪp'tɒgrəfi/ n. criptografía f.

crystal /'krɪstl/ n. cristal m.

crystalline /'krɪstlɪn/ a. cristalino, transparente.

crystallize /'krɪstl,aiz/ v. cristalizar.

cub /kʌb/ n. cachorro m.

Cuban /'kyubən/ n. & a. cubano -na.

cube /kyub/ n. cubo m.

cubic /'kyubɪk/ a. cúbico.

cubicle /'kyubɪkəl/ n. cubículo m.

cubic measure medida de capacidad f.

cubism /'kyubɪzəm/ n. cubismo m.

cuckoo /'kuku/ n. cuco m.

cucumber /'kyukʌmbər/ n. pepino m.

cuddle /'kʌdl/ v. abrazar.

cudgel /'kʌdʒəl/ n. palo m.

cue /kyu/ n. apunte m.; (billiards) taco m.

cuff /kʌf/ n. puño de camisa. **c. links,** gemelos.

cuisine /kwɪ'zin/ n. arte culinario m.

culinary /'kyulə,neri/ a. culinario.

culminate /'kʌlmə,neit/ v. culminar.

culmination /,kʌlmə'neiʃən/ n. culminación f.

culpable /'kʌlpəbəl/ a. culpable.

culprit /'kʌlprɪt/ n. criminal; delincuente m. & f.

cult /kʌlt/ n. culto m.

cultivate /'kʌltə,veit/ v. cultivar.

cultivated /'kʌltə,veitɪd/ a. cultivado.

cultivation /,kʌltə'veiʃən/ n. cultivo m.; cultivación f.

cultivator /'kʌltə,veitər/ n. cultivador -ra.

cultural /'kʌltʃərəl/ a. cultural.

culture /ˈkʌltʃər/ n. cultura f.

cultured /ˈkʌltʃərd/ a. culto.

cumbersome /ˈkʌmbərsəm/ a. pesado, incómodo.

cumulative /ˈkyumyəlϑtɪv/ a. acumulativo.

cunning /ˈkʌnɪŋ/ a. **1.** astuto. —n. **2.** astucia f.

cup /kʌp/ n. taza, jícara f.

cupboard /ˈkʌbərd/ n. armario, aparador m.

cupidity /kyuˈpɪdɪti/ n. avaricia f.

curable /ˈkyurəbəl/ a. curable.

curator /kyuˈreitər/ n. guardián -ana.

curb /kərb/ n. **1.** freno m. —v. **2.** refrenar.

curd /kərd/ n. cuajada f.

curdle /ˈkərdl/ v. cuajarse, coagularse.

cure /kyur/ n. **1.** remedio m. —v. **2.** curar, sanar.

curfew /ˈkərfyu/ n. toque de queda m.

curio /ˈkyuri,ou/ n. objeto curioso.

curiosity /ˌkyuriˈɒsɪti/ n. curiosidad f.

curious /ˈkyuriəs/ a. curioso.

curl /kərl/ n. **1.** rizo m. —v. **2.** rizar.

curly /ˈkərli/ a. rizado.

currant /ˈkərənt/ n. grosella f.

currency /ˈkərənsi/ n. circulación f.; dinero m.

current /ˈkərənt/ a. & n. corriente f.

current events /ɪˈvɛnts/ actualidades f.pl.

currently /ˈkərəntli/ adv. corrientemente.

curriculum /kəˈrɪkyələm/ n. plan de estudio m.

curse /kərs/ n. **1.** maldición f. —v. **2.** maldecir.

cursor /ˈkərsər/ n. cursor m.

cursory /ˈkərsəri/ a. sumario.

curt /kərt/ a. brusco.

curtail /kərˈteil/ v. reducir; restringir.

curtain /ˈkərtn/ n. cortina f.; Theat. telón m.

curtsy /ˈkərtsi/ n. **1.** reverencia f. —v. **2.** hacer una reverencia.

curvature /ˈkərvətʃər/ n. curvatura f.

curve /kərv/ n. **1.** curva f. —v. **2.** encorvar.

cushion /ˈkuʃən/ n. cojín m.; almohada f.

cuspidor /ˈkʌspɪˌdor/ n. escupidera f.

custard /ˈkʌstərd/ n. flan m.; natillas f.pl.

custodian /kʌˈstoudiən/ n. custodio m.

custody /ˈkʌstədi/ n. custodia f.

custom /ˈkʌstəm/ n. costumbre f.

customary /ˈkʌstəˌmɛri/ a. acostumbrado, usual.

customer /ˈkʌstəmər/ n. cliente m. & f.

customhouse /ˈkʌstəmˌhaus/ **customs** n. aduana f.

customs duty /ˈkʌstəmz/ derechos de aduana m.pl.

customs officer /ˈkʌstəmz/ agente de aduana m. & f.

cut /kʌt/ n. **1.** corte m.; cortada f., tajada f.; (printing) grabado m. —v. **2.** cortar; tajar.

cute /kyut/ a. mono, lindo.

cut glass cristal tallado m.

cuticle /ˈkyutɪkəl/ n. cutícula f.

cutlery /ˈkʌtləri/ n. cuchillería f.

cutlet /ˈkʌtlɪt/ n. chuleta f.

cutter /ˈkʌtər/ n. cortador -ra; Naut. cúter m.

cutthroat /ˈkʌtˌθrout/ n. asesino -na.

cyberpunk /ˈsaibər,pʌŋk/ n. ciberpunk m. & f.

cyberspace /ˈsaibər,speis/ n. ciberespacio m.

cyclamate /ˈsaiklə,meit, ˈsɪklə-/ n. ciclamato m.

cycle /ˈsaikəl/ n. ciclo m.

cyclist /ˈsaiklɪst/ n. ciclista m. & f.

cyclone /ˈsaikloun/ n. ciclón m., huracán m.

cyclotron /ˈsaiklə,tron, ˈsɪklə-/ n. ciclotrón m.

cylinder /ˈsɪlɪndər/ n. cilindro m.

cylindrical /sɪˈlɪndrɪkəl/ a. cilíndrico.

cymbal /ˈsɪmbəl/ n. címbalo m.

cynic /ˈsɪnɪk/ n. cínico -ca.

cynical /ˈsɪnɪkəl/ a. cínico.

cynicism /ˈsɪnə,sɪzəm/ n. cinismo m.

cypress /ˈsaiprəs/ n. ciprés m. **c. nut,** piñuela f.

cyst /sɪst/ n. quiste m.

D

dad /dæd/ *n.* papá *m.*, papito *m.*

daffodil /'dæfədɪl/ *n.* narciso *m.*

dagger /'dægər/ *n.* puñal *m.*

dahlia /'dælyə/ *n.* dalia *f.*

daily /'deɪli/ *a.* diario, cotidiano.

daintiness /'deɪntɪnɪs/ *n.* delicadeza *f.*

dainty /'deɪnti/ *a.* delicado.

dairy /'dɛəri/ *n.* lechería, quesería *f.*

dais /'deɪɪs/ *n.* tablado *m.*

daisy /'deɪzi/ *n.* margarita *f.*

dale /deɪl/ *n.* valle *m.*

dally /'dæli/ *v.* holgar; perder el tiempo.

dam /dæm/ *n.* presa *f.*; dique *m.*

damage /'dæmɪdʒ/ *n.* **1.** daño *m.* —*v.* **2.** dañar.

damask /'dæməsk/ *n.* damasco *m.*

damn /dæm/ *v.* condenar.

damnation /dæm'neɪʃən/ *n.* condenación *f.*

damp /dæmp/ *a.* húmedo.

dampen /'dæmpən/ *v.* humedecer.

dampness /'dæmpnɪs/ *n.* humedad *f.*

damsel /'dæmzəl/ *n.* doncella *f.*

dance /dæns/ *n.* **1.** baile *m.*; danza *f.* —*v.* **2.** bailar.

dance hall salón de baile *m.*

dancer /'dænsər/ *n.* bailador -ra; (professional) bailarín -na.

dancing /'dænsɪŋ/ *n.* baile *m.*

dandelion /'dændl,aɪən/ *n.* amargón *m.*

dandruff /'dændrəf/ *n.* caspa *f.*

dandy /'dændi/ *n.* petimetre *m.*

danger /'deɪndʒər/ *n.* peligro *m.*

dangerous /'deɪndʒərəs/ *a.* peligroso.

dangle /'dæŋgəl/ *v.* colgar.

Danish /'deɪnɪʃ/ *a.* danés -sa; dinamarqués -sa.

dapper /'dæpər/ *a.* gallardo.

dare /dɛər/ *v.* atreverse, osar.

daredevil /'dɛər,dɛvəl/ *n.* atrevido *m.*, -da *f.*

daring /'dɛərɪŋ/ *a.* **1.** atrevido. —*n.* **2.** osadía *f.*

dark /dɑrk/ *a.* **1.** obscuro; moreno. —*n.* **2.** obscuridad *f.*

darken /'dɑrkən/ *v.* obscurecer.

darkness /'dɑrknɪs/ *n.* obscuridad *f.*

darkroom /'dɑrk,rum, -,rʊm/ *n.* cámara obscura *f.*

darling /'dɑrlɪŋ/ *a.* & *n.* querido -da, amado -da.

darn /dɑrn/ *v.* zurcir.

darning needle /'dɑrnɪŋ/ aguja de zurcir *f.*

dart /dɑrt/ *n.* dardo *m.*

dartboard /'dɑrt,bɔrd/ *n.* diana *f.*

dash /dæʃ/ *n.* arranque *m.*; *Punct.* guión *m.*

data /'deɪtə/ *n.* datos *m.*

database /'deɪtəbeɪs/ *n.* base de datos *m.*

data processing /'prɒsɛsɪŋ/ proceso de datos *m.*

date /deɪt/ *n.* fecha *f.*; (engagement) cita *f.*; (fruit) dátil *m.*

daughter /'dɔtər/ *n.* hija *f.*

daughter-in-law /'dɔ,tər ɪn lɔ/ *n.* nuera *f.*

daunt /dɔnt, dɑnt/ *v.* intimidar.

dauntless /'dɔntlɪs/ *a.* intrépido.

davenport /'dævən,pɔrt/ *n.* sofá *m.*

dawn /dɔn/ *n.* **1.** alba, madrugada *f.* —*v.* **2.** amanecer.

day /deɪ/ *n.* día *m.* **good d.,** buenos días.

daybreak /'deɪ,breɪk/ *n.* alba, madrugada *f.*

daydream /'deɪ,drim/ *n.* fantasía *f.*

daylight /'deɪ,laɪt/ *n.* luz del día.

daze /deɪz/ *v.* aturdir.

dazzle /'dæzəl/ *v.* deslumbrar.

deacon /'dikən/ *n.* diácono *m.*

dead /dɛd/ *a.* muerto.

deaden /'dɛdn/ *v.* amortecer.

dead end atolladero *m.* (impasse); callejón sin salida *m.* (street).

deadline /'dɛd,laɪn/ *n.* fecha límite *f.*

deadlock /'dɛd,lɒk/ *n.* paro *m.*

deadly /'dɛdli/ *a.* mortal.

deaf /dɛf/ *a.* sordo.

deafen /'dɛfən/ *v.* ensordecer.

deafening /'dɛfənɪŋ/ *a.* ensordecedor.

deaf-mute /dɛf 'myut/ *n.* sordomudo *m.*

deafness /'dɛfnɪs/ *n.* sordera *f.*

deal /dil/ *n.* **1.** trato *m.*; negociación *f.* **a great d., a good d.,** mucho. —*v.* **2.** tratar; negociar.

dealer /'dilər/ *n.* comerciante *m.*, (at cards) tallador -ra.

dean /din/ *n.* decano -na.

dear /dɪər/ a. querido; caro.

dearth /dɜrθ/ n. escasez f.

death /dɛθ/ n. muerte f.

death certificate partida de defunción f.

deathless /'dɛθlɪs/ a. inmortal.

debacle /də'bakəl/ n. desastre m.

debase /dɪ'beɪs/ v. degradar.

debatable /dɪ'beɪtəbəl/ a. discutible.

debate /dɪ'beɪt/ n. **1.** debate m. —v. **2.** disputar, deliberar.

debauch /dɪ'bɔtʃ/ v. corromper.

debilitate /dɪ'bɪlɪˌteɪt/ v. debilitar.

debit /'dɛbɪt/ n. débito m.

debit balance saldo deudor m.

debonair /ˌdɛbə'nɛər/ a. cortés; alegre, vivo.

debris /deɪ'bri/ n. escombros m.pl.

debt /dɛt/ n. deuda f. **get into d.** endeudarse.

debtor /'dɛtər/ n. deudor -ra.

debug /di'bʌg/ v. depurar, limpiar.

debunk /dɪ'bʌŋk/ v. desacreditar; desenmascarar.

debut /deɪ'byu/ n. debut, estreno m.

debutante /ˌdɛbyuˌtɑnt/ n. debutante f.

decade /'dɛkeɪd/ n. década f.

decadence /'dɛkədəns/ n. decadencia f.

decadent /'dɛkədənt/ a. decadente.

decaffeinated /di'kæfɪˌneɪtɪd/ a. descafeinado.

decalcomania /dɪˌkælkə'meɪniə/ n. calcomanía f.

decanter /dɪ'kæntər/ n. garrafa f.

decapitate /dɪ'kæpɪˌteɪt/ v. descabezar.

decay /dɪ'keɪ/ n. **1.** descaecimiento m.; (dental) caries f. —v. **2.** decaer; (dental) cariarse.

deceased /dɪ'sist/ a. muerto, difunto.

deceit /dɪ'sit/ n. engaño m.

deceitful /dɪ'sitfəl/ a. engañoso.

deceive /dɪ'siv/ v. engañar.

December /dɪ'sɛmbər/ n. diciembre m.

decency /'disənsi/ n. decencia f.; decoro m.

decent /'disənt/ a. decente.

decentralize /di'sɛntrəˌlaɪz/ v. descentralizar.

deception /dɪ'sɛpʃən/ n. decepción f.

deceptive /dɪ'sɛptɪv/ a. deceptivo.

decibel /'dɛsəˌbɛl/ n. decibelio m.

decide /dɪ'saɪd/ v. decidir.

decimal /'dɛsəməl/ a. decimal.

decipher /dɪ'saɪfər/ v. descifrar.

decision /dɪ'sɪʒən/ n. decisión f.

decisive /dɪ'saɪsɪv/ a. decisivo.

deck /dɛk/ n. cubierta f.

deck chair tumbona f.

declamation /ˌdɛklə'meɪʃən/ n. declamación f.

declaration /ˌdɛklə'reɪʃən/ n. declaración f.

declarative /dɪ'klærətɪv/ a. declarativo.

declare /dɪ'klɛər/ v. declarar.

declension /dɪ'klɛnʃən/ n. declinación f.

decline /dɪ'klaɪn/ n. **1.** decadencia f. —v. **2.** decaer; negarse; Gram. declinar.

decompose /ˌdikəm'pouz/ v. descomponer.

decongestant /ˌdikən'dʒɛstənt/ n. descongestionante m.

decorate /'dɛkəˌreɪt/ v. decorar, adornar.

decoration /ˌdɛkə'reɪʃən/ n. decoración f.

decorative /'dɛkərətɪv/ a. decorativo.

decorator /'dɛkəˌreɪtər/ n. decorador -ra.

decorous /'dɛkərəs/ a. correcto.

decorum /dɪ'kɔrəm/ n. decoro m.

decrease /dɪ'kris/ v. disminuir.

decree /dɪ'kri/ n. decreto m.

decrepit /dɪ'krɛpɪt/ a. decrépito.

decry /dɪ'kraɪ/ v. desacreditar.

dedicate /'dɛdɪˌkeɪt/ v. dedicar; consagrar.

dedication /ˌdɛdɪ'keɪʃən/ n. dedicación; dedicatoria f.

deduce /dɪ'dus/ v. deducir.

deduction /dɪ'dʌkʃən/ n. rebaja; deducción f.

deductive /dɪ'dʌktɪv/ a. deductivo.

deed /did/ n. acción; hazaña f.

deem /dim/ v. estimar.

deep /dip/ a. hondo, profundo.

deepen /'dipən/ v. profundizar, ahondar.

deep freeze congelación m.

deeply /'dipli/ adv. profundamente.

deer /dɪər/ n. venado, ciervo m.

deface /dɪ'feɪs/ v. mutilar.

defamation /ˌdɛfə'meɪʃən/ n. calumnia f.

defame /dɪ'feɪm/ v. difamar.

demolish

default /dɪ'fɔlt/ n. **1.** defecto m.
—v. **2.** faltar.

defeat /dɪ'fit/ n. **1.** derrota f. —v.
2. derrotar.

defeatism /dɪ'fitɪzəm/ n. derrotismo m.

defect /'difɛkt, dɪ'fɛkt/ n. defecto m.

defective /dɪ'fɛktɪv/ a. defectivo.

defend /dɪ'fɛnd/ v. defender.

defendant /dɪ'fɛndənt/ n. acusado -da.

defender /dɪ'fɛndər/ n. defensor -ra.

defense /dɪ'fɛns/ n. defensa f.

defensive /dɪ'fɛnsɪv/ a. defensivo.

defer /dɪ'fɜr/ v. aplazar; deferir.

deference /'dɛfərəns/ n. deferencia f.

defiance /dɪ'faɪəns/ n. desafío m.

defiant /dɪ'faɪənt/ a. desafiador.

deficiency /dɪ'fɪʃənsi/ n. defecto m.

deficient /dɪ'fɪʃənt/ a. deficiente.

deficit /'dɛfəsɪt/ n. déficit, descubierto m.

defile /dɪ'faɪl/ n. **1.** desfiladero m. —v. **2.** profanar.

define /dɪ'faɪn/ v. definir.

definite /'dɛfənɪt/ a. exacto; definitivo.

definitely /'dɛfənɪtli/ adv. definitivamente.

definition /,dɛfə'nɪʃən/ n. definición f.

definitive /dɪ'fɪnɪtɪv/ a. definitivo.

deflation /dɪ'fleɪʃən/ n. desinflación f.

deflect /dɪ'flɛkt/ v. desviar.

deform /dɪ'fɔrm/ v. deformar.

deformity /dɪ'fɔrmɪti/ n. deformidad f.

defraud /dɪ'frɔd/ v. defraudar.

defray /dɪ'freɪ/ v. costear.

defrost /dɪ'frɔst/ v. descongelar.

deft /dɛft/ a. diestro.

defy /dɪ'faɪ/ v. desafiar.

degenerate /a dɪ'dʒɛnərɪt; v -,reɪt/ a. **1.** degenerado. —v. **2.** degenerar.

degeneration /dɪ,dʒɛnə'reɪʃən/ n. degeneración f.

degradation /,dɛgrɪ'deɪʃən/ n. degradación f.

degrade /dɪ'greɪd/ v. degradar.

degree /dɪ'gri/ n. grado m.

deign /deɪn/ v. condescender.

deity /'diɪti/ n. deidad f.

dejected /dɪ'dʒɛktɪd/ a. abatido.

dejection /dɪ'dʒɛkʃən/ n. tristeza f.

delay /dɪ'leɪ/ n. **1.** retardo m., demora f. —v. **2.** tardar, demorar.

delegate /n 'dɛlɪgɪt; v -,geɪt/ n. **1.** delegado -da. —v. **2.** delegar.

delegation /,dɛlɪ'geɪʃən/ n. delegación f.

delete /dɪ'lit/ v. suprimir, tachar.

deliberate /a dɪ'lɪbərɪt; v -ə,reɪt/ a. **1.** premeditado. —v. **2.** deliberar.

deliberately /dɪ'lɪbərɪtli/ adv. deliberadamente.

deliberation /dɪ,lɪbə'reɪʃən/ n. deliberación f.

deliberative /dɪ'lɪbərətɪv/ a. deliberativo.

delicacy /'dɛlɪkəsi/ n. delicadeza f.

delicate /'dɛlɪkɪt/ a. delicado.

delicious /dɪ'lɪʃəs/ a. delicioso.

delight /dɪ'laɪt/ n. deleite m.

delightful /dɪ'laɪtfəl/ a. deleitoso.

delinquency /dɪ'lɪŋkwənsi/ a. delincuencia f.

delinquent /dɪ'lɪŋkwənt/ a. & n. delincuente. m. & f.

delirious /dɪ'lɪriəs/ a. delirante.

deliver /dɪ'lɪvər/ v. entregar.

deliverance /dɪ'lɪvərəns/ n. liberación; salvación f.

delivery /dɪ'lɪvəri/ n. entrega f.; Med. parto m.

delude /dɪ'lud/ v. engañar.

deluge /'dɛlyudʒ/ n. inundación f.

delusion /dɪ'luʒən/ n. decepción f.; engaño m.

delve /dɛlv/ v. cavar, sondear.

demagogue /'dɛmə,gɒg/ n. demagogo -ga.

demand /dɪ'mænd/ n. **1.** demanda f. —v. **2.** demandar; exigir.

demarcation /,dimɑr'keɪʃən/ n. demarcación f.

demeanor /dɪ'minər/ n. conducta f.

demented /dɪ'mɛntɪd/ a. demente, loco.

demilitarize /di'mɪlɪtə,raɪz/ v. desmilitarizar.

demobilize /di'moubə,laɪz/ v. desmovilizar.

democracy /dɪ'mɒkrəsi/ n. democracia f.

democrat /'dɛmə,kræt/ n. demócrata -m. & f.

democratic /,dɛmə'krætɪk/ a. democrático.

demolish /dɪ'mɒlɪʃ/ v. demoler.

demon /'dimən/ n. demonio m.

demonstrate /'dɛmən,streit/ v. demostrar.

demonstration /,dɛmən'streiʃən/ n. demostración f.

demonstrative /də'mɒnstrətiv/ a. demostrativo.

demoralize /di'mɔrə,laiz/ v. desmoralizar.

demure /di'myʊr/ a. modesto, serio.

den /dɛn/ n. madriguera, caverna f.

denature /di'neitʃər/ v. alterar.

denial /di'naiəl/ n. negación f.

denim /'dɛnəm/ n. dril, tela vaquera.

Denmark /'dɛnmɑrk/ n. Dinamarca f.

denomination /di,nɒmə'neiʃən/ n. denominación f.

denote /di'nout/ v. denotar.

denounce /di'nauns/ v. denunciar.

dense /dɛns/ a. denso, espeso; estúpido.

density /'dɛnsiti/ n. densidad f.

dent /dɛnt/ n. **1.** abolladura f. —v. **2.** abollar.

dental /'dɛntl/ a. dental.

dentist /'dɛntist/ n. dentista m. & f.

dentistry /'dɛntəstri/ n. odontología f.

denture /'dɛntʃər/ n. dentadura f.

denunciation /di,nʌnsi'eiʃən/ n. denunciación f.

deny /di'nai/ v. negar, rehusar.

deodorant /di'oudərənt/ n. desodorante m.

depart /di'pɑrt/ v. partir; irse, marcharse.

department /di'pɑrtmənt/ n. departamento m.

departmental /di,pɑrt'mɛntl/ a. departamental.

department store grandes almacenes m.pl.

departure /di'pɑrtʃər/ n. salida; desviación f.

depend /di'pɛnd/ v. depender.

dependability /di,pɛndə'biliti/ n. confiabilidad f.

dependable /di'pɛndəbəl/ a. confiable.

dependence /di'pɛndəns/ n. dependencia f.

dependent /di'pɛndənt/ a. & n. dependiente m. & f.

depict /di'pikt/ v. pintar; representar.

deplete /di'plit/ v. agotar.

deplorable /di'plɔrəbəl/ a. deplorable.

deplore /di'plɔr/ v. deplorar.

deport /di'pɔrt/ v. deportar.

deportation /,dipɔr'teiʃən/ n. deportación f.

deportment /di'pɔrtmənt/ n. conducta f.

depose /di'pouz/ v. deponer.

deposit /di'pɒzit/ n. **1.** depósito m. (of money); yacimiento (of ore, etc.) m. —v. **2.** depositar.

depositor /di'pɒzitər/ n. depositante m. & f.

depot /'dipou/ n. depósito m.; (railway) estación f.

depravity /di'præviti/ n. depravación f.

deprecate /'dɛpri,keit/ v. deprecar.

depreciate /di'priʃi,eit/ v. depreciar.

depreciation /di,priʃi'eiʃən/ n. depreciación f.

depredation /,dɛprə'deiʃən/ n. depredación f.

depress /di'prɛs/ v. deprimir; desanimar.

depression /di'prɛʃən/ n. depresión f.

deprive /di'praiv/ v. privar.

depth /dɛpθ/ n. profundidad f, hondura f.

depth charge carga de profundidad f.

deputy /'dɛpyəti/ n. diputado -da.

deride /di'raid/ v. burlar.

derision /di'riʒən/ n. burla f.

derivation /,dɛrə'veiʃən/ n. derivación f.

derivative /di'rivətiv/ a. derivativo.

derive /di'raiv/ v. derivar.

dermatologist /,dɜrmə'tɒlədʒist/ n. dermatólogo -ga.

derogatory /di'rɒgə,tɔri/ a. derogatorio.

derrick /'dɛrik/ n. grúa f.

descend /di'sɛnd/ v. descender, bajar.

descendant /di'sɛndənt/ n. descendiente m. & f.

descent /di'sɛnt/ n. descenso m.; origen m.

describe /di'skraib/ v. describir.

description /di'skripʃən/ n. descripción f.

descriptive /di'skriptiv/ a. descriptivo.

desecrate /'dɛsɪ,kreit/ v. profanar.

desert /n 'dɛzərt; v dɪ'zɜrt/ n. 1. desierto m. —v. 2. abandonar.

deserter /dɪ'zɜrtər/ n. desertor -ra.

desertion /dɪ'zɜrʃən/ n. deserción f.

deserve /dɪ'zɜrv/ v. merecer.

design /dɪ'zaɪn/ n. 1. diseño m. —v. 2. diseñar.

designate /'dɛzɪg,neit/ v. señalar, apuntar; designar.

designation /,dɛzɪg'neiʃən/ n. designación f.

designer /dɪ'zainər/ n. diseñador -ra; (technical) proyectista m. & f.

designer clothes, designer clothing ropa de marca f.

desirability /dɪ,zaiərə'bɪliti/ n. conveniencia f.

desirable /dɪ'zaiərəbəl/ a. deseable.

desire /dɪ'zaiər/ n. 1. deseo m. —v. 2. desear.

desirous /dɪ'zaiərəs/ a. deseoso.

desist /dɪ'sɪst/ v. desistir.

desk /dɛsk/ n. escritorio m.

desk clerk recepcionista m. & f.

desktop computer /'dɛsk,tɒp/ computadora de sobremesa f., ordenador de sobremesa f.

desolate /a 'dɛsəlɪt; v -,leit/ a. desolado. —v. 2. desolar.

desolation /,dɛsə'leiʃən/ n. desolación, ruina f.

despair /dɪ'spɛər/ n. 1. desesperación f. —v. 2. desesperar.

despatch /dɪ'spætʃ/ **dispatch** n. 1. despacho m.; prontitud f. —v. 2. despachar.

desperado /,dɛspə'rɑdoʊ/ n. bandido m.

desperate /'dɛspərɪt/ a. desesperado.

desperation /,dɛspə'reiʃən/ n. desesperación f.

despicable /dɪ'spɪkəbəl/ a. vil.

despise /dɪ'spaiz/ v. despreciar.

despite /dɪ'spait/ prep. a pesar de.

despondent /dɪ'spɒndənt/ a. abatido; desanimado.

despot /'dɛspət/ n. déspota m. & f.

despotic /dɛs'pɒtɪk/ a. despótico.

dessert /dɪ'zɜrt/ n. postre m.

destination /,dɛstə'neiʃən/ n. destinación f.

destine /'dɛstɪn/ v. destinar.

destiny /'dɛstəni/ n. destino m.

destitute /'dɛstɪ,tut/ a. destituido, indigente.

destitution /,dɛstɪ'tuʃən/ n. destitución f.

destroy /dɪ'strɔi/ v. destrozar, destruir.

destroyer /dɪ'strɔiər/ n. destruidor -ra; (naval) destructor m.

destruction /dɪ'strʌkʃən/ n. destrucción f.

destructive /dɪ'strʌktɪv/ a. destructivo.

desultory /'dɛsəl,tɔri/ a. inconexo; casual.

detach /dɪ'tætʃ/ v. separar, desprender.

detachment /dɪ'tætʃmənt/ n. Mil. destacamento; desprendimiento m.

detail /dɪ'teil/ n. 1. detalle m. —v. 2. detallar.

detain /dɪ'tein/ v. detener.

detect /dɪ'tɛkt/ v. descubrir.

detection /dɪ'tɛkʃən/ n. detección f.

detective /dɪ'tɛktɪv/ n. detective m. & f.

détente /dei'tɑnt/ n. distensión f.; Pol. détente.

detention /dɪ'tɛnʃən/ n. detención; cautividad f.

deter /dɪ'tɜr/ v. disuadir.

detergent /dɪ'tɜrdʒənt/ n. & a. detergente m.

deteriorate /dɪ'tiəriə,reit/ v. deteriorar.

deterioration /dɪ,tiəriə'reiʃən/ n. deterioración f.

determination /dɪ,tɜrmə'neiʃən/ n. determinación f.

determine /dɪ'tɜrmɪn/ v. determinar.

deterrence /dɪ'tɜrəns/ n. disuasión f.

detest /dɪ'tɛst/ v. detestar.

detonate /'dɛtn,eit/ v. detonar.

detour /'dituər/ n. desvío m. v. desviar.

detract /dɪ'trækt/ v. disminuir.

detriment /'dɛtrəmənt/ n. detrimento m., daño m.

detrimental /,dɛtrə'mɛntl/ a. dañoso.

devaluate /di'vælyu,eit/ v. depreciar.

devastate /'dɛvə,steit/ v. devastar.

develop /dɪ'vɛləp/ v. desarrollar; Phot. revelar.

developing nation /dɪˈvɛləpɪŋ/ nación en desarrollo.

development /dɪˈvɛləpmənt/ n. desarrollo m.

deviate /ˈdiviˌeit/ v. desviar.

deviation /ˌdiviˈeiʃən/ n. desviación f.

device /dɪˈvais/ n. aparato; artificio m.

devil /ˈdɛvəl/ n. diablo, demonio m.

devious /ˈdiviəs/ a. desviado.

devise /dɪˈvaiz/ v. inventar.

devoid /dɪˈvɔid/ a. desprovisto.

devote /dɪˈvout/ v. dedicar, consagrar.

devoted /dɪˈvoutɪd/ a. devoto.

devotee /ˌdɛvəˈti/ n. aficionado -da.

devotion /dɪˈvouʃən/ n. devoción f.

devour /dɪˈvaur/ v. devorar.

devout /dɪˈvaut/ a. devoto.

dew /du/ n. rocío, sereno m.

dexterity /dɛkˈstɛrɪti/ n. destreza f.

dexterous /ˈdɛkstrəs/ a. diestro.

diabetes /ˌdaiəˈbitis/ n. diabetes f.

diabolic /ˌdaiəˈbɒlɪk/ a. diabólico.

diadem /ˈdaiəˌdɛm/ n. diadema f.

diagnose /ˈdaiəgˌnous/ v. diagnosticar.

diagnosis /ˌdaiəgˈnousis/ n. diagnóstico m.

diagonal /daiˈægənl/ n. diagonal f.

diagram /ˈdaiəˌgræm/ n. diagrama m.

dial /ˈdaiəl/ n. **1.** cuadrante m., carátula f. —v. **2. dial up** marcar.

dialect /ˈdaiəˌlɛkt/ n. dialecto m.

dialing code /ˈdaiəlɪŋ/ prefijo m.

dialogue /ˈdaiəˌlɔg/ n. diálogo m.

dial tone señal de marcar f.

diameter /daiˈæmɪtər/ n. diámetro m.

diamond /ˈdaimənd/ n. diamante, brillante m.

diaper /ˈdaipər/ n. pañal m.

diarrhea /ˌdaiəˈriə/ n. diarrea f.

diary /ˈdaiəri/ n. diario m.

diathermy /ˈdaiəˌθɜrmi/ n. diatermia f.

dice /dais/ n. dados m.pl.

dictate /ˈdikteit/ n. **1.** mandato m. —v. **2.** dictar.

dictation /dikˈteiʃən/ n. dictado m.

dictator /ˈdikteitər/ n. dictador -ra.

dictatorship /dikˈteitərˌʃip/ n. dictadura f.

diction /ˈdikʃən/ n. dicción f.

dictionary /ˈdikʃəˌnɛri/ n. diccionario m.

die /dai/ n. **1.** matriz f.; (game) dado m. —v. **2.** morir.

diet /ˈdaiit/ n. dieta f.

dietary /ˈdaiiˌtɛri/ a. dietético.

dietitian /ˌdaiiˈtiʃən/ n. & a. dietético -ca.

differ /ˈdifər/ v. diferir.

difference /ˈdifərəns/ n. diferencia f. **to make no d.,** no importar.

different /ˈdifərənt/ a. diferente, distinto.

differential /ˌdifəˈrɛnʃəl/ n. diferencial f.

differentiate /ˌdifəˈrɛnʃiˌeit/ v. diferenciar.

difficult /ˈdifiˌkʌlt/ a. difícil.

difficulty /ˈdifiˌkʌlti/ n. dificultad f.

diffident /ˈdifidənt/ a. tímido.

diffuse /dɪˈfyuz/ v. difundir.

diffusion /dɪˈfyuʒən/ n. difusión f.

dig /dig/ v. cavar.

digest /n /ˈdaidʒɛst; v dɪˈdʒɛst, dai-/ n. **1.** extracto m. —v. **2.** digerir.

digestible /dɪˈdʒɛstəbəl, dai-/ a. digerible.

digestion /dɪˈdʒɛstʃən, dai-/ n. digestión f.

digestive /dɪˈdʒɛstiv, dai-/ a. digestivo.

digital /ˈdidʒitl/ a. digital.

digitalis /ˌdidʒiˈtælis/ n. digital f.

dignified /ˈdignəˌfaid/ a. digno.

dignify /ˈdignəˌfai/ v. dignificar.

dignitary /ˈdigniˌtɛri/ n. dignatario -ria.

dignity /ˈdigniti/ n. dignidad f.

digress /dɪˈgrɛs, dai-/ v. divagar.

digression /dɪˈgrɛʃən, dai-/ n. digresión f.

dike /daik/ n. dique m.

dilapidated /dɪˈlæpiˌdeitid/ a. dilapidado.

dilapidation /dɪˌlæpiˈdeiʃən/ n. dilapidación f.

dilate /daiˈleit/ v. dilatar.

dilatory /ˈdiləˌtɔri/ a. dilatorio.

dilemma /dɪˈlɛmə/ n. dilema m.

dilettante /ˌdiliˈtɑnt/ n. diletante m. & f.

diligence /ˈdilidʒəns/ n. diligencia f.

diligent /'dılıdʒənt/ a. diligente, aplicado.

dilute /dı'lut, dai-/ v. diluir.

dim /dım/ a. 1. oscuro. —v. 2. oscurecer.

dimension /dı'menʃən/ n. dimensión f.

diminish /dı'mınıʃ/ v. disminuir.

diminution /,dımə'nuʃən/ n. disminución f.

diminutive /dı'mınyətıv/ a. diminutivo.

dimness /'dımnıs/ n. oscuridad f.

dimple /'dımpəl/ n. hoyuelo m.

din /dın/ n. alboroto, estrépito m.

dine /dain/ v. comer, cenar.

diner /'dainər/ n. coche comedor m.

dingy /'dındʒi/ a. deslucido, deslustrado.

dining room /'dainıŋ/ comedor m.

dinner /'dınər/ n. comida, cena f.

dinosaur /'dainə,sɔr/ n. dinosauro m.

diocese /'daiəsıs/ n. diócesis f.

dip /dıp/ v. sumergir, hundir.

diphtheria /dıf'θıəriə/ n. difteria f.

diploma /dı'ploumə/ n. diploma m.

diplomacy /dı'plouməsi/ n. diplomacia f.

diplomat /'dıplə,mæt/ n. diplomático -ca.

diplomatic /,dıplə'mætık/ a. diplomático.

dipper /'dıpər/ n. cucharón m.

dire /dairʳ/ a. horrendo.

direct /dı'rɛkt, dai-/ a. 1. directo. —v. 2. dirigir.

direction /dı'rɛkʃən, 'dai-/ n. dirección f.

directive /dı'rɛktıv, dai-/ n. directiva f.

directly /dı'rɛktli, dai-/ adv. directamente.

director /dı'rɛktər, dai-/ n. director -ra.

directory /dı'rɛktəri, dai-/ n. rectorio m., guía f.

dirigible /'dırıdʒəbəl/ n. dirigible m.

dirt /dərt/ n. basura f.; (earth) tierra f.

dirt-cheap /'dərt 'tʃip/ a. tirado.

dirty /'dərti/ a. sucio.

dis /dıs/ v. Colloq. ofender, faltar al respeto.

disability /,dısə'bılıti/ n. inhabilidad f.

disable /dıs'eibəl/ v. incapacitar.

disabuse /,dısə'byuz/ v. desengañar.

disadvantage /,dısəd'væntıdʒ/ n. desventaja f.

disagree /,dısə'gri/ v. desconvenir; disentir.

disagreeable /,dısə'griəbəl/ a. desagradable.

disagreement /,dısə'grimənt/ n. desacuerdo m.

disappear /,dısə'pıər/ v. desaparecer.

disappearance /,dısə'pıərəns/ n. desaparición f.

disappoint /,dısə'pɔint/ v. disgustar, desilusionar.

disappointment /,dısə'pɔintmənt/ n. disgusto m., desilusión f.

disapproval /,dısə'pruvəl/ n. desaprobación f.

disapprove /,dısə'pruv/ v. desaprobar.

disarm /dıs'arm/ v. desarmar.

disarmament /dıs'arməmənt/ n. desarme m.

disarrange /,dısə'reindʒ/ v. desordenar; desarreglar.

disaster /dı'zæstər/ n. desastre m.

disastrous /dı'zæstrəs/ a. desastroso.

disavow /,dısə'vau/ v. repudiar.

disavowal /,dısə'vauəl/ n. repudiación f.

disband /dıs'bænd/ v. dispersarse.

disbelieve /,dısbı'liv/ v. descreer.

disburse /dıs'bərs/ v. desembolsar, pagar.

discard /dı'skard/ v. descartar.

discern /dı'sɜrn/ v. discernir.

discerning /dı'sɜrnıŋ/ a. discernidor, perspicaz.

discernment /dı'sɜrnmənt/ n. discernimiento m.

discharge /dıs'tʃardʒ/ v. descargar; despedir.

disciple /dı'saipəl/ n. discípulo -la.

disciplinary /'dısəplə,neri/ a. disciplinario.

discipline /'dısəplın/ n. disciplina f.

disclaim /dıs'kleim/ v. repudiar.

disclaimer /dıs'kleimər/ n. negación f.

disclose /dı'sklouz/ v. revelar.

disclosure /dı'sklouʒər/ n. revelación f.

disco /'dıskou/ n. discoteca f.

discolor /dɪsˈkʌlər/ v. descolorar.

discomfort /ˌdɪsˈkʌmfərt/ n. incomodidad f.

disconcert /ˌdɪskənˈsərt/ v. desconcertar.

disconnect /ˌdɪskəˈnɛkt/ v. desunir; desconectar.

disconnected /ˌdɪskəˈnɛktɪd/ a. desunido.

disconsolate /dɪsˈkɒnsəlɪt/ a. desconsolado.

discontent /ˌdɪskənˈtɛnt/ n. descontento m.

discontented /ˌdɪskənˈtɛntɪd/ a. descontento.

discontinue /ˌdɪskənˈtɪnyu/ v. descontinuar.

discord /ˈdɪskɔrd/ n. discordia f.

discordant /dɪsˈkɔrdənt/ a. disonante.

discotheque /ˈdɪskəˌtɛk/ n. discoteca f.

discount /ˈdɪskaunt/ n. descuento m.

discourage /dɪsˈkɜrɪdʒ/ v. desalentar, desanimar.

discouragement /dɪsˈkɜrɪdʒmənt/ n. desaliento, desánimo m.

discourse /ˈdɪskɔrs/ n. discurso m.

discourteous /dɪsˈkɜrtiəs/ a. descortés.

discourtesy /dɪsˈkɜrtəsi/ n. descortesía f.

discover /dɪsˈkʌvər/ v. descubrir.

discoverer /dɪsˈkʌvərər/ n. descubridor -ra.

discovery /dɪsˈkʌvəri/ n. descubrimiento m.

discreet /dɪˈskrit/ a. discreto.

discrepancy /dɪˈskrɛpənsi/ n. discrepancia f.

discretion /dɪˈskrɛʃən/ n. discreción f.

discriminate /dɪˈskrɪmɪˌneɪt/ v. distinguir. **d. against** discriminar contra.

discrimination /dɪˌskrɪməˈneɪʃən/ n. discernimiento m.; discriminación f.

discuss /dɪˈskʌs/ v. discutir.

discussion /dɪˈskʌʃən/ n. discusión f.

disdain /dɪsˈdeɪn/ n. **1.** desdén m. —v. **2.** desdeñar.

disdainful /dɪsˈdeɪnfəl/ a. desdeñoso.

disease /dɪˈziz/ n. enfermedad f., mal m.

disembark /ˌdɪsɛmˈbɑrk/ v. desembarcar.

disentangle /ˌdɪsɛnˈtæŋgəl/ v. desenredar.

disfigure /dɪsˈfɪgyər/ v. desfigurar.

disgrace /dɪsˈgreɪs/ n. **1.** vergüenza; deshonra f. —v. **2.** deshonrar.

disgraceful /dɪsˈgreɪsfəl/ a. vergonzoso.

disguise /dɪsˈgaɪz/ n. **1.** disfraz m. —v. **2.** disfrazar.

disgust /dɪsˈgʌst/ n. **1.** repugnancia —v. **2.** fastidiar; repugnar.

dish /dɪʃ/ n. plato m.

dishearten /dɪsˈhɑrtn/ v. desanimar; descorazonar.

dishonest /dɪsˈɒnɪst/ a. deshonesto.

dishonesty /dɪsˈɒnəsti/ n. deshonestidad f.

dishonor /dɪsˈɒnər/ n. **1.** deshonra f. —v. **2.** deshonrar.

dishonorable /dɪsˈɒnərəbəl/ a. deshonroso.

dishwasher /ˈdɪʃˌwɒʃər/ n. lavaplatos m.

disillusion /ˌdɪsɪˈluʒən/ n. **1.** desengaño m. —v. **2.** desengañar.

disinfect /ˌdɪsɪnˈfɛkt/ v. desinfectar.

disinfectant /ˌdɪsɪnˈfɛktənt/ n. desinfectante m.

disinherit /ˌdɪsɪnˈhɛrɪt/ v. desheredar.

disintegrate /dɪsˈɪntəˌgreɪt/ v. desintegrar.

disinterested /dɪsˈɪntəˌrɛstɪd, -trɪstɪd/ a. desinteresado.

disk /dɪsk/ n. disco m.

disk drive disquetera f.

diskette /dɪˈskɛt/ n. disquete m.

disk jockey pinchadiscos m. & f.

dislike /dɪsˈlaɪk/ n. **1.** antipatía f. —v. **2.** no gustar de.

dislocate /ˈdɪsloʊˌkeɪt/ v. dislocar.

dislodge /dɪsˈlɒdʒ/ v. desalojar; desprender.

disloyal /dɪsˈlɔɪəl/ a. desleal; infiel.

disloyalty /dɪsˈlɔɪəlti/ n. deslealtad f.

dismal /ˈdɪzməl/ a. lúgubre.

dismantle /dɪsˈmæntl/ v. desmantelar, desmontar.

dismay /dɪsˈmeɪ/ n. **1.** consternación f. —v. **2.** consternar.

dismiss /dɪsˈmɪs/ v. despedir.

dismissal /dɪsˈmɪsəl/ n. despedida f.

dismount /dɪsˈmaunt/ v. apearse, desmontarse.

disobedience /ˌdɪsəˈbidiəns/ n. desobediencia f.

disobedient /ˌdɪsəˈbidiənt/ a. desobediente.

disobey /ˌdɪsəˈbei/ v. desobedecer.

disorder /dɪsˈɔrdər/ n. desorden m.

disorderly /dɪsˈɔrdərli/ a. desarreglado, desordenado.

disown /dɪsˈoun/ v. repudiar.

dispassionate /dɪsˈpæʃənɪt/ a. desapasionado; templado.

dispatch /dɪsˈpætʃ/ n. **1.** despacho m. —v. **2.** despachar.

dispel /dɪsˈpel/ v. dispersar.

dispensary /dɪsˈpensəri/ n. dispensario m.

dispensation /ˌdɪspənˈseiʃən/ n. dispensación f.

dispense /dɪsˈpens/ v. dispensar.

dispersal /dɪsˈpərsəl/ n. dispersión f.

disperse /dɪsˈpərs/ v. dispersar.

displace /dɪsˈpleis/ v. dislocar.

display /dɪsˈplei/ n. **1.** despliegue m., exhibición f. —v. **2.** desplegar, exhibir.

displease /dɪsˈpliz/ v. disgustar; ofender.

displeasure /dɪsˈpleʒər/ n. disgusto, sinsabor m.

disposable /dɪsˈpouzəbəl/ a. disponible; desechable.

disposal /dɪsˈpouzəl/ n. disposición f.

dispose /dɪsˈpouz/ v. disponer.

disposition /ˌdɪspəˈzɪʃən/ n. disposición f.; índole f., genio m.

dispossess /ˌdɪspəˈzes/ v. desposeer.

disproportionate /ˌdɪsprəˈpɔrʃənɪt/ a. desproporcionado.

disprove /dɪsˈpruv/ v. confutar.

dispute /dɪsˈpyut/ n. **1.** disputa f. —v. **2.** disputar.

disqualify /dɪsˈkwɒləˌfai/ v. inhabilitar.

disregard /ˌdɪsrɪˈgɑrd/ n. **1.** detención f. —v. **2.** desatender.

disrepair /ˌdɪsrɪˈpeər/ n. descompostura f.

disreputable /dɪsˈrepyətəbəl/ a. desacreditado.

disrespect /ˌdɪsrɪˈspekt/ n. falta de respeto, f., desacato m.

disrespectful /ˌdɪsrɪˈspektfəl/ a. irrespetuoso.

disrobe /dɪsˈroub/ v. desvestir.

disrupt /dɪsˈrʌpt/ v. romper; desbaratar.

dissatisfaction /ˌdɪssætɪsˈfækʃən/ n. descontento m.

dissatisfy /dɪsˈsætɪsˌfai/ v. descontentar.

dissect /dɪˈsekt/ v. disecar.

dissemble /dɪˈsembəl/ v. disimular.

disseminate /dɪˈseməˌneit/ v. diseminar.

dissension /dɪˈsenʃən/ n. disensión f.

dissent /dɪˈsent/ n. **1.** disensión f. —v. **2.** disentir.

dissertation /ˌdɪsərˈteiʃən/ n. disertación f.

dissimilar /dɪˈsɪmələr/ a. desemejante.

dissipate /ˈdɪsəˌpeit/ v. disipar.

dissipation /ˌdɪsəˈpeiʃən/ n. disipación f.; libertinaje m.

dissolute /ˈdɪsəˌlut/ a. disoluto.

dissolution /ˌdɪsəˈluʃən/ n. disolución f.

dissolve /dɪˈzɒlv/ v. disolver; derretirse.

dissonant /ˈdɪsənənt/ a. disonante.

dissuade /dɪˈsweid/ v. disuadir.

distance /ˈdɪstəns/ n. distancia f. **at a d., in the d.,** a lo lejos.

distant /ˈdɪstənt/ a. distante, lejano.

distaste /dɪsˈteist/ n. disgusto, sinsabor m.

distasteful /dɪsˈteistfəl/ a. desagradable.

distill /dɪsˈtɪl/ v. destilar.

distillation /ˌdɪstɪˈleiʃən/ n. destilación f.

distillery /dɪsˈtɪləri/ n. destilería f.

distinct /dɪsˈtɪŋkt/ a. distinto.

distinction /dɪsˈtɪŋkʃən/ n. distinción f.

distinctive /dɪsˈtɪŋktɪv/ a. distintivo; característico.

distinctly /dɪsˈtɪŋktli/ adv. distintamente.

distinguish /dɪsˈtɪŋgwɪʃ/ v. distinguir.

distinguished /dɪsˈtɪŋgwɪʃt/ a. distinguido.

distort /dɪsˈtɔrt/ v. falsear; torcer.

distract /dɪsˈtrækt/ v. distraer.

distraction /dɪsˈtrækʃən/ n. distracción f.

distraught /dɪˈstrɔt/ a. aturrullado; demente.

distress /dɪˈstrɛs/ n. **1.** dolor m. —v. **2.** afligir.

distressing /dɪˈstrɛsɪŋ/ a. penoso.

distribute /dɪˈstrɪbyut/ v. distribuir.

distribution /ˌdɪstrəˈbyuʃən/ n. distribución f.; reparto m.

distributor /dɪˈstrɪbyətər/ n. distribuidor -ra.

district /ˈdɪstrɪkt/ n. distrito m.

distrust /dɪsˈtrʌst/ n. **1.** desconfianza f. —v. **2.** desconfiar.

distrustful /dɪsˈtrʌstfəl/ a. desconfiado; sospechoso.

disturb /dɪˈstɜrb/ v. incomodar; inquietar.

disturbance /dɪˈstɜrbəns/ n. disturbio m.

disturbing /dɪˈstɜrbɪŋ/ a. inquietante.

ditch /dɪtʃ/ n. zanja f.; foso m.

divan /dɪˈvæn/ n. diván m.

dive /daɪv/ n. **1.** clavado m.; *Colloq.* leonera f. —v. **2.** echar un clavado; bucear.

diver /ˈdaɪvər/ n. buzo m.

diverge /dɪˈvɜrdʒ/ v. divergir.

divergence /dɪˈvɜrdʒəns/ n. divergencia f.

divergent /dɪˈvɜrdʒənt/ a. divergente.

diverse /dɪˈvɜrs/ a. diverso.

diversion /dɪˈvɜrʒən/ n. diversión f.; pasatiempo m.

diversity /dɪˈvɜrsɪti/ n. diversidad f.

divert /dɪˈvɜrt/ v. desviar; divertir.

divest /dɪˈvɛst/ v. desnudar, despojar.

divide /dɪˈvaɪd/ v. dividir.

dividend /ˈdɪvɪˌdɛnd/ n. dividendo m.

divine /dɪˈvaɪn/ a. divino.

divinity /dɪˈvɪnɪti/ n. divinidad f.

division /dɪˈvɪʒən/ n. división f.

divorce /dɪˈvɔrs/ n. **1.** divorcio m. —v. **2.** divorciar.

divorcee /dɪvɔrˈseɪ/ n. divorciado -da.

divulge /dɪˈvʌldʒ/ v. divulgar, revelar.

dizziness /ˈdɪzɪnɪs/ n. vértigo, mareo m.

dizzy /ˈdɪzi/ a. mareado.

DNA *abbr.* (deoxyribonucleic acid) ADN (ácido deoxirribonucleico) m.

do /du/ v. hacer.

docile /ˈdɒsəl/ a. dócil.

dock /dɒk/ n. **1.** muelle m. **dry d.,** astillero m. —v. **2.** entrar en muelle.

doctor /ˈdɒktər/ n. médico m.; doctor -ra.

doctorate /ˈdɒktərɪt/ n. doctorado m.

doctrine /ˈdɒktrɪn/ n. doctrina f.

document /ˈdɒkyəmənt/ n. documento m.

documentary /ˌdɒkyəˈmɛntəri/ a. documental.

documentation /ˌdɒkyəmənˈteɪʃən/ n. documentación f.

dodge /dɒdʒ/ n. **1.** evasión f. —v. **2.** evadir.

dodgem /ˈdɒdʒɪm/ n. coche de choque m.

doe /doʊ/ n. gama f.

dog /dɒg/ n. perro -a.

dogma /ˈdɔgmə/ n. dogma m.

dogmatic /dɔgˈmætɪk/ a. dogmático.

dogmatism /ˈdɔgməˌtɪzəm/ n. dogmatismo m.

doily /ˈdɔɪli/ n. servilletita f.

doleful /ˈdoʊlfəl/ a. triste.

doll /dɒl/ n. muñeca -co.

dollar /ˈdɒlər/ n. dólar m.

dolorous /ˈdoʊlərəs/ a. lastimoso.

dolphin /ˈdɒlfɪn/ n. delfín m.

domain /doʊˈmeɪn/ n. dominio m.

dome /doʊm/ n. domo m.

domestic /dəˈmɛstɪk/ a. doméstico.

domesticate /dəˈmɛstɪˌkeɪt/ v. domesticar.

domicile /ˈdɒməˌsaɪl/ n. domicilio m.

dominance /ˈdɒmənəns/ n. dominación f.

dominant /ˈdɒmənənt/ a. dominante.

domination /ˌdɒməˈneɪʃən/ v. dominar.

domination /ˌdɒməˈneɪʃən/ n. dominación f.

domineer /ˌdɒməˈnɪər/ v. dominar.

domineering /ˌdɒməˈnɪərɪŋ/ a. tiránico, mandón.

dominion /dəˈmɪnyən/ n. dominio; territorio m.

domino /ˈdɒməˌnoʊ/ n. dominó m.

donate /ˈdoʊneɪt/ v. donar; contribuir.

donation /doʊˈneɪʃən/ n. donación f.

donkey /'dɒŋki/ n. asno, burro m.

doom /dum/ n. **1.** perdición, ruina f. —v. **2.** perder, ruinar.

door /dɔr/ n. puerta f.

doorman /'dɔr,mæn, -mən/ n. portero m.

doormat /'dɔr,mæt/ n. felpudo m.

doorway /'dɔr,wei/ n. entrada f.

dope /doup/ n. Colloq. narcótico m.; idiota m.

dormant /'dɔrmənt/ a. durmiente; inactivo.

dormitory /'dɔrmɪ,tɔri/ n. dormitorio m.

dosage /'dousɪdʒ/ n. dosificación f.

dose /dous/ n. dosis f.

dot /dɒt/ n. punto m.

dotted line /'dɒtɪd/ línea de puntos f.

double /'dʌbəl/ a. **1.** doble. —v. **2.** duplicar.

double bass /beis/ contrabajo m.

double-breasted /'dʌbəl 'brestɪd/ a. cruzado.

double-cross /'dʌbəl 'krɔs/ v. traicionar.

doubly /'dʌbli/ adv. doblemente.

doubt /daut/ n. **1.** duda f. —v. **2.** dudar.

doubtful /'dautfəl/ a. dudoso, incierto.

doubtless /'dautlɪs/ a. **1.** indudable. —adv. **2.** sin duda.

dough /dou/ n. pasta, masa f.

doughnut /'dounət, -,nʌt/ n. buñuelo m.

dove /dʌv/ n. paloma f.

dowager /'dauədʒər/ n. viuda (con título) f.

down /daun/ a. **1.** abajo. —prep. **2.** d. the street, etc. calle abajo, etc.

downcast /'daun,kæst/ a. cabizbajo.

downfall /'daun,fɔl/ n. ruina f., perdición f.

downhearted /'daun'hɑrtɪd/ a. descorazonado.

download /'daun,loud/ v. bajar, descargar.

downpour /'daun,pɔr/ n. chaparrón m.

downright /'daun,rait/ a. absoluto, completo.

downriver /'daun'rɪvər/ adv. aguas abajo, río abajo.

downstairs /'daun'steərz/ adv. **1.** abajo. —n. **2.** primer piso.

downstream /'daun'strim/ adv. aguas abajo, río abajo.

downtown /'daun'taun/ adv. al centro, en el centro.

downward /'daunwərd/ a. **1.** descendente. —adv. **2.** hacia abajo.

dowry /'dauri/ n. dote f.

doze /douz/ v. dormitar.

dozen /'dʌzən/ n. docena f.

draft /dræft/ n. **1.** dibujo m.; Com. giro m.; Mil. conscripción f. —v. **2.** dibujar; Mil. reclutar.

draftee /dræf'ti/ n. conscripto m.

draft notice notificación de reclutamiento f.

drag /dræg/ v. arrastrar.

dragon /'drægən/ n. dragón m.

drain /drein/ n. **1.** desaguadero m. —v. **2.** desaguar.

drainage /'dreinɪdʒ/ n. drenaje m.

drain board escurridero m.

drama /'drɑmə, 'dræmə/ n. drama m.

dramatic /drə'mætɪk/ a. dramático.

dramatics /drə'mætɪks/ n. dramática f.

dramatist /'dræmətɪst, 'drɑmə-/ n. dramaturgo -ga.

dramatize /'dræmə,taiz, 'drɑmə-/ v. dramatizar.

drape /dreip/ n. cortinas f.pl. —v. vestir; adornar.

drapery /'dreipəri/ n. colgaduras f.pl.; ropaje m.

drastic /'dræstɪk/ a. drástico.

draw /drɔ/ v. dibujar; atraer. **d. up,** formular.

drawback /'drɔ,bæk/ n. desventaja f.

drawer /drɔr/ n. cajón m.

drawing /'drɔɪŋ/ n. dibujo m.; rifa f.

dread /drɛd/ n. **1.** terror m. —v. **2.** temer.

dreadful /'drɛdfəl/ a. terrible.

dreadfully /'drɛdfəli/ adv. horrendamente.

dream /drim/ n. **1.** sueño, ensueño m. —v. **2.** soñar.

dreamer /'drimər/ n. soñador -ra; visionario -ia.

dreamy /'drimi/ a. soñador, contemplativo.

dreary /'drɪəri/ a. monótono y pesado.

dredge /drɛdʒ/ n. **1.** rastra f. —v. **2.** rastrear.

dregs /drɛgz/ n. sedimento m.

drench /drɛntʃ/ v. mojar.

dress /drɛs/ n. **1.** vestido; traje m. —v. **2.** vestir.

dresser /'drɛsər/ n. (furniture) tocador.

dressing /'drɛsɪŋ/ n. Med. curación f.; (cookery) relleno m., salsa f.

dressing gown bata f.

dressing table tocador m.

dressmaker /drɛs,meikər/ n. modista m. & f.

drift /drɪft/ n. **1.** tendencia f.; Naut. deriva f. —v. **2.** Naut. derivar; (snow) amontonarse.

drill /drɪl/ n. **1.** ejercicio m.; Mech. taladro m. —v. **2.** Mech. taladrar.

drink /drɪŋk/ n. **1.** bebida f. —v. **2.** beber, tomar.

drinkable /'drɪŋkəbəl/ a. potable, bebible.

drip /drɪp/ v. gotear.

drive /draiv/ n. **1.** paseo m. —v. **2.** impeler; Auto. guiar, conducir.

drive-in (movie theater) /'draiv ,ɪn/ n. autocine, autocinema m.

driver /'draivər/ n. conductor -ra; chofer m. **d.'s license,** permiso de conducir.

driveway /'draiv,wei/ n. entrada para coches.

drizzle /'drɪzəl/ n. **1.** llovizna f. —v. **2.** lloviznar.

dromedary /'drɒmɪ,dɛri/ n. dromedario m.

droop /drup/ v. inclinarse.

drop /drɒp/ n. **1.** gota f. —v. **2.** soltar; dejar caer.

dropout /'drɒp,aut/ n. joven que abandona sus estudios.

dropper /'drɒpər/ n. cuentagotas f.

dropsy /'drɒpsi/ n. hidropesía f.

drought /draut/ n. sequía f.

drove /drouv/ n. manada f.

drown /draun/ v. ahogar.

drowse /drauz/ v. adormecer.

drowsiness /'drauzinɪs/ n. somnolencia f.

drowsy /'drauzi/ a. soñoliento.

drudge /drʌdʒ/ n. ganapán m.

drudgery /'drʌdʒəri/ n. trabajo penoso.

drug /drʌg/ n. **1.** droga f. —v. **2.** narcotizar.

drug addict drogadicto -ta, toxicómano -na m. & f.

druggist /'drʌgɪst/ n. farmacéutico -ca, boticario -ria.

drugstore /'drʌg,stɔr/ n. farmacia, botica, droguería f.

drum /drʌm/ n. tambor m.

drummer /'drʌmər/ n. tambor m.

drumstick /'drʌm,stɪk/ n. palillo m.; Leg. pierna f.

drunk /drʌŋk/ a. & n. borracho, -a.

drunkard /'drʌŋkərd/ n. borrachón m.

drunken /'drʌŋkən/ a. borracho; ebrio.

drunkenness /'drʌŋkənnɪs/ n. embriaguez f.

dry /drai/ a. **1.** seco, árido. —v. **2.** secar.

dry cell n. pila seca f.

dry cleaner tintorero -ra.

dryness /'drainɪs/ n. sequedad f.

dual /'duəl/ a. doble.

dubious /'dubiəs/ a. dudoso.

duchess /'dʌtʃɪs/ n. duquesa f.

duck /dʌk/ n. **1.** pato m. —v. **2.** zambullir; (avoid) esquivar.

duct /dʌkt/ n. canal m.

due /du/ a. **1.** debido; Com. vencido. —n. **2.** dues cuota f.

duel /'duəl/ n. duelo m.

duelist /'duəlɪst/ n. duelista m.

duet /du'ɛt/ n. dúo m.

duke /duk/ n. duque m.

dull /dʌl/ a. apagado, desteñido; sin punta; Fig. pesado, soso.

dullness /'dʌlnɪs/ n. estupidez; pesadez f.; deslustre m.

duly /'duli/ adv. debidamente.

dumb /dʌm/ a. mudo; Colloq. estúpido.

dumbwaiter /'dʌm,weitər/ n. montaplatos m.

dumfound /dʌm'faund/ v. confundir.

dummy /'dʌmi/ n. maniquí m.

dump /dʌmp/ n. **1.** depósito m. —v. **2.** descargar.

dune /dun/ n. duna f.

dungeon /'dʌndʒən/ n. calabozo m.

dunk /dʌŋk/ v. mojar.

dupe /dup/ v. engañar.

duplicate /a, n 'duplikɪt; v -,keit/ a. & n. **1.** duplicado m. —v. **2.** duplicar.

duplication /,dupli'keiʃən/ n. duplicación f.

duplicity /du'plisiti/ n. duplicidad f.

durability /,durə'bɪliti/ n. durabilidad f.

durable /'durəbəl/ a. durable, duradero.

duration /du'reiʃən/ n. duración f.

duress /dʊˈrɛs/ n. compulsión f.; encierro m.

during /ˈdʊrɪŋ/ prep. durante.

dusk /dʌsk/ n. crepúsculo m.

dusky /ˈdʌski/ a. oscuro; moreno.

dust /dʌst/ n. 1. polvo m. —v. 2. polvorear; despolvorear.

dusty /ˈdʌsti/ a. empolvado.

Dutch /dʌtʃ/ a. holandés -sa.

dutiful /ˈdutəfəl/ a. respetuoso.

dutifully /ˈdutəfəli/ adv. respetuosamente, obedientemente.

duty /ˈduti/ n. deber m.; Com. derechos m.pl.

duty-free /ˈduti ˈfri/ a. libre de derechos.

dwarf /dwɔrf/ n. 1. enano -na. —v. 2. achicar.

dwell /dwɛl/ v. habitar, residir. **d. on,** espaciarse en.

dwelling /ˈdwɛlɪŋ/ n. morada, casa f.

dwindle /ˈdwɪndl/ v. disminuirse.

dye /dai/ n. 1. tintura f. —v. 2. teñir.

dyer /ˈdaiər/ n. tintorero -ra.

dynamic /daiˈnæmɪk/ a. dinámico.

dynamite /ˈdainəˌmait/ n. dinamita f.

dynamo /ˈdainəˌmou/ n. dínamo m.

dynasty /ˈdainəsti/ n. dinastía f.

dysentery /ˈdɪsənˌtɛri/ n. disentería f.

dyslexia /dɪsˈlɛksiə/ n. dislexia f.

dyslexic /dɪsˈlɛksɪk/ a. disléxico.

dyspepsia /dɪsˈpɛpʃə/ n. dispepsia f.

E

each /itʃ/ a. 1. cada. —pron. 2. cada uno -na. **e. other,** el uno al otro.

eager /ˈigər/ a. ansioso.

eagerly /ˈigərli/ adv. ansiosamente.

eagerness /ˈigərnɪs/ n. ansia f.

eagle /ˈigəl/ n. águila f.

ear /iər/ n. oído m.; (outer) oreja f.; (of corn) mazorca f.

earache /ˈiərˌeik/ n. dolor de oído m.

earl /ɜrl/ n. conde m.

early /ˈɜrli/ a. & adv. temprano.

earn /ɜrn/ v. ganar.

earnest /ˈɜrnɪst/ a. serio.

earnestly /ˈɜrnɪstli/ adv. seriamente.

earnings /ˈɜrnɪŋz/ n. ganancias f.pl.; Com. ingresos m.pl.

earphone /ˈiərˌfoun/ n. auricular m.

earring /ˈiərˌrɪŋ/ n. pendiente, arete m.

earth /ɜrθ/ n. tierra f.

earthquake /ˈɜrθˌkweik/ n. terremoto m.

ease /iz/ n. 1. reposo m.; facilidad f. —v. 2. aliviar.

easel /ˈizəl/ n. caballete m.

easily /ˈizəli/ adv. fácilmente.

east /ist/ n. oriente, este m.

Easter /ˈistər/ n. Pascua Florida.

eastern /ˈistərn/ a. oriental.

eastward /ˈistwərd/ adv. hacia el este.

easy /ˈizi/ a. fácil.

eat /it/ v. comer.

eau de Cologne /ˈou də kəˈloun/ colonia f.

eaves /ivz/ n. socarrén m.

ebb /ɛb/ n. 1. menguante f. —v. 2. menguar.

ebony /ˈɛbəni/ n. ébano m.

eccentric /ɪkˈsɛntrɪk/ a. excéntrico.

eccentricity /ˌɪksɛnˈtrɪsɪti/ n. excentricidad f.

ecclesiastic /ɪˌkliziˈæstɪk/ a. & n. eclesiástico f.

echelon /ˈɛʃəˌlɒn/ n. escalón f.

echo /ˈɛkou/ n. eco m.

eclipse /ɪˈklɪps/ n. 1. eclipse m. —v. 2. eclipsar.

ecological /ˌɛkəˈlɒdʒɪkəl/ a. ecológico.

ecology /ɪˈkɒlədʒi/ n. ecología f.

economic /ˌɛkəˈnɒmɪk, ˌikə-/ a. económico.

economical /ˌɛkəˈnɒmɪkəl, ˌikə-/ a. económico.

economics /ˌɛkəˈnɒmɪks, ˌikə-/ n. economía política.

economist /ɪˈkɒnəmɪst/ n. economista m. & f.

economize /ɪˈkɒnəˌmaiz/ v. economizar.

economy /ɪˈkɒnəmi/ n. economía f.

ecstasy /ˈɛkstəsi/ n. éxtasis f.

Ecuadorian /ˌɛkwəˈdɔriən/ a. & n. ecuatoriano -na.

ecumenical /ˌɛkyuˈmɛnɪkəl/ a. ecuménico.

eczema /'ɛksəmə/ n. eczema f.

eddy /'ɛdi/ n. **1.** remolino m. —v. **2.** remolinar.

edge /ɛdʒ/ n. **1.** filo; borde m. —v. **2. e. one's way,** abrirse paso.

edible /'ɛdəbəl/ a. comestible.

edict /'idɪkt/ n. edicto m.

edifice /'ɛdəfɪs/ n. edificio m.

edify /'ɛdə,faɪ/ v. edificar.

edition /ɪ'dɪʃən/ n. edición f.

editor /'ɛdɪtər/ n. redactor -ra.

editorial /,ɛdɪ'tɔriəl/ n. editorial m. & a. editorial m. **e. board,** consejo de redacción m. **e. staff,** redacción f.

educate /'ɛdʒu,keɪt/ v. educar.

education /,ɛdʒu'keɪʃən/ n. instrucción; enseñanza f.

educational /,ɛdʒu'keɪʃənl/ a. educativo.

educator /'ɛdʒu,keɪtər/ n. educador -ra, pedagogo -ga.

eel /il/ n. anguila f.

efface /ɪ'feɪs/ v. tachar.

effect /ɪ'fɛkt/ n. **1.** efecto m. **in e.,** en vigor. —v. **2.** efectuar, realizar.

effective /ɪ'fɛktɪv/ a. eficaz; efectivo; en vigor.

effectively /ɪ'fɛktɪvli/ adv. eficazmente.

effectiveness /ɪ'fɛktɪvnɪs/ n. efectividad f.

effectual /ɪ'fɛktʃuəl/ a. eficaz.

effeminate /ɪ'fɛmənɪt/ a. afeminado.

efficacy /'ɛfɪkəsi/ n. eficacia f.

efficiency /ɪ'fɪʃənsi/ n. eficiencia f.

efficient /ɪ'fɪʃənt/ a. eficaz.

efficiently /ɪ'fɪʃəntli/ adv. eficazmente.

effigy /'ɛfɪdʒi/ n. efigie f.

effort /'ɛfərt/ n. esfuerzo m.

effrontery /ɪ'frʌntəri/ n. impudencia f.

effusive /ɪ'fyusɪv/ a. efusivo.

egg /ɛg/ n. huevo m. **fried e.,** huevo frito. **soft-boiled e.,** h. pasado por agua. **scrambled eggs,** huevos revueltos.

eggplant /'ɛg,plænt/ n. berenjena f.

egg white clara de huevo f.

egoism /'igou,ɪzəm/ **egotism** n. egoísmo m.

egoist /'igouɪst/ **egotist** n. egoísta m. & f.

egotism /'igə,tɪzəm/ n. egotismo m.

egotist /'igətɪst/ n. egotista m. & f.

Egypt /'idʒɪpt/ n. Egipto m.

Egyptian /ɪ'dʒɪpʃən/ a. & n. egipcio -ia.

eight /eɪt/ a. & pron. ocho.

eighteen /'eɪ'tin/ a. & pron. dieciocho.

eighth /eɪtθ, eɪθ/ a. octavo.

eightieth /'eɪtiɪθ/ a. octogésimo m.

eighty /'eɪti/ a. & pron. ochenta.

either /'iðər/ a. & pron. **1.** cualquiera de los dos. —adv. **2.** tampoco. —conj. **3. either... or,** o... o.

ejaculate /ɪ'dʒækyə,leɪt/ v. exclamar; eyacular.

ejaculation /ɪ,dʒækyə'leɪʃən/ n. eyaculación f.

eject /ɪ'dʒɛkt/ v. expeler; eyectar.

ejection /ɪ'dʒɛkʃən/ n. expulsión f.; eyección f.

elaborate /a ɪ'læbərɪt; v -ə,reɪt/ a. **1.** elaborado. —v. **2.** elaborar; ampliar.

elapse /ɪ'læps/ v. transcurrir; pasar.

elastic /ɪ'læstɪk/ a. & n. elástico m.

elasticity /ɪlæ'stɪsɪti/ n. elasticidad f.

elate /ɪ'leɪt/ v. exaltar.

elation /ɪ'leɪʃən/ n. exaltación f.

elbow /'ɛlbou/ n. codo m.

elder /'ɛldər/ a. **1.** mayor. —n. **2.** anciano -na.

elderly /'ɛldərli/ a. de edad.

eldest /'ɛldɪst/ a. mayor.

elect /ɪ'lɛkt/ v. elegir.

election /ɪ'lɛkʃən/ n. elección f.

elective /ɪ'lɛktɪv/ a. electivo.

electorate /ɪ'lɛktərɪt/ n. electorado m.

electric /ɪ'lɛktrɪk/ **electrical** a. eléctrico.

electrician /ɪlɛk'trɪʃən/ n. electricista m. & f.

electricity /ɪlɛk'trɪsɪti/ n. electricidad f.

electrocardiogram /ɪ,lɛktrou'kardiə,græm/ n. electrocardiograma m.

electrocute /ɪ'lɛktrə,kyut/ v. electrocutar.

electrode /ɪ'lɛktroud/ n. electrodo m.

electrolysis /ɪlɛk'trɒləsɪs/ n. trólisis f.

electron /ɪ'lɛktrɒn/ n. electrón m.

electronic /ɪlɛkˈtrɒnɪk/ a. electrónico.

electronics /ɪlɪkˈtrɒnɪks/ n. electrónica f.

elegance /ˈɛlɪgəns/ n. elegancia f.

elegant /ˈɛlɪgənt/ a. elegante.

elegy /ˈɛlɪdʒi/ n. elegía f.

element /ˈɛləmənt/ n. elemento m.

elemental /ˌɛləˈmɛntl/ a. elemental.

elementary /ˌɛləˈmɛntəri/ a. elemental.

elephant /ˈɛləfənt/ n. elefante -ta.

elevate /ˈɛləˌveɪt/ v. elevar.

elevation /ˌɛləˈveɪʃən/ n. elevación f.

elevator /ˈɛləˌveɪtər/ n. ascensor m.

eleven /ɪˈlɛvən/ a. & pron. once.

eleventh /ɪˈlɛvənθ/ a. undécimo.

eleventh hour último minuto m.

elf /ɛlf/ n. duende m.

elicit /ɪˈlɪsɪt/ v. sacar; despertar.

eligibility /ˌɛlɪdʒəˈbɪlɪti/ n. elegibilidad f.

eligible /ˈɛlɪdʒəbəl/ a. elegible.

eliminate /ɪˈlɪməˌneɪt/ v. eliminar.

elimination /ɪˌlɪməˈneɪʃən/ n. eliminación f.

elixir /ɪˈlɪksər/ n. elixir m.

elk /ɛlk/ n. alce m., anta m.

elm /ɛlm/ n. olmo m.

elocution /ˌɛləˈkyuʃən/ n. elocución f.

elongate /ɪˈlɒŋgeɪt/ v. alargar.

elope /ɪˈloup/ v. fugarse.

eloquence /ˈɛləkwəns/ n. elocuencia f.

eloquent /ˈɛləkwənt/ a. elocuente.

eloquently /ˈɛləkwəntli/ adv. elocuentemente.

else /ɛls/ adv. más. **someone e.,** otra persona. **something e.,** otra cosa. **or e.,** de otro modo.

elsewhere /ˈɛlsˌwɛər/ adv. en otra parte.

elucidate /ɪˈlusɪˌdeɪt/ v. elucidar.

elude /ɪˈlud/ v. eludir.

elusive /ɪˈlusɪv/ a. evasivo.

emaciated /ɪˈmeɪʃiˌeɪtɪd/ a. demacrado, enflaquecido.

e-mail /ˈiˌmeɪl/ n. correo electrónico m.

emanate /ˈɛməˌneɪt/ v. emanar.

emancipate /ɪˈmænsəˌpeɪt/ v. emancipar.

emancipation /ɪˌmænsəˈpeɪʃən/ n. emancipación f.

emancipator /ɪˈmænsəˌpeɪtər/ n. libertador -ra.

embalm /ɛmˈbɑm/ v. embalsamar.

embankment /ɛmˈbæŋkmənt/ n. malecón, dique m.

embargo /ɛmˈbɑrgou/ n. embargo m.

embark /ɛmˈbɑrk/ v. embarcar.

embarrass /ɛmˈbærəs/ v. avergonzar; turbar.

embarrassing /ɛmˈbærəsɪŋ/ a. penoso, vergonzoso.

embarrassment /ɛmˈbærəsmənt/ n. turbación; vergüenza f.

embassy /ˈɛmbəsi/ n. embajada f.

embellish /ɛmˈbɛlɪʃ/ v. hermosear, embellecer.

embellishment /ɛmˈbɛlɪʃmənt/ n. embellecimiento m.

embezzle /ɛmˈbɛzəl/ v. desfalcar, malversar.

emblem /ˈɛmbləm/ n. emblema m.

embody /ɛmˈbɒdi/ v. incorporar; personificar.

embrace /ɛmˈbreɪs/ n. **1.** abrazo m. —v. **2.** abrazar.

embroider /ɛmˈbrɔɪdər/ v. bordar.

embroidery /ɛmˈbrɔɪdəri, -dri/ n. bordado m.

embryo /ˈɛmbriˌou/ n. embrión m.

embryonic /ˌɛmbriˈɒnɪk/ a. embrionario.

emerald /ˈɛmərəld/ n. esmeralda f.

emerge /ɪˈmɜrdʒ/ v. salir.

emergency /ɪˈmɜrdʒənsi/ n. emergencia f.

emergency brake freno de auxilio m.

emergency exit salida de urgencia f.

emergency landing aterrizaje forzoso m.

emergent /ɪˈmɜrdʒənt/ a. emergente.

emery /ˈɛməri/ n. esmeril m.

emetic /ɪˈmɛtɪk/ n. emético n.

emigrant /ˈɛmɪgrənt/ a. & n. emigrante m. & f.

emigrate /ˈɛmɪˌgreɪt/ v. emigrar.

emigration /ˌɛməˈgreɪʃən/ n. emigración f.

eminence /ˈɛmənəns/ n. altura; eminencia f.

eminent /ˈɛmənənt/ a. eminente.

emissary /ˈɛməˌsɛri/ n. emisario m.

emission /ɪˈmɪʃən/ n. emisión f.

emit /ɪˈmɪt/ v. emitir.

emolument /ɪˈmɒlyəmənt/ n. emolumento m.

emotion /ɪˈmoʊʃən/ n. emoción f.

emotional /ɪˈmoʊʃənl/ a. emocional; sentimental.

emperor /ˈɛmpərər/ n. emperador m.

emphasis /ˈɛmfəsɪs/ n. énfasis m. or f.

emphasize /ˈɛmfəˌsaɪz/ v. acentuar, recalcar.

emphatic /ɛmˈfætɪk/ a. enfático.

empire /ˈɛmpaɪr/ n. imperio m.

empirical /ɛmˈpɪrɪkəl/ a. empírico.

employ /ɛmˈplɔɪ/ v. emplear.

employee /ɛmˈplɔɪi/ n. empleado -da.

employer /ɛmˈplɔɪər/ n. patrón -ona.

employment /ɛmˈplɔɪmənt/ n. empleo m.

employment agency agencia de colocaciones f.

empower /ɛmˈpaʊər/ v. autorizar.

emptiness /ˈɛmptɪnɪs/ n. vaciedad; futilidad f.

empty /ˈɛmpti/ a. **1.** vacío. —v. **2.** vaciar.

emulate /ˈɛmyəˌleɪt/ v. emular.

emulsion /ɪˈmʌlʃən/ n. emulsión f.

enable /ɛnˈeɪbəl/ v. capacitar; permitir.

enact /ɛnˈækt/ v. promulgar, decretar.

enactment /ɛnˈæktmənt/ n. ley f., estatuto m.

enamel /ɪˈnæməl/ n. **1.** esmalte m. —v. **2.** esmaltar.

enamored /ɪˈnæmərd/ a. enamorado.

enchant /ɛnˈtʃænt/ v. encantar.

enchantment /ɛnˈtʃæntmənt/ n. encanto m.

encircle /ɛnˈsɜrkəl/ v. circundar.

enclose /ɛnˈkloʊz/ v. encerrar. **enclosed,** (in letter) adjunto.

enclosure /ɛnˈkloʊʒər/ n. recinto m.; (in letter) incluso m.

encompass /ɛnˈkʌmpəs/ v. circundar.

encounter /ɛnˈkaʊntər/ n. **1.** encuentro m. —v. **2.** encontrar.

encourage /ɛnˈkɜrɪdʒ/ v. animar.

encouragement /ɛnˈkɜrɪdʒmənt/ n. estímulo m.

encroach /ɛnˈkroʊtʃ/ v. usurpar; meterse.

encryption /ɛnˈkrɪpʃən/ n. encriptación f., cifrado m.

encyclical /ɛnˈsɪklɪkəl/ n. encíclica f.

encyclopedia /ɛnˌsaɪkləˈpidiə/ n. enciclopedia f.

end /ɛnd/ n. **1.** fin, término; cabo; extremo; (aim) propósito m. —v. **2.** acabar; terminar.

endanger /ɛnˈdeɪndʒər/ v. poner en peligro.

endear /ɛnˈdɪər/ v. hacer querer.

endeavor /ɛnˈdɛvər/ n. **1.** esfuerzo m. —v. **2.** esforzarse.

ending /ˈɛndɪŋ/ n. conclusión f.

endless /ˈɛndlɪs/ a. sin fin.

endocrine gland /ˈɛndəkrɪn/ glándula endocrina f.

endorse /ɛnˈdɔrs/ v. endosar; apoyar.

endorsement /ɛnˈdɔrsmənt/ n. endoso m.

endow /ɛnˈdaʊ/ v. dotar, fundar.

endowment /ɛnˈdaʊmənt/ n. dotación f., fundación f.

endurance /ɛnˈdʊrəns/ n. resistencia f.

endure /ɛnˈdʊr/ v. soportar, resistir, aguantar.

enema /ˈɛnəmə/ n. enema; lavativa f.

enemy /ˈɛnəmi/ n. enemigo -ga.

energetic /ˌɛnərˈdʒɛtɪk/ a. enérgico.

energy /ˈɛnərdʒi/ n. energía f.

enervate /ˈɛnərˌveɪt/ v. enervar.

enervation /ˌɛnərˈveɪʃən/ n. enervación f.

enfold /ɛnˈfoʊld/ v. envolver.

enforce /ɛnˈfɔrs/ v. ejecutar.

enforcement /ɛnˈfɔrsmənt/ n. ejecución f.

engage /ɛnˈgeɪdʒ/ v. emplear; ocupar.

engaged /ɛnˈgeɪdʒd/ a. (to marry) prometido.

engagement /ɛnˈgeɪdʒmənt/ n. combate; compromiso; contrato m.; cita f.

engine /ˈɛndʒən/ n. máquina f. (railroad) locomotora f.

engineer /ˌɛndʒəˈnɪər/ n. ingeniero -ra; maquinista m.

engineering /ˌɛndʒəˈnɪərɪŋ/ n. ingeniería f.

England /ˈɪŋglənd/ n. Inglaterra f.

English /ˈɪŋglɪʃ/ a. & n. inglés -esa.

English Channel Canal de la Mancha m.

Englishman /ˈɪŋglɪʃmən/ n. inglés m.

Englishwoman /ˈɪŋglɪʃwʊmən/ n. inglesa f.

engrave /enˈgreiv/ v. grabar.

engraver /enˈgreivər/ n. grabador m.

engraving /enˈgreiviŋ/ n. grabado m.

engross /enˈgrous/ v. absorber.

enhance /enˈhæns/ v. aumentar en valor; realzar.

enigma /əˈnigmə/ n. enigma m.

enigmatic /ˌenigˈmætɪk/ a. enigmático.

enjoy /enˈdʒɔi/ v. gozar de; disfrutar de. **e. oneself,** divertirse.

enjoyable /enˈdʒɔiəbəl/ a. agradable.

enjoyment /enˈdʒɔimənt/ n. goce m.

enlarge /enˈlɑrdʒ/ v. agrandar; ampliar.

enlargement /enˈlɑrdʒmənt/ n. ensanchamiento m., ampliación f.

enlarger /enˈlɑrdʒər/ n. amplificador m.

enlighten /enˈlaitn/ v. informar.

enlightenment /enˈlaitnmənt/ n. esclarecimiento m.; cultura f.

enlist /enˈlist/ v. reclutar; alistarse.

enlistment /enˈlistmənt/ n. alistamiento m.

enliven /enˈlaivən/ v. avivar.

enmesh /enˈmeʃ/ v. entrampar.

enmity /ˈenmiti/ n. enemistad f.

enormity /iˈnɔrmiti/ n. enormidad f.

enormous /iˈnɔrməs/ a. enorme.

enough /iˈnʌf/ a. & adv. bastante. **to be e.,** bastar.

enrage /enˈreidʒ/ v. enfurecer.

enrich /enˈritʃ/ v. enriquecer.

enroll /enˈroul/ v. registrar; matricularse.

enrollment /enˈroulmənt/ n. matriculación f.

ensign /ˈensən/ n. bandera f.; (naval) subteniente m.

enslave /enˈsleiv/ v. esclavizar.

ensue /enˈsu/ v. seguir, resultar.

entail /enˈteil/ v. acarrear, ocasionar.

entangle /enˈtæŋgəl/ v. enredar.

enter /ˈentər/ v. entrar.

enterprise /ˈentərˌpraiz/ n. empresa f.

enterprising /ˈentərˌpraiziŋ/ a. emprendedor.

entertain /ˌentərˈtein/ v. entretener; divertir.

entertainment /ˌentərˈteinmənt/ n. entretenimiento m.; diversión f.

enthrall /enˈθrɔl/ v. esclavizar; cautivar.

enthusiasm /enˈθuziˌæzəm/ n. entusiasmo m.

enthusiast /enˈθuziˌæst, -ist/ n. entusiasta m. & f.

enthusiastic /enˌθuziˈæstik/ a. entusiasmado.

entice /enˈtais/ v. inducir.

entire /enˈtaiər/ a. entero.

entirely /enˈtaiərli/ adv. enteramente.

entirety /enˈtaiərti/ n. totalidad f.

entitle /enˈtaitl/ v. autorizar; (book) titular.

entity /ˈentiti/ n. entidad f.

entrails /ˈentreilz/ n. entrañas f.pl.

entrance /ˈentrəns/ n. entrada f.

entrance examination examen de ingreso m.

entrant /ˈentrənt/ n. competidor -ra.

entreat /enˈtrit/ v. rogar, suplicar.

entreaty /enˈtriti/ n. ruego m., súplica f.

entrench /enˈtrentʃ/ v. atrincherar.

entrust /enˈtrʌst/ v. confiar.

entry /ˈentri/ n. entrada f.; Com. partida f.

entry blank hoja de inscripción f.

enumerate /iˈnuməˌreit/ v. enumerar.

enumeration /iˌnuməˈreiʃən/ n. enumeración f.

enunciate /iˈnʌnsiˌeit/ v. enunciar.

enunciation /iˌnʌnsiˈeiʃən/ n. enunciación f.

envelop /enˈveləp/ v. envolver.

envelope /ˈenvəˌloup/ n. sobre m.; cubierta f.

enviable /ˈenviəbəl/ a. envidiable.

envious /ˈenviəs/ a. envidioso.

environment /enˈvairənmənt/ n. ambiente m.

environmentalist /enˌvairənˈmentlist/ n. ambientalista, ecologista m. & f.

environmental protection /enˌvairənˈmentəl/ protección del ambiente.

environs /enˈvairənz/ n. alrededores m.

envoy /'ɛnvɔɪ/ n. enviado m.

envy /'ɛnvɪ/ n. **1.** envidia f. —v. **2.** envidiar.

eon /'iən/ n. eón m.

ephemeral /ɪ'fɛmərəl/ a. efímero m.

epic /'ɛpɪk/ a. **1.** épico. —n. **2.** epopeya f.

epicure /'ɛpɪ,kyʊr/ n. epicúreo m.

epidemic /,ɛpɪ'dɛmɪk/ a. **1.** epidémico. —n. **2.** epidemia f.

epidermis /,ɛpɪ'dɜrmɪs/ n. epidermis f.

epigram /'ɛpɪ,græm/ n. epigrama m.

epilepsy /'ɛpə,lɛpsɪ/ n. epilepsia f.

epilogue /'ɛpə,lɔg/ n. epílogo m.

episode /'ɛpə,soʊd/ n. episodio m.

epistle /ɪ'pɪsəl/ n. epístola f.

epitaph /'ɛpɪ,tæf/ n. epitafio m.

epithet /'ɛpə,θɛt/ n. epíteto m.

epitome /ɪ'pɪtəmɪ/ n. epítome m.

epoch /'ɛpək/ n. época, era f.

Epsom salts /'ɛpsəm/ n.pl. sal de la Higuera f.

equal /'ikwəl/ a. & n. **1.** igual m. —v. **2.** igualar; equivaler.

equality /ɪ'kwɒlɪtɪ/ n. igualdad f.

equalize /'ikwə,laɪz/ v. igualar.

equanimity /,ikwə'nɪmɪtɪ/ n. ecuanimidad f.

equate /ɪ'kweɪt/ v. igualar.

equation /ɪ'kweɪʒən/ n. ecuación f.

equator /ɪ'kweɪtər/ n. ecuador m.

equatorial /,ikwə'tɔrɪəl/ a. ecuatorial

equestrian /ɪ'kwɛstrɪən/ n. **1.** jinete m. —a. **2.** ecuestre.

equilibrium /,ikwə'lɪbrɪəm/ n. equilibrio m.

equinox /'ikwə,nɒks/ n. equinoccio m.

equip /ɪ'kwɪp/ v. equipar.

equipment /ɪ'kwɪpmənt/ n. equipo m.

equitable /'ɛkwɪtəbəl/ a. equitativo.

equity /'ɛkwɪtɪ/ n. equidad, justicia f.

equivalent /ɪ'kwɪvələnt/ a. & n. equivalente m.

equivocal /ɪ'kwɪvəkəl/ a. equívoco, ambiguo.

era /'ɪərə, 'ɛrə/ n. era, época, edad f.

eradicate /ɪ'rædɪ,keɪt/ v. extirpar.

erase /ɪ'reɪs/ v. borrar.

eraser /ɪ'reɪsər/ n. borrador m.

erasure /ɪ'reɪʃər/ n. borradura f.

erect /ɪ'rɛkt/ a. **1.** derecho, erguido. —v. **2.** erigir.

erection /ɪ'rɛkʃən/ **erectness** n. erección f.

ermine /'ɜrmɪn/ n. armiño m.

erode /ɪ'roʊd/ v. corroer.

erosion /ɪ'roʊʒən/ n. erosión f.

erotic /ɪ'rɒtɪk/ a. erótico.

err /ɜr, ɛr/ v. equivocarse.

errand /'ɛrənd/ n. encargo, recado m.

errant /'ɛrənt/ a. errante.

erratic /ɪ'rætɪk/ a. errático.

erroneous /ə'roʊnɪəs/ a. erróneo.

error /'ɛrər/ n. error m.

erudite /'ɛryʊ,daɪt/ a. erudito.

erudition /,ɛryʊ'dɪʃən/ n. erudición f.

eruption /ɪ'rʌpʃən/ n. erupción, irrupción f.

erysipelas /,ɛrə'sɪpələs/ n. erisipela f.

escalate /'ɛskə,leɪt/ v. escalar; intensificarse.

escalator /'ɛskə,leɪtər/ n. escalera mecánica f.

escapade /'ɛskə,peɪd/ n. escapada; correría f.

escape /ɪ'skeɪp/ n. **1.** fuga, huída f. **fire e.,** escalera de salvamento. —v. **2.** escapar; fugarse.

eschew /ɛs'tʃu/ v. evadir.

escort /n 'ɛskɔrt; v ɪ'skɔrt/ n. **1.** escolta f. —v. **2.** escoltar.

escrow /'ɛskroʊ/ n. plica f.

escutcheon /ɪ'skʌtʃən/ n. escudo de armas m.

esophagus /ɪ'sɒfəgəs/ n. esófago m.

esoteric /,ɛsə'tɛrɪk/ a. esotérico.

especially /ɪ'spɛʃəli/ adv. especialmente.

espionage /'ɛspɪə,nɑʒ/ n. espionaje m.

espresso /ɛ'sprɛsoʊ/ n. café exprés, f.

essay /'ɛseɪ/ n. ensayo m.

essayist /'ɛseɪɪst/ n. ensayista m. & f.

essence /'ɛsəns/ n. esencia f.; perfume m.

essential /ə'sɛntʃəl/ a. esencial.

essentially /ə'sɛntʃəli/ adv. esencialmente.

establish /ɪ'stæblɪʃ/ v. establecer.

establishment /ɪ'stæblɪʃmənt/ n. establecimiento m.

estate /ɪ'steɪt/ n. estado m.; hacienda f.; bienes m.pl.

esteem /ɪ'stim/ n. **1.** estima f. —v. **2.** estimar.

estimable /'estəməbəl/ a. estimable.

estimate /n 'estəmɪt; v -,meɪt/ v. **1.** cálculo; presupuesto m. —v. **2.** estimar.

estimation /,estə'meɪʃən/ n. estimación f.; cálculo m.

estrange /ɪ'streɪndʒ/ v. extrañar; enajenar.

estuary /'estʃu,eri/ n. estuario m.

etch /etʃ/ v. grabar al agua fuerte.

etching /'etʃɪŋ/ n. aguafuerte.

eternal /ɪ'tɜrnl/ a. eterno.

eternity /ɪ'tɜrnɪti/ n. eternidad f.

ether /'iθər/ n. éter m.

ethereal /ɪ'θɪəriəl/ a. etéreo.

ethical /'eθɪkəl/ a. ético.

ethics /'eθɪks/ n. ética f.

ethnic /'eθnɪk/ a. étnico.

etiquette /'etɪkɪt/ n. etiqueta f.

etymology /,etə'mɒlədʒi/ n. etimología f.

eucalyptus /,yukə'lɪptəs/ n. eucalipto m.

eugenic /yu'dʒenɪk/ a. eugenésico.

eugenics /yu'dʒenɪks/ n. eugenesia f.

eulogize /'yulə,dʒaɪz/ v. elogiar.

eulogy /'yulədʒi/ n. elogio m.

eunuch /'yunək/ n. eunuco m.

euphonious /yu'founiəs/ a. eufónico.

Europe /'yurəp/ n. Europa f.

European /,yurə'piən/ a. & n. europeo -pea.

euthanasia /,yuθə'neɪʒə, -ʒiə, -ziə/ n. eutanasia f.

evacuate /ɪ'vækyu,eɪt/ v. evacuar.

evade /ɪ'veɪd/ v. evadir.

evaluate /ɪ'vælyu,eɪt/ v. evaluar.

evaluation /ɪ,vælyu'eɪʃən/ n. valoración f.

evangelist /ɪ'vændʒəlɪst/ n. evangelista m. & f.

evaporate /ɪ'væpə,reɪt/ v. evaporarse.

evaporation /ɪ,væpə'reɪʃən/ n. evaporación f.

evasion /ɪ'veɪʒən/ n. evasión f.

evasive /ɪ'veɪsɪv/ a. evasivo.

eve /iv/ n. víspera f.

even /'ivən/ a. **1.** llano; igual. —adv. **2.** aun; hasta. **not e.,** ni siquiera.

evening /'ivnɪŋ/ n. noche, tarde f. **good e.!** ¡buenas tardes! ¡buenas noches!

evening class clase nocturna f.

evenness /'ivənnɪs/ n. uniformidad f.

even number número par m.

event /ɪ'vent/ n. acontecimiento, suceso m.

eventful /ɪ'ventfəl/ a. memorable.

eventual /ɪ'ventʃuəl/ a. eventual.

ever /'evər/ adv. alguna vez; (after not) nunca. **e. since,** desde que.

everlasting /,evər'læstɪŋ/ a. eterno.

every /'evri/ a. cada, todos los.

everybody /'evri,bɒdi, -,bʌdi/ pron. todo el mundo; cada uno.

everyday /'evri,deɪ/ a. ordinario, de cada día.

everyone /'evri,wʌn/ pron. todo el mundo; cada uno; cada cual.

everything /'evri,θɪŋ/ pron. todo m.

everywhere /'evri,wεər/ adv. por todas partes, en todas partes.

evict /ɪ'vɪkt/ v. expulsar.

eviction /ɪ'vɪkʃən/ n. evicción f.

evidence /'evɪdəns/ n. evidencia f.

evident /'evɪdənt/ a. evidente.

evidently /'evɪdəntli/ adv. evidentemente.

evil /'ivəl/ a. **1.** malo; maligno. —n. **2.** mal m.

evince /ɪ'vɪns/ v. revelar.

evoke /ɪ'vouk/ v. evocar.

evolution /,evə'luʃən/ n. evolución f.

evolve /ɪ'vɒlv/ v. desenvolver; desarrollar.

ewe /yu/ n. oveja f.

exact /ɪg'zækt/ a. **1.** exacto. —v. **2.** exigir.

exacting /ɪg'zæktɪŋ/ a. exigente.

exactly /ɪg'zæktli/ adv. exactamente.

exaggerate /ɪg'zædʒə,reɪt/ v. exagerar.

exaggeration /ɪg,zædʒə'reɪʃən/ n. exageración f.

exalt /ɪg'zɔlt/ v. exaltar.

exaltation /,egzɔl'teɪʃən/ n. exaltación f.

examination /ɪg,zæmə'neɪʃən/ n. examen m.; (legal) interrogatorio m.

examine /ɪg'zæmɪn/ v. examinar.

example /ɪg'zæmpəl/ n. ejemplo m.

exasperate /ɪg'zæspə,reɪt/ v. exasperar.

exasperation /ɪgˌzæspəˈreɪʃən/ n. exasperación f.

excavate /ˈɛkskəˌveɪt/ v. excavar, cavar.

exceed /ɪkˈsid/ v. exceder.

exceedingly /ɪkˈsidɪŋli/ adv. sumamente, extremadamente.

excel /ɪkˈsɛl/ v. sobresalir.

excellence /ˈɛksələns/ n. excelencia f.

Excellency /ˈɛksələnsi/ n. (title) Excelencia f.

excellent /ˈɛksələnt/ a. excelente.

except /ɪkˈsɛpt/ prep. **1.** salvo, excepto. —v. **2.** exceptuar.

exception /ɪkˈsɛpʃən/ n. excepción f.

exceptional /ɪkˈsɛpʃənl/ a. excepcional.

excerpt /ˈɛksɜrpt/ n. extracto.

excess /ɪkˈsɛs, ˈɛksɛs/ n. exceso m.

excessive /ɪkˈsɛsɪv/ a. excesivo.

exchange /ɪksˈtʃeɪndʒ/ n. **1.** cambio; canje m. **stock e.,** bolsa f. **telephone e.,** central telefónica. —v. **2.** cambiar, canjear, intercambiar.

exchangeable /ɪksˈtʃeɪndʒəbəl/ a. cambiable.

exchange rate tipo de cambio m.

excise /n. ˈɛksaɪz; v. ɪkˈsaɪz/ n. **1.** sisa f. —v. **2.** extirpar.

excite /ɪkˈsaɪt/ v. agitar; provocar; emocionar.

excitement /ɪkˈsaɪtmənt/ n. agitación, conmoción f.

exciting /ɪkˈsaɪtɪŋ/ a. emocionante.

exclaim /ɪkˈskleɪm/ v. exclamar.

exclamation /ˌɛkskləˈmeɪʃən/ n. exclamación f.

exclamation mark punto de admiración m.

exclude /ɪkˈsklud/ v. excluir.

exclusion /ɪkˈskluʒən/ n. exclusión f.

exclusive /ɪkˈsklusɪv/ a. exclusivo.

excommunicate /ˌɛkskəˈmyuniˌkeɪt/ v. excomulgar, descomulgar.

excommunication /ˌɛkskəˌmyuniˈkeɪʃən/ n. excomunión f.

excrement /ˈɛkskrəmənt/ n. excremento m.

excruciating /ɪkˈskruʃiˌeɪtɪŋ/ a. penosísimo.

exculpate /ˈɛkskʌlˌpeɪt/ v. exculpar.

excursion /ɪkˈskɜrʒən/ n. excursión, jira f.

excuse /n. ɪkˈskyus; v. ɪkˈskyuz/ n. **1.** excusa f. —v. **2.** excusar, perdonar, disculpar; dispensar.

execrable /ˈɛksɪkrəbəl/ a. execrable.

execute /ˈɛksɪˌkyut/ v. ejecutar.

execution /ˌɛksɪˈkyuʃən/ n. ejecución f.

executioner /ˌɛksɪˈkyuʃənər/ n. verdugo m.

executive /ɪgˈzɛkyətɪv/ n. & a. ejecutivo m.

executor /ɪgˈzɛkyətər/ n. testamentario m.

exemplary /ɪgˈzɛmpləri/ a. ejemplar.

exemplify /ɪgˈzɛmpləˌfaɪ/ v. ejemplificar.

exempt /ɪgˈzɛmpt/ a. **1.** exento. —v. **2.** exentar.

exercise /ˈɛksərˌsaɪz/ n. **1.** ejercicio m. —v. **2.** ejercitar.

exert /ɪgˈzɜrt/ v. esforzar.

exertion /ɪgˈzɜrʃən/ n. esfuerzo m.

exhale /ɛksˈheɪl/ v. exhalar.

exhaust /ɪgˈzɔst/ n. **1.** Auto. escape m. —v. **2.** agotar.

exhaustion /ɪgˈzɔstʃən/ n. agotamiento m.

exhaustive /ɪgˈzɔstɪv/ a. exhaustivo.

exhaust pipe tubo de escape m.

exhibit /ɪgˈzɪbɪt/ n. **1.** exhibición, exposición f. —v. **2.** exhibir.

exhibition /ˌɛksəˈbɪʃən/ n. exhibición f.

exhilarate /ɪgˈzɪləˌreɪt/ v. alegrar; estimular.

exhort /ɪgˈzɔrt/ v. exhortar.

exhortation /ˌɛgzɔrˈteɪʃən/ n. exhortación f.

exhume /ɪgˈzum/ v. exhumar.

exigency /ˈɛksɪdʒənsi/ n. exigencia f., urgencia f.

exile /ˈɛgzaɪl/ n. **1.** destierro m., (person) desterrado m. —v. **2.** desterrar.

exist /ɪgˈzɪst/ v. existir.

existence /ɪgˈzɪstəns/ n. existencia f.

existent /ɪgˈzɪstənt/ a. existente.

exit /ˈɛgzɪt, ˈɛksɪt/ n. salida f.

exodus /ˈɛksədəs/ n. éxodo m.

exonerate /ɪgˈzɒnəˌreɪt/ v. exonerar.

exorbitant /ɪgˈzɔrbɪtənt/ a. exorbitante.

exorcise /'eksɔr,saiz/ v. exorcizar.

exotic /ig'zɒtik/ a. exótico.

expand /ik'spænd/ v. dilatar; ensanchar.

expanse /ik'spæns/ n. espacio m.; extensión f.

expansion /ik'spænʃən/ n. expansión f.

expansion slot ranura de expansión f.

expansive /ik'spænsiv/ a. expansivo.

expatiate /ik'speiʃi,eit/ v. espaciarse.

expatriate /n, a eks'peitriit; v eks'peitri,eit/ n. & a. **1.** expatriado m. —v. **2.** expatriar.

expect /ik'spekt/ v. esperar; contar con.

expectancy /ik'spektənsi/ n. esperanza f.

expectation /,ekspek'teiʃən/ n. esperanza f.

expectorate /ik'spektə,reit/ v. expectorar.

expediency /ik'spidiənsi/ n. conveniencia f.

expedient /ik'spidiənt/ a. **1.** oportuno. —n. **2.** expediente m.

expedite /'ekspi,dait/ v. acelerar; despachar.

expedition /,ekspi'diʃən/ n. expedición f.

expel /ik'spel/ v. expeler; expulsar.

expend /ik'spend/ v. desembolsar, expender.

expenditure /ik'spendit ʃər/ n. desembolso; gasto m.

expense /ik'spens/ n. gasto m.; costa f.

expensive /ik'spensiv/ a. caro, costoso.

expensively /ik'spensivli/ adv. costosamente.

experience /ik'spiəriəns/ n. **1.** experiencia f. —v. **2.** experimentar.

experienced /ik'spiəriənst/ a. experimentado, perito.

experiment /n ik'sperəmənt; v -,ment/ n. **1.** experimento m. —v. **2.** experimentar.

experimental /ik,sperə'mentl/ a. experimental.

expert /'ekspɜrt/ a. & n. experto -ta.

expertise /,ekspər'tiz/ n. pericia f.

expiate /'ekspi,eit/ v. expiar.

expiration /,ekspə'reiʃən/ n. expiración f.

expiration date fecha de caducidad f.

expire /ik'spaiər/ v. expirar; Com. vencerse.

explain /ik'splein/ v. explicar.

explanation /,eksplə'neiʃən/ n. explicación f.

explanatory /ik'splænə,tori/ a. explicativo.

expletive /'eksplitiv/ n. **1.** interjección f. —a. **2.** expletivo.

explicit /ik'splisit/ a. explícito, claro.

explode /ik'sploud/ v. estallar, volar; refutar.

exploit /ik'sploit/ n. **1.** hazaña f. —v. **2.** explotar.

exploitation /,eksploi'teiʃən/ n. explotación f.

exploration /,eksplə'reiʃən/ n. exploración f.

exploratory /ik'splorə,tori/ a. exploratorio.

explore /ik'splor/ v. explorar.

explorer /ik'splorər/ n. explorador -ra.

explosion /ik'splouʒən/ n. explosión f.

explosive /ik'splousiv/ a. explosivo.

export /n 'eksport; v ik'sport/ n. **1.** exportación f. —v. **2.** exportar.

exportation /,ekspor'teiʃən/ n. exportación f.

expose /ik'spouz/ v. exponer; descubrir.

exposition /,ekspə'ziʃən/ n. exposición f.

expository /ik'spozi,tori/ a. expositivo.

expostulate /ik'spostʃə,leit/ v. altercar.

exposure /ik'spouʒər/ n. exposición f.

expound /ik'spaund/ v. exponer, explicar.

express /ik'spres/ a. & n. **1.** expreso m. **e. company,** compañía de porteo. —v. **2.** expresar.

expression /ik'spreʃən/ n. expresión f.

expressive /ik'spresiv/ a. expresivo.

expressly /ik'spresli/ adv. expresamente.

expressman /ik'spresmən, -,mæn/ n. empresario de expresos m.

expressway /ik'spres,wei/ n. autopista f.

expropriate /eks'proupri,eit/ v. expropriar.

expulsion /ɪk'spʌlʃən/ n. expulsión f.

expunge /ɪk'spʌndʒ/ v. borrar, expurgar.

expurgate /'ekspər,geit/ v. expurgar.

exquisite /ɪk'skwɪzɪt/ a. exquisito.

extant /'ekstənt/ a. existente.

extemporaneous /ɪk,stempə'reiniəs/ a. improvisado.

extend /ɪk'stend/ v. extender.

extension /ɪk'stenʃən/ n. extensión f.

extensive /ɪk'stensiv/ a. extenso.

extensively /ɪk'stensivli/ adv. extensamente.

extent /ɪk'stent/ n. extensión f.; grado m. **to a certain e.,** hasta cierto punto.

extenuate /ɪk'stenyu,eit/ v. extenuar.

exterior /ɪk'stɪəriər/ a. & n. exterior m.

exterminate /ɪk'stɜrmə,neit/ v. exterminar.

extermination /ɪk,stɜrmə'neiʃən/ n. exterminio m.

external /ɪk'stɜrnl/ a. externo, exterior.

extinct /ɪk'stɪŋkt/ a. extinto.

extinction /ɪk'stɪŋkʃən/ n. extinción f.

extinguish /ɪk'stɪŋgwɪʃ/ v. extinguir, apagar.

extol /ɪk'stoul/ v. alabar.

extort /ɪk'stɔrt/ v. exigir dinero sin derecho.

extortion /ɪk'stɔrʃən/ n. extorsión f.

extra /'ekstrə/ a. 1. extraordinario; adicional. —n. 2. (newspaper) extra m.

extract /n 'ekstrækt; v ɪk'strækt/ n. 1. extracto m. —v. 2. extraer.

extraction /ɪk'strækʃən/ n. extracción f.

extraneous /ɪk'streiniəs/ a. extraño; ajeno.

extraordinary /ɪk'strɔrdn,eri/ a. extraordinario.

extravagance /ɪk'strævəgəns/ n. extravagancia f.

extravagant /ɪk'strævəgənt/ a. extravagante.

extreme /ɪk'strim/ a. & n. extremo m.

extremity /ɪk'stremɪti/ n. extremidad f.

extricate /'ekstrɪ,keit/ v. desenredar.

exuberant /ɪg'zubərənt/ a. exuberante.

exude /ɪg'zud/ v. exudar.

exult /ɪg'zʌlt/ v. regocijarse.

exultant /ɪg'zʌltnt/ a. triunfante.

eye /ai/ n. 1. ojo m. —v. 2. ojear.

eyeball /'ai,bɔl/ n. globo del ojo.

eyebrow /'ai,brau/ n. ceja f.

eyeglasses /'ai,glæsɪz/ n. lentes m.pl.

eyelash /'ai,læʃ/ n. pestaña f.

eyelid /'ai,lɪd/ n. párpado m.

eyeliner /'ai,lainər/ n. lápiz de ojos m.

eye shadow n. sombra de ojos f.

eyesight /'ai,sait/ n. vista f.

F

fable /'feibəl/ n. fábula; ficción f.

fabric /'fæbrɪk/ n. tejido m., tela f.

fabricate /'fæbrɪ,keit/ v. fabricar.

fabulous /'fæbyələs/ a. fabuloso.

façade /fə'sɑd/ n. fachada f.

face /feis/ n. 1. cara f. **make faces,** hacer muecas. —v. 2. encararse con. **f. the street,** dar a la calle.

facet /'fæsɪt/ n. faceta f.

facetious /fə'siʃəs/ a. chistoso.

facial /'feiʃəl/ n. 1. masaje facial m. —a. 2. facial.

facile /'fæsɪl/ a. fácil.

facilitate /fə'sɪlɪ,teit/ v. facilitar.

facility /fə'sɪlɪti/ n. facilidad f.

facsimile /fæk'sɪməli/ n. facsímile m.

fact /fækt/ n. hecho m. **in f.,** en realidad.

faction /'fækʃən/ n. facción f.

factor /'fæktər/ n. factor m.

factory /'fæktəri/ n. fábrica f.

factual /'fæktʃuəl/ a. verdadero.

faculty /'fækəlti/ n. facultad f.

fad /fæd/ n. boga; novedad f.

fade /feid/ v. desteñirse; (flowers) marchitarse.

fail /feil/ n. 1. **without f.,** sin falla. —v. 2. fallar; fracasar. **not to f. to,** no dejar de.

failure /'feilyər/ n. fracaso m.

faint /feint/ a. 1. débil; vago;

pálido. —*n.* **2.** desmayo *m.* —*v.*
3. desmayarse.

faintly /'feintli/ *adv.* débilmente;
indistintamente.

fair /feər/ *a.* **1.** razonable, justo;
(hair) rubio; (weather) bueno.
—*n.* **2.** feria *f.*

fairly /'feərli/ *adv.* imparcial-
mente; regularmente; claramente;
bellamente.

fairness /'feərnis/ *n.* justicia *f.*

fair play juego limpio *m.*

fairway /'feər,wei/ *n.* (golf) calle
f.

fairy /'feəri/ *n.* hada *f.*, duende *m.*

faith /feiθ/ *n.* fe; confianza *f.*

faithful /'feiθfəl/ *a.* fiel.

fake /feik/ *a.* **1.** falso; postizo.
—*n.* **2.** imitación; estafa *f.* —*v.* **3.**
imitar; fingir.

faker /'feikər/ *n.* imitador *m.*;
farsante *m.*

falcon /'fɔlkən/ *n.* halcón *m.*

fall /fɔl/ *n.* **1.** caída; catarata *f.*;
(season) otoño *m.*; (in price) baja
f. —*v.* **2.** caer; bajar. **f. asleep,**
dormirse; **f. in love,** enamorarse.

fallacious /fə'leiʃəs/ *a.* falaz.

fallacy /'fæləsi/ *n.* falacia *f.*

fallible /'fæləbəl/ *a.* falible.

fallout /'fɔl,aut/ *n.* lluvia radiac-
tiva, polvillo radiactivo.

fallow /'fælou/ *a.* sin cultivar;
barbecho.

false /fɔls/ *a.* falso; postizo.

falsehood /'fɔlshud/ *n.* falsedad;
mentira *f.*

falseness /'fɔlsnis/ *n.* falsedad,
perfidia *f.*

false teeth /tiθ/ dentadura postiza
f.

falsetto /fɔl'setou/ *n.* falsete *m.*

falsification /,fɔlsəfɪ'keiʃən/ *n.*
falsificación *f.*

falsify /'fɔlsəfai/ *v.* falsificar.

falter /'fɔltər/ *v.* vacilar; (in
speech) tartamudear.

fame /feim/ *n.* fama *f.*

familiar /fə'milyər/ *a.* familiar;
conocido. **be f. with,** estar fami-
liarizado con.

familiarity /fə,mili'æriti/ *n.* familiaridad *f.*

familiarize /fə'milyə,raiz/ *v.*
familiarizar.

family /'fæməli/ *n.* familia; especie *f.*

family name apellido *m.*

family tree árbol genealógico *m.*

famine /'fæmin/ *n.* hambre; carestía *f.*

famished /'fæmiʃt/ *a.* hambriento.

famous /'feiməs/ *a.* famoso, célebre.

fan /fæn/ *n.* abanico; ventilador
m. (sports) aficionado -da.

fanatic /fə'nætik/ *a. & n.* fanático
-ca.

fanatical /fə'nætikəl/ *a.* fanático.

fanaticism /fə'nætə,sizəm/ *n.*
fanatismo *m.*

fanciful /'fænsifəl/ *a.* caprichoso;
fantástico.

fancy /'fænsi/ *a.* **1.** fino, elegante.
f. foods, novedades *f.pl.* —*n.* **2.**
fantasía *f.*; capricho *m.* —*v.* **3.**
imaginar.

fanfare /'fænfeər/ *n.* fanfarria *f.*

fang /fæŋ/ *n.* colmillo *m.*

fan heater estufa de aire *f.*

fantastic /fæn'tæstik/ *a.* fantástico.

fantasy /'fæntəsi/ *n.* fantasía *f.*

FAQ /fæk/ *n.* (Frequently Asked
Questions) preguntas más fre-
cuentes *f.pl.*

far /far/ *a.* **1.** lejano, distante.
—*adv.* **2.** lejos. **how f.,** a qué distancia. **as f. as,** hasta. **so f., thus
f.,** hasta aquí.

farce /fars/ *n.* farsa *f.*

fare /feər/ *n.* pasaje *m.*

farewell /,feər'wel/ *n.* **1.** despedida *f.* **to say f.** despedirse.
—*interj.* **2.** ¡adiós!

farfetched /'far'fetʃt/ *a.* forzado,
inverosímil.

farm /farm/ *n.* **1.** granja; hacienda
f. —*v.* **2.** cultivar, labrar la tierra.

farmer /'farmər/ *n.* labrador,
agricultor *m.*

farmhouse /'farm,haus/ *n.* hacienda, alquería *f.*

farming /'farmiŋ/ *n.* agricultura
f.; cultivo *m.*

fart /fart/ *n. Colloq.* pedo *m.*

fascinate /'fæsə,neit/ *v.* fascinar,
embelesar.

fascination /,fæsə'neiʃən/ *n.* fascinación *f.*

fascism /'fæʃ,izəm/ *n.* fascismo
m.

fashion /'fæʃən/ *n.* **1.** moda; costumbre; guisa *f.* **be in f.,** estilarse. —*v.* **2.** formar.

fashionable /'fæʃənəbəl/ *a.* de
moda, en boga.

fashion show desfile de modas, pase de modelos *m.*

fast /fæst/ *a.* **1.** rápido, veloz; (watch) adelantado; (color) firme. —*adv.* **2.** ligero, de prisa. —*n.* **3.** ayuno *m.* —*v.* **4.** ayunar.

fasten /'fæsən/ *v.* afirmar; atar; fijar.

fastener /'fæsənər/ *n.* asegurador *m.*

fastidious /fæ'stɪdiəs/ *a.* melindroso.

fat /fæt/ *a.* **1.** gordo. —*n.* **2.** grasa, manteca *f.*

fatal /'feitl/ *a.* fatal.

fatality /fei'tæliti/ *n.* fatalidad *f.*

fatally /'feitli/ *adv.* fatalmente.

fate /feit/ *n.* destino *m.*; suerte *f.*

fateful /'feitfəl/ *a.* fatal; ominoso.

father /'fɑðər/ *n.* padre *m.*

fatherhood /'fɑðər,hʊd/ *n.* paternidad *f.*

father-in-law /'fɑ,ðər ɪn lɔ/ *n.* suegro *m.*

fatherland /'fɑðər,lænd/ *n.* patria *f.*

fatherly /'fɑðərli/ *a.* paternal. —*adv.* **2.** paternalmente.

fathom /'fæðəm/ *n.* **1.** braza *f.* —*v.* **2.** sondar; *Fig.* penetrar en.

fatigue /fə'tig/ *n.* **1.** fatiga *f.*, cansancio *m.* —*v.* **2.** fatigar, cansar.

fatten /'fætn/ *v.* engordar, cebar.

faucet /'fɔsɪt/ *n.* grifo *m.*, llave *f.*

fault /fɔlt/ *n.* culpa *f.*; defecto *m.* **at f.,** culpable.

faultless /'fɔltlɪs/ *a.* sin tacha, perfecto.

faultlessly /'fɔltlɪsli/ *adv.* perfectamente.

faulty /'fɔlti/ *a.* defectuoso, imperfecto.

fauna /'fɔnə/ *n.* fauna *f.*

favor /'feivər/ *n.* **1.** favor *m.* —*v.* **2.** favorecer.

favorable /'feivərəbəl/ *a.* favorable.

favorite /'feivərɪt/ *a.* & *n.* favorito -ta.

favoritism /'feivəri,tɪzəm/ *n.* favoritismo *m.*

fawn /fɔn/ *n.* **1.** cervato *m.* —*v.* **2.** halagar, adular.

fax /fæks/ *n.* **1.** fax *m.* —*v.* **2.** mandar un fax.

faze /feiz/ *v.* desconcertar.

fear /fɪər/ *n.* **1.** miedo, temor *m.* —*v.* **2.** temer.

fearful /'fɪərfəl/ *a.* temeroso, medroso.

fearless /'fɪərlɪs/ *a.* intrépido; sin temor.

fearlessness /'fɪərlɪsnɪs/ *n.* intrepidez *f.*

feasible /'fizəbəl/ *a.* factible.

feast /fist/ *n.* banquete *m.*; fiesta *f.*

feat /fit/ *n.* hazaña *f.*; hecho *m.*

feather /'fɛðər/ *n.* pluma *f.*

feature /'fitʃər/ *n.* **1.** facción *f.*; rasgo *m.*; (movies) película principal *f.*, largometraje *m.* —*v.* **2.** presentar como atracción especial.

February /'fɛbru,ɛri, 'fɛbyu-/ *n.* febrero *m.*

federal /'fɛdərəl/ *a.* federal.

federation /,fɛdə'reiʃən/ *n.* confederación, federación *f.*

fee /fi/ *n.* honorarios *m.pl.*

feeble /'fibəl/ *a.* débil.

feeble-minded /'fibəl 'maindɪd/ *a.* imbécil.

feebleness /'fibəlnɪs/ *a.* debilidad *f.*

feed /fid/ *n.* **1.** pasto *m.* —*v.* **2.** alimentar; dar de comer. **fed up with,** harto de.

feedback /'fid,bæk/ *n.* feedback *m.*, retroalimentación *f.*

feel /fil/ *n.* **1.** sensación *f.* —*v.* **2.** sentir; palpar. **f. like,** tener ganas de.

feeling /'filɪŋ/ *n.* sensación; sentimiento.

feign /fein/ *v.* fingir.

felicitate /fɪ'lɪsɪ,teit/ *v.* felicitar.

felicitous /fɪ'lɪsɪtəs/ *a.* feliz.

felicity /fɪ'lɪsɪti/ *n.* felicidad *f.*, dicha *f.*

feline /'filain/ *a.* felino.

fellow /'fɛlou/ *n.* compañero; socio *m.*; *Colloq.* tipo *m.*

fellowship /'fɛlou,ʃɪp/ *n.* compañerismo; (for study) beca *f.*

felon /'fɛlən/ *n.* reo *m.* & *f.*, felón -ona.

felony /'fɛləni/ *n.* felonía *f.*

felt /fɛlt/ *n.* fieltro *m.*

felt-tipped pen /'fɛlt ,tɪpt/ rotulador *m.*

female /'fimeil/ *a.* & *n.* hembra *f.*

feminine /'fɛmənɪn/ *a.* femenino.

feminist /'fɛmənɪst/ *a.* & *n.* feminista *a.* & *f.*

fence /fɛns/ *n.* **1.** cerca *f.* —*v.* **2.** cercar.

fender /'fɛndər/ *n.* guardabarros *m.pl.*

ferment /n 'fɜrmɛnt; v fər'mɛnt/

n. **1.** fermento *m.; Fig.* agitación *f.* —*v.* **2.** fermentar.

fermentation /ˌfɜrmenˈteiʃən/ *n.* fermentación *f.*

fern /fɜrn/ *n.* helecho *m.*

ferocious /fəˈrouʃəs/ *a.* feroz, fiero.

ferociously /fəˈrouʃəsli/ *adv.* ferozmente.

ferocity /fəˈrɒsɪti/ *n.* ferocidad *f.*, fiereza *f.*

Ferris wheel /ˈferɪs/ rueda de feria *f.*

ferry /ˈferi/ *n.* transbordador *m.*, barca de transporte.

fertile /ˈfɜrtl/ *a.* fecundo; (land) fértil.

fertility /fərˈtɪliti/ *n.* fertilidad *f.*

fertilization /ˌfɜrtləˈzeiʃən/ *n.* fertilización *f.*

fertilize /ˈfɜrtlˌaiz/ *v.* fertilizar, abonar.

fertilizer /ˈfɜrtlˌaizər/ *n.* abono *m.*

fervency /ˈfɜrvənsi/ *n.* ardor *m.*

fervent /ˈfɜrvənt/ *a.* fervoroso.

fervently /ˈfɜrvəntli/ *adv.* fervorosamente.

fervid /ˈfɜrvɪd/ *a.* férvido.

fervor /ˈfɜrvər/ *n.* fervor *m.*

fester /ˈfestər/ *v.* ulcerarse.

festival /ˈfestəvəl/ *n.* fiesta *f.*

festive /ˈfestɪv/ *a.* festivo.

festivity /feˈstɪvɪti/ *n.* festividad *f.*

festoon /feˈstun/ *n.* **1.** festón *m.* —*v.* **2.** festonear.

fetch /fetʃ/ *v.* ir por; traer.

fete /feit/ *n.* **1.** fiesta *f.* —*v.* **2.** festejar.

fetid /ˈfetɪd/ *a.* fétido.

fetish /ˈfetɪʃ/ *n.* fetiche *m.*

fetter /ˈfetər/ *n.* **1.** grillete *m.* —*v.* **2.** engrillar.

fetus /ˈfitəs/ *n.* feto *m.*

feud /fyud/ *n.* riña *f.*

feudal /ˈfyudl/ *a.* feudal.

feudalism /ˈfyudlˌɪzəm/ *n.* feudalismo *m.*

fever /ˈfivər/ *n.* fiebre *f.*

feverish /ˈfivərɪʃ/ *a.* febril.

feverishly /ˈfivərɪʃli/ *adv.* febrilmente.

few /fyu/ *a.* pocos. **a. f.,** algunos, unos cuantos.

fiancé, fiancée /ˌfianˈsei/ *n.* novio -via.

fiasco /fiˈæskou/ *n.* fiasco *m.*

fiat /ˈfiət/ *n.* fiat *m.*, orden *f.*

fib /fɪb/ *n.* **1.** mentira *f.* —*v.* **2.** mentir.

fiber /ˈfaibər/ *n.* fibra *f.*

fibrous /ˈfaibrəs/ *a.* fibroso.

fickle /ˈfɪkəl/ *a.* caprichoso.

fickleness /ˈfɪkəlnɪs/ *n.* inconstancia *f.*

fiction /ˈfɪkʃən/ *n.* ficción *f.;* (literature) novelas *f.pl.*

fictitious /fɪkˈtɪʃəs/ *a.* ficticio.

fidelity /fɪˈdelɪti/ *n.* fidelidad *f.*

fidget /ˈfɪdʒɪt/ *v.* inquietar.

field /fild/ *n.* campo *m.*

field trip viaje de estudios *m.*

fiend /find/ *n.* demonio *m.*

fiendish /ˈfindɪʃ/ *a.* diabólico, malvado.

fierce /fɪərs/ *a.* fiero, feroz.

fiery /ˈfaiəri/ *a.* ardiente.

fiesta /fiˈestə/ *n.* fiesta *f.*

fife /faif/ *n.* pífano *m.*

fifteen /ˈfifˈtin/ *a. & pron.* quince.

fifteenth /ˈfifˈtinθ/ *n. & a.* décimoquinto.

fifth /fifθ/ *a.* quinto.

fifty /ˈfifti/ *a. & pron.* cincuenta.

fig /fɪg/ *n.* higo *m.* **f. tree,** higuera *f.*

fight /fait/ *n.* **1.** lucha, pelea *f.* —*v.* **2.** luchar, pelear.

fighter /ˈfaitər/ *n.* peleador -ra, luchador -ra.

figment /ˈfɪgmənt/ *n.* invención *f.*

figurative /ˈfɪgyərətɪv/ *a.* metafórico.

figuratively /ˈfɪgyərətɪvli/ *adv.* figuradamente.

figure /ˈfɪgyər/ *n.* **1.** figura; cifra *f.* —*v.* **2.** figurar; calcular.

filament /ˈfɪləmənt/ *n.* filamento *m.*

file /fail/ *n.* **1.** archivo *m.;* (instrument) lima *f.;* (row) fila *f.* —*v.* **2.** archivar; limar.

file cabinet archivador *m.*

filial /ˈfɪliəl/ *a.* filial.

filigree /ˈfɪləˌgri/ *n.* filigrana *f.*

fill /fɪl/ *v.* llenar.

fillet /ˈfɪlɪt/ *n.* filete *m.*

filling /ˈfɪlɪŋ/ *n.* relleno *m.;* (dental) empastadura *f.* **f. station,** gasolinera *f.*

film /fɪlm/ *n.* **1.** película *f.,* film *m.* —*v.* **2.** filmar.

filter /ˈfɪltər/ *n.* **1.** filtro *m.* —*v.* **2.** filtrar.

filth /fɪlθ/ *n.* suciedad, mugre *f.*

filthy /ˈfɪlθi/ *a.* sucio.

fin /fɪn/ *n.* aleta *f.*

final /ˈfainl/ *a.* **1.** final, último. —*n.* **2.** examen final. **finals** (sports) final *f.*

finalist /'fainlist/ n. finalista m. & f.

finally /'fainli/ adv. finalmente.

finances /'fainænsəz/ n. recursos, fondos m.pl.

financial /fi'nænʃəl/ a. financiero.

financier /,finən'siər, ,fainən-/ n. financiero -ra.

find /faind/ n. **1.** hallazgo m. —v. **2.** hallar; encontrar. **f. out,** averiguar, enterarse, saber.

fine /fain/ a. **1.** fino; bueno. —adv. **2.** muy bien. —n. **3.** multa f. —v. **4.** multar.

fine arts /arts/ bellas artes f.pl.

finery /'fainəri/ n. gala f., adorno m.

finesse /fi'nɛs/ n. **1.** artificio m. —v. **2.** valerse de artificio.

finger /'fiŋgər/ n. dedo m.

finger bowl n. enjuagatorio m.

fingernail /'fiŋgər,neil/ n. uña f.

fingerprint /'fiŋgər,print/ n. **1.** impresión digital f. —v. **2.** tomar las impresiones digitales.

finicky /'finiki/ a. melindroso.

finish /'finiʃ/ n. **1.** conclusión f. —v. **2.** acabar, terminar.

finished /'finiʃt/ a. acabado.

finite /'fainait/ a. finito.

fir /fɜr/ n. abeto m.

fire /faiʰr/ n. **1.** fuego; incendio m. —v. **2.** disparar, tirar; *Colloq.* despedir.

fire alarm n. alarma de incendio f.

firearm /'faiʰr,arm/ n. arma de fuego.

firecracker /'faiʰr,krækər/ n. triquitraque m., buscapiés m., petardo m.

firefly /'faiʰr,flai/ n. luciérnaga f.

fireman /'faiʰr,mən/ n. bombero m.; (railway) fogonero m.

fireplace /'faiʰr,pleis/ n. hogar, fogón m.

fireproof /'faiʰr,pruf/ a. incombustible.

fireside /'faiʰr,said/ n. hogar, fogón m.

fireworks /'faiʰr,wɜrks/ n. fuegos artificiales.

firm /fɜrm/ a. **1.** firme. —n. **2.** firma, empresa f.

firmness /'fɜrmnis/ n. firmeza f.

first /fɜrst/ a. & adv. primero. **at f.,** al principio.

first aid primeros auxilios.

first-class /'fɜrst 'klæs/ a. de primera clase.

fiscal /'fiskəl/ a. fiscal.

fish /fiʃ/ n. **1.** (food) pescado m.; (alive) pez m. —v. **2.** pescar.

fisherman /'fiʃərmən/ n. pescador m.

fishhook /'fiʃ,hʊk/ n. anzuelo m.

fishing /'fiʃiŋ/ n. pesca f. **go f.,** ir de pesca.

fishmonger /'fiʃ,mʌŋgər/ n. pescadero m.

fish store pescadería f.

fission /'fiʃən/ n. fisión f.

fissure /'fiʃər/ n. grieta f., quebradura f.; fisura.

fist /fist/ n. puño m.

fit /fit/ a. **1.** capaz; justo. —n. **2.** corte, talle m.; *Med.* convulsión f. —v. **3.** caber; quedar bien, sentar bien.

fitful /'fitfəl/ a. espasmódico; caprichoso.

fitness /'fitnis/ n. aptitud; conveniencia f.

fitting /'fitiŋ/ a. **1.** conveniente. **be f.,** convenir. —n. **2.** ajuste m.

fitting room probador m.

five /faiv/ a. & pron. cinco.

five-day work week /faiv 'dei/ semana inglesa f.

fix /fiks/ n. **1.** apuro m. —v. **2.** fijar; arreglar; componer, reparar.

fixation /fik'seiʃən/ n. fijación f.; fijeza f.

fixed /fikst/ a. fijo.

fixture /'fikstʃər/ n. instalación; guarnición f.

flabby /'flæbi/ a. flojo.

flaccid /'flæksid, 'flæsid/ a. flojo; flácido.

flag /flæg/ n. bandera f.

flagellant /'flædʒələnt/ n. & a. flagelante m.

flagon /'flægən/ n. frasco m.

flagrant /'fleigrənt/ a. flagrante.

flagrantly /'fleigrəntli/ adv. notoriamente.

flair /flɛər/ n. aptitud especial f.

flake /fleik/ n. **1.** escama f.; copo de nieve. —v. **2.** romperse en láminas.

flamboyant /flæm'bɔiənt/ a. flamante, llamativo.

flame /fleim/ n. **1.** llama f. —v. **2.** llamear.

flaming /'fleimiŋ/ a. llameante, flamante.

flamingo /flə'miŋgou/ n. flamenco m.

flammable /'flæməbəl/ a. inflamable.

flank /flæŋk/ n. **1.** ijada f.; Mil. flanco m. —v. **2.** flanquear.

flannel /'flænl/ n. franela f.

flap /flæp/ n. **1.** cartera f. —v. **2.** aletear; sacudirse.

flare /fleər/ n. **1.** llamarada f. —v. **2.** brillar; Fig. enojarse.

flash /flæʃ/ n. **1.** resplandor m.; (lightning) rayo, relámpago m.; Fig. instante m. —v. **2.** brillar.

flashcube /'flæʃ,kyub/ n. cubo de flash m.

flashlight /'flæʃ,lait/ n. linterna (eléctrica).

flashy /'flæʃi/ a. ostentoso.

flask /flæsk/ n. frasco m.

flat /flæt/ a. **1.** llano; (tire) desinflado. —n. **2.** llanura f.; apartamento m.

flatness /'flætnɪs/ n. llanura f.

flatten /'flætn/ v. aplastar, allanar; abatir.

flatter /'flætər/ v. adular, lisonjear.

flatterer /'flætərər/ n. lisonjero -ra; zalamero -ra.

flattery /'flætəri/ n. adulación, lisonja f.

flaunt /flɔnt/ v. ostentar.

flavor /'fleivər/ n. **1.** sabor m. —v. **2.** sazonar.

flavoring /'fleivərɪŋ/ n. condimento m.

flaw /flɔ/ n. defecto m.

flax /flæks/ n. lino m.

flay /flei/ v. despellejar; excoriar.

flea /fli/ n. pulga f.

flea market rastro m.

fleck /flɛk/ n. **1.** mancha f. —v. **2.** varetear.

flee /fli/ v. huir.

fleece /flis/ n. **1.** vellón m. —v. **2.** esquilar.

fleet /flit/ a. **1.** veloz. —n. **2.** flota f.

fleeting /'flitɪŋ/ a. fugaz, pasajero.

flesh /flɛʃ/ n. carne f.

fleshy /'flɛʃi/ a. gordo; carnoso.

flex /flɛks/ n. **1.** doblez m. —v. **2.** doblar.

flexibility /,flɛksə'bɪlɪti/ n. flexibilidad f.

flexible /'flɛksəbəl/ a. flexible.

flier /'flaiər/ n. aviador -ra.

flight /flait/ n. vuelo m.; fuga f.

flight attendant n. azafata f.; ayudante de vuelo m.

flimsy /'flɪmzi/ a. débil.

flinch /flɪntʃ/ v. acobardarse.

fling /flɪŋ/ v. lanzar.

flint /flɪnt/ n. pedernal m.

flip /flɪp/ v. lanzar.

flippant /'flɪpənt/ a. impertinente.

flippantly /'flɪpəntli/ adv. impertinentemente.

flirt /flɜrt/ n. **1.** coqueta f. —v. **2.** coquetear, flirtear.

flirtation /flɜr'teiʃən/ n. coqueteo m.

float /flout/ v. flotar.

flock /flɒk/ n. **1.** rebaño m. —v. **2.** congregarse.

flog /flɒg/ v. azotar.

flood /flʌd/ n. **1.** inundación f. —v. **2.** inundar.

floor /flɔr/ n. **1.** suelo, piso m. —v. **2.** derribar.

floppy disk /'flɒpi/ floppy, m., disquete, m.

floral /'flɔrəl/ a. floral.

florid /'flɔrɪd/ a. florido.

florist /'flɔrɪst/ n. florista m. & f.

flounce /flauns/ n. **1.** (sewing) volante m. —v. **2.** pernear.

flounder /'flaundər/ n. rodaballo m.

flour /flauər/ n. harina f.

flourish /'flɜrɪʃ/ n. **1.** Mus. floreo m. —v. **2.** florecer; prosperar; blandir.

flow /flou/ n. **1.** flujo m. —v. **2.** fluir.

flow chart organigrama m.

flower /'flauər/ n. **1.** flor f. —v. **2.** florecer.

flowerpot /'flauər,pɒt/ n. maceta f.

flowery /'flauəri/ a. florido.

fluctuate /'flʌktʃu,eit/ v. fluctuar.

fluctuation /,flʌktʃu'eiʃən/ n. fluctuación f.

flue /flu/ n. humero m.

fluency /'fluənsi/ n. fluidez f.

fluent /'fluənt/ a. fluido; competente.

fluffy /'flʌfi/ a. velloso.

fluid /'fluid/ a. & n. fluido m.

fluidity /flu'ɪdɪti/ n. fluidez f.

fluoroscope /'flʊrə,skoup/ n. fluoroscopio m.

flurry /'flɜri/ n. agitación f.

flush /flʌʃ/ a. **1.** bien provisto. —n. **2.** sonrojo m. —v. **3.** limpiar con un chorro de agua; sonrojarse.

flute /flut/ n. flauta f.

flutter /'flʌtər/ n. **1.** agitación f. —v. **2.** agitarse.

flux /flʌks/ n. flujo m.

fly /flai/ n. **1.** mosca f. —v. **2.** volar.

flying saucer /'flaiiŋ/ platillo volante m.

foam /foum/ n. **1.** espuma f. —v. **2.** espumar.

focal /'foukəl/ a. focal.

focus /'foukəs/ n. **1.** enfoque m. —v. **2.** enfocar.

fodder /'fɒdər/ n. forraje m., pienso m.

foe /fou/ n. adversario -ria, enemigo -ga.

fog /fɒg/ n. niebla f.

foggy /'fɒgi/ a. brumoso.

foil /fɔil/ v. frustrar.

foist /fɔist/ v. imponer.

fold /fould/ n. **1.** pliegue m. —v. **2.** doblar, plegar.

foldable /'fouldəbəl/ a. plegable.

folder /'fouldər/ n. circular m.; (for filing) carpeta f.

folding /'fouldiŋ/ a. plegable.

foliage /'foulidʒ/ n. follaje m.

folio /'fouli,ou/ n. infolio; folio m.

folklore /'fouk,lɔr/ n. folklore m.

folks /fouks/ n. gente; familia f.

follicle /'fɒlikəl/ n. folículo m.

follow /'fɒlou/ v. seguir.

follower /'fɒlouər/ n. partidario -ria.

folly /'fɒli/ n. locura f.

foment /ou'mɛnt/ v. fomentar.

fond /fɒnd/ a. cariñoso, tierno. **be f. of,** ser aficionado a.

fondle /'fɒndl/ v. acariciar.

fondly /'fɒndli/ adv. tiernamente.

fondness /'fɒndnis/ n. afición f.; cariño m.

food /fud/ n. alimento m.; comida f.

foodie /'fudi/ n. Colloq. gastrónomo -ma, gourmet m. & f.

food poisoning /'pɔizəniŋ/ intoxicación alimenticia f.

foodstuffs /'fud,stʌfs/ n.pl. comestibles, víveres m.pl.

fool /ful/ n. tonto -ta; bobo -ba; bufón -ona. —v. engañar.

foolhardy /'ful,hɑrdi/ a. temerario.

foolish /'fuliʃ/ a. bobo, tonto, majadero.

foolproof /'ful,pruf/ a. seguro.

foot /fut/ n. pie m.

footage /'futidʒ/ n. longitud en pies.

football /'fut,bɔl/ n. fútbol, balompié m.

footbridge /'fut,bridʒ/ n. puente para peatones m.

foothold /'fut,hould/ n. posición establecida.

footing /'futiŋ/ n. base f., fundamento m.

footlights /'fut,laits/ n.pl. luces del proscenio.

footnote /'fut,nout/ n. nota al pie de una página.

footpath /'fut,pæθ/ n. sendero m.

footprint /'fut,print/ n. huella f.

footstep /'fut,stɛp/ n. paso m.

footstool /'fut,stul/ n. escañuelo m., banqueta f.

fop /fɒp/ n. petimetre m.

for /fɔr; unstressed fər/ prep. **1.** para; por. **as f.,** en cuanto a. **what f.,** ¿para qué? —conj. **2.** porque, pues.

forage /'fɔridʒ/ n. **1.** forraje m. —v. **2.** forrajear.

foray /'fɔrei/ n. correría f.

forbear /fɔr'bɛər/ v. cesar; abstenerse.

forbearance /fɔr'bɛərəns/ n. paciencia f.

forbid /fər'bid/ v. prohibir.

forbidding /fər'bidiŋ/ a. repugnante.

force /fɔrs/ n. **1.** fuerza f. —v. **2.** forzar.

forced landing /fɔrst/ aterrizaje forzoso m.

forceful /'fɔrsfəl/ a. fuerte; enérgico.

forcible /'fɔrsəbəl/ a. a la fuerza; enérgico.

ford /fɔrd/ n. **1.** vado m. —v. **2.** vadear.

fore /fɔr/ a. **1.** delantero. —n. **2.** delantera f.

fore and aft de popa a proa.

forearm /'fɔr'ɑrm/ n. antebrazo m.

forebears /'fɔr,bɛərz/ n.pl. antepasados m.pl.

forebode /fɔr'boud/ v. presagiar.

foreboding /fɔr'boudiŋ/ n. presentimiento m.

forecast /'fɔr,kæst/ n. **1.** pronóstico m.; profecía f. —v. **2.** pronosticar.

forecastle /'fouksəl/ n. Naut. castillo de proa.

forefathers /'for,fɑðərz/ n. antepasados m.pl.

forefinger /'for,fɪŋgər/ n. índice m.

forego /for'gou/ v. renunciar.

foregone /for'gɔn/ a. predeterminado.

foreground /'for,graund/ n. primer plano.

forehead /'forɪd/ n. frente f.

foreign /'forɪn/ a. extranjero.

foreign aid n. ayuda exterior f.

foreigner /'forənər/ n. extranjero -ra; forastero -ra.

foreleg /'for,leg/ n. pierna delantera.

foreman /'formən/ n. capataz, jefe de taller m.

foremost /'for,moust/ a. **1.** primero. —adv. **2.** en primer lugar.

forenoon /'for,nun/ n. mañana f.

forensic /fə'rɛnsɪk/ a. forense.

forerunner /'for,rʌnər/ n. precursor -ra.

foresee /for'si/ v. prever.

foreshadow /for'ʃædou/ v. prefigurar, anunciar.

foresight /'for,sait/ n. previsión f.

forest /'forɪst/ n. bosque m.; selva f.

forestall /for'stɔl/ v. anticipar; prevenir.

forester /'forəstər/ n. silvicultor -ra; guardamontes m.pl. & f.pl.

forestry /'forəstri/ n. silvicultura f.

foretell /for'tɛl/ v. predecir.

forever /for'ɛvər/ adv. por siempre, para siempre.

forevermore /for,ɛvər'mor/ adv. siempre.

forewarn /for'worn/ v. advertir, avisar.

foreword /'for,wərd/ n. prefacio m.

forfeit /'forfɪt/ n. **1.** prenda; multa f. —v. **2.** perder.

forfeiture /'forfɪtʃər/ n. decomiso m., multa f.; pérdida f.

forgather /for'gæðər/ v. reunirse.

forge /fordʒ/ n. **1.** fragua f. —v. **2.** forjar; falsear.

forger /'fordʒər/ n. forjador -ra; falsificador -ra.

forgery /'fordʒəri/ n. falsificación f.

forget /for'gɛt/ v. olvidar.

forgetful /for'gɛtfəl/ a. olvidadizo.

forgive /for'gɪv/ v. perdonar.

forgiveness /for'gɪvnɪs/ n. perdón m.

fork /fork/ n. **1.** tenedor m.; bifurcación f. —v. **2.** bifurcarse.

forlorn /for'lorn/ a. triste.

form /form/ n. **1.** forma f.; (document) formulario m. —v. **2.** formar.

formal /'forməl/ a. formal; ceremonioso. **f. dance,** baile de etiqueta. **f. dress,** traje de etiqueta.

formality /for'mælɪti/ n. formalidad f.

formally /'forməli/ adv. formalmente.

format /'formæt/ n. formato m.

formation /for'meɪʃən/ n. formación f.

formative /'formətɪv/ a. formativo.

formatting /'formætɪŋ/ n. formateo m.

former /'formər/ a. anterior; antiguo. **the f.,** aquél.

formerly /'formərli/ adv. antiguamente.

formidable /'formɪdəbəl/ a. formidable.

formless /'formlɪs/ a. sin forma.

formula /'formyələ/ n. fórmula f.

formulate /'formyə,leit/ v. formular.

formulation /,formy'leɪʃən/ n. formulación f.; expresión f.

forsake /for'seik/ v. abandonar.

fort /fort/ n. fortaleza f.; fuerte m.

forte /'fortei/ a. & adv. Mus. forte; fuerte.

forth /forθ/ adv. adelante. **back and f.,** de aquí allá. **and so f.,** etcétera.

forthcoming /'forθ'kʌmɪŋ/ a. futuro, próximo.

forthright /'forθ,rait/ a. franco.

forthwith /,forθ'wɪθ/ adv. inmediatamente.

fortification /,fortəfɪ'keɪʃən/ n. fortificación f.

fortify /'fortə,fai/ v. fortificar.

fortissimo /for'tɪsə,mou/ a. & adv. Mus. fortísimo.

fortitude /'fortɪ,tud/ n. fortaleza; fortitud f.

fortnight /'fort,nait/ n. quincena f.

fortress /'fortrɪs/ n. fuerte m., fortaleza f.

fortuitous /for'tuɪtəs/ a. fortuito.

fortunate /'fortʃənɪt/ a. afortunado.

fortune /ˈfɔrtʃən/ n. fortuna; suerte f.

fortune-teller /ˈfɔrtʃən ˌtelər/ n. sortílego -ga, adivino -na.

forty /ˈfɔrti/ a. & pron. cuarenta.

forum /ˈfɔrəm/ n. foro m.

forward /ˈfɔrwərd/ a. **1.** delantero; atrevido. —adv. **2.** adelante. —v. **3.** trasmitir, reexpedir.

foster /ˈfɔstər/ a. **1. f. child,** hijo adoptivo. —v. **2.** fomentar; criar.

foul /faul/ a. sucio; impuro.

found /faund/ v. fundar.

foundation /faunˈdeiʃən/ n. fundación f.; (of building) cimientos m.pl.

founder /ˈfaundər/ n. **1.** fundador -ra. —v. **2.** irse a pique.

foundry /ˈfaundri/ n. fundición f.

fountain /ˈfauntn/ n. fuente f.

fountain pen pluma estilográfica, plumafuente f.

four /fɔr/ a. & pron. cuatro.

fourteen /ˈfɔrˈtin/ a. & pron. catorce.

fourth /fɔrθ/ a. & n. cuarto m.

fowl /faul/ n. ave f.

fox /fɒks/ n. zorro -rra.

fox-trot /ˈfɒks,trɒt/ n. foxtrot m.

foxy /ˈfɒksi/ a. astuto.

foyer /ˈfɔiər/ n. salón de entrada.

fracas /ˈfreikəs, ˈfrækəs/ n. riña f.

fraction /ˈfrækʃən/ n. fracción f.

fracture /ˈfræktʃər/ n. **1.** fractura, rotura f. —v. **2.** fracturar, romper.

fragile /ˈfrædʒəl/ a. frágil.

fragment /ˈfrægmənt/ n. fragmento, trozo m.

fragmentary /ˈfrægmən,teri/ a. fragmentario.

fragrance /ˈfreigrəns/ n. fragancia f.

fragrant /ˈfreigrənt/ a. fragante.

frail /freil/ a. débil, frágil.

frailty /ˈfreilti/ n. debilidad f., fragilidad f.

frame /freim/ n. **1.** marco; armazón; cuadro; cuerpo m. —v. **2.** fabricar; formar; encuadrar.

frame-up /ˈfreim ˌʌp/ n. Colloq. conspiración f.

framework /ˈfreim,wɜrk/ n. armazón m.

France /fræns/ n. Francia f.

franchise /ˈfræntʃaiz/ n. franquicia f.

frank /fræŋk/ a. **1.** franco. —v. **2.** carta franca. —v. **3.** franquear.

frankfurter /ˈfræŋkfərtər/ n. salchicha f.

frankly /ˈfræŋkli/ adv. francamente.

frankness /ˈfræŋknɪs/ n. franqueza f.

frantic /ˈfræntɪk/ a. frenético.

fraternal /frəˈtɜrnl/ a. fraternal.

fraternity /frəˈtɜrnɪti/ n. fraternidad f.

fraternization /ˌfrætərnəˈzeiʃən/ n. fraternización f.

fraternize /ˈfrætər,naiz/ v. confraternizar.

fratricide /ˈfrætrɪ,said/ n. fratricida m. & f.; fratricidio m.

fraud /frɔd/ n. fraude m.

fraudulent /ˈfrɔdʒələnt/ a. fraudulento.

fraudulently /ˈfrɔdʒələntli/ adv. fraudulentamente.

fraught /frɔt/ a. cargado.

freak /frik/ n. rareza f.; monstruosidad.

freckle /ˈfrekəl/ n. peca f.

freckled /ˈfrekəld/ a. pecoso.

free /fri/ a. **1.** libre; gratis. —v. **2.** libertar, librar.

freedom /ˈfridəm/ n. libertad f.

freeze /friz/ v. helar, congelar.

freezer /ˈfrizər/ n. heladora f.

freezing point /ˈfrizɪŋ/ punto de congelación m.

freight /freit/ n. **1.** carga f.; flete m. —v. **2.** cargar; fletar.

freighter /ˈfreitər/ n. Naut. fletador m.

French /frentʃ/ a. & n. francés -esa.

Frenchman /ˈfrentʃmən/ n. francés m.

Frenchwoman /ˈfrentʃ,wumən/ n. francesa f.

frenzied /ˈfrenzid/ a. frenético.

frenzy /ˈfrenzi/ n. frenesí m.

frequency /ˈfrikwənsi/ n. frecuencia f.

frequency modulation /ˌmɒdʒə-ˈleiʃən/ modulación de frequencia.

frequent /ˈfrikwənt/ a. frecuente.

frequently /ˈfrikwəntli/ adv. frecuentemente.

fresco /ˈfreskou/ n. fresco.

fresh /freʃ/ a. fresco. **f. water,** agua dulce.

freshen /ˈfreʃən/ v. refrescar.

freshness /ˈfreʃnɪs/ n. frescura f.

fret /fret/ n. quejarse, irritarse; Mus. traste m.

fretful /ˈfretfəl/ a. irritable.

fretfully /'frɛtfəli/ *adv.* de mala gana.

fretfulness /'frɛtfəlnis/ *n.* mal humor.

friar /'fraiər/ *n.* fraile *m.*

fricassee /ˌfrikə'si/ *n.* fricasé *m.*

friction /'frikʃən/ *n.* fricción *f.*

Friday /'fraidei/ *n.* viernes *m.*
Good F., Viernes Santo *m.*

fried /fraid/ *a.* frito.

friend /frɛnd/ *n.* amigo *m.*

friendless /'frɛndlis/ *a.* sin amigos.

friendliness /'frɛndlinis/ *n.* amistad *f.*

friendly /'frɛndli/ *a.* amistoso.

friendship /'frɛndʃip/ *n.* amistad *f.*

fright /frait/ *n.* susto *m.*

frighten /'fraitn/ *v.* asustar, espantar.

frightful /'fraitfəl/ *a.* espantoso.

frigid /'fridʒid/ *a.* frígido; frío.

frill /fril/ *n.* (sewing) lechuga *f.*

fringe /frindʒ/ *n.* fleco; borde *m.*

frisky /'friski/ *a.* retozón.

fritter /'fritər/ *n.* fritura *f.*

frivolity /fri'vɒliti/ *n.* frivolidad *f.*

frivolous /'frivələs/ *a.* frívolo.

frivolousness /'frivələsnis/ *n.* frivolidad *f.*

frock /frɒk/ *n.* vestido de mujer. **f. coat,** levita *f.*

frog /frɒg/ *n.* rana *f.*

frolic /'frɒlik/ *n.* **1.** retozo *m.* —*v.* **2.** retozar.

from /frʌm, *unstressed* frəm/ *prep.* de; desde.

front /frʌnt/ *n.* frente; (of building) fachada *f.* **in f. of,** delante de.

frontal /'frʌntl/ *a.* frontal.

front door puerta principal *f.*

frontier /frʌn'tiər/ *n.* frontera *f.*

front seat asiento delantero *m.*

frost /frɔst/ *n.* helada, escarcha *f.*

frosty /'frɔsti/ *a.* helado.

froth /frɔθ/ *n.* espuma *f.*

frown /fraun/ *n.* **1.** ceño *m.* —*v.* **2.** fruncir el entrecejo.

frowzy /'frauzi/ *a.* desaliñado.

frozen /'frouzən/ *a.* helado; congelado.

fructify /'frʌktə,fai/ *v.* fructificar.

frugal /'frugəl/ *a.* frugal.

frugality /fru'gæliti/ *n.* frugalidad *f.*

fruit /frut/ *n.* fruta *f.*; (benefits) frutos *m.pl.* **f. tree,** árbol frutal.

fruitful /'frutfəl/ *a.* productivo.

fruition /fru'iʃən/ *n.* fruición *f.*

fruitless /'frutlis/ *a.* inútil, en vano.

fruit salad macedonia de frutas *f.*

fruit store frutería *f.*

frustrate /'frʌstreit/ *v.* frustrar.

frustration /frʌ'streiʃən/ *n.* frustración *f.*

fry /frai/ *v.* freír.

fuel /'fyuəl/ *n.* combustible *m.*

fugitive /'fyudʒitiv/ *a. & n.* fugitivo -va.

fugue /fyug/ *n.* fuga *f.*

fulcrum /'fulkrəm/ *n.* fulcro *m.*

fulfill /ful'fil/ *v.* cumplir.

fulfillment /ful'filmənt/ *n.* cumplimiento *m.*; realización *f.*

full /ful/ *a.* lleno; completo; pleno.

full name nombre y apellidos.

fullness /'fulnis/ *n.* plenitud *f.*

fulminate /'fʌlmə,neit/ *v.* volar; fulminar.

fulmination /ˌfʌlmə'neiʃən/ *n.* fulminación; detonación *f.*

fumble /'fʌmbəl/ *v.* chapucear.

fume /fyum/ *n.* **1.** humo *m.* —*v.* **2.** humear.

fumigate /'fyumi,geit/ *v.* fumigar.

fumigator /'fyumi,geitər/ *n.* fumigador *m.*

fun /fʌn/ *n.* diversión *f.* **to make f. of,** burlarse de. **to have f.,** divertirse.

function /'fʌŋkʃən/ *n.* **1.** función *f.* —*v.* **2.** funcionar.

functional /'fʌŋkʃənl/ *a.* funcional.

fund /fʌnd/ *n.* fondo *m.*

fundamental /ˌfʌndə'mɛntl/ *a.* fundamental.

funeral /'fyunərəl/ *n.* funeral *m.*

funeral home, funeral parlor funeraria *f.*

fungus /'fʌŋgəs/ *n.* hongo *m.*

funnel /'fʌnl/ *n.* embudo *m.*; (of ship) chimenea *f.*

funny /'fʌni/ *a.* divertido, gracioso. **to be f.,** tener gracia.

fur /fər/ *n.* piel *f.*

furious /'fyuriəs/ *a.* furioso.

furlough /'fərlou/ *n.* permiso *m.*

furnace /'fərnis/ *n.* horno *m.*

furnish /'fərniʃ/ *v.* surtir, proveer; (a house) amueblar.

furniture /'fərnitʃər/ *n.* muebles *m.pl.*

furrow /'fʌrou/ *n.* **1.** surco *m.* —*v.* **2.** surcar.

further /'fərðər/ *a. & adv.* **1.** más. —*v.* **2.** adelantar, fomentar.

furthermore /'fərðər,mor/ adv. además.

fury /'fyʊri/ n. furor m.; furia f.

fuse /fyuz/ n. **1.** fusible m. —v. **2.** fundir.

fuss /fʌs/ n. **1.** alboroto m. —v. **2.** preocuparse por pequeñeces.

fussy /'fʌsi/ a. melindroso.

futile /'fyutḷ/ a. fútil.

future /'fyutʃər/ a. **1.** futuro. —n. **2.** porvenir m.

futurology /,fyutʃə'rolədʒi/ n. futurología f.

fuzzy logic /'fʌzi/ lógica matizada f.

FYI abbr. (For Your Information) para su información.

G

gag /gæg/ n. chiste m.; mordaza f.

gaiety /'geiiti/ n. alegría f.

gain /gein/ n. **1.** ganancia f. —v. **2.** ganar.

gait /geit/ n. paso m.

gale /geil/ n. ventarrón m.

gall /gɔl/ n. hiel f.; Fig. amargura f.; descaro m.

gallant /'gælənt, gə'lænt, -'lɑnt/ a. **1.** galante. —n. **2.** galán m.

gallery /'gæləri/ n. galería f.; Theat. paraíso m.

gallon /'gælən/ n. galón m.

gallop /'gæləp/ n. **1.** galope m. —v. **2.** galopar.

gallows /'gælouz/ n. horca f.

gamble /'gæmbəl/ n. **1.** riesgo m. —v. **2.** jugar, aventurar.

game /geim/ n. juego m.; (match) partida f.; (hunting) caza f.

gang /gæŋ/ n. cuadrilla; pandilla f.

gangster /'gæŋstər/ n. rufián m.

gap /gæp/ n. raja f.

gape /geip/ v. boquear.

garage /gə'rɑʒ/ n. garaje m.

garbage /'gɑrbidʒ/ n. basura f.

garden /'gɑrdn̩/ n. jardín m.; (vegetable) huerta f.

gardener /'gɑrdnər/ n. jardinero -ra.

gargle /'gɑrgəl/ n. **1.** gárgara f. —v. **2.** gargarizar.

garland /'gɑrlənd/ n. guirnalda f.

garlic /'gɑrlık/ n. ajo m.

garment /'gɑrmənt/ n. prenda de vestir.

garrison /'gærəsən/ n. guarnición f.

garter /'gɑrtər/ n. liga f.; ataderas f.pl.

gas /gæs/ n. gas m.

gasohol /'gæsə,hɔl, -,hɒl/ n. gasohol m.

gasoline /,gæsə'lin/ n. gasolina f.

gasp /gæsp/ n. **1.** boqueada f. —v. **2.** boquear.

gas station gasolinera f.

gate /geit/ n. puerta; entrada; verja f.

gather /'gæðər/ v. recoger; inferir; reunir.

gaudy /'gɔdi/ a. brillante; llamativo.

gauge /geidʒ/ n. **1.** manómetro, indicador m. —v. **2.** medir; estimar.

gaunt /gɔnt/ a. flaco.

gauze /gɔz/ n. gasa f.

gay /gei/ a. **1.** alegre; homosexual. —n. **2.** homosexual.

gaze /geiz/ n. **1.** mirada f. —v. **2.** mirar con fijeza.

gear /gıər/ n. engranaje m. **in g.,** en juego.

gearshift /'gıər,ʃıft/ n. palanca de cambio f.

gem /dʒem/ n. joya f.

gender /'dʒendər/ n. género m.

general /'dʒenərəl/ a. & n. general m.

generality /,dʒenə'ræliti/ n. generalidad f.

generalize /'dʒenərə,laiz/ v. generalizar.

generation /,dʒenə'reiʃən/ n. generación f.

generator /'dʒenə,reitər/ n. generador m.

generosity /,dʒenə'rɒsiti/ n. generosidad f.

generous /'dʒenərəs/ a. generoso.

genetic /dʒə'nɛtık/ a. genético.

genial /'dʒinyəl/ a. genial.

genius /'dʒinyəs/ n. genio m.

genocide /'dʒenə,said/ n. genocidio m.

gentle /'dʒentḷ/ a. suave; manso; benigno.

gentleman /'dʒentḷmən/ n. señor; caballero m.

gentleness /'dʒentḷnıs/ n. suavidad f.

genuine /'dʒenyuın/ a. genuino.

genuineness /'dʒɛnyuɪnnɪs/ n. pureza f.

geographical /,dʒiə'græfɪkəl/ a. geográfico.

geography /dʒi'ɒɡrəfi/ n. geografía f.

geometric /,dʒiə'mɛtrɪk/ a. geométrico.

geranium /dʒə'reiniəm/ n. geranio m.

germ /dʒɜrm/ n. germen; microbio m.

German /'dʒɜrmən/ a. & n. alemán -mana.

Germany /'dʒɜrməni/ n. Alemania f.

gesticulate /dʒɛ'stɪkyə,leit/ v. gesticular.

gesture /'dʒɛstʃər/ n. **1.** gesto m. —v. **2.** gesticular, hacer gestos.

get /gɛt/ v. obtener; conseguir; (become) ponerse. **go and g.,** ir a buscar; **g. away,** irse; escaparse; **g. together,** reunirse; **g. on,** subirse; **g. off,** bajarse; **g. up,** levantarse; **g. there,** llegar.

ghastly /'gæstli/ a. pálido; espantoso.

ghost /goust/ n. espectro, fantasma m.

giant /'dʒaiənt/ n. gigante m.

gibberish /'dʒɪbərɪʃ/ n. galimatías, m.

gift /gɪft/ n. regalo, don; talento m.

gigabyte /'gɪgə,bait, 'dʒɪg-/ n. giga m.

gild /gɪld/ v. dorar.

gin /dʒɪn/ n. ginebra f.

ginger /'dʒɪndʒər/ n. jengibre m.

gingerbread /'dʒɪndʒər,brɛd/ n. pan de jengibre.

gingham /'gɪŋəm/ n. guinga f.

gird /gɜrd/ v. ceñir.

girdle /'gɜrdl/ n. faja f.

girl /gɜrl/ n. muchacha, niña, chica f.

give /gɪv/ v. dar; regalar. **g. back,** devolver. **g. up,** rendirse; renunciar.

giver /'gɪvər/ n. dador -ra; donador -ra.

glacier /'gleiʃər/ n. glaciar; ventisquero m.

glad /glæd/ a. alegre, contento. **be g.,** alegrarse.

gladly /'glædli/ adj. con mucho gusto.

gladness /'glædnɪs/ n. alegría f.; placer m.

glamor /'glæmər/ n. encanto m.; elegancia f.

glamorous /'glæmərəs/ a. encantador; elegante.

glamour /'glæmər/ n. encanto m.; elegancia f.

glance /glæns/ n. **1.** vistazo m., ojeada f. —v. **2.** ojear.

gland /glænd/ n. glándula f.

glare /glɛər/ n. **1.** reflejo; brillo m. —v. **2.** deslumbrar; echar miradas indignadas.

glass /glæs/ n. vidrio; vaso m.; **(eyeglasses),** lentes, anteojos m.pl.

gleam /glim/ n. **1.** fulgor m. —v. **2.** fulgurar.

glee /gli/ n. alegría f.; júbilo m.

glide /glaid/ v. deslizarse.

glimpse /glɪmps/ n. **1.** vislumbre, vistazo m. —v. **2.** vislumbrar, ojear.

glisten /'glɪsən/ n. **1.** brillo m. —v. **2.** brillar.

glitter /'glɪtər/ n. **1.** resplandor m. —v. **2.** brillar.

globe /gloub/ n. globo; orbe m.

gloom /glum/ n. oscuridad; tristeza f.

gloomy /'glumi/ a. oscuro; sombrío, triste.

glorify /'glɔrə,fai/ v. glorificar.

glorious /'glɔriəs/ a. glorioso.

glory /'glɔri/ n. gloria, fama f.

glossary /'glɒsəri/ n. glosario m.

glove /glʌv/ n. guante m.

glove compartment guantera f.

glow /glou/ n. **1.** fulgor m. —v. **2.** relucir; arder.

glucose /'glukous/ n. glucosa f.

glue /glu/ n. **1.** cola f., pegamento m. —v. **2.** encolar, pegar.

glum /glʌm/ a. de mal humor.

glutton /'glʌtn/ n. glotón -ona.

gnarl /narl/ n. nudo m.

gnat /næt/ n. jején m.

gnaw /nɔ/ v. roer.

GNP (abbr. **gross national product**), **PNB** (producto nacional bruto).

go /gou/ v. ir, irse. **g. away,** irse, marcharse. **g. back,** volver, regresar. **g. down,** bajar. **g. in,** entrar. **g. on,** seguir. **g. out,** salir. **g. up,** subir.

goal /goul/ n. meta f.; objeto m.

goalkeeper /'goul,kipər/ n. guardameta mf.

goat /gout/ n. cabra f.

goblet /'gɒblɪt/ n. copa f.

God /gɒd/ n. Dios m.

gold /gould/ n. oro m.

golden /'gouldən/ a. áureo.

gold-plated /'gould ,pleitid/ a. chapado en oro.

golf /golf/ n. golf m.

golf course campo de golf m.

golfer /'golfər/ n. golfista m. & f.

good /gud/ a. **1.** bueno. —n. **2.** bienes m.pl.; Com. géneros m.pl.

good-bye /'gud'bai/ n. **1.** adiós m. —interj. **2.** ¡adiós!; ¡hasta la vista!, ¡hasta luego! **say g. to**, despedirse de.

goodness /'gudnɪs/ n. bondad f.

goodwill /'gud'wɪl/ n. buena voluntad. f.

goose /gus/ n. ganso m.

gooseberry /'gus,bɛri/ n. uva crespa f.

gooseneck /'gus,nɛk/ n. **1.** cuello de cisne m. —a. **2.** curvo.

goose step /'gus,stɛp/ paso de ganso m.

gore /gɔr/ n. **1.** sangre f. —v. **2.** acornear.

gorge /gɔrdʒ/ n. **1.** gorja f. —v. **2.** engullir.

gorgeous /'gɔrdʒəs/ a. magnífico; precioso.

gorilla /gə'rɪlə/ n. gorila m.

gory /'gɔri/ a. sangriento.

gosling /'gɒzlɪŋ/ n. gansarón m.

gospel /'gɒspəl/ n. evangelio m.

gossamer /'gɒsəmər/ n. **1.** telaraña f. —a. **2.** delgado.

gossip /'gɒsəp/ n. **1.** chisme m. —v. **2.** chismear.

Gothic /'gɒθɪk/ a. gótico.

gouge /gaudʒ/ n. **1.** gubia f. —v. **2.** escoplear.

gourd /gɔrd/ n. calabaza f.

gourmand /gur'mɑnd/ n. glotón m.

gourmet /gur'mei/ a. gastrónomo -ma.

govern /'gʌvərn/ v. gobernar.

governess /'gʌvərnɪs/ n. aya, institutriz f.

government /'gʌvərnmənt, -ərmənt/ n. gobierno m.

governmental /,gʌvərn'mɛntl, ,gʌvər-/ a. gubernamental.

governor /'gʌvərnər/ n. gobernador -ra.

governorship /'gʌvərnər,ʃɪp/ n. gobernatura f.

gown /gaun/ n. vestido m. **dressing g.**, bata f.

grab /græb/ v. agarrar, arrebatar.

grace /greis/ n. gracia; gentileza; merced f.

graceful /'greisfəl/ a. agraciado.

graceless /'greislɪs/ a. réprobo; torpe.

gracious /'greiʃəs/ a. gentil, cortés.

grackle /'grækəl/ n. grajo m.

grade /greid/ n. **1.** grado; nivel m.; pendiente; nota; calidad f. —v. **2.** graduar.

grade crossing n. paso a nivel m.

gradual /'grædʒuəl/ a. gradual, paulatino.

gradually /'grædʒuəli/ adv. gradualmente.

graduate /n 'grædʒuɪt; v -,eit/ n. **1.** graduado -da, diplomado -da. —v. **2.** graduar; diplomarse.

graft /græft/ n. **1.** injerto m.; soborno público. —v. **2.** injertar.

graham /'greiəm/ a. centeno; acemita.

grail /greil/ n. grial m.

grain /grein/ n. grano; cereal m.

grain alcohol n. alcohol de madera m.

gram /græm/ n. gramo m.

grammar /'græmər/ n. gramática f.

grammarian /grə'mɛəriən/ n. gramático -ca.

grammar school n. escuela elemental f.

grammatical /grə'mætɪkəl/ a. gramatical.

gramophone /'græmə,foun/ n. gramófono m.

granary /'greinəri/ n. granero m.

grand /grænd/ a. grande, ilustre; estupendo.

grandchild /'græn,tʃaild/ n. nieto -ta.

granddaughter /'græn,dɔtər/ n. nieta f.

grandee /græn'di/ n. noble m.

grandeur /'grændʒər/ n. grandeza f.

grandfather /'græn,fɑðər/ n. abuelo m.

grandiloquent /græn'dɪləkwənt/ a. grandílocuo.

grandiose /'grændi,ous/ a. grandioso.

grand jury jurado de acusación, jurado de juicio m.

grandly /'grændli/ adv. grandiosamente.

grandmother /'græn,mʌðər/ n. abuela f.

grand opera ópera grande f.

grandparents /'grænd,peərənts/ n. abuelos m.pl.

grandson /'græn,sʌn/ n. nieto m.

grandstand /'græn,stænd/ n. andanada f.; tribuna f.

grange /greindʒ/ n. granja f.

granger /'greindʒər/ n. labriego m.

granite /'grænɪt/ n. granito m.

granny /'græni/ n. abuelita f.

grant /grænt/ n. **1.** concesión; subvención f. —v. **2.** otorgar; conceder; conferir. **take for granted,** tomar por cierto.

granular /'grænjələr/ a. granular.

granulate /'grænjə,leit/ v. granular.

granulation /,grænjə'leiʃən/ n. granulación f.

granule /'grænjul/ n. gránulo m.

grape /greip/ n. uva f.

grapefruit /'greip,frut/ n. toronja f.

grape harvest vendimia f.

grapeshot /'greip,ʃɒt/ n. metralla f.

grapevine /'greip,vain/ n. vid; parra f.

graph /græf/ n. gráfica f.

graphic /'græfɪk/ a. gráfico.

graphite /'græfait/ n. grafito m.

graphology /græ'fɒlədʒi/ n. grafología f.

grapple /'græpəl/ v. agarrar.

grasp /græsp/ n. **1.** puño; comprender; conocimiento m. —v. **2.** empuñar, agarrar; comprender.

grasping /'græspɪŋ/ a. codicioso.

grass /græs/ n. hierba f.; (marijuana) marijuana f.

grasshopper /'græs,hɒpər/ n. saltamontes m.

grassy /'græsi/ a. herboso.

grate /greit/ n. reja f.

grateful /'greitfəl/ a. agradecido.

gratify /'grætɪ,fai/ v. satisfacer.

grating /'greitɪŋ/ n. **1.** enrejado m. —a. **2.** discordante.

gratis /'grætɪs/ adv. & a. gratis.

gratitude /'grætɪ,tud/ n. agradecimiento m.

gratuitous /grə'tuɪtəs/ adj. gratuito.

gratuity /grə'tuɪti/ n. propina f.

grave /greiv/ a. **1.** grave. —n. **2.** sepultura; tumba f.

gravel /'grævəl/ n. cascajo m.

gravely /'greivli/ adv. gravemente.

gravestone /'greiv,stoun/ n. lápida sepulcral f.

graveyard /'greiv,yɑrd/ n. cementerio m.

gravitate /'grævɪ,teit/ v. gravitar.

gravitation /,grævɪ'teiʃən/ n. gravitación f.

gravity /'grævɪti/ n. gravedad; seriedad f.

gravure /grə'vyur/ n. fotograbado m.

gravy /'greivi/ n. salsa f.

gray /grei/ a. gris; (hair) cano.

grayish /'greiɪʃ/ a. pardusco.

gray matter substancia gris f.

graze /greiz/ v. rozar; (cattle) pastar.

grazing /'greizɪŋ/ a. pastando.

grease /gris/ n. **1.** grasa f. —v. **2.** engrasar.

greasy /'grisi/ a. grasiento.

great /greit/ a. grande, ilustre; estupendo.

Great Dane /dein/ n. mastín danés m.

great-grandfather /,greit 'græn,fɑðər/ n. bisabuelo.

great-grandmother /,greit 'græn,mʌðər/ n. bisabuela.

greatness /'greitnɪs/ n. grandeza f.

Greece /gris/ n. Grecia f.

greed /grid/ **greediness** n. codicia, voracidad f.

greedy /'gridi/ a. voraz.

Greek /grik/ a. & n. griego -ga.

green /grin/ a. & n. verde m.

greens, n. verduras f.pl.

greenery /'grinəri/ n. verdor m.

greenhouse /'grin,haus/ n. invernáculo m.

greenhouse effect n. efecto invernáculo m.

greet /grit/ v. saludar.

greeting /'gritɪŋ/ n. saludo m.

gregarious /grɪ'gɛəriəs/ a. gregario; sociable.

grenade /grɪ'neid/ n. granada; bomba f.

greyhound /'grei,haund/ n. galgo m.

grid /grid/ n. parrilla f.

griddle /'gridl/ n. tortera f.

griddlecake /'gridl,keik/ n. tortita de harina f.

gridiron /'grid,aiərn/ n. parrilla f.; campo de fútbol m.

grief /grif/ n. dolor m.; pena f.

grievance /'grivəns/ n. pesar; agravio m.

grieve /griv/ v. afligir.

grievous /'grivəs/ a. penoso.

grill /gril/ n. **1.** parrilla f. —v. **2.** asar a la parrilla.

grillroom /ˈgril,rum, -,rʊm/ n. parrilla f.

grim /grim/ a. ceñudo.

grimace /ˈgriməs/ n. **1.** mueca f. —v. **2.** hacer muecas.

grime /graim/ n. mugre f.

grimy /ˈgraimi/ a. sucio; mugroso.

grin /grin/ n. **1.** sonrisa f. —v. **2.** sonreír.

grind /graind/ v. moler; afilar.

grindstone /ˈgraind,stoun/ n. amoladera f.

gringo /ˈgriŋgou/ n. gringo; yanqui m.

grip /grip/ n. **1.** maleta f. —v. **2.** agarrar.

gripe /graip/ v. **1.** agarrar. —n. **2.** asimiento m., opresión f.

grippe /grip/ n. gripe f.

grisly /ˈgrizli/ a. espantoso.

grist /grist/ n. molienda f.

gristle /ˈgrisəl/ n. cartílago m.

grit /grit/ n. arena f.; entereza f.

grizzled /ˈgrizəld/ a. tordillo.

groan /groun/ n. **1.** gemido m. —v. **2.** gemir.

grocer /ˈgrousər/ n. abacero m.

grocery /ˈgrousəri/ n. tienda de comestibles, abacería f.; (Carib.) bodega f.

grog /grɒg/ n. brebaje m.

groggy /ˈgrɒgi/ a. medio borracho; vacilante.

groin /grɔin/ n. ingle f.

groom /grum/ n. (of horses) establero; (at wedding) novio m.

groove /gruv/ n. **1.** estría f. —v. **2.** acanalar.

grope /group/ v. tentar; andar a tientas.

gross /grous/ a. **1.** grueso; grosero. —n. **2.** gruesa f.

grossly /ˈgrousli/ adv. groseramente.

gross national product producto nacional bruto m.

grossness /ˈgrousnis/ n. grosería f.

grotesque /grouˈtɛsk/ a. grotesco.

grotto /ˈgrɒtou/ n. gruta f.

grouch /grautʃ/ n. gruñón; descontento m.

ground /graund/ n. tierra f.; terreno; suelo; campo; fundamento m.

ground floor planta baja f.

groundhog /ˈgraund,hɔg/ n. marmota f.

groundless /ˈgraundlis/ a. infundado.

groundwork /ˈgraund,wɜrk/ n. base f., fundamento m.

group /grup/ n. **1.** grupo m. —v. **2.** agrupar.

groupie /ˈgrupi/ n. persona aficionada que acompaña a un grupo de música moderna.

grouse /graus/ v. quejarse.

grove /grouv/ n. arboleda f.

grovel /ˈgrɒvəl/ v. rebajarse; envilecerse.

grow /grou/ v. crecer; cultivar.

growl /graul/ n. **1.** gruñido m. —v. **2.** gruñir.

grown /groun/ a. crecido; desarrollado.

grownup /ˈgroun,ʌp/ n. adulto -ta.

growth /grouθ/ n. crecimiento m.; vegetación f.; Med. tumor m.

grub /grʌb/ n. gorgojo m., larva f.

grubby /ˈgrʌbi/ a. gorgojoso, mugriento.

grudge /grʌdʒ/ n. rencor m. **bear a g.,** guardar rencor.

gruel /ˈgruəl/ n. **1.** atole m. —v. **2.** agotar.

gruesome /ˈgrusəm/ a. horripilante.

gruff /grʌf/ a. ceñudo.

grumble /ˈgrʌmbəl/ v. quejarse.

grumpy /ˈgrʌmpi/ a. gruñón; quejoso.

grunt /grʌnt/ v. gruñir.

guarantee /ˌgærənˈti/ n. **1.** garantía f. —v. **2.** garantizar.

guarantor /ˈgærən,tɔr/ n. fiador -ra.

guaranty /ˈgærən,ti/ n. garantía f.

guard /gɑrd/ n. **1.** guardia m. & f. —v. **2.** vigilar.

guarded /ˈgɑrdid/ a. cauteloso.

guardhouse /ˈgɑrd,haus/ n. prisión militar f.

guardian /ˈgɑrdiən/ n. guardián -ana.

guardianship /ˈgɑrdiən,ʃip/ n. tutela f.

guardsman /ˈgɑrdzmən/ n. centinela m.

guava /ˈgwɑvə/ n. guayaba f.

gubernatorial /ˌgubərnəˈtɔriəl/ a. gubernativo.

guerrilla /gəˈrilə/ n. guerrilla f.; guerrillero m.

guess /gɛs/ n. **1.** conjetura f. —v. **2.** adivinar; Colloq. creer.

guesswork /'gɛs,wɜrk/ n. conjetura f.

guest /gɛst/ n. huésped m. & f.

guest room alcoba de huéspedes f., alcoba de respeto f., cuarto para invitados m.

guffaw /gʌ'fɔ/ n. risotada f.

guidance /'gaidns/ n. dirección f.

guide /gaid/ n. **1.** guía m. & f. —v. **2.** guiar.

guidebook /'gaid,bʊk/ n. guía f.

guided tour /'gaidid/ visita explicada, visita programada, visita con guía f.

guideline /'gaid,lain/ n. pauta f.

guidepost /'gaid,poʊst/ n. poste indicador m.

guild /gild/ n. gremio m.

guile /gail/ n. engaño m.

guillotine /'gilə,tin/ n. **1.** guillotina f. —v. **2.** guillotinar.

guilt /gilt/ n. culpa f.

guiltily /'giltəli/ adv. culpablemente.

guiltless /'giltlis/ a. inocente.

guilty /'gilti/ a. culpable.

guinea fowl /'gini/ gallina de Guinea f.

guinea pig /'gini/ cobayo m., conejillo de Indias m.

guise /gaiz/ n. modo m.

guitar /gi'tɑr/ n. guitarra f.

guitarist /gi'tɑrist/ n. guitarrista m. & f.

gulch /gʌltʃ/ n. quebrada f.

gulf /gʌlf/ n. golfo m.

gull /gʌl/ n. gaviota f.

gullet /'gʌlit/ n. esófago m.; zanja f.

gullible /'gʌləbəl/ a. crédulo.

gully /'gʌli/ n. barranca f.

gulp /gʌlp/ n. **1.** trago m. —v. **2.** tragar.

gum /gʌm/ n. **1.** goma f.; Anat. encía f. **chewing g.,** chicle m. —v. **2.** engomar.

gumbo /'gʌmboʊ/ n. quimbombó m.

gummy /'gʌmi/ a. gomoso.

gun /gʌn/ n. fusil, revólver m.

gunboat /'gʌn,boʊt/ n. cañonero m.

gunman /'gʌnmən/ n. bandido m.

gunner /'gʌnər/ n. artillero m.

gun permit licencia de armas f.

gunpowder /'gʌn,paʊdər/ n. pólvora f.

gunshot /'gʌn,ʃɒt/ n. escopetazo m.

gunwale /'gʌnl/ n. borda f.

gurgle /'gɜrgəl/ n. **1.** gorgoteo m. —v. **2.** gorgotear.

guru /'gʊru, gʊ'ru/ n. gurú m.

gush /gʌʃ/ n. **1.** chorro m. —v. **2.** brotar, chorrear.

gusher /'gʌʃər/ n. pozo de petróleo m.

gust /gʌst/ n. soplo m.; ráfaga f.

gustatory /'gʌstə,tɔri/ a. gustativo.

gusto /'gʌstoʊ/ a. gusto; placer m.

gusty /'gʌsti/ a. borrascoso.

gut /gʌt/ n. intestino m., tripa f.

gutter /'gʌtər/ n. canal; zanja f.

guttural /'gʌtərəl/ a. gutural.

guy /gai/ n. tipo m.

guzzle /'gʌzəl/ v. engullir; tragar.

gym /dʒim/ n. gimnasio m.

gymnasium /dʒim'noʊziəm/ n. gimnasio m.

gymnast /'dʒimnæst/ n. gimnasta m. & f.

gymnastic /dʒim'næstik/ a. gimnástico.

gymnastics /dʒim'næstiks/ n. gimnasia f.

gynecologist /,gaini'kɒlədʒist/ n. ginecólogo, -ga m. & f.

gynecology /,gaini'kɒlədʒi/ n. ginecología f.

gypsum /'dʒipsəm/ n. yeso m.

Gypsy /'dʒipsi/ a. & n. gitano -na.

gyrate /'dʒaireit/ v. girar.

gyroscope /'dʒairə,skoʊp/ n. giroscopio m.

H

habeas corpus /'heibiəs 'kɔrpəs/ habeas corpus m.

haberdasher /'hæbər,dæʃər/ n. camisero m.

haberdashery /'hæbər,dæʃəri/ n. camisería f.

habiliment /hə'biləmənt/ n. vestuario m.

habit /'hæbit/ n. costumbre f., hábito m. **be in the h. of,** estar acostumbrado a; soler.

habitable /'hæbitəbəl/ a. habitable.

habitat /'hæbi,tæt/ n. habitación f., ambiente m.

habitation /ˌhæbɪ'teiʃən/ n. habitación f.

habitual /hə'bɪtʃuəl/ a. habitual.

habituate /hə'bɪtʃu,eit/ v. habituar.

habitué /hə'bɪtʃu,ei/ n. parroquiano m.

hack /hæk/ n. **1.** coche de alquiler. —v. **2.** tajar.

hacker /'hækər/ n. pirata m. & f.

hackneyed /'hæknid/ a. trillado.

hacksaw /'hæk,sɔ/ n. sierra para cortar metal f.

haddock /'hædək/ n. merluza f.

haft /hæft/ n. mango m.

hag /hæg, hɑg/ n. bruja f.

haggard /'hægərd/ a. trasnochado.

haggle /'hægəl/ v. regatear.

hail /heil/ n. **1.** granizo; (greeting) saludo m. —v. **2.** granizar; saludar.

Hail Mary /'mɛəri/ Ave María m.

hailstone /'heil,stoun/ n. piedra de granizo f.

hailstorm /'heil,stɔrm/ n. granizada f.

hair /hɛər/ n. pelo; cabello m.

haircut /'hɛər,kʌt/ n. corte de pelo.

hairdo /'hɛər,du/ n. peinado m.

hairdresser /'hɛər,drɛsər/ n. peluquero m.

hair dryer /'draiər/ secador de pelo, secador m.

hairpin /'hɛər,pɪn/ n. horquilla f.; gancho m.

hair's-breadth /'hɛərz,brɛdθ/ n. ancho de un pelo m.

hairspray /'hɛərsprei/ n. aerosol para cabello.

hairy /'hɛəri/ a. peludo.

halcyon /'hælsiən/ n. **1.** alcedón m. —a. **2.** tranquilo.

hale /heil/ a. sano.

half /hæf/ a. **1.** medio. —n. **2.** mitad f.

half-and-half /'hæf ən 'hæf/ a. mitad y mitad.

half-baked /'hæf 'beikt/ a. medio crudo.

half-breed /'hæf ,brid/ n. mestizo m.

half brother n. medio hermano m.

half-hearted /'hæf'hɑrtɪd/ a. sin entusiasmo.

half-mast /'hæf 'mæst/ a. & n. media asta m.

halfpenny /'heipəni/ n. medio penique m.

halfway /'hæf'wei/ adv. a medio camino.

half-wit /'hæf ,wɪt/ n. bobo m.

halibut /'hæləbət/ n. hipogloso m.

hall /hɔl/ n. corredor m.; (for assembling) sala f. **city h.,** ayuntamiento m.

hallmark /'hɔl,mɑrk/ n. marca del contraste f.

hallow /'hælou/ v. consagrar.

Halloween /ˌhælə'win/ n. víspera de Todos los Santos f.

hallucination /hə,lusə'neiʃən/ n. alucinación f.

hallway /'hɔl,wei/ n. pasadizo m.

halo /'heilou/ n. halo m.; corona f.

halt /hɔlt/ a. **1.** cojo. —n. **2.** parada f. —v. **3.** parar. —interj. **4.** ¡alto!

halter /'hɔltər/ n. cabestro m.

halve /hæv/ v. dividir en dos partes.

halyard /'hælyərd/ n. driza f.

ham /hæm/ n. jamón m.

hamburger /'hæm,bɜrgər/ n. albóndiga f.

hamlet /'hæmlɪt/ n. aldea f.

hammer /'hæmər/ n. **1.** martillo m. —v. **2.** martillar.

hammock /'hæmək/ n. hamaca f.

hamper /'hæmpər/ n. canasta f., cesto m.

hamstring /'hæm,strɪŋ/ n. **1.** tendón de la corva m. —v. **2.** desjarretar.

hand /hænd/ n. **1.** mano f. **on the other h.,** en cambio. —v. **2.** pasar. **h. over,** entregar.

handbag /'hænd,bæg/ n. cartera f.

handball /'hænd,bɔl/ n. pelota f.

handbook /'hænd,bʊk/ n. manual m.

handbrake /'hændbreik/ n. freno de mano m.

handcuff /'hænd,kʌf/ n. esposa v. esposar.

handful /'hændfʊl/ n. puñado m.

handicap /'hændi,kæp/ n. desventaja f.

handicraft /'hændi,kræft/ n. artífice m.; destreza manual.

handiwork /'hændi,wɜrk/ n. artefacto m.

handkerchief /'hæŋkərtʃɪf/ n. pañuelo m.

handle /'hændl/ n. **1.** mango m. —v. **2.** manejar.

hand luggage equipaje de mano m.

handmade /ˈhændˈmeid/ a. hecho a mano.

handmaid /ˈhændˌmeid/ n. criada de mano, sirvienta f.

hand organ organillo m.

handsome /ˈhænsəm/ a. guapo; hermoso.

hand-to-hand /ˈhænd tə ˈhænd/ adv. de mano a mano.

handwriting /ˈhændˌraitɪŋ/ n. escritura f.

handy /ˈhændi/ a. diestro; útil; a la mano.

hang /hæŋ/ v. colgar; ahorcar.

hangar /ˈhæŋər/ n. hangar m.

hangdog /ˈhæŋˌdɔg/ a. & n. camastrón m.

hanger /ˈhæŋər/ n. colgador, gancho m.

hanger-on /ˈhæŋər ˈɒn/ n. dependiente; mogollón m.

hang glider /ˈglaidər/ aparato para vuelo libre, delta, el delta.

hanging /ˈhæŋɪŋ/ n. **1.** ahorcadura f. —a. **2.** colgante.

hangman /ˈhæŋmən/ n. verdugo m.

hangnail /ˈhæŋˌneil/ n. padrastro m.

hang out v. enarbolar.

hangover /ˈhæŋˌouvər/ n. resaca f.

hangup /ˈhæŋʌp/ n. tara (psicológica) f.

hank /hæŋk/ n. madeja f.

hanker /ˈhæŋkər/ v. ansiar; apetecer.

haphazard. /ˈhæpˈhæzərd/ a. casual.

happen /ˈhæpən/ v. acontecer, suceder, pasar.

happening /ˈhæpənɪŋ/ n. acontecimiento m.

happiness /ˈhæpinɪs/ n. felicidad; dicha f.

happy /ˈhæpi/ a. feliz; contento; dichoso.

happy-go-lucky /ˈhæpi gou ˈlʌki/ a. & n. descuidado m.

harakiri /ˈhærəˈkiəri/ n. harakiri (suicidio japonés) m.

harangue /həˈræŋ/ n. **1.** arenga f. —v. **2.** arengar.

harass /ˈhærəs/ v. acosar; atormentar.

harbinger /ˈhɑrbɪndʒər/ n. presagio m.

harbor /ˈhɑrbər/ n. **1.** puerto; albergue m. —v. **2.** abrigar.

hard /hɑrd/ a. **1.** duro; difícil. —adv. **2.** mucho.

hard coal antracita m.

hard disk disco duro m.

harden /ˈhɑrdn/ v. endurecer.

hard-headed /ˈhɑrd ˈhɛdɪd/ a. terco.

hard-hearted /ˈhɑrd ˈhɑrtɪd/ a. empedernido.

hardiness /ˈhɑrdinɪs/ n. vigor m.

hardly /ˈhɑrdli/ adv. apenas.

hardness /ˈhɑrdnɪs/ n. dureza; dificultad f.

hardship /ˈhɑrdʃɪp/ n. penalidad f.; trabajo m.

hardware /ˈhɑrdˌwɛər/ n. hardware m.; (computer) quincalla f.

hardwood /ˈhɑrdˌwʊd/ n. madera dura f.

hardy /ˈhɑrdi/ a. fuerte, robusto.

hare /hɛər/ n. liebre f.

harebrained /ˈhɛərˌbreind/ a. tolondro.

harelip /ˈhɛərˌlɪp/ n. **1.** labio leporino m. —a. **2.** labihendido.

harem /ˈhɛərəm/ n. harén m.

hark /hɑrk/ v. escuchar; atender.

Harlequin /ˈhɑrləkwɪn/ n. arlequín m.

harlot /ˈhɑrlət/ n. ramera f.

harm /hɑrm/ n. **1.** mal, daño; perjuicio m. —v. **2.** dañar.

harmful /ˈhɑrmfəl/ a. dañoso.

harmless /ˈhɑrmlɪs/ a. inocente.

harmonic /hɑrˈmɒnɪk/ a. armónico m.

harmonica /hɑrˈmɒnɪkə/ n. armónica f.

harmonious /hɑrˈmouniəs/ a. armonioso.

harmonize /ˈhɑrməˌnaiz/ v. armonizar.

harmony /ˈhɑrməni/ n. armonía f.

harness /ˈhɑrnɪs/ n. arnés m.

harp /hɑrp/ n. arpa f.

harpoon /hɑrˈpun/ n. arpón m.

harridan /ˈhɑridn/ n. vieja regañona f.

harrow /ˈhærou/ n. **1.** rastro m.; grada f. —v. **2.** gradar.

harry /ˈhæri/ v. acosar; pillar.

harsh /hɑrʃ/ a. áspero.

harshness /ˈhɑrʃnɪs/ n. aspereza f.

harvest /ˈhɑrvɪst/ n. **1.** cosecha f. —v. **2.** cosechar.

hash /hæʃ/ n. picadillo m.

hashish /ˈhæʃɪʃ/ n. haxis m.

hasn't /ˈhæzənt/ v. no tiene (neg. + tener).

hassle /ˈhæsəl/ n. lío m., molestia f.; controversia f.

hassock /ˈhæsək/ n. cojín m.

haste /heist/ n. prisa f.

hasten /ˈheisən/ v. apresurarse, darse prisa.

hasty /ˈheisti/ a. apresurado.

hat /hæt/ n. sombrero m.

hat box /hæt ˌbɒks/ sombrerera f.

hatch /hætʃ/ n. **1.** Naut. cuartel m. —v. **2.** incubar; Fig. tramar.

hatchery /ˈhætʃəri/ n. criadero m.

hatchet /ˈhætʃɪt/ n. hacha pequeña.

hate /heit/ v. **1.** odio m. —v. **2.** odiar, detestar.

hateful /ˈheitfəl/ a. detestable.

hatred /ˈheitrɪd/ n. odio m.

haughtiness /ˈhɔtinis/ n. arrogancia f.

haughty /ˈhɔti/ a. altivo.

haul /hɔl/ n. **1.** (fishery) redada f. —v. **2.** tirar, halar.

haunch /hɔntʃ/ n. anca f.

haunt /hɔnt/ n. **1.** lugar frecuentado. —v. **2.** frecuentar, andar por.

have /hæv; unstressed həv, əv/ v. tener; haber.

haven /ˈheivən/ n. puerto; asilo m.

haven't /ˈhævənt/ v. no tiene (neg. + tener).

havoc /ˈhævək/ n. ruina f.

hawk /hɔk/ n. halcón m.

hawker /ˈhɔkər/ n. buhonero m.

hawser /ˈhɔzər/ n. cable m.

hawthorn /ˈhɔˌθɔrn/ n. espino m.

hay /hei/ n. heno m.

hay fever n. fiebre del heno f.

hayfield /ˈheiˌfild/ n. henar m.

hayloft /ˈheiˌlɔft/ n. henil m.

haystack /ˈheiˌstæk/ n. hacina de heno f.

hazard /ˈhæzərd/ n. **1.** azar m. —v. **2.** aventurar.

hazardous /ˈhæzərdəs/ a. peligroso.

haze /heiz/ n. niebla f.

hazel /ˈheizəl/ n. avellano m.

hazelnut /ˈheizəlˌnʌt/ avellana f.

hazy /ˈheizi/ a. brumoso.

he /hi/ pron. él m.

head /hed/ n. **1.** cabeza f.; jefe m. —v. **2.** dirigir, encabezar.

headache /ˈhedˌeik/ n. dolor de cabeza m.

headband /ˈhedˌbænd/ n. venda para cabeza f.

headfirst /ˈhedˈfɜrst/ adv. de cabeza.

headgear /ˈhedˌgɪr/ n. tocado m.

headlight /ˈhedˌlait/ n. linterna delantera f., farol de tope m.

headline /ˈhedˌlain/ n. encabezado m.

headlong /ˈhedˌlɔŋ/ a. precipitoso.

head-on /ˈhed ˈɒn/ adv. de frente.

headphones /ˈhedˌfounz/ n.pl. auriculares m.pl.

headquarters /ˈhedˌkwɔrtərz/ n. jefatura f.; Mil. cuartel general.

headstone /ˈhedˌstoun/ n. lápida mortuoria f.

headstrong /ˈhedˌstrɔŋ/ a. terco.

headwaiter /ˈhedˈweitər/ n. jefe de comedor m. & f.

headwaters /ˈhedˌwɔtərz/ n. cabeceras f.pl.

headway /ˈhedˌwei/ n. avance m., progreso m.

headwork /ˈhedˌwɜrk/ n. trabajo mental m.

heady /ˈhedi/ a. impetuoso.

heal /hil/ v. curar, sanar.

health /helθ/ n. salud f.

healthful /ˈhelθfəl/ a. saludable.

healthy /ˈhelθi/ a. sano; salubre.

heap /hip/ n. montón m.

hear /hɪər/ v. oír. **h. from**, tener noticias de. **h. about, h. of**, oír hablar de.

hearing /ˈhɪərɪŋ/ n. oído m.

hearing aid n. audífono m.

hearsay /ˈhɪərˌsei/ n. rumor m.

hearse /hɜrs/ n. ataúd m.

heart /hɑrt/ n. corazón; ánimo m. **by h.**, de memoria. **have h. trouble** padecer del corazón.

heartache /ˈhɑrtˌeik/ n. angustia f.

heart attack ataque cardíaco, infarto, infarto de miocardio m.

heartbreak /ˈhɑrtˌbreik/ n. angustia f.; pesar m.

heartbroken /ˈhɑrtˌbroukən/ a. acongojado.

heartburn /ˈhɑrtˌbɜrn/ n. acedía f., ardor de estómago m.

heartfelt /ˈhɑrtˌfelt/ a. sentido.

hearth /hɑrθ/ n. hogar m., chimenea f.

heartless /ˈhɑrtlis/ a. empedernido.

heartsick /ˈhɑrtˌsik/ a. desconsolado.

heart-stricken /ˈhɑrt ˈstrɪkən/ a. afligido.

heart-to-heart /ˈhɑrt tə ˈhɑrt/ adv. franco; sincero.

hearty /ˈhɑrti/ a. cordial; vigoroso.

heat /hit/ n. **1.** calor; ardor m.; calefacción f. —v. **2.** calentar.

heated /ˈhitɪd/ a. acalorado.

heater /ˈhitər/ n. calentador m.

heath /hiθ/ n. matorral m.

heathen /ˈhiðən/ a. & n. pagano -na.

heather /ˈhɛðər/ n. brezo m.

heating /ˈhitɪŋ/ n. calefacción f.

heatstroke /ˈhitˌstrouk/ n. insolación f.

heat wave onda de calor f.

heave /hiv/ v. tirar.

heaven /ˈhɛvən/ n. cielo m.

heavenly /ˈhɛvənli/ a. divino.

heavy /ˈhɛvi/ a. pesado; oneroso.

Hebrew /ˈhibru/ a. & n. hebreo -ea.

hectic /ˈhɛktɪk/ a. turbulento.

hedge /hɛdʒ/ n. seto m.

hedgehog /ˈhɛdʒˌhɔg/ n. erizo m.

hedonism /ˈhidnˌɪzəm/ n. hedonismo m.

heed /hid/ n. **1.** cuidado m. —v. **2.** atender.

heedless /ˈhidlɪs/ a. desatento; incauto.

heel /hil/ n. talón m.; (of shoe) tacón m.

heifer /ˈhɛfər/ n. novilla f.

height /hait/ n. altura f.

heighten /ˈhaitn/ v. elevar; exaltar.

heinous /ˈheinəs/ a. nefando.

heir /ɛr/ **heiress** n. heredero -ra.

helicopter /ˈhɛlɪˌkɔptər/ n. helicóptero m.

heliotrope /ˈhiliəˌtroup/ n. heliotropo m.

helium /ˈhiliəm/ n. helio m.

hell /hɛl/ n. infierno m.

Hellenism /ˈhɛləˌnɪzəm/ n. helenismo m.

hellish /ˈhɛlɪʃ/ a. infernal.

hello /hɛˈlou/ interj. ¡hola!; (on telephone) aló; bueno.

helm /hɛlm/ n. timón m.

helmet /ˈhɛlmɪt/ n. yelmo, casco m.

helmsman /ˈhɛlmzmən/ n. limonero m.

help /hɛlp/ n. **1.** ayuda f. **help!** ¡socorro! —v. **2.** ayudar. **h. one-** self, servirse. **can't help (but),** no poder menos de.

helper /ˈhɛlpər/ n. ayudante m.

helpful /ˈhɛlpfəl/ a. útil; servicial.

helpfulness /ˈhɛlpfəlnɪs/ n. utilidad f.

helpless /ˈhɛlplɪs/ a. imposibilitado.

hem /hɛm/ n. **1.** ribete m. —v. **2.** ribetear.

hemisphere /ˈhɛmɪˌsfɪər/ n. hemisferio m.

hemlock /ˈhɛmˌlɔk/ n. abeto m.

hemoglobin /ˈhiməˌgloubɪn/ n. hemoglobina f.

hemophilia /ˌhiməˈfɪliə/ n. hemofilia f.

hemorrhage /ˈhɛmərɪdʒ/ n. hemorragia f.

hemorrhoids /ˈhɛməˌrɔidz/ n. hemorroides f.pl.

hemp /hɛmp/ n. cáñamo m.

hemstitch /ˈhɛmˌstɪtʃ/ n. **1.** vainica f. —v. **2.** hacer una vainica.

hen /hɛn/ n. gallina f.

hence /hɛns/ adv. por lo tanto.

henceforth /ˌhɛnsˈfɔrθ/ adv. de aquí en adelante.

henchman /ˈhɛntʃmən/ n. paniaguado m.

henna /ˈhɛnə/ n. alheña f.

hepatitis /ˌhɛpəˈtaitɪs/ n. hepatitis f.

her /hɜr/ unstressed hər, ər/ a. **1.** su. —pron. **2.** ella; la; le.

herald /ˈhɛrəld/ n. heraldo m.

heraldic /hɛˈrældɪk/ a. heráldico.

heraldry /ˈhɛrəldri/ n. heráldica f.

herb /ɜrb; esp. Brit. hɜrb/ n. yerba, hierba f.

herbaceous /hɜrˈbeiʃəs, ɜr-/ a. herbáceo.

herbarium /hɜrˈbɛəriəm, ɜr-/ n. herbario m.

herd /hɜrd/ n. **1.** hato, rebaño m. —v. **2.** reunir en hatos.

here /hɪər/ adv. aquí; acá.

hereafter /hɪərˈæftər/ adv. en lo futuro.

hereby /hɪərˈbai/ adv. por éstas, por la presente.

hereditary /həˈrɛdɪˌtɛri/ a. hereditario.

heredity /həˈrɛdɪti/ n. herencia f.

herein /hɪərˈɪn/ adv. aquí dentro; incluso.

heresy /ˈhɛrəsi/ n. herejía f.

heretic /ˈhɛrɪtɪk/ a. **1.** herético. —n. **2.** hereje m. & f.

heretical /həˈretɪkəl/ a. herético.

heretofore /ˌhɪərtəˈfɔr/ adv. hasta ahora.

herewith /hɪərˈwɪθ/ adv. con esto, adjunto.

heritage /ˈherɪtɪdʒ/ n. herencia f.

hermetic /hərˈmetɪk/ a. hermético.

hermit /ˈhɜrmɪt/ n. ermitaño m.

hernia /ˈhɜrniə/ n. hernia f.

hero /ˈhɪərou/ n. héroe m.

heroic /hɪˈrouɪk/ a. heroico.

heroically /hɪˈrouɪkəli/ adv. heroicamente.

heroin /ˈherouɪn/ n. heroína f.

heroine /ˈherouɪn/ n. heroína f.

heroism /ˈherouˌɪzəm/ n. heroísmo m.

heron /ˈherən/ n. garza f.

herring /ˈherɪŋ/ n. arenque m.

hers /hɜrz/ pron. suyo, de ella.

herself /hərˈself/ pron. sí, sí misma, se. **she h.,** ella misma. **with h.,** consigo.

hertz /hɜrts/ n. hertzio m.

hesitancy /ˈhezɪtənsi/ n. hesitación f.

hesitant /ˈhezɪtənt/ a. indeciso.

hesitate /ˈhezɪˌteɪt/ v. vacilar.

hesitation /ˌhezɪˈteɪʃən/ n. duda; vacilación f.

heterogeneous /ˌhetərəˈdʒiniəs/ a. heterogéneo.

heterosexual /ˌhetərəˈsekʃuəl/ a. heterosexual.

hexagon /ˈheksəˌgɒn/ n. hexágono m.

hibernate /ˈhaɪbərˌneɪt/ v. invernar.

hibernation /ˌhaɪbərˈneɪʃən/ n. invernada f.

hibiscus /haɪˈbɪskəs/ n. hibisco m.

hiccup /ˈhɪkʌp/ n. **1.** hipo m. —v. **2.** tener hipo.

hickory /ˈhɪkəri/ n. nogal americano m.

hidden /ˈhɪdn/ a. oculto; escondido.

hide /haɪd/ n. **1.** cuero m.; piel f. —v. **2.** esconder; ocultar.

hideous /ˈhɪdiəs/ a. horrible.

hide-out /ˈhaɪd ˌaut/ n. escondite m.

hiding place /ˈhaɪdɪŋ/ escondrijo m.

hierarchy /ˈhaɪəˌrɑrki/ n. jerarquía f.

high /haɪ/ a. alto, elevado; (in price) caro.

highbrow /ˈhaɪˌbrau/ n. erudito m.

highfalutin /ˌhaɪfəˈlutn/ a. pomposo, presumido.

high fidelity de alta fidelidad.

highlighter /ˈhaɪˌlaɪtər/ n. marcador m.

highly /ˈhaɪli/ adv. altamente; sumamente.

high school escuela secundaria f.

highway /ˈhaɪˌweɪ/ n. carretera f.; camino real m.

hijacker /ˈhaɪˌdʒækər/ n. secuestrador, pirata de aviones m.

hike /haɪk/ n. caminata f.

hilarious /hɪˈleəriəs/ a. alegre, bullicioso.

hilarity /hɪˈlærɪti/ n. hilaridad f.

hill /hɪl/ n. colina f.; cerro m.; **down h.,** cuesta abajo. **up h.,** cuesta arriba.

hilly /ˈhɪli/ a. accidentado.

hilt /hɪlt/ n. puño m. **up to the h.,** a fondo.

him /hɪm/ pron. él; lo; le.

himself /hɪmˈself/ pron. sí, sí mismo; se. **he h.,** él mismo. **with h.,** consigo.

hinder /ˈhɪndər/ v. impedir.

hindmost /ˈhaɪndˌmoust/ a. último.

hindquarter /ˈhaɪndˌkwɔrtər/ n. cuarto trasero m.

hindrance /ˈhɪndrəns/ n. obstáculo m.

hinge /hɪndʒ/ n. **1.** gozne m. —v. **2.** engoznar. **h. on,** depender de.

hint /hɪnt/ n. **1.** insinuación f.; indicio m. —v. **2.** insinuar.

hip /hɪp/ n. cadera f.

hippopotamus /ˌhɪpəˈpɒtəməs/ n. hipopótamo m.

hire /haɪ^r/ v. alquilar.

his /hɪz; unstressed ɪz/ a. **1.** su. —pron **2.** suyo, de él.

Hispanic /hɪˈspænɪk/ a. hispano.

hiss /hɪs/ n. silbar, sisear.

historian /hɪˈstɔriən/ n. historiador m.

historic /hɪˈstɔrɪk/ **historical** a. histórico.

history /ˈhɪstəri/ n. historia f.

histrionic /ˌhɪstriˈɒnɪk/ a. histriónico.

hit /hɪt/ n. **1.** golpe m.; Colloq. éxito m.; (Internet) hit m. —v. **2.** golpear.

hitch /hɪtʃ/ v. amarrar; enganchar.

hitchhike /ˈhɪtʃˌhaɪk/ v. hacer autostop.

hitchhiker /'hɪt∫,haikər/ n. autostopista f.

hitchhiking /'hɪt∫,haikɪŋ/ n. autostop m.

hither /'hɪðər/ adv. acá, hacia acá.

hitherto /'hɪðər,tu/ adv. hasta ahora.

hive /haiv/ n. colmena f.

hives /haivz/ n. urticaria f.

hoard /hɔrd/ n. 1. acumulación f. —v. 2. acaparar; atesorar.

hoarse /hɔrs/ a. ronco.

hoax /houks/ n. 1. engaño m. —v. 2. engañar.

hobby /'hɒbi/ n. afición f., pasatiempo m.

hobgoblin /hɒb,gɒblɪn/ n. trasgo m.

hobnob /hɒb,nɒb/ v. tener intimidad.

hobo /'houbou/ n. vagabundo m.

hockey /'hɒki/ n. hockey m.

ice-h., hockey sobre hielo.

hod /hɒd/ n. esparavel m.

hodgepodge /'hɒdʒ,pɒdʒ/ n. baturrillo m.; mezcolanza f.

hoe /hou/ n. 1. azada f. —v. 2. cultivar con azada.

hog /hɒg/ n. cerdo, puerco m.

hoist /hɔist/ n. 1. grúa f., elevador m. —v. 2. elevar, enarbolar.

hold /hould/ n. 1. presa f.; agarro m.; Naut. bodega f. **to get h. of,** conseguir, apoderarse de. —v. 2. tener; detener; sujetar; celebrar.

holder /'houldər/ n. tenedor m. **cigarette h.,** boquilla f.

holdup /'hould,ʌp/ n. salteamiento m.

hole /houl/ n. agujero; hoyo; hueco m.

holiday /'hɒli,dei/ n. día de fiesta.

holiness /'houlinɪs/ n. santidad f.

Holland /'hɒlənd/ n. Holanda f.

hollow /'hɒlou/ a. 1. hueco. —n. 2. cavidad f. —v. 3. ahuecar; excavar.

holly /'hɒli/ n. acebo m.

hollyhock /'hɒli,hɒk/ n. malva real f.

holocaust /'hɒlə,kɔst/ n. holocausto m.

hologram /'hɒlə,græm/ n. holograma m.

holography /hə'lɒgrəfi/ n. holografía f.

holster /'houlstər/ n. pistolera f.

holy /'houli/ a. santo.

holy day disanto m.

Holy See Santa Sede f.

Holy Spirit Espíritu Santo m.

Holy Week Semana Santa f.

homage /'hɒmɪdʒ/ n. homenaje m.

home /houm/ n. casa, morada f; hogar m. **at h.,** en casa. **to go h.,** ir a casa.

home appliance electrodoméstica m.

home computer ordenador doméstico m., computadora doméstica f.

homeland /'houm,lænd/ n. patria f.

homely /'houmli/ a. feo; casero.

home rule n. autonomía f.

homesick /'houm,sɪk/ a. nostálgico.

homespun /'houm,spʌn/ a. casero; tocho.

homeward /'houmwərd/ adv. hacia casa.

homework /'houm,wɜrk/ n. deberes m.pl.

homicide /'hɒmə,said/ n. homicida m. & f.

homily /'hɒməli/ n. homilía f.

homogeneous /,houmə'dʒiniəs/ a. homogéneo.

homogenize /hə'mɒdʒə,naiz/ v. homogeneizar.

homosexual /,houmə'sekʃuəl/ n. & a. homosexual m.

Honduras /hɒn'durəs/ n. Honduras f.

hone /houn/ n. 1. piedra de afilar f. —v. 2. afilar.

honest /'ɒnɪst/ a. honrado, honesto; sincero.

honestly /'ɒnɪstli/ adv. honradamente; de veras.

honesty /'ɒnəsti/ n. honradez, honestidad f.

honey /'hʌni/ n. miel f.

honeybee /'hʌni,bi/ n. abeja obrera f.

honeymoon /'hʌni,mun/ n. luna de miel f.

honeysuckle /'hʌni,sʌkəl/ n. madreselva f.

honor /'ɒnər/ n. 1. honra f.; honor m. —v. 2. honrar.

honorable /'ɒnərəbəl/ a. honorable; ilustre.

honorary /'ɒnə,reri/ a. honorario.

hood /hud/ n. capota; capucha f.; Auto. cubierta del motor.

hoodlum /'hudləm/ n. pillo m., rufián m.

hoodwink /'hud,wɪŋk/ v. engañar.

hoof /huf/ *n.* pezuña *f.*

hook /huk/ *n.* **1.** gancho *m.* —*v.* **2.** enganchar.

hooligan /ˈhuligən/ *n.* gamberro -rra.

hoop /hup/ *n.* cerco *m.*

hop /hɒp/ *n.* **1.** salto *m.* —*v.* **2.** saltar.

hope /houp/ *n.* **1.** esperanza *f.* —*v.* **2.** esperar.

hopeful /ˈhoupfəl/ *a.* lleno de esperanzas.

hopeless /ˈhouplɪs/ *a.* desesperado; sin remedio.

horde /hɔrd/ *n.* horda *f.*

horehound /ˈhɔrˌhaund/ *n.* marrubio *m.*

horizon /həˈraizən/ *n.* horizonte *m.*

horizontal /ˌhɔrəˈzɒntl̩/ *a.* horizontal.

hormone /ˈhɔrmoun/ *n.* hormón *m.*

horn /hɔrn/ *n.* cuerno *m.*; (music) trompa *f.*; *Auto.* bocina *f.*

hornet /ˈhɔrnɪt/ *n.* avispón *m.*

horny /ˈhɔrni/ *a.* córneo; calloso.

horoscope /ˈhɔrəˌskoup/ *n.* horóscopo *m.*

horrendous /həˈrɛndəs/ *a.* horrendo.

horrible /ˈhɔrəbəl/ *a.* horrible.

horrid /ˈhɔrɪd/ *a.* horrible.

horrify /ˈhɔrəˌfai/ *v.* horrorizar.

horror /ˈhɔrər/ *n.* horror *m.*

horror film película de terror *f.*

hors d'oeuvre /ɔr ˈdɜrv/ *n.* entremés *m.*

horse /hɔrs/ *n.* caballo *m.* **to ride a h.,** cabalgar.

horseback /ˈhɔrsˌbæk/ *n.* **on h.,** a caballo. **to ride h.,** montar a caballo.

horseback riding equitación *f.*

horsefly /ˈhɔrsˌflai/ *n.* tábano *m.*

horsehair /ˈhɔrsˌhɛər/ *n.* pelo de caballo *m.*; tela de crin *f.*

horseman /ˈhɔrsmən/ *n.* jinete *m.*

horsemanship /ˈhɔrsmənˌʃɪp/ *n.* manejo *m.*, equitación *f.*

horsepower /ˈhɔrsˌpauər/ *n.* caballo de fuerza *m.*

horse race carrera de caballos *f.*

horseradish /ˈhɔrsˌrædɪʃ/ *n.* rábano picante *m.*

horseshoe /ˈhɔrsˌʃu/ *n.* herradura *f.*

hortatory /ˈhɔrtəˌtɔri/ *a.* exhortatorio.

horticulture /ˈhɔrtɪˌkʌltʃər/ *n.* horticultura *f.*

hose /houz/ *n.* medias *f.pl*; (garden) manguera *f.*

hosiery /ˈhouʒəri/ *n.* calcetería *f.*

hospitable /ˈhɒspɪtəbəl/ *a.* hospitalario.

hospital /ˈhɒspɪtl̩/ *n.* hospital *m.*

hospitality /ˌhɒspɪˈtælɪti/ *n.* hospitalidad *f.*

hospitalization /ˌhɒspɪtl̩ɪˈzeiʃən/ *n.* hospitalización *f.*

hospitalize /ˈhɒspɪtl̩ˌaiz/ *v.* hospitalizar.

host /houst/ *n.* anfitrión *m.*, dueño de la casa; *Relig.* hostia *f.*

hostage /ˈhɒstɪdʒ/ *n.* rehén *m.*

hostel /ˈhɒstl̩/ *n.* hostería *f.*

hostelry /ˈhɒstl̩ri/ *n.* fonda *f.*, parador *m.*

hostess /ˈhoustɪs/ *n.* anfitriona *f.*, dueña de la casa.

hostile /ˈhɒstl̩/ *a.* hostil.

hostility /hɒˈstɪlɪti/ *n.* hostilidad *f.*

hot /hɒt/ *a.* caliente; (sauce) picante. **to be h.,** tener calor; (weather) hacer calor.

hotbed /ˈhɒtˌbɛd/ *n.* estercolero *m.* *Fig.* foco *m.*

hot dog perrito caliente *m.*

hotel /houˈtɛl/ *n.* hotel *m.*

hotelier /ˌoutlˈyei, ˌhoutlˈɪər/ *n.* hotelero -ra.

hot-headed /ˈhɒt ˈhɛdɪd/ *a.* turbulento, alborotadizo.

hothouse /ˈhɒtˌhaus/ *n.* invernáculo *m.*

hot-water bottle /ˈhɒt ˈwɔtər/ bolsa de agua caliente *f.*

hound /haund/ *n.* **1.** sabueso *m.* —*v.* **2.** perseguir; seguir la pista.

hour /auər/ *n.* hora *f.*

hourglass /ˈauərˌglæs/ *n.* reloj de arena *m.*

hourly /ˈauərli/ *a.* **1.** por horas. —*adv.* **2.** a cada hora.

house /*n* haus; *v* hauz/ *n.* **1.** casa *f.*; *Theat.* público *m.* —*v.* **2.** alojar, albergar.

housefly /ˈhausˌflai/ *n.* mosca ordinaria *f.*

household /ˈhausˌhould/ *n.* familia; casa *f.*

housekeeper /ˈhausˌkipər/ *n.* ama de llaves.

housemaid /ˈhausˌmeid/ *n.* criada *f.*, sirvienta *f.*

housewife /ˈhausˌwaif/ *n.* ama de casa.

hydraulic

housework /'haus,wɜrk/ n. tareas domésticas.

hovel /'hʌvəl/ n. choza f.

hover /'hʌvər/ v. revolotear.

hovercraft /'hʌvər,kræft/ n. aerodeslizador m.

how /hau/ adv. cómo. **h. much,** cuánto. **h. many,** cuántos. **h. far,** a qué distancia.

however /hau'evər/ adv. como quiera; sin embargo.

howl /haul/ n. **1.** aullido m. —v. **2.** aullar.

HTML abbr. (HyperText Markup Language) Lenguaje de Marcado de Hipertexto m.

hub /hʌb/ n. centro m.; eje m. **h. of a wheel,** cubo de la rueda m.

hubbub /'hʌbʌb/ n. alboroto m., bulla f.

hue /hyu/ n. matiz m.; color m.

hug /hʌg/ n. **1.** abrazo m. —v. **2.** abrazar.

huge /hyudʒ/ a. enorme.

hulk /hʌlk/ n. casco de buque m.

hull /hʌl/ n. **1.** cáscara f.; (naval) casco m. —v. **2.** decascarar.

hum /hʌm/ n. **1.** zumbido m. —v. **2.** tararear; zumbar.

human /'hyumən/ a. & n. humano -na.

human being ser humano m.

humane /hyu'mein/ a. humano, humanitario.

humanism /'hyumə,nɪzəm/ n. humanidad f.; benevolencia f.

humanitarian /hyu,mænɪ'tɛəriən/ a. humanitario.

humanity /hyu'mænɪti/ n. humanidad f.

humanly /'hyumənli/ a. humanamente.

humble /'hʌmbəl/ a. humilde.

humbug /'hʌm,bʌg/ n. farsa f., embaucador m.

humdrum /'hʌm,drʌm/ a. monótono.

humid /'hyumɪd/ a. húmedo.

humidity /hyu'mɪdɪti/ n. humedad f.

humiliate /hyu'mɪli,eit/ v. humillar.

humiliation /hyu,mɪli'eiʃən/ n. mortificación f.; bochorno m.

humility /hyu'mɪlɪti/ n. humildad f.

humor /'hyumər/ n. **1.** humor; capricho m. —v. **2.** complacer.

humorist /'hyumərɪst/ n. humorista m.

humorous /'hyumərəs/ a. divertido.

hump /hʌmp/ n. joroba f.

humpback /'hʌmp,bæk/ n. jorobado m.

humus /'hyuməs/ n. humus m.

hunch /hʌntʃ/ n. giba f.; (idea) corazonada f.

hunchback /'hʌntʃ,bæk/ n. jorobado m.

hundred /'hʌndrɪd/ a. & pron. **1.** cien, ciento. **200,** doscientos. **300,** trescientos. **400,** cuatrocientos. **500,** quinientos. **600,** seiscientos. **700,** setecientos. **800,** ochocientos. **900,** novecientos. —n. **2.** centenar m.

hundredth /'hʌndrɪdθ/ n. & a. centésimo m.

Hungarian /hʌŋ'gɛəriən/ a. & n. húngaro -ra.

Hungary /'hʌŋgəri/ Hungría f.

hunger /'hʌŋgər/ n. hambre f.

hunger strike huelga de hambre f.

hungry /'hʌŋgri/ a. hambriento. **to be h.,** tener hambre.

hunt /hʌnt/ n. **1.** caza f. —v. **2.** cazar. **h. up,** buscar.

hunter /'hʌntər/ n. cazador m.

hunting /'hʌntɪŋ/ n. caza f. **to go h.,** ir de caza.

hurdle /'hɜrdl/ n. zarzo m., valla f.; dificultad f.

hurl /hɜrl/ v. arrojar.

hurricane /'hɜri,kein/ n. huracán m.

hurry /'hɜri/ n. **1.** prisa f. **to be in a h.,** tener prisa. —v. **2.** apresurar; darse prisa.

hurt /hɜrt/ n. **1.** daño, perjuicio m. —v. **2.** dañar; lastimar; doler; ofender.

hurtful /'hɜrtfəl/ a. perjudicial, dañino.

hurtle /'hɜrtl/ v. lanzar.

husband /'hʌzbənd/ n. marido, esposo m.

husk /hʌsk/ n. **1.** cáscara f. —v. **2.** descascarar.

husky /'hʌski/ a. fornido.

hustle /'hʌsəl/ v. empujar.

hustle and bustle ajetreo m.

hut /hʌt/ n. choza f.

hyacinth /'haiəsɪnθ/ n. jacinto m.

hybrid /'haibrɪd/ a. híbrido.

hydrangea /hai'dreindʒə/ n. hortensia f.

hydraulic /hai'drɔlɪk/ a. hidráulico.

hydroelectric /,haidrou'lɛktrɪk/ a. hidroeléctrico.

hydrogen /'haidrədʒən/ n. hidrógeno m.

hydrophobia /,haidrə'foubiə/ n. hidrofobia. f.

hydroplane /'haidrə,plein/ n. hidroavión m.

hydrotherapy /,haidrə'θɛrəpi/ n. hidroterapia f.

hyena /hai'inə/ n. hiena f.

hygiene /'haidʒin/ n. higiene f.

hygienic /,haidʒi'ɛnɪk/ a. higiénico.

hymn /hɪm/ n. himno m.

hymnal /'hɪmnl/ n. himnario m.

hype /haip/ n. Colloq. **1.** bomba publicitario f. —v. **2.** promocionar a bombo y platillo.

hypercritical /,haipər'krɪtɪkəl/ a. hipercrítico.

hyperlink /'haipər,lɪŋk/ n. (Internet) hiperenlace m.

hypermarket /'haipər,mɑrkɪt/ n. hipermercado m.

hypertension /,haipər'tɛnʃən/ n. hipertensión f.

hypertext /'haipər,tɛkst/ n. (Internet) hipertexto m.

hyphen /'haifən/ n. guión m.

hyphenate /'haifə,neit/ v. separar con guión.

hypnosis /hɪp'nousis/ n. hipnosis f.

hypnotic /hɪp'nɒtɪk/ a. hipnótico.

hypnotism /'hɪpnə,tɪzəm/ n. hipnotismo m.

hypnotize /'hɪpnə,taiz/ v. hipnotizar.

hypochondria /,haipə'kɒndriə/ n. hipocondría f.

hypochondriac /,haipə'kɒndri,æk/ n. & a. hipocondríaco m.

hypocrisy /hɪ'pɒkrəsi/ n. hipocresía f.

hypocrite /'hɪpəkrɪt/ n. hipócrita m. & f.

hypocritical /,hɪpə'krɪtɪkəl/ a. hipócrita.

hypodermic /,haipə'dɜrmɪk/ a. hipodérmico.

hypotenuse /hai'pɒtŋ,us/ n. hipotenusa f.

hypothesis /hai'pɒθəsɪs/ n. hipótesis f.

hypothetical /,haipə'θɛtɪkəl/ a. hipotético.

hysterectomy /,hɪstə'rɛktəmi/ n. histerectomía f.

hysteria /hɪ'stɛriə/ **hysterics** /hɪ'stɛrɪks/ n. histeria f.

hysterical /hɪ'stɛrɪkəl/ a. histérico.

I

I /ai/ pron. yo.

iambic /ai'æmbɪk/ a. yámbico.

ice /ais/ n. hielo m.

iceberg /'aisbɜrg/ n. iceberg m.

icebox /'ais,bɒks/ n. refrigerador m.

ice cream helado, mantecado m.; **i.-c. cone**, barquillo de helado; **i.-c. parlor** heladería f.

ice cube cubito de hielo m.

ice skate patín de cuchilla m.

icon /'aikɒn/ n. icón m.

icy /'aisi/ a. helado; indiferente.

idea /ai'diə/ n. idea f.

ideal /ai'diəl/ a. ideal.

idealism /ai'diə,lɪzəm/ n. idealismo m.

idealist /ai'diəlɪst/ n. idealista m. & f.

idealistic /ai,diə'lɪstɪk/ a. idealista.

idealize /ai'diə,laiz/ v. idealizar.

ideally /ai'diəli/ adv. idealmente.

identical /ai'dɛntɪkəl/ a. idéntico.

identifiable /ai,dɛntɪ'faiəbəl/ a. identificable.

identification /ai,dɛntəfɪ'keiʃən/ n. identificación f. **i. papers**, cédula de identidad f.

identify /ai'dɛntə,fai/ v. identificar.

identity /ai'dɛntɪti/ n. identidad f.

ideology /,aidi'ɒlədʒi/ n. ideología f.

idiocy /'ɪdiəsi/ n. idiotez f.

idiom /'ɪdiəm/ n. modismo m.; idioma m.

idiot /'ɪdiət/ n. idiota m. & f.

idiotic /,ɪdi'ɒtɪk/ a. idiota, tonto.

idle /'aidl/ a. desocupado; perezoso.

idleness /'aidlnɪs/ n. ociosidad, pereza f.

idol /'aidl/ n. ídolo m.

idolatry /ai'dɒlətri/ n. idolatría f.

idolize /'aidl,aiz/ v. idolatrar.

idyl /'aidl/ n. idilio m.

idyllic /ai'dɪlɪk/ a. idílico.

if /ɪf/ *conj.* si. **even if,** aunque.
ignite /ɪg'naɪt/ *v.* encender.
ignition /ɪg'nɪʃən/ *n.* ignición *f.*
ignoble /ɪg'noubəl/ *a.* innoble, indigno.
ignominious /ˌɪgnə'mɪniəs/ *a.* ignominioso.
ignoramus /ˌɪgnə'reɪməs/ *n.* ignorante *m.*
ignorance /'ɪgnərəns/ *n.* ignorancia *f.*
ignorant /'ɪgnərənt/ *a.* ignorante. **to be i. of,** ignorar.
ignore /ɪg'nɔr/ *v.* desconocer, pasar por alto.
ill /ɪl/ *a.* enfermo, malo.
illegal /ɪ'ligəl/ *a.* ilegal.
illegible /ɪ'lɛdʒəbəl/ *a.* ilegible.
illegibly /ɪ'lɛdʒəbli/ *a.* ilegiblemente.
illegitimacy /ˌɪlɪ'dʒɪtəməsi/ *n.* ilegitimidad *f.*
illegitimate /ˌɪlɪ'dʒɪtəmɪt/ *a.* ilegítimo; desautorizado.
illicit /ɪ'lɪsɪt/ *a.* ilícito.
illiteracy /ɪ'lɪtərəsi/ *n.* analfabetismo *m.*
illiterate /ɪ'lɪtərɪt/ *a.* & *n.* analfabeto -ta.
illness /'ɪlnɪs/ *n.* enfermedad, maldad *f.*
illogical /ɪ'lɒdʒɪkəl/ *a.* ilógico.
illuminate /ɪ'lumə,neɪt/ *v.* iluminar.
illumination /ɪ,lumə'neɪʃən/ *n.* iluminación *f.*
illusion /ɪ'luʒən/ *n.* ilusión *f.*; ensueño *m.*
illusive /ɪ'lusɪv/ *a.* ilusivo.
illustrate /'ɪlə,streɪt/ *v.* ilustrar; ejemplificar.
illustration /ˌɪlə'streɪʃən/ *n.* ilustración *f.*; ejemplo; grabado *m.*
illustrative /ɪ'lʌstrətɪv/ *a.* ilustrativo.
illustrious /ɪ'lʌstriəs/ *a.* ilustre.
ill will *n.* malevolencia *f.*
image /'ɪmɪdʒ/ *n.* imagen, estatua *f.*
imagery /'ɪmɪdʒri/ *n.* imaginación *f.*
imaginable /ɪ'mædʒənəbəl/ *a.* imaginable.
imaginary /ɪ'mædʒə,nɛri/ *a.* imaginario.
imagination /ɪ,mædʒə'neɪʃən/ *n.* imaginación *f.*
imaginative /ɪ'mædʒənətɪv/ *a.* imaginativo.

imagine /ɪ'mædʒɪn/ *v.* imaginarse, figurarse.
imam /ɪ'mɑm/ *n.* imán *m.*
imbecile /'ɪmbəsɪl/ *n.* & *a.* imbécil *m.*
imitate /'ɪmɪ,teɪt/ *v.* imitar.
imitation /ˌɪmɪ'teɪʃən/ *n.* imitación *f.*
imitative /'ɪmɪ,teɪtɪv/ *a.* imitativo.
immaculate /ɪ'mækyəlɪt/ *a.* inmaculado.
immanent /'ɪmənənt/ *a.* inmanente.
immaterial /ˌɪmə'tɪəriəl/ *a.* inmaterial; sin importancia.
immature /ˌɪmə'tʃʊr/ *a.* inmaturo.
immediate /ɪ'midɪt/ *a.* inmediato.
immediately /ɪ'midɪtli/ *adv.* inmediatamente.
immense /ɪ'mɛns/ *a.* inmenso.
immerse /ɪ'mɜrs/ *v.* sumergir.
immigrant /'ɪmɪgrənt/ *n.* & *a.* inmigrante *m.* & *f.*
immigrate /'ɪmɪ,greɪt/ *v.* inmigrar.
imminent /'ɪmənənt/ *a.* inminente.
immobile /ɪ'moubəl/ *a.* inmóvil.
immoderate /ɪ'mɒdərɪt/ *a.* inmoderado.
immodest /ɪ'mɒdɪst/ *a.* inmodesto; atrevido.
immoral /ɪ'mɔrəl/ *a.* inmoral.
immorality /ˌɪmə'rælɪti/ *n.* inmoralidad *f.*
immorally /ɪ'mɔrəli/ *adv.* licenciosamente.
immortal /ɪ'mɔrtl/ *a.* inmortal.
immortality /ˌɪmɔr'tælɪti/ *n.* inmortalidad *f.*
immortalize /ɪ'mɔrtl,aɪz/ *v.* inmortalizar.
immune /ɪ'myun/ *a.* inmune.
immunity /ɪ'myunɪti/ *n.* inmunidad *f.*
immunize /'ɪmyə,naɪz/ *v.* inmunizar.
impact /'ɪmpækt/ *n.* impacto *m.*
impair /ɪm'pɛər/ *v.* empeorar, perjudicar.
impale /ɪm'peɪl/ *v.* empalar.
impart /ɪm'pɑrt/ *v.* impartir, comunicar.
impartial /ɪm'pɑrʃəl/ *a.* imparcial.
impatience /ɪm'peɪʃəns/ *n.* impaciencia *f.*
impatient /ɪm'peɪʃənt/ *a.* impaciente.
impede /ɪm'pid/ *v.* impedir, estorbar.

impediment /ɪmˈpɛdəmənt/ n. impedimento m.

impel /ɪmˈpɛl/ v. impeler.

impenetrable /ɪmˈpɛnɪtrəbəl/ a. impenetrable.

impenitent /ɪmˈpɛnɪtənt/ n. & a. impenitente m.

imperative /ɪmˈpɛrətɪv/ a. imperativo.

imperceptible /ˌɪmpərˈsɛptəbəl/ a. imperceptible.

imperfect /ɪmˈpərfɪkt/ a. imperfecto.

imperfection /ˌɪmpərˈfɛkʃən/ n. imperfección f.

imperial /ɪmˈpɪriəl/ a. imperial.

imperialism /ɪmˈpɪriəˌlɪzəm/ n. imperialismo m.

imperious /ɪmˈpɪriəs/ a. imperioso.

impersonal /ɪmˈpərsənļ/ a. impersonal.

impersonate /ɪmˈpərsəˌneɪt/ v. personificar; imitar.

impersonation /ɪmˌpərsəˈneɪʃən/ n. personificación f.; imitación f.

impertinence /ɪmˈpərtņəns/ n. impertinencia f.

impervious /ɪmˈpərviəs/ a. impermeable.

impetuous /ɪmˈpɛtʃuəs/ a. impetuoso.

impetus /ˈɪmpɪtəs/ n. ímpetu m., impulso m.

impinge /ɪmˈpɪndʒ/ v. tropezar; infringir.

implacable /ɪmˈplækəbəl/ a. implacable.

implant /ɪmˈplænt/ v. implantar; inculcar.

implement /ˈɪmpləmənt/ n. herramienta f.

implicate /ˈɪmplɪˌkeɪt/ v. implicar; embrollar.

implication /ˌɪmplɪˈkeɪʃən/ n. inferencia f.; complicidad f.

implicit /ɪmˈplɪsɪt/ a. implícito.

implied /ɪmˈplaɪd/ a. implícito.

implore /ɪmˈplɔr/ v. implorar.

imply /ɪmˈplaɪ/ v. significar; dar a entender.

impolite /ˌɪmpəˈlaɪt/ a. descortés.

import /n ˈɪmpɔrt; v ɪmˈpɔrt/ n. **1.** importación f. —v. **2.** importar.

importance /ɪmˈpɔrtņs/ n. importancia f.

important /ɪmˈpɔrtņt/ a. importante.

importation /ˌɪmpɔrˈteɪʃən/ n. importación f.

importune /ˌɪmpɔrˈtun/ v. importunar.

impose /ɪmˈpouz/ v. imponer.

imposition /ˌɪmpəˈzɪʃən/ n. imposición f.

impossibility /ɪmˌpɑsəˈbɪlɪti/ n. imposibilidad f.

impossible /ɪmˈpɑsəbəl/ a. imposible.

impotence /ˈɪmpətəns/ n. impotencia f.

impotent /ˈɪmpətənt/ a. impotente.

impregnable /ɪmˈprɛgnəbəl/ a. impregnable.

impregnate /ɪmˈprɛgneɪt/ v. impregnar; fecundizar.

impresario /ˌɪmprəˈsɑriˌou/ n. empresario m.

impress /ɪmˈprɛs/ v. impresionar.

impression /ɪmˈprɛʃən/ n. impresión f.

impressive /ɪmˈprɛsɪv/ a. imponente.

imprison /ɪmˈprɪzən/ v. encarcelar.

imprisonment /ɪmˈprɪzənmənt/ n. prisión, encarcelación f.

improbable /ɪmˈprɑbəbəl/ a. improbable.

impromptu /ɪmˈprɑmptu/ a. extemporáneo.

improper /ɪmˈprɑpər/ a. impropio.

improve /ɪmˈpruv/ v. mejorar; progresar.

improvement /ɪmˈpruvmənt/ n. mejoramiento; progreso m.

improvise /ˈɪmprəˌvaɪz/ v. improvisar.

impudent /ˈɪmpyədənt/ a. descarado.

impugn /ɪmˈpyun/ v. impugnar.

impulse /ˈɪmpʌls/ n. impulso m.

impulsive /ɪmˈpʌlsɪv/ a. impulsivo.

impunity /ɪmˈpyunɪti/ n. impunidad f.

impure /ɪmˈpyur/ a. impuro.

impurity /ɪmˈpyurɪti/ n. impureza f.; deshonestidad f.

impute /ɪmˈpyut/ v. imputar.

in /ɪn/ prep. **1.** en; dentro de. —adv. **2.** adentro.

inadvertent /ˌɪnədˈvərtņt/ a. inadvertido.

inalienable /ɪnˈeɪlyənəbəl/ a. inalienable.

inane /ɪˈneɪn/ a. mentecato.

inaugural /ɪnˈɔgyərəl/ a. inaugural.

inaugurate /ɪnˈɔːɡjəˌreɪt/ v. inaugurar.

inauguration /ɪnˌɔːɡjəˈreɪʃən/ n. inauguración f.

Inca /ˈɪŋkə/ n. inca m.

incandescent /ˌɪnkənˈdɛsənt/ a. incandescente.

incantation /ˌɪnkænˈteɪʃən/ n. encantación f., conjuro m.

incapacitate /ˌɪnkəˈpæsɪˌteɪt/ v. incapacitar.

incarcerate /ɪnˈkɑːrsəˌreɪt/ v. encarcelar.

incarnate /ɪnˈkɑːrnɪt/ a. encarnado; personificado.

incarnation /ˌɪnkɑːrˈneɪʃən/ n. encarnación f.

incendiary /ɪnˈsɛndiˌɛri/ a. incendiario.

incense /ɪnˈsɛns/ n. **1.** incienso m. —v. **2.** indignar.

incentive /ɪnˈsɛntɪv/ n. incentivo m.

inception /ɪnˈsɛpʃən/ n. comienzo m.

incessant /ɪnˈsɛsənt/ a. incesante.

incest /ˈɪnsɛst/ n. incesto m.

inch /ɪntʃ/ n. pulgada f.

incidence /ˈɪnsɪdəns/ n. incidencia f.

incident /ˈɪnsɪdənt/ n. incidente m.

incidental /ˌɪnsɪˈdɛntl/ a. incidental.

incidentally /ˌɪnsɪˈdɛntli/ adv. incidentalmente; entre paréntesis.

incinerate /ɪnˈsɪnəˌreɪt/ v. incinerar.

incinerator /ɪnˈsɪnəˌreɪtər/ n. incinerador m.

incipient /ɪnˈsɪpiənt/ a. incipiente.

incision /ɪnˈsɪʒən/ n. incisión f.; cortadura f.

incisive /ɪnˈsaɪsɪv/ a. incisivo; mordaz.

incisor /ɪnˈsaɪzər/ n. incisivo m.

incite /ɪnˈsaɪt/ v. incitar, instigar.

inclination /ˌɪnkləˈneɪʃən/ n. inclinación f.; declive m.

incline /ɪnˈkleɪn/ v ɪnˈklaɪn/ n. **1.** pendiente f. —v. **2.** inclinar.

inclose /ɪnˈkloʊz/ v. incluir.

include /ɪnˈkluːd/ v. incluir, englobar.

including /ɪnˈkluːdɪŋ/ prep. incluso.

inclusive /ɪnˈkluːsɪv/ a. inclusivo.

incognito /ˌɪnkɒɡˈniːtoʊ/ a. & adv. incógnito m.

income /ˈɪnkʌm/ n. renta f.; ingresos m.pl.

income tax impuesto sobre la renta f.

incomparable /ɪnˈkɒmpərəbəl/ a. incomparable.

inconvenience /ˌɪnkənˈviːnyəns/ n. **1.** incomodidad f. —v. **2.** incomodar.

inconvenient /ˌɪnkənˈviːnyənt/ a. incómodo.

incorporate /ɪnˈkɔːrpəˌreɪt/ v. incorporar; dar cuerpo.

incorrigible /ɪnˈkɔːrɪdʒəbəl/ a. incorregible.

increase /ɪnˈkriːs/ v. crecer; aumentar.

incredible /ɪnˈkrɛdəbəl/ a. increíble.

incredulity /ˌɪnkrɪˈduːlɪti/ n. incredulidad f.

incredulous /ɪnˈkrɛdʒələs/ a. incrédulo.

increment /ˈɪnkrəmənt/ n. incremento m., aumento m.

incriminate /ɪnˈkrɪməˌneɪt/ v. incriminar.

incrimination /ɪnˌkrɪməˈneɪʃən/ n. incriminación f.

incrust /ɪnˈkrʌst/ v. incrustar.

incubator /ˈɪnkyəˌbeɪtər/ n. incubadora f.

inculcate /ɪnˈkʌlkeɪt/ v. inculcar.

incumbency /ɪnˈkʌmbənsi/ n. incumbencia f.

incumbent /ɪnˈkʌmbənt/ a. obligatorio; colocado sobre.

incur /ɪnˈkɜːr/ v. incurrir.

incurable /ɪnˈkyʊrəbəl/ a. incurable.

indebted /ɪnˈdɛtɪd/ a. obligado; adeudado.

indeed /ɪnˈdiːd/ adv. verdaderamente, de veras. **no i.,** de ninguna manera.

indefatigable /ˌɪndɪˈfætɪɡəbəl/ a. incansable.

indefinite /ɪnˈdɛfənɪt/ a. indefinido.

indefinitely /ɪnˈdɛfənɪtli/ adv. indefinidamente.

indelible /ɪnˈdɛləbəl/ a. indeleble.

indemnify /ɪnˈdɛmnəˌfaɪ/ v. indemnizar.

indemnity /ɪnˈdɛmnɪti/ n. indemnificación f.

indent /ɪnˈdɛnt/ n. **1.** diente m., mella f. —v. **2.** indentar, mellar.

indentation /ˌɪndɛnˈteɪʃən/ n. indentación f.

independence /ˌɪndɪˈpɛndəns/ n. independencia f.

independent /ˌɪndɪˈpɛndənt/ a. independiente.

in-depth /ˈɪn ˈdɛpθ/ adj. en profundidad.

index /ˈɪndɛks/ n. índice m.; (of book) tabla f.

index card ficha f.

index finger dedo índice m.

India /ˈɪndiə/ n. India f.

Indian /ˈɪndiən/ a. & n. indio -dia.

indicate /ˈɪndɪˌkeɪt/ v. indicar.

indication /ˌɪndɪˈkeɪʃən/ n. indicación f.

indicative /ɪnˈdɪkətɪv/ a. & n. indicativo m.

indict /ɪnˈdaɪt/ v. encausar.

indictment /ɪnˈdaɪtmənt/ n. (law) sumaria; denuncia f.

indifference /ɪnˈdɪfərəns/ n. indiferencia f.

indifferent /ɪnˈdɪfərənt/ a. indiferente.

indigenous /ɪnˈdɪdʒənəs/ a. indígena.

indigent /ˈɪndɪdʒənt/ a. indigente, pobre.

indigestion /ˌɪndɪˈdʒɛstʃən/ n. indigestión f.

indignant /ɪnˈdɪgnənt/ a. indignado.

indignation /ˌɪndɪgˈneɪʃən/ n. indignación f.

indignity /ɪnˈdɪgnɪti/ n. indignidad f.

indirect /ˌɪndəˈrɛkt/ a. indirecto.

indiscreet /ˌɪndɪˈskrit/ a. indiscreto.

indiscretion /ˌɪndɪˈskrɛʃən/ n. indiscreción f.

indiscriminate /ˌɪndɪˈskrɪmənɪt/ a. promiscuo.

indispensable /ˌɪndɪˈspɛnsəbəl/ a. indispensable.

indisposed /ˌɪndɪˈspouzd/ a. indispuesto.

individual /ˌɪndəˈvɪdʒuəl/ a. & n. individuo m.

individuality /ˌɪndəˌvɪdʒuˈælɪti/ n. individualidad f.

individually /ˌɪndəˈvɪdʒuəli/ adv. individualmente.

indivisible /ˌɪndəˈvɪzəbəl/ a. indivisible.

indoctrinate /ɪnˈdɒktrəˌneɪt/ v. doctrinar, enseñar.

indolent /ˈɪndələnt/ a. indolente.

indoor /ˈɪnˌdɔr/ a. **1.** interior. **indoors** —adv. **2.** en casa; bajo techo.

indorse /ɪnˈdɔrs/ v. endosar.

induce /ɪnˈdus/ v. inducir, persuadir.

induct /ɪnˈdʌkt/ v. instalar, iniciar.

induction /ɪnˈdʌkʃən/ n. introducción f.; instalación f.

inductive /ɪnˈdʌktɪv/ a. inductivo; introductor.

indulge /ɪnˈdʌldʒ/ v. favorecer. **i. in**, entregarse a.

indulgence /ɪnˈdʌldʒəns/ n. indulgencia f.

indulgent /ɪnˈdʌldʒənt/ a. indulgente.

industrial /ɪnˈdʌstriəl/ a. industrial.

industrialist /ɪnˈdʌstriəlɪst/ n. industrial m.

industrial park polígono industrial m.

industrious /ɪnˈdʌstriəs/ a. industrioso, trabajador.

industry /ˈɪndəstri/ n. industria f.

inedible /ɪnˈɛdəbəl/ a. incomible.

ineligible /ɪnˈɛlɪdʒəbəl/ a. inelegible.

inept /ɪnˈɛpt/ a. inepto.

inert /ɪnˈɜrt/ a. inerte.

inertia /ɪnˈɜrʃə/ n. inercia f.

inevitable /ɪnˈɛvɪtəbəl/ a. inevitable.

inexpensive /ˌɪnɪkˈspɛnsɪv/ a. económico.

inexplicable /ˌɪnˈɛksplɪkəbəl/ a. inexplicable.

infallible /ɪnˈfæləbəl/ a. infalible.

infamous /ˈɪnfəməs/ a. infame.

infamy /ˈɪnfəmi/ n. infamia f.

infancy /ˈɪnfənsi/ n. infancia f.

infant /ˈɪnfənt/ n. nene m.; criatura f.

infantile /ˈɪnfənˌtaɪl/ a. infantil.

infantry /ˈɪnfəntri/ n. infantería f.

infatuated /ɪnˈfætʃuˌeɪtɪd/ a. infatuado.

infatuation /ɪnˌfætʃuˈeɪʃən/ a. encaprichamiento m.

infect /ɪnˈfɛkt/ v. infectar.

infection /ɪnˈfɛkʃən/ n. infección f.

infectious /ɪnˈfɛkʃəs/ a. infeccioso.

infer /ɪnˈfɜr/ v. inferir.

inference /ˈɪnfərəns/ n. inferencia f.

inferior /ɪnˈfɪəriər/ a. inferior.

infernal /ɪnˈfɜrnl/ a. infernal.

inferno /ɪnˈfɜrnou/ n. infierno m.

inquest

infest /ɪnˈfest/ v. infestar.

infidel /ˈɪnfɪdl/ n. **1.** infiel m. & f.; pagano -na. —a. **2.** infiel.

infidelity /ˌɪnfɪˈdelɪti/ n. infidelidad f.

infiltrate /ɪnˈfɪltreit/ v. infiltrar.

infinite /ˈɪnfənɪt/ a. infinito.

infinitesimal /ˌɪnfɪnɪˈtesəməl/ a. infinitesimal.

infinitive /ɪnˈfɪnɪtɪv/ n. & a. infinitivo m.

infinity /ɪnˈfɪnɪti/ n. infinidad f.

infirm /ɪnˈfɜrm/ a. enfermizo.

infirmary /ɪnˈfɜrməri/ n. hospital m., enfermería f.

infirmity /ɪnˈfɜrmɪti/ n. enfermedad f.

inflame /ɪnˈfleim/ v. inflamar.

inflammable /ɪnˈflæməbəl/ a. inflamable.

inflammation /ˌɪnfləˈmeiʃən/ n. inflamación f.

inflammatory /ɪnˈflæməˌtɔri/ a. inflamante; Med. inflamatorio.

inflate /ɪnˈfleit/ v. inflar.

inflation /ɪnˈfleiʃən/ n. inflación f.

inflection /ɪnˈflekʃən/ n. inflexión f.; (of the voice) modulación de la voz f.

inflict /ɪnˈflɪkt/ v. infligir.

infliction /ɪnˈflɪkʃən/ n. imposición f.

influence /ˈɪnfluəns/ n. **1.** influencia f. —v. **2.** influir en.

influential /ˌɪnfluˈenʃəl/ a. influyente.

influenza /ˌɪnfluˈenzə/ n. gripe f.

influx /ˈɪnflʌks/ n. afluencia f.

inform /ɪnˈfɔrm/ v. informar. **i. oneself,** enterarse.

informal /ɪnˈfɔrməl/ a. informal.

information /ˌɪnfərˈmeiʃən/ n. informaciones f.pl.

information technology n. informática f.

infrastructure /ˈɪnfrəˌstrʌktʃər/ n. infraestructura f.

infringe /ɪnˈfrɪndʒ/ v. infringir.

infuriate /ɪnˈfyuriˌeit/ v. enfurecer.

ingenious /ɪnˈdʒinyəs/ a. ingenioso.

ingenuity /ˌɪndʒəˈnuɪti/ n. ingeniosidad f.; destreza f.

ingredient /ɪnˈɡridiənt/ n. ingrediente m.

inhabit /ɪnˈhæbɪt/ v. habitar.

inhabitant /ɪnˈhæbɪtənt/ n. habitante m. & f.

inhale /ɪnˈheil/ v. inhalar.

inherent /ɪnˈhɪərənt/ a. inherente.

inherit /ɪnˈherɪt/ v. heredar.

inheritance /ɪnˈherɪtəns/ n. herencia f.

inhibit /ɪnˈhɪbɪt/ v. inhibir.

inhibition /ˌɪnɪˈbɪʃən/ n. inhibición f.

inhuman /ɪnˈhyumən/ a. inhumano.

inimical /ɪˈnɪmɪkəl/ a. hostil.

inimitable /ɪˈnɪmɪtəbəl/ a. inimitable.

iniquity /ɪˈnɪkwɪti/ n. iniquidad f.

initial /ɪˈnɪʃəl/ a. & n. inicial f.

initiate /ɪˈnɪʃiˌeit/ v. iniciar.

initiation /ɪˌnɪʃiˈeiʃən/ n. iniciación f.

initiative /ɪˈnɪʃiətɪv/ n. iniciativa f.

inject /ɪnˈdʒekt/ v. inyectar.

injection /ɪnˈdʒekʃən/ n. inyección f.

injunction /ɪnˈdʒʌŋkʃən/ n. mandato m.; (law) embargo m.

injure /ˈɪndʒər/ v. herir; lastimar; ofender.

injurious /ɪnˈdʒuriəs/ a. perjudicial.

injury /ˈɪndʒəri/ n. herida; afrenta f.; perjuicio m.

injustice /ɪnˈdʒʌstɪs/ n. injusticia f.

ink /ɪŋk/ n. tinta f.

inland /ˈɪnlænd/ a. **1.** interior. —adv. **2.** tierra adentro.

inlet /ˈɪnlet/ n. entrada f.; ensenada f.; estuario m.

inmate /ˈɪnˌmeit/ n. residente m. & f.; (of a prison) preso -sa.

inn /ɪn/ n. posada f.; mesón m.

inner /ˈɪnər/ a. interior. **i. tube,** cámara de aire.

innocence /ˈɪnəsəns/ n. inocencia f.

innocent /ˈɪnəsənt/ a. inocente.

innocuous /ɪˈnɒkyuəs/ a. innocuo.

innovation /ˌɪnəˈveiʃən/ n. innovación f.

innuendo /ˌɪnyuˈendou/ n. insinuación f.

innumerable /ɪˈnumərəbəl/ a. innumerable.

inoculate /ɪˈnɒkyəˌleit/ v. inocular.

inoculation /ɪˌnɒkyəˈleiʃən/ n. inoculación f.

input /ˈɪnˌput/ n. aducto m., ingreso m.; entrada f.

inquest /ˈɪnkwest/ n. indagación f.

inquire /ɪnˈkwaɪˀr/ v. preguntar; inquirir.

inquiry /ɪnˈkwaɪˀri/ n. pregunta; investigación f.

inquisition /ˌɪnkwəˈzɪʃən/ n. escudriñamiento m.; (church) Inquisición f.

insane /ɪnˈseɪn/ a. loco. **to go i.,** perder la razón; volverse loco.

insanity /ɪnˈsænɪti/ n. locura f., demencia f.

inscribe /ɪnˈskraɪb/ v. inscribir.

inscription /ɪnˈskrɪpʃən/ n. inscripción; dedicatoria f.

insect /ˈɪnsɛkt/ n. insecto m.

insecticide /ɪnˈsɛktəˌsaɪd/ n. & a. insecticida m.

inseparable /ɪnˈsɛpərəbəl/ a. inseparable.

insert /ɪnˈsɔrt/ v. insertar, meter.

insertion /ɪnˈsɔrʃən/ n. inserción f.

inside /ˌɪnˈsaɪd/ a. & n. **1.** interior m. —adv. **2.** adentro, por dentro. **i. out,** al revés. —prep. **3.** dentro de.

insidious /ɪnˈsɪdiəs/ a. insidioso.

insight /ˈɪnˌsaɪt/ n. perspicacia f.; comprensión f.

insignia /ɪnˈsɪɡniə/ n. insignias f.pl.

insignificance /ˌɪnsɪɡˈnɪfɪkəns/ n. insignificancia f.

insignificant /ˌɪnsɪɡˈnɪfɪkənt/ a. insignificante.

insinuate /ɪnˈsɪnyuˌeɪt/ v. insinuar.

insinuation /ɪnˌsɪnyuˈeɪʃən/ n. insinuación f.

insipid /ɪnˈsɪpɪd/ a. insípido.

insist /ɪnˈsɪst/ v. insistir.

insistence /ɪnˈsɪstəns/ n. insistencia f.

insistent /ɪnˈsɪstənt/ a. insistente.

insolence /ˈɪnsələns/ n. insolencia f.

insolent /ˈɪnsələnt/ a. insolente.

insomnia /ɪnˈsɒmniə/ n. insomnio m.

inspect /ɪnˈspɛkt/ v. inspeccionar, examinar.

inspection /ɪnˈspɛkʃən/ n. inspección f.

inspector /ɪnˈspɛktər/ n. inspector -ora.

inspiration /ˌɪnspəˈreɪʃən/ n. inspiración f.

inspire /ɪnˈspaɪˀr/ v. inspirar.

install /ɪnˈstɔl/ v. instalar.

installation /ˌɪnstəˈleɪʃən/ n. instalación f.

installment /ɪnˈstɔlmənt/ n. plazo m.

instance /ˈɪnstəns/ n. ocasión f. **for i.,** por ejemplo.

instant /ˈɪnstənt/ a. & n. instante m.

instantaneous /ˌɪnstənˈteɪniəs/ a. instantáneo.

instant coffee café soluble m.

instantly /ˈɪnstəntli/ adv. al instante.

instead /ɪnˈstɛd/ adv. en lugar de eso. **i. of,** en vez de, en lugar de.

instigate /ˈɪnstɪˌɡeɪt/ v. instigar.

instill /ɪnˈstɪl/ v. instilar.

instinct /ˈɪnstɪŋkt/ n. instinto m. **by i.** por instinto.

instinctive /ɪnˈstɪŋktɪv/ a. instintivo.

instinctively /ɪnˈstɪŋktɪvli/ adv. por instinto.

institute /ˈɪnstɪˌtut/ n. **1.** instituto m. —v. **2.** instituir.

institution /ˌɪnstɪˈtuʃən/ n. institución f.

instruct /ɪnˈstrʌkt/ v. instruir.

instruction /ɪnˈstrʌkʃən/ n. instrucción f.

instructive /ɪnˈstrʌktɪv/ a. instructivo.

instructor /ɪnˈstrʌktər/ n. instructor -ora.

instrument /ˈɪnstrəmənt/ n. instrumento m.

instrumental /ˌɪnstrəˈmɛntl/ a. instrumental.

insufficient /ˌɪnsəˈfɪʃənt/ a. insuficiente.

insular /ˈɪnsələr/ a. insular; estrecho de miras.

insulate /ˈɪnsəˌleɪt/ v. aislar.

insulation /ˌɪnsəˈleɪʃən/ n. aislamiento m.

insulator /ˈɪnsəˌleɪtər/ n. aislador m.

insulin /ˈɪnsəlɪn/ n. insulina f.

insult /n. ˈɪnsʌlt; v. ɪnˈsʌlt/ n. **1.** insulto m. —v. **2.** insultar.

insuperable /ɪnˈsupərəbəl/ a. insuperable.

insurance /ɪnˈʃurəns/ n. seguro m.

insure /ɪnˈʃur, -ˈʃɔr/ v. asegurar.

insurgent /ɪnˈsɔrdʒənt/ a. & n. insurgente m. & f.

insurrection /ˌɪnsəˈrɛkʃən/ n. insurrección f.

intact /ɪnˈtækt/ a. intacto.

intangible /ɪnˈtændʒəbəl/ a. intangible, impalpable.

integral /ˈɪntɪgrɪl/ a. íntegro.

integrate /ˈɪntɪˌgreɪt/ v. integrar.

integrity /ɪnˈtɛgrɪti/ n. integridad f.

intellect /ˈɪntlˌɛkt/ n. intelecto m.

intellectual /ˌɪntlˈɛktʃuəl/ a. & n. intelectual m. & f.

intelligence /ɪnˈtɛlɪdʒəns/ n. inteligencia f.

intelligence quotient /ˈkwouʃənt/ coeficiente intelectual m.

intelligent /ɪnˈtɛlɪdʒənt/ a. inteligente.

intelligible /ɪnˈtɛlɪdʒəbəl/ a. inteligible.

intend /ɪnˈtɛnd/ v. pensar; intentar; destinar.

intense /ɪnˈtɛns/ a. intenso.

intensify /ɪnˈtɛnsəˌfaɪ/ v. intensificar.

intensity /ɪnˈtɛnsɪti/ n. intensidad f.

intensive /ɪnˈtɛnsɪv/ a. intensivo.

intensive-care unit /ɪnˈtɛnsɪvˈkɛər/ unidad de cuidados intensivos, unidad de vigilancia intensiva f.

intent /ɪnˈtɛnt/ n. intento m.

intention /ɪnˈtɛnʃən/ n. intención f.

intentional /ɪnˈtɛnʃənl/ a. intencional.

intercede /ˌɪntərˈsid/ v. interceder.

intercept /ˌɪntərˈsɛpt/ v. interceptar; detener.

interchange /ˌɪntərˈtʃɛndʒ/ v. intercambiar.

interchangeable /ˌɪntərˈtʃɛindʒəbəl/ a. intercambiable.

intercourse /ˈɪntərˌkɔrs/ n. tráfico m.; comunicación f.; coito m.

interest /ˈɪntərɪst/ n. **1.** interés m. —v. **2.** interesar.

interesting /ˈɪntərəstɪŋ/ a. interesante.

interest rate n. tipo de interés m.

interface /ˈɪntərˌfeɪs/ n. interfaz f.

interfere /ˌɪntərˈfɪər/ v. entrometerse, intervenir. **i. with,** estorbar.

interference /ˌɪntərˈfɪərəns/ n. intervención f.; obstáculo m.

interior /ɪnˈtɪəriər/ a. interior.

interject /ˌɪntərˈdʒɛkt/ v. interponer; intervenir.

interjection /ˌɪntərˈdʒɛkʃən/ n. interjección f.; interposición f.

interlude /ˈɪntərˌlud/ n. intervalo

m.; Theat. intermedio m.; (music) interludio m.

intermediary /ˌɪntərˈmidiˌɛri/ n. intermediario -ria.

intermediate /ˌɪntərˈmidiˌeɪt/ a. intermedio.

interment /ɪnˈtɜrmənt/ n. entierro.

intermission /ˌɪntərˈmɪʃən/ n. termisión f.; Theat. entreacto m.

intermittent /ˌɪntərˈmɪtnt/ a. intermitente.

intern /ɪnˈtɜrn/ n. **1.** interno -na, internado -da. —v. **2.** internar.

internal /ɪnˈtɜrnl/ a. interno.

international /ˌɪntərˈnæʃənl/ a. internacional.

internationalism /ˌɪntərˈnæʃənlˌɪzəm/ n. internacionalismo m.

Internet, the /ˈɪntərˌnɛt/ n. el Internet m.

interpose /ˌɪntərˈpouz/ v. interponer.

interpret /ɪnˈtɜrprɪt/ v. interpretar.

interpretation /ɪnˌtɜrprɪˈteɪʃən/ n. interpretación f.

interpreter /ɪnˈtɜrprɪtər/ n. intérprete m. & f.

interrogate /ɪnˈtɛrəˌgeɪt/ v. interrogar.

interrogation /ɪnˌtɛrəˈgeɪʃən/ n. interrogación; pregunta f.

interrogative /ˌɪntəˈrɒgətɪv/ a. terrogativo.

interrupt /ˌɪntəˈrʌpt/ v. interrumpir.

interruption /ˌɪntəˈrʌpʃən/ n. interrupción f.

intersect /ˌɪntərˈsɛkt/ v. cortar.

intersection /ˌɪntərˈsɛkʃən/ n. intersección f.; (street) bocacalle f.

intersperse /ˌɪntərˈspɜrs/ v. entremezclar.

interval /ˈɪntərvəl/ n. intervalo m.

intervene /ˌɪntərˈvin/ v. intervenir.

intervention /ˌɪntərˈvɛnʃən/ n. intervención f.

interview /ˈɪntərˌvyu/ n. **1.** entrevista f. —v. **2.** entrevistar.

interviewer /ˈɪntərˌvyuər/ n. entrevistador -ora m. & f.

intestine /ɪnˈtɛstɪn/ n. intestino m.

intimacy /ˈɪntəməsi/ n. intimidad; familiaridad f.

intimate /ˈɪntəmɪt/ a. **1.** íntimo, familiar. —n. **2.** amigo -ga íntimo -ma. —v. **3.** insinuar.

intimidate /ɪn'tɪmɪ,deɪt/ v. intimidar.

intimidation /ɪn,tɪmɪ'deɪʃən/ n. intimidación f.

into /'ɪntu; unstressed -tʊ, -tə/ prep. en, dentro de.

intonation /,ɪntoʊ'neɪʃən/ n. entonación f.

intone /ɪn'toʊn/ v. entonar.

intoxicate /ɪn'tɒksɪ,keɪt/ v. embriagar.

intoxication /ɪn,tɒksɪ'keɪʃən/ n. embriaguez f.

intravenous /,ɪntrə'vinəs/ a. intravenoso.

intrepid /ɪn'trɛpɪd/ a. intrépido.

intricacy /'ɪntrɪkəsi/ n. complejidad f.; enredo m.

intricate /'ɪntrɪkɪt/ a. intrincado; complejo.

intrigue /ɪn'trig; n. also 'ɪntrig/ n. **1.** intriga f. —v. **2.** intrigar.

intrinsic /ɪn'trɪnsɪk/ a. intrínseco.

introduce /,ɪntrə'dus/ v. introducir; (a person) presentar.

introduction /,ɪntrə'dʌkʃən/ n. presentación; introducción f.

introductory /,ɪntrə'dʌktəri/ a. introductor; preliminar. **i. offer,** ofrecimiento de presentación m.

introvert /'ɪntrə,vɜrt/ n. & a. introvertido -da.

intrude /ɪn'trud/ v. entremeterse.

intruder /ɪn'trudər/ n. intruso -sa.

intuition /,ɪntu'ɪʃən/ n. intuición f.

intuitive /ɪn'tuɪtɪv/ a. intuitivo.

inundate /'ɪnən,deɪt/ v. inundar.

invade /ɪn'veɪd/ v. invadir.

invader /ɪn'veɪdər/ n. invasor -ra.

invalid /ɪn'vælɪd/ a. & n. inválido -da.

invariable /ɪn'vɛəriəbəl/ a. invariable.

invasion /ɪn'veɪʒən/ n. invasión f.

invective /ɪn'vɛktɪv/ n. **1.** invectiva f. —a. **2.** ultrajante.

inveigle /ɪn'veɪgəl/ v. seducir.

invent /ɪn'vɛnt/ v. inventar.

invention /ɪn'vɛnʃən/ n. invención f.

inventive /ɪn'vɛntɪv/ a. inventivo.

inventor /ɪn'vɛntər/ n. inventor -ra.

inventory /'ɪnvən,tɔri/ n. inventario m.

invertebrate /ɪn'vɜrtəbrɪt/ n. & a. invertebrado m.

invest /ɪn'vɛst/ v. investir; Com. invertir.

investigate /ɪn'vɛstɪ,geɪt/ v. investigar.

investigation /ɪn,vɛstɪ'geɪʃən/ n. investigación f.

investment /ɪn'vɛstmənt/ n. inversión f.

investor /ɪn'vɛstər/ n. inversor -ra.

inveterate /ɪn'vɛtərɪt/ a. inveterado.

invidious /ɪn'vɪdiəs/ a. abominable, odioso, injusto.

invigorate /ɪn'vɪgə,reɪt/ v. vigorizar, fortificar.

invincible /ɪn'vɪnsəbəl/ a. invencible.

invisible /ɪn'vɪzəbəl/ a. invisible.

invitation /,ɪnvɪ'teɪʃən/ n. invitación f.

invite /ɪn'vaɪt/ v. invitar, convidar.

invocation /,ɪnvə'keɪʃən/ n. invocación f.

invoice /'ɪnvɔɪs/ n. factura f.

invoke /ɪn'voʊk/ v. invocar.

involuntary /ɪn'vɒlən,tɛri/ a. involuntario.

involve /ɪn'vɒlv/ v. envolver; implicar.

involved /ɪn'vɒlvd/ a. complicado.

invulnerable /ɪn'vʌlnərəbəl/ a. invulnerable.

inward /'ɪnwərd/ adv. hacia adentro.

inwardly /'ɪnwərdli/ adv. interiormente.

iodine /'aɪə,daɪn/ n. iodo m.

IQ abbr. CI (coeficiente intelectual) m.

irate /aɪ'reɪt/ a. encolerizado.

Ireland /'aɪərlənd/ n. Irlanda f.

iris /'aɪrɪs/ n. Anat. iris m.; (botany) flor de lis f.

Irish /'aɪrɪʃ/ a. irlandés.

irk /ɜrk/ v. fastidiar.

iron /'aɪərn/ n. **1.** hierro m.; (appliance) plancha f. —v. **2.** planchar.

ironical /aɪ'rɒnɪkəl/ a. irónico.

ironing board /'aɪərnɪŋ/ tabla de planchar f.

irony /'aɪrəni/ n. ironía f.

irrational /ɪ'ræʃənl/ a. irracional; ilógico.

irregular /ɪ'rɛgyələr/ a. irregular.

irregularity /ɪ,rɛgyə'lærɪti/ n. irregularidad f.

irrelevant /ɪ'rɛləvənt/ a. ajeno.

irresistible /,ɪrɪ'zɪstəbəl/ a. irresistible.

irresponsible /ˌɪrɪˈspɒnsəbəl/ a. irresponsable.

irreverent /ɪˈrɛvərənt/ a. irreverente.

irrevocable /ɪˈrɛvəkəbəl/ a. irrevocable.

irrigate /ˈɪrɪˌgeit/ v. regar; Med. irrigar.

irrigation /ˌɪrɪˈgeiʃən/ n. riego m.

irritability /ˌɪrɪtəˈbɪliti/ n. irritabilidad f.

irritable /ˈɪrɪtəbəl/ a. irritable.

irritant /ˈɪrɪtnt/ n. & a. irritante m.

irritate /ˈɪrɪˌteit/ v. irritar.

irritation /ˌɪrɪˈteiʃən/ n. irritación f.

island /ˈailənd/ n. isla f.

isolate /ˈaisəˌleit/ v. aislar.

isolation /ˌaisəˈleiʃən/ n. aislamiento m.

isosceles /aiˈsɒsəˌliz/ a. isósceles.

issuance /ˈɪʃuəns/ n. emisión f.; publicación f.

issue /ˈɪʃu/ n. **1.** emisión; edición; progenie f.; número m.; punto en disputa. —v. **2.** emitir; publicar.

isthmus /ˈɪsməs/ n. istmo m.

it /ɪt/ pron. ello; él, ella; lo, la.

Italian /ɪˈtælyən/ a. & n. italiano -na.

Italy /ˈɪtli/ n. Italia f.

itch /ɪtʃ/ n. **1.** picazón f. —**2.** picar.

item /ˈaitəm/ n. artículo; detalle m.; inserción f.; Com. renglón m.

itemize /ˈaitəˌmaiz/ v. detallar.

itinerant /aiˈtɪnərənt/ n. **1.** viandante m. —a **2.** ambulante.

itinerary /aiˈtɪnəˌreri/ n. itinerario m.

its /ɪts/ a. su.

itself /ɪtˈsɛlf/ pron. sí; se.

ivory /ˈaivəri/ n. marfil m.

ivy /ˈaivi/ n. hiedra f.

J

jab /dʒæb/ n. **1.** pinchazo m. —v. **2.** pinchar.

jack /dʒæk/ n. (for lifting) gato m.; (cards) sota f.

jackal /ˈdʒækəl/ n. chacal m.

jackass /ˈdʒækˌæs/ n. asno m.

jacket /ˈdʒækɪt/ n. chaqueta f.; saco m.

jack-of-all-trades /ˈdʒæk əv ɔl ˈtreidz/ n. estuche f.

jade /dʒeid/ n. (horse) rocín m.; (woman) picarona f.; (mineral) jade m.

jaded /ˈdʒeidɪd/ a. rendido.

jagged /ˈdʒægɪd/ a. mellado.

jaguar /ˈdʒægwɑr/ n. jaguar m.

jail /dʒeil/ n. cárcel f.

jailer /ˈdʒeilər/ n. carcelero m.

jam /dʒæm/ n. **1.** conserva f.; aprieto, apretón m. —v. **2.** apiñar, apretar; trabar.

janitor /ˈdʒænɪtər/ n. portero m.

January /ˈdʒænyuˌɛri/ n. enero m.

Japan /dʒəˈpæn/ n. Japón m.

Japanese /ˌdʒæpəˈniz/ a. & n. japonés -esa.

jar /dʒɑr/ n. **1.** jarro m. —v. **2.** chocar; agitar.

jargon /ˈdʒɑrgən/ n. jerga f.

jasmine /ˈdʒæzmɪn/ n. jazmín m.

jaundice /ˈdʒɔndɪs/ n. ictericia f.

jaunt /dʒɔnt/ n. paseo m.

javelin /ˈdʒævlɪn/ n. jabalina f.

jaw /dʒɔ/ n. quijada f.

jay /dʒei/ n. grajo m.

jazz /dʒæz/ n. jazz m.

jealous /ˈdʒɛləs/ a. celoso. **to be j.,** tener celos.

jealousy /ˈdʒɛləsi/ n. celos m.pl.

jeans /dʒinz/ n. vaqueros, tejanos m.pl.

jeer /dʒɪər/ n. **1.** burla f., mofa f. —v. **2.** burlar, mofar.

jelly /ˈdʒɛli/ n. jalea f.

jellyfish /ˈdʒɛliˌfɪʃ/ n. aguamar m.

jeopardize /ˈdʒɛpərˌdaiz/ v. arriesgar.

jeopardy /ˈdʒɛpərdi/ n. riesgo m.

jerk /dʒɜrk/ n. **1.** sacudida f. —v. **2.** sacudir.

jerky /ˈdʒɜrki/ a. espasmódico.

Jerusalem /dʒɪˈrusələm/ n. Jerusalén m.

jest /dʒɛst/ n. **1.** broma f. —v. **2.** bromear.

jester /ˈdʒɛstər/ n. bufón -ona; burlón -ona.

Jesuit /ˈdʒɛʒuɪt/ a. & n. jesuíta m.

Jesus Christ /ˈdʒizəs ˈkraist/ n. Jesucristo m.

jet /dʒɛt/ n. chorro m.; (gas) mechero m.

jet lag /dʒɛt læg/ n. defase horario m., inadaptación horaria f.

jetsam /ˈdʒɛtsəm/ n. echazón f.

jettison /ˈdʒɛtəsən/ v. echar al mar.

jetty /ˈdʒɛti/ n. muelle m.

Jew /dʒu/ n. judío -día.

jewel /'dʒuəl/ n. joya f.

jeweler /'dʒuələr/ n. joyero -ra.

jewelry /'dʒuəlri/ n. joyas f.pl. **j. store,** joyería f.

Jewish /'dʒuɪʃ/ a. judío.

jib /dʒɪb/ n. Naut. foque m.

jiffy /'dʒɪfi/ n. instante m.

jig /dʒɪg/ n. jiga f. **j-saw,** sierra de vaivén f.

jilt /dʒɪlt/ v. dar calabazas.

jingle /'dʒɪŋgəl/ n. **1.** retintín m.; rima pueril f. —v. **2.** retiñir.

jinx /dʒɪŋks/ n. **1.** aojo m. —v. **2.** aojar.

jittery /'dʒɪtəri/ a. nervioso.

job /dʒɒb/ n. empleo m.

jobber /'dʒɒbər/ n. destajista m. & f., corredor m.

jockey /'dʒɒki/ n. jockey m.

jocular /'dʒɒkyələr/ a. jocoso.

jog /dʒɒg/ n. empujoncito m. v. empujar; estimular. **j. along,** ir a un trote corto.

join /dʒɔɪn/ v. juntar; unir.

joiner /'dʒɔɪnər/ n. ebanista m.

joint /dʒɔɪnt/ n. juntura f.

jointly /'dʒɔɪntli/ adv. conjuntamente.

joke /dʒouk/ n. **1.** broma, chanza f.; chiste m. —v. **2.** bromear.

joker /'dʒoukər/ n. bromista m. & f.; comodín m.

jolly /'dʒɒli/ a. alegre, jovial.

jolt /dʒoult/ n. **1.** sacudido m. —v. **2.** sacudir.

jonquil /'dʒɒŋkwɪl/ n. junquillo m.

jostle /'dʒɒsəl/ v. empujar.

journal /'dʒɜrnl/ n. diario m.; revista f.

journalism /'dʒɜrnl,ɪzəm/ n. periodismo m.

journalist /'dʒɜrnlɪst/ n. periodista m. & f.

journey /'dʒɜrni/ n. **1.** viaje m.; jornada f. —v. **2.** viajar.

journeyman /'dʒɜrnimən/ n. jornalero m., oficial m.

jovial /'dʒouviəl/ a. jovial.

jowl /dʒaul/ n. carrillo m.

joy /dʒɔɪ/ n. alegría f.

joyful /'dʒɔɪfəl/ **joyous** a. alegre, gozoso.

jubilant /'dʒubələnt/ a. jubiloso.

jubilee /'dʒubə,li/ n. jubileo m.

Judaism /'dʒudi,ɪzəm/ n. judaísmo m.

judge /dʒʌdʒ/ n. **1.** juez m. & f. —v. **2.** juzgar.

judgment /'dʒʌdʒmənt/ n. juicio m.

judicial /dʒuˈdɪʃəl/ a. judicial.

judiciary /dʒuˈdɪʃiˌeri/ a. judiciario.

judicious /dʒuˈdɪʃəs/ a. juicioso.

jug /dʒʌg/ n. jarro m.

juggle /'dʒʌgəl/ v. escamotear.

juice /dʒus/ n. jugo, zumo m.

juicy /'dʒusi/ a. jugoso.

July /dʒu'laɪ/ n. julio m.

jumble /'dʒʌmbəl/ n. **1.** revoltijo m. —v. **2.** arrebujar, revolver.

jump /dʒʌmp/ n. **1.** salto m. —v. **2.** saltar, brincar.

junction /'dʒʌŋkʃən/ n. confluencia f.; (railway) empalme m.

juncture /'dʒʌŋktʃər/ n. juntura f.; coyuntura f.

June /dʒun/ n. junio m.

jungle /'dʒʌŋgəl/ n. jungla, selva f.

junior /'dʒunyər/ a. menor; más joven. **Jr.,** hijo.

juniper /'dʒunəpər/ n. enebro m.

junk /dʒʌŋk/ n. basura f.

junket /'dʒʌŋkɪt/ n. **1.** leche cuajada f. —v. **2.** festejar.

junkie /'dʒʌŋki/ n. Colloq. yonqui m. & f., toxicómano -na.

junk mail n. porpaganda indeseada f., correo basura m.

jurisdiction /,dʒʊrɪs'dɪkʃən/ n. jurisdicción f.

jurisprudence /,dʒʊrɪs'prudns/ n. jurisprudencia f.

jurist /'dʒʊrɪst/ n. jurista m. & f.

juror /'dʒʊrər/ n. jurado -da.

jury /'dʒʊri/ n. jurado m.

just /dʒʌst/ a. **1.** justo; exacto. —adv. **2.** exactamente; (only) sólo. **j. now,** ahora mismo. **to have j.,** acabar de.

justice /'dʒʌstɪs/ n. justicia f.; (person) juez m. & f.

justifiable /'dʒʌstə,faiəbəl/ a. justificable.

justification /,dʒʌstəfɪ'keiʃən/ n. justificación f.

justify /'dʒʌstə,fai/ v. justificar.

jut /dʒʌt/ v. sobresalir.

jute /dʒut/ n. yute m.

juvenile /'dʒuvənl/ a. juvenil.

juvenile delinquency delincuencia de menores, delincuencia juvenil f.

K

kaleidoscope /kə'laidə,skoup/ n. calidoscopio m.

kangaroo /,kæŋgə'ru/ n. canguro m.

karakul /'kærəkəl/ n. caracul m.

karat /'kærət/ n. quilate m.

karate /kə'rɑti/ n. karate m.

keel /kil/ n. **1.** quilla f. —v. **2. to k. over,** volcarse.

keen /kin/ a. agudo; penetrante.

keep /kip/ v. mantener, retener; guardar; preservar. **k. on,** seguir, continuar.

keeper /'kipər/ n. guardián m.

keepsake /'kip,seik/ n. recuerdo m.

keg /kɛg/ n. barrilito m.

kennel /'kɛnl/ n. perrera f.

kerchief /'kɜrtʃɪf/ n. pañuelo m.

kernel /'kɜrnl/ n. pepita f.; grano m.

kerosene /'kɛrə,sin/ n. kerosén m.

ketchup /'kɛtʃəp/ n. salsa de tomate f.

kettle /'kɛtl/ n. caldera, olla f.

kettledrum /'kɛtl,drʌm/ n. tímpano m.

key /ki/ n. llave f.; (music) clave f.; (piano) tecla f.

keyboard /'ki,bɔrd/ n. teclado m.

keyhole /'ki,houl/ n. bocallave f.

keypad /'ki,pæd/ n. teclado m.

khaki /'kæki/ a. caqui.

kick /kɪk/ n. **1.** patada f. —v. **2.** patear; Colloq. quejarse.

kid /kɪd/ n. **1.** cabrito m.; Colloq. niño -ña, chico -ca. —v. **2.** Colloq. bromear.

kidnap /'kɪdnæp/ v. secuestrar.

kidnaper /'kɪdnæpər/ n. secuestrador -ora.

kidnaping /'kɪdnæpɪŋ/ n. rapto, secuestro m.

kidney /'kɪdni/ n. riñón m.

kidney bean n. frijol m.

kill /kɪl/ v. matar.

killer /'kɪlər/ n. matador -ora.

killjoy /'kɪldʒɔi/ n. aguafiestas m. & f.

kiln /kɪl/ n. horno m.

kilogram /'kɪlə,græm/ n. kilogramo m.

kilohertz /'kɪlə,hɜrts/ n. kilohercio m.

kilometer /kɪ'lɒmɪtər/ n. kilómetro m.

kilowatt /'kɪlə,wɒt/ n. kilovatio m.

kin /kɪn/ n. parentesco m.; parientes m.pl.

kind /kaind/ a. **1.** bondadoso, amable. —n. **2.** género m.; clase f. **k. of,** algo, un poco.

kindergarten /'kɪndər,gɑrtn/ n. kindergarten m.

kindle /'kɪndl/ v. encender.

kindling /'kɪndlɪŋ/ n. encendimiento m. **k.-wood,** leña menuda f.

kindly /'kaindli/ a. bondadoso.

kindness /'kaindnɪs/ n. bondad f.

kindred /'kɪndrɪd/ n. parentesco m.

kinetic /kɪ'nɛtɪk/ a. cinético.

king /kɪŋ/ n. rey m.

kingdom /'kɪŋdəm/ n. reino m.

king prawn n. langostino m.

kink /kɪŋk/ n. retorcimiento m.

kinky /'kɪŋki/ a. Colloq. pervertidillo; (hair) rizado.

kiosk /'kiɒsk/ n. kiosco m.

kiss /kɪs/ n. **1.** beso m. —v. **2.** besar.

kitchen /'kɪtʃən/ n. cocina f.

kite /kait/ n. cometa f.

kitten /'kɪtn/ n. gatito m.

kleptomania /,klɛptə'meiniə/ n. cleptomanía f.

kleptomaniac /,klɛptə'meiniæk/ n. cleptómano -na.

klutz /klʌts/ n. Colloq. torpe, patoso -sa.

knack /næk/ n. don m., destreza f.

knapsack /'næp,sæk/ n. alforja f.

knead /nid/ v. amasar.

knee /ni/ n. rodilla f.

kneecap /'ni,kæp/ n. rodillera, rótula f.

kneel /nil/ v. arrodillarse.

knickers /'nɪkərz/ n. calzón corto m., pantalones m.pl.

knife /naif/ n. cuchillo m.

knight /nait/ n. caballero m.; (chess) caballo m.

knit /nɪt/ v. tejer.

knob /nɒb/ n. tirador m.

knock /nɒk/ n. **1.** golpe m.; llamada f. —v. **2.** golpear; tocar, llamar.

knot /nɒt/ n. **1.** nudo; lazo m. —v. **2.** anudar.

knotty /'nɒti/ a. nudoso.

know /nou/ v. saber; (a person) conocer.

knowledge /'nɒlɪdʒ/ n. conocimiento, saber m.

knuckle /'nʌkəl/ n. nudillo m. **k. bone**, jarrete m. **to k. under**, ceder a.

Koran /kə'ran/ n. Corán m.

Korea /kə'riə/ n. Corea f.

Korean /kə'riən/ a. & n. coreano.

L

label /'leibəl/ n. 1. rótulo m. —v. 2. rotular; designar.

labor /'leibər/ n. 1. trabajo m.; la clase obrera. —v. 2. trabajar.

laboratory /'læbrə,tɔri/ n. laboratorio m.

laborer /'leibərər/ n. trabajador, obrero m.

laborious /lə'bɔriəs/ a. laborioso, difícil.

labor union gremio obrero, sindicato m.

labyrinth /'læbərɪnθ/ n. laberinto m.

lace /leis/ n. 1. encaje m.; (of shoe) lazo m. —v. 2. amarrar.

lacerate /'læsə,reit/ v. lacerar, lastimar.

laceration /,læsə'reiʃən/ n. laceración f., desgarro m.

lack /læk/ n. 1. falta f. **l. of respect**, desacato m. —v. 2. faltar, carecer.

lackadaisical /,lækə'deizikəl/ a. indiferente; soñador.

laconic /lə'kɒnɪk/ a. lacónico.

lacquer /'lækər/ n. 1. laca f., barniz m. —v. 2. laquear, barnizar.

lactic /'læktɪk/ a. láctico.

lactose /'læktous/ n. lactosa f.

ladder /'lædər/ n. escalera f.

ladle /'leidl/ n. 1. cucharón m. —v. 2. servir con cucharón.

lady /'leidi/ n. señora, dama f.

ladybug /'leidi,bʌg/ n. mariquita f.

lag /læg/ n. 1. retraso m. —v. 2. quedarse atrás.

lagoon /lə'gun/ n. laguna f.

laid-back /'leid 'bæk/ a. de buen talante, ecuánime, pacífico.

laity /'leiiti/ n. laicado m.

lake /leik/ n. lago m.

lamb /læm/ n. cordero m.

lame /leim/ a. 1. cojo; estropeado. —v. 2. estropear, lisiar; incapacitar.

lament /lə'mɛnt/ n. 1. lamento m. —v. 2. lamentar.

lamentable /lə'mɛntəbəl/ a. lamentable.

lamentation /,læmən'teiʃən/ n. lamento m.; lamentación f.

laminate /'læmə,neit/ a. laminado. v. laminar.

lamp /læmp/ n. lámpara f.

lampoon /læm'pun/ n. 1. pasquín m. —v. 2. pasquinar.

lance /læns/ n. 1. lanza f. —v. 2. Med. abrir.

land /lænd/ n. 1. país m.; tierra f. **native l.**, patria f. —v. 2. desembarcar; (plane) aterrizar.

landholder /'lænd,houldər/ n. hacendado -da.

landing /'lændɪŋ/ n. (of stairs) descanso, descansillo m.; (ship) desembarcadero m.; (airplane) aterrizaje m.

landlady /'lænd,leidi/ **landlord** n. propietario -ria.

landmark /'lænd,mɑrk/ n. mojón m., señal f.; rasgo sobresaliente m.

landscape /'lænd,skeip/ n. paisaje m.

landslide /'lænd,slaid/ n. derrumbe m.

lane /lein/ n. senda f.

language /'læŋgwɪdʒ/ n. lengua f., idioma m.; lenguaje m.

languid /'læŋgwɪd/ a. lánguido.

languish /'læŋgwɪʃ/ v. languidecer.

languor /'læŋgər/ n. languidez f.

lanky /'læŋki/ a. larguirucho; desgarbado.

lanolin /'lænlɪn/ n. lanolina f.

lantern /'læntərn/ n. linterna f.; farol m.

lap /læp/ n. 1. regazo m.; falda f. —v. 2. lamer.

lapel /lə'pɛl/ n. solapa f.

lapse /læps/ n. 1. lapso m. —v. 2. pasar; decaer; caer en error.

laptop computer /'læp,tɒp/ ordenador portátil m.

larceny /'lɑrsəni/ n. ratería f.

lard /lɑrd/ n. manteca de cerdo f.

large /lɑrdʒ/ a. grande.

largely /'lɑrdʒli/ *adv.* ampliamente; mayormente; muy.

largo /'lɑrgou/ *n.* & *a. Mus.* largo *m.*

lariat /'læriət/ *n.* lazo *m.*

lark /lɑrk/ *n.* (bird) alondra *f.*

larva /'lɑrvə/ *n.* larva *f.*

laryngitis /ˌlærənˈdʒaitɪs/ *n.* laringitis *f.*

larynx /'lærɪŋks/ *n.* laringe *f.*

lascivious /ləˈsɪviəs/ *a.* lascivo.

laser /'leɪzər/ *n.* láser *m.*

lash /læʃ/ *n.* **1.** azote, latigazo *m.* —*v.* **2.** azotar.

lass /læs/ *n.* doncella *f.*

lassitude /'læsɪˌtud/ *n.* lasitud *f.*

lasso /'læsou/ *n.* **1.** lazo *m.* —*v.* **2.** enlazar.

last /læst/ *a.* **1.** pasado; (final) último. **at l.**, por fin. **l. but one,** penúltimo. **l. but two,** antepenúltimo. —*v.* **2.** durar.

lasting /'læstɪŋ/ *a.* duradero.

latch /lætʃ/ *n.* aldaba *f.*

late /leit/ *a.* **1.** tardío; (deceased) difunto. **to be l.,** llegar tarde. —*adv.* **2.** tarde.

lately /'leitli/ *adv.* recientemente.

latent /'leitnt/ *a.* latente.

lateral /'lætərəl/ *a.* lateral.

lather /'læðər/ *n.* **1.** espuma de jabón. —*v.* **2.** enjabonar.

Latin /'lætn/ *n.* latín *m.*

Latin America /əˈmɛrɪkə/ Hispanoamérica, América Latina *f.*

Latin American hispanoamericano -na.

latitude /'lætɪˌtud/ *n.* latitud *f.*

latrine /ləˈtrin/ *n.* letrina *f.*

latter /'lætər/ *a.* posterior. **the l.,** éste.

lattice /'lætɪs/ *n.* celosía *f.*

laud /lɔd/ *v.* loar.

laudable /'lɔdəbəl/ *a.* laudable.

laudanum /'lɔdnəm/ *n.* láudano *m.*

laudatory /'lɔdəˌtɔri/ *a.* laudatorio.

laugh /læf/ *n.* **1.** risa, risotada *f.* —*v.* **2.** reír. **l. at,** reírse de.

laughable /'læfəbəl/ *a.* risible.

laughter /'læftər/ *n.* risa *f.*

launch /lɔntʃ/ *n.* **1.** *Naut.* lancha *f.* —*v.* **2.** lanzar.

launder /'lɔndər/ *v.* lavar y planchar la ropa.

laundry /'lɔndri/ *n.* lavandería *f.*

laundryman /'lɔndriˌmæn/ *n.* lavandero -ra.

laureate /'lɔriit/ *n.* & *a.* laureado -da.

laurel /'lɔrəl/ *n.* laurel *m.*

lava /'lɑvə/ *n.* lava *f.*

lavatory /'lævəˌtɔri/ *n.* lavatorio *m.*

lavender /'lævəndər/ *n.* lavándula *f.*

lavish /'lævɪʃ/ *a.* **1.** pródigo. —*v.* **2.** prodigar.

law /lɔ/ *n.* ley *f.*; derecho *m.*

lawful /'lɔfəl/ *a.* legal.

lawless /'lɔlɪs/ *a.* sin ley.

lawn /lɔn/ *n.* césped; prado *m.*

lawn mower /'mouər/ *n.* cortacésped *m.* & *f.*

lawsuit /'lɔˌsut/ *n.* pleito *m.*

lawyer /'lɔyər/ *n.* abogado *m.* & *f.*

lax /læks/ *a.* flojo, laxo.

laxative /'læksətɪv/ *n.* purgante *m.*

laxity /'læksɪti/ *n.* laxidad *f.*; flojedad *f.*

lay /lei/ *a.* **1.** secular. —*v.* **2.** poner.

layer /'leiər/ *n.* capa *f.*

layman /'leimən/ *n.* lego, seglar *m.*

lazy /'leizi/ *a.* perezoso.

lead /lɛd, lid/ *n.* **1.** plomo *m.*; *Theat.* papel principal. **to take the l.,** tomar la delantera. —*v.* **2.** conducir; dirigir.

leaden /'lɛdn/ *a.* plomizo; pesado; abatido.

leader /'lidər/ *n.* líder *m.* & *f.*; jefe *m.* & *f.*; director -ora.

leadership /'lidərˌʃɪp/ *n.* dirección *f.*

leaf /lif/ *n.* hoja *f.*

leaflet /'liflɪt/ *n. Bot.* hojilla *f.*; folleto *m.*

league /lig/ *n.* liga; (measure) legua *f.*

leak /lik/ *n.* **1.** escape; goteo *m.* —*v.* **2.** gotear; *Naut.* hacer agua.

leakage /'likɪdʒ/ *n.* goteo *m.*, escape *m.*, pérdida *f.*

leaky /'liki/ *a.* llovedizo, resquebrajado.

lean /lin/ *a.* **1.** flaco, magro. —*v.* **2.** apoyarse, arrimarse.

leap /lip/ *n.* **1.** salto *m.* —*v.* **2.** saltar.

leap year *n.* año bisiesto *m.*

learn /lɜrn/ *v.* aprender; saber.

learned /'lɜrnɪd/ *a.* erudito.

learning /'lɜrnɪŋ/ *n.* erudición *f.*, instrucción *f.*

lease /lis/ *n.* **1.** arriendo *m.* —*v.* **2.** arrendar.

leash /liʃ/ *n.* **1.** correa *f.* —*v.* **2.** atraillar.

least /list/ *a.* menor; mínimo. **the l.,** lo menos. **at l.,** por lo menos.

leather /'lɛðər/ *n.* cuero *m.*

leathery /'lɛðəri/ *a.* coriáceo.

leave /liv/ *n.* **1.** licencia *f.* **to take l.,** despedirse. —*v.* **2.** dejar; (depart) salir, irse. **l. out,** omitir.

leaven /'lɛvən/ *n.* **1.** levadura *f.* —*v.* **2.** fermentar, imbuir.

lecherous /'lɛtʃərəs/ *a.* lujurioso.

lecture /'lɛktʃər/ *n.* conferencia *f.*

lecturer /'lɛktʃərər/ *n.* conferencista *m. & f.*; catedrático -ca.

ledge /lɛdʒ/ *n.* borde *m.*; capa *f.*

ledger /'lɛdʒər/ *n.* libro mayor *m.*

lee /li/ *n.* sotavento *m.*

leech /litʃ/ *n.* sanguijuela *f.*

leek /lik/ *n.* puerro *m.*

leer /lɪər/ *v.* mirar de soslayo.

leeward /'liwərd/ *a.* sotavento.

left /lɛft/ *a.* izquierdo. **the l.,** la izquierda. **to be left,** quedarse.

left-handed /'lɛft 'hændɪd/ *a.* zurdo.

leftist /'lɛftɪst/ *n.* izquierdista *m. & f.*

leftovers /'lɛft,ouvərz/ *n.* sobras *f.pl.*

leg /lɛg/ *n.* pierna *f.*

legacy /'lɛgəsi/ *n.* legado *m.*, herencia *f.*

legal /'ligəl/ *a.* legal.

legalize /'ligə,laiz/ *v.* legalizar.

legation /lɪ'geiʃən/ *n.* legación, embajada *f.*

legend /'lɛdʒənd/ *n.* leyenda *f.*

legendary /'lɛdʒən,dɛri/ *a.* legendario.

legible /'lɛdʒəbəl/ *a.* legible.

legion /'lidʒən/ *n.* legión *f.*

legislate /'lɛdʒɪs,leit/ *v.* legislar.

legislation /,lɛdʒɪs'leiʃən/ *n.* legislación *f.*

legislator /'lɛdʒɪs,leitər/ *n.* legislador -ra.

legislature /'lɛdʒɪs,leitʃər/ *n.* legislatura *f.*

legitimate /lɪ'dʒɪtəmɪt/ *a.* legítimo.

legume /'lɛgyum/ *n.* legumbre *f.*

leisure /'liʒər/ *n.* desocupación *f.*; horas libres.

leisurely /'liʒərli/ *a.* **1.** deliberado. —*adv.* **2.** despacio.

lemon /'lɛmən/ *n.* limón *m.*

lemonade /,lɛmə'neid/ *n.* limonada *f.*

lend /lɛnd/ *v.* prestar.

length /lɛŋkθ/ *n.* largo *m.*; duración *f.*

lengthen /'lɛŋkθən/ *v.* alargar.

lengthwise /'lɛŋkθ,waiz/ *adv.* a lo largo.

lengthy /'lɛŋkθi/ *a.* largo.

lenient /'liniənt/ *a.* indulgente.

lens /lɛnz/ *n.* lente *m. or f.*

Lent /lɛnt/ *n.* cuaresma *f.*

Lenten /'lɛntn/ *a.* cuaresmal.

lentil /'lɛntɪl/ *n.* lenteja *f.*

leopard /'lɛpərd/ *n.* leopardo *m.*

leotard /'liə,tɑrd/ *n.* mallas *f.pl.*

leper /'lɛpər/ *n.* leproso -sa.

leprosy /'lɛprəsi/ *n.* lepra *f.*

lesbian /'lɛzbiən/ *n.* lesbiana *f.*

lesion /'liʒən/ *n.* lesión *f.*

less /lɛs/ *a. & adv.* menos.

lessen /'lɛsən/ *v.* disminuir.

lesser /'lɛsər/ *a.* menor; más pequeño.

lesson /'lɛsən/ *n.* lección *f.*

lest /lɛst/ *conj.* para que no.

let /lɛt/ *v.* dejar; permitir; arrendar.

letdown /'lɛt,daun/ *n.* decepción *f.*

lethal /'liθəl/ *a.* letal.

lethargic /lə'θɑrdʒɪk/ *a.* letárgico.

lethargy /'lɛθərdʒi/ *n.* letargo *m.*

letter /'lɛtər/ *n.* carta; (of alphabet) letra *f.*

letterhead /'lɛtər,hɛd/ *n.* membrete *m.*

lettuce /'lɛtɪs/ *n.* lechuga *f.*

leukemia /lu'kimiə/ *n.* leucemia *f.*

levee /'lɛvi, lɛ'vi/ *n.* recepción *f.*

level /'lɛvəl/ *a.* **1.** llano, nivelado. —*n.* **2.** nivel *m.*; llanura *f.* —*v.* **3.** allanar; nivelar.

lever /'lɛvər/ *n.* palanca *f.*

levity /'lɛvɪti/ *n.* levedad *f.*

levy /'lɛvi/ *v.* **1.** leva *f.* —*v.* **2.** imponer.

lewd /lud/ *a.* lascivo.

lexicon /'lɛksɪ,kɒn/ *n.* léxico *m.*

liability /,laiə'bɪlɪti/ *n.* riesgo *m.*; obligación *f.*

liable /'laiəbəl/ *a.* sujeto; responsable.

liaison /li'eizən/ *n.* vinculación *f.*, enlace *m.*; concubinaje *m.*

liar /'laiər/ *n.* embustero -ra.

libel /'laibəl/ *n.* **1.** libelo *m.* —*v.* **2.** difamar.

libelous /'laibələs/ *a.* difamatorio.

liberal /'lıbərəl/ *a.* liberal; generoso.

liberalism /'lıbərə,lızəm/ *n.* liberalismo *m.*

liberality /,lıbə'rælıti/ *n.* liberalidad *f.*

liberate /'lıbə,reit/ *v.* libertar.

liberty /'lıbərti/ *n.* libertad *f.*

libidinous /lı'bıdnəs/ *a.* libidinoso.

librarian /lai'brɛəriən/ *n.* bibliotecario -ria.

library /'lai,brɛri/ *n.* biblioteca *f.*

libretto /lı'brɛtou/ *n.* libreto *m.*

license /'laisəns/ *n.* licencia *f.*; permiso *m.*

licentious /lai'sɛnfəs/ *a.* licencioso.

lick /lık/ *v.* lamer.

licorice /'lıkərıf, 'lıkrıf, 'lıkərıs/ *n.* regaliz *m.*

lid /lıd/ *n.* tapa *f.*

lie /lai/ *n.* **1.** mentira *f.* —*v.* **2.** mentir. **l. down,** acostarse, echarse.

lieutenant /lu'tɛnənt/ *n.* teniente *m.*

life /laif/ *n.* vida *f.*

lifeboat /'laif,bout/ *n.* bote salvavidas *m.*

life buoy boya *f.*

lifeguard /'laif,gard/ socorrista *m.* & *f.*

life insurance seguro de vida *m.*

life jacket chaleco salvavidas *m.*

lifeless /'laiflıs/ *a.* sin vida.

life preserver /prı'zɜrvər/ salvavidas *m.*

lifestyle /'laifstail/ *n.* modo de vida *m.*

lift /lıft/ *v.* levantar, alzar, elevar.

ligament /'lıgəmənt/ *n.* ligamento *m.*

ligature /'lıgətfər/ *n.* ligadura *f.*

light /lait/ *a.* **1.** ligero; liviano; (in color) claro. —*n.* **2.** luz; candela *f.* —*v.* **3.** encender; iluminar.

light bulb bombilla *f.*

lighten /'laitn/ *v.* aligerar; aclarar; iluminar.

lighter /'laitər/ *n.* encendedor *m.*

lighthouse /'lait,haus/ *n.* faro *m.*

lightness /'laitnıs/ *n.* ligereza; agilidad *f.*

lightning /'laitnıŋ/ *n.* relámpago *m.*

like /laik/ *a.* **1.** semejante. —*prep.* **2.** como. —*v.* **3.** **I like...** me gusta, me gustan... **I should like,** quisiera.

likeable /'laikəbəl/ *a.* simpático, agradable.

likelihood /'laikli,hud/ *n.* probabilidad *f.*

likely /'laikli/ *a.* probable; verosímil.

liken /'laikən/ *v.* comparar; asemejar.

likeness /'laiknıs/ *n.* semejanza *f.*

likewise /'laik,waiz/ *adv.* igualmente.

lilac /'lailək/ *n.* lila *f.*

lilt /lılt/ *n.* **1.** cadencia alegre *f.* —*v.* **2.** cantar alegremente.

lily /'lıli/ *n.* lirio *m.*

lily of the valley muguete *m.*

limb /lım/ *n.* rama *f.*

limber /'lımbər/ *a.* flexible. **to l. up,** ponerse flexible.

limbo /'lımbou/ *n.* limbo *m.*

lime /laim/ *n.* cal *f.*; (fruit) limoncito *m.*, lima *f.*

limestone /'laim,stoun/ *n.* piedra caliza *f.*

limewater /'laim,wɔtər/ *n.* agua de cal *f.*

limit /'lımıt/ *n.* **1.** límite *m.* —*v.* **2.** limitar.

limitation /,lımı'teifən/ *n.* limitación *f.*

limitless /'lımıtlıs/ *a.* ilimitado.

limousine /'lımə,zin/ *n.* limusina *f.*

limp /lımp/ *n.* **1.** cojera *f.* —*a.* **2.** flojo. —*v.* **3.** cojear.

limpid /'lımpıd/ *a.* límpido.

line /lain/ *n.* **1.** línea; fila; raya *f.*; (of print) renglón *m.* —*v.* **2.** forrar; rayar.

lineage /'lınıdʒ/ *n.* linaje *m.*

lineal /'lınıəl/ *a.* lineal.

linear /'lınıər/ *a.* linear, longitudinal.

linen /'lınən/ *n.* lienzo, lino *m.*; ropa blanca.

liner /'lainər/ *n.* vapor *m.*

linger /'lıŋgər/ *v.* demorarse.

lingerie /,lanʒə'rei/ *n.* ropa blanca *f.*

linguist /'lıŋgwıst/ *n.* lingüista *m.* & *f.*

linguistic /lıŋ'gwıstık/ *a.* lingüístico.

liniment /'lınəmənt/ *n.* linimento *m.*

lining /'lainıŋ/ *n.* forro *m.*

link /lıŋk/ *n.* **1.** eslabón; vínculo *m.* —*v.* **2.** vincular.

linoleum /lı'nouliəm/ *n.* linóleo *m.*

linseed /'lɪn,sid/ n. linaza f.; simiente de lino f.

lint /lɪnt/ n. hilacha f.

lion /'laɪən/ n. león m.

lip /lɪp/ n. labio m.

liposuction /'lɪpə,sʌkʃən, 'laɪpə-/ n. liposucción f.

lipstick /'lɪp,stɪk/ n. lápiz de labios.

liqueur /lɪ'kɜr/ n. licor m.

liquid /'lɪkwɪd/ a. & n. líquido m.

liquidate /'lɪkwɪ,deɪt/ v. liquidar.

liquidation /,lɪkwɪ'deɪʃən/ n. liquidación f.

liquor /'lɪkər/ n. licor m.

lisp /lɪsp/ n. 1. ceceo m. —v. 2. cecear.

list /lɪst/ n. 1. lista f. —v. 2. registrar.

listen (to) /'lɪsən/ v. escuchar.

listless /'lɪstlɪs/ a. indiferente.

litany /'lɪtṇi/ n. letanía f.

liter /'litər/ n. litro m.

literal /'lɪtərəl/ a. literal.

literary /'lɪtə,rɛri/ a. literario.

literate /'lɪtərɪt/ a. alfabetizado.

literature /'lɪtərətʃər/ n. literatura f.

litigant /'lɪtɪgənt/ n. & a. litigante m. & f.

litigation /,lɪtɪ'geɪʃən/ n. litigio, pleito m.

litter /'lɪtər/ n. 1. litera f.; cama de paja. —v. 2. poner en desorden.

little /'lɪtḷ/ a. pequeño; (quantity) poco.

little finger meñique m.

liturgical /lɪ'tɜrdʒɪkəl/ a. litúrgico.

liturgy /'lɪtərdʒi/ n. liturgia f.

live /a laɪv; v lɪv/ a. 1. vivo. —v. 2. vivir.

livelihood /'laɪvli,hʊd/ n. subsistencia f.

lively /'laɪvli/ a. vivo; rápido; animado.

liver /'lɪvər/ n. hígado m.

livery /'lɪvəri/ n. librea f.

livestock /'laɪv,stɒk/ n. ganadería f.

livid /'lɪvɪd/ a. lívido.

living /'lɪvɪŋ/ a. 1. vivo. —n. 2. sustento m. **to earn (make) a living,** ganarse la vida.

living room salón m.

lizard /'lɪzərd/ n. lagarto m., lagartija f.

llama /'lɑmə/ n. llama f.

load /loʊd/ n. 1. carga f. —v. 2. cargar.

loaf /loʊf/ n. 1. pan m. —v. 2. holgazanear.

loam /loʊm/ n. marga f.

loan /loʊn/ n. 1. préstamo m. —v. 2. prestar.

loathe /loʊð/ v. aborrecer, detestar.

loathsome /'loʊðsəm/ a. repugnante.

lobby /'lɒbi/ n. vestíbulo m.

lobe /loʊb/ n. lóbulo m.

lobster /'lɒbstər/ n. langosta f.

local /'loʊkəl/ a. local.

local area network red local f.

locale /loʊ'kæl/ n. localidad f.

locality /loʊ'kælɪti/ n. localidad f., lugar m.

localize /'loʊkə,laɪz/ v. localizar.

locate /'loʊkeɪt/ v. situar; hallar.

location /loʊ'keɪʃən/ n. sitio m.; posición f.

lock /lɒk/ n. 1. cerradura f.; (pl.) cabellos m.pl. —v. 2. cerrar con llave.

locker /'lɒkər/ n. cajón m.; ropero m.

locket /'lɒkɪt/ n. guardapelo m.; medallón m.

lockjaw /'lɒk,dʒɔ/ n. trismo m.

locksmith /'lɒk,smɪθ/ n. cerrajero -ra.

locomotive /,loʊkə'moʊtɪv/ n. locomotora f.

locust /'loʊkəst/ n. cigarra f., saltamontes m.

locution /loʊ'kyuʃən/ n. locución f.

lode /loʊd/ n. filón m., veta f.

lodge /lɒdʒ/ n. 1. logia f.; (inn) posada f. —v. 2. fijar; alojar, morar.

lodger /'lɒdʒər/ n. inquilino m.

lodging /'lɒdʒɪŋ/ n. alojamiento m.

loft /lɔft/ n. desván, sobrado m.

lofty /'lɔfti/ a. alto; altivo.

log /lɔg/ n. tronco de árbol; Naut. barquilla f.

loge /loʊʒ/ n. palco m.

logic /'lɒdʒɪk/ n. lógica f.

logical /'lɒdʒɪkəl/ a. lógico.

loin /lɔɪn/ n. lomo m.

loincloth /'lɔɪn,klɔθ/ n. taparrabos m.

loiter /'lɔɪtər/ v. haraganear.

lone /loʊn/ a. solitario.

loneliness /'loʊnlinɪs/ n. soledad f.

lonely, /'loʊnli/ **lonesome** a. solo y triste.

lonesome /'lounsəm/ a. solitario, aislado.

long /lɔŋ/ a. **1.** largo. **a l.** time, mucho tiempo. —adv. **2.** mucho tiempo. **how l.,** cuánto tiempo. **no longer,** ya no. —v. **3. l.** for, anhelar.

long-distance call /'lɔŋ 'dɪstəns/ conferencia interurbana f.

longevity /lɒn'dʒɛvɪti/ n. longevidad f.

long-haired /'lɔŋ 'hɛərd/ a. melenudo.

longing /'lɔŋɪŋ/ n. anhelo m.

longitude /'lɒndʒɪ,tud/ n. longitud m.

look /lʊk/ n. **1.** mirada f.; aspecto m. —v. **2.** parecer; mirar. **l. at,** mirar. **l. for,** buscar. **l. like,** parecerse a. **l. out!,** ¡cuidado! **l. up,** buscar; ir a ver, venir a ver.

looking glass /'lʊkɪŋ/ espejo m.

loom /lum/ n. **1.** telar m. —v. **2.** asomar.

loop /lup/ n. vuelta f.

loophole /'lup,houl/ n. aspillera f.; Fig. callejuela, evasiva f., efugio m.

loose /lus/ a. suelto; flojo.

loose change suelto m.

loosen /'lusən/ v. soltar; aflojar.

loot /lut/ n. **1.** botín m., saqueo m. —v. **2.** saquear.

lopsided /'lɒp'saidɪd/ a. desequilibrado.

loquacious /lou'kweiʃəs/ a. locuaz.

lord /lɔrd/ n. señor m.; (Brit. title) lord m.

lordship /'lɔrdʃɪp/ n. señorío m.

lose /luz/ v. perder. **l. consciousness,** perder el conocimiento.

loss /lɔs/ n. pérdida f.

lost /lɔst/ a. perdido.

lot /lɒt/ n. suerte f. **building l.,** solar m. **a lot (of), lots of,** mucho.

lotion /'louʃən/ n. loción f.

lottery /'lɒtəri/ n. lotería f.

loud /laud/ a. **1.** fuerte; ruidoso. —adv. **2.** alto.

loudspeaker /'laud,spikər/ n. altavoz m.

lounge /laundʒ/ n. sofá m.; salón de fumar m.

louse /laus/ n. piojo m.

love /lʌv/ n. **1.** amor m. **in l.,** enamorado. **to fall in l.,** enamorarse. **l. at first sight,** flechazo m. —v. **2.** querer; amar; adorar.

lovely /'lʌvli/ a. hermoso.

lover /'lʌvər/ n. amante m. & f.

low /lou/ a. bajo; vil.

low-cut /'lou 'kʌt/ a. escotado.

lower /'louər/ v. bajar; (in price) rebajar.

lower-case letter /'louər 'keis/ minúscula f.

lowly /'louli/ a. humilde.

low neckline /'nɛk,lain/ escote m.

loyal /'lɔiəl/ a. leal, fiel.

loyalist /'lɔiəlɪst/ n. lealista m. & f.

loyalty /'lɔiəlti/ n. lealtad f.

lozenge /'lɒzɪndʒ/ n. pastilla f.

lubricant /'lubrɪkənt/ n. lubricante m.

lubricate /'lubrɪ,keit/ v. engrasar, lubricar.

lucid /'lusɪd/ a. claro, lúcido.

luck /lʌk/ n. suerte; fortuna f.

lucky /'lʌki/ a. afortunado. **to be l.,** tener suerte.

lucrative /'lukrətɪv/ a. lucrativo.

ludicrous /'ludɪkrəs/ a. ridículo.

luggage /'lʌgɪdʒ/ n. equipaje m.

lukewarm /'luk,wɔrm/ a. tibio.

lull /lʌl/ n. **1.** momento de calma. —v. **2.** calmar.

lullaby /'lʌlə,bai/ n. arrullo m.

lumbago /lʌm'beigou/ n. lumbago m.

lumber /'lʌmbər/ n. madera f.

luminous /'lumənəs/ a. luminoso.

lump /lʌmp/ n. protuberancia f.; (of sugar) terrón m.

lump sum suma global f.

lunacy /'lunəsi/ n. locura f.

lunar /'lunər/ a. lunar.

lunatic /'lunətɪk/ a. & n. loco -ca.

lunch, luncheon /lʌntʃ; 'lʌntʃhən/ n. **1.** merienda f., almuerzo m. —v. **2.** merendar, almorzar.

lunch box /'lʌntʃ,bɒks/ fiambrera f.

lung /lʌŋ/ n. pulmón m.

lunge /lʌndʒ/ n. **1.** estocada, arremetida f. —v. **2.** dar un estocada, arremeter.

lure /lur/ v. atraer.

lurid /'lurɪd/ a. sensacional; espeluznante.

lurk /lɜrk/ v. esconderse; espiar.

luscious /'lʌʃəs/ a. sabroso, delicioso.

lust /lʌst/ n. sensualidad; codicia f.

luster /'lʌstər/ n. lustre m.

lustful /'lʌstfəl/ a. sensual, lascivo.

lusty /'lʌsti/ a. vigoroso.

lute /lut/ n. laúd m.

Lutheran /'luθərən/ n. & a. luterano -na.

luxuriant /lʌg'ʒuriənt/ a. exuberante, frondoso.

luxurious /lʌg'ʒuriəs/ a. lujoso.

luxury /'lʌkʃəri/ n. lujo m.

lying /'laiiŋ/ a. mentiroso.

lymph /limf/ n. linfa f.

lynch /lintʃ/ v. linchar.

lyre /laiᵊr/ n. lira f.

lyric /'lirik/ a. lírico.

lyricism /'lirə,sizəm/ n. lirismo m.

M

macabre /mə'kabrə/ a. macabro.

macaroni /,mækə'rouni/ n. macarrones m.

machine /mə'ʃin/ n. máquina f.

machine gun ametralladora f.

machinery /mə'ʃinəri/ n. maquinaria f.

machinist /mə'ʃinist/ n. maquinista m. & f., mecánico m.

macho /'matʃou/ a. machista.

mackerel /'mækərəl/ n. escombro m.

macro /'mækrou/ n. (computer) macro m.

mad /mæd/ a. loco; furioso.

madam /'mædəm/ n. señora f.

mafia /'mafiə/ n. mafia f.

magazine /'mægə'zin/ n. revista f.

magic /'mædʒik/ a. **1.** mágico. —n. **2.** magia f.

magician /mə'dʒiʃən/ n. mágico m.

magistrate /'mædʒə,streit/ n. magistrado -da.

magnanimous /mæg'nænəməs/ a. magnánimo.

magnate /'mægneit/ n. magnate m.

magnesium /mæg'niziəm/ n. magnesio m.

magnet /'mægnit/ n. imán f.

magnetic /mæg'nɛtik/ a. magnético.

magnificence /mæg'nifəsəns/ n. magnificencia f.

magnificent /mæg'nifəsənt/ a. magnífico.

magnify /'mægnə,fai/ v. magnificar.

magnifying glass /'mægnə,faiiŋ/ lupa f.

magnitude /'mægni,tud/ n. magnitud f.

magpie /'mæg,pai/ n. hurraca f.

mahogany /mə'hɒgəni/ n. caoba f.

maid /meid/ n. criada f. **old m.,** solterona f.

maiden /'meidn/ a. soltera.

mail /meil/ n. **1.** correo m. **air m.,** correo aéreo. **by return m.,** a vuelta de correo. —v. **2.** echar al correo.

mailbox /'meil,bɒks/ n. buzón m.

mailman /'meil,mæn/ n. cartero m.

maim /meim/ v. mutilar.

main /mein/ a. principal.

mainframe /'mein,freim/ n. componente central de una computadora.

mainland /'mein,lænd/ n. continente m.

maintain /mein'tein/ v. mantener; sostener.

maintenance /'meintənəns/ n. mantenimiento; sustento m.; conservación f.

maître d' /,meit'ər di, ,meitrə, ,metrə/ n. jefe de sala m. & f.

maize /meiz/ n. maíz m.

majestic /mə'dʒɛstik/ a. majestuoso.

majesty /'mædʒəsti/ n. majestad f.

major /'meidʒər/ a. **1.** mayor. —n. **2.** Mil. comandante m.; (study) especialidad f.

majority /mə'dʒɔrɪti/ n. mayoría f.

make /meik/ n. **1.** marca f. —v. **2.** hacer; fabricar; (earn) ganar.

maker /'meikər/ n. fabricante m.

makeshift /'meik,ʃift/ a. provisional.

make-up /'meik,ʌp/ n. cosméticos m.pl.

malady /'mælədi/ n. mal m., enfermedad f.

malaria /mə'lɛəriə/ n. paludismo m.

male /meil/ a. & n. macho m.

malevolent /mə'lɛvələnt/ a. malévolo.

malice /'mælis/ n. malicia f.

malicious /mə'liʃəs/ a. malicioso.

malign /mə'lain/ v. **1.** difamar. —a. **2.** maligno.

malignant /mə'lignənt/ a. maligno.

malnutrition /,mælnu'trɪʃən/ n. desnutrición f.

malt /mɔlt/ n. malta f.

mammal /'mæməl/ n. mamífero m.

man /mæn/ n. hombre; varón m. v. tripular.

manage /'mænɪdʒ/ v. manejar; dirigir; administrar; arreglárselas. **m. to,** lograr.

management /'mænɪdʒmənt/ n. dirección, administración f.

manager /'mænɪdʒər/ n. director -ora.

mandate /'mændeit/ n. mandato m.

mandatory /'mændə,tɔri/ a. obligatorio.

mandolin /'mændlɪn/ n. mandolina f.

mane /mein/ n. crines f.pl.

maneuver /mə'nuvər/ n. **1.** maniobra f. —v. **2.** maniobrar.

manganese /'mæŋgə,nis, -,niz/ n. manganeso m.

manger /'meindʒər/ n. pesebre m.

mangle /'mæŋgəl/ n. **1.** rodillo, exprimidor m. —v. **2.** mutilar.

manhood /'mænhʊd/ n. virilidad f.

mania /'meiniə/ n. manía f.

maniac /'meini,æk/ a. & n. maníaco -ca; maníaco -ca.

manicure /'mænɪ,kyʊr/ n. manicura f.

manifest /'mænə,fest/ a. & n. **1.** manifiesto m. —v. **2.** manifestar.

manifesto /,mænə'festoʊ/ n. manifiesto m.

manifold /'mænə,foʊld/ a. **1.** muchos. —n. **2.** Auto. tubo múltiple.

manipulate /mə'nɪpyə,leit/ v. manipular.

mankind /'mæn'kaind/ n. humanidad f.

manly /'mænli/ a. varonil.

manner /'mænər/ n. manera f., modo m. **manners,** modales m.pl.

mannerism /'mænə,rɪzəm/ n. manerismo m.

mansion /'mænʃən/ n. mansión f.

mantel /'mæntl/ n. manto de chimenea.

mantle /'mæntl/ n. manto m.

manual /'mænyuəl/ a. & n. manual m.

manufacture /,mænyə'fæktʃər/ v. fabricar.

manufacturer /,mænyə'fæktʃərər/ n. fabricante m.

manufacturing /,mænyə-'fæktʃərɪŋ/ n. fabricación f.

manure /mə'nʊr/ n. abono, estiércol m.

manuscript /'mænyə,skrɪpt/ n. manuscrito m.

many /'meni/ a. muchos. **how m.,** cuántos. **so m.,** tantos. **too m.,** demasiados. **as m. as,** tantos como.

map /mæp/ n. mapa m.

maple /'meipəl/ n. arce m.

mar /mɑr/ v. estropear; desfigurar.

marble /'mɑrbəl/ n. mármol m.

march /mɑrtʃ/ n. **1.** marcha f. —v. **2.** marchar.

March /mɑrtʃ/ n. marzo m.

mare /mɛr/ n. yegua f.

margarine /'mɑrdʒərɪn/ n. margarina f.

margin /'mɑrdʒɪn/ n. margen m. or f.

marijuana /,mærə'wɑnə/ n. marijuana f.

marine /mə'rin/ a. **1.** marino. —n. **2.** soldado de marina.

mariner /'mærənər/ n. marinero m.

marionette /,mæriə'nɛt/ n. marioneta f.

marital /'mærɪtl/ a. marital.

maritime /'mærɪ,taim/ a. marítimo.

mark /mɑrk/ n. **1.** marca f. —v. **2.** marcar.

market /'mɑrkɪt/ n. mercado m. **meat m.,** carnicería f. **stock m.,** bolsa f. v. comercializar.

marmalade /'mɑrmə,leid/ n. mermelada f.

maroon /mə'run/ a. & n. color rojo oscuro. v. dejar abandonado.

marquis /'mɑrkwɪs/ n. marqués m.

marriage /'mærɪdʒ/ n. matrimonio m.

marriage certificate partida de matrimonio f.

married /'mærid/ a. casado. **to get m.,** casarse.

marrow /'mæroʊ/ n. médula f.; substancia f.

marry /'mæri/ v. casarse con; casar.

marsh /marʃ/ n. pantano m.

marshal /'marʃəl/ n. mariscal m.

marshmallow /'marʃ,melou/ n. malvarisco m.; bombón de altea m.

martial /'marʃəl/ a. marcial. **m. law,** gobierno militar.

martyr /'martər/ n. mártir m. & f.

martyrdom /'martərdəm/ n. martirio m.

marvel /'marvəl/ n. **1.** maravilla f. —v. **2.** maravillarse.

marvelous /'marvələs/ a. maravilloso.

mascara /mæ'skærə/ n. rimel m.

mascot /'mæskɒt/ n. mascota f.

masculine /'mæskyəlin/ a. masculino.

mash /mæʃ/ v. majar. **mashed potatoes,** puré de papas m.

mask /mæsk/ n. máscara f.

mason /'meisən/ n. albañil m.

masquerade /,mæskə'reid/ n. mascarada f.

mass /mæs/ n. masa f.; *Relig.* misa f. **to say m.,** cantar misa. **m. production,** producción en serie.

massacre /'mæsəkər/ n. **1.** carnicería, matanza f. —v. **2.** matar atrozmente, destrozar.

massage /mə'saʒ/ n. **1.** masaje m.; soba f. —v. **2.** sobar.

masseur /mə'sər/ n. masajista m. & f.

massive /'mæsiv/ a. macizo, sólido.

mast /mæst/ n. palo, árbol m.

master /'mæstər/ n. **1.** amo; maestro m. —v. **2.** domar, dominar.

masterpiece /'mæstər,pis/ n. obra maestra f.

master's degree /'mæstərz/ maestría f.

mastery /'mæstəri/ n. maestría f.

mat /mæt/ n. **1.** estera f.; palleta f. —v. **2.** enredar.

match /mætʃ/ n. **1.** igual m; fósforo m.; (sport) partida, contienda f.; (marriage) noviazgo; casamiento. —v. **2.** ser igual a; igualar.

matchbox /'mætʃ,bɒks/ n. caja de cerillas, caja de fósforos f.

mate /meit/ n. **1.** consorte m. & f.; compañero -ra. —v. **2.** igualar, casar.

material /mə'tɪəriəl/ a. & n. material m. **raw materials,** materias primas.

materialism /mə'tɪəriə,lɪzəm/ n. materialismo m.

materialize /mə'tɪəriə,laiz/ v. materializar.

maternal /mə'tɜrnl/ a. materno.

maternity /mə'tɜrnɪti/ n. maternidad f.

maternity hospital maternidad f.

mathematical /,mæθə'mætɪkəl/ a. matemático.

mathematics /,mæθə'mætɪks/ n. matemáticas f.pl.

matinee /,mætn'ei/ n. matiné f.

matrimony /'mætrə,mouni/ n. matrimonio m.

matron /'meitrən/ n. matrona; directora f.

matter /'mætər/ n. **1.** materia f.; asunto m. **what's the m.?,** ¿qué pasa? —v. **2.** importar.

mattress /'mætrɪs/ n. colchón m.

mature /mə'tʃur/ a. **1.** maduro. —v. **2.** madurar.

maturity /mə'tʃurɪti/ n. madurez f.

maudlin /'mɔdlɪn/ a. sentimental en exceso; sensiblero.

maul /mɔl/ v. aporrear.

maxim /'mæksɪm/ n. máxima f.

maximum /'mæksəməm/ a. & n. máximo.

may /mei/ v. poder.

May /mei/ n. mayo m.

maybe /'meibi/ adv. quizá, quizás, tal vez.

mayonnaise /,meiə'neiz/ n. mayonesa f.

mayor /'meiər/ n. alcalde m. alcaldesa f.

maze /meiz/ n. laberinto m.

me /mi/ pron. mí; me. **with me,** conmigo.

meadow /'medou/ n. prado m.; vega f.

meager /'migər/ a. magro; pobre.

meal /mil/ n. comida; (flour) harina f.

mean /min/ a. **1.** bajo; malo. —n. **2.** medio (see also **means**). —v. **3.** significar; querer decir.

meander /mi'ændər/ v. (river) serpentear; (person) deambular.

meaning /'minɪŋ/ n. sentido, significado m.

meaningless /'minɪŋlɪs/ a. sin sentido.

means /minz/ n.pl. medios, recursos m. **by all m.,** sin falta. **by no**

m., de ningún modo. **by m. of,** por medio de.

meanwhile /'mɛʒər/ *adv.* mientras tanto.

measles /'mizəlz/ *n.* sarampión *m.*

measure /'mɛʒər/ *n.* **1.** medida *f.;* (music) compás *m.* —*v.* **2.** medir.

measurement /'mɛʒərmənt/ *n.* medida, dimensión *f.*

meat /mit/ *n.* carne *f.*

mechanic /mə'kænɪk/ *n.* mecánico *m.* & *f.*

mechanical /mə'kænɪkəl/ *a.* mecánico.

mechanism /'mɛkə,nɪzəm/ *n.* mecanismo *m.*

mechanize /'mɛkə,naiz/ *v.* mecanizar.

medal /'mɛdl/ *n.* medalla *f.*

meddle /'mɛdl/ *v.* meterse, entremeterse.

mediate /'midi,eit/ *v.* mediar.

medical /'mɛdɪkəl/ *a.* médico.

medicine /'mɛdəsɪn/ *n.* medicina *f.*

medicine chest botiquín *m.*

medieval /,midi'ivəl/ *a.* medieval.

mediocre /,midi'oukər/ *a.* mediocre.

mediocrity /,midi'ɒkrɪti/ *n.* mediocridad *f.*

meditate /'mɛdɪ,teit/ *v.* meditar.

meditation /,mɛdɪ'teiʃən/ *n.* meditación *f.*

Mediterranean /,mɛdɪtə'reiniən/ *n.* Mediterráneo *m.*

medium /'midiəm/ *a.* **1.** mediano, medio. —*n.* **2.** medio *m.*

medley /'mɛdli/ *n.* mezcla *f.,* ensalada *f.*

meek /mik/ *a.* manso; humilde.

meekness /'miknɪs/ *n.* modestia *f.;* humildad *f.*

meet /mit/ *a.* **1.** apropiado. —*n.* **2.** concurso *m.* —*v.* **3.** encontrar; reunirse; conocer.

meeting /'mitɪŋ/ *n.* reunión *f.;* mitin *m.*

megahertz /'mɛgə,hɜrts/ *n.* megahercio *m.*

megaphone /'mɛgə,foun/ *n.* megáfono *m.*

melancholy /'mɛlən,kɒli/ *a.* **1.** melancólico. —*n.* **2.** melancolía *f.*

mellow /'mɛlou/ *a.* suave; blando; maduro.

melodious /mə'loudiəs/ *a.* melodioso.

melodrama /'mɛlə,dramə/ *n.* melodrama *m.*

melody /'mɛlədi/ *n.* melodía *f.*

melon /'mɛlən/ *n.* melón *m.*

melt /mɛlt/ *v.* derretir.

meltdown /'mɛlt,daun/ *n.* fundición resultante de un accidente en un reactor nuclear.

member /'mɛmbər/ *n.* socio -ia; miembro *m.* **m. of the crew,** tripulante *m.* & *f.*

membership /'mɛmbər,ʃɪp/ *n.* número de miembros.

membrane /'mɛmbrein/ *n.* membrana *f.*

memento /mə'mɛntou/ *n.* recuerdo *m.*

memoir /'mɛmwɑr/ *n.* memoria *f.*

memorable /'mɛmərəbəl/ *a.* memorable.

memorandum /,mɛmə'rændəm/ *n.* memorándum, volante *m.*

memorial /mə'mɔriəl/ *a.* **1.** conmemorativo. —*n.* **2.** memorial *m.*

memorize /'mɛmə,raiz/ *v.* aprender de memoria.

memory /'mɛməri/ *n.* memoria *f.;* recuerdo *m.*

menace /'mɛnɪs/ *n.* **1.** amenaza *f.* —*v.* **2.** amenazar.

mend /mɛnd/ *v.* reparar, remendar.

menial /'miniəl/ *a.* **1.** servil. —*n.* **2.** sirviente -ta.

meningitis /,mɛnɪn'dʒaitɪs/ *n.* meningitis *f.*

menopause /'mɛnə,pɔz/ *n.* menopausia *f.*

menstruation /,mɛnstru'eiʃən/ *n.* menstruación *f.*

menswear /'mɛnz,wɛər/ *n.* ropa de caballeros *f.*

mental /'mɛntl/ *a.* mental.

mental disorder trastorno mental *m.*

mentality /mɛn'tælɪti/ *n.* mentalidad *f.*

menthol /'mɛnθɔl/ *n.* mentol *m.*

mention /'mɛnʃən/ *n.* **1.** mención *f.* —*v.* **2.** mencionar.

menu /'mɛnyu/ *n.* menú *m.,* lista *f.*

mercantile /'mɜrkən,til/ *a.* mercantil.

mercenary /'mɜrsə,nɛri/ *a.* & *n.* mercenario -ria.

merchandise /'mɜrtʃən,daiz/ *n.* mercancía *f.*

merchant /'mɜrtʃənt/ *n.* **1.** mercante. —*n.* **2.** comerciante *m.*

merciful /'mərsɪfəl/ a. misericordioso, compasivo.

merciless /'mərsɪlɪs/ a. cruel, inhumano.

mercury /'mərkyəri/ n. mercurio m.

mercy /'mərsi/ n. misericordia; merced f.

mere /mɪər/ a. mero, puro.

merely /'mɪərli/ adv. solamente; simplemente.

merge /mərdʒ/ v. unir, combinar.

merger /'mərdʒər/ n. consolidación, fusión f.

meringue /məˈræŋ/ n. merengue m.

merit /'merɪt/ n. **1.** mérito m. —v. **2.** merecer.

meritorious /ˌmerɪˈtɔriəs/ a. meritorio.

mermaid /'mərˌmeid/ n. sirena f.

merriment /'merɪmənt/ n. regocijo m.

merry /'meri/ a. alegre, festivo.

merry-go-round /'meri gou ˌraund/ n. caballitos m. pl.; tiovivo m.

mesh /meʃ/ n. malla f.

mess /mes/ n. **1.** lío m.; confusión f.; Mil. salón comedor; rancho m. —v. **2. m. up**, ensuciar; enredar.

message /'mesɪdʒ/ n. mensaje, recado m.

messenger /'mesəndʒər/ n. mensajero -ra.

messy /'mesi/ a. confuso; desarreglado.

metabolism /məˈtæbəˌlɪzəm/ n. metabolismo m.

metal /'metl/ n. metal m.

metallic /məˈtælɪk/ a. metálico.

metaphysics /ˌmetəˈfɪzɪks/ n. metafísica f.

meteor /'mitiər/ n. meteoro m.

meteorology /ˌmitiəˈrɒlədʒi/ n. meteorología f.

meter /'mitər/ n. contador, medidor; (measure) metro m.

method /'meθəd/ n. método m.

meticulous /məˈtɪkyələs/ a. meticuloso.

metric /'metrɪk/ a. métrico.

metropolis /mɪˈtrɒpəlɪs/ n. metrópoli f.

metropolitan /ˌmetrəˈpɒlɪtn/ a. metropolitano.

Mexican /'meksɪkən/ a. & n. mexicano -na.

Mexico /'meksɪˌkou/ n. México m.

mezzanine /'mezəˌnin/ n. entresuelo m.

microbe /'maikroub/ n. microbio m.

microchip /'maikrouˌtʃɪp/ n. microchip m.

microfiche /'maikrəˌfiʃ/ n. microficha f.

microfilm /'maikrəˌfɪlm/ n. microfilm m.

microform /'maikrəˌfɔrm/ n. microforma f.

microphone /'maikrəˌfoun/ n. micrófono m.

microscope /'maikrəˌskoup/ n. microscopio m.

microscopic /ˌmaikrəˈskɒpɪk/ a. microscópico.

mid /mɪd/ a. medio.

middle /'mɪdl/ a. & n. medio m. **in the m. of,** en medio de, a mediados de.

middle-aged /eidʒd/ a. de edad madura.

Middle East Medio Oriente m.

middle finger dedo corazón m.

midget /'mɪdʒɪt/ n. enano -na.

midnight /'mɪdˌnait/ n. medianoche f.

midwife /'mɪdˌwaif/ n. comadrona, partera f.

might /mait/ n. poder m., fuerza f.

mighty /'maiti/ a. poderoso.

migraine /'maigrein/ n. migraña f.; jaqueca f.

migrate /'maigreit/ v. emigrar.

migration /maiˈgreiʃən/ n. emigración f.

migratory /'maigrəˌtɔri/ a. migratorio.

mild /maild/ a. moderado, suave; templado.

mildew /'mɪlˌdu/ n. añublo m., moho m.

mile /mail/ n. milla f.

mileage /'mailɪdʒ/ n. kilometraje m.

militant /'mɪlɪtənt/ a. militante.

militarism /'mɪlɪtəˌrɪzəm/ n. militarismo m.

military /'mɪlɪˌteri/ a. militar.

militia /mɪˈlɪʃə/ n. milicia f.

milk /mɪlk/ n. **1.** leche f. —v. **2.** ordeñar.

milk chocolate chocolate con leche m.

milkman /'mɪlkˌmæn/ n. lechero m.

milk shake batido m.

milky /'mɪlki/ a. lácteo; lechoso.

mill /mɪl/ n. **1.** molino m.; fábrica f. —v. **2.** moler.

miller /'mɪlər/ n. molinero -ra.

millimeter /'mɪlə,mitər/ n. milímetro m.

milliner /'mɪlənər/ n. sombrerero -ra.

millinery /'mɪlə,nɛri/ n. sombrerería f.

million /'mɪlyən/ n. millón m.

millionaire /,mɪlyə'nɛər/ n. millonario -ria.

mimic /'mɪmɪk/ n. **1.** mimo -ma. —v. **2.** imitar.

mind /maɪnd/ n. **1.** mente; opinión f. —v. **2.** obedecer. **never m.,** no se ocupe.

mindful /'maɪndfəl/ a. atento.

mine /maɪn/ pron. **1.** mío. —n. **2.** mina f. —v. **3.** minar.

miner /'maɪnər/ n. minero m.

mineral /'mɪnərəl/ a. & n. mineral m.

mineral water agua mineral f.

mine sweeper /'maɪn,swipər/ dragaminas f.

mingle /'mɪŋgəl/ v. mezclar.

miniature /'mɪniətʃər/ n. miniatura f.

miniaturize /'mɪniətʃə,raɪz/ v. miniaturizar.

minibus /'mɪni,bʌs/ n. microbús m.

minicab /'mɪni,kæb/ n. microtaxi m.

minimize /'mɪnə,maɪz/ v. menospreciar.

minimum /'mɪnəməm/ a. & n. mínimo m.

mining /'maɪnɪŋ/ n. minería f.

minister /'mɪnəstər/ n. **1.** ministro -tra; *Relig.* pastor m. —v. **2.** ministrar.

ministry /'mɪnəstri/ n. ministerio m.

mink /mɪŋk/ n. visón m.; (fur) piel de visón m.

minor /'maɪnər/ a. **1.** menor. —n. **2.** menor de edad.

minority /mɪ'nɔrɪti/ n. minoría f.

minstrel /'mɪnstrəl/ n. juglar m.

mint /mɪnt/ n. **1.** menta f.; casa de moneda. —v. **2.** acuñar.

minus /'maɪnəs/ prep. menos.

minute /a. maɪ'nut; n. 'mɪnɪt/ a. **1.** minucioso. —n. **2.** minuto, momento m.

miracle /'mɪrəkəl/ n. milagro m.

miraculous /mɪ'rækyələs/ a. milagroso.

mirage /mɪ'rɑʒ/ n. espejismo m.

mire /maɪᵊr/ n. lodo m.

mirror /'mɪrər/ n. espejo m.

mirth /mɜrθ/ n. alegría; risa f.

misbehave /,mɪsbɪ'heɪv/ v. portarse mal.

miscellaneous /,mɪsə'leɪniəs/ a. misceláneo.

mischief /'mɪstʃɪf/ n. travesura, diablura f.

mischievous /'mɪstʃəvəs/ a. travieso, dañino.

miser /'maɪzər/ n. avaro -ra.

miserable /'mɪzərəbəl/ a. miserable; infeliz.

miserly /'maɪzərli/ a. avariento, tacaño.

misfortune /mɪs'fɔrtʃən/ n. desgracia f., infortunio, revés m.

misgiving /mɪs'gɪvɪŋ/ n. recelo m., desconfianza f.

mishap /'mɪshæp/ n. desgracia f., contratiempo m.

mislay /mɪs'leɪ/ v. perder.

mislead /mɪs'lid/ v. extraviar, despistar; pervertir.

misplaced /mɪs'pleɪst/ a. extraviado.

mispronounce /,mɪsprə'naʊns/ v. pronunciar mal.

miss /mɪs/ n. **1.** señorita f. —v. **2.** perder; echar de menos, extrañar. **be missing,** faltar.

missile /'mɪsəl/ n. proyectil m.

mission /'mɪʃən/ n. misión f.

missionary /'mɪʃə,nɛri/ n. misionero -ra.

mist /mɪst/ n. niebla, bruma f.

mistake /mɪ'steɪk/ n. equivocación f.; error m. **to make a m.,** equivocarse.

mistaken /mɪ'steɪkən/ a. equivocado.

mister /'mɪstər/ n. señor m.

mistletoe /'mɪsəl,toʊ/ n. muérdago m.

mistreat /mɪs'trit/ v. maltratar.

mistress /'mɪstrɪs/ n. ama; señora; concubina f.

mistrust /mɪs'trʌst/ v. desconfiar; sospechar.

misty /'mɪsti/ a. nebuloso, brumoso.

misunderstand /,mɪsʌndər'stænd/ v. entender mal.

misuse /mɪs'yuz/ v. maltratar; abusar.

mite /maɪt/ n. pizca f., blanca f.

mitten /'mɪtn/ n. mitón, confortante m.

mix /mɪks/ v. mezclar. **m. up,** confundir.

mixer /'mɪksər/ (for food), n. batidora f.

mixture /'mɪkstʃər/ n. mezcla, mixtura f.

mix-up /'mɪks,ʌp/ n. confusión f.

moan /moun/ n. 1. quejido, gemido m. —v. 2. gemir.

mob /mob/ n. muchedumbre f.; gentío f.

mobilization /,moubələ'zeiʃən/ n. movilización f.

mobilize /'moubə,laiz/ v. movilizar.

mock /mok/ v. burlar.

mockery /'mokəri/ n. burla f.

mod /mod/ a. a la última; en boga.

mode /moud/ n. modo m.

model /'modl/ n. 1. modelo m. —v. 2. modelar.

modem /'moudəm/ n. módem m.

moderate /a 'modərɪt; v -ə,reit/ a. 1. moderado. —v. 2. moderar.

moderation /,modə'reiʃən/ n. moderación; sobriedad f.

modern /'modərn/ a. moderno.

modernize /'modər,naiz/ v. modernizar.

modest /'modɪst/ a. modesto.

modesty /'modəsti/ n. modestia f.

modify /'modə,fai/ v. modificar.

modulate /'modʒə,leit/ v. modular.

moist /moist/ a. húmedo.

moisten /'moisən/ v. humedecer.

moisture /'moistʃər/ n. humedad f.

moisturize /'moistʃə,raiz/ v. hidratar.

molar /'moulər/ n. molar m.

molasses /mə'læsɪz/ n. melaza f.

mold /mould/ n. 1. molde; moho m. —v. 2. moldar, formar; enmohecerse.

moldy /'mouldi/ a. mohoso.

mole /'moulei/ n. lunar m.; (animal) topo m.

molecule /'molɪ,kyul/ n. molécula f.

molest /mə'lest/ v. molestar.

mollify /'molə,fai/ v. molificar.

moment /'moumənt/ n. momento m.

momentary /'moumən,teri/ a. momentáneo.

momentous /mou'mentəs/ a. importante.

monarch /'monərk/ n. monarca m. & f.

monarchy /'monərki/ n. monarquía f.

monastery /'monə,steri/ n. monasterio m.

Monday /'mʌndei/ n. lunes m.

monetary /'moni,teri/ a. monetario.

money /'mʌni/ n. dinero m. **m. order,** giro postal.

mongrel /'mʌŋgrəl/ n. 1. mestizo m. —a. 2. mestizo, cruzado.

monitor /'monitər/ n. amonestador m.; (computer) consola f., pantalla f.

monk /mʌŋk/ n. monje m.

monkey /'mʌŋki/ n. mono -na.

monocle /'monəkəl/ n. monóculo m.

monologue /'monə,ləg/ n. monólogo m.

monopolize /mə'nopə,laiz/ v. monopolizar.

monopoly /mə'nopəli/ n. monopolio m.

monosyllable /'monə,sɪləbəl/ n. monosílabo m.

monotone /'monə,toun/ n. monotonía f.

monotonous /mə'notnəs/ a. monótono.

monotony /mə'notni/ n. monotonía f.

monsoon /mon'sun/ n. monzón m.

monster /'monstər/ n. monstruo m.

monstrosity /mon'strositi/ n. monstruosidad f.

monstrous /'monstrəs/ a. monstruoso.

month /mʌnθ/ n. mes m.

monthly /'mʌnθli/ a. mensual.

monument /'monyəmənt/ n. monumento m.

monumental /,monyə'mentl/ a. monumental.

mood /mud/ n. humor m.; Gram. modo m.

moody /'mudi/ a. caprichoso, taciturno.

moon /mun/ n. luna f.

moonlight /'mun,lait/ n. luz de la luna.

moonlighting /'mun,laitɪŋ/ n. pluriempleo m.

moor /mur/ n. **1.** párano m. —v. **2.** anclar.

Moor /mur/ n. moro -ra.

mop /mɒp/ n. **1.** fregasuelos m., fregona f., (S.A.) trapeador m. —v. **2.** fregar, (S.A.) trapear.

moped /'mou,ped/ n. (vehicle) velomotor m.

moral /'mɔrəl/ a. **1.** moral. —n. **2.** moraleja f. **morals,** moralidad f.

morale /mə'ræl/ n. espíritu m.

moralist /'mɔrəlıst/ n. moralista m. & f.

morality /mə'rælıti/ n. moralidad, ética f.

morbid /'mɔrbɪd/ a. mórbido.

more /mɔr/ a. & adv. más. **m. and m.,** cada vez más.

moreover /mɔr'ouvər/ adv. además.

morgue /mɔrg/ n. necrocomio m.

morning /'mɔrnɪŋ/ n. mañana f. **good m.,** buenos días.

Morocco /mə'rɒkou/ n. Marruecos m.

morose /mə'rous/ a. malhumorado.

morphine /'mɔrfin/ n. morfina f.

morsel /'mɔrsəl/ n. bocado m.

mortal /'mɔrtl̩/ a. & n. mortal m. & f.

mortality /mɔr'tælıti/ n. mortalidad f.

mortar /'mɔrtər/ n. mortero m.

mortgage /'mɔrgɪdʒ/ n. **1.** hipoteca f. —v. **2.** hipotecar.

mortify /'mɔrtə,faɪ/ v. mortificar.

mosaic /mou'zeɪk/ n. & a. mosaico m.

mosque /mɒsk/ n. mezquita f.

mosquito /mə'skitou/ n. mosquito m.

moss /mɔs/ n. musgo m.

most /moust/ a. **1.** más. —adv. **2.** más; sumamente. —pron. **3.** m. of, la mayor parte de.

mostly /'moustli/ adv. principalmente; en su mayor parte.

motel /mou'tel/ n. motel m.

moth /mɔθ/ n. polilla f.

mother /'mʌðər/ n. madre f.

mother-in-law /'mʌðər ɪn ,lɔ/ n. suegra f.

motif /mou'tif/ n. tema m.

motion /'mouʃən/ n. **1.** moción f.; movimiento m. —v. **2.** hacer señas.

motionless /'mouʃənlıs/ a. inmóvil.

motion picture película f.

motivate /'moutə,veɪt/ v. motivar.

motive /'moutɪv/ n. motivo m.

motor /'moutər/ n. motor m.

motorboat /'moutər,bout/ n. lancha motora f., autobote, motorbote m., gasolinera f.

motorcycle /'moutər,saɪkəl/ n. motocicleta f.

motorcyclist /'moutər,saɪklıst/ n. motociclista m. & f.

motorist /'moutərıst/ n. motorista m. & f.

motto /'motou/ n. lema m.

mound /maund/ n. terrón; montón m.

mount /maunt/ n. **1.** monte m.; (horse) montura f. —v. **2.** montar; subir.

mountain /'mauntn̩/ n. montaña f.

mountaineer /,mauntn̩'ɪər/ n. montañés m.

mountainous /'mauntn̩əs/ a. montañoso.

mourn /mɔrn/ v. lamentar, llorar; llevar luto.

mournful /'mɔrnfəl/ a. triste.

mourning /'mɔrnɪŋ/ n. luto; lamento m.

mouse /maus/ n. ratón, ratoncito m.

mouth /mauθ/ n. boca f.; (of river) desembocadura f.

mouthwash /'mauθ,wɒʃ/ n. enjuague bucal m.

movable /'muvəbəl/ a. movible, movedizo.

move /muv/ n. **1.** movimiento m.; mudanza f. —v. **2.** mover; mudarse; emocionar, conmover. **m. away,** quitar; alejarse; mudarse.

movement /'muvmənt/ n. movimiento m.

movie /'muvi/ n. película f. **m. theater, movies,** cine m.

moving /'muvɪŋ/ a. conmovedor; persuasivo.

mow /mou/ v. guadañar, segar.

Mr. /'mɪstər/ title. Señor (Sr.).

Mrs. /'mɪsəz/ title. Señora (Sra.).

much /mʌtʃ/ a. & adv. mucho. **how m.,** cuánto: so m., tanto. **too m.,** demasiado. **as m. as,** tanto como.

mucilage /'myusəlɪdʒ/ n. mucílago m.

mucous /'myukəs/ a. mucoso.

mucous membrane n. membrana mucosa f.

mud /mʌd/ n. fango, lodo m.

muddy /'mʌdi/ a. **1.** lodoso; turbio. —v. **2.** ensuciar; enturbiar.

muff /mʌf/ n. manguito m.

muffin /'mʌfɪn/ n. panecillo m.

mug /mʌg/ n. cubilete m.

mugger /'mʌgər/ n. asaltante m. & f.

mulatto /mə'lætou/ n. mulato m.

mule /myul/ n. mula f.

mullah /'mʌlə/ n. mullah m.

multicultural /,mʌlti'kʌltʃərəl, ,mʌltai-/ a. multicultural.

multinational /,mʌlti'næʃənl, ,mʌltai-/ a. multinacional.

multiple /'mʌltəpəl/ a. múltiple.

multiplication /,mʌltəplɪ'keiʃən/ n. multiplicación f.

multiplicity /,mʌltə'plɪsɪti/ n. multiplicidad f.

multiply /'mʌltəplɪ/ v. multiplicar.

multitasking /,mʌlti'tæskɪŋ, ,mʌltai-/ n. multitarea f.

multitude /'mʌltɪ,tud/ n. multitud f.

mummy /'mʌmi/ n. momia f.

mumps /mʌmps/ n. paperas f.pl.

municipal /myu'nɪsəpəl/ a. municipal.

munificent /myu'nɪfəsənt/ a. munífico.

munitions /myu'nɪʃənz/ n. municiones m.pl.

mural /'myʊrəl/ a. & n. mural m.

murder /'mɜrdər/ n. **1.** asesinato; homicidio m. —v. **2.** asesinar.

murderer /'mɜrdərər/ n. asesino -na.

murmur /'mɜrmər/ n. **1.** murmullo m. —v. **2.** murmurar.

muscle /'mʌsəl/ n. músculo m.

muscular /'mʌskyələr/ a. muscular.

muse /myuz/ n. **1.** musa f. —v. **2.** meditar.

museum /myu'ziəm/ n. museo m.

mushroom /'mʌʃrum/ n. seta f., hongo m.

music /'myuzɪk/ n. música f.

musical /'myuzɪkəl/ a. musical; melodioso.

musician /myu'zɪʃən/ n. músico -ca.

Muslim /'mʌzlɪm/ a. & n. musulmano.

muslin /'mʌzlɪn/ n. muselina f.; percal m.

mussel /'mʌsəl/ n. mejillón m.

must /mʌst/ v. deber; tener que.

mustache /'mʌstæʃ/ n. bigotes m.pl.

mustard /'mʌstərd/ n. mostaza f.

muster /'mʌstər/ n. **1.** Mil. revista f. —v. **2.** reunir, juntar.

mute /myut/ a. & n. mudo -da.

mutilate /'myut,leit/ v. mutilar.

mutiny /'myutnɪ/ n. **1.** motín m. —v. **2.** amotinarse.

mutt /mʌt/ n. Colloq. chucho m.

mutter /'mʌtər/ v. refunfuñar, gruñir.

mutton /'mʌtn/ n. carnero m.

mutual /'myutʃuəl/ a. mutuo.

muzzle /'mʌzəl/ n. **1.** hocico m.; bozal m. —v. **2.** embozar.

my /mai/ a. mi.

myriad /'mɪriəd/ n. miríada f.

myrtle /'mɜrtl/ n. mirto m.

myself /mai'self/ pron. mí, mí mismo; me. **I m.,** yo mismo.

mysterious /mɪ'stiriəs/ a. misterioso.

mystery /'mɪstəri/ n. misterio m.

mystic /'mɪstɪk/ a. místico.

mystify /'mɪstə,fai/ v. confundir.

myth /mɪθ/ n. mito m.

mythical /'mɪθɪkəl/ a. mítico.

mythology /mɪ'θɒlədʒi/ n. mitología f.

N

nag /næg/ n. **1.** jaca f. —v. **2.** regañar; sermonear.

nail /neil/ n. **1.** clavo m.; (finger) uña f. **n. polish,** esmalte para las uñas. —v. **2.** clavar.

naïve /nɑ'iv/ a. ingenuo.

naked /'neikɪd/ a. desnudo.

name /neim/ n. **1.** nombre m.; reputación f. —v. **2.** nombrar, mencionar.

namely /'neimli/ adv. a saber; es decir.

namesake /'neim,seik/ n. tocayo m.

nanny /'næni/ n. niñera f.

nap /næp/ n. siesta f. **to take a n.,** echar una siesta.

naphtha /'næfθə, 'næp-/ n. nafta f.

napkin /'næpkɪn/ n. servilleta f.

narcissus /nɑr'sɪsəs/ n. narciso m.

narcotic /nɑr'kɒtɪk/ a. & n. narcótico m.

narrate /'næreit/ v. narrar.

narrative /'nærətɪv/ *a.* **1.** narrativo. —*n.* **2.** cuento, relato *m.*

narrow /'nærou/ *a.* estrecho, angosto. **n.-minded,** intolerante.

nasal /'neɪzəl/ *a.* nasal.

nasty /'næsti/ *a.* desagradable.

nation /'neɪʃən/ *n.* nación *f.*

national /'næʃənl/ *a.* nacional.

nationalism /'næʃənl,ɪzəm/ *n.* nacionalismo *m.*

nationality /,næʃə'nælɪti/ *n.* nacionalidad *f.*

nationalization /,næʃənlə'zeɪʃən/ *n.* nacionalización *f.*

nationalize /'næʃənl,aɪz, 'næʃnə,laɪz/ *v.* nacionalizar.

native /'neɪtɪv/ *a.* **1.** nativo. —*n.* **2.** natural; indígena *m. & f.*

nativity /nə'tɪvɪti/ *n.* natividad *f.*

natural /'nætʃərəl/ *a.* natural.

naturalist /'nætʃərəlɪst/ *n.* naturalista *m. & f.*

naturalize /'nætʃərə,laɪz/ *v.* naturalizar.

naturalness /,nætʃərəlnɪs/ *n.* naturalidad *f.*

nature /'neɪtʃər/ *n.* naturaleza *f.*; índole *f.*; humor *m.*

naughty /'nɔti/ *a.* travieso, desobediente.

nausea /'nɔziə, -ʒə/ *n.* náusea *f.*

nauseous /'nɔʃəs/ *a.* nauseoso.

nautical /'nɔtɪkəl/ *a.* náutico.

naval /'neɪvəl/ *a.* naval.

nave /neɪv/ *n.* nave *f.*

navel /'neɪvəl/ *n.* ombligo *m.*

navigable /'nævɪgəbəl/ *a.* navegable.

navigate /'nævɪ,geɪt/ *v.* navegar.

navigation /,nævɪ'geɪʃən/ *n.* navegación *f.*

navigator /'nævɪ,geɪtər/ *n.* navegante *m. & f.*

navy /'neɪvi/ *n.* marina *f.*

navy blue azul marino *m.*

near /nɪər/ *a.* **1.** cercano, próximo. —*adv.* **2.** cerca. —*prep.* **3.** cerca de.

nearby /'nɪər'baɪ/ *a.* **1.** cercano. —*adv.* **2.** cerca.

nearly /'nɪərli/ *adv.* casi.

nearsighted /'nɪər,saɪtɪd/ *a.* corto de vista.

neat /nit/ *a.* aseado; ordenado.

neatness /'nitnɪs/ *n.* aseo *m.*

nebulous /'nɛbyələs/ *a.* nebuloso.

necessary /'nɛsə,sɛri/ *a.* necesario.

necessity /nə'sɛsɪti/ *n.* necesidad *f.*

neck /nɛk/ *n.* cuello *m.*

necklace /'nɛklɪs/ *n.* collar *m.*

necktie /'nɛk,taɪ/ *n.* corbata *f.*

nectar /'nɛktər/ *n.* néctar *m.*

nectarine /,nɛktə'rin/ *n.* nectarina *f.*

need /nid/ *n.* **1.** necesidad; (poverty) pobreza *f.* —*v.* **2.** necesitar.

needle /'nidl/ *n.* aguja *f.*

needless /'nidlɪs/ *a.* innecesario, inútil.

needy /'nidi/ *a.* indigente, necesitado, pobre.

nefarious /nɪ'fɛəriəs/ *a.* nefario.

negative /'nɛgətɪv/ *a.* negativo. *n.* negativa *f.*

neglect /nɪ'glɛkt/ *n.* **1.** negligencia *f.*; descuido *m.* —*v.* **2.** descuidar.

negligee /,nɛglɪ'ʒeɪ/ *n.* negligé *m.*, bata de casa *f.*

negligent /'nɛglɪdʒənt/ *a.* negligente, descuidado.

negligible /'nɛglɪdʒəbəl/ *a.* insignificante.

negotiate /nɪ'goʊʃi,eɪt/ *v.* negociar.

negotiation /nɪ,goʊʃi'eɪʃən/ *n.* negociación *f.*

Negro /'nigrou/ *n.* negro -ra.

neighbor /'neɪbər/ *n.* vecino -na.

neighborhood /'neɪbər,hʊd/ *n.* vecindad *f.*

neither /'niðər, 'naɪ-/ *a. & pron.* **1.** ninguno de los dos. —*adv.* **2.** tampoco. —*conj.* **3.** **neither... nor,** ni... ni.

neon /'niɒn/ *n.* neón *m.* **n. light,** tubo neón *m.*

nephew /'nɛfyu/ *n.* sobrino *m.*

nerve /nɜrv/ *n.* nervio *m.*; *Colloq.* audacia *f.*

nervous /'nɜrvəs/ *a.* nervioso.

nervous breakdown /'breɪk,daʊn/ crisis nerviosa *f.*

nest /nɛst/ *n.* nido *m.*

net /nɛt/ *a.* **1.** neto. —*n.* **2.** red *f.* **hair n.,** albanega, redecilla *f.* *v.* redar; *Com.* ganar.

netiquette /'nɛtɪkɪt/ *n.* etiqueta de la red *f.*

netting /'nɛtɪŋ/ *n.* red *m.*; obra de malla *f.*

network /'nɛt,wɜrk/ *n.* (radio) red radiodifusora.

neuralgia /nʊ'rældʒə/ *n.* neuralgia *f.*

neurology /nʊ'rɒlədʒi/ *n.* neurología *f.*

neurotic /nʊ'rɒtɪk/ *a.* neurótico.

neutral /'nutrəl/ a. neutral.

neutrality /nu'træliti/ n. neutralidad f.

neutron /'nutrɒn/ n. neutrón m.

neutron bomb bomba de neutrones f.

never /'nevər/ adv. nunca, jamás; **n. mind,** no importa.

nevertheless /,nevərðə'les/ adv. no obstante, sin embargo.

new /nu/ a. nuevo.

newbie /'nubi/ n. Colloq. novato -ta, inexperto -ta.

news /nuz/ n. noticias f.pl.

newsboy /'nuz,bɔi/ n. vendedor -ra de periódicos.

news bulletin boletín informativo m.

news flash n. noticia de última hora f.

newsgroup /'nuz,grup/ n. grupo de discusion m.

newsletter /'nuz,letər/ n. hoja informativa f.

newspaper /'nuz,peipər/ n. periódico m.

New Testament Nuevo Testamento m.

new year n. año nuevo m.

next /nekst/ a. **1.** próximo; siguiente; contiguo. —adv. **2.** luego, después. **n. door,** al lado. **n. to,** al lado de la.

next-to-the-last /'nekst tə ðə 'læst/ a. penúltimo.

nibble /'nibəl/ v. picar.

nice /nis/ a. simpático, agradable; amable; hermoso; exacto.

nick /nik/ n. muesca f., picadura f. **in the n. of time,** a punto.

nickel /'nikəl/ n. níquel m.

nickname /'nik,neim/ n. **1.** apodo, mote m. —v. **2.** apodar.

nicotine /'nikə,tin/ n. nicotina f.

niece /nis/ n. sobrina f.

niggardly /'nigərdli/ a. mezquino.

night /nait/ n. noche f. **good n.,** buenas noches. **last n.,** anoche. **n. club,** cabaret m.

nightclub /'nait,klʌb/ n. cabaret m.

nightclub owner cabaretero -ra m. & f.

nightgown /'nait,gaun/ n. camisa de dormir.

nightingale /'naitṇ,geil, 'naitiṇ-/ n. ruiseñor m.

nightly /'naitli/ adv. todas las noches.

nightmare /'nait,meər/ n. pesadilla f.

night school escuela nocturna f.

night watchman vigilante nocturno m.

nimble /'nimbəl/ a. ágil.

nine /nain/ a. & pron. nueve.

nineteen /'nain'tin/ a. & pron. diecinueve.

ninety /'nainti/ a. & pron. noventa.

ninth /nainθ/ a. noveno.

nipple /'nipəl/ n. teta f.; pezón m.

nitrogen /'naitrədʒən/ n. nitrógeno m.

no /nou/ a. **1.** ninguno. **no one,** nadie. —adv. **2.** no.

nobility /nou'biliti/ n. nobleza f.

noble /'noubəl/ a. & n. noble m.

nobleman /'noubəlmən/ n. noble m.

nobody /'nou,bɒdi/ pron. nadie.

nocturnal /nɒk'tɜrnl/ a. nocturno.

nocturne /'nɒktɜrn/ n. nocturno m.

nod /nɒd/ n. **1.** seña con la cabeza. —v. **2.** inclinar la cabeza; (doze) dormitar.

no-frills /nou 'frilz/ a. sin extras.

noise /nɔiz/ n. ruido m.

noiseless /'nɔizlis/ a. silencioso.

noisy /'nɔizi/ a. ruidoso.

nominal /'nɒmənl/ a. nominal.

nominate /'nɒmə,neit/ v. nombrar.

nomination /,nɒmə'neiʃən/ n. nombramiento m., nominación f.

nominee /,nɒmə'ni/ n. candidato -ta.

nonaligned /,nɒnə'laind/ (in political sense) n. no alineado.

nonchalant /,nɒnʃə'lɒnt/ a. indiferente.

noncombatant /,nɒnkəm'bætnt/ n. no combatiente m.

noncommittal /,nɒnkə'mitl/ a. evasivo; reservado.

nondescript /'nɒndi'skript/ a. difícil de describir.

none /nʌn/ pron. ninguno.

nonentity /nɒn'entiti/ n. nulidad f.

nonpartisan /nɒn'pɑrtəzən/ a. sin afiliación f.

non-proliferation /,nɒnprə,lifə-'reiʃən/ n. no proliferación m.

nonsense /'nɒnsens/ n. tontería f.

nonsmoker /nɒn'smoukər/ n. no fumador -dora.

noodle /'nudl/ n. fideo m.

noon /nun/ *n.* mediodía *m.*

noose /nus/ *n.* lazo corredizo *m.*; dogal *m.*

nor /nɔr/ *unstressed* nər/ *conj.* ni.

normal /'nɔrməl/ *a.* normal.

north /nɔrθ/ *n.* norte *m.*

North America /ə'mɛrɪkə/ Norte América *f.*

North American *a. & n.* norteamericano -na.

northeast /,nɔrθ'ist; *Naut.* ,nɔr-/ *n.* nordeste *m.*

northern /'nɔrðərn/ *a.* septentrional.

North Pole *n.* Polo Norte *m.*

northwest /,nɔrθ'wɛst; *Naut.* ,nɔr-/ *n.* noroeste *m.*

Norway /'nɔrwei/ *n.* Noruega *f.*

Norwegian /nɔr'widʒən/ *a. & n.* noruego -ga.

nose /nouz/ *n.* nariz *f.*

nosebleed /'nouz,blid/ *n.* hemorragia nasal *f.*

nostalgia /nɒ'stældʒə/ *n.* nostalgia *f.*

nostril /'nɒstrəl/ *n.* ventana de la nariz; (pl.) narices *f.pl.*

not /nɒt/ *adv.* no. **n. at all,** de ninguna manera. **n. even,** ni siquiera.

notable /'noutəbəl/ *a.* notable.

notary /'noutəri/ *n.* notario *m.*

notation /nou'teiʃən/ *n.* notación *f.*

notch /nɒtʃ/ *n.* muesca *f.*; corte *m.*

note /nout/ *n.* **1.** nota *f.*; apunte *m.* —*v.* **2.** notar.

notebook /'nout,bʊk/ *n.* libreta *f.*, cuaderno *m.*

noted /'noutid/ *a.* célebre.

notepaper /'nout,peipər/ *n.* papel de notas *m.*

noteworthy /'nout,wɜrði/ *a.* notable.

nothing /'nʌθɪŋ/ *pron.* nada.

notice /'noutis/ *n.* **1.** aviso *m.*; noticia *f.* —*v.* **2.** observar, fijarse en.

noticeable /'noutisəbəl/ *a.* notable.

notification /,noutəfɪ'keiʃən/ *n.* notificación *f.*

notify /'noutə,fai/ *v.* notificar.

notion /'nouʃən/ *n.* noción; idea *f.*; (pl.) novedades *f.pl.*

notoriety /,noutə'raiiti/ *n.* notoriedad *f.*

notorious /nou'tɔriəs/ *a.* notorio.

noun /naun/ *n.* nombre, sustantivo *m.*

nourish /'nɜrɪʃ/ *v.* nutrir, alimentar.

nourishment /'nɜrɪʃmənt/ *n.* nutrimento; alimento *m.*

novel /'nɒvəl/ *a.* **1.** nuevo, original. —*n.* **2.** novela *f.*

novelist /'nɒvəlist/ *n.* novelista *m. & f.*

novelty /'nɒvəlti/ *n.* novedad *f.*

November /nou'vɛmbər/ *n.* noviembre *m.*

novena /nou'vinə/ *n.* novena *f.*

novice /'nɒvis/ *n.* novicio -cia, novato -ta.

novocaine /'nouvə,kein/ *n.* novocaína *f.*

now /nau/ *adv.* ahora. **n. and then,** de vez en cuando. **by n.,** ya. **from n. on,** de ahora en adelante. **just n.,** ahorita. **right n.,** ahora mismo.

nowadays /'nauə,deiz/ *adv.* hoy día, hoy en día, actualmente.

nowhere /'nou,wɛər/ *adv.* en ninguna parte.

nozzle /'nɒzəl/ *n.* boquilla *f.*

nuance /'nuɑns/ *n.* matiz *m.*

nuclear /'nukliər/ *a.* nuclear.

nuclear energy energía nuclear *f.*

nuclear warhead /'wɔr,hɛd/ cabeza nuclear *f.*

nuclear waste desechos nucleares *m.pl.*

nucleus /'nukliəs/ *n.* núcleo *m.*

nude /nud/ *a.* desnudo.

nuisance /'nusəns/ *n.* molestia *f.*

nuke /nuk/ *n.* bomba atómica *f.*

nullify /'nʌplə,fai/ *v.* anular.

number /'nʌmbər/ *n.* **1.** número *m.*; cifra *f.*; **license n.,** matrícula *f.* —*v.* **2.** numerar, contar.

numeric /nu'mɛrɪk/ **numerical** *a.* numérico.

numeric keypad /nu'mɛrɪk/ teclado numérico *m.*

numerous /'numərəs/ *a.* numeroso.

nun /nʌn/ *n.* monja *f.*

nuptial /'nʌpʃəl/ *a.* nupcial.

nurse /nɜrs/ *n.* **1.** enfermera *f.*; (child's) niñera *f.* —*v.* **2.** criar, alimentar, amamantar; cuidar.

nursery /'nɜrsəri/ *n.* cuarto destinado a los niños; *Agr.* plantel, criadero *m.*

nursery school jardín de infancia *m.*

nurture /'nɔrtʃər/ v. nutrir.

nut /nʌt/ n. nuez f.; *Mech.* tuerca f.

nutcracker /'nʌt,krækər/ n. cas canueces m.

nutrition /nu'trɪʃən/ n. nutrición f.

nutritious /nu'trɪʃəs/ a. nutritivo.

nylon /'nailɒn/ n. nilón m.

nymph /nɪmf/ n. ninfa f.

O

oak /ouk/ n. roble m.

oar /ɔr/ n. remo m.

OAS abbr. (Organization of American States) OEA (Organización de los Estados Americanos) f.

oasis /ou'eisis/ n. oasis m.

oat /out/ n. avena f.

oath /ouθ/ n. juramento m.

oatmeal /'out,mil/ n. harina de avena f.

obedience /ou'bidiəns/ n. obediencia f.

obedient /ou'bidiənt/ a. obediente.

obese /ou'bis/ a. obeso, gordo.

obey /ou'bei/ v. obedecer.

obituary /ou'bɪtʃu,ɛri/ n. obituario m.

object /n 'ɒbdʒɪkt; v əb'dʒɛkt/ n. **1.** objeto m.; *Gram.* complemento m. —v. **2.** oponerse; objetar.

objection /əb'dʒɛkʃən/ n. objeción f.

objectionable /əb'dʒɛkʃənəbəl/ a. censurable.

objective /əb'dʒɛktɪv/ a. & n. objetivo m.

obligation /,ɒblɪ'geiʃən/ n. obligación f.

obligatory /ə'blɪgə,tɔri/ a. obligatorio.

oblige /ə'blaidʒ/ v. obligar; complacer.

oblique /ə'blik/ a. oblicuo.

obliterate /ə'blɪtə,reit/ v. borrar; destruir.

oblivion /ə'blɪviən/ n. olvido m.

oblong /'ɒb,lɒŋ/ a. oblongo.

obnoxious /əb'nɒkʃəs/ a. ofensivo, odioso.

obscene /əb'sin/ a. obsceno, indecente.

obscure /əb'skyur/ a. **1.** obscuro. —v. **2.** obscurecer.

observance /əb'zɜrvəns/ n. observancia f.; ceremonia f.

observation /,ɒbzɜr'veiʃən/ n. observación f.

observatory /əb'zɜrvə,tɔri/ n. observatorio m.

observe /əb'zɜrv/ v. observar; celebrar.

observer /əb'zɜrvər/ n. observador -ra.

obsession /əb'sɛʃən/ n. obsesión f.

obsolete /,ɒbsə'lit/ a. anticuado.

obstacle /'ɒbstəkəl/ n. obstáculo m.

obstetrician /,ɒbstɪ'trɪʃən/ n. obstétrico -ca, tocólogo -ga m. & f.

obstinate /'ɒbstənɪt/ a. obstinado, terco.

obstruct /əb'strʌkt/ v. obstruir, impedir.

obstruction /əb'strʌkʃən/ n. obstrucción f.

obtain /əb'tein/ v. obtener, conseguir.

obtuse /əb'tus/ a. obtuso.

obviate /'ɒbvi,eit/ v. obviar.

obvious /'ɒbviəs/ a. evidente, obvio.

occasion /ə'keiʒən/ n. **1.** ocasión f. —v. **2.** ocasionar.

occasional /ə'keiʒənl/ a. ocasional.

occult /ə'kʌlt/ a. oculto.

occupant /'ɒkyəpənt/ n. ocupante m. & f.; inquilino -na.

occupation /,ɒkyə'peiʃən/ n. ocupación f.; empleo m.

occupy /'ɒkyə,pai/ v. ocupar; emplear.

occur /ə'kɜr/ v. ocurrir.

occurrence /ə'kɜrəns/ n. ocurrencia f.

ocean /'ouʃən/ n. océano m.

o'clock /ə'klɒk/ **it's one o.**, es la una. **it's two o.**, son las dos, etc. **at... o.**, a las...

octagon /'ɒktə,gɒn/ n. octágono m.

octave /'ɒktɪv/ n. octava f.

October /ɒk'toubər/ n. octubre m.

octopus /'ɒktəpəs/ n. pulpo m.

oculist /'ɒkyəlɪst/ n. oculista m. & f.

odd /ɒd/ a. impar; suelto; raro.

odd number número impar m.

odious /'oudiəs/ a. odioso.

odor /'oudər/ n. olor m.; fragancia f.

of /əv/ prep. de.

off /ɔf/ adv. (see under verb: **stop off, take off,** etc.)

offend /ə'fɛnd/ v. ofender.

offender /ə'fɛndər/ n. ofensor -ra; delincuente m. & f.

offense /ə'fɛns/ n. ofensa f.; crimen m.

offensive /ə'fɛnsɪv/ a. **1.** ofensivo. —**2.** ofensiva f.

offer /'ɔfər/ n. **1.** oferta f. —v. **2.** ofrecer.

offering /'ɔfərɪŋ/ n. oferta f.

office /'ɔfɪs/ n. oficina f.; despacho m.; oficio, cargo m.

officer /'ɔfəsər/ n. oficial m. & f. **police o.,** agente de policía m. & f.

official /ə'fɪʃəl/ a. **1.** oficial m. & f., funcionario -ria.

officiate /ə'fɪʃi,eɪt/ v. oficiar.

officious /ə'fɪʃəs/ a. oficioso.

offspring /'ɔf,sprɪŋ/ n. hijos m.pl.; progenie f.

often /'ɔfən/ adv. muchas veces, a menudo. **how o.,** con qué frecuencia.

oil /ɔɪl/ n. **1.** aceite; óleo; petróleo m. —v. **2.** aceitar; engrasar.

oil refinery /rɪ'faɪnəri/ destilería de petróleo f.

oil tanker /'tæŋkər/ petrolero m.

oily /'ɔɪli/ a. aceitoso.

ointment /'ɔɪntmənt/ n. ungüento m.

okay /'ou'keɪ, ,ou'keɪ/ adv. bien; de acuerdo.

old /ould/ a. viejo; antiguo. **o. man, o. woman,** viejo -ja.

old-fashioned /'ould 'fæʃənd/ a. fuera de moda, anticuado.

Old Testament Antiguo Testamento m.

olive /'ɔlɪv/ n. aceituna, oliva f.

ombudsman /'ɔmbədzmən/ n. ombudsman f.

omelet /'ɔmlɪt/ n. tortilla de huevos.

omen /'oumən/ n. agüero m.

ominous /'ɔmənəs/ a. ominoso, siniestro.

omission /ou'mɪʃən/ n. omisión f.; olvido m.

omit /ou'mɪt/ v. omitir.

omnibus /'ɔmnə,bʌs/ n. ómnibus m.

omnipotent /ɔm'nɪpətənt/ a. omnipotente.

on /ɔn/ prep. **1.** en, sobre, encima de. —adv. **2.** adelante.

once /wʌns/ adv. una vez. **at o.,** en seguida. **o. in a while,** de vez en cuando.

one /wʌn/ a. & pron. uno -na.

one-armed bandit /'wʌn 'armd/ tragaperras f.

oneself /wʌn'sɛlf/ pron. sí mismo -ma; se. **with o.,** consigo.

onion /'ʌnyən/ n. cebolla f.

on-line /'ɔn 'laɪn/ a. conectado.

only /'ounli/ a. **1.** único, solo. —adv. **2.** sólo, solamente.

onward /'ɔnwərd/ adv. adelante.

opal /'oupəl/ n. ópalo m.

opaque /ou'peɪk/ a. opaco.

open /'oupən/ a. **1.** abierto; franco. **o. air,** aire libre. —v. **2.** abrir.

opening /'oupənɪŋ/ n. abertura f.

opera /'ɔpərə/ n. ópera f. **o. glasses,** anteojos de ópera; gemelos m.pl.

operate /'ɔpə,reɪt/ v. operar.

operation /,ɔpə'reɪʃən/ n. operación f. **to have an o.,** operarse, ser operado.

operative /'ɔpərətɪv/ a. eficaz, operativo.

operator /'ɔpə,reɪtər/ n. operario -ria. **elevator o.,** ascensorista m. & f. **telephone o.,** telefonista m. & f.

operetta /,ɔpə'rɛtə/ n. opereta f.

ophthalmic /ɔf'θælmɪk, ɔp-/ a. oftálmico.

opinion /ə'pɪnyən/ n. opinión f.

opponent /ə'pounənt/ n. antagonista m. & f.

opportune /,ɔpər'tun/ a. oportuno.

opportunism /,ɔpər'tunɪzəm/ n. oportunismo m.

opportunity /,ɔpər'tunɪti/ n. ocasión, oportunidad f.

oppose /ə'pouz/ v. oponer.

opposite /'ɔpəzɪt/ a. **1.** opuesto, contrario. —prep. **2.** al frente de. —n. **3.** contrario m.

opposition /,ɔpə'zɪʃən/ n. oposición f.

oppress /ə'prɛs/ v. oprimir.

oppression /ə'prɛʃən/ n. opresión f.

oppressive /ə'prɛsɪv/ a. opresivo.

optic /'ɔptɪk/ a. óptico.

optical disc /'ɔptɪkəl 'dɪsk/ disco óptico m.

optical illusion /ɒptɪkəl/ ilusión de óptica f.

optician /ɒptɪʃən/ n. óptico -ca.

optics /ɒptɪks/ n. óptica f.

optimism /ɒptə,mɪzəm/ n. optimismo.

optimistic /ɒptəˈmɪstɪk/ a. optimista.

option /ɒpʃən/ n. opción, elección f.

optional /ɒpʃənl/ a. discrecional, facultativo.

optometry /ɒpˈtɒmɪtri/ n. optometría f.

opulent /ɒpyələnt/ a. opulento.

or /ɔr/ conj. o, (before if-, ho-) u.

oracle /ɔrəkəl/ n. oráculo m.

oral /ɔrəl/ a. oral, vocal.

orange /ɔrɪndʒ/ n. naranja f.

orange juice jugo de naranja, zumo de naranja f.

orange squeezer /skwizər/ n. exprimidora de naranjas f.

oration /ɔˈreɪʃən/ n. discurso m.; oración f.

orator /ɔrətər/ n. orador -ra.

oratory /ɔrə,tɔri/ n. oratoria f.; (church) oratorio m.

orbit /ɔrbɪt/ n. órbita f.

orchard /ɔrtʃərd/ n. huerto m.

orchestra /ɔrkəstrə/ n. orquesta f. **o. seat,** butaca f.

orchid /ɔrkɪd/ n. orquídea f.

ordain /ɔrˈdeɪn/ v. ordenar.

ordeal /ɔrˈdil/ n. prueba f.

order /ɔrdər/ n. orden, m. or f.; clase f.; Com. pedido m. **in o. that,** para que. v. ordenar; mandar; pedir.

order blank hoja de pedidos f.

orderly /ɔrdərli/ a. ordenado.

ordinance /ɔrdnəns/ n. ordenanza f.

ordinary /ɔrdn,ɛri/ a. ordinario.

ordination /,ɔrdnˈeɪʃən/ n. ordenación f.

ore /ɔr/ n. mineral m.

organ /ɔrgən/ n. órgano m.

organdy /ɔrgəndi/ n. organdí m.

organic /ɔrˈgænɪk/ a. orgánico.

organism /ɔrgə,nɪzəm/ n. organismo m.

organist /ɔrgənɪst/ n. organista m. & f.

organization /,ɔrgənəˈzeɪʃən/ n. organización f.

organize /ɔrgə,naɪz/ v. organizar.

orgy /ɔrdʒi/ n. orgía f.

orient /ɔriənt/ n. **1.** oriente m. —v. **2.** orientar.

Orient /ɔriənt/ n. Oriente m.

Oriental /,ɔriˈɛntl/ a. oriental.

orientation /,ɔriənˈteɪʃən/ n. orientación f.

origin /ɔrɪdʒɪn/ n. origen m.

original /əˈrɪdʒənl/ a. & n. original m.

originality /ə,rɪdʒəˈnælɪti/ n. originalidad f.

ornament /n ɔrnəmənt; v -,mɛnt/ n. **1.** ornamento m. —v. **2.** ornamentar.

ornamental /,ɔrnəˈmɛntl/ a. ornamental, decorativo.

ornate /ɔrˈneɪt/ a. ornado.

ornithology /,ɔrnəˈθɒlədʒi/ n. ornitología f.

orphan /ɔrfən/ a. n. huérfano -na.

orphanage /ɔrfənɪdʒ/ n. orfanato m.

orthodox /ɔrθə,dɒks/ a. ortodoxo.

ostentation /,ɒstɛnˈteɪʃən/ n. ostentación f.

ostentatious /,ɒstɛnˈteɪʃəs/ a. ostentoso.

ostrich /ɒstrɪtʃ/ n. avestruz f.

other /ʌðər/ a. & pron. otro. **every o. day,** un día sí otro no.

otherwise /ʌðər,waɪz/ adv. de otra manera.

ought /ɔt/ v. deber.

ounce /aʊns/ n. onza f.

our /aʊər; unstressed ɑr/ **ours** a. & pron. nuestro.

ourselves /ɑrˈsɛlvz/ pron. nosotros -as; mismos -as; nos.

oust /aʊst/ v. desalojar.

ouster /aʊstər/ n. desahucio m.

out /aʊt/ adv. **1.** fuera, afuera. **out of,** fuera de. —prep. **2.** por.

outbreak /aʊt,breɪk/ n. erupción f.

outcast /aʊt,kæst/ n. paria m. & f.

outcome /aʊt,kʌm/ n. resultado m.

outdoors /,aʊtˈdɔrz/ adv. fuera de casa; al aire libre.

outer /aʊtər/ a. exterior, externo.

outfit /aʊt,fɪt/ n. **1.** equipo; traje m. —v. **2.** equipar.

outgrowth /aʊt,groʊθ/ n. resultado m.

outing /aʊtɪŋ/ n. paseo m.

outlaw /aʊt,lɔ/ n. **1.** bandido m. —v. **2.** proscribir.

outlet /aʊtlɛt/ n. salida f.

outline /aʊt,laɪn/ n. **1.** contorno;

esbozo *m.*; silueta *f.* —*v.* **2.** esbozar.

outlive /,aut'lɪv/ *v.* sobrevivir.

out-of-court settlement /'autəv,kɔrt/ arreglo pacífico *m.*

out-of-date /'aut əv 'deit/ *a.* anticuado.

out of focus *a.* desenfocado.

outpost /'aut,poust/ *n.* puesto avanzado.

output /'aut,put/ *n.* capacidad *f.*; producción *f.*

outrage /'autreidʒ/ *n.* **1.** ultraje *m.*; atrocidad *f.* —*v.* **2.** ultrajar.

outrageous /aut'reidʒəs/ *a.* atroz.

outrun /,aut'rʌn/ *v.* exceder.

outside /a, prep, adv 'aut'said; n 'aut'said/ *a. & n.* **1.** exterior *m.* —*adv.* **2.** afuera, por fuera. —*prep.* **3.** fuera de.

outskirt /'aut,skɜrt/ *n.* borde *m.*

outward /'autwərd/ *adv.* hacia afuera.

outwardly /'autwərdli/ *adv.* exteriormente.

oval /'ouvəl/ *a.* **1.** oval, ovalado. —*n.* **2.** óvalo *m.*

ovary /'ouvəri/ *n.* ovario *m.*

ovation /ou'veiʃən/ *n.* ovación *f.*

oven /'ʌvən/ *n.* horno *m.*

over /'ouvər/ *prep.* **1.** sobre, encima de; por. —*adv.* **2. o. here,** aquí. **o. there,** allí, por allí. **to be o.,** estar terminado.

overcoat /'ouvər,kout/ *n.* abrigo, sobretodo *m.*

overcome /,ouvər'kʌm/ *v.* superar, vencer.

overdose /'ouvər,dous/ *n.* sobredosis *f.*

overdue /,ouvər'du/ *a.* retrasado.

overflow /n 'ouvər,flou; v ,ouvər'flou/ *n.* **1.** inundación *f.* —*v.* **2.** inundar.

overhaul /,ouvər'hɔl/ *v.* reparar.

overhead /'ouvər'hɛd/ *adv.* arriba, en lo alto.

overkill /'ouvər,kɪl/ *n.* efecto mayor que el pretendido.

overlook /,ouvər'luk/ *v.* pasar por alto.

overnight /'ouvər'nait/ *adv.* **to stay or stop o.,** pasar la noche.

overpower /,ouvər'pauər/ *v.* vencer.

overrule /,ouvər'rul/ *v.* predominar.

overrun /,ouvər'rʌn/ *v.* invadir.

oversee /,ouvər'si/ *v.* superentender.

oversight /'ouvər,sait/ *n.* descuido *m.*

overt /ou'vɜrt/ *a.* abierto.

overtake /,ouvər'teik/ *v.* alcanzar.

overthrow /n 'ouvər,θrou; v ,ouvər'θrou/ *n.* **1.** trastorno *m.* —*v.* **2.** trastornar.

overture /'ouvərtʃər/ *n. Mus.* obertura *f.*

overturn /,ouvər'tɜrn/ *v.* trastornar.

overview /'ouvər,vyu/ *n.* visión de conjunto *f.*

overweight /'ouvər,weit/ *a.* demasiado pesado.

overwhelm /,ouvər'wɛlm/ *v.* abrumar.

overwork /,ouvər'wɜrk/ *v.* trabajar demasiado.

owe /ou/ *v.* deber. **owing to,** debido a.

owl /aul/ *n.* búho *m.*, lechuza *f.*

own /oun/ *a.* **1.** propio. —*v.* **2.** poseer.

owner /'ounər/ *n.* dueño -ña. *f.*

ox /ɒks/ *n.* buey *m.*

oxygen /'ɒksidʒən/ *n.* oxígeno *m.*

oxygen tent tienda de oxígeno *f.*

oyster /'ɔistər/ *n.* ostra *f.*

P

pace /peis/ *n.* **1.** paso *m.* —*v.* **2.** pasearse. **p. off,** medir a pasos.

pacific /pə'sɪfɪk/ *a.* pacífico.

Pacific Ocean Océano Pacífico *m.*

pacifier /'pæsə,faiər/ *n.* pacificador *m.*; (baby p.) chupete *m.*

pacifism /'pæsə,fizəm/ *n.* pacifismo *m.*

pacifist /'pæsəfist/ *n.* pacifista *m. & f.*

pacify /'pæsə,fai/ *v.* pacificar.

pack /pæk/ *n.* **1.** fardo; paquete

m.; (animals) muta *f.* **p. of cards,** baraja *f.* —*v.* **2.** empaquetar; (baggage) empacar.

package /'pækidʒ/ *n.* paquete, bulto *m.*

package tour viaje todo incluido *m.*

pact /pækt/ *n.* pacto *m.*

pad /pæd/ *n.* **1.** colchoncillo *m.* **p. of paper,** bloc de papel. —*v.* **2.** rellenar.

paddle /'pædl/ n. **1.** canalete m. —v. **2.** remar.

padlock /'pæd,lɒk/ n. candado m.

pagan /'peigən/ a. & n. pagano -na.

page /peidʒ/ n. página f.; (boy) paje m.

pageant /'pædʒənt/ n. espectáculo m.; procesión f.

pail /peil/ n. cubo m.

pain /pein/ n. dolor m. **to take pains,** esmerarse.

painful /'peinfəl/ a. doloroso; penoso.

pain killer /'pein,kɪlər/ analgésico m.

paint /peint/ n. **1.** pintura f. —v. **2.** pintar.

painter /'peintər/ n. pintor -ra.

painting /'peintiŋ/ n. pintura f.; cuadro m.

pair /pɛər/ n. **1.** par m.; pareja f. —v. **2.** parear. **p. off,** emparejarse.

pajamas /pə'dʒɑməz, -'dʒæməz/ n. pijama m.

palace /'pælis/ n. palacio m.

palatable /'pælətəbəl/ a. sabroso, agradable.

palate /'pælit/ n. paladar m.

palatial /pə'leiʃəl/ a. palaciego, suntuoso.

pale /peil/ a. pálido. **to turn pale,** palidecer.

paleness /'peilnis/ n. palidez f.

palette /'pælit/ n. paleta f.

pallbearer /'pɔl,bɛərər/ n. portador del féretro, portaféretro m.

pallid /'pælid/ a. pálido.

palm /pɑm/ n. palma f. **p. tree,** palmera f.

palpitate /'pælpi,teit/ v. palpitar.

paltry /'pɔltri/ a. miserable.

pamper /'pæmpər/ v. mimar.

pamphlet /'pæmflit/ n. folleto m.

pan /pæn/ n. cacerola f.

panacea /,pænə'siə/ n. panacea f.

Pan-American /,pænə'mɛrikən/ a. panamericano.

pane /pein/ n. hoja de vidrio f.; cuadro m.

panel /'pænl/ n. tablero m.

pang /pæŋ/ n. dolor; remordimiento m.

panic /'pænik/ n. pánico m.

panorama /,pænə'ræmə, -'rɑmə/ n. panorama m.

pant /pænt/ v. jadear.

panther /'pænθər/ n. pantera f.

pantomine /'pæntə,maim/ n. pantomima f.; mímica f.

pantry /'pæntri/ n. despensa f.

pants /pænts/ n. pantalones, m.pl.

panty hose /'pænti,houz/ n. pantys, pantimedias f.pl. (medias hasta la cintura).

papal /'peipəl/ a. papal.

paper /'peipər/ n. papel; periódico; artículo m.

paperback /'peipər,bæk/ n. libro en rústica m.

paper clip sujetapapeles m.

paper cup vaso de papel m.

paper hanger /'peipər,hæŋər/ empapelador -ra.

paper money papel moneda m.

paperweight /'peipər,weit/ n. pisapapeles m.

papier-mâché /,peipərmə'ʃei, pɑ,pyei-/ n. cartón piedra m.

paprika /pæ'prikə, pə-, pa-, 'pæprikə/ n. pimentón m.

par /pɑr/ n. paridad f.; Com. par f.

parable /'pærəbəl/ n. parábola f.

parachute /'pærə,ʃut/ n. paracaídas m.

parade /pə'reid/ n. **1.** desfile m.; procesión f. —v. **2.** desfilar.

paradise /'pærə,dais/ n. paraíso m.

paradox /'pærə,dɒks/ n. paradoja f.

paraffin /'pærəfin/ n. parafina f.

paragraph /'pærə,græf/ n. párrafo m.

parakeet /'pærə,kit/ n. perico m.

parallel /'pærə,lɛl/ a. **1.** paralelo. —v. **2.** correr parejas con.

paralysis /pə'ræləsis/ n. parálisis f.

paralyze /'pærə,laiz/ v. paralizar.

paramedic /,pærə'mɛdik/ n. paramédico -ca.

parameter /pə'ræmitər/ n. parámetro m.

paramount /'pærə,maunt/ a. supremo.

paraphrase /'pærə,freiz/ n. **1.** paráfrasis f. —v. **2.** parafrasear.

paraplegic /,pærə'plidʒik/ n. parapléjico -ca.

parasite /'pærə,sait/ n. parásito m.

parboil /'pɑr,bɔil/ v. sancochar.

parcel /'pɑrsəl/ n. paquete m. **p. of land,** lote de terreno.

parchment /'pɑrtʃmənt/ n. pergamino m.

pardon /'pɑrdn/ n. **1.** perdón m. —v. **2.** perdonar.

pare /pɛər/ v. pelar.

parentage /'pɛərəntɪdʒ, 'pær-/ n. origen m.; extracción f.

parenthesis /pə'rɛnθəsɪs/ n. paréntesis m.

parents /'pɛərənts/ n. padres m.pl.

parish /'pærɪʃ/ n. parroquia f.

Parisian /pə'rɪʒən, -'rɪʒən, -'rɪziən/ a. & n. parisiense m. & f.

parity /'pærɪti/ n. igualdad f., paridad f.

park /pɑrk/ n. **1.** parque m. —v. **2.** estacionar.

parking lot /'pɑrkɪŋ/ n. estacionamiento, aparcamiento m.

parking meter /'pɑrkɪŋ/ parquímetro m.

parking space /'pɑrkɪŋ/ estacionamiento, aparcamiento m.

parkway /'pɑrk,weɪ/ n. bulevar m.; autopista f.

parley /'pɑrli/ n. conferencia f.; Mil. parlamento m.

parliament /'pɑrləmənt/ n. parlamento m.

parliamentary /,pɑrlə'mɛntəri, -tri; sometimes ,pɑrlyə-/ a. parlamentario.

parlor /'pɑrlər/ n. sala f., salón m.

parochial /pə'roukiəl/ a. parroquial.

parody /'pærədi/ n. **1.** parodia f. —v. **2.** parodiar.

parole /pə'roul/ n. **1.** palabra de honor f.; Mil. santo y seña. —v. **2.** poner en libertad bajo palabra.

paroxysm /'pærək,sɪzəm/ n. paroxismo m.

parrot /'pærət/ n. loro, papagayo m.

parsimony /'pɑrsə,mouni/ n. parsimonia f.

parsley /'pɑrsli/ n. perejil m.

parson /'pɑrsən/ n. párroco m.

part /pɑrt/ n. **1.** parte f.; Theat. papel m. —v. **2.** separarse, partirse. **p. with,** desprenderse de.

partake /pɑr'teik/ v. tomar parte.

partial /'pɑrʃəl/ a. parcial.

participant /pɑr'tɪsəpənt/ n. participante m. & f.

participate /pɑr'tɪsə,peit/ v. participar.

participation /pɑr,tɪsə'peiʃən/ n. participación f.

participle /'pɑrtə,sɪpəl, -səpəl/ n. participio m.

particle /'pɑrtɪkəl/ n. partícula f.

particular /pər'tɪkyələr/ a. & n. particular m.

parting /'pɑrtɪŋ/ n. despedida f.

partisan /'pɑrtəzən, -sən/ a. & n. partidario -ria.

partition /pɑr'tɪʃən, pər-/ n. tabique m. v. dividir, partir.

partly /'pɑrtli/ adv. en parte.

partner /'pɑrtnər/ n. socio -cia; compañero -ra.

partridge /'pɑrtrɪdʒ/ n. perdiz f.

party /'pɑrti/ n. tertulia, fiesta f.; grupo m.; (political) partido m.

pass /pæs/ n. **1.** pase; (mountain) paso m. —v. **2.** pasar. **p. away,** fallecer.

passable /'pæsəbəl/ a. transitable; regular.

passage /'pæsɪdʒ/ n. pasaje; (corridor) pasillo m.

passé /pæ'sei/ a. anticuado.

passenger /'pæsəndʒər/ n. pasajero -ra.

passenger ship buque de pasajeros m.

passerby /'pæsər'bai/ n. transeúnte m. & f.

passion /'pæʃən/ n. pasión f.

passionate /'pæʃənit/ a. apasionado.

passive /'pæsɪv/ a. pasivo.

passport /'pæsport/ n. pasaporte m.

password /'pæs,wərd/ n. código m., clave m.; contraseña f.

past /pæst/ a. & n. **1.** pasado m. —prep. **2.** más allá de; después de.

paste /peist/ n. **1.** pasta f. —v. **2.** empastar; pegar.

pasteurize /'pæstʃə,raiz/ v. pasteurizar.

pastime /'pæs,taim/ n. pasatiempo m.; diversión f.

pastor /'pæstər/ n. pastor m.

pastrami /pə'strɑmi/ n. pastrón m.

pastry /'peistri/ n. pastelería f.

pasture /'pæstʃər/ n. **1.** pasto m.; pradera f. —v. **2.** pastar.

pat /pæt/ n. **1.** golpecillo m. **to stand p.,** mantenerse firme. —v. **2.** dar golpecitos.

patch /pætʃ/ n. **1.** remiendo m. —v. **2.** remendar.

patent /'pætnt/ a. & n. **1.** patente m. —v. **2.** patentar.

patent leather /'pætnt, 'pætn/ charol m.

paternal /pə'tɜrnl/ *a.* paterno, paternal.

paternity /pə'tɜrnɪti/ *n.* paternidad *f.*

path /pæθ/ *n.* senda *f.*

pathetic /pə'θetɪk/ *a.* patético.

pathology /pə'θɒlədʒi/ *n.* patología *f.*

pathos /'peɪθɒs/ *n.* rasgo conmovedor *m.*

patience /'peɪʃəns/ *n.* paciencia *f.*

patient /'peɪʃənt/ *a.* **1.** paciente. —*n.* **2.** enfermo -ma, paciente *m.* & *f.*

patio /'pæti,oʊ/ *n.* patio *m.*

patriarch /'peɪtri,ɑrk/ *n.* patriarca *m.*

patriot /'peɪtriət/ *n.* patriota *m.* & *f.*

patriotic /,peɪtri'ɒtɪk/ *a.* patriótico.

patriotism /'peɪtri,tɪzəm/ *n.* patriotismo *m.*

patrol /pə'troʊl/ *n.* **1.** patrulla *f.* —*v.* **2.** patrullar.

patrolman /pə'troʊlmən/ *n.* vigilante *m.*; patrullador *m.*

patron /'peɪtrən/ *n.* patrón *m.*

patronize /'peɪtrə,naɪz/ *v.* condescender; patrocinar; ser cliente de.

pattern /'pætərn/ *n.* modelo *m.*

pauper /'pɔpər/ *n.* indigente *m.* & *f.*

pause /pɔz/ *n.* **1.** pausa *f.* —*v.* **2.** pausar.

pave /peɪv/ *v.* pavimentar. **p. the way,** preparar el camino.

pavement /'peɪvmənt/ *n.* pavimento *m.*

pavilion /pə'vɪlyən/ *n.* pabellón *m.*

paw /pɔ/ *n.* **1.** pata *f.* —*v.* **2.** tear.

pawn /pɔn/ *n.* **1.** prenda *f.*; (chess) peón de ajedrez *m.* —*v.* **2.** empeñar.

pay /peɪ/ *n.* **1.** pago; sueldo, salario *m.*; —*v.* **2.** pagar. **p. back,** pagar; vengarse de. **p. cash,** pagar en metálico.

payee /peɪ'i/ *n.* destinatario -ria *m.* & *f.*

payment /'peɪmənt/ *n.* pago *m.*; recompensa *f.*

pay phone teléfono público *m.*

pea /pi/ *n.* guisante *m.*

peace /pis/ *n.* paz *f.*

peaceable /'pisəbəl/ *a.* pacífico.

peaceful /'pisfəl/ *a.* tranquilo.

peach /pitʃ/ *n.* durazno, melocotón *m.*

peacock /'pi,kɒk/ *n.* pavo real *m.*

peak /pik/ *n.* pico, cumbre; máximo *m.*

peal /pil/ *n.* repique; estruendo *m.* **p. of laughter,** risotada *f.*

peanut /'pi,nʌt/ *n.* maní, cacahuete *m.*

pear /pɛər/ *n.* pera *f.*

pearl /pɜrl/ *n.* perla *f.*

peasant /'pɛzənt/ *n.* campesino -na.

pebble /'pɛbəl/ *n.* guija *f.*

peck /pɛk/ *n.* **1.** picotazo. —*v.* **2.** picotear.

peckish /'pɛkɪʃ/ *a.* tener un poco de hambre.

peculiar /pɪ'kyulyər/ *a.* peculiar.

pecuniary /pɪ'kyuni,ɛri/ *a.* pecuniario.

pedagogue /'pɛdə,gɒg/ *n.* pedagogo -ga.

pedagogy /'pɛdə,goʊdʒi, -,gɒdʒi/ *n.* pedagogía *f.*

pedal /'pɛdl/ *n.* pedal *m.*

pedant /'pɛdnt/ *n.* pedante *m.* & *f.*

peddler /'pɛdlər/ *n.* buhonero *m.*

pedestal /'pɛdəstl/ *n.* pedestal *m.*

pedestrian /pə'dɛstriən/ *n.* peatón *m.*

pedestrian crossing paso de peatones *m.*

pediatrician /,pidiə'trɪʃən/ *n.* pediatra *m.* & *f.*

pediatrics /,pidi'ætrɪks/ *n.* puericultura *f.*

pedigree /'pɛdɪ,gri/ *n.* genealogía *f.*

peek /pik/ *n.* **1.** atisbo *m.* —*v.* **2.** atisbar.

peel /pil/ *n.* **1.** corteza *f.*; (fruit) pellejo *m.* —*v.* **2.** descortezar; pelar.

peep /pip/ *n.* **1.** ojeada *f.* —*v.* **2.** mirar, atisbar.

peer /pɪər/ *n.* **1.** par *m.* —*v.* **2.** mirar fijamente.

peg /pɛg/ *n.* clavija; estaquilla *f.*; gancho *m.*

pelt /pɛlt/ *n.* **1.** pellejo *m.* —*v.* **2.** apedrear; (rain) caer con fuerza.

pelvis /'pɛlvɪs/ *n.* pelvis *f.*

pen /pɛn/ *n.* pluma *f.*; corral *m.* **fountain p.,** pluma fuente.

penalty /'pɛnlti/ *n.* pena; multa *f.*; castigo *m.*

penance /'pɛnəns/ *n.* penitencia *f.* **to do p.,** penar.

penchant /'pentʃənt/ n. propensión f.

pencil /'pensəl/ n. lápiz m.

pencil sharpener /'ʃɑrpənər/ sacapuntas m.

pending /'pendɪŋ/ a. pendiente.
to be p., pender.

penetrate /'peni,treit/ v. penetrar.

penetration /,peni'treiʃən/ n. penetración f.

penicillin /,penə'sılın/ n. penicilina f.

peninsula /pə'nınsələ, -'nınsyələ/ n. península f.

penitent /'penitənt/ n. & a. penitente m. & f.

penknife /'pen,naif/ n. cortaplumas f.

penniless /'penɪlɪs/ a. indigente.

penny /'peni/ n. penique m.

pension /'penʃən/ n. pensión f.

pensive /'pensiv/ a. pensativo.

penultimate /pɪ'nʌltəmɪt/ a. penúltimo.

penury /'penyəri/ n. penuria f.

people /'pipəl/ n. **1.** gente f.; (of a nation) pueblo m. —v. **2.** poblar.

pepper /'pepər/ n. pimienta f.; (plant) pimiento m.

per /pər; unstressed pər/ prep. por.

perambulator /pər'æmbyə,leitər/ n. cochecillo de niño m.

perceive /pər'siv/ v. percibir.

percent /pər'sent/ adv. por ciento.

percentage /pər'sentɪdʒ/ n. porcentaje m.

perceptible /pər'septəbəl/ a. perceptible.

perception /pər'sepʃən/ n. percepción f.

perch /pɜrtʃ/ n. percha f.; (fish) perca f.

perdition /pər'dɪʃən/ n. perdición f.

peremptory /pə'remptəri/ a. perentorio, terminante.

perennial /pə'reniəl/ a. perenne.

perfect /a. 'pɜrfɪkt; v. pər'fekt/ a. **1.** perfecto. —v. **2.** perfeccionar.

perfection /pər'fekʃən/ n. perfección f.

perfectionist /pər'fekʃənɪst/ a. & n. perfeccionista m. & f.

perforation /,pɜrfə'reiʃən/ n. perforación f.

perform /pər'fɔrm/ v. hacer; ejecutar; Theat. representar.

performance /pər'fɔrməns/ n. ejecución f.; Theat. representación f.

perfume /n. 'pɜrfyum; v. pər'fyum/ n. **1.** perfume m.; fragancia f. —v. **2.** perfumar.

perfunctory /pər'fʌŋktəri/ a. perfunctorio, superficial.

perhaps /pər'hæps/ adv. quizá, quizás, tal vez.

peril /'perəl/ n. peligro m.

perilous /'perələs/ a. peligroso.

perimeter /pə'rɪmɪtər/ n. perímetro m.

period /'pɪəriəd/ n. período m.; Punct. punto m.

periodic /,pɪəri'ɒdɪk/ a. periódico.

periodical /,pɪəri'ɒdɪkəl/ n. revista f.

periphery /pə'rɪfəri/ n. periferia f.

perish /'perɪʃ/ v. perecer.

perishable /'perɪʃəbəl/ a. perecedero.

perjury /'pɜrdʒəri/ n. perjurio m.

permanent /'pɜrmənənt/ a. permanente. **p. wave,** ondulado permanente.

permeate /'pɜrmi,eit/ v. penetrar.

permissible /pər'mɪsəbəl/ a. permisible.

permission /pər'mɪʃən/ n. permiso m.

permit /n. 'pɜrmɪt; v. pər'mɪt/ n. **1.** permiso m. —v. **2.** permitir.

pernicious /pər'nɪʃəs/ a. pernicioso.

perpendicular /,pɜrpən'dɪkyələr/ n. & a. perpendicular f.

perpetrate /'pɜrpɪ,treit/ v. perpetrar.

perpetual /pər'petʃuəl/ a. perpetuo.

perplex /pər'pleks/ v. confundir.

perplexity /pər'pleksɪti/ n. perplejidad f.

persecute /'pɜrsɪ,kyut/ v. perseguir.

persecution /,pɜrsɪ'kyuʃən/ n. persecución f.

perseverance /,pɜrsə'vɪərəns/ n. perseverancia f.

persevere /,pɜrsə'vɪər/ v. perseverar.

persist /pər'sɪst/ v. persistir.

persistent /pər'sɪstənt/ a. persistente.

person /'pɜrsən/ n. persona f.

personage /'pɜrsənɪdʒ/ n. personaje m.

personal /'pɜrsənəl/ a. personal.

personality /,pɜrsə'nælɪti/ n. personalidad f.

personnel /,pɜrsə'nɛl/ *n.* personal *m.*

perspective /pər'spɛktɪv/ *n.* perspectiva *f.*

perspiration /'pɜrspə'reɪʃən/ *n.* sudor *m.*

perspire /pər'spaɪər/ *v.* sudar.

persuade /pər'sweɪd/ *v.* persuadir.

persuasive /pər'sweɪsɪv/ *a.* persuasivo.

pertain /pər'teɪn/ *v.* pertenecer.

pertinent /'pɜrtnənt/ *a.* pertinente.

perturb /pər'tɜrb/ *v.* perturbar.

peruse /pə'ruz/ *v.* leer con cuidado.

pervade /pər'veɪd/ *v.* penetrar; llenar.

perverse /pər'vɜrs/ *a.* perverso.

perversion /pər'vɜrʒən/ *n.* perversión *f.*

pessimism /'pɛsə,mɪzəm/ *n.* pesimismo *m.*

pester /'pɛstər/ *v.* molestar; fastidiar.

pesticide /'pɛstə,saɪd/ *n.* pesticida *m.*

pestilence /'pɛstləns/ *n.* pestilencia *f.*

pet /pɛt/ *n.* **1.** favorito -ta.; animal doméstico *m.* —*v.* **2.** mimar.

petal /'pɛtl/ *n.* pétalo *m.*

petition /pə'tɪʃən/ *n.* **1.** petición, súplica *f.* —*v.* **2.** pedir, suplicar.

petrify /'pɛtrə,faɪ/ *v.* petrificar.

petroleum /pə'troʊliəm/ *n.* petróleo *m.*

petticoat /'pɛti,koʊt/ *n.* enagua *f.*

petty /'pɛti/ *a.* mezquino, insignificante.

petulant /'pɛtʃələnt/ *a.* quisquilloso.

pew /pyu/ *n.* banco de iglesia *m.*

pewter /'pyutər/ *n.* peltre *m.*

phantom /'fæntəm/ *n.* espectro, fantasma *m.*

pharmacist /'fɑrməsɪst/ *n.* farmacéutico *m.*, boticario -ria.

pharmacy /'fɑrməsi/ *n.* farmacia, botica *f.*

phase /feɪz/ *n.* fase *f.*

pheasant /'fɛzənt/ *n.* faisán *m.*

phenomenal /fɪ'nɒmənl/ *a.* fenomenal.

phenomenon /fɪ'nɒmə,nɒn/ *n.* fenómeno *f.*

philanthropy /fɪ'lænθrəpi/ *n.* filantropía *f.*

philately /fɪ'lætli/ *n.* filatelia *f.*

philosopher /fɪ'lɒsəfər/ *n.* filósofo -fa.

philosophical /,fɪlə'sɒfɪkəl/ *a.* filosófico.

philosophy /fɪ'lɒsəfi/ *n.* filosofía *f.*

phlegm /flɛm/ *n.* flema *f.*

phlegmatic /flɛg'mætɪk/ *a.* flemático.

phobia /'foʊbiə/ *n.* fobia *f.*

phone /foʊn/ *n.* teléfono *m.*

phonetic /fə'nɛtɪk/ *a.* fonético.

phonograph /'foʊnə,græf/ *n.* fonógrafo *m.*

phosphorus /'fɒsfərəs/ *n.* fósforo *m.*

photocopier /'foʊtə,kɒpiər/ *n.* fotocopiadora *f.*

photocopy /'foʊtə,kɒpi/ *n.* **1.** fotocopia *f.* —*v.* **2.** fotocopiar.

photoelectric /,foʊtoʊɪ'lɛktrɪk/ *a.* fotoeléctrico.

photogenic /,foʊtə'dʒɛnɪk/ *a.* fotogénico.

photograph /'foʊtə,græf/ *n.* **1.** fotografía *f.* —*v.* **2.** fotografiar; retratar.

photography /fə'tɒgrəfi/ *n.* fotografía *f.*

phrase /freɪz/ *n.* **1.** frase *f.* —*v.* **2.** expresar.

physical /'fɪzɪkəl/ *a.* físico.

physician /fɪ'zɪʃən/ *n.* médico *m.* & *f.*

physics /'fɪzɪks/ *n.* física *f.*

physiology /,fɪzi'ɒlədʒi/ *n.* fisiología *f.*

physiotherapy /,fɪzioʊ'θerəpi/ *n.* fisioterapia *f.*

physique /fɪ'zik/ *n.* físico *m.*

pianist /pi'ænɪst, 'piənɪst/ *n.* pianista *m.* & *f.*

piano /pi'ænoʊ/ *n.* piano *m.*

picayune /,pɪkə'yun/ *a.* insignificante.

piccolo /'pɪkə,loʊ/ *n.* flautín *m.*

pick /pɪk/ *n.* **1.** pico *m.* —*v.* **2.** escoger. **p. up,** recoger.

picket /'pɪkɪt/ *n.* piquete *m.*

pickle /'pɪkəl/ *n.* **1.** salmuera *f.*; encurtido *m.* —*v.* **2.** escabechar.

pickpocket /'pɪk,pɒkɪt/ *n.* cortabolsas *m.* & *f.*

picnic /'pɪknɪk/ *n.* picnic *m.*

picture /'pɪktʃər/ *n.* **1.** cuadro; retrato *m.*; fotografía *f.*; (movie) película *f.* —*v.* **2.** imaginarse.

picturesque /,pɪktʃə'rɛsk/ *a.* pintoresco.

pie /paɪ/ *n.* pastel *m.*

piece /pis/ n. pedazo m.; pieza f.

pieceworker /'pis,wɜrkər/ n. destajero -ra, destajista m. & f.

pier /piər/ n. muelle m.

pierce /piərs/ v. perforar; pinchar; traspasar.

piety /'paiiti/ n. piedad f.

pig /pig/ n. puerco, cerdo, lechón m.

pigeon /'pidʒən/ n. paloma f.

pigeonhole /'pidʒən,houl/ n. casilla f.

pigment /'pigmənt/ n. pigmento m.

pile /pail/ n. **1.** pila f.; montón m.; Med. hemorroides f.pl. —v. **2.** amontonar.

pilfer /'pilfər/ v. ratear.

pilgrim /'pilgrim/ n. peregrino -na, romero -ra.

pilgrimage /'pilgrəmidʒ/ n. romería f.

pill /pil/ n. píldora f.

pillage /'pilidʒ/ n. **1.** pillaje m. —v. **2.** pillar.

pillar /'pilər/ n. columna f.

pillow /'pilou/ n. almohada f.

pillowcase /'pilou,keis/ n. funda de almohada f.

pilot /'pailət/ n. **1.** piloto m. & f. —v. **2.** pilotar.

pimple /'pimpəl/ n. grano m.

pin /pin/ n. alfiler; broche m.; Mech. clavija f. —v. **2.** prender. **p. up,** fijar.

pinafore /'pinə,fɔr/ n. delantal (de niña) m.

pinch /pintʃ/ n. **1.** pellizco m. —v. **2.** pellizcar.

pine /pain/ n. pino m. —v. **2.** **p. away,** languidecer. **p. for,** anhelar.

pineapple /'pai,næpəl/ n. piña f., ananás m.pl.

pink /piŋk/ a. rosado.

pinky /'piŋki/ n. meñique m.

pinnacle /'pinəkəl/ n. pináculo m.; cumbre f.

pint /paint/ n. pinta f.

pioneer /,paiə'niər/ n. pionero -ra.

pious /'paiəs/ a. piadoso.

pipe /paip/ n. pipa f.; tubo; (of organ) cañón m.

pipeline /'paip,lain/ n. oleoducto m.

piper /'paipər/ n. flautista m. & f.

piquant /'pikənt/ a. picante.

pirate /'pairət/ n. pirata m.

pistol /'pistl/ n. pistola f.

piston /'pistən/ n. émbolo, pistón m.

pit /pit/ n. hoyo m.; (fruit) hueso m.

pitch /pitʃ/ n. **1.** brea f.; grado de inclinación; (music) tono m.; —v. **2.** lanzar; (ship) cabecear.

pitchblende /'pitʃ,blend/ n. pechblenda f.

pitcher /'pitʃər/ n. cántaro m.; (baseball) lanzador -ra.

pitchfork /'pitʃ,fɔrk/ n. horca f.; tridente m.

pitfall /'pit,fɔl/ n. trampa f., hoya cubierta f.

pitiful /'pitifəl/ a. lastimoso.

pitiless /'pitilis/ a. cruel.

pituitary gland /pi'tui,teri/ glándula pituitaria f.

pity /'piti/ n. **1.** compasión, piedad f. **to be a p.,** ser lástima. —v. **2.** compadecer.

pivot /'pivət/ n. **1.** espiga f., pivote m.; punto de partida m. —v. **2.** girar sobre un pivote.

pizza /'pitsə/ n. pizza f.

placard /'plækard/ n. **1.** cartel m. —v. **2.** fijar carteles.

placate /'pleikeit/ v. aplacar.

place /pleis/ n. **1.** lugar, sitio, puesto m. —v. **2.** colocar, poner.

placid /'plæsid/ a. plácido.

plagiarism /'pleidʒə,rizəm/ n. plagio m.

plague /pleig/ n. **1.** plaga, peste f. —v. **2.** atormentar.

plain /plein/ a. **1.** sencillo; puro; evidente. —n. **2.** llano m.

plaintiff /'pleintif/ n. demandante m. & f.

plan /plæn/ n. **1.** plan, propósito m. —v. **2.** planear; planear; planificar. **p. on,** contar con.

plane /plein/ n. **1.** plano; (tool) cepillo m. —v. **2.** allanar; acepillar.

planet /'plænit/ n. planeta m.

planetarium /,plæni'teəriəm/ n. planetario m.

plank /plæŋk/ n. tablón m.

planning /'plæniŋ/ n. planificación f.

plant /plænt/ n. **1.** mata, planta f. —v. **2.** sembrar, plantar.

plantation /plæn'teiʃən/ n. plantación f. **coffee p.,** cafetal m.

planter /'plæntər/ n. plantador m.; hacendado m.

plasma /'plæzmə/ n. plasma m.

plaster /'plæstər/ n. **1.** yeso; emplasto *m.* —*v.* **2.** enyesar; emplastar.

plastic /'plæstɪk/ *a.* plástico.

plate /pleɪt/ *n.* **1.** plato *m.*; plancha de metal. —*v.* **2.** planchear.

plateau /plæ'tou/ *n.* meseta *f.*

platform /'plætfɔrm/ *n.* plataforma *f.*

platinum /'plætnəm/ *n.* platino *m.*

platitude /'plætɪ,tud/ *n.* perogrullada *f.*

platter /'plætər/ *n.* fuente *f.*, platel *m.*

plaudit /'plɔdɪt/ *n.* aplauso *m.*

plausible /'plɔzəbəl/ *a.* plausible.

play /pleɪ/ *n.* **1.** juego *m.*; *Theat.* pieza *f.* —*v.* **2.** jugar; (music) tocar; *Theat.* representar. **p. a part,** hacer un papel.

player /'pleɪər/ *n.* jugador -ra; (music) músico -ca.; *Theat.* actor *m.*, actriz *f.*

playful /'pleɪfəl/ *a.* juguetón.

playground /'pleɪ,graund/ *n.* campo de deportes; patio de recreo.

playmate /'pleɪ,meɪt/ *n.* compañero -ra de juego.

playwright /'pleɪ,raɪt/ *n.* dramaturgo -ga.

plea /pli/ *n.* ruego *m.*; súplica *f.*; (legal) declaración *f.*

plead /plid/ *v.* suplicar; declararse. **p. a case,** defender un pleito.

pleasant /'plɛzənt/ *a.* agradable.

please /pliz/ *v.* gustar, agradar. **Pleased to meet you,** Mucho gusto en conocer a Vd. —*adv.* **2.** por favor. **Please...** Haga el favor de..., Tenga la bondad de..., Sírvase...

pleasure /'plɛʒər/ *n.* gusto, placer *m.*

pleat /plit/ *n.* **1.** pliegue *m.* —*v.* **2.** plegar.

plebiscite /'plɛbə,saɪt/ *n.* plebiscito *m.*

pledge /plɛdʒ/ *n.* **1.** empeño *f.* —*v.* **2.** empeñar.

plentiful /'plɛntɪfəl/ *a.* abundante.

plenty /'plɛnti/ *n.* abundancia *f.* **p. of,** bastante. **p. more,** mucho más.

pleurisy /'plʊrəsi/ *n.* pleuritis *f.*

pliable /'plaɪəbəl/ **pliant** /'plaɪənt/ *a.* flexible.

pliers /'plaɪərz/ *n.pl.* alicates *m.pl.*

plight /plaɪt/ *n.* apuro, aprieto *m.*

plot /plɒt/ *n.* **1.** conspiración; (of

a story) trama; (of land) parcela *f.* —*v.* **2.** conspirar; tramar.

plow /plau/ *n.* **1.** arado *m.* —*v.* **2.** arar.

pluck /plʌk/ *n.* **1.** valor *m.* —*v.* **2.** arrancar; desplumar.

plug /plʌg/ *n.* **1.** tapón; *Elec.* enchufe *m.* **spark plug,** bujía *f.* —*v.* **2.** tapar.

plum /plʌm/ *n.* ciruela *f.*

plumage /'plumɪdʒ/ *n.* plumaje *m.*

plumber /'plʌmər/ *n.* fontanero -era, plomero -era.

plume /plum/ *n.* pluma *f.*

plump /plʌmp/ *a.* regordete.

plunder /'plʌndər/ *n.* **1.** botín *m.*; despojos *m.pl.* —*v.* **2.** saquear.

plunge /plʌndʒ/ *v.* zambullir; precipitar.

plural /'plʊrəl/ *a. & n.* plural *m.*

plus /plʌs/ *prep.* más.

plutocrat /'plutə,kræt/ *n.* plutócrata *m. & f.*

pneumatic /nʊ'mætɪk/ *a.* neumático.

pneumonia /nʊ'mounyə/ *n.* pulmonía *f.*

poach /poutʃ/ *v.* (eggs) escalfar; invadir; cazar en vedado.

pocket /'pɒkɪt/ *n.* **1.** bolsillo *m.* —*v.* **2.** embolsar.

pocketbook /'pɒkɪt,bʊk/ *n.* cartera *f.*

podiatry /pə'daɪətri/ *n.* podiatría *f.*

poem /'pouəm/ *n.* poema *m.*

poet /'pouɪt/ *n.* poeta *m. & f.*

poetic /pou'ɛtɪk/ *a.* poético.

poetry /'pouɪtri/ *n.* poesía *f.*

poignant /'pɔɪnyənt/ *a.* conmovedor.

point /pɔɪnt/ *n.* **1.** punta *f.*; punto *m.* —*v.* **2.** apuntar. **p. out,** señalar.

pointed /'pɔɪntɪd/ *a.* puntiagudo; directo.

pointless /'pɔɪntlɪs/ *a.* inútil.

poise /pɔɪz/ *n.* **1.** equilibrio *m.*; serenidad *f.* —*v.* **2.** equilibrar; estar suspendido.

poison /'pɔɪzən/ *n.* **1.** veneno *m.* —*v.* **2.** envenenar.

poisonous /'pɔɪzənəs/ *a.* venenoso.

poke /pouk/ *n.* **1.** empuje *m.*, hurgonada *f.* —*v.* **2.** picar; haronear.

Poland /'poulənd/ *n.* Polonia *f.*

polar /'poulər/ *a.* polar.

pole /poul/ *n.* palo *m.*; *Geog.* polo *m.*

polemical /pə'lɛmɪkəl/ *a.* polémico.

police /pə'lis/ *n.* policía *f.*

policeman /pə'lismən/ *n.* policía *m.*

policy /'pɒləsi/ *n.* política *f.* **insurance p.,** póliza de seguro.

Polish /'pɒlɪʃ/ *a. & n.* polaco -ca.

polish /'pɒlɪʃ/ *n.* **1.** lustre *m.* —*v.* **2.** pulir, lustrar.

polite /pə'laɪt/ *a.* cortés.

politic /'pɒlɪtɪk/ **political** *a.* político.

politician /ˌpɒlɪ'tɪʃən/ *n.* político -ca.

politics /'pɒlɪtɪks/ *n.* política *f.*

poll /poul/ *n.* encuesta *f.;* (pl.) urnas *f.pl.*

pollen /'pɒlən/ *n.* polen *m.*

pollute /pə'lut/ *v.* contaminar.

pollution /pə'luʃən/ *n.* contaminación *f.*

polo /'poulou/ *n.* polo *m.*

polyester /ˌpɒli'ɛstər/ *n.* poliéster *m.*

polygamy /pə'lɪgəmi/ *n.* poligamia *f.*

polygon /'pɒliˌgɒn/ *n.* polígono *m.*

pomp /pɒmp/ *n.* pompa *f.*

pompous /'pɒmpəs/ *a.* pomposo.

poncho /'pɒntʃou/ *n.* poncho *m.*

pond /pɒnd/ *n.* charca *f.*

ponder /'pɒndər/ *v.* ponderar, meditar.

ponderous /'pɒndərəs/ *a.* ponderoso, pesado.

pontiff /'pɒntɪf/ *n.* pontífice *m.*

pontoon /pɒn'tun/ *n.* pontón *m.*

pony /'pouni/ *n.* caballito *m.*

ponytail /'pouniˌteil/ *n.* cola de caballo *f.*

poodle /'pudl/ *n.* caniche *m.*

pool /pul/ *n.* charco *m.* **swimming p.,** piscina *f.*

poor /pur/ *a.* pobre; (not good) malo.

pop /pɒp/ *n.* chasquido *m.*

popcorn /'pɒpˌkɔrn/ *n.* rosetas de maíz, palomitas de maíz *f.pl.*

pope /poup/ *n.* papa *m.*

poppy /'pɒpi/ *n.* amapola *f.*

popsicle /'pɒpsɪkəl/ *n.* polo *m.*

popular /'pɒpyələr/ *a.* popular.

popularity /ˌpɒpyə'lærɪti/ *n.* popularidad *f.*

population /ˌpɒpyə'leɪʃən/ *n.* población *f.*

porcelain /'pɔrsəlɪn/ *n.* porcelana *f.*

porch /pɔrtʃ/ *n.* pórtico *m.;* galería *f.*

pore /pɔr/ *n.* poro *m.*

pork /pɔrk/ *n.* carne de puerco.

pornography /pɔr'nɒgrəfi/ *n.* pornografía *f.*

porous /'pɔrəs/ *a.* poroso, esponjoso.

port /pɔrt/ *n.* puerto; *Naut.* babor *m.* **p. wine,** oporto *m.*

portable /'pɔrtəbəl/ *a.* portátil.

portal /'pɔrtl/ *n.* portal *m.*

portend /pɔr'tɛnd/ *v.* pronosticar.

portent /'pɔrtɛnt/ *n.* presagio *m.,* portento *m.*

porter /'pɔrtər/ *n.* portero *m.*

portfolio /pɔrt'fouliˌou/ *n.* cartera *f.*

porthole /'pɔrtˌhoul/ *n.* porta *f.*

portion /'pɔrʃən/ *n.* porción *f.*

portly /'pɔrtli/ *a.* corpulento.

portrait /'pɔrtrɪt/ *n.* retrato *m.*

portray /pɔr'trei/ *v.* pintar.

Portugal /'pɔrtʃəgəl/ *n.* Portugal *m.*

Portuguese /ˌpɔrtʃə'giz/ *a. & n.* portugués -esa.

pose /pouz/ *n.* **1.** postura; actitud *f.* —*v.* **2.** posar. **p. as,** pretender ser.

position /pə'zɪʃən/ *n.* posición *f.*

positive /'pɒzɪtɪv/ *a.* positivo.

possess /pə'zɛs/ *v.* poseer.

possession /pə'zɛʃən/ *n.* posesión *f.*

possessive /pə'zɛsɪv/ *a.* posesivo.

possibility /ˌpɒsə'bɪlɪti/ *n.* posibilidad *f.*

possible /'pɒsəbəl/ *a.* posible.

post /poust/ *n.* **1.** poste; puesto *m.* —*v.* **2.** fijar; situar; echar al correo.

postage /'poustɪdʒ/ *n.* porte de correo. **p. stamp,** sello *m.*

postal /'poustl/ *a.* postal.

post card tarjeta postal.

poster /'poustər/ *n.* cartel, letrero *m.*

posterior /pɒ'stɪəriər/ *a.* posterior.

posterity /pɒ'stɛrɪti/ *n.* posteridad *f.*

postgraduate /poust'grædʒuɪt/ *a. & n.* postgraduado -da.

postmark /'poustˌmɑrk/ *n.* matasellos *m.*

post office correos *m.pl.*

postpone /poust'poun/ *v.* posponer, aplazar.

postscript /'poust,skrɪpt/ n. posdata f.

posture /'pɒstʃər/ n. postura f.

pot /pɒt/ n. olla, marmita; (marijuana) hierba f.
flower p., tiesto, m.

potassium /pə'tæsɪəm/ n. potasio m.

potato /pə'teɪtou/ n. patata, papa f. **sweet p.,** batata f.

potent /'poutn̩t/ a. potente, poderoso.

potential /pə'tɛnʃəl/ a. & n. potencial f.

potion /'pouʃən/ n. poción, pócima f.

pottery /'pɒtəri/ n. alfarería f.

pouch /pautʃ/ n. saco m.; bolsa f.

poultry /'poultri/ n. aves de corral.

pound /paund/ n. **1.** libra f. —v. **2.** golpear.

pour /pɔr/ v. echar; verter; llover a cántaros.

poverty /'pɒvərti/ n. pobreza f.

powder /'paudər/ n. **1.** polvo m.; (gun) pólvora f. —v. **2.** empolvar; pulverizar.

power /'pauər/ n. poder m.; potencia f.

powerful /'pauərfəl/ a. poderoso, fuerte.

powerless /'pauərlɪs/ a. impotente.

practical /'præktɪkəl/ a. práctico.

practical joke inocentada f.

practically /'præktɪkli/ adv. casi; prácticamente.

practice /'præktɪs/ n. **1.** práctica f.; costumbre; clientela f. —v. **2.** practicar; ejercer.

practiced /'præktɪst/ a. experto.

practitioner /præk'tɪʃənər/ n. practicante m. & f.

pragmatic /præg'mætɪk/ a. pragmático.

prairie /'prɛəri/ n. llanura; S.A. pampa f.

praise /preiz/ n. **1.** alabanza f. —v. **2.** alabar.

prank /præŋk/ n. travesura f.

prawn /prɔn/ n. gamba f.

pray /prei/ v. rezar; (beg) rogar.

prayer /'preiər/ n. oración; súplica f., ruego m.

preach /pritʃ/ v. predicar; sermonear.

preacher /'pritʃər/ n. predicador m.

preamble /'pri,æmbəl/ n. preámbulo m.

precarious /prɪ'kɛəriəs/ a. precario.

precaution /prɪ'kɔʃən/ n. precaución f.

precede /prɪ'sid/ v. preceder, anteceder.

precedent /n. 'prɛsɪdənt/, a. prɪ'sidn̩t/ n. & a. precedente m.

precept /'prisɛpt/ n. precepto m.

precinct /'prisɪŋkt/ n. recinto m.

precious /'prɛʃəs/ a. precioso.

precipice /'prɛsəpɪs/ n. precipicio m.

precipitate /prɪ'sɪpɪ,teɪt/ v. precipitar.

precise /prɪ'sais/ a. preciso, exacto.

precision /prɪ'sɪʒən/ n. precisión f.

preclude /prɪ'klud/ v. evitar.

precocious /prɪ'kouʃəs/ a. precoz.

precooked /pri'kukt/ a. precocinado.

predatory /'prɛdə,tɔri/ a. de rapiña, rapaz.

predecessor /'prɛdə,sɛsər/ n. predecesor -ra, antecesor -ra.

predicament /prɪ'dɪkəmənt/ n. dificultad f.; apuro m.

predict /prɪ'dɪkt/ v. pronosticar, predecir.

predictable /prɪ'dɪktəbəl/ a. previsible.

predilection /,prɛdl̩'ɛkʃən/ n. predilección f.

predispose /,pridɪ'spouz/ v. predisponer.

predominant /prɪ'dɒmənənt/ a. predominante.

prefabricate /pri'fæbrɪ,keit/ v. fabricar de antemano.

preface /'prɛfɪs/ n. prefacio m.

prefer /prɪ'fɜr/ v. preferir.

preferable /'prɛfərəbəl/ a. preferible.

preference /'prɛfərəns/ n. preferencia f.

prefix /'prifɪks/ n. **1.** prefijo m. —v. **2.** prefijar.

pregnant /'prɛgnənt/ a. preñada.

prehistoric /,prihɪ'stɔrɪk/ a. prehistórico.

prejudice /'prɛdʒədɪs/ n. prejuicio m.

prejudiced /'prɛdʒədɪst/ a. (S.A.) prejuiciado.

preliminary /prɪ'lɪmə,nɛri/ a. preliminar.

print

prelude /ˈprɛljud/ n. preludio m.

premature /ˌprɪməˈtʃʊr/ a. prematuro.

premeditate /prɪˈmɛdɪˌteɪt/ v. premeditar.

premier /prɪˈmɪər/ n. primer ministro.

première /prɪˈmɪər/ n. estreno m.

premise /ˈprɛmɪs/ n. premisa f.

premium /ˈprimiəm/ n. premio m.

premonition /ˌprɛməˈnɪʃən/ n. presentimiento m.

prenatal /prɪˈneɪtl/ a. prenatal.

preparation /ˌprɛpəˈreɪʃən/ n. preparativo m.; preparación f.

preparatory /prɪˈpærəˌtɔri/ a. preparatorio. p. to, antes de.

prepare /prɪˈpɛər/ v. preparar.

preponderant /prɪˈpɒndərənt/ a. preponderante.

preposition /ˌprɛpəˈzɪʃən/ n. preposición f.

preposterous /prɪˈpɒstərəs/ a. prepóstero, absurdo.

prerequisite /prɪˈrɛkwəzɪt/ n. requisito previo.

prerogative /prɪˈrɒgətɪv/ n. prerrogativa f.

prescribe /prɪˈskraɪb/ v. prescribir; Med. recetar.

prescription /prɪˈskrɪpʃən/ n. prescripción f.; Med. receta f.

presence /ˈprɛzəns/ n. presencia f.; porte m.

present /a, n ˈprɛzənt; v prɪˈzɛnt/ a. 1. presente. to be present at, asistir a. —n. 2. presente; (gift) regalo m. at p., ahora, actualmente. for the p., por ahora. —v. 3. presentar.

presentable /prɪˈzɛntəbəl/ a. presentable.

presentation /ˌprɛzənˈteɪʃən/ n. presentación f.; introducción f.; Theat. representación f.

presently /ˈprɛzəntli/ adv. luego; dentro de poco.

preservative /prɪˈzɜrvətɪv/ a. & n. preservativo m.

preserve /prɪˈzɜrv/ n. 1. conserva f.; (hunting) vedado m. —v. 2. preservar.

preside /prɪˈzaɪd/ v. presidir.

presidency /ˈprɛzɪdənsi/ n. presidencia f.

president /ˈprɛzɪdənt/ n. presidente -ta.

press /prɛs/ n. 1. prensa f. —v. 2. apretar; urgir; (clothes) planchar.

pressing /ˈprɛsɪŋ/ a. urgente.

pressure /ˈprɛʃər/ n. presión f.

pressure cooker /ˈkʊkər/ cocina de presión f.

prestige /prɛˈstiʒ/ n. prestigio m.

presume /prɪˈzum/ v. presumir, suponer.

presumptuous /prɪˈzʌmptʃuəs/ a. presuntuoso.

presuppose /ˌprisəˈpouz/ v. presuponer.

pretend /prɪˈtɛnd/ v. fingir. p. to the throne, aspirar al trono.

pretense /prɪˈtɛns, ˈpritɛns/ n. pretensión f.; fingimiento m.

pretension /prɪˈtɛnʃən/ n. pretensión f.

pretentious /prɪˈtɛnʃəs/ a. presumido.

pretext /ˈpritɛkst/ n. pretexto m.

pretty /ˈprɪti/ a. 1. bonito, lindo. —adv. 2. bastante.

prevail /prɪˈveɪl/ v. prevalecer.

prevailing /prɪˈveɪlɪŋ/ prevalent a. predominante.

prevalent /ˈprɛvələnt/ a. predominante.

prevent /prɪˈvɛnt/ v. impedir; evitar.

prevention /prɪˈvɛnʃən/ n. prevención f.

preventive /prɪˈvɛntɪv/ a. preventivo.

preview /ˈpriˌvyu/ n. vista anticipada f.

previous /ˈpriviəs/ a. anterior, previo.

prey /preɪ/ n. presa f.

price /praɪs/ n. precio m.

priceless /ˈpraɪslɪs/ a. sin precio.

prick /prɪk/ n. 1. punzada f. —v. 2. punzar.

pride /praɪd/ n. orgullo m.

priest /prist/ n. sacerdote, cura m.

prim /prɪm/ a. estirado, remilgado.

primary /ˈpraɪmɛri/ a. primario, principal.

prime /praɪm/ a. 1. primero. —n. 2. flor f. —v. 3. alistar.

prime minister primer ministro m. & f.

primitive /ˈprɪmɪtɪv/ a. primitivo.

prince /prɪns/ n. príncipe m.

Prince Charming Príncipe Azul

princess /ˈprɪnsɪs/ n. princesa f.

principal /ˈprɪnsəpəl/ a. 1. principal. —n. 2. principal m. & f.; director -ra.

principle /ˈprɪnsəpəl/ n. principio m.

print /prɪnt/ n. 1. letra de molde

f.; (art) grabado *m.* —*v.* **2.** imprimir, estampar.

printer /'prɪntər/ *n.* impresora *f.*

printing /'prɪntɪŋ/ *n.* impresión; **p. office,** imprenta *f.*

printing press prensa *f.*

printout /'prɪnt,aʊt/ *n.* impreso producido por una computadora, impresión *f.*

priority /praɪ'ɔrɪti/ *n.* prioridad, precedencia *f.*

prism /'prɪzəm/ *n.* prisma *m.*

prison /'prɪzən/ *n.* prisión, cárcel *f.*

prisoner /'prɪzənər/ *n.* presidiario -ria, prisionero -ra, preso -sa.

pristine /'prɪstɪn/ *a.* inmaculado.

privacy /'praɪvəsi/ *n.* soledad *f.*

private /'praɪvɪt/ *a.* **1.** particular. —*n.* **2.** soldado raso. **in p.,** en particular.

privation /praɪ'veɪʃən/ *n.* privación *f.*

privet /'prɪvɪt/ *n.* ligustro *m.*

privilege /'prɪvəlɪdʒ/ *n.* privilegio *m.*

privy /'prɪvi/ *n.* letrina *f.*

prize /praɪz/ *n.* **1.** premio *m.* —*v.* **2.** apreciar, estimar.

probability /,prɒbə'bɪlɪti/ *n.* probabilidad *f.*

probable /'prɒbəbəl/ *a.* probable.

probate /'proʊbeɪt/ *a.* testamentario.

probation /proʊ'beɪʃən/ *n.* prueba *f.;* probación *f.;* libertad condicional *f.*

probe /proʊb/ *n.* **1.** indagación *f.* —*v.* **2.** indagar; tentar.

probity /'proʊbɪti/ *n.* probidad *f.*

problem /'prɒbləm/ *n.* problema *m.*

procedure /prə'sidʒər/ *n.* procedimiento *m.*

proceed /prə'sid/ *v.* proceder; proseguir.

process /'prɒsɛs/ *n.* proceso *m.*

procession /prə'sɛʃən/ *n.* procesión *f.*

proclaim /proʊ'kleɪm/ *v.* proclamar, anunciar.

proclamation /,prɒklə'meɪʃən/ *n.* proclamación *f.;* decreto *m.*

procrastinate /proʊ'kræstə,neɪt/ *v.* dilatar.

procure /proʊ'kyʊr/ *v.* obtener, procurar.

prodigal /'prɒdɪgəl/ *n. & a.* pródigo -ga.

prodigy /'prɒdɪdʒi/ *n.* prodigio *m.*

produce /prə'dus/ *v.* producir.

product /'prɒdʌkt/ *n.* producto *m.*

production /prə'dʌkʃən/ *n.* producción *f.*

productive /prə'dʌktɪv/ *a.* productivo.

profane /prə'feɪn/ *a.* **1.** profano. —*v.* **2.** profanar.

profanity /prə'fænɪti/ *n.* profanidad *f.*

profess /prə'fɛs/ *v.* profesar; declarar.

profession /prə'fɛʃən/ *n.* profesión *f.*

professional /prə'fɛʃənl/ *a. & n.* profesional *m. & f.*

professor /prə'fɛsər/ *n.* profesor -ra; catedrático -ca.

proficient /prə'fɪʃənt/ *a.* experto, proficiente.

profile /'proʊfaɪl/ *n.* perfil *m.*

profit /'prɒfɪt/ *n.* **1.** provecho *m.;* ventaja *f.; Com.* ganancia *f.* —*v.* **2.** aprovechar; beneficiar.

profitable /'prɒfɪtəbəl/ *a.* provechoso, ventajoso, lucrativo.

profiteer /,prɒfɪ'tɪər/ *n.* **1.** explotador -ra. —*v.* **2.** explotar.

profound /prə'faʊnd/ *a.* profundo, hondo.

profuse /prə'fyus/ *a.* pródigo; profuso.

prognosis /prɒg'noʊsɪs/ *n.* pronóstico *m.*

program /'proʊgræm/ *n.* programa *m.*

progress /*n.* 'prɒgrɛs; *v.* prə'grɛs/ *n.* **1.** progresos *m.pl.* **in p.,** en marcha. —*v.* **2.** progresar; marchar.

progressive /prə'grɛsɪv/ *a.* progresivo; progresista.

prohibit /proʊ'hɪbɪt/ *v.* prohibir.

prohibition /,proʊə'bɪʃən/ *n.* prohibición *f.*

prohibitive /proʊ'hɪbɪtɪv/ *a.* prohibitivo.

project /*n.* 'prɒdʒɛkt; *v.* prə'dʒɛkt/ *n.* **1.** proyecto *m.* —*v.* **2.** proyectar.

projectile /prə'dʒɛktɪl/ *n.* proyectil *m.*

projection /prə'dʒɛkʃən/ *n.* proyección *f.*

projector /prə'dʒɛktər/ *n.* proyector *m.*

proliferation /prə,lɪfə'reɪʃən/ *n.* proliferación *f.*

prolific /prə'lɪfɪk/ *a.* prolífico.

prologue /'proʊlɔg/ *n.* prólogo *m.*

prolong /prə'lɔŋ/ v. prolongar.

prominent /'prɑmənənt/ a. prominente; eminente.

promiscuous /prə'mɪskyuəs/ a. promiscuo.

promise /'prɑmɪs/ n. **1.** promesa f. —v. **2.** prometer.

promote /prə'mout/ v. fomentar; estimular; adelantar; promocionar.

promotion /prə'mouʃən/ n. promoción f.; adelanto m.

prompt /prɑmpt/ a. **1.** puntual. —v. **2.** impulsar; Theat. apuntar. —adv. **3.** pronto.

promulgate /'prɑməl,geit/ v. promulgar.

pronoun /'prou,naun/ n. pronombre m.

pronounce /prə'nauns/ v. pronunciar.

pronunciation /prə,nʌnsi'eiʃən/ n. pronunciación f.

proof /pruf/ n. prueba f.

proof of purchase certificado de compra m.

proofread /'pruf,rid/ v. corregir pruebas.

prop /prɑp/ n. **1.** apoyo, m. —v. **2.** sostener.

propaganda /,prɑpə'gændə/ n. propaganda f.

propagate /'prɑpə,geit/ v. propagar.

propel /prə'pɛl/ v. propulsar.

propeller /prə'pɛlər/ n. hélice f.

propensity /prə'pɛnsɪti/ n. tendencia f.

proper /'prɑpər/ a. propio; correcto.

property /'prɑpərti/ n. propiedad f.

prophecy /'prɑfəsi/ n. profecía f.

prophesy /'prɑfə,sai/ v. predecir, profetizar.

prophet /'prɑfɪt/ n. profeta m.

prophetic /prə'fɛtɪk/ a. profético.

propitious /prə'pɪʃəs/ a. propicio.

proponent /prə'pounənt/ n. & a. proponente f.

proportion /prə'pɔrʃən/ n. proporción f.

proportionate /prə'pɔrʃənɪt/ a. proporcionado.

proposal /prə'pouzəl/ n. propuesta; oferta f.; (marriage) declaración f.

propose /prə'pouz/ v. proponer; pensar; declararse.

proposition /,prɑpə'zɪʃən/ n. proposición f.

proprietor /prə'praiətər/ n. propietario -ria, dueño -ña.

propriety /prə'praiɪti/ n. corrección f., decoro m.

prosaic /prou'zeiɪk/ a. prosaico.

proscribe /prou'skraib/ v. proscribir.

prose /prouz/ n. prosa f.

prosecute /'prɑsɪ,kyut/ v. acusar, procesar.

prospect /'prɑspɛkt/ n. perspectiva; esperanza f.

prospective /prə'spɛktɪv/ a. anticipado, presunto.

prosper /'prɑspər/ v. prosperar.

prosperity /prə'spɛrɪti/ n. prosperidad f.

prosperous /'prɑspərəs/ a. próspero.

prostate gland /'prɑsteit/ glándula prostática f.

prostitute /'prɑstɪ,tut/ n. **1.** prostituta f. —v. **2.** prostituir.

prostrate /'prɑstreit/ a. **1.** postrado. —v. **2.** postrar.

protect /prə'tɛkt/ v. proteger; amparar.

protection /prə'tɛkʃən/ n. protección f.; amparo m.

protective /prə'tɛktɪv/ a. protector.

protector /prə'tɛktər/ n. protector -ora.

protégé /'proutə,ʒei/ n. protegido -da.

protein /'proutin, -tiin/ n. proteína f.

protest /n. 'proutɛst; v. prə'tɛst, 'proutɛst/ n. **1.** protesta f. —v. **2.** protestar.

Protestant /'prɑtəstənt/ a. & n. protestante m. & f.

protocol /'proutə,kɔl/ n. protocolo m.

proton /'proutɒn/ n. protón m.

protract /prou'trækt/ v. alargar, demorar.

protrude /prou'trud/ v. salir fuera.

protuberance /prou'tubərəns/ n. protuberancia f.

proud /praud/ a. orgulloso.

prove /pruv/ v. comprobar.

proverb /'prɑvərb/ n. proverbio, refrán m.

provide /prə'vaid/ v. proporcionar; proveer.

provided /prə'vaidid/ *conj.* con tal que.

providence /'prɒvidəns/ *n.* providencia *f.*

province /'prɒvins/ *n.* provincia *f.*

provincial /prə'vinʃəl/ *a.* **1.** provincial. —*n.* **2.** provinciano -na.

provision /prə'viʒən/ *n.* **1.** provisión *f.*; (pl.) comestibles *m.pl.* —*v.* **2.** abastecer.

provocation /,prɒvə'keiʃən/ *n.* provocación *f.*

provoke /prə'vouk/ *v.* provocar.

prowess /'praʊis/ *n.* proeza *f.*

prowl /praʊl/ *v.* rondar.

prowler /'praʊlər/ *n.* merodeador -dora *m.* & *f.*

proximity /prɒk'simiti/ *n.* proximidad *f.*

proxy /'prɒksi/ *n.* delegado -da. **by p.,** mediante apoderado.

prudence /'prudns/ *n.* prudencia *f.*

prudent /'prudnt/ *a.* prudente, cauteloso.

prune /prun/ *n.* ciruela pasa *f.*

pry /prai/ *v.* atisbar; curiosear; *Mech.* alzaprimar.

psalm /sɑm/ *n.* salmo *m.*

pseudonym /'sudnim/ *n.* seudónimo *m.*

psychedelic /,saiki'dɛlik/ *a.* psiquedélico.

psychiatrist /si'kaiətrist, sai-/ *n.* psiquiatra *m.* & *f.*

psychiatry /si'kaiətri, sai-/ *n.* psiquiatría *f.*

psychoanalysis /,saikouə'næləsis/ *n.* psicoanálisis *m.*

psychoanalyst /,saikou'ænḷist/ *n.* psicoanalista *m.* & *f.*

psychological /,saikə'lɒdʒikəl/ *a.* psicológico.

psychology /sai'kɒlədʒi/ *n.* psicología *f.*

psychosis /sai'kousis/ *n.* psicosis *f.*

ptomaine /'toumein/ *n.* tomaína *f.*

pub /pʌb/ *n.* bar *m.*

public /'pʌblik/ *a.* & *n.* público *m.*

publication /,pʌbli'keiʃən/ *n.* publicación; revista *f.*

publicity /pʌ'blisiti/ *n.* publicidad *f.*

publicity agent publicista *m.* & *f.*

publish /'pʌbliʃ/ *v.* publicar.

publisher /'pʌbliʃər/ *n.* editor -ora.

pudding /'pudiŋ/ *n.* pudín *m.*

puddle /'pʌdl/ *n.* charco, lodazal *m.*

Puerto Rican /'pwɛrtə 'rikən, 'pɔr-/ *a.* & *n.* puertorriqueño -ña.

Puerto Rico /'pwɛrtə rikou, 'pɔrtə/ Puerto Rico *m.*

puff /pʌf/ *n.* **1.** soplo *m.*; (of smoke) bocanada *f.* **powder p.,** polvera *f.* —*v.* **2.** jadear; echar bocanadas. **p. up,** hinchar; *Fig.* engreír.

pugnacious /pʌg'neiʃəs/ *a.* pugnaz.

puh-lease! /pʌ 'liz/ ¡Favor!

pull /pul/ *n.* **1.** tirón *m.*; *Colloq.* influencia *f.* —*v.* **2.** tirar; halar.

pulley /'puli/ *n.* polea *f.*, motón *m.*

pulmonary /'pʌlmə,neri/ *a.* pulmonar.

pulp /pʌlp/ *n.* pulpa *f.*; (of fruit) carne *f.*

pulpit /'pulpit, 'pʌl-/ *n.* púlpito *m.*

pulsar /'pʌlsɑr/ *n.* pulsar *m.*

pulsate /'pʌlseit/ *v.* pulsar.

pulse /pʌls/ *n.* pulso *m.*

pump /pʌmp/ *n.* **1.** bomba *f.* —*v.* **2.** bombear. **p. up,** inflar.

pumpkin /'pʌmpkin/ *n.* calabaza *f.*

pun /pʌn/ *n.* juego de palabras.

punch /pʌntʃ/ *n.* **1.** puñetazo; *Mech.* punzón; (beverage) ponche *m.* —*v.* **2.** dar puñetazos; punzar.

punch bowl ponchera *f.*

punctual /'pʌŋktʃuəl/ *a.* puntual.

punctuate /'pʌŋktʃu,eit/ *v.* puntuar.

puncture /'pʌŋktʃər/ *n.* **1.** pinchazo *m.*, perforación *f.* —*v.* **2.** pinchar, perforar.

pungent /'pʌndʒənt/ *a.* picante, pungente.

punish /'pʌniʃ/ *v.* castigar.

punishment /'pʌniʃmənt/ *n.* castigo *m.*

punitive /'pyunitiv/ *a.* punitivo.

puny /'pyuni/ *a.* encanijado.

pupil /'pyupəl/ *n.* alumno -na; *Anat.* pupila *f.*

puppet /'pʌpit/ *n.* muñeco *m.*

puppy /'pʌpi/ *n.* perrito -ta.

purchase /'pɜrtʃəs/ *n.* **1.** compra *f.* —*v.* **2.** comprar.

purchasing power /'pɜrtʃəsiŋ/ poder adquisitivo *m.*

pure /pyur/ *a.* puro.

purée /pyu'rei/ *n.* puré *m.*

purge /pɜrdʒ/ *v.* purgar.

purify /'pyʊrə,faɪ/ v. purificar.
puritanical /,pyʊrɪ'tænɪkəl/ a. puritano.
purity /'pyʊrɪti/ n. pureza f.
purple /'pərpəl/ a. **1.** purpúreo. —2. púrpura f.
purport /pər'pɔrt/ v. par'pɔrt/ n. **1.** significación f. —v. **2.** significar.
purpose /'pərpəs/ n. propósito m. **on p.,** de propósito.
purr /pɜr/ v. ronronear.
purse /pɜrs/ n. bolsa f.
pursue /pər'su/ v. perseguir.
pursuit /pər'sut/ n. caza f.; busca;

ocupación f. **p. plane,** avión de caza m.
push /pʊʃ/ n. **1.** empuje; impulso m. —v. **2.** empujar.
put /pʊt/ v. poner, colocar. **p. away,** guardar. **p. in,** meter. **p. off,** dejar. **p. on,** ponerse. **p. out,** apagar. **p. up with,** aguantar.
putrid /'pyutrɪd/ a. podrido.
putt /pʌt/ n. (golf) golpe corto m.
puzzle /'pʌzəl/ n. **1.** enigma; rompecabezas m. —v. **2.** dejar perplejo. **p. out,** descifrar.
pyramid /'pɪrəmɪd/ n. pirámide f.
pyromania /,paɪrə'meɪniə/ n. piromanía f.

Q

quack /kwæk/ n. **1.** (doctor) curandero -ra; (duck) graznido m. —v. **2.** graznar.
quadrangle /'kwɒd,ræŋgəl/ n. cuadrángulo m.
quadraphonic /,kwɒdrə'fɒnɪk/ a. cuatrifónico.
quadruped /'kwɒdrʊ,pɛd/ a. & n. cuadrúpedo m.
quail /kweɪl/ n. **1.** codorniz f. —v. **2.** descorazonarse.
quaint /kweɪnt/ a. curioso.
quake /kweɪk/ n. **1.** temblor m. —v. **2.** temblar.
qualification /,kwɒləfɪ'keɪʃən/ n. requisito m.; (pl.) preparaciones f.pl.
qualified /'kwɒlə,faɪd/ a. calificado, competente; preparado.
qualify /'kwɒlə,faɪ/ v. calificar, modificar; llenar los requisitos.
quality /'kwɒlɪti/ n. calidad f.
quandary /'kwɒndəri, -dri/ n. incertidumbre f.
quantity /'kwɒntɪti/ n. cantidad f.
quarantine /'kwɔrən,tin, 'kwɒr-, ,kwɔrən'tin, ,kwɒr-/ n. cuarentena f.
quarrel /'kwɔrəl, 'kwɒr-/ n. **1.** riña, disputa f. —v. **2.** reñir, disputar.
quarry /'kwɔri, 'kwɒri/ n. cantera; (hunting) presa f.
quarter /'kwɔrtər/ n. cuarto m.; (pl.) vivienda f.
quarterly /'kwɔrtərli/ a. **1.** trimestral. —adv. **2.** por cuartos.
quartet /kwɔr'tɛt/ n. cuarteto f.
quartz /kwɔrts/ n. cuarzo m.
quasar /'kweɪzar/ n. cuasar m.
quaver /'kweɪvər/ v. temblar.

queen /kwin/ n. reina f.; (chess) dama f.
queer /kwɪər/ a. extraño, raro.
quell /kwɛl/ v. reprimir.
quench /kwɛntʃ/ v. apagar.
query /'kwɪəri/ n. **1.** pregunta f. —v. **2.** preguntar.
quest /kwɛst/ n. busca f.
question /'kwɛstʃən/ n. **1.** pregunta, cuestión f. **q. mark,** signo de interrogación. —v. **2.** preguntar; interrogar; dudar.
questionable /'kwɛstʃənəbəl/ a. dudoso.
questionnaire /,kwɛstʃə'nɛər/ n. cuestionario m.
quiche /kiʃ/ n. quiche f.
quick /kwɪk/ a. rápido.
quicken /'kwɪkən/ v. acelerar.
quicksand /'kwɪk,sænd/ n. arena movediza.
quiet /'kwaɪɪt/ a. **1.** quieto, tranquilo; callado. **be q., keep q.,** callarse. —n. **2.** calma; quietud f. —v. **3.** tranquilizar. **q. down,** callarse; calmarse.
quilt /kwɪlt/ n. colcha f.
quinine /'kwaɪnaɪn/ n. quinina f.
quintet /kwɪn'tɛt/ n. Mus. quinteto m.
quip /kwɪp/ n. **1.** pulla f. —v. **2.** echar pullas.
quit /kwɪt/ v. dejar; renunciar a. **q. doing** (etc.) dejar de hacer (etc.).
quite /kwaɪt/ adv. bastante; completamente. **not q.,** no precisamente; no completamente.
quiver /'kwɪvər/ n. **1.** aljaba f.; temblor m. —v. **2.** temblar.

quixotic /kwɪkˈsɒtɪk/ a. quijotesco.

quorum /ˈkwɔrəm/ n. quórum m.

quota /ˈkwoutə/ n. cuota f.

quotation /kwouˈteɪʃən/ n. citación; Com. cotización f. **q. marks**, comillas f.pl.

quote /kwout/ v. citar; Com. cotizar.

R

rabbi /ˈræbaɪ/ n. rabí, rabino m.

rabbit /ˈræbɪt/ n. conejo m.

rabble /ˈræbəl/ n. canalla f.

rabid /ˈræbɪd/ a. rabioso.

rabies /ˈreɪbiz/ n. hidrofobia f.

race /reɪs/ n. 1. raza; carrera f. —v. 2. echar una carrera; correr de prisa.

race track /ˈreɪsˌtræk/ hipódromo m.

rack /ræk/ n. 1. (cooking) pesebre m.; (clothing) colgador m. —v. 2. atormentar.

racket /ˈrækɪt/ n. 1. (noise) ruido m.; (tennis) raqueta f.; (graft) fraude organizado.

radar /ˈreɪdɑr/ n. radar m.

radiance /ˈreɪdiəns/ n. brillo m.

radiant /ˈreɪdiənt/ a. radiante.

radiate /ˈreɪdiˌeɪt/ v. irradiar.

radiation /ˌreɪdiˈeɪʃən/ n. irradiación f.

radiator /ˈreɪdiˌeɪtər/ n. calorífero m.; Auto. radiador m.

radical /ˈrædɪkəl/ a. & n. radical m.

radio /ˈreɪdiˌou/ n. radio m. or f. **r. station**, estación radiodifusora f.

radioactive /ˌreɪdiouˈæktɪv/ a. radioactivo.

radio cassette radiocasete m.

radish /ˈrædɪʃ/ n. rábano m.

radium /ˈreɪdiəm/ n. radio m.

radius /ˈreɪdiəs/ n. radio m.

raffle /ˈræfəl/ n. 1. rifa, lotería f. —v. 2. rifar.

raft /ræft/ n. balsa f.

rafter /ˈræftər/ n. viga f.

rag /ræg/ n. trapo m.

ragamuffin /ˈrægəˌmʌfɪn/ n. galopín m.

rage /reɪdʒ/ n. 1. rabia f. —v. 2. rabiar.

ragged /ˈrægɪd/ a. andrajoso; desigual.

raid /reɪd/ n. Mil. correría f.

rail /reɪl/ n. baranda f.; carril m. **by r.**, por ferrocarril.

railroad /ˈreɪlˌroud/ n. ferrocarril m.

rain /reɪn/ n. 1. lluvia f. —v. 2. llover.

rainbow /ˈreɪnˌbou/ n. arco iris m.

raincoat /ˈreɪnˌkout/ n. impermeable m.; gabardina f.

rainfall /ˈreɪnˌfɔl/ n. precipitación f.

rainy /ˈreɪni/ a. lluvioso.

raise /reɪz/ n. 1. aumento m. —v. 2. levantar, alzar; criar.

raisin /ˈreɪzɪn/ n. pasa f.

rake /reɪk/ n. 1. rastro m. —v. 2. rastrillar.

rally /ˈræli/ n. 1. reunión f. —v. 2. reunirse.

ram /ræm/ n. carnero m.

ramble /ˈræmbəl/ v. vagar.

ramp /ræmp/ n. rampa f.

rampart /ˈræmpɑrt/ n. terraplén m.

ranch /ræntʃ/ n. rancho m.

rancid /ˈrænsɪd/ a. rancio.

rancor /ˈræŋkər/ n. rencor m.

random /ˈrændəm/ a. fortuito. **at r.**, a la ventura.

range /reɪndʒ/ n. 1. extensión f.; alcance m.; estufa; sierra f.; terreno de pasto. —v. 2. recorrer; extenderse.

rank /ræŋk/ a. 1. espeso; rancio. —n. 2. fila f.; grado m. —v. 3. clasificar.

ransack /ˈrænsæk/ v. saquear.

ransom /ˈrænsəm/ n. 1. rescate m. —v. 2. rescatar.

rap /ræp/ n. 1. golpecito m. —v. 2. golpear.

rapid /ˈræpɪd/ a. rápido.

rapist /ˈreɪpɪst/ n. violador -dora m. & f.

rapport /ræˈpɔr/ n. armonía f.

rapture /ˈræptʃər/ n. éxtasis m.

rare /rɛər/ a. raro; (of food) a medio cocer.

rascal /ˈræskəl/ n. pícaro, bribón m.

rash /ræʃ/ a. 1. temerario. —n. 2. erupción f.

raspberry /ˈræzˌbɛri/ n. frambuesa f.

rat /ræt/ n. rata f.

rate /reit/ *n.* **1.** velocidad; tasa *f.*; precio *m.*; (of exchange; of interest) tipo *m.* **at any r.,** de todos modos. —*v.* **2.** valuar.

rather /'ræðər/ *adv.* bastante; más bien, mejor dicho.

ratify /'rætə,fai/ *v.* ratificar.

ratio /'reiʃou/ *n.* razón; proporción *f.*

ration /'ræʃən, 'reiʃən/ *n.* **1.** ración *f.* —*v.* **2.** razonar.

rational /'ræʃənl/ *a.* racional.

rattle /'rætl/ *n.* **1.** ruido *m.*; matraca *f.* **r. snake,** culebra de cascabel, serpiente de cascabel *f.* —*v.* **2.** matraquear; rechinar.

raucous /'rɔkəs/ *a.* ronco.

ravage /'rævidʒ/ *v.* pillar; destruir; asolar.

rave /reiv/ *v.* delirar; entusiasmarse.

ravel /'rævəl/ *v.* deshilar.

raven /'reivən/ *n.* cuervo *m.*

ravenous /'rævənəs/ *a.* voraz.

raw /rɔ/ *a.* crudo; verde.

ray /rei/ *n.* rayo *m.*

rayon /'reiɒn/ *n.* rayón *m.*

razor /'reizər/ *n.* navaja de afeitar. **r. blade,** hoja de afeitar.

reach /ritʃ/ *n.* **1.** alcance *m.* —*v.* **2.** alcanzar.

react /ri'ækt/ *v.* reaccionar.

reaction /ri'ækʃən/ *n.* reacción *f.*

reactionary /ri'ækʃə,neri/ *a.* **1.** reaccionario. —*n.* **2.** *Pol.* retrógrado *m.*

read /rid/ *v.* leer.

reader /'ridər/ *n.* lector -ra; libro de lectura *m.*

readily /'rɛdli/ *adv.* fácilmente.

reading /'ridɪŋ/ *n.* lectura *f.*

ready /'rɛdi/ *a.* listo, preparado; dispuesto.

ready-cooked /'rɛdi ,kʊkt/ *a.* precocinado.

real /riəl/ *a.* verdadero; real.

real estate bienes inmuebles, *m.pl.*

real-estate agent /'riəl ɪ'steit/ agente inmobiliario *m.*, agente inmobiliaria *f.*

realist /'riəlɪst/ *n.* realista *m.* & *f.*

realistic /,riə'lɪstɪk/ *a.* realista.

reality /ri'ælɪti/ *n.* realidad *f.*

realization /,riələ'zeiʃən/ *n.* comprensión; realización *f.*

realize /'riə,laiz/ *v.* darse cuenta de; realizar.

really /'riəli/ *adv.* de veras; en realidad.

realm /rɛlm/ *n.* reino; dominio *m.*

reap /rip/ *v.* segar, cosechar.

rear /riər/ *a.* **1.** posterior. —*n.* **2.** parte posterior. —*v.* **3.** criar; levantar.

reason /'rizən/ *n.* **1.** razón; causa *f.*; motivo *m.* —*v.* **2.** razonar.

reasonable /'rizənəbəl/ *a.* razonable.

reassure /,riə'ʃʊr/ *v.* calmar, tranquilizar.

rebate /'ribeit/ *n.* rebaja *f.*

rebel /*n.* 'rɛbəl, *v.* rɪ'bɛl/ *n.* **1.** rebelde *m.* & *f.* —*v.* **2.** rebelarse.

rebellion /rɪ'bɛlyən/ *n.* rebelión *f.*

rebellious /rɪ'bɛlyəs/ *a.* rebelde.

rebirth /ri'bɜrθ/ *n.* renacimiento *m.*

rebound /rɪ'baund/ *v.* repercutir; resaltar.

rebuff /rɪ'bʌf/ *n.* **1.** repulsa *f.* —*v.* **2.** rechazar.

rebuke /rɪ'byuk/ *n.* **1.** reprensión *f.* —*v.* **2.** reprender.

rebuttal /rɪ'bʌtl/ *n.* refutación *f.*

recalcitrant /rɪ'kælsɪtrənt/ *a.* recalcitrante.

recall /rɪ'kɔl/ *v.* recordar; acordarse de; hacer volver.

recapitulate /,rikə'pɪtʃə,leit/ *v.* recapitular.

recede /ri'sid/ *v.* retroceder.

receipt /rɪ'sit/ *n.* recibo *m.*; (com., pl.) ingresos *m.pl.*

receive /rɪ'siv/ *v.* recibir.

receiver /rɪ'sivər/ *n.* receptor *m.*

recent /'risənt/ *a.* reciente.

recently /'risəntli/ *adv.* recién.

receptacle /rɪ'sɛptəkəl/ *n.* receptáculo *m.*

reception /rɪ'sɛpʃən/ *n.* acogida; recepción *f.*

receptionist /rɪ'sɛpʃənɪst/ *n.* recepcionista *m.* & *f.*

receptive /rɪ'sɛptɪv/ *a.* receptivo.

recess /'rises, rɪ'ses/ *n.* nicho; retiro; recreo *m.*

recipe /'rɛsəpi/ *n.* receta *f.*

recipient /rɪ'sɪpiənt/ *n.* recibidor -ra, recipiente *m.* & *f.*

reciprocate /rɪ'sɪprə,keit/ *v.* corresponder; reciprocar.

recite /rɪ'sait/ *v.* recitar.

reckless /'rɛklɪs/ *a.* descuidado; imprudente.

reckon /'rɛkən/ *v.* contar; calcular.

reclaim /rɪ'kleim/ *v.* reformar; *Leg.* reclamar.

recline /rɪ'klain/ *v.* reclinar; recostar.

recognition /ˌrekəgˈniʃən/ n. reconocimiento m.

recognize /ˈrekəgˌnaiz/ v. reconocer.

recoil /ˈriˌkɔil; v. riˈkɔil/ n. **1.** culatada f. —v. **2.** recular.

recollect /ˌrekəˈlɛkt/ v. recordar, acordarse de.

recommend /ˌrekəˈmend/ v. recomendar.

recommendation /ˌrekəmənˈdeiʃən/ n. recomendación f.

recompense /ˈrekəmˌpens/ n. **1.** recompensa f. —v. **2.** recompensar.

reconcile /ˈrekənˌsail/ v. reconciliar.

recondition /ˌrikənˈdiʃən/ v. reacondicionar.

reconsider /ˌrikənˈsidər/ v. considerar de nuevo.

reconstruct /ˌrikənˈstrʌkt/ v. reconstruir.

record /n. ˈrekərd, v. riˈkɔrd/ n. **1.** registro, (sports) record m. **phonograph r.,** disco m. —v. **2.** registrar.

record player tocadiscos m.

recount /riˈkaunt/ v. relatar; contar.

recover /riˈkʌvər/ v. recobrar; restablecerse.

recovery /riˈkʌvəri/ n. recobro m.; recuperación f.

recruit /riˈkrut/ n. **1.** recluta m. —v. **2.** reclutar.

rectangle /ˈrekˌtæŋgəl/ n. rectángulo m.

rectify /ˈrektəˌfai/ v. rectificar.

recuperate /riˈkupəˌreit/ v. recuperar.

recur /riˈkɜr/ v. recurrir.

recycle /riˈsaikəl/ v. reciclar.

red /red/ a. rojo, colorado.

redeem /riˈdim/ v. redimir, rescatar.

redemption /riˈdempʃən/ n. redención f.

redhead /ˈredˌhed/ n. pelirrojo -ja.

red mullet /ˈmʌlit/ salmonete m.

reduce /riˈdus/ v. reducir.

reduction /riˈdakʃən/ n. reducción f.

reed /rid/ n. caña f., S.A. bejuco m.

reef /rif/ n. arrecife, escollo m.

reel /ril/ n. **1.** aspa f., carrete m. —v. **2.** aspar.

refer /riˈfɜr/ v. referir.

referee /ˌrefəˈri/ n. árbitro m. & f.

reference /ˈrefərəns/ n. referencia f.

refill /n. ˈriˌfil; v. riˈfil/ n. **1.** relleno m. —v. **2.** rellenar.

refine /riˈfain/ v. refinar.

refinement /riˈfainmənt/ n. refinamiento m.; cultura f.

reflect /riˈflekt/ v. reflejar; reflexionar.

reflection /riˈflekʃən/ n. reflejo m.; reflexión f.

reflex /ˈrifleks/ a. reflejo.

reform /riˈfɔrm/ n. **1.** reforma f. —v. **2.** reformar.

reformation /ˌrefərˈmeiʃən/ n. reformación f.

refractory /riˈfræktəri/ a. refractario.

refrain /riˈfrein/ n. **1.** estribillo m. —v. **2.** abstenerse.

refresh /riˈfreʃ/ v. refrescar.

refreshment /riˈfreʃmənt/ n. refresco m.

refrigerator /riˈfridʒəˌreitər/ n. refrigerador m.

refuge /ˈrefyudʒ/ n. refugio m.

refugee /ˌrefyuˈdʒi/ n. refugiado -da.

refund /n. ˈriˌfʌnd; v. riˈfʌnd/ n. **1.** reembolso m. —v. **2.** reembolsar.

refusal /riˈfyuzəl/ n. negativa f.

refuse /n. ˈrefyus; v riˈfyuz/ n. **1.** basura f. —v. **2.** negarse, rehusar.

refute /riˈfyut/ v. refutar.

regain /riˈgein/ v. recobrar. **r. consciousness,** recobrar el conocimiento.

regal /ˈrigəl/ a. real.

regard /riˈgɑrd/ n. **1.** aprecio; respeto m. **with r. to,** con respecto a. —v. **2.** considerar; estimar.

regarding /riˈgɑrdiŋ/ prep. en cuanto a, acerca de.

regardless (of) /riˈgɑrdlis/ a pesar de.

regent /ˈridʒənt/ n. regente m. & f.

regime /rəˈʒim, rei-/ n. régimen m.

regiment /n. ˈredʒəmənt; v. -ˌment/ n. **1.** regimiento m. —v. **2.** regimentar.

region /ˈridʒən/ n. región f.

register /ˈredʒəstər/ n. **1.** registro m. **cash r.,** caja registradora f. —v. **2.** registrar; matricularse; (a letter) certificar.

registration /ˌredʒəˈstreiʃən/ n. registro m.; matrícula f.

regret /rɪ'grɛt/ n. **1.** pena f. —v. **2.** sentir, lamentar.

regular /'rɛgyələr/ a. regular; ordinario.

regularity /,rɛgyə'lærɪti/ n. regularidad f.

regulate /'rɛgyə,leit/ v. regular.

regulation /,rɛgyə'leiʃən/ n. regulación f.

regulator /'rɛgyə,leitər/ n. regulador m.

rehabilitate /,rihə'bɪli,teit, ,riə-/ v. rehabilitar.

rehearse /rɪ'hɜrs/ v. repasar; *Theat.* ensayar.

reheat /ri'hit/ v. recalentar.

reign /rein/ n. **1.** reino, reinado m. —v. **2.** reinar.

reimburse /,riɪm'bɜrs/ v. reembolsar.

rein /rein/ n. **1.** rienda f. —v. **2.** refrenar.

reincarnation /,riɪnkɑr'neiʃən/ n. reencarnación f.

reindeer /'rein,dɪər/ n. reno m.

reinforce /,riɪn'fɔrs, -'fours/ v. reforzar.

reinforcement /,riɪn'fɔrsmənt, -'fours-/ n. refuerzo m.; armadura f.

reiterate /ri'ɪtə,reit/ v. reiterar.

reject /rɪ'dʒɛkt/ v. rechazar.

rejoice /rɪ'dʒɔis/ v. regocijarse.

rejoin /rɪ'dʒɔin/ v. reunirse con; replicar.

rejuvenate /rɪ'dʒuvə,neit/ v. rejuvenecer.

relapse /v. rɪ'læps; n. also 'rilæps/ v. **1.** recaer. —n. **2.** recaída f.

relate /rɪ'leit/ v. relatar, contar; relacionar. **r. to,** llevarse bien con.

relation /rɪ'leiʃən/ n. relación f.; pariente m. & f.

relative /'rɛlətɪv/ a. **1.** relativo. —n. **2.** pariente m. & f.

relativity /,rɛlə'tɪvɪti/ n. relatividad f.

relax /rɪ'læks/ v. descansar; relajar.

relay /rilei; v. also rɪ'lei/ n. **1.** relevo m. —v. **2.** retransmitir.

release /rɪ'lis/ n. **1.** liberación f. —v. **2.** soltar.

relent /rɪ'lɛnt/ v. ceder.

relevant /'rɛləvənt/ a. pertinente.

reliability /rɪ,laiə'bɪlɪti/ n. veracidad f.

reliable /rɪ'laiəbəl/ a. responsable; digno de confianza.

relic /'rɛlɪk/ n. reliquia f.

relief /rɪ'lif/ n. alivio; (sculpture) relieve m.

relieve /rɪ'liv/ v. aliviar.

religion /rɪ'lɪdʒən/ n. religión f.

religious /rɪ'lɪdʒəs/ a. religioso.

relinquish /rɪ'lɪŋkwɪʃ/ v. abandonar.

relish /'rɛlɪʃ/ n. **1.** sabor; condimento m. —v. **2.** saborear.

reluctant /rɪ'lʌktənt/ a. renuente.

rely /rɪ'lai/ v. **r. on,** confiar en; contar con; depender de.

remain /rɪ'mein/ v. **1.** (pl.) restos m.pl. —v. **2.** quedar, permanecer.

remainder /rɪ'meindər/ n. resto m.

remark /rɪ'mɑrk/ n. **1.** observación f. —v. **2.** observar.

remarkable /rɪ'mɑrkəbəl/ a. notable.

remedial /rɪ'midiəl/ a. reparador.

remedy /'rɛmɪdi/ n. **1.** remedio m. —v. **2.** remediar.

remember /rɪ'mɛmbər/ v. acordarse de, recordar.

remembrance /rɪ'mɛmbrəns/ n. recuerdo m.

remind /rɪ'maind/ v. **r. of,** recordar.

reminisce /,rɛmə'nɪs/ v. pensar en o hablar de cosas pasadas.

remiss /rɪ'mɪs/ a. remiso; flojo.

remit /rɪ'mɪt/ v. remitir.

remorse /rɪ'mɔrs/ n. remordimiento m.

remote /rɪ'mout/ a. remoto.

remote control mando a distancia m.

removal /rɪ'muvəl/ n. alejamiento m.; eliminación f.

remove /rɪ'muv/ v. quitar; remover.

renaissance /,rɛnə'sɑns/ n. renacimiento m.

rend /rɛnd/ v. hacer pedazos; separar.

render /'rɛndər/ v. dar; rendir; *Theat.* interpretar.

rendezvous /'rɑndə,vu, -dei-/ n. cita f.

rendition /rɛn'dɪʃən/ n. interpretación, rendición f.

renege /rɪ'nɪg, -'nɛg/ v. renunciar; faltar a su palabra, no cumplir una promesa.

renew /rɪ'nu, -'nyu/ v. renovar.

renewal /rɪ'nuəl, -'nyu-/ n. renovación; *Com.* prórroga f.

renounce /rɪ'nauns/ v. renunciar a.

renovate /'rɛnə,veɪt/ v. renovar.

renown /rɪ'naun/ n. renombre m., fama f.

rent /rɛnt/ n. **1.** alquiler m. —v. **2.** arrendar, alquilar.

repair /rɪ'pɛər/ n. **1.** reparo m. —v. **2.** reparar.

repairman /rɪ'pɛər,mæn/ n. técnico m.

repatriate /rɪ'peɪtri,eɪt/ v. repatriar.

repay /rɪ'peɪ/ v. pagar; devolver.

repeat /rɪ'pit/ v. repetir.

repel /rɪ'pɛl/ v. repeler, repulsar.

repent /'rɪpənt, rɪ'pɛnt/ v. arrepentirse.

repentance /rɪ'pɛntns, -'pɛntəns/ n. arrepentimiento m.

repercussion /,ripər'kʌʃən, ,rɛpər-/ n. repercusión f.

repertoire /'rɛpər,twar/ n. repertorio m.

repetition /,rɛpɪ'tɪʃən/ n. repetición f.

replace /rɪ'pleɪs/ v. reemplazar.

replenish /rɪ'plɛnɪʃ/ v. rellenar; surtir de nuevo.

reply /rɪ'plaɪ/ n. **1.** respuesta f. —v. **2.** replicar; contestar.

report /rɪ'pɔrt, -'pourt/ n. **1.** informe m. —v. **2.** informar, contar; denunciar; presentarse.

reporter /rɪ'pɔrtər, -'pour-/ n. repórter m. & f., reportero -ra.

repose /rɪ'pouz/ n. **1.** reposo m. —v. **2.** reposar; reclinar.

reprehensible /,rɛprɪ'hɛnsəbəl/ a. reprensible.

represent /,rɛprɪ'zɛnt/ v. representar.

representation /,rɛprɪzɛn'teɪʃən, -zən-/ n. representación f.

representative /,rɛprɪ'zɛntətɪv/ a. **1.** representativo. —n. **2.** representante m. & f.

repress /rɪ'prɛs/ v. reprimir.

reprimand /'rɛprə,mænd, -,mɑnd/ n. **1.** regaño m. —v. **2.** regañar.

reprisal /rɪ'praɪzəl/ n. represalia f.

reproach /rɪ'proutʃ/ n. **1.** reproche m. —v. **2.** reprochar.

reproduce /,riprə'dus, -'dyus/ v. reproducir.

reproduction /,riprə'dʌkʃən/ n. reproducción f.

reproof /rɪ'pruf/ n. censura f.

reprove /rɪ'pruv/ v. censurar, regañar.

reptile /'rɛptɪl, -taɪl/ n. reptil m.

republic /rɪ'pʌblɪk/ n. república f.

republican /rɪ'pʌblɪkən/ a. & n. republicano -na.

repudiate /rɪ'pyudi,eɪt/ v. repudiar.

repulsive /rɪ'pʌlsɪv/ a. repulsivo, repugnante.

reputation /,rɛpyə'teɪʃən/ n. reputación; fama f.

repute /rɪ'pyut/ n. **1.** reputación f. —v. **2.** reputar.

request /rɪ'kwɛst/ n. **1.** súplica f., ruego m. —v. **2.** pedir; rogar, suplicar.

require /rɪ'kwaɪər/ v. requerir; exigir.

requirement /rɪ'kwaɪərmənt/ n. requisito m.

requisite /'rɛkwəzɪt/ a. **1.** necesario. —n. **2.** requisito m.

requisition /,rɛkwə'zɪʃən/ n. requisición f.

rescind /rɪ'sɪnd/ v. rescindir, anular.

rescue /'rɛskyu/ n. **1.** rescate m. —v. **2.** rescatar.

research /rɪ'sɜrtʃ, 'risɜrtʃ/ n. investigación f.

researcher /rɪ'sɜrtʃər/ n. investigador -dora.

resemble /rɪ'zɛmbəl/ v. parecerse a, asemejarse a.

resent /rɪ'zɛnt/ v. resentirse de.

reservation /,rɛzər'veɪʃən/ n. reservación f.

reserve /rɪ'zɜrv/ n. **1.** reserva f. —v. **2.** reservar.

reservoir /'rɛzər,vwar, -,vwɔr, -,vɔr, 'rɛzə-/ n depósito; tanque m.

reside /rɪ'zaɪd/ v. residir, morar.

residence /'rɛzɪdəns/ n. residencia, morada f.

resident /'rɛzɪdənt/ n. residente m. & f.

residue /'rɛzɪ,du/ n. residuo m.

resign /rɪ'zaɪn/ v. dimitir; resignar.

resignation /,rɛzɪg'neɪʃən/ n. dimisión; resignación f.

resist /rɪ'zɪst/ v. resistir.

resistance /rɪ'zɪstəns/ n. resistencia f.

resolute /'rɛzə,lut/ a. resuelto.

resolution /,rɛzə'luʃən/ n. resolución f.

resolve /rɪ'zɒlv/ v. resolver.

resonant /'rɛzənənt/ a. resonante.

resort /rɪ'zɔrt/ n. **1.** recurso; expediente m. **summer r.,** lugar de veraneo. —v. **2.** acudir, recurrir.

resound /rɪ'zaund/ v. resonar.

resource /'risɔrs/ n. recurso m.

respect /rɪ'spɛkt/ n. **1.** respeto m. **with r. to,** con respecto a. —v. **2.** respetar.

respectable /rɪ'spɛktəbəl/ a. respetable.

respectful /rɪ'spɛktfəl/ a. respetuoso.

respective /rɪ'spɛktɪv/ a. respectivo.

respiration /ˌrɛspə'reɪʃən/ n. respiración f.

respite /'rɛspɪt/ n. pausa, tregua f.

respond /rɪ'spɒnd/ v. responder.

response /rɪ'spɒns/ n. respuesta f.

responsibility /rɪˌspɒnsə'bɪlɪti/ n. responsabilidad f.

responsible /rɪ'spɒnsəbəl/ a. responsable.

responsive /rɪ'spɒnsɪv/ a. sensible a.

rest /rɛst/ n. **1.** descanso; reposo m.; (music) pausa f. **the r.,** el resto, lo demás; los demás. —v. **2.** descansar; recostar.

restaurant /'rɛstərɒnt, -tə,rɒnt, -trɒnt/ n. restaurante m.

restful /'rɛstfəl/ a. tranquilo.

restitution /ˌrɛstɪ'tuʃən, -'tyu-/ n. restitución f.

restless /'rɛstlɪs/ a. inquieto.

restoration /ˌrɛstə'reɪʃən/ n. restauración f.

restore /rɪ'stɔr, -'stour/ v. restaurar.

restrain /rɪ'streɪn/ v. refrenar.

restraint /rɪ'streɪnt/ n. limitación, restricción f.

restrict /rɪ'strɪkt/ v. restringir, limitar.

rest room aseos m.pl.

result /rɪ'zʌlt/ n. **1.** resultado m. —v. **2.** resultar.

resume /rɪ'zum/ v. reasumir; empezar de nuevo.

résumé /'rɛzʊ,meɪ/ n. resumen m.

resurgent /rɪ'sɜrdʒənt/ a. resurgente.

resurrect /ˌrɛzə'rɛkt/ v. resucitar.

resuscitate /rɪ'sʌsɪ,teɪt/ v. resucitar.

retail /'riteɪl/ n. **at r.,** al por menor.

retain /rɪ'teɪn/ v. retener.

retaliate /rɪ'tæli,eɪt/ v. vengarse.

retard /rɪ'tɑrd/ v. retardar.

retention /rɪ'tɛnʃən/ n. retención f.

reticent /'rɛtəsənt/ a. reticente.

retire /rɪ'taɪər/ v. retirar.

retirement /rɪ'taɪrmənt/ n. jubilación f.

retort /rɪ'tɔrt/ n. **1.** réplica; Chem. retorta f. —v. **2.** replicar.

retreat /rɪ'trit/ n. **1.** retiro m.; Mil. retirada, retreta f. —v. **2.** retirarse.

retribution /ˌrɛtrə'byuʃən/ n. retribución f.

retrieve /rɪ'triv/ v. recobrar.

return /rɪ'tɜrn/ n. **1.** vuelta f., regreso; retorno m. **by r. mail,** a vuelta de correo. —v. **2.** volver, regresar; devolver.

reunion /ri'yunyən/ n. reunión f.

rev /rɛv/ n. **1.** revolución f. —v. **2.** (motor) acelerar.

reveal /rɪ'vil/ v. revelar.

revelation /ˌrɛvə'leɪʃən/ n. revelación f.

revenge /rɪ'vɛndʒ/ n. venganza f. **to get r.,** vengarse.

revenue /'rɛvən,yu, -ə,nu/ n. renta f.

revere /rɪ'vɪər/ v. reverenciar, venerar.

reverence /'rɛvərəns, 'rɛvrəns/ n. **1.** reverencia f. —v. **2.** reverenciar.

reverend /'rɛvərənd, 'rɛvrənd/ a. **1.** reverendo. —n. **2.** pastor m.

reverent /'rɛvərənt, 'rɛvrənt/ a. reverente.

reverse /rɪ'vɜrs/ a. **1.** inverso. —n. **2.** revés, inverso m. —v. **3.** invertir; revocar.

revert /rɪ'vɜrt/ v. revertir.

review /rɪ'vyu/ n. **1.** repaso m.; revista f. —v. **2.** repasar; Mil. revistar.

revise /rɪ'vaɪz/ v. revisar.

revision /rɪ'vɪʒən/ n. revisión f.

revival /rɪ'vaɪvəl/ n. reavivamiento m.

revive /rɪ'vaɪv/ v. avivar; revivir, resucitar.

revoke /rɪ'vouk/ v. revocar.

revolt /rɪ'voult/ n. **1.** rebelión f. —v. **2.** rebelarse.

revolting /rɪ'voultɪŋ/ a. repugnante.

revolution /ˌrɛvə'luʃən/ n. revolución f.

revolutionary /ˌrɛvə'luʃə,nɛri/ a. & n. revolucionario -ria.

revolve /rɪ'vɒlv/ v. girar; dar vueltas.

revolver /rɪ'vɒlvər/ n. revólver m.

revolving door /rɪ'vɒlvɪŋ/ puerta giratoria f.

reward /rɪ'wɔrd/ n. **1.** pago m.; recompensa f. —v. **2.** recompensar.

rhetoric /'rɛtərɪk/ n. retórica f.

rheumatism /'rumə,tɪzəm/ n. reumatismo m.

rhinoceros /raɪ'nɒsərəs/ n. rinoceronte m.

rhubarb /'rubɑrb/ n. ruibarbo m.

rhyme /raɪm/ n. **1.** rima f. —v. **2.** rimar.

rhythm /'rɪðəm/ n. ritmo m.

rhythmical /'rɪðmɪkəl/ a. rítmico.

rib /rɪb/ n. costilla f.

ribbon /'rɪbən/ n. cinta f.

rib cage caja torácica f.

rice /raɪs/ n. arroz m.

rich /rɪtʃ/ a. rico.

rid /rɪd/ v. librar. **get r. of**, deshacerse de, quitarse.

riddle /'rɪdl/ n. enigma; rompecabezas m.

ride /raɪd/ n. **1.** paseo (a caballo, en coche, etc.) m. —v. **2.** cabalgar; ir en coche.

ridge /rɪdʒ/ n. cerro m.; arruga f.; (of a roof) caballete m.

ridicule /'rɪdɪ,kyul/ n. **1.** ridículo m. —v. **2.** ridiculizar.

ridiculous /rɪ'dɪkyələs/ a. ridículo.

riding /'raɪdɪŋ/ n. equitación f.

riding school picadero m.

rifle /'raɪfəl/ n. **1.** fusil m. —v. **2.** robar.

rig /rɪg/ v. **1.** aparejo m. —v. **2.** aparejar.

right /raɪt/ a. **1.** derecho; correcto. **to be r.**, tener razón. —adv. **2.** bien, correctamente. **r. here**, etc., aquí mismo, está bien, muy bien. **all r.**, está bien, muy bien. —n. **3.** derecho m.; justicia f. **to the r.**, a la derecha. —v. **4.** corregir; enderezar.

righteous /'raɪtʃəs/ a. justo.

rigid /'rɪdʒɪd/ a. rígido.

rigor /'rɪgər/ n. rigor m.

rigorous /'rɪgərəs/ a. riguroso.

rim /rɪm/ n. margen m. or f.; borde m.

ring /rɪŋ/ n. **1.** anillo m.; sortija f.; círculo m.; campaneo m. —v. **2.** cercar; sonar; tocar.

ring finger dedo anular m.

rinse /rɪns/ v. enjuagar, lavar.

riot /'raɪət/ n. motín; alboroto m.

rip /rɪp/ n. **1.** rasgadura f. —v. **2.** rasgar; descoser.

ripe /raɪp/ a. maduro.

ripen /'raɪpən/ v. madurar.

ripoff /'rɪp,ɔf/ n. robo, atraco m.

ripple /'rɪpəl/ n. **1.** onda f. —v. **2.** ondear.

rise /raɪz/ n. **1.** subida f. —v. **2.** ascender; levantarse; (moon) salir.

risk /rɪsk/ n. **1.** riesgo m. —v. **2.** arriesgar.

rite /raɪt/ n. rito m.

ritual /'rɪtʃuəl/ a. & n. ritual m.

rival /'raɪvəl/ n. rival m. & f.

rivalry /'raɪvəlri/ n. rivalidad f.

river /'rɪvər/ n. río m.

rivet /'rɪvɪt/ n. **1.** remache, roblón m. —v. **2.** remachar, roblar.

road /roud/ n. camino m.; carretera f.

roadside /'roud,saɪd/ n. borde de la carretera m.

roam /roum/ v. vagar.

roar /rɔr, rour/ n. **1.** rugido, bramido m. —v. **2.** rugir, bramar.

roast /roust/ n. **1.** asado m. —v. **2.** asar.

rob /rɒb/ v. robar.

robber /'rɒbər/ n. ladrón -na.

robbery /'rɒbəri/ n. robo m.

robe /roub/ n. manto m.

robin /'rɒbɪn/ n. petirrojo m.

robust /rou'bʌst, 'roubʌst/ a. robusto.

rock /rɒk/ n. **1.** roca, peña f.; (music) rock m., música (de) rock f. —v. **2.** mecer; oscilar.

rocker /'rɒkər/ n. mecedora f.

rocket /'rɒkɪt/ n. cohete m.

rocking chair /'rɒkɪŋ/ mecedora f.

Rock of Gibraltar /dʒɪ'brɔltər/ Peñón de Gibraltar m.

rocky /'rɒki/ a. pedregoso.

rod /rɒd/ n. varilla f.

rodent /'roudnt/ n. roedor m.

rogue /roug/ n. bribón, pícaro m.

roguish /'rougɪʃ/ a. pícaro.

role /roul/ n. papel m.

roll /roul/ **1.** rollo m.; lista f.; panecillo m. **to call the r.**, pasar lista. —v. **2.** rodar. **r. up**, enrollar. **r. up one's sleeves**, arremangarse.

roller /'roulər/ n. rodillo, cilindro m.

roller skate patín de ruedas m.

Roman /'roumən/ a. & n. romano -na.

romance /rou'mæns, 'roumæns/ a.

1. románico. —**2.** romance *m.*; amorío *m.*

romantic /rou'mæntɪk/ *a.* romántico.

romp /rɒmp/ *v.* retozar; jugar.

roof /ruf, rʊf/ *n.* **1.** techo *m.*; —*v.* **2.** techar.

room /rum, rʊm/ *n.* **1.** cuarto *m.*, habitación *f.*; lugar *m.* —*v.* **2.** alojarse.

roommate /'rum,meit, 'rʊm-/ *n.* compañero -ra de cuarto.

rooster /'rustər/ *n.* gallo *m.*

root /rut/ *n.* raíz *f.* **to take r.**, arraigar.

rootless /'rutlɪs/ *a.* desarraigado.

rope /roup/ *n.* cuerda, soga *f.*

rose /rouz/ *n.* rosa *f.*

rosy /'rouzi/ *a.* róseo, rosado.

rot /rɒt/ *n.* **1.** putrefacción *f.* —*v.* **2.** pudrirse.

rotary /'routəri/ *a.* giratorio; rotativo.

rotate /'routeit/ *v.* girar; alternar.

rotation /rou'teiʃən/ *n.* rotación *f.*

rotten /'rɒtn/ *a.* podrido.

rouge /ruʒ/ *n.* colorete *m.*

rough /rʌf/ *a.* áspero; rudo; grosero; aproximado.

round /raund/ *a.* **1.** redondo. **r. trip**, viaje de ida y vuelta. —*n.* **2.** ronda *f.*; (boxing) asalto *m.*

rouse /rauz/ *v.* despertar.

rout /raut, rut/ *n.* **1.** derrota *f.* —*v.* **2.** derrotar.

route /rut, raut/ *n.* ruta, vía *f.*

routine /ru'tin/ *n.* **1.** rutinario. —*n.* **2.** rutina *f.*

rove /rouv/ *v.* vagar.

rover /'rouvər/ *n.* vagabundo -da.

row /rou/ *n.* **1.** fila *f.* —*v.* **2.** *Naut.* remar.

rowboat /'rou,bout/ *n.* bote de remos.

rowdy /'raudi/ *a.* alborotado.

royal /'rɔiəl/ *a.* real.

royalty /'rɔiəlti/ *n.* realeza *f.*; (pl.) regalías *f.pl.*

rub /rʌb/ *v.* frotar. **r. against**, rozar. **r. out**, borrar.

rubber /'rʌbər/ *n.* goma *f.*; caucho *m.*; (pl.) chanclos *m.pl.*, zapatos de goma.

rubbish /'rʌbɪʃ/ *n.* basura *f.*; (nonsense) tonterías *f.pl.*

ruby /'rubi/ *n.* rubí *m.*

rudder /'rʌdər/ *n.* timón *m.*

ruddy /'rʌdi/ *a.* colorado.

rude /rud/ *a.* rudo; grosero; descortés.

rudiment /'rudəmənt/ *n.* rudimento *m.*

rudimentary /,rudə'mɛntəri, -tri-/ *a.* rudimentario.

rue /ru/ *v.* deplorar; lamentar.

ruffian /'rʌfiən, 'rʌfyən/ *n.* rufián, bandolero *m.*

ruffle /'rʌfəl/ *n.* **1.** volante fruncido. —*v.* **2.** fruncir; irritar.

rug /rʌg/ *n.* alfombra *f.*

rugged /'rʌgɪd/ *a.* áspero; robusto.

ruin /'ruɪn/ *n.* **1.** ruina *f.* —*v.* **2.** arruinar.

ruinous /'ruənəs/ *a.* ruinoso.

rule /rul/ *n.* **1.** regla *f.* **as a r.**, por regla general. —*v.* **2.** gobernar; mandar; rayar.

ruler /'rulər/ *n.* gobernante *m.* & *f.*; soberano -na; regla *f.*

rum /rʌm/ *n.* ron *m.*

rumble /'rʌmbəl/ *v.* retumbar.

rumor /'rumər/ *n.* rumor *m.*

rumpus /'rʌmpəs/ *n.* lío, jaleo, escandalo *m.*

run /rʌn/ *v.* correr; hacer correr. **r. away**, escaparse. **r. into**, chocar con.

runner /'rʌnər/ *n.* corredor -ra; mensajero -ra.

runner-up /'rʌnər 'ʌp/ *n.* subcampeón -ona.

runproof /'rʌnpruf/ *a.* indesmallable.

rupture /'rʌptʃər/ *n.* **1.** rotura; hernia *f.* —*v.* **2.** reventar.

rural /'rʊrəl/ *a.* rural, campestre.

rush /rʌʃ/ *n.* **1.** prisa *f.*; *Bot.* junco *m.* —*v.* **2.** ir de prisa.

rush hour hora punta *f.*

Russia /'rʌʃə/ *n.* Rusia *f.*

Russian /'rʌʃən/ *a. & n.* ruso -sa.

rust /rʌst/ *n.* **1.** herrumbre *f.* —*v.* **2.** aherrumbrarse.

rustic /'rʌstɪk/ *a.* rústico.

rustle /'rʌsəl/ *n.* **1.** susurro *m.* —*v.* **2.** susurrar.

rusty /'rʌsti/ *a.* mohoso.

rut /rʌt/ *n.* surco *m.*

ruthless /'ruθlɪs/ *a.* cruel, inhumano.

rye /rai/ *n.* centeno *m.*

rye bread pan de centeno *m.*

S

saber /ˈseibər/ n. sable m.

sable /ˈseibəl/ n. cebellina f.

sabotage /ˈsæbəˌtɑʒ/ n. sabotaje m.

sachet /sæˈʃei/ n. perfumador m.

sack /sæk/ n. **1.** saco m. —v. **2.** Mil. saquear.

sacred /ˈseikrid/ a. sagrado, santo.

sacrifice /ˈsækrəˌfais/ n. **1.** sacrificio m. —v. **2.** sacrificar.

sacrilege /ˈsækrəlidʒ/ n. sacrilegio m.

sad /sæd/ a. triste.

saddle /ˈsædl/ n. **1.** silla de montar. —v. **2.** ensillar.

sadness /ˈsædnis/ n. tristeza f.

safe /seif/ a. **1.** seguro; salvo. —n. **2.** caja de caudales.

safeguard /ˈseifˌgɑrd/ n. **1.** salvaguardia m. —v. **2.** proteger, poner a salvo.

safety /ˈseifti/ n. seguridad, protección f.

safety belt cinturón de seguridad m.

safety pin imperdible m.

safety valve /vælv/ válvula de seguridad f.

sage /seidʒ/ a. **1.** sabio, sagaz. —n. **2.** sabio m.; Bot. salvia f.

sail /seil/ n. **1.** vela f.; paseo por mar. —v. **2.** navegar; embarcarse.

sailboat /ˈseilˌbout/ n. barco de vela.

sailor /ˈseilər/ n. marinero m.

saint /seint/ n. santo -ta.

sake /seik/ n. **for the s. of,** por; por el bien de.

salad /ˈsæləd/ n. ensalada f. **s. bowl,** ensaladera f.

salad dressing aliño m.

salary /ˈsæləri/ n. sueldo, salario m.

sale /seil/ n. venta f.

salesman /ˈseilzmən/ n. vendedor m.; viajante de comercio.

sales tax /seilz/ impuesto sobre la venta.

saliva /səˈlaivə/ n. saliva f.

salmon /ˈsæmən/ n. salmón m.

salt /sɔlt/ a. **1.** salado. —n. **2.** sal f. —v. **3.** salar.

salute /səˈlut/ n. **1.** saludo m. —v. **2.** saludar.

salvage /ˈsælvidʒ/ v. salvar; recobrar.

salvation /sælˈveiʃən/ n. salvación f.

salve /sæv/ n. emplasto, ungüento m.

same /seim/ a. & pron. mismo. **it's all the s.,** lo mismo da.

sample /ˈsæmpəl/ n. **1.** muestra f. —v. **2.** probar.

sanatorium /ˌsænəˈtɔriəm/ n. sanatorio m.

sanctify /ˈsæŋktəˌfai/ v. santificar.

sanction /ˈsæŋkʃən/ n. **1.** sanción f. —v. **2.** sancionar.

sanctity /ˈsæŋktiti/ n. santidad f.

sanctuary /ˈsæŋktʃuˌeri/ n. santuario, asilo m.

sand /sænd/ n. arena f.

sandal /ˈsændl/ n. sandalia f.

sandpaper /ˈsændˌpeipər/ n. papel de lija m.

sandwich /ˈsændwitʃ, ˈsæn-/ n. emparedado, sándwich m.

sandy /ˈsændi/ a. arenoso; (color) rufo.

sane /sein/ a. cuerdo; sano.

sanitary /ˈsæniˌteri/ a. higiénico, sanitario. **s. napkin,** toalla sanitaria.

sanitation /ˌsæniˈteiʃən/ n. saneamiento m.

sanity /ˈsæniti/ n. cordura f.

Santa Claus /ˈsæntə klɔz/ Papá Noel m.

sap /sæp/ n. savia f.; Colloq. estúpido, bobo m. —v. agotar.

sapphire /ˈsæfaiᵊr/ n. zafiro m.

sarcasm /ˈsɑrkæzəm/ n. sarcasmo m.

sardine /sɑrˈdin/ n. sardina f.

sash /sæʃ/ n. cinta f.

satellite /ˈsætlˌait/ n. satélite m.

satellite dish antena parabólica f.

satin /ˈsætn/ n. raso m.

satire /ˈsætaiᵊr/ n. sátira f.

satisfaction /ˌsætisˈfækʃən/ n. satisfacción f.; recompensa f.

satisfactory /ˌsætisˈfæktəri/ a. satisfactorio.

satisfy /ˈsætisˌfai/ v. satisfacer. **be satisfied that...,** estar convencido de que.

saturate /ˈsætʃəˌreit/ v. saturar.

Saturday /ˈsætərˌdei/ n. sábado m.

sauce /sɔs/ n. salsa; compota f.

saucer /ˈsɔsər/ n. platillo m.

saucy /'sɔsɪ/ a. descarado, insolente.

sauna /'sɔnə/ n. sauna f.

sausage /'sɔsɪdʒ/ n. salchicha f.

savage /'sævɪdʒ/ a. & n. salvaje m. & f.

save /seiv/ v. **1.** salvar; guardar; ahorrar, economizar. —prep. **2.** salvo, excepto.

savings /'seiviŋz/ n. ahorros m.pl.

savings account cuenta de ahorros m.

savings bank caja de ahorros f.

savior /'seivyər/ n. salvador -ora.

savor /'seivər/ n. **1.** sabor m. —v. **2.** saborear.

savory /'seivəri/ a. sabroso.

saw /sɔ/ n. **1.** sierra f. —v. **2.** aserrar.

saxophone /'sæksə,foun/ n. saxofón, saxófono, m.

say /sei/ v. decir; recitar.

saying /'seiiŋ/ n. dicho, refrán m.

scaffold /'skæfəld/ n. andamio; (gallows) patíbulo m.

scald /skɔld/ v. escaldar.

scale /skeil/ n. **1.** escala; (of fish) escama f.; (pl.) balanza f. —v. **2.** escalar; escamar.

scalp /skælp/ n. pericráneo m. v. escalpar.

scan /skæn/ v. hojear, repasar; (poetry) escandir; (computer) escanear, digitalizar.

scandal /'skændl/ n. escándalo m.

scanner /'skænər/ n. escáner m.

scant /skænt/ a. escaso.

scar /skɑr/ n. cicatriz f.

scarce /skɛərs/ a. escaso; raro.

scarcely /'skɛərsli/ adv. & conj. apenas.

scare /skɛər/ n. **1.** susto m. —v. **2.** asustar. **s. away,** espantar.

scarf /skɑrf/ n. pañueleta, bufanda f.

scarlet /'skɑrlɪt/ n. escarlata f.

scarlet fever escarlatina f.

scatter /'skætər/ v. esparcir; dispersar.

scavenger /'skævɪndʒər/ n. basurero m.

scenario /sɪ'nɛəri,ou, -'nɑr-/ n. escenario m.

scene /sin/ n. vista f., paisaje m.; Theat. escena f. **behind the scenes,** entre bastidores.

scenery /'sinəri/ n. paisaje m.; Theat. decorado m.

scent /sɛnt/ n. **1.** olor, perfume;

(sense) olfato m. —v. **2.** perfumar; Fig. sospechar.

schedule /'skɛdʒul, -ʊl, -uəl/ n. **1.** programa, horario m. —v. **2.** fijar la hora para.

scheme /skim/ n. **1.** proyecto; esquema m. —v. **2.** intrigar.

scholar /'skɒlər/ n. erudito -ta; becado -da.

scholarship /'skɒlər,ʃɪp/ n. beca; erudición f.

school /skul/ n. **1.** escuela f.; colegio m.; (of fish) banco m. —v. **2.** enseñar.

sciatica /saɪ'ætɪkə/ n. ciática f.

science /'saɪəns/ n. ciencia f.

science fiction ciencia ficción.

scientific /,saɪən'tɪfɪk/ a. científico.

scientist /'saɪəntɪst/ n. científico -ca.

scissors /'sɪzərz/ n. tijeras f.pl.

scoff /skɔf, skɒf/ v. mofarse, burlarse.

scold /skould/ v. regañar.

scoop /skup/ n. **1.** cucharón m.; cucharada f. —v. **2. s. out,** recoger, sacar.

scope /skoup/ n. alcance; campo m.

score /skɔr/ n. **1.** tantos m.pl.; (music) partitura f. —v. **2.** marcar, hacer tantos.

scorn /skɔrn/ n. **1.** desprecio m. —v. **2.** despreciar.

scornful /'skɔrnfəl/ a. desdeñoso.

Scotland /'skɒtlənd/ n. Escocia f.

Scottish /'skɒtɪʃ/ a. escocés.

scour /skaʊⁿr/ v. fregar, estregar.

scourge /skɜrdʒ/ n. azote m.; plaga f.

scout /skaʊt/ n. **1.** explorador -ra. —v. **2.** explorar, reconocer.

scramble /'skræmbəl/ n. **1.** rebatiña f. —v. **2.** bregar. **scrambled eggs,** huevos revueltos.

scrap /skræp/ n. **1.** migaja f.; pedacito m.; Colloq. riña f. **s. metal,** hierro viejo m. **s. paper,** papel borrador. —v. **2.** desechar; Colloq. reñir.

scrapbook /'skræp,bʊk/ n. álbum de recortes m.

scrape /skreip/ n. **1.** lío, apuro m. —v. **2.** raspar; (feet) restregar.

scratch /skrætʃ/ n. **1.** rasguño m. —v. **2.** rasguñar; rayar.

scream /skrim/ n. **1.** grito, chillido m. —v. **2.** gritar, chillar.

screen /skrin/ n. biombo m.; (for

window) tela metálica; (movie) pantalla f.

screw /skru/ n. **1.** tornillo m. —v. **2.** atornillar.

screwdriver /'skru,draivər/ n. destornillador m.

scribble /'skrɪbəl/ v. hacer garabatos.

scroll /skroul/ n. **1.** rúbrica f.; rollo de papel.

scroll bar n. barra de enrollar f.

scrub /skrʌb/ v. fregar, estregar.

scruple /'skrupəl/ n. escrúpulo m.

scrupulous /'skrupyələs/ a. escrupuloso.

scuba diving /'skubə 'daivɪŋ/ submarinismo m.

sculptor /'skʌlptər/ n. escultor -ra.

sculpture /'skʌlptʃər/ n. **1.** escultura f. —v. **2.** esculpir.

scythe /saið/ n. guadaña f.

sea /si/ n. mar m. or f.

seabed /'si,bɛd/ n. lecho marino m.

sea breeze brisa marina f.

seafood /'si,fud/ n. mariscos m.pl.

seal /sil/ n. **1.** sello m.; (animal) foca f. —v. **2.** sellar.

seam /sim/ n. costura f.

seamy /'simi/ a. sórdido.

seaplane /'si,plein/ n. hidroavión m.

seaport /'si,pɔrt/ n. puerto de mar.

search /sɜrtʃ/ n. **1.** registro m. **in s. of,** en busca de. —v. **2.** registrar. **s. for,** buscar.

search engine motor de búsqueda m., buscador m., indexador de información m.

seasick /'si,sɪk/ a. mareado. **to get s.,** marearse.

season /'sizən/ n. **1.** estación f., sazón; temporada f. —v. **2.** sazonar.

seasoning /'sizənɪŋ/ n. condimento m.

season ticket abono m.

seat /sit/ n. asiento m.; residencia, sede f.; Theat. localidad f. **s. belt,** cinturón de seguridad. —v. **2.** sentar. **be seated,** sentarse.

seaweed /'si,wid/ n. alga, alga marina f.

second /'sɪkənd/ a. & n. **1.** segundo m. —v. **2.** apoyar, segundar.

secondary /'sɛkən,dɛri/ a. secundario.

secret /'sikrɪt/ a. & n. secreto m.

secretary /'sɛkrɪ,tɛri/ n. secretario -ria; Govt. ministro -tra; (furniture) papelera f.

sect /sɛkt/ n. secta f.; partido m.

section /'sɛkʃən/ n. sección, parte f.

sectional /'sɛkʃənl/ a. regional, local.

secular /'sɛkyələr/ a. secular.

secure /sɪ'kyur/ a. **1.** seguro. —v. **2.** asegurar; obtener; Fin. garantizar.

security /sɪ'kyurɪti/ n. seguridad; garantía f.

sedative /'sɛdətɪv/ a. & n. sedativo m.

seduce /sɪ'dus/ v. seducir.

see /si/ v. ver; comprender. **s. off,** despedirse de. **s. to,** encargarse de.

seed /sid/ n. **1.** semilla f. —v. **2.** sembrar.

seek /sik/ v. buscar. **s. to,** tratar de.

seem /sim/ v. parecer.

seep /sip/ v. colarse.

segment /'sɛgmənt/ n. segmento m.

segregate /'sɛgrɪ,geit/ v. segregar.

seize /siz/ v. agarrar; apoderarse de.

seldom /'sɛldəm/ adv. rara vez.

select /sɪ'lɛkt/ a. **1.** escogido, selecto. —v. **2.** elegir, seleccionar.

selection /sɪ'lɛkʃən/ n. selección f.

selective /sɪ'lɛktɪv/ a. selectivo.

selfish /'sɛlfɪʃ/ a. egoísta.

selfishness /'sɛlfɪʃnɪs/ n. egoísmo m.

sell /sɛl/ v. vender.

semester /sɪ'mɛstər/ n. semestre m.

semicircle /'sɛmi,sɜrkəl/ n. semicírculo m.

semolina /,sɛmə'linə/ n. sémola f.

senate /'sɛnɪt/ n. senado m.

senator /'sɛnətər/ n. senador -ra.

send /sɛnd/ v. mandar, enviar; (a wire) poner. **s. away,** despedir. **s. back,** devolver. **s. for,** mandar buscar. **s. off,** expedir. **s. word,** mandar recado.

senile /'sinail/ a. senil.

senior /'sinyər/ a. mayor; más viejo. **Sr.,** padre.

senior citizen persona de edad avanzada.

sensation /sɛnˈseɪʃən/ n. sensación f.

sensational /sɛnˈseɪʃənl/ a. sensacional.

sense /sɛns/ n. 1. sentido; juicio m. —v. 2. percibir; sospechar.

sensible /ˈsɛnsəbəl/ a. sensato, razonable.

sensitive /ˈsɛnsɪtɪv/ a. sensible; sensitivo.

sensual /ˈsɛnʃuəl/ a. sensual.

sentence /ˈsɛntns/ n. 1. frase; Gram. oración; Leg. sentencia f. —v. 2. condenar.

sentiment /ˈsɛntəmənt/ n. sentimiento m.

sentimental /ˌsɛntəˈmɛntl/ a. sentimental.

separate /a. ˈsɛpərɪt; v. -ˌreɪt/ a. 1. separado; suelto. —v. 2. separar, dividir.

separation /ˌsɛpəˈreɪʃən/ n. separación f.

September /sɛpˈtɛmbər/ n. septiembre m.

sequence /ˈsikwəns/ n. serie f. **in s.,** seguidos.

serenade /ˌsɛrəˈneɪd/ n. 1. serenata f. —v. 2. dar serenata a.

serene /səˈrin/ a. sereno; tranquilo.

sergeant /ˈsɑrdʒənt/ n. sargento m.

serial /ˈsɪəriəl/ a. en serie, de serie.

series /ˈsɪəriz/ n. serie f.

serious /ˈsɪəriəs/ a. serio; grave.

sermon /ˈsɜrmən/ n. sermón m.

serpent /ˈsɜrpənt/ n. serpiente f.

servant /ˈsɜrvənt/ n. criado -da; servidor -ra.

serve /sɜrv/ v. servir.

server /ˈsɜrvər/ n. servidor m.

service /ˈsɜrvɪs/ n. 1. servicio m. **at the s. of,** a las órdenes de. **be of s.,** servir; ser útil. —v. 2. Auto. reparar.

service station estación de servicio f.

session /ˈsɛʃən/ n. sesión f.

set /sɛt/ a. 1. fijo. —n. 2. colección f.; (of a game) juego; Mech. aparato m.; Theat. decorado m. —v. 3. poner; colocar; fijar; (sun) ponerse. **s. forth,** exponer. **s. off, s. out,** salir. **s. up,** instalar; establecer.

settle /ˈsɛtl/ v. solucionar; arreglar; establecerse.

settlement /ˈsɛtlmənt/ n. caserío m.; arreglo; acuerdo m.

settler /ˈsɛtlər/ n. poblador -ra.

seven /ˈsɛvən/ a. & pron. siete.

seventeen /ˈsɛvənˈtin/ a. & pron. diecisiete.

seventh /ˈsɛvənθ/ a. séptimo.

seventy /ˈsɛvənti/ a. & pron. setenta.

sever /ˈsɛvər/ v. desunir; romper.

several /ˈsɛvərəl/ a. & pron. varios.

severance pay /ˈsɛvərəns/ indemnización de despido.

severe /səˈvɪər/ a. severo; grave.

severity /səˈvɛrɪti/ n. severidad f.

sew /sou/ v. coser.

sewer /ˈsuər/ n. cloaca f.

sewing /ˈsouɪŋ/ n. costura f.

sewing basket costurero m.

sewing machine máquina de coser f.

sex /sɛks/ n. sexo m.

sexism /ˈsɛksɪzəm/ n. sexismo m.

sexist /ˈsɛksɪst/ a. & n. sexista m. & f.

sexton /ˈsɛkstən/ n. sacristán m.

sexual /ˈsɛkʃuəl/ a. sexual.

shabby /ˈʃæbi/ a. haraposo, desaliñado.

shade /ʃeɪd/ n. 1. sombra f.; tinte m.; (window) transparente m. —v. 2. sombrear.

shadow /ˈʃædou/ n. sombra f.

shady /ˈʃeɪdi/ a. sombroso; sospechoso.

shaft /ʃæft/ n. (columna) fuste; Mech. asta f.

shake /ʃeɪk/ v. sacudir; agitar; temblar. **s. hands with,** dar la mano a.

shallow /ˈʃælou/ a. poco hondo; superficial.

shame /ʃeɪm/ n. 1. vergüenza f. **be a s.,** ser una lástima. —v. 2. avergonzar.

shameful /ˈʃeɪmfəl/ a. vergonzoso.

shampoo /ʃæmˈpu/ n. champú m.

shape /ʃeɪp/ n. 1. forma f.; estado m. —v. 2. formar.

share /ʃɛər/ n. 1. parte; (stock) acción f. 2 —v. 2. compartir.

shareholder /ˈʃɛərˌhouldər/ n. accionista m. f.

shareware /ˈʃɛərˌwɛər/ n. programas compartidos m.pl.

shark /ʃɑrk/ n. tiburón m.

sharp /ʃɑrp/ a. agudo; (blade) afilado.

sharpen /ˈʃɑrpən/ v. aguzar; afilar.

shatter /ˈʃætər/ v. estrellar; hacer pedazos.

shave /ʃeiv/ n. **1.** afeitada f. —v. **2.** afeitarse.

shawl /ʃɔl/ n. rebozo, chal m.

she /ʃi/ pron. ella f.

sheaf /ʃif/ n. gavilla f.

shear /ʃiər/ v. cizallar.

shears /ʃiərz/ n. cizallas f.pl.

sheath /ʃiθ/ n. vaina f.

shed /ʃɛd/ n. **1.** cobertizo m. —v. **2.** arrojar, quitarse.

sheep /ʃip/ n. oveja f.

sheet /ʃit/ n. sábana f.; (of paper) hoja f.

shelf /ʃɛlf/ n. estante, m., repisa f.

shell /ʃɛl/ n. **1.** cáscara; (sea) concha f.; Mil. proyectil m. —v. **2.** desgranar; bombardear.

shellac /ʃəˈlæk/ n. laca f.

shelter /ˈʃɛltər/ n. **1.** albergue; refugio m. —v. **2.** albergar; amparar.

shepherd /ˈʃɛpərd/ n. pastor m.

sherry /ˈʃɛri/ n. jerez m.

shield /ʃild/ n. **1.** escudo m. —v. **2.** amparar.

shift /ʃift/ n. **1.** cambio; (work) turno m. —v. **2.** cambiar, mudar. **s. for oneself,** arreglárselas.

shine /ʃain/ n. **1.** brillo, lustre m. —v. **2.** brillar; (shoes) lustrar.

shiny /ʃaini/ a. brillante, lustroso.

ship /ʃip/ n. **1.** barco m., nave f. —v. **2.** embarcar; Com. enviar.

shipment /ˈʃipmənt/ n. envío f.; embarque m.

shirk /ʃɑrk/ v. faltar al deber.

shirt /ʃɑrt/ n. camisa f.

shiver /ˈʃivər/ n. **1.** temblor m. —v. **2.** temblar.

shock /ʃɒk/ n. **1.** choque m. —v. **2.** chocar.

shoe /ʃu/ n. zapato m.

shoelace /ˈʃuˌleis/ n. lazo m.; cordón de zapato.

shoemaker /ˈʃuˌmeikər/ n. zapatero m.

shoot /ʃut/ v. tirar; (gun) disparar. **s. away, s. off,** salir disparado.

shop /ʃɒp/ n. tienda f.

shopping /ˈʃɒpiŋ/ n. **to go s.,** hacer compras, ir de compras.

shop window escaparate m.

shore /ʃɔr/ n. orilla; playa f.

short /ʃɔrt/ a. corto; breve; (in stature) pequeño, bajo. **a s. time,** poco tiempo. **in s.,** en suma.

shortage /ˈʃɔrtidʒ/ n. escasez; falta f.

shorten /ˈʃɔrtn/ v. acortar, abreviar.

shortly /ˈʃɔrtli/ adv. en breve, dentro de poco.

shorts /ʃɔrts/ n. calzoncillos m.pl.

shot /ʃɒt/ n. tiro, disparo m.

shoulder /ˈʃouldər/ n. **1.** hombro m. —v. **2.** asumir; cargar con.

shoulder blade n. omóplato m., paletilla f.

shout /ʃaut/ n. **1.** grito m. —v. **2.** gritar.

shove /ʃʌv/ n. **1.** empujón m. —v. **2.** empujar.

shovel /ˈʃʌvəl/ n. **1.** pala f. —v. **2.** traspalar.

show /ʃou/ n. **1.** ostentación f.; Theat. función f.; espectáculo m. —v. **2.** enseñar, mostrar; verse. **s. up,** destacarse; Colloq. asomar.

shower /ˈʃauər/ n. **1.** chubasco m.; (bath) ducha f. v. ducharse.

shrapnel /ˈʃræpnl/ n. metralla f.

shrewd /ʃrud/ a. astuto.

shriek /ʃrik/ n. **1.** chillido m. —v. **2.** chillar.

shrill /ʃril/ a. chillón, agudo.

shrimp /ʃrimp/ n. camarón m.

shrine /ʃrain/ n. santuario m.

shrink /ʃriŋk/ v. encogerse, contraerse. **s. from,** huir de.

shroud /ʃraud/ n. **1.** mortaja f. —v. **2.** Fig. ocultar.

shrub /ʃrʌb/ n. arbusto m.

shudder /ˈʃʌdər/ n. **1.** estremecimiento m. —v. **2.** estremecerse.

shun /ʃʌn/ v. evitar, huir de.

shut /ʃʌt/ v. cerrar. **s. in,** encerrar. **s. up,** Colloq. callarse.

shutter /ˈʃʌtər/ n. persiana f.

shy /ʃai/ a. tímido, vergonzoso.

sick /sik/ a. enfermo. **s. of,** aburrido de, cansado de.

sickness /ˈsiknis/ n. enfermedad f.

side /said/ n. **1.** lado; partido m.; parte f.; Anat. costado m. —v. **2.** s. with, ponerse del lado de.

sidewalk /ˈsaidˌwɔk/ n. acera, vereda f.

siege /sidʒ/ n. asedio m.

sieve /siv/ n. cedazo m.

sift /sift/ v. cerner.

sigh /sai/ n. **1.** suspiro m. —v. **2.** suspirar.

skim

sight /sait/ n. vista f.; punto de interés m. **lose s. of**, perder de vista. —v. **2.** divisar.

sign /sain/ n. **1.** letrero; señal, seña f. —v. **2.** firmar. **s. up**, inscribirse.

signal /'sɪgnl/ n. **1.** señal f. —v. **2.** hacer señales.

signature /'sɪgnətʃər/ n. firma f.

significance /sɪg'nɪfikəns/ n. significación f.

significant /sɪg'nɪfikənt/ a. significativo.

significant other pareja m. & f.

signify /'sɪgnə,fai/ v. significar.

silence /'sailəns/ n. **1.** silencio m. —v. **2.** hacer callar.

silent /'sailənt/ a. silencioso; callado.

silk /sɪlk/ n. seda f.

silken /'sɪlkən/ **silky** a. sedoso.

sill /sɪl/ n. umbral de puerta m., solera f.

silly /'sɪli/ a. necio, tonto.

silo /'sailou/ n. silo m.

silver /'sɪlvər/ n. plata f.

silver-plated /'sɪlvər 'pleitid/ a. chapado en plata.

silverware /'sɪlvər,wɛər/ n. vajilla de plata f.

similar /'sɪmələr/ a. semejante, parecido.

similarity /,sɪmə'læriti/ n. semejanza f.

simple /'sɪmpəl/ a. sencillo, simple.

simplicity /sɪm'plɪsiti/ n. sencillez f.

simplify /'sɪmplə,fai/ v. simplificar.

simulate /'sɪmyə,leit/ v. simular.

simultaneous /,saimǝl'teiniǝs/ a. simultáneo.

sin /sɪn/ n. **1.** pecado m. —v. **2.** pecar.

since /sɪns/ adv. **1.** desde entonces. —prep. **2.** desde. —conj. **3.** desde que; puesto que.

sincere /sɪn'sɪər/ a. sincero.

sincerely /sɪn'sɪərli/ adv. sinceramente.

sincerity /sɪn'sɛriti/ n. sinceridad f.

sinew /'sɪnyu/ n. tendón m.

sinful /'sɪnfəl/ a. pecador.

sing /sɪŋ/ v. cantar.

singe /sɪndʒ/ v. chamuscar.

singer /'sɪŋər/ n. cantante m. & f.

single /'sɪŋgəl/ a. solo; (room)

sencillo; (unmarried) soltero. **s. room**, habitación individual.

singular /'sɪŋgyələr/ a. & n. singular m.

sinister /'sɪnəstər/ a. siniestro.

sink /sɪŋk/ n. **1.** fregadero m. —v. **2.** hundir; Fig. abatir.

sinner /'sɪnər/ n. pecador -ra.

sinuous /'sɪnyuəs/ a. sinuoso.

sinus /'sainəs/ n. seno m.

sip /sɪp/ n. **1.** sorbo m. —v. **2.** sorber.

siphon /'saifən/ n. sifón m.

sir /sɜr/ title. señor.

siren /'sairən/ n. sirena f.

sirloin /'sɜrlɔin/ n. solomillo m.

sisal /'saisəl, 'sɪsəl/ n. henequén m.

sister /'sɪstər/ n. hermana f.

sister-in-law /'sɪstərɪn,lɔ/ n. cuñada f.

sit /sɪt/ v. sentarse; posar. **be sitting**, estar sentado. **s. down**, sentarse. **s. up**, incorporarse; quedar levantado.

site /sait/ n. sitio, local m.

sitting /'sɪtɪŋ/ n. sesión f. a. sentado.

situate /'sɪtʃu,eit/ v. situar.

situation /,sɪtʃu'eiʃən/ n. situación f.

sit-up /'sɪt ,ʌp/ n. abdominal m.

six /sɪks/ a. & pron. seis.

sixteen /'sɪks'tin/ a. & pron. dieciséis.

sixth /sɪksθ/ a. sexto.

sixty /'sɪksti/ a. & pron. sesenta.

size /saiz/ n. tamaño f.; (of shoe, etc.) número m.; talla f.

sizing /'saizɪŋ/ n. upreso m.; sisa, cola de retazo f.

skate /skeit/ n. **1.** patín m. —v. **2.** patinar.

skateboard /'skeit,bɔrd/ n. monopatín m.

skein /skein/ n. madeja f.

skeleton /'skelitn/ n. esqueleto m.

skeptic /'skeptɪk/ n. escéptico -ca.

skeptical /'skeptɪkəl/ a. escéptico.

sketch /skɛtʃ/ n. **1.** esbozo m. —v. **2.** esbozar.

ski /ski/ n. **1.** esquí m. —v. **2.** esquiar.

skid /skɪd/ n. **1.** resbalar. —n. **2.** varadera f.

skill /skɪl/ n. destreza, habilidad f.

skillful /'skɪlfəl/ a. diestro, hábil.

skim /skɪm/ v. rasar; (milk) desnatar. **s. over, s. through**, hojear.

skin /skɪn/ *n.* **1.** piel; (of fruit) corteza *f.* —*v.* **2.** desollar.

skin doctor dermatólogo -ga *m. & f.*

skip /skɪp/ *n.* **1.** brinco *m.* —*v.* **2.** brincar. **s. over,** pasar por alto.

skirmish /'skɜrmɪʃ/ *n.* escaramuza *f.*

skirt /skɜrt/ *n.* falda *f.*

skull /skʌl/ *n.* cráneo *m.*

skunk /skʌŋk/ *n.* zorrillo *m.*

sky /skaɪ/ *n.* cielo *m.*

skylight /'skaɪˌlaɪt/ *n.* tragaluz *m.*

skyscraper /'skaɪˌskreɪpər/ *n.* rascacielos *m.*

slab /slæb/ *n.* tabla *f.*

slack /slæk/ *a.* flojo; descuidado.

slacken /'slækən/ *v.* relajar.

slacks /slæks/ *n.* pantalones flojos.

slam /slæm/ *n.* **1.** portazo *m.* —*v.* **2.** cerrar de golpe. **slamming on the brakes,** frenazo *m.*

slander /'slændər/ *n.* **1.** calumnia *f.* —*v.* **2.** calumniar.

slang /slæŋ/ *n.* jerga *f.*

slant /slænt/ *n.* **1.** sesgo *m.* —*v.* **2.** sesgar.

slap /slæp/ *n.* **1.** bofetada, palmada *f.* —*v.* **2.** dar una bofetada.

slash /slæʃ/ *n.* **1.** cuchillada *f.* —*v.* **2.** acuchillar.

slat /slæt/ *n.* **1.** tablilla *f.* —*v.* **2.** lanzar.

slate /sleɪt/ *n.* **1.** pizarra *f.*; lista de candidatos. —*n.* **2.** destinar.

slaughter /'slɔtər/ *n.* **1.** matanza *f.* —*v.* **2.** matar.

slave /sleɪv/ *n.* esclavo -va.

slavery /'sleɪvəri/ *n.* esclavitud *f.*

Slavic /'slɑvɪk/ *a.* eslavo.

slay /sleɪ/ *v.* matar, asesinar.

sled /slɛd/ *n.* trineo *m.*

sleek /slik/ *a.* liso y brillante.

sleep /slip/ *n.* **1.** sueño *m.* **to get much s.,** dormir mucho. —*v.* **2.** dormir.

sleeping car /'slipɪŋ/ coche cama.

sleeping pill /'slipɪŋ/ pastilla para dormir, somnífero *m.*

sleepy /'slipi/ *a.* soñoliento. **to be s.,** tener sueño.

sleet /slit/ *n.* **1.** cellisca *f.* —*v.* **2.** cellisquear.

sleeve /sliv/ *n.* manga *f.*

slender /'slɛndər/ *a.* delgado.

slice /slaɪs/ *n.* **1.** rebanada *f.*; (of meat) tajada *f.* —*v.* **2.** rebanar; tajar.

slide /slaɪd/ *v.* resbalar, deslizarse.

slide rule regla de cálculo *f.*

slight /slaɪt/ *n.* **1.** desaire *m.* —*a.* **2.** pequeño; leve. —*v.* **3.** desairar.

slim /slɪm/ *a.* delgado.

slime /slaɪm/ *n.* lama *f.*

sling /slɪŋ/ *n.* **1.** honda *f.*; *Med.* cabestrillo *m.* —*v.* **2.** tirar.

slink /slɪŋk/ *v.* escabullirse.

slip /slɪp/ *n.* **1.** imprudencia; (garment) combinación *f.*; (of paper) trozo *m.*; ficha *f.* —*v.* **2.** resbalar; deslizar. **s. up,** equivocarse.

slipper /'slɪpər/ *n.* chinela *f.*

slippery /'slɪpəri/ *a.* resbaloso.

slit /slɪt/ *n.* **1.** abertura *f.* —*v.* **2.** cortar.

slogan /'sloʊgən/ *n.* lema *m.*

slope /sloʊp/ *n.* **1.** declive *m.* —*v.* **2.** inclinarse.

sloppy /'slɒpi/ *a.* desaliñado, chapucero.

slot /slɒt/ *n.* ranura *f.*

slot machine tragaperras *f.*

slouch /slaʊtʃ/ *n.* **1.** patán *m.* —*v.* **2.** estar gacho.

slovenly /'slʌvənli/ *a.* desaliñado.

slow /sloʊ/ *a.* **1.** lento; (watch) atrasado. —*v.* **2. s. down, s. up,** retardar; ir más despacio.

slowly /'sloʊli/ *adv.* despacio.

slowness /'sloʊnɪs/ *n.* lentitud *f.*

sluggish /'slʌgɪʃ/ *a.* perezoso, inactivo.

slum /slʌm/ *n.* barrio bajo *m.*

slumber /'slʌmbər/ *n.* **1.** sueño *m.* —*v.* **2.** dormitar.

slur /slɜr/ *n.* **1.** estigma *m.* —*v.* **2.** menospreciar.

slush /slʌʃ/ *n.* fango *m.*

sly /slaɪ/ *a.* taimado. **on the s.** a hurtadillas.

smack /smæk/ *n.* **1.** manotada *f.* —*v.* **2.** manotear.

small /smɔl/ *a.* pequeño.

small letter minúscula *f.*

smallpox /'smɔlˌpɒks/ *n.* viruela *f.*

smart /smɑrt/ *a.* **1.** listo; elegante. —*v.* **2.** escocer.

smash /smæʃ/ *v.* aplastar; hacer pedazos.

smear /smɪər/ *n.* **1.** mancha; difamación *f.* —*v.* **2.** manchar; difamar.

smell /smɛl/ *n.* **1.** olor; (sense) olfato *m.* —*v.* **2.** oler.

smelt /smɛlt/ *n.* **1.** eperlano *m.* —*v.* **2.** fundir.

smile /smaɪl/ *n.* **1.** sonrisa *f.* —*v.* **2.** sonreír.

smite /smaɪt/ *v.* afligir; apenar.

smock /smɒk/ *n.* camisa de mujer *f.*

smoke /smouk/ n. **1.** humo m.
—v. **2.** fumar; (food) ahumar.

smokestack /'smouk,stæk/ n. chimenea f.

smolder /'smouldər/ v. arder sin llama.

smooth /smuð/ a. **1.** liso; suave; tranquilo.—v. **2.** alisar.

smother /'smʌðər/ v. sofocar.

smug /smʌg/ a. presumido.

smuggle /'smʌgəl/ v. pasar de contrabando.

snack /snæk/ n. bocadillo m.

snag /snæg/ n. nudo; obstáculo m.

snail /sneil/ n. caracol m.

snake /sneik/ n. culebra, serpiente f.

snap /snæp/ n. **1.** trueno m.—v. **2.** tronar; romper.

snapshot /'snæp,ʃɒt/ n. instantánea f.

snare /snɛər/ n. trampa f.

snarl /snɑrl/ n. **1.** gruñido m.—v. **2.** gruñir; (hair) enredar.

snatch /snætʃ/ v. arrebatar.

sneak /snik/ v. ir, entrar, salir (etc.) a hurtadillas.

sneaker /'snikər/ n. sujeto ruín m. zapatilla de tenis.

sneer /snɪər/ n. **1.** mofa f.—v. **2.** mofarse.

sneeze /sniz/ n. **1.** estornudo m. —v. **2.** estornudar.

snicker /'snɪkər/ n. risita m.

snob /snɒb/ n. esnob m.

snore /snɔr/ n. **1.** ronquido m.—v. **2.** roncar.

snow /snou/ n. **1.** nieve f.—v. **2.** nevar.

snowball /'snou,bɔl/ n. bola de nieve f.

snowdrift /'snou,drɪft/ n. ventisquero m.

snowplow /'snou,plau/ n. quitanieves m.

snowstorm /'snou,stɔrm/ n. nevasca f.

snub /snʌb/ v. desairar.

snug /snʌg/ a. abrigado y cómodo.

so /sou/ adv. **1.** así; (also) también. **so as to,** para. **so that,** para que. **so... as,** tan... como. **so... that,** tan... que.—conj. **2.** así es que.

soak /souk/ v. empapar.

soap /soup/ n. **1.** jabón m.—v. **2.** enjabonar.

soap powder jabón en polvo m.

soar /sɔr/ v. remontarse.

sob /sɒb/ n. **1.** sollozo m.—v. **2.** sollozar.

sober /'soubər/ a. sobrio; pensativo.

sociable /'souʃəbəl/ a. sociable.

social /'souʃəl/ a. **1.** social.—n. **2.** tertulia f.

socialism /'souʃə,lɪzəm/ n. socialismo m.

socialist /'souʃəlɪst/ a. & n. socialista m. & f.

society /sə'saiɪti/ n. sociedad; compañía f.

sociological /,sousiə'lɒdʒɪkəl/ a. sociológico.

sociologist /,sousi,ɒlədʒɪst/ n. sociólogo -ga m. & f.

sociology /,sousi'ɒlədʒi/ n. sociología f.

sock /sɒk/ n. **1.** calcetín; puñetazo m. —v. **2.** dar un puñetazo a.

socket /'sɒkɪt/ n. cuenca f.; Elec. enchufe m.

sod /sɒd/ n. césped m.

soda /'soudə/ n. soda; Chem. sosa f.

sodium /'soudiəm/ n. sodio m.

sofa /'soufə/ n. sofá m.

soft /sɒft/ a. blando; fino; suave.

soft drink bebida no alcohólica.

soften /'sɒfən/ v. ablandar; suavizar.

software /'sɒft,wɛər/ n. software m., programa m.

soil /sɔil/ n. **1.** suelo m.—v. **2.** ensuciar.

sojourn /'soudʒɜrn/ n. morada f., estancia f.

solace /'sɒlɪs/ n. **1.** solaz m.—v. **2.** solazar.

solar /'soulər/ a. solar.

solar system sistema solar m.

solder /'sɒdər/ v. **1.** soldar.—n. **2.** soldadura f.

soldier /'souldʒər/ n. soldado m. & f.

sole /soul/ n. **1.** suela f.; (of foot) planta f.; (fish) lenguado m.—a. **2.** único.

solemn /'sɒləm/ a. solemne.

solemnity /sə'lɛmnɪti/ n. solemnidad f.

solicit /sə'lɪsɪt/ v. solicitar.

solicitous /sə'lɪsɪtəs/ a. solícito.

solid /'sɒlɪd/ a. & n. sólido m.

solidify /sə'lɪdə,fai/ v. solidificar.

solidity /sə'lɪdɪti/ n. solidez f.

solitary /'sɒlɪ,tɛri/ a. solitario.

solitude /'sɒlɪ,tud/ n. soledad f.

solo /'soulou/ *n.* solo *m.*

soloist /'soulouɪst/ *n.* solista *m.* & *f.*

soluble /'sɒlyəbəl/ *a.* soluble.

solution /sə'luʃən/ *n.* solución *f.*

solve /sɒlv/ *v.* solucionar; resolver.

solvent /'sɒlvənt/ *a.* solvente.

somber /'sɒmbər/ *a.* sombrío.

some /sʌm, *unstressed* səm/ *a.* & *pron.* algo (de), un poco (de); alguno; (pl.) algunos, unos.

somebody, someone /'sʌmbɒdi, 'sʌm,wʌn/ *pron.* alguien.

somehow /'sʌm,hau/ *adv.* de algún modo.

someone /'sʌm,wʌn/ *n.* alguien o alguno.

somersault /'sʌmər,sɒlt/ *n.* salto mortal *m.*

something /'sʌm,θɪŋ/ *pron.* algo, alguna cosa.

sometime /'sʌm,taim/ *adv.* alguna vez.

sometimes /'sʌm,taimz/ *adv.* a veces, algunas veces.

somewhat /'sʌm,wʌt/ *adv.* algo, un poco.

somewhere /'sʌm,wɛər/ *adv.* en (*or* a) alguna parte.

son /sʌn/ *n.* hijo *m.*

song /sɒŋ/ *n.* canción *f.*

son-in-law /'sʌn ɪn ,lɔ/ *n.* yerno *m.*

soon /sun/ *adv.* pronto. **as s. as possible,** cuanto antes. **sooner or later,** tarde o temprano. **no sooner... than,** apenas... cuando.

soot /sut/ *n.* hollín *m.*

soothe /suð/ *v.* calmar.

soothingly /'suðɪŋli/ *adv.* tiernamente.

sophisticated /sə'fɪstɪ,keitɪd/ *a.* sofisticado.

sophomore /'sɒfə,mɔr/ *n.* estudiante de segundo año *m.*

soprano /sə'prænou/ *n.* soprano *m.* & *f.*

sorcery /'sɔrsəri/ *n.* encantamiento *m.*

sordid /'sɔrdɪd/ *a.* sórdido.

sore /sɔr/ *n.* 1. llaga *f.* —*a.* 2. lastimado; *Colloq.* enojado. **to be s.,** doler.

sorority /sə'rɔrɪti, -'rɒr-/ *n.* hermandad de mujeres *f.*

sorrow /'sɒrou/ *n.* pesar, dolor *m.*, aflicción *f.*

sorrowful /'sɒrəfəl/ *a.* doloroso; afligido.

sorry /'sɒri/ *a.* **to be s.,** sentir, lamentar. **to be s. for,** compadecer.

sort /sɔrt/ *n.* 1. tipo *m.*; clase, especie *f.* **s. of,** algo, un poco. —*v.* 2. clasificar.

soul /soul/ *n.* alma *f.*

sound /saund/ *a.* 1. sano; razonable; firme. —*a.* 2. sonido *m.* —*v.* 3. sonar; parecer.

soundproof /'saund,pruf/ *a.* insonorizado. *v.* insonorizar.

soundtrack /'saund,træk/ *n.* banda sonora *f.*

soup /sup/ *n.* sopa *f.*

sour /sauər/ *a.* agrio; ácido; rancio.

source /sɔrs/ *n.* fuente; causa *f.*

south /sauθ/ *n.* sur *m.*

South Africa /'æfrɪkə/ Sudáfrica *f.*

South African *a.* & *n.* sudafricano.

South America /ə'mɛrɪkə/ Sud América, América del Sur.

South American *a.* & *n.* sudamericano -na.

southeast /,sauθ'ist/ *Naut.* ,sau-/ *n.* sudeste *m.*

southern /'sʌðərn/ *a.* meridional.

South Pole *n.* Polo Sur *m.*

southwest /,sauθ'wɛst/ *Naut.* ,sau-/ *n.* sudoeste *m.*

souvenir /,suvə'nɪər/ *n.* recuerdo *m.*

sovereign /'sɒvrɪn/ *n.* soberano -na.

sovereignty /'sɒvrɪnti/ *n.* soberanía *f.*

Soviet Russia Rusia Soviética *f.*

sow /n.* sau; *v.* sou/ *n.* 1. puerca *f.* —*v.* 2. sembrar.

space /speis/ *n.* 1. espacio *m.* —*v.* 2. espaciar.

space out *v.* escalonar.

spaceship /'speis,ʃɪp/ *n.* nave espacial, astronave *f.*

space shuttle /'ʃʌtl/ *n.* transbordador espacial *m.*

spacious /'speiʃəs/ *a.* espacioso.

spade /speid/ *n.* 1. laya; (cards) espada *f.* —*v.* 2. layar.

spaghetti /spə'geti/ *n.* espaguetis *m.pl.*

Spain /spein/ *n.* España *f.*

span /spæn/ *n.* 1. tramo *m.* —*v.* 2. extenderse sobre.

Spaniard /'spænyərd/ *n.* español -ola.

Spanish /'spænɪʃ/ *a.* & *n.* español -ola.

spoil

spank /spæŋk/ v. pegar.
spanking /'spæŋkɪŋ/ n. tunda, zumba f.
spar /spɑr/ v. altercar.
spare /spɛər/ a. **1.** de repuesto. —v. **2.** perdonar; ahorrar; prestar. **have... to s.,** tener... de sobra.
spare tire neumático de recambio m.
spark /spɑrk/ n. chispa f.
sparkle /'spɑrkəl/ n. **1.** destello m. —v. **2.** chispear. **sparkling wine,** vino espumoso.
spark plug /spɑrk,plʌg/ n. bujía f.
sparrow /'spærou/ n. gorrión m.
sparse /spɑrs/ a. esparcido.
spasm /'spæzəm/ n. espasmo m.
spasmodic /spæz'mɒdɪk/ a. espasmódico.
spatter /'spætər/ v. salpicar; manchar.
speak /spik/ v. hablar.
speaker /'spikər/ n. conferencista m. & f.
spear /spɪər/ n. lanza f.
spearmint /'spɪər,mɪnt/ n. menta romana f.
special /'spɛʃəl/ a. especial. **s. delivery,** entrega inmediata, entrega urgente.
specialist /'spɛʃəlɪst/ n. especialista m. & f.
specialty /'spɛʃəlti/ n. especialidad f.
species /'spiʃiz, -siz/ n. especie f.
specific /spɪ'sɪfɪk/ a. específico.
specify /'spɛsə,faɪ/ v. especificar.
specimen /'spɛsəmən/ n. espécimen m.; muestra f.
spectacle /'spɛktəkəl/ n. espectáculo m.; (pl.) lentes, anteojos m.pl.
spectacular /spɛk'tækyələr/ a. espectacular, aparatoso.
spectator /'spɛkteitər/ n. espectador -ra.
spectrum /'spɛktrəm/ n. espectro m.
speculate /'spɛkyə,leit/ v. especular.
speculation /,spɛkyə'leiʃən/ n. especulación f.
speech /spitʃ/ n. habla f.; lenguaje; discurso m. **part of s.,** parte de la oración.
speechless /'spitʃlɪs/ a. mudo.
speed /spid/ n. **1.** velocidad; rapidez f. —v. **2. s. up,** acelerar, apresurar.

speed limit velocidad máxima f.
speedometer /spi'dɒmɪtər/ n. velocímetro m.
speedy /'spidi/ a. veloz, rápido.
spell /spɛl/ n. **1.** hechizo; rato; Med. ataque m. —v. **2.** escribir; relevar.
spelling /'spɛlɪŋ/ n. ortografía f.
spend /spɛnd/ v. gastar; (time) pasar.
spendthrift /'spɛnd,θrɪft/ a. & n. pródigo; manirroto m.
sphere /sfɪər/ n. esfera f.
spice /spais/ n. **1.** especia f. —v. **2.** especiar.
spider /'spaidər/ n. araña f.
spider web telaraña f.
spike /spaik/ n. alcayata f.; punta f., clavo m.
spill /spɪl/ v. derramar. n. caída f., vuelco m.
spillway /'spɪl,wei/ n. vertedero m.
spin /spɪn/ v. hilar; girar.
spinach /'spɪnɪtʃ/ n. espinaca f.
spine /spain/ n. espina dorsal f.
spinet /'spɪnɪt/ n. espineta m.
spinster /'spɪnstər/ n. solterona f.
spiral /'spairəl/ a. & n. espiral f.
spire /spaiər/ n. caracol m., espiral f.
spirit /'spɪrɪt/ n. espíritu; ánimo m.
spiritual /'spɪrɪtʃuəl/ a. espiritual.
spiritualism /'spɪrɪtʃuə,lɪzəm/ n. espiritismo m.
spirituality /,spɪrɪtʃu'ælɪti/ n. espiritualidad f.
spit /spɪt/ v. escupir.
spite /spait/ n. despecho m. **in s. of,** a pesar de.
splash /splæʃ/ n. **1.** salpicadura f. —v. **2.** salpicar.
splendid /'splɛndɪd/ a. espléndido.
splendor /'splɛndər/ n. esplendor m.
splice /splais/ v. **1.** empalmar. n. **2.** empalme m.
splint /splɪnt/ n. tablilla f.
splinter /'splɪntər/ n. **1.** astilla f. —v. **2.** astillar.
split /splɪt/ n. **1.** división f. —v. **2.** dividir, romper en dos.
splurge /splɜrdʒ/ v. **1.** fachendear. —v. **2.** fachenda f.
spoil /spɔil/ n. **1.** (pl.) botín m. —v. **2.** echar a perder; (a child) mimar.

spoke /spouk/ n. rayo (de rueda) m.

spokesman /'spouksmən/ n. portavoz m. & f.

spokesperson /'spouks,pərsən/ n. portavoz m. & f.

sponge /spʌndʒ/ n. esponja f.

sponsor /'spɒnsər/ n. **1.** patrocinador m. —v. **2.** patrocinar; costear.

spontaneity /,spɒntə'niiti, -'nei-/ n. espontaneidad f.

spontaneous /spɒn'teiniəs/ a. espontáneo.

spool /spul/ n. carrete m.

spoon /spun/ n. cuchara f.

spoonful /'spunful/ n. cucharada f.

sporadic /spə'rædik/ a. esporádico.

sport /spɔrt/ n. deporte m.

sport jacket chaqueta deportiva f.

sports center /spɔrts/ pabellón de deportes, polideportivo m.

sportsman /'spɔrtsmən/ n. **1.** deportivo. —n. **2.** deportista m. & f.

spot /spɒt/ n. **1.** mancha f.; lugar, punto m. —v. **2.** distinguir.

spouse /spaus/ n. esposo -sa.

spout /spaut/ n. **1.** chorro; (of teapot) pico m. —v. **2.** correr a chorro.

sprain /sprein/ n. **1.** torcedura f., esguince m. —v. **2.** torcerse.

sprawl /sprɔl/ v. tenderse.

spray /sprei/ n. **1.** rociada f. —v. **2.** rociar.

spread /spred/ n. **1.** propagación; extensión; (for bed) colcha f. —v. **2.** propagar; extender.

spreadsheet /'spred,ʃit/ n. hoja de cálculo f.

spree /spri/ n. parranda f.

sprig /sprig/ n. ramita f.

sprightly /'spraitli/ a. garboso.

spring /spriŋ/ n. resorte, muelle m.; (season) primavera f.; (of water) manantial m.

springboard /'spriŋ,bɔrd/ n. trampolín m.

spring onion cebolleta f.

sprinkle /'spriŋkəl/ v. rociar; (rain) lloviznar.

sprint /sprint/ n. carrera f.

sprout /spraut/ n. retoño m.

spry /sprai/ a. ágil.

spun /spʌn/ a. hilado.

spur /spər/ n. **1.** espuela f. **on the s. of the moment,** sin pensarlo. —v. **2.** espolear.

spurious /'spyuriəs/ a. espurio.

spurn /spərn/ v. rechazar, despreciar.

spurt /spərt/ n. **1.** chorro m.; esfuerzo supremo. —v. **2.** salir en chorro.

spy /spai/ **1.** espía m. & f. —v. **2.** espiar.

squabble /'skwɒbl/ n. **1.** riña f. —v. **2.** reñir.

squad /skwɒd/ n. escuadra f.

squadron /'skwɒdrən/ n. escuadrón m.

squalid /'skwɒlɪd/ a. escuálido.

squall /skwɔl/ n. borrasca f.

squalor /'skwɒlər/ n. escualidez f.

squander /'skwɒndər/ v. malgastar.

square /skwɛər/ a. **1.** cuadrado. —n. **2.** cuadrado m.; plaza f.

square dance n. contradanza f.

squat /skwɒt/ v. agacharse.

squeak /skwik/ n. **1.** chirrido m. —v. **2.** chirriar.

squeamish /'skwimiʃ/ a. escrupuloso.

squeeze /skwiz/ n. **1.** apretón m. —v. **2.** apretar; (fruit) exprimir.

squirrel /'skwərəl/ n. ardilla f.

squirt /skwərt/ n. **1.** chisguete m. —v. **2.** jeringar.

stab /stæb/ n. **1.** puñalada f. —v. **2.** apuñalar.

stability /stə'bilɪti/ n. estabilidad f.

stabilize /steibə,laiz/ v. estabilizar.

stable /'steibəl/ a. **1.** estable, equilibrado. —n. **2.** caballeriza f.

stack /stæk/ n. **1.** pila f. —v. **2.** apilar.

stadium /'steidiəm/ n. estadio m.

staff /stæf/ n. personal m. **editorial s.,** cuerpo de redacción. **general s.,** estado mayor.

stag /stæg/ n. ciervo m.

stage /steidʒ/ n. **1.** etapa f.; *Theat.* escena f. —v. **2.** representar.

stagflation /stæg'fleiʃən/ n. estagflación.

stagger /'stægər/ v. (teeter) tambalear; (space out) escalonar.

stagnant /'stægnənt/ a. estancado.

stagnate /'stægneit/ v. estancarse.

stain /stein/ n. **1.** mancha f. —v. **2.** manchar.

stainless steel /'steinlis/ acero inoxidable m.

staircase /'stɛər,keis/ *n.* escalera *f.*

stairs *n.* escalera *f.*

stake /steik/ *n.* estaca; (bet) apuesta *f.* **at s.,** en juego; en peligro.

stale /steil/ *a.* rancio.

stalemate /'steil,meit/ *n.* estancación *f.*; tablas *f.pl.*

stalk /stɔk/ *n.* caña *f.*; (of flower) tallo *m. v.* acechar.

stall /stɔl/ *n.* 1. tenderete; (for horse) pesebre *m.* —*v.* 2. demorar; (motor) atascar.

stallion /'stælyən/ *n. S.A.* garañón *m.*

stalwart /'stɔlwərt/ *a.* fornido.

stamina /'stæmənə/ *n.* vigor *m.*

stammer /'stæmər/ *v.* tartamudear.

stamp /stæmp/ *n.* 1. sello *m.,* estampilla *f.* —*v.* 2. sellar.

stamp collecting /kə'lɛktɪŋ/ filatelia *f.*

stampede /stæm'pid/ *n.* estampida *f.*

stand /stænd/ *n.* 1. puesto *m.;* posición; (speaker's) tribuna; (furniture) mesita *f.* —*v.* 2. estar; estar de pie; aguantar. **s. up,** pararse, levantarse.

standard /'stændərd/ *a.* 1. normal, corriente. —*n.* 2. norma *f.* **s. of living,** nivel de vida.

standardize /'stændər,daiz/ *v.* uniformar.

standing /'stændɪŋ/ *a.* fijo; establecido.

standpoint /'stænd,pɔint/ *n.* punto de vista *m.*

staple /'steipəl/ *n.* materia prima *f.;* grapa *f.*

stapler /'steiplər/ *n.* grapadora *f.*

star /stɑr/ *n.* estrella *f.*

starboard /'stɑrbərd/ *n.* estribor *m.*

starch /stɑrtʃ/ *n.* almidón *m.;* (in diet) fécula *f.* —*v.* 2. almidonar.

stare /stɛər/ *v.* mirar fijamente.

stark /stɑrk/ *a.* 1. severo. —*adv.* 2. completamente.

start /stɑrt/ *n.* 1. susto; principio *m.* —*v.* 2. comenzar, empezar; salir; poner en marcha; causar.

startle /'stɑrtl/ *v.* asustar.

starvation /stɑr'veiʃən/ *n.* hambre *f.*

starve /stɑrv/ *v.* morir de hambre.

state /steit/ *n.* 1. estado *m.* —*v.* 2. declarar, decir.

statement /'steitmənt/ *n.* declaración *f.*

stateroom /'steit,rum/ *n.* camarote *m.*

statesman /'steitsmən/ *n.* estadista *m.*

static /'stætik/ *a.* 1. estático. —*n.* 2. estática *f.*

station /'steiʃən/ *n.* estación *f.*

stationary /'steiʃə,nɛri/ *a.* estacionario, fijo.

stationery /'steiʃə,nɛri/ *n.* papel de escribir.

statistics /stə'tistiks/ *n.* estadística *f.*

statue /'stætʃu/ *n.* estatua *f.*

stature /'stætʃər/ *n.* estatura *f.*

status /'steitəs, 'stætəs/ *n.* condición, estado *m.*

statute /'stætʃut/ *n.* ley *f.*

staunch /stɔntʃ/ *a.* fiel; constante.

stay /stei/ *n.* 1. estancia; visita *f.* —*v.* 2. quedar, permanecer; parar, alojarse. **s. away,** ausentarse. **s. up,** velar.

steadfast /'stɛd,fæst/ *a.* inmutable.

steady /'stɛdi/ *a.* 1. firme; permanente; regular. —*v.* 2. sostener.

steak /steik/ *n.* biftec, bistec *m.*

steal /stil/ *v.* robar. **s. away,** escabullirse.

stealth /stɛlθ/ *n.* cautela *f.*

steam /stim/ *n.* vapor *m.*

steamboat /'stim,bout/ **steamer, steamship** *n.* vapor *m.*

steel /stil/ *n.* 1. acero *m.* —*v.* 2. **s. oneself,** fortalecerse.

steep /stip/ *a.* escarpado, empinado.

steeple /'stipəl/ *n.* campanario *m.*

steer /stɪər/ *n.* 1. buey *m.* —*v.* 2. guiar, manejar.

stellar /'stɛlər/ *a.* astral.

stem /stɛm/ *n.* 1. tallo *m.* —*v.* 2. parar. **s. from,** emanar de.

stencil /'stɛnsəl/ *n.* 1. estarcido. —*v.* 2. estarcir.

stenographer /stə'nɒgrəfər/ *n.* estenógrafo -fa.

stenography /stə'nɒgrəfi/ *n.* taquigrafía *f.*

step /stɛp/ *n.* 1. paso *m.;* medida *f.;* (stairs) escalón *m.* —*v.* 2. pisar. **s. back,** retirarse.

stepladder /'stɛp,lædər/ *n.* escalera de mano *f.*

stereophonic /,stɛriə'fɒnik/ *a.* estereofónico.

stereotype /'stɛrɪə,taip/ *n.* **1.** estereotipo *m.* —*v.* **2.** estereotipar.

sterile /'stɛrɪl/ *a.* estéril.

sterilize /'stɛrə,laiz/ *v.* esterilizar.

sterling /'stɜrlɪŋ/ *a.* esterlina, genuino.

stern /stɜrn/ *n.* **1.** popa *f.* —*a.* **2.** duro, severo.

stethoscope /'stɛθə,skoup/ *n.* estetoscopio *m.*

stevedore /'stivɪ,dɔr/ *n.* estibador *m.*

stew /stu/ *n.* **1.** guisado *m.* —*v.* **2.** estofar.

steward /'stuərd/ *n.* camarero.

stewardess /'stuərdɪs/ *n.* azafata *f.*, aeromoza *f.*

stick /stɪk/ *n.* **1.** palo, bastón *m.* —*v.* **2.** pegar; (put) poner, meter.

sticky /'stɪki/ *a.* pegajoso.

stiff /stɪf/ *a.* tieso; duro.

stiffness /'stɪfnɪs/ *n.* tiesura *f.*

stifle /'staifəl/ *v.* sofocar; *Fig.* suprimir.

stigma /'stɪgmə/ *n.* estigma *m.*

still /stɪl/ *a.* **1.** quieto; silencioso. **to keep s.,** quedarse quieto. —*adv.* **2.** todavía, aún; no obstante. —*n.* **3.** alambique *m.*

stillborn /'stɪl,bɔrn/ *a.* & *a.* nacido -da muerto -ta.

still life *n.* naturaleza muerta *f.*

stillness /'stɪlnɪs/ *n.* silencio *m.*

stilted /'stɪltɪd/ *a.* afectado, artificial.

stimulant /'stɪmyələnt/ *a.* & *n.* estimulante *m.*

stimulate /'stɪmyə,leit/ *v.* estimular.

stimulus /'stɪmyələs/ *n.* estímulo *m.*

sting /stɪŋ/ *n.* **1.** picadura *f.* —*v.* **2.** picar.

stingy /'stɪndʒi/ *a.* tacaño.

stir /stɜr/ *n.* **1.** conmoción *f.* —*v.* **2.** mover. **s. up,** conmover; suscitar.

stitch /stɪtʃ/ *n.* **1.** puntada *f.* —*v.* **2.** coser.

stock /stɒk/ *n.* surtido *f.*; raza *f.*; (finance) acciones. *f.pl.* **in s.,** en existencia. **to take s. in,** tener fe en.

stock exchange bolsa *f.*

stockholder /'stɒk,houldər/ *n.* accionista *m.* & *f.*

stocking /'stɒkɪŋ/ *n.* media *f.*

stockyard /'stɒk,yɑrd/ *n.* corral de ganado *m.*

stodgy /'stɒdʒi/ *a.* pesado.

stoical /'stouɪkəl/ *a.* estoico.

stole /stoul/ *n.* estola *f.*

stolid /'stɒlɪd/ *a.* impasible.

stomach /'stʌmək/ *n.* estómago *m.*

stomachache /'stʌmək,eik/ *n.* dolor de estómago *m.*

stone /stoun/ *n.* piedra *f.*

stool /stul/ *n.* banquillo *m.*

stoop /stup/ *v.* encorvarse; *Fig.* rebajarse. espaldas encorvadas *f.pl.*

stop /stɒp/ *n.* **1.** parada *f.* **to put a s. to,** poner fin a. —*v.* **2.** parar; suspender; detener; impedir. **s. doing** (etc.), dejar de hacer (etc.).

stopgap /'stɒp,gæp/ *n.* recurso provisional *m.*

stopover /'stɒp,ouvər/ *n.* parada *f.*

stopwatch /'stɒp,wɒtʃ/ *n.* cronómetro *m.*

storage /'stɔrɪdʒ/ *n.* almacenaje *m.*

store /stɔr/ *n.* **1.** tienda; provisión *f.* **department s.,** almacén *m.* —*v.* **2.** guardar; almacenar.

store window escaparate *m.*

stork /stɔrk/ *n.* cigüeña *f.*

storm /stɔrm/ *n.* tempestad, tormenta *f.*

stormy /'stɔrmi/ *a.* tempestuoso.

story /'stɔri/ *n.* cuento; relato *m.*; historia *f.* **short s.,** cuento.

stout /staut/ *a.* corpulento.

stove /stouv/ *n.* hornilla; estufa *f.*

straight /streit/ *a.* **1.** recto; derecho. —*adv.* **2.** directamente.

straighten /'streitn/ *v.* enderezar. **s. out,** poner en orden.

straightforward /,streit'fɔrwərd/ *a.* recto, sincero.

strain /strein/ *n.* **1.** tensión *f.* —*v.* **2.** colar.

strainer /'streinər/ *n.* colador *m.*

strait /streit/ *n.* estrecho *m.*

strand /strænd/ *n.* **1.** hilo *m.* —*v.* **2. be stranded,** encallarse.

stranger /'streindʒər/ *n.* extranjero -ra; forastero -ra; desconocido -da.

strangle /'stræŋgəl/ *v.* estrangular.

strap /stræp/ *n.* correa *f.*

stratagem /'strætədʒəm/ *n.* estratagema *f.*

sublime

strategic /strə'tidʒɪk/ a. estratégico.

strategy /'strætɪdʒɪ/ n. estrategia f.

stratosphere /'strætə,sfɪər/ n. estratosfera f.

straw /strɔ/ n. paja f.

strawberry /'strɔ,berɪ/ n. fresa f.

stray /streɪ/ a. 1. vagabundo. —v. 2. extraviarse.

streak /strik/ n. 1. racha; raya f.; lado m. —v. 2. rayar.

stream /strim/ n. corriente f.; arroyo m.

street /strit/ n. calle f.

streetcar /'strit,kɑr/ n. tranvía m.

street lamp /'strit,læmp/ n. farol m.

strength /strɛŋkθ, strɛŋθ/ n. fuerza m.

strengthen /'strɛŋkθən, 'strɛŋ-/ v. reforzar.

strenuous /'strɛnyuəs/ a. estrenuo.

streptococcus /,strɛptə'kɒkəs/ n. estreptococo m.

stress /strɛs/ n. 1. tensión f.; énfasis m. —v. 2. recalcar; acentuar.

stretch /strɛtʃ/ n. 1. trecho m. **at one s.,** de un tirón. —v. 2. tender; extender; estirarse.

stretcher /'strɛtʃər/ n. camilla f.

strew /stru/ v. esparcir.

stricken /'strɪkən/ a. agobiado.

strict /strɪkt/ a. estricto; severo.

stride /straɪd/ n. 1. tranco m.; (fig., pl.) progresos. —v. 2. andar a trancos.

strife /straɪf/ n. contienda f.

strike /straɪk/ n. 1. huelga f. —v. 2. pegar; chocar con; (clock) dar.

striker /'straɪkər/ n. huelguista m. & f.

string /strɪŋ/ n. cuerda f.; cordel m.

string bean n. habichuela f.

stringent /'strɪndʒənt/ a. estricto.

strip /strɪp/ n. 1. tira f. —v. 2. despojar; desnudarse.

stripe /straɪp/ n. raya f.; Mil. galón m.

strive /straɪv/ v. esforzarse.

stroke /strouk/ n. 1. golpe m.; (swimming) brazada f.; Med. ataque m. **s. of luck,** suerte f.

stroll /stroul/ n. 1. paseo m. —v. 2. pasearse.

stroller /'stroulər/ n. vagabundo m.; cochecito (de niño) m.

strong /strɔŋ/ a. fuerte.

stronghold /'strɔŋ,hould/ n. fortificación f.

structure /'strʌktʃər/ n. estructura f.

struggle /'strʌgəl/ n. 1. lucha f. —v. 2. luchar.

strut /strʌt/ n. 1. pavonada f. —v. 2. pavonear.

stub /stʌb/ n. 1. cabo; (ticket) talón m. —v. 2. **s. on one's toes,** tropezar con.

stubborn /'stʌbərn/ a. testarudo.

stucco /'stʌkou/ n. 1. estuco m. —v. 2. estucar.

student /'studnt/ n. alumno -na, estudiante -ta.

studio /'studi,ou/ n. estudio m.

studious /'studiəs/ a. aplicado; estudioso.

study /'stʌdɪ/ n. 1. estudio m. —v. 2. estudiar.

stuff /stʌf/ n. 1. cosas f.pl. —v. 2. llenar; rellenar.

stuffing /'stʌfɪŋ/ n. relleno m.

stumble /'stʌmbəl/ v. tropezar.

stump /stʌmp/ n. cabo; tocón; muñón m.

stun /stʌn/ v. aturdir.

stunt /stʌnt/ n. 1. maniobra sensacional f. —v. 2. impedir crecimiento.

stupendous /stu'pɛndəs/ a. estupendo.

stupid /'stupɪd/ a. estúpido.

stupidity /stu'pɪdɪtɪ/ n. estupidez f.

stupor /'stupər/ n. estupor m.

sturdy /'stɜrdɪ/ a. robusto.

stutter /'stʌtər/ v. 1. tartamudear. —n. 2. tartamudeo m.

sty /staɪ/ n. pocilga f.; Med. orzuelo.

style /staɪl/ n. estilo m.; moda f.

stylish /'staɪlɪʃ/ a. elegante; a la moda.

suave /swɑv/ a. afable, suave.

subconscious /sʌb'kɒnʃəs/ a. subconsciente.

subdue /səb'du/ v. dominar.

subject /n. 'sʌbdʒɪkt; v. səb'dʒɛkt/ n. 1. tema m.; (of study) materia f.; Pol. súbdito -ta; Gram. sujeto m. —v. 2. someter.

subjugate /'sʌbdʒə,geɪt/ v. sojuzgar, subyugar.

subjunctive /səb'dʒʌŋktɪv/ a. & n. subjuntivo m.

sublimate /'sʌblə,meɪt/ v. sublimar.

sublime /sə'blaɪm/ a. sublime.

submarine /ˌsʌbməˈrin/ a. & n. submarino m.

submerge /səbˈmɜrdʒ/ v. sumergir.

submission /səbˈmɪʃən/ n. sumisión f.

submit /səbˈmɪt/ v. someter.

subnormal /sʌbˈnɔrməl/ a. subnormal.

subordinate /a, n səˈbɔrdənɪt; v -dn̩ˌeit/ a. & n. **1.** subordinado -da. —v. **2.** subordinar.

subscribe /səbˈskraɪb/ v. aprobar; abonarse.

subscriber /səbˈskraɪbər/ n. abonado -da m. & f.

subscription /səbˈskrɪpʃən/ n. abono m.

subsequent /ˈsʌbsɪkwənt/ a. subsiguiente.

subservient /səbˈsɜrviənt/ a. servicial.

subside /səbˈsaɪd/ v. apaciguarse, menguar.

subsidy /ˈsʌbsɪdi/ n. subvención f.

subsoil /ˈsʌbˌsɔɪl/ n. subsuelo m.

substance /ˈsʌbstəns/ n. substancia f.

substantial /səbˈstænʃəl/ a. substancial; considerable.

substitute /ˈsʌbstɪˌtut/ a. **1.** substitutivo. —n. **2.** substituto -ta. —v. **3.** substituir.

substitution /ˌsʌbstɪˈtuʃən/ n. substitución f.

subterfuge /ˈsʌbtərˌfyudʒ/ n. subterfugio m.

subtitle /ˈsʌbˌtaɪtl̩/ n. subtítulo m.

subtle /ˈsʌtl̩/ a. sutil.

subtract /səbˈtrækt/ v. substraer.

suburb /ˈsʌbɜrb/ n. suburbio m.; (pl.) afueras f.pl.

subversive /səbˈvɜrsɪv/ a. subversivo.

subway /ˈsʌbˌweɪ/ n. metro m.

succeed /səkˈsid/ v. lograr, tener éxito; (in office) suceder a.

success /səkˈsɛs/ n. éxito m.

successful /səkˈsɛsfəl/ a. próspero; afortunado.

succession /səkˈsɛʃən/ n. sucesión f.

successive /səkˈsɛsɪv/ a. sucesivo.

successor /səkˈsɛsər/ n. sucesor -ra; heredero -ra.

succor /ˈsʌkər/ n. **1.** socorro m. —v. **2.** socorrer.

succumb /səˈkʌm/ v. sucumbir.

such /sʌtʃ/ a. tal.

suck /sʌk/ v. chupar.

suction /ˈsʌkʃən/ n. succión f.

sudden /ˈsʌdn̩/ a. repentino, súbito. **all of a s.,** de repente.

suds /sʌdz/ n. jabonaduras f.pl.

sue /su/ v. demandar.

suffer /ˈsʌfər/ v. sufrir; padecer.

suffice /səˈfaɪs/ v. bastar.

sufficient /səˈfɪʃənt/ a. suficiente.

suffocate /ˈsʌfəˌkeit/ v. sofocar.

sugar /ˈʃʊgər/ n. azúcar m.

sugar bowl azucarero m.

suggest /səgˈdʒɛst/ v. sugerir.

suggestion /səgˈdʒɛstʃən/ n. sugerencia f.

suicide /ˈsuəˌsaid/ n. suicidio m.; (person) suicida m. & f. **to commit s.,** suicidarse.

suit /sut/ n. **1.** traje; (cards) palo; (law) pleito m. —v. **2.** convenir a.

suitable /ˈsutəbəl/ a. apropiado; que conviene.

suitcase /ˈsutˌkeis/ n. maleta f.

suite /swit/ n. serie f., séquito m.

suitor /ˈsutər/ n. pretendiente m.

sullen /ˈsʌlən/ a. hosco.

sum /sʌm/ n. **1.** suma f. —v. **2. s. up,** resumir.

summarize /ˈsʌməˌraiz/ v. resumir.

summary /ˈsʌməri/ n. resumen m.

summer /ˈsʌmər/ n. verano m.

summon /ˈsʌmən/ v. llamar; (law) citar.

summons /ˈsʌmənz/ n. citación f.

sumptuous /ˈsʌmptʃuəs/ a. suntuoso.

sun /sʌn/ n. **1.** sol m. —v. **2.** tomar el sol.

sunbathe /ˈsʌnˌbeið/ v. tomar el sol.

sunburn /ˈsʌnˌbɜrn/ n. quemadura de sol.

sunburned /ˈsʌnˌbɜrnd/ a. quemado por el sol.

Sunday /ˈsʌndei/ n. domingo m.

sunken /ˈsʌŋkən/ a. hundido.

sunny /ˈsʌni/ a. asoleado. **s. day,** día de sol. **to be s.,** (weather) hacer sol.

sunshine /ˈsʌnˌʃain/ n. luz del sol.

suntan /ˈsʌnˌtæn/ n. bronceado m. **s. lotion,** loción bronceadora f., bronceador m.

superb /sʊˈpɜrb/ a. soberbio.

superficial /ˌsupərˈfɪʃəl/ a. superficial.

superfluous /sʊˈpɜrfluəs/ a. superfluo.

superhuman /ˌsupər'hyumən/ a. sobrehumano.

superintendent /ˌsuprɪn'tɛndənt/ n. superintendente m. & f.; (of building) conserje m.; (of school) director -ra general.

superior /sə'pɪriər/ a. & n. superior m.

superiority /sə͵pɪrɪ'ɔriti/ n. superioridad f.

superlative /sə'pərlətɪv/ a. superlativo.

supernatural /ˌsupər'nætʃərəl/ a. sobrenatural.

supersede /ˌsupər'sid/ v. reemplazar.

superstar /ˈsupər͵star/ n. superestrella m. & f.

superstition /ˌsupər'stɪʃən/ n. superstición f.

superstitious /ˌsupər'stɪʃəs/ a. supersticioso.

supervise /ˈsupər͵vaɪz/ v. supervisar.

supper /ˈsʌpər/ n. cena f.

supplement /ˈsʌpləmənt/ n. 1. suplemento m. —v. 2. suplementar.

supply /sə'plaɪ/ n. 1. provisión f.; Com. surtido m.; Econ. existencia f. —v. 2. suplir; proporcionar.

support /sə'pɔrt/ n. 1. sustento; apoyo m. —v. 2. mantener; apoyar.

suppose /sə'pouz/ v. suponer. **be supposed to,** deber.

suppository /sə'pɒzɪ͵tɔri/ n. supositorio m.

suppress /sə'prɛs/ v. suprimir.

suppression /sə'prɛʃən/ n. supresión f.

supreme /sə'prim/ a. supremo.

sure /ʃʊr, ʃɜr/ a. seguro, cierto. **for s.,** con seguridad. **to make s.,** asegurarse.

surety /ˈʃʊrti, ˈʃɜr-/ n. garantía f.

surf /sɜrf/ n. 1. oleaje m. —v. 2. (Internet) navegar; (sport) surfear.

surface /ˈsɜrfɪs/ n. superficie f.

surfboard /ˈsɜrf͵bɔrd/ n. tabla de surf f.

surfer /ˈsɜrfər/ n. (Internet) usuario -ria, navegante m. & f.; (sport) surfero -ra.

surge /sɜrdʒ/ v. surgir.

surgeon /ˈsɜrdʒən/ n. cirujano -na.

surgery /ˈsɜrdʒəri/ n. cirugía f.

surmise /sər'maɪz/ v. suponer.

surmount /sər'maunt/ v. vencer.

surname /ˈsɜr͵neɪm/ n. apellido m.

surpass /sər'pæs/ v. superar.

surplus /ˈsɜrpləs/ a. & n. sobrante m.

surprise /sər'praɪz, sə-/ n. 1. sorpresa —v. 2. sorprender. **I am surprised...,** me extraña...

surrender /sə'rɛndər/ n. 1. rendición f. —v. 2. rendir.

surround /sə'raund/ v. rodear, circundar.

surveillance /sər'veiləns/ n. vigilancia f.

survey /n. 'sɜrvei; v. sər'vei/ n. 1. examen; estudio m. —v. 2. examinar; (land) medir.

survival /sər'vaivəl/ n. supervivencia f.

survive /sər'vaiv/ v. sobrevivir.

susceptible /sə'sɛptəbəl/ a. susceptible.

suspect /v. sə'spɛkt; n. 'sʌspɛkt/ v. 1. sospechar. —n. 2. sospechoso m.

suspend /sə'spɛnd/ v. suspender.

suspense /sə'spɛns/ n. incertidumbre f. **in s.,** en suspenso.

suspension /sə'spɛnʃən/ n. suspensión f.

suspension bridge n. puente colgante m.

suspicion /sə'spɪʃən/ n. sospecha f.

suspicious /sə'spɪʃəs/ a. sospechoso.

sustain /sə'stein/ v. sustentar; mantener.

swallow /ˈswɒlou/ n. 1. trago m.; (bird) golondrina f. —v. 2. tragar.

swamp /swɒmp/ n. 1. pantano m. —v. 2. Fig. abrumar.

swan /swɒn/ n. cisne m.

swap /swɒp/ n. 1. trueque m. —v. 2. cambalachear.

swarm /swɔrm/ n. enjambre m.

swarthy /ˈswɔrði/ a. moreno.

sway /swei/ n. 1. predominio m. —v. 2. bambolearse; Fig. influir en.

swear /swɛər/ v. jurar. **s. off,** renunciar a.

sweat /swɛt/ n. 1. sudor m. —v. 2. sudar.

sweater /ˈswɛtər/ n. suéter m.

sweatshirt /ˈswɛt͵ʃɜrt/ n. sudadera f.

Swede /swid/ n. sueco -ca.

Sweden /ˈswidn̩/ n. Suecia f.

Swedish /'swidɪʃ/ a. sueco.

sweep /swip/ v. barrer.

sweet /swit/ a. **1.** dulce; amable, simpático. —n. **2.** (pl.) dulces m.pl.

sweetheart /'swit,hɑrt/ n. novio -via.

sweetness /'switnɪs/ n. dulzura f.

sweet-toothed /'swit ,tuθt/ a. goloso.

swell /swɛl/ a. **1.** Colloq. estupendo, excelente. —n. **2.** (of the sea) oleada f. —v. **3.** hincharse; aumentar.

swelter /'swɛltər/ v. sofocarse de calor.

swift /swɪft/ a. rápido, veloz.

swim /swɪm/ n. **1.** nadada f. —v. **2.** nadar.

swimming /'swɪmɪŋ/ n. natación f.

swimming pool alberca f, piscina f.

swindle /'swɪndḷ/ n. **1.** estafa f. —v. **2.** estafar.

swine /swaɪn/ n. puercos m.pl.

swing /swɪŋ/ n. **1.** columpio m. **in full s.,** en plena actividad. —v. **2.** mecer; balancear.

swirl /swɜrl/ n. **1.** remolino m. —v. **2.** arremolinar.

Swiss /swɪs/ a. & n. suizo -za.

switch /swɪtʃ/ n. **1.** varilla f.; Elec. llave f., conmutador m.;

(railway) cambiavía m. —v. **2.** cambiar; trocar.

switchboard /'swɪtʃ,bɔrd/ n. cuadro conmutador m., centralita f.

Switzerland /'swɪtsərlænd/ n. Suiza f.

sword /sɔrd/ n. espada f.

syllable /'sɪləbəl/ n. sílaba f.

symbol /'sɪmbəl/ n. símbolo m.

sympathetic /,sɪmpə'θɛtɪk/ a. compasivo. **to be s.,** tener simpatía.

sympathy /'sɪmpəθi/ n. lástima; condolencia f.

symphony /'sɪmfəni/ n. sinfonía f.

symptom /'sɪmptəm/ n. síntoma m.

synagogue /'sɪnə,gɒg/ n. sinagoga f.

synchronize /'sɪŋkrə,naɪz/ v. sincronizar.

syndicate /'sɪndɪkɪt/ n. sindicato m.

syndrome /'sɪndroum, -drəm/ n. síndrome m.

synonym /'sɪnənɪm/ n. sinónimo m.

synthetic /sɪn'θɛtɪk/ a. sintético.

syringe /sə'rɪndʒ/ n. jeringa f.

syrup /'sɪrəp, 'sɜr-/ n. almíbar; Med. jarabe m.

system /'sɪstəm/ n. sistema m.

systematic /,sɪstə'mætɪk/ a. sistemático.

T

tabernacle /'tæbər,nækəl/ n. tabernáculo m.

table /'teɪbəl/ n. mesa; (list) tabla f.

tablecloth /'teɪbəl,klɔθ/ n. mantel m.

table of contents /'kɒntɛnts/ índice de materias m.

tablespoon /'teɪbəl,spun/ n. cuchara f.

tablespoonful /'teɪbəlspun,fʊl/ n. cucharada f.

tablet /'tæblɪt/ n. tableta; Med. pastilla f.

tack /tæk/ n. tachuela f.

tact /tækt/ n. tacto m.

tag /tæg/ n. etiqueta f, rótulo m.

tail /teɪl/ n. cola f, rabo m.

tailor /'teɪlər/ n. sastre m.

take /teɪk/ v. tomar; llevar. **t. a bath,** bañarse. **t. a shower,** ducharse. **t. away,** quitar. **t. off,** quitarse. **t. out,** sacar. **t. long,** tardar mucho.

tale /teɪl/ n. cuento m.

talent /'tælənt/ n. talento m.

talk /tɔk/ n. **1.** plática, habla f.; discurso m. —v. **2.** hablar.

talkative /'tɔkətɪv/ a. locuaz.

tall /tɔl/ a. alto.

tame /teɪm/ a. **1.** manso, domesticado. —v. **2.** domesticar.

tamper /'tæmpər/ v. **t. with,** entremeterse en.

tampon /'tæmpɒn/ n. tampón m.

tan /tæn/ a. **1.** color de arena. —v. **2.** curtir; tostar. n. bronceado.

tangerine /,tændʒə'rin/ n. clementina f.

tangible /'tændʒəbəl/ a. tangible.

tangle /'tæŋgəl/ n. **1.** enredo m. —v. **2.** enredar.

tank /tæŋk/ n. tanque m.

tap /tæp/ n. **1.** golpe ligero. —v. **2.** golpear ligeramente; decentar.

tape /teɪp/ n. cinta f.

tape recorder /rɪˈkɔrdər/ magnetófono m., grabadora f.

tapestry /ˈtæpəstriː/ n. tapiz m.; tapicería f.

tar /tɑr/ n. 1. brea f. —v. 2. embrear.

target /ˈtɑrgɪt/ n. blanco m.

tarnish /ˈtɑrnɪʃ/ n. 1. deslustre f. —v. 2. deslustrar.

tarpaulin /tɑrˈpɔlɪn, ˈtɑrpəlɪn/ n. lona f.

task /tæsk/ n. tarea f.

taste /teɪst/ n. 1. gusto; sabor m. —v. 2. gustar; probar. **t. of,** saber a.

tasty /ˈteɪstiː/ a. sabroso.

tattoo /tæˈtuː/ v. tatuar.

taut /tɔt/ a. tieso.

tavern /ˈtævərn/ n. taberna f.

tax /tæks/ n. 1. impuesto m. —v. 2. imponer impuestos.

tax collector n. recaudador -ra m. & f.

taxi /ˈtæksiː/ n. taxi, taxímetro m. **t. driver,** taxista m. & f.

taxpayer /ˈtæksˌpeɪər/ n. contribuyente m. & f.

tax reform reforma tributaria f.

tax return declaración de la renta f.

tea /tiː/ n. té m.

teach /tiːtʃ/ v. enseñar.

teacher /ˈtiːtʃər/ n. maestro -tra, profesor -ra.

team /tiːm/ n. equipo m.; pareja f.

tear /tɪər/ n. 1. rasgón m.; lágrima f. —v. 2. rasgar, lacerar. **t. apart,** separar.

tease /tiːz/ v. atormentar; embromar.

teaspoon /ˈtiːˌspuːn/ n. cucharita f.

technical /ˈteknɪkəl/ a. técnico.

technician /tekˈnɪʃən/ n. técnico -ca m. & f.

technique /tekˈniːk/ n. técnica f.

technology /tekˈnɒlədʒiː/ n. tecnología f.

teddy bear /ˈtediː/ oso de felpa m.

tedious /ˈtiːdiəs/ a. tedioso.

telegram /ˈteliˌgræm/ n. telegrama m.

telegraph /ˈteliˌgræf/ n. 1. telégrafo m. —v. 2. telegrafiar.

telephone /ˈteləˌfoun/ n. 1. teléfono m. **t. book,** directorio telefónico. —v. 2. telefonear; llamar por teléfono.

telescope /ˈteləˌskoup/ n. 1. telescopio m. —v. 2. enchufar.

television /ˈteləˌvɪʒən/ n. televisión f.

tell /tel/ v. decir; contar; distinguir.

temper /ˈtempər/ n. 1. temperamento, genio m. —v. 2. templar.

temperament /ˈtempərəmənt, -prəmənt/ n. temperamento.

temperamental /ˌtempərəˈmentl̩, -prəˈmen-/ a. sensitivo, emocional.

temperance /ˈtempərəns/ n. moderación; sobriedad f.

temperate /ˈtempərɪt/ a. templado.

temperature /ˈtempərətʃər/ n. temperatura f.

tempest /ˈtempɪst/ n. tempestad f.

tempestuous /temˈpestʃuəs/ a. tempestuoso.

temple /ˈtempəl/ n. templo m.

temporary /ˈtempəˌreriː/ a. temporal, temporario.

tempt /tempt/ v. tentar.

temptation /tempˈteɪʃən/ n. tentación f.

ten /ten/ a. & pron. diez.

tenant /ˈtenənt/ n. inquilino -na.

tend /tend/ v. tender. **t. to,** atender.

tendency /ˈtendənsiː/ n. tendencia f.

tender /ˈtendər/ a. 1. tierno. —v. 2. ofrecer.

tenderness /ˈtendərnɪs/ n. ternura f.

tennis /ˈtenɪs/ n. tenis m.

tennis court cancha de tenis, pista de tenis f.

tenor /ˈtenər/ n. tenor m.

tense /tens/ a. 1. tenso. —n. 2. *Gram.* tiempo m.

tent /tent/ n. tienda, carpa f.

tenth /tenθ/ a. décimo.

term /tɜrm/ n. 1. término; plazo m. —v. 2. llamar.

terminal /ˈtɜrmənl̩/ n. terminal f.

terrace /ˈterəs/ n. terraza f.

terrible /ˈterəbəl/ a. terrible, espantoso; pésimo.

territory /ˈterɪˌtoriː/ n. territorio m.

terror /ˈterər/ n. terror, espanto, pavor m.

test /test/ n. 1. prueba f.; examen m. —v. 2. probar; examinar.

testament /ˈtestəmənt/ n. testamento m.

testify /ˈtestəˌfaɪ/ v. atestiguar, testificar.

testimony /ˈtestəˌmouniː/ n. testimonio m.

test tube tubo de ensayo *m.*

text /tɛkst/ *n.* texto; tema *m.*

textbook /'tɛkst,bʊk/ *n.* libro de texto.

textile /'tɛkstail/ *a.* **1.** textil. —*n.* **2.** tejido *m.*

texture /'tɛkstʃər/ *n.* textura *f.*; tejido *m.*

than /ðæn, ðɛn; *unstressed* ðən, ən/ *conj.* que; de.

thank /θæŋk/ *v.* agradecer, dar gracias; **thanks, the, you,** gracias.

thankful /'θæŋkfəl/ *a.* agradecido; grato.

that /ðæt; *unstressed* ðət/ *a.* **1.** ese, aquel. —*dem. pron.* **2.** ése, aquél; eso, aquello. —*rel. pron. & conj.* **3.** que.

the /*stressed* ði; *unstressed before a consonant* ðə, *unstressed before a vowel* ði/ *art.* el, la, los, las; lo.

theater /'θiatər/ *n.* teatro *m.*

theft /θɛft/ *n.* robo *m.*

their /ðɛər; *unstressed* ðər/ *a.* su.

theirs /ðɛərz/ *pron.* suyo, de ellos.

them /ðɛm; *unstressed* ðəm, əm/ *pron.* ellos, ellas; los, las; les.

theme /θim/ *n.* tema; *Mus.* motivo *m.*

themselves /ðəm'sɛlvz, ˌðɛm-/ *pron.* sí, sí mismos -as. **they th.,** ellos mismos, ellas mismas. **with th.,** consigo.

then /ðɛn/ *adv.* entonces, después; pues.

thence /ðɛns/ *adv.* de allí.

theology /θi'ɒlədʒi/ *n.* teología *f.*

theory /'θiəri/ *n.* teoría *f.*

there /ðɛər; *unstressed* ðər/ *adv.* allí, allá, ahí. **there is, there are,** hay.

therefore /'ðɛər,fɔr/ *adv.* por lo tanto, por consiguiente.

thermometer /θər'mɒmɪtər/ *n.* termómetro *m.*

thermostat /'θɜrmə,stæt/ *n.* termostato *m.*

they /ðei/ *pron.* ellos, ellas.

thick /θɪk/ *a.* espeso, grueso, denso; torpe.

thicken /'θɪkən/ *v.* espesar, condensar.

thief /θif/ *n.* ladrón -na.

thigh /θai/ *n.* muslo *m.*

thimble /'θɪmbəl/ *n.* dedal *m.*

thin /θɪn/ *a.* **1.** delgado; fino; claro; escaso. —*v.* **2.** enrarecer; adelgazar.

thing /θɪŋ/ *n.* cosa *f.*

thingamabob /'θɪŋəmə,bɒb/ *n. Colloq.* chisme *m.*

think /θɪŋk/ *v.* pensar; creer.

thinker /'θɪŋkər/ *n.* pensador -ra.

third /θɜrd/ *a.* tercero.

Third World Tercer Mundo *m.*

thirst /θɜrst/ *n.* sed *f.*

thirsty /'θɜrsti/ *a.* sediento. **to be th.,** tener sed.

thirteen /'θɜr'tin/ *a. & pron.* trece.

thirty /'θɜrti/ *a. & pron.* treinta.

this /ðɪs/ *a.* **1.** este. —*pron.* **2.** éste; esto.

thoracic cage /θɔ'ræsɪk/ *n.* caja torácica *f.*

thorn /θɔrn/ *n.* espina *f.*

thorough /'θɜroʊ/ *a.* completo; cuidadoso.

though /ðoʊ/ *adv.* **1.** sin embargo. —*conj.* **2.** aunque. **as th.,** como si.

thought /θɔt/ *n.* pensamiento *m.*

thoughtful /'θɔtfəl/ *a.* pensativo; considerado.

thousand /'θaʊzənd/ *a. & pron.* mil.

thread /θrɛd/ *n.* hilo *m.*; (of screw) rosca *f.*

threat /θrɛt/ *n.* amenaza *f.*

threaten /'θrɛtn̩/ *v.* amenazar.

three /θri/ *a. & pron.* tres.

thrift /θrɪft/ *n.* economía, frugalidad *f.*

thrill /θrɪl/ *n.* **1.** emoción *f.* —*v.* **2.** emocionar.

thrive /θraiv/ *v.* prosperar.

throat /θroʊt/ *n.* garganta *f.*

throne /θroʊn/ *n.* trono *m.*

through /θru/ *prep.* **1.** por; a través de; por medio de. —*a.* **2.** continuo. **th. train,** tren directo. **to be th.,** haber terminado.

throughout /θru'aʊt/ *prep.* **1.** por todo, durante todo. —*adv.* **2.** en todas partes; completamente.

throw /θroʊ/ *n.* **1.** tiro *m.* —*v.* **2.** tirar, lanzar. **th. away,** arrojar. **th. out,** echar.

thrust /θrʌst/ *n.* **1.** lanzada *f.* —*v.* **2.** empujar.

thumb /θʌm/ *n.* dedo pulgar, pulgar *m.*

thumbtack /'θʌm,tæk/ *n.* chincheta *f.*

thunder /'θʌndər/ *n.* **1.** trueno *m.* —*v.* **2.** tronar.

Thursday /'θɜrzdei/ *n.* jueves *m.*

thus /ðʌs/ *adv.* así, de este modo.

thwart /θwɔrt/ *v.* frustrar.

ticket /'tɪkɪt/ n. billete, boleto m.
t. window, taquilla f. **round trip t.,** billete de ida y vuelta.

tickle /'tɪkəl/ v. **1.** cosquilla f. —v. **2.** hacer cosquillas a.

ticklish /'tɪklɪʃ/ a. cosquilloso.

tide /taɪd/ n. marea f.

tidy /'taɪdi/ a. **1.** limpio, ordenado. —v. **2.** poner en orden.

tie /taɪ/ n. **1.** corbata f.; lazo; (game) empate m. —v. **2.** atar; anudar.

tier /tɪər/ n. hilera f.

tiger /'taɪgər/ n. tigre m.

tight /taɪt/ a. apretado; tacaño.

tighten /'taɪtn/ v. estrechar, apretar.

tile /taɪl/ n. teja f.; azulejo m.

till /tɪl/ prep. **1.** hasta. —conj. **2.** hasta que. —n. **3.** cajón m. —v. **4.** cultivar, labrar.

tilt /tɪlt/ n. **1.** inclinación; justa f. —v. **2.** inclinar; justar.

timber /'tɪmbər/ n. **1.** madera f.; (beam) madero m.

time /taɪm/ n. tiempo m.; vez f.; (of day) hora f.; v. cronometrar.

timetable /'taɪm,teɪbəl/ n. horario, itinerario m.

time zone huso horario m.

timid /'tɪmɪd/ a. tímido.

timidity /tɪ'mɪdɪti/ n. timidez f.

tin /tɪn/ n. estaño m.; hojalata f. **t. can,** lata f.

tin foil papel de estaño m.

tint /tɪnt/ n. **1.** tinte m. —v. **2.** teñir.

tiny /'taɪni/ a. chiquito, pequeñito.

tip /tɪp/ n. **1.** punta; propina f. —v. **2.** inclinar; dar propina a.

tire /taɪər/ n. **1.** llanta, goma f.; neumático m. —v. **2.** cansar.

tired /taɪərd/ a. cansado.

tissue /'tɪʃu/ n. tejido m. **t. paper,** papel de seda.

title /'taɪtl/ n. **1.** título m. —v. **2.** titular.

to /tu/ unstressed tʊ, tə/ prep. **1.** para.

toast /toʊst/ n. **1.** tostada f.; (drink) brindis m. —v. **2.** tostar; brindar.

toaster /'toʊstər/ n. tostador m.

tobacco /tə'bækoʊ/ n. tabaco m. **t. shop,** tabaquería f.

toboggan /tə'bɒgən/ n. tobogán m.

today /tə'deɪ/ adv. hoy.

toe /toʊ/ n. dedo del pie.

together /tə'gɛðər/ a. **1.** juntos. —adv. **2.** juntamente.

toil /tɔɪl/ n. **1.** trabajo m. —v. **2.** afanarse.

toilet /'tɔɪlɪt/ n. tocado; excusado; retrete m. **t. paper,** papel higiénico.

token /'toʊkən/ n. señal f.

tolerance /'tɒlərəns/ n. tolerancia f.

tolerate /'tɒlə,reɪt/ v. tolerar.

toll-free number /toʊl 'fri/ teléfono gratuito m.

tomato /tə'meɪtoʊ/ n. tomate m.

tomb /tum/ n. tumba f.

tomorrow /tə'mɒroʊ/ adv. mañana. **day after t.,** pasado mañana.

ton /tʌn/ n. tonelada f.

tone /toʊn/ n. tono m.

tongue /tʌŋ/ n. lengua f.

tonic /'tɒnɪk/ n. tónico m.

tonight /tə'naɪt/ adv. esta noche.

tonsil /'tɒnsəl/ n. amígdala f.

too /tu/ adv. también. **t. much,** demasiado. **t. many,** demasiados.

tool /tul/ n. herramienta f.

tooth /tuθ/ n. diente m.; (back) muela f.

toothache /'tuθ,eɪk/ n. dolor de muela.

toothbrush /'tuθ,brʌʃ/ n. cepillo de dientes.

toothpaste /'tuθ,peɪst/ n. crema dentífrica, pasta dentífrica.

top /tɒp/ n. **1.** parte de arriba. —v. **2.** cubrir; sobrepasar.

topic /'tɒpɪk/ n. S.A. tópico m.

topical /'tɒpɪkəl/ a. tópico.

torch /tɔrtʃ/ n. antorcha f.

torment /n. 'tɔrmɛnt; v. tɔr'mɛnt/ n. **1.** tormento m. —v. **2.** atormentar.

torrent /'tɔrənt/ n. torrente m.

torture /'tɔrtʃər/ n. **1.** tortura f. —v. **2.** torturar.

toss /tɒs/ v. tirar; agitar.

total /'toʊtl/ a. **1.** total, entero. —n. **2.** total m.

touch /tʌtʃ/ n. **1.** tacto m. **in t.,** en comunicación. —v. **2.** tocar; conmover.

tough /tʌf/ a. tosco; tieso; fuerte.

tour /tʊr/ n. **1.** viaje m. —v. **2.** viajar.

tourist /'tʊrɪst/ n. turista m. & f. a. turístico.

tournament /'tʊrnəmənt/ n. torneo m.

tow /tou/ n. **1.** remolque m. —v. **2.** remolcar.

toward /tɔrd, tə'wɔrd/ prep. hacia.

towel /'tauəl/ n. toalla f.

tower /'tauər/ n. torre f.

town /taun/ n. pueblo m.

town meeting cabildo abierto m.

tow truck grúa f.

toy /tɔi/ n. **1.** juguete m. —v. **2.** jugar.

trace /treis/ n. **1.** vestigio; rastro m. —v. **2.** trazar; rastrear; investigar.

track /træk/ n. **1.** huella, pista f.

race t., hipódromo m. —v. **2.** rastrear.

tract /trækt/ n. trecho; tracto m.

tractor /'træktər/ n. tractor m.

trade /treid/ n. **1.** comercio, negocio; oficio; canje m. —v. **2.** comerciar, negociar; cambiar.

trader /'treidər/ n. comerciante m.

tradition /trə'dɪʃən/ n. tradición f.

traditional /trə'dɪʃənl/ a. tradicional.

traffic /'træfɪk/ n. **1.** tráfico m. —v. **2.** traficar.

traffic jam atasco, embotellamiento m.

traffic light semáforo m.

tragedy /'trædʒɪdi/ n. tragedia f.

tragic /'trædʒɪk/ a. trágico.

trail /treil/ n. **1.** sendero, rastro m. —v. **2.** rastrear; arrastrar.

train /trein/ n. **1.** tren m. —v. **2.** enseñar; disciplinar; (sport) entrenarse.

traitor /'treitər/ n. traidor -ora.

tramp /træmp/ n. **1.** caminata f.; vagabundo m. —v. **2.** patear.

tranquil /'træŋkwɪl/ a. tranquilo.

tranquilizer /'træŋkwə,laizər/ n. tranquilizante m.

tranquillity /træŋ'kwɪlɪti/ n. tranquilidad f.

transaction /træn'sækʃən/ n. transacción f.

transfer /n. 'trænsfər, v. træns'fər/ n. **1.** traslado m.; boleto de transbordo. —v. **2.** trasladar, transferir.

transform /træns'fɔrm/ v. transformar.

transfusion /træns'fyuʒən/ n. transfusión f.

transistor /træn'zɪstər/ n. transistor m.

transition /træn'zɪʃən/ n. transición f.

translate /træns'leit/ v. traducir.

translation /træns'leiʃən/ n. traducción f.

transmit /træns'mɪt/ v. transmitir.

transparent /træns'pɛərənt/ a. transparente.

transport /n. 'trænsport, v. træns'pɔrt/ n. **1.** transporte m. —v. **2.** transportar.

transportation /,trænspər'teiʃən/ n. transporte m.

transsexual /træns'sɛkʃuəl/ a. & n. transexual m. & f.

transvestite /træns'vestait/ n. travestí m. & f.

trap /træp/ n. **1.** trampa f. —v. **2.** atrapar.

trash /træʃ/ n. desecho m.; basura f.

trash can cubo de la basura m.

travel /'trævəl/ n. **1.** tráfico m.; (pl.) viajes m.pl. —v. **2.** viajar.

travel agency agencia de viajes f.

traveler /'trævələr/ n. viajero -ra.

traveler's check /'trævələrz/ cheque de viaje m.

tray /trei/ n. bandeja f.

tread /trɛd/ n. **1.** pisada f.; (of a tire) cubierta f. —v. **2.** pisar.

treason /'trizən/ n. traición f.

treasure /'trɛʒər/ n. tesoro m.

treasurer /'trɛʒərər/ n. tesorero -ra.

treasury /'trɛʒəri/ n. tesorería f.

treat /trit/ v. tratar; convidar.

treatment /'tritmənt/ n. trato, tratamiento m.

treaty /'triti/ n. tratado, pacto m.

tree /tri/ n. árbol m.

tremble /'trɛmbəl/ v. temblar.

tremendous /trɪ'mɛndəs/ a. tremendo.

trench /trɛntʃ/ n. foso m.; Mil. trinchera f.

trend /trɛnd/ n. **1.** tendencia f. —v. **2.** tender.

trespass /'trɛspəs, -pæs/ v. traspasar; violar.

triage /tri'ɑʒ/ n. clasificación de los heridos después del combate.

trial /'traiəl/ n. prueba f.; Leg. proceso, juicio m.

triangle /'trai,æŋgəl/ n. triángulo m.

tribulation /,tribyə'leiʃən/ n. tribulación f.

tributary /'tribyə,teri/ a. & n. tributario m.

tribute /'tribyut/ n. tributo m.

tyrant

trick /trɪk/ n. **1.** engaño m.; maña f.; (cards) baza f. —v. **2.** engañar.

trifle /ˈtraɪfəl/ n. **1.** pequeñez f. —v. **2.** juguetear.

trigger /ˈtrɪgər/ n. gatillo m.

trim /trɪm/ a. **1.** ajustado; acicalado. —n. **2.** adorno m. —v. **3.** adornar; ajustar; cortar un poco.

trinket /ˈtrɪŋkɪt/ n. bagatela, chuchería f.

trip /trɪp/ n. **1.** viaje m. —v. **2.** tropezar.

triple /ˈtrɪpəl/ a. **1.** triple —v. **2.** triplicar.

tripod /ˈtraɪpɒd/ n. trípode f.

trite /traɪt/ a. banal.

triumph /ˈtraɪəmf/ n. **1.** triunfo m. —v. **2.** triunfar.

triumphant /traɪˈʌmfənt/ a. triunfante.

trivial /ˈtrɪviəl/ a. trivial.

trolley /ˈtrɒli/ n. tranvía m.

trombone /trɒmˈboʊn/ n. trombón m.

troop /trup/ n. tropa f.

trophy /ˈtroʊfi/ n. trofeo m.

tropical /ˈtrɒpɪkəl/ a. trópico.

tropics /ˈtrɒpɪks/ n. trópico m.

trot /trɒt/ n. **1.** trote m. —v. **2.** trotar.

trouble /ˈtrʌbəl/ n. **1.** apuro m.; congoja f.; aflicción f. —v. **2.** molestar; afligir.

troublesome /ˈtrʌbəlsəm/ a. penoso, molesto.

trough /trɒf/ n. artesa f.

trousers /ˈtraʊzərz/ n. pantalones, calzones m.pl.

trout /traʊt/ n. trucha f.

truce /trus/ n. tregua f.

truck /trʌk/ n. camión m.

true /tru/ a. verdadero, cierto, verdad.

truffle /ˈtrʌfəl/ n. trufa f.

trumpet /ˈtrʌmpɪt/ n. trompeta, trompa f.

trunk /trʌŋk/ n. baúl m.; (of a tree) tronco m.

trust /trʌst/ n. **1.** confianza f. —v. **2.** confiar.

trustworthy /ˈtrʌstˌwərði/ a. digno de confianza.

truth /truθ/ n. verdad f.

truthful /ˈtruθfəl/ a. veraz.

try /traɪ/ n. **1.** prueba f.; ensayo m. —v. **2.** tratar; probar; ensayar; Leg. juzgar. **t. on,** probarse.

T-shirt /ˈtiˌʃərt/ n. camiseta f.

tub /tʌb/ n. tina f.

tube /tub/ n. tubo m.

tuberculosis /tʊˌbərkyəˈloʊsɪs/ n. tuberculosis f.

tuck /tʌk/ n. **1.** recogido m. —v. **2.** recoger.

Tuesday /ˈtuzdeɪ/ n. martes m.

tug /tʌg/ n. **1.** tirada f.; (boat) remolcador m. —v. **2.** tirar de.

tuition /tuˈɪʃən/ n. matrícula, colegiatura f.

tumble /ˈtʌmbəl/ n. **1.** caída f. —v. **2.** caer, tumbar; voltear.

tumult /ˈtumʌlt/ n. tumulto f., alboroto m.

tuna /ˈtuni/ n. atún m.

tune /tun/ n. **1.** tono m.; melodía, canción f. —v. **2.** templar.

tunnel /ˈtʌnl/ n. túnel m.

turf /tərf/ n. césped m.

Turkey /ˈtərki/ n. Turquía f.

Turkish /ˈtərkɪʃ/ a. turco.

turmoil /ˈtərmɔɪl/ n. disturbio m.

turn /tərn/ n. **1.** vuelta f.; giro; turno m. —v. **2.** volver, tornear, girar; **t. into,** transformar. **t. around,** volverse. **t. on,** encender; abrir. **t. off, t. out,** apagar.

turnip /ˈtərnɪp/ n. nabo m.

turret /ˈtərɪt/ n. torrecilla f.

turtle /ˈtərtl/ n. tortuga f.

turtleneck sweater /ˈtərtlˌnɛk/ jersey de cuello alto m.

tutor /ˈtutər/ n. **1.** tutor -ra. —v. **2.** enseñar.

tweezers /ˈtwizərz/ n.pl. pinzas f.pl.

twelve /twɛlv/ a. & pron. doce.

twenty /ˈtwɛnti/ a. & pron. veinte.

twice /twaɪs/ adv. dos veces.

twig /twɪg/ n. varita; ramita f.; vástago m.

twilight /ˈtwaɪˌlaɪt/ n. crepúsculo m.

twin /twɪn/ n. gemelo -la.

twine /twaɪn/ n. **1.** guita f. —v. **2.** torcer.

twinkle /ˈtwɪŋkəl/ v. centellear.

twist /twɪst/ v. torcer.

two /tu/ a. & pron. dos.

type /taɪp/ n. **1.** tipo m. —v. **2.** escribir a máquina.

typewriter /ˈtaɪpˌraɪtər/ n. máquina de escribir.

typhoid fever /ˈtaɪfɔɪd/ fiebre tifoidea.

typical /ˈtɪpɪkəl/ a. típico.

typist /ˈtaɪpɪst/ n. mecanógrafo -fa.

tyranny /ˈtɪrəni/ n. tiranía f.

tyrant /ˈtaɪrənt/ n. tirano -na.

U

udder /'ʌdər/ n. ubre f.

UFO abbr. (unidentified flying object) OVNI m. (objeto volador no identificado).

ugly /'ʌgli/ a. feo.

Ukraine /yu'krein/ n. Ucrania f.

Ukrainian /yu'kreiniən/ a. & n. ucranio.

ulcer /'ʌlsər/ n. úlcera f.

ulterior /ʌl'tɪəriər/ a. ulterior.

ultimate /'ʌltəmɪt/ a. último.

ultrasonic /ˌʌltrə'sɒnɪk/ a. ultrasónico.

umbrella /ʌm'brɛlə/ n. paraguas m. **sun u.,** quitasol m.

umpire /'ʌmpaɪər/ n. árbitro m.

unable /ʌn'eibəl/ a. incapaz. **to be u.,** no poder.

unanimous /yu'nænəməs/ a. unánime.

uncertain /ʌn'sɜrtn/ a. incierto, inseguro.

uncle /'ʌŋkəl/ n. tío m.

unconscious /ʌn'kɒnʃəs/ a. inconsciente; desmayado.

uncover /ʌn'kʌvər/ v. descubrir.

undeniable /ˌʌndɪ'naiəbəl/ a. innegable.

under /'ʌndər/ adv. **1.** debajo, abajo. —prep. **2.** bajo, debajo de.

underestimate /ˌʌndər'estəˌmeit/ v. menospreciar; subestimar.

undergo /ˌʌndər'gou/ v. sufrir.

underground /'ʌndərˌgraund/ a. subterráneo; clandestino.

underline /'ʌndərˌlain/ v. subrayar.

underneath /ˌʌndər'niθ/ adv. **1.** por debajo. —prep. **2.** debajo de.

undershirt /'ʌndərˌʃɜrt/ n. camiseta f.

understand /ˌʌndər'stænd/ v. entender, comprender.

undertake /ˌʌndər'teik/ v. emprender.

underwear /'ʌndərˌwɛr/ n. ropa interior.

undo /ʌn'du/ v. deshacer; desatar.

undress /ʌn'drɛs/ v. desnudar, desvestir.

uneasy /ʌn'izi/ a. inquieto.

uneven /ʌn'ivən/ a. desigual.

unexpected /ˌʌnik'spɛktid/ a. inesperado.

unfair /ʌn'fɛər/ a. injusto.

unfit /ʌn'fit/ a. incapaz; inadecuado.

unfold /ʌn'fould/ v. desplegar; revelar.

unforgettable /ˌʌnfər'gɛtəbəl/ a. inolvidable.

unfortunate /ʌn'fɔrtʃənit/ a. desafortunado, desgraciado.

unfurnished /ʌn'fɜrnɪʃt/ a. desamueblado.

unhappy /ʌn'hæpi/ a. infeliz.

uniform /'yunəˌfɔrm/ a. & n. uniforme m.

unify /'yunəˌfai/ v. unificar.

union /'yunyən/ n. unión f. **labor u.,** sindicato de obreros.

unique /yu'nik/ a. único.

unisex /'yunəˌsɛks/ a. unisex.

unit /'yunɪt/ n. unidad f.

unite /yu'nait/ v. unir.

United Nations /yu'naitid 'neiʃənz/ Naciones Unidas f.pl.

United States /yu'naitid 'steits/ Estados Unidos m.pl.

unity /'yuniti/ n. unidad f.

universal /ˌyunə'vɜrsəl/ a. universal.

universe /'yunəˌvɜrs/ n. universo m.

university /ˌyunə'vɜrsɪti/ n. universidad f.

unleaded /ʌn'lɛdid/ a. sin plomo.

unless /ʌn'lɛs/ conj. a menos que, si no es que.

unlike /ʌn'laik/ a. disímil.

unload /ʌn'loud/ v. descargar.

unlock /ʌn'lɒk/ v. abrir.

unplug /ʌn'plʌg/ v. desenchufar.

unpopular /ʌn'pɒpyələr/ a. impopular.

unreasonable /ʌn'rizənəbəl/ a. desrazonable.

unscrew /ʌn'skru/ v. desatornillar.

untie /ʌn'tai/ v. desatar; soltar.

until /ʌn'til/ prep. **1.** hasta. —conj. **2.** hasta que.

unusual /ʌn'yuʒuəl/ a. raro, inusitado.

up /ʌp/ adv. **1.** arriba. —prep. **2. u. the street,** etc. calle arriba, etc.

uphold /ʌp'hould/ v. apoyar; defender.

upholster /ʌp'houlstər, ə'poul-/ v. entapizar.

upload /ʌp,loud/ n. **1.** ascenso de archivos m. —v. **2.** subir, cargar.

upon /ə'pɒn/ prep. sobre, encima de.

upper /'ʌpər/ a. superior.

upper-case letter /ˈʌpər ˈkeɪs 'letter/ mayúscula f.

us /ʌs/ pron. nosotros -as; nos.

upright /ˈʌpˌraɪt/ a. derecho, recto.

upriver /ʌpˈrɪvər/ adv. río arriba.

uproar /ˈʌpˌrɔr/ n. alboroto, tumulto m.

upset /n. ˈʌpˌset; v. ʌpˈset/ n. 1. trastorno m. —v. 2. trastornar.

upsetting /ʌpˈsetɪŋ/ a. inquietante.

upstream /ʌpˈstrim/ adv. aguas arriba, contra la corriente, río arriba.

uptight /ˈʌpˈtaɪt/ a. (psicológicamente) tenso, tieso.

upward /ˈʌpwərd/ adv. hacia arriba.

urge /ɜrdʒ/ n. 1. deseo m. —v. 2. instar.

urgency /ˈɜrdʒənsi/ n. urgencia f.

urgent /ˈɜrdʒənt/ a. urgente. **to be u.,** urgir.

use /n. yus; v. yuz/ n. 1. uso m. —v. 2. usar, emplear. **u. up,** gastar, agotar. **be used to,** estar acostumbrado a.

useful /ˈyusfəl/ a. útil.

useless /ˈyuslɪs/ a. inútil, inservible.

user-friendly /ˈyuzər ˈfrendli/ a. amigable.

username /ˈyuzərˈneɪm/ n. nombre de usuario m.

usher /ˈʌʃər/ n. 1. acomodador -ora. —v. 2. introducir.

usual /ˈyuʒuəl/ a. usual.

utensil /yuˈtensəl/ n. utensilio m.

utmost /ˈʌtˌmoʊst/ a. sumo, extremo.

utter /ˈʌtər/ a. 1. completo. —v. 2. proferir; dar.

utterance /ˈʌtərəns/ n. expresión f.

V

vacancy /ˈveɪkənsi/ n. vacante f.

vacant /ˈveɪkənt/ a. desocupado, libre.

vacation /veɪˈkeɪʃən/ n. vacaciones f.pl.

vaccinate /ˈvæksəˌneɪt/ v. vacunar.

vacuum /ˈvækyʊm/ n. vacuo, vacío m. **v. cleaner,** aspiradora f.

vagrant /ˈveɪgrənt/ a. & n. vagabundo- da.

vague /veɪg/ a. vago.

vain /veɪn/ a. vano; vanidoso. **in v.,** en vano.

valiant /ˈvælyənt/ a. valiente.

valid /ˈvælɪd/ a. válido.

valley /ˈvæli/ n. valle m.

valor /ˈvælər/ n. valor m.

valuable /ˈvælyuəbəl/ a. valioso. **to be v.,** valer mucho.

value /ˈvælyu/ n. 1. valor, importe m. —v. 2. valorar; estimar.

van /væn/ n. furgoneta f.

vandal /ˈvændl/ n. vándalo m.

vandalism /ˈvændlˌɪzəm/ n. vandalismo m.

vanish /ˈvænɪʃ/ v. desaparecer.

vanity /ˈvænɪti/ n. vanidad f. **v. case,** polvera f.

vanquish /ˈvæŋkwɪʃ/ v. vencer.

vapor /ˈveɪpər/ n. vapor m.

variation /ˌvɛəriˈeɪʃən/ n. variación f.

varicose vein /ˈværɪˌkoʊs/ variz f.

variety /vəˈraɪɪti/ n. variedad f.

various /ˈvɛəriəs/ a. varios; diversos.

varnish /ˈvɑrnɪʃ/ n. 1. barniz m. —v. 2. barnizar.

vary /ˈvɛəri/ v. variar; cambiar.

vase /veɪs, veɪz, vɑz/ n. florero; jarrón m.

vasectomy /væˈsɛktəmi/ n. vasectomía f.

vassal /ˈvæsəl/ n. vasallo m.

vast /væst/ a. vasto.

vat /væt/ n. tina f., tanque m.

VAT /væt/ n. IVA (impuesto sobre el valor añadido).

vault /vɔlt/ n. bóveda f.

vegetable /ˈvɛdʒtəbəl/ a. & n. vegetal m.; (pl.) legumbres, verduras f.pl.

vehement /ˈviəmənt/ a. vehemente.

vehicle /ˈviɪkəl/ n. vehículo m.

veil /veɪl/ n. 1. velo m. —v. 2. velar.

vein /veɪn/ n. vena f.

velocity /vəˈlɒsɪti/ n. velocidad f.

velvet /ˈvɛlvɪt/ n. terciopelo m.

Venetian /vəˈniʃən/ a. & n. veneciano.

vengeance /ˈvɛndʒəns/ n. venganza f.

Venice /ˈvɛnɪs/ n. Venecia f.

vent /vɛnt/ n. apertura f.

ventilate /ˈvɛntlˌeɪt/ v. ventilar.

venture /'vɛntʃər/ n. ventura f.

verb /vərb/ n. verbo m.

verbose /vər'bous/ a. verboso.

verdict /'vərdɪkt/ n. veredicto, fallo m.

verge /vərdʒ/ n. borde m.

verify /'vɛrə,faɪ/ v. verificar.

versatile /'vərsətl/ a. versátil.

verse /vərs/ n. verso m.

version /'vərʒən/ n. versión f.

vertical /'vərtɪkəl/ a. vertical.

very /'vɛri/ a. **1.** mismo. —adv. **2.** muy.

vessel /'vɛsəl/ n. vasija f.; barco m.

vest /vɛst/ n. chaleco m.

veteran /'vɛtərən/ a. & n. veterano -na.

veto /'vitou/ n. veto m.

vex /vɛks/ v. molestar.

via /'vaɪə, 'viə/ prep. por la vía de; por.

viaduct /'vaɪə,dʌkt/ n. viaducto m.

vibrate /'vaɪbreɪt/ v. vibrar.

vibration /vaɪ'breɪʃən/ n. vibración f.

vice /vaɪs/ n. vicio m.

vicinity /vɪ'sɪnɪti/ n. vecindad f.

vicious /'vɪʃəs/ a. vicioso.

victim /'vɪktəm/ n. víctima f.

victor /'vɪktər/ n. vencedor -ora.

victorious /vɪk'tɔriəs/ a. victorioso.

victory /'vɪktəri/ n. victoria f.

video camera /'vɪdi,ou/ videocámara f.

videoconference /'vɪdiou,kɒnfərəns/ videoconferencia f.

videodisc /'vɪdiou,dɪsk/ n. videodisco m.

video game /'vɪdi,ou/ videojuego m.

videotape /'vɪdiou,teɪp/ n. vídeo m., magnetoscopio m.

view /vyu/ n. **1.** vista f. —v. **2.** ver.

viewpoint /'vyu,pɔɪnt/ n. punto de vista m.

vigil /'vɪdʒəl/ n. vigilia, vela f.

vigilant /'vɪdʒələnt/ a. vigilante.

vigor /'vɪgər/ n. vigor m.

vile /vaɪl/ a. vil, bajo.

village /'vɪlɪdʒ/ n. aldea f.

villain /'vɪlən/ n. malvado -da.

vindicate /'vɪndɪ,keɪt/ v. vindicar.

vine /vaɪn/ n. parra, vid f.

vinegar /'vɪnɪgər/ n. vinagre m.

vintage /'vɪntɪdʒ/ n. vendimia f.

violate /'vaɪə,leɪt/ v. violar.

violation /,vaɪə'leɪʃən/ n. violación f.

violence /'vaɪələns/ n. violencia f.

violent /'vaɪələnt/ a. violento.

violin /,vaɪə'lɪn/ n. violín m.

virgin /'vərdʒɪn/ n. virgen f.

virile /'vɪrəl/ a. viril.

virtual /'vərtʃuəl/ a. virtual.

virtual memory memoria virtual f.

virtual reality realidad virtual f.

virtue /'vərtʃu/ n. virtud f.

virtuous /'vərtʃuəs/ a. virtuoso.

virus /'vaɪrəs/ n. virus m.

visa /'vizə/ n. visa f.

visible /'vɪzəbəl/ a. visible.

vision /'vɪʒən/ n. visión f.

visit /'vɪzɪt/ n. **1.** visita f. —v. **2.** visitar.

visitor /'vɪzɪtər/ n. visitante m. & f.

visual /'vɪʒuəl/ a. visual.

vital /'vaɪtl/ a. vital.

vitality /vaɪ'tælɪti/ n. vitalidad, energía vital f.

vitamin /'vaɪtəmɪn/ n. vitamina f.

vivacious /vɪ'veɪʃəs/ a. vivaz.

vivid /'vɪvɪd/ a. vivo; gráfico.

vocabulary /vou'kæbyə,lɛri/ n. vocabulario m.

vocal /'voukəl/ a. vocal.

vodka /'vɒdkə/ n. vodca f.

vogue /voug/ n. boga; moda f. **be in vogue** estilarse.

voice /vɔɪs/ n. **1.** voz f. —v. **2.** expresar.

voice mail correo de voz m.

voice recognition reconocimiento de voz m.

void /vɔɪd/ a. **1.** vacío. —n. **2.** vacío m. —v. **3.** invalidar.

voltage /'voultɪdʒ/ n. voltaje m.

volume /'vɒlyum/ n. volumen; tomo m.

voluntary /'vɒlən,tɛri/ a. voluntario.

volunteer /,vɒlən'tɪər/ n. **1.** voluntario -ria. —v. **2.** ofrecerse.

vomit /'vɒmɪt/ v. vomitar.

vote /vout/ n. **1.** voto m. —v. **2.** votar.

voter /'voutər/ n. votante m. & f.

vouch /vautʃ/ v. **v. for,** garantizar.

vow /vau/ n. **1.** voto m. —v. **2.** jurar.

vowel /'vauəl/ n. vocal f.

voyage /'vɔɪɪdʒ/ n. viaje m.

vulgar /'vʌlgər/ a. vulgar; común; soez.

vulnerable /'vʌlnərəbəl/ a. vulnerable.

W X Y Z

wade /weid/ v. vadear.

wag /wæg/ v. menear.

wage /weidʒ/ n. **1.** (pl.) sueldo, salario m. —v. **2. w. war,** hacer guerra.

wagon /'wægən/ n. carreta f.

wail /weil/ n. **1.** lamento, gemido m. —v. **2.** lamentar, gemir.

waist /weist/ n. cintura f.

wait /weit/ n. **1.** espera f. —v. **2.** esperar. **w. for,** esperar. **w. on,** atender.

waiter /'weitər/ **waitress** n. camarero -ra.

waiting room /'weitiŋ/ sala de espera.

wake /weik/ v. **w. up,** despertar.

walk /wɔk/ n. **1.** paseo m.; vuelta; caminata f.; modo de andar. —v. **2.** andar; caminar; ir a pie.

wall /wɔl/ n. pared; muralla f.

wallcovering /'wɔl,kʌvəriŋ/ n. tapizado de pared m.

wallet /'wɒlit/ n. cartera f.

wallpaper /'wɔl,peipər/ n. **1.** empapelado m. —v. **2.** empapelar.

walnut /'wɔl,nʌt/ n. nuez f.

waltz /wɔlts/ n. vals m.

wander /'wɒndər/ v. vagar.

want /wɒnt/ n. **1.** necesidad f. —v. **2.** querer.

war /wɔr/ n. guerra f.

ward /wɔrd/ n. **1.** Pol. barrio m.; (hospital) cuadra f. —v. **2. w. off,** parar.

warehouse /'wɛər,haus/ n. almacén m.

wares /wɛərz/ n. mercancías f.pl.

warlike /'wɔr,laik/ a. belicoso.

warm /wɔrm/ a. caliente; Fig. caluroso. **to be w.,** tener calor; (weather) hacer calor. —v. **2.** calentar.

warmth /wɔrmθ/ n. calor m.

warn /wɔrn/ v. advertir.

warning /'wɔrniŋ/ n. aviso m.

warp /wɔrp/ v. alabear.

warrant /'wɔrənt, 'wɒr-/ v. justificar.

warrior /'wɔriər/ n. guerrero -ra.

warship /'wɔr,ʃip/ n. navío de guerra, buque de guerra m.

wash /wɒʃ/ v. lavar.

washing machine /'wɒʃiŋ/ máquina de lavar, lavadora f.

wasp /wɒsp/ n. avispa f.

waste /weist/ n. **1.** gasto m.; desechos m.pl. —v. **2.** gastar; perder.

watch /wɒtʃ/ n. **1.** reloj m.; Mil. guardia f. —v. **2.** observar, mirar. **w. for,** esperar. **w. out for,** tener cuidado con. **w. over,** guardar; velar por.

watchful /'wɒtʃfəl/ a. desvelado.

watchmaker /'wɒtʃ,meikər/ n. relojero -ra.

watchman /'wɒtʃmən/ n. sereno m.

water /'wɔtər/ n. **1.** agua f. **w. color,** acuarela f. —v. **2.** aguar.

waterbed /'wɔtər,bɛd/ n. cama de agua f.

waterfall /'wɔtər,fɔl/ n. catarata f.

watering can /'wɔtəriŋ/ regadera f.

waterproof /'wɔtər,pruf/ a. impermeable.

wave /weiv/ n. **1.** onda; ola f. —v. **2.** ondear; agitar; hacer señas.

waver /'weivər/ v. vacilar.

wax /wæks/ n. **1.** cera f. —v. **2.** encerar.

way /wei/ n. camino; modo m., manera f. **in a w.,** hasta cierto punto. **a long w.,** muy lejos. **by the w.,** a propósito. **this w.,** por aquí. **that w.,** por allí. **which w.,** por dónde.

we /wi/ pron. nosotros -as.

weak /wik/ a. débil.

weaken /'wikən/ v. debilitar.

weakness /'wiknis/ n. debilidad f.

wealth /wɛlθ/ n. riqueza f.

wealthy /'wɛlθi/ a. adinerado.

wean /win/ v. destetar.

weapon /'wɛpən/ n. arma f.

wear /wɛər/ n. **1.** uso; desgaste m.; (clothes) ropa f. —v. **2.** usar, llevar. **w. out,** gastar; cansar.

weary /'wiəri/ a. cansado, rendido.

weather /'wɛðər/ n. tiempo m.

weave /wiv/ v. tejer.

weaver /'wivər/ n. tejedor -ra.

web /wɛb/ n. tela f.

Web /wɛb/ n. (Internet) malla f., telaraña f.; web m.

wedding /'wɛdiŋ/ n. boda f.

wedge /wɛdʒ/ n. cuña f.

Wednesday /'wɛnzdei/ n. miércoles m.

weed /wid/ *n.* maleza *f.*

week /wik/ *n.* semana *f.*

weekday /'wik,deɪ/ *n.* día de trabajo.

weekend /'wik,ɛnd/ *n.* fin de semana.

weekly /'wikli/ *a.* semanal.

weep /wip/ *v.* llorar.

weigh /weɪ/ *v.* pesar.

weight /weɪt/ *n.* peso *m.*

weightless /'weɪtlɪs/ *a.* ingrávido.

weightlessness /'weɪtlɪsnɪs/ *n.* ingravidez *f.*

weird /wɪərd/ *a.* misterioso, extraño.

welcome /'wɛlkəm/ *a.* **1.** bienvenido. **you're w.,** de nada, no hay de qué. —*n.* **2.** acogida, bienvenida *f.* —*v.* **3.** acoger, recibir bien.

welfare /'wɛl,fɛər/ *n.* bienestar *m.*

well /wɛl/ *a.* **1.** sano, bueno. —*adv.* **2.** bien; pues. —*n.* **3.** pozo *m.*

well-done /'wɛl 'dʌn/ *a.* (food) bien cocido.

well-known /'wɛl 'noʊn/ *a.* bien conocido.

well-mannered /'wɛl 'mænərd/ *a.* educado.

west /wɛst/ *n.* oeste, occidente *m.*

western /'wɛstərn/ *a.* occidental.

westward /'wɛstwərd/ *adv.* hacia el oeste.

wet /wɛt/ *a.* **1.** mojado. **to get w.,** mojarse. —*v.* **2.** mojar.

whale /weɪl/ *n.* ballena *f.*

what /wʌt; *unstressed* wət/ *a.* **1.** qué; cuál. —*interrog. pron.* **2.** qué. —*rel. pron.* **3.** lo que.

whatever /wʌt'ɛvər/ *a.* **1.** cualquier. —*pron.* **2.** lo que; todo lo que.

wheat /wit/ *n.* trigo *m.*

wheel /wil/ *n.* rueda *f.* **steering w.,** volante *m.*

when /wɛn; *unstressed* wən/ *adv.* **1.** cuándo. —*conj.* **2.** cuando.

whenever /wɛn'ɛvər/ *conj.* siempre que, cuando quiera que.

where /wɛər/ *adv.* **1.** dónde, adónde. —*conj.* **2.** donde.

wherever /wɛər'ɛvər/ *conj.* dondequiera que, adondequiera que.

whether /'wɛðər/ *conj.* si.

which /wɪtʃ/ *a.* **1.** qué. —*interrog. pron.* **2.** cuál. —*rel. pron.* **3.** que; el cual; lo cual.

whichever /wɪtʃ'ɛvər/ *a. & pron.* cualquiera que.

while /waɪl/ *conj.* **1.** mientras; mientras que. —*n.* **2.** rato *m.*

whip /wɪp/ *n.* **1.** látigo *m.* —*v.* **2.** azotar.

whipped cream /wɪpt/ nata batida *f.*

whirl /wɜrl/ *v.* girar.

whirlpool /'wɜrl,pul/ *n.* vórtice *m.*

whirlwind /'wɜrl,wɪnd/ *n.* torbellino *m.*

whisk broom /wɪsk/ escobilla *f.*

whisker /'wɪskər/ *n.* bigote *m.*

whiskey /'wɪski/ *n.* whisky *m.*

whisper /'wɪspər/ *n.* **1.** cuchicheo *m.* —*v.* **2.** cuchichear.

whistle /'wɪsəl/ *n.* **1.** pito; silbido *m.* —*v.* **2.** silbar.

white /waɪt/ *a.* **1.** blanco. —*n.* **2.** (of egg) clara *f.*

who /hu/ **whom** *interrog. pron.* **1.** quién. —*rel. pron.* **2.** que; quien.

whoever /hu'ɛvər/ **whomever** *pron.* quienquiera que.

whole /hoʊl/ *a.* **1.** entero. **the wh.,** todo el. —*n.* **2.** totalidad *f.* **on the wh.,** por lo general.

wholesale /'hoʊl,seɪl/ *a.* **1.** al por mayor. **at wh.,** al por mayor.

wholesaler /'hoʊl,seɪlər/ *n.* mayorista *m. & f.*

wholesome /'hoʊlsəm/ *a.* sano, saludable.

wholly /'hoʊli/ *adv.* enteramente.

whose /huz/ *interrog. adj.* **1.** de quién. —*rel. adj.* **2.** cuyo.

why /waɪ/ *adv.* por qué; para qué.

wicked /'wɪkɪd/ *a.* malo, malvado.

wickedness /'wɪkɪdnɪs/ *n.* maldad *f.*

wide /waɪd/ *a.* **1.** ancho; extenso. —*adv.* **2.** **w. open,** abierto de par en par.

widen /'waɪdn/ *v.* ensanchar; extender.

widespread /'waɪd'sprɛd/ *a.* extenso.

widow /'wɪdoʊ/ *n.* viuda *f.*

widower /'wɪdoʊər/ *n.* viudo *m.*

width /wɪdθ/ *n.* anchura *f.*

wield /wild/ *v.* manejar, empuñar.

wife /waɪf/ *n.* esposa, señora, mujer *f.*

wig /wɪg/ *n.* peluca *f.*

wild /waɪld/ *a.* salvaje; bárbaro.

wilderness /'wɪldərnɪs/ *n.* desierto *m.*

wildlife /'waɪld,laɪf/ *n.* fauna silvestre *f.*

will /wɪl/ *n.* **1.** voluntad *f.*; testamento *m.* —*v.* **2.** querer; determinar; *Leg.* legar.

willful /'wɪlfəl/ *a.* voluntarioso; premeditado.

willing /'wɪlɪŋ/ *a.* **to be w.**, estar dispuesto.

willingly /'wɪlɪŋli/ *adv.* de buena gana.

wilt /wɪlt/ *v.* marchitar.

win /wɪn/ *v.* ganar.

wind /wɪnd/ *n.* wind; *v.* waind/ *n.* **1.** viento *m.* —*v.* **2.** torcer; dar cuerda a.

windmill /'wɪnd,mɪl/ *n.* molino de viento *m.*

window /'wɪndou/ *n.* ventana *f.*; (of car) ventanilla *f.*; (of shop or store) escaparate *m.*

windshield /'wɪnd,ʃild/ *n.* parabrisas *m.*

windy /'wɪndi/ *a.* ventoso. **to be w.**, (weather) hacer viento.

wine /wain/ *n.* vino *m.*

wing /wɪŋ/ *n.* ala *f.*; *Theat.* bastidor *m.*

wink /wɪŋk/ *n.* **1.** guiño *m.* —*v.* **2.** guiñar.

winner /'wɪnər/ *n.* ganador -ra.

winter /'wɪntər/ *n.* invierno *m.*

wipe /waip/ *v.* limpiar; (dry) secar. **w. out,** destruir.

wire /waiər/ *n.* **1.** alambre; hilo; telegrama *m.* —*v.* **2.** telegrafiar.

wireless /'waiərlɪs/ *n.* telégrafo sin hilos.

wisdom /'wɪzdəm/ *n.* juicio *m.*; sabiduría *f.*

wise /waiz/ *a.* sensato, juicioso; sabio.

wish /wɪʃ/ *n.* **1.** deseo; voto *m.* —*v.* **2.** desear; querer.

wit /wɪt/ *n.* ingenio *m.*, sal *f.*

witch /wɪtʃ/ *n.* bruja *f.*

with /wɪθ, wɪð/ *prep.* con.

withdraw /wɪð'drɔ, wɪθ-/ *v.* retirar.

wither /'wɪðər/ *v.* marchitar.

withhold /wɪθ'hould, wɪð-/ *v.* tener; suspender.

within /wɪð'ɪn, wɪθ-/ *adv.* **1.** dentro, por dentro. —*prep.* **2.** dentro de; en.

without /wɪð'aut, wɪθ-/ *adv.* **1.** fuera, por fuera. —*prep.* **2.** sin.

witness /'wɪtnɪs/ *n.* **1.** testigo; testimonio *m.* & *f.* —*v.* **2.** presenciar; atestar.

witty /'wɪti/ *a.* ingenioso, gracioso, ocurrente.

wizard /'wɪzərd/ *n.* hechicero *m.*

woe /wou/ *n.* dolor *m.*; pena *f.*

wolf /wulf/ *n.* lobo -ba.

woman /'wumən/ *n.* mujer *f.*

womb /wum/ *n.* entrañas *f.pl.*, matriz *f.*

wonder /'wʌndər/ *n.* **1.** maravilla *f.*; admiración *f.* **for a w.,** por milagro. **no w.,** no es extraño. —*v.* **2.** preguntarse; maravillarse.

wonderful /'wʌndərfəl/ *a.* maravilloso; estupendo.

woo /wu/ *v.* cortejar.

wood /wud/ *n.* madera *f.*; (for fire) leña *f.*

wooden /'wudn/ *a.* de madera.

wool /wul/ *n.* lana *f.*

word /wɜrd/ *n.* **1.** palabra *f.* **the words** (of a song), la letra. —*v.* **2.** expresar.

word processing /'prɒsɛsɪŋ/ procesamiento de textos *m.*

word processor /'prɒsɛsər/ procesador de textos *m.*

work /wɜrk/ *n.* **1.** trabajo *m.*; (of art) obra *f.* —*v.* **2.** trabajar; obrar; funcionar.

worker /'wɜrkər/ *n.* trabajador -ra; obrero -ra.

workman /'wɜrkmən/ *n.* obrero *m.*

work station estación de trabajo *f.*

work week /'wɜrk,wik/ semana laboral *f.*

world /wɜrld/ *n.* mundo *m.* **w. war,** guerra mundial.

worldly /'wɜrldli/ *a.* mundano.

worldwide /'wɜrld'waid/ *a.* mundial.

worm /wɜrm/ *n.* gusano *m.*

worn /wɔrn/ *a.* usado. **w. out,** gastado; cansado, rendido.

worrisome /'wɜrisəm/ *a.* inquietante.

worry /'wɜri/ *n.* **1.** preocupación *f.* —*v.* **2.** preocupar.

worrying /'wɜriɪŋ/ *a.* inquietante.

worse /wɜrs/ *a.* peor. **to get w.,** empeorar.

worship /'wɜrʃɪp/ *n.* **1.** adoración *f.* —*v.* **2.** adorar.

worst /wɜrst/ *a.* peor.

worth /wɜrθ/ *a.* **1. to be w.,** valer. —*n.* **2.** valor *m.*

worthless /'wɜrθlɪs/ *a.* sin valor.

worthy /'wɜrði/ *a.* digno.

wound /wund/ *n.* **1.** herida *f.* —*v.* **2.** herir.

wrap /ræp/ *n.* **1.** (pl.) abrigos *m.pl.* —*n.* **2.** envolver.

wrapping /'ræpɪŋ/ *n.* cubierta *f.*

wrath /ræθ/ *n.* ira, cólera *f.*

wreath /riθ/ *n.* guirnalda; corona *f.*

wreck /rɛk/ *n.* **1.** ruina *f.*; accidente *m.* —*v.* **2.** destrozar, arruinar.

wrench /rɛntʃ/ *n.* llave *f.* **monkey w.**, llave inglesa.

wrestle /'rɛsəl/ *v.* luchar.

wretched /'rɛtʃɪd/ *a.* miserable.

wring /rɪŋ/ *v.* retorcer.

wrinkle /'rɪŋkəl/ *n.* **1.** arruga *f.* —*v.* **2.** arrugar.

wrist /rɪst/ *n.* muñeca *f.* **w. watch**, reloj de pulsera.

write /raɪt/ *v.* escribir. **w. down**, apuntar.

writer /'raɪtər/ *n.* escritor -ra.

writhe /raɪð/ *v.* contorcerse.

writing paper /'raɪtɪŋ/ papel de escribir *m.*

wrong /rɔŋ/ *a.* **1.** equivocado; incorrecto. **to be w.**, equivocarse; no tener razón. —*adv.* **2.** mal, incorrectamente. —*n.* **3.** agravio *m.* **right and w.**, el bien y el mal. —*v.* **4.** agraviar, ofender.

WWW *abbr.* (World Wide Web) malla mundial *f.*

x-ray /'ɛks,reɪ/ *n.* **1.** rayo X *m.*, radiografía, *f.* —*v.* **2.** radiografiar.

xylophone /'zaɪlə,foʊn/ *n.* xilófono *m.*

yacht /yɒt/ *n.* yate *m.*

yard /yɑrd/ *n.* patio, corral *m.*; (measure) yarda *f.*

yarn /yɑrn/ *n.* hilo.

yawn /yɔn/ *n.* **1.** bostezo *m.* —*v.* **2.** bostezar.

year /yɪər/ *n.* año *m.*

yearly /'yɪərli/ *a.* anual.

yearn /yɜrn/ *v.* anhelar.

yell /yɛl/ *n.* **1.** grito *m.* —*v.* **2.** gritar.

yellow /'yɛloʊ/ *a.* amarillo.

yes /yɛs/ *adv.* sí.

yesterday /'yɛstər,deɪ/ *adv.* ayer.

yet /yɛt/ *adv.* todavía, aún.

Yiddish /'yɪdɪʃ/ *n.* yídish *m.*

yield /yild/ *v.* producir; ceder.

yogurt /'yoʊgərt/ *n.* yogur *m.*

yoke /youk/ *n.* yugo *m.*

yolk /youk/ *n.* yema *f.*

you /yu; *unstressed* yʊ, yə/ *pron.* usted, (pl.) ustedes; lo, la, los, las; le, les; (familiar) tú, (pl.) vosotros -as; ti; te, (pl.) os. **with y.**, contigo, con usted.

young /yʌŋ/ *a.* joven.

youngster /'yʌŋstər/ *n.* muchacho -cha *m.* & *f.*

your /yʊr, yər; *unstressed* yər/ *a.* su; (familiar) tu; (pl.) vuestro.

yours /yʊrz, yərz/ *pron.* suyo; (familiar) tuyo; (pl.) vuestro.

yourself -selves /yʊr'sɛlf, yər-yər-/ *pron.* sí; se; (familiar) ti; te. **with y.**, consigo; contigo. **you y.**, usted mismo, ustedes mismos; tú mismo, vosotros mismos.

youth /yuθ/ *n.* juventud *f.*; (person) joven *m.* & *f.*

youth club club juvenil *m.*

youthful /'yuθfəl/ *a.* juvenil.

yuppie /'yʌpi/ *n.* yuppie *m.* & *f.*

zap /zæp/ *v.* desintegrar, aniquilar.

zeal /zil/ *n.* celo, fervor *m.*

zealous /'zɛləs/ *a.* celoso, fervoroso.

zero /'zɪəroʊ/ *n.* cero *m.*

zest /zɛst/ *n.* gusto *m.*

zip code /zɪp/ número de distrito postal.

zipper /'zɪpər/ *n.* cremallera *f.*

zone /zoʊn/ *n.* zona *f.*

zoo /zu/ *n.* jardín zoológico.

Spanish Irregular Verbs

Infinitive	Present	Future	Preterit	Past Part.
andar	ando	andaré	anduve	andado
caber	quepo	cabré	cupe	cabido
caer	caigo	caeré	caí	caído
conducir	conduzco	conduciré	conduje	conducido
dar	doy	daré	di	dado
decir	digo	diré	dije	dicho
estar	estoy	estaré	estuve	estado
haber	he	habré	hube	habido
hacer	hago	haré	hice	hecho
ir	voy	iré	fui	ido
jugar	juego	jugaré	jugué	jugado
morir	muero	moriré	morí	muerto
oir	oigo	oiré	oí	oído
poder	puedo	podré	pude	podido
poner	pongo	pondré	puse	puesto
querer	quiero	querré	quise	querido
saber	sé	sabré	supe	sabido
salir	salgo	saldré	salí	salido
ser	soy	seré	fui	sido
tener	tengo	tendré	tuve	tenido
traer	traigo	traeré	traje	traído
valer	valgo	valdré	valí	valido
venir	vengo	vendré	vine	venido
ver	veo	veré	vi	visto

Las formas del verbo inglés

1. Se forma la 3ª persona singular del tiempo presente exactamente al igual que el plural de los sustantivos, añadiendo **-es** o **-s** a la forma sencilla según las mismas reglas, así:

(1)	teach	pass	wish	fix	buzz
	teaches	passes	wishes	fixes	buzzes

(2)	place	change	judge	please	freeze
	places	changes	judges	pleases	freezes

(3a)	find	sell	clean	hear	love	buy	know
	finds	sells	cleans	hears	loves	buys	knows

(3b)	think	like	laugh	stop	hope	meet	want
	thinks	likes	laughs	stops	hopes	meets	wants

(4)	cry	try	dry	carry	deny
	cries	tries	dries	carries	denies

Cinco verbos muy comunes tienen 3ª persona singular irregular:

(5)	go	do	say	have	be
	goes	does	says	has	is

2. Se forman el tiempo pasado y el participio de modo igual, añadiendo a la forma sencilla la terminación **-ed** o **-d** según las reglas que siguen:

(1) Si la forma sencilla termina en **-d** o **-t**, se le pone **-ed** como sílaba aparte:

end	fold	need	load
ended	folded	needed	loaded

want	feast	wait	light
wanted	feasted	waited	lighted

(2) Si la forma sencilla termina en cualquier otra consonante, se añade también **-ed** pero sin hacer sílaba aparte:

(2a)	bang	sail	seem	harm	earn	weigh
	banged	sailed	seemed	harmed	earned	weighed

(2b)	lunch	work	look	laugh	help	pass
	lunched	worked	looked	laughed	helped	passed

(3) Si la forma sencilla termina en **-e**, se le pone sólo **-d**:

(3a)	hate	taste	waste	guide	fade	trade
	hated	tasted	wasted	guided	faded	traded

(3b)	free	judge	rule	name	dine	scare
	freed	judged	ruled	named	dined	scared

(3c)	place	force	knife	like	hope	base
	placed	forced	knifed	liked	hoped	based

(4) Una **-y** final que sigue a cualquier consonante se cambia en **-ie** al añadir la **-d** del pasado/participio:

cry	try	dry	carry	deny
cried	tried	dried	carried	denied

3. Varios verbos muy comunes forman el tiempo pasado y el participio de manera irregular. Pertenecen a tres grupos.

(1) Los que tienen una sola forma irregular para tiempo pasado y participio, como los siguientes:

bend	bleed	bring	build	buy	catch	creep	deal
bent	bled	brought	built	bought	caught	crept	dealt

dig	feed	feel	fight	find	flee	get	hang
dug	fed	felt	fought	found	fled	got	hung

have	hear	hold	keep	lead	leave	lend	lose
had	heard	held	kept	led	left	lent	lost

make	mean	meet	say	seek	sell	send	shine
made	meant	met	said	sought	sold	sent	shone

shoot	sit	sleep	spend	stand	strike	sweep	teach
shot	sat	slept	spent	stood	struck	swept	taught

(2) Los que tienen una forma irregular para el tiempo pasado y otra forma irregular para el participio, como los siguientes:

be	beat	become	begin	bite
was	beat	became	began	bit
been	beaten	become	begun	bitten

blow	break	choose	come	do
blew	broke	chose	came	did
blown	broken	chosen	come	done

draw	drink	drive	eat	fall
drew	drank	drove	ate	fell
drawn	drunk	driven	eaten	fallen

fly	forget	freeze	give	go
flew	forgot	froze	gave	went
flown	forgotten	frozen	given	gone

grow	hide	know	ride	ring
grew	hid	knew	rode	rang
grown	hidden	known	ridden	rung

rise	run	see	shake	shrink
rose	ran	saw	shook	shrank
risen	run	seen	shaken	shrunk

sing	sink	speak	steal	swear
sang	sank	spoke	stole	swore
sung	sunk	spoken	stolen	sworn
swim	tear	throw	wear	write
swam	tore	threw	wore	wrote
swum	torn	thrown	worn	written

(3) Los que no varían del todo, la forma sencilla funcionando también como pasado/participio; entre éstos son de mayor frecuencia:

bet	burst	cast	cost	cut
hit	hurt	let	put	quit
read	set	shed	shut	slit
spit	split	spread	thrust	wet

El plural del sustantivo inglés

A la forma singular se añade la terminación **-es** o **-s** de acuerdo con las reglas siguientes.

(1) Si el singular termina en **-ch, -s, -sh, -x** o **-z**, se le pone **-es** como sílaba aparte:

match	glass	dish	box	buzz
matches	glasses	dishes	boxes	buzzes

(2) Si el singular termina en **-ce, -ge, -se** o **-ze**, se le pone una **-s** que con la vocal precedente forma sílaba aparte:

face	page	house	size
faces	pages	houses	sizes

(3) Una **-y** final que sigue a cualquier consonante se cambia en **-ie** a ponérsele la **-s** del plural:

sky	city	lady	ferry	penny
skies	cities	ladies	ferries	pennies

(4) Los siguientes sustantivos comunes tienen plural irregular:

man	woman	child	foot	mouse	goose
men	women	children	feet	mice	geese
wife	knife	life	half	leaf	deer
wives	knives	lives	halves	leaves	deer

Weights and Measures/Pesos y Medidas

Spanish/ English	1 centímetro	=	.3937 inches
	1 metro	=	39.37 inches
	1 kilómetro	=	.621 mile
	1 centigramo	=	.1543 grain
	1 gramo	=	15.432 grains
	1 kilogramo	=	2.2046 pounds
	1 tonelada	=	2.204 pounds
	1 centilitro	=	.338 ounces
	1 litro	=	1.0567 quart (liquid); .908 quart (dry)
	1 kilolitro	=	264.18 gallons
English/ Spanish	1 inch	=	2.54 centímetros
	1 foot	=	.305 metros
	1 mile	=	1.61 kilómetros
	1 grain	=	.065 gramos
	1 pound	=	.455 kilogramos
	1 ton	=	.907 toneladas
	1 ounce	=	2.96 centilitros
	1 quart	=	1.13 litros
	1 gallon	=	4.52 litros

Days of the Week/Días de la Semana

Sunday	domingo	**Thursday**	jueves
Monday	lunes	**Friday**	viernes
Tuesday	martes	**Saturday**	sábado
Wednesday	miércoles		

Months/Meses

January	enero	**July**	julio
February	febrero	**August**	agosto
March	marzo	**September**	septiembre
April	abril	**October**	octubre
May	mayo	**November**	noviembre
June	junio	**December**	diciembre

Useful Phrases/Locuciones Útiles

Good day, Good morning.   Buenos días.
Good afternoon.   Buenas tardes.
Good night, Good evening.   Buenas noches.
Hello.   ¡Hola!
Welcome!   ¡Bienvenido!
See you later.   Hasta luego.
Goodbye.   ¡Adiós!
How are you?   ¿Cómo está usted?
I'm fine, thank you.   Estoy bien, gracias.
I'm pleased to meet you.   Mucho gusto en
   conocerle.
May I introduce… Quisiera presentar…
Thank you very much.   Muchas gracias.
You're welcome.   De nada *or* No hay de qué.
Please.   Por favor.
Excuse me.   Con permiso.
Good luck.   ¡Buena suerte!
To your health.   ¡Salud!

Please help me.   Ayúdeme, por favor.
I don't know.   No sé.
I don't understand.   No entiendo.
Do you understand?   ¿Entiende usted?
I don't speak Spanish.   No hablo español.
Do you speak English?   ¿Habla usted inglés?
How do you say . . . in Spanish?   ¿Cómo se dice
   . . . en español?
What do you call this?   ¿Cómo se llama esto?
Speak slowly, please.   Hable despacio, por favor.
Please repeat.   Repita, por favor.
I don't like it.   No me gusta.
I am lost.   Ando perdido; Me he extraviado.

What is your name?   ¿Cómo se llama usted?
My name is . . . Me llamo . . .
I am an American.   Soy norteamericano.
Where are you from?   ¿De dónde es usted?
I'm from… Soy de…

How is the weather? ¿Qué tiempo hace?

It's cold (hot) today. Hace frío (calor) hoy.

What time is it? ¿Qué hora es?

How much is it? ¿Cuánto es?

It is too much. Es demasiado.

What do you wish? ¿Qué desea usted?

I want to buy . . . Quiero comprar . . .

May I see something better? ¿Podría ver algo mejor?

May I see something cheaper? ¿Podría ver algo menos caro?

It is not exactly what I want. No es exactamente lo que quiero.

I'm hungry. Tengo hambre.

I'm thirsty. Tengo sed.

Where is there a restaurant? ¿Dónde hay un restaurante?

I have a reservation. Tengo una reservación.

I would like… Quisiera…; Me gustaría…

Please give me… Por favor, déme usted…

Please bring me… Por favor, tráigame usted…

May I see the menu? ¿Podría ver el menú?

The bill, please. La cuenta, por favor.

Is service included in the bill? ¿El servicio está incluido en la cuenta?

Where is there a hotel? ¿Dónde hay un hotel?

Where is the post office? ¿Dónde está el correo?

Is there any mail for me? ¿Hay correo para mí?

Where can I mail this letter? ¿Dónde puedo echar esta carta al correo?

Take me to… Lléveme a…

I believe I am ill. Creo que estoy enfermo.

Please call a doctor. Por favor, llame al médico.

Please call the police. Por favor, llame a la policía.

I want to send a telegram. Quiero poner un telegrama.

As soon as possible. Cuanto antes.

Round trip. Ida y vuelta.

Please help me with my luggage. Por favor, ayúdeme con mi equipaje.

Where can I get a taxi? ¿Dónde se puede encontrar un taxi?

What is the fare to… ¿Cuánto es el pasaje hasta…?

Please take me to this address. Por favor, lléveme a esta dirección.

Where can I change my money? ¿Dónde puedo cambiar mi dinero?

Where is the nearest bank? ¿Dónde está el banco más cercano?

Can you accept my check? ¿Puede aceptar usted mi cheque?

Do you accept traveler's checks? ¿Aceptan cheques de viaje?

What is the postage? ¿Cuánto es el franqueo?

Where is the nearest drugstore? ¿Dónde está la farmacia más cercana?

Where is the men's (women's) room? ¿Dónde está el servicio de caballeros (de señoras)?

Please let me off at… Por favor, déjeme bajar en…

Right away. ¡Pronto!

Help. ¡Socorro!

Who is it? ¿Quién es?

Just a minute! ¡Un momento no más!

Come in. ¡Pase usted!

Pardon me. Disculpe usted.

Stop. ¡Pare!

Look out. ¡Cuidado!

Hurry. ¡De prisa! or ¡Dése prisa!

Go on. ¡Siga!

To (on, at) the right. A la derecha.

To (on, at) the left. A la izquierda.

Straight ahead. Adelante.